NON-LEAGUE DIRECTORY 1987

EDITOR
TONY WILLIAMS

SPONSORED
BY
COMPOSITE GRANDSTANDS

Published by Tony Williams
and distributed by
The Hamlyn Publishing Group Limited
Rushden, Northants, England

ISBN-1-869833-03-1

Printed by Sovereign Printing Group, Sidmouth, Devon

Paper supplied by St Regis Company (UK) Ltd. Silver Mill, Devon

Front Cover: Altrincham and England Captain
John Davison, crashes in a free kick during Altrincham's Fourth Round F.A. Cup tie against York City. Photo John Rooney

EDITORIAL PREFACE

Last season I highlighted the fact that my annual publication featuring our national winter sport outside the Football League had been published by no less than five different organisations. Well in it's ninth year I am now personally publishing 'The Official F.A. Non-League Directory' and I am pleased to be able to report that last year's request for help with order form distribution worked and over 60 pages have been added.

We also welcome new sponsors who I am sure will be of great use to nearly all club officials who are reading this book. 'Composite Grandstands' have set up a team of consultants who can advise club Chairmen and Secretaries just how best they can improve their facilities, the most economical way to go about the work and how to raise the funds. This service is offered for nothing so I feel sure this is going to be of tremendous help to many clubs.

My aim is to develop this 'Directory' until we can include 1,000 pages covering football from senior district leagues right through to a future six page a club 'special' section on the G.M. Vauxhall Conference. This will not take long to achieve if everyone who is reading this introduces the book to all their friends who are 'non-league' enthusiasts. Please write to the Editorial office if you want order forms, or even if you would like officially to act as an agent for the book in your area. We already have a very knowledgable and concientious 'team' of contributors and the book would soon be able to grow if we could set up an equally efficient distribution 'team'. Please let me know if you have any ideas.

While thanking all at The Football Association for their continued encouragement and support I would like to point out once more that the views expressed in this book are not necessarily those of The Football Association. *Tony Williams.*

Editor:	Tony Williams
Assistant Editor:	George Brown
Executive Editorial Committee:	Tony Williams, George Brown, Adrian Titcombe and Steve Clark
Editorial Office:	2 Elder Cottages, Hatch Beauchamp, Taunton, Somerset
Senior Editorial Team:	Leo Hoenig (Photos and County Cup Feature), Eric Marsh (Senior Photographer) Colin Startup (Statistics), Steve Whitney (Players Records) Peter Burrin (Photos), John Rooney (Photos), Bill Mitchell (Admin.).
Contributors:	Paul Walker (Daily Star), Paul Newman (The Times), Tony Incenzo (Pyramid), Ian Runham (Wirral Programme Club) David Stacey (Football Programme Directory) Mike Berry, Allan Jenkins, Chris Foote-Wood, Jim Blackstone, Chris Sandeman, Mark Herron, David Shute and Nick Robinson

ACKNOWLEDGEMENTS

The thought of compiling a book which is made up of entries from about 800 different sources gives one a very severe 'sinking feeling'.

However, the response from the League Secretaries, the club enthusiasts, the public and of course the certified 'non-league nutters' always lifts me up and makes me realise the whole operation is well worth while. More than that — it's positively exhilerating at times as one realises just how many people really love the game of football. If only those people received as much publicity as the press insist on giving to sports personnel in trouble.

I must thank all League Secretaries once again for the tremendous support they give the publication despite being overworked themselves. This year, having taken on all the responsibilities of publisher, I also really appreciate the advice and very professional work put by the Typesetters, Printers and Paper suppliers. Their names all feature on 'the credits' pages as do the superb 'teams' of editorial contributors. They are backed up by other helpers who collect regional club information and these include Jeremy Biggs, Peter Bentley and Norman Matthews.

The Press too have been very kind to our efforts over the years. Whether it was an amusing feature in the Observer, a kind mention in a Frank Keating Guardian article (as shown on the back cover of this Directory) or a short but valued review in the regional papers. They are all appreciated, Thank You.

I have been very proud of the fact that The Football Association have been happy for the publication to be listed on their 'official' list and the help from all the staff at the F.A. offices has always been given cheefully. This support is a great boost when the pressure is on!

Circulars will be sent to all clubs but I suggest you read about the company and if you think they can help you with your particular problems then contact them as soon as possible.

A SPECIAL THANK YOU!

When compiling a book that receives contributions of varying size and style from about 800 sources the job of the typesetter is extremely difficult. So I would especially like to thank the quite superb staff of Sovereign Printing for masterminding this years 'jig-saw' and also show my appreciation to a very helpful team of typesetters which included: Busby Typesetting and Design, Exeter; Exe Valley Dataset, Exeter, Vine, Gorfin Ltd., Exmouth; Arnold Desmond, Langport; Typecast, Yeovil; Pronto Print and Barnicotts, Taunton and South West Typesetting Service, Sidmouth.

COMPOSITE GRANDSTANDS

As I mentioned in my Editorial Preface, Composite Grandstands have set up a unique consultancy service for all football clubs who want to improve their facilities in any way. Advice will be given to club officials to show how they can develop facilities to make money for clubs all year round. They will also show them the most economical way of building and how money can be raised to complete the work.

CONTENTS

SPECTATOR SAFETY IS PERHAPS THE GREATEST CHALLENGE FACING BRITISH FOOTBALL. BUT HOW CAN CLUBS ADDRESS THE PROBLEM WITHIN A SENSIBLE BUDGET?

COMPOSITE GRANDSTANDS IS A SPECIALIST COMPANY OFFERING AN ECONOMICAL SOLUTION.

MAKING A STAND FOR SAFETY

Building a stand is a major commitment for any football club...

Of course safety is important, but so too is overall cost. There's also the sheer scale of the project in terms of paperwork, organisation and planning.

After extensive research, Composite Grandstands has designed a complete package to provide safe and flexible spectator accommodation at lower cost than traditional 'one-off' stands.

Moreover, the company can handle the entire operation from planning permission and stand erection to electrics, plumbing and the installation of under-stand facilities. Clubs may choose as much or as little of this package as they require.

CONCRETE FOR SAFETY

All Composite Grandstands accommodation is built around a frame of pre-cast reinforced concrete.

In tests, the Composite Grandstands System was shown to exceed the requirements set out in the Home

Office's 'Guide to Safety at Sports Grounds.'

ECONOMY WITHOUT COMPROMISE

Composite Grandstands facilities are constructed from a wide range of proven standard components.

The large-scale pre-casting of these components ensures an economical solution. In addition, there are none of the costs and delays associated with on-site casting.

Yet the system provides so many options that the end result is tailored to the needs of the individual club.

In this way, Composite Grandstands ensures an economical solution without compromise on safety, appearance or long-term flexibility.

DESIGNED TO GROW

The 'components' approach also means that it's a simple matter to extend facilities when finance permits or additional accommodation is required. ▶

MAKING A STAND FOR SAFETY (continued)

fig. 1

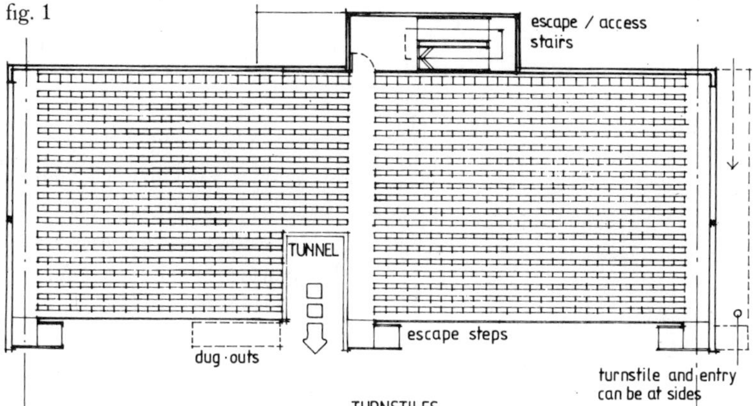

fig. 2

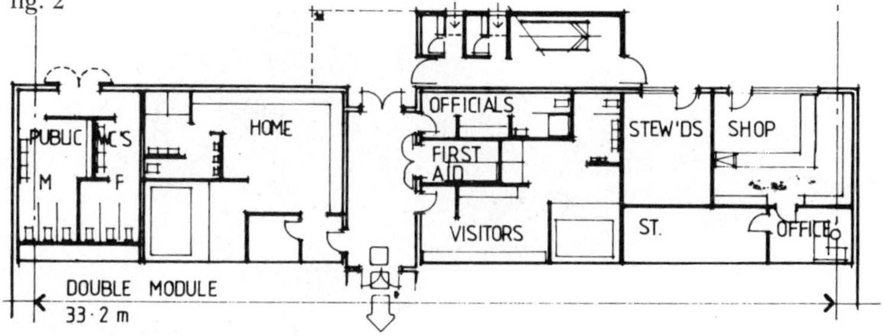

fig. 3

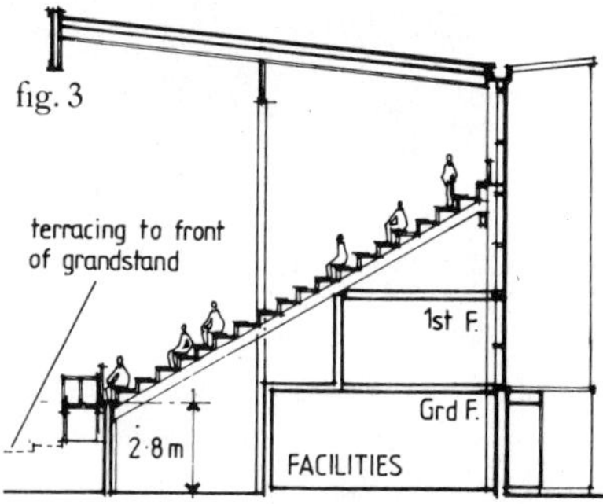

fig. 4

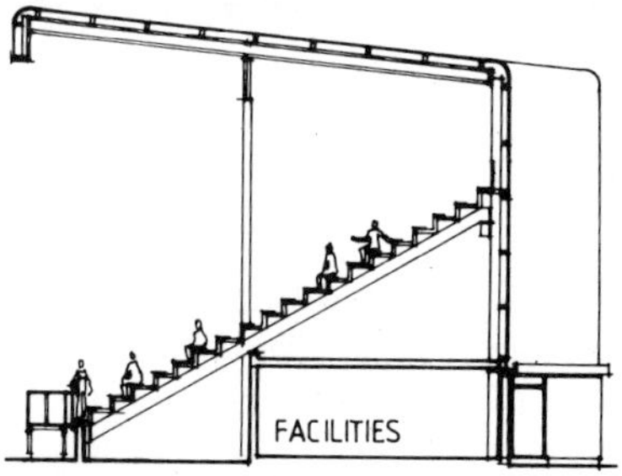

FLEXIBILITY. THE KEY TO ALL THE BEST PLANS

The basic unit of the versatile Composite Grandstands system is a stand with seating for 196 people. The illustration left (fig. 1) shows how such units can be combined.

The under-stand area can be used for changing facilities, officials accommodation and so on (fig. 2).

Alternatively, the space could be used for shops or offices; or left empty and fitted out at a later date.

Units can also provide two-storey accommodation (fig. 3), or be adjusted to suit the club's requirements (fig. 4).

A WINNING APPEARANCE

For most clubs, looks are important. Composite Grandstands can provide glazing, seating and coloured cladding. The company can also install fully-fitted under-stand facilities.

A COMPLETE SERVICE

Composite Grandstands is a subsidiary of Composite Holdings Limited, set up specifically to serve the sports and leisure market.

Composite Grandstands offers a complete building package, including site work, assistance with grants, planning permission and building regulations.

Clubs can choose as much or as little of this package as they wish. For a full consultation – without obligation – call Ted Langford on 0703 616712.

Or write to:
Composite Grandstands Limited,
Omega House, Southampton Road,
Eastleigh, Hants., SO5 5PB.

NON LEAGUE PHOTOGRAPHS OF THE YEAR

An exciting time for me each year is sorting out the wide range of photos sent in by 'Non-League' Football enthusiasts who tour the country throughout the season. Our 'senior photographer' is Eric Marsh who covers a wide range of games and supplies very comprehensive captions (although I wish he would stop phoning me at 7.30 in the morning to discuss them!). Without doubt the most travelled is Leo Hoenig who also has the eye for the picturesque. Peter Burrin certainly spots the 'funnies' and this year we seen to have had more photographic contributors than ever before. Thank you all very much. This section and the amusing ones that follow later on, are a tribute to all the photographers who tour the country in all weathers.

The atmosphere doesn't exist but the clarity and the superb action has been beautifully presented by Peter Burrin who caught Wembley's Mark Davis crashing home a superb goal past Boreham Wood goalkeeper Steve Walduck. This wins him 'The Best Non-League Action Photo of the Year' title.

For excitement you do need atmosphere and for a Non-League club there is nothing like playing at a League Club ground. When that ground is as famous as the Baseball Ground, Derby and it happens to be reasonably full, then a goal for 'the underdogs' is even more memorable. Leo Hoenig captured just this when he caught Ken McKenna at the top of his leap to head Telfort United's F.A. Cup equaliser in the 2nd Round match. This wins Leo 'The Most Exciting Non-League Photo of the Year'.

THE YEAR OF THE VOLLEY

Some excellent photos of crashing volleys have reached us from all over the country here are just a few.

The Dorset News feature Weymouth's leading scorer Mick Doherty as he just fails to get over his close range shot.

Hampton's Chris Hills fires in a piledriver which hits the Leatherhead goalkeeper. This action along with many more from Hampton's matches was sent in by Andrew Eggleton.

Still wearing the white shirt and dark shorts and firing in from the right is Barrow's Walter Nesbitt. His shot is watched by ex Barrow players Ken Gordon (left) and Steve Brooks of Morecambe in their A.T.S. Cup quarter Final won 4-0 by Barrow. This photo was supplied by Phil Yelland and taken by the North Western Evening Mail.

GOAL!

One of the Gola League's success stories last season was Enfield's Carl Richards. Here Tom Scott, who supplied some excellent action, shows Carl's second goal of his third hat trick (all away from home) scored at Scarborough.

A different view but well 'snapped' all the same. The Vauxhall Opel League score their winner at Burton Albion against The Multipart League and a proud League Secretary catches the action for posterity! Thank you Nick Robinson.

In darkest December it's not easy to capture the clearest of pictures. Indeed this one from Peter Burrin would have been outstanding in better light but he still shows Wembley's Tony Waugh scoring a delightful goal at Leytonstone.

BRAVERY IN THE BOX

You need courage to win the ball in the goal area and here Eric Marsh shows how Halesowen goalkeeper Alan Pemberton dives in to gain possession in the F.A. Vase against Southall.

Sutton United's Supporters Club Secretary Dave Farebrother who produces such superb magazines for his club, also takes good photos and in this one he caught Mark Golley making a spectacular attempt at a volley in the Uxbridge goalmouth in the A.C. Delco Final.

Probably the most consistent photographer in Non-League Football as far as quality is concerned is last years winner, Althrincham's John Rooney. Here he featured England and 'Alty' captain John Davison trying a diving header against Cheltenham Town. Unfortunately with photographers who only follow one client its difficult to use many of their photos but John's contributions are always first class.

HISTORY IS ABOUT TO BE MADE

It amazed me that the decision taken last season, which will probably have more effect on English football than any other since the introduction of professionalism, was virtually ignored by the National Press.

The decision to introduce a scheme of one up and one down between the Gola (now the G.M. Vauxhall Conference) and the Fourth Division has changed the attitude of 95% of clubs in this country.

Senior Semi-Professional football had put its own house in order by steadily developing a sensible 'pyramid' system of promotion and relegation which enabled any ambitious club in the country to work its way through 'the ranks provided it won its matches and possessed facilities of the required standard.

This whole operation didn't just form itself overnight. A lot of soul searching, sacrifice and negotiating around boardroom tables took place before to-day's pattern was set up. During those days a tremendous amount of responsibility was taken on by The Football Association's Adrian Titcombe. He covered thousands of miles as he spent hours talking to League officials about their place in a new national scheme. Often a place which didn't immediately appeal! It certainly wasn't easy to please everyone but in the end an acceptable format developed.

At the same time as Adrian Titcombe was helping the whole of football, there emerged a driving force who undoubtable inspired the cream of Semi-Professional Football to put it's own house very much in order. Jim Thompson, Maidstone's chairman, took up the reigns as leader of the Alliance Football League at the top of the pyramid and has campaigned for his member clubs with a single mindedness that has brought great progress.

Enterprising sponsorships, weekend conventions at the end of the season, leading the way with allocation of points, high standards of administration and an acceptance into the football pools: all these things plus the very healthy appearance of member club's grounds and their performances in the F.A. Cup frightened the Third and Fourth Division clubs to death. Perhaps Jim had inadvertantly been too successful! Whatever it was, having accepted Wigan Athletic and Wimbledon, The Football League suddenly closed ranks and after the inception of The Alliance and its very sensible pyramid not one new club was voted in.

Negotiations continued with The Football League of course but it wasn't until the big clubs (who had always agreed with an Alliance 'link' in public but had never pushed for it when it mattered) decided they wanted a Super League or a showdown with The Football League. Then, at last, the vital link — that suddenly everyone seemed to agree with — became reality.

Jim Thompson and his excellent committee and clubs must have felt elated. Adrian Titcombe and his colleagues at The Football Association must have been tremendously satisfied.

And I must say that, having had the priviledge of setting up the first Non-League sponsorship for Rothmans (with Jimmy Hill's idea of three points for a win), having been able to help encourage the introduction of Semi-professional Internationals and having 'nagged' away about automatic promotion and relegation with the Fourth Division since the First F.A. Non-League Football Annual nine years ago, I am very very pleased indeed!

This season will see the most competetive challenge for that all important top place in the new 'G.M. Vauxhall Conference'. I only hope that 'silly money' isn't paid to players who may neither be worth it nor may work for it. Such quality clubs as Altrincham, Enfield and Telford United have already proved their worth consistently over the last seven years and I hope it is their standards that their colleagues will attempt to emulate, while at the same time aiming for The Football League.

Last season saw a superb Enfield side deservedly take the Gola championships, a vintage Altrincham complete a very professional season's work with a place in the F.A. Cup Fourth Round (including a victory at First Division Birmingham City) and a Trophy triumph at Wembley and a quite remarkable Welsh Cup 'run' by Kidderminster Harriers who lost in the final to Wrexham after a replay, having beaten Newport County, Swansea City and Hereford United. Bangor City from the Multipart League also hit the headlines with a first round European Cup Winners victory over Fredrikstad of Norway and a very plucky and respectable 0-3 defeat by the 'giants' of Atletico Madrid over two legs.

This is what the game should be about! A happy day out for young and old as Weymouth fans look forward to the match Photo: Dorset News

Barrow continued their up and down connection with the senior competition but, with Ray Wilkie now in charge, who will bet against them bouncing straight back from the Multipart League? Wycombe Wanderers found the consistency needed just too much to survive in last season's Gola League but they were desperately unlucky to lose their star goalscorer half way through the season and to be the only one of four clubs on 36 points to go down on goal difference. However this means that Sutton United, another excellent club with fine traditions, will have their chance in the national competition.

Dartford, after all sorts of internal problems, lost most of their staff and their senior place to Welling United, one of the pyramid's success stories who will be looking forward to proving themselves at the senior level while the evergreen John Bartley, who has scored more goals than any other current semi-professional, will be a player to watch.

5,348!

One of the most amazing phenomenons of modern semi-professional football is the position where Yeovil Town find themselves. They were last season's best supported club outside the Football League and actually attracted 5,348 to an ordinary Vauxhall Opel League match against Sutton United but they are not yet in with a chance of challenging for a League place.

Worcester City too, with superb support, cannot get out of the Southern League and the message here is that you can sign all the big names available but, if the team work isn't right, results don't come. Hopefully for the good of this level of football both these famous and exciting clubs will get things right this year and we will see then back where they belong.

The only black cloud over the pyramid system at present is the link between the very successful Multipart League and its extremely well administered 'feeder leagues' the North West Counties and Northern Counties (East). Hopefully this will be sorted out soon.

Talking of the North West Counties; what a tremendous record Clitheroe have set up, having won the third, second and first Division championships in consecutive years.

In general, Gola League clubs dominated the F.A. Trophy although Leek Town certainly enjoyed themselves but the interesting statistic was highlighted by the attendances. While the Trophy games were still well supported, the F.A. Vase games attracted excellent crowds, culminating with a Wembley Final attendance superior to that recorded for their 'big brothers in the Trophy Final.

WELL DONE WALES!

Sadly the Four Nations Tournament wasn't held this year but special congratulations should go to the Welsh side who beat the pride of English Semi-Professional football 3-1 in an excellent match at Merthyr.

In general, attendances (especially those in cup football) held up while I should imagine more clubs than ever before raised funds to improve their grounds. The spirit within practically all Semi-Professional clubs is still one of great comradeship while everyone is still dedicated to progression on and off the field.

As I have said year after year, this level of football gives you the dedicated competitiveness, the comfortable facilities with ample food and drink plus the spirit and hospitality for which I am sure all football lovers are looking.

As clubs in such competitions as the London Spartan, Central Midlands and Wessex Leagues set out on their way to the top, at least they know that the route is open to them and we all know that they should enjoy themselves on the way.

Tony Williams.

A FUNNY THING HAPPENED ON THE WAY TO THE CLUBHOUSE!

Linesman: Am I seeing things?

Referee: (Bob French) Now just watch it No.8, I know you're there.

(Wembley's Dave Moynihan) No. 8: Just looking for a ball Ref!

Look out Robert Maxwell is here! (Southend Manor F.C. Photo Robert Errington)

Fancy letting a winning goal in with two minutes to go especially when we had been such an attraction (Banbury lose at Chalfont St. Peter)
Photo: Bob Imber

Don't you think they should have built a proper tunnel? (Weymouth v Dorchester)

Was it something we ate in the pre match meal (Enfield before Altrincham Semi-Final)
Photo: Andy Cussell

You see I'm the danger man! Godalming Town v Farnham Town
Photo: Eric Marsh

Look Boss any fella with three arms can send you the wrong way. (Frickley Athletic v Hyde United in Friendly). Photo Chris Goodale

Excuse me Pal, do you fancy a 'sliced brown' (Enfield v Northwich) Photo: Tom Scott

Do you think they ought to have put the hedge behind the stand? (Action at Barking, with John Bolle challenging a visiting keeper)

O.K. No. 11 you think it's 10 yards, but if you don't move back you'll be in the glasshouse (Danson v Banstead Athletic) Photo: Nick Robinson

How can you fail to give a penalty Ref? (Calne Town v Hungerford Town) Photo: Leo Hoenig

If you can't see it Ref you must be blind! (Berks & Bucks Cup Final Aylesbury v Wycombe)
Photo Shaun Twitchen

Two minutes gone and he's got cramp! (Hungerford v Dorking)
Photo Newbury Weekly News

I'm sure we shouldn't have seven in the wall on the half way line! (Royston in wall v Heybridge Swifts).
Photo Martyn Annetts Mid-Anglia Newspapers

ONE FOR THE READERS

The best two captions for this photo will earn the senders a free copy of next years Directory (Danson v Banstead Athletic in F.A. Vase).
Photo Nick Robinson

Poor Blackpool, have been beaten twice at home by Altrincham in the F.A. Cup in the last two seasons. Here their defence can only watch as Jeff enjoys another special 'Alty moment to remember'. Photo John Rooney.

PLAYER OF THE YEAR
Jeff Johnson
(Altrincham and England)

When deciding on a 'Player of the Year' one often turns to goalscorers as the obvious candidates but, despite last season producing a number of excellent achievements notably the incredible record of Kim Casey, there was no doubt that the award should go to a man who was expected to retire from senior semi-professional football and who had achieved just about everything there was to achieve in our level of football.

JEFF JOHNSON probably had his most momentous season of all at the age of 36 as he enjoyed Altrincham's F.A. Cup run which included a victory on the ground of a First Division club and an F.A. Trophy triumph at Wembley. He also played again for England and finished his career at the top.

Having worked at close quarters with Jeff during the Four Nations Tournament both at home and abroad I would describe him as a classic strong silent type who doesn't suffer fools easily. He has been completely dedicated to his club and country and he always gives 150%. It was no surprise that, however Jeff had been playing in domestic football just before an International Tournament, the England manager would always want him in the squad.

During the year I received a letter from an Altrincham supporter who described how he felt about Jeff's contribution to Alty's perpetual success. I am sure he speaks for all Altrincham supporters.

STATISTICAL ANALYSIS

Altrincham debut: 4th December 1976 v Gainsborough Trinity (Home)

Total Appearances: 481 (+7 sub)

Total Goals: 142

Season by Season:

1976-77:	35 apps	11 goals	(forward)
1977-78:	60 apps	35 goals	(forward)
1978-79:	58 apps	30 goals	(forward)
1979-80:	53 apps	11 goals	(midfield)
1980-81:	54 apps	11 goals	(midfield)
1981-82:	58 apps	13 goals	(midfield)
1983-84:	32 apps	10 goals	(midfield)
1984-85:	41 apps	4 goals	(defence)
1985-86:	46 apps	3 goals	(defence)

Honours

Player of the Year

Hyde Utd:	74-75, 75-76
Altrincham:	77-78, 79-80, 85-86
A.P.L. Championships:	79-80, 80-81
F.A. Trophy Winners:	77-78, 85-86
A.P.L. Cup Winners:	80-81
Ches. Sen. Cup Winners:	81-82
A.P.L. Shield Winners:	81-82
N.P.L. Shield Winners:	79-80
International Caps:	15
Goals:	3

MERIT AWARD WINNERS

KIM CASEY (Kidderminster): Wherever Kim has played he has scored goals. Having represented England schools at Under 18 level he has enjoyed his football successes mainly under the management of Graham Allner. His prolific goalscoring feats have benefited A.P. Leamington and of course Kidderminster Harriers. His full total last season was 73 and these goals brought him England Semi-Pro recognition and caps. You can hardly call Kidderminster Harriers outsiders but watch out for them in the 'Conference' next season and don't miss a chance to see Kim Casey.

PAUL SHIRTLIFF (Frickley Athletic): When players leave the Football League having sampled life right at the top it is always a nice surprise when they still show enthusiasm for the game at semi-professional level. Paul Shirtliff had a spell at Sheffield Wednesday where he left his brother to the excitement of the First Division, and last season his outstanding full back performances earned him a place in the England side and of course helped his club to their best ever season.

CYRIL WHITESIDE (Chairman of Clitheroe F.C.): For those of us outside Lancashire the remarkable performances of the Clitheroe club who have won the championships of the North West Counties, Divisions Three, Two and One in consecutive seasons, has probably gone unnoticed, However, anyone in the game will recognise just what hard work and dedication is needed to achieve this record at any level and over the last three years Chairman Cyril Whiteside has led this memorable ascent.

BARRIE WILLIAMS (Football Manager, Sutton United): Last season saw the Surrey club pick up their usual quota of silverware as the Vauxhall-Opel Championship, The A.C. Delco Cup and County Senior Cup were won. With promotion accepted into the New G.M. Vauxhall Conference the club is about to set out on yet another exciting stage of it's history and in the last years Barrie Williams has been it's guiding light as far as football matters were concerned. His personal standards reflect in the attitudes of his players, coaching staff and even the superb Sutton supporters. The club is a credit to the game.

REGIONAL CLUB AWARDS

North East: GATESHEAD. When a club suffers relegation it often takes a few seasons before the bruises heal. To lose ones place in the Gola League as Gateshead did, means a very big difference to life, as the 'National' atmosphere is lost weekly routine could become a little flat. However Gateshead stormed into the fray last season and fought off challenges from firstly Morecombe and then Marine while also leaving quality clubs such as Gainsborough Trinity and Burton Albion a long way behind. With a superb stadium it can only be hoped that in their next spell in senior semi-professional football the public will give them the impetus to do the North East proud.

North West: ALTRINCHAM. If a semi-professional club takes on First Division opposition in the Third Round of the F.A. Cup away from home you can hardly expect a good result. so when Altrincham beat Birmingham City and no-one really seemed to be surprised it speaks volumes for the non-league club. Altrincham are the aristocrats of their level of the game and they had the experience and attitude necessary to cope with this cup run and storm straight into a Trophy campaign which finished trimphantly at Wembley.

Captain of Kidderminster Harriers in their best ever season has been Graham Mackenzie. He is seen here crashing a dangerous ball into the Wrexham penalty area during the Welsh Cup Final in North Wales. Graham also finished at the top of his clubs appearance chart in their memorable centenary season. Photo Leo Hoenig.

Midlands: KIDDERMINSTER HARRIERS. A club that scores 203 goals in a season and reaches the Final of the Welsh Cup must be good to watch. The fact that it was the Harriers Centenary was also appropriate as they also won two County Cups. The club staged a Semi-Professional International and two of their star strikers, Kim Casey (73 goals) and Paul Davies (44 goals) won caps, so all in all it was not surprising that attendances were doubled in the second half of the season.

Eastern Counties: WISBECH TOWN. As someone who has been closely connected with a club who has failed twice at the semi-final stage of the F.A. Vase, I know how the Wisbech personnel must be feeling this summer. However it is still a superb achievement for the club from The Eastern Counties to reach this stage twice and also to attract such excellent crowds during their cup 'runs'. Hopefully the club will go from strength to strength and will use the experience of the last two seasons as a stepping stone to success.

Home Counties: ENFIELD: Just as Liverpool annd Manchester United are expected to win something in senior football so are Enfield and Altrincham in their level of the game. Eddie McCluskey is a very intelligent manager who knows the semi-professional game inside out and you won't see him wasting good fees or salaries on players who are not 100%. Last season the quality of football produced placed them way above everyone else and if they lost out a fraction in the blood and thunder of cup games, I can only forcast they will get that aspect of their game right next season. Enfield were worthy Gola Champions.

West of England and Wales: BARRY TOWN. We have included Wales in this area this year which possibly is unfortunate for Exmouth Town who won the Western League Title again but the tremendous season enjoyed by Barry Town certainly deserves recognition. They completed their Abacus Welsh League Season unbeaten after 32 games and won the championship for the fourth consecutive year. The club's move from the Southern League seems to have rejuvinated all personel although it may be difficult to keep this impetus up.

Arthur Clark (League Chairman) on right and Graham Falconer (Drybrough) sign a new three-year sposorship deal.

INTERNATIONAL AND F.A. REPRESENTATIVE FOOTBALL

FA REPRESENTATIVE COMMITTEE

Match Committee: B. Mulrenan Chairman: C. G. Oakes
Vice-Chairman: A. E. Brown; B. Clark; F. Hannah;
Lt.-Cdr. H. A. Sheppard; C. H. Wilcox

A YEAR OF REBUILDING

Since the abolition of the 'amateur' the climax to the season for England Senior semi-professional players has become the 'Four Nations Tournament'. After a sad gap when there were no honours for the 'Non-League' stars the competition started in England in 1979 and since then Holland, Italy and Scotland have joined in the lively and enjoyable 'battle'.

This year the Italians, because their season's duration was modified to improve preparation for the World Cup, were unable to agree dates and sadly the tournament was postponed.

Perhaps this may have suited England manager Kevin Verity who invited Mick Wadsworth, the F.A.'s North West Regional Coach to join him as assistant and was due for some rebuilding to a side that had faded under pressure against the Scots in Holland in 1985.

Mid-season weather hardly helped his cause, however, and only five F.A. XI games could be used as England trials. When the Welsh encounter had to be faced, Kevin had a number of established players injured, but his new-look team certainly should have put the game out of our opponents grasp well before the incredible heroics of the two Welsh heroes.

How Tom Morgan the Aberystwyth winger failed to become a Football League Club regular is beyond me, and his general performance and quite incredible goal will be long remembered by everyone at Merthyr when Wales recorded an excellent victory on a very wet evening. If one outstanding performance wasn't enough, the local club's goalkeeper Gary Wager turned on a display that reminded one of John Swannell in his early years. (For the younger readers John was England Amateurs' goalkeeper in a record-breaking 64 games whose display for Hendon against Whitley Bay at Sunderland in 1966 has long been rated as one of the all- time great displays). Sadly, only a few hundred saw Gary flying around his goalmouth with great skill and bravery. Over 20,000 were at Roker Park.

England's two games against the Republic of Ireland brought more satisfactory results and a chance for Kevin Verity to 'blood' a number of new names to the England scene. Hopefully, with a better winter for preparation and the experience gained this season, the England team will be difficult to beat in Scotland next June. Why not take a week's holiday and enjoy some excellent football, happy company and breathtaking Scottish countryside by spending seven days at the tournament?

My thanks goes to Paul Walker who has loyally followed the England team for 'The Daily Star', and has not only submitted excellent reports on England matches but has given the semi- professional game much appreciated excellent coverage in his national newspaper throughout recent seasons.

Tony Williams

F.A. REPRESENTATIVE XI
RESULTS 1976-86

F.A. XI v Cambridge University

		FA XI	CU
1966/77 Cambridge Utd.	W	1	0
1977/78 Cambridge Utd.	W	4	0
1978/79 Cambridge Utd.	W	6	1
1979/80 Cambridge City	W	2	1
1980/81 Cambridge City	D	1	1
1981/82 Cambridge Utd.	D	1	1
1982/83 Cambridge City	L	1	2
1983/84 Cambridge Utd.	L	0	2
1984/85 Cambridge Utd.	D	3	3
1085/86 Cambridge City	D	0	0

F.A. XI v Oxford University

		FA XI	OU
1976/77 Oxford Utd.	W	1	0
1977/78 Oxford Utd.	W	4	0
1978/79 Oxford City	W	3	1
1079/80 Oxford City	W	6	1
1980/81 Witney Town	W	3	1
1981/82 Oxford City	L	0	2
1982/83 Oxford City	W	7	0
1983/84 Oxford City	W	7	2
1984/85 Witney Town	W	4	2

F.A. XI v London University

		FA XI	LU
1975/76 Kingstonian	W	4	1
1976/77 Wealdstone	W	3	0
1977/78 Met. Police	W	2	0
1978/79 Harrow Bor.	W	5	1
1979/80 Hayes	W	3	0
1980/81 Sutton Utd.	W	3	1
1982/83 Tooting & M	W	7	0
1983/84 Dagenham	W	4	1

F.A. XI v British Colleges Sports Association

		FA XI	BC
1975/76 Cheltenham T.	L	0	1
1976/77 Cheltenham T.	W	4	0
1977/78 Cheltenham T.	L	0	1
1979/80 Stafford Rg.	W	2	0
1980/81 Cancelled due to bad weather			
1981/82 Nuneaton B.	W	4	3
1092/83 York City	W	4	1
1983/84 Cheltenham T.	W	4	2
1984/85 Cheltenham T.	D	1	1
1985/86 Kidderminster H.	D	0	0

F. A. v Royal Air Force

		FA XI	RAF
1975/76 Wealdstone	W	2	1

F.A. XI v Combined Services

		FA XI	CS
1976/77 Army Stadium	D	2	2
1977/78 Aldershot	D	1	1
1978/79 Aldershot	D	1	1
1979/80 Aldershot	L	1	2
1980/81 Aldershot	D	1	1
1982/83 Aldershot	L	0	2
1983/84 Aldershot	W	3	2

F.A. XI v South West Counties

		FA XI	SWC
1977/78 Exeter City	L	O	1
1978/79 Southampton	W	1	0
1979/80 Bath City	W	5	1
1981/82 Swindon	W	2	1
1983/84 Southampton	L	2	3

F.A. v Isthmian League

		FA XI	IL
1979/80 Dagenham	L	0	3
1984/85 Met. Police	W	2	1
1985/86 Met. Police	L	2	4

F.A. XI v Western League

		FA XI	WL
1980/81 Frome Town	D	0	0
1982/83 Frome Town	D	2	2
1984/85 Taunton Town	W	2	0

F.A. XI v Northern League

		FA XI	NL
1976/77 Blyth Spartans	L	2	3
1977/78 Consett	L	2	3
1978/79 North Shields	L	0	2
1979/80 Blyth Spartans	L	1	3
1980/81 Consett	D	0	0
1981/82 North Shields	W	2	0
1982/83 Bishop Auck.	D	1	1
1983/84 Darlington	L	0	1
1984/85 Blyth Spartans	L	0	1
1985/86 Whitby Town	W	1	0

F.A. XI v Northern Premier League

		FA XI	NPL
1980/81 Runcorn	D	0	0
1981/82 Gainsbgh. T.	D	1	1
1982/83 Burton Albion	D	3	3
1983/84 Barrow	L	0	2
1984/85 Stafford Rang.	L	1	2
1985/86 Witton Albion	W	1	0

F.A. XI v Amateur Football Alliance

		FA XI	AFA
1975/76 Dulwich	W	4	0
1976/77 Leytonstone	D	2	2
1977/78 Wealdstone	W	4	1
1978/79 Met. Police	W	5	2
1979/80 Met. Police	W	2	1
1980/81 Met. Police	W	5	1
1981/82 Harrow Borgh	D	1	1
1982/83 Enfield	W	2	1
1984/85 Sutton Utd.	L	0	2

F.A. XI v Universities Athletic Union

		FA XI	UAU
1975/76 York City	D	2	2
1976/77 York City	D	2	2
1977/78 Altrincham	W	2	1
1978/79 Alrincham	D	1	1
1079/80 Altrincham	W	4	2
1980/81 Cancelled due to weather			
1981/82 Altrincham	W	3	0
1982/83 Nuneaton B	W	4	0
1983/84 Altrincham	W	5	0
1984/85 Worcester City	D	0	0

F.A. XI v British Police

		FA XI	BP
1979/80 Bramshill	D	1	1
1980/81 Bramshill	W	1	0
1982/83 Bramshill	W	2	0

F.A. XI v Jersey F.A.

		FA XI	JFA
1980/81 St. Hellier	W	3	0

F.A. XI v Lincolnshire F.A.

		FA XI	LFA
1980/81 Boston Utd.	D	0	0

F.A. XI v Middlesex F.A.

		FA XI	MCFA
1983/84 Harrow Bor	D	0	0

F.A. XI v Oxfordshire F.A.

		FA XI	OCFA
1983/84 Oxford City	W	3	1

F.A. XI v Cambridgeshire F.A.

		FA XI	CFA
1984/85 Cambridge Utd.	W	2	1

F.A. v English Schools F.A. (U-18)

		FA XI	ESFA
1984/85 Boston United	L	3	4

F.A. XI v Suffolk F.A.

		FA XI	SFA
1984/85 Ipswich Town	W	4	3

F.A. Representative Matches 1985-86

F.A. XI 2 (Ferguson, Link) Vauxhall-Opel League 4

Andy Pape (Enfield), David Jacques (Dartford), Steve McCargo (Wealdstone), Paul Bowgett (Wealdstone), Anton Vircavs (Sycombe Wanderers). Ian Ferguson (Maidstone United), Tony Burman (Dartford), Duncan Horton (Maidstone United), Declan Link (Wycombe Wanderers), Micky Dingwall (Dartford), Colin Barnes (Maidstone United). Reserves: John Glover (Maidstone United) for Link.

F.A. XI 0 Cambridge University 0

Stephen Foyster (Gorleston). Simon Haigh (Ortonians), Paul Magee (61 F.C. Luton), Mel Mattless (Wisbech Town), Jim Jackson (Bourne Town), Jamie Brightly (Wisbech Town), John Hines (Holbeach Town), Steve Russell (Vauxhall Motors), Peter Jackson (Thringstone), Gary Grogan (Cambridge City), Andy Hollis (Ramsey Town). Substitutes: Keith Moore (Cambridge City) for Magee. Des Perry (Thringstone) for Hollis.

F.A. XI 1 (Williams) The Multipart League 0
David Ryan (Northwich Victoria), Antone Joseph (Telford United) [Captain], Stephen Nelson (Northwich Victoria), Alec Davies (Stalybridge Celtic), Neil Williams (Warrington Town), Gary Butterworth (Stalybridge Celtic), Doug Newton (Altrincham), Peter Conning (Altrincham), Frank Dolan (Warrington Town), Ray Redshaw (Northwich Victoria), Steve Blake (Stalybridge Celtic). Substitute: Neil Cook (Warrington Town).

F.A. XI 1 (Semley) Drybroughs Northern League 0
Tony Harrison (Gateshead), Paul Stanley (Matlock Town), Neil Thompson (Scarborough), Russ Wilcox (Frickley Athletic), Malcolm Wright (Frickley Athletic), Mark Rhodes (Matlock Town), Gary Clayton (Burton Albion), Peter Howey (Frickley Athletic), David Hoyland (Gainsborough Trinity), Alan Semley (Matlock Town), Paul Wilson (Frickley Athletic). Substitute: Ian Helliwell (Matlock Town) for Hoyland.

F.A. XI 0 British Polytechnics Sports Association 0
M. Martin (Bedworth United), P. Cooper (Bromsgrove Rovers), M. Woodall (Kidderminster Harriers), S. Jackson (Bedworth United), A. Kurila (Bromsgrove Rovers), M. Hazelwood (Dudley Town), A. O'Dowd (Kidderminster Harriers) [Captain], M. Gavin (Kidderminster Harriers), M. Tuoy (Kidderminster Harriers), M. Dunkley (Bromsgrove Rovers), R. Shilvock (Bromsgrove Rovers). Substitutes: C. Moss (Stourbridge) for Hazelwood, A. Reece (Stourbridge) for Kurila, M. Lander (Gloucester City) for O'Down, C. Jones (Kidderminster Harriers) for Jackson.

THE INTERNATIONAL SEASON

England Semi-Professional Team Manager, Kevin Verity, named the following Squad of 16 players as well as Non-travelling reserves to play Wales at Merthyr on Tuesday 18th March.

A. Pape (Enfield), D. Richardson **(Maidstone United)**, D. Constantine **(Witton Albion)**, J. Davison **(Altrincham)**, D. Howell **(Enfield)**, J. Johnson **(Altrincham)**, R. Wilcox **(Frickley Athletic)**, A. Joseph **(Telford United)**, S. Smithers **(Nuneaton Borough)**, M. Stephens **(Sutton United)**, P. Walker **(Blyth Spartans)**, N. Ashford **(Enfield)**, K. Casey **(Kidderminster Harriers)**, P. Davies **(Kidderminster Harriers)**, C. Richards **(Enfield)**, P. Wilson **(Frickley Athletic)**.
Non-travelling reserves: R. Fearon **(Sutton United)**, P. Bowgett **(Wealdstone)**, K. Brown **(Bath City)**, R. Dawson **(Kettering Town)**, T. Agana **(Weymouth)**, D. Buchanan **(Blyth Spartans)**, M. Doherty **(Weymouth)**, S. Tapley **(Wealdstone)**.

Wales 3, England 1

by Paul Walker, *Daily Star*

England fielded six new caps in the semi-pro international against Wales at Merthyr Tydfil on March 18th but finished rather surprisingly beaten 3-1.

They were confronted by an exceptional display by Welsh 'keeper **Gary Wager**, playing on his home pitch, but wasted a string of chances.

Wales, however, deserve full praise for a quality team performance in appalling conditions.

England boss **Kevin Verity** gave first caps to Frickley pair **Russ Wilcox** and **Paul Wilson**, Blyth's midfield man **Paul Walker** (no relation) and the free-scoring Kidderminster strikers **Kim Casey** and **Paul Davies**, plus Weymouth's **Mick Doherty,** a second half substitute.

It was also interesting to note that Maidstone 'keeper **Derek Richardson**, who has been out of favour for the previous seven internationals, started the game, with **Andy Pape**, who won his place in Holland the previous summer, coming on as a second half substitute.

Full-back **Dave Constantine**, who had played much of the season in the N.W. Counties League for Stalybridge, retained his position following a move into the higher grade Multipart League with Witton Albion.

England started in fine style as **Wilson's** left wing run and cross ended with **Davies** turning his shot over the top, and then **Wilson**, himself, hit a post.

Casey, who last wore an England shirt for the Under-18 schools side, was put clear after 39 minutes, but was thwarted by a fine challenge from **Wager** who again did enough five minutes from the break to deny **Wilson**, also on a clear run at goal.

England should have been two or three ahead, but found themselves one down at the break. **Tom Morgan**, the Aberystwyth winger who caused England no end of trouble at Newtown two years previously, got away on the right and crossed for Cwmbran striker **Mark Grypton** to score on his debut.

Five minutes after the break it was two. and England were really in trouble.

It was a goal fit to win any match, an absolute cracker from **Morgan**. A lightening break from defence saw **Morgan** running on to **Paul Preece's** fine pass and from fully 30 yards he confounded everyone with a brilliant volley over the advancing **Richardson**.

England, to their credit, came straight back and a **Casey** cross caused Skipper **Derek Redwood** to make a mistake on the far post and let in **Davies** to score.

The veteran **Jeff Johnson** came on for Walker to win his 16th England cap while **Pape** took over from **Richardson**.

Casey could have equalised after 66 minutes, but **Wager** again saved superbly at his feet and the Welsh were home and dry a minute later when **Jim Smith** was allowed to pick his way through a packed area to net the third from close range.

Weymouth's **Mick Doherty** got his first cap as **Casey's** replacement, and then **Wager** pulled off two spectacular saves from long range free-kicks from skipper **John Davison**, winning his 22nd cap to increase his own international record.

Davison's Altrincham club mate, **Johnson**, had a couple of brave efforts before **Anton Joseph** replaced **Micky Stephen's**, back in the side after a four-year absence, with just three minutes left.

Wales, though, were now in full command and deserved victors which said much for boss **Terry Casey's** planning and organisation. It was nice, too, to see **Casey** and **Verity**, old friends from their days when both were F.A. regional coaches, sitting in the stand discussing the game.

Casey was once assistant manager to Howard Wilkinson for the ENGLAND team, before returning to Wales as director of coaching. Victory for him, his second against England on Welsh soil, must have been particularly sweet.

Wales: Gary Wager (Merthyr); Derek Redwood (Barry), Bryn Jones (Colwyn Bay), Ray Merrill (Lex), Dave Humphries (Aberystwyth); Tom Morgan (Aberystwyth), Alan Sullivan (Barry), Jim Smith (Colwyn Bay), Paul Preece (Sully); Garry Davies (Sully), Mark Grypton (Cwmbran). Substitutes: Ian Sutton (Sully) for Grypton. Bob Smith (Barry) for Davies.

England: Derek Richardson (Maidstone); Dave Constantine (Witton), David Howell (Enfield), Russ Wilcox (Frickley), John Davison (Altrincham); Mickey Stephens (Sutton United), Paul Walker (Blyth), Tim Smithers (Nuneaton); Kim Casey (Kidderminster), Paul Wilson (Frickley), Paul Davies (Kidderminster).

Substitutes: Jeff Johnson (Altrincham) for Walker. Andy Pape (Enfield) for Richardson. Mick Doherty (Weymouth) for Casey. Anton Joseph (Telford) for Stephens.

FOOTNOTE: The game also marked **Mick Wadsworth's** international debut... as England's assistant manager.

Wadsworth had been a free-scoring striker with Frickley and Gainsborough before gaining recognition as coach to Barnsley's youth team.

He was appointed N.W. regional F.A. coach during last season, and snapped up by Verity to assist with the England set-up.

England's Irish Win Double

A season that looked like fizzling out when the Four Nations Tournament was called off, ended for England's semi-pro side with two wins in three days against the Republic of Ireland.

The two Irish dates were organised at short notice to fill the gap left by the postponed tournament in Scotland, and proved to be a significant and enjoyable weekend for both squads, based at the Post House Hotel, Great Barr.

The Irish, who only play one game a season (against the Scots) at this level, sent over their all-amateur junior side, managed by the likeable **Martin Lynch**.

The level of opposition was hard to judge beforehand, and although they were technically inferior throughout, they made up for their lack of experience with brave, gutsy showings in both matches... leading in both!

For England boss **Kevin Verity**, it was another couple of steps in a transition period. Over the weekend he gave six players their first caps, to make it 11 over the three games England played during the season.

It was also nice to see previously unfashionable clubs getting their players through to the top level. Frickley's excellent season was mirrored by the fact that they had three new caps, with defenders **Russ Wilcox** and **Paul Shirtliff** making their mark, along with **Paul Wilson**.

Kidderminster's fre-scoring front pair **Kim Casey** and **Paul Davies** made their debuts, along with Weymouth's strikers **Tony Agana** and **Mick Doherty**. Blyth, too, had a couple of lads to keep up the tradition set by **David Clarke**, with **Paul Walker** and **David Buchanan** making their first appearances.

Stafford's **Gary Simpson** played in both games against thge Irish, while Burton's **Gary Clayton** played well in the second game.

Verity now has a large pool of players, that he knows would do England proud when Scotland finally stage the 'Four Nations' Tournament' next Spring.

One sad note was the end of **Jeff Johnson's** international career. At 35 he had won a Trophy winner's medal again, turned in brilliant performances in Altrincham's famous Cup run, and was given two more caps against Ireland to make his final total 17.

In semi-retirement at club level now, he had been determined to end his season in an England shirt, and it was tragic that a serious knee injury curtailed his last match at Nuneaton. He will be sadly missed. Well done, Jeff, you did your country proud.

England 2 (Johnson Casey) Republic of Ireland 1 (Tracey) (at Kidderminster 24th May 1985)

England made desperately hard work of winning the first match 2-1 at Kidderminster on 24th May.

They dominated the match after giving away a silly goal after just two minutes, and it wasn't until 11 minutes from time that they finally forced their way level.

Then, with five minutes to go, **Kim Casey** sent his home fans wild with the winner, his first goal for his country and 74th of an amazing season for the stocky striker.

Two new caps were in boss **Kevin Verity's** starting line-up, and two more got their chance as substitutes.

In right back **Paul Shirtliff** we witnessed one of the most impressive debuts you could ask for in an England shirt. The Frickley defender, who had been forced to pull out of the squad for the game in Wales through work commitments, grabbed his chance the second time around with both hands.

His tackling and distribution were first class and one stunning run from his own half which ended with a 30-yarder against the post suggests that the No. 2 shirt is his for a long time to come.

Upfront Enfield's top scorer **Carl Richards** got his first chance, and showed remarkable ball control and mobility for a big man, keeping the Irish best player-centre half **Martin Kerr**, fully occupied.

The Irish got off to a dream start with a second minute goal, following a horrific mix-up between 'keeper **Andy Pape** and his Enfield colleague **David Howell**.

Pape threw the ball out to **Howell**, who, under pressure, stepped into the area to push it back. **Pape** picked the ball up and was penalised because he had received the ball back without it going out of the box. **Eddie Doyle** tapped the free kick to **John Tracey**, and he cracked a six yard shot past the wall.

From then on **Pape** didn't have a thing to do as England drove forward. **Jeff Johnson**, had an overhead kick clear the bar following **Micky Stephens'** corner, **Casey** had a shot deflected wide by **Declan Daly** and skipper **John Davison** blasted wide from 20 yards.

Richards, Russ Wilcox, Johnson again, and **Noel Ashford** all went close, but the battling Irish held on until the break.

The chances kept coming, and **Verity** must have felt he was watching a re-run of the Welsh game a few months earlier.

Eire keeper Gary Mattews punches clear from Noel Asford

Photo: Leo Hoenig

The England squad before the Eire International at Nuneaton

Photo: Leo Hoenig

Tony Agana, one of the 'finds' of the season from Weymouth, scores England's winner at Nuneaton

Photo: Leo Hoenig

A goal for Frickley centre back Russ Wilcox (who has since signed for Northampton Town) as England equalise against Eire at Nuneaton

Photo: Leo Hoenig

Casey (twice), **Shirtliff**, and **Wilcox** all had good openings. **Gary Simpson** came on for his debut to replace **Stephens** after 62 minutes and set about inspiring England, who had begun to look a little frustrated and ragged.

The equaliser finally came after 79 minutes. **Paul Walker's** curling corner to the near post was nodded in by **Johnson,** and before the re-start **Walker** was replaced by his Blyth team mate **David Buchanan**, for his first international.

With five minutes to go the deserved winner arrived. Johnson's long throw was touched on by **Wilcox**, and **Casey** gleefully headed home from close range.

There was time for **Buchanan** to force his way clear, only for **John Grace** to save bravely at his feet. The inevitable **Casey** saw his shot from the rebound kicked off the line by **Daly**.

England: Pape (Enfield); Shirtliff (Frickley), Wilcox (Frickley), Howell (Enfield), Davison (Altrincham); Stephens (Sutton Utd.), Walker (Blyth), Johnson (Altrincham); Casey (Kidderminster), Richards (Enfield), Ashford (Enfield). Substitutes: Simpson (Stafford) for Stephens, Buchanan (Blyth) for Walker.

Republic of Ireland: John Grace (Tolka Rovers); Tom Williams (Cherry Orchard), Declan Daly (St. Mary's Cork), Martin Kerr (St. Francis), Colm Grace (St. Kevin's Boys); John Tracey (St. Kevin's Boys), Eddie Doyle (St. Francis), Mark Shaw (Tolka Rovers); Mick Dunne (St. Kevin's Boys), John Young (Wicklow), Tom Dillon (Glenmore Celtic). Substitutes: Paul Kearns (East Wall Utd.) for Young.

England 2 (Wilcox, Agana)
Republic of Ireland 1 (Doyle)
(at Nuneaton 26th May)

England won the second match by the same score, and once again went behind early on, following a goalkeeping mistake.

Ashford had seen a flicked header from **Davison's** corner knocked off the line by **Williams**, and **Derek Richardson** had needed to be down sharply to block a snap shot from **Shaw**. But after 22 minutes the big Maidstone 'keeper dropped a cross from **Kerr**, and **Eddie Doyle** was able to turn the ball into the empty net.

England this time didn't take long drawing level. After 33 minutes a curling **Davison** corner was hooked into the roof of the net by the cultured **Wilcox**, for his first goal for his country.

All that happened while England were down to ten men as **Johnson** received treatment. He lasted four more minutes before his six year England career ended with him limping off to be replaced by **Stephens**.

Lynch had a low drive well held, and **Richardson** made amends for his error with a spectacular point blank block from **Tracey's** piledriver, as the Irish showed far more attacking flair than in the first match.

Tony Agana had throughout looked capable of exposing the Irish right flank, and he almost scored when **David Howell** sent him away, only to stab wide under pressure.

Matthews did well to save at **Buchanan's** feet before **Agana** won the match with a stunning run past three men, ending with a 63rd minute chip over the 'keeper.

Howell went off with a pulled hamstring to be replaced by **Walker**, as **Ogana** and **Wilcox** went close to the third. **Casey** got on with 17 minutes left for **Buchanan** and threatened in typical fashion, but England played out time with reasonable ease.

England: Richardson (Maidstone); **Shirtliff** (Frickley), **Howell** (Enfield), **Wilcox** (Frickley), **Davison** (Altrincham); **Johnson** (Altrincham), **Clayton** (Burton), **Simpson** (Stafford); **Ashford** (Enfield), **Buchanan** (Blyth), **Agana** (Weymouth). Substitutes: **Stephens** (Sutton) for **Johnson**; **Walker** (Blyth) for **Howell**; **Casey** (Kidderminster) for **Buchanan**.

Republic of Ireland: Gary Matthews (Usher Celtic); **Williams**, **Daly**, **Kerr**, **Grace**; **Tracey**, **Doyle**, **Shaw**; **Arthur Monks** (Usher Celtic), **Finton Lynch**, **Kerns**. Substitutes: **Eric Fitzpatrick** (Glasnevin) for **Grace**; **Tony Byrne** (St. Columbans) for **Shaw**; **Austin Ricken** (Temple Athletic) for **Monks**; **Jimmy Kelly** (Killavilla) for **Doyle**.

English Semi-Professional International Caps 1979-1986 (max 26)

David Adamson (Boston United) 79 v S.H. 80 v I.S.H. (5)
Jim Arnold (Stafford Rangers) 79 v S.H. (2)
Tony Agana (Weymouth) 86 v R.I (1)
Noel Ashford (Enfield) 82 v G.H.S. 83 v I.H.S. 84 v W.H.S.I. 85 v W.1(sub) 86 v Rep. Ireland; R.I (14)
Keith Barrett (Enfield) 81 v H.S.1. 82 v G.I.H.S. 83 v I.H.S. 84 v W.(sub)H.S. 85 v I.H.S. (16)
David Buchanan (Blyth) 86 v R.I(sub)R.1 (2)
Kim Casey (Kidderminster) 86 v W, R.I; R.I(sub) (3)
Kevin Charlton (Telford) 85 v W.I. (2)
David Clarke (Blyth Spartans) 80 v I.S.(sub)H 81 v H.S.1 82 v I.H.S. 83 v H.S. 84 v H.S.1. (14)
David Constantine (Altrincham) 85 v 1.H.S. 86 v W. (4)
Alan Cordice (Wealdstone) 83 v 1.H.S. 84 v W.S.(sub)I.(sub)85 I.H.S. (9)
Paul Culpin (Nuneaton Borough) 84 v W 85 v W.(sub)I.H.S. (5)
Paul Davies (Kidderminster) 86 v W (1)
John Davison (Altrincham) 79 v S.H. 80 v I.S. 81 v H.S.I. 82 v G.I.H.S. 83 v I.H.S. 84 v W.H.I.S. 85 v I.H.S. 86 v W.R.1, R.I (23)
John Denham (Northwich Victoria) 80 v H. (1)
Phil Derbyshire (Mossley) 83 v H.(sub)S.(sub)(2)
Mick Doherty (Weymouth) 86 v W.(sub.) (1)
Trevor Finnegan (Weymouth) 81 v H.S. (2)
John Glover (Maidstone United) 85 v W.I.H.S. (4)
Kenny Hill (Maidstone United) 80 v I.S.H. (3)
Gary Hooley (Frickley) 85 v W. (1)
Keith Houghton (Blyth Spartans) 79 v S. (1)
Barry Howard (Altrincham) 81 v H.S.I. 82 v G.I.H.S. (7)
David Howell (Enfield) 85 v H.(sub)S.(sub) 86 v W. R.I; (4)
Nicky Ironton (Enfield) 83 v H.(sub) 84 v W. (2)
Tony Jennings (Enfield) 79 v S.H. 80 v I.S.H. 81 v H.S.I. 82 v G.I.H.S. (12)
Jeff Johnson (Altrincham) 81 v S.I. 82 v G.I.H.S. 83 v I.H.S. 84 v H.S.I. 85 v I.H.S. 86 v W. (sub). R.I; R.I(17)
Anton Joseph (Telford United) 84 v S.(sub) 85 v W.I.H.S. 86 v W. (sub) (8)
Paul Mayman (Northwich Victoria) 80 v I.S. (2)
Neil Merrick (Weymouth) 80 v I.(sub)S.(2)
Stewart Mell (Burton) 85 v W. (1)
Trevor Morley (Nuneaton Borough) 84 v W.H.S.I. 85 v W.S.(sub)(6)
Les Mutrie (Blyth Spartans) 79 v S.H. 80 v I.S.H.(5)
Mark Newson (Maidstone United) 84 v W.H.S.I. 85 v W.(5)
Doug Newton (Burton) 85 v W.H.S. (3)
Eamon O'Keefe (Mossley) 79 v S.H. (2)
Frank Ovard (Maidstone United) 81 v H.(sub)S.(sub) I.(sub)(3)
Andy Pape (Harrow) 85 v W.(sub)H.S. 86 v W. (sub). R.I.(5)
Brian Parker (Yeovil Town) 80 v S.(1)
Trevor Peake (Nuneaton Borough) 79 v S.H. (2)
David Pearce (Harrow Borough) 84 v I.(sub)(1)
Brendan Phillips (Nuneaton B., Kettering) 79 v S.H. 80 v S.(sub)H.(4)
Gary Philips (Barnet) 82 v G. (1)
Carl Richards (Enfield) 86 v R.I. (1)
Derek Richardson (Maidstone United) 83 v I. 84 v W. 86 v W. R.I. (4)
Peter Robinson (Blyth Spartans) 83 v I.H.S. 84 v W.I. 85 v W. (6)
John Rogers (Altrincham) 81 v H.S.I. 82 v I.(sub)S.(5)
Neil Sellars (Scarbough) 81 v H.S.I. 82 v G.H.(sub)S. 83 v I.H.S.(9)
Paul Shirtlife (Frickley) 86 v R.1; R.I. (2)
Gordon Simmonite (Boston Utd.) 79 v S.(sub)H.(sub) 80 v I.S.H.(5)
Gary Simpson (Stafford) 86 v R.I. R.I. (2)
Tim Smithers (Nuneaton) 85 v W.(sub)I. 86 v W. (3)
Alan Smith (Alvechurch) 82 v G.I.S. (3)
Ian Smith (Mossley) 80 v I.S.H.(sub)(3)
Ossie Smith (Runcorn) 84 v W. (1)
Mickey Stephens (Sutton United) 82 v G.S.(sub) 86 v W, R.I; R.I (sub)(5)
Bob Stockley (Nuneaton Borough) 80 v H. (1)
Peter Taylor (Maidstone) 84 v H.S.I. (3)
Brian Thompson (Yeovil Town & Maidstone United) 79 v S.H. 81 v H.S.I. 82 v I.H.S. 83 v I.H.S. 84 v W.H.S.I.(15)
Tony Turner (Telford) 85 v W.(1)
David Waite (Enfield) 82 v G. (1)
Paul Walker (Blyth) 86 v W, R.I; R.I.(sub) (2)
Paul Wilson (Frickley) 86 v W (1)
Mark Ward (Northwich Victoria) 83 v S.(sub) (1)
John Watson (Wealdstone, Scarborough & Maidstone) 79 v S.(sub)H. 80 v I.S.H. 81 v H.S.I. 82 v I.H.S. 83 v I.H.S. 84 v W.(sub)H.S.I. (18)
Barry Whitbread (Runcorn, Altrincham) 79 v S.H. 80 v I.S.H. 81 v I. (6)
Russ Wilcox (Frickley) 86 v W, R.I; R.I. (2)
Colin Williams (Scarborough & Telford) 81 v H.S. 82 v I. 83 v I.H.S. 84 v H.S.I. 85 v I.H.S. (12)
Paul Wilson (Fricklay A.) 86 v W (1)

International Players to join Football League Clubs since playing for England

Jim Arnold (Blackburn Rovers, Everton)
Paul Culpin (Coventry City)
Keith Houghton (Carlisle United)
Trevor Morley (Northampton Town)
Les Mutrie (Hull City)
Mark Newson (Bournemouth)
Eamonn O'Keefe (Everton)
Frank Ovard (Gillingham)
Trevor Peake (Lincoln City, Coventry City)
Brendan Philips (Mansfield Town)
Gary Phillips (Brentford)
Carl Richards (Bournemouth, Enfield)
Peter Robinson (Rochdale and Hartlepool United)
John Rogers (Wigan Athletic)
Gordon Simmonite (Blackpool, Lincoln City)
Alan Smith (Leicester City)
Brian Thompson (Mansfield Town)
Mark Ward (Oldham Athletic, West Ham United)
Russ Wilcox (Northampton Tn, Frickley Ath)

England Goalscorers

John Davison	(Altrincham)	5(all pens)
Colin Williams	(Scar'bro & Telford)	5
Jeff Johnson	(Altrincham)	4
Paul Culpin	(Nuneaton)	4
Noel Ashford	(Enfield)	4
Dave Adamson	(Boston United)	3(2 pens)
Keith Barrett	(Enfield)	2
Alan Cordice	(Wealdstone)	2
Kenny Hill	(Maidstone U)	2
Les Mutrie	(Blyth Spartans)	2
John Watson	(Wealdstone, Scar'bro & Maidstone U)	2
Barry Whitbread	(Altrincham)	2
Tony Agana	(Weymouth)	1
Kim Casey	(Kidderminster)	1
Paul Davies	(Kidderminster)	1
Eamonn O'Keefe	(Mossley)	1
'Own Goal'		1
Peter Robinson	(Blyth Spartans)	1
Neil Sellars	(Scarborough)	1
Ian Smith	(Mossley)	1
Ossie Smith	(Runcorn)	1
Kenny Stephens	(Sutton United)	1
Russ Wilcox	(Frickley)	1

FOUR NATIONS TOURNAMENTS 1979-85

1979 (England)
Knock-out basis, England won final.

	P	W	D	L	F	A	Pts
1980 (Holland)							
Scotland	3	2	1	0	7	2	5
England	3	2	0	1	6	5	4
Italy	3	0	2	1	2	4	2
Holland	3	0	1	2	3	7	1
1981 (Italy)							
England	3	1	2	0	3	1	4
Italy	3	1	2	0	2	1	4
Scotland	3	0	3	0	2	2	3
Holland	3	0	0	3	1	4	0
1982 (Scotland)							
Scotland	3	1	2	0	5	4	4
England	3	1	2	0	2	1	4
Italy	3	0	2	1	4	6	2
Holland	3	1	0	2	5	5	2
1983 (England)							
England	3	3	0	0	10	1	6
Scotland	3	1	1	1	7	6	4
Holland	3	1	1	1	6	4	3
Italy	3	0.	0	0	3	8	0
1984 (Italy)							
Italy	3	2	1	0	4	1	5
England	3	1	1	1	5	4	3
Holland	3	1	1	1	8	8	3
Scotland	3	0	1	2	2	6	1
1985 (Holland)							
Scotland	3	2	0	1	4	4	4
England	3	1	1	1	6	5	3
Italy	3	1	1	1	4	4	3
Holland	3	1	0	2	4	5	2

International Caps per Club

(figure in brackets is number of internationals per club. Main figure is amount of caps players have won with club).

Altrincham (6)	58	Runcorn (2)	6
Enfield (7)	53	Weymouth (4)	6
Maidstone United (8)	42	Frickley Ath. (4)	5
Blyth Spartans (6)	31	Burton Albion (3)	5
Nuneaton Borough (6)	19	Harrow B. (2)	4
Telford United (4)	18	Kidderminster (2)	4
Scarborough (3)	16	Yeovil (2)	3
Wealdstone (2)	14	Stafford R. (2)	3
Boston United (2)	10	Alvechurch (1)	3
Mossley (3)	7	Kettering T. (1)	2
Sutton United (1)	7	Barnet (1)	1
Northwich Victoria (4)	6		

Other Results

v. WALES

	E	W
1984 Newtown	1	2
1985 Telford	1	0
1986 Merthyr	1	3

v. REP. of IRELAND

	E	ROI
1986 Kidderminster	2	1
1986 Nuneaton	2	1

OVERALL RECORD

P26 W15 D6 L5 F48 A27

England's Team v Holland in 1979

Tony Jennings, Barry Whitbread, Brian Thompson, John Davison, Jim Arnold, Eamonn O'Keefe, Brendan Phillips, John Watson, Les Mutrie, Dave Adamson, Trevor Peake, Gordon Simmonite, Stuart Chapman, Keith Houghton, Roy Clayton, Brian Parker.

Enfields defence brings Barrow's Colin Cowperthwaite to his knees as another goal attempt fails!

Congratulations Altrincham, winners of the 1986 F.A. Challenge Trophy at Wembley Stadium — the Electric Scoreboard says it all!

F. A. CHALLENGE TROPHY

F. A. CHALLENGE TROPHY
Committee: E. G. Powell (Chairman), G. A. Jones, Vice-Chairman; C. D. Bullen; A. Clarke; G. T. Evans; J. V. Hayward; T. Myatt; G. Thompson; J. C. Thompson; N. White

GOLA LEAGUE DOMINATE AGAIN

The system of allocating exemptions takes into account a Club's performance in the Trophy itself as well as the previous seasons's League record, so the Competition really takes off with the entry of the leading lights in the First Round Proper. Of course, those Clubs who have battled through the qualifying rounds from the Preliminary in early September, might take issue and this season there were four of them. Western League champions **Saltash United** went down to **Dartford** by the odd goal in three while **Tilbury** were edged out by **Slough Town**. **Grays Athletic** overcame **Uxbridge**, who like them, were making their first appearance in the Trophy having been 'promoted' from the Vase, while **Leek Town** of the North West Counties League, who last reached this stage in 1973, scored a surprise replay win over **Rhyl** (Multipart League).

For the first time the Gola League had its full complement of 22 in the Competition Proper but seven of their number went no further. All their F.A. Cup exploits counted for nothing as **Telford United**, in front of the biggest gate of the Round, slumped to a 4-2 home defeat by Multipart Leaguers **Southport**, while **Bath City** could not survive the trip to **Chelmsford** for whom ex-England star Peter Taylor scored from the penalty spot. The other five casualties suffered at the hands of fellow Gola Leaguers. Last year's beaten Finalists **Boston United** whose up and down season had already seen the departure of Manager Arthur Mann conceded five at **Kidderminster**, and **Maidstone United** struggling in the relegation zone would have enjoyed the 3-0 defeat of third placed **Weymouth**. Holders **Wealdstone** faced **Welling United** convincing leaders of the Southern League whom they had defeated en route to Wembley and Wainwright's goal was sufficient to repeat the job. Other ties worthy of note saw Vauxhall-Opel title chasers **Sutton United** succumb to Jeffrey's penalty for **Kettering**, while **Bishop Auckland** won the North-East "Match of the Day" against **Blyth Spartans**. **Worcester City** anxious to make an immediate return to the Gola League, crashed 5-2 to Southern League rivals **Crawley Town**.

A crowd of close to a thousand saw **Leek** continue their winning ways in the Second Round with another Multipart victim **Macclesfield Town** who were then in top spot. The other Preliminary Round survivors **Grays Athletic** found Southern League **Chelmsford** too strong going down 3-1 in a replay in front of more than twelve hundred fans. The Round's biggest crowd was at **Southport** for the second replay with **Scarborough** and the majority of the two thousand would have been delighted with Owen's winner for the home side.

After grabbing all the headlines with their mid-week Cup defeat of Birmingham City, **Altrincham** will not have relished the visit of **Bangor City**, Finalists in 1984, for fear of an anti-climax. However, they had little cause for worry for despite conceding an early goal, their 6-1 victory included a Paul Reid hat-trick. There were three all-Gola clashes. Trophy holders **Wealdstone** once again repeated one of last seasons's victories, this time against **Frickley Athletic** while leaders **Enfield's** 3-2 defeat of **Maidstone** left the latter free to concentrate on the fight against relegation. **Dagenham**, the most successful Trophy Club over the past ten years or so, fielded Dunwell and Horan, survivors of the 1980 winning team as well as three other Wembley winners – Sullivan (Bishops Stortford 1981) and Taylor and Jacobs (Enfield 1982). Indeed, both Sullivan and Taylor had scored their side's winning goal. None of this prevented **Cheltenham's** Powell notching the game's solitary goal **South Bank's** 3-1 win at **Dartford** was notable for the home teams lack of a specialist 'keeper being forced to fill in with central defender McCayna, himself less than one hundred per cent fit.

The Third Round coincided with the arrival of the snow and ice which was to disrupt even the Fourth Round. One of the few ties to be played on the appointed Saturday was at **Enfield** where **Chelmsford City** were the visitors. Spectators arriving a mere eighty seconds late will have missed King and Richard's goals for the home team and after eighteen minutes Hinds made it 3-0. A Taylor shot from outside the box reduced the deficit before the interval and Thrift pulled another back soon afterwards. Enfield's Ironton was dismissed for a second caution but the ten men extended their lead in the seventy

Three of Semi Professionals best known names. Altrincham and England captain John Davison, ex - Manchester United and Birmingham City goalkeeper. Jeff Wealands and Player of the year Jeff Johnson meets Sir Matt Busby.
Photo: John Rooney

first minute through Hinds but Owens immediately grabbed the third for Chelmsford who went in search of an equaliser. The result hung in the balance until a fine individual effort from Richards three minutes from time made it 5-3 to round off an exciting afternoon for the crowd of nearly fifteen hundred.

The Round was further prolonged by the fact that apart from **Enfield** only **Runcorn** and **Altrincham** won at the first attempt. The longest running tie saw under-dogs **Leek** force three draws with **Wycombe Wanderers** (including an amazing 5-5 first replay) before the Gola Leaguers outlasted them 1-0 in a fourth encounter at Worcester. **Kidderminster Harriers** were in an impressive streak of form and the 6-1 replay defeat of **Southport** included yet another hat-trick for Casey.

Wealdstone were one of the last to go into action and they could not make home advantage tell against the resilient **South Bank** who hung on for a goal-less draw. The Northern League side may not have previously been given sufficient credit for their win at **Dartford** but they enhanced their reputation further as a late goal in the replay earned them a 2-1 victory over the holders.

In the only Quarter-Final tie played on schedule, **Kidderminster** faced **Runcorn** having defeated them in a Gola League match the previous week. However, the Casey-Davies scoring machine did not function on this occasion and Runcorn reached the Semi-Finals albeit courtesy of a freak own-goal due to the blustery conditions. **Enfield** made the long trek to **South Bank** but in front of a crowd in excess of two thousand turned in their customary professional performance and came away with a 2-1 win. **Altrincham's** greater experience stood them in good stead for the visit to **Cheltenham** where two goals from Ellis brought a second successive Semi-Final for the conquerors of Birmingham City. The remaining tie at **Kettering** proved to be the only one at which the home supporters went away happy and **Wycombe's** weariness may have been a contributory factor to their 2-1 defeat.

The Semi-Final draw paired most peoples' favourites **Enfield**, who were looking to emulate **Wealdstone's** fine Trophy/Gola double, with old rivals **Altrincham** who were naturally out to avenge their 1982 Final defeat. The latter's determination was apparent in the first leg at Southbury Road and by keeping a particularly close watch on leading scorer Richards, they restricted the home side's chances before taking the lead through Newton's penalty early in the second half. Despite missing opportunities to increase their lead and the late equaliser from Docker, Altrincham will have been well satisfied with their afternoons work. The return leg saw **Enfield** start confidently with the best chances falling to them. However, stout work by the 'Alty' defence kept the score sheet blank and after the interval their attack began to pose more problems. Ellis got the all important breakthrough and Newton's second penalty of the Tie in the dying minutes, settled the issue, shattering Enfield's double dreams.

The other Semi-Final was a tense affair, typical of such occasions, with both sides determined to avoid costly errors in the first leg. **Kettering** were clearly intent on returning home without a deficit to take full advantage of an anticipated bumper attendance. Their celebrations as the match ended goalless suggested they could almost see the Twin Towers and a week later, four thousand excited fans assembled to witness their team's triumph. However, a stirring display by **Runcorn's** keeper McBride, despite being handicapped by an early injury, along with his back four, absorbed everything **Kettering,** who included ex-England star Dave Watson in their side, could throw at them and when the home team pressed forward with insufficient caution Mather duly punished them. Skipper Smith's header for number two sealed **Kettering's** fate and set up an intriguing all Cheshire Final.

ADRIAN TITCOMBE
The Football Association's Administrative Secretary.
This review was first published in the F.A. Trophy Final Programme

Llanelli keeper Peter Fearn saves well at Bristol Manor Farm in the Preliminary Round. Photo: Eric Marsh.

Tom Hammond of Farnborough tips a last minute effort from visiting Gosport over the bar and the home side go through into the Second Qualifying Round.

Photo: Eric Marsh.

Mangotsfield's Jim Billings goes close against Taunton. However, Taunton drew and won the replay at home after extra time.

Photo: Mike Brown.

Saltsbury score from a penalty against Maesteg Park and the goalkeeper doesn't quite 'read' the situation.

F.A. TROPHY ROUND BY ROUND RESULTS

PRELIMINARY ROUND

Best Attendance
V. S. Rugby v Ilkeston Town (Replay) 301
Best Home Victory
V. S. Rugby v Ilkeston Town 10-0
Best Away Victory
Redditch United v Hednesford Town 2-4
Result of the Round
V. S. Rugby v Ilkeston Town 10-0

RESULTS	Sc.	Att.
Lancaster City v Accrington Stanley	0-0	119
Leyland Motors v Glossop	3-1	81
Curzon Ashton v Penrith	2-0	79
Ilkeston Town v V. S. Rugby	1-1	192
Hednesford Town v Redditch United	0-0	233
Spalding United v Leek Town	0-0	122
Caernarfon Town v Leicester United	1-0	101
Clapton v Leyton-Wingate	1-1	83
Chesham United v Finchley	1-1	110
Grays Athletic v Witney Town	2-2	171
St. Albans City v Oxford City	1-2	179
Sheppey United v Metropolitan Police	0-0	140
Tilbury v Wembley (at Aveley)	3-1	40
Maidenhead United v Walton & Hersham	3-0	78
Chatham Town v Thanet United	2-0	108
Chard Town v Minehead	1-0	72
Bristol Manor Farm v Llanelli	0-0	70
Maesteg Park v Weston-Super-Mare	1-0	36
Saltash United v Poole Town	3-0	148
REPLAYS		
Accrington Stanley v Lancaster City	4-4	236
V. S. Rugby v Ilkeston Town	10-0	301
Redditch United v Hednesford Town	2-4	228
Leek Town v Spalding United	3-0	185
Leyton-Wingate v Clapton	5-0	71
Finchley v Chesham United	3-1	42
Witney Town v Grays Athletic	3-4	153
Metropolitan Police v Sheppey United	2-3	45
Llanelli v Bristol Manor Farm	3-1	64
2nd REPLAY		
Accrington Stanley v Lancaster City	2-2	250
3rd REPLAY		
Lancaster City v Accrington Stanley	4-2	166

1st QUALIFYING ROUND

Best Attendance
Shepshed Charterhouse v Bootle (Replay) 498
Best Home Victory
Brandon United v Horwich R.M.I. 9-1
Best Away Victory
Alvechurch v Worksop Town 1-4
Result of the Round
Brandon United v Horwich R.M.I. 9-1

RESULTS	Sc.	Att.
Crook Town v Goole Town	1-2	154
Billingham Town v Morecambe	1-1	88
Workington v Denaby United	2-1	265
Gretna v Lancaster City	4-1	95
Billingham Synthonia v Curzon Ashton	3-0	23
Congleton Town v Tow Law Town	0-2	112
Ryhope CA v Netherfield	6-1	86
Consett v Bridlington Trinity	0-3	112
Whitley Bay v Bedlington Terriers	1-0	239
Brandon United v Horwich RMI	9-1	180
Leyland Motors v Horden CW	7-0	135
Southport v Burscough	2-1	303
Chester le Street v Peterlee Newtown	3-0	158
Formby v Ferryhill Athletic	3-2	90
Prescot Cables v Shildon	1-1	58
V. S. Rugby v Winsford United	5-2	389
Oldbury United v Caernarfon Town	2-4	61
South Liverpool v Alfreton Town	0-1	110
Sutton Coldfield Town v Leek Town	0-0	233
Stourbridge v Hednesford Town	1-2	216
Arnold v Mossley	0-1	162
Alvechurch v Worksop Town	1-4	273
Buxton v Sutton Town	4-1	222
Stalybridge Celtic v Moor Green	4-0	366
Bootle v Shepshed Charterhouse	4-4	110
Eastwood Town v Radcliffe Borough	1-1	138
Oswestry Town v Gainsborough Trinity	0-3	240
Colwyn Bay v Belper Town	1-1	202
Dudley Town v Heanor Tn (at Bilston Tn.)	3-0	143
Finchley v Leyton-Wingate	1-3	92
Grays Athletic v Hampton	0-0	188
Banbury United v Burnham & Hillingdon	3-2	125
Hayes v Uxbridge	1-3	294
Basildon United v Harlow Town	2-2	121
Staines Town v Boreham Wood	2-0	107
Aylesbury United v Wellingborough Town (at R.A.F. Halton)	3-1	224
Oxford City v Aveley	2-1	113
Hitchin Town v Dunstable	1-2	250
Billericay Town v Walthamstow Avenue	5-1	437
Cambridge City v Bedworth United	2-2	160
Hertford Town v Corby Town	2-5	69
Tilbury v Hornchurch	1-0	78
RS Southampton v Andover	3-0	120
Farnborough Town v Gosport Borough	3-0	394
Sittingbourne v Chatham Town	4-0	202
Woking v Maidenhead United	4-5	195
Ashford Town v Bromley	0-0	294
Gravesend & Northfleet v Sheppey United	1-2	341
Bognor Regis Town v Tonbridge AFC	3-0	301
Folkestone v Lewes	0-1	328
Basingstoke Tn. v Tooting & Mitcham Utd.	1-0	320
Dover Athletic v Fareham Town	0-3	246
Epsom & Ewell v Kingstonian	5-1	252
Waterlooville v Canterbury City	3-1	112
Hastings United v Leatherhead (Walkover for Leatherhead)		
Clandown v Mangotsfield United	0-2	84
Bideford v Trowbridge Town	2-1	232
Saltash United v Forest Green Rovers	3-1	127
Barry Town v Frome Town	3-2	238
Melksham Town v Chard Town	3-2	161
Llanelli v Dorchester Town	1-1	94
Salisbury v Maesteg Park	4-1	210
Bridgend Town v Barnstaple Town	4-1	115
Ton Pentre v Taunton Town	0-3	311
REPLAY		
Morecambe v Billingham Town	2-0	303
Shildon v Prescot Cables	2-1	102
Leek Town v Sutton Coldfield Town	2-1	271
Shepshed Charterhouse v Bootle	3-1	498
Radcliffe Borough v Eastwood Town	5-1	230
Belper Town v Colwyn Bay	3-2	236
Hampton v Grays Athletic	0-1	132
Harlow Town v Basildon United	0-1	77
Bedworth United v Cambridge City	2-1	160
Bromley v Ashford Town	3-0	262
Dorchester Town v Llanelli	2-1	127

2nd QUALIFYING ROUND

Best Attendance
V. S. Rugby v Basildon United (Replay) 554
Best Home Victory
Corby Town v Oxford City 6-1
Best Away Victory
No victory by more than two goals.
Result of the Round
Shepshed Charterhouse v Gainsborough Trinity (Replay) 5-1

RESULTS	Sc.	Att.
Formby v Gretna	1-1	
Workington v Brandon United	5-4	287
Whitley Bay v Chester le Street	3-1	147
Ryhope CA v Bridlington Trinity	3-1	98
Goole Town v Leyland Motors	0-1	175
Tow Law Town v Southport	1-3	155
Billingham Synthonia v Morecambe	0-2	116
Mossley v Shildon	3-0	298
Worksop Town v Alfreton Town	2-3	440
Radcliffe Borough v Belper Town	2-0	230
Leek Town v Buxton	3-2	503
Stalybridge Celtic v Hednesford Town	2-1	412

Hampton's Ricky Waires comes close with a crashing close range drive against Grays Athletic.
Photo: Andrew Eggleton

Action from the Ashford v Bromley Cup Tie. The visiting keeper, Sullivan, catches a corner.
Photo: Nick Robinson

North West Counties League club Leek Towen had a great run in the Trophy and here we see action from their home game against Macclesfield which they won 2-1.

Action from the South Back v Whitby Town match in the First Round.
Photo: Leo Hoening.

Gainsborough Trinity v Shepshed Char	1-1	336
Caernarfon Town v Dudley Town	0-2	125
Billericay Town v Banbury United	2-0	404
Basildon United v V. S. Rugby	0-0	151
Corby Town v Oxford City	6-1	344
Aylesbury United v Bedworth United (at R.A.F. Halton)	0-2	233
Uxbridge v Staines Town	3-1	302
Grays Athletic v Dunstable	6-2	174
Tilbury v Leyton-Wingate	3-1	116
Sheppey United v Sittingbourne	2-1	436
Fareham Town v Waterlooville	1-1	169
Maidenhead United v Bognor Regis Town	1-2	130
Lewes v Bromley	1-2	156
Epsom & Ewell v Basingstoke Town	3-0	265
Farnborough Town v Leatherhead	4-1	462
Salisbury v Bideford	2-0	266
Melksham Town v Saltash United	1-3	205
RS Southampton v Bridgend Town	1-1	96
Mangotsfield United v Taunton Town	1-1	83
Dorchester Town v Barry Town	4-1	189

REPLAYS

Gretna v Formby	3-0	82
Shepshed Char v Gainsborough Trinity	5-1	403
V. S. Rugby v Basildon United	4-0	554
Waterlooville v Fareham Town	3-2	296
Bridgend Town v RS Southampton	3-0	78
Taunton Town v Mangotsfield United	2-1 *	166

3rd QUALIFYING ROUND

Best Attendance
Yeovil Town v Saltash United 1,315
Best Home Victory
Bridgend Town v Taunton Town 6-1
Best Away Victory
Gloucester City v Worcester City 0-4
Result of the Round
Yeovil Town 1 Saltash United 2

RESULTS	Sc.	Att.
Chorley v Blyth Spartans	0-2	311
Ryhope CA v Spennymoor United	2-1	246
Morecambe v Gretna	1-1	481
Southport v Gateshead	2-0	446
Leyland Motors v Whitby Town	1-3	694
Whitley Bay v South Bank	0-3	108
North Shields v Workington	1-1	316
Barrow v Mossley	0-0	412
Bedworth United v Alfreton Town	1-1	115
Leek Town v Dudley Town	2-1	257
Leamington v Rhyl	1-2	187
Shepshed Charterhouse v Matlock Town	2-1	403
Stalybridge Celtic v Hyde United	1-3	958
Radcliffe Borough v Willenhall Town	2-2	167
Burton Albion v Grantham	3-0	588
Corby Town v Witton Albion	1-0	341
Chelmsford City v Bognor Regis Town	3-0	643
Slough Town v Bromley	1-0	431
Farnborough Town v Crawley Town	0-3	375
Hendon v Workington Town	0-1	154
Bishops Stortford v Croydon	2-1	220
Billericay Town v Sheppey United	2-4	396
Waterlooville v Carshalton Athletic	4-3	154
Uxbridge v Barking	2-0	211
Windsor & Eton v Leytonstone/Ilford	5-0	277
Epsom & Ewell v Grays Athletic	2-2 +	182
V. S. Rugby v Tilbury	0-1	437
Dorchester Town v Weymouth	3-5	945
Yeovil Town v Saltash United	1-2	1315
Bridgend Town v Taunton Town	6-1	86
Gloucester City v Worcester City	0-4	486
Merthyr Tydfil v Salisbury	1-1	300

REPLAYS

Gretna v Morecambe	1-2	189
Workington v North Shields	2-0	308
Mossley v Barrow	2-4 *	270
Alfreton Town v Bedworth United	2-3	181
Willenhall Town v Radcliffe Borough	3-1	253
Grays Athletic v Epsom & Ewell	3-2	164
Salisbury v Merthyr Tydfil	2-1	372

1st ROUND PROPER

Best Attendance
Telford United v Southport 1,133
Best Home Victory
Frickley Athletic v Bedworth United (Replay) 5-0
Best Away Victory
Shepshed Charterhouse v Bromsgrove Rovers (Replay) 1-4
Result of the Round
Telford United v Southport 2-4

RESULTS	Sc.	Att.
Kidderminster Harriers v Boston United	5-2	582
Rhyl v Leek Town	1-1	272
Hyde United v Corby Town	0-2	372
Ryhope CA v Altrincham	1-3	714
Northwich Victoria v Workington	1-0	679
Scarborough v Barrow	2-1	803
Bishops Auckland v Blyth Spartans	2-0	474
Bedworth United v Frickley Athletic	1-1	289
Stafford Rangers v Nuneaton Borough	1-0	837
Runcorn v Marine	2-0	698
Bangor City v Willenhall Town	1-0	395
Bromsgrove Rovers v Shepshed C'house	1-1	529
Kings Lynn v Macclesfield Town	1-1	419
Telford United v Southport	2-4	1,133
Morecambe v Burton Albion	0-2	394
South Bank v Whitby Town	1-1	536
Cheltenham Town v Fisher Athletic	3-0	857
Dulwich Hamlet v Windsor & Eton	1-1	193
Slough Town v Tilbury	1-0	403
Sutton United v Kettering Town	0-1	773
Maidstone United v Weymouth	3-0	635
Chelmsford City v Bath City	2-1	830
Bishops Stortford v Wokingham Town	2-0	332
Grays Athletic v Uxbridge	2-1	271
Crawley Town v Worcester City	5-2	756
Enfield v Waterlooville	3-0	612
Worthing v Salisbury	1-0	387
Dagenham v Sheppey United	3-0	472
Saltash United v Dartford	1-2	363
Barnet v Wycombe Wanderers	0-1	660
Wealdstone v Welling United	1-0	629
Bridgend Town v Harrow Borough	2-2	112

REPLAYS

Leek Town v Rhyl	3-2	404
Frickley Athletic v Bedworth United	5-0	674
Shepshed C'House v Bromsgrove Rovers	1-4	611
Macclesfield Town v Kings Lynn	3-0	308
Whitby Town v South Bank	1-2	594
Windsor & Eton v Dulwich Hamlet	2-1	318
Harrow Borough v Bridgend Town	1-2	390

2nd ROUND PROPER

Best Attendance
Southport v Scarborough (2nd replay) 2,000
Best Home Victory
Altringcham v Bangor City 6-1
Best Away Victory
Corby Town v Kidderminster Harriers 0-4
Result of the Round
Stafford Rangers v Bishops Auckland 0-1

RESULTS	Sc.	Att.
Corby Town v Kidderminster Harriers	0-4	865
Leek Town v Macclesfield Town	2-1	934
Altrincham v Bangor City	6-1	1,011
Bishops Stortford v Northwich Victoria	2-0	682
Scarborough v Southport	0-0	1.048
Stafford Rangers v Bishops Auckland	0-1	1,060
Wealdstone v Frickley Athletic	2-1	815
Windsor & Eton v Runcorn	0-1	452
Burton Albion v Bromsgrove Rovers	1-0	1,129
Dartford v South Bank	1-3	507
Dagenham v Cheltenham Town	0-1	499
Slough Town v Kettering Town	1-2	870
Enfield v Maidstone United	3-2	1,019
Grays Athletic v Chelmsford City	1-1	972
Crawley Town v Wycombe Wanderers	0-2	1,250
Worthing v Bridgend Town	1-0	356

REPLAYS

Southport v Scarborough	1-1	1,084
Chelmsford City v Grays Athletic	3-1	1,226

2nd REPLAY

Southport v Scarborough	1-0	2,000

Wycombe's Lester saves bravely from Kettering's Ian Grawley.

Surrounded by Bridgend defenders, Micky Edmunds crashes home one of his 40 goals last season to put Worthing into the Third Round of the F.A. Trophy.

Photo: Micky Edmonds

Maidstone's Micky Joyce puts Weymouth goalkeeper, Len Bond, under heavy pressure during second half action in the F.A. Trophy match played at Maidstone on Saturday, 21st December, 1985.

Photo: Photo-News

Steve King scores for Enfield after 17 seconds in their 5 - 3 victory over Chelmsford in the 3rd Round of the F.A. Trophy.
Photo: Thomas Scott

Third Round

Altrincham 1 (Chesters) **Bishops Auckland 0** Attendance 756
Altrincham: Wealands, Gardner, Densmore, Johnson, Farrelly, Conning, Ellis, Davison, Reid, Chesters, Anderson, (Newton (D)).
Bishops Auckland: Owers, Newton (M), Barker, Varty, Blair, Lormor, Pearson (M), Person (WM), Linacre, Grady, Dunn (Newton (D)).

Cheltenham Town 0 Bishops Stortford 0 Attendance 1,151
Cheltenham Town: Hards, Baverstock, Baddeley, Blackler, Cornes, Brooks, Hughes, Jordan, Boyland, Abbley, Powell, (Willetts).
Bishops Stortford: Taylor (M), Wickenden, Goodchild, Tomkins, Hull, Hopkins, Flynn, Nunn, Hardy, Taylor (K), Newbury, (Reading).

Enfield 5 (Hinds 2, Richards 2, King) **Chelmsford 3** (Taylor, Owers, Thrift) Attendance 1,445
Enfield: Pape, Barrett, Hayzelden, Cooper, Gray, Ironton, Hinds, Duffield, Ashford, Richards, King, (Flint).
Chelmsford City: Keeley, Lee, Johnson, Oliver, Makin, Taylor, Owers, Foley, Lazarus, Pountney, Thrift, (Entwistle).

Runcorn 2 (Skeete, Carter) **Burton Albion 0** Attendance 856
Runcorn: McBride, Rowlands, Roberts, Jones, Skeete, Smith, Crompton (S), Crompton (A), Carter, Mather, Imrie, (Holden).
Burton Albion: New, McJannett, Kamara, Vaughan, Essex, Saunders, Kersley, Clayton, Mell, Edmunds, Hall, (Simms).

Southport 1 (King) **Kidderminster Harriers 1** (Casey). Attendance 1,902
Southport: Evans, Reid, King, Naden, Carr, Owens, Teale, Quinn, Coleman, Mutch, McCormack, (Brady).
Kidderminster Harriers: Garner, Buckland, Barton, Boxall, Jones, Woodall, Mackenzie, Casey, Davies, Tuohy, Gavin, (Richards).

Wealdstone 0 South Bank 0 Attendance 451
Wealdstone: Iles, Tapley, McCargo, Byatt, Bowgett, Wainwright, Doyle, Holmes, Cordice, Graves, Donnellan, (Jones).
South Bank: Gormley, Lynch, Taylor, Howley, Hartley, Roberts, Butler, Malone, Boylan, Sills, Lilley, (Burton).

Worthing 0 Kettering Town 0 Attendance 602
Worthing: Steele, Norlund, Cox, Vessey, Raynsford, Saunders, Lelliott, Dove, Tiltman, Edmonds, Foreman, (Taylor).
Kettering Town: Harrison, Thacker, Hines, Dawson, Fee, Wood, Wharton, Kabia, Smith, Jeffrey, Harrison, (Crawley).

Wycombe Wanderers 2 (Read, Dell) **Leek Town 2** (Morgan 2). Attendance 417
Wycombe Wanderers: Lester, Toll, Riley, Burgess, Vircavs, Collins, West, Read, Dell, Blochel, Stanley, (Macmahon).
Leek Town: Deaville, Robson, Goldstraw, McMullen, Sromek, Mellor, O'Connor, Griffiths, Morgan, Mallaburn, France, (Proctor).

THIRD ROUND REPLAYS

Bishops Stortford 1 (Hardy pen.) **Cheltenham Town 3** (Boyland 2, Brooks) Attendance 595
Bishops Stortford: Taylor, Wickenden, Goodchild, Tomkins, Hull, Hopkins, Flynn, Nunn, Hardy, Whitton, Newbury, (Reading).
Cheltenham Town: Hards, Hughes, Baddeley, Collicutt, Cornes, Brooks, Willetts, Baverstock, Boyland, Abbley, Powell, (Jordan).

Kettering Town 2 (Smith, Jeffrey) **Worthing 1** (Edmonds) Attendance 1,365
Kettering Town: Harrison (M), Thacker, Hines, Dawson, Fee, Wood, Wharton, Dabia, Smith, Jeffrey, Harrison (A), (Crawley).
Worthing: Steele, Norlund, Cox, Vessey, Raynsford, Rogerson, Lelliott, Dove, Saunders, Edmonds; Foreman, (O'Sullivan).

Kidderminster Harriers 6 (Casey 3, Davies 2, Buckland) **Southport 1** Attendance 1,113
Kidderminster Harriers: Campbell, Buckland, Barton, Boxall, Jones, Woodall, Mackenzie, Casey, Davies, Tuohy, Gavin, (Richards).
Southport: Evans, Reid, King, Naden, Stungeon, Owens, Teale, Brady, Coleman, Mutch, McCormack, (Hunter).

Leek Town 5 (Robson pen., McMullen, O'Connor, Mallaburn, France) **Wycombe Wanderers 5** (Read 2, Dell, Blochel, Stanley). Attendance 1,081
Leek Town: Deaville, Robson, Goldstraw, McMullen, Sromek, Mellor, O'Connor, Griffiths, Morgan, Mallaburn, France, (Proctor).
Wycombe Wanderers: Lester, Collins, Toll, Burgess, Vircavs, Fairchild, West, Read, Dell, Blochel, Stanley, (Harman).

South Bank 2 Wealdstone 1 (Graves) Attendance 451
Wealdstone: Iles, Tapley McCargo, Jones, Bowgett, Wainwright, Doyle, Holmes, Cordice, Graves, Donnellan, (Tonge).
South Bank: Gormley, Lynch, Taylor, Howley, Hartley, Roberts, Butler, Malone, Boylan, Sills, Lilley, (Burton).

THIRD ROUND SECOND REPLAY †

Leek Town 1 (O'Connor) **Wycombe Wanderers 1** (Stanley) Attendance 696
Leek Town: Deaville, Robson, Goldstraw, McMullen, Sromek, Mellor, O'Connor, Griffiths, Morgan, Mallaburn, France, (Proctor).
Wycombe Wanderers: Lester, Collins, Toll, Burgess, Vircavs, Harman, West, Read, Dell, Blochel, Stanley, (Fairchild).

THIRD ROUND THIRD REPLAY †

Wycombe Wanderers 1 (West) **Leek Town 0** Attendance 690
Wycombe Wanderers: Lester, Riley, Pearce, Burgess, Vircavs, Harman, West, Read, Dell, Blochel, Stanley, (Fairchild).
Leek Town: Deaville, Robson, Goldstraw, McMullen, Sromek, Mellor, O'Connor, Griffiths, Morgan, Mallaburn, France, (Proctor).

† Played at St. George's Lane, Worcester.

The moment of truth? The camera catches Kidderminster's Clive Boxall's outstretched hand knocking the ball away from the head of Runcorn's Ossie Smith. Runcorn scored from the resultant penalty helping them to a 2 - 1 win in the FK.A. Trophy quarter final at the Harriers ground. Steve Skeete (Runcorn) No.10 on the left and Harrier's Chris Jones are in attendance.

Fourth Round

Cheltenham Town 0 Altrincham 2 (Ellis 2) Attendance 2,200
Cheltenham Town: Hards, Hughes, Baddeley, Collicutt, Cornes, Brooks, Willetts, Baverstock, Boyland, Abbley, Powell, (Jordan).
Altrincham: Wealands, Gardner, Densmore, Ellis, Farrelly, Conning, Newton, Davison, Reid, Buxton, Anderson, (Chesters).

Kettering Town 2 (Smith, one o.g.) **Wycombe Wanderers 1** (Read) Attendance 2,312
Kettering Town: Harrison, Thacker, Hines, Dawson, Fee, Wood, Wharton, Kabia, Smith, Jeffrey, Harrison, (Crawley).
Wycombe Wanderers: Lester, Toll, Price, Burgess, Vircavs, Collins, West, Read, Dell, Blochel, Stanley, (Harman).

Kidderminster Harriers 1 (Tuohy) **Runcorn 2** (Lee Pen, Richards o.g.) Attendance 2,015
Kidderminster Harriers: Campbell, Buckland, Barton, Boxall, Jones, Woodall, Mackenzie, Casey, Davies, Tuohy, Richards, (Rosegreen).
Runcorn: McBride, Rowlands, Roberts, Jones, Fraser, Smith, Lee, Imrie, Carter, Skeete, Carradus, (Mather).

South Bank 0 Enfield 2 (Hinds, one o.g.) Attendance 2,384
South Bank: Gormley, Lynch, Taylor, Malone, Hartley, Roberts, Butler, Connor, Boylan, Sills, Lilley, (Burton).
Enfield: Pape, Barrett, Hayzelden, Docker, Howell, Ironton, Hinds, Duffield, Ashford, Richards, King, (Flint).

Dave Burgess of Wycombe powers in an header during their 2 - 1 defeat by Kettering Town in the 4th Round of the F.A. Trophy.
Photo: Shaun Twitchen

Semi-Finals 1st Legs

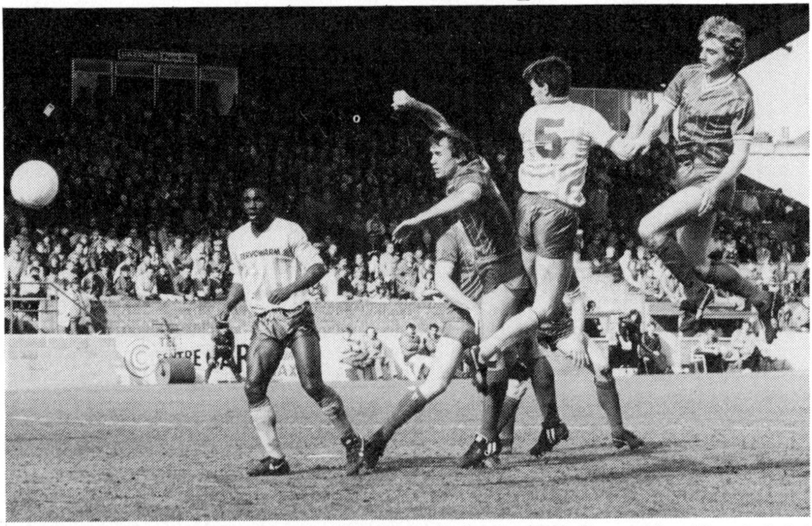

Runcorn Weekly News photographer Stuart Bogg's highly praised action shot of Bobby Fraser and Dave Watson in the 2nd leg of the F.A. Trophy semi-final at Kettering, Runcorn won 2 - 0.

ENFIELD 1 (Docker) **ALTRINCHAM 1** (Newton 1 pen) Attendance: 1,804
Enfield: Pape, Barrett, Hayzelden, Cooper, Howell, Docker, Hinds, Duffield, Ashford, Richards, King (Flint).
Altrincham: Wealands, Gardner, Densmore, Johnson, Farrelly, Conning, Newton, Davison, Reid, Ellis, Anderson (Buxton).

RUNCORN 0 KETTERING TOWN 0 Attendence: 2,023
Runcorn: McBride, Lee, Roberts, Jones, Fraser, Smith, Crompton (S), Crompton (A), Imrie, Brockbank, Carradus (Rowland).
Kettering Town: Harrison (M), Thacker, Timothy, McIlwayne, Dawson, Wood, Wharton, Kadia, Crawley, Jeffrey, Harrison (A), (Keast).

Ossie Smith gets the second goal for Runcorn in their 2 - 0 win over Kettering in the 2nd leg of the F.A. Trophy semi-final.
Photo: W. Leigh

Doug Newton, England's Semi-Professional International, who joined 'Alty' from Burton Albion follows up his successful penalty kick and celebrates as his side take a 2-0 lead.
Photo: John Rooney

Semi-Final 2nd Legs

ALTRINCHAM 2 (Newton 1 pen, Ellis 1) **ENFIELD 0** Attendence: 2,134
Altrincham: Wealands, Gardner, Densmore, Johnson, Farrelly, Conning, Newton, Davison, Reid, Ellis, Anderson, (Buxton)
Enfield: Pape, Barrett, Hayzelden, Ironton, Howell, Docker, Hinds, Duffield, Ashford, Richards, King, (Flint).

KETTERING Town 0 RUNCORN 2 (Smith, Mather) Attendence: 4,032
Kettering Town: Harrison (M), Thacker, McIlwain, Dawson, Watson, Wood, Wharton, Kabia, Smith, Jeffrey, Harrison (A), (Crawley).
Runcorn: McBride, Rowlands, Lee, Jones, Fraser, Smith, Crompton (S), Imrie, Carter, Mather, Carrodus, (Crompton (A)).

F.A. TROPHY — ROUND-BY-ROUND TO WEMBLEY

First Round

Altrincham.......... 3
*Ryhops C.A. 1

*Bangor City........ 1
Willenhall........... 0

*Stafford R. 1
Nuneaton B........ 0

*Bishop Auckland 2
Blyth Spartans.... 0

*Dagenham.......... 3
Sheapey Utd....... 0

*Cheltenham T..... 3
Fisher Ath. 0

*Bishop Storford.. 2
Wokingham 0

*Northwich Vic.... 1
Workington........ 0

*Wealdstone 1
Welling Utd........ 0

*Bedworth Utd. 1,0
Frickley Ath. ... 1,5

*Saltash Utd. 1
Dartford............. 2

*South Bank 1,2
Whitby T......... 1,1

*Enfield 3
Waterlooville...... 0

*Maidstone Utd... 3
Weymouth 0

*Grays Ath. 2
Uxbridge T......... 1

*Chelmsford C..... 2
Bath City............ 1

*Worthing............ 1
Sailsbury 0

*Bridgend T. 2,2
Harrow B. 2,1

*Slough Town...... 1
Tilbury 0

*Sutton Utd. 0
Kettering T......... 1

*Crawley Town.... 5
Worcester C. 2

*Barnet 0
Wycombe W....... 1

*Rhyl 1,2
Leek Town 1,3

*Kings Lynn 1,0
Macclesfield T. 1,3

*Scarborough....... 2
Barrow 1

*Telford Utd. 2
Southport........... 4

*Hyde Utd. 0
Corby Town....... 2

*Kidderminster H. 5
Boston Utd. 2

*Morecambe 0
Burton Alb. 2

*Bromsgrove R. 1,4
Shepshed C...... 1,1

*Dulwich 1,1
Windsor & E. .. 1,2

*Marine 0
Runcorn.............. 2

Second Round

***Altrincham.......... 6**
Bangor City........ 1

*Stafford R. 0
Bishop Auckland... 1

*Dagenham.......... 0
Cheltenham T..... 1

*Bishop Storford.. 2
Northwich Vic.... 0

*Wealdstone 2
Frickley Ath. 1

*Dartford............. 1
South Bank 3

*Enfield 3
Maidstone Utd... 2

*Grays Ath. 1,1
Chelmsford C.. 1,3

*Worthing............ 1
Bridgend T. 0

*Slough Town...... 1
Kettering T......... 2

*Crawley Town.... 0
Wycombe W....... 2

*Leek Town 2
Macclesfield T.... 1

*Scarborough. 0,1,0
Southport....0,1,1

*Corby Town....... 0
Kidderminster H. 4

*Burton Alb. 1
Bromsgrove R. ... 0

*Windsor & E. 0
Runcorn.............. 1

Third Round

***Altrincham.......... 1**
Bishop Auckland...0

*Cheltenham T.. 0,3
Bishop Storford0,1

*Wealdstone 0,1
South Bank 0,2

*Enfield 5
Chelmsford C..... 3

*Worthing......... 0,1
Kettering T......... 2

*Wycombe W2,5,1,1
Leek Town .2,5,1,0

*Southport...... 1,1
Kidderminster H. 1

Burton Alb......... 0
Runcorn.............. 2

Fourth Round

Altrincham.......... 2
*Cheltenham T..... 0

*South Bank 0
Enfield 1.0

*Kettering T......... 2
Wycombe W....... 1

*Kidderminster H. 1
Runcorn.............. 2

Semi-Final

Altrincham....... 1,2
Enfield............. 1,0

1st Leg at Enfield
2nd Leg at Altrincham

Kettering Town0,0
Runcorn........... 0,2

1st Leg at Runcorn
2nd Leg at Kettering

Final

Altrinham 1
Runcorn.............. 0

*** Indicates club drawn at home**

Altrincham's Professionalism Decisive

Altrincham (1) 1 Farrelly (43mins) **Runcorn (0) 0**

You had to feel a little sorry for Runcorn in the FA Trophy Final on May 17th.

The hard working Cheshire side had finally reached Wembley, after three agonising semi-final defeats. But when they got there, they walked straight into Altrincham at their most professional.

The streak of sheer quality that has set Altrincham apart from the rest for so long, revealed itself in this, their third final in eight years.

They left their local rivals, and closest friends, frustrated and well beaten – despite the 1-0 scoreline – on what should have been their greatest day.

Runcorn came to Wembley with conviction, a well drilled side, and all the heart in the world. The met a Robins side knowing just too much about the big occassion.

Birmingham City and a host of other Football League clubs have suffered at Altrincham's hands, so Runcorn are in good company.

Only an excellent display by 'Keeper Ray McBride, and fine performances by central defenders Bobby Fraser and Graham Jones, stopped Altrincham getting the goals to underline their superiority.

Runcorn were always going to make it hard. In the four previous meetings between the sides during the season, three had been drawn with the Linnets winning the other. And having conceded just one goal in their run to the final, Runcorn were never likely to keel over.

For a brief early spell they must have encouraged their fans. But the sum total of their efforts was one shot, a 30 yarder from John Imrie that flashed a yard wide of 'keeper Jeff Wealans' right hand post.

Ronnie Ellis had hoooked over from a Paul Reid flick, and Steve Crompton had been booked for elbowing Jeff Johnson, as Altricham's grip on the game tightened.

Runcorn had high hopes of their twin strikers.Mark Carter, a final loser with Bangor two seasons previously, and Dave Mather – two goal hero of Telford's win in '83 – got little joy against the 35 year old Johnson, in his third final, and Paul Cuddy.

Cuddy had been brought into the side after spending three months struggling to overcome a shin injury, and that cost the unlucky Doug Newton his place in the eleven. Sadly the England semi-pro cap didn't even get on as substitute.

When the Robins goal did come after 43 minutes it was richly deserved. The excellent Phil Gardner put Gary Anderson away on the right, and from his pulled back cross, full back Mike Farrelly crashed in a shot that hit the bar, bounced down and spun viciously high into the roof of the net.

A minute later Johnson almost marked his last appearance at Wembley with a killer goal. Ellis this time drove in the cross, and Johnson's stinging low hook was miraculously clutched on the line by McBride – the save of the match!

Altrincham came out after the break to play some superb, controlled possession soccer, backed up by a well drilled offside trap.

Well done John Rooney who has produced superb photos of Altrincham year after year. This time he caught the goalmouth expressions as the only goal of the game, from Mike Farrelly, sails into the corner of Runcorn's net. Altrincham also became the first 'Non-League' club to have a full page colour team photo in 'Match' magazine during the season curtesy of John Rooney.

Altrincham to Wembley

Round	Opponents	Venue	Result	Scorers
1st Round	**Ryhope C.A.** (Northern First)	Away	3-1	Anderson 2, Reid
2nd Round	**Bangor City** (Multipart)	Home	6-1	Reid 3, Davison2, Chesters
3rd Round	**Bishop Auckland** (Northern First)	Home	1-0	Chesters
4th Round	**Cheltenham Town** (Gola)	Away	2-0	Ellis 2
Semi-Final				
1st Leg	**Enfield** (Gola)	Away	1-1	Newton (pen)
2nd Leg	**Enfield**	Home	2-0	Ellis, Newton (pen)

Matches played: 6 goals for: 15 against: 3

Runcorn to Wembley

Round	Opponents	Venue	Result	Scorers
1st Round	**Marine** (Multipart)	Home	2-0	Mather, Crompton S.
2nd Round	**Windsor & Eaton** (Vauxhall-Opel)	Away	1-0	Carter
3rd Round	**Burton Albion** (Multipart)	Home	2-0	Skeete, Carter
4th Round	**Kidderminster Harriers** (Gola)	Away	2-1	Lee (pen), own goal
Semi-Final				
1st Leg	**Kettering Town** (Gola)	Home	0-0	
2nd Leg	**Kettering Town**	Away	2-0	Mather, Smith

Matches played: 6 Goals for: 9 against: 1

Altrincham celebrate their Wembley triumph. Photo: John Rooney.

Reid, in his third final in four years – the previous two were with Northwich – had a shot on the turn deflected wide, but the goals wouldn't come.

This gave Runcorn heart and they slowly forced their way into the game. The ex-Manchester City and Aston Villa star Frank Carrodus – at 36 probably playing his last big match-tried hard to create the chances, but Altrincham's Gardner and skipper John Davison had such a grip on midfield, the task was beyond him.

Alan Crompton came on to replace his namesake Steve, and Davison found himself booked for a foul on Imrie. One goal was never enough for comfort, but Altrincham still had a measure of authority that kept Runcorn at arms length.

Clincally and efficiently they played out time, and their boss John King ended as the first man to skipper and manage a side to Trophy final glory.

Altrincham have learned to live and prosper in the shadows of Old Trafford, so it was somewhat fitting that Davison should step up to recieve the Trophy from Sir Matt Busby at the end.

The only sad spot was the size of the crowd 15,700. The parochial nature of the match had seen it virtually ignored in the south, and the dreadful weather in the north on the morning of the game probably stopped many from travelling.

Runcorn boss John Williams had seen the only major trophy he has not won snatched from him, but he paid tribute to Altrincham at the end, and no doubt vowed to be back one day to put matters right.

Altrincham, having earlier in the season gone further in the FA Cup than they had even managed previously, added the Trophy as well. Their fourth place in the Gola League wasn't enough to stop Enfield deservedly taking the title and going forward to contest League membership.

But it all added fuel to the Moss Lane side's obsessive campaign to make it into the Fourth Division. One day they'll succeed, few will doubt that.

Paul Walker, DAILY STAR.

Altrincham: Wealands, Gardner, Densmore, Johnson, Farrelly, Conning, Cuddy, Davison (captain), Reid, Ellis, Anderson, Substitute: Newton.
Runcorn: McBride, Lee, Roberts, Jones, Fraser, Smith (captain), Crompton S, Crompton A, Imrie, Carter, Mather, Carrodus.

F.A. CHALLENGE TROPHY FINALS 1970-85

1970 *(Attendance: 28,000)*
Macclesfield Town 2 (Lyons, Fidler B.) **Telford United 0** Referee: K. Walker
Macclesfield Town: Cooke, Sievwright, Bennett, Collins, Roberts, Lyons, Fidler B, Young, Corfield, Fidler D.
Telford United: Irvine, Harris, Croft, Flowers, Coton, Ray, Fudge, Hart, Bentley, Murray, Jagger.

1971 *(Attecdance: 29,500)*
Telford United 3 (Owen, Bentley, Fudge) **Hillingdon 2** (Reeve, Bishop) Referee: D. Smith
Teleford United: Irvine, Harris, Croft, Ray, Coton, Carr, Fudge, Owen, Bentley, Jagger, Murray.
Hillingdon: Lowe, Batt, Langley, Higginson, Newcombe, Moore. Fairchild, Bishop, Carter, Knox.

1972 *(Attendance: 24,000)*
Stafford Rangers 3 (Williams (2), Cullerton (1)) **Barnet 0** Referee: P. Partridge
Stafford Rangers: Aleksic, Chadwick, Clayton, Sargeant, Aston, Machin, Cullerton, Chapman, Williams, Bayley, Jones.
Barnet: McClelland, Lye, Jenkins, Ward, Embrey, King, Powell, Ferry, Easton, Plume.

1973 *(Attendance: 23,000)*
Scarborough 2 (Leask, Thompson) **Wigan Athletic 1** (Rogers) aet Referee: H. Hackney
Scarborough: Garrow, Appleton, Shoulder, Dunn, Siddle, Fagan, Donoghue, Franks, Leask (Barmby), Thompson, Hewitt.
:Wigan Athletic: Reeves, Morris, Sutherland, Taylor, Jackson, Gillibrand, Clements, Oates (McCunnell), Rogers, King, Worswick.

1974 *(Attendance: 19,000)*
Morecambe 2 (Richmond, Sutton) **Dartford 1** (Cunningham) Referee: B. Homewood
Morecambe: Coates, Pearson, Bennett, Sutton, Street, Baldwin, Done, Webber, Roberts (Galley), Kershaw, Richmond.
Dartford: Morton, Read, Payne, Carr, Burns, Binks, Light, Glozier, Robinson (Hearne), Cunningham, Halleday.

1975 *(Attendance: 21,000)*
Matlock Town 4 (Oxley, Dawson, T. Fenoughty, N. Fenoughty) **Scarborough 0** Referee: K. Styles
Matlock Town: Fell. McKay, Smith, Stuart, Dawson, Swan, Oxley, Fenoughty N, Scott, Fenoughty T, Fenoughty M.
Scarborough: Williams, Hewitt, Rettit, Dunn, Marshall, Todd, Houghton, Woodall, Davidson, Barnby, Aveyard.

1976 *(Attencance: 21,000)*
Scarborough 3 (Woodall, Abbey, Marshall pen) **Stafford Rangers 2** (Jones 2) aet Referee: R. Challis
Scarborough: Barnard, Jackson, Marshall, Dunn (H), Ayre, (Donoghue), Dunn (H.A.), Dale, Barmby, Woodall, Abbey, Hilley.
Stafford Rangers: Arnold, Ritchie, Richards, Sargeant, Seddon, Morris Chapman, Lowe, Jones, Hutchison, Chadwick.

1977 *(Attendance: 20,500)*
Scarborough 2 (Dunn pen, Abbey) **Dagenham 1** (Harris) Referee: G. Courtney
Scarborough: Chapman, Smith, Marshall (Barmby), Dunn, Ayre, Deere, Aveyard, Donoghue, Woodall, Abbey, dunn.
Dagenham: Huttley, Wellman, Currie P, Dunwell, Moore, Currie W, Harkins, Saul, Fox, Harris, Holder.

1978 *(Attendance: 20,000)*
Altrincham 3 (King, Johnson, Rogers) **Leatherhead 1** (Cook) Referee: A. Grey
Altrincham: Eales, Allan, Crossley, Baily, Owens, King, Morris, Heathcote, Johnson, Rogers, Davison (Flkaherty).
*Leatherhead:*Swannell, Cooper, Eaton, Davies, Reis, Malley, Cook, Salkeld, Kelly, Baker, Boyle (Bailey).

1979 *(Attendance: 32,000)*
Stafford Rangers 2 (Wood A. 2) **Kettering Town 0** Referee: D. Richardson
Stafford Rangers: Arnold, Wood F, Willis, Sargeant, Ritchie, Seeker, Chapman, Wood A, Cullerton, Chadwick (Jones).
Kettering Town: Lane, Ashby, Lee, Easthall, Dixey, Suddards, Flannagan, Kellock, Phipps, Clayton, Evans (Hughes).

1980 *(Attendence: 26,000)*
Dagenham 2 *(Duck, Maycock)* **Mossley 1** (Smith) Referee: K. Baker
Dagenham: Huttley, Willman, Scales, Dunwell, Moore, Durrell, Maycock, Horan, Duck, Kidd, Jones (Holder).
Mossley: Fitton, Brown, Vaughan, Gorman, Salter, Polliot, Smith, Moore, Skeete, O'Connor, Keelan (Wilson).

1981 *(Attendance: 22,578)*
Bishop's Stortford 1 (Sullivan) **Sutton United 0** Referee: J. Warrall
Bishop's Stortford: Moore, Blackman (Capt), Brame, Amith (Worrell), Bradford, Abery, Sullivan, Knapman, Radford, Simmonds, Mitchell.
Sutton United: Collyer, Rogers, Green, Rains J. (Capt), Rains T, Stephens (Sunnucks), Waldon, Pritchard, Cornwell, Parsons, Dennis.

1982 *(Attendence: 18,678)*
Enfield 1 (taylor) **Altrincham 0** Referee: B. Stevens
Enfield: J. Jacobs, K. Barrett, J. Tone, J. Jennings, D. Waite, N. Ironton, N. Ashford, P. Taylor, L. Holmes, S. Oliver (D. Flint), S. King.
Altrincham: J. Connaughton, I. Crossley, J. Davison, M. Bailey, P. Cuddy, J. King (B. Whitbread), S. Allan, G. Heathcote, J. Johnson, J. Rogers, B. Howard.

1983 *(Attendence: 22,071)*
Telford 2 (Mather 2) **Northwuch Victoria 1** (Bennett) Referee: B. Hill
Telford United: Charlton, Lewis, Turner, Mayman (Joseph), Walker (Capt), Eaton, Williams, Mather, Hogan, Alcock.
Northwich Victoria: Ryan, Fretwell, Murphy, Jones (Capt), Forshsaw, Ward, Anderson, Abel (Bennett), Reid, Chesters, Wilson.

Two Special Trophy Photos

A desperate lunging tackle fails to prevent Bishop Stortford's Sullivan scoring the winner against Sutton United in 1981.
Photo: Mike Eason

Dave Mather, who played at Wembley again for Runcorn last season, Scores Telford United's first goal against Northwich Victoria 1983.
Photo: Mike Joss

1984 *(Attendance: 14,200 Replay: 5,805)*
Northwich Victoria 1 (Chesters) **Bangor City 1** (Whelan)
Northwich Victoria 2 (Chesters pen, Anderson) **Bangor City 1** (Lunn) Referee: John Martin
Northwich Victoria: Ryan, Fretwell, Dean, Jones (Capt), Forshaw (Power 65 minutes), Bennett, Anderson, Abel, Reid, Chesters, Wilson.
Bangor City: Letheren, Cavanagh, Gray, Whelan, Banks, Lunn, Urquhart, Morris, Carter (Chap), Howat, Sutcliffe (Westwood 105 minutes). (Teams the same for both games).

1985 *(Attendance: 20,775)*
Wealdstone 2 (Graham, Holmes) **Boston United 1** Cook) Referee: J. Bray
Wealdstone: Iles, Perkins, Bowgett, Byatt, Davies, Greenaway, Holmes, Wainwright, Donnellan, Graham, (N. Cordice, 89 mins), A. Cordice.
Boston United: Blackwell, Casey, Ladd, Creane, O'Brien, Thommson, Lavereick, (Mallender, 78 mins), Simpson, Gilbert, Lee, Cook.

F.A. TROPHY CLUB RECORDS

	Points 69-73	73-74	74-75	75-76	76-77	77-78	78-79	79-80	80-81	81-82	82-83	83-84	84-85	Total
Scarborough	15pts	F	W	W	1	2	1	1	QF	3	1	2	2	52
Stafford R.	19pts	1	F	2	2	W	1	2	1	1	–	QF	2	48
Dagenham	0pts	QF	3	F	QF	SF	W	2	3	SF	SF	1	2	47
Altrincham	3pts	1	–	SF	W	1	3	QF	F	3	1	SF	W	46
Telford U.	21pts	3	2	1	–	–	1	–	3	W	QF	2	1	45
Bangor C.	13pts.	1	1	2	3	1	2	SF	1	3	F	2	2	42
Enfield	0pts	3	SF	1	2	QF	1	1	W	QF	1	SF	SF	39
Northwich Vic.	6pts	2	1	1	1	2	1	3	SF	F	W	1	2	38
Weymouth	12pts	3	2	QF	2	2	3	2	1	3	1	1	1	37
Dartford	14pts	1	1	2	2	–	1	SF	2	QF	1	1	2	36
Runcorn	0pts	–	SF	3	SF	SF	1	1	3	1	2	QF	F	36
Boston U.	6pts	2	1	1	2	3	SF	2	1	QF	1	F	1	35
Burton Alb.	11pts	SF	2	2	1	–	3	1	1	1	–	2	3	32
Matlock T.	8pts	W	3	3	3	1	2	1	–	1	1	2	–	32
Worcester C.	13pts	1	1	–	1	2	1	QF	QF	2	1	1	1	32
Kettering T.	8pts	2	1	2	1	F	1	2	1	1	–	1	SF	31
Morecambe	15pts	2	3	QF	1	1	2	1	–	–	–	1	1	31
Yeovil T.	13pts	1	1	2	1	QF	3	2	1	1	2	–	–	31
Barnet	14pts	–	–	1	–	–	3	–	–	2	QF	3	1	28
Macesfield T.	21pts	1	1	2	–	–	1	–	–	–	–	–	2	28
Mossley	9pts	3	–	–	–	–	F	QF	3	2	1	–	–	28
Kidderminster H.	9pts	–	1	1	–	1	1	1	QF	1	3	1	QF	27
Nuneaton Bor.	7pts	–	–	QF	2	1	QF	1	1	2	3	1	1	27
Chorley	8pts	–	–	QF	2	2	2	1	2	2	2	1	–	26
Wycombe W.	0pts	–	–	2	2	3	2	2	SF	2	2	2	QF	26
Bromsgrove R.	10pts	1	QF	1	1	–	–	–	–	–	3	3	2	25
Burnham & Hillingdon*	16pts	2	QF	1	1	1	–	–	–	–	–	–	–	25
Grantham	13pts	2	2	1	1	1	1	–	–	–	2	1	–	24
Chelmsford C.	15pts	1	1	–	–	–	–	–	–	–	3	–	3	23
Merthyr Tydfil	6pts	1	2	1	QF	–	2	–	2	–	2	2	–	22
Slough T.	0pts	–	3	SF	2	2	1	1	3	1	1	1	2	22
Barrow	4pts	1	1	–	–	2	QF	1	1	3	2	1	1	21
Bishop's Stortford	0pts	1	2	1	–	–	–	W	QF	1	1	1	3	21
Blyth Spartans	0pts	1	–	1	1	2	QF	3	2	QF	1	1	1	21
Maidstone U.	2pts	–	–	–	1	3	1	1	2	3	2	QF	2	21
Bishop Auckland	0pts	1	2	1	–	QF	1	–	3	1	1	3	3	20
Cheltenham T.	2pts	2	–	1	1	3	2	1	1	1	–	2	QF	20
Buxton	16pts	1	1	–	–	–	–	–	1	–	–	–	–	19
Lancaster C.	4pts	3	3	1	2	2	1	1	2	–	–	–	–	19
Marine	0pts	–	–	1	1	2	3	2	1	1	SF	2	1	19
Leatherhead	0pts	2	2	1	F	3	2	1	1	–	–	–	–	18
Sutton U.	0pts	1	1	–	1	1	–	F	3	2	1	1	1	18
Wealdstone	3pts	–	–	–	–	–	–	–	2	1	1	W	3	17
Bath C.	2pts	–	–	1	–	1	3	1	1	1	2	3	1	16
Tooting & Mitcham U.	0pts	1	QF	3	3	1	2	1	1	–	–	–	–	16
Dulwich H.	0pts	–	1	–	–	–	QF	1	1	2	3	2	1	15
Goole T.	2pts	QF	2	–	3	1	–	2	–	1	–	–	–	15
Hendon	0pts	1	2	3	3	1	1	–	2	–	2	–	–	15
Spennymoor U.	0pts	–	–	2	SF	2	1	1	1	2	1	–	–	15
Stourbridge	12pts	1	1	–	–	–	–	–	–	–	–	1	–	15
Witton Alb.	5pts	–	–	2	–	3	–	1	3	–	1	–	–	15
Dover Ath.	8pts	2	1	1	–	1	1	–	–	–	–	–	–	14
Frickley Ath.	0pts	–	–	1	2	–	–	–	1	–	3	QF	2	13
Banbury U.	8pts	1	1	1	1	–	–	–	–	–	–	–	–	12
Gainsborough Tr.	6pts	–	2	–	1	1	2	–	–	–	–	–	–	12
Harrow Bor.	0pts	–	–	–	1	1	–	–	–	SF	1	3	1	12
King's Lynn	5pts	1	1	–	–	2	–	–	–	1	–	1	1	12
Minehead	5pts	–	–	2	1	2	–	1	1	–	–	–	–	12
South Liverpool	7pts	2	1	1	–	–	–	–	–	–	1	–	–	12
Thanet U.	4pts	2	2	1	–	3	–	–	–	–	–	–	–	12
Winsford U.	2pts	1	–	1	QF	1	1	2	–	–	–	–	–	12
Woking	0pts	–	–	–	1	1	SF	1	2	1	–	1	–	12
Burscough	7pts	2	1	–	–	–	–	–	–	1	–	–	–	11
Leytonstone/Ilford*	0pts	3	–	–	–	–	–	3	–	2	2	1	–	11
Stalybridge Celtic	3pts	–	–	–	–	1	2	1	1	2	–	1	–	11
Whitby T.	0pts	–	–	–	2	1	–	–	–	1	QF	1	1	10

W = 7 F = 6 SF = 5 QF = 4

Leytonstone/Ilford – 74/75 performance relates to Ilford before the amalgamation.
Burnham & Hillingdon – performances prior to 85/86 relate to Hillingdon before the amalgamation.
Bedford T. (35). Wigan Ath. (27), Hastings U. (22), Romford (18), Wimbledon (18), Atherstone P. (12), Gateshead U. (12) and Hereford U. (10) no longer compete in the F.A. Trophy.

THE OFFICIAL F.A. CUP FOOTBALL COMPUTER GAME

Featuring all the 92 League Clubs and the following Non-League Clubs: Altrincham, Bangor City, Barnet, Bath City, Bishop Auckland, Blyth Spartans, Boston United, Chelmsford City, Dartford, Enfield, Gainsborough Trinity, Gateshead, Maidstone United, Northwich Victoria, Nuneaton Borough, Runcorn, Scarborough, Stafford Rangers, Sutton United, Telford United, Tooting & Mitcham United, Walthamstow Avenue, Wealdstone, Weymouth, Worcester City, Wycombe Wanderers, Yeovil Town. Each player can also enter a Non-League club in addition to the above from the First Round Proper through to the Final. Authentic form can be influenced by you if you are a good manager. Round-by-round results and realistic cup draws for every round. You can play against the computer yourself or up to eight people can attempt to take their teams to Wembley. The game gives hours of fun and is equally enjoyed by League or Non-League fans. The idea and real life form from Tony Williams. Published by Virgin Games. Available on Amstrad CPC464/664/6128, Commodore 64/128, Spectrum 48K (£7.95) postage free. These games are available from Tony Williams, 2 Elder Cottages, Hatch Beauchamp, Taunton, Somerset TA3 6TH with cheque or postal order for £7.95 made payable to Tony Williams.

F. A. CHALLENGE VASE

Committee: C. C. Oakes (Chairman), J. R. Plumbe, J. Barter, A. Burbidge, J. E. Davey, W. G. Halsey, R. W. Kiddell, J. M. Ryder, D. Henson.

When today's two Finalists finally booked their Wembley spots I am sure their supporters will have heaved vast sighs of relief. Fans of the beaten Semi-Finalists will have taken little consolation from the achievement of reaching the last four, although it is possible this may change with the passage of time. It is a brutal fact of soccer life that whilst the losing Finalists will have earned themselves a place in the history of the competition, few other than their most ardent supporters will remember the identity of those who failed at the penultimate stage.

Wisbech Town by virtue of their Second Leg defeat at home to **Southall** have, much to their chagrin, joined an exclusive group of clubs who have tasted that most bitter pill in two successive seasons. Last year they twice held eventual winners **Halesowen Town** to a draw before succumbing by the odd goal in three in a replay.

Friar Lane Old Boys missed out in the first two competitions, while **Farnborough Town** were unfortunate enough to be paired with **Billericay Town** in 1976 and 1977. Two other clubs have a pair of Semi-Final failures to their name – **Hungerford Town**, who on both occasions were beaten in their home leg, and **Irthlingborough Diamonds**, whose frustration will be more acute having also suffered three Quarter-Final defeats.

For another three clubs, the pain of Semi-Final defeat was wiped out by success the following year. **Stamford's** disappointment against **Epsom & Ewell** in the inaugural season of the Vase was soon forgotten even if they did come off second best to Billericay at Wembley, and **Barton Rovers** defeat by **Sheffield** in 1977 did not matter despite the following year's loss in the Final to **Blue Star**. The latter had qualified for Wembley at the expense of **Almondsbury Greenway** who had the smiles restored to their faces twelve months later even after **Billericay** completed their third victory in four years. Such was the tension that the Almondsbury Chairman could not bear to watch and spent the Second Leg at **Whickham** pacing outside the ground.

Whickham themselves took two years to put the record straight and in fact, ran out winners at Wembley with a 3-2 extra-time victory over **Willenhall Town**. This match was also notable for the fact that Willenhall used three goalkeepers. In the lead when first choice keeper Newton was stretchered off, leading goal scorer Matthews first of all went between the posts before he was replaced by Woodall. Matthews himself wore three different numbers during the game.

There are many theories about the most appropriate tactics for two-legged contests but statistics suggest that it is important to make the most of home advantage. Of the 24 Finalists to-date only two have lost in front of their own fans. In 1978 **Barton Rovers** were able to make up a single goal home deficit in the Second Leg to force a replay in which they overcame **Hungerford** while **Forest Green Rovers** were not unduly concerned at the 1-0 Second Leg defeat having already booked their Wembley place with a 4-1 win at **Blue Star**.

It does not seem to matter whether a club is drawn to play at home first or second for there have been twelve examples of each. Of more significance is winning, or at least avoiding defeat, in the First Leg for only three Finalists have managed to overcome this handicap. In 1977 **Billericay** trailed **Farnborough** by two goals but swept to Wembley with a resounding 6-0 win in the second encounter.

The following season **Barton Rovers** survived despite losing the First Leg in which they also had home advantage, while last season **Fleetwood Town** lost 3-2 at **Exmouth** but put things to right a week later. **Halesowen**, however, seem to be intent on starting a new trend having drawn both legs for the past two seasons, relying on neutral ground replays for ultimate victory.

Every season the Vase provides a fine blend of established clubs and first timers. Five of the clubs who reached the last eight in 1985 were in the hunt at this year's Fourth Round stage though beaten Finalists **Fleetwood Town** had already suffered defeat at the hands of **Blue Star** (the reverse of last season's encounter), while **Exmouth's** exit at home to **Moreton Town** will have been both a surprise and a disappointment to their fans. **Halesowen** emphatically disposed of **Sheffield** (Finalists in 1977), **Blue Star** moved on smoothly at the expense of **North Ferriby** and **Wisbech's** defeat of **Hinckley Athletic** drew the biggest gate of the Round – 1162. Of those with no real pedigree in the competition, **Havant Town** thrust themselves into the spotlight with their 10-0 annihilation of **Sholing Sports, Southall** aaccounted for Vase stalwards **Barton Rovers** and the impressive Vauxhall-Opel outfit **Stevenage Borough** matched their League form with their win at **Sharpness**.

Another large crowd witnessed **Wisbech's** Fifth Round 1-0 victory over Eastern League rivals **Sudbury Town** and **Halesowen** took their customary large support to **Tamworth** where they recorded a 2-0 victory. Perhaps the biggest upset came at **Hucknall** where **Blue Star** went out to a controversial late penalty, but **Havant's** win at **Buckingham**, top of the United Counties League, erased any suggestion that the previous Round's result had been a fluke.

The Sixth Round was disrupted by February's snow and ice but **Warrington Town** who had progressed thus far without attracing a great deal of attention and **Southall**, ignoring **Stevenage's** reputation, soon booked their spots in the last four.

The Semi-Final draw kept the experienced **Halesowen** and **Wisbech** sides apart and when both recorded 5-1 Quarter-Final victories, most pundits had them marked down as favourites for the Final. First Leg draws away from home made this outcome all the more likely. **Wisbech** however were totally unnerved by the occasion and two goals shortly before the interval and another immediately after, saw the well- drilled **Southall** virtually home and dry. Even with their usual enthusiastic support **Halesowen** found **Warrington** a tough nut to crack and were forced into extra time when they soon regained the lead. Reading the results the next morning, most people were confronted by the prospect of a **Southall** v **Halesowen** Final. Whether there exists in the Sunday press some secret admiration for Halesowen is still unclear but it eventually transpired that Warrington's late equaliser had been largely ignored. Like it or not **Halesowen** had to travel to **Telford** the following Tuesday where once again they faced stubborn resistance from the North-West Counties side before running out 6-3 victors, giving themselves the opportunity of becoming only the second team to retain the Vase.

The quality of football in the Non-League ranks is increasingly in evidence by virtue not only of the regular F.A. Cup exploits of the likes of Altrincham and Telford but also the number of players who have established themselves in the Football League after initially making a name for themselves in the Semi- Professional game. **Alan Devonshire (Southall), Pau Mariner (Chorley), Graham Roberts (Weymouth)** and **Kerry Dixon (Dunstable)** have all gained Full International honours in recent seasons. The latter in fact topped the Southern League goal scoring charts for 1979/80 and made three appearances for its Representative side.

Leicester's Alan Smith was a member of the England Under-21 Squad very soon after winning Semi-Pro caps while with **Alvechurch**, **Jim Arnold (Stafford Rangers)** and **Gary Phillips (Barnet)** both kept goal for England before moving into the League while **Graham Pearce** could only have dreamed of a Cup Final appearance until Brighton snapped him up from **Barnet**. Centre- backs **Steve Thompson (Charlton), Alan Walker (Milwall), Trevor Peake (Coventry)** and **Eric Young (Brighton)** made their names at **Boston**, **Telford**, **Nuneaton** and **Slough** respectively. **Mark Ward**, who has hit the headlines with West Ham this season, appeared in the 1983 Trophy Final for **Northwich Victoria**.

ADRIAN TITCOMBE

The Football Association's Administrative Secretary.

This review was first published in the F.A. Vase Final Programme

F. A. VASE ROUND BY ROUND RESULTS

EXTRA PRELIMINARY ROUND
Best Attendance
Canvey Island v St. Neots Town 160
Best Home Victory
Darwen v Alnwick Town 5-0
Best Away Victory
Daisy Hill v Liversedge 1-5
Result of the Round
Harrisons v Long Buck by 0-1

RESULTS	Sc.	Att.
Darwen v Alnwick Town	5-0	50
Langley Park Welfare v Newton Aycliffe	4-1	45
Shotton Comrades v Ponteland United	0-2	15
Dudley Welfare v Murton	0-3	110
Tees Components v Bridlington Town	3-2	36
Annfield Plain v Northallerton Town	1-2 *	62
Daisy Hill v Liversedge	1-5	40
Merseyside Police v Ashton Town (Walkover for Merseyside Police)		
Rossington Main v Kirkby Town	1-3	50
Borrowash Victoria v Harworth CI	2-0	69
Kiverton Park v Urmston Town (Walkover for Kiverton Park)		
Barnton v Keyworth United	0-2	41
Welwyn G. C. v Leighton Town	1-2	53
Chasetown v Hurley Daw MW	0-3	63
Harrisons v Long Buckby	0-1	75
Brackley Town v Westfields	1-0	85
Armitage v Hinckley Town	0-3	40
Leavesden Hospital v Ortonians	5-1	66
Langford v Halstead Town	0-3	70
Pennant v St. Ives Town	2-0	32
Mirrless Blackstone v E. Thurrock United	0-2	75
Eynesbury Rovers v Shefford Town	1-0	100
Hanwell Town v Rayners Lane	3-2	65
Canvey Island v St. Neots Town	3-1	160
St. Margaretsbury v Gt. Shelford (at Ware)	2-0	125
Danson (Bexley Boro.) v Portsmouth RN (Match awarded to Danson (Bexley Boro.))	0-3	45
Peacehaven & Telscombe v Shoreham	3-3	105
Haywards Heath v Fleet Town	2-0	46
Wigmore Athletic v Lymington Town	1-2	14
Farleigh Rovers v Molesey	0-1	25
Greenwich Borough v Havant Town	1-3	58
Yeading v Petersfield United	3-2	70
Amesbury Tn. v Swanage Tn. & Herston	0-4	48
Abingdon United v Blandford United	4-0	45
Harrow Hill v Avon St. Philips	1-2	35
Robinsons Drg v Lydbrook Athletic	2-0	132
Brislington v Bristol St. George (at Keynsham)	2-1	78
Dawlish Town v St. Blazey	1-0	50
Wadebridge Town v Tiverton Town	4-1	90
REPLAY		
Shoreham v Peacehaven & Telscombe	2-1	95

PRELIMINARY ROUND
Best Attendance
Stevenage Borough v Ware 415
Best Home Victory
Banstead Athletic v Dansan 6-0
Best Away Victory
Brockenhurst v Westbury United 0-4
Sawbridgeworth v March Town United 0-4
Nantwich Town v Kirkby Town 0-4
Result of the Round
Hounslow v Shillington 1-3

RESULTS	Sc.	Att.
Cleator Motor Celtic v Rowntree Mack.	1-1	201
Tees Components v Coundon TT	0-2	30
Esh Winning v Yorkshire Amateurs	0-1	34
Farsley Celtic v Harrogate RA	2-2	165
Seaton Delaval St. v Willington	2-1	28
Evenwood Town v Washington	1-3	29
South Shields v Tadcaster Albion	0-1	47
Wingate v Marchon	3-1	45
Nunthorpe Athletic v Darwen	0-1	70
Easington Colliery v Northallerton Town	5-0	50
Ashington v West Allotment Celtic	2-3	60
Norton & Stockton Ancients v York RI	1-0	24
Murton v Durham City	3-2	123
Seaham CW Red Star v Ponteland United	3-1	70
Langley Pk. Welfare v W. Auckland Town	3-0	65
Darlington CB v Armthorpe Welfare	0-2	106
Wren Rovers v Bentley Victoria	3-2 *	42
Maltby MW v St. Dominics	0-2	28
Liversedge v Bradley Rangers	3-2 *	24
Emley v Maine Road	2-1	172
Rylands v Rossendale United	1-3	42
Fryston CW v Maghull	1-2 *	16
Heswall v Burnley Belvedere	1-2	47
Atherton Collieries v Cheadle Town	3-0	40
Garforth Town v Lytham (Walkover for Garforth Town)		
Merseyside Police v Grimethorpe MW	3-2	97
Ford Motors v Nelson	1-2	6
Waterloo Dock v Skelmersdale United	5-1	65
Linotype v BSC Parkgate	2-2	25
Woolley MW v Ellesmere Port & Neston	0-2	70
Sheffield v Kiveton Park	2-0 *	49
Irlam Town v Prestwich Heys	2-0	68
Harrogate Town v Keyworth United	3-0	166
Ossett Town v Thackley	1-2	70
Nantwich Town v Kirkby Town	0-4	114
Hatfield Main v Atherton LR	0-3	40
Borrowash Vic. v Mexborough Tn. Ath.	3-1	36
Pilkington Recreation v Droylsden	1-2	56
Ashton United v Chadderton	1-3	108
N. Ferriby United v Kimberley Town	5-2	55
Brigg Town v Graham St. Prims	2-1	40
Hall Road Rangers v Stapenhill	1-2 *	84
Louth United v Oakham United	1-0	45
Clipstone Welfare v Gresley Rovers	1-2	88
Immingham Town v Barton Town	1-0	31
Retford Town v Long Eaton United (Walkover for Long Eaton United)		
Newhall United v Bourne Town	2-0	54
Arnold Kingswell v Boston	2-1	56
Stratford Town v Desborough Town	1-2 *	78
Tamworth v Malvern Town	4-1	352
Walsall Borough v Long Buckby	0-3	54
Rushden Town v Friar Lane OB	1-4	119
Lye Town v Hurley Daw MW	2-3	121
Boldmere St. Michaels v Blakenall	2-0	50
Birstall United v Solihull Borough	4-1	85
Evesham United v Eastwood Hanley	4-3 *	101
Coleshill Town v Smethwick Highfield	3-0	40
Hinckley Athletic v West Midlands Police	3-1	170
Paget Rangers v Wolverhampton United	4-1	35
Tividale v Mile Oak Rovers	0-1	44
Anstey Nomads v Bilston Town	1-2	132
Highgate United v Coventry Sporting	0-1	30
Wednesfield Social v Racing Club Warwick	2-0	57
Hinckley Town v GKN Sankey	3-1	35
Northfield Town v Oldswinford	3-2	50
Brackley Town v Bridgnorth Town	1-2	68
Rushall Olympic v Oadby Town	1-3	98
Wolverton Town v Brereton Social	1-1	65
Brantham Athletic v Harwich & Parkeston	1-3	75
Somersham Town v Brightlingsea United	2-1	100
Diss Town v Yaxley	0-1	118
Halstead Town v Watton United	4-3	85
Histon v East Thurrock United	1-3	78
Ely City v Lowestoft Town	1-0	97
Holbeach United v Witham Town	0-2	59
Newmarket Town v Eynesbury Rovers (at Eynesbury Rovers)	2-4	65
Hadleigh United v Canvey Island	1-0	50
Clacton Town v Stowmarket Town	0-3	118
Bowers United v Maldon Town	2-1	96
Felixstowe Town v Ransomes	1-2	50
Thetford Town v Chatteris Town	2-3	81
Haverhill Rovers v Soham. Town Rangers	0-0	108
Sawbridgeworth v March Town United	0-4	60
Saffron Walden Town v Pennant	3-1	125
Feltham v Bicester Town	1-0	46
Amersham Town v Wootton Blue Cross	2-4	27
Chalfont St. Peter v Newport Pagnell Tn.	3-2	79
Cheshunt v Norsemen	2-1	50
Arlesey Town v St. Margaretsbury	0-0	55
Winslow United v Beconsfield United	0-3	52

	Sc.	Att.
Stevenage Borough v Ware	6-1 *	415
Sixty-One v Hanwell Town	1-2	15
Ruislip Manor v Eaton Bray United	0-0	61
Maidenhead Town v Old Esthameians	4-1	45
Leighton Town v Winchmore Hill	3-0	94
Woodford Town v Potton United	0-2	49
Hounslow v Shillington	1-3	104
Ashcroft Co-op v Leavesden Hospital	0-1 *	30
Vauxhall Motors v Berkhamsted Town	2-3	51
Haringey Borough v Hazells (Aylesbury)	2-3	25
Milton Keynes Borough v Letchworth GC	1-2	37
Pirton v Hoddesdon Town	3-2	30
Ampthill Town v Edgware	3-3	110
Royston Town v Tring Town	1-1	75
Southall v Kingsbury Town	1-1	86
Brimsdown Rovers v Northwood	1-2	55
Flackwell Heath v Stotfold	2-1 *	100
Ringmer v Rainham Town	2-1	61
Malden Town v Shoreham	2-4	30
Yeading v Beckenham Town	5-0	84
Redhill v Hastings Town	2-3	207
Whitstable Town v Hailsham Town	2-0	45
Eastbourne United v Beckton United	1-2	63
Merstham v Faversham Town	2-1	62
Erith & Belvedere v Malden Vale	0-2	74
Burgess Hill Town v Deal Town	2-1	44
Herne Bay v Slade Green	3-2	85
Chertsey Town v West Wickham	1-0 *	55
Swanley Town v Eastbourne Town	1-3	41
East Grinstead v Molesey	0-1	59
Darenth Heathside v Egham Town	0-1	41
Havant Town v Horley Town	3-0	92
Hythe Town v Midland Bank	2-1	60
Danson (Bexley Boro) v Banstead Athletic	3-3	65
Godalming Town v Horsham	2-1	105
Pirelli General v Lancing	4-1	30
Frimley Green v Cobham	0-1	16
Horndean v Chichester City	2-0	62
Chobham v Pagham	2-2	58
Wick v Farnham Town	2-0	50
Littlehampton Town v Camberley Town	2-5 *	81
Southwick v Horsham YMCA	4-0	99
Dorking v Haywards Heath	2-0	90
Didcot Town v Romsey Town	2-3 *	57
Whitehawk v Lymington Town	1-1	81
Portfield v Eastleigh	0-3	54
Arundel v Ash United	1-3	50
Portway Bristol v Calne Town	1-2	35
Avon (Bradford) v Wimborne Town	2-3	50
Welton Rovers v Thame United	2-0	90
Brockenhurst v Westbury United	0-4	68
Warminster Town v Odd Down Athletic	2-0	100
Supermarine v Port of Bristol	2-1 *	45
Backwell United v Avon St. Philips	4-0	35
Lawrence Weston Hallen v Keynsham Tn.	0-1	21
Yate Town v Glastonbury	1-0	84
Chippenham Town v Swanage Town & Herston	3-0	154
Wantage Town v Cirencester Town	4-2	37
Brislington v Hungerford Town	0-1	104
Wellington v Cinderford Town	2-4 *	95
Moreton Town v Radstock Town	2-0	66
Robinsons DRG v Fairford Town	1-1	75
Paulton Rovers v Clevedon Town	2-3	77
Thatcham Town v Abingdon United	0-0	95
Wallingford Town v Pegasus Juniors	4-3	42
Larkhall Athletic v Clanfield	2-1	68
Newquay v Flight Refuelling	1-3	145
Bridport v Ottery St. Mary	3-1	142
Hengrove Athletic v Dawlish Town	3-1	55
Wadebridge Town v Shepton Mallet Town	0-1	74
REPLAYS		
Rowntree Mack. v Cleator Moor Celtic	4-1	68
Harrogate RA v Farsley Celtic	1-2	170
BSC Parkgate v Linotype	1-0	38
Brereton Social v Wolverton Town	3-1	100
Soham Town Rangers v Haverhill Rovers	3-2 *	135
St. Margaretsbury v Arlesey Town	1-1	118
Eaton Bray United v Ruislip Manor	1-0	48
Edgware v Ampthill Town	0-1	56
Tring Town v Royston Town	1-2	93
Kingsbury Town v Southall	0-1	50
Banstead Athletic v Danson (Bexley Boro)	6-0	88
Pagham v Chobham (at Bognor Regis Tn)	1-1	196
Lymington Town v Whitehawk	3-2	96
Fairford Town v Robinsons DRG	3-1 *	48
Abingdon United v Thatcham Town	1-2 *	42
2nd REPLAYS		
Arlesey Town v St. Margaretsbury	0-1 *	120
Pagham v Chobham	4-0	198

FIRST ROUND

Best Attendance
Stevenage Borough v Flackwell Heath 475
Best Home Victory
Brereton Social v Coleshill Town 5-1
Barton Rovers v Hadleigh United 4-0
Eaton Bray United v Maidenhead Town 4-0
Best Away Victory
Burnley Belvedere v Borrowash Victoria 0-8
Result of the Round
Burnley Belvedere v Borrowash Victoria 0-8

RESULTS	Sc.	Att.
Seaton Delaval St. v Wingate	3-2 *	37
Easington Colliery v Langley Park Welfare	1-2	74
Coundon TT v Rowntree Mackintosh	2-2	30
Seaham CW Red Star v Ossett Albion	3-2 *	200
Eppleton CW v Armthorpe Welfare	4-1 *	67
Washington v Murton	1-1	120
Darwen v West Allotment Celtic	0-1	80
Yorkshire Amateurs v Farsley Celtic	2-0	139
Tadcaster Albion v Norton & Stockton Ancients	4-1	79
Hallam v Guiseley	2-6	226
Waterloo Dock v Wren Rovers	5-4 *	40
Rossendale United v Chadderton	0-1	116
Harrogate Town v St. Dominics	1-3	174
Burnley Belvedere v Borrowash Victoria	0-8	50
Frecheville Community v BSC Parkgate	0-0	42
Irlam Town v Emley	1-0	120
Droylsden v Sheffield	0-3	83
Nelson v Kirkby Town	1-8	22
Ellesmere Port & Nelson v Liversedge	3-0	13
Warrington Town v Atherton Collieries	2-0	63
Maghull v Garforth Town	1-0	82
Thackley v Clitheroe	2-2	149
Atherton LR v Merseyside Police	2-0	89
Appleby Frodingham v Friar Lane OB	3-2 *	51
Gresley Rovers v Immingham Town	4-3 *	302
Brigg Town v Newhall United	2-1	59
Skegness Town v Stapenhill	3-0	95
Louth United v Long Eaton United	3-2	60
Arnold Kingswell v North Ferriby United	1-3	25
Rothwell Town v Long Buckby	0-1	110
Hurley Daw MW v Bridgnorth Town	0-3	67
Mile Oak Rovers v Northfield Town	1-1	58
Oadby Town v Paget Rangers	3-1	38
Bilston Town v Birstall United	3-1	121
Hinckley Town v Wigston Fields	4-2	70
Hinckley Athletic v Wednesfield Social	4-2	204
Brereton Social v Coleshill Town	5-1	48
Tamworth v Evesham United	0-0	385
Coventry Sporting v Boldmere St. Michaels	3-0	30
Gorleston v Somersham Town	3-0	160
Yaxley v Baldock Town	0-1	150
(Match awarded to Yaxley FC due to Baldock Town playing a suspended player)		
Stowmarket Town v March Town United	3-3	204
Barton Rovers v Hadleigh United	4-0 *	109
Bowers United v East Thurrock United	2-0	132
Soham Tn. Rangers v Great Yarmouth Tn.	2-3	75
Eynesbury Rovers v Chatteris Town	2-0	125
Bury Town v Witham Town	0-1	123
Harwich & Parkeston v Ely City	0-1	122
Ransomes v Halstead Town	2-3	68
Desborough Town v St. Margaretsbury	0-4	120
Northwood v Hazells (Aylesbury)	4-1	65
Royston Town v Cheshunt	3-3	109
Ampthill Town v Hemel Hempstead	3-1	112
Beaconsfield United v Potton United	0-1	30

Cinderford Town won this match at Wellington 4-2 after extra time

Photo: Mike Brown

Ortonians score first with a penalty but lose 1-5, away to Leavesden Hospital.

Photo: David Shute

A great chance goes begging as Martin Duffy has his effort saved during a Farnham attack at Wick.

Photo: Eric Marsh.

	Sc.	Att.
Tiptree United v Chalfont St. Peter	0-2	60
Shillington v Berkhamsted Town	2-1	65
Pirton v Southall	0-2	33
Letchworth GC v Feltham	0-1	62
Stevenage Borough v Flackwell Heath	3-2	475
Leavesden Hospital v Wootton Blue Cross	1-2 *	80
Eaton Bray United v Maidenhead Town	4-0	55
Hanwell Town v Leighton Town	2-0	117
Camberley Town v Hythe Town	3-1	30
Cobham v Horndean	2-1	40
Beckton United v Romsey Town	4-1 *	40
Pirelli General v Malden Vale	3-2	15
Havant Town v Herne Bay	2-1	79
Lymington Town v Eastleigh	0-2	100
Ringmer v Chertsey Town	3-2	134
Southwick v Cray Wanderers	5-2	202
Burgess Hill Town v Molesey	0-1	108
Whyteleafe v Wick	2-1	82
Egham Town v Whitstable Town	0-2	52
Merstham v Ash United	3-2 *	64
Dorking v Yeading	0-1	110
Banstead Athletic v Tunbridge Wells	2-4	36
Pagham v Three Bridges	2-2	96
Shoreham v Eastbourne Town	0-2	85
Sholing Sports v Godalming Town	2-0	148
AFC Totton v Hastings Town	2-1	160
Crockenhill v Alma Swanley	2-2	139
Sharpness v Devizes Town	3-0	121
Hungerford Town v Calne Town	1-1	113
Warminster Town v Shepton Mallet Town	0-2	60
Thatcham Town v Wimborne Town	2-1	100
Backwell United v Bridport	0-2	40
Almondsbury Greenway v Cinderford Tn.	0-2	66
Clevedon Town v Westbury United	4-1	78
Hengrove Athletic v Fairford Town	0-1	70
Wantage Town v Larkhill Athletic	1-2	49
Moreton Town v Welton Rovers	3-0	66
Torrington v Keynsham Town	2-1	127
Supermarine v Yate Town	2-4	55
Wallingford Town v Abingdon Town	0-3	65
Flight Refuelling v Chippenham Town	0-3	90

Saffron Walden receive a bye into the 2nd Round.

REPLAYS

Rowntree Mackintosh v Coundon TT	0-1	72
Murton v Washington	1-3	154
BSC Parkgate v Frecheville Community	2-2	40
Clitheroe v Thackley	1-0	415
Northfield Town v Mile Oak Rovers	3-1	95
Evesham United v Tamworth	3-5 *	203
March Town United v Stowmarket Town	2-4	152
Cheshunt v Royston Town	2-1 *	95
Three Bridges v Pagham	1-4	135
Alma Swanley v Crockenhill	2-0	145
Calne Town v Hungerford	1-2	145

2nd REPLAY

Frecheville Community v BSC Parkgate	5-2	40

(at Staveley Works)

SECOND ROUND

Best Attendance
Halesowen Town v Brereton Social 737
Best Home Victory
Wisbech Town v Ely City 5-1
Best Away Victory
Appleby Frodingham v Borrowash Victoria 0-5
Result of the Round
Blue Star v Fleetwood 3-1

RESULTS	Sc.	Att.
Tadcaster Albion v Clitheroe	0-3	154
Seaham CW Red Star v Whickham	0-1	100
W Allotment Celtic v Yorkshire Amateurs	2-1	160
Eppleton CW Red Star v Guiseley	0-2	101
Sheffield v Frecheville Community	1-0 *	62
Seaton Delaval St v Guisborough Town	0-4	70
Washington v North Ferriby United	2-5	100
Blue Star v Fleetwood Town	3-1	509
Coundon TT v Langley Park Welfare	3-0	45
Irlam Town v Hucknall CW	0-2	120
Maghull v Ellesmere Port & Neston	1-1	44
Louth United v Waterloo Dock	2-3	123

	Sc.	Att.
Bridgnorth Town v Chadderton	2-1 *	105
Appleby Frodingham v Borrowash Vic	0-5	34
St Dominics v Lincoln United	2-1	90
Skegness Town v Staveley Works	0-1	60
Rainworth MW v Brigg Town	0-2	128
Wythenshawe Amateurs v Kirkby Town	1-1	72
Warrington Town v Atherton LR	1-0	54
Atherstone United v Northfield Town	1-0	162
Bilston Town v Shifnal Town	4-2	95
Halesowen Town v Brereton Social	2-1 *	737
Hinckley Town v Long Buckby	1-0	100
Coventry Sporting v Stamford	2-1	60
Hinckley Athletic v Gresley Rovers	3-0	207
Oadby Town v Tamworth	0-1	250
Saffron Walden Town v Potton United	2-1	133
Beckton United v Gorleston	2-1	31
Buckingham Town v Eaton Bray United	1-0	155
Molesey v Sudbury Town	0-3	65
Barton Rovers v Bowers United	1-0	127
Shillington v Yaxley	1-0	102
Collier Row v Wootton Blue Cross	3-1	106
Ampthill Town v St Margaretsbury	0-2	100
Irthlingborough D v Great Yarmouth T	3-1 *	135
Southall v Feltham	2-2	78
Stowmarket Town v Witham Town	0-1	220
Cheshunt v Stansted	2-1	85
Northwood v Harefield United	1-1	94
Hanwell Town v Eynesbury Rovers	1-0	86
Chalfont St Peter v Stevenage Borough	2-3	134
Braintree Town v Halstead Town	4-1	275
Ely City v Wisbech Town	2-2	174
Heybridge Swifts v Wivenhoe Town	1-0	130
Havant Town v Merstham	2-1	60
Camberley Town v Tunbridge Wells	3-3	50
Cobham v Ringmer	1-0	85
Sholing Sports v Yeading	1-0	229
Bracknell Town v Eastbourne Town	3-2	62
Eastleigh v Alma Swanley	1-0	80
Corinthian-Casuals v Newport IOW	1-2	93
Marlow v Southwick	1-2	75
Steyning Town v Pagham	3-0	120
Pirelli General v AFC Totton	0-2	73
Whitstable Town v Whyteleafe	0-2	55
Larkhall Athletic v Abingdon Town	1-2	77
Thatcham Town v Shortwood United	2-1	71
Clevedon Town v Fairford Town	4-2	79
Bridport v Moreton Town	2-3	165
Yate Town v Torrington	1-3	120
Sharpness v Old Georgians	4-0	139
Cinderford Town v Chippenham Town	0-1	165
Newbury Town v Exmouth Town	1-4	134
Shepton Mallet Town v Hungerford Town	2-3	60

REPLAYS

Ellesmere Port & Neston v Maghull	4-1	50
Kirkby Town v Wythenshawe Amateurs	1-2	42
Feltham v Southall	1-3	101
Harefield United v Northwood	3-5 *	88
Wisbech Town v Ely City	5-0	502
Tunbridge Wells v Camberley Town	5-5	154

SECOND REPLAY

Camberley Town v Tunbridge Wells	3-1	88

(After abandoned match)

THIRD ROUND

Best Attendance
Hinckley Athletic v Hinckley Town 553
Best Home Victory
Southall v Hanwell Town 5-0
Best Away Victory
Cheshunt v Barton Rovers 0-4
Cobham v Abingdon Town 0-4
Result of the Round
Exmouth Town v Moreton Town 0-2
Hucknall CW v Coventry Sporting 3-0

RESULTS	Sc.	Att.
Sheffield v Ellesmere Port & Neston	2-0	66
Whickham v Waterloo Dock	0-1	210
North Ferriby United v Guisborough Tn.	3-3	120
Clitheroe v St. Dominics	0-0	343
Coundon TT v West Allotment Celtic	2-1	90

The result of the round was this 8-0 away victory by Borrowash Victoria at Burnley Belvedere. Here the striped forwards cause more trouble for the Belvedere defence.

Photo: Leo Hoenig.

Cobham about to score their winner against Ringmer.

Photo: Eric Marsh.

Famous name Corinthian Casuals going through difficult times, lose 1-2 to Newport (Isle of Wight). Here a Casuals defender is left grounded as Glen Buck moves into the penalty area at the Wimbledon Park Stadium.

Photo: Leo Hoenig.

	Sc.	Att.
Warrington Tn v Wythenshawe Amateurs	2-1	71
Blue Star v Guiseley	0-0	171
Hinckley Athletic v Hinckley Town	3-2	553
Brigg Town v Halesowen Town	1-2	280
Hucknall CW v Coventry Sporting	3-0	180
Bridgnorth Town v Atherstone United	0-1	220
Staveley Works v Bilston Town	2-2	120
Borrowash Victoria v Tamworth	3-3	251
Southall v Hanwell Town	5-0	80
Irthlingborough Diamonds v Collier Row	0-2	213
Northwood v Heybridge Swifts	2-2	60
St. Margaretsbury v Wisbech Town	0-1	327
Shillington v Saffron Walden Town	1-0	115
Buckingham Town v Witham Town	1-0	175
Cheshunt v Barton Rovers	0-4	95
Beckton United v Stevenage Borough	0-3	110
Sudbury Town v Braintree Town	3-1	436
Whyteleafe v Steyning Town	3-2	110
Bracknell Town v Southwick	4-1	73
Havant Town v AFC Totton	2-1	60
Camberley Town v Eastleigh	0-0	75
Sholing Sports v Newport IOW	3-1	140
Cobham v Abingdon Town	0-4	92
Thatcham Town v Hungerford Town	4-2 *	250
Chippenham Town v Clevedon Town	3-0	123
Torrington v Sharpness	1-3	128
Exmouth Town v Moreton Town	0-2	276

REPLAYS

Guisborough Town v North Ferriby United	0-2	176
St. Dominics v Clitheroe	4-2	98
Guiseley v Blue Star	0-3	363

	Sc.	Att.
Bilston Town v Staveley Works	2-1	135
Tamworth v Borrowash Victoria	2-1	524
Heybridge Swifts v Northwood	2-0	160
Eastleigh v Camberley Town	0-1	96

FOURTH ROUND

Best Attendance
Wisbech Town v Hinckley Athletic 1,162
Best Home Victory
Havant Town v Sholing Sports 10-0
Best Away Victory
No Victory by more than a two goal margin
Result of the Round
Havant Town v Sholing Sports 10-0
Chippenham Town v Abingdon Town 5-6*

RESULTS

	Sc.	Att.
Atherstone United v Bilston Town	4-1	323
Halesowen Town v Sheffield	8-1	917
Wisbech Town v Hinckley Athletic	1-0	1,162
Blue Star v North Ferriby United	2-1	382
Coundon TT v Tamworth	1-1	140
Waterloo Dock v Warrington Town	0-2	104
Hucknall CW v St. Dominics	5-4	460
Thatcham Town v Heybridge Swifts	1-0	230
Moreton Town v Whyteleafe	0-2	181
Havant Town v Sholing Sports	10-0	106
Sharpness v Stevenage Borough	0-2	291
Camberley Town v Bracknell Town	1-0	190
Shillington v Buckingham Town	0-1	295
Collier Row v Sudbury Town	1-2	262
Chippenham Town v Abingdon Town	5-6 *	220
Southall v Barton Rovers	2-0	191

REPLAY

Tamworth v Coundon TT	4-0	637

For the last two season's Exmouth Town have won Vase matches in Newbury. Last season it was 4-1, the previous year 6-5 and each year Mel Pym (seen scoring here) was amongst the goals. The unlucky goalkeeper on this occasion was Mark Whiffen.

Photo: Newbury Weekly News.

Moreton Town, following their superb 2-0 victory at Exmouth, were suprisingly beaten by Whyteleafe. Here the home players surround Whyteleafe's Grant.

Photo: David Shute.

One of its best Vase games of the season! Hucknall Colliery Welfare Beat St. Dominicss 5-4 and here Steve Dykes crashed home Colliery's second.

Photo: Brian Pickering.

Fifth Round

Buckingham Town 0 Havant Town 1 (Laidlaw) Attendance 357
Buckingham Town: (Gilbert, Ellis, Hatton, Elley, Blayluck, Laidlaw, Gee, Aldworth, Plumbley (T), Plumbley (Trevor), Rapley, (Sorrell))
Havant Town: (Hopps, Kinston, Robinson, Heap, Roberts, Pittam, Russell, Heeley, Larkins, Butterworth, Frost, (Hodge)).

Camberley Town 3 (Price 2, Kerbey) **Thatcham Town 2** (Upton 2) Attendance 375
Camberley Town: Dupree, Hutchins, Turner, Moynihan, Hutton, Kerbey, Price, Windiate, Bishop, Steele, Atkins, (Clark).
Thatcham Town: Birks, Cook, Warrick, Penny, Martin, Chard, Prior, Upton (P), Stephens, Stirland, Mooney, (Upton (C)).

Hucknall Colly Wel 1 (Dykes) **Blue Star 0** Attendance 670
Hucknall Colly Wel: Bull, Beeby, Newton, Chamberlain, Harrod, Priestley, Hare, Grantham, Hannah, Dawkins, Dykes, (Towle).
Blue Star: Goodwin, Scott, Swinburn, Reach, Magee, Scaife, Hampton, Wicks, Todd, Crumplin, Bragan, (Carver).

Southall 2 (Dennison, Rowe) **Abingdon Town 0** Attendance 165
Southall: Bridges, James, Jones, McGovern, Holland, Powell, Richmond, Dennison, Ferdinand, Rowe, Pierre, (Stevens).
Abingdon Town: Lymer, Allen, Appleton, Alens, Sutton, Lever, LsMsden, O'Hanlon, Berry, Spittle, Sunderland, (Flanagan).

Tamworth 0 Halesowen 2 (Heath, one o.g.) Attendandce 1,940
Tamworth: Kendall, Lockett, Ward (I), Atkins, Brown, Hayward, Ward (S), Heath, Maddocks, Crompton, Reeves, Jones, (Fox).
Halesowen Town: Pemberton, Moore, Sherwood, Lacey, Randle, Heath, Penn, Moss, Woodhouse, Joinson (P), Joinson (L), (Smith).

Warrington Town 3 (Copeland, Dolan, Reid) **Atherstone United 1** (Pugh) Attendance 324
Warrington Town: Cunneely, Alcock, Williams, Hunter, Copeland, Cook, Hughes, Dolan, Kinsey, Price, Reid, (Mather).
Atherstone United: Spencer, Bennetts, Peacock, Boneham, Olner, Wilcox, Parker, Brotherton, Brain, Farmer, Fallow, (Pugh).

Whyteleafe 1 (Grant) **Stevenage Borough 4** (Gittings 2, Adcroft, Marshall pen.) Attendance 521
Whyteleafe: Borrelli, Berry, Mahoney, Purvis, Richardson, Rose, Wilgoss, Kaidi, Flemington, Grant, Goodwin, (Nelson).
Stevenage Borough: Gallagher, Honey, Marshall, Tyler, Watkins, Armsby, Adcroft, Pirie, Myers, Gittings, Driver, (Shadbolt).

Wisbech Town 1 (Rider G.) **Sudbury Town 0** Attendance 1,108
Wisbech Town: Hudson, Jones, Rider (W), Ward, Mattless, Rider (G), Gale, Brighty, Garner (W), Waddicor, Tyler, (Garner (C)).
Sudbury Town: Peatfield, Hubbard, Thorpe, Barker, Elden, Smythe, Haddool, Barber, Davis, Smith, Taylor, (Norrissey).

Sixth Round

Halesowen Town 5 (Joinson P. 2, Joinson L. 2, Sherwood 1 pen.) **Camberley Town 1** (Price) Attendance 1,700
Halesowen Town: Pemberton, Moore, Sherwood, Lacey, Randle, Heath, Penn, Moss, Woodhouse, Joinson (P), Joinson (L), (Weston).
Camberley Town: Dupree, Hutchins, Turner, Berkij, Hutton, Kerbey, Clark Windiate, Price, Steele, Atkins, (Bishop).

Havant Town 1 (Rapley) **Wisbech Town 5** (Waddicor 3, Rider, Brighty) Attendance 561
Havant Town: Gilbert, Ellis, Hatton, Elley, Blaylock, Laidlaw, Gee, Aldworth, Plumbley (Tony), Plumbley (Trevor), Rapley, (Sorrell).
Wisbech Town: Hudson, Jones, Rider (W), Ward, Mattless, Rider (G), Gale, Brighty, Alexander, Waddicor, Garner, (Hanslip).

Southall 2 (James 2) **Stevenage Borough 0** Attendance 1,109
Southall: Bridges, James, Holland, McGovern, Croad, Richardson, Richmond, Sweales, Ferdinand, Rowe, Pierre, (Dennison).
Stevenage Borough FC: Gallagher, Honey, Marshall, Tyler, Watkins, Gittings (P), Johnson, Pirie, Armsby, Gittings (M), Myers, (Shadbolt).

Warrington Town 3 (Dolan, Price, Kinsley) **Hucknall CW 1** (Harrod) Attendance 1,144
Warrington Town: Cunneely, Gratton, Williams, Hunter, Copeland, Cook, Hughes, Dolan, Price, Kinsey Reid, (Stokes).
Hucknall Colly. Wel.: Bull, Beeby, Newton, Chamberlain, Harrod, Priestley, Hare, Grantham, Hannah, Dawkins, Dykes, (Towle).

Semi-Finals First Legs

Southall 2 (Holland, Ferdinand) **Wisbech Town 2** (Waddicor, Mitchell) Attendance 1,038
Southall: MacKenzie, James, Holland, McGovern, Croad, Powell, Richmond, Sweales, Ferdinand, Rowe, Pierre, (Richardson).
Wisbech Town: Hudson, Jones, Rider (W), Ward, Mattless, Rider (G), Gale, Brighty, Alexander, Waddicor, Garner, (Mitchell).

Warrington Town 1 (Hunter) **Halesowen Town 1** (Joinson L.) Attendance 2,120
Warrington Town: Cunneely, Gratton, Williams, Hunter, Copeland, Cook, Hughes, Dolan, Price, Kinsey, Reid, (Stokes).
Halesowen Town: Pemberton, Moore, Sherwood, Lacey, Randle, Heath, Penn, Moss, Woodhouse, Joinson (P.), Joinson (L.), (Rhoet).

Semi-Final Second Legs

Wisbech Town 1 (Mitchell) **Southall 3** (Ferdinand 2, Powell) Attendance 3,216
Wisbech Town: Hudson, Jones, Rider (W), Ward, Mattless, Rider (G), Gale, Brighty, Alexander, Waddicor, Mitchell, (Tyler).
Southall: Bridges, James, Holland, McGovern, Croad, Powell, Richmond, Richardson, Ferdinand, Rowe, Pierre, (Sweales).

Halesowen Town 3 (Joinson L. 2, Joinson P. 1) Warrington Town 3 (Hughes 2, Kinsey 1) **Attendance 3,035**
Halesowen Town: Coldicott, Moore, Sherwood, Lacey, Randle, Heath, Penn, Moss, Woodhouse, Joinson P, Joinson L, (Smith).
Warrington Town: Cunneely, Gratton, Williams, Hunter, Copeland, Cook, Hughes, Dolan, Kinsey, Price, Henderson, (Stokes).

Semi-Final Replay

Halesowen Town 6 (Lacey, Moss, Joinson P, Smith, Joinson L 2) **Warrington Town 3** (Kinsey 2, Henderson 1) (played at Telford Utd) Attendance 2,511
Halesowen Town: Coldicott, Moore, Sherwood, Lacey, Randle, Heath, Penn, Moss, Woodhouse, Joinson P, Joinson L, (Smith).
Warrington Town: Cunneely, Gratton, Williams, Hunter, Copeland, Cook, Hughes, Dolan, Kinsey, Price, Henderson, (Stokes).

CELEBRATIONS!

Lee Joinson's equaliser has the travelling hordes in ecstasy.

Photo: David Shute

Waddicor (No. 10) gives Wisbech Town an early lead at Southall in the 1st leg of the semi-final of the F.A. Vase.

Photo: Eric Marsh

A tense moment in front of the Warrington goalmouth as Lee Joinson lobs just over in the semi-final 1st leg.
Photo: David Shute

The dark shirted players of Wisbech in front of a superb attendance of 3,216 sadly disappointed their supporters by losing in the semi-final for the second time. Here Southall captain Steve Croad reaches the ball first but all neutrals will hope that it will be third time lucky for the Eastern club.

Paul Joinson scores a valuable replay goal past Warrington Town's Graham Cuneely.

F.A. VASE — ROUND-BY-ROUND TO WEMBLEY

Third Round

Halesowen T. 2
*Brigg Town 1

*Sheffield 2
Ellesmere Port 0

*Coundon T.T. 2
W. Allotment C. 1

*Borrowash V. 3,1
Tamworth 3,2

*Camberley T. 0,1
Eastleigh 0,0

*Bracknell T. 4
Southwick 1

*Thatcham T. §4
Hungerford T. 2

Northwood 2,0
Hayebridge S. 2,2

*Whickham 0
Waterloo Dock 1

*Warrington T. 2
Wythonshaw A. 1

*Bridgnorth T. 0
Atherstone Utd 1

*Staveley W. 2,1
Bilston T. 2,2

*Hucknall C.W. 3
Coventry Sp. 0

*Clitheroe 0,2
St Dominics 0,4

*Blue Star 0,3
Guiseley 0,0

*N. Ferriby U. 3,2
Guisborough T. 3,0

*Shillington 1
Saffron W.T. 0

*Buckingham T. 1
Witham T. 0

*Havant Town 2
AFC Totton 1

Sholing Sports 3
Newport (I.O.W.) 1

*St. Margb'ry 0
Wisbech Town 1

*Hinckley Ath. 3
Hinckley T. 2

*Irthlingboro D. 0
Collier Row 2

*Sudbury T. 3
Braintree A. 1

*Exmouth T. 0
Moreton T. 2

*Whyteleafe 3
Steyning 2

*Torrington 1
Sharpness 3

*Beckton U. 0
Stevenage B. 3

*Chippenham T. 3
Clevedon T. 0

*Cobham 0
Abingdon T. 4

*Cheshunt 0
Barton R. 4

*Hanwell T. 0
Southall 5

Fourth Round

***Halesowen T. 8**
Sheffield 1
*Coundon T.T. §1,0
Tamworth 1,4
*Camberley T. 1
Bracknell T. 0
*Thatcham T. 1
Hayebridge S. 0
*Waterloo Dock 0
Warrington T. 2
*Atherstone Utd 4
Bilson T. 1
*Hucknall C.W. 5
St Dominics 4
*Blue Star 2
N. Ferriby Utd. 1
Guisborough T. 3,0
*Shillington 0
Buckingham T. 1
*Havant Town 10
Sholing Sports 0
*Wisbech Town 1
Hinckley Ath. 0
*Collier Row 1
Sudbury T. 2
*Moreton T. 0
Whyteleafe 2
*Sharpness 1
Stevenage B. 2
*Chippenham T. §5
Abingdon T. 6
Barton R. 0
***Southall 2**

Fifth Round

Halesowen T. 2
*Tamworth 0
*Camberley T. 3
Thatcham T. 2
*Warrington T. 3
Atherstone Utd. 1
*Hucknall C.W. 1
Blue Star 0
*Buckingham T. 0
Havant Town 1
*Wisbech Town 1
Sudbury T. 0
*Whyteleafe 1
Stevenage B. 4
Abingdon T. 0
***Southall 2**

Sixth Round

***Halesowen T. 5**
Camberley T. 1
*Warrington T. 3
Hucknall C.W. 1
*Havant Town 1
Wisbech Town 1
Stevenage B. 0
***Southall 2**

Semi-Final

Halesowen T. 1,3,6
1st Leg at Warrington
2nd Leg at Halesowen
Replay at Telford Utd
Warrington T. 1,3,3

Wisbech Town. 2,1
1st Leg at Southall
2nd Leg at Wisbech
Southall 2,3

Final

HALESOWEN TOWN 3
SOUTHALL 0

*** Indicates club drawn at home**
§ denotes after extra time.

Superb Halesowen Support Rewarded

Halesowen 3 Southall 0

(Moss 2, Joinson, L.) Att: 18,340

This year's FA Vase Final at Wembley was memorable for a number of reasons.

Halesowen beccame only the second team in the competition's history to retain the trophy. Amazingly, the match attracted a record crowd – 18,340 – and record receipts of £58,539.

And in underdogs Southall, the occasion boasted probably the youngest ever manager to lead a side out at Wembley in 30 year old Gordon Barlett, complete with his left arm in plaster after a recent break!

The fact that that Halesowen kept the trophy was none too surprising. Their domination of the event in the 80's now rivals

The record crowd was almost totally a result of the Black Country club's amazing charisma. At least 15,000 of their fans headed down from the Midlands.

Southall's arrival in the final, their first match at Wembley since 1944, when, would you believe, they played a Middlesex Red Cross Cup Final there, had cast doubts on the gate being anywhere near a record.

The West London club, 115 years old, have seen the community around their Western Road ground change dramatically in the past two decades. Their traditional support has melted away to be replaced by one of the country's largest Asian communities.

What was good to see, though, was little groups of Asian lads decked out in red and white . . . Southall can glean great encouragement for the future in that!

Halesowen's side was predictably packed with Wembley 'veterans', this being their third final in four seasons. Only young 'keeper Alan Pemberton and full back Neil Moore, were on their first trips to the stadium. The rest had seen it all before!

Spare a thought though for veteran Don Smith. He was hoping for his fourth Wembley trip – all Halesowen's plus one for Willenhall – but at the last minute John Rhodes was preferred as substiture.

Southall had no one who had played at the stadium before, but set about unsettling the favourites from ther start. Les Ferdinand had a snap shot from 20 yards wide, and but for a brave save by Pemberton at Paul Sweales' feet after a bad Ian Sherwood miskick, Southall would have turned their early promise into goals.

Bruce Rowe, a constant threat up front for Southall, went closest after 29 minutes. A Les Randle back pass and Sherwood error allowed the winger the chance to round Pemberton, but the shot was scrambled away.

Southall then suffered one of several pieces of bad luck. Rowe was harshly penalised on the line for a tackle, and Richard Heath thumped over the free kick.

Mard Lacey headed back, Paul Joinson nodded it on, and there was Geoff Moss to head Halesowen ahead.

Four minutes after the break Southall thought they were level. Sweales had played in a cross and Rowe slid the ball home from a few feet, only to be given offside.

Southall kept going forward and it was taking all Halesowen's big match experience to keep in control. The turning point came after 67 minutes when from Rowe's cross, Roland Peirre sent in apower header that was miraculously saved by Pemberton. A goal then, and Southall considered they would have won.

The traditional group photo but it will give enjoyment for years to come when the scrap books come out!

Photo: Eric Marsh

Geoff Moss scores his second and Halesowen Town's third in a memorable afternoon for the West Midlands.
Photo: Birmingham Post & Mail

But eight minutes later the game was drifting away from them. Halesowen were spreading the play well, and when Lee Joinson got down the left, he squeezed a shot under Stuart Mackenzie, only for the ball to hit the post and role agonisingly along the line. More bad luck for Southall, because as Rob Holland tried to clear, he managed only to turn the ball over his own line.

Joinson made it clear afterwards that the goal was his, and Holland wold not want an own goal on his record in an otherwise splendid show.

Southall threw on substitute Randy Richmond for John Powell, but Halesowen were not going to lose their grip now, and began to look the fine side they are.

After 77 minutes Heath cracked a shot against a post and Lee Joinson's effort from the rebound was blocked on the line by Mackensie. But Moss was on hand to force the ball inches over the line, and an astute linesman immediatly signalled the third.

Rhodes got his taste of Wembley with five minutes left as Randle's substitute, and John Woodhouse was soon bounding up the steps to claim the trophy again.

Halesowen were good winners in the end, but the scoreline was cruel on Southall, and as Bartlett said afterwards: "They lost on their first trip to Wembley, we've got to show we can come back and do what they have done". Brave words on a bitter day.

Halesowen knew it was not as good a performance as the victory over Fleetwood a year earlier, but they once again showed they are a club with great ambitions and potential, who had only being held back from progress through the Pyramid because of varying problems with their ground.

Halesowin: Pemberton, Moore, Lacey, Randle (Rhodes), Sherwood, Heath, Penn, Woodhouse, P. Joinson, Moss, L. Joinson.
Southall: Mackenzie, James, McGovern, Croad, Holland, Powell (Richmond), Pierre, Richardson, Sweales, Ferdinand, Rowe.
Referee: Mr. D. Scott (Burnley).

Paul Walker, DAILY STAR

RESULTS OF PREVIOUS FINALS 1975-1985

1975 (*Attendance:* 9,500)
Hoddesdon Town 2 (Sedgwick 2) **Epsom & Ewell 1** (Wales) Referee: R. Toseland
Hoddesdon Town: Galvin, Green, Hickey, Maybury, Stevenson, Wilson, Bishop, Picking, Sedgwick, Nathan, Schofield.
Epsom & Ewell: Page, Bennett, Webb, Wales, Worby, Jones, O'Connell, Walker, Tuite, Eales, Lee.

1976 (*Attendance:* 11,858)
Billericay Town 1 (Aslett) **Stamford 0** *aet* Referee: Alan Robinson
Billericay Town: Griffiths, Payne, Bone, Coughlan, Geddes, Aslett, Clayden, Scott, Smith.
Stamford: Johnson, Kwiatkowski, Marchant, Crawford, Downs, Hird, Barnes, Walpole, Smith, Russell, Brosdhurst.

1977 (*Attendance* 14,000)
Billericay Town 1 (Clayden) **Sheffield 1** (Coughlan og) *aet* Referee: J. Worrall
Billericay Town: Griffiths, Payne, Bone, Coughlan, Pullin, Scott, Wakefield, Aslett, Clayden, Woodhouse, McQueen. Sub: Whettell.
Sheffield: Wing, Gilbody, Lodge, Hardisty, Watts, Skelton, Kay, Travis, Pugh, Thornhill, Haines. Sub: Strutt.

Replay at Nottingham Forest (*Attendance:* 3,482)
Billericay Town 2 (Aslett, Woodhouse) **Sheffield 1** (Thornhill) Referee: T. Morris
Billericay Town: Griffiths, Payne, Pullin, Whettell, Bone, McQueen, Woodhouse, Aslett, Clayden, Scott, Wakefield.
Sheffield: Wing, Gilbody, Lodge, Strutt, Watts, Skelton, Kay, Travis, Pugh, Thornhill, Haines.

1978 (*Attendance:* 16,391)
Blue Star 2 (Dunn, Crumplin) Referee: C. Seel
Blue Star: Halbert, Feenan, Thompson, Davidson, S. Dixon, Beynon, Storey, P. Dixon, Crumplin, Callaghan, Dunn. Sub: Diamond.
Barton Rovers: Blackwell, Stephens, Crossley, Evans, Harris, Dollimore, Dunn, Harnaman, Fossey, Turner, Smith. Sub: Cox.

1979 (*Attendance:* 17,500)
Billericay Town 4 (Young 3, Clayden) **Almondsbury Greenway 1** (Price) Referee: N. Midgeley
Billericay Town: Norris, Blackaller, Bingham, Whettall, Bone, Reeves, Pullin, Scott, Clayden, Young, Groom. Sub: Carrigan.
Almondsbury Greenway: Hamilton, Bowers, Scarrett, Sullivan, Tudor, Wookey, Bowers, Shehean, Kerr, Butt, Price. Sub: Kilbaine.

1980 (*Attendance* 11,500)
Stamford 2 (Alexander, McGowan) **Guisborough Town 0** **Referee: R. Lewis**
Stamford: Johnson, Kwiatowski, Ladd, McGowan, I. Bliszczak, Mackin, Broadhurst, Hall, Czarnecki, Potter, Alexander. Sub: S. Bliszczak.
Guisborough Town: Cutter, Scott, Thornton, Angus, Maltby, Percy, Skelton, Coleman, McElvaney, Sills, Dilworth. Sub: Harrison.

1981 (*Attendance:* 12,000)
Whickham 3 (Scott, Williamson, Peck og) *aet* **Willenhall Town 2** (Smith, Stringer) Referee: K. Walmsley
Whickham: Thompson, Scott, Knox, Williamson, Cook, Ward, Carroll, Diamond, Cawthra, Robertson, Turnbull. Sub: Allon.
Willenhall Town: Newton, White, Dams, Woodall, Heath, Fox, Peck, Price, Matthews, Smith, Stringer. Sub: Trevor.

1982 (*Attendance:* 12,500)
Forest Green Rovers 3 (Leitch 2, Norman) **Rainworth Miners' Welfare 0** Referee: B. Daniels
Forest Green Rovers: Moss, Norman, Day, Turner, Higgins, Jenkins, Burns, Guest, Millard, Leitch, Doughty. Sub: Dangerfield.
Rainworth Miners' Welfare: Watson, Hallam, Hodgson, Slater, Sterland, Oliver, Knowles, Raine, Radzki, Reah, Comerford. Sub: Robinson.

1983 (*Attendance:* 13,700)
VS Rugby 1 (Crawley) **Halesowen Town 0** Referee: T. Bune
VS Rugby: Burton, McGinty, Harrison, Preston, Knox, Evans, Ingram, Setchell, Owen, Beecham, Crawley. Sub: Haskins.
Halesowen Town: Coldicott, Penn, Edmonds, Lacey, Randle, Shilvock, Hazlewood, Moss, Woodhouse, Joinson E, Joinson L. Sub: Smith.

1984 (*Attendance:* 8,125)
Stansted 3 (Holt, Gillard, Reading) **Stamford 2** (Waddicor, Allen) Referee: C. Downey
Stansted: Coe, Williams, Hilton, Simpson, Cooper, Reading, Callanan, Holt, Reeves, Doyle, Gillard, (Williams).
Stamford: Parslow, Smitheringale, Blades, McIlwain, Lyon, Mackin, Genovese, Waddicor, Allen, Robson, Beech, (Chapman).

1985 (*Attendance:* 16,715)
Halesowen 3 (Moss, Joinson L. 2) **Fleetwood Town 1** (Moran) Referee: D. Scott
Halesowen: Coldicott, Penn, Sherwood, Warner, Randle, Heath, Hazlewood, Moss (Smith), Woodhouse, P Joinson, L Joinson.
Fleetwood: Dobson, Moran, Hadgraft, Strachan, Robinson, Milligan, Hall, Trainor, Taylor (Whitehouse), Cain, Kennerley.

F.A. VASE CLUB RECORD

Total	73-74	74-75	75-76	76-77	77-78	78-79	79-80	80-81	81-82	82-83	83-84	84-85	Total
Stamford	S-F	F	3	3	2	W	4	2	3	F	3	2	55
Blue Star		2	5	W	3	4	3	S-F	5	3	Q-F	5	53
Barton R.		Q-F	S-F	F	Q-F	2	2	S-F	3	2	1	4	48
Halesowen T.		1	1	4	3	2	3	3	F	3	W	W	48
Irthlingborough D.				Q-F	5	Q-F	S-F	Q-F	4	S-F	4	3	48
Friar Lane O.B.	S-F	S-F	4	5	5	4	4	2	3	2	1	1	45
Billericay T.	2	W	W	5	W	Q-F							43
Hungerford T.	1	5	4	S-F	2	S-F	5	2	2	1	1	3	40
Buckingham T.		1	5	4	2	3	2	5	4	5	3	5	39
Leyton Wingate	Q-F	2	2	2	5	5	2	4	2	Q-F	3		39
Burnham & Hittingdon		4	4	Q-F	3	4	4	2	S-F	2	2		38
Molesey	5	5	4	2	4	5	2	Q-F	3		–	2	38
Almondsbury Gr.			5	S-F	F	4	4	3	2	2	1	1	37
Lincoln U.	Q-F	4	2	3	4	2	3	2	2	3	4	2	37
Whickham					S-F	3	W	2	2	S-F	2	3	36
Alma Swanley			4	4	3	4	Q-F	2	2	2	3	2	32
Hallam		4	4	3	2	3	5	4	3	2	1	1	32
Windsor & Eaton	1	3	1	1	4	Q-F	S-F	4	5				32
Farnborough T.	Q-F	S-F	S-F	5	Q-F								31
Guiseley		2	3	1	1	4	Q-F	2	2	5	2	3	31
Newbury T.	1	1	–	4	3	5	3	3	3	4	2	2	31
Cray W.	1	1	3	2	1	Q-F	5	2	3	2	3	1	30
Frecheville C.A.	1	1	–	Q-F	2	4	2	4	4	2	2	2	30
Willenhall T.				3	Q-F	5	F	Q-F	2				30
Hinckley Ath.	1	1	4	4	4	2	2	3	1	2	1	4	29
Sheffield	4	3	F	2	3	2	1	–	–	1	1	4	29
Basildon U.	3	4	2	1	2	3	Q-F	2	3	2			28
Eastbourne U.	1	1	3	5	Q-F	2	2	3	1	–	4	–	28
Forest Green R.	3	1	1	3	2	2	–	W	Q-F				28
Guisborough T.					–	F	3	5	4	2	3	3	28
Whyteleafe	2	1	1	2	1	2	5	3	2	2	2	5	28
Wigston Fields			Q-F	2	2	5	4	2	2	2	2	1	28
Bracknell T.	3	5	2		–	1	–	1	5	3	3	4	27
Kempston R.	5	1	3	4	2	3	5	2	2	–			27
Leeds Ashley Road	3	5	4	3	3	2	3	2	2				27
Warrington T.	1	1	3	4	1	1	–	2	–	4	3	S-F	27
Abingdon T.	2	5	1	2	2	1	–	–	3	4	1	5	26
Grays Ath.				4	3	4	2	4	3	4	2		26
Heybridge Swifts	2	2	–	3	1	1	1	1	4	4	3	4	26
Skegness T.				2	4	3	3	5	2	2	3	2	26
Cheshunt					5	3	4	Q-F			4	3	25
Marlow	5	2	1	–	–	1	3	3	3	2	3	2	25
Newport (I.O.W.)			2	2	2	4	2	2	1	4	3	3	25
Tunbridge Wells	4	4	2	1	4	–	–	1	–	3	4	2	25
V. S. Rugby	2	2	1	1	–	1	–	1	W	4	3		25
Devizes T.			2			3	Q-F	3	4	3	2	1	24
Egham T.	2	3	2	3	2	1	3	1	1	1	4	1	24
Harefield U.	2	2	–	2	–	2	3	2	2	3	4	2	24
Irlam T.	4	1	2	2	2	1	1	5	1	2	1	2	24
Ossett Alb.			2	2	3	2	3	4	3	2	2	1	24
Tring T.	3	4	5	2	3	2	1		1	1	2	–	24
Winterton R.			Q-F	4	5	2	2	2	2	1	–		24
Prescot Cables	1	5	3	5	4	3	2						23
Rainworth M.W.						–	–	F	3	5	5	2	23
Shepshed Ch.				–	S-F	4	2	2	Q-F	2			23
Staveley Works				–	–	2	3	3	4	Q-F	2	3	23
Blakenall	4	2	5	3	2	1	1	2	–	–	2	–	22
Brigg T.	2	4	2	4	1	2	1	1	1	–	1	3	22
Coventry Sp.	3	3	–	1	2	–	5	1	–	2	2	3	22
Eastbourne T.	4	5	3	3	2	1	–	2	–	–	–	2	22
Haringey Bor.	1	2	2	Q-F	4	2	2	2	1	–	–	–	22
Hemel Hempstead	1	3	3	–	–	3	–	5	2	3	1	1	22
Hoddesdon T.	W	1	3	2	2	1	1	–	1	1	–	–	22
Shifnal T.						3	3	4	4	4	2	2	22
Stansted	1	1	1	1	1	–	–	1	1	W	3	2	22
Bridgnorth T.	1	5	1	2	1	3	–	–	2	3	–	3	21
Crockenhill	4	3	1		1	2	–	–	3	4	2	1	21
Gorleston						4	3	4	3	2	3	2	21
Gosport Bor.	3	4	Q-F	3	5								21
Malvern T.	4	3	4	2	2	1	2	1	–	2	–	–	21
Rushden T.			3	3	3	3	3	2	2	1	1	–	21
Sholing Sp.			1	1	1	–	3	4	2	2	3	4	21
Brandon U.					–	2	–	2	Q-F	Q-F	4		20
Eastleigh		2	1	3	–	1	1	–	4	3	2	3	20
Epping T.	1	3	5	3	3	2	1	–	2	–	–		20
Evesham U.	3	4	1	2	1	4	–	–	2	–	2	1	20
Gt. Yarmouth T.							4	2	S-F	3	2	2	20
Rainham T.	2	2	–	5	2	3	2	3	1	–	–	–	20
Southall							3	4	2	2	1	F	20
Uxbridge			2	2	3	2	2	1	1	4	3		20

W = 10 F = 8 S-F = 7 Q-F = 6

THE START

THE FINISH

The F.A. Vase started last season on Saturday 31st August. In the top photo by Leo Hoenig he has caught Darwen's Paul Roberts (No 11) after he has put over a centre in his side's 5-0 victory over Alnwick. It's not too difficult to work out who is celebrating as the competition comes to an end at Wembley on Saturday 26th April. The photo was taken by Bob Thomas.

F.A. CHALLENGE CUP

F.A. CHALLENGE CUP
Committee: L. Smart (Chairman), E. A. Brown (Vice-Chairman), H. W. Alcock, W.T Annable, W. S. G. Needham, Dr. J. O'Hara, F. J. Pdeart, S. Seymour, A. L. Smith, P. Rushton, J. R. Smith.

First Division Scalp for Altrincham

At the beginning of every season every senior Non League club secretly hopes for a little luck in the F.A. Cup which will change their finanfcial fortunes and public image overnight.

This year when the Fourth Qualifying Round was reached and that all important victory was needed for a place with the big brothers from the Football League, some of the regulars were back in contention but there were heart stopping moments ahead for *Peterlee Newtown, Gresley Rovers, St Helens Town, Hastings Town* and **Ton Pentre** who didn't get through. And for *Fareham Town*, **Aylesbury United,** *Macclesfield Town* and *Frickley Athletic* who confounded even their own supporters by featuring in the First Round Proper.

The Gola League big boys also entered at this stage and some intriguing ties were presented when the draw was made. Little *Halesowen Town* kings on the F.A. Vase scene, followed by massive support, had to travel to *Frickley* and achieved a creditable draw before losing at home. One of the results of the round was achieved by *Bognor Regis* in another all 'non-league' tie at *Enfield* where they won 2-0.

Creditable draws against League opposition were achieved by *Morecambe* at York, *Windsor & Eton* at home to Toquay, *V.S. Rugby* at home to Orient, *Bishops Stortford* at home to Peterborough and Dartford at Bournemouth while unexpected draw was also achieved by *Aylesbury United* at *Slough United.*

The Non-League F.A. all 'Champions' *Yeovil Town* only lost in the last few minutes against Hereford United and *Nuneaton Bouough* were just piped by famous Burnley 2-3 at home. However th pride of place went to Gola League new boys *Wycombe Wanderers* who beat Colchester United 2-0 at Loakes Park, specialists *Telford United* who beat Stockport County away 1-0 and *Dagenham* who eliminated Cambridge United 2-0 at home.

Altrincham had quietly eased through with an away win at Chorley but now they were drawn away to Blackpool, thus giving the 'Seasiders' a chance to avenge last seasons defeat. This was not to be however and goals from Reid and **Anderson** saw 'Alty' through along with *Frickley Athletic* who won 1-0 at high flying Hartlepool while *Slough Town* acheived a creditable draw at Orient and *Runcorn* held Wigan Athletic at home.

After replays, this left *Altrincham* drawn away at Birmingham City, *Frickley Athletic* at hame with a local 'derby' against Rotherham United and *Wycombe Wanderers* with a long journey to York in the Second Round.

The weather delayed some ties and by the time that *Altrincham* travelled to St Andrews, *Frickley* and *Wycombe Wanderers* had finished their excellent F.A. Cup runs. First Division Birmingham City were having a bad time but for some national daily reporters to suggest that *Altrincham* should win away to a First Division club managed by **Ron Saunders** was surley taking things too far.

The strange thing about the actual game was the fact that *'Alty'* showed far more understanding of the blustery conditions and changed their tactics accordingly at half time. The non-leaguers mid field dominated, they looked more professional and in the end surprised no one at the ground when they ran out 2-1 winners.

When talking about the winning goal to **Bob Wilson** on BBC Breakfast Television the next morning, **John King** described the scorer as "Ghosting past two defenders, drawing the keeper and placing the ball coolly in the net; but I thought it was an 'own goal,'" said **Bob**, "Yes it was," replied **John**, "a cracker"!

When the Fourth Round Draw was announced, York City couldn't believe their luck, after home ties against non-league opposition from *Morecambe, Whitby Town* and *Wycombe Wanderers,* who had they got? Yes, *Altrincham.* The league side didn't underestimate their visitors and qualified for another visit from Linerpool in the Fifth Round.

Another eventful season for Non-League Clubs in the F.A. Cup had come to an end but *Altrincham's* victory over First Division opposition will always be remembered and it couldn't have come at a better time, as the League Clubs decided on the merits of automatic promotion from the senior Semi-Professional League. Well done and thank you *'Alty'!*

Tony Williams

The End of the Road.

After a superb F.A. Cup run Altrincham met their match at York. Here Semi-Professional 'Player of the Year' Jeff Johnson challenges two City players in their Fourth Round battle.

Photo: John Rooney

The special atmosphere of the F.A. Cup. A cold evening with the players skating around in the gloom. But can the potential 'giantkillers' manage a win. On this occasion there was no fairy story as Bournemouth won their replay at Dartford 2-0.

Photo: David Hills

PRELIMINARY ROUND

Best Attendance
Stevenage Borough v Leamington 375
Best Home Victory
Gresley Rovers v Friar Lane OB 8-0
Best Away Victory
Royston Town v March Town United 2-7
Result of the Round
Gresley Rovers v Friar Lane OB 8-0

RESULTS	Sc.	Att.
Ferryhill Athletic v West Auckland Town	2-2	61
Bridlington Trinity v Netherfield	4-0	56
Farsley Celtic v Seaham CW Red Star	2-0	139
Langley Park Welfare v Horden CW	2-6	71
Evenwood Tn v Crook Tn (at Crook Tn)	1-5	81
Ashington v Durham City	0-2	55
Eppleton CW v Yorkshire Amateurs	5-1	71
Lancaster City v Willington	1-0	138
Shildin v Esh Winning	3-1	65
Easington Colliery v Billingham Town	2-3	72
Thackley v Fleetwood Town	0-1	200
Garforth Town v Northallerton Town	1-2	138
Norton & Stockton ANC v Shotton Comrades	1-1	14
Rossendale United v Guiseley	1-0	130
Accrington Stanley Darwen	2-0	296
Chadderton v Ashton United	2-2	130
Emley v Belper Town	1-1	170
Nantwich Town v Glossop	1-0	119
Warrington Town v Eastwood Town	3-1	102
Caernarfon Town v Congleton Town	1-1	209
Leek Town v Armitage	0-0	162
Colwyn Bay v Leyland Motors	3-1	259
Ilkeston Town v Lincoln United	5-0	149
Radcliffe Borough v North Ferriby United	2-2	171
Heanor Tn v Boldmere St Michaels (at BSM)	0-2*	45
Arnold v Shifnal Town (at Eastwood Tn)	4-0	119
Spalding United v Coventry Sporting (tie awarded to Spalding United)	1-2*	129
Oldswinford v Highgate United	2-1	44
Gresley Rovers v Friar Lane OB	8-0	210
Desborough Town v Oldbury United	2-3	105
Bolton v Atherstone United	0-2	64
Lye Town v Sutton C Tn (at Sutton C Tn)	2-1	171
Paget Rangers v Rushall Olympic	2-2	50
Wellingbough Town v Wigston Fields	4-0	101
Stevenage Borough v Leamington	2-1	375
Blakenall v Tamworth	0-4	101
Rothwell Town v Hemel Hempstead	3-3	73
Holbeach United v Rushden Town	1-1	86
Royston Town v March Town United	2-7	120
Sudbury Town v Tiptree United	2-0	147
Chatteris Town v Newmarket Town	0-3	85
Stowmarket v Flackwell Heath	3-0	145
Histon v Soham Town Rangers	3-0	116
Chalfont St Peter v Banbury United	2-1	107
Lowestoft Town v Bury Town	2-0	214
Great Yarmouth Tn v Burnham & Hillingdon	2-0	286
Wootton Blue Cross v Woodford Town	0-1	99
St Albans City v Wolverton Town	1-1	216
Barton Rovers v Chesham United	2-1	119
Harwich & Parkeston v Hoddesdon Town	2-3*	110
Hampton v Chertsey Town	2-0	144
Chatham Town v Southall	1-1	116
Uxbridge v Corinthian-Casuals	3-0	172
Clapton v Leytonstone/Ilford (tie awarded to Leytonstone/Ilford)	3-2	94
Edgware v Erith & Belvedere	1-1	100
Crockenhill v Hounslow	0-1	93
Kingsbury Town v Leyton-Wingate	1-1	65
Fleet Town v Sheppey United	0-2	35
Tilbury v Maidenhead United (at Aveley)	2-0	35
Rainham Town v Littlehampton Town	1-2	40
Thanet United v Chichester City	3-1	207
Camberley Town v Bromley	2-2	75
Hailsham Town v Dorking	4-4	100
Ringmer v Whitstable Town	2-1	100
Horley Town v Walton & Hersham	0-5	50
Three Bridges v Lewes	2-3	106
Tonbridge AFC v Horsham	3-0	266
Hastings Town v Burgess Hill Town	1-0	357
Horsham YMCA v Whyteleafe	0-3	52
Eastbourne United v Dover Athletic	4-2	141
Deal Town v Southwick	1-4	56
Lancing v Hythe Town	0-3	116
Ashford Town v Faversham Town	5-1	164
Horndean v Calne Town	1-1	75
Devizes Town v Pagham	2-2	58
Brockenhurst v Warminster Town	1-3	76
Newbury Town v Meldsham Town	2-1	156
AFC Totton v Shling Sports	2-0	171
Bristol Manor farm v Chard Town	2-0	70
Bridgend Town v Poole Town	0-1	120
Winbourne Town v Weston-Super-Mare	2-5	176
Welton Rovers v Mangotsfield United	1-3	100
Maesteg Park v Forest Green Rovers	0-1	43
Dorchester Town v Clandown	0-0	121
Llanelli v Minehead	2-3	158
Saltash United v Barnstable Town	1-0	112
Shortwood United v Sharpness	1-1	200
St Blazey v Shepton Mallet Town	1-0	147
Glastonbury v Exmouth Town	0-5	114
Ottery St Mary v Torring ton	1-0	101

REPLAYS		
West Auckland v Ferryhill Athletic	1-2	105
Shotton Comrades v Norton & Stockton ANC	2-2	32
Ashton United v Chadderton	2-1	221
Belper Town v Emley	0-1	200
Congleton Town v Caernarfon Town	1-0	172
Armittage v Leek Town	0-2	130
North Ferriby United v Radcliffe Borough	1-2	86
Rushall Olympic v Paget Rangers	3-0	100
Hemel Hempstead v Rothwell Town	1-0	81
Rushden Town v Holbeach United	3-3	161
Wolverton Town v St Alban City	0-2	140
Harefield United v Hertford Town	3-0	120
Southall v Chatham Town	2-0	110
Erith & Belvedere v Edgware	1-0	100
Leyton-Wingate v Kingsbury Town	3-0	131
Bromley v Camberley Town	4-0	150
Dorking v Hailsham Town	3-0	150
Calne Town v Horndean	0-0	90
Pagham v Devizes Town	4-1	140
Clandown v Dorchester Town	0-0	95
Sharpness v Shortwood United	1-1	160

2nd REPLAY		
Shotton Comrades v Norton & Stockton ANC	5-2	20
Rushden Town v Holbeach United	1-0	148
Horndean v Calene Town	2-1	115
Dorchester Town v Clandown	1-2	129
Sharpness v Shortwood United	5-1	130

1st QUALIFYING ROUND

Best Attendance
Cheltenham Town v Minehead (replay) 933
Best Home Victory
Marine v Sutton Town (replay)6-0
Alfreton Town v Bourne Town 6-0
Best Away Victory
Dorking v Welling United 1-7
Result of the Round
Brandon United v Barrow 5-0

RESULTS	Sc.	Att.
Bridlington Trinity v Alnwick Town	1-0	36
Ferryhill Athletic v Bishop Auckland	0-3	140
Brandon United v Barrow	5-0	121
Blue Star v Guisborough Town	2-1	140
Horden CW v Crook Town	2-3	78
Farsley Celtic v Blyth Spartans	1-2	418
Bridlington Town v Scareborough	0-1	612
Ryhope CA v Whitley Bay	1-3	75
Eppleton CW v Spennymoor United	2-4	70
Durham City v Chester-Le-Street	2-3	144
Billingham Synthonia v Gateshead	0-4	111
South Bank v Darlington CB	4-0	73
Shildon v Billingham Town	1-2	56
Lancaster City v Gretna	0-4	136
Harrogate Town v Morecambe	0-2	182

Tow Law Town v Consett	1-0	164
Northallerton Town v Shotton Comrades	1-2	75
Fleetwood Town v North Shields	2-2	302
Wingate v Workington	4-2	36
Penrith v Peterlee Newtown	1-3	90
Accrngton Stanley v Droylsden	4-1	330
Rossendale United v Mossley	1-2	114
Prescot Cables v Runcorn	1-2	380
Burscough v Armthorpe Welfare	1-1	119
Emley v Nantwich Town	1-0	181
Ashton United v Stalybridge Celtic	0-1	520
Bootle v Chorley	0-1	125
Southport v Clitheroe	4-2	339
Congleton Town v Curzon Ashton	1-0	143
Warrington Town v Formby	1-3	50
Skelmersdale United v Horwich RMI	2-2	110
Rhyl v Wren Rovers	3-1	311
Colwyn Bay v St Helens Town	0-3	249
Leek Town v Winsford United	2-0	211
Eastwood Hanley v Hyde United	0-0	221
Oswestry Town v GKN Sankey	1-1	276
Radcliffe Borough v Ossett Albion	0-0	184
Ilkeston Town v Buxton	2-2	197
Sutton Town v Marine	2-2	164
Goole Town v Skegness Town	3-2	162
Arnold v Tividale	6-1	174
Boldmere St Michaels v South Liverpool	1-1	95
Leicester United v Witton Albion	0-1	102
Denaby United v Long Eaton United	0-0	92
Winford v Gresley Rovers	2-2	49
Spalding United v Matlock Town	2-2	186
Brigg Town v Worksop Town	0-1	160
Alfreton Town v Bourne Town	6-0	144
Atherstone United v Bilston Town	3-3	173
Oldbury United v Grantham	1-1	73
Bromsgrove Rovers v Gainsbough Trinity	1-1	339
Bridgnorth Town v Mile Oak Rovers	0-1	124
Rushall Olympeic v Wellingborough Town	0-2	87
Lye Town v Stafford Rangers	1-3	509
Irthlingborough Dia v Shepshed Charterhouse	3-2	205
Halesowen Town v Racing Club Warwick	2-0	507
Tamworth v Walsall Borough	2-1	414
Stevenage Borough v Kidderminster Harriers	2-0	644
Wisbech Town v Dudley Town	2-0	438
Hednesford Town v Milton Keynes Bourough	2-1	356
Rushden Town v March Town United	2-3	137
Hemel Hempstead v Nuneaton Borough	1-3	205
Hinckley Athletic v Wollenhall Town	2-1	248
Moor Green v Wednesfield Social	5-0	123
Newmarket Town v Stamford (at Stamford)	1-6	155
Sudbury Town v Stourbridge	0-0	274
Berkhamsted Town v Bedworth United	0-0	91
Witney Town v Saffron Walden Town	3-0	130
Histon v Finchley	3-1	68
Stowmarket v VS Rugby	2-2	278
Letchworth Garden City v Corby Town	2-3	124
Hitchin Town v Haverhill Rovers	1-1	248
Lowestoft Town v Braintree Town	1-2	195
Chalfont St Peter v Kings Lynn	1-1	125
Basildon United v Alvechurch	1-3	124
Barking v Cheshunt	4-1	89
Woodford Town v St Albans City	1-0	106
Great Yarmouth Town v Heybridge Swifts	0-1	173
Felixstowe Town v Gorleston	4-0	70
Harlow Town v Cambridge City	2-1	191
Hoddesdon Town v Dunstable	1-3	98
Barton Rovers v Walthamstow Avenue	1-2	160
Abingdon Town v Tring Town	0-1	123
Wembely v Boreham Wood	2-0	65
Hampton v Southall	3-1	155
Harefield United v Aveley	0-0	65
Arlesey Town v Aylesbury United	1-2	110
Grays Athletic v Burnham (walkover for Grays Athletic)		
Leytonstone/Ilford v Marlow	0-2	87
Uxbridge v Buckingham Town	0-1	219
Ware v Billericay Town	1-0	134
Chelmsford city v Alma Swanley	2-0	312
Hounslow v Leyton-Wingate	1-2	78
Erith & Beledere v Crawley Town	1-1	184
Baldock Town v Harrow Borough	0-2	192
Egham Town v Hornchurch	1-1	58
Tilbury v Tunbridge Wells (at Grays Athletic)	2-1	152
Sheppey United v Fisher Athletic	1-1	207
Bracknell Town v Hayes	1-1	120
Leatherhead v Redhill	0-2	241
Thanet United v Bromley	2-2	299
Littlehampton Town v Gravesend & Northfleet (at Gravesend & Nothfleet)	1-2*	242
Ruislip Manor v Hendon	1-0	161
Sutton United v Beckinham Town	5-0	268
Ringmer v Woking	1-3	130
Dorking v Welling United	1-7	150
Merstham v Slough Town	0-4	220
Staines Town v Molesey	3-1	105
Lewes v Tonbridge AFC	0-1	211
Walton & Hersham v Hastings United (walkover for Walton & Hersham)		
Herne Bay v Carshalton Athletic	1-5	120
Kingstonian v Whitehawk	1-0	179
Whyteleafe v Eastbourne United	2-1	118
Hastings Town v Epsom & Ewell	2-1	384
Cray Wanderers v Canterbury City	1-1	90
Sittingbourne v Banstead Athletic	1-2	171
Hythe Town v Ashford Town	1-0	300
Southwick v Folkestone	1-1	181
Haywards Heath v Croydon	3-5	105
Dulwich Hamlet v Eastbourne Town	3-1	180
Pagham v Petersfield United	2-0	103
Horndean v Tooting & Mitcham United	2-3	191
Newport IOW v Metropolitan Police	3-2	198
Worthing v Waterlooville	3-0	265
Newbury Town v AFC Totton	3-3	135
Warminster Town v Wokingham Town	1-1	150
Arundel v Basingstoke Town	1-3	132
Fareham Town v Salisbury	2-2	179
Poole town v Weston-super-Mare	5-1	169
Bristol Manor farm v Gosport Borough	1-1	73
Andover v Hungerford Town	1-3	158
Oxford City v Malvern Town	7-2	88
Forest Green Rovers v Clandown	0-1	179
Mangotsfield United v Frome Town	1-3	110
Reddich United v RS Southhampton	1-1	235
Gloucester city v Ton Pentre	0-0	246
Saltash United v Sharpness	1-2	173
Minehead v Cheltenham Town	1-1	216
Trowbridge Town v Chippenham Town	1-3	405
Exmouth Town v Ottery St Mary	2-0	150
St Blazey v Clevedon Town	2-4	120
Bideford v Merthyr Tydfil	1-1	260
Bath City v Taunton Town	4-1	406

REPLAYS

North Shieds v Fleetwood Town	2-1	411
Armthorpe Welfare v Burscough	0-1	250
Horwich RMI v Skelmersdale United	3-0	227
Hyde United v Eastwood Hanley	1-2	405
GKN Sankey v Oswestry Town	1-0	305
Ossett Albion v Radcliffe Borough	0-3	78
Buxton v Ilkeston Town	4-1	217
Marine v Sutton Town	6-0	147
South Liverpool v Boldmere St Michaels	5-0	159
Long Eaton United v Denaby United	1-0	35
Gresley Rovers v Oldswinford	5-3	210
Matlock Town v Spalding United	0-0	390
Bilston Town v Atherstone United	0-2	130
Grantham v Oldbury United	2-1	196
Gainsborough Trinity v Bromsgrove Rovers	1-2	347
Stourbridge v Sudbury Town	1-0	167
Bedworth United v Berkhamsted Town	1-2	98
VS Rugby v Stowmarket	3-2	397
Haverhill Rovers v Hitchin Town	0-0	185
Kings Lynn v Chalfont St Peter	1-2	630
Aveley v Harefield United	2-0	40
Crawley Town v Erith & Belvedere	3-0	316
Hornchurch v Egham Town	0-1*	69
Fisher Athletic v Sheppey United	2-2	78
Hayes v Bracknell Town	2-1	97
Bromley v Thanet United	2-1	150
Canterbury City v Cray Wanderers	5-0	66
Folkestone v Southwick	1-1	248

A picturesque view of the St. Blazey ground during their 1-0 victory over Shepton Mallet.

(Photo: Leo Hoenig)

Two of Hampshire's most successful clubs clash and A.F.C. Totton's home advantage sees them through by 2-0. Here Dene (No.8) scores the first goal through the legs of the Sholing Sports goalkeeper.

(Photo: David Shute)

Action from Brigg Town's 1-0 away victory at Worksop.

(Photo: Leo Hoenig)

A goal for Wokingham Town in their 3-2 replay victory at home to Warminster Town.

(Photo: Eric Marsh)

AFC Totton v Newbury Town	2-0	268
Wokingham Town v Warminster Town	3-2	189
Salisbury v Fareham Town	0-5	291
Gosport Borough v Bristol Manor Farm	2-2	227
RS Southampton v Redditch United	3-2	159
Ton Pentre v Gloucester City	3-3	326
Cheltenham Town v Minehead	1-2	933
Paulton Rovers v Barry Town	0-2	244
Merthyr Tydfil v Bideford	1-1	280

2nd REPLAY

Matlock Town v Spalding United	3-2*	371
Hitchin Town v Haverhill Rovers	3-0	362
Sheppey United v Fisher Athletic	0-4	302
Southwick v Folkestone	3-1*	355
Gosport Borough v Bristol Manor Farm	4-3	490
Ton Pentre v Gloucester City	2-1	460
Bideford v Merthyr Tydfil	2-0	302

2nd QUALIFYING ROUND

Best Attendance
Halesowen Town v Stafford Rangers 1,453
Best Home Victory
Runcorn v Accrington Stanley (Replay) 9-1
Best Away Victory
Egham Town v Crawley Town 0-6
Result of the Round
Halesowen Town v Stafford Rangers 3-2

RESULTS	Sc.	Att.
Bridlington Trinity v Brandon United	6-2	120
Blue Star v Bishop Auckland	1-3	430
Crook Town v Scarborough	0-1	397
Whitley Bay v Blyth Spartans	1-2	541
Spennymoor United v Gateshead	1-2	331
South Bank v Chester-Le-Street	2-0	122
Billingham Town v Morecambe	0-5	145
Tow Law Town v Gretna	0-1	181
Shotton Comrades v Wingate	0-2	62
Peterlee Newtown v North Shields	2-1	84
Accrington Stanley v Runcorn	1-1	840
Burscough v Mossley	0-3	200
Emley v Chorley	1-4	449
Southport v Stalybridge celtic	2-0	415
Congleton Town v Horwich RMI	2-2	194
Rhyl v Formby	5-0	321
St Helens Town v Eastwood Hanley	2-0	142
GKN Sankey v Leek Town	1-1	55
Radcliffe Borough v Marine	0-4	308
Goole Town v Buxton	3-1	212
Arnold v Witton Albion	0-2	276
Long Eaton United v South Liverpool	2-3	130
Gresley Rovers v Worksop Town	1-0	450
Alfreton Town v Matlock Town	2-0	499
Atherstone United v Bromsgrove Rovers	4-0	248
Mile Oak Rovers v Grantham	1-3	96
Wellingborough Town v Irthlingborough Dia	1-1	352
Halesowen Town v Stafford Rangers	3-2	1453
Tamworth v Wisbech Town	2-1	541
Hednesford Town v Kidderminster Harriers	1-5	557
March Town United v Hinckley Athletic	1-2	158
Moor Green v Nuneaton Borough	1-4	388
Stamford v Berkhamsted Town	3-0	193
Witney Town v Stourbridge	0-0	145
Histon v Corby Town	0-1	235
Hitchin Town v VS Rugby	0-0	409
Braintree Town v Alvechurch	2-1	271
Barking v Chalfont St Peter	0-2	64
Woodford Town v Felixstowe Town	3-1	78
Harlow Town v Heybridge Swifts	1-0	134
Dunstable v Tring Town	3-2	122
Wembley v Walthamstow Avenue	1-3	118
Hampton v Aylesbury United	0-1	183
Grays Athletic v Aveley	2-1	311
Marlow v Ware	2-3	85
Chelmsford City v Buckingham Town	1-0	524
Leyton-Wingate v Harrow Borough	2-2	97
Egham Town v Crawley Town	0-6	152
Tilbury v Hayes	0-0	113
Redhill v Fisher Athletic	0-2	244
Bromley v Ruislip Manor	3-2	200
Sutton United v Gravesend & Northfleet	0-1	458
Woking v Slough Town	1-5	302
Staines Town v Welling United	0-3	182
Tonbridge AFC v Carshalton Athletic	0-2	348
Kingstonian v Walton & Hersham	3-1	244
Whyteleafe v Canterbury City	1-2	152
Banstead Athletic v Hastings Town	0-1	136
Hythe Town v Croydon	1-5	356
Dulwich Hamlet v Southwick	1-1	209
Pagham v Newport IOW	3-5	213
Worthing v Tooting & Mitcham United	5-1	444
AFC Totton v Basingstoke Town	1-1	257
Fareham Town v Woking Town	1-0	130
Poole Town v Hungerford Town	3-2	209
Oxford City v Gosport Borough	2-1	99
Clandown v RS Southampton	1-2	105
Ton Pentre v Frome Town	2-1	490
Sharpness v Chippenham Town	2-3	305
Barry Town v Minehead	5-1	280
Exmouth Town v Bideford	2-1	278
Bath City v Clevedon Town	1-0	515

REPLAYS

Runcorn v Accrington Stanley	9-1	625
Horwich RMI v Congleton Town	2-0	160
Leek Town v GKN Sankey	5-4*	317
Irthlingborough Dia v Wellingborough Town	4-2	371
Stourbridge v Witney Town	1-0	209
VS Rugby v Hitchin Town	3-1	671
Harrow Borough v Leyton-Wingate	2-3	251
Southwick v Dulwich Hamlet	2-1	342
Basingstoke Town v AFC Totton	1-2	380
Hayes v Tilbury	1-2	211

3rd QUALIFYING ROUND

Best Attendance
Nuneaton Borough v Hinckley Athletic 1,526
Best Home Victory
South Liverpool v Witton Albion 5-0
Best Away Victory
Goole Town v Marine 0-5
Result of the Round
RS Southampton v Ton Pentre (replay) 1-2

RESULTS	Sc.	Att.
Bishop Auckland v Bridlington Trinity	3-2	334
Blyth Spartans v Scarborough	1-1	1,100
South Bank v Gateshead	2-2	283
Gretna v Morecambe	0-2	179
Peterlee Newtown v Wingate	2-1	139
Mossley v Runcorn	0-2	704
Southport v Chorley	1-3	578
Rhyl v Horwich RMI	2-0	371
Leek Town v St Helens Town	0-1	343
Goole Town v Marine	0-5	346
South Liverpool v Witton Albion	5-0	245
Alfreton Town v Gresley Rovers	0-1	445
Grantham v Athertstone United	0-2	395
Halesowen Town v Irthingborough Diamonds	2-2	1,153
Kidderminster Harriers v Tamworth	4-3	747
Nuneaton Borough v Hinckley Athletic	0-0	1,526
Stourbridge v Stamford	4-0	224
VS Rugby v Corby Town	2-0	909
Chalfont St Peter v Braintree Town	1-1	239
Harlow Town v Woodford Town	3-0	161
Walthamstow Avenue v Dunstable	0-0	139
Grays Athletic v Aylesbury United	2-2	291
Chelmsford City v Ware	1-0	626
Crawley Town v Leyton-Wingate	2-3	570
Fisher Athletic v Tilbury	2-1	256
Gravesend & Northfleet v Bromley	2-3	600
Welling United v Slough Town	0-0	688
Kingstonian v Carshalton Athletic	2-0	231
Hastings Town v Canterbury City	3-0	542
Southwick v Croydon	0-1	344
Worthing v Newport IOW	4-0	599
Fareham Town v AFC Totton	0-0	205

Above, Slough Town's Devon Petty in possession against Woking (reverting to their famous red and white halves for this match).

Left, Heads up! Two of the season's most successful clubs early in the season, met in the Third Qualifying Round. After a 2-2 draw Barry Town beat Chippenham away 1-0.
Photos: Eric Marsh

Oxford City v Poole Town	4-1	165
Ton Pentre v RS Southampton	1-1	505
Barry Town v Chippenham Town	2-2	436
Bath City v Exmouth Town	2-0	613

REPLAYS

Scarborough v Blyth Spartans	3-1	1,323
Gateshead v South Bank	1-1	409
Irthlingborough Diamonds v Halesowen Town	1-2	677
Hinckley Athletic v Nuneaton Borough	0-1	1,249
Braintree Town Chalfont St Peter	2-0	547
Dunstable v Walthamstow Avenue	2-0	181
Aylesbury United v Grays Athletic (at Tring Town FC)	1-0	301
Slough Town v Welling United	2-1	751
AFC Totton v Fareham Town	0-3	495
RS Southampton v Ton Pentre	1-2	247
Chippenham Town v Barry Town	0-1	527

2nd REPLAY

Gateshead v South Bank	1-2	404

4th QUALIFYING ROUND

Best Attendance
Barnet v Enfield 1,841
Best Home Victory
Dagenham v Atherstone United 5-1
Best Away Victory
Barnet v Enfield 0-7
Result of the Round
Barnet v Enfield 0-7

RESULTS	Sc.	Att.
Frickley Athletic v Northwich Victoria	2-1	961
Bangor City v South Liverpool	1-1	714
Whitby Town v Peterlee Newtown	2-2	696
Scarborough v Bishop Auckland	4-1	1,733
Morecambe v St Helens Town	1-1	756
Chorley v Marine	4-2	674
Macclesfield Town v South Bank	3-1	637
Rhyl v Runcorn	0-2	904
Barnet v Enfield	0-7	1,841
Dagenham v Atherstone United	5-1	550
Dunstable v Nuneaton Borough	0-2	628
Leyton-Wingate v Gresley Rovers	2-0	294
Wycombe Wanderers v Burton Albion	1-0	1,157
Chelmsford City v Kettering Town	1-0	1,319
Stourbridge v VS Rugby	1-1	685
Halesowen Town v Braintree Town	2-1	1,650
Kidderminster Harriers v Bishops Stortford	3-4	726
Aylesbury United v Harlow Town (at RAF Halton)	0-0	634
Dartford v Worcester City	2-0	609
Yeovil Town v Barry Town	4-1	1,679
Farnborough Town v Hastings Town	3-2	595
Slough Town v Kingstonian	2-2	631
Bath City v Croydon	4-1	815
Fisher Athletic v Fareham Town	1-2	201
Bromley v Maidstone United	0-2	1,008
Worthing v Bognor Regis Town	1-2	1,536
Ton Pentre v Weymouth	1-3	1,122
Windsor & Eton v Oxford City	2-2	415

REPLAYS

South Liverpool v Bangor City	3-2*	869
Peterlee Newtown v Whitby Town	0-1	1,050
St Helens Town v Morecambe	0-1	1,146
VS Rugby v Stourbridge	3-1	1,383
Harlow Town v Aylesbury United	1-2	315
Kingstonian v Slough Town	1-1	610
Oxford City v Windsor & Eton	0-1	859

REPLAY

Slough Town v Kingstonian	2-1	1,012

1st ROUND PROPER

Best Attendance at a Non-League Club Ground
Yeovil Town v Hereford United 4,533
Result of the Round
Wycombe Wanderers v Colchester United 2-0

FIRST ROUND RESULTS

	Sc.	Att.
Notts County v **Scarborough**	6-1	5,621
Macclesfield Town v Hartlepool United	1-2	2,366
Tranmere Rovers v Chesterfield	2-2	2,252
Walsall v Preston North End	7-3	4,035
Halifax Town v Scunthorpe United	1-3	1,501
York City v **Morecambe**	0-0	3,696
Wrexham v Bolton Wanderers	3-1	2,738
Lincoln City v Blackpool	0-1	2,596
Frickley Athletic v **Halesowen Town**	1-1	1,720
Mansfield Town v Port Vale	1-1	5,207
Whitby Town v **South Liverpool**	1-0	1,200
Stockport County v **Telford Uninted**	0-1	2,994
Derby County v Crewe Alexandra	5-1	11,047
Rotherham United v Wolverhampton Wanderers	6-0	3,507
Bury v Chester City	2-0	3,424
Rochdale v Darlington	2-1	2,153
Chorley v **Altrincham**	0-2	1,827
Runcorn v **Boston United**	2-2	1,315
Nuneaton Borough v Burnley	2-3	3,182
Wigan Athletic v Doncaster Rovers	4-1	3,315
Brentford v Bristol Rovers	1-3	4,716
Chelmsford City v **Weymouth**	1-0	2,070
Yeovil Town v Hereford United	2-4	4,533
Swansea City v **Leyton-Wingate**	2-0	3,295
Windsor & Eton v Torquay United	1-1	1306
Enfield v **Bognor Regis Town**	0-2	1,340
Swindon Town v Bristol City	0-0	10,468
Reading v **Wealdstone**	1-0	6,460
VS Rugby v Orient	2-2	2,724
Southend United v Newport County	0-1	3,343
Farnborough Town v **Bath City**	0-4	1,324
Fareham Town v **maidstone United**	0-3	800
Bishops Stortford v Peterborough United	2-2	1,981
AFC Bournemouth v **Dartford**	0-0	3,499
Wycombe Wanderers v Colchester United	2-0	3,089
Gillingham v Northampton Town	3-0	3,991
Exeter City v Cardiff City	2-1	2,772
Slough Town v **Aylesbury United**	2-2	1,051
Dagenham v Cambridge United	2-1	1,351
Plymouth Argyle v Aldershot	1-0	7,209
Notts County v Scarborough	6-1	5621

REPLAYS

Chesterfield v Tranmere Rovers	0-1	2,950
Morecambe v York City (at Manchester City FC)	0-2	1,305
Halesowen Town v **Frickley Athletic**	1-1	1,720
Port Vale v Mansfield Town	1-0	6,749
Boston United v **Runcorn**	1-1	2,158
Torquay United v **Windsor & Eton**	3-0	1,429
Bristol City v Swindon Town	4-2	8,979
Orient v **VS Rugby**	4-1	2,311
Peterborough United v **Bishops Stortford**	3-1	2,778
Dartford v Bournemouth	0-2	2,555
Aylesbury United v **Slough Town** (at Tring Town FC)	2-5	1,448

2nd REPLAYS

Runcorn v **Boston United**	4-1	2,525

NON-LEAGUE CLUB'S MATCH DETAILS

Best Attendance at a Non-League Club Ground
Yeovil Town v Hereford United 4,533
Result of the Round
Wycombe Wanderers v Colchester United 2-0

Bishop Stortford (1) 2 (Hardy 25, 70)
Peterborough (2) 2 (Hull, og 17, Worrall 35) Att: 2,000
Bishop Stortford: Taylor M, Wickenden, Tomkins, Knapman, Hull, Hopkins, Staunton, Flynn, Hardy, Nunn, Newbury (sub. Taylor K).
Peterborough: Turner, Paris, Pike, Quow, Slack, Holmes, Kowalski, Fuccillo, Gallagher, Shepherd, Worrsall.
Referee: K. Barratt (Coventry)

Bournemouth (0) 0
Dartford (0) 0 Att: 3,499
Bournemouth: Smeulders, Heffernan, Sulley, Newson, Brown R, Shaw, Driscoll, Russeil, Clarke, Howlett, Morrell.
Dartford: Mallett, Jaques, Brown D, Pamthlett, Gibson, Cowley, Reeves, Stewart, Dingwall, Burman, Robinson.
Referee: C. Downey (Hounslow).

Chelmsford (0) 1 (Pountney 82)
Weymouth (0) 0 Att: 2,041
Chelmsford: Keeley, Lee, Spittle, Markin, Oliver, Taylor, Johnson, Foley, Lazarus, Owers, Pountney.
Weymouth: Bond, Steele, Rogers P, Coombes, Bourne, Iannone, Borthwick, Rogers M, Clarridge, Doherty, Agana.
Referee: D. Hedges (Oxford)

Chorley (0) 0
Altrincham (1) 2 (Reid 12, Anderson 62) Att: 1,827
Chorley: Pierce, Gardner, Hughes, Hanson, Silous, Westwell, Liptrot (sub. Gay), Haslam, Edwards, Buttler, McLachlan.
Altrincham: Wealands, Gardner Jonhson, Edwards, Cuddy, Farrelly, Conning, Densmore, Reid, Chesterton, Anderson (sub. Newton).
3*Referee:* D. Hutchinson (Harrogate)

Dagenham (0) 2 (Sullivan 50, Scott 63)
Cambridge (0) 1 (Crown 80) Att: 1,351
Dagenham: Jacobs, Coles, Day, Risk, Dunwell, Taylor, Cox, Scott, Manderson, Sullivan, Cowell.
Cambridge: Hansbury, Clark, Scott, Finney, Downman, Bennett, Sinton, (sub. Massey),Spriggs, Cooper, Comfort, Crown.
Referee: P. Vanes (Warley)

Enfield (0) 0
Bognor Regis (1) 2 (Cooper 21, Clements 56) Att: 1,340
Enfield: Rape, Barrett, Hayzelden, Cooper, Howell (sub Gray), Docker, Drummy, Ironton, Ashford, Flint, King.
Bognor: Sperring, Crumplin, Bird, Burtenshaw, Gill, Pullen M, Manley, Pullen P, Gladding, Clements, Cooper.
Referee: A. Seville (Birmingham)

Fareham (0) 0
Maidstone (0) 3 (Cugley 48,87, Barnes 68) Att: 800
Fareham: Grant, Davies, Watt, North (sub. Clapp), Bye, Wilkes, Bartlett, Andrews, McIntyre, Long, Tindal.
Maidstone: Richardson, Thompson, Borg, Crowe, Pittway, Donn, Hill, Fergusson, Cugley, Barnes, Tiltman.
Referee: A. Buksh (London)

Farnborough (0) 0
Bath (0) 4 (Chandler 50, Palmer, pen 55, Ricketts 69, Bodin 85) Att: 1,324
Farnborough: Osgood, Walden, Baker, Broome, Dorherty, Chester, Turkington, Bolton, Jones, Morris, Nilson (sub. Cowlishaw).
Bath: Mogg, Palmer, Fulbrook, Sherwood, Ricketts, Barton, Brown, Bodin, Sinleton, Chandler, Payne.
Referee: D. Vickers (Ilford)

Paul Reid puts Altrincham ahead against Chorley at the very impressive Victory Park.

(Photo: John Rooney)

Halesowen Town did well to draw at Frickley but then lost 1-3 at home. A Frickley Forward heads for goal in the replay.

(Photo: Leo Hoenig)

Another good crowd, this time at Gillingham where the visitors are Bognor Regis and Geoff Cooper is about to score the visitor's goal from a penalty in their 1-6 defeat'

(Photo Leo Hoenig)

Nuneaton (0) 2 (Bennyworth 75, Murphy 82)
Burnley (2) 3 (Malley 15, Denvine 43, 89) Att: 4,500
Nuneaton: Bythe, Carr, Gibson, Bennyworth, Thurman, Smithers, McGoldrick, Murphy, Hamil, Denyer, Brown.
Burnley: Neenan, Hird, Heesom, Divine, Haggarty, Deakin, Grewcock, Malley, Taylor, Parker, Hoskin.
Referee: B. Hill (Kettering)

Reading (0) 1 (Horrix, pen 58)
Wealdstone (0) 0 Att: 7,169
Reading: Westwood, Peters, Richardson, Beavon, Hicks, Wood, Burvill, Horrix, Senior, Bremner, Gilkes.
Wealdstone: Isles, Tapley, McCargo, Byatt, Bowgett, Wainwright, Greenaway, Holmes, Donnellan, Graham, (sub. Jones), Doyle.
Referee: Hutchinson (Harrogate)
Sendings off: Burvill (Reading), Bowgett and Doyle (Wealdstone)

Frickley (0) 1 (Bishop 74)
Halesowen (1) 1 (Joinson P, 41) Att: 1,720
Frickley: Maxted, Shirtliff, Daniels, Wilcox, Wright, Bishop, Marshall (sub. Noteman), Howey, Wilson, Mallender, Foley.
Halesowen: Pemberton, Moore, Sherwood, Lacey, Randle, Penn, Heath, Moss, Woodhouse, Joinson P, Joinson L (sub. Smith).
Referee: M. Scott (Nottingham)

Macclesfield (0) 1 (Askey 57)
Hartlepool (1) 2 (Shoulder 40, 47) Att: 3,000
Macclesfield: Zelem, Fielding, Fairclough, Griffiths, Hardman, Shaw, Kersley, Tobin, Askey, Hall, Mountford.
Hartlepool: Blackburn, Nobbs, Chambers, Hogan, Smith, Linighan, Proudlock, Borthwick, Walker, Shoulder.
Referee: K. Walmsley (Blackpool)

Runcorn (1) 2 (Smith 5,57)
Boston (1) 2 (Casey 19, Nuttell 55) Att: 1,315
Runcorn: Eales, Rowland, Roberts, Jones, Fraser, Smith, Crompton S, Imrie, Skeete (sub. Crompton A.), Mather, Carrodus.
Boston: Blackwell, Casey, Stenson, Czuzman, Creane, Ladd, Laverick, Nuttell, Thomson, Cook, Gilbert.
Referee: T. Mills (Barnsley)

Slough (2) 2 (Dodds 16, White 38)
Aylesbury (1) 2 Botterill 42, Hercules 80) Att: 1,051
Slough: Cox, Norman, Harris, Knight, Bateman, White, Petty, Jacobs, Dodds, Woodley (sub. Kiely) Wilson.
Aylesbury: Baker, Mead, James, Saunders, Bougouneau, Hackett, Botterill, Coffill, Hercules, Campbell, Shrieves (sub. Pronger).
Referee: I. Hemley (Ampthil)

Stockport (0) 0
Telford (1) 1 (McGinty, pen 31) Att: 2,994
Stockport: Salmon, Rutter, Sherlock, Chapman, Wiliams B, Mathewson, Hodkinson, Hendrie, leonard, Sword Mossman.
Telford: Charlton, McGinty B, Turner, Barnett, Mann Joseph, Williams C, Stringer, Hogan, Alcock.
Referee: T. Holbrook (Wolverhampton)
Sending off: Rutter (Stockport)

Swansea (1) 2 (Waddle 16, Williams 50)
Leyton-windgate (0) 0 Att: 3,29
Swansea: Rimmer, Hough, Sullivan, Gibbins, Harrison McHale, Williams, Randell, Emmanuel, Waddle, Pasco (sub. Melville).
Leyton Wingate: Tucker, Taylor, Wood, Mavin Hamberger, O'Hehir, Bee, Lane, heselden, Rhoden (sub Warwick), Baxter.
Referee: M. James (Horsham)
Sending off: Hamberger (Leyton-Wingate)

VS Rugby (1) 2 (Downes 41, 77)
Orient (1) 2 (Brooks 9, pen 79) Att: 2,500
Rugby: Marsden, Potter, Harrison, Knox, Geddes, Gorman, Ingram, Carmichael, Norris, Conway, Downes.
Orient: Wells, Hales, Dickenson, Sussex (sub. Castle), Cunningham, Cornwall, Mountford, Brooks, Jones,Shinners, Juryeff.
Referee: D. Reeves (Uxbridge)

Whitby (0) 1 (Hankin 61)
South Liverpool (0) 0 Att: 1,200
Whitby: Harvey, Scott L, Scott J, Fell, Johnson, March, Balcombe, Watson, Hankin (sub. Sharkey), Omoni, Gray.
South Liverpool: Hughes, Higgins, Thompson, Iro, Carroll, Billing, Kilshaw, Baker, Rice, Joel, Whitbread (sub. Atwere).
Referee: L. Dilkes (Mossley)

Windsor and Eton (0) 1 (Woods 78)
Torquay (1) 1 (Durham 2) Att: 1,477
Windsor and Eton: Michell K, Walsh, Woodcraft (sub. Michell J), Hill, Woods, Dennis, Huxley, Barton, Davis, Yates, Franks.
Torquay: Fry, Pugh, Dawkins, Fowler (sub. Viney), Compton, Crowe, Crabbe, Walsh, Loram, Durham, Wheeldon.
Referee: J. Martin (Alton)

Wycombe (2) 2 (West 3, Read 40)
Colchester (0) 0 Att: 3,018
Wycombe: Lester, Collins, Riley, Burgess, Vircavs, McMahon, West, Read, Dell, Link, Stanley.
Colchester: Chamberlain, Hedman, Farell, Reeves, Game, Houston, Groves, Parkinson, Turner, Adcock, English, Tony.
Referee: E. Scales (Ware)

Yeovil (1) 2 (Smith 18, McGinlay 66)
Hereford (2) 4
(Carter 13, 86, 89, Kearns 45) Att: 4,533
Yeovil: James K, Linney, Kember, Craig, Thorpe, Gow, James P, Smith, Pearson, Ritchie, McGinlay.
Hereford: Rose, Price, Pejic, Halliday, Cegieiske, Maddy, Harvey, Delve, Wells, Kearns, Carter.
Referee: J. Deakin (Llantwit Major)

York (0) 0
Morcambe (0)0 Att: 3,692
York: Leaning, Senior, Hay, Sbragia, MacPhail, Haslegrave, Ford, Banton, Walwyn, Mills, Canham (sub. Houchen).
Morecambe: McDonnell, Jones, Kennedy, Brooks, Gordon, Balm, Thornton, Sayer, Galley, Walsh, Gill.
Referee: K. Lupton (Stockton)

Notts County (3) 6 (Hunt 20, Harkouk 28, 29, 79, Young 68, McParland 75)
Scarborough (0) 1
(Burke, pen 74) Att: 5,621
Notts County: Leonard, Richards, Clarke, Benjamin, Sims, Yates, McParland, Goodwin, Young, Harkouk, Hunt.
Scarborough: Crawford, Dennis, Thompson, Dunn, Hartley (sub. Burke), Coleby, Davis, Sellars, Bowman. Wintergill, Wiggan.
Referee: R. Banks (Manchester))

FIRST ROUND REPLAYS

Aylesbury (2) 2 (Champbell 2, 34)
Slough (1) 5 (Woodley 31,
White 59, Dodds 60, 70, Kiely 88) Att: 1,000
Aylesbury: Baker, Mead, James, Saunders, Bougouneau, Hackett, Botterill, Coffill, Hercules, Campbell, Pronger.
Slough: Cox, Norman, Gardam, Knight, Bateman, White, Petty, Jacobs, Dodds, Woodley (sub. Kiely), Wilson.
Referee: I. Hemley (Amphill)

Another impressive view of Chorley's ground as Gary Pierce clears an Altrincham attack.

(Photo: Leo Hoenig)

Brian Greenaway in possession at Reading opposing Stuart Beavon. The high flying League club on with a penalty by Horrix.

Exciting goalmouth action in the Windsor & Eton v Torquay United cup tie which was drawn.

Dartford (0) 0
Bournemouth (2) 2
(Clarke 20, Newson 30) Att: 2,555
Dartford: Mallett, Jacques, Brown, Phamphlett, Gibson, Cowley (sub. McCayna), Reeves, Stewart, Dingwall, Burman, Robinson.
Bournemouth: Smeulders, Heffernan, Sulley, Newson, Brown, Nightingale, O'Driscoll, Russell, Clarke, Thompson, Morrell.
Referee: C. Downey (Hounslow)

Halesowen (1) 1 Sherwood, pen 10)
Frickley (1) 3
(Bishop 28, Wilson 67, Wilcox, pen 83 Att: 2,973
Halesowen: Pemberton, Moore, Sherwood, Lacy, Randle, Heath, Penn, Moss, Woodhouse, Joinson P, Joinson L.
Frickley: Maxted, Shirtliff, Marshall, Wilcox, Wright, Bishop, Noteman, Howley, Wilson, Mallender, Foley.
Referee: M. Scott (Nottingham)

Morecambe (0) 0
YORK (2) 2 (Sbragia 2, Walwyn 10) Att; 1,305
(at Maine Road)
Morecambe: McDonnell, Jones, Kennedy, Brooks, Gordon, Balm, Thornton, Sayer, Galley, Walsh (sub. Large), Gill.
York: Leaning, Senoir, Hay, Sbragia, MacPhail, Mills, Ford, Banton, Welwyn, Houchen, Pearce.
Referee: K. Lupton (Stockton)

Orient (3) 4 (Jones 17, Castle 32, Juryeff 38, Brooks 46)
VS Rugby (0) 1 (Gorman 63) Att:2,311
Orient: Wells, Hales, Dickenson, John, Mountford, Cornwell, Godfrey (sub. Harvey), Brooks, Jones, Castle, Juryeff.
VS Rugby: Lawrence, Potter, Harrison, Knox, Geddes, Gorman, Ingram, Carmicheal, Norris, Conway, Downes.
Referee: D. Reeves (Uxbridge)

Torquay (1) 3 (Walsh 38, 75, loram 68)
Windsor & Eton (0) 0 Att: 1,429
Torquay: Fry, Pugh, Dawkins,Wheeldon, Compton, Crowe, Crabbe, Walsh, Loram, Durham, Smith.
Windsor: Mitchell K, Walsh, Mitchell J, Hill, Woods, Dinnis, Huxley, Baron (sub. Craker), Davis, Yates, Franks.
Referee: R. Groves (Weston-Super-Mare)

Boston (1) 1 (Gilbert 28)
Runcorn (0) 1 (Carter 51)
After exta-time Att: 2,158
Boston: Blackwell, Casey, Stenson, Czuzman, Creane, Muttell, Laverick (sub. Harrison), Thomson, White, Cook, Gilbert.
Runcorn: McBride, Rowland, Roberts, Jones, Fraser, Smith, Crompton S.Imrie (sub. Cromton A), Carter, Mather, Carrodus.
Referee: T. Mills (Barnsley)

Peterborough (1) 3 (Cassidy 24, Gallagher 85, Kowalski 87)
Brishop's Stortford (0) 1 (Flynn 60) Att: 2,778
Peterborough: Turner, Paris, Pike, Cassidy, Slack, Holmes, Kowalski, Fuccillo, Gallagher, Shepherd (sub. Kelly), Worrall.
Bishop's Stortford: Taylor M, Wickenden, Tomkins, Knapman, Hull, Hopkins, Staunton, Flynn, Hardy, Nunn, Taylor K, (sub. Newbury).
Referee: K. Barratt (Coventry)

SECOND REPLAY NOV. 25

Runcorn (1) 4 (Mather 44, Carter 57, 68, Crompton S, 62)
Boston (0) 1 (Gilbert 66) Att: 2,525
Runcorn: McBride, Rowlands, Roberts, Jones, Fraser, Smith, Crompton S, Imrie, Carter, Mather, Carrodus.
Boston: Blackwill, Casey, Stenson, Czuzman, Crean, Hasrrison, Thomson, Nuttell, White (sub. Ladd), Cook, Gilbert.
Referee: J. Lloyd (Wrexham)

A great save by Dartford's Mallett as Bournemouth turn on pressure in their replay at Watling St.
(Photo: David Mills)

Oh we do like to be beside The Seaside!

Gary Anderson scores the winner to eliminate Blackpool away for the second year in succession.

Is everybody happy?

Photos: John Rooney

SECOND ROUND

Best Attendance at a Non-League Club Ground
Runcorn v Wigan Athletic 4,500
Result of the Round
Hartlepool United v Frickley Athletic

Hartlepool United v **Frickley Athletic**	0-1	4,807
Blackpool v **Altrincham**	1-2	5,037
Port Vale v Walsall	0-0	11,736
Notts County v Wrexham	2-2	4,673
Rotherham United v Burnley	4-1	4,264
Runcorn v Wigan Athletic	1-1	3,310
York City v **Whitby Town**	3-1	6,229
Derby County v **Telford United**	6-1	12,291
Scunthorpe United v Rochdale	2-2	2,868
Tranmere Rovers v Bury	1-1	3,398
Gillingham v **Bognor Regis Town**	6-1	4,228
Wycombe Wanderers v **Chelmsford City**	2-0	3,816
Plymouth Argyle v **Maidstone United**	3-0	7,597
Orient v **Slough Town**	2-2	3,450
Reading v Hereford United	2-0	6,096
Newport County v Torquay United	1-1	2,283
Bristol City v Exeter City	1-2	8,065
Swansea City v Bristol Rovers	1-2	4,230
Peterborough United v **Bath City**	1-0	3,388
AFC Bournemouth v **Dagenham**	4-1	3,336

REPLAYS

Walsall v Port Vale	2-1	5,671
Wrexham v Notts County	0-3	2,645
Wigan Athletic v **Runcorn**	4-0	3,390
Rochdale v Scunthorpe United	2-1	5066
Bury v Tranmere Rovers	2-1	3,137
Slough Town v Orient	2-3	6,086

NON-LEAGUE CLUB'S MATCH DETAILS

Bournemouth (2) 4 (O'Druscikk 16, Thompson 37, Brown 61, Clarke 66)
Dagenham (1) 1 (Cox 27) Att: 3,336
Bournemouth: Smeulders, Heffernan, Sulley, Newson, Brown, Beck, O'Drisoll, Russell, Clarke, Thompson, Morrell.
Dagenham: Jacobs, Coles, Baxter, Risk, Dunwell, Taylor, Cox, Scott, Horan, Sullivan (sub. Day), Powell.
Referee: D. Reeves (Uxbridge)

Blackpool (0) 1 (Stewart 60)
Altrincham (1) 2
(Reid 22, Anderson 86) Att: 5,037
Blackpool: O'Rourke, Walsh, Stonehouse, Hetzke, Greenall, Davis, Deary, Stewart, Windridge, Dyer.
Altrincham: Wealands, Edwards, Densmore, Johnson, Cuddy, Farrelly, Gardner, Conning, Reid, Ellis, Anderson.
Referee: T. Simpson (Sowerby Bridge)

Gillingham (3) 6 (Cascarino 2, 13, Robinson 40, Shearer 50, Cochrane 65, Hales 80)
Bognor (0) 1 (Cooper, pen 69) Att: 4,228
Gillingham: Hillyard, Sage, Elsey, Oakes, Weatherly, Robinson, Cochrane, Shearer, Hales, Collins, Cascarino.
Bognor: Sperring, Crumplin, Bird, Burtenshaw (sub. Clarke), Gill, Pullen M, Manley, Pullen P, Gladding, Clements, Cooper.
Referee: D. Axcell (Southend)

Hartlepool (0) 0
Frickley (0) 1 (Wilson 79) Att: 4,100
Hartlepool: Blackburn, Nobbs, Chambers, Robinson, Smith, Linighan, Honour, Shoulder, Borthwick (sub. Dobson), Walker, Gollogly.
Frickley: Maxted, Shirtliff, Marshall, Wilcox, Wright, Bishop, Noteman, Howey, Wilson, Mallender, Hatto.
Referee: D. Scott (Burnley)

Orient (0) 2 Cornwell 55, Juryeff 64)
Slough (2) 2 (Dodds, Wilson 26) Att: 3,450
Orient: Wells, Hales, Dickenson, Sussex, Sitton, Cornwell, Foster, Brooks, Shinners, Golfrey, Juryeff.
Slough: Way, Norman, Harris, Knight, Bateman, White, Petty, Jacobs, Dodds, kiely (sub. Landeg), Wilson.
Referee: D Hedges (Oxford)

Peterborough (0) 1 (Gallagher 53)
Bath (0) 0 Att: 3,388
Peterborough: Turner, Paris, Pike, Cassidy, Wile, Slack, Kowalski, Fuccillo, Gallagher, Kelly, Worrall.
Bath: Mogg, Palmer, Barton, Sherwood, Pratt, Adams (sub. Taylor), Chandler, Brown, Bodin, Singleton, Payne.
Referee: A. Ward (London)

Plymouth (2) 3 (Cooper L. 12, Nelson 29, Summerfield 84)
Maidstone (0) 0 Att: 7,597
Plymouth: Crudgington, Nisbet, Cooper L, Goodyear, McElhinney, Cooper S, Clayton, Nelson.
Maidstone: Richardson, Thompson, Borg, Pittaway, Glover, Fergusson, Hill, Reynolds, Cugley, Barnes, Tilman (sub. Joyce).
Referee: R. Milford (Bristol)

Runcorn (1) 1 (Mather 45)
Wigan (0) 1 (Knowles 74) Att: 4,500
Runcorn: McBride, Rowlands, Roberts, Jones, Fraser, Smith, Crompton, Imrie, Carter, Mather (sub. Skeet), Carrodus.
Wigan: Trunks, Butler, Knowles, Kelly, Cribley, Mathven, Lowe, Barrow, Newell (sub. Aspinall), Langley, Griffiths.
Referee: J. Key (Rotherham)

Wycombe (1) 2 (Read 14, McMahon 55)
Chelmsford (0) 0 Att: 3,816
Wycomge: Lester, Collins, Riley, Burgess, Virvacs, McMahon, West, Read, Dell, Blochell, Stanley.
Chelmsford: Keeley, Lee, Johnson, Oliver, Makin, Taylor, Owers (sub. Thrift), Foley, Lazarus, Glynn, Pountney.
Referee: M. Bodenham (Brighton)

York (1) 3 (Ford 7, Walwyn 74, Pearce 79,)
Whitby (0) 1 (Watson 59) Att: 6,225
York: Leaning, Hood, Hay, McAughtrie, MacPhail, Mills, Ford, Banton, Walwyn, Houchen, Pearce.
Whitby: Harvey, Scott L, Scott J, Dale, Sell, March (sub. Johnson), Watson, Gray Balcombe, Omoni, Sharkey.
Referee: G. Aplin (Kendal)

Derby (1) 6 (Gregory 32,Chandler 50, 63, 84, Micklewhite 73, 82)
Telford (1) 1 (Mckenna 45) Att: 12,267
Derby: Wallington, Blades, Buckley, Williams, hindmarch, McClaren, Michlewhite, Christie, Davison, Gregory (sub. Garner), Chandler.
Telford: Charlton, McGinlay, Turner, Barrnett, Eaton, Haldon, Joseph, Williams, Mckenna, Hogan, Alcock.
Referee: R. Nixon (West Kirby)

Slough (1) 2 (White 43, Harris, pen 85)
Orient (1) 3
(Juryeff 19, Godgfrey 63, Shinner 71) Att: 3,200
Slough: Way, Norman (sub. Woodley), Harris, Knight, Bateman, White, Petty, Jacobs, Dodds, Kiely, Wilson.
Orient: Wells, Hales, Dickenson, Brookes, Shinners, Godfrey, Juryeff (sub. Mountford).
Referee: D. Hwsfwa (Oxford)

Wigan (2) 4 (Methven 5, Newell 69, Jones, og 82)
Runcorn (0) 0 Att: 3,390
Wigan: Tunks, Butler, Knowles, Kelly, Cribley (sub. Aspinall), Methven, Lowe, Barrow, Newell, Langley, Griffiths.
Runcorn:, McBride, Rowland, Roberts, Jones, Fraser, Smith, Crompton, Imrie, (sub. Holdin), Carter, Mather, Carrodus.
Referee: G. Aplin (Kendal)

THIRD ROUND

Frickley (0) 1 (Bishop 82)
Rotherham (2) 3
Gooding 14, Pugh 31, Tynan 75) Att: 5, 932
Frickley: Maxed, Shirtleff, Marshall, Wilcox (sub. Hatto), Wright, Gill, Bishop, Howey, Mallender, Foley.
Rotherham: O'Hanlon, Barnsley, Dungworth, Gooding, Smith, Pickering, Birch, Emerson, Tynan, Trusson, Pugh.
Referee: R. Nixon (West Kirby)

York (1) 2 (Walwyn 41, 61)
Wycombe Wanderers (0) 0 Att: 5,532
York: Leaning, Senior, Hood, McAughtrie, MacPhail, Haslegrave, Ford, Banton, Walwyn, Houchen, Canham.
Wycombe: Lester, Collins, Riley, Burgess, Vircavs, McMahon, West, Read, Dell, Blochel, Stanley.
Referee: D. Allison (Lancaster)

Birmingham (0) 1 (Hopkins 67)
Altrincham (0) 2
(Ellis 64, Hopkins, og 74 Att: 6,636
Birmingham: Seaman, Ranson, Dicks, Hagan, Armstrong, Kuhl (sub. Wright), Bremner, Roberts, Kennedy, Platnauer, Hopkins.
Altrincham: Wealands, Gardner, Densmore, Johnson, Cuddy, Conning, Ellis (sub. Farrelly), Davison, Reid, Chester, Anderson.
Referee: K. Hackett (Sheffield)

FOURTH ROUND

York (0) 2 (Banton 67, Ford 80)
Altrincham (0) 0 **Att. 8.834**
York: Leaning, Senior, Hood, McAughtrie, MacPhail, Mills, Ford, Banton, Walwyn, Houchen, Canham.
Altrincham: Wealands, Gardner, Densmore, Johnson, Cuddy, Conning, Ellis, Davison, Reid, Chesters, Anderson.
Referee: G. Tyson (Sunderland)

'Two Historic Goals'

'The Equaliser'. A Ronnie Ellis volley crashes through a packed Birmingham City defence to make the score 1- 1.
(Photo: John Rooney)

A beautifully placed and absolutely vital 'goal' but sadly for First Division Birmingham City's Robert Hopkins, it's in his own net and Altrincham record a famous victory.
(Photo: John Rooney)

A great moment as Wycombe Wanderers, having held top of the First Division Middlesborough until the last minute of their Third Round Replay in 1975, are clapped off the field in front of 30,000. The winning goal was scored by David Armstrong and there's Graeme Souness applauding on the right.

F.A. CUP NON LEAGUE TABLE 1925-1986

	1st	2nd	3rd	4th	5th	P	W	D	L	F	A	Seasons
Yeovil T.	20	9	8	–	1	83	29	16	38	106	146	38
Weymouth	21	7	2	1	–	61	14	6	31	67	127	31
Blyth Spartans	14	9	1	–	1	59	15	19	25	77	117	25
Kettering T.	21	7	2	–	–	59	11	18	30	74	122	30
Scarborough	20	8	4	–	–	59	16	11	32	79	134	32
Altrincham	7	5	6	1	–	50	20	11	19	64	68	19
Barnet	18	4	4	–	–	49	12	10	27	65	110	26
Boston U.	18	5	4	–	–	49	13	9	27	70	106	27
Enfield	11	8	2	1	–	49	15	12	22	76	85	22
Telford U.	17	5	–	1	1	46	12	9	25	60	97	24
Wycombe W.	15	6	2	–	–	46	10	13	23	50	72	23
Bath C.	8	8	4	–	–	43	17	5	21	65	72	20
Chelmsford C.	14	7	1	1	–	43	12	7	24	57	84	23
Dartford	14	7	2	–	–	41	11	7	23	60	86	23
Walthamstow Ave.	10	8	–	1	–	41	12	10	19	73	83	19
Bishop Auckland	8	8	–	1	–	38	11	8	19	62	79	17
Rhyl	15	3	2	1	–	38	12	5	21	39	85	21
Gainsborough Tr.	10	10	–	–	–	36	11	5	20	47	69	20
Thanet U.	10	6	2	–	–	34	10	6	18	47	89	18
Folkestone T.	11	4	2	–	–	32	8	7	17	44	72	17
Nuneaton Bor.	11	3	2	–	–	31	7	8	16	35	48	16
Gravesend & N.*	12	4	–	1	–	28	7	4	17	33	61	17
Leytonstone/Ilford*	17	5	–	–	–	28	5	1	22	35	71	22
Grantham	8	6	1	–	–	27	8	3	16	39	61	15
Workington	13	1	1	1	–	27	6	4	17	35	60	17
Bangor C.	9	4	–	–	–	23	4	6	13	28	53	13
Crook T.	9	4	1	–	–	23	6	3	14	32	69	14
Dagenham	8	4	1	–	–	23	6	4	13	19	34	13
Hendon	10	3	1	–	–	23	5	4	14	28	53	14
King's Lynn	7	5	1	–	–	23	7	3	13	25	51	13
Spennymoor U.	8	4	1	–	–	23	6	4	13	27	58	13
Worcester C.	5	2	1	1	–	23	7	7	19	33	36	9
Cheltenham T.	13	1	1	–	–	22	3	3	16	26	56	15
Runcorn	5	4	1	–	–	22	6	6	10	31	47	10
Corinthian Casuals*	7	–	6	2	–	21	2	4	15	24	56	15
Maidstone U.	1	2	3	–	–	21	8	7	6	30	29	6
Northwich Vic.	4	3	–	1	–	21	6	7	8	32	33	8
Morecambe	11	1	1	–	–	20	3	4	13	12	35	13
Merthyr Tydfil	7	4	–	–	–	19	4	4	11	26	47	11
Tooting & Mitcham	5	2	1	1	–	19	7	3	9	26	30	9
Wealdstone	10	1	1	–	–	19	3	4	12	15	36	12
Bishops Stortford	5	2	1	–	–	18	4	6	8	25	36	8

Sutton U.	6	1	–	1	–	18	4	5	9	18	40	8
Hitchin T.	5	1	1	–	–	17	3	7	7	22	31	7
Stafford R.	6	2	–	1	–	17	5	3	9	15	23	9
Goole T.	8	1	1	–	–	16	3	3	10	16	34	10
Leatherhead	2	3	–	1	–	16	6	4	6	16	21	6
Dulwich H.	13	–	–	–	–	15	0	2	13	17	53	13
Slough T.	3	4	–	–	–	15	5	3	7	21	29	7
South Liverpool	4	4	–	–	–	15	4	3	8	19	33	8
Bromley	5	3	–	–	–	14	3	2	9	24	40	8
Kidderminster H.	9	1	–	–	–	14	1	3	10	13	31	10
Lancaster C.	8	2	–	–	–	14	2	2	10	11	37	10
Leyton-Wingate*	6	3	–	–	–	14	3	2	9	14	36	9
Macclesfield T.	9	–	1	–	–	14	2	3	9	18	37	10
Netherfield	6	2	–	–	–	14	2	4	8	20	40	8
North Shields	8	2	–	–	–	14	2	1	11	18	48	10
Burton Alb.	6	–	2	–	–	13	4	1	8	13	31	8
Frickley Ath.	6	1	1	–	–	13	3	2	8	14	27	8
Newport (I.O.W.)	6	2	–	–	–	13	2	1	10	8	47	8
Poole T.	6	–	1	–	–	13	2	4	7	14	32	7
Barking	2	4	–	–	–	12	4	2	6	11	21	6
Burnham & Hillingdon	5	1	1	–	–	12	3	2	7	13	30	7
Marine	4	2	–	–	–	12	2	4	6	19	31	6
Mossley	6	2	–	–	–	12	2	2	8	7	25	8
Shildon	6	1	–	–	–	12	1	4	7	11	30	7
Dorchester T.	3	3	–	–	–	11	3	2	6	19	27	6
Hayes	7	1	–	–	–	11	1	2	8	10	26	8
Witton Alb.	5	2	–	–	–	11	2	2	7	15	22	7
Minehead	4	2	–	–	–	10	2	2	6	12	20	6
Stalybridge Celtic	7	1	–	–	–	10	1	1	8	13	31	8
Woking	5	1	–	–	–	10	1	3	6	16	30	6

*Gravesend & N. – includes Northfleet U. (13). Leytonstone/Ilford – includes Leytonstone (13) and Ilford (13). Corinthian Casuals – includes Corinthians (18). Leyton-Wingate – includes Leyton (13).

The following clubs have been excluded –

(a) Hereford U. (53), Wigan Ath. (43), Peterborough U. (36), Wimbledon (34), Scunthorpe U. (17), Oxford U. (15) and Gillingham (10) are all now league clubs.

(b) Gateshead U. (36), Guildford and Dorking U. (35), Bedford T. (34), Romford (23), Stockton (15), Hastings U. (14) and Gateshead (10) are all defunct.

Another famous face. It's Kenny Dalglish heading in Liverpool's second goal against Altrincham at Anfield in 1981. Again, the attendance exceeded 30,000.

NEW LIFE BREATHED INTO FOOTBALL

by Paul Newman of The Times

The year 1986 will go down in the history of English football as one of the most significant in the game's development. The sweeping structural changes to which the Football League finally agreed not only averted — temporarily at least — the threat of a "Super League", but also promised to breath new life into a sport which had been ailing for too long.

Amongst all the reforms which the League adopted, the one which may have the most widespread effect is the one setting up a promotion and relegation link between the Fourth Division and the GM Vauxhall Conference. From the end of the 1986-87 season, the Conference champions will automatically win promotion to the Fourth Division, provided their facilities are considered acceptable.

New Names, New Faces

The consequences of this revolutionary change will be felt deeply both within the Football League and outside. For the 92 League clubs, there is the regular promise of new names, new faces and new grounds. In reaching the First Division and enjoying considerable cup success, new League clubs like Oxford United and Wimbledon have brought great interest to the game over the last 10 years; there is no reason why the likes of Altrincham and Telford United cannot go on to emulate them.

To the regret of some of its members, but to the satisfaction of nearly everyone else, the Fourth Division will no longer be a safe haven for those clubs apparently content to accept their annual cash hand-out from the League but unable or unwilling to contribute positively to the game.

For up to half the Fourth Division clubs, their season has until now been effectively over by Christmas, except perhaps for the hope of progress in the Freight Rover Trophy. The usually meaningless and half-hearted attempt to avoid re-election will henceforth be replaced by a determined effort to keep clear of the relegation position.

And although the season will have a painful end for one club, the others will surely benefit from the interest that the new situation will generate. Moreover, the relegated club will immediately have the chance to win back their place the following season; the likes of Barrow and Southport never had that opportunity when they were voted out of the Fourth Division.

Injustices

Yet it is outside the Football League that the effects of this fundamental change will be most keenly felt. The consequences for the GM Vauxhall Conference will be obviouss. The championship will no longer be an end in itself but a door to a whole new world; the chance of "doing a Wimbledon or an Oxford".

The future of the Conference clubs will be in their own hands and no longer at the mercy of the Football League's annual election. There will be no repetition of the injustices done over the last decade to Altrincham and Maidstone United, who both did well in re-election polls but then won fewer votes when they returned with an even stronger case a year later.

The most obvious and immediate result seems certain to be an even more intense struggle for the Conference championship. As chairmen and boards of directors will be prepared to spend more money on their squads in the hope of gaining promotion, so the trend from professional to semi-professional football is likely to accelerate, raising still further the standards at part-time level.

Will we be seeing Altrincham scoring goals like this one (by Paul Reid in the F.A. Cup at Blackpool) on League Grounds in the 1987-88 season.

Photo: John Rooney

Ground improvements will also continue, for there could surely be no greater disappointment for a club than to win the championship and then be refused entry into the Four Division because of inadequate facilities.

The two-way influx of new clubs into the Conference will itself create added interest. If clubs like Enfield, Kidderminster Harriers and Wycombe Wanderers have brought fresh impetus in recent years, what would clubs such as Preston North End and Burnley provide?

In wider terms, the pyramid of football will be greatly strengthened everywhere. cracks had developed over the last couple of years, largely because it had been claimed in some quarters that the system was not working at the highest level. Now, can any ambitious club afford not to be in the pyramid?

Even some clubs in the Drybroughs Northern League, who have had sound geographical reasons for remaining outside the structure, must surely be wondering how long they can remain in isolation. Many of their older members may still say they are happy with their present status, but will their League in future be able to attract any new, young clubs with limitless horizons?

Ambitious New Clubs

The wind of change will blow through every league in the pyramid. For example, every one of the 170 or so clubs in the highest divisions of each of the Southern League's nine feeders could—facilities permitting—be only four years away from joining the Football League. Promotion in successive seasons to the Southern League regional division, premier division, GM Vauxhall Conference and Fourth Division may sound a tall order, but in the light of the achievements in recent years of Welling United, Fisher Athletic, Shepshed Charterhouse, Caernarfon Town, Gateshead, Harrow Borough, Farnborough Town and Windsor and Eton, such progress is far from impossible.

Indeed, it will now be possible for a totally new club to reach the Football League within a decade of its formation. As the likes of R.S. Southampton, Stevenage Borough and Corinthian have shown recently, ambitious new clubs can quickly enter the upper levels of the pyramid, and having done so anything is now possible.

All these fascinating thoughts will bring new interest to the game and real hope for the future. The fight for automatic promotion to the Fourth Division, led by the GM Vauxhall Conference in general and by their chairman Jim Thompson in particular, may have been a long and difficult one, but history will show that it was truly worthwhile.

INTRODUCTION TO THE CLUB AND LEAGUE SECTION

Every year we try to include one or two fresh ways of presenting our basic information and hopefully this year you will find 'The Directory' reasonably easy to follow and our liberal supply of photographic content should keep the general appearance lively.

Last year we gave four pages to each of the, then Gola League clubs and this year's book will contain basically the same features: revue of the past season, players background, action photo, last season's match details a ground and team photo (where available) and club details. Not all clubs can provide suitable photos and sometimes when copy is received in a different layout to the one required, there just isn't time to re-arrange it. However, I must say the efficient co-operation of all the Conference Club officials this year gives the impression they are all potential Football League club executives and I hope to give them six pages each next year.

The three major feeder Leagues below the tip of the Pyramid have been given a whole page of their own in this Directory but the slight problem here is that it has sometimes been very difficult to obtain photos to complete their pages as we would wish. I am sure that when club officials realise they are getting extra space they will ensure that photos get through to us in the future.

In different years we also find that certain areas of the country seem to take varying amounts of interest in the publication. This year we are attempting to give reasonable coverage to Wales and Scotland although one or two smaller leagues may have reduced coverage. However, I hope you will enjoy the excellent COUNTY CUP Section painstakingly compiled by Leo Hoenig and may I underline the fact that if the Directory continues to reach new readers every year (and you can help greatly by introducing it to any semi-professional football fanatics you know) I am aiming at increasing the pages to eventually reach the 1,000 mark and then we can surely give the sort of comprehensive coverage we dream about, to ALL COMPETITIONS OUTSIDE THE LEAGUE.

Ideas, distribution help or contributions (photographic and editorial) are always welcome but in the meantime I do hope you enjoy this years presentation.

Tony Williams

THE PYRAMID

The North East clubs have in general turned down the chance of joining the pyramid as the travelling time and costs would be too great. However, a few teams such as Gatehead and Scarborough have qualified for the top national Division by joining the Multipart League (or as it was known, The Northern Premier League). The Drybrough's Northern League has recently grown to two divisions and most of the progressive clubs in the area graduating from the Vaux Wearside and The McEwans Northern Alliance have done so by greatly improving their facilities, but now there is a chance of real progress into The Football League maybe one or two more North Eastern clubs may wish to step onto the ladder.

Promotion and relegation arrangements between leagues shown above, vary from area to area but at least most are automatic, although the Multipart League is the last (now the Football League have opened their doors) to come to settled arrangements at the foot of their competition.

THE PYRAMID

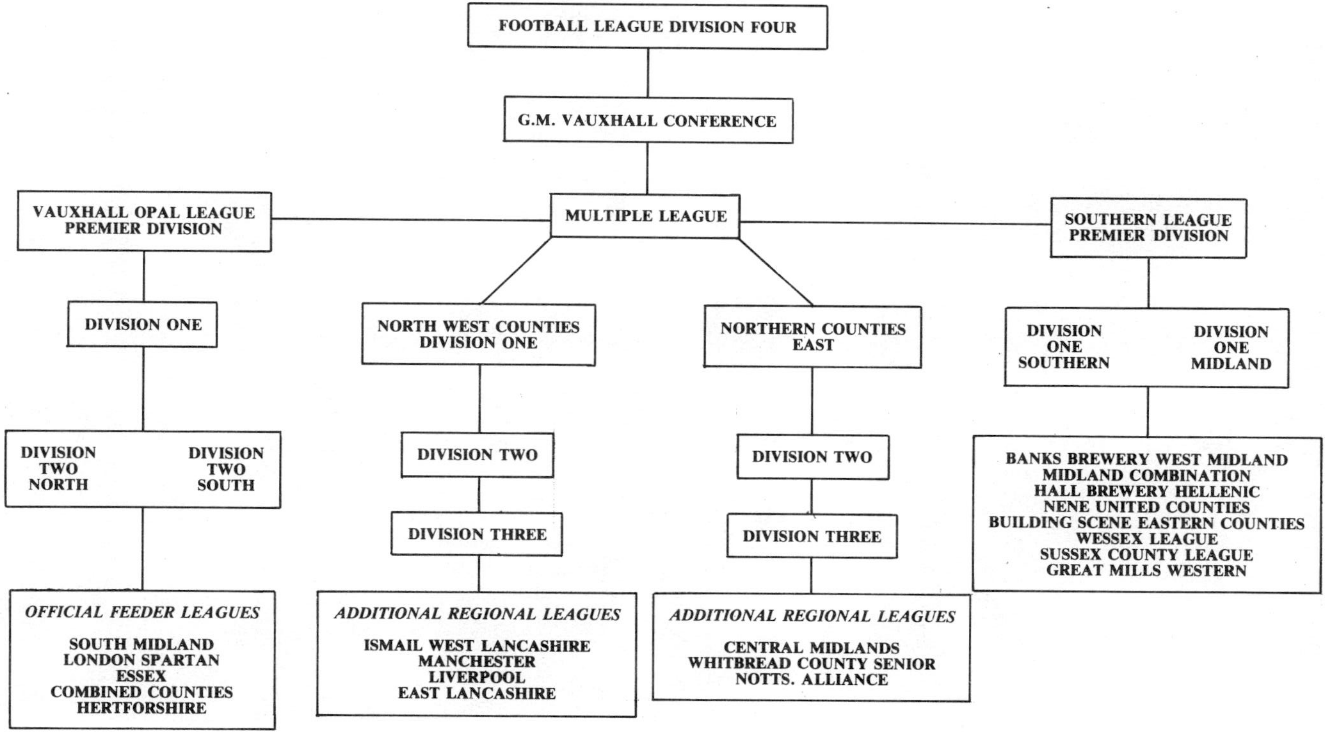
FOOTBALL LEAGUE DIVISION FOUR
G.M. VAUXHALL CONFERENCE
MULTIPLE LEAGUE
VAUXHALL OPAL LEAGUE PREMIER DIVISION
DIVISION ONE
DIVISION TWO NORTH
DIVISION TWO SOUTH
OFFICIAL FEEDER LEAGUES
SOUTH MIDLAND
LONDON SPARTAN
ESSEX
COMBINED COUNTIES
HERTFORSHIRE
NORTH WEST COUNTIES DIVISION ONE
DIVISION TWO
DIVISION THREE
ADDITIONAL REGIONAL LEAGUES
ISMAIL WEST LANCASHIRE
MANCHESTER
LIVERPOOL
EAST LANCASHIRE
NORTHERN COUNTIES EAST
DIVISION TWO
DIVISION THREE
ADDITIONAL REGIONAL LEAGUES
CENTRAL MIDLANDS
WHITBREAD COUNTY SENIOR
NOTTS. ALLIANCE
SOUTHERN LEAGUE PREMIER DIVISION
DIVISION ONE SOUTHERN
DIVISION ONE MIDLAND
BANKS BREWERY WEST MIDLAND
MIDLAND COMBINATION
HALL BREWERY HELLENIC
NENE UNITED COUNTIES
BUILDING SCENE EASTERN COUNTIES
WESSEX LEAGUE
SUSSEX COUNTY LEAGUE
GREAT MILLS WESTERN

WHO WILL BE JOINING THE FOOTBALL LEAGUE IN 1987?

On past form three of the favourites for this season's Championship and a place in the Fourth Division would be ENFIELD: Carl Richards, who has already moved into The League with Bournemouth, scores against Chelmsford City. Photo: J. Vass

ALTRINCHAM'S Paul Reid crashes home a smart volley against Wycombe Wanderers. Photo: John Rooney

Action from Bath City's visit to Maidstone. Photo: David Hills

VAUXHALL CONFERENCE

Chairman: J C Thomson
Secretary: P D Hunter, 24 Barnehurst Road, Bexleyheath, Kent
Tel: 0322 22616 (business) 0322 521116 (home)

AN EXCITING SEASON AHEAD

With Enfield firmly established in most people's minds as probable Champions the Gola League's main source of end of season excitement stemmed from the battle to avoid relegation.

In the end the outcome just couldn't have been closer as four teams finished level and Maidstone United, Dagenham (with four points from the last two away matches) and Nuneaton avoiding the drop purely thanks to goal difference!

Poor Wycombe Wanderers returned to the Vauxhall Opal League after just one season of 'national' football and over the season's form must feel very unlucky. There's no doubt the loss of star striker Declan Link, who accepted a job in America halfway through the season, certainly ruined their remarkable goalscoring record.

Taking the place of Wanderers, Dartford and Barrow are Gateshead, who showed great resilience and spirit to bounce straight back after relegation, plus two new boys in Welling United (with non-league footballs most prolific goalscorer, John Bartley) and the very competent and well administered Sutton United.

Two of the big success stories of the league last season were previously unfashionable Frickley Athletic and Kidderminster Harriers. Frickley followed an F.A. Cup run ro the second round with their best ever position in the league (Runners-Up) and had three players capped for England.

Kidderminster Harriers who celebrated their Centenary hit tremendous form in the second half of the season. Graham Allner their very intelligent and shrewd manager, backed by skipper Graham Mackenzie and Kim Casey (who had followed him throughout a very successful five years in Midland football) stormed to the Welsh Cup Final, eliminating Newport County, Swansea City and Hereford United on the way. They lost in a replay to Wrexham but Kim Casey (73 goals) and Paul Davies (44 goals) both played for England. Third place and a County Cup triumph completed an excellent season and look out for impressive ground improvements at Aggborough.

Altrinchams exploits are given their rightful prominence elsewhere in the Directory but their victory at First Division Birmingham City just couldn't have been better timed. The whole of the Pyramid should be grateful to 'Alty' for underlining the quality to be found outside the league.

When talking of quality one has to come back to Enfield, where Eddie McClusky has consistently produced sides capable of very special football. Carl Richards their star goalscorer has taken Colin Clarkes' place at Bournemouth but no doubt the Enfield Club will be quite capable of filling the gap and they will be challenging for honours again next season.

The coming campaign will probably be one of the most memorable in the history of the game outside the Football League. One club will be moving up subject to their facilities and what a battle it will be for that place!

The new G.M. Vauxhall Conference wiith superb sponsorship features should enjoy a thrilling campaign. These clubs are undoubtedly the best in non-league circles (they dominated the FA Trophy) with another all 'Gola' final last season between Altrincham and Runcorn, and I wouldn't be surprised to see a record number of clubs from the Conference in the third round of the FA Cup next season.

The new GMAC Challenge Cup (League Cup) is a wonderful addition to the calendar and I'm sure that we will all have a superb season to remember for years to come.

History is about to be made! T.W.

	Home						Away					
	P	W	D	L	F	A	W	D	L	F	A	Pts
Enfield	42	15	4	2	48	20	12	6	3	46	27	76
Frickley	42	16	4	1	46	21	9	6	6	32	29	69
Kidderminster	42	12	4	5	51	28	12	3	6	48	34	67
Altrincham	42	14	3	4	42	27	8	8	5	28	22	63
Weymouth	42	11	8	2	43	24	8	7	6	32	36	61
Runcorn	42	11	6	4	40	17	8	8	5	30	27	60
Stafford	42	10	7	4	30	22	9	6	6	31	32	60
Telford	42	13	5	3	42	24	5	5	11	26	42	51
Kettering	42	11	6	4	37	24	4	9	8	18	29	49
Wealdstone	42	10	5	6	35	28	6	4	11	22	28	47
Cheltenham	42	13	4	4	47	27	3	7	11	22	42	46
Bath	42	5	8	8	28	25	8	3	10	25	29	45
Boston	42	11	5	5	41	26	5	2	14	25	50	44
Barnet	42	9	4	8	32	23	4	7	10	24	37	41
Scarborough	42	10	4	7	35	31	3	7	11	19	35	40
Northwich	42	5	6	10	24	25	5	6	10	18	29	37
Maidstone	42	7	9	5	35	29	2	7	12	22	37	36
Nuneaton	42	8	3	10	27	27	5	2	14	31	46	36
Dagenham	42	6	7	8	23	29	4	5	12	25	37	36
Wycombe	42	7	6	8	30	35	3	7	11	25	49	36
Dartford	42	7	6	8	36	33	1	3	17	15	49	26
Barrow	42	5	6	10	26	34	2	2	17	15	52	24

Points scoring: Home win = 2 pts; Away win = 3 pts; Draw = 1 pt.

BOB LORD CHALLENGE TROPHY

First Round

Stafford Rangers	0-1	Barrow	0-1
Northwich Victoria	1-0	Frickley Athletic	0-4
Telford United	3-2	Boston United	1-1
Weymouth	3-1	Wycombe Wand.	4-2
Cheltenham	5-1	Kettering Town	1-0
Dagenham	0-0	Barnet	3-2

Second Round

Stafford Rangers	1-1	Nuneaton Boro	2-1
Scarborough	3-2	Altringham	0-2
Telford United	1-0	Frickley Athletic	0-4
Kidderminster H.	1-4	Runcorn	3-8
Weymouth	3-2	Wealdstone	1-1
Enfield	1-1	Dartford	1-2
Cheltenham	2-3	Maidstone United	0-1
Bath City	0-1	Barnet	1-1

Third Round

Stafford Rangers	2	Altringham	0
Frickley Athletic	2	Runcorn	6
Weymouth	8	Dartford	1
Maidstone United	0	Barnet	2

Semi-Finals

Stafford Rangers 0-2 Runcorn 0-1
attandance @ Stafford 987
attendance @ replay Runcorn 697

Weymouth 0 Barnet 1
attendance @ Weymouth 801

Final

Stafford Rangers 2-1 Barnet 1-0
1st Leg Attendance 1,370 2nd Leg Attendance 1,037

Winners for 1985/86 season
STAFFORD RANGERS F.C. 3-1 on aggregate

Noel Ashford goes close v. Altrincham. Photo: J. Vass

GOLA LEAGUE 1979-86

	P	W	D	L	F	A	Pts*	%	Best Position	Seasons
1 Enfield	210	109	49	52	427	262	267	63.5	1st	81-86
2 Runcorn	210	102	59	49	327	267	263	62.6	1st	81-86
3 Altrincham	286	142	65	79	476	323	349	61.0	1st (2)	79-86
4 Weymouth	286	126	71	89	445	363	323	56.4	2nd	79-86
5 Kidderminster Harriers	126	55	29	42	232	197	139	55.1	3rd	83-86
6 Maidstone United	286	115	85	86	442	334	315	55.0	1st	79-86
7 Wealdstone	244	97	72	75	355	297	266	54.5	1st	79-81, 82-86
8 Scarborough	286	109	91	86	407	379	309	54.0	3rd	79-86
9 Telford United	286	119	71	96	415	396	309	54.0	3rd	79-86
10 Northwich V	286	113	77	96	373	334	303	52.9	4th	79-86
11 Boston United	286	113	74	99	454	440	300	52.4	4th	79-86
12 Frickley Athletic	248	101	58	89	385	376	260	52.4	2nd	80-86
13 Nuneaton Boro	244	94	65	85	377	324	253	51.8	2nd (2)	79-81, 82-86
14 Cheltenham Town	42	16	11	15	69	69	43	51.1	11th	85-86
15 Bath City	286	109	73	104	367	364	291	50.8	4th	79-86
16 Worcester City	244	93	58	93	347	376	244	50.0	3rd	79-85
17 Kettering Town	286	98	78	110	430	441	274	47.9	2nd	79-86
18 Dagenham	210	68	57	85	281	328	193	45.9	5th	81-86
19 Gravesend & N	118	40	28	50	148	168	108	45.7	5th	79-82
20 Barnet	286	91	66	129	332	412	248	43.3	9th	79-86
21 Stafford Rangers	202	53	68	81	246	289	174	43.0	7th	79-83, 85-86
22 Barrow	244	73	61	110	290	371	207	42.4	8th	79-83, 84-86
23 Bangor City	160	44	45	71	201	273	133	41.5	9th	79-81, 82-84
24 Dartford	126	35	31	60	157	197	101	40.0	3rd	81-82, 84-86
25 Gateshead	84	21	25	38	110	155	67	39.8	16th	83-85
26 Yeovil Town	244	70	53	121	324	444	193	39.5	12th	79-85
27 Wycombe W	42	10	13	19	55	84	33	39.2	20th	85-86
28 Trowbridge T	126	29	25	72	127	239	83	32.9	17th	81-84
29 Leamington	118	21	32	65	119	234	74	31.3	16th	79-82
30 Redditch United	38	5	8	25	26	69	18	23.6	20th	79-80

* 2pts for a win
1pt for a draw

THE GOLA LEAGUE RESULTS
1985/86 SEASON

Home Team																						
Altrincham		2-0	2-0	1-2	1-3	4-1	3-1	0-0	1-4	1-0	2-2	2-1	1-0	2-1	7-4	1-1	2-0	1-3	1-0	1-0	2-1	4-3
Barnet	2-2		4-1	1-0	3-0	2-2	4-1	2-0	1-0	1-2	3-0	3-1	3-3	1-0	0-1	1-2	1-0	0-2	1-2	1-0	2-2	0-1
Barrow	0-1	0-1		1-1	2-1	2-2	1-0	1-2	1-2	2-2	1-0	3-4	1-1	1-2	2-0	0-4	2-4	0-1	1-0	1-1	3-4	1-1
Bath City	0-2	1-1	6-0		2-0	1-1	1-1	2-0	0-2	1-2	1-1	2-4	1-1	0-0	0-3	0-1	0-0	0-1	3-0	2-3	2-2	3-1
Boston United	1-3	1-2	2-1	1-1		1-2	3-1	3-0	1-2	0-3	4-1	2-1	2-2	3-0	3-2	2-1	2-1	1-1	2-2	1-0	5-0	1-1
Cheltenham Town	2-0	2-1	2-0	1-2	2-1		2-2	3-1	2-0	1-1	5-1	2-6	2-1	2-0	5-3	1-1	1-0	2-0	1-1	1-2	0-1	4-2
Dagenham	1-3	2-1	3-0	0-1	2-2	1-3		2-1	0-2	0-0	1-0	0-1	0-0	1-0	3-2	2-3	0-0	1-1	1-4	0-2	2-2	1-1
Dartford	3-2	5-3	3-2	1-2	0-1	3-3	1-1		2-3	1-2	0-2	5-1	1-1	2-0	0-1	0-1	1-1	3-3	2-1	1-2	1-1	1-0
Enfield	1-1	1-0	4-0	3-1	3-0	1-0	3-1	1-0		3-1	1-1	2-2	1-3	1-0	3-2	2-0	4-0	3-1	4-0	1-0	4-4	2-3
Frickley Athletic	0-0	3-3	2-0	2-1	5-1	2-1	3-2	1-0	1-4		3-0	3-1	2-0	1-0	2-2	3-1	2-1	3-0	3-1	2-1	1-0	2-2
Kettering Town	2-2	1-1	4-2	2-0	2-1	2-1	0-2	2-2	2-1	2-0		2-2	2-0	2-1	1-4	0-0	0-0	0-1	4-0	2-1	0-2	4-1
Kidderminster Harriers	0-2	0-2	2-1	3-1	3-2	5-1	2-0	4-1	1-2	1-1	0-0		3-1	2-2	2-1	2-4	5-1	1-1	3-0	3-1	1-2	8-2
Maidstone United	1-2	2-2	0-0	3-2	1-2	1-0	2-1	3-0	3-3	3-2	0-0	2-1		0-1	5-1	1-1	1-1	2-4	4-4	0-1	0-0	1-1
Northwich Victoria	0-1	0-1	0-1	1-2	3-4	3-1	0-1	2-0	2-2	2-3	0-0	0-0	1-0		0-3	1-1	0-0	2-0	0-1	2-2	0-1	4-0
Nuneaton Borough	0-0	4-1	0-1	2-3	0-1	0-1	1-2	3-1	1-5	0-1	0-3	0-3	1-0	1-3		1-0	3-1	3-0	1-1	0-0	3-0	3-0
Runcorn	2-1	0-0	3-1	2-0	3-1	5-0	1-1	5-0	1-1	2-2	0-1	0-2	3-0	2-3	3-1		0-0	3-2	1-0	1-1	1-2	2-1
Scarborough	1-0	3-1	3-1	2-1	2-1	1-0	2-1	1-1	1-3	2-3	2-3	3-5	2-0	0-0	2-1	1-1		2-4	3-1	0-1	1-1	0-1
Stafford Rangers	1-1	0-0	1-0	1-0	2-1	2-0	3-0	5-1	1-1	0-0	0-0	3-2	2-1	1-2	2-0	1-1	0-3		0-3	2-1	2-3	1-1
Telford United	2-1	2-2	3-1	1-0	2-1	3-0	2-1	2-1	2-2	2-1	2-2	0-1	2-4	4-0	1-1	2-3	1-0	0-0		2-1	4-1	3-1
Wealdstone	2-2	2-0	4-0	0-1	7-2	0-0	0-4	2-1	2-4	2-0	3-1	0-3	3-2	0-0	1-0	1-1	0-3	2-3	1-1		1-0	2-0
Weymouth	0-0	4-2	3-2	0-0	0-0	0-0	2-1	2-1	2-2	2-3	1-0	1-2	2-0	2-2	2-0	5-2	4-1	1-1	5-2	4-2		1-1
Wycombe Wanderers	0-1	2-0	1-1	1-4	4-1	3-3	1-1	3-2	1-0	1-3	0-0	2-5	2-2	1-1	2-0	0-1	2-1	2-4	1-2	1-0	0-3	

Highest Aggregate Scores

Altrincham .... 7 v Nuneaton B 4
9.11 85

Kidderminster H ... 8 v Wycombe W 2
24.4.86

Weymouth .... 8 v Dartford 1
B.L.T. 12.2.86

Runcorn .... 8 v Kidderminster H ...1
B.L.T. 27.11.85

Largest Home Wins

Runcorn .... 8 v Kidderminster H ...1
B.L.T. 27.11.85

Weymouth .... 8 v Dartford 1
B.L.T. 12.2.86

Kidderminster H ... 8 v Wycombe W 2
24.4.86

Wealdstone .... 7 v Boston U 2
22.10.85

Bath City .... 6 v Barrow 0
14.12.85

Largest Away Wins

Nuneaton Boro .... 1 v Enfield 5
2.12.85

Wealdstone .... 0 v Dagenham 4
15.10.85

Wycombe W ...... 2 v Kidderminster H ... 5
5.4.86

Scarborough ...... 3 v Kidderminster H ... 5
25.1.86

Enfield's England International goalkeeper Andy Pape wins this duel with Altrincham's Mike Farrelly during the Gola League clash in March. The 4-1 win for the North Londoners virtually killed off Altrincham's championship hopes Photo: John Rooney

Barnet defend in numbers against Northwich Victoria at Underhill Photo: Alan Bunce

Boston United's Derek Bell heads in at the far post against visitors Cheltenham Town

ALLIANCE PREMIER LEAGUE AVERAGE HOME ATTENDANCES

(1) = Best Supported Club

	1979-80	1980-81	1981-82	1982-83	1983-84	1984-85	1985-86
Altrincham	1,945 (2)	1,772 (1)	1,181 (4)	1,039 (82)	1,060 (6)	1,054 (4)	1,022 (5)
Bangor City	791 (16)	471 (19)		724 (16)	540 (20)		—
Barnet	752 (17)	694 (15)	756 (16)	656 (19)	703 (12)	740 (14)	710 (12)
Barrow	873 (15)	669 (16)	725 (18=)	546 (21)		782 (12=)	473 (21)
Bath City	956 (13)	898 (12)	874 (13)	738 (15)	635 (14)	650 (17)	571 (17)
Boston United	1,699 (5)	1,157 (6)	1,097 (7)	1,264 (3)	1,005 (9)	1,139 (3)	1,301 (1)
Cheltenham T							1,021 (6)
Dagenham			907 (12)	648 (20)	575 (17)	604 (19)	542 (19)
Dartford			725 (18=)			651 (16)	466 (22)
Enfield			769 (15)	841 (G)	574 (18)	633 (18)	767 (9)
Frickley Ath		548 (18)	466 (21)	444 (22)	426 (21)	430 (21)	505 (20)
Gateshead					289 (22)	253 (22)	—
Gravesend	1,022 (11)	949 (11)	914 (11)				
Kettering T	1,939 (4)	1,673 (2)	1,244 (2)	1,030 (8=)	1,017 (8)	1,108 (5)	1,062 (4)
Kidderminster H					605 (16)	676 (15)	762 (10)
A.P. Leamington	506 (19)	440 (20)	340 (22)				
Maidstone U	916 (14)	848 (13)	813 (14)	1,440 (1)	1,060 (5)	839 (8)	698 (14)
Northwich V	1,465 (7)	1,088 (8)	921 (10)	1,415 (2)	1,082 (3)	808 (11)	686 (15)
Nuneaton B	1,309 (9)	986 (10)		921 (10)	1,057 (7)	930 (7)	736 (11)
Redditch U	358 (20)						—
Runcorn			1,060 (8)	719 (17)	618 (15)	468 (20)	567 (18)
Scarborough	2,224 (1)	1,663 (3)	1,827 (1)	1,081 (7)	922 (10)	782 (12=)	666 (16)
Telford U	957 (12)	716 (14)	1,179 (5)	1,083 (6)	1,075 (4)	1,106 (6)	1,109 (2)
Trowbridge T			626 (20)	695 (18)	572 (19)		—
Stafford R	1,155 (10)	1,146 (7)	934 (9)	812 (13)			1,089 (3)
Wealdstone	653 (18)	646 (15)		828 (12)	667 (13)	826 (10)	700 (13)
Weymouth	1,333 (8)	1,032 (9)	732 (17)	808 (14)	758 (11)	830 (9)	822 (7)
Worcester C	1,941 (3)	1,406 (4)	1,235 (3)	1,122 (5)	1,201 (1)	1,187 (2)	—
Wycombe W							775 (8)
Yeovil T	1,582 (6)	1,352 (2)	1,167 (6)	1,139 (4)	1,115 (2)	1,297 (1)	—

AGGREGATE ATTENDANCES

	1979-80	80-81	81-82	82-83	83-84	84-85	85-86
Altrincham	36,947	33,676	24,791	21,811	22,252	22,127	21,454
Bangor City	15,022	8,948	—	15,210	11,336	—	—
Barnet	14,277	13,193	15,879	13,773	14,758	15,539	14,911
Barrow	16,581	12,708	15,233	11,463	—	16,425	9,934
Bath City	18,149	17,057	18,348	15,506	13,343	13,655	11,998
Boston United	32,270	21,990	23,028	26,543	21,103	23,913	27,319
Cheltenham Town							21,443
Dagenham	—	—	19,045	13,614	12,053	12,685	11,374
Dartford	—	—	15,221	—	—	13,665	9,785
Enfield	—	—	16,142	17,670	12,047	13,293	16,114
Frickley Athletic	—	10,411	9,784	9,331	8,940	9,037	10,602
Gateshead	—	—	—	—	6,062	5,307	—
Gravesend & N	19,408	18,039	19,184	—	—	—	—
Kettering Town	36,837	31,791	26,103	21,629	21,347	23,269	22,306
Kidderminster H	—	—	—	—	12,707	14,191	15,995
Maidstone United	17,388	16,115	17,078	30,242	22,260	17,616	14,657
Northwich Vic	27,823	20,663	19,346	21,384	22,721	16,975	14,414
Nuneaton Boro	24,858	18.743	—	19,342	22,187	19,524	15,462
A. P. Leamington	9,598	8,361	7,148	—	—	—	—
Redditch	6,790	—	—	—	—	—	—
Runcorn	—	—	22,266	15,092	12,986	9,828	11,915
Scarborough	42,242	31,791	38,360	22,709	19,357	16,427	13,994
Telford United	18,181	13,595	24,762	22,739	22,584	23,219	23,288
Trowbridge Town	—	—	13,150	14,604	12,011	—	—
Stafford Rangers	21,927	21,773	19,607	17,049	—	—	22,875
Wealdstone	12,393	12,282	—	17,387	14,015	17,352	14,690
Weymouth	25,321	19,602	15,380	16,964	15,919	17,421	17,260
Worcester C	36,864	26,718	25,930	23,562	25,216	24,931	—
Wycombe Wanderers							16,279
Yeovil Town	30,049	25,686	24,057	23,927	23,421	27,226	—
							Total 358,067

Leading Goalscorers:

	League	B.L.T.	Hat tricks	Total
Kim Casey (Kidderminster H)	36	2	2	38
Mark Carter (Runcorn)	22	7	4	29
Mick Doherty (Weymouth)	25	3	1	28
Carl Richards (Enfield)	28	—	2	28
Nicky Evans (Barnet)	20	4	2	24
Paul Davies (Kidderminster H)	21	—	—	21
Gary Hooley (Frickley Athletic incl. 7 for Scarborough)	20	—	—	20
Mark Boyland (Cheltenham)	16	3	—	19
Stephen Claridge (Weymouth)	10	8	1	18
Ken McKenna (Telford United)	18	—	—	18
Paul Wilson (Frickley Athletic)	18	—	1	18
Tony Agana (Weymouth)	13	7	1	17
Graham Bennett (Stafford Rangers incl. 10 for Altrincham)	17	—	1	17
Tony Burman (Dartford)	14	2	1	16
David Gilbert (Boston United)	16	—	—	16
Frank Murphy (Nuneaton Borough)	15	1	—	16
Bob Mountain (Stafford Rangers)	11	4	1	15
Colin Cowperthwaite (Barrow)	15	—	1	15
Noel Ashford (Enfield)	13	1	1	14
Phil Derbyshire (Stafford Rangers)	12	2	—	14
David Singleton (Bath City)	14	—	1	14
Tim Smithers (Nuneaton Borough)	14	—	—	14
Chris Townsend (Cheltenham Town)	14	—	2	14

Highest Scorers

S. Claridge (Weymouth)	4 v Dartford	B.L.T.	12.2.86
D. Singleton (Bath City)	4 v Barrow	League	14.12.85
S. Skeete (Runcorn)	4 v Kidderminster	League	27.11.85
C. Townsend (Cheltenham Town)	4 v Nuneaton Boro	League	19.4.86

SPONSORSHIP AWARDS SEASON

Club	Championship Awards £	Initial Payment £	Monthly Jackpot £	TOTAL £
Enfield	3,000	1,000	1,581.39	5,581.39
Frickley Athletic	2,000	1,000	1,729.51	4,729.51
Kidderminster H	1,000	1,000	1,772.17	3,772.17
Barnet		1,000	1,459.66	2,459.66
Weymouth		1,000	1,399.85	2,399.85
Runcorn		1,000	1,162.69	2,162.69
Cheltenham T		1,000	1,112.65	2,112.65
Stafford R		1,000	1,052.43	2,052.43
Wealdstone		1,000	1,025.64	2,025.64
Telford United		1,000	937.69	1,937.69
Nuneaton Boro		1,000	894.35	1,894.35
Maidstone U		1,000	852.23	1,852.23
Altrincham		1,000	777.27	1,777.27
Boston United		1,000	777.13	1,777.13
Kettering Town		1,000	765.87	1,765.87
Northwich V		1,000	563.19	1,563.19
Bath City		1,000	527.13	1,527.13
Scarborough		1,000	489.93	1,489.93
Dartford		1,000	470.08	1,470.08
Wycombe W		1,000	456.34	1,456.34
Dagenham		1,000	192.31	1,192.31
Barrow		1,000	—	1,000.00

The Real Mackenzie Whisky MANAGER OF THE MONTH AWARDS

1985		
September	John King	Altrincham
October	Eddie McCluskey	Enfield
November	John Williams	Runcorn
December	Sean Marshall	Frickley Athletic
1986		
January	John Williams	Runcorn
February	Graham Allner	Kidderminster Harriers
March	Eddie McCluskey	Enfield
April	Ron Reid	Stafford Rangers

League Manager of the Year Award:
To be announced at the A.G.M.

Since the start of the Mackenzie Whisky sponsorship in 1979/80 season, the total awards to individual managers are:

Eddie McCluskey	Enfield	6
John Williams	Runcorn	5
Stan Storton	Telford United	4

GOLA LEAGUE—PAST CHAMPIONS

Max Pts	Season	1st	2nd	3rd	4th
76	1979/80	56 Altrincham	54 Weymouth	49 Worcester C	45 Boston U
76	1980/81	54 Altrincham	51 Kettering T	47 Scarborough	45 Northwich V
126	1981/82	93 Runcorn	86 Enfield	77 Telford U	71 Worcester C
126	1982/83	84 Enfield	83 Maidstone U	79 Wealdstone	72* Runcorn
105	1983/84	70 Maidstone U	69 Nuneaton Boro	65 Altrincham	62* Wealdstone
105	1984/85	62 Wealdstone	58 Nuneaton Boro	57* Dartford	57 Bath C
105	1985/86	76 Enfield	69 Frickley Ath	67 Kidderminster H	63 Altrincham

* goal average/difference

BEST ATTENDANCES 1979-86

	1979-80	1980-81	1981-82	1982-83	1983-84	1984-85	1985-86
Altrincham	2,670 v Worcester C	2,864 v Yeovil T	1,472 v Enfield	1,712 v Runcorn	1,488 v Runcorn	1,454 v Wealdstone	1,340 v Enfield
Bangor City	1,500 v Altrincham	800 v Altrincham	—	1,256 v Northwich V	722 v Altrincham	—	—
Barnet	1,028 v Scarborough	969 v Wealdstone	1,404 v Enfield	1,702 v Enfield	1,499 v Enfield	1,349 v Enfield	1,455 v Enfield
Barrow	2,027 v Yeovil T	1,361 v Altrincham	1,212 v Runcorn	757 v Stafford	—	1,731 v Scarborough	845 v Maidstone
Bath City	1,840 v Yeovil T	—	2,015 v Trowbridge	1,804 v Trowbridge	1,139 v Trowbridge	808 v Yeovil T	758 v Wycombe W
Boston United	2,284 v Altrincham	—	1,456 v Kettering	1,612 v Enfield	1,357 v Runcorn	1,402 v Kettering	2,067 v Wealdstone
Cheltenham Town	—	—	—		—	—	1,311 v Weymouth
Dagenham	—	—	1,227 v Yeovil	1,243 v Enfield	928 v Enfield	878 v Wealdstone	836 v Enfield
Dartford	—	—	1,182 v Gravesend	—	—	913 v Kettering	892 v Maidstone
Enfield	—	—	1,376 v Runcorn	1,377 v Barnet	1,096 v Barnet	1,021 v Barnet	1,112 v Wycombe W
Frickley A	—	789 v Altrincham	760 v Altrincham	656 v Boston U	683 v Nuneaton B	988 v Altrincham	787 v Scarborough
Gateshead	—	—	—	—	710 v Wealdstone	425 v Worcester C	—
Gravesend	1,438 v Altrincham	1,518 v Maidstone	2,051 v Dartford	—	—	—	—
Kettering T	2,867 v Altrincham	2,608 v Boston U	1,623 v Bath C	1,598 v Enfield	1,390 v Scarborough	1,345 v Enfield	1,255 v Altrincham
Kidderminster	—	—	—	—	872 v Runcorn	1,370 v Telford U	1,441 v Frickley A
A.P. Leamington	968 v Northwich V	650 v Worcester C	544 v Worcester C	—	—	—	—
Maidstone U	1,706 v Gravesend	1,151 v Gravesend	1,125 v Dartford	2,452 v Wealdstone	2,502 v Telford U	1,553 v Maidstone U	854 v Dartford
Northwich V	2,394 v Altrincham	2,530 v Altrincham	1,674 v Runcorn	1,018 v Telford U	1,641 v Altrincham	1,152 v Runcorn	1,224 v Altrincham
Nuneaton B	1,970 v Kettering T	1,506 v Stafford R	—	1,640 v Stafford R	1,057 v Maidstone	1,113 v Kidderminster	1,034 v Kidderminster
Redditch U	936 v Worcester C	—	—	—	—	—	—
Runcorn	—	—	1,682 v Enfield	1,220 v Northwich V	826 v Telford U	944 v Northwich V	970 v Northwich V
Scarborough	3,120 v Kettering T	2,225 v Kettering T	2,920 v Enfield	1,772 v Boston U	1,500 v Kettering	1,526 v Telford U	1,299 v Altrincham
Telford U	1,506 v Northwich V	955 v Worcester	1,825 v Runcorn	1,370 v Enfield	1,336 v Kettering T	1,335 v Yeovil T	1,557 v Enfield
Trowbridge	—	—	1,056 v Bath C	1,439 v Bath C	1,967 v Bath C	—	—
Stafford R	2,104 v Kettering	1,599 v Kettering	1,359 v Dartford	—	—	—	1,958 v Telford
Wealdstone	976 v Nuneaton	1,080 v Barnet	—	1,725 v Enfield	865 v Enfield	1,004 v Frickley A	1,323 v Enfield
Weymouth	2,818 v Yeovil T	2,113 v Yeovil T	1,614 v Yeovil T	1,656 v Yeovil T	1,452 v Yeovil T	1,004 v Yeovil T	1,501 v Enfield
Worcester C	2,405 v Weymouth	2,254 v Bath	1,763 v Runcorn	1,704 v Altrincham	2,165 v Kidderminster	2,258 v Kidderminster	—
Wycombe W	—	—	—	—	—	—	1,068 v Enfield
Yeovil T	4,872 v Weymouth	2,457 v Weymouth	2,276 v Weymouth	2,299 v Weymouth	1,597 v Runcorn	2,102 v Weymouth	—

ALTRINCHAM

Gola League 4th **F.A. Trophy** W **F.A. Cup** 4th Rd **C.S.C.** 2nd Rd **Bob Lord Trophy** 3rd Rd

Altrincham: *Back Row (left to right): Paul Cuddy, Jeff Wealands, Jeff Johnson, Phil Jackson, Mike Farrelly. Middle Row: Ewan Simpson (Physiotherapist), Paul Reid, Peter Conning, Phil Gardner, Doug Newton, Ronnie Ellis, Gary Anderson, Stan Allen (Coach). Front Row: John King (Manager), Damien Looker, Steve Buxton, John Davison, Peters Densmore and George Rooney (Assistant Manager).*
Photo: John Rooney

THE GREATEST SEASON?

Altrincham crowned yet another memorable season with victory in the F.A. Trophy final at Wembley only four months after their greatest ever F.A. Cup run had come to an end in the 4th round at York City.

The season also saw two notable departures from Moss Lane, with chairman Noel White moving onto the board of directors at Liverpool after 25 years with the Robins, while manager John King resigned 24 hours after the Wembley victory and subsequently swapped jobs with Runcorn boss John Williams.

F.A. Cup glory is now part of Altrincham's folklore, but last season the Robins surpassed even their previous notable exploits by reaching the 4th round for the first time (this after reaching the 3rd round on 6 previous occasions). To get that far they had to come from a goal down to beat 1st division Birmingham City on their own ground, after adding insult to injury in the previous round when they returned to Bloomfield Road to beat Blackpool for the second successive season, one of Altrincham's 12 wins against football league opposition in the F.A. Cup—a total only challenged by Yeovil Town in non-league football.

Mick Farrelly's shot is on its way into the back of Bath City's net to put Altrincham level at 1-1.
Photo: John Rooney

The Robins were at their best throughout the F.A. Trophy run, sweeping through the early rounds to face a tough semi-final test against Enfield who had sent them crashing to their biggest league defeat at Moss Lane for many years only two weeks earlier.

But Altrincham's cup expertise took them through that test—and made up for the agony of going out in the previous year's semi-final while leaving Enfield to suffer that bitter disappointment for the second successive season—before Mike Farrelly's spectacular goal clinched a final victory over the Robins' friends and neighbours from Runcorn.

Altrincham's Gola League hopes had been dashed during a three month spell at the start of 1986 after they had led the table at various times in September, October, November and December. However between January and March, cup commitments meant that the Robins played only seven league games in three months (winning only two of them), before the season ended on that high note at Wembley.

The F.A. Trophy final climaxed a run of 13 games that brought nine victories and only one defeat (ironically at Runcorn), and took Altrincham into 4th place in the final table—their fifth top five placing in the seven seasons since the formation of the Alliance Premier League.

ALTRINCHAM SQUAD 1986

Goalkeepers
Jeff Wealands: Darlington (28), Hull City (240), Birmingham City (102), Manchester United (7), Oldham Athletic (10), Preston North End (4)
Phil Jackson: Cheadle Town

Defenders
Paul Cuddy: Chorley, Bolton Wanderers, Huddersfield Town, Rochdale (1)
John Davison: Burnley, Altrincham, Bangor City
Peter Densmore: Liverpool, Ford Motors
Mike Farrelly: Preston North End (82)

Midfield
Gary Anderson: Altrincham, South Liverpool
Peter Conning: Liverpool, Wigan Athletic
Phil Gardner: Everton
Doug Newton: Chesterfield, Eastwood, Alfreton, Belper, Burton Albion

Forwards
Ronnie Ellis: Buscough, Winsford United, Runcorn
Damian Looker: West Kirkby
Paul Reid: Nantwich Town, Northwich Victoria

Publications

Copies of 'All the King's Men', a 48 page souvenir brochure produced to mark Altrincham's appearance in the F.A. Trophy final at Wembley are available from the club by sending a remittance for £1.50, payable to Altrincham Football Club, to the club's Pools Office at Moss Lane, Altrincham, Cheshire, WA15 8AP.

ALTRINCHAM GOLA LEAGUE SEASON 1985-6

Venue	Opponents	Result	Scorers	Att.
H	Kettering Town	D 2-2	Johnson, Chesters	1059
A	Kidderminster Harriers	W 2-0	Reid (2)	811
H	Wycombe Wanderers	W 4-3	Reid, Conning (2), Anderson	1006
A	Frickley Athletic	D 0-0		363
A	Barnet	D 2-2	Aspinall, Ellis	648
H	Frickley Athletic	W 1-0	Bennett	940
H	Weymouth	W 3-1	Bennett (2), Ellis	1012
A	Scarborough	L 0-1		1299
H	Dartford	D 0-0		1009
H	Scarborough	W 2-0	Bennett (2)	1023
A	Wealdstone	D 2-2	Bennett, Farrelly	854
A	Northwich Victoria	W 2-1	Bennett (2)	1224
H	Bath City	L 1-2	Farrelly	1063
H	Telfford United	W 1-0	E. Edwards	969
A	Kettering Town	D 2-2	Aspinall, Reid	1253
H	Kidderminster Harriers	W 2-1	Gardner, Bennett	1013
A	Maidstone United	W 2-1	Anderson, Newton (pen)	717
H	Wealdstone	W 1-0	Conning	1151
A	Dagenham	W 3-1	Reid, Newton (pen), Anderson	582
A	**Scarborough (BLT)**	**L 2-3**	**Reid, Davison**	**623**
H	Nuneaton Borough	W 7-4	Reid (3), Chesters, Davison, Anderson, Conning	1118
A	**Chorley (FAC)**	**W 2-0**	**Reid, Anderson**	**1827**
H	Boston United	L 1-3	Bennett	1264
H	**Scarborough (BLT)**	**W 2-0**	**McMahon, Anderson aet**	**823**
A	Enfield	D 1-1	Chesters	945
A	**Blackpool (FAC)**	**W 2-1**	**Reid, Anderson**	**5037**
H	Stafford Rangers	L 1-3	E. Edwards	1152
A	**Ryhope CA (FAT)**	**W 3-1**	**Anderson (2), Reid**	**750**
A	Barrow	W 1-0	Chesters	745
A	Telford United	L 1-2	Newton (pen)	1012
H	Cheltenham Town	W 4-1	Buxton (pen), Davison, Chesters, Conning	1012
A	**Birmingham City (FAC)**	**W 2-1**	**Elliss, Hopkins (o.g.)**	**6636**
H	**Bangor City (FAT)**	**W 6-1**	**Davison (2 pens), Reid (3), Chesters**	**1211**
A	**York City (FAC)**	**L 0-2**		**8834**
H	**General Chemicals (CSC)**	**W 4-0**	**Reid, Anderson, Gardner, Johnson**	**502**
A	Dartford	L 2-3	Davison (pen), Chesters	379
H	**Runcorn (CSC)**	**D 2-2**	**Johnson, Farelly**	**774**
H	**Bishop Auckland (FAT)**	**W 1-0**	**Chesters**	**756**
A	**Runcorn (CSC)**	**D 0-0**	**aet**	**500**
H	**Stafford Rangers (BLT)**	**L 0-2**		**614**
H	Barnet	W 2-0	Newton, Ellis	789
A	**Cheltenham Town (FAT)**	**W 2-0**	**Ellis (2)**	**2196**
H	Enfield	L 1-4	Anderson	1340
A	Weymouth	D 0-0		830
A	**Enfield (FAT s.f.)**	**D 1-1**	**Newton (pen)**	**1804**
A	Cheltenham Town	L 0-2		1113
H	**Enfield (FAT s.f.)**	**W 2-0**	**Ellis, Newton (pen)**	**2134**
A	Stafford Rangers	D 1-1	Reid	1041
H	Runcorn	D 1-1	Anderson	1021
A	Bath City	W 2-0	Reid (2)	669
H	Barrow	W 2-0	Davison, Conning	831
A	Runcorn	L 1-2	Ellis	988
H	Northwich Victoria	W 2-1	Newton, Scott (o.g.)	1013
H	Dagenham	W 3-1	Anderson, Looker, Newton	652
H	Maidston United	W 1-0	Conning	1017
A	Nuneaton Borough	D 0-0		829
A	Wycombe Wanderers	W 1-0	Pearce (o.g.)	544
A	Boston United	W 3-1	Newton (2), Ellis	1094
N	**Runcorn (FAT final)**	**W 1-0**	**Farrelly**	**15700**

BLT = Bob Lord Trophy
FAT = F.A. Trophy
FAC = F.A. Cup

Appearances:
(max 59); Reid 58, Anderson 52, Gardner 50 + 1, Wealands 49, Johnson 48 + 2, Davison 47 + 1, Conning 46 + 4, Farrelly 45 + 6, Ellis 41 + 3, Cuddy 39, Densmore 33, Newton 26 + 4, Edwards E. 24, Chesters 22 + 2, McMahon 18 + 3, Bennett 17 + 1, Jackson 8, Fagan 6 + 1, Buxton 5 + 6, Aspinall 5 + 2, Edwards L. 4 + 2, Looker 4, Dance 2, Dyke 1 + 1, McMullen 1, Dunne 0 + 1. The following players were named as substitute for first team matches but not used: Grant (2), Davies M. and Cunningham.

Goalscorers:
League (70); Reid 11, Bennett 10, Newton 8, Anderson 7, Conning 7, Chesters 6, Ellis 5, Davison 4, Aspinall 2, Edwards E. 2, Farrelly 2, Buxton 1 (pen), Gardner 1, Johnson 1, Looker 1. Own goals 2
Cups (33); Reid 8, Anderson 6, Ellis 4, Davison 3 (2 pens), Chesters 2, Farrelly 2, Johnson 2, McMahon 2, Newton 2, Gardner 1. Own goals 1

Altrincham's Moss Lane ground photographed from the roof of the north-west headquarters of British Gas Photo: John Rooney

ALTRINCHAM

President: Noel White
Chairman: Gerry Berman
Manager: John Williams
Asst. Manager: Stan Allan
Coach:
Physiotherapist: Ewan Simpson

Secretary: David Baldwin
Address & Tel. No. Moss Lane, Altrincham, Cheshire, WA15 8AP. Tel: 061 928 1045
Commercial Manager: Steve Hartley
Address & Tel. No. Moss Lane, Altrincham, Cheshire, WA15 8AP. Tel: 061 928 6905
Press Officer & Tel. No. Paul Brady, Tel: 061 928 8103 (H) or 061 234 3179 (B, messages only)
Address and Tel. No. of ground: Moss Lane, Altrincham, Cheshire, WA 15 8AP. Tel: 061 928 1045
Simple ground directions: ½ mile from town centre, bus/rail interchange along Moss Lane **Club shop:**
No. of seats: 1,000 **Covered accommodation:** 5,000 **Capacity:** 10,000 **Floodlights:** Yes
Year formed: 1903 **Nickname:** The Robins **Club sponsor:**

Previous names: None
Previous grounds: Pollits Field 1903-05
Day for midweek home matches: Tuesday

Club colours: Red & white stripes/black/red
Change colours: All yellow
Club metal badges: Yes

Record attendance: 35,530 v Everton, F.A. Cup 3rd rd replay at Old Trafford **Year** 1975. At Moss Lane; 10,275 (est) Altrincham Boys v Sunderland Boys, English Schools Shield 3rd Rd 28th February 1925
Best performance in: F.A. Cup: 4th Rd 1985-86
F.A. Trophy: Winners 1978 and 1986, Finalists 1982
Previous Leagues: Manchester, Lancashire Combination, Cheshire, Northern Premier
Clubhouse details:
Present players with Football League experience: Jeff Wealands (Darlington, Hull City, Birmingham City, Manchester United, Oldham Athletic, Preston North End). Mike Farrelly (Preston North End), Paul Cuddy (Rochdale)
Past players who progressed into the Football League: Graham Barrow (Wigan 1981), Frank Carrodus (Manchester City 1969), Robert Dale (Bury 1951), Brian Green (Exeter City 1962), John Hughes (Stockport County 1976), Steve Johnson (Bury 1977), Joe Kennedy (West Bromwich Albion 1948), Stan March (Port Vale 1959), Charlie Mitten (Halifax Town 1965), Brian Phillips (Middlesborough 1954), Eric Robinson (West Bromwich Albion 1957), John Rogers (Wigan Athletic 1982), Nelson Stiffle (Chesterfield 1954), Jeff Street (Barrow 1969)
Record transfer fee paid: To Runcorn for Barry Whitbread
Record transfer fee received: From Wigan Athletic for Graham Barrow
Programme details: 24 pages 35p (available on subscription)
Programme editor: Paul Brady

Club Captain (1985-86): John Davison
Player of the Year (1985-86): Jeff Johnson

Local newspapers & Tel. No. Altrincham and Sale Guardian, Tel: 061 928 3737; Sale and Altrincham Messenger, 061 477 5636; Manchester Evening News, 061 832 7200
Major Honours: Alliance Premier League Champions (2), F.A. Trophy Winners (2), Alliance Premier League Cup Winners, Alliance Premier League Shield Winners, Northern Premier League Cup Winners, Cheshire League Champions (2), Cheshire League Cup Winners (3), Cheshire Senior Cup Winners (4)

BARNET

Gola League 14th **F.A. Trophy** 1st Rd **F.A. Cup** 4th Qual Rd **H.S.C.** Winners **Bob Lord Trophy** Runners-up

Barnet F.C.

BARNET DEFENCE IMPRESSIVE

Barnet beginning a season without Barry Fry just didn't seem right but five draws and a win in the first seven league games was a steady start and with Nicky Evans averaging a goal a game, the supporters must have felt reasonably optimistic. Indeed a slight set-back at home against Frickley was quickly followed by three victories in a row and progress was being steadily made in the Bob Lord Trophy as well.

Consistency was missing however and although Dagenham, Bath City, Maidstone and Weymouth (away) were impressively sent packing in the League Trophy, Gola League form varied.

Very brief involvement was 'enjoyed' in the F.A. Cup, where Barnet were unfortunate enough to meet Enfield on top form, and in the F.A Trophy when they lost at home to Wycombe Wanderers.

Manager Roger Thompson stepped down and as things didn't seem to be too settled in deepest Kent, where Barry Fry and Maidstone United were still trying to get used to each other, it wasn't really surprising when it was announced that Barry would be returning to Underhill.

With a reasonably safe position in the league (Barnet eventually finished 14th) Barry was able to get the adrenalin flowing again as two cup competitions entered their final rounds.

The Herts Senior Cup was won without conceding a goal and in two stirring legs of the Bob Lord Trophy, Stafford Rangers won both games by the odd goal 2-1 and 1-0.

Even more heartening was the form shown in the last four home league matches which were all won, again without conceding a goal. If this can be kept up then we will be seeing a 'bubbling Barry' again and Barnet will certainly be a happy place to visit.

BARNET SQUAD 1986

Goalkeepers
Steve Humphries: Kettering Town, Leicester City, Oldham Athletic, Cardiff City (1), Wrexham (2), Vancouver Whitecaps (Can), Doncaster Rovers (13), Leicester City
Steve Waller: Enfield, Boreham Wood, Arsenal, Brighton

Defenders
Glyn Creaser: Newport Pagnell, Wolverton Town, Kettering Town, Wolverton Town
Steve Whitworth: Mansfield Town (80-2), Bolton Wanderers (67), Sunderland (83), Leicester City (353)
Kevin Thomas: Hitchin Town, Waterlows
Peter Brown: Tring Town, Aylesbury United, Napier City Rovers (N.Z.), Wimbledon (55-3), Chelsea
Gordon Smith: Wolves (38-3), Tottenham Hotspur (38-1), Aston Villa (79), St Johnston (112-8), Rangers BC

Midfield
Eddie Stein: Dagenham, Harrow Borough, Edgware
Barry Little: Dagenham, Gillingham, Charlton Athletic (2-1)
Dave Sansom: Fisher Athletic, Tooting & Mitcham, Crystal Palace
John Margerrison: Wealdstone, Boreham Wood, Kansas City (USA), Orient (80-6), Fulham (71-9), Tottenham Hotspur
Paul Wimbleton: Portsmouth (10)
Nigel Johnson: Wealdstone, Luton Town

Forwards
Robert Codner: Dagenham, Leicester City, Orient
Nicky Evans: Kettering Town, Peterborough United, Q.P.R.
David Pearce: Harrow Borough, Wealdstone, Millwall (1)
Steve Ragan: Maidstone United, Dagenham, Barnet, Hillingdon, Barnet, Tottenham Hotspur
John Neal: Millwall (6-1)

Phil Gardner finds the Barnet net during this Altrincham attack but this effort was ruled out for an earlier infringement. Photo: John Rooney

BARNET GOLA LEAGUE SEASON 1985-6

Venue	Opponents	Result	Scorers	Att.
A	Telford Unitd	D 2-2	Creaser, Evans	1233
H	Wycombe Wanderers	L 0-1		1061
A	Staffford Rangers	D 0-0		1168
H	Maidstone United	D 3-3	Evans (3)	602
H	Altrincham	D 2-2	Sansom (2)	648
A	Maidstone United	D 2-2	Baldry, Evans	673
A	Kidderminster	W 2-0	Evans (2)	548
H	Frickley Athletic	L 1-2	Sansom	513
A	Boston United	W 2-1	Hayes, Sansom	1325
H	Dartford	W 2-0	Baldry, Codner	761
A	Barrow	W 1-0	Hayes	341
A	Weymouth	L 2-4	Neal, Sansom	800
H	Dagenham	W 4-1	Little (2), Parker, Creaser	1014
A	Scarborough	L 1-3	Sansom	749
A	Nuneaton Borough	L 1-4	Sansom	786
H	Northwich Victoria	W 1-0	Codner	687
H	Kidderminster	L 0-1		631
H	Cheltenham Town	D 2-2	Pearce, Evans	659
A	Wealdstone	L 0-2		947
A	Kettering Town	D 1-1	Codner	1103
H	Runcorn	L 1-2	Codner	620
H	Wealdstone	W 1-0	Evans	902
H	Enfield	L 0-1		1455
A	Dartford	L 3-5	Evans (2), Sansom	539
H	Weymouth	D 2-2	Evans, Margerrison	638
H	Boston United	W 3-0	Codern, Evans, Sansom	598
A	Cheltenham Town	L 1-2	Stein	598
A	Enfield	L 0-1		772
A	Frickley Athletic	D 3-3	Evans (2), Sansom	518
A	Altrincham	L 0-2		1003
A	Dagenham	L 1-2	Sansom	539
A	Wycombe Wanderers	L 0-2		832
A	Bath City	D 1-1	Evans	604
H	Barrow	W 4-1	Evans (3), Little	614
A	Runcorn	D 0-0		400
H	Nuneaton Borough	L 0-1		678
H	Stafford Rangers	L 0-2		547
H	Telford United	L 1-2	Johnson	583
A	Northwich Victoria	W 1-0	Little	474
H	Scarborough	W 1-0	Codner	561
H	Bath City	W 1-0	Evans	442
H	Kettering Town	W 3-0	Sansom (2), Johnson	622

Cup Details

H	**Enfield (FAC)**	**L 0-7**		**1841**
H	**Wycombe Wanderers (FAT)**	**L 0-1**		**882**
H	**Dagenham (BLT)**	**W 3-2**	**Evans (2), Codner**	**606**
A	**Dagenham (BLT)**	**D 0-0**		**502**
H	**Bath City (BLT)**	**D 1-1**	**Davis**	**425**
A	**Bath City (BLT)**	**W 1-0**	**Pearce**	**388**
H	**Maidstone United (BLT)**	**W 2-0**	**Margerrison, Mahoney**	**314**
A	**Weymouth (BLT s.f.)**	**W 1-0**	**Evans**	**870**
A	**Stafford Rangers (BLT final)**	**L 1-2**	**Evans**	**1340**
H	**Stafford Rangers (BLT final)**	**L 0-1**		**1087**
A	**Tring Town (HSC)**	**W 2-0**	**Evans (2)**	**112**
A	**St Albans City (HSC)**	**W 1-0**	**Pearce**	**482**
A	**Hitchin Town (HSC s.f.)**	**W 2-0**	**Pearce (2)**	**220**
N	**Stevenage (HSC final)**	**W 4-0**	**Sansom (2), Brown, Creaser**	**800**

FAC = F.A. Cup
FAT = F.A. Trophy
BLT = Bob Lord Trophy
HSC = Herts Senior Cup

Appearances:
Humphries 41, Whitworth 39, Little 36 + 3, Brown 36, Sansom 35 + 3, Stein 35 + 1, Creaser 35, Evans 31 + 1, Codner 29+ 4, Margerrison 25 + 2, Baldry 18 + 2, Smith 17, O'Neill 13, Parker 10 + 10, Goodchild 9 + 3, Johnson 9, Wimbleton 8, Lacey 6, Pearce 5 + 2, Thomas 4 + 2, Cox 4 + 1, McAllister 4, Neal 3 + 5, Mahoney 3 + 1, Hayes 3, Ragan 1 + 3, Beattie 1, Davis 1, Waller 1, Campbell 0 + 1, Taylor 0 + 1

Goalscorers:
(56); Evans 20, Sansom 13, Codner 6, Little 4, Baldry 2, Creaser 2, Hayes 2, Johnson 2, Margerrison 1, Neal 1, Parker 1, Pearce 1, Stein 1

A terrace behind one of the goals at Underhill Photo: Alan Bunce

BARNET

President: C. Whitta
Chairman: Stan Flashman
Manager: Barry Fry
Asst. Manager:
Player/Coach: Steve Whitworth
Physiotherapist: Paul Loman
Secretary: Bryan Ayres
Address & Tel. No. 01 440 0277
Social Club Secretary: Gaynor Perrett
Address & Tel. No. 01 441 6932
Press Officer & Tel. No. Bryan Ayres. 01 440 0277
Address and Tel. No. of ground: Barnet Lane, Underhill, Barnet, Herts. 01 441 6932. Match information 01 449 4173
Simple ground directions: At the foot of Barnet Hill on London side A1000 **Club shop:**
No. of seats: 884 **Covered accommodation:** 5,500 **Capacity:** 10,000 **Floodlights:** Yes
Year formed: 1888 **Nickname:** The Bees **Club sponsor:** David Godwin Plumbing Supplies
Previous names: None
Previous grounds: None
Day for midweek home matches: Tuesday
Club colours: Amber/black
Change colours: All red
Club metal badges: Yes
Record attendance: 14,000 v Wycombe Wanderers F.A. Amateur Cup **Year:** 1949
Best performance in: **F.A. Cup:** 1972-73, 1981-82 v Brighton 3rd Rd replay
F.A. Trophy: 1971-72 Finalists
Previous Leagues: Athenian, Southern, Gola
Clubhouse details: Social Club
Present players with Football League experience: S. Humphries, W. Baldy, J. Margerrison, P. Brown, E. Stein, N. Evans, S. Whitworth, G. Roberts
Past players who progressed into the Football League: Colin Powell, Gary Borthwick, Graham Pearce, Russell Townsend, Colin Barnes, Gary Phillips
Record transfer fee paid: £4,000 Stuart Atkins (Kettering)
Record transfer fee received: £35,000 Graham Pearce (Brighton)
Programme details: 32 pages, 35p
Programme editor: Tony Holmes
Club Captain (1985-86): Peter Brown
Player of the Year (1985-86): Nicky Evans/Steve Humphries
Local newspapers & Tel. No. Barnet Press, Barnet Advertiser, Barnet Independent, Hendon & Finchley Times. Local radio stations: Capital, L.B.C., BBC Radio Bedfordshire
Major Honours: F.A. Amateur Cup (Winners 1945-46), F.A. Amateur Cup (runners-up twice, 1947-48, 1958-59), F.A. Trophy (runners-up 1971-72), Athenian League (Winners seven times, 1930-31, 1931-32, 1946-47, 1947-48, 1958-59, 1963-64, 1964-65), Souther Leagie Div 1 (1965-66), Southern Leagie Div 1 South (1976-77), Southern League Cup (1971-72)

BATH CITY

Gola League 11th **F.A. Trophy** 1st Rd **F.A. Cup** 2nd Rd **S.P.C.** W **Bob Lord Trophy** 1st Rd

Bath City 1985/86

A STEADY SEASON

The prospect of ground sharing with Bristol Rovers at Twerton Park probably dominated proceedings last season but Bobby Jones' side enjoyed a steady season while keeping within a strict budget.

While other clubs around them seemed to be spending freely without necessarily making progress, City finished half way up the league, won the Somerset Professional Cup by beating Yeovil Town in both legs of the final and reached the first round of the F.A. Cup.

Following an impressive string of victories against Taunton Town, Exmouth Town, Croydon and Farnborough 4-0 away, a close battle was fought at Peterborough where just a single goal let the league club through to start a good run of their own.

David Mogg was again outstanding in goal while Dave Singleton headed the goalscoring lists. Supporters also welcomed back old favourite Graham Withey who having scored goals for Bristol Rovers, Coventry City and Cardiff City since he left Twerton helped out at the end of season and scored in seven of the last fourteen matches.

Good management and sensible 'housekeeping' by the directors may keep the club solvent but now the extra revenue from Bristol Rovers improving finances even more, fans may well be expecting a top of the table challenge. Only two seasons ago Bath City were the Gola League's nomination for a place in the Football League, this season a repeat of that would mean a Division Four place. Competition will be intense but an improvement in support could make all the difference. Surely the City of Bath should be able to average at least 1,000 for home matches and perhaps this would inspire City back to the top. T.W.

BATH CITY

Goalkeepers
David Mogg: Bristol City, Atvidaberg (Swe), Bristol City

Defenders
Gary Fulbrook: Swindon Town (1)
David Palmer: Bristol Rovers (1)
Mike Pratt: Newport County (9-2)
Jeff Sherwood: Bristol Rovers (18), Bath City, Taunton Town
Paul Bodin: Cardiff City (75-4), Newport County, Chelsea
Richard Crowley: Frome Town

Midfield
Paul Stevens: Bristol City (147-3)
Keith Brown: Bristol Rovers (7)
Phil Barton: Blackburn Rovers
Brian O'Donnell: Poole Town, Blacktown City (Aus), Torquay United (19), AFC Bournemouth (13), Blacktown City (Aus), Bristol Rovers, AFC Bournemouth
Martin Grimshaw: Local
Martin Wheeler: Clevedon Town, Bath City, Clevedon Town

Forwards
Ricky Chandler: Bristol City (61-13)
David Payne: Local
Dave Singleton: Weymouth, Tauton Town
Mark Wright: Local
Mike Adams: Bristol Rovers (1)

David Palmer (Bath City) scores from 'spot' in beating the Hampshire Club 4-0 in 1st round F.A. Cup 16.11.85 Photo: Eric Marsh

Action versus Bristol Rovers at Twerton Park.

BATH CITY GOLA LEAGUE SEASON 1985-6

Venue	Opponents	Result	Scorers	Att.
H	Northwich V	D 0-0		668
A	Maidstone United	L 2-3	Grimshaw (2)	548
A	Barrow	D 1-1	Bodin	425
H	Nuneaton B	L 0-2		547
H	**Taunton T (FAC)**	**W 4-1**	**Payne, Brown, Adams, Wright**	**404**
A	Nuneaton B	W 3-2	Brown, Bodin, Smithers (o.g.)	926
A	Boston United	D 1-1	Wright	1334
H	Kidderminster Harriers	L 2-4	Stevens, Adams	587
A	Runcorn	L 0-2		507
A	Kidderminster Harriers	L 1-3	Adams	648
H	Clevedon Town	W 1-0	Clarke (o.g.)	515
H	Stafford Rangers	L 0-1		484
A	Altrincham	W 2-1	Crowley, Grimshaw	1063
A	Stafford Rangers	L 0-1		1196
H	**Exmouth (FAC)**	**W 2-0**	**Payne, Grimshaw**	**613**
H	Telford	W 3-0	Singleton (2), Barton	593
A	Enfield	L 1-3	Singleton	770
H	Cheltenham	D 1-1	Adams	737
H	**Croydon (FAC)**	**W 4-1**	**Singleton (2), Barton, Ricketts**	**815**
H	Scarborough	D 0-0		530
A	**Barnet (BLT)**	**D 1-1**	**Fulbrook**	**425**
A	Scarborough	L 1-2	Palmer (pen)	726
A	**Farnborough (FAC)**	**W 4-0**	**Chandler, Ricketts**	**1324**
A	Cheltenham	W 2-1	Singleton, Brown	875
H	Wycombe Wanderers	W 3-1	Bodin, Singleton, Ricketts	758
H	**Barnet (BLT)**	**L 0-1**		**388**
H	Dagenham	D 1-1	Payne	570
A	**Peterborough (FAC)**	**L 0-1**		**3388**
H	Barrow	W 6-0	Singleton 4, Brown, Bodin	504
A	**Chelmsford (FAT)**	**L 1-2**	**Palmer (pen)**	**803**
A	Weymouth	D 0-0		950
H	Maidstone	D 1-1	Bodin	534
A	Dagenham	W 1-0	Bodin (pen)	505
H	**Shepton Mallet (SC)**	**W 5-1**	**Bodin (3, 1 pen), Payne, Ricketts**	**169**
A	Telford	L 0-1		1050
H	Wealdstone	L 2-3	Wheeler, Palmer	521
H	Weymouth	D 2-2	Adams, Withey	454
H	Boston	W 2-0	Chandler, Withey	598
H	Frickley	L 1-2	Payne	417
H	**Taunton (SC)**	**W 2-0**	**Chandler, Withey**	**196**
A	Northwich	W 2-1	Chandler, Wheeler	615
H	Barnet	D 1-1	Singleton	604
H	Wycombe	W 4-1	Singleton 3, Burgess (o.g.)	
A	Wealdstone	W 1-0	Withey	
H	**Yeovil (SC)**	**W 1-0**	**Withey**	**779**
H	Dartford	W 2-0	Withey, Singleton	570
H	Altrincham	L 0-2		669
H	Kettering	D 1-1	Withey	402
H	Frickley	L 1-2	Bodin	592
A	**Yeovil (SC)**	**W 2-1**		
H	Runcorn	L 0-1		652
A	Yeovil	W 2-0	Bodin, Payne	1320
H	Enfield	L 0-2		522
A	Barnet	L 0-1		442
H	Frickley	H 1-2	Bodin	552

FAC = F.A. Cup
BLT = Bob Lord Trophy
FAT = F.A. Trophy
SC = Somerset Cup

Appearances: League
41 — Mogg, 40 — Bodin, 38 — Payne, 35 — Adams, Sherwood, 34 — Chandler, 33 — Brown, 31 — Stevens, 30 — Singleton, 25 — Fulbrook, Pratt, 18 — Barton, 15 — Wheeler, 14 — Withey, 13 — Crowley, O'Donnell, Ricketts, 11 — Grimshaw, 7 — Wright, 2 — Smith, Taylor, 1 — Casey, George, Miles, Sowter, Stroud, Tilley.

Cup
13 — Mogg, Payne, Sherwood, 12 — Bodin, 11 — Chandler, Singleton, 9 — Adams, Barton, 8 — Brown, Pratt, 7 — Fulbrook, Ricketts, 6 — Stevens, 5 — Palmer, 3 — Crowley, Withey, 2 — George, Grimshaw, O'Donnell, Taylor, Wright, 1 — Miles, Stroud, Tilley.

Goalscorers: League
13 — Singleton, 7 — Bodin, 6 — Withey, 4 — Adams, 3 — Brown, Grimshaw, 2 — Chandler, Palmer, Payne, Wheeler, O.G., 1 — Barton, Crowley, Ricketts, Stevens, Wright.

Cup
5 — Bodin, 4 — Payne, 3 — Ricketts, 2 — Chandler, Palmer, Withey, 1 — Adams, Barton, Brown, Fulbrook, Grimshaw, Wright, O.G.

Twerton Park, Bath 1986

BATH CITY

President: R.G. Williams F.R.S.A.
Chairman: T.P. Richards
Manager: Bobby Jones
Asst. Manager:
Coach: Mike Lyons
Physiotherapist: D. Monks

Secretary: Ann Cunningham
Address & Tel. No. Twerton Park, Bath BA2 1DB. Tel 0225 23087

Commercial Manager: Graham Bowen
Address & Tel. No. c/o Club

Press Officer & Tel. No.
Address and Tel. No. of ground: Twerton Park, Bath. Tel Bath 23087
Simple ground directions: Situated just off the main A36. Lower Bristol Road approx. 1¾ miles from the city centre
Club shop: No
No. of seats: 600 **Covered accommodation:** 5,000 **Capacity:** 20,000 **Floodlights:** Yes
Year formed: 1889 **Nickname:** City **Club sponsor:** Avongraphics Bristol
Previous names: None
Previous grounds: Lambridge
Day for midweek home matches: Tuesday
Club colours: Black/white
Change colours: Red
Club metal badges: Yes
Record attendance: 18,020 v Brighton, F.A. Cup **Year:** 1960
Best performance in: **F.A. Cup:** 1963-4 v Bolton Wanderers 3rd Round Replay
F.A. Trophy: 1979-80 3rd Round
Previous Leagues: Southern
Clubhouse details: 'Sportsman' 11 a.m.-2.30 p.m. and 6.30 p.m.-10.30 p.m. F.O.B. Club 7.30 p.m.-10.30 p.m.
Present players with Football League experience: Mike Adams, Keith Brown, Druid Palmer, Jeff Sherwood (Bristol Rovers), Ricky Chandler, David Mogg
Past players who progressed into the Football League: Alan Skirton (Arsenal), Tony Book (Plymouth, Man. City), Ken Allen (Bournemouth), Peter Rogers, Martin Rogers (Exeter), Richard Bourne (Torquay), Dave Wiffil (Man. City), G. Withey (Bristol R., Coventry, Cardiff), Stan Mortensen (Blackpool)
Record transfer fee paid: £7,000 to Minehead for Brian Durbin
Record transfer fee received: £25,000 Dave Wiffil (Manchester City)
Programme details: 22 pages, 30p
Programme editor:
Club Captain (1985-86): Jeff Sherwood
Player of the Year (1985-86): Jeff Sherwood
Local newspapers & Tel. No. Bath Evening Chronicle, Bath 63051
Major Honours: Southern League (2), League Cup, Somerset Premier Cup (12), Anglo-Italian Cup Finalists

BOSTON UNITED

Gola League 13th **F.A. Trophy** 1st Rd proper **F.A. Cup** 1st Rd proper **L.S.C.** 1st Rd
Bob Lord Trophy 1st Rd

Boston United: *Back Row (L-R): Gavin Ottewell, Brian Thomson, Gerald Creane, Derek Nuttall, Devan White, Ian Ladd, Bob Lee (now left the club), Arthur Mann (now with Telford), Paul Hooks, Ray O'Brien (caretaker manager), Don Robinson (trainer).*
Front Row: Chris Cook, David Gilbert, David Stenson, Kevin Blackwell, Paul Casey, Andy Harrison, Mick Laverick

WHEN WILL THE SLEEPING GIANT AWAKE?

Boston United, F.A. Trophy finalists in the previous season failed to propel the same momentum into their Gola League campaign and the season was sadly one of anticlimax and disappointment. Having made a sound start to the campaign when a couple of away victories kept them in contention with the pacesetters, The Pilgrims dropped down the league during a turbulent October.

Out of 21 points available only two were acredited to their tally. Ironically during this depressing period Boston produced one of their most impressive displays beating Lincoln City 4-0 in the Lincolnshire County Cup Final. As they slipped down the table, the drastic measure of sacking manager Arthur Mann was taken. His assistant Ray O'Brien, the former Notts County and Eire International was invited to take over.

After successfully coming through his probationary period, O'Brien was then appointed in full control, as results improved.

York Street again became a bastion, and the home run of success contributed to erasing any threat of relegation. One of O'Brien's first decisions was to release Bob Lee, who was only a shadow of the player who scored 27 goals the previous season.

Twin striker Chris Cook then had a succession of partners, none of whom seem to complement him. Boston's problems were twin-fold. They had difficulty scoring, while conceeding goals with enormous regularity, giving them one of the worst defensive records in the league.

This was no reflection of keeper Kevin Blackwell. Not only was he the club's only ever present, he forced himself into the reckoning for England's semi-professional squad. Boston had no success at all in the cup competitions. Excempt until the first round proper of the F.A. Cup, Runcorn beat them after two replays. Kidderminster were too strong in the F.A. Trophy, while Telford were superior in the Bob Lord Trophy.

Despite their problems in making an impact, The Pilgrims still managed to be the best supported team in the league.

An average of 1,301 were attracted through the turnstiles and into the beautifully appointed York Street ground, the envy of many football league clubs.

2,067 watched the game against Wealdstone, the highest single gate of the season. With the facilities and support available it is surprising Boston have still to win an honour at the highest non-league level. This season, perhaps, the sleeping giant will show his strength.

BOSTON UNITED SQUAD 1986

Goalkeepers
Kevin Blackwell: Barnet, Barton Rovers, Bedford Town

Defenders
Ray O'Brien: Notts County (323-30), Manchester United, Shelbourne)
Ian Ladd: Corby Town, Stamford, Bourne Town, Notts County (1)
Gerard Creane: Yaro (Finland), Tsun Wan (Hong Kong), Lincoln City (7)
Paul Casey: Sheffield United (25-1)
Derrick Nuttell: Local
Mick Czuczman: Skegness Town, Hull City, York City (17), Grimsby Town (9), San Jose Earthquakes (USA), Stockport County (36-7), Scunthorpe United (116-1), Grimsby Town (114-6), Preston North End

Midfield
David Stenson: Spalding United, Manawate United (N.Z.), Retford Town, Rotherham United
Mick Laverick: York City (41-6), Huddersfield Town (74-9), Southend United (110-18), Mansfield Town (89-13)
Gavin Ottewell: Hucknall C.W.
David Gilbert: Scunthorpe United (1), Lincoln City (30-1)
Brian Thomson: King's Lynn, Corby Town, Mansfield Town (63-1), West Ham United, Morcambe

Forwards
Dominic Genovese: Nuneaton Borough, Boston United, Stamford
Chris Cook: Local
Paul Hooks: Derby County (48-4), Notts County (173-30)
Chris Townsend: Arnold
Derek Bell: Scunthorpe United (23-7), Chesterfield (17-3), Lincoln City (83-33), Barnsley (46-20), Halifax Town (112-21)

A 'goal' for Derek Bell against Kidderminster Harriers is disallowed for offside

BOSTON UNITED GOLA LEAGUE SEASON 1985-6

Venue	Opponents	Result	Scorers	Att.
H	**Grimsby Town (LSC)**	**W 5-3**		**707**
A	**Grantham (LSC)**	**D 2-2**		
H	Nuneaton Borough	W 3-2	Hooks, Cook, Hilbert (pen)	1304
H	Stafford Rangers	D 1-1	Cook	1483
A	Dartford	W 1-0	Creane	439
H	Wealdstone	W 1-0	O.G.	2067
A	Weymouth	D 0-0		886
H	Bath City	D 1-1	Thomson	1334
H	Enfield	L 1-2	Lee	1345
A	Northwich Victoria	W 4-3	Hooks 2, Ladd, Cook	710
H	**Telford United (BLT)**	**D 1-1**		**1163**
H	Barnet	L 1-2	Gilbert	1325
A	**Telford United (BLT)**	**L 2-3**		**1053**
A	Dagenham	D 2-2	Cook	521
H	Frickley Athletic	L 0-3		1303
A	Enfield	L 0-3		777
A	Barrow	L 1-2	Gilbert	412
A	Wealdstone	L 2-7	Nuttell, Cook	628
H	Telford United	D 2-2	Laverick (pen), O.G.	1029
H	**Lincoln City (LSC final)**	**W 4-0**		**1398**
A	Frickley Athletic	L 1-5	White	569
H	Runcorn	W 2-1	Cook	1172
A	**Runcorn (FAC)**	**D 2-2**		**1315**
H	**Runcorn (FAC)**	**D 1-1**		**2158**
A	**Altrincham**	**W 3-1**	**Gilbert 2, White**	**1264**
A	**Runcorn (FAC)**	**L 1-4**		**2525**
A	Kidderminster Harriers	L 2-3	Nuttell, Townsend	512
H	Scarborough	W 2-1	Czuczmzn	1238
H	Northwich Victoria	W 3-0	Gilbert 2, Thomson	1281
A	Wycombe Wanderers	L 1-4	Gilbert (pen)	741
A	Nuneaton Borough	W 1-0	Townsend	590
A	**Kidderminster Harriers (FAT)**	**L 2-5**		**582**
H	Kettering Town	W 4-1	Townsend 3, Laverick	1553
A	Kettering Town	L 1-3	Cook	1952
H	Dagenham	W 3-0	Hooks, Cook, Gilbert (pen)	1202
H	Dartford	W 3-0	Laverick, Cook, Gilbert	1226
A	Barnet	L 0-3		598
A	Telford United	L 1-2	Hooks	895
H	Wycombe Wanderers	D 1-1	Cook	1231
A	Bath City	L 0-2		598
H	Maidstone United	D 2-2		1032
H	Barrow	W 2-1	Gilbert 2 (pen)	1096
A	Cheltenham Town	L 1-2	Creane	847
A	Maidstone United	W 2-1	Bell 2	621
H	Weymouth	W 5-0	Bell 2, Nuttell, Cook, Gilbert (pen)	1385
A	Scarborough	L 1-2	Gilbert (pen)	644
H	Cheltenham Town	L 1-2	Bell	1303
H	Kidderminster Harriers	W 2-1	Hooks, Gilbert (pen)	1316
A	Stafford Rangers	L 1-2	Nuttell	1130
A	Runcorn	L 0-3		476
H	Altrincham	L 1-3	Gilbert	1094

LSC =
BLT = Bob Lord Trophy
FAC = F.A. Cup
FAT = F.A. Trophy

Appearances:
League (42), Cup (9); Blackwell 51, Creane 48, Thomson 47, Cook 47, Gilbert 47, Casey 44, Stewson 39, Nuttell 36, Ladd 33, Hooks 31, Czuczman 28, Laverick 19, Harrison 17, Lee 15, Townsend 11, Ottewell 10, Bell 8, Simpson 8, Mann 7, Dewyer 5, White 5, O'Brien 3, Genovese 2

Goalscorers:
(87); Gilbert 19, Cook 18, Nuttell 8, Hooks 6, Bell 5, Townsend 5, Creane 4, Laverick 4, Czuczman 3, Thomson 3, O.G. 3, Ladd 2, Lee 2, White 2, Casey 1, Dewyer 1, Harrison 1

Main Stand, York Street Ground

BOSTON UNITED

President:
Chairman: P. Malkinson
Manager: Ray O'Brien
Asst. Manager:
Coach:
Physiotherapist: Dr L.D. Taffinder
Secretary: John Blackwell
Address & Tel. No. 14-16 Spain Place, Boston. 0205 65652 (H), 0205 64406 (B)
Commercial Manager: John Blackwell
Address & Tel. No. As above
Press Officer & Tel. No. Club office
Address and Tel. No. of ground: York Street Ground, Boston. 0205 65524/5. Match days only
Simple ground directions: Two minutes walk from town centre **Club shop:** Yes
No. of seats: 2,000 **Covered accommodation:** All **Capacity:** 15,000 **Floodlights:** Yes, Mercury Halide
Year formed: 1934 **Nickname:** Pilgrims **Club sponsor:** Burdens Tractors
Previous names: Boston Town, Boston Swifts
Previous grounds: None
Day for midweek home matches: Wednesday
Club colours: Amber/black
Change colours: White & red
Club metal badges: Yes + embroidered ones
Record attendance: 10,086 v Corby Town **Year:** Unknown
Best performance in: **F.A. Cup:** 1955-6 Tottenham, 1973-4 v Derby Co. 3rd Rd
F.A. Trophy: 1979-80 losing semi-finalists
Previous Leagues: Central Alliance, Midland Counties, United Counties, West Midlands, Northern Prem.
Clubhouse details: Open every day except Tuesday. 7-11 p.m. Friday, Saturday 11-3 p.m. Sunday 12-2pm. Live entertainment, darts, dominoes. Tel: 0205 62967.
Present players with Football League experience: D. Gilbert, P. Casey, G. Creane, R. O'Brien, D. Bell
Past players who progressed into the Football League: J. Smith (Colchester, Blackburn, Birmingham), S. Thompson (Lincoln City), B. Phillips (Mansfield Town), G. Simmonite (Blackpool), S. Garner (Blackburn Rovers)
Record transfer fee paid: £10,000 Brendan Phillips (Mansfield Town)
Record transfer fee received: £15,000 B. Phillips (Mansfield), S. Thompson (Lincoln), G. Simmonite (Blackpool)
Programme details: 16 pages, 35p, photographs
Programme editors: Nick Thompson and John Blackwell
Club Captain (1985-86): Gerald Creane
Player of the Year (1985-86): David Gilbert
Local newspapers & Tel. No. Lincolnshire Standard 0205 65001, Boston Target, 0205 50220, Boston Choice, Lincs Echo 0522 26101, Local radio stations: Radio Lincoln, Hereward Radio
Major Honours: United Counties League, West Midlands League (2), N.P.L. (4) & Runners-up, N.P.L. Cup (2) & Runners-up, N.P.L. Shield (3), N.P.L. Champs v S.L. Champs (2) & Runners-up

CHELTENHAM TOWN

Gola League 11th **F.A. Trophy** Q.F. **F.A. Cup** 1st Qual Rd **Bob Lord Trophy** 2nd Rd
N.G.S.P. Cup Finalists

Cheltenham Town: *Back Row: C. Boxall, N. Gazzard, N. Hards, S. Martyn, T. Harris, K. Baddeley (now Kidderminster), S. Doughty, K. Willetts, N. Goff, M. Boyland (now Forest Green) Middle Row: D. Smith (commercial), B. Williams (trainer), D. Lewis (assistant manager), N. Jordan, P. Collicutt, C. Smith, R. Baverstock, M. Blackler, B. Hughes, S. Brooks, S. Cornes, J. Murphy (manager), D. Parrott (general Manager) Front Row: D. Hudd, J. Turner, F. Touhey (directors), K. Rushworth (president), A.Hayward (chairman), R. Burge (director), R. Woodward (general secretary/director)*

Cheltenham opened their first season in the top flight of non-league football with a line-up boosted by the signings of goalkeeper Neil Hards from neighbours Gloucester City and the Witney Town pair Martin Blackler and Steve Brooks. The first competitive game brought another trophy to Whaddon Road, when the Robins as Southern League champions beat Fisher Athletic (Bill Dellow Cup winners) by 3-2 in the Southern League Championship match.

Any hopes of a lucrative F.A. Cup run were dashed in the 1st qualifying round, when, following a 1-1 draw at Minehead, two goals by Matt Lazenby saw the Western Leaguers score a shock 2-1 win in the replay. This was compensated by a fine run in the F.A. Trophy. Victories over Fisher, Dagenham and Bishop Stortford (after a replay) took them into the quarter finals for the very first time where a crowd of 2,196 saw Altrincham triumph at Whaddon Road with two Ronnie Ellis goals.

In the league a steady start took them into a mid-table position, before a spell from 19 October to 8 January which brought only five points from eight games. However a fine run in over the last two months of the season brought them into a creditable eleventh position. This spell brought to prominence young striker Chris Townsend, who scored hat-tricks on successive Saturdays and linked up well with leading scorer Mark Boyland.

Goalkeeper Neil Hards was both the players' and supporters' 'Player of the Year', while Brian Hughes completed 115 consecutive games since joining the Robins from Torquay in August 1984. The major problem of the season was a succession of injuries to the central defenders culminating in a broken leg suffered by Stuart Cornes which resulted in Tim Bayliffe rejoining the Club he first played for as a seventeen-year-old.

CHELTENHAM TOWN SQUAD 1986

Goalkeepers
Neil Hards: Gloucester City, Wimbledon, Plymouth Argyle
Les White: Local

Defenders
Kevin Baddeley: Wealdstone, Swindon Town, Bristol City
Stuart Cornes: Hereford United
Paul Collicutt: Trowbridge Town, Swindon Town
Martin Blackler: Whitney Town, Swindon Town

Midfield
Ray Baverstock: Swindon Town
Steve Brooks: Witney Town
Steve Abbley: Witney Town, Swindon Town
Nick Jordan: Moreton Town

Forwards
Mark Boyland: Banbury United, Witney Town, Oxford City
Kevin Willetts: Sharpness
Chris Townsend: Newport County
John Powell: Corby Town, Kidderminster Harriers, Nottm Forest

A Cheltenham Town leg appears to try and (assist) Mark Boyland in this tussle during the recent home game against Boston United Photo: Mike Halford

CHELTENHAM TOWN GOLA LEAGUE SEASON 1985-6

Venue	Opponents	Result	Scorers	Att.
H	Fisher Athletic	W 3-2	Hughes (2), Baverstock	802
H	Maidstone United	W 2-1	Brooks, Hughes	1082
A	Weymouth	D 0-0		1001
A	Enfield	L 0-1		597
H	Telford	D 1-1	Boyland	1157
A	**Minehead (F.A. Cup)**	**D 1-1**	**O.G.**	**216**
H	**Minehead (F.A. Cup)**	**L 1-2**	**Jordan**	**933**
H	Wealdstone	L 1-2	Boyland	982
A	**Kettering (B.L.T.)**	**W 1-0**	**Boyland**	**920**
A	Dagenham	W 3-1	Cornes, Brooks, Hughes	528
H	**Kettering (B.L.T.)**	**W 5-1**	**Blackler, Brooks (2), Boyland (2)**	**1293**
A	Barrow	D 2-2	Boyland (2)	517
H	Weymouth	L 0-1		1311
H	Frickley	D 1-1	Hughes	1007
A	Nuneaton	W 1-0	Boyland	707
H	Stafford	W 2-0	Cornes, Hughes	1223
A	Wycombe Wanderers	D 3-3	Brooks, Willetts, Abbley	825
H	Kettering	W 5-1	Hughes (2), Smith, Boyland (2)	1221
A	Bath City	D 1-1	Gazzard	737
A	Runcorn	L 0-5		620
H	**Maidstone (B.L.T.)**	**L 2-3**	**Smith, Willetts**	**874**
H	Dagenham	D 2-2	Townsend, Jordan	913
H	**Gloucester City (N.G.S.C.)**	**W 7-1**	**Cornes, Brooks (2), Hughes, Abbley, Townsend, O.G.**	**753**
H	Bath City	L 1-2	Townsend	875
A	Barnet	D 2-2	Cornes, Abbley	659
A	**Maidstone United (B.L.T.)**	**L 0-1**		**293**
H	**Runcorn**	**D 1-1**	**Boyland**	**1086**
A	**Dartford**	**D 3-3**	**Brooks,Smith,Boyland**	**441**
H	**Fisher Athletic (F.A.T.)**	**W 3-0**	**Hughes, Boyland, Jordan**	**857**
A	Kidderminster	L 1-5	Boyland	1102
H	Northwich	W 2-0	Boyland, Powell	898
A	Altrincham	L 1-4	Cornes	1012
A	Dagenham	W 1-0	Powell	499
H	Barnet	W 2-1	Boyland, Abbley	1090
A	Northwich	L 1-3	Brooks	521
H	**Bishops Stortf'd (F.A.T.)**	**D 0-0**		**1201**
A	Maidstone	L 0-1		650
H	Barrow	W 2-0	Abbley, Powell	719
A	**Bishops Stortf'd (F.A.T.)**	**W 3-1**	**Brooks, Boyland (2)**	**590**
A	Wealdstone	D 0-0		708
H	**Altrincham (F.A.T.)**	**L 0-2**		**2196**
H	Boston	W 2-1	Brooks, Abbley	847
A	Scarborough	L 0-1		452
H	Kidderminster	L 2-6	Townsend (2)	1274
H	Altrincham	W 2-0	Willetts, Powell	1113
A	Stafford	L 0-2		927
H	Scarborough	W 5-1	Townsend (2), Boyland (2), Powell	887
H	Enfield	W 2-0	Brooks, Boyland	1196
A	Boston	W 2-1	Brooks, Boyland	1303
A	Telford	L 0-3		1083
H	Nuneaton	W 5-3	Townsend 4, Powell	939
H	Dartford	W 3-1	Baverstock, Brooks (2)	727
H	WycombeWanderers	W 4-2	Townsend (3), Abbley	994
H	**Forest Green (N.G.S.C.)**	**L 1-1**	**aet. Lost 3-4 on pens**	**691**
A	Kettering	L 1-2	Bayliffe	532
A	Frickley	L 1-2	Townsend	575

Appearances:
League and Cup (56 games); Hughes, Boyland 56, Abbley, Hards 55, Baverstock, Brooks 53, Jordan 50, Cornes 44, Baddeley, Willetts 34, Blackler 33, Townsend 26, Powell 24, Collicutt, Boxall 22, Smith 19, Gazzard 11, Bayliffe 8, Brown, Aizlewood 4, Doughty, Lockwood, White, Whelen 1

Goalscorers:
League (69 goals); Boyland 16, Townsend 14, Brooks 10, Hughes, Abbley 6, Powell 5, Corner 4, Smith, Willetts 2, Baverstock, Jordan, Gazzard, Bayliffe 1.
Cups (28 goals); Boyland 6, Brooks 5, Hughes 4, Jordan 2, Cornes, Baverstock, Abbley, Blackler, Smith, Willetts, Townsend, Powell 1. Opponents 3

Cheltenham Town's 1200 seater stand at their Waddon Road ground.

CHELTENHAM TOWN

President: K. Rushworth JP
Chairman: A W Hayward
Player/Manager: John Murphy
Asst. Manager: Dave Lewis
Coach:
Physiotherapist: Bert Williams

Secretary: Reg Woodward
Address & Tel. No. 23 Enfield Villas, Winchcombe, Glos. GL54 5QH. 0242 602261 (H), 0242 516328 (B)
Dep. Secretary: Ken Turner, 0242 522514 (H), 0242 521491 ext. 2717 (B)
Commercial Manager: Dennis Smith
Address & Tel. No. 0242 573558

Press Officer & Tel. No.
Address and Tel. No. of ground: Whaddon Road, Cheltenham, Glos. GL52 5NA.Tel 0242 513397/521974
Simple ground directions: Situated NE side of Cheltenham, approx. 1 mile from town centre, off A46 (Prestbury Road)
Club shop: Yes
No. of seats: 1,200 **Covered accommodation:** 8,000 **Capacity:** 13,000 **Floodlights:** Yes
Year formed: 1892 **Nickname:** The Robins **Club sponsor:** Whitbread
Previous names: None
Previous grounds: None
Day for midweek home matches: Wednesday
Club colours: Red & white stripes
Change colours: All white
Club metal badges: Yes
Record attendance: 8,326 v Reading in F.A. Cup 1st Round **Year:** 1956
Best performance in: F.A. Cup: 1933-4 v Blackpool 3rd Round, lost 3-1
F.A. Trophy: 1985-6 Qtr Finals
Previous Leagues: Glos. Northern Senior, Birmingham Combination
Clubhouse details: Open 7 nights a week. 3 bars, clubroom, lounge and Robin's Nest function room. Nest and clubroom available for private hire. Open before and after Saturday matches
Present players with Football League experience: Steve Abbley (Swindon), Kevin Baddeley (Bristol City, Swindon), Ray Baverstock (Swindon), Stuart Cornes (Hereford), Brian Hughes (Swindon, Torquay), Neil Hards (Plymouth, Wimbledon)
Past players who progressed into the Football League: James Currier (Bolton W), Jack Wheeler (Birmingham C), Peter Goring (Arsenal), Peter Rushworth (Leicester C), Roy Shiner (Huddersfield T), Tim Ward (Derby C), Ray Bishop (Cardif C), Jack Haycox (Newport C), Jack Bowles (Stockport C), Roy Hill (Newport C), Ernie Thornley (Bristol C), Reg Watts (Bristol C), Jimmy Heal (Doncaster R), John McIlvenny (Bristol R), Peter Hauser (Chester), Paul Collicutt (Swindon T), Paul Tester (Shrewsbury T)
Record transfer fee paid: £3,000 joint-fee for Gary Fleet and Dave Lewis (Nuneaton Boro' 1979); £2,000 Gary Stevens (Alvechurch 1983)
Record transfer fee received: £1,500 Roy Shiner (Huddersfield 1951); £10,000 Paul Tester (Shrewsbury 1983)
Programme details: 16 pages, 20p
Club Captain (1985-86): Ray Baverstock
Programme editor:
Player of the Year (1985-86): Neil Hards
Local newspapers & Tel. No. Gloucestershire Echo 0242 526261. Local radio station 'Severn Sound' gives match coverage/live reports from h & a games
Major Honours: Champions; Southern League 1984-85, Southern League Cup, Southern League Merit Cup, Southern League Championship Match Winners, Gloucestershire Senior Cup (North) (24), Southern League Midland Divn Winners 1982-83

DAGENHAM

Gola League 19th | **F.A. Trophy** 2nd Rd | **F.A. Cup** 2nd Rd | **E.S.C.** 1st Rd | **Bob Lord Trophy** 1st Rd

Photo: David Hill

EXCITING FINISH — BUT TOO WORRYING TO ENJOY

Last season was another very disappointing one for Dagenham supporters. For the second successive season we came perilously close to being relegated from the Gola League and had little joy in the cup competition.

In the F.A. Cup, we defeated a gallant Atherstone United 5-1, and then gained our third ever victory over a football league side in the Cup when we beat Cambridge United 2-1. In the second round we were paired with AFC Bournemouth, who proved to be an extremely good all round side, although the 4-1 scoreline did not do justice to the brave efforts of the Dagenham lads.

The F.A. Trophy saw us lose at home to a late Cheltenham Town goal in the second round and in the Essex Senior Cup we crashed out at the first hurdle to Harlow Town.

In the Gola League we finished 19th and escaped relegation only by goal difference. Although we must admit that our lack of finishing power was evident throughout the season, it must not be overlooked that we suffered some cruel luck through injuries to key players.

We lost both central defenders for long periods at vital times during the season. Alan Campbell played only six league matches before missing the rest of the season with a damaged knee and an operation on his back; and then Alan Risk was hospitalised with a hernia operation and missed 14 games. Other injuries and suspensions depleated the side so much so that on several occasions the team was picked from the fittest players registered.

The league campaign saw only ten points gained from the opening 14 matches including three away to last season's champions, Wealdstone. At this stage Ken Knighton left the club due to business commitments in the Bristol area and Tony Jennings took over the reins. His team lost only once in the next seven games, collecting a total of ten points. We then lost the next four games, had a short revival when we lost 1 in 5, and followed this by losing the next five.

This gave us seven games, six of them away, in which to work miracles and avoid the drop which seemed almost certain. An away draw at Dartford was noteworthy because it saw the return of Alan Risk. Three points at Kettering were welcome, but only one point from the two following games did not help our cause. Fortunately the other bottom sides were also losing, some heavily. A trip to Wycombe saw us gain a welcome point, which left us needing four points from the last two away trips to stay up.

The first of these games was at Northwich and saw right back Frank Coles netting the only goal of the game deep into injury time to give us three vital points. A draw only was needed at Runcorn the following day to save us. After just 45 seconds goalkeeper John Jacobs, testing the strength of the strong wind, scored direct from a drop-kick. The next 89 minutes were nail-biting, but Runcorn could only equalise and we therefore obtained the point required to ensure Gola League football at Victoria Road during 1986/87 season.

It was an exciting finish to a long season, but too worrying to enjoy.

DAGENHAM SQUAD 1986

Goalkeepers
John Jacobs: Enfield, Dagenham, Bishop's Stortford, Enfield, Leytonstone, Ilford, Barking, Chelsea
Darren Williams: East Ham United

Defenders
Paul Baxter: Enfield, Leytonstone/Ilford, Crystal Palace (1), Tottenham Hotspur
Alan Campbell: Barnet, Hendon, Finchley
Alan Day: Billericay Town, Heybridge Swifts, Billercay Town, East Thurrock United
Clive Day: Aldershot (60), Mansfield Town, Fulham (10)
Tommy Horan: Leytonstone/Ilford, Dagenham, West Ham United
Alan Risk: Gravesend & Northfleet, Orient, Coventry

Midfield
Frank Coles: Leytonstone/Ilford, Charlton A
Joe Dunwell: Chelmsford City, Tilbury
Richard Head: Harlow Town
Steve Scott: Leytonstone/Ilford, Cheshunt
Paul Taylor: Enfield, Barking, Orient, Arsenal

Forwards
Devon Gayle: Walthamstow Av., Hendon, Cheshunt, Dagenham, Hendon
David Pearce: Barnet, Harrow Borough, Millwall
Terry Sullivan: Dartford, Bishops Stortford
Paul Turnpenny: Walthamstow Avenue

DAGENHAM GOLA LEAGUE SEASON 1985-6

Venue	Opponents	Result	Scorers	Att.
A	Kidderminster Harriers	L 0-2		623
H	Dartford	W 2-1	Cox, Whitton	779
A	Telford United	L 1-2	Whitton	1012
H	Weymouth	D 2-2	Cox (2)	554
H	Wycombe Wanderers	D 1-1	Whitton	584
A	Weymouth	L 1-2	McCombe	746
A	Scarborough	L 1-2	Whitton	630
A	**Barnet (BLT)**	**L 2-3**	**Cox, Scott S.**	**606**
H	Cheltenham Town	L 1-3	Cox	528
H	**Barnet (BLT)**	**D 0-0**		**462**
H	Kettering Town	W 1-0	Cox	536
A	Enfield	L 1-3	Cox (pen)	664
H	Boston United	D 2-2	Coles, Taylor	521
H	Enfield	L 0-2		836
A	Barnet	L 1-4	Dunwell	1014
A	Wealdstone	W 4-0	Manderson (3), Powell	782
H	Nuneaton Borough	W 3-2	Cox (2), Powell	548
H	**Atherstone United (FAC)**	**W 5-1**	**Risk (2), Dunwell, Powell, Scott S.**	**550**
H	Altrincham	L 1-3	Powell	582
H	**Harlow Town (ESC)**	**L 1-2**	**Scott S.**	**250**
A	Cheltenham Town	D 2-2	Taylor (2)	913
H	**Cambridge United (FAC)**	**W 2-1**	**Scott S., Sullivan**	**1351**
H	Maidstone United	D 0-0		598
H	Northwich Victoria	W 1-0	O.G.	539
A	Bath City	D 1-1	Scott (S)	570
A	**AFC Bournemouth (FAC)**	**L 1-4**	**Cox**	**3336**
A	Nuneaton Borough	W 2-1	Cox, Taylor	639
H	**Sheppey United (FAC)**	**W 3-0**	**Scott S. (2), Sullivan**	**472**
A	Boston United	L 0-3		1202
H	Wealdstone	L 0-2		462
H	Bath City	L 0-1		505
H	**Cheltenham Town (FAT)**	**L 0-1**		**499**
A	Maidstone United	L 1-2	Pearce	457
H	Stafford Rangers	D 1-1	Gayle	419
H	Barnet	W 2-1	Taylor (2)	539
H	Barrow	W 3-1	Day A.	784
A	Stafford Rangers	L 1-3		448
H	Frickley Athletic	D 0-0	Head, Scott S.	450
A	Frickley Athletic	L 2-3		594
H	Kidderminster Harriers	L 0-1	Gayle (2, pen)	486
A	Barrow	L 0-1		365
H	Telford United	L 1-4	Scott S.	462
H	Runcorn	L 2-3	Gayle (2)	474
A	Dartford	D 1-1	Taylor	399
A	Kettering Town	W 2-0	Gayle, Taylor	896
A	Altrincham	L 1-3	Taylor	652
H	Scarborough	D 0-0		426
A	Wycombe Wanderers	D 1-1	Gayle	537
A	Northwich Victoria	W 1-0	Coles	367
A	Runcorn	D 1-1	Jacobs	629

FAC = F.A. Cup
FAT = F.A. Trophy
BLT = Bob Lord Trophy
ESC = Essex Senior Cup

Appearances:
(All matches); Scott S. 60, Day C. 58, Coles 56, Dunwell 55, Horan 54, Taylor 54, Jacobs 50, Sullivan 47, Risk 43, Cox 38, Manderson 29, Baxter 25, McCombe 23, Whitton 23, Gayle 21, Banfield 20, Head 19, Powell 19, Turnpenny 19, Williams 19, Day A. 16, Campbell 15, Pearce 14, Scott C. 8, Timson 7, Cribb 6, Boniface 5, Giles 5, Browne 3, Murphy 3, Daniel 2, Harmeston 2, Jobson 2, Reber 2, Reeves 2, Waters 2, Armstrong 1, Beadle 1, Blackhall 1, Capper 1, Cowley 1, Emmerson 1, Flynn 1, Kelly 1, Kidney 1, Lindsay 1, Mahoney 1, Ryan 1, Tucker 1, Wilkinson 1

Goalscorers:
(All matches); Scott S. 12, Cox 11, Taylor 9, Gayle 8, McCombe 5, Sullivan 5, Whitton 5, Dunwell 4, Manderson 4, Powell 4, Head 3, Turnpenny 3, Coles 2, Risk 2, Boniface 1, Capper 1, Cribb 1, Day A. 1, Flynn 1, Harmeston 1, Jacobs 1, Kidney 1, Pearce 1, O.G. 1

A floodlit view of Dagenhams main stand Photo: David Hills

DAGENHAM

President: Vic Sparrow
Chairman: Norman Sparrow
Manager: Tony Jennings
Asst. Manager:
Coach: Norman Milne
Physiotherapist: Ken Steggles

Secretary: Fred H. Hawthorn
Address & Tel. No. c/o Dagenham F.C. 01 592 7194 (evenings)

Commercial Manager: Mrs Elaine Coney
Address & Tel. No. 01 593 3864

Press Officer & Tel. No. Bill Bridges, Hornchurch 58879
Address and Tel. No. of ground: Victoria Road Ground, Dagenham, Essex, RM10 7XL. 01 592 1549 (Reception), 01 592 7194 (office)
Simple ground directions: On A1112 between A12 and A13. By rail, LT District Line to Dagenham East. Turn left out of station. Victoria Road is the fifth turning on the left
Club shop: Yes
No. of seats: 500 **Covered accommodation:** 5,000 **Capacity:** 9,000 **Floodlights:** Yes
Year formed: 1949 **Nickname:** The Daggers **Club sponsor:**
Previous names: None
Club colours: All red
Previous grounds: The Arena, Old Dagenham Park
Change colours: All yellow
Day for midweek home matches: Monday
Club metal badges: Yes, £1.50 incl. p & p
Record attendance: 7,100 v Reading F.A. Cup **Year:** 1968
Best performance in: **F.A. Cup:** 1984-5 Third Rd v Carlisle United
F.A. Trophy: 1979-80 Winners
Previous Leagues: Metropolitan, Delphian, Corinthian, Athenian, Isthmian
Clubhouse details: Four bars, two halls, offices etc. Various entertainment throughout the year. Open every day, normal 'pub' hours
Present players with Football League experience: Clive Day
Past players who progressed into the Football League: M. Lazarus (Orient, QPR etc), J. Compton (Chelsea, Ipswich), A. Marshall (Colchester), E. May (Southend, Wrexham, Swansea), M. Newman (West Ham), Peter Kitchen (Chester), Danny Greaves (Cambridge Utd), Dave Hubbick (Colchester)
Record transfer fee paid: To Harrow Borough for Eddie Stein
Record transfer fee received: For George Duck and Steven Jones (Exchange)
Programme details: 35p
Club Captain (1985-86): Various
Programme editor: Fred Hawthorn
Player of the Year (1985-86): Tommy Horan
Local newspapers & Tel. No. Post 01 593 8100, Advertiser 0708 66044. Local radio stations: LBC, Capital Radio, Essex
Major Honours: F.A. Challenge Trophy & Runners-up, F.A. Amateur Cup Runners-up (2), London Senior Cup & Runners-up (2), Essex Senior Cup (6) & Runners-up (4), Isthmian League Premier Division Runners-up (2)

ENFIELD

Gola League 1st **F.A. Trophy** S.F. **F.A. Cup** 1st Rd **M.S.C.** 1st Rd
Bob Lord Trophy 2nd Rd

Enfield: *Back Row (L-R): Keith Barrett, David Flint, Andy Pape, Neil Baxter (physiotherapist), Eddie McCluskey (manager), Dave Jones (trainer), Mark Poultney, John Cooper, David Martin, Dave Howell Middle Row: Martin Duffield, Carl Richards, Nigel Gray, Noel Ashford, Paul Baxter, Mark Furneaux Front Row: Steve King, Keith Hayzelden, Phil Stacey, John Decker, Dermot Drummy* Photo: North London & Hamps Newspapers Ltd

CHAMPIONS AGAIN

Enfield were just about everyone's choice as the best footballing side in the Gola League last season and as such, Eddie McCluskey's side were rewarded with the Championship.

While producing consistently outstanding performances in the league, highlighted by their 4-1 victory at Altrincham, Enfield found the cup competitions less profitable. A good run in the Trophy ended at the semi-final stage for the second consecutive year, giving Alty a little revenge. But surprise defeats in the F.A. Cup, at home to Bognor Regis Town, the County Cup away to Finchley, and over two legs to Dartford were disappointing.

However the good days were far more frequent than the bad and the consistent goalscoring of Carl Richards and the delightful football played throughout the season must have brought immense pleasure to the Enfield regulars.

Keith Hayzeldon on the ball against Frickley Athletic Photo: J. Vass

This season will really sort out the men from the boys as all ambitious clubs strengthen their sides in a bid to claim the first automatic promotion place into the Fourth Divison. If the professionalism and sheer class showed on and off the field at Enfield over the last six years is anything to go by, it will take a very special club to prevent them making that place their own.

Last season's side contained England Internationals Keith Barrett, Andy Pape, David Howell, Carl Richards and Noel Ashford, Nicky Ironton, while Eddie McCluskey has kept his squad consistently challenging for honours by sensible additions each year. No doubt he will again have 'plugged' any gaps that needed strengthening and with the experienced off-the-field team having worked together under chairman Tommy Unwin for many years now, they must be the best equipped club to take up the next G.M. Vauxhall Conference challenge this season.

T.W.

ENFIELD

Goalkeepers
Andy Pape: Feltham, QPR, Charlton, Ikast (Den), Harrow Borough
Mark Poultney*: Local

Defenders
Keith Barrett: Barking, Tottenham Hotspur
Keith Hayzelden: Leytonstone-Ilford, Fulham
Nigel Gray: Orient, Brentford, Swindon
Dave Howell: Harow Borough, Hillingdon, Fulham
Phil Stacey: Leytonstone-Ilford
Mark Furneaux: Local
David Martin: Tottenham Hotspur

Midfield
Dermot Drummy: Hendon, Arsenal
Peter Hinds: Local
John Cooper: Helsingborg (Swe), Tottenham Hotspur
Martin Duffield: QPR
Nicky Ironton: Barking, QPR
John Docker*: Barnet, Notts Co., QPR

Forwards
David Flint: Leyton County
Noel Ashford: Fulham, Barking
Carl Richards: Dulwich Hamlet
Steve King: Leytonstone-Ilford
Mark Buglione: Local

Steve King scores v Chelmsford City in the F.A. Trophy **Photo: J. Vass**

ENFIELD GOLA LEAGUE SEASON 1985-6

Venue	Opponents	Result	Scorers	Att.
A	Frickley Athletic	W 4-1	Howell, Duffield, King (2)	426
A	**Wealdstone (MSCF)**	**L 2-4**	**Ashford (2)**	**805**
H	Cheltenham Town	W 1-0	Howell	597
A	Kettering Town	L 1-2	King	1354
A	Northwich Victoria	D 2-2	Ashford, Richards	785
H	Kettering Town	D 1-1	King	570
H	Barrow	W 4-0	Docker, Duffield, Richards (2)	546
A	Boston United	W 2-1	Docker, King	1345
A	Stafford Rangers	D 1-1	Hayzelden (pen)	1226
H	Dartford	W 1-0	Ashford	631
A	Wycombe Wanderers	L 0-1		1068
H	Dagenham	W 3-1	Drummy, O.G.	664
H	Telford United	W 4-0	Duffield (2), Richards (2)	728
A	Dagenham	W 2-0	Duffield, Ironton	836
A	Wealdstone	W 4-2	Howell, Richards, King (2)	1323
H	Boston United	W 3-0	Ironton (2), Ashford	777
H	Bath City	W 3-1	Ironton, Richards, King	770
A	**Barnet (FAC)**	**W 7-0**	**Hayzelden, Ironton, Ashford, Richards (3), King**	**1841**
A	Weymouth	D 2-2	Howell, Flint	1506
H	**Dartford (BLT)**	**L 1-2**	**Flint**	**646**
H	**Bognor R (FAC)**	**L 0-2**		**1340**
A	**Finchley (MSC)**	**L 0-2**		**150**
A	Runcorn	D 1-1	Ashford	679
A	**Dartford (BLT)**	**D 1-1**	**Ashford**	**495**
H	Altrincham	D 1-1	Richards	945
A	Nuneaton Borough	W 5-1	Drummy, Ashford (3), Richards	753
A	Kidderminster	W 2-1	Drummy, Flint	649
A	Maidstone United	D 3-3	Ashford, Richards (2)	715
H	Weymouth	D 4-4	Ironton, Ashford, Richards, Flint	808
H	**Waterlooville (FAT)**	**W 3-0**	**Ironton, Duffield, Richards**	**610**
A	Barnet	W 1-0	Richards	1455
H	Stafford Rangers	W 3-1	Ironton (2), Drummy	1016
H	Kidderminster	D 2-2	Richards, O.G.	801
H	**Maidstone (FAT)**	**W 3-2**	**Ashford (2), Richards**	**1019**
H	Wycombe Wanderers	L 2-3	Duffield (pen), King	1112
H	Runcorn	W 2-0	Hinds, Richards	696
H	**Chelmsford (FAT)**	**W 5-3**	**Hinds (2), Richards (2), King**	**1445**
H	Barnet	W 1-0	Ashford	772
A	Dartford	W 3-2	Richards (3)	381
H	Nuneaton Borough	W 3-2	Hinds, Dufffield (pen), Richards	826
A	**South Bank (FAT)**	**W 2-0**	**Hinds, O.G.**	**2384**
A	Altrincham	W 4-1	Hinds, Duffield, Richards (2)	1340
A	Barrow	W 2-1	Ashford (2)	363
A	Scarborough	W 3-1	Richards (3)	726
H	**Altrincham (FAT s.f.)**	**D 1-1**	**Docker**	**1804**
A	**Altrincham (FAT s.f.2)**	**L 0-2**		**2134**
A	Cheltenham Town	L 0-2		1196
H	Frickley Athletic	W 3-1	Howell, Ashford, Richards	915
H	Northwich Victoria	W 1-0	O.G.	781
H	Maidstone United	L 1-3	Howell	805
A	Telford United	D 2-2	Duffield (pen), Richards	1557
H	Wealdstone	W 1-0	Richards	1024
A	Bath City	W 2-0	Hinds, Buglione	522
H	Scarborough	W 4-0	Stacey, Hinds, Flint, King	710

MSC = Middlesex Senior Cup
FAC = F.A. Cup
BLT = Bob Lord Trophy
FAT = F.A. Trophy

Appearances:
League (42), Cup (12); Pape 53, King 52 + 1, Barrett 50 + 1, Richards 50 + 1, Duffield 47, Ashford 45 + 1, Hayzelden 40, Cooper 37 + 1, Ironton 36 + 1, Drummy 35 + 3, Howell 35 + 1, Docker 32 + 3, Gray 28 + 4, Hinds 18 + 4, Flint 16 + 15, Stacey 7 + 3, Furneaux 6 + 1, Radovic 3 + 3, Baxter 2, Buglione 1, Poultney 1, Martin 0 + 1

Goalscorers:
League (94), Cup (25); Richards 35, Ashford 19 (2 pens), King 12, Duffield 10 (4 pens), Ironton 9, Hinds 8, Howell 6, Flint 5, Drummy 4, Docker 3, Buglione 1, Hayzelden 1 (1 pen), Stacey 1, O.G. 5

The Stadium, Enfield

ENFIELD

President:
Chairman: Tom Unwin
Manager: Eddie McCluskey
Asst. Manager:
Coach: Ian Wolstenholme
Physiotherapist: Neil Baxter

Secretary: K.Wortley
Address & Tel. No. 9 Smarts Green, Cheshunt, Herts EN7 6BB. 97 20169

Commercial Manager: J. Jefferson
Address & Tel. No. 25 Bycullah Road, Enfield

Press Officer & Tel. No. John Jefferson 01 363 6273
Address and Tel. No. of ground: The Stadium, Southbury Road, Enfield, Middx. 01 363 2858
Simple ground directions: Train to Enfield Town (any bus passes ground). Train to Southbury 5 minutes walk
Club shop: Yes
No. of seats: 1850 **Covered accommodation:** All 4 sides **Capacity:** 7,500 **Floodlights:** Yes
Year formed: 1900 **Nickname:** None **Club sponsor:** Sampson Coaches
Previous names: None
Previous grounds: Cherry Orchard Lane
Day for midweek home matches: Tuesday
Club colours: All white/blue trim
Change colours: All yellow
Club metal badges: Yes
Record attendance: 35,000 v Barnsley F.A. Cup 4th Rd at Spurs **Year:** 1981
Best performance in: F.A. Cup: 1980-1 4th Rd replay
F.A. Trophy: 1981-2 Winners
Previous Leagues: Athenian, Isthmian
Clubhouse details: Club bar open every lunchtime and evening, snacks available. Starlight night club, cabaret, dine and dance as per programme. Tel. 363 3127 or 363 2858
Present players with Football League experience: John Cooper, Nigel Gray, Martin Duffield
Past players who progressed into the Football League: Peter Feeley (Chelsea), Terry Hurlock (Brentford)
Record transfer fee paid: None available
Record transfer fee received: None available
Programme details: 32 pages, 40p
Programme editor: Ken Brazier and Lee Harding
Club Captain (1985-86): Noel Ashford
Player of the Year (1985-86): Carl Richards
Local newspapers & Tel. No. Enfield Gazette 01 441 3003, Enfield Independent, Enfield Advertiser
Major Honours: F.A. Trophy, F.A. Amateur Cup, Isthmian League, Athenian League, Middlesex Senior Cup, London Senior Cup, Alliance Champions, Alliance Charity Shield, Gola League Champions

FRICKLEY ATHLETIC

Gola League R.U. | **F.A. Trophy** 3rd Rd | **F.A. Cup** 3rd Rd | **S.S.C.** Winners

Frickley Athletic: *Back Row (L-R): P. Wilson, S. Daniels, W. Hoteman, T. Meeham, M. Wright, S. Marshall, A. Semley. Front Row: Gary Hatto, P. Shirtliff, P. Howey, C. Bishop, G. Mallender.* Photo: John Womack

Season 1985-86 got off to a bad start when the team found themselves four goals down with the season only 40 minutes old, this was at Westfield Lane against Enfield, who later finished as champions. The second half was an improvement with the goal flood being stopped and the Blues scoring a consolation goal. From this point a steady improvement took place and the team were undefeated for the next three games, they then lost the next two. After these defeats the gradual improvement continued and they went seven games before losing at Telford. After the defeat at Telford they bounced back to beat Boston 5-1 in the next game.

The season continued to improve with a good 2-1 win against Northwich Victoria in the Fourth Qualifying round of the F.A. Cup. In the First Round Proper draw of the F.A. Cup things looked favourable with the club being drawn at home to Halesowen Town. The Blues however got a shock with the quality of the Halesowen side and could only manage a draw. The replay however was entirely different when in front of a crowd of 2973 the Blues dominated the game and came away 3-1 winners, to go into the Second Round draw for the second year in succession.

Touchline action during Frickley's visit to Enfield. Photo: J. Vass

The draw this time was not favourable and once again the team had to travel to the North East this time to play Hartlepool.

This game started with the Pool throwing everything they had at the Blue's but the defence held out and after about twenty minutes the game levelled out. Shortly after this the Blues were awarded a penalty, but once again Lady Luck was against them and this ideal opportunity to take the lead was missed. As the game wore on and it started to appear as if a replay was on the cards the Blues started to take the control of the game and in the 74th minute Paul Wilson was on hand to blast the winning goal into the Hartlepool net from close range, to take the Blues into the Third Round for the first time in their history.

Although the draw favoured the Blues it was not to be their day and on conditiosn more favourable to ice skating than football Rotherham adapted themselves better and came out on top 3-1. Once again the Blues missed a penalty.

Frickley returned to the domestic scene of league football and continued with the steady climb up the league table, with the climax coming in the very last game of the season.

The team had to win the game which was at Bath City to finish runners-up, a draw would only give them third place. The team took the lead after about 4 minutes but Bath equalised a short while later, and it was not until the 83rd minute that the Blues regained the lead which in turn gave them the runners-up spot.

Sandwiched somewhere between the F.A. Cup glory and the end of season climax the team also managed to win the Sheffield Senior Challenge Cup (County Cup).

FRICKLEY ATHLETIC SQUAD 1985-86

Goalkeepers
Tommy Meehan: Sheffield Utd, Barnsley, Worksop
Paul Maxted: Pontefract Colliery

Defenders
Paul Shirtliff: Sheffield Wednesday, Northampton (England)
Sean Marshall: Scarborough (England Schools)
Steve Daniels: Doncaster
Mally Wright: Scarborough, Leeds, Ashley Road
Steve Myley: Sheffield Wednesday, Worksop Town, Chesterfield
Colin Bishop: Local

Midfield
Barry Gill: Barnsley, Scarborough
Peter Howey: Newport County, Leeds, Huddersfiled, Scarborough
Russ Wilcox: Doncaster, Cambridge Utd, (England)
Gary Mallender: Sheffield Utd, Boston Utd

Forwards
Paul Wilson: Denaby Utd (England)
Gary Hodley: Altrincham, Scarborough (England)
Wayne Noteman: Harrogate Town
Gary Hatto: Huddersfield, Doncaster
Martin Clark: Pontefract Colliery
Alan Semley: Matlock Town
Will Foley: York City

Paul Wilson challenging Gary Mallender of Rotherham United in the F.A. Cup Second Round.
South Yorkshire Times

FRICKLEY ATHLETIC GOLA LEAGUE SEASON 1985-6

Venue	Opponents	Result	Scorers	Att.
H	Enfield	L 1-4	Hoyland	624
A	Barrow	D 2-2	Hoyland, Hatto	585
H	Kidderminster H.	W 3-1	Hoyland, Wilson, Hatto	312
H	Altrincham	D 0-0		363
A	Wealdstone	L 0-2		702
A	Altrincham	L 0-1		940
H	Dartford	W 1-0	Hatto	325
H	**Northwich V. (BLT1/1)**	**L 0-1**		**389**
A	Barnet	W 2-1	Hoyland, Wilcox	523
A	**Northwich V. (BLT1/2)**	**W 4-0**	**Bishop (2), Hoyland (2)**	**660**
H	Maidstone United	W 2-0	Noteman, Clark	476
H	Barrow	W 2-0	Noteman, Howey	466
A	Cheltenham T.	D 1-1	Hatto	1007
A	Boston United	W 3-0	Wilson (3)	1330
H	Stafford Rangers	W 3-0	Wilson, Wilcox (2)	587
A	Telford United	L 1-2	Howey	1013
H	**Northwich V. (FAC4q)**	**H 2-1**	**Noteman, Mallender**	**961**
H	Boston United	W 5-1	Wilson (2), Foley (3)	569
H	**Telford United (BLT2/1)**	**W 4-0**	**McGinty (og), Foley (2), Noteman**	**573**
H	**Sheffield Cen. (SSC1)**	**W 5-1**	**Bishop, Hatto (2), Wilson, Shirtliff**	**207**
A	Kettering Town	L 0-2		768
H	**Halesowen Town (FAC1)**	**D 1-1**	**Bishop**	**1720**
H	**Halesowen Town (FAC1r)**	**W 3-1**	**Bishop, Wilson, Wilcox**	**2973**
H	Nuneaton Borough	D 2-2	Shirtliff, Wilson	587
A	**Telford United (BLT2/2)**	**L 0-1**		**626**
A	Dartford	W 2-1	Wilson, Hooley	465
A	**Hartlepool United (FAC2)**	**W 1-0**	**Wilson**	**4100**
A	**Dearne Community (SSC2)**	**W 5-3**	**Gill, Hatto, Hooley (3)**	**284**
A	Northwich V.	W 3-2	Wright, Hooley, Foley	660
A	**Bedworth United (FAT1)**	**D 1-1**	**Foley**	**298**
H	Scarborough	W 2-1	Mallender, Hooley	787
H	**Bedworth United (FAT1r)**	**W 5-0**	**Foley (2), Noteman, Gill, Wilson**	**674**
H	**Rotherham United (FAC3)**	**L 1-3**	**Bishop**	**5923**
A	**Treeton Welfare (SSC3)**	**W 4-1**	**Wright, Hatto, Mallender (2)**	**319**
A	Runcorn	D 2-2	Hooley Wilcox	351
A	**Wealdstone (FAT2)**	**L 1-2**	**Wilcox**	**841**
H	Northwich V.	W 1-0	Howey	517
A	Stafford Rangers	A 0-0		925
A	Maidstone United	L 2-3	Wilcox, Bishop	541
H	**Worksop T. (SSC Semi)**	**W 3-0**	**Noteman, Hooley, Hatto**	**540**
A	**Runcorn (BLT3)**	**L 2-6**	**Mallender, Hotte**	**427**
A	Scarborough	W 3-2	Hooley (2), Coleby (og)	392
H	Barnet	D 3-3	Hooley, Wilson, Wilcox	518
H	Bath City	W 2-1	Howey, Wilson	417
H	Wycombe Wanderers	D 2-2	Burgess (og), Wilcox	537
H	Telford United	W 3-1	Wilson, Howey, Wilcox	419
A	Dagenham	D 0-0		448
H	Dagenham	W 3-2	Hooley, Wilson, Noteman	450
H	Wealdstone	W 2-1	Hooley, Wilcox	535
A	Wycombe Wanderers	D 3-1	Wilson, Wilcox, Mallender	862
H	Weymouth	W 1-0	Noteman	550
***N**	**Crookes (SSC Final)**	**W 2-0**	**Wilcox, Hooley**	**625**
A	Enfield	L 1-3	Noteman	715
A	Nuneaton Borough	L 1-0	Hatto	762
A	Weymouth	W 3-0	Wright, Howey, Wilson	892
H	Runcorn	W 3-1	Wilcox, Wilson, Hooley	610
H	Kettering Town	W 3-0	Wilcox, Wilson, Hooley	576
A	Kidderminster H.	D 1-1	Hooley	1237
H	Cheltenham Town	H 2-1	Gill, Wilson	575
A	Bath City	W 2-1	Noteman, Hooley	631

* — At Worksop Town FC

Goalscorers:
Wilson 22, Hooley 18, Wilcox 15, Hatto 10, Foley 9, Bishop 7, Howey 6, Hoyland 6, Mallender 6, Gill 3, Wright 3, Shirtliff 2, Clark 1, Hotte 1, Own Goals 3.

FRICKLEY ATHLETIC

President: M. Twiby
V. Chairman: J. Barber
Manager: Sean Marshall, York (0904) 34300
Asst. Manager:
Coach:
Physiotherapist:
Press Officer & Tel. No. P. Maylor
Secretary: R.L. Bates
Address & Tel. No. South Elmshall (0977) 44575
Commercial Manager: F. Wilcox (Full Time)
Address & Tel. No.
Address and Tel. No. of ground: Westfield Lane, South Elmshall, Pontefract, W. Yorks
Simple ground directions: A 63 (North) From A1 to South Elmshall, Westfield Lane, Turn left opposite Westfield Hotel down Oxford Street.
Club shop: Yes
No. of seats: 850 **Covered accommodation:** 2,000 **Capacity:** 8,500 **Floodlights:** Yes
Year formed: 1910 **Nickname:** The Blues **Club sponsor:** Reading Bailey
Previous names: Frickley Colliery
Previous grounds:
Day for midweek home matches: Tuesday
Club colours: Blue
Change colours: All White or Yellow and Red
Club metal badges: Yes
Record attendance:
Best performance in: F.A. Cup:
F.A. Trophy:
Previous Leagues: Sheffield County, Yorkshire, Midland, Cheshire County, Northern Premier
Clubhouse details: Social Club outside Ground
Present players with Football League experience: Barry Gill, Sean Marshall, Tommy Meehan, Russ Wilcox, Mally Wright, Phil Campbell, Peter Howey, Steve Daniels, Will Foley.
Recent players who progressed into the Football League: Derek Downing, Graham Reed, Will Foley
Record transfer fee paid: £1,500 Dave Smith
Record transfer fee received: £7,000 Peter Howey (Scarborough)
Programme details: 30 pages 25p
Programme editor: R.L. Bates (Sec)
Club Captain (1985-86): Mally Wright
Player of the Year (1985-86): Russ Wilcox 1985-86
Local newspapers & Tel. No. South Yorkshire Times, Hemsworth and South Elmshall Express
Major Honours: Midland League Cup, Sheffield Senior Cup (3), Gola League Runners Up

GATESHEAD

Multipart League Winners **F.A. Trophy** 1st Rd **F.A. Cup** 3rd Rd **S.S.C.** Winner

Gateshead: *Back Row (L-R): P. Doolan, P. O'Hagan, D. Mitchinson, S. Smith, D. Parnaby, M. Fagan, D. Bell.* *Front Row: S. Higgins, B. Wardrobe, R. Hulse, P. Hampson, J. Robson, K McNall, M. Henderson, B. Stimpson.*

After relegation at the end of 1984-85 it would have been quite natural for the Tynesiders to take a while to regain confidence and find their feet. After winning 2-0 at Witton in the opening match however, Gateshead went on to lose only once in their first ten league matches to establish themselves as early front runners.

Strenthened by new signings Stimpson and Smith the defence had a more solid look to it, while McNall especially was scoring with great regularity. Only Macclesfield seemed capable of posing a threat during the first third of the season. Even the long term absence of Parnaby the club captain and Donaldson the previous season's top scorer did not pose problems for a team riding high.

Injury and loss of form caused a slump in the Tynesiders' results in mid-season during which period they suffered their only home defeats of the season — against rivals Macclesfield and bogey side Workington. Macclesfield though suffered a greater collapse in the second half of the season allowing Morecambe to establish themselves as the Geordies' main rivals.

In mid March, Gateshead began a run of twelve games with only one defeat but less than a fornight later were rocked when Chairman/Manager Ray Wilkie quit the club to join Gola League Strugglers Barrow. Within days of Wilkie's departure the caretaker managerial team had to prepare for the crunch match against Morecambe. Slack defensive play gave the Shrimps a 2-1 half time lead but in the second half Gateshead showed their character and team spirit, which were their halmarks all season, to hit three goals and effectively kill off their rivals promotion hopes.

By the time Gateshead had clinched promotion in the last home game, an incredible 15 players had scored in the League showing the club's strength in depth. Donaldson, back from injury, scored seven in his last ten appearances.

Sadly the Tynesiders League from was not reflected in the cups where a disastrous run of defeats against lesser teams continued.. For the record Won 2 drawn 2 lost 4 was the final, tally, certainly 'concentrating on the League' is a much phrase in Gateshead.

GATESHEAD

Goalkeepers
Simon Smith: Whitley Bay, Newcastle United

Defenders
Paul Dooland: Local
Steve Higgins: Local
Mike Fagan: Consett, Hartlepool (41-1), Carlisle United
Dave Parnaby: Durham City, Whitey Town, Willington
Dave Mitchinson: Takapuna City (N.Z.), Blyth Spartans, Gateshead, Whitley Bay
Paul O'Hagan: Sunderland
Barrie Stimpson: Hartlepool (18), Chesterfield (27), Hartlepool (68-2)

Midfield
Bryan Robson: Carlisle United (11-1), Sunderland (12-3), Chelsea (15-3), Carlisle United (48-21), Sunderland (52-23), West Ham (107-47), Sunderland (90-34), West Ham (120-47), Newcastle United (206-81)
Kevin Pugh: Darlington (7), Gateshead, Newcastle United (1)
Justin Robson: Newcastle United
Derek Bell: Blue Star, Newcastle United
Barry Wardrobe: Hartlepool (27-17

Forwards
Keith McNall: Crook Town
Ian Donaldson: North Shields, Ashington
Martin Henderson: Durham City, Crook Town
Les Mutrie: Hartlepool (18-4), Colchester United (14-2), Hull City (115-49), Blyth Spartans, Carlisle United (5), Gateshead, Ashington

Terry Hibbitt (then captain, now manager) lifts the N.P.L. Championship Trophy back in 1983.

GATESHEAD MULTIPART LEAGUE RECORD 1985-6

Venue	Opponents	Result	Scorers
A	Witton Albion	W 2-0	McNall (2)
A	Workington	L 2-4	Mitchinson, Henderson
A	Chorley	D 1-1	Bell
H	Gainsborough Trinity	W 4-0	Stimpson, Bell, Robson J, McNall
A	**Billingham Synthonia (FAC)**	**W 4-0**	**McNall (2), Bell, Henderson**
H	**Worksop Town**	**W 2-0**	**McNall, Henderson**
A	**Burton Albion**	**W 3-1**	**Davies, Bell, Higgins**
A	**Worksop Town**	**W 2-1**	**Davies, Robson J**
H	**Rhyl**	**W 5-1**	**Parnaby, Robson J, Bell, Stimpson, McNall**
A	**Goole Town**	**W 2-0**	**Davies, Higgins**
A	**Spennymoor United (FAC)**	**W 2-1**	**Henderson, Davies**
H	Matlock Town	D 2-2	Henderson, Robson J
A	Macclesfield Town	L 0-1	
H	Buxton	W 5-0	McNall (3), Henderson
A	**South Bank (FAC)**	**D 2-2**	**McNall, Mitchinson**
H	**South Bank (FAC)**	**D 1-1**	**McNall**
H	Hyde United	D 1-1	Davies
H	**South Bank (FAC)**	**L 1-2**	**Henderson**
H	Goole Town	W 2-0	McNall, Bell
H	Macclesfield Town	L 1-3	Henderson
A	Buxton	W 5-1	McNall (2), Stimpson (2), Own Goal
A	**Chorley (NPLC)**	**L 1-2**	**Robson B**
H	**Marine**	**D 1-1**	**Fagan**
A	**Gainsborough Trinity**	**D 2-2**	**McNall, Henderson**
A	**Southport**	**L 1-3**	**Mitchinson**
H	**Witton Albion**	**W 2-0**	**McNall (2)**
A	**Southport (FAC)**	**L 0-2**	
H	Bangor City	W 3-0	McNall, Bell, Stimpson
H	**Chorley (NPLC)**	**L 1-3**	**Robson J**
H	Workington	L 0-2	
H	Horwich RMI	W 3-1	McNall, Fagan, Davies
H	South Liverpool	W 1-0	Robson J
A	South Liverpool	W 2-1	Henderson, Fagan
A	Caernarfon Town	D 2-2	Lowe, Davies
A	Morecambe	L 0-2	
H	Southport	W 3-1	Lowe, Donaldson, McNall
A	Mossley	D 0-0	
A	Marine	L 1-3	McNall
H	Mossley	W 2-0	McNall, Bell
H	Chorley	W 1-0	Donaldson
H	Burton Albion	W 2-0	Wardrobe, Robson J
H	Morecombe	W 4-2	Mitchinson, McNall, Hulse, Henderson
A	Bangor City	W 2-0	Stimpson (2)
A	Horwich RMI	L 1-2	McNall
H	Caernarfon Town	W 3-2	McNall, Donaldson, Parnaby
A	Oswestry Town	W 1-0	Donaldson
A	Rhyl	W 3-2	Donaldson(2), Stimpson

Appearances: (42 League and 8 Cup-ties)
Smith 50, Doolan 49, Fagan 49, Stimpson 48, McNall 46, Robson J 45, Henderson 42 + 1, Bell 41, Mitchinson 39 + 1, Davieș 32 + 4, Higgins 25 + 1, Parnaby 20 + 3, Donaldson 15 + 1, Wardrobe 11 + 2, Hampson 11, Robson B 6 + 1, Lowe 6, Hulse 5 + 2, Ord 2 + 1, O'Hagan 2, O'Donnell 0 + 1

Goalscorers: (League (85)
McNall 23, Stimpson 10, Henderson 9, Bell 7, Donaldson 7, Robson J 7, Davies 6, Fagan 3, Mitchinson 3, Higgins 2, Lowe 2, Parnaby 2, Hampson 1, Hulse 1, Wardrobe 1, Own Goal 1, Cups (11) McNall 4, Henderson 3, Bell 1, Davies 1, Mitchinson 1, Robson B1

GATESHEAD

President: J.C Thomas
Chairman: E.J. Hall
Manager: T.A. (Terry) Hibbitt
Asst. Manager: G. Ramshaw
Coach:
Physiotherapist: P. Garvie

Secretary: J.L. Battla
Address & Tel. No. 27 Earlswood Avenue, Gateshead, NE9 GAH 091 487 8782 (H) 091 487 8822 x 6221 (B)

Commercial Manager: E.J. Hall
Address & Tel. No. Gateshead Football Social Club, Sunderland Road, Gateshead NE10 OBU, 091 477 6464 (phone number may change

Press Officer & Tel. No.
Address and Tel. No. of ground: International Stadium, Neilson Road, Gateshead NE10 0EF 091-478 3883 (Gateshead FC direct line)
Simple ground directions: From North/South A6127 to town centre then A6115 (South Shields/sunderland) for about one mile. Ground left at first traffic lights. By public transport: Metro to Gateshead Stadium Station turn right out of station then right at main road.
Club shop: Yes
No. of seats: 7,300 **Covered accommodation:** 3,300 **Capacity:** 14,000 **Floodlights:** Yes
Year formed: 1977 **Nickname:Tynesiders** **Club sponsor:**
Previous names: Gateshead FC Ltd was formed to replace Gateshead United whi in turn had replaced Gateshead AFC Ltd in 1973
Club colours: White Shirts, Navy Shorts
Previous grounds:
Change colours: Red Shirts, White Shorts
Day for midweek home matches: Wednesday
Club metal badges: Yes
Record attendance: 5012 v Newcastle Utd, testemonial 20 August 1984 (Gateshead AFC record: 20,752 v Lincoln City 1937)
Best performance in: F.A. Cup:
F.A. Trophy:
Previous Leagues: Northern Premier 1977-83, Alliance Premier 1983-85, Northern Premier 1985-86
Clubhouse details:
Present players with Football League experience: Derek Bell (Newcastle), Mick Fagan (Hartlepool), Terry Hibbitt (Leeds, Newcastle, Birmingham) Barry Wardrobe (Hartlepool)
Past players who progressed into the Football League: O. Williams (Southampton, Stockport, Port Vale), J. McGinley (Sunderland, Lincoln), L. Pearson (Hull) K. Dodds (Hartlepool)
Record transfer fee paid: £1,000 to Sunderland for J. McGinley
Record transfer fee received: £3,000 from Sunderland for J McGinley
Programme details: 20 pages 25p (1985-86)
Club Captain (1985-86): David Parnaby
Programme editor: Harry Gaffing 091 487 3307 (H)
Player of the Year (1985-86): Barrie Stimpson
Local newspapers & Tel. No. Gatehead Post 091 447 3245 Journal and Evening Chronicle 091 232 7500, Radio: Metro, 091 488 3131, BBC: 091 281 4243
Major Honours: Northern Premier League Champions

KETTERING TOWN

Gola League 9th **F.A. Trophy** S.F. **F.A. Cup** 4th Qual Rd **C.S.C.** W
Bob Lord Trophy 1st Rd

Kettering Town: *Back Row (L-R): Mark Geeson (physio), Richard Dawson, Alan McIlwain, Keith Alexander, Mark Harrison, Greg Fee, Ian Crawley, Ian Wood, Malcolm Watts (assistant). Front Row (L-R): Doug Keast, Steve Hines, John Sellers, Jim Kabia, David Needham (manager), David Wharton, Mark Smith, Tim Thacker, Billy Jeffrey*

Last season proved to be a topsy turvey affair for Kettering. A great start lifted morale and four wins with three draws in the first seven games brought thirteen goals and high hopes for the campaign ahead

This impresseive start was immediately followed by fourteen games without a win and left everyone thoroughly bewildered. They had made an exit from three cup competitions including the F.A. Cup and where was it all leading?

However three straight League wins put the club back into the right frame of mind for the F.A. Trophy and a tremendous result was acheived against a very confident Sutton United side.

While Kettering did win the County Cup against Corby Town, the highlight of the season had to be their Trophy run, for after the defeat of Sutton, 'The Poppies' followed up by defeating two more highly placed Vauxhall-Opel League clubs in Slough Town (away) and Worthing, after drawing away.

Keeping the Vauxhall-Opel connection, the next club drawn were newly promoted Wycombe Wanderers and perhaps Kettering were lucky to catch them on the rebound as they had just completed a four game marathon with Leek Town in the previous round. An excellent crowd of 2,312 turned out on a chilly evening to see the home side recover from an early deficit and qualify for the Semi-Finals with a 2-1 victory.

To avoid both Enfield and Altrincham with Semi Final draw could be described as lucky but when the club left is of the quality of Runcorn, there really wasn't much to feel elated about. Or would Runcorn freeze again as they had done in three previous Semi-Finals? Perhpaps Runcorn felt they were never meant to reach Wembley?

Those sentiments were certainly considered when the first leg resulted in a 0-0 draw at Runcorn but as Kettering threw everything at the Cheshire club in the second leg the experienced visiting strikers won the game on the break and a dream was shattered.

A sound 9th position was achieved in the league however, the Trophy run did the club a lot of good on and off the field and in Ian Crawley Kettering may have a striker capable of a lot of goals in the seasons ahead. T.W.

KETTERING TOWN SQUAD 1986

Goalkeepers
Mark Harrison: South Africa, Stoke City (8), Port Vale (78), Notts Forest

Defenders
Tim Thacker: Shepshed Charterhouse, Grantham, Notts County
Greg Fee: Bradford City (7)
Ian Wood: King's Lynn, Wellingboro', Boston United, Aldershot (14), Mansfield (149)
Steve Hines: King's Lynn, Stamford, Grantham, Notts Forest
Alan McIlwain: Stamford, Corby Town
John Sellers: Manchester United, Kettering Town

Midfield
Dave Wharton: Shepshed Charterhouse, Eastwood Town
Dick Dawson: Gainsboro' Trinity, Scarborough Town, Chesterfield (12-1), Doncaster (43-14), Rotherham (24-3)
Billy Jeffrey: Northampton (45-4), Blackpool (14-1), Oxford (314-24)
Andy Harrison: Boston United, Burton Albion, New Zealand, Burton Albion
Doug Keast: Shepshed Charterhouse, Hibs

Forwards
Keith Alexander: King's Lynn, Corby, Grantham, Spalding, Stamford, Boston United, Boston F.C.
Mark Smith: Shepshed Charterhouse, Kettering, Buxton, Worksop, Burton Albion, Gainsboro' Trinity, Sheffield United
Ian Crawley: VS Rugby, Nuneaton, Bedworth
Jim Kabia: Burton Albion, Stafford, Boston United, Chesterfield, Derby County

Ian Crawley's magnificent strike rockets past the Wycombe defenders for his first goal

KETTERING TOWN GOLA LEAGUE SEASON 1985-6

Venue	Opponents	Result	Scorers	Att.
A	Altrincham	D 2-2	McGowan (2)	1059
H	Northwich V	W 2-1	McGowan, Watson	1367
A	Nuneaton B	W 3-0	Kabia, Watson, Crawley	1016
H	Enfield	W 2-1	Jeffrey, Shrieves	1354
H	Maidstone United	W 2-0	Keast (2)	1459
A	Enfield	D 1-1	Keast	570
A	Telford United	D 2-2	Keast, Watson	1147
H	**Cheltenham Town (BLT)**	**L 0-1**		**920**
A	**Cheltenham Town (BLT)**	**L 1-5**	**Crawley**	**1293**
A	Dagenham	L 0-1		536
H	Kidderminster H	D 2-2	Crawley, Fee	1015
H	Stafford R	L 0-1		1207
A	Kidderminster H	D 0-0		579
H	Altrincham	D 2-2	McGowan, Smith	1255
H	Dartford	D 2-2	Jeffrey (2)	1016
A	Cheltenham T	L 1-5	Smith	1221
A	**Chelmsford C (FAC)**	**L 0-1**		**1319**
H	**Northampton T (MCF)**	**L 1-2**	**Smith**	**1456**
A	Maidstone United	D 0-0		753
H	Frickley Athletic	W 2-0	Smith, Fee	768
H	Barrow	W 4-2	Keast (2), Fee, Hines	984
H	Wealdstone	W 2-1	Smith (2)	1047
A	Northwich V	D 0-0		519
H	Barnet	D 1-1	Smith	1103
A	Wealdstone	L 1-3	Kabia	653
A	**Sutton U (FAT)**	**W 1-0**	**Jeffrey**	**773**
A	Boston United	L 1-4	Crawley	1553
H	Bath C	W 2-0	Jeffrey, Hines	951
H	Boston United	W 3-1	Crawley (3)	1951
H	Scarborough	D 0-0		1348
A	Barrow	L 0-1		487
A	**Slough T (FAT)**	**W 2-1**	**Fee, Smith**	**871**
H	Telford	W 4-0	Dawson, Kabia, Smith, Jeffrey	1074
A	Weymouth	L 0-1		720
A	**Worthing (FAT)**	**D 0-0**		**602**
H	**Worthing (FAT)**	**W 2-1**	**Smith, Jeffrey**	**1365**
H	Weymouth	L 0-2		999
A	Dartford	W 2-0	Kabia, Jeffrey	456
H	**Wycombe Wanderers (FAT)**	**W 2-1**	**Smith, O.G.**	**2312**
H	**Wellingborough T (CSC s.f.)**	**W 1-0**	**Smith**	**278**
A	**Runcorn (CSC)**	**W 1-0**	**Smith**	**565**
A	**Runcorn (FAT s.f.)**	**D 0-0**		**2023**
H	**Runcorn (FAT s.f.)**	**L 0-2**		**4032**
H	Nuneaton B	L 1-4	Crawley	733
H	Wycombe Wanderers	W 4-1	Crawley (2), Thacker, Jeffrey	662
A	Scarborough	W 3-2	Crawley (2), Kabia	520
H	Dagenham	L 0-2		896
A	Bath C	D 1-1	Kabia	402
H	Runcorn	D 0-0		583
A	Frickley Athletic	L 0-3		576
A	**Corby Town (CSC)**	**W 1-0**	**Keast**	**836**
H	Cheltenham T	W 2-1	Keast, Jeffrey	532
A	Wycombe Wanderers	D 0-0		715
A	Barnet	L 0-3		622
A	Stafford R	D 0-0		851

BLT = Bob Lord Trophy
FAC = F.A. Cup
MCF =
FAT = F.A. Trophy
CSC =

Appearances:
Jeffrey 55, Thacker 54, Wharton 47 + 1, Kabia 46 + 3, Fee 43 + 1, Dawson 38 + 4, Harrison M. 38, Crawley 31 + 9, McIlwain 29 + 1, Hines 29 + 3, Smith 28 + 3, Wood 27, Keast 25 + 2, Harrison A. 25, McGowan 17, Alexander 16 + 10, Sellers 15 + 1, Watson 14, Boyd 13, Gould 7 + 5, Shrieves 4 + 5, Goodwin 3, Torrence 1, Radford 0 + 4

Goalscorers:
League (55); Crawley 11, Smith 8, Jeffrey 8, Keast 7, Kabia 6, McGowan 4, Watson 3, Fee 3, Hines 2, Shrieves 1, Dawson 1, Thacker 1
Cups (11); Smith 5, Jeffrey 2, Crawley 1, Fee 1, Keast 1, O.G. 1

KETTERING TOWN

President:
Chairman: C. Gingell
Manager: D. Needham
Asst. Manager: J. Nixon
Coach:
Physiotherapist: M. Geeson
Press Officer & Tel. No.

Secretary: R. Abraham
Address & Tel. No. 68 Cornwall Road, Kettering. K. 522159
Commercial Manager: G. Ellitson
Address & Tel. No. 2 St Marks Close, Rushden. Rushden 313106

Address and Tel. No. of ground: Rockingham Road, Kettering. Tel: 83028
Simple ground directions: On A6003 Kettering-Oakham
Club shop: Yes
No. of seats: 1,800 **Covered accommodation:** 7,000 **Capacity:** 13,000 **Floodlights:** Yes
Year formed: 1876 **Nickname:** **Club sponsor:** Milas
Previous names: None
Previous grounds: None
Day for midweek home matches: Wednesday
Club colours: All red
Change colours: All yellow
Club metal badges: Yes
Record attendance: 11,526. **Year:** 1947
Best performance in: **F.A. Cup:** 1968-69, 1976-7 3rd Rd
F.A. Trophy: 1978-9 Beaten finalists
Previous Leagues: Midland, Southern, Northampton, Birmingham, Central Alliance
Clubhouse details: Small clubhouse at the ground
Present players with Football League experience: M. Harrison (Stoke City, Port Vale), Billy Jeffrey (Oxford, Blackpool, Northampton), Jim Kabia (Derby, Chesterfield), Dave Watson (Notts County, Sunderland, Manchester City, Southampton, Derby, Notts County), Greg Fee (Bradford City), Richard Dawson (Chesterfield), Ian Wood (Mansfield, Aldershot)
Past players who progressed into the Football League: B. Kellock (Peterborough), G. Wood (Notts County), D. Longhurst (Notts Forest), S. Enderby (Ipswich), S. Fallon (Cambridge United), J. Sellers (Manchester United), A. Rodgers (Plymouth), M. Forster (Northampton), J. Brown (Chesterfield), S. Conroy (Rochdale)
Record transfer fee paid: Nuneaton Borough for Brendan Phillips
Record transfer fee received: Boston United for Brendan Phillips
Programme details: 36 pages, 35p
Programme editor:
Club Captain (1985-86): D. Wharton
Player of the Year (1985-86): D. Wharton
Local newspapers & Tel. No. Evening Telegraph. K. 81111
Major Honours: Trophy finalists, Southern League winners, Southern League Cup winners, County Cup winners, S.L. Merit Cup winners

KIDDERMINSTER HARRIERS

Gola League 3rd **F.A. Trophy** Q.F. **F.A. Cup** 4th Qual Rd **Welsh Cup** Finalists
Worcs. S.C. Winners **Staffs S.C.** Finalists **Bob Lord Trophy** 2nd Rd

Kidderminster Harriers: *Back Row (L-R): Micky Tuohy, Chris Jones, Tim Garner, Trevor Campbell, Paul Davies, Russell Bradley. Middle Row: Alan Morris, Martin Woodall, Adrian O'Dowd, Clive Boxall, Mark Buckland, Mark Rosegreen, Jack Chapman (physio). Front Row: Graham Allner (general manager), Martin Gavin, John Barton, Graham Mackenzie (captain), Kim Casey, Archie Richards, Brian Kenning (coach)*

Not many clubs in their Centenary Year can finish the season with two County Cup Finals with crowds around 2,000 for each match, winning against Bromsgrove Rovers with three goals in the last eight minutes after trailing by two goals; and two Cup Finals with Wrexham in the Welsh Cup (before crowds of over 5,000 for each match) before losing in the replay—and then finishing the season with a non-league international match between England and Eire.

So much for Kidderminster Harriers in a fantastic season with no less than 76 matches!

Records were beaten at regular intervals. A record individual goal scoring feat by Kim Casey with 73 goals in his first season with the club. A record number of goals in the Gola League (99). A run of eighteen matches without defeat. And gates in the second half of the season doubling those in the first half of the season. And the best position in the Harriers three seasons in the Gola League. If only the earlier results had been better!

Disappointments in losing to Bishops Stortford in the F.A. Cup and losing to Runcorn in the quarter finals of the F.A. Trophy.

Changes during the season with the signings of Clive Boxall and Adrian O'Dowd, and the inclusion of Trevor Campbell in goal when Tim Garner was injured, and Campbell kept his place when Garner was fit to resume.

John Powell, following a successful testimonial season, moved on to Cheltenham after a tremendous career with the Harriers.

Trustees Savings Bank were superb sponsors—and talking of sponsors—the Harriers received more money than any other team for their goal scoring exploits. And talking of goals—203 for and 114 against—if it is goals you are after—the name is Kidderminster Harriers!

KIDDERMINSTER HARRIERS SQUAD 1986

Goalkeepers
Tim Garner: A.P. Leamington, Nuneaton Borough, Northampton Town
Trevor Campbell: Crystal Palace, Redditch, Sutton Coldfield

Defenders
John Horne: Walsall (16-1), Aston Villa
John Barton: Everton (20), Derby County (69), Worcester City, Stourbridge
Mark Buckland: Wolverhampton Wanderers, A.P. Leamington, Cheltenham Town
Chris Jones: Stourbridge, Bilston, Telford United
Archie Richards: Alvechurch, Weymouth, Telford, Kettering, Stafford Rangers
Alan Kurila: Birmingham City, Bedford, Bromsgrove Rovers (signed in closed season for 1986-87)

Midfield
Graham Mackenzie: A.P. Leamington, Cheltenham, Wycombe Wanderers
Martin Gavin: Bristol City, Telford United, Bromsgrove Rovers, Bilston
Clive Boxall: Cheltenham, A.P. Leamington
Adrian O'Dowd: Aston Villa, Oxford, Banbury United, Alvechurch
Martin Woodall: A.P. Leamington, Willenhall, Cheltenham, Walsall, W.B.A., Tipton Town

Forwards
Paul Davies: SCHerakles (Holland), Trowbridge Town, Cardiff City (2)
Kim Casey: Gloucester, A.P. Leamington, Sutton Coldfield
Micky Tuohy: Worcester City, Walsall, Redditch United, Southend United (21-4)
Mark Rosegreen: A.P. Leamington
Russell Bradley: Notts Forest, Alvechurch, Dudley Town

Kidderminster Harriers defender Chris Jones leaps high to head goalwards in the first meeting of Kidderminster Harriers and Wrexham in the Welsh Cup Final at Wrexham when the match ended in a 1-1 draw after extra time

KIDDERMINSTER HARRIERS GOLA LEAGUE SEASON 1985-6

Venue	Opponents	Result	Scorers
H	**Leek Town (SSC final)**	**W 5-1**	**Davies, Mackenzie, Barton, Gavin, O.G.**
H	**Moor Green (TSB)**	**W 4-0**	**Davies (3), Powell**
A	**Leek Town (SSC final)**	**W 2-0**	**Casey, Davies**
H	Dagenham	W 2-0	Casey (2)
H	Altrincham	L 0-2	
A	Frickley Athletic	L 1-3	Casey
H	Northwick Victoria	D 2-2	Davies, Casey
A	**Stevenage (FAC)**	**W 2-0**	**Davies, Rosegreen**
A	Northwich Victoria	D 0-0	
H	Barnet	L 0-2	
A	Bath City	W 4-2	Buckland (3), Powell
H	**Montgomery (WC)**	**W 2-0**	**Powell, Buckland**
H	Bath City	W 3-1	Casey (2), Tuohy
A	**Hednesford (FAC)**	**W 5-1**	**Tuohy (3), Davies, Mackenzie**
A	Kettering Town	D 2-2	Ollis, Powell
A	Dartford	L 1-5	Mackenzie
H	Kettering Town	D 0-0	
H	**Tamworth (FAC)**	**W 4-3**	**Tuohy (2), Casey (2)**
A	Altrincham	L 1-2	Casey
H	Weymouth	L 1-2	Woodall
A	**Telford United (MBC)**	**W 5-2**	**Casey (3), Mackenzie, Davies**
H	**Bishops Stortford (FAC)**	**L 3-4**	**Casey (2), Gavin**
H	Nuneaton Borough	W 2-1	Tuohy, Rosegreen
A	**Chirk (WC)**	**D 2-2**	**Buckland, Powell**
H	**Runcorn (BLC)**	**L 1-4**	**O'Dowd**
H	**Chirk (WC)**	**W 10-1**	**Davies (3), Casey (3), Buckland (2), Gavin, Kavanagh**
A	Barnet	W 1-0	Casey
H	Telford United	W 3-0	Casey (2), Davies
H	**Shrewsbury Town (WC)**	**W 3-1**	**Horne, Casey, Davies**
A	Stafford Rangers	L 2-3	Davies (2)
A	**Runcorn (BLC)**	**L 3-8**	**O'Dowd (2), Casey**
H	Boston United	W 3-2	Tuohy, Casey, O.G.
H	Enfield	L 1-2	Davies
H	**Worcester City (MBC)**	**W 3-0**	**Davies (2), O'Dowd**
A	Maidstone United	L 1-2	Tuohy
H	**Armitage (SSC)**	**W 6-0**	**Rosegreen (2), Smith, Powell, O'Dowd, Buckland**
H	**Boston United (FAT)**	**W 5-2**	**Casey (2), Davies, Tuohy, O.G.**
H	Cheltenham Town	W 5-1	Casey (2), Davies, Tuohy, Mackenzie
H	Scarborough	W 5-1	Davies (2), Tuohy (2), Gavin
A	Weymouth	W 2-1	Casey (2)
A	Enfield	D 2-2	O'Dowd, Casey
A	**Newport County (WC)**	**D 3-3**	**Davies, Tuohy, Casey**
A	**Corby Town (FAT)**	**W 4-0**	**Casey (2), Davies, Woodall**
H	**Dudley Town (WSC)**	**W 3-0**	**Casey (2), O'Dowd**
A	Scarborough	W 5-3	Casey (2), Davies, Tuohy, Buckland
H	Barrow	W 2-1	Davies, Casey
H	**Newport County (WC)**	**W 2-1**	**Davies, Casey**
A	**Southport (FAT)**	**D 1-1**	**Casey**
A	**Swansea City (WC)**	**D 1-1**	**Casey**
H	Maidstone United	W 3-1	Casey (2), Davies
H	**Southport (FAT)**	**W 6-1**	**Casey (3), Davies (2), Buckland**
A	Runcorn	W 2-0	Davies, O'Dowd
H	**Swansea City (WC)**	**W 4-0**	**Casey (3), O.G.**
H	**Runcorn (FAT)**	**L 1-2**	**Tuohy**
H	Stafford Rangers	D 1-1	Davies
A	Telford United	W 1-0	O.G.
A	**Stoke City (SSC)**	**L 0-2**	
H	Wealdstone	W 3-1	Jones, Davies, O'Dowd
A	Wealdstone	W 3-0	Mackenzie, Casey, O'Dowd
A	Cheltenham Town	W 6-2	Casey (3), Mackenzie, Davies, Tuohy
H	Dartford	W 4-1	Casey (2), Jones, Davies
A	Dagenham	W 1-0	Casey
H	**Halesowen Town (WSC)**	**W 4-3**	**Casey (2), Davies, Tuohy**
A	Wycombe Wanderers	W 5-2	Casey (2), Davies, Tuohy, O'Dowd
H	**Hereford United (WC s.f.)**	**W 4-1**	**Casey (2), Davies (2)**
A	Nuneaton Borough	W 3-0	Casey, Jones, O.G.
H	Runcorn	L 2-4	Casey, Tuohy
A	Boston United	L 1-2	Casey
A	**Hereford United (WC s.f.)**	**L 1-3**	**Tuohy**
H	Wycombe Wanderers	W 8-2	Casey (3), Davies (2), O'Dowd (2), Jones
H	Frickley Athletic	D 1-1	Buckland
A	Barrow	W 4-3	Davies (2), Buckland, Tuohy
A	**Bromsgrove Rovers (WSC final)**	**D 0-0**	
H	**Bromsgrove Rovers (WSC final)**	**W 3-2**	**Casey (2), Boxall**
A	**Wrexham (WC final)**	**D 1-1**	**Casey**
H	**Wrexham (WC final)**	**L 1-2**	**Casey**

SSC = Staffordshire Senior Cup
TSB = TSB Trophy
FAC = F.A. Cup
WC = Welsh Cup

MBC = M & B Cup
BLC = Bob Lord Cup
FAT = F.A. Trophy
WSC = Worcestershire Senior Cup

KIDDERMINSTER HARRIERS

President:
Chairman: David Reynolds
Manager: Graham Allner
Asst. Manager: John Barton
Coach: Brian Kenning
Physiotherapist: Jack Chapman
Secretary: Ray Mercer
Address & Tel. No. Kidderminster 0562 67934 (B) 67450 (H)
Commercial Manager: Nick Savage
Address & Tel. No. Kidderminster 3931
Press Officer & Tel. No. Ray Mercer
Address and Tel. No. of ground: Aggborough, Hoo Road, Kidderminster (0562) 3931
Simple ground directions: From M5 North/Midlands A456 (Halesowen). From South/West Kidderminster turn-off (Worcester)
Club shop: Yes
No. of seats: 500 **Covered accommodation:** 4,000 **Capacity:** 10,000 **Floodlights:** Yes
Year formed: 1886 **Nickname: The Harriers** **Club sponsor:** Trustee Savings Bank
Previous names: None
Previous grounds: None
Day for midweek home matches: Monday
Club colours: Red shirts, red shorts
Change colours: White shirts/shorts
Club metal badges: Yes
Record attendance: 9,155 v Hereford United **Year:** 1948
Best performance in: F.A. Cup: 1935 v Workington 2nd Round
F.A. Trophy: 1981-2 v Wycombe W Quarter-final
1985-86 Runcorn Quarter-final
Previous Leagues: Birmingham, West Midland, Birmingham Comb, Southern, Worcestershire Comb
Clubhouse details: Open 7 days a week. Adjoins football ground. All star cabaret, ballroom dancing disco, bingo, snooker, darts, etc. Vice Presidents Club open daily.
Present players with Football League experience: Martin Gavin (Bristol City), Tim Garner (Northampton Town), Paul Davies (Cardiff City), Micky Tuohy (Walsall and Southend), Mark Buckland (Wolverhampton Wanderers), John Barton (Everton and Derby County), Adrian O'Dowd (Aston Villa and Oxford)
Past players who progressed into the Football League: Gerry Hitchins (Aston Villa, Cardiff, Inter Milan, England), K. Keelan (Norwich), Trevor Meredith (Burnley), Tony Cunningham (Barnsley), Paul McGhee (QPR, Preston, Eire)
Record transfer fee paid: Mick Williams £3,000 from Redditch; Mick Tuohy £3,000 from Worcester C
Record transfer fee received: John Powell £3,000, Peter Wassell £3,000, Gerry Hitchens £2,000
Programme details: 24 pages, 40p
Programme editor:
Club Captain (1985-86): Graham Mackenzie
Player of the Year (1985-86): Kim Casey
Clubman of the Year: Micky Tuohy
Local newspapers & Tel. No. Kidderminster Times/Shuttle (K. 3606), Kidderminster Chronicle (K. 753377, Kidderminster Source (K. 69951), Worcester Evening News, Express & Star, Birmingham Evening Mail
Major Honours: Worcester Senior Cup (16), Welsh Cup Finalists 1985-86, Birmingham Senior Cup (7), Staffs Senior Cup (3), West Midland League Champions (3) & League Cup (4), Birmingham League Champions (3) & League Cup (3), Southern League Cup

---

Appearances:
Mackenzie 74, Barton 70, Casey 68, Tuohy 67, Davies 64, Woodall 62, Buckland 61, Jones 50, Campbell 47, Gavin 47, O'Dowd 45, Boxall 33, Richards 32, Garner 29, Rosegreen 24, Horne 23, Kavanagh 23, Powell 18, Ollis 14, Bradley 9, Judd 1, Smith 1

Goalscorers:
Casey 73, Davies 44, Tuohy 22, O'Dowd 13, Buckland 12, Mackenzie 7, O.G. 6, Powell 6, Gavin 4, Jones 4, Rosegreen 4, Woodall 2, Barton 1, Boxall 1, Horne 1, Kavanagh 1, Ollis 1, Smith 1.

MAIDSTONE UNITED

Gola League 17th | **F.A. Trophy** 2nd Rd | **F.A. Cup** 2nd Rd | **K.S.C.** 1st Rd
Bob Lord Trophy 3rd Rd

Maidstone United: *Front Row (L-R): Eddie Boulton, Paul Weston, Russell Debnam, Simon Brown, Andrew Baker, Dave Moorekite (youth team manager), Billy Thompson, Peter Randall, Trevor Mitchell, Ricky Harris, Michael Roganon, Andy Pearson. Middle Row 1 (L-R): Mick Goodwin, Mark Anthony, Tony Reynolds, Colin Barnes, John Clover, Mick Mercer (secretary), Barry Fry (manager), Jim Thompson (chairman), John Baxter (vice-chairman), Geoff Pearson (director), Brian Thompson (club captain), Mark Hill, Ian Fergusson, Graham Humphrey, Stephen Rex. Middle Row 2 (L-R): Charlie Wagstaff (kit manager), Tony Weston (reserve team manager), Dave Griffin, Bobby Moore, Steve Ward, Julian Farmer, Kevin Waugh, Steve Campbell, Graham Stonestreet, Mick Hoad, Mark Jones, Mario Lembo, David Larr, Bernie Holden (youth team trainer), Frank Brooks (first team manager). Back Row (L-R): Jason Payne Wheeler, Chris Reeves, Mick Wens, Gerry Pearson, Clive Green, Derek Richardson, Mick Crowe, Lee Smizt, Steve Brinkman, Nigel Down, Neil Curley, Mick Pittaway, Richard Tiltman.*

A SEASON OF STRUGGLE

A number of new players were signed during the summer to strengthen the squad, but for a number of reasons a settled side never materialized and it became obvious that a serious challenge at the top of the Gola League would be unlikely, as failure in the forward line to score even reasonably consistently led to many drawn games and subsequently defeats.

More players were signed by manager Barry Fry in an effort to push the club up the league table but fifteenth spot was the best reached and it was only in the F.A. Cup that a glimmer of success appeared when the second round proper was reached only to see a disappointing performance end in a 3-0 defeat at Plymouth.

1985/86 was then definitely a season of what might have been, and towards the end there was a very serious risk of the club being relegated for the first time in its history, their Gola League place only being secured on the last Saturday of the playing season. A month before the end of the season, Barry Fry was relieved of team responsibilities and these were taken over by coach, John Ryan. Fry declined the club's offer to remain as general manager and tendered his resignation to end an eighteen month association with the club that had seen many players come and go, but little to cheer supporters used to greater success.

The return from Durban, South Africa of Bill Williams as general manager for the 1986/87 season to work with John Ryan who stays as team manager, is eagerly anticipated, for it was Williams who led the club to the brink of the Football League in 1984. With automatic promotion into the Fourth Division now a reality, the club will be looking to be challenging for the Gola League title this season.

The dangers of not having depth of quality in the playing squad and relying on loan players in key positions will have been noted and the traumatic effect of enduring a relegation struggle for much of the season, will not be an experience anyone at Maidstone United will be too keen to relive.

MAIDSTONE UNITED SQUAD 1986

Goalkeepers
Derek Richardson: Coventry City, Sheffield United (42), Q.P.R. (31), Chelsea

Defenders
Brian Thompson: Mansfield Town (9), Yeovil Town, Sunderland
Mark Hill: Wycombe Wanderers, Brentford (56-3), Q.P.R.
John Glover: Nuneaton Borough, Bedford Town, Dulwich Hamlet
David Carr: Torquay United (34), Lincoln City (168-4), Luton Town (43)
Mike Pittaway: Barnet, Arsenal()
Micky Crowe: Hasting United, Gravesend, Glentworth, Dartford, Dartford, Faversham, Brentford, Gillingham

Midfield
Tony Reynolds: Ashford Town, Folkestone Town
Bobby Fisher: Brentford (49), Cambridge United (42), Orient (314-4)
George Borg: Dartford, Wycombe Wanderers, Carolina Lighting (USA), Dulwich, Hamlet, Leytonstone and Ilford, Millwall
Nigel Donn: Orient (27-2), Gillingham (6)
Duncan Horton: Chatham Town, Charlton Athletic

Forwards
Micky Joyce: Sutton United
Steve Mahoney: Barnet, Hitchin Town, Hertford Town, Stevenage
Mark Cooper: Cambridge United (25-5)
Colin Barnes: Yeovil Town, Torquay United (41-10), Barnet, Hitchin Town
Ian Fergusson: Barnet, Baldock Town, Wimbledon, Brentford

Mickey Joyce goes for goal during his first Gola League season

Keeper Lee Smelt covered by Brian Thompson clutches the ball in one of his early season appearances for Maidstone against Bath City

MAIDSTONE UNITED SEASON 1985-6
(GOLA LEAGUE ONLY)

Venue	Opponents	Result	Scorers	Att.
A	Cheltenham Town	L 1-2	Tiltman	1082
H	Bath City	W 3-2	Cugley (2), Barnes	662
H	Scarborough	D 1-1	Reynolds	655
A	Barnet	D 3-3	Hill, Barnes, Reynolds	602
A	Kettering Town	L 0-2		1459
H	Barnet	D 2-2	Barnes (pen), Reynolds	673
A	Runcorn	L 0-3		444
H	Telford United	D 4-4	Butler, Barnes, Tiltman, Joyce	719
H	Wealdstone	L 0-1		819
A	Frickley Athletic	L 0-2		476
A	Wealdstone	L 2-3	Glover, Butler	770
H	Nuneaton Borough	W 5-1	Butler (2), Borg, Reynolds, Joyce	735
H	Wycombe Wanderers	D 1-1	Borg	770
A	Northwich Victoria	L 0-1		643
A	Weymouth	L 0-2		820
H	Altrincham	L 1-2	Cugley	717
H	Kettering Town	D 0-0		753
A	Barrow	D 1-1	Tiltman	891
A	Dagenham	D 0-0		598
H	Weymouth	D 0-0		621
A	Stafford Rangers	L 1-2	Barnes	1035
H	Enfield	D 3-3	Fisher, Joyce, Barnes	715
H	Kidderminster Harriers	W 2-1	Glover (2)	678
A	Dartford	D 1-1	Thompson	892
A	Bath City	D 1-1	Reynolds	534
A	Wycombe Wanderers	D 2-2	Thompson, Hill	794
H	Dagenham	W 2-1	Fergusson (pen), Cooper	754
H	Frickley Athletic	W 3-2	Glover (2), Reynolds	541
A	Kidderminster Harriers	L 1-3	Churchill	819
H	Cheltenham Town	W 1-0	Barnes	650
A	Boston United	D 2-2	Butler (2)	1036
A	Telford United	W 4-2	Butler (3), Barnes	955
A	Nuneaton Borough	L 0-1		541
H	Runcorn	D 1-1	Farmer	713
H	Boston United	L 1-2	Pittaway (pen)	621
H	Stafford Rangers	L 2-4	Joyce (2)	719
H	Northwich Victoria	L 0-1		646
A	Scarborough	L 0-2		587
H	Barrow	D 0-0		631
A	Enfield	W 3-1	Joyce (2), Mahoney	805
A	Altrincham	L 0-1		1017
H	Dartford	W 3-0	Churchill, Torrance, Joyce	854

Appearances:
League (42), Cup Ties (9): Richardson 46, Horton 41, Barnes 39, Hill 37, Thompson 35, Borg 33, Glover 33, Joyce 31, Fergusson 30, Reynolds 30, Donn 24, Pittaway 23, Crowe 19, Tiltman 18, Butler 17, Fisher 15, Cugley 13, Millett 9, Carr 8, Torrance 8, Churchill 7, Bates 6, Brinkman 5, Cooper 5, Smelt 5, Farmer 4, Mahoney 4, Baldry 3, Green 2, Pearson, A. 1, Pearson, G. 1.

Goalscorers:
League (57): Butler 9, Barnes 8, Joyce 8, Reynolds 6, Glover 5, Cugley 3, Tiltman 3, Borg 2, Churchill 2, Hill 2, Thompson 2, Cooper 1, Farmer 1, Fergusson 1, Fisher 1, Mahoney 1, Torrance 1, Pittaway 1.
Cups (15): Barnes 7, Cugley 2, Joyce 2, Butler 1, Crowe 1, Donn 1, Fergusson 1.

The Stadium, Maidstone

Maidstone defending during their 3-2 home win against Bath City Photo: David Hills

MAIDSTONE UNITED

President:
Chairman: J. C. Thompson
General Manager: Bill Williams
Team Manager: John Ryan
Coach:
Medical Officer: D. M. Gatha, L.R.C.P., M.R.C.S.
Press Officer & Tel. No. M. R. Mercer (54403)

Secretary: M. K. Mercer
Address & Tel. No. As stadium. 54403 (B)

Commercial Manager: Bernie Holden
Address & Tel. No. c/o Club (54403)

Address and Tel. No. of ground: The Stadium, London Road, Maidstone, Kent ME 16 ODT. Tel 54403
Simple ground directions: M20 to junction (Maidstone West), London Road to Maidstone Ground on left—1 mile from town centre **Club shop:** Yes
No. of seats: 700 **Covered accommodation:** 2,000 **Capacity:** 15,000 **Floodlights:** Yes
Year formed: 1897 **Nickname:** Stones **Club sponsor:** Rootes
Previous names: Maidstone Invicta **Club colours:** Amber/black
Previous grounds: None **Change colours:** Blue/white
Day for midweek home matches: Wednesday **Club metal badges:** Yes
Record attendance: 10,591 v Charlton F.A. Cup 3rd Round replay **Year:** 1979
Best performance in: **F.A. Cup:** 1979 v Charlton 3 Round
1984 v Darlington 3rd Round
F.A. Trophy: 1979 v Kettering 3rd Round proper
1983 v Boston Utd 3rd Round proper
Previous Leagues: East Kent, Thames & Medway Comb., Kent, Corinthian, Athenian, Isthmian, Southern
Clubhouse details: Open every night. Greyhound racing and other entertainments. Catering available.
Present players with Football League experience: Derek Richardson, Nigel Donn, Bobby Fisher, Mark Hill, Duncan Horton, Brian Thompson, Colin Barnes, George Borg
Past players who progressed into the Football League: David Sadler, John Ryan, Neil Ayrton, Tony Weston, Mark Newson
Record transfer fee paid: £8,000 to Yeovil for Clive Green
Record transfer fee received: £8,000 from Welling United for John Bartley
Programme details: 16 pages, 30p **Club Captain (1985-86):** Brian Thompson
Programme editor: Mick Mercer **Player of the Year (1985-86):** Derek Richardson
Local newspapers & Tel. No. Kent Messenger, Maidstone 77880. Adscene Maidstone 679047
Major Honours: Southern League Div 1 South, Kent Senior Cup (13), East Kent League (2), Kent League (2), Winners Alliance Premier

NORTHWICH VICTORIA

Gola League 16th **F.A. Trophy** 1st Rd **F.A. Cup** 2nd Rd **C.S.C.** R.U. **Bob Lord Trophy** 1st Rd

Eddie Bishop scores for Northwich Vics in their 3-1 Cheshire Senior cup defeat at Altrincham by arch-rivals Runcorn.

THE END OF AN ERA

In a season of many disappointments a lot of people were saddened at the departure from the Drill field of Stalwart Ken Jones.

Many thought that Ken, in his 18th season, could go on to achieve that magic 1000 appearances for the Vics but it wasn't to be. Manager Terry Murphy seemed intent on bringing his own players to the club and after Jones' departure to Carnarvon Town and the transfer of Graham Abel to Chester City only four of the F.A.Trophy wining team remained.

Supporters hopes for a good season were raised by an impressive 4-0 win over local rivals Witton Albion in a pre-season charity shield match. On paper the opening fixtures of the League programme looked difficult and so they proved to be, it wasn't until the 7th game against Nuneaton at home that Vics registered their first win of the season

Although outnumbered the lone Northwich striker powers in a header at Barnet Photo: Alan Bunce

In the next game Vics gained a 1-0 1st leg victory at Frickley Athletic in the Bob Lord Trophy, but were beaten 4-0 at home in the 2nd Leg. With three league wins in October Vics took on Frickley again, this time in the F.A. Cup 4th Qualifying Round only to be denied again by the Yorkshiremen, losing 2-1. Drawn at home to Workington in the F.A. Trophy First Round Vics were under pressure to do well after their Cup dismissed and poor league form.

A crowd of under 700 saw Vics run out 1-0 winners, their reward being a tough trip to Bishops Stortford in the 2nd round. Vics hopes of a third Wembley appearance were ended when after a hard fought game in Hertfordshire the home side won 2-0.

Now out of both major cup competitions Vics had to try and improve thier league position with this in mind Manager Terry Murphy signed experienced Central defender Bob Scott who played for Crewe Athletic for many years, this allowed Captain Glyn Stephens to revert to his more familiar midfield role.

On March 22nd after losing 3-0 at home to Nuneaton Terry Murphy resigned his position saying he felt he could do no more to improve the clubs position. Recent signing Bob Scott and Assistant Manager Mike Pejic were put in charge of team affairs until the end of the season with the brief to keep Vics in the league. this they achieved by one point the 1-0 Victory at Maidstone on 5th April being one of the most important results of the season.

In the Cheshire Senior Cup Final Vics played Runcorn at Altrincham F.C. only to go down 3-1, a Bob Scott own goal optimizing a season to forget. One piece of silverware did remain in the boardroom however, this being the District Senior Cup, The Greens defeating a spirited Winsford United side 2-0.

NORTHWICH VICTORIA

Goalkeepers
David Ryan: Southport (23), Manchester United

Defenders
Tony Murphy: Bangor City, Runcorn
David Young: Wrexham, Wigan Athletic, Tranmere Rovers
John Price: Winsford United
Steve Nelson: Leek Town, Crewe Alexandra, Stoke City
Bob Scott: Crewe Alexandra (238-15), Rochdale (71-3), Hartlepool (37), Wrexham (19)
Seamus Heath: Tranmere Rovers (17), Wrexham (32-1), Luton Town

Midfield
Glyn Stephens: Horwich RMI, Wigan Athletic, Altrincham
Eddie Bishop: Local
Mark Emmerson: Wrexham
Mark Ferguson: Scarborough, Tranmere Rovers (87-13)
Paul Bennett: Telford United, Northwich Victoria, Port Vale (30-1)
Marshall Burke: Scarborough, Tranmere Rovers (3), Lincoln City (50-7), Blackburn Rovers (39-7), Leeds United, Burnley (24-5)

Forwards
Ray Redshaw: Auckland (N.Z.), Wigan Athletic (4), Northwich Victoria, Horwich RMI, Glossop, Southport, Hyde United, Glossop, Prestwich Heys
Mark Dunn: Local
Darren Lloyd: Local
Don Page: Stafford Rangers, Altricham, South Liverpool
Rory Blease: Chester City (4), Caernorfon Town

Northwich Victoria's long-serving goalkeeper Dave Ryan receives the club's 'Player of the Year' award from Chester City manager Harry McNally. The superbly consistent Ryan has only missed a handful of games in nine seasons at the Drill Field.

NORTHWICH VICTORIA GOLA LEAGUE SEASON 1985-6

Venue	Opponents	Result	Scorers	Att.
A	Bath	D 0-0		668
A	Kettering	L 1-2	Horton	1367
H	Wealdstone	D 2-2	Smith (2)	810
A	Kidderminster	D 2-2	Bishop, Smith	450
H	Enfield	D 2-2	Bishop, Smith	785
H	Kidderminster	D 0-0		714
A	Nuneaton	W 3-1	Murphy, Craven, Blease	702
A	**Frickley (B.L.T.)**	**W 1-0**	**Redshaw**	**389**
H	Boston Utd.	L 3-2	Abel, Stephens, Redshaw	710
H	**Frickley (B.L.T.)**	**L 0-4**		**660**
A	Altrincham	L 1-2	Bishop	1224
A	Weymouth	D 2-2	Bishop, Nelson	836
A	Barrow	W 2-1	Redshaw (2)	300
H	Maidstone	W 1-0	Redshaw	667
H	Wycombe W.	W 4-0	Craven, Redshaw (2), Armstrong	787
A	**Frickley (F.A.C.)**	**L 1-2**	**Horton**	**971**
H	Scarborough	D 0-0		666
A	Wealdstone	D 0-0		757
A	Barnet	L 0-1		687
H	Stafford	W 2-0	Redshaw (2)	701
H	Barrow	L 0-1		620
A	Dagenham	L 0-1		539
A	Wycombe W.	D 1-1	Redshaw	662
H	Kettering	D 0-0		519
A	Boston	L 0-3		1281
H	Frickley	L 2-3	Stephens, Bennett	631
H	**Workington (F.A.T.)**	**W 1-0**	**Power**	**679**
A	Runcorn	W 3-2	Bishop, Bennett, Dunn	970
H	Runcorn	D 1-1	Redshaw	1202
A	Cheltenham	L 0-2		898
A	**B. Stortford (F.A.T.)**	**L 0-2**		**682**
A	Frickley	L 0-1		517
H	Cheltenham	W 3-1	Bennett, Page, Dunn	521
A	Scarborough	D 0-0		540
H	Weymouth	L 0-1		588
A	Stafford	W 2-1	Page, Burke	926
H	Bath City	L 1-2	Page	615
H	Nuneaton	L 0-3		610
A	Telford	L 0-4		1200
H	Telford	L 0-1		641
A	Maidstone	W 1-0	Redshaw	646
H	Dartford	W 2-0	Scott, Redshaw	556
A	Altrincham	L 1-2	Page	1013
A	Enfield	L 0-1		761
H	Barnet	L 0-1		474
H	Dagenham	L 0-1		367

Appearances: (Max 47)
Ryan 47, Nelson 46, Stephens 46, Murphy 41, Bishop 38, Redshaw 38, Young 33, Craven 27, Aspinall 24, Bennett 22, Heath 20, Blease 19, Abel 18, Horton 17, Page 17, Burke 14, Smith 13, Scott 10, Armstrong 9, Dean 7, Dunn 7, Emmerson 7, Price 6, Pye 6, Branhall 5, Jones 5, Woods 4, Power 3, Lloyd 2, Doherty 1, Mundy 1, Pevic 1.

Goalscorers: (38 League and 3 Cup)
Redshaw 12, Bishops, Smith 4, Page 3, Stephens 3, Craven 2, Dunn 2, Horton 2, Armstrong, Bennett, Blease, Burke, Murphy, Nelson, Power, Scott 1 Each.

Action at the Drill Field against Weymouth

NORTHWICH VICTORIA

President: Mr J. Horton
Chairman: D.R. Nuttall
Manager: S. Pearson
Asst. Manager:
Coach:
Physiotherapist: Ron Reddy
Press Officer & Tel. No.

Secretary: I. Merrill.
"Harlow", Glebe Road, Cuddington, Northwich
Ches. CW8 2LR. 0606 882260 (H)

Commercial Manager: D. Thomas
Address & Tel. No. c/o Club

Address and Tel. No. of ground:
Simple ground directions: Leave the M6 at junction 19. Turn right. After approx 4 miles at second roundabout. Ground on right immediately before traffic lights (¾ mile). Alongside bus station **Club shop:** Yes
No. of seats: 660 **Covered accommodation:** 3,500 **Capacity:** 10,000 **Floodlights:** Yes
Year formed: 1874 **Nickname:** The Vics **Club sponsor:**Sandbury Construction
Previous names: **Club colours:** Green/White/Green
Previous grounds: **Change colours:** Claret/Blue
Day for midweek home matches: Wednesday **Club metal badges:** Yes
Record attendance: 28,635 v Oldham Athletic at Maine Road. 1977
Best performance in: F.A. Cup: 1976-77 4th Round Proper
F.A. Trophy: 1983-84 Winners
Previous Leagues: Football League Div II, Manchester, Cheshire, Northern Premier
Clubhouse details:
Present players with Football League experience: Dave Ryan (Southport), Roy Redshaw (Wigan), Nigel Smith (Stockport), Dave Constantine (Bury), Dave Young (Transmere)
Past players who progressed into the Football League: Frank Corrigan (Wigan), Jim Walker (Chester), Billy Meredith, (Manchester City), Mark Ward (Oldham), Graham Abel (Chester City)
Record transfer fee paid: £5,000 for Colin Williams from Telford
Record transfer fee received: £12,000 for Mark Ward (Oldham A)
Programme details: **Club Captain (1985-86):** Glyn Stephens
Programme editor: Dave Millington **Player of the Year (1985-86):** Dave Ryan
Local newspapers & Tel. No. Northwich Guardian 0606 3333, Northwich Chronicle 0606 2272
Major Honours: Cheshire F.A. Senior Cup (15), Manchester League, Cheshire League, N.P.L. Cup, N.P.L. Runners-up, N.P.L. Cup Runners-up, Staffordshire Senior Cup (2), Alliance Premier League Cup, Alliance Premier League Shield, F.A. Trophy Finalists, F.A. Trophy Winners 1983-84

NUNEATON BOROUGH

Gola League 18th **F.A. Trophy** 1st Rd **F.A. Cup** 1st Rd **B.S.C.** 4th Rd replay
Bob Lord Trophy 2nd Rd.

Nuneaton Borough: *Back Row (L-R); J. Holmes (manager), R. Grant, M. Thurman, W. Gibson, A. Harris, F. Murphy, R. Dixey, L. Morrison, J. Rudkin*
Front Row (L-R); E. Carr, M. Hutchinson, T. Smithers, E. McGoldrizt, A. McGranaghan, L. Donoghue Photo: Courtesy Nuneaton & Bedworth Trader

BOROUGH SURVIVE

Following the success of the previous two seasons 1985-86 proved to be one of survival for the 'Borough'. With the pre-season departures of manager Graham Carr to Northampton Town along with players Trevor Morley and Richard Hill for a combined £30,000 fee and Paul Culpin to Coventry City, Nuneaton also had the setback of losing club skipper Richard Dixey with a pelvic injury early on in the season, his last match being in October, in the 1-5 defeat at Maidstone.

Former Ipswich and Mansfield Town Stalwart Peter Morris was appointed manager during the close season. Despite a fine run in the F.A. Cup that took in four qualifying rounds Borough's league position gradually deteriorated and following a 1-2 defeat at Kidderminster Harriers on 28th October, Morris was relieved of his responsibilities, the team lying in 21st position having taken 9 points from fourteen league games. Richard Dixey, for the second time in 6 months took over the reins as caretaker manager appropriately enough in time for the first round cup tie against his former club Burnley. A crowd of 3182 saw Boro' come back from a two goal deficit, but a cruel last minute goal from the fourth division club deprived Nuneaton of a well deserved replay. Just over a week later Jimmy Holmes took over as player manager making his debut in a 1-2 Bob Lord Trophy defeat at Stafford Rangers.

After losing five league matches in January, Nuneaton found themselves bottom of the table with 15 points from 27 matches and relegation looked certain. The turning point came on February 1st when 3rd placed Weymouth were defeated 3-0 at Manor Park. This proved to be the start of a haul of 21 points from the last fifteen matches which saw Nuneaton retain their Gola League status.

During the course of the season, Boro' in their rebuilding plans included four former internationals in their colours. Trevor Whymark of England, Les Cartwright of Wales, Jim Blyth of Scotland and Republic of Ireland player Jim Holmes. Keeper Jim Blyth's injury sustained at Stafford in November cleared the way for two youth keepers, Mick Beale and Alan Harris to show their potential but with the situation critical Jim Holmes went back to Tottenham to sign 3rd choice custodian at White Hart Lane, Peter Corder for £1,000. Striker Lance Morrison was recruited before the transfer deadline, a £4,000 fee to Alvechurch securing his signature. Lance's goal at Telford on the last of the season proved invaluable as Boro' gained the point needed to stay up in the top flight.

NUNEATON BOROUGH SQUAD 1985-86

Goalkeepers
Peter Corder: Tottenham Hotspur, Peterborough United
Alan Harris: Local

Defenders
Everton Carr: Rochdale (9), Halifax Town (43), Leicester City (14)
Willie Gibson: Leicester City (28)
Richard Dixey: Scarborough, Kettering Town, Burnley (2), Stockport County (14)
Ian Bennyworth: Gainsborough Trinity, Hull City (1)
Jim Holmes: Coventry City (128-7), Tottenham Hotspur (82-2), Vancouver Whitecaps, Leicester City, Brentford, Torquay United, Peterborough United (as player/assistant manager)

Midfield
Eddie McGoldrick: Kettering Town
Tim Smithers: Oxford United (119-7)
Mick Thurman: Local
Mark Hutchinson: Leicester City, Carlisle United

Forwards
Frank Murphy: Kettering Town, Desborough Town, Corby Town
Lance Morrison: Moorgreen, Alvechurch
Trevor Parr: Boston United, Peterborough United
Dave Kenney: Local

Peter Denyer's first goal coming up, against Barnet, as he rockets the ball home with a powerful header Photo: Nuneaton & Bedworth Trader

NUNEATON BOROUGH GOLA LEAGUE SEASON 1985-6

Venue	Opponents	Result	Scorers	Att.
A	Boston United	L 2-3	Murphy, Denyer	1304
A	Scarborough	L 1-2	Dixey	673
H	Kettering Town	L 0-3		1016
A	Bath City	W 2-0	Murphy, Denyer	547
H	Bath City	L 2-3	Dixey, Denyer	926
H	Northwich Victoria	L 1-3	Murphy	702
A	Dartford	W 1-0	Smithers	463
H	Wealdstone	D 0-0		851
H	Runcorn	W 1-0	Whalley	845
A	Wycombe Wanderers	L 0-2		786
A	Maidstone United	L 1-5	Murphy	735
H	Cheltenham Town	L 0-1		707
A	Dagenham	L 2-3	Bennyworth, Murphy	548
A	Kidderminster Harriers	L 1-2	Genovese	672
H	Barnet	W 4-1	Denyer (2), Murphy (pen), Brown	786
A	Altrincham	L 4-7	Murphy (2, 1 pen), Brown, Hamill	1118
A	Frickley Athletic	D 2-2	Murphy, Smithers	587
H	Telford United	D 1-1	Whalley	741
H	Enfield	L 1-5	Smithers	753
H	Dagenham	L 1-2	Hamill	639
H	Boston United	L 0-1		573
H	Wycombe Wanderers	W 3-0	Hutchinson, Smithers, Thurman	649
A	Wealdstone	L 0-1		754
H	Barrow	L 0-1		590
A	Stafford Rangers	L 0-2		1079
A	Weymouth	L 0-2		734
A	Runcorn	L 1-3	Murphy	426
H	Weymouth	W 3-0	Smithers, Holmes (pen), Parr	369
A	Enfield	L 2-3	Smithers (2 pen)	898
H	Maidstone United	W 1-0	Smithers (pen)	541
H	Stafford Rangers	W 3-0	Smithers (pen), Murphy, Gibson	729
A	Northwich Victoria	W 3-0	Hutchinson (2), McGoldrick	610
H	Scarborough	W 3-1	Holmes (2), Murhpy	621
A	Barrow	L 0-2		376
A	Barnet	W 1-0	Murphy	678
A	Kettering	W 4-1	Smithers (2), Bennyworth, Murphy	733
H	Kidderminster Harriers	L 0-3		1034
H	Frickley Athletic	L 0-1		762
A	Cheltenham	L 3-5	Smithers (2, 1 pen), Murphy	939
H	Dartford	W 3-1	Smithers (pen), Morrison, McGoldrick	778
H	Altrincham	D 0-0		829
A	Telford	D 1-1	Morrison	1230

Cup Results 1985-86

A	**Hemel Hempstead (FAC)**	**W 3-1**	**McGoldrick, Genovese, Murphy**	**205**
A	**Moor Green (FAC)**	**W 4-1**	**Genovese (2), Smithers (pen), McGoldrick**	**338**
H	**Hinckley Athletic (FAC)**	**D 0-0**		**1526**
A	**Hinckley Athletic (FAC)**	**W 1-0**	**Smithers**	**1296**
A	**Dunstable (FAC)**	**W 2-0**	**Murphy (2)**	**628**
H	**Burnley (FAC)**	**L 2-3**	**Bennyworth, Murphy**	**3182**
H	**West Midland Police (BSC)**	**W 3-0**	**Whalley (2), Genovese**	**107**
H	**Highgate United (BSC)**	**W 4-1**	**Whalley (2), Genovese (2)**	**308**
H	**Dudley Town (BSC)**	**D 2-2**	**Hamill (pen), Kenney**	**167**
A	**Dudley Town (BSC)**	**L 0-1**	**aet**	**221**
H	**Stafford Rangers (BLT)**	**D 1-1**	**Murphy (pen)**	**578**
A	**Stafford Rangers (BLT)**	**L 1-2**	**Hamill**	**777**
A	**Bedworth United (MBC)**	**W 4-3**	**Murphy (2), Parr, Holmes**	**323**
H	**Kettering Town (MBC)**	**W 1-0**	**Morrison**	**184**
A	**Stafford Rangers (FAT)**	**L 0-1**		**837**

FAC = F.A. Cup
BSC = Birmingham Senior Cup
BLT = Bob Lord Trophy
MBC = M & B Cup
FAT = F.A. Trophy

Appearances:
League (42), Cup Ties (15); Smithers 57, Goldrick 55, Gibson 53, Murphy 47 + 4, Bennyworth 47 + 1, Thurman 46 + 6, Carr 46 + 2, Hutchinson 34 + 17, Homes 23 + 3, Parr 22 + 2, Blyth 21, Hamill 18 + 7, Whalley 18 + 2, Corder 17, Morrison 15, Denyer 27
Genovese 14 + 7, Dixey 14, Beale 12, Harris 7, Armstrong 6 + 1, Cartwright 5, Kenney 4 + 16, Brown 4 + 4, Fry 3 + 1, Trickett 2 + 4, Johnston 2 + 6, Manning 2 + 4, Hormantschuk 2 + 1, Hardwick 1 + 6, Bailey 1 + 4, Bradley 1 + 4, Bancroft 1 + 2, Burke 0 + 1, Phillips 0 + 1

Goalscorers:
League (58), Cup (28); Murphy 22, Smithers 16, Genovese 7, Whalley 6, Denyer 5, Hamill 4, Hilmes 4, McGoldrick 4, Bennyworth 3, Hutchinson 3, Morrison 3, Brown 2, Dixey 2, Parr 2, Gibson 1, Kenney 1, Thurman 1

The impressive terrace behind the Beaumont Road end goal at Manor Park Photo: W.N. Mather

NUNEATON BOROUGH

President: A. Scattergood
Chairman: Noel Kelly
Manager: Jim Holmes
Asst. Manager:
Coach:
Secretary: Dr John Evans
Address & Tel. No. Nuneaton 348416 (H), 0203 617231 (B)
Commercial Manager:
Address & Tel. No. Nuneaton 385738
Physiotherapist: D. Looms
Press Officer & Tel. No. Secretary
Address and Tel. No. of ground: Manor Park, Beaumont Road, Nuneaton
Simple ground directions: Manor Park is at the northern end of Queens Road, the main street in the town centre
Club shop: Yes, manager Geoff Cooke 0203 328623
No. of seats: 450 **Covered accommodation:** 5,000 **Capacity:** 18,500 **Floodlights:** Yes
Year formed: 1937 **Nickname:** The Boro **Club sponsor:** None
Previous names: None
Previous grounds: None
Day for midweek home matches: Monday
Club colours: Blue/white stripes/white
Change colours: Yellow
Club metal badges: Yes
Record attendance: 22,114 v Rotherham United F.A. Cup 3rd Rd **Year:** 1967
Best performance in: **F.A. Cup:** 1949-50, 1966-7 Third Rd
F.A. Trophy: 1976-7, 1979-80 Quarter Finals
Previous Leagues: Central Amateur, Birmingham Comb, Birmingham, Southern, Alliance, Premier
Clubhouse details: Open match days, evenings, Sunday lunchtime (Nuneaton 383152)
Present players with Football League experience: Tim Smithers, Everton Carr, Peter Corder, Richard Dixey, Willie Gibson, Jim Holmes, Mark Hutchinson
Past players who progressed into the Football League: George Dewis (Leicester C) 1946, Alf Wood (Cov. C) 1946, Eric Betts (Walsall) 1949, Ken Plant (Bury) 1950, Frank Upton (Northampton) 1953, George Catleugh (Watford) 1954, Mike Gibson (Shrewsbury) 1960, Mickey Harland (Oxford) 1963, Barry Holbutt (Walsall) 1965, Ken Satchwell (Walsall) 1965, Terry Bell (Hartlepool) 1966, Alan Moreton (Fulham) 1970, Wayne Thomas (K.S.V. Baunatal) 1978, Kirk Stephens (Luton T.) 1978, Trevor Peake (Lincoln City) 1979, Paul Sugrue (Man City) 1980, Malcon Shotton (Oxford) 1980, Tim Smithers (Oxford) 1980, Dean Thomas (Wimbledon) 1981, Paul Richardson (Derby C.) 1984, Paul Culpin (Coventry) 1985, Richard Hill (Northampton) 1985, Trevor Morley (Northampton) 1985
Record transfer fee paid: £9,500 for Richard Dixey to Scarborough
Record transfer fee received: £25,800 from Lincoln City for Trevor Peake, Paul Culpin £50,000 to Coventry City
Programme details: 20 pages, 35p
Programme editor: Geoff Cooke
Club Captain (1985-86):
Player of the Year (1985-86):
Local newspapers & Tel. No. Nuneaton Evening Tribune (Nun 382251), Coventry Evening Telegraph (Cov 25588), Nuneaton Observer (Nun 383636), Nuneaton Trader
Major Honours: Birmingham League (North), Birmingham League Div 1, Southern League Inter-Zone, Southern League Midlands, Birmingham Senior Cup

RUNCORN AFC

Gola League 6th **F.A. Trophy** Runners-up **F.A. Cup** 2nd Rd proper **C.S.C.** Winners
Bob Lord Trophy S.F.
J.C. Thompson Championship Shield: Winners (1984-5 Champions v Bob Lord winners)

Runcorn: *Back Row (L-R): P. Rowlands, S. Skeete, R. McBride, G. Jones, P. Goodwin (trainer), R. Fraser, P. Eales, S. Crompton, S. Holden Middle Row: A. Brockbank, A. Lee, J. Imrie, M. Roberts, O. Smith (captain), M. Carter, D. Mather, A. Crompton, F. Carrodus, S. Joel Front Row: A. Stringer*, H. Braverman*, P. Bredican*, W.J. King (acting chairman), J. Williams (manager), T. Baker*, D. Robinson*, S. Jones*, G.H. Worrall* (secretary)* Photo: W. Leigh
* Directors

WEMBLEY AT LAST!

Having failed at the semi-final stage consistently over the years, everyone connected with Runcorn Football Club must have feared the worst when they were held to a draw by Kettering at home in the semi-final first leg last season.

However, a superb rearguard action at Kettering made a dream come true! The Final, a local 'derby' with Altrincham, was a closely contested battle with the more cup hardened 'Alty' just taking the trophy. Since then the clubs have swapped managers so John Williams' vastly successful spell at Canal Street closes amidst very happy memories.

Last season's side was built along John's usual 'no nonsense' lines; solid uncompromising defence with quick direct counter-attacking capabilities. Mark Carter finished as top scorer but was given fine support from the experienced Cromptons (Steve and Alan), skipper Ossie Smith and another giant member of the Skeete family, 27 year-old Steven.

Steve Holden also featured well amongst the goalscorers during the season but the signing of one of the Gola League's star marksmen Dave Mather was one of the manager's shrewdest moves. The ex-Telford favourite scored 14 goals including a vital semi-final contribution.

No semi-professional team can consistently do well without a hard core of experienced players and the Runcorn defence certainly supported this theory and with ex-league star Frank Carrodus also in midfield they were a daunting proposition for any young opposition. This strength was shown consistently in the cups as the second round proper of the F.A. Cup was reached (this included a creditable draw with Wigan Athletic) along with the Bob Lord semi-finals and a triumph in the Cheshire Senior Cup which brought victories over Altrincham and Northwich Victoria in the last two ties. The club also won the Jim Thompson Championship Shield when they (as Bob Lord Cup Holders) beat Champions, Wealdstone.

If you add a creditable 6th place in the league, the club had every right to feel proud of their efforts over their 71 game season! T.W.

RUNCORN SQUAD 1986

Goalkeepers
Ray McBride: Vauxhall Motors, Port Sunlight, Stork

Defenders
Mick Roberts: Winsford United, Mossley, Oldham Athletic
Bobby Fraser: Winsford United, Portmadog, Holyhead, Marine, Skelmersdale United, Tranmere Rovers, Liverpool
Graham Jones: Stockport County (35-2), Torquay United (110-5), Luton Town (39)
Paul Rowlands: Heswall, Cammel Laird, Heswall, West Kirby
Andy Lee: Tranmere, Stafford Rangers, Cambridge United, Bangor Cty

Midfield
Andy Brockbank: Blackpool (28-1)
John Imrie: Buxton, Bury, Barnsley
Ossie Smith: Altrincham, Manchester United
Alan Crompton: Wigan Athletic (13), Blackburn Rovers (4), Sunderland

Forwards
Mark Carter: Bangor City, South Liverpool, Liverpool
Steve Joel: Winsford United, Portmadog
Dave Mather: South Liverpool Bangor City, Telford
Steve Crompton: Wolves, Hereford, Worcester
Frank Carrodus: Manchester City, Aston Villa, Bury, Birmingham, Wrexham
Steve Skeete: Stalybridge C, Congleton, Prescot, Burscough, Mossley
Steve Halden: Blackpool Mech, Blackpool Rangers, Wren Rovers

Runcorn striker Mark Carter, top scorer at the Canal Street club with 35 goals last season, gives the Linnets a head start in the 3-0 home victory over Maidstone United
Photo: James Coogan, Runcorn Weekly News

RUNCORN GOLA LEAGUE SEASON 1985-6

Venue	Opponents	Result	Scorers	Att.
A	Wycombe Wanderers	W 1-0	Holden	1036
H	Telford United	W 1-0	Holden	737
H	Weymouth	L 2-1	Fraser	534
H	Stafford Rangers	W 3-0	Carter (2), Smith	561
A	**Prescot C (FAC)**	**W 2-1**	**Kettle, Holden**	**300**
A	Stafford Rangers	D 1-1	Crompton S.	989
H	Maidstone United	W 3-0	Crompton A., Carter, Carrodus	444
A	**Wealdstone (JTS)**	**W 7-6**	**Kettle (2), Jones, Imrie, Carter, Carrodus, Parker**	
H	Bath City	W 2-0	Imrie, Carter	507
A	Nuneaton	W 1-0		836
A	**Accrington Stanley (FAC)**	**D 1-1**	**Crompton**	**840**
H	**Accrington (FAC)**	**W 9-1**	**Skeetes (3), Carter, Crompton A., Crompton S., Roberts,Smith, Kettle**	**625**
H	Wealdstone	D 1-1	Skeete	624
A	Scarborough	D 1-1	Holden	
A	**Mossley (FAC)**	**W 2-0**	**Smith (2)**	**704**
H	Barrow	W 3-1	Smith, Imrie, Crompton A.	556
A	Dartford	W 1-0	Skeete	
A	**Rhyl (FAC)**	**W 2-0**	**Imrie, Mather**	
H	Cheltenham	W 5-0	Smith, Imrie, Skeete, Mather, Carter	620
A	**Kidderminster Harriers (BLT)**	**W 4-1**	**Holden (3), Carter**	
A	Boston	L 2-1	Mather	
H	**Boston (FAC)**	**D 2-2**	**Smith (2)**	**1315**
A	**Boston (FAC)**	**D 1-1**	**Carter**	**2315**
H	Enfield	D 1-1	Carter	679
H	**Boston (FAC)**	**W 4-1**	**Carter (2), Crompton S., Mather**	**2525**
H	**Kidderminster (BLT)**	**W 8-1**	**Carter (3), Skeete (4), Holden**	
A	Cheltenham	D 1-1	Imrie	
H	**Wigan Athletic (FAC)**	**D 1-1**	**Mather**	**3310**
A	**Wigan Athletic (FAC)**	**L 4-0**		**3390**
A	Barnet	W 2-0	Mather (2)	
H	**Marine (FAT)**	**W 2-0**	**Crompton S., Mather**	**698**
H	Northwich Victoria	L 3-2	Carter, Holden	970
A	Northwich Victoria	D 1-1	Carter	
A	Telford United	W 3-2	Smith (2), Carter	
H	Frickley	D 2-2	Carter (2)	351
A	Windsor & Eaton	W 1-0	Carter	427
A	Barrow	W 4-0	Carter (3), Mather	
A	**Warrington T (CSC)**	**W**		
H	Nuneaton	W 3-1	Holden (2), Skeete	426
A	Enfield	L 2-0		
H	**Burton A (FAT)**	**W 2-0**	**Skeete, Carter**	**856**
A	**Altrincham (CSC)**	**D**		
H	**Frickley (BLT)**	**W 6-2**	**Carter (3), Crompton S., Fraser, Joel**	**351**
H	**Altrincham (CSC)**			
H	Kidderminster	L 2-0		613
A	**Kidderminster (FAT)**	**W 2-1**	**Lee, O.G.**	**2015**
H	**Stafford (BLT)**	**D 0-0**		**697**
A	**Witton A (CSC)**			
A	**Stafford (BLT)**	**L 2-1**	**Lee**	
A	Maidstone	D 1-1	Imrie	
H	**Witton A (CSC)**			
H	Kettering T	L 1-0		565
H	Scarborough	D 0-0		451
H	**Kettering (FAT)**	**D 0-0**		**2500**
H	Barnet	D 0-0		374
A	**Kettering (FAT)**	**W 2-0**	**Smith, Mather**	
H	Wycombe Wanderers	W 2-1	Lee, Crompton S.,	515
A	Altrincham	D 1-1	Skeete	
A	Dagenahm	W 3-2	Lee, Carter, Skeete	
A	Kidderminster	W 4-2	Lee, Carter (3)	908
H	Altrincham	W 2-1	Crompton A., Gardner (o.g.)	988
A	Frickley	L 3-1	Carter	
A	Kettering	D 0-0		
A	Weymouth	L 5-2	Carter, Mather	
A	Bath City	W 1-0	Pratt (o.g.)	
H	Boston United	W 3-0	Lee, Skeete, Holden	476
H	Dartford	W 5-0	Imrie (2), Crompton A., Skeete, Carter	375
A	**Northwich (CSC final)**	**W 3-1**		
A	Wealdstone	D 1-1	Holden	
H	Dagenham	D 1-1	Carter	629
A	**Wembley (FAT final)**	**L 1-0**		

FAC = F.A. Cup
JTS = J.C. Thompson Shield
BLT = Bob Lord Trophy
FAT = F.A.Trophy
CSC = Cheshire Senior Cup

RUNCORN

President:
Chairman: W.J. King
Manager: John King
Asst. Manager:
Coach:
Physiotherapist: P. Goodwin

Secretary: G.H. Worrall
Address & Tel. No. 09285 60076 (B), 09285 64052 (H)

Commercial Director: P.B. Redican
Address & Tel. No. 09285 76454

Press Officer & Tel. No. W.J. King 0253 32131 (B), 0244 336059 (H)
Address and Tel. No. of ground: Canal Street, Runcorn. Tel (09285) 60076
Simple ground directions: From M56 follow signs for Runcorn Old Town. From M62 follow signs for Runcorn & Widnes Bridge, then Runcorn Old Town
Club shop: Yes
No. of seats: 400 **Covered accommodation:** 2,000 **Capacity:** 7,000 **Floodlights:** Yes
Year formed: 1918 **Nickname:** Linnets **Club sponsor:**
Previous names: None
Previous grounds: None
Day for midweek home matches: Tuesday
Club colours: Green/yellow/green
Change colours: White/black
Club metal badges: Yes
Record attendance: 10,111 v Preston North End **Year:** 1939
Best performance in: **F.A. Cup:** 1939 v Preston North End 3rd Round
F.A. Trophy: 1985-86 Finalists
Best Performance Trophy: 1985-86 Runners-up
Previous Leagues: Cheshire County, Northern Premier
Clubhouse details: Next to ground, open every day. Functions by arrangement (09285 75858). VIP lounge by boardroom
Present players with Football League experience: A. Crompton (Wigan, A. Brockbank (Blackpool), G. Jones (Luton, Torquay), A. Lee (Tranmere Rovers, Cambridge United), F. Carrodus
Past players who progressed into the Football League: J. Cumbes (Aston Villa)
Record transfer fee paid: Not disclosed
Record transfer fee received: Not disclosed
Programme details: 24 pages, 35p
Programme editor: R. Pickering, D. Rose
Club Captain (1985-86): Ossie Smith
Player of the Year (1985-86): Mark Carter
Local newspapers & Tel. No. Runcorn Weekly News 09285 717979, Runcorn World 050 423 3303
Major Honours: Cheshire League (3), Cheshire Senior Cup (9), Cheshire Bowl, Northern Premier League (2), Northern Premier League Cup (3), Northern Premier League Shield (2), Alliance Premier League, Bob Lord Trophy (2), Jim Thompson League Championship Shield

---

Appearances:
Jones 66, Smith 66, Imrie 66, Roberts 64, Fraser 62, Carter 59, Crompton S. 59, Rowlands 58, McBride 57, Holden 54, Skeete 53, Crompton A. 51, Carrodus 50, Mather 47, Lee 35, Eales 13, Brookbank 13, Kettle 12, Parker 9, Joel 6, Hirst 5, Thomas 2

Goalscorers:
Carter 45, Skeete 23, Mather 14, Holden 13, Smith 12, Lee 9, Crompton S. 8, Crompton A. 8, Imrie 8, Fraser 3, Kettle 2, Joel 2, Roberts 1, Carrodus 1

SCARBOROUGH

Gola League | **F.A. Trophy** 2nd Rd | **F.A. Cup** 1st Rd | **N.R.S.C.** S.F.
Bob Lord Trophy 1st Rd

Happy Days! Scarborough meet Dagenham at Wembley in 1977 to record their third F.A. Trophy success

A SEASON OF UPS AND DOWNS

Scarborough began the season with great hopes, following the revival of the previous year under the managership of Harry Dunn. Five wins and two drawn matches seemed to confirm these hopes and by mid-September a fine win over Altrincham saw the club riding high at the top of the league. In spite of having to play through the qualifying rounds they reached the first round proper of the F.A. Cup with a series of sterling performances against Bridlington Town, Crook, Blyth Spartans and Bishop Auckland, before going out to Notts County away. Within a few weeks, the season which had begun so well was in tatters with a disastrous run of eleven matches without a win, including being dispatched from the trophy by Southport of the Multipart League (after two replays). March arrived with the threat of relegation looming, but fortunately enough points were accumulated to avoid the ignominious drop. Even the North Riding Senior Cup slipped from the club's grasp with a home defeat at the hands of York City. A season which had begun with so much promise ended on a dismal note.

Within a month Harry Dunn departed as manager to be replaced by Neil Warnock.

Who, When and Where? The clue is that its FA Trophy action at Scarborough! Photo: Denis Dobson

Phil Stacey scores against Scarborough with Peter Hirds in support Photo: Thomas Scott

Ray Baverstock is in control as a Scarborough attack breaks down in the recent Gola league match Photo: Michael Halford

SCARBOROUGH GOLA LEAGUE SEASON 1985-6

Venue	Opponents	Result	Scorers	Att.
H	Dartford	D 1-1	Wiggan	656
H	Nuneaton Boro	W 2-1	Hooley (2, 1 pen)	673
A	Maidstone United	D 1-1	Bowman D.	655
H	Barrow	W 3-1	Hooley, Rose (2)	655
A	**Bridlington Town (FAC)**	**W 1-0**	**Hooley**	**650**
A	Barrow	W 4-2	Hooley (2, 1 pen), Rose, Bowman D.	409
H	Dagenham	W 2-1	Bowman D., Thompson	630
H	Altrincham	W 1-0	Bowman D.	1299
A	Weymouth	L 1-4	Hooley	750
A	Altrincham	L 0-2		1023
A	**Crook Town (FAC)**	**W 1-0**	**Sellers**	**369**
H	Wycombe Wanderers	L 1-2	Hooley	805
H	Runcorn	D 1-1	Thompson	770
A	**Blyth Spartans (FAC)**	**D 1-1**	**Wiggan**	**1100**
H	**Blyth Spartans (FAC)**	**W 3-1**	**Bowman (2), Thompson**	**1323**
H	Barnet	W 3-1	Burke, Ferguson, Wiggan	749
H	**Bishop Auckland (FAC)**	**W 4-1**	**Burke (pen), Hartley, Dawson, Wiggan**	**1773**
A	Northwich Vic.	D 0-0		666
A	Bath City	D 0-0		530
H	**Altrincham (BLT)**	**W 3-2**	**Bowman D. (3)**	**623**
A	Bath City	W 2-1	Burke, Wintersgill	726
A	**Notts County (FAC)**	**L 1-6**	**Burke (pen)**	**5621**
A	Telford	L 0-1		948
A	**Altrincham (BLT)**	**L 0-2**		**823**
A	Boston United	L 1-2	Bowman D.	1258
A	Stafford Rangers	W 3-0	Wintersgill (2), Hartley	1164
H	Telford United	W 3-1	Dawson, Rose, Wiggan	669
H	**Barrow (FAT)**	**W 2-1**	**Ferguson, Thompson**	**803**
A	Frickley Athletic	L 1-2	Rose	787
A	Kidderminster	L 1-5	Hartley	727
A	Kettering Town	D 0-0		1348
H	Wealdstone	L 0-1		726
H	**Southport (FAT)**	**D 0-0**		**1048**
A	**Southport (FAT)**	**D 1-1**	**aet Hartley**	**1084**
H	Kidderminster Harriers	L 3-5	Burke (2), Sellers	543
A	**Southport (FAT)**	**L 0-1**		**1612**
A	Wycombe Wanderers	L 1-2	Burke	680
H	Northwich Victoria	D 0-0		618
A	Barnet			
H	Frickley Athletic	L 2-3	Thompson, Sellers	480
A	**Middlesborough (NRSC)**	**W 2-1**	**Omoni, Thompson**	**50**
A	Dartford	D 1-1	Dawson	431
H	Weymouth	D 1-1	Thompson	537
H	Cheltenham	W 1-0	Thompson (pen)	452
H	Enfield	L 1-3	Hartley	726
A	Runcorn	D 0-0		451
A	Nuneaton Borough	L 1-3	Phillips	621
H	Boston United	W 2-1	Mitchell, Fairless	644
H	**York City (NRSC s.f.)**	**L 1-4**	**Fairless**	**692**
A	Wealdstone	W 3-0	Haire (2), Hartley	503
A	Cheltenham	L 1-5	Haire	887
H	Maidstone United	W 2-0	Thompson, Cooper	587
H	Kettering	L 2-3	Dawson, Haire	520
H	Stafford Rangers	L 2-4	Philips, o.g.	559
A	Dagenham	D 0-0		
A	Barnet	W 1-0		
A	Enfield	W 4-0		

SCARBOROUGH SQUAD 1985-86

Goalkeepers
Dave Coleby: Whitby Town, Chesterfield, Burnley
Dave Chapman: Pickering Town, Old Malton, Whitby Town, Scarborough, Pickering Town, Selby Town

Defenders
Kenny Dennis: Peterborough United
Graham Hartley: Local
Geoff Bowman: Local
Neil Thompson: Hull City (31), Notts Forest
Richard Dawson: York City (5)
Harry Dunn: York City (5)
Ken Mitchell: Seaham Red Star, Darlington (13-1), Newcastle United (66-2)

Midfield
Stuart Coleby: Whitby Town, Nunthorpe Athletic
Neil Sellers: Goole Town, Bridlington Town, Hull City
Dave Wintersgill: Gresley Rovers, Tornavon pallo (Fin), Wolves (4)
Phil Omoni: Whitby Town, Shildon, Billingham Town, Nunthorpe Athletic
Lee Cooper: Local
Brendan Phillips: Corby Town, Shepshed, Charterhouse, Burton Albion, Nuneaton Borough, Scarborough, Nuneaton Borough, Boston United, Mansfield Town (17), Boston United, Kettering Town, Nuneaton Borough, Burton Albion, Peterborough United (1), Leicester City

Forwards
Keith Fairless: Peterlee Newton
David Bowman: Local
Nigel Rose: Frickley Athletic, Scarborough
Garry Haire: Darlington (19-2), Bradford City (49-13), Oxford United
Pat Olney: Bangor City, Preston North End, Manchester United
Trenton Wiggan: Gainsborough Trinity, Sheffield United (24-2)

SCARBOROUGH

President: David Jenkinson
Chairman: Mr B Adamson
Manager: Neil Warnock
Asst. Manager:
Trainer: Geoff Bowman
Doctor: Dr A.F. Chico
Secretary: J.T. Crawford, M.Ed.,
Address & Tel. No. 22 Barmoor Close, Scalby, Scarborough. 0723 365655
Commercial Manager: Dave Gibbin
Address & Tel. No. Scarborough F.C. Development Assoc., 97 Victoria Road, Scarborough. 0723 369211
Press Officer & Tel. No. B. Adamson, 4 Prospect Park, Scarborough. (0723) 367977
Address and Tel. No. of ground: Athletic Ground, Seamer Road, Scarborough. 0723 375094
Simple ground directions: A64 main trunk road from York. ¼ mile on left past Plaxtons coach factory
Club shop: Yes
No. of seats: 864 **Covered accommodation:** 4,000 **Capacity:** 10,000
Floodlights: Yes
Year formed: 1879 **Nickname:** The Boro
Club sponsor:
Previous names: None
Previous grounds: None
Day for midweek home matches: Wednesday
Club colours: All red
Change colours: Blue
Club metal badges: Yes
Record attendance: 11,124 v Luton Town **Year:** 1938
Best performance in: **F.A. Cup:** 1938, 1976, 1978 3rd Rd
F.A. Trophy: 1973, 1976, 1977 Winners. 1975 Runners-up
Previous Leagues: Northern, Yorkshire, North Eastern, Midland, Northern Premier
Clubhouse details: Fully licensed bar, concert room, dance floor
Present players with Football League experience: C. Podd (Halifax), R. Dawson (York), N. Thompson (Hull), P. Olney (Manchester United)
Past players who progressed into the Football League: W. Ayre (Hartlepool), S. Deere (Scarborough), C. Appleton (Leicester)
Record transfer fee paid: £12,000 for John Watson
Record transfer fee received: £10,000 from Nuneaton for R. Dixey
Programme details: 20 pages, 25p
Programme editor: Keith Crowe
Club Captain (1985-86): Richard Dawson
Player of the Year (1985-86): Neil Thompson
Local newspapers & Tel. No. Scarborough Evening News 0723 363636. The Mercury
Major Honours: F.A. Trophy (3) & Runners-up, Bob Lord Trophy, Northern Premier League Runners-up, Northern Premier League Cup, Vaux Floodlight League (2), Yorkshire League Cup, North Eastern League, North Eastern League Cup, Midland League, North Riding Senior Cup (16)

SUTTON UNITED

Vauxhall-Opel League Champions **F.A. Trophy** 1st Rd **F.A. Cup** 2nd Rd Qual Rd
AC Delco Cup Winners **Surrey Senior Cup** Winners

Sutton United: *Back Row (L-R); Wally Birchmore (matchday assistant), Danny Keenan (physio), Steve Bangs, Paul McKinnon, Mark Golley, Paul Rogers, Nigel Golley, Tony Rains, Lenny Dennis, Dave Wall (club liaison officer), Barrie Williams (club football manager). Front Row (L-R): Steve Tutt, Phil Dawson, John Rains (captain), Micky Stephens, Ron Fearon. Absent from photo: Larry Pritchard (first team manager), Roger Mackay, Mike Cornwell, Paul Thornton*

Promotion to the GM-Vauxhall Conference this season was the icing on the cake for Sutton United players and supporters who saw the club retain the Vauxhall-Opel League Championship with an increased points total, win the Surrey Senior Cup for the fourth time in succession (a county record) and add the AC Delco Cup for good measure.

This superb repeat success vindicated Sutton's decision not to take the chance of Gola League football a year earlier. Although that decision disappointed many people at the time, the club had felt that they were not yet fully prepared, in terms of finance or facilities, to take on such a commitment, the main uncertainty being discussions with the local council on taking over the running of the Gander Green Lane ground for themselves.

In the event not only was agreement with the council successfully concluded, but on the field Sutton enjoyed their most successful season ever—the culmination of a remarkable run of success since Barrie Williams, ably supported by popular former player Larry Pritchard, took over as manager eight seasons ago.

Sutton's hopes of retaining the Vauxhall-Opel title started quietly enough, and by early November they lay only 7th in the table, but then eight league wins on the trot saw them comfortably to the top of the table by the turn of the year. The main disappointment was early exits from both the F.A. Cup and Trophy.

But it was the emergence of Yeovil as contenders for the title that really brought excitement to the season. While Sutton were extending their unbeaten league record to 24 games, Yeovil had taken over at the top and were looking equally unstoppable in their bid to go straight back into the Alliance. When the two clubs met in a potential title-decider at Huish on 22 April, a phenomenal 5,348 fans turned out—surely a record in recent years for a non-league game.

Sutton lost that pulsating match 2-0 but still had the chance to take the title if they could win five out of an absurdly demanding six games in the last ten days of the season, the inheritance of postponements during February's big freeze (only one, ironically on Sutton's own ground). It was here that the side's character really came to the fore and they **did** win five of the six, a slip by Yeovil in the meantime extending the final winning margin to four points.

In the process Sutton also topped 100 league goals for the second season in a row, finishing with 109. In all matches United fans were treated to 171 goals, with Paul McKinnon notching a record 53 of them.

The close season has seen Sutton busily preparing to meet the new and exciting challenge of the GM-Vauxhall Conference with almost £50,000 invested in improvements to the already well-equipped Gander Green Lane facilities. These include new covered terracing on one side, refurbished terracing behind one goal, a hard-surface training area and a new press box.

SUTTON UNITED

Goalkeepers
Ron Fearon: San Diego Sockers, Reading (86), Dover, QPR
Rick Collier: Crawley, Carshalton, Sutton United, Staines, Sutton United, Crawley, Redhill

Defenders
Roger Mackay: Hendon, Hayes, Slough Town, Mansfield, Coventry
Paul Estall: Leatherhead
John Rains: Bromley, Fulham
Tony Rains: Fulham, Sutton United youth
Ned Metaxa: Woking, Oxford University
Micky Barker: Croydon

Midfield
Mark Golley: Crystal Palace
Nigel Golley: Whyteleafe, Crystal Palace
Micky Stephens: Youth team
Phil Dawson: Youth team, Wimbledon
Neil Robson: Youth team
Steve Tutt: Local, Chelsea, Fulham

Forwards
Lenny Dennis: Dulwich, Bromley, Orient, Crystal Palace
Mike Cornwell: Worthing, Sutton United, Horsham, Eastbourne United
Paul McKinnon: Tegs (Sweden), Sutton United, Trelleborg (Sweden), Sutton United, Ryoden (Hong Kong), Sutton United, Malmo (Sweden), Sutton United, Woking, Chelsea
Paul Rogers: Youth team
Paul Thornton: Youth team

Sutton's only competitive meeting with a Gola League side last season came in the F.A. Trophy 1st Round when Kettering Town were 1-0 victors at Gander Green Lane. Here Sutton's Mike Cornwell (light shirt) rides a tackle from Kettering centre-half Greg Fee, with fellow striker Paul McKinnon in close attendance Photo: Sutton Herald

SUTTON UNITED VAUXHALL-OPEL LEAGUE SEASON 1985-6

Venue	Opponents	Result	Scorers	Att.
A	Hampton (fr)	W 2-0	Rains T., McKinnon	
H	Wealdstone (fr)	W 2-1	Mackay, Dawson	
H	Chelmsford City (fr)	W 4-1	Rains J., (2), Golley M., Rogers	
H	**Maidstone United (DPT)**	**D 2-2**	**L 1-3 pens. McKinnon (2)**	
H	**Wycombe Wanderers (DCS)**	**L 1-3**	**McKinnon**	
H	Enfield (fr)	D 3-3	McKinnon (2), Golley M.,	
A	Farnborough Town	L 2-3	McKinnon, Golley N.,	
H	Walthamstow Avenue	D 3-3	Rogers (2), Golley N.,	301
H	Hayes	W 3-1	Golley M. (3)	295
A	Hitchin Town	L 1-2	McKinnon	
H	**Beckenham Town (FAC)**	**W 5-0**	**McKinnon (2), Golley N., Rains J., Stephens**	**358**
H	Hendon	W 3-0	Thornton, Rains J., Golley M. (pen)	300
H	Carshalton Athletic	D 2-2	Thornton (2)	526
A	Billericay Town	W 2-1	McKinnon (pen), Golley M.	
A	Kingstonian	W 4-2	Archbold 2, McKinnon, Thornton	
H	**Gravesend & N (FAC)**	**L 0-1**		
H	Worthing	D 0-0		365
H	Bishop's Stortford	W 4-1	Thornton, Golley M., Rains J., McKinnon	343
H	**Bognor Regis T (ACD)**	**D 3-3**	**aet. McKinnon (3, 1 pen)**	
A	Bognor Regis T	L 0-2		
A	**Bognor Regis T (ACD)**	**W 3-1**	**McKinnon (2), Dennis**	
H	Tooting & M	D 0-0		464
A	Barking	W 2-0	Cornwell (2)	
A	Epsom & Ewell	D 2-2	Dennis, Rains J.	447
H	Wokingham Town	W 5-0	McKinnon (3), Dennis (2)	300
H	Dulwich Hamlet	W 6-1	Golley M. (2), Dennis (2), Stephens, Cornwell	449
H	Billericay Town	W 3-2	Dennis, McKinnon, Golley M.	372
H	Slough Town	W 4-1	Golley M., (2), Stephens, McKinnon (pen)	438
A	**Maidenhead United (ACD)**	**W 5-3**	**McKinnon (3), Golley N. (2)**	
A	Harrow Borough	W 3-0	Dennis (2), McKinnon (pen)	
A	Dulwich Hamlet	W 2-1	Thornton, Dennis	
H	Epsom & Ewell	W 3-1	Golley M., Rains J., Tutt	505
A	**Carshalton Ath (ACD)**	**W 2-0**	**Golley M., Thornton**	
H	**Kettering Town (FAT)**	**L 0-1**		**770**
A	Carshalton Athletic	W 4-1	Dennis (3, 1 pen), Cornwell	
H	**Croydon (SSC)**	**D 1-1**	**Cornwell**	**460**
A	Hayes	D 1-1	Golley M. (pen)	
A	**Croydon (SSC)**	**W 3-1**	**Cornwell, Dawson, Rains J.**	
H	Farnborough Town	D 1-1	Golley M.	521
A	Hendon	W 2-1	Dennis, Golley M. (pen)	
A	**Carshalton Ath (SSC)**	**W 5-3**	**Dennis (3), McKinnon, Golley M.**	
A	**Harrow Borough (ACD)**	**W 5-3**	**McKinnon (2), Dennis, Stephens, Golley M.**	
A	**Kingstonian (SSC s.f.)**	**W 4-1**	**Dennis (2), KcKinnon (2)**	
H	Yeovil Town	W 3-1	McKinnon (2, 1 pen), Dawson	1333
A	**Hampton (ACD s.f.)**	**L 0-1**		
H	Barking	D 1-1	Rains J.	347
H	Bognor Regis T	W 6-0	McKinnon (2), Golley M., Rains J., Cornwell, Dennis	270
A	Tooting & Mitcham United	W 5-1	McKinnon (3), Cornwell, Dennis	425
A	Slough Town	W 1-0	Dennis	553
H	Windsor & Eton	W 5-0	Cornwell, Dennis, Golley M., Bangs, Stephens	458
N	**Chertsey Town (SSC final)**	**W 2-0**	**McKinnon, Golley M.**	
H	**Hampton (ACD s/f)**	**W 2-1**	**aet. Thornton, McKinnon (pen)**	
A	Bishop's Stortford	W 6-0	McKinnon (2, 1 pen), Dennis (2), Goley M., Robson	
H	**Hampton (ACD s/f)**	**W 3-1**	**Golley M., Vagg (o.g.), Hollands (o.g.)**	
A	Worthing	W 2-0	Golley M., McKinnon	394
H	Croydon	W 3-2	McKinnon (pen), Rains T., Dennis	328
H	Hitchin Town	W 4-1	McKinnon, Cornwell, Rains J., Rogers	481
A	Yeovil Town	L 0-2		5348
A	Wokingham Town	W 3-1	Dennis (2), Thornton	
H	Harrow Borough	W 2-0	How (o.g.), McKinnon	503
A	Croydon	L 0-1		
A	Walthamstow Avenue	W 1-0	McKinnon	
H	Kingstonian	W 2-0	McKinnon, Dennis	671
A	Windsor & Eton·	W 3-0	McKinnon (2, 1 pen), Thornton	
N	**Uxbridge (ACD final)**	**W 3-1**	**McKinnon (2), Dennis**	**1052**
A	**Crystal Palce (SBS)**	**L 2-3**	**Thornton, Dennis**	

ACD = AC Delco Cup
SSC = Surrey Senior Cup
DPT = Dick Prichard Trophy
DCS = Dylon Charity Shield
SBS = Surrey FA Benevolent Shield

The main stand at Sutton's Gander Green Lane ground, where almost £50,000 worth of improvements have been made to facilities since the beginning of 1986 in anticipation of moving to the GM-Vauxhall Conference

SUTTON UNITED

President: Andrew Letts
Chairman: Petery Molloy
Club Football Manager: Barrie Williams
First Team Manager: Larry Pritchard
Reserve Team Manager: Ken Ireland
Youth Team Manager: Ted Shepherd

Secretary: Ralph Carr
Address & Tel. No. 8 Shelley Close, Banstead, Surrey Burgh Heath 58103 (H)
Commercial Manager: Barry Aplin
Address & Tel. No. 6 Mellow Close, Banstead, Surrey. Burgh Heath 53939 (H)

Physiotherapist: Danny Keenan
Press Officer & Tel. No. Simon Clennell. Tel 01 720 6754
Address and Tel. No. of ground: Borough Sports Ground, Gander Green Lane, Sutton, Surrey. 01 644 4440
Simple ground directions: Gander Green Lane crosses the Sutton by-pass (A217) about one mile south of Rose Hill roundabout. Heading from London, turn left at traffic lights by 'Gander' pub. From M25 (Junction 8, Reigate Hill interchange), head north along A217 for approx. 8 miles, cross A232 then turn right by 'Gander'. Rail: West Sutton station
Club shop: Yes, Tony Dolbear, 17 Hilbert Rd., Cheam, Surrey
No. of seats: 1,000 **Covered accommodation:** 2,000 **Capacity:** 10,000 **Floodlights:** Yes
Year formed: 1898 **Nickname:** U's **Club sponsor:** Business Press International
Previous names: Sutton Association FC and Sutton Guild Rovers FC merged in 1898
Previous grounds: Manor Lane, 1898-1911

Day for midweek home matches: Tuesday

Club colours: All amber with chocolate trim
Change colours: All white with chocolate and amber trim
Club metal badges: Yes, £1.40 each plus post from Club Shop (Tony Dolbear)

Record attendance: 14,000 v Leeds Utd., F.A. Cup 4th Rd **Year:** 1970
Best performance in: **F.A. Cup:** 1969-70 4th Rd
F.A. Trophy: 1980-81 Finalists
Previous Leagues: Herald, Surrey Junior, Southern Suburban, Athenian, Vauxhall-Opel
Clubhouse details: Three bars plus conference/meeting rooms, open lunchtimes and evenings, 7 days a week. Available for private hire. Steward: Brenda Reed 01 644 4440
Present players with Football League experience: Ron Fearon (Reading)
Past players who progressed into the Football League: Charlie Vaughan (Charlton), Billy Robinson (C. Palace), Tony Barton (Fulham), Mike Pentecost (Fulham), John Faulkner (Leeds), Micky Fillery (Chelsea), Steve Galloway (Crystal Palace)
Record transfer fee paid: Paul McKinnon to Malmo, Sweden
Record transfer fee received: Paul McKinnon from Malmo, Sweden
Programme details: 28 pages, 30p
Programme editor: Simon Clennell
Club Captain (1985-86): John Rains
Player of the Year (1985-86): Paul McKinnon
Local newspapers & Tel. No. Sutton Herald 01 643 4351, Sutton & Cheam Advertiser 01 668 4111, Sutton Borough Guardian 01 661 0002
Major Honours: F.A. Amateur Cup Finalists (2), Anglo-Italian Tournament Winners & Runners-up (2), F.A. Trophy Finalists, Isthmian League Champions (3) & Runners-up (3), Athenian League Champions (3) & Runners-up, London Senior Cup Winners (2), Surrey Senior Cup Winners (9) & Runners-up (8), AC Delco Cup Winners (3) and Runners-up

---

Appearances:
League (42), Cup (20); Golley M. 61 + 1, Fearon 61, Rains T. 61, Rains J. 59, McKinnon 52, Mackay 51, Stephens 49 + 1, Bangs 48, Dawson 47 + 1, Dennis 45, Cornwell 37 + 1, Golley N. 29 + 6, Rogers 21 + 4, Thornton 15 + 5, Archbold 11 + 2, Metz 10 + 1, Tutt 9 + 3, Robson 5 + 2, Kidd 4 + 3, Metaxa 4 + 1, Estall 2, Collier 1, Barker 0 + 2

Goalscorers:
League (109); McKinnon 28, Dennis 23, Golley M. 19, Cornwell 8, Thornton 8, Rains J. 7, Rogers 3, Stephens 3, Archbold 2, Golley N. 2, Bangs 1, Dawson 1, Rains T. 1, Robson 1, Tutt 1, own goals 1
Cups (51); McKinnon 22, Dennis 9, Golley M. 5, Golley N. 3, Thornton 3, Cornwell 2, Rains J. 2, Stephens 2, Dawson 1, own goals 2

STAFFORD RANGERS

Gola League 7th **F.A. Trophy** 2nd Rd **F.A. Cup** 2nd Qual Rd **S.S.C.** 2nd Rd
Bob Lord Trophy Winners

Stafford Rangers: *Back Row: P. Derbyshire, M. Hanchard, P. Upton, P. Titley, M. Gill, F. Wood   Middle Row: B. Whittaker (physio), P Carr, D. Field, G. Simpson, P. Pritchard, G. Bennett. M. Meddings (assistant manager), R. Walters (trainer)   Front Row: P. Johnson, B. Lowe, J. Ridley, R. Reid (manager), K. Beech, K. Mooney, R. Mountain*

To win a trophy in their first season back in semi-professional's premier competition must have been very satisfying to all concerned at Marston Road.

Having won the Northern Premier League Championship Shield at the beginning of the season, Gola League football didn't immediately come easy to Rangers who took five league games to find their feet and eventually got off the mark with their first victory against newcomers Wycombe Wanderers.

However, despite the disappointment of an F.A. Cup defeat at Halesowen in front of 1,453, league form became much steadier and with nine away victories during the season a creditable seventh place was achieved.

Phil Derbyshire in action against Cheltenham Photo: Staffs Newsletter/Advertiser

Port Vale knocked Rangers out of the County Cup but it was the Bob Lord Trophy which produced the season's highlights. Barrow, Nuneaton Borough and Altrincham were beaten on the way to the semi-finals where Runcorn were eliminated after a replay. This presented a two legged final against Barnet and two straight victories brought the trophy back to Staffordshire.

Ron Reid built a sound side as the campaign developed and England semi-pro international Phil Derbyshire finished as top scorer, closely followed by Bobby Mountain an interesting signing who has a tremendous goal scoring record behind him in his days at Matlock Town.

Stafford Rangers have an excellent non-league pedigree and who knows, they are quite capable, with a superb ground and good support, to raise their game and push for that treasured Football League place.

STAFFORD RANGERS SQUAD 1986

Goalkeepers
David Field: Hednesford Town
Philip Pritchard: Stoke City

Defenders
Paul Johnson: Altrincham, Chester (21-1), Stoke City (60)
Kevin Mooney: Tranmere Rovers (25-3), Telford United, Bury (1), Bangor City
John Ridley: Leicester, Chesterfield, Port Vale
Phil Titley: Armitage, Chasetown, Great Wyrley
Paul Upton: Bedworth United, Coventry Sporting
Fraser Wood: Kidderminster Harriers, Stafford Rangers, Tipton

Midfield
Ken Beech: Port Vale, Walsall, Peterborough
Peter Carr: Burton Albion, Gainsborough Trinity, Rotherham United (36-3)
Philip Derbyshire: Altrincham, Mossley, Avro F.C., Stalybridge, Celtic
Martyn Gill: Mossley, Frickley Athletic, Bridlington Trinity, Worsborough
Barry Lowe: Nuneaton Borough, Worcester City, Nuneaton Borough, Worcester City, Weymouth, Stafford Rangers
Gary Simpson: Stoke City, Boston United

Forwards
Graham Bennett: Bangor City, Bridgend Town, Barry Town, Altrincham
Martin Hanchard: Stoke City
Bobby Mountain: Huddersfield, Matlock Town, Alfreton Town
Donald Page: Altrincham, Northwich Victoria

Graham Bennett challenges in the Cheltenham goalmouth. Photo: Staff Newsletter/Advertiser

STAFFORD RANGERS GOLA LEAGUE SEASON 1985-6

Venue	Opponents	Result	Scorers	Att.
H	**Marine (NPL Shield)**	**W 3-2**	**Hanchard, Gill, Beech**	**918**
H	Weymouth	L 2-3	Page, Hanchard	1168
A	Boston United	D 1-1	Hanchard	1483
H	Barnet	D 0-0		1168
A	Runcorn	L 0-3		561
A	**Lye Town (FAC)**	**W 3-1**	**Page, Youll, Beech**	**508**
H	Runcorn	D 1-1	Page	989
A	Wycombe Wanderers	W 4-2	Derbyshire, Hanchard (pen), Gill, Beech	767
A	**Barrow (BLT)**	**W 1-0**	**Ridley**	**400**
H	Enfield	D 1-1	Derbyshire (pen)	1228
H	**Barrow (BLT)**	**W 1-0**	**Page**	**797**
A	**Halesowen Town (FAC)**	**L 2-3**	**Derbyshire, Gill**	**1453**
A	Bath City	W 1-0	Gill	484
A	Kettering Town	W 1-0	Derbyshire	1207
H	Bath City	W 1-0	Upton	1196
A	Cheltenham Town	L 0-2		1223
A	Frickley Athletic	L 0-3		587
H	Wealdstone	W 2-1	Tapley (o.g.), Page	1123
A	Barrow	W 1-0	Derbyshire	427
H	**Port Vale (SSC)**	**D 1-1**	**Derbyshire (pen)**	**729**
A	**Nuneaton B (BLT)**	**D 1-1**	**Power**	**578**
A	Dartford	D 3-3	Carr, Derbyshire (pen), Page	468
A	Northwich Victoria	L 0-2		701
H	Kidderminster Harriers	W 3-2	Derbyshire, Mountain (2)	1273
H	**Nuneaton B (BLT)**	**W 2-1**	**Mountain, Page**	**777**
H	Maidstone United	W 2-1	Mountain, Derbyshire	1035
A	**Port Vale (SSC)**	**L 0-1**		**894**
H	Scarborough	L 0-3		1164
A	Altrincham	W 3-1	Derbyshire, Gardner (o.g.), Ridley	1152
H	**Nuneaton Borough (FAT)**	**W 1-0**	**Hanchard**	**857**
A	Telford United	D 0-0		1483
H	Telford United	L 0-3		1958
A	Enfield	L 1-3	Beech	1018
H	Nuneaton B	W 2-0	Ridley, Mountain	1076
H	**Bishop Auckland (FAT)**	**L 0-1**		**1060**
A	Weymouth	D 1-1	Simpson	900
H	Frickley Athletic	D 0-0		872
A	Dagenham	D 1-1	Hanchard (pen)	419
A	Oswestry Town (Fr.)	W 5-1	Derbyshire, Hanchard (3), Bennett	90
A	**Altrincham (BLT)**	**W 2-0**	**Hanchard, Mountain**	**615**
H	Northwich Victoria	L 1-2	Hanchard	926
A	**Runcorn (BLT s.f.)**	**D 0-0**		**697**
A	Kidderminster Harriers	D 1-1	Bennett	1064
H	**Runcorn (BLT)**	**W 2-1**	**Derbyshire (2, 1 pen)**	**987**
A	Nuneaton Borough	L 0-3		729
H	Dagenham	W 3-1	Bennett (2), Upton	784
H	Dartford	W 5-1	Mountain (3), Bennett, Derbyshire	1011
H	Barrow	W 1-0	Hanchard	922
H	Wycombe Wanderers	D 1-1	Simpson	1035
A	Maidstsone United	W 4-2	Bennett, Simpson, Carr, Mountain	719
H	Cheltenham Town	W 2-0	Carr, Mountain	1035
H	Altrincham	D 1-1	Derbyshire	1041
A	Barnet	W 2-0	Bennett (2)	547
H	**Barnet (BLT)**	**W 2-1**	**Lowe, Mountain**	**1379**
H	Scarborouogh	W 4-2	Derbyshire (2), Gill, Mountain	459
A	**Barnet (BLT)**	**W 1-0**	**Mountain**	**1087**
H	Boston United	W 2-1	Bennett, Carr	1130
A	Wealdstone	W 3-2	Mountain, Carr, Hanchard	304
H	Stoke City (Test.)	L 1-0		851
H	Kettering Town	D 0-0		

NPL Shield = Northern Premier League Shield
FAC = F.A. Cup
BLT = Bob Lord Trophy
SSC = Staffs Senior Cup
FAT = F.A. Trophy

Appearances:
Ridley 57, Carr 57, Beech 55, Titley 55, Johnson 53, Field 50, Lowe 50, Upton 50, Derbyshire 47, Gill 46, Hanchard 34, Simpson 33, Page 31, Mountain 29, Wood 22, Bennett 18, Youll 8, Cross 7, Pritchard 7, Lodge 6, Brown 6, Mooney 5, Power 5, Austin 4, Kelly 2

Goalscorers:
Derbyshire 15, Mountain 14, Hanchard 8, Page 6, Bennett 5, Carr 4, Gill 4, Simpson 4, Beech 3, Ridley 3, Lowe 1, Power 1, Upton 1, Youll 1

The main stand at Rangers' fine Marston Road Ground.

STAFFORD RANGERS

President: R.N. Heath
Chairman: R.J. Burrill
Manager: Ron Reid 0742 471017 (H)
Asst. Manager:
Coach:
Physiotherapist: Mr P.S.B. Whittaker

Secretary: Mrs Angela Meddings
Address & Tel. No. 49 Cresswell Grove, Stafford ST18 9QP

Commercial Manager:
Address & Tel. No.

Press Officer & Tel. No. Angela Meddings 0785 52339
Address and Tel. No. of ground: Marston Road, Stafford. 0785 42750
Simple ground directions: Leave at exit 14 off M6 motorway to the A34 into Stafford. First turn left over railway bridge into Co-operative Street. Ground at the end of this street **Club shop:** Yes
No. of seats: 426 **Covered accommodation:** 3,000 **Capacity:** 9,500 **Floodlights:** Yes
Year formed: 1876 **Nickname:** The Boro **Club sponsors:** Various
Previous names: None
Previous grounds: Lammascotes
Day for midweek home matches: Tuesday
Club colours: Black/white stripes
Change colours: Yellow
Club metal badges: Yes
Record attendance: 8,523 v Rotherham **Year:** 1975
Best performance in: F.A. Cup: 1973-4 v Peterborough 4th Rd
F.A. Trophy: 1971-2 and 1978-9 Winners
Previous Leagues: Birmingham & Dist., North Staffs, Birmingham Comb., Cheshire, Alliance, Premier
Clubhouse details: Open daily. Bar, snacks, Saturday night entertainment
Present players with Football League experience: J. Ridley, K. Beech
Past players who progressed into the Football League: M. Aleksic (Tottenham), J. Arnold (Blackburn), R. Williams (Port Vale), M. Cullerton (Port Vale), Ken Barnes (Man C.), McIllvenny (WBA), E.Cameron (Exeter), G. Bullock (Barnsley), K. Mottershead (Doncaster), A. Lee (Tranmere)
Record transfer fee paid: £10,000 T. Dance
Record transfer fee received: £20,000 J. Arnold
Programme details: 30p
Programme editor: Angela Meddings
Club Captain (1985-86): K. Beech
Player of the Year (1985-86): John Ridley
Local newspapers & Tel. No. Stafford Newsletter 57700, Express & Star 52192. Sentinel 51139. Local radio stations: Beacon Radio, Radio Stoke, Signal Radio
Major Honours: Birmingham Combination League, Birmingham & District League, Northern Premier League (2), Staffs Senior Cup (7), Cheshire League Cup, F.A. Trophy (2), Bob Lord Trophy

TELFORD UNITED

Gola League 8th **F.A. Trophy** 1st Rd **F.A. Cup** 2nd Rd **S.S.C.** 1st Rd
Bob Lord Trophy 2nd Rd

Telford United: *Back Row: Kevin Charlton, John McGinty, Arthur Mann, Ken McKenna, Steve Ecton, Mark Hancock, Colin Williams, John Alcock, Len Lloyd.*
Front Row: Paul Jackson, Eddie Hogan, Tony Turner, Dave Barnett, Anton Joseph.

QUIET SEASON LEADS TO OPTIMISM

Compared with recent years the 1985/86 season of Telford United was tame and ordinary, rather disappointing in fact; yet at the very end there was surprisingly more cause for optimism than at the corresponding stages of those F.A. Cup-dominated terms. On those occasions, once the excellent cup displays had come to an end the team's league performances were at best ordinary and, at times, alarming as the season drew to a close; 1985-86 saw no real exploits in glamour competitions and, for quite a while, nothing to be over-pleased about in Gola League matters either, but a remarkable upturn in performances over the last ten games brought the season to an end on a successful and optimistic note.

Early season displays made it clear that some deficiences needed to be rectified quickly and it was not long before midfielder Hogan was coaxed out of 'retirement' to put some pattern into the team's play. Defensive frailties were also proving difficult to eradicate for various reasons and the team stuttered along with 'Jeckyll and Hyde' home and away fortunes. Away

success did not arrive until the F.A. Cup tie at Stockport; this fortunate result misled some of the national press into believing that another cup story was about to begin but those close to the Club realised this was never a possibility. The second round visit to Derby, tough enough in any event, was made all the harder by the absence of the then first-choice central defenders and the end result was predictable and inevitable. Shortly afterwards Southport ended any hopes in the F.A. Trophy.

The period around New Year saw playing resources stretched to the limit and several half-forgotten and new players were called upon to temporarily fill the breach; surprisingly home performances did not suffer during this spell and indeed the first away league success was gained at Stafford. In general, however, the security of points from the team's travels had always meant that the lower reaches of the table were never too far away and, following a four-match succession of defeats, including one dreadful home display against Maidstone (who thereby gained their first away win), the possibility of relegation was at its strongest.

As if stung into action by this threat, the Club seemed to be transformed during the course of one week. Former captain Kevin Lewis, who had left to manage Leek Town at the end of the previous season, returned as assistant manager to Stan Storton whose previous long-time accomplice, Brian Daintith, had parted company with the Club several months earlier. With him Lewis brought midfield player Tony Griffiths and the arrival of this duo, together with a blunt appraisal of the situation, saw a different attitude and style of play from then onwards. Griffiths solved what had been a problem position throughout and the team instantly had a new dimension to its attacking game. Victory at the then comfortably positioned Wycombe Wanderers in the first game of the new set-up saw the start of an enterprising and confident ten-match unbeaten run to the season's end and an eventual position of eighth in the table—dizzy heights by comparison to two months or so previously.

So the season ended on that optimistic note—as this is read we should know whether such optimision was well-founded.

TELFORD UNITED SQUAD 1986

Goalkeepers
Kevin Charlton: Bangor City, Hereford United (52), AFC Bournemouth (21), Wolves
Trevor Dance: Altrincham, Stafford Rangers, Port Vale (84)

Defenders
John McGinty: V.S. Rugby, Coventry Sporting
Tony Turner: Nuneaton Borough, Hednesford Town, Stop Out Wellington (N.Z.), Hednesford Town
Steve Eaton: Northwich Victoria, Tranmere Rovers (1)
Mike Hancock: Van Leer
Harry Wiggins: Local
Liam Halton: Bedworth United
Mark Greenaway: Oswestry Town, Halifax Town (16-1)

Midfield
Paul Mayman: Northwich Victoria, Nantwich Town, Crewe Alexandra (43-3)
Dave Barnett: Stafford Rangers, Bangor City, Oldham Athletic
Eddie Hogan: Nuneaton Borough, Telford United, Redditch United, Derby County
Antone Joseph: Weymouth, Cardiff City
Tony Griffiths: Leek Town, Port Vale, Leek Town
Jon Sille: Dartford, Maidstone United, Dagenham, St. Albans City, Kingstonian, Hertford Town

Forwards
Colin Williams: Scarborough, Northwich Victoria, Telford United, Northwich Victoria, Droylsden, Oldham Athletic
John Alcock: Eastwood, Hanley
John Stringer: Runcorn, Barnton
Ken McKenna: Tranmere Rovers, Everton
Kevin Sheldon: Leek Town, Burton Albion, Wigan Athletic (39-1), Stoke City (15)

Colin Williams

TELFORD UNITED GOLA LEAGUE SEASON 1985-6

Venue	Opponents	Result	Scorers	Att.
H	Barnet	D 2-2	Stringer, Williams	1233
A	Runcorn	L 0-1		
H	Dagenham	W 2-1	McKenna (2)	1012
A	Cheltenham Town	D 1-1	McKenna	
A	Dartford	L 1-2	McKenna	
H	Kettering Town	D 2-2	McKenna, O.G.	1151
H	**Oswestry Town (SSC)**	**L 2-3**	**Barnett, McKenna**	**778**
A	Maidstone United	D 4-4	McKenna 62), Alcock, O.G.	
A	**Boston United (BLT)**	**D 1-1**	**Williams**	
H	Weymouth	W 4-1	McKenna 62), Williams, Stringer	1113
H	**Boston United (BLT)**	**W 3-2**	**McGinty, Bennett, Hogan**	**1053**
A	Enfield	L 0-4		
A	Altrincham	L 0-1		
H	Barrow	W 3-1	Barnett, Williams, Alcock	1162
A	Bath City	L 0-3		
H	Frickley Athletic	W 2-1	Williams, McKenna	1013
H	**Kidderminster (MBC)**	**L 2-5**	**McGinty, McKenna**	**778**
A	Boston United	D 2-2	McKenna, Hogan	
H	Dartford	W 2-1	Stringer (2)	1073
A	**Frickley Athletic (BLT**	**L 0-4**		
A	Weymouth	L 2-5	Williams, Hogan	
A	**Stockport County (FAC)**	**W 1-0**	**McGinty**	**2994**
A	Kidderminster	L 0-3		
H	Scarborough	W 1-0	McKenna	948
H	**Frickley Athletic (BLT)**	**W 1-0**	**Williams**	**626**
A	Nuneaton B	D 1-1	McKenna	
A	**Derby County (FAC)**	**L 1-6**	**McKenna**	**12267**
A	Scarborough	L 1-3	Stringer	
H	**Southport (FAT)**	**L 2-4**	**Williams, Hogan**	**1133**
H	Stafford R	D 0-0		1481
H	Altrincham	W 2-1	McGinty, Hogan	1012
A	Stafford R	W 3-0	McGinty, McKenna (2)	
H	Wealdstone	W 2-1	Sheldon, McKenna	943
H	Runcorn	L 2-3	Sheldon, Joseph	1291
H	Bath C	W 1-0	Williams	1050
A	Kettering Town	L 0-4		
H	Boston United	W 2-1	Williams, McKenna	895
A	Barrow	L 0-1		
H	Maidstone United	L 2-4	McGinty, O.G.	955
H	Kidderminster	L 0-1		1011
A	Frickley Athletic	L 1-3	McGinty	
A	Wycombe Wanderers	W 2-1	Williams (2)	
H	Northwich V	W 4-0	McGinty, Griffiths, Stringer, Hogan	1009
A	Nortwich V	W 1-0	McGinty	
A	Dagenham	W 4-1	Griffiths, Halton, Hancock, Stringer	
A	Wealdstone	D 1-1	Stringer	
H	Cheltenham Town	W 3-0	Halton, Stringer (2)	1083
A	Barnet	W 2-1	McGinty, Griffiths	
H	Wycombe Wanderers	W 3-1	Halton, Williams, McKenna	1066
H	Enfield	D 2-2	Hogan, Joseph	1557
H	Nuneaton B	D 1-1	Stringer	1230

SSC = Shropshire Senior Cup
BLT = Bob Lord Trophy
MBC = M & B Cup
FAC = F.A. Cup
FAT = F.A. Trophy

Appearances:
League (42), Cup Ties (9); McGinty 49 + 2, Williams 48 + 2, Alcock 43, Hogan 42 + 1, Wiggins 39 + 3, Charlton 38 + 1, Turner 37 + 3, Joseph 36 + 3, McKenna 30 + 6, Halton 29 + 6, Stringer 28 + 6, Barnett 28 + 1, Eaton 26 + 5, Hancock 25 + 1, Dance 12, Griffiths 10, Jackson 8, Bennett 7 + 3, Mann 7 + 1, Jackson 5 + 1, Arnot 3 + 1, Ellison 2, Mayman 2, Shildon 2, Sille 2, Bowles 1, Whittingham 1, Mather 0 + 7, Edwards 0 + 1

Goalscorers:
League (68), Cup Ties (13); McKenna 21, Williams 13, Stringer 11, McGinty 10, Hogan 8, Griffiths 3, Hatton 3, Opponents 3, Barnett 2, Joseph 2, Sheldon 2, Alcock 1, Bennet 1, Hancock 1

TELFORD UNITED

President:
Chairman: G.E. Smith
Manager: Stan Storton
Asst. Manager:
Coach: Kevin Lewis
Physiotherapist: S. Day

Secretary: M.J. Ferriday
Address & Tel. No. 199 Trench Road, Telford TF2 7DX. (0952) 605193

Commercial Manager: D. Harris
Address & Tel. No.

Press Officer & Tel. No. Secretary
Address and Tel. No. of ground: Buck's Head Ground, Watling Street, Wellington, Telford, Shropshire. (0952) 3838
Simple ground directions: Situated on the B5061 (formerly main A5) in the Wellington district of north Telford. Leave M54 at Junction 6
Club shop: Yes
No. of seats: 1,200 **Covered accommodation:** 3,000 **Capacity:** 10,000 **Floodlights:** Yes
Year formed: 1877 **Nickname:** Lillywhites **Club sponsor:** Maxell
Previous names: Wellington Town (until 1969)
Previous grounds: None
Day for midweek home matches: Tuesday
Club colours: White with blue/red trim/blue/white
Change colours: Blue/white/red
Club metal badges: Yes
Record attendance: 13,000 v Shrewsbury Town **Year:** 1935
Best performance in: **F.A. Cup:** 4th Round, 1983-84; 5th Round, 1984-85
F.A. Trophy: 1970-71, 1982-83 Winners; 1969-70 Runners-up
Previous Leagues: Birmingham, Cheshire, Southern
Clubhouse details: Match days and selected other hours
Present players with Football League experience: Kevin Charlton, Paul Mayman, Steve Exton, Trevor Dance
Past players who progressed into the Football League: Graham French (Luton), Alan Walker (Lincoln)
Record transfer fee paid: £10,000 for Paul Mayman to Northwich Victoria
Record transfer fee received: Alan Walker (£20,000 to Lincoln)
Programme details: 24 pages, 30p
Programme editor: B.G. Bagnall
Club Captain (1985-86): Tony Turner
Player of the Year (1985-86): Harry Wiggins
Local newspapers & Tel. No. Shropshire Star 0952 44377. Telford Journal 0952 56262
Major Honours: F.A. Challenge Trophy & Runners-up, Southern League Cup, Welsh Cup (3), Birmingham League (3), Birmingham League Cup, Cheshire League (3) & Runners-up (2), Birmingham Senior Cup, Walsall Senior Cup, Shropshire Senior Cup (30)

WEALDSTONE

Gola League 10th **F.A. Trophy** 3rd Rd (after replay) **F.A. Cup** 1st Rd proper **M.S.C.** 1st Rd
Bob Lord Trophy 2nd Rd **Capital League** Runners-up

A QUIETER SEASON

At the end of Wealdstones' historic 'double' season, it was accepted that their amazing feat would be very difficult to repeat, or even to match. Wealdstone found this to be so, by finishing a rather disappointing 10th position in the league. The turning point in the season was without doubt the cold spell in February, when, like most clubs, Wealdstone were on ice for a month. Immediately prior to the snow they had probably their best spell winning nine out of eleven matches and moving into the top three in the league. But the resumption in March found Wealdstone struggling to score goals and a usually watertight defence more than generous on several occasions. Only one victory against Weymouth (a last minute winner at that!) was achieved from the last sixteen matches.

One player doesn't make a team (Maradonna excepted), but the loss of Alan Cordice, the England striker, through a serious knee injury certainly had an adverse effect. Cordice ironically injured his knee in a freak accident during a reserve game when he crashed into a wall behind the goal while chasing an elusive throughball. Players of Cordice's calibre are very rare in non-league football and many teams breathed a sigh of relief when they saw that the name—A. Cordice—was absent from the team sheet. Wealdstone's pattern of play—geared around a fully fit no. 9 was therefore disrupted. Alternatives were tried but lack of goals always prevailed.

Initially few changes were made to the double winning side—only Mark Graves reclaiming his place from Andy Graham who never recaptured any of the form that culminated in him scoring that memorable Wembley goal. Full back Steve Perkins was forced to retire through injury, but shrewd shopping by manager Brian Hall meant that the replacement—Steve Tapley signed from Fulham—was ready to impress. He had a super season and deservedly won the players' 'Player of the Year' award. The evergreen Robin Wainwright at 34 and in his seventh season for The Stones had his best ever year—scoring many vital goals and even 4 in one match against Boston United (a 7-2 win resulted) and he won both the Supporters Club and the Vice-President's 'Player of the Year' award.

Wealdstone's hold on the F.A. Trophy slipped when they lost narrowly to a highly underrated South Bank. In the F.A. Cup a creditable performance saw a 1-0 defeat at Reading who were seventeen points clear in the third division at the time.

Manager Brian Hall gained a great deal, though, from the season and the coming season with a league position at stake will surely see Wealdstone challenging.

WEALDSTONE SQUAD 1986

Goalkeepers
Bob Iles: Chelsea (14), Weymouth, Poole Town, AFC Bournemouth
Les Cleevely: Crystal Palace
Paul Jones: Wimbledon

Defenders
Steve Perkins: Wimbledon (52), QPR (2), Chelsea
Paul Bowgett: Wimbledon (41), Tottenham Hotspur, Letchworth Garden City
Dennis Byatt: Northampton Town (47-3), Peterborough United (3), Fulham
Steve McCargo: Local
Vince Jones: Watford & Bedmond
Chris Seagraves: Grimsby Town (38), Liverpool
Doug McClure: Wimbledon
Steve Tapley: Fulham

Midfield
Brian Geenaway: Fulham (85-8)
Robin Wainwright: Hillingdon Borough, Cambridge United, Northampton Town (32-5), Millwall (4), Luton Town (16-3)
Lee Holmes: Dartford, Enfield, Brentford (28-6), Haringey Borough, Edmonton, West Ham United
Neil Cordice: Northampton Town (8-1), Wycombe Wanderers
Gary Donnellan: Reading (44-5), Watford, Chelsea
Robin O'Keefe: Vauxhall Motors
Derek Doyle: Harrow Borough, Brentford, Southall, Hayes

Forwards
Alan Cordice: Norwich City, Maidenhead United
Mark Graves: Plymouth Argyle (33-3)
Andy Graham: Lancaster City, Hyde United
Keith Tonge: Cheshunt

Lee Holmes scoring v Frickley in the F.A. Trophy, watched by Mark Graves

WEALDSTONE GOLA LEAGUE SEASON 1985-6

Venue	Opponents	Result	Scorers	Att.
H	Barrow	W 4-0	Greenaway, Holmes (2), Graves	756
A	**Enfield (MSC)**	**W 4-2**	**Holmes, Cordice A., Graves, Cordice N.**	**805**
A	Northwich	D 2-2	McCargo, Donnellan	810
A	Boston	L 0-1		2067
H	Frickley Athletic	W 2-0	Holmes (2)	702
A	Cheltenham	W 2-1	Cordice A., Doyle	982
H	Runcorn	L 2-2	Holmes, Doyle, (L 3-5 on pen)	531
A	Nuneaton	D 0-0		851
A	Maidstone	W 1-0	Doyle	814
H	Altrincham	D 2-2	Graves, Doyle	854
H	Maidstone	W 3-2	Wainwright, Graves, Cordice N.	770
A	Runcorn	D 1-1	Holmes	624
A	Dartford	W 2-1	Bowgett, Cordice N.	622
H	Enfield	L 2-4	Graves, Graham	1323
H	Dagenham	L 0-4		781
A	Stafford	L 1-2	Graham	1123
H	Boston	W 7-2	Wainwright(4), Greenaway, Graves (2)	623
A	Altrincham	L 0-1		1151
H	Northwich	D 0-0		752
A	**Weymouth (BLT)**	**D 1-1**	**Cordice N.**	**402**
H	Wycombe	W 2-0	Jones, Graham	925
A	**Reading (FAC)**	**L 0-1**		**6460**
H	**Kingsbury (MSC)**	**L 1-3**	**Donnellan**	**186**
A	Kettering	L 1-2	Cordice N.	1057
A	**Weymouth (BLT)**	**L 2-3**	**Wainwright, Holmes**	**600**
H	Barnet	W 2-0	Wainwright, Greenaway	947
H	Kettering	W 3-1	Wainwright, Graham, Cordice N.	653
H	**Welling United (FAT)**	**W 1-0**	**Wainwright**	**629**
A	Barnet	L 0-1		907
H	Nuneaton	W 1-0	Bowgett	754
A	Telford	L 1-2	Holmes	943
A	Dagenham	W 2-0	Byatt, Donnellan	462
A	Scarborough	W 1-0	Cordice N.	767
H	**Frickley Athletic (FAT)**	**W 2-1**	**Wainwright, Holmes**	**815**
H	Dartford	W 2-1	Jones, Cordice N.	717
A	Bath	W 3-2	Wainwright, Greenaway, Doyle	521
H	**South Bank (FAT)**	**D 0-0**		**451**
A	**South Bank (FAT)**	**L 1-2**	**Graves**	**1147**
H	Cheltenham Town	D 0-0		708
A	Weymouth	L 2-4	Greenaway, Graves	775
A	Kidderminster	L 1-3	Graves	907
H	Kidderminster	L 0-3		620
A	Frickley Athletic	L 1-2	Doyle	535
H	Bath	L 0-1		610
H	Scarborough	L 0-3		503
H	Weymouth	W 1-0	Graham	434
H	Telford	D 1-1	Graham	
A	Wycombe Wanderers	L 0-1		889
A	Barrow	D 1-1	O.G.	402
A	Enfield	L 0-1		
H	Stafford Rangers	L 2-3	McCargo, Graves	304
H	Runcorn	D 1-1	Graves	408

MSC = Middlesex Senior Cup
BLT = Bob Lord Trophy
FAC = F.A. Cup
FAT = F.A. Trophy

Appearances:
League (42), Cup (11): Wainwright 52, Tapley 50, Bowgett 48, Iles 48, Holmes 45, McCargo 43, Greenaway 42, Graves 40, Doyle 33, Donnellan 32, Cordice N. 31, Byatt 30, Cordice A. 18, Graham 15, Jones 14, Perkins 12, McClure 8, Jones P. 3, O'Keefe 2, Seagraves 2, Cleaveley 1, Davies, Elliott 1, Tonge 1

Goalscorers:
Graves 21, Holmes 16, Wainwright 14, Cordice N. 11, Donnellan 11, Doyle 11, Graham 13, Greenaway 6, Jones 4, O'Keefe 4, Cordice 3, Tonge 4, Bowgett 2, McCargo 2, Iles 1, Byatt 1, Hall 1, O.G. 1

The main stand at Lower Mead stadium

WEALDSTONE

President: G.D. Morritt
Chairman: D.G. Morritt
Manager: Brian Hall
Asst. Manager:
Coach: Les Reed
Physiotherapist: Arnold Reed
Secretary: Peter Braxton, Wealdstone F.C.
Address & Tel. No. Station Road, Harrow HA1 2TU. 01 427 4064
Commercial enquiries: Barbara Vane
Address & Tel. No. 01 427 4064
Press Officer & Tel. No. D. Free, 01 863 1313. Ext. 4128
Address and Tel. No. of ground: Lower Mead Stadium, Station Road, Harrow, Middlesex. 01 427 4064
Simple ground directions: Station Road (town centre). Rear of EMI (ABC) cinema. Entrance by car park sign. A409 route from Junction 5 on M1. A312 via Hayes M3 & M4
Club shop: Yes
No. of seats: 496 **Covered accommodation:** 6,400 **Capacity:** 9,400 **Floodlights:** Yes
Year formed: 1900 **Nickname:** Royal Stones **Club sponsor:** Morritt Homes
Previous names: None
Club colours: Royal blue
Previous grounds: College Farm, Belmont Road, Wealdstone
Change colours: All red
Day for midweek home matches: Tuesday
Club metal badges: Yes
Record attendance: 13,504 v Leytonstone F.A. Amateur Cup **Year:** 1949
Best performance in: **F.A. Cup:** 1977-8 v QPR 3rd Rd
F.A. Trophy: Winners 1984-5
Previous Leagues: Spartan, Athenian, Isthmian, Southern
Clubhouse details: 3 bars plus Directors' bar and Vice-Presidents' bar. Dance hall and restaurant
Present players with Football League experience: R. Iles, D. Byatt, P. Bowgett, B. Wainwright, N. Cordice, B. Greenaway, S. Tapley, A. Cordice, G. Donnellan, M. Graves, D. McClure, L. Holmes
Past players who progressed into the Football League: Charlie Sells, Colin Franks, Tommy McGee, Bobby Ryan, Eddie Smith, Phil White, Francis Joseph, Stuart Pearce
Record transfer fee paid: £5,000 to Trowbridge (joint fee) for Terry & Derek Evans, summer 1974
Record transfer fee received: £25,000 from Coventry City for Stuart Pearce, November 1983
Programme details: 24 pages, 35p
Programme editor: D. Free
Club Captain (1985-86): Paul Bowgett
Player of the Year (1985-86): Robin Wainwright
Local newspapers & Tel. No. Harrow Observer, 01 427 4404
Major Honours: Amateur Cup Winners, Southern League (Div 1, sth) Champions, Southern League (sthn div) Champions, Southern League Shield Winners, Southern League Cup Winners, Southern League Challenge Cup Winners, Athenian League Champions, Gola League Champions, F.A. Trophy Winners, Middlesex Senior Cup Winners (10 times)

WELLING UNITED

Gola League	F.A. Trophy	F.A. Cup	C.S.C.	Bob Lord Trophy

Back Row: (Left to Right), Nicky Brigden (coach), Paul Sawyer, Gary Abbott, Kevin Shoemake, Nigel Ransome, Ian Starkey, Stuart White.
Front Row: John Parry, Louis Robinson, Neil Clemmence, Ray Burgess, John Bartley (Missing: David Smith and Adrian Lemoine)

WELLING'S SEASON TO REMEMBER

Welling completed a rise from Sunday football to Gola League, as they walked away with the Southern League, some 23 points ahead of nearest rivals Chelmsford City. Included in this was the Southern League points record of 93, a generous 95 goals for (19 more than any other club), and a miserly 31 against (9 less than any other club), whilst the nearest challenger to a goal difference of +64 was Chelmsford's +27.

It was Welling's form in the new year that won them the Championship as they took 55 points from a possible 60, following a goalless draw at King's Lynn on New Year's Day. Nearest rivals Chelmsford and Worcester kept up the chase until Easter, when the Wings won 3 games in 4 days to move 15 points clear.

Any reasonable doubt over the destination of the title was removed with a 3-0 victory over Chelmsford, the following week, which left Welling needing two points from six games to be certain. On April 12th United drew 3-3 at Crawley, but that proved to be enough as Chelmsford and Worcester lost to Alvechurch and Fisher respectively. If anyone thought the side would let up, they were proved embarrassingly wrong as Welling won their final five matches including two wins over Gravesend which condemned the Fleet to relegation.

During the run in Welling had two gates of over 1000, a record 1,413 for the visit of local rivals Fisher on Good Friday, and 1,317 for second placed Chelmsford eight days later.

The only shadow over Welling's title win, was a rumour that was spread nationally that the club's ground would not be up to Gola League standard. However, the club completed all necessary ground improvements by May 1st, when the ground was passed fit, and Welling were assured of promotion.

The Wings celebrated by beating Dover 2-0 in the Kent Senior Cup Final at Gillingham four days later to complete the double.

John Bartley, the club's record-breaking striker, hit 57 goals in 55 matches during the season, but still failed to make the England non-league squad. During the league match at R. S. Southampton on 22nd February the remarkable striker scored his 500th goal from the club, the goals being spread over two spells at Welling.

So this remarkable club, run by brothers Graham and Barrie Hobbins, now join the cream of non-league soccer, aiming to silence the sceptics who predict that they will make a rapid return from when they came.

WELLING UNITED SQUAD 1986

Goalkeepers
Kevin Shoemake: Harlow Town, Chelmsford City, Orient
Alan Rogers: Tunbridge Wells, Welling United, Bromley, Carshalton Athletic, Eastbourne United

Defenders
Paul Sawyer: Local
Adrian Lemoine: Maidstone United
Ian Starkey: Dartford, Bromley, Maidstone United
Nigel Ranson: Local
Paul Summersby: Local

Midfield
Ray Burgess: Local
Stuart White: Gillingham, Charlton Athletic (apprentice)
John Parry: Millwall (apprentice)
Neil Clemmence: Dartford
Ian Crouch: Local

Forwards
John Bartley: Maidstone United, Kuipio ELO (Finland), Millwall, Welling United
Gary Abbott: Local
David Smith: Dartford
Shaun Adams: Local
Jeff Ross: Ashford Town

Hectic goalmouth action at last season's Top of the Table clash with Fisher Athletic which attracted a record crowd.

WELLING UNITED'S SOUTHERN LEAGUE SEASON 1985-6

Venue	Opponents	Result	Scorers	Att.
H	Shepshed Charterhouse	W 1-0	Abbot	403
A	Willenhall Town	D 1-1	Bartley	205
A	**Thanet United (BDC)**	**W 2-0**	**Bartley (2)**	**150**
A	**Dorking (FAC)**	**W 7-1**	**Bartley (5, 1 pen), Smith, Abbot**	**100**
H	Witney Town	W 6-1	Sawyer, Abbott, White (2), Burgess, Bartley (pen)	365
H	**Canterbury City (BDC)**	**W 2-0**	**Bartley (2)**	**331**
A	Fareham Town	W 4-1	Bartley, Crouch, Smith (2)	125
A	**Sheppey United (BDC)**	**W 3-1**	**Smith, Crouch, Bartley**	**133**
A	**Staines Town (FAC)**	**W 3-0**	**Allan, Crouch, Bartley**	**182**
A	**Canterbury City (BDC)**	**L 0-1**		**100**
A	Worcester City	L 1-3	Crouch	921
H	**Slough Town (FAC)**	**D 0-0**		**688**
A	**Slough Town (FAC)**	**L 1-2**	**Bartley**	**751**
H	**Thanet United (BDC)**	**W 2-0**	**Bartley, Parry**	**152**
H	Gosport Borough	W 3-0	Bartley (2), Ransom	359
H	**Sheppey United (BDC)**	**W 3-1**	**Parry, Bartley, White**	**278**
A	Corby Town	W 3-1	Bartley (2), Sawyer	400
A	Chelmsford City	L 0-2		741
H	King's Lynn	W 3-0	White, Bartley, Smith	389
H	Folkestone	W 4-2	Bartley, Abbott, Jolley (O.G.), Smart (O.G.)	395
A	Bedworth United	D 0-0		100
A	**Canterbury City (KSC)**	**W 1-0**	**White**	**—**
H	Alvechurch	W 3-1	White, Bartley, Smith	412
A	**Crawley Town (BDC)**	**L 0-3**		**400**
A	Basingstoke Town	W 1-0	Smith (pen)	325
H	Aylesbury United	D 2-2	Smith (2)	380
A	Dudley Town	W 3-0	Bartley (2), Smith	200
H	Willenhall Town	D 0-0		488
A	**Wealdstone (FAT)**	**L 0-1**		**622**
H	Crawley Town	W 2-1	Bartley (2)	637
A	King's Lynn	D 0-0		505
A	Fisher Athletic	W 3-1	Ransom, Bartley (2)	525
H	Fareham Town	W 3-0	Smith, Bartley, Ransom	289
H	Bedworth United	W 2-1	White, Abbott	600
H	**Kingstonian (LSC)**	**W 2-0**	**Adams, White**	**350**
A	Witney Town	W 3-2	Bartley (2, 1 pen), Smith	190
H	**Fisher Athletic (KSC)**	**W 2-0**	**Crouch, Bartley (pen)**	**682**
H	Dudley Town	W 2-1	Bartley (2)	482
A	R.S. Southampton	W 3-1	Ransom, Bartley (2)	200
H	Worcester City	L 1-2	Bartley	649
H	**Gravesend & Northfleet (KSC s.f.)**	**W 3-1**	**Bartley, Smith (pen), Parry**	**525**
A	Folkestone	W 4-1	Abbott, Bartley (2, 1 pen), Smith	350
H	Corby Town	W 5-1	Ransom, Bartley (3), Smith	400
H	R.S. Southampton	W 4-0	Bartley, Parry (2), Abbott	530
H	Fisher Athletic	W 2-0	White, Wilkins (O.G.)	1413
A	Alvechurch	W 3-0	Abbot (2), Bartley	240
A	Gosport Borough	W 1-0	White	250
H	Chelmsford City	W 3-0	Abbott, Bartley (2)	1317
A	Crawley Town	D 3-3	Parry, Bartley, White	500
A	Gravesend & Northfleet	W 3-0	Starkey, White, Clemmence	612
H	Basingstoke Town	W 5-0	Bartley (4), Parry	831
A	Aylesbury United	W 3-1	Smith (2), Bartley	189
A	Shepshed Charterhouse	W 3-1	Abbott (2), Bartley	—
H	Gravesend & Northfleet	W 2-1	Bartley, Smith	700
G*	**Dover Athletic (KSC, Final)**	**W 2-0**	**Abbott (2)**	**971**

* Gillingham F.C.
BDC = Bill Dellow (Southern League) Cup
FAC = F.A. Cup
FAT = F.A. Trophy
LSC = London Senior Cup
KSC = Kent Senior Cup

Appearances:
League (38), Cup (17); Bartley 55, Lemoine 55, Ransom 55, Sawyer 55, Starkey 52, White 52, Smith 50 + 1, Burgess 50, Abbott 47 + 1, Clemmence 37 + 3, Shoemake 27, Parry 18 + 1, Rogers 16, Crouch 14 + 9, Jessop 12, Allan 6 + 4, Ross 2 + 5, Adams 2 + 4, Ryan 0 + 1, Joseph 0 + 1.

Goalscorers:
League (95); Bartley 41 (3 pens), Smith 15 (1 pen), Abbott 11, White 9, Ransom 5, Parry 4, Own goals 3, Crouch 2, Sawyer 2, Burgess 1, Clemmence 1, Starkey 1
Cup (33); Bartley 16 (2 pens), Abbott 3, Parry 3, Smith 3 (1 pen), White 3, Crouch 3, Adams 1, Allan 1

A view of the Main Stand at Park View Road.

WELLING UNITED

President: Eric Brackstone
Chairman: Paul Websdale
Manager: Graham Hobbins
Asst. Manager:
Coach: Nicky Brigden
Physiotherapist: P. Fitchett

Secretary: Barrie Hobbins
Address & Tel. No. c/o Club (01 301 1196 H & B)
Commercial Manager: Secretary
Address & Tel. No. As secretary
Press Officer & Tel. No. As secretary

Address and Tel. No. of ground: Park View Road, Welling, Kent DA 16 1SY (01 301 1196)
Simple ground directions: Ten minutes' walk from Welling Station. Ground on main road, two minutes' walk from Welling High Street
Club shop: Yes
No. of seats: 500 **Covered accommodation:** 1,000 **Capacity:** 6,500 **Floodlights:** Yes
Year formed: 1963 **Nickname:** The Wings **Club sponsor:** Bettabuys of Sidcup
Previous names: None
Previous grounds: Butterfly Lane, Eltham
Day for midweek home matches: Wednesday
Club colours: All red
Change colours: All sky blue
Club metal badges: Yes
Record attendance: 1,413 v Fisher Athletic, Southern League, 1985-86
Best performance in: **F.A. Cup:** 1979-80, 4th Qual Rd
F.A. Vase: 1979-80, 3rd Rd
F.A. Trophy: 1984-85, 3rd Rd proper
Previous Leagues: Spartan, Athenian, Southern
Clubhouse details: Lounge with bar, pool table, darts, television, open evenings, weekend functions
Present players with Football League experience: John Bartley (Millwall)
Past players who progressed into the Football League: Paul Barron (Plymouth, Arsenal, Crystal Palace, WBA, QPR), John Bartley (Millwall), Andy Townsend (Southampton), Ian Thompson (Bournemouth)
Record transfer fee paid: £8,000 for John Bartley (Maidstone United)
Record transfer fee received: £13,500 for Andy Townsend (Weymouth)
Programme details: 16 pages, 30p
Programme editor: Secretary
Club Captain (1985-86): Nigel Ransom
Player of the Year (1985-86): John Bartley
Local newspapers & Tel. No. Kentish Times (01 303 2229)
Major Honours: London Spartan League Cup (1977-78), Kent Youth Cup (6), Southern League Champions (1985-86), Kent Senior Cup Winners (1985-86)

WEYMOUTH

Gola League 5th **F.A. Trophy** 1st Rd **F.A. Cup** 1st Rd **Dorset S.G.** W **Bob Lord Trophy** S.F.

Weymouth: *Back Row (L-R): R. Lucas (physio), M. Rogers, G. Dine, A. Coombes, T. Agana, R. Bourne, A. Iannone, L. Bond, A. Doidge, M. Greeno, P. Rogers. Front Row (L-R): M. Hirst, S. Claridge, P. Arnold (Captain), M. Doherty, G. Borthwick, G. Ayles, Daniel Steadman (mascot)* Photo: Dorset News

Weymouth can look back on the 1985/86 season with a great deal of satisfaction. After their disappointing league performances of the previous season they enjoyed considerable success in the league and up until March were well in contention for the League Championship. Several poor performances however, during the period of the heavy grounds spoilt their chances of actually winning the championship and in the end they had to settle for a rather disappointing fifth position.

Brian Godfrey has however assembled an exciting attacking squad and the signatures of non-league international Gary Simpson from Stafford and mid-fielder Tom Jones, from Farnborough could be the missing links to a championship winning side.

The Cup competitions, apart from the County Cup which they won for the second year running, were again disappointing. A disappointing defeat in the F.A. Cup first round at the hands of southern league Chelmsford was followed by an even more disappointing defeat at Maidstone in the first round of the F.A. Trophy. Sooner or later it is hoped that they may have a run in the F.A. Trophy and who knows next season may be the year.

Steve Claridge—Weymouth's £10,000 signing from Bournemouth in action

Apart from the activity on the football field Weymouth were involved in negotiations off the field regarding the possibility of moving to a new ground. After months and months of deliberation it was agreed that Weymouth would move to a new ground at the end of the 1986/87 season which would be on the site of the old Wessex Speedway Stadium. The existing ground would be taken over and used as a supermarket. The new ground will be built to the highest possible standards and will consist of a main pitch and a practice pitch. All facilities will be first class and suitable to take Weymouth into the Football League should the opportunity ever arise. Indeed, 1986/87 could be an exciting year of Weymouth's history.

They have assembled a squad good enough to beat the best and should promotion to the Football League be attained simultaneously with the transfer to the new ground, this would indeed be an exciting period.

WEYMOUTH SQUAD 1986

Goalkeepers
Len Bond: Exeter City (138), Brentford (122), St. Louis Stars (USA), Bristol City (30)

Defenders
Hedley Steele: Dorchester Town, Exeter City
Ashley Doidge: Local
Paul Arnold: Southampton
Richard Bourne: Torquay United (68-7), Bath City, Colchester United (4), Ramsgate
Martyn Rogers: Exeter City (122-5), Bath City, Bristol City

Midfield
Anniello Iannone: Dunstable
Gary Borthwick: Yeovil Town, Weymouth, Yeovil Town, AFC Bournemouth (74-4), Barnet, Aylesbury United, Southend United, Portsmouth
Peter Rogers: Exeter City (205-39), Bath City
Pat Russell: Salisbury
Ashley Coombes: Poole Town, Wimborne Town
Martyn Hirst: Bristol City (40-1), Bath City
David McMannus: Dorchester Town

Forwards
Mike Doherty: Yeovil Town, Slough Town, Reading (26-5), Basingstoke Town, Hounslow, Harrow Borough, Wigan Athletic, Southampton
Tony Agana: Welling United
Steve Claridge: AFC Bournemouth (6-1), Fareham Town, Portsmouth
Clive Southern: Dorchester Town

Chris Steadman, Secretary Weymouth

Weymouth away to St Pauls, Jersey Dorset Senior Cup

Tony Agnew, Weymouth's England non-league international in action

WEYMOUTH GOLA LEAGUE SEASON 1985-6

Venue	Opponents	Result	Scorers	Att.
A	Stafford Rangers	W 3-2	Southern, Doherty, Iannone	1168
H	Cheltenham Town	D 0-0		1043
A	Runcorn	W 2-1	Doherty (2, 1 pen)	534
A	Dagenham	D 2-2	Doherty (2)	554
H	Boston United	D 0-0		866
H	Dagenham	W 2-1	Iannone, Doherty	730
A	Altrincham	L 1-3	Claridge	1089
A	**Wycombe Wanderers (BLT)**	**W 3-1**	**Claridge, Doherty (2)**	**667**
H	Scarborough	W 4-1	Claridge, Doherty (3)	830
H	**Wycombe Wanderers (BLT)**	**W 4-2**	**Claridge, Russell, Agana, O.G.**	**740**
A	Telford United	L 1-4	Claridge	1129
A	Cheltenham Town	W 1-0	Coombes	1312
H	Northwich Victoria	D 2-2	Claridge, Agana	836
H	Barnet	W 4-2	Doidge, Iannone, Claridge, Agana	800
A	Wycombe Wanderers	W 3-0	Coombes, Borthwick, Doherty	1001
H	Maidstone United	W 2-0	Doherty, Doidge	835
A	Kidderminster Harriers	W 2-1	Southern (2)	610
A	**Tom Pentre (FAC)**	**W 3-1**	**P. Rogers, Iannone, Doherty**	**1162**
H	Enfield	D 2-2	Iannone, Agana	1501
A	**St Pauls, Jersey (DSC)**	**W 3-1**	**Doherty (2), Doidge**	**207**
A	**Wealdstone (BLT)**	**D 1-1**	**Claridge**	
H	Telford United	W 5-2	Claridge (2), Agana (2), Doherty	850
A	**Chelmsford City (FAC)**	**L 0-1**		**2100**
A	Maidstone United	D 0-0		
H	**Wealdstone (BLT)**	**W 3-2**	**Claridge, Doherty, O.G.**	**760**
A	**Dorchester Town (FAT)**	**W 5-3**	**Steele, Coombes, Doherty (2), Agana**	
H	Dartford	W 2-1	Doherty, Agana	830
H	**Blandford United (DSC)**	**W 7-0**		
A	Enfield	D 4-4	Iannone, Claridge, Doherty, Agana	
A	**Maidstone United (FAT)**	**L 0-3**		
H	Bath City	D 0-0		1004
H	Kidderminster Harriers	L 1-2	Agana	670
A	Barnet	D 2-2	Doherty, Steele	
H	Nuneaton Borough	W 2-0	Iannone, Doherty	734
H	Stafford Rangers	D 1-1	Doherty	900
A	Nuneaton Borough	L 0-3		
H	Wycombe Wanderers	D 1-1	Agana	630
H	**Dartford (BLT)**	**W 8-1**	**Hirst, Claridge (4), Agana (3)**	**385**
H	Kettering Town	W 1-0	Hirst	720
A	Bath City	D 2-2	Hirst, Claridge	
A	Northwich Victoria	W 1-0	Doherty	
A	**Sturminster (DSC)**	**W 2-0**	**Hirst, Bourne**	**350**
A	Kettering Town	W 2-0	Hirst, Doherty	
H	Wealdstone	W 4-2	Doherty (2),Bourne, Agana	732
A	Scarborough	D 1-1	Bourne	
H	Altrincham	D 0-0		830
H	**Barnet (BLT)**	**L 0-1**		**801**
A	Boston United	L 0-5		
A	Dartford	D 1-1	Chesters	
A	Frickley Athletic	L 0-1		
A	Wealdstone	L 0-1		
A	Barrow	W 4-3	Chesters (3), Agana	
H	Frickley Athletic	L 2-3	Bourne, Doherty	660
H	Runcorn	W 5-2	Doherty (2), Agana (2), Claridge	705
A	**Wimborne (DSC Final)**	**W 8-0**	**Agana (2), Doherty (2), Claridge (2), Coombes, Greeno**	
H	Barrow	W 3-2	Bourne, Iannone, Doherty	660

BLT = Bob Lord Trophy
FAC = F.A. Cup
DSC = Dorset Senior Cup
FAT = F.A. Trophy

Appearances:
Doherty 52, Agana 50, Arnold 50, Iannone 50, Borthwick 49, Claridge 46, P. Rogers 45, Bond 43, M. Rogers 38, Steele 35, Bourne 32, Coombes 27, Hirst 19, Doidge 11, George 8, Chesters 5, Russell 5, Southern 4, Greeno 1, Roberts 1.

Goalscorers:
Doherty 31, Agana 18, Claridge 18, Iannone 8, Bourne 4, Chesters 4, Hirst 4, Coombes 3, Southern 3, Doidge 2, Steele 2, Rogers 1, Russell 2.

An aerial view of The Recreation Ground, Weymouth

WEYMOUTH

President:
Chairman: A. Source
Manager: Brian Godfrey
Asst. Manager: S. Bell
Physiotherapist: R. Lucas

Secretary: C.W. Steadman
Address & Tel. No. 0305 785558

Commercial Manager: R. Russell
Address & Tel. No. 0305 784133

Press Officer & Tel. No. A. Source. Weymouth 785558
Address and Tel. No. of ground: Recreation Ground, Newstead Road, Weymouth, Dorset. Weymouth 785558
Simple ground directions: Through main town St. Thomas Street (one way) over town bridge turn right, ground straight in front.
Club shop: Yes
No. of seats: 520 **Covered accommodation:** 6,500 **Capacity:** 10,000 **Floodlights:** Yes
Year formed: 1890 **Nickname:** The Terras **Club sponsor:** Daihatsu
Previous names: None
Club colours: White shirt with terra cotta and blue stripe, claret shorts, white socks with claret and blue rings
Previous grounds: None
Change colours: Claret and blue shirts, sky blue shorts, sky blue socks
Day for midweek home matches: Wednesday
Club metal badges: Yes
Record attendance: 12,512 v Yeovil **Year:** 1948
Best performance in: **F.A. Cup:** 1961-2 v Preston North End 4th Round
F.A. Trophy: 1973-4, 1976-7, 1979-80 Quarter-Final
Previous Leagues: Western, Southern
Clubhouse details: Public house and club adjoining the ground—no longer run by the Club. Open during all games
Present players with Football League experience: M. Rogers, R. Bourne, P. Arnold, H.Steele, B. Godfrey, L. Bond, P. Rogers, S. Claridge, M. Hirst, C. Chesters
Past players who progressed into the Football League: R. Pickett, R. Fogg, A. Smith, B. Hutchinson, T. Spratt, T. Gulliver, R. Hall, R. Iles, G. Roberts, M. Cave, D. Fry, A. Beer, B. Carter, N. Townsend, W. Holt, P. Leggett, S. Northover, A. Townsend
Record transfer fee paid: £6,000 for G. Roberts from Dorchester Town 1979-80
Record transfer fee received: £85,000 for G. Roberts from Tottenham Hotspur 1979-80
Programme details: 16 pages, 40p
Club Captain (1985-86): Paul Arnold
Programme editor: The Secretary
Player of the Year (1985-86): Tony Agana
Local newspapers & Tel. No. Dorset Evening Echo 0305 784804. Western Gazette
Major Honours: Southern Premier League (2) & Runners-up (3), Western League (5) & Runners-up (3), Southern League Cup (1) & Runners-up (4), Alliance Premier League Runners-up, Bob Lord Trophy (Alliance League Cup)

VAUXHALL-OPEL FOOTBALL LEAGUE

President: B. D. East, BSc *Chairman:* A. C. F. Turvey
Secretary: N. R. Robinson, 226 Rye Lane, Peckham, London SE15 4NL
Tel: 01 639 5726 (B); 01 653 3903 (H)

SUTTON UNITED MOVE UP

In a very exciting climax to this season we saw Sutton United retain the Championship of the League in grand style, despite losing to challengers Yeovil Town at the Huish at the end of April, in front of more than 5,000 spectators. At the second time of asking, Sutton decided to tread the path that Wycombe Wanderers trod at the end of season 1984/85 and have chosen to go to the GM Vauxhall Conference, and we wish them well. Wycombe Wanderers made the return journey and we do welcome them back and there can be little doubt that Wycombe will be going all out to go straight back again although Yeovil will contest this.

At the other end of the table we saw Billericay Town and Epsom & Ewell relegated to Division 1 and if those Clubs have anything to do with it it will not be too long before they grace the Premier Division once again.

In Division 1 St Albans City became Champions in fine style winning 7-1 at Lewes on the final day of the season, and the runners-up, Bromley, achieved their feat despite having a considerable number of games to play in the last few weeks of the season. This really was a very closely fought division, with five or six clubs vying for promotion as the season came to an exciting climax and as the others fell by the wayside.

At the other end of Division 1 we experienced a problem yet again with regionalised Divisions 2, because the four relegated clubs, Aveley, Hornchurch, Harlow Town and Chesham United all came within the 'north' geographical division for Division 2; by moving Harefield United and Chalfont St Peter to the 'south' division we have been

We heard the sad news of the death of Sir Stanley Rous in the close season. Sir Stanley had a tremendous love of the game of football but his contribution to the Non-League scene was massive. He was a dear friend to so many and I for one have many treasured memories of the great man passing on advice for my publications and indeed the original sponsorship schemes for Rothmans. Sir Stanley watched an average of two games a week throughout last season and I imagine we would all envy him his fitness to the last in a happy life that contributed so much for all of us involved in football. In this photo, taken by Peter Burrin, Sir Stanley shakes hands with Monty Hyams, joint President of Hendon with Bobby Butlin, on left, when Hendon held a special dinner to mark the 70 years in which the two gentlemen had been connected with Hendon.

The Vauxhall-Opel's first all weather pitch at the Felthams Arena. Photo: Peter Burrin

able to accommodate all four clubs in the 'north' division for next season. In that North Division it was virtually a two horse race for the majority of the season, with the real question being as to whether it would be Stevenage Borough or Kingsbury Town who finished as champions. As things turned out it was Stevenage who pipped Kingsbury for the top spot. In Division 2, newcomers Southwick took the title after a marvellous start to the season when they were unbeaten in league and cup matches until the end of September. They will be joined in Division 1 next season by Bracknell Town, who are another side who have achieved tremendous progress in a relatively short period of time and who now face probably their hardest task yet as they go into the highest sphere of football at which they have ever played.

We welcome from the Combined Counties Football League Chertsey Town, who return after just one season having been relegated at the end of the 1984/85 season, Collier Row, from the London Spartan Football League and Wivenhoe Town from the Essex Football League to Division 2 North. This means that for next season we will run with 22 clubs in Division 2 North and 21 clubs in Division 2 South and there is just one vacancy left.

It is to be hoped that at the end of this forthcoming season we will see our one vacancy being filled and promotion and relegation with our feeder leagues becoming a reality.

In the A.C. Delco Cup, which replaced the Hitachi Cup as the league's own cup competition, the final reverted to a one-off match at a neutral venue after three years of being two-legged, and over 1,100 people saw Sutton United do 'the double' by defeating Uxbridge from Division 1 by 3 goals to 1.

We look forward to a season at the beginning of which we bring in floodlighting level requirements for all clubs and at the end of which we bring in a brand new ground grading system.

THE VAUXHALL-OPEL FOOTBALL LEAGUE SEASON 1985-86
PREMIER DIVISION

LEAGUE TABLE

	Pl	W	D	L	Gf	Ga	Pts
Sutton United	42	29	8	5	109	39	95
Yeovil Town	42	28	7	7	92	48	91
Farnborogh Town	42	23	8	11	90	50	77
Croydon	42	23	7	12	70	50	76
Harrow Borough	42	21	8	13	76	66	71
Slough Town	42	18	8	16	66	68	62
Bishop's Stortford	42	17	10	15	55	61	61
Kingstonian	42	15	15	12	57	56	60
Dulwich Hamlet	42	17	9	16	64	79	60
Wokingham Town	42	16	10	16	67	64	58
Windsor & Eaton	42	17	7	18	58	75	58
Tooting & Mitcham U.	42	14	11	17	65	76	53
Walthamstow Avenue	42	12	14	16	69	70	50
Worthing	42	13	10	19	72	82	49
Bognor Regis Town	42	15	6	21	63	70	*48
Hayes	42	10	17	15	36	42	47
Hitchin Town	42	11	14	17	53	69	47
Barking	42	11	13	18	45	55	46
Hendon	42	10	13	19	59	77	43
Carlshalton Athletic	42	9	13	20	56	79	40
Billericay Town	42	9	12	21	59	78	39
Epsom & Ewell	42	8	12	22	63	90	36

* 3 points deducted by league

RESULTS

Barking		0-0	2-2	0-2	3-0	1-2	1-1	2-1	2-3	2-0	1-0	2-0	1-1	1-2	4-3	0-2	1-2	1-0	2-2	1-2	3-0	0-0
Billericay Town	2-1		0-0	3-3	3-3	1-1	2-1	0-0	1-2	1-1	1-2	1-4	1-0	1-3	2-3	1-2	3-4	0-2	3-1	3-1	2-3	0-2
Bishops Stortford	2-1	0-0		4-0	2-1	2-1	0-1	2-1	0-1	1-0	0-2	3-2	2-0	2-0	0-3	0-6	2-1	2-0	2-5	3-2	0-1	0-1
Bognor Regis Town	0-1	1-0	1-1		6-0	0-2	3-1	1-1	0-1	4-1	3-0	1-1	0-2	3-3	3-0	2-0	2-1	3-2	0-1	2-1	0-3	3-1
Carshalton Athletic	3-1	1-2	1-2	1-2		0-2	2-0	2-1	1-0	0-1	2-0	1-1	2-3	0-0	1-1	1-4	1-2	1-1	2-1	1-0	3-1	1-1
Croydon	0-1	2-1	2-0	2-0	2-1		1-1	3-1	3-2	1-3	1-0	1-1	2-0	4-1	1-0	1-0	0-4	2-3	5-2	2-0	3-4	4-1
Dulwich Hamlet	1-1	1-3	2-5	3-1	2-1	1-1		5-3	2-1	1-4	1-0	0-0	1-0	2-3	0-1	1-2	2-2	1-1	1-2	1-0	2-2	1-1
Epsom & Ewell	3-0	0-2	0-2	1-0	2-2	1-2	0-3		0-1	1-3	1-0	5-3	3-3	3-2	2-1	2-2	1-2	1-2	2-3	2-4	3-3	2-2
Farnborough Town	0-0	4-0	1-0	2-1	4-2	0-2	6-1	2-3		6-0	1-1	5-0	6-0	0-0	2-1	3-2	2-3	3-2	2-1	0-1	3-2	1-2
Harrow Borough	0-0	1-1	3-1	3-2	3-2	2-1	3-0	3-0	1-3		1-0	3-2	2-0	1-3	4-2	0-3	1-1	2-2	4-1	1-1	3-2	3-2
Hayes	1-1	2-2	0-0	1-2	1-1	0-0	0-2	0-0	2-0	2-1		1-1	1-1	4-1	0-1	1-1	2-1	2-1	0-0	3-1	0-3	0-1
Hendon	2-1	4-2	1-1	1-0	2-3	0-2	1-3	3-0	1-5	1-3	0-0		2-3	1-1	1-1	1-2	1-1	1-2	2-0	1-2	2-2	1-2
Hitchin Town	0-0	2-2	1-1	2-1	1-1	1-1	1-2	2-1	1-1	3-2	2-2	2-2		0-0	0-1	2-1	0-0	2-0	1-2	0-2	4-1	1-3
Kingstonian	2-0	2-2	1-1	2-1	1-0	0-2	1-2	2-2	2-2	1-0	0-0	3-0	2-0		1-1	2-4	2-1	2-1	2-3	2-2	1-1	0-1
Slough Town	2-0	4-3	1-0	1-0	2-1	0-0	1-2	4-4	2-3	0-0	0-2	1-4	1-2	3-2		0-1	4-1	1-0	3-1	1-1	3-1	2-3
Sutton United	1-1	3-2	4-1	6-0	2-2	3-2	6-1	3-1	1-1	2-0	3-1	3-0	4-1	2-0	4-1		0-0	3-3	5-0	5-0	0-0	3-1
Totg & Mitcham Unt.	3-1	3-2	1-2	1-0	2-2	0-4	3-4	2-2	2-2	1-4	2-0	0-1	1-0	1-1	2-3	1-5		2-2	1-3	3-2	4-2	0-2
Walthamstow Avenue	3-2	2-0	1-3	5-2	2-2	1-0	7-2	2-2	0-5	3-2	0-0	0-2	3-3	0-1	1-2	0-1	0-0		4-1	0-0	4-2	2-2
Windsor & Eaton	1-0	2-3	0-0	3-2	3-3	2-0	1-0	2-1	1-2	0-3	0-0	4-0	1-4	1-0	0-0	0-3	2-1	1-0		0-3	1-0	2-2
Wokingham Town	1-1	2-0	2-2	1-2	2-0	2-3	1-2	3-1	2-1	1-2	0-2	3-3	3-0	0-0	4-0	1-3	3-1	2-2	2-0		3-3	2-1
Worthing	0-1	2-1	6-2	2-2	3-1	2-0	2-3	2-3	1-1	4-0	0-0	0-2	2-1	0-1	2-1	0-2	0-2	2-2	3-1	1-2		2-5
Yeovil Town	3-1	1-0	2-0	3-2	5-1	5-0	3-1	3-0	1-0	2-2	2-1	2-1	3-1	1-2	3-4	2-0	3-0	2-1	2-1	3-0	5-0	

Paul McKinnon's 53rd goal of the season for Sutton United v Uxbridge in the A.C. Delco Cup Final

A. C. DELCO CUP 1984/85

First Round

Ruislip Manor	1	Epsom & Ewell	2	A.E.T
Bishop Storford	2	Basildon Utd	0	
Hornchurch	0	Flackwell Heath	1	
Dulwich Hamlet	2	Saffron Walden T.	1	
Oxford City	3	Wokingham Town	2	
Tilbury	3 & 1	Walthamstowe Ave	3 & 3	
Uxbridge	2	Woking	1	
Feltham	1	Hendon	3	
Croydon	1	Hungerford Town	0	
Leyton-Wingate	1	Chesham Utd	0	
Hayes	5	Aveley	0	
Newbury Town	0 & 2	Finchley	0 & 3	
Farnborough T.	9	Harlow Town	3	
Grays Ath.	2	Worthing	1	
Staines Town	3	Wolverton Town	1	
Walton & Hersham	2	Southwick	1	
Leatherhead	4	Boreham Wood	3	
Wembley	2	Kingstonian	4	
Harefield Utd.	0	Whyteleafe	1	
Metropolitan Police	1	Hitchin Town	0	
Stevenage Borough	1	Barking	4	
Hampton	3	Toting & Mitcham U	0	
Lewes	2	St. Albans City	3	
Petersfield Utd	4	Tring Town	3	A.E.T.
Southall	0	Harrow Borough	3	
Dorking	3	Banstead Ath.	1	
Billericay Town	3	Leytonstone-Ilford	2	
Carshalton Ath.	3	Bracknell Town	0	
Slough Town	3	Bromley	1	A.E.T.
Yeovil Town	2 & 1	Maidenhead Utd	2 & 3	A.E.T.
Sutton Utd	3 & 3	Bognor Regis Town	3 & 1	

Second Round

Epsom & Ewell	3	Bishops Stortford	1	
Flackwell Heath	1	Dulwich Hamlet	3	
Oxford City	4	Walthamstow Ave.	1	
Uxbridge	1	Hendon	0	
Croydon	2	Leyton-Wingate	1	A.E.T.
Hayes	1	Finchley	0	A.E.T.
Farnborough Town	3	Grays Ath.	2	
Staines Town	3	Walton & Hersham	2	
Leatherhead	2	Kingstonian	1	
Whyteleafe	1	Metropolitan Police	2	A.E.T.
Barking	0	Hampton	1	
Lewes	2	St. Albans City	1	
Petersfield Utd.	0	Harrow Borough	1	
Dorking	1	Billericay Town	0	
Carshalton Ath.	2 & 2	Slough Town	2 & 0	
Maidenhead Utd.	3	Sutton Utd.	5	

Third Round

Epsom & Ewell	3	Dulwich Hamlet	2	A.E.T.
Oxford City	1	Uxbridge	3	
Croydon	1	Hayes	3	
Farnborough Town	7	Staines Town	1	
Leatherhead	5	Metropolitan Police	3	
Hampton	3	Lewes	2	
Harrow Borough	5	Dorking	1	
Carshalton Ath.	0	Sutton Utd.	2	

Fourth Round

Epsom & Ewell	1 & 2	Uxbridge	1 & 4	
Hayes	1	Farnborough Town	2	
Leatherhead	0 & 0	Hampton	0 & 2	A.E.T.
Harrow Borough	3	Sutton Utd.	2	

Semi-Final

†Uxbridge	6	†Farnborough T.	3
†Hampton	3	†Sutton Utd.	5

Final

Uxbridge	1	Sutton Utd.	3

†*Played on Aggregate*

The Happy Winners—Sutton United Photo: Davy Farebrother

(Est. 1880) BARKING (Nickname: The Blues)

President: J. Poneskis
Joint Chairmen: J. Poneskis & P. Thomson
Manager: Bobby Arber
Ass. Man: Fred Beaumont
Physiotherapist: John Sewters

Secretary: J. R. Wilson
Address & Tel. No: 24 Colenso Road, Ilford, 1GZ 7AH

Commercial Manager:
Press Officer: M. Roberts

Ground Address & Tel. No: Mayesbrook Park, Lodge Ave., Dagenham.
Capacity: 4,200 **Covered accommodation:** 600 **Seating:** 200 **Floodlights:** Yes
Simple ground directions: A13 to Thatched House roundabout, exit A1153 (Lodge Ave.) Mayesbrook Park 1 Mile on left. Or 162 Bus from Barking Station.
Clubhouse details: Two large Bars, open every lunch time & evening.
Programme details: 12 pages **Editor:** M. Roberts **Club metal badges:** No
Local Newspaper(s): Dagenham & Barking Advertiser, Barking & Dagenham Post

Club colours: Blue & white, Blue Shorts **Change colours:** White or Yellow
Midweek match day: Tuesday **Previous Leagues:** South Essex CGE., London League, Athenian League
Record transfer fee paid:
Record transfer fee received:
Record attendance: (At Mayesbrook) 1972 v Aldershot, F.A. Cup 2nd Round 1978
Senior honours/best performance: Isthmian League Champions 1979. F.A. Cup 2nd Round, 5 times (1927, 1978, 1979, 1981, 1983), London Senior Cup (4 times), Essex Senior Cup (5 times), Athenian League Champions (1), London League Champions (1), South Essex League Champions (1)
Past players (who progressed to Football League): J. Williams (Plymouth Arg.), L. Abrahams (Charlton Ath.), K. Hitchcock (Notts. F.), E. Nwagiobi (Luton)

SEASON 1985/86
League posn: 18th **A.C. Delco Cup:** 2nd Rd. **County Cup:** London 1st Rd. Essex Semi-Final
F.A. Trophy: 3rd Qual **F.A. Cup:** 2nd Qual
Club Captain: Liam Gallagher **Player of the Year:** (Joint) Mervyn Cawston, Geoff Spooner
Leading Goalscorers:
Neil Satchell 11
Jon Bolle 8
Nick Phillips 7

Hat-tricks:
None

Penalties: 6
Pllilips 2, Berwick 2, Warterfall 1, McNeil 1.

Most appearances: Paul Watts 62, Robert Waferfall 56, Mervyn Cawston 49

Goalkeepers
Mervyn Cawston: Woodford Town, Southend United (198), Chicago Sting (USA), Gillingham (19), Norwich City (4)

Defenders
Robert Waterfall: Clapton, Orient
Paul Watts: Local
Liam Gallagher: Walthamstow Avenue, Queen of the South
Geoff Spooner: Billericay Town, Barking, Dagenham
Keith Elley: Bishop's Stortford, Dagenham, Enfield, Leytonstone & Ilford, Enfield, Tottenham Hotspur, West Ham United
Paul Robinson: Hendon, Barking, Blackburn Rovers

Midfield
Trevor Burke: Grays Athletic, Gravesend, Barking, Danson, Gravesend, Dartford, Bromley, Crystal Palace
Gary Anderson: Woodford Town, Billericay Town, Chelmsford City, Maidstone United, Barking, Northampton Town, Tottenham Hotspur
Nigel McNeil: Clapton, West Ham United
Nicky Phillips: Coventry City (5)
Dennis Bailey: Watford

Forwards
Joe Simmonds: Bishop's Stortford, Dartford, Bishop's Stortford, Bigog Copenhagen (Den), Tottenham Hotspur
Jon Bolle: Clapton, Dagenham, Orient
Peter Berwick: Clapton, Beckton United, Oxford City, East Ham United
Paul Cockayne: Woodford Town, Barking, Hornchurch, Billericay Town, Hendon
Neil Satchell: Dartford, Enfield, Clapton, East Ham United

Back Row (L-R): Robert Waterfall, Liam Gallagher, Geoff Spooner, Mervyn Cawston, Neil Satchell, Billy Goldstone, Henry Clark Front Row (L-R): Peter Berwick, Gary Seymour, Paul Watts, John Harrison, Les Whitton

(Est. 1883) BOGNOR REGIS TOWN F.C. (Nickname: The Rocks)

President: F. R. Butlin
Chairman: S. J. Rowlands

Manager: Jack Pearce. Tel. (0705) 816803(H)
Ass. Man: D. Probee
Physiotherapist: S. Robinson

Secretary: T. N. Grasty
Address & Tel. No: 'Timberleys' West Drive, Elmer Beach, Bognor Regis, West Sussex PO22 7TS. Tel. (024369) 3248(H) 777829(B)
Commercial Manager: Jack. Pearce
Press Officer: Jack Pearce

Ground Address & Tel. No: Nyewood Lane, Bognor Regis, West Sussex PO21 2TY. B.R.(0243) 822325
Capacity: 6,000 **Covered accommodation:** 3,000 **Seating:** 200 **Floodlights:** yes
Simple ground directions: Follow seafront westwards from Pier, past Aldwick shopping centre, left into Nyewood Lane.
Clubhouse details: Members Bars (normal opening hours) Available private hire.
Programme details: 32 page 25p **Editor:** Jack Pearce **Club metal badges:** Yes
Local Newspaper(s): Bognor Regis Post 865241, Bognor Observer 864267, Brighton Argus 606799, Portsmouth News 64488
Club colours: White/Green/White **Change colours:** All Yellow
Midweek match day: Monday **Previous Leagues:** West Sussex, Sussex County, Southern
Record transfer fee paid: None
Record transfer fee received: None
Record attendance: 3,642 v Swansea City 1st Round F.A. Cup Replay 1984–85
Senior honours/best performance: Sussix Senior Cup (7), Souther League Runners-up, Southern League Merit Cup, Southern League Cup Finalists, Berger Isth League Div 1 Runners-up. F.A. Cup 1984-85 2nd Round, F.A. Trophy 1980-1 1st Round Proper.
Past players (who progressed to Football League): Ernie Randall (Chelsea), Andy Wood (Brentford)

SEASON 1985/86
League posn: 15th **A.C. Delco Cup:** 1st Rd. **County Cup:** Semi-Final
F.A. Trophy: **F.A. Cup:** 2nd Rd. Proper
Club Captain: Mick Pullen **Player of the Year:** Aistair Sperring
Leading Goalscorers: Geoff Cooper 17
Hat-tricks:
Penalties:
Most appearances: M. Pullen (55), P. Pullen (55)

BOGNOR REGIS TOWN

Goalkeepers
Alistair Sperring: Reading, Southampton

Defenders
Mick Pullen: Local
Graham Marriner: Gravesend, Portsmouth
Mark Bird: Local
John Crumplin: Portsmouth, Bognor Regis Town
Neil Turnbull: Local
Billy Gill: Local
Kevin Hotson: Littlehampton Town

Midfield
Paul Pullen: Local
Russell Burtenshaw: Crawley Town, Dagenham, Wimbledon, Southampton
Mark Vickers: Local
Nick Manley: Pagham, Bognor Regis Town
Simon Price: Portfield
David Poole: Southampton, Bognor Regis Town

Forwards
Kevin Clements: Portsmouth
Geoff Cooper: Local
Dave Gladding: Local
Peter Clarke: Horndean

The Bognor Regis goalkeeper saves despite pressure from the visiting Yeovil Town attack
Photo: Eric Marsh

(Est. 1874) BISHOP'S STORTFORD (Nickname: Blues or Bishop's)

President: E. A. Bentley
Chairman: James L. M. Gill
Manager: T. Coakley
Coach: P. Feary
Physiotherapist: Dusty Miller

Secretary: James L. M. Gill
Address & Tel. No: 71, Warwick Road, Bishop's Stortford. Tel. (0279) 53569(H) (01) 588 7633(B)
Commercial Manager: E. A. Bentley. Tel. (0279) 54237(B)
Press Officer: V. Woodcock. Tel. (0279) 870424(H), Roydon 3421(B)

Ground Address & Tel. No: George Wilson Stadium, Rhodes Avenue, Bishop's Stortford. Tel. (0279) 54140
Capacity: 6,000 **Covered accommodation:** 1,500 . **Seating:** 228 **Floodlights:** Yes
Simple ground directions: M11 to junction 8, A120 to Bishop's Stortford, from Station 800 yards.

Clubhouse details: Open Match days, training nights or private functions. Two Bars three tea Bars.
Programme details: 12 page 25p **Editor:** S. Haylock **Club metal badges:** Yes
Local Newspaper(s): Bishop's Stortford Gazette, Citizen, Herts & Essex Observer

Club colours: Blue/White stripes/White shorts & Socks **Change colours:** All Yellow
Midweek match day: Tuesday **Previous Leagues:** Herts County, Delphian, Atheniam
Record transfer fee paid: Club does not disclose any fees
Record transfer fee received: Club does not disclose andy fees
Record attendance: 6,000 v Peterborough F.A. Cup 2nd Round 1972. 6,000 v Middlesbrough F.A. Cup
Senior honours/best performance: F.A. Trophy. F.A. Amateur Cup, London Senior Cup, Herts Senior Cup, Isthmian League Div 1, East Anglian Cup, Herts Charity Cup, Courage Eastern Floodlight Cup.
Past players (who progressed to Football League): P. Phillips (Luton Town)

SEASON 1985/86
League posn: 7th **A.C. Delco Cup:** 2nd Rd. **County Cup:** Qt. Final
F.A. Trophy: 3rd Rd. (Replay) **F.A. Cup:** 1st Rd. (Replay)
Club Captain: Phil Hopkins **Player of the Year:** M. Nunn
Leading Goalscorers: D. Hardy **Hat-tricks:** **Penalties:** **Most Appearances:** Colin Hull

BISHOP'S STORTFORD

Goalkeepers
Martin Taylor: Epping Town, Woodford Town, Hendon, Charlton Athletic, Arsenal
Eddie Coe: Stansted, Harlow Town, St Albans City

Defenders
Andy Goodchild: Barnet, Boreham Wood, Tottenham Hotspur
Ray Wickenden: Harlow Town, Southend United, Q.P.R.
Colin Hull: Watford
Micky Bright: Marldon Town, Chelmsford City, Orient
Lenny Tomkins: Hornchurch, Chelmsford City, Gravesend, Toronto Whitecaps (Can), Crystal Palace (20)
John Knapman: Dagenham, Bishop's Stortford, Enfield, Walthamstow Avenue, Bromley, Torquay United

Midfield
Roger Avery: Cambridge United (1)
Phil Hopkins: Walthamstow Avenue, Chelmsford City, Colchester United
Micky Nunn: Hitchin Town, Westmills, Hoddesdon Town, Ware, Cambridge United
Owen Griffiths: Dartford, Tilbury, Harlow Town
Tony Flynn: East Thurrock United, Aveley, Clapton, Aveley

Forwards
Kevin Newbury: Maldon Town
Pat Staunton: Clapton
Duncan Hardy: Barnet, Cheshunt, Hendon, Cheshunt, Finchley
Les Whitton: Dagenham, Croydon, Oxford City, Woodford Town

Cheltenham Town defenders Stuart Cornes and goalkeeper Neil Hards are challenged by Duncan Hardy and Kenny Taylor of Bishop's Stortford in the F.A. Trophy
Photo: Herts & Essex Observer

(Est. 1892) BROMLEY (Nickname: Lillywhites)

President: Elect G. T. Ransom
Chairman: G. T. Ransom
Manager: Trevor Ford
Ass. Man/Coach: Colin Powell
Physiotherapist:

Secretary: J. M. Cooper
Address & Tel. No: 185, Burnt Ash Lane, Bromley, Kent. Tel. (01) 857 3961(H) (01) 659 6918(B)
Commercial Manager: K. Cafferty. Tel. (0732) 843022
Press Officer: John Fiorini. Tel. (01) 460 9013(H) (01) 736 3435(B)

Ground Address & Tel. No: Hayes Lane, Bromley. Tel. (01) 460 5291
Police Limit Capacity: 8,500 **Covered accommodation:** 4,000 **Seating:** 2,000 **Floodlights:** Yes
Simple ground directions: Bromley South (BR). 146 and 119 Buses Pass ground. M25 junction 4 take A21 Bromley

Clubhouse details: Open Match days, and private functions.
Programme details: 20 page (at least) **Editor:** Gus Johnson **Club metal badges:** Yes
Local Newspaper(s): Bromley Times. Tel. (01) 300 1234. Bromley Advertiser. Tel. 668 4811

Club colours: White shirts/Black shorts **Change colours:** Red shirts/Black shorts
Midweek match day: Tuesday **Previous Leagues:** Athenian, London, Kent, Spartan
Record transfer fee paid: Not disclosed
Record transfer fee received: Not disclosed
Record attendance: 12,00 Bromley v Nigerian XI 1950
Senior honours/best performance: Istmian League 5 aside Tournament winners for "Prince Philip Cup" 1979, F.A. Amateur Cup (3), London Senior Cup (3), Isthmian League Champs (4), Kent Senior Cup Winners (2), Kent Amateur Cup Winners (11), Athenian League Champs (3), London League (2), Spartan League (2).
Past players (who progressed to Football League): Roy Merryfield (Chelsea), Stan Charlton (Arsenal), Ron Heckman (Ley. Orie3nt – Crystal Palace), John Gregory (West Ham – Scunthorpe), Bill Lloyd (Millwall), Brian Kinsey (Charlton), Harold Hobbis (Pre war Charlton and England).

SEASON 1985/86
Vauxhall-Opel Div. 1 League posn: 2nd **A.C. Delco Cup:** 1st Rd. **County Cup:** London Sen. 1st Rd. Kent Sen, 2nd Rd.
F.A. Trophy: 3rd Rd. Qual. **F.A. Cup:** 4th Qual. lost 2-0 Maidstone
Club Captain: Paul Edwards **Player of the Year:** Nicky Sullivan.(Goal Keeper)

Leading Goalscorers:	Hat-tricks:	Penalties:	Most Appearances:
Gary Flemington 25		12	Max 57 full
Brian Gregory 22			Nicky Sullivan 55
Neil Missen 13			Paul Edwards 55

Goalkeepers
Nicky Sullivan: Tooting & Mitcham United, Woking, Arsenal

Defenders
Brian Frampton: Local
John Roles: Sutton United, Portsmouth, Southampton
Paul Edwards: Dulwich Hamlet, Bromley
Steve Ward: Tooting & Mitcham United
Wayne Draper: Local

Midfield
Neil Missen: Arsenal, Millwall
Ian Young: Gillingham
Alan Scotting: Gillingham (2)
Graham Brenton: Local
Jeff Fuller: Local
Dick Tydeman: Dagenham, Chatham Town, Peterborough United (29), Gillingham (76-2), Charlton Athletic (158-7), Gillingham (295-13)

Forwards
Terry Young: Local
Gary Flemington: Croydon, Sutton United, Redhill
Paul Hanifan: Local
Brian Gregory: Sheppey United, Crawley Town, Dartford, Dover, Gravesend, Maidstone United, Weymouth, Luton Town, Thanet United, Gillingham

Bromley F.C. Photo: Bromley Advertiser

(Est. 1905) CARSHALTON ATHLETIC (Nickname. The Robins)

President: Bill Cooper
Chairman: Trevor Cripps
Manager: Billy Smith
Ass. Man/Coach: Ron King
Physiotherapist: George Gates

Secretary: Vic Thompson
Address & Tel. No: 11 Poulton Ave., Sutton, Surrey SM1 3PZ. Tel. (644) 6402(H)
Commercial Manager:
Press Officer: Martin Roper (01) 643 6747

Ground Address & Tel. No: War Memorial Sports Ground, Colston Ave., Carshalton, Surrey. Tel. (01) 642 8658 (Club) (01) 643 1618 (Boardroom)
Capacity: 8,000 **Covered accommodation:** 5,000 **Seating:** 250 **Floodlights:** Yes
Simple ground directions: B.R. (Southern Region) to Carshalton Station, turn rught from station approach, Colston Avenue first left, ground entrance 150 yards on right. L.T. 157 busto Wrythe Green, adjacent to Wrythe Lane ground entrance
Clubhouse details: Club open every evening, Sat., Sun. lunchtimes, Licensed bar, snacks available match days. Gaming machines, computer games, darts, pool & Snooker. Live music Sat., Sun. evenings, men's dars Mon., Wed., Fri., lady's darts Thur.
Programme details: 16 page 30p **Editor:** Andy Hill (01) 643 4824 **Club metal badges:** £1.00 + postage from club shop
Local Newspaper(s): Wallington & Carshalton Advertiser 01-643 6953, Wallinton & Carshalton Times 01-643 4351

Club colours: Maroon/White shorts (maroon stripe)/Maroon **Change colours:** White (maroon trim)/White/White
Midweek match day: Tuesday **Previous Leagues:** London, Surrey Sen., Corinthian, Athenian
Record transfer fee paid: £1,500 to Tooting & Mitcham United for Desmond Dennis
Record transfer fee received: £3,500 from :Culwich Hamlet for Gary Allen
Record attendance: 8,000 v Totting & Mitcham 1951
Senior honours/best performance: Isthmian League Div 2 Runners-up, Corinthian League Champions (2), Surrey Senior League Runners-up (2), Surrey Senior Shield & Finalists (2), Surrey Senior Cup Finalests./F.A. Cup 1982/3 2nd Round Proper v Torquay United (A) 1-4, F.A. Trophy 1980/81 3rd Round Proper v Mossley (H) 0-3.
Past players (who progressed to Football League): Ernie Taylor (Newcastle United, Blackpool, Manchester United), Billy Barragon (Q.P.R.), Alan Eagles (Leyton Orient), Frank George (Leyton Orient), Roy Lunnes (Crystal Palace), Jock McDonald (Notts. County), Derek Razzell (Q.P.R.), Terry Stacey (Plymouth Argyle), Ron Walker (Watford), Nobby Warren (Exeter City), Tommy Williams (Colchester United), Gus Ceaser (Arsenal)

SEASON 1985/86
League posn: **A.C. Delco Cup:** **Lon. Semi. County Cup:** 2 Rd. Proper **F.A. Trophy:** 3rd Qual **F.A. Cup:** 3rd Qual
Club Captain: Tony Maurice **Player of the Year:** Gary Mitchell

Leading Goalscorers:	**Hat-tricks:**	**Penalties:**	**Most appearances:**
Jon Warden 26		G. Mitchell 2	G. Mitchell 60
Trevor Smith 15		J. Raffington 2	C. Oakley 58
			J. Raffington 55

Goalkeepers
Colin Oakley: Sheffield United

Defenders
Gary Mitchell: Local
Phil Smith: Leatherhead, Banstead Athletic, Sutton United, Wimbledon
Tony Maurice: Millwall
Keith Oakley: Crystal Palace
Andy Cullum: Leatherhead, Dorking, Kingstonian, Crystal Palace
John Raffington: Epsom & Ewell, Carshalton Athletic, Croydon

Midfield
Chris Dibble: Kuopio ELO (Fin), Leatherhead, Wealdstone, Wimbledon (8), Millwall (63-5)
Simon Constable: Port Hacking (AVS), Hampton, Dorking, Walton & Hersham, Staines Town, Walton & Hersham
Gary Marchant: Local
Bradley Maltese: Leatherhead
Gavin Mayoss: Tooting & Mitcham
Mark Dodman: Leatherhead

Forwards
Trevor Smith: Bromley, Crawley Town, Gravesend, Crawley Town, Dulwich Hamlet
Jon Warden: Croydon, Tooting & Mitcham, Croydon
Paul Williams: Leatherhead, Woking, Brentford, Chelsea (1)
John Archbold: Sutton United, Dover Athletic, Gravesend, Chelmsford City
John McDaide: Slough Town
Paul Holder: Leatherhead, Carshalton Athletic, Dorking, Leatherhead, Dorking, Epsom & Ewell, Woking

This is a 1985 Team photo and there have been many changes at Colston Avenue since then but sorry we haven't received one from last season.

(Est. 1953) CROYDON F.C. (Nickname. Blues.)

President: C. R. Waters
Chairmen: J. H. Milsted. JP., FI., Ceram.
Manager: Adrian Hill
Ass. Man/Coach: Micky Stratford
Physiotherapist: Dennis Kenny
Secretary: Eddie Dukelow
Address & Tel. No: Horsham. Tel. (0403) 56745
Commercial Manager:
Press Officer: Geoff Brown. Tel. (01) 656 1022
Ground Address & Tel. No: Croydon Sports Arena, Albert Road, South Norwood, London SE 25. Tel. (01) 654 8555 (Clubhouse), (01) 654 5524 (Ground)
Capacity: 8,000 **Covered accommodation:** 450 **Seating:** 450 **Floodlights:** Yes
Simple ground directions: By train to East Croydon or Norwood junction stations, to Belmont or Dundee Road, Walk doen either road, Ground at botton.
Clubhouse details: 250 people licenced bar, Snacks available, Dancing, Disco's, Bingo, Private functions lounge bar available for – Private hire, open lunchtime and every night. Tel. (01) 654 8555.
Programme details: 20 page 25p **Editor:** Dave West **Club metal badges:** £1.20
Local Newspaper(s): Croydon Advertiser (01) 668 4111
Club Colours: Light Blue shirts & socks dark Blue shorts **Change colours:** All Red
Midweek match day: Monday/Tuesday **Previous Leagues:** Surrey Senior, Spartan, Athenian
Record transfer fee paid: Steve Brown
Record transfer fee received: Steve Brown
Record attendance: 9,815 v Millwall, F.A. Cup 2nd Round (At Crystal Palace Ground)
Senior honours/best performance: Surrey Senior Cup. F.A. Cup 1979/80 2nd Round v Millwall 1-1, Replay 2-3 A.E.T. F.A. Trophy 1981/82 1982/83 2nd Round Proper.
Past players (who progressed to Football League): Peter Bonetti

SEASON 1985/86
League posn: 4th **A.C. Delco Cup:** 3rd Rd. **County Cup:** 1st Rd. **F.A. Trophy:** 3rd Qual **F.A. Cup:** 4th Qual
Club Captain: Stuart Hemsley **Player of the Year:** Paul Gbogidi

Leading Goalscorers:	**Hat-tricks:**	**Penalties:**	**Most appearances:**
Steve Hill 20	Steve Milton	Mark Denton 10	Steve Dungey 52 (Keeper)
Mark Denton 14			Stuart Hemsley 52
Steve Milton 121			

Goalkeepers
Steve Dungey: Farleigh Rovers

Defenders
Tony Jasper: Local
Mark Denton: Dulwich Hamlet, Chelsea
Graeme Wadley: Wimbledon
Stuart Hemsley: Local
Barry Constable: Sutton United, Croydon
Andy Blythe: Local
Russell Harmsworth: Epsom & Ewell, Croydon, Redhill, Wimbledon

Midfield
Mick Stratford: Epsom & Ewell, Sutton United, Epsom & Ewell, Kingstonian, Woking, Slough Town
Paul Gbogidi: Local
Alec Jackson: Dulwich Hamlet, Chelsea
Tony Boorman: Epsom & Ewell, Crockenhill
Ian Paterson: Local
Micky Gillam: Local

Forwards
Steve Milton: Epsom & Ewell, Redhill, West Ham United
Steve Hill: Epsom & Ewell, Hampton, Molesey, Sutton United, Slough Town, Harrow Borough
Ian Simpson: Local
Murray Jones: Epsom & Ewell, Wellington United, Southend United
Barry Blackman: Local

Action from Croydon's F.A. Cup Tie at Hythe Town

(Est. 1893) DULWICH HAMLET (Nickname 'The Hamlet')

President: Tommy Jover Esq.
Chairman: David J. Milsted
General Manager: Allen Batsford
Man/Coach: Micky Leach
Physiotherapist: Caroline Brouwer

Secretary: Terry Stephens
Tel. No: 01-542 8905

Commercial Manager: Paul Rickaby. 01-693 4177
Press Officer: John Lawrence. 01-733 6385

Ground Address & Tel. No: Champion Hill Ground, Dog Kennel Hill, London SE22. 01-274 5187
Capacity: 16,000 **Covered accommodation:** 10,000 **Seating:** 1,500 **Floodlights:** Yes
Simple ground directions: East Dulwich Station, Denmark Hill then 10 minute walk. Herne Hill then 37 bus stops near ground. Also 184 from Elephant & castle and 185 from Victoria.

Clubhouse details: Three bars on match days and one bar every day. Live music, Thur, Fri, Sat and Sun.
Programme details: 20 pages **Editor:** J. Lawrence **Club metal badges:** Yes
Local Newspaper(s): South London Press. 01-769 444, S.E. London & Kentish Mercury 01-692 1122

Club colours: Pink/Blue **Change colours:** Yellow
Midweek match day: Monday **Previous Leagues:** Camberwell, Southern Suburban, Dulwich
Record transfer fee paid: T. Eames G. Allen
Record transfer fee received: E. Nwajiobi
Record attendance: 20,744 Kingstonian v Stockton, F.A. Amateur Cup Final
Senior honours/best performance: Istmian League (4) Div 1, F.A. Amateur Cup (4), London Senior Cup (4) Surrey Senior Cup (16). / F.A. 13 times to 1st Round Proper (last occasoin 1948-49). F.A. Trophy 1979-80 Quarter-Final

Past players (who progressed to Football League): W. Bellamy (Tottenham, A. Solly (Arsenal), J. Mossley (Milwall), E. Tower (Milwall), G. Pearce (Plymouth), R. Crisp (Watford), J. Ryan (Charlton), E. Nwajiobi (Luton Town).

SEASON 1985/86
League posn: 9th **A.C. Delco Cup:** **County Cup:** 1st Round **F.A. Trophy:** **F.A. Cup:**

Goalkeepers
Peter Dale: Carshalton Athletic

Defenders
Billy Edwards: Tooting & Mitcham, Leatherhead, Tooting & Mitcham, Bromley, Maidstone United, Wimbledon (21-2), Walton & Hersham, Tottenham Hotspur
Bob Pittaway: Hendon, Walthamstow Avenue, Tooting & Mitcham, Barnet, Tooting & Mitcham, Dartford, Chelmsford City, Millwall, Charlton Athletic
Paul O'Gorman: Corinthian Casuals, Croydon, Brighton, Charlton Athletic
Micky Brookman: Bromley, Croydon, Fulham, Q.P.R.
Stuart Farnell: Local
Colin Coldspring: Corinthian Casuals
Reg Gaston: Epsom & Ewell, Bromley, Croydon, Bromley, Croydon

Midfield
Lee Akers: Carshalton Athletic
Gary Hogan: Local
Steve Tomlin: Bromley
Martin Nolan: Chelsea
Micky Leach: Leatherhead, Cambridge United (19-1), Q.P.R. (313-61)
Bobby Armitt: Corinthian Casuals, Luton Town, Southampton

Forwards
Steve Parsons: Wembley, Hayes, Orient (36-6), Wimbledon (94-19), Walton & Hersham
Andy Perry: Local
Paul Harding: Carshalton Athletic, Epsom & Ewell, Sutton United, Whyteleafe
Eddie Martin: Tottenham Hotspur
Conrad Kane: Bromley, Dulwich Hamlet, Merstham
Bernie Merron: Corinthian Casuals, Molesey, Bromley, Croydon

Bernie Merron

(Est. 1967) FARNBOROUGH TOWN (Nickname. The 'Boro')

President:
Chairmen: Ron Wallace
Manager: Ted Pearce
Ass. Man/Coach: Colin Lippiatt/Kevin Leahy
Physiotherapist:

Secretary: Garry Ward
Address & Tel. No: 25 Teal Crescent, Kempshot, Basingstoke, Hants. Tel. (Basingstoke) 22252
Commercial Manager:
Press Officer: Paul Johnstone. Tel. (Farnborough) 516061

Ground Address & Tel. No: John Roberts Broucd, Cherrywood Road, Farnborough. Tel 541469 / 545553
Capacity: 4,000 **Covered accommodation:** 400 **Seating:** 310 **Floodlights:** Yes
Simple ground directions: From M3 (junction 4) along A325 turn right into Prospect Avenue, second right into Cherrywood Road, 20-30 minutes walk from Farmborough, Farnborough North & Frimley stations. Alder Valley bus routes 439 & 440 pass ground.
Clubhouse details: Large bar open every evening & Saturday/Sunday lunchtimes.
Programme details: 32 page 30p **Editor:** Mick Keith & Keith Wickham **Club metal badges:** Yes
Local Newspaper(s): Farnborough News (0252) 28221
Club Colours: Yellow/Blue/Yellow
Change colours: White/White/Red
Midweek match day: Tuesday
Previous Leagues: Surrey Senior, Spartan, London Spartan, Athenian
Record transfer fee paid:
Record transfer fee received:
Record attendance: 3,000 v Billericay Town (F.A. Vase Semi-Final) 1977
Senior honours/best performance: Isthmian League Division 1 Champions, Isthmian League division 2 Champions, Athenian League Division 2 Champions. Spartan League Champions (4). Spartan League Cup (2). Hants Senior Cup (4). F.A. Vase Semi-Finals (2)
Past players (who progressed to Football League):

SEASON 1985/86
League posn: 3rd **A.C. Delco Cup:** Semi-Final **County Cup:** Winners **F.A. Trophy:** 3rd Qual **F.A. Cup:** 1st Rd. Proper
Club Captain: Richard Walden **Player of the Year:** Tommy Jones

Leading Goalscorers:	**Hat-tricks:**	**Penalties:**	**Most appearances:**
Jimmy Bolton 33	Jimmy Bolton 2	Richard Walden 5	Tony Carter 58*
Tommy Jones 23	Tommy Jones 2	Tommy Jones 1	Tommy Jones 58*
Brian Broome 14			Mark Turkington 57

(* Ever Present)

Goalkeepers
Tom Hammond: Local
Steve Osgood: Local

Defenders
Richard Walden: Newport County (151-2), Sheffield Wednesday (100-1), Aldershot (405-16)
Tony Carter: Local
Tony Doherty: Woking, Slough Town, Basingstoke Town, Harrow Borough, Buscough, Wigan Athletic, Cardiff City, Everton
Keith Baker: Cobham, Egham Town, Hounslow, Southall, Staines Town
Robin Gosnell: Slough Town, Hungerford Town, Farnborough Town, Maidenhead United

Midfield
Brian Broome: Wycombe Wanderers, Farnborough Town, Camberley Town
Micky Milsom: Andover, Basingstoke Town, Woking, Farnborough Town, Aldershot
Freddie Jones: Camberley Town, Woking
Mark Turkington: Leatherhead, Farnborough Town, Charlton Athletic, Chelsea

Forwards
Tommy Jones: Woking, Farnborouough Town, Chelsea
Brian Perkins: Leatherhead, Carshalton F.C.
Jimmy Bolton: Tooting & Mitcham, Farnborough Town, Wimbledon, Hillingdon, Tottenham Hotspur
Glyn Cowlishaw: Chelmsford City, Worksop Town, Chelmsford City, Heybridge Swifts, Maidenhead United

Farnborough Town F.C. Photo: Eric Marsh

(Est. 1933) HARROW BOROUGH (Nickname. The 'Boro')

President: E. G. May
Chairmen: P. K. Rogers
Manager: Keith Chamberlin
Ass. Man/Coach: Trevor How/Alan Randall
Physiotherapist: George Price

Secretary: B. Rogers
Address & Tel. No: 21 Ludlow Close, South Harrow, Middlesex HA2 8SR. Tel. (01) 422 8606(H) (01) 422 5221(B)
Commercial Manager: T. Connor c/o Club
Press Officer: Tony Burroughs. Tel. (01) 845 9438

Ground Address & Tel. No: Earlsmead, Carlyon Auenue, South Harrow, Middlesex HA2 8SS. Tel. (01) 422 5989 (Foyer), (01) 422 5221 (Office).
Capacity: 4,750 **Covered accommodation:** 2 sides **Seating:** 200 **Floodlights:** Yes
Simple ground directions: LTE stations Northolt (central line) then by 140 or 282 bus, South Harrow (Piccadilly line) then H1 or 114 bus.
Clubhouse details: Open seven days a week normal licencing hours. Four bars, ballroom, games room, varied entertainment venue for major sporting & social events.
Programme details: 24 page 30p **Editor:** M. Gibbs **Club metal badges:** Yes
Local Newspaper(s): Harrow Observer (01) 422 4404
Club Colours: All Red
Change colours: All Yellow
Midweek match day: Tuesday
Previous Leagues: Harrow a Dist, Spartan, West Middle Comb., Delphian, Athenian
Record transfer fee paid: To Dagenham for George Duck & Steve Jones
Record transfer fee received: £15,000 Chris Huchings (Chelsea)
Record attendance: 3,000 F.A. Cup v Wealdstone 1946
Senior honours/best performance: Isthmian League Champions, 2nd Round F.A. Cup, Semi-Finalists F.A. Trophy, Middlesex Senior Cup Winners, Middlesex Charity Cup Winners
Past players (who progressed to Football League): Terry Eden (Raith R.), Denis Russell (Arsenal), Ron Shaw (Torquay), Micky Bottoms (Q.P.R.), Mel Lucas (Leyton Orient, Wales), Dave Bassett (Wimbledon), David Kemp (Crystal Palace), Gary Borthwick (Bournemouth), Chyris Hutchings (Chelsea), Mick Dohety (Reading), Tom Carpenter (Watford), Robert Rosarie (Norwich), Benny Laryea (Torquay Utd.)

SEASON 1985/86
League posn: 5th **A.C. Delco Cup:** Quart. Final **County Cup:** Semi-Final **F.A. Trophy:** 1st Rd. **F.A. Cup:** 2nd Qual Rd
Club Captain: Trevor How
Player of the Year: Lawrie Holmes

Leading Goalscorers:	Hat-tricks:	Penalties:	Most appearances:
L. Holmes 40	S. Long	R. Johnson 9	T. How 65, S. Bateman 65
S. Long 33	L. Holmes 1	S. Long 3	R. Johnson 64, S. Ennanuel 63
S. Emmanuel 13			L. Holmes 63, S. Long 62

Goalkeepers
Les Currell: Slough Town, Harrow Borough, Wealdstone, Harrow Borough, Chelsea
Ken Lavender: Harefield United, Q.P.R., Southall, Wealdstone

Defenders
Colin Payne: Local
Robbie Johnson: Hayes, Brentford (2), Arsenal
Trevor How: Wycombe Wanderers, Aylesbury United, Watford (91-2)
Steve Bateman: Everton, Hemel Hempstead
Ray Duffy: Hanwell Town, Wembley, Harrow Borough

Midfield
Paul Dawson: Brentford
Paul Morris: Hillingdon
Steve Smith: Hendon, Harrow Borough
Steve Emmanuel: Staines Town, Harrow Borough, Watford, Wolves
Russell Townsend: Finchley, Boreham Wood, Barnet, Northampton Town (12-1), Barnet, Arsenal

Forwards
Steve Long: Wycombe Wanderers, Burton Albion
Lawrence Holmes: Harlow Town, Edgware
Sean Baker: Finchley, Barnet, Maidstone United, Tottenham Hotspur, Boreham Wood
Tim Vincent: Ruislip Manor, Harrow Borough
Steve Goodwin: Stafford Rangers, Leek Town

Back Row: *Ray Duffy, Robbie Johnson, Lawrie Holmes, Keith Chamberlin (manager), Mark Adams, Paul Dawson, Colin Payne.*
Front Row: *Steve Myers (kit manager), Trevor How, Rjussell Townsend, Steve Bateman, Neil Deamer, Kenny Lavender, Paul Morris, Steve Long, Alan Randall (Coach).*

(Est. 1909) HAYES (Nickname. The 'Missioners')

President: L. Lovering
Chairman: D. L. W. Goodall
Manager: George Goode
Ass. Man/Coach:
Physiotherapist: Cliff Cobb

Secretary: J. Price
Address & Tel. No: 10 Minterne Waye, Hayes, Middlesex. Tel. (01) 848 0743 (H). (01) 200 2322 (B).
Commercial Manager: Emile Van Laer. Tel. (01) 573 0018
Press Officer: Trevor Griffith. Tel. (Ruislip 08956 72771)

Ground Address & Tel. No: Church Road, Hayes, Middlesex. Tel. (01) 573 4598 (Ground), (01) 573 0933 (Clubhouse).
Capacity: 9,000 **Covered accommodation:** 2,000 **Seating:** 450 **Floodlights:** Yes
Simple ground directions: 1 mile Hayes Town centre. Close M4 and A4020 (Uxbridge Road). Also buses pass ground.
Clubhouse details: Open every evening and Saturday and Sunday lunchtimes. Snacks, Dance hall, Bar and Kitchen Facklties, Large car park, Full time steward.
Programme details: 20 page 30p **Editor:** Kevin Watts **Club metal badges:** Yes
Local Newspaper(s): Hayes Gazette. Tel. 0895 37161
Club Colours: Gold and Red **Change colours:** All White
Midweek match day: Tuesday **Previous Leagues:** Great Western, Suburban, Spartan and Athenian
Record transfer fee paid: £3,000 to Kingstonian for Graham Drake
Record transfer fee received: £10,000 from W.B.A. for Cyrille Regis
Record attendance: 7,000 v Bromley Amateur Cup (1952)
Senior honours/best performance: Past winners of Athenian, Great Western Suburban, Spartan Leagues, Amateur Cup finalists 1930-1, seni-finalists 1956-7. London Senior Cup (2), Middlesex Senior Cup (8), Middlesex Charity Cup (14), London Charity Cup (1), London Challenge Cup Finalists (1), Hitachi Cup Finalists (1)./F.A. Cup 1972-3 v Reading 2nd Round, 0-0 and 0-1, F.A. Trophy 1978-9 Quarter-Final
Past players (who progressed to Football League): Les Smith (Aston Villa, England), Tony Alleman (Switzerland), Robin Friday (Reading), Cyrille Regis (W.B.A., England)

SEASON 1985/86
League posn: 16th **A.C. Delco Cup:** Quart Final **County Cup:** S/Final **F.A. Trophy:** 1st Qual Rd **F.A. Cup:** 2nd Qual Rd
Club Captain: Reg Leather **Player of the Year:** Paul Hyde – 2nd year running

Leading Goalscorers:	Hat-tricks:	Penalties:	Most appearances:	
Byron Walton 19	None	Dave Silman 5	Glen Hayward 62	(Max possible 62)
		Kevin Tilley 2		
		Reg Leather 1		

Goalkeepers
Paul Hyde: Hillingdon

Defenders
Peter Bartlett: Epsom & Ewell, Hampton, Leatherhead, Hampton
Mark Harrison: Local
Dave Silman: Harrow Borough, Walthamstow Avenue, Brentford (1), Wolves
Kevin Tilley: Wycombe Wanderers, Hayes, Aylesbury United, Maidstone United, Wimbledon (13), Q.P.R.
Reg Leather: Southall, Leatherhead, Hayes, Woking, Hillingdon, Hayes, Q.P.R.

Midfield
Harry Manoe: Harrow Borough, Ruislip Manor, Southall, Hayes
Noel Fletcher: Addlestone, Woking
Mark Lovell: Local
Glen Hayward: Brentford, Hounslow
Steve Corey: Addlestone

Forwards
Rob Smale: St Albans City
John Regan: Southall, Harefield United
Gary Dolling: Local
Byron Walton: Wokingham Town, Hayes, Aylesbury United, Millwall
Greg West: Whitstable Town, Harrow Borough, Wembley, Hillingdon
Keith Dunmore: Local

Hayes F.C.

(Est. 1908) HENDON (Nickname. 'Dons or Greens')

Joint Presidents: M. Hyams, R. Butlin
Chairman: C. Geary
Manager: Ted Hardy
Ass. Man/Coach: Micky Janes
Physiotherapist: Sally Geater

Secretary: D. Stanley
Address & Tel. No: 17 Old Vicarage Gardens, Markyate, St. Albans, Herts. AL3 8PW. Tel. Luton (0582) 840707
Commercial Manager: Contact bar manager
Press Officer: D. Stanley

Ground Address & Tel. No: Claremont Road, Cricklewood, London NW2 1AE. Tel. (01) 455 9185
Capacity: 8,000 **Covered accommodation:** 5,500 **Seating:** 500 **Floodlights:** Yes
Simple ground directions: Golders Green Station then 226 bus to Claremont Road. Brent Cross Station then walk coming from East 1st left after Brent Cross flyover on North Circular Road.
Clubhouse details: Two bars open during normal licensing hours and match days. Entertainment on Friday and Saturday evenings
Programme details: 32 page 30p **Editor:** P. Dean. Tel (01) 450 7585 **Club metal badges:** Yes
Local Newspaper(s): Hendon Times. Tel. (01) 203 0411

Club Colours: Green shirts/socks, White shorts
Change colours: All White
Midweek match day: Tuesday
Previous Leagues: Athenian League
Record transfer fee paid: £1,500 to Harrow Borough for G. Duck
Record transfer fee received: £2,500 from Enfield for D. Drummy
Record attendance: 8,000 F.A. Cup 1953-54
Senior honours/best performance: European Amateur Champs, F.A. Amateur Cup (3), Runners-up (2), Isthmian League (2), Tunners-up (3), Isthmian Keague Cup, Athenian League (3), Middlesex Senior Cup (11), London Senior Cup (2), F.A. Cup 1973-74 v Newcastle Utd. 3rd Round lost replay at Watford, F.A. Trophy 1976-77, 1977-78 3rd Round
Past players (who progressed to Football League): Roy Stroud (West Ham), Peter Shearing (Plymouth), Jeff Harris (Leyton Orient), Peter Anerson (Luton)

SEASON 1985/86
League posn: 19th **A.C. Delco Cup:** 2nd Rd. **County Cup:** Winners **F.A. Trophy:** 3rd Qual Rd **F.A. Cup:** 1st Qual Rd
Club Captain: Roger Wade
Player of the Year: Colin Tate

Leading Goalscorers:	**Hat-tricks:**	**Penalties:**	**Most appearances:**
Colin Tate 21	None	Colin Tate 2, Mark Adams 1	Colin Tate 51
Danny Worley 5		Steve Newing 1, Stene Wilkins 1	Andy O'Brien 51
			Phil Gridelet 47

Goalkeepers
Lee Hunter: Walthamstow Avenuw, West Ham United

Defenders
Andy O'Brien: Local
Tommy Murphy: Harrow Borough, Wembley, Hendon, Wealdstone, Luton Town
Steve Newing: Local
Phil Gridelet: Watford
Tony Gibson: Dartford, Dagenham, Enfield, Ilford, Bishop's Stortford, Enfield
Paul Curran: Local
Paul Shields: Wembley, Hendon, Edgware Town, Kingsbury Town, Slough Town

Midfield
Roger Wade: St Albans City, Dagenham, Enfield, Leytonstone & Ilford, Tottenham Hotspur
Derek Brown: Dartford
Peter Stapleton: Local
Steve Wilkins: Chesham United, Hayes, Walthamstow Avenue, Chelsea
Billy Beeson: Clacton Town

Forwards
Mark Adams: Chesham United, Kingstonian, Hendon, Wealdstone
Gary Allen: Boreham Wood, Dulwich Hamlet, Carshalton Athletic, Birmingham City
Erskine Smart: Local
David Clark: Dartford, Charlton Athletic
Colin Tate: Slough Town, Wycombe Wanderers, Oxford City, Hampton, St Albans City, Hayes, Southall, Brentford, Q.P.R.
Kenny Page: Local
Danny Worley: Local

Back Row
Left to Right: *K. Barker (kitman), Mick Kiely, Phil Gridelet, Danny Worley, Bryan Kelly, Roy Drake, Andy O'Brien, David Clark, Tony Gibson, Ted Hardy (manager).*
Front Row
Left to Right: *Micky Janes (asst. manager), John Knapman, Colin Tate, Roger Wade (captain), Bobby Harding, Erskine Smart, Derek Brown, Goal-keeper Mark Broughton missing from photo.*

(Est. 1865) HITCHIN TOWN (Nickname. The 'Canaries')

President: J. Dawson
Chairman: G. A. Lincoln

Manager: Alan West
Ass. Man/Coach: Steve Gear
Physiotherapist: Mick Walker

Secretary: C. B. C. Buck
Address & Tel. No: 19 Baliol Road, Hitchin, Hertfordshire SG5 1TT. Tel. Hitchin (0462) 59152 Home and Ansaphone service
Commercial Manager: Basil Plews. Tel. (0462) 894945
Press Officer: D. C. Birdsey. Tel. Hitchin (0462) 51887

Ground Address & Tel. No: Fishpond's Road, Hitchin, Herts SG5 1NU. Tel. Hitchin (0462) 59028 & 34483
Capacity: 6,000 **Covered accommodation:** 500 **Seating:** 500 **Floodlights:** Yes
Simple ground directions: 1 mile Town Centre & Station A1(M) + A6202 + A600 + A505:-M1 + A505 + A600 + A505: Brentford A600 + A505: Cambridge A505:.
Clubhouse details: Boardroom, Lounge, Kitchen 2 Bars open every night, midday lunches and snacks
Programme details: 28 page 30p **Editor:** C. B. C. Buck **Club metal badges:** Yes
Local Newspaper(s): Hitchin Gazette and Express, Weekend Mirror. Tel. (0462) 59651. Hichin Comet. Tel. (0462) 31666

Club Colours: Yellow/Green/Yellow
Midweek match day: Tuesday
Record transfer fee paid: £1,000
Record transfer fee received: £3,500
Record attendance: 7,878

Change colours: Green/Yellow/Green
Previous Leagues: South Eastern, Spartan, Athenian

Senior honours/best performance: F.A. Amateur Cup Semi-Finalists 2, Herts Sinior Cup 18, London Senior Cup & Runner-up, Isthmian League & Athenian League runners-up, Spartan
Past players (who progressed to Football League): Reg Smith, C. J. Walker, W. R. Odell, S. R. Foss, R. Stevens, T. Clark, G. Goodyear, L. Garwood, P. Burridge, R. Kitchener, D, Bunpstead, M. Dixon, D. Pacey, D. Hille, G. Ley, R. Morton, D. Castle, G. Goodeve, B. Robinson

SEASON 1985/86
League posn: 17th **A.C. Delco Cup:** 1st Rd. **County Cup:** S/Finals **F.A. Trophy:** 1st Qual **F.A. Cup:** 2nd Qual
Club Captain: Steve Fountain **Player of the Year:** Ian Lindsay

Leading Goalscorers:	**Hat-tricks:**	**Penalties:**	**Most appearances:**
Mick Every 14	None	S. Fountain 10	Steve Fountain 57
Ian Lindsay 12		Alan West 2	Tony Luff 55
Steve Fountain 11			Ian Lindsay 54

Goalkeepers
Tony Luff: Bedford Town

Defenders
John Woodward: Hendon, Hitchin Town, Luton Town
Steve Fountain: Barton Rovers, Letchworth Garden City, Milton Keynes City, Kempston Rovers, Bedford Town, Charlton Athletic
David McDermott: Local
Ronnie Lawson: Baldock Town, Hitchin Town
Stuart Harding: Barton Rovers, Dunstable, Barton Rovers

Midfield
David Taylor: Barton Rovers
Alan West: Millwall (58-4), Minnesota Kicks (USA), Luton Town (285-16), Burnley (44-3)
Ian Lindsay: Rushden Town, Wellingborough Town, Kempston Rovers, Bedford Town
Colin Cardines: Bishop's Stortford, Letchworth Garden City
Steve Miller: Local
Nick Holloway: Local

Forwards
Paul Grant: Morecambe, Hitchin Town, Bedford Town
Lee Payne: Local
Mark Thomas: Barton Rovers, Luton Town
Mick Every: Baldock Town, Hitchin Town, Cambridge City
Richard Gander: Penrith
Mark Burke: Luton Town, Q.P.R.
Paul Giggle: Pirton, Baldock Town, Hitchin Town, Letchworth Garden City, Hitchin Town

Hitchin Town F.C.

0(Est. 1885) KINGSTONIAN (Nickname 'K's')

President: E. A. Croker
Chairman: F. R. Jones

Manager: Chris Kelly
Ass. Man/Coach: Micky Cook / Keith Mead
Physiotherapist: Kevin

Secretary: Mrs M. W. Rowat
Address & Tel. No: 11 Eastbury Road, Kingston upon Thames. 01-546 5538 (H) 01-546 4116 (B)

Commercial Manager:
Press Officer: Derek Guppy (Bagshot 73737) (H) Ashford 51100 (B)

Ground Address & Tel. No: Richmond Road, Kinston upon Thames, Surrey. 01-546 4116
Capacity: 6,500 **Covered accommodation:** **Seating:** 1,200 **Floodlights:** Yes
Simple ground directions: On main A307 Kingston-Richmond Road, about one mile from town centre. Entrance in Richmond Road, Thorpe Road and Earle Gardens.

Clubhouse details: Open every evening and Sunday lunchtime. Large hall for dances, dinners, meetings, socials, etc.
Programme details: Available on subscription, 32 pages, 25p**Editors:** John Trevor (Chertsey 61790)33Club metal badges: Yes
Local Newspaper(s): Surrey Comet 01-546 2261, Kingston Informer 01-546 2522

Club colours: Red & White hoops/Black **Change colours:** All White
Midweek match day: Tuesday **Previous Leagues:** Kingston and District, West Surrey, Southern Suburban, Athenian
Record transfer fee paid: Alan Morton, Dave Alexander (Woking), Jester Williams (Stains Town)
Record transfer fee received: Giles Stille (Brighton)
Record attendance: Not known
Senior honours/best performance: F.A. Amateur Cup Winners, Finalists; Isthmian League (2), Runners-up (2); Hitachi Cup Finalists; London Senior Cup (2) Finalists (5); Surrey Senior Cup (11), Finalists (5) / F.A. Cup 1926, 1930, 1932/33 First Round Proper; F.A. Trophy 1977/78 3rd Qualifying Round

Past players (who progressed to Football League): Giles Stille (Brighton), John Lacy (Tottenham Hotspur)

Goalkeepers
John Power: Limerick City

Defenders
Ian Armstrong: Feltham, Willesden, Kingstonian
Darren Bird: Local
Kevin O'Donoghue: Banstead Athletic, Hounslow, Feltham, Molesey
Ken Greig: Local
Micky Preston: Leatherhead, Woking, Sutton United, Kingstonian
Kevin Wedderburn: Wimbledon

Midfield
Terry Eames: Leatherhead, Walton & Hersham, Leatherhead, Dulwich Hamlet, Wimbledon (47-1), Crystal Palace
Martin Nelmes: Local
Gary Dodd: Farnborough Town, Westfield
Andy Wallace: Metropolitan Police
Gary Seward: Clapton, Harrow Borough, Wembley, KPT Kuopian (Fin), Oulun Pallosevra (Fin), Blackpool (1)
Chris Kelly: Leatherhead, Millwall, Leatherhead, Sutton United, Tooting & Mitcham, Epsom & Ewell

Forwards
Kim/Connett: Bromley, Walthamstow Avenue, Tooting & Mitcham, Dulwich Hamlet, Charlton Athletic, Dulwich Hamlet
Richard Parkin: Farnborough Town, Addlestone, Egham Town, Epsom & Ewell, Camberley
Larry Galvin: Local
Jester Williams: Staines Town
Maurice Cox: Woking, Hillingdon, Huddersfield Town (4-1), Torquay United (62-13)
Martin Taylor: Local
John Martin: Egham Town, Walton & Hersham, Kingstonian, Hampton, Kingstonian

Chris Kelly is now manager of Kingstonian Football Club and in his heyday 'Budgie' or 'The Leatherhead Lip', as he was known when Leatherhead were enjoying superb F.A. Cup runs, modestly told the media just what was in store for the League Clubs.
What made Chris very special was the fact that he scored the promised goals to back up his 'confidence', indeed the solo effort from the half way line against Brighton was one of the all time great moments caught on television. This photo is from that game (Look at the crowd) Hopefully he will make just as much a success of management and as I signed him for Epsom once I will take all the credit! T.W.

A spectacular overhead shot for Chris Kelly at Brighton

(Est. 1908) ST. ALBANS CITY (Nickname. The 'Saints'

President: Mick Challis
Chairman: Tony Berry
Manager: John Mitchell
Ass. Man/Coach: Peter Lawrence
Physiotherapist: Beverley Long
Secretary: Ron Mann
Address & Tel. No: 91 Cavan Drive, St. Albans, Herts. AL3 6HP. Tel. (0727) 50886 (H&B)
Commercial Manager: Barry O'Donovan
Press Officer: David Tavemer. Tel. (0727) 67858
Ground Address & Tel. No: Clarence Park, Hatfield Road, St. Albans Herts. Tel. (0727) 64296
Capacity: 8,000 **Covered accommodation:** 1,500 **Seating:** 1,000 **Floodlights:** Yes
Simple ground directions: 200 yards from St. Albans City station
Clubhouse details: Bar and Boardroom for 200
Programme details: 20 page 25p **Editors:** R. Stanton/T. Edwards**Club metal badges:** Yes
Local Newspaper(s): Herts Advertiser, St. Albans Observer, St. Albans Review

Club Colours: All Yellow
Midweek match day: Tuesday
Change colours: All Royal Blue
Previous Leagues: Herts County, Sparton, Athenian
Record transfer fee paid: None
Record transfer fee received: £500 John Mitchell (Fulham), J. Mawhinney (Letchworth)
Record attendance: 9,745 v Southall, F.A. Cup (Amateur) 3rd Round replay 1925-26
Senior honours/best performance: Isthmian League. (3), Sparton League, Athenian League (2), London Senior Cup, Herts Senior Cup A.F.A. Cup, Herts Charity Cup (22), F.A. Amateur Cup Semi-Finalists (4), F.A. Cup 1968-69 v Walsall, 1980-81 v Tarquay
Past players (who progressed to Football League): J. Mitchell
SEASON 1985/86
League posn: 1st **A.C. Delco Cup:** 2nd Rd. **County Cup:** Qtr Finals **F.A. Trophy:** 1st Qual **F.A. Cup:** 1st Qual
Club Captain: John Watt
Player of the Year: Cary Keen

Leading Goalscorers:	Hat-tricks:	Penalties:	Most appearances:
Steve Perrin 23	Steve Perrin 3	John Watt 5	Mick Pearson 51 (Goalkeeper)
Gary Keen 17			John Watt 51 (Captain)
John Watt 16			

Goalkeepers
Mark Pearson: Oxford City, Hampton, Tring Town

Defenders
Rob Dowie: Cheshunt, Hatfield Town, Bishop's Stortford
Mark Vidgen: Tring Town, St Albans City
Alan Paradise: Letchworth Garden City, Leavesden
Steve Shea:
Gary Keen: Wycombe Wanderers
Nigel Wilson:

Midfield
John Watt: Oxford City, Hillingdon, Chesham United, Maidenhead United, Hayes, Hillingdon, Watford
Steve Oliver: Local
Richard White: Local
Ian Dowie: Cheshunt
Mick O'Shea: Boreham Wood

Forwards
Steve Perrin: Hillingdon, Wycombe Wanderers, Northampton Town (22-5), Hillingdon, Portsmouth (28-3), Plymouth Argyle (35-6), Crystal Palace (48-11), Wycombe Wanderers
Martin Gurney: Local
Neil Jeffreys: Local
Mark Biggins: Maidenhead United, Feltham, Hanwell Town, Hampton

From left to right, standing: *Steve Perrin, Ian Dowie, Terry Benning, Mick Pearson, Rob Dowie, Neil Jeffery, Alan Paradise and John Mitchell (Manager).*
From Left to right, seated: *Nigel Wilson, Steve Oliver, John Watt, Mick O'Shea, Garry Keen, Martin Gurney*

(Est. 1890) SLOUGH TOWN (Nickname. The Rebels)

President: Gordon W. Greig
Chairman: Mervyn H. Jones
Manager: Alan Davies
Ass. Man/Coach: Alan Humphries
Physiotherapist: Kevin McGoldrick
Secretary: Tony Abbott
Address & Tel. No: 138 St. Paul's Avenue, Slough, SL2 5ER. Tel. (0753) 20881 (H&B)
Commercial Manager: None
Press Officer: John Tebbit. Tel. (0753) 21156 (H)
Ground Address & Tel. No: Wexham Park Stadium, Wexham Road, Slough SL2 5QR. Tel. (0753) 23358/26738 & 23359 (Answerphone)
Capacity: 8,000 **Covered accommodation:** 650 **Seating:** 395 **Floodlights:** Yes
Simple ground directions: Turn off A4 towards Uxbridge (A412). At first traddic-lighhs turn left into Broadmark Road and at the end turn right into Wwxham Road. Bround approx. 1 mile on left.
Clubhouse details: Lounge, games and Tv room and main hall (seat 350 for meals). Regular entertainment, food available.
Programme details: 20 page 30p **Editor:** Richard Lewis. **Club metal badges:** Yes
Local Newspaper(s): Slough & Eton Observer. Tel. (0753) 75155. Windsor, Slough & Eton Express. Tel. (0753) 869651. Midweed Editins of Observer & Express. Slough Leader.
Club Colours: Amber Shirts, Navy Shorts/Socks.
Change colours: All White
Midweek match day: Tuesday
Previous Leagues: Southern Alliance, Berks & Bucks, Great Western Suburban, Spartan, Herts & Middx. Corinthian, Athenian
Record transfer fee paid: £3,000 Frank Parsons
Record transfer fee received: £2,200 Eric Young. (Brighton & H.)
Record attendance: 8,940 v Pegasus, Amateur Cup, 1953 (Dolphin Stadium), 5,000 v Millwall, F.A. Cup, 1982 (Wrexham Park)
Senior honours/best performance: F.A. Cup 1970-71 v Barnet 0-1, 1978-79 v Yeovil 0-1, 1985-6 v Orient 2-2, 2-3. All in 2nd Round proper, F.A. Trophu 1976-77 v Dagenham 0-2, 2-3 Semi-Final, F.A. Amateur Cup 1972-73 Finalists v Walton & H. 0-1
Past players (who progressed to Football League): Paul Barron, David Kemp, Roy Davies, Mickey Droy, Eric Young
SEASON 1985/86
League posn: 6th **A.C. Delco Cup:** 2nd Rd. **County Cup:** 2nd Rd. **F.A. Trophy:** 2nd Proper **F.A. Cup:** 2nd Proper
Club Captain: Derek Harris
Player of the Year: Jeff Bateman

Leading Goalscorers:	Hat-tricks:	Penalties:	Most appearances:
Rowan Dodds 18	Ken Wilson 1	Derek Harris 10	Keith White 59
Keith White 14	Rowan Dodds 1		Ken Wilson 59
Ken Wilson, Derek Harris 11			Rowan Dodds 57

Rowan Dodds scored nine goals in the 1985/86 F.A. Cup Comp., understood to be the highest munber of goals scored by one person in that competition for that season.

Goalkeepers
Graham Cox: Aldershot (12), South Ascot, Wokingham Town, Addlestone, Hillingdon
Chris Way: Wycombe Wanderers

Defenders
Jeff Bateman: Hillingdon, Harefield United, North Greenford United
Paul Gardam: Local
Steve Norman: Wokingham Town, Slough Town, Wycombe Wanderers, Molesley, Slough Town
Tony Knight: Harrow Borough, Wembley, Hillingdon
Derek Harris: Harrow Borough, Maidenhead United, Wycombe Wanderers, Southall

Midfield
Keith White: Burnham, Chelsea
Jimmy Jacobs: Hillingdon, Wycombe Wanderers, Northampton Town, Wycombe Wanderers
James Hartridge: Local
Steve Playle: Local

Forwards
Rowan Dodds: Local
Jimmy Brown: Wokingham Town, Hillingdon, Wokingham Town
Devon Petty: Hillingdon, Slough Town, Molesey, Slough Town, Southampton
Ken Wilson: Wycombe Wanderers, Hounslow, Walton & Hersham

Slough Town in action at Croydon

TOOTING & MITCHAM

President:
Chairman: J. Payne
Manager: D. Donaldson
Asst. Manager:
Coach:
Physiotherapist: Brian Mayo
Press Officer & Tel. No. F. Jannaway. 01 648 7240
Secretary: A.T. Gaitt
Address & Tel. No. 196 Hamilton Avenue, North Cheam, Surrey SM3 9DT. 01 641 2374
Commercial Manager:
Address & Tel. No.
Address and Tel. No. of ground: Sandy Lane, Mitcham, Surrey. 01 648 3248
Simple ground directions: Turning off Streatham Road, Mitcham near the 'Swan'
No. of seats: 1,990 **Covered accommodation:** 1,990 **Capacity:** 8,000
Year formed: 1932 **Nickname:** Terrors
Club shop:
Floodlights: Yes
Club sponsor:
Previous names:
Previous grounds:
Day for midweek home matches: Tuesday
Club colours: Black/white
Change colours: All light blue
Club metal badges: No
Record attendance: 14,500 v Nottingham Forest, F.A. Cup 3rd Rd **Year:** 1958-59
Best performance in: F.A. Cup:
F.A. Trophy:
Previous Leagues: London/Athenian
Clubhouse details: Mon-Thurs 6.30-10.30 pm. Fri 6.30-11 pm. Sat 1-00-6.30 pm. Sun 12-2 pm, 7.00-10.30 pm
Present players with Football League experience:
Past players who progressed into the Football League: A. Stepney, D. Bumstead, V. Akers, H. Smith, P. Hasty, C. Fairweather
Record transfer fee paid: R. Knowles (Wimbledon)
Record transfer fee received: H. Smith (Luton Town), C. Fairweather (Wimbledon)
Programme details: 16 pages, 25p
Programme editor: P. Garrard
Club Captain (1985-86): J. Bryant
Player of the Year (1985-86): J. Hamlet
Local newspapers & Tel. No. Mitcham News, 01 672 1077
Major Honours: Isthmian League (2), Athenian League (2), Surrey Senior Cup (8), London Senior Cup (4)

League 12th **F.A. Trophy** 1st Qual Rd **F.A. Cup** 2nd Qual **A.C. Delco Cup** 1st Rd **County Cup** 2nd Rd

Goalkeepers
David Taylor: Local

Defenders
Martin Lewis: Dulwich Hamlet, Croydon, Dulwich Hamlet, Wimbledon
Danny Godwin: Dulwich Hamlet, Wimbledon, Chelsea
Jeff Bryant: Crawley Town, Tooting & Mitcham, Gravesend, AFC Bournemouth (16-2), Wimbledon (73-9), Fulham
Andy Edwards: Dulwich Hamlet, Thanet United, Crawley Town, Bromley
David Shepherd: Borough Road College
Geo Inglesizs: Local
Alan Roughan: Dulwich Hamlet, Cheshunt, Hendon, Dulwich Hamlet, Kingstonian
John Roberts: Local

Midfield
Martin Morgan: Dulwich Hamlet, Tooting & Mitcham, Dulwich Hamlet, Carshalton Athletic, Dulwich Hamlet
Paul Haverson: Enfield, Kettering Town, Wimbledon (28-2), Q.P.R.
Neil Norman: Hendon, Dulwich Hamlet
Peter Kingston: Dulwich Hamlet, Carshalton Athletic, Fisher Athletic
Pat Carolan: Dulwich Hamlet, Carshalton Athletic

Forwards
Jeff Hamlet: Wimbledon
Ossie Bayram: Fisher Athletic, Dulwich Hamlet
Clevere Forde: Harrow Borough, Wealdstone, Plymouth Argyle (5), Hounslow
Sean Priddle: Wimbledon, Crewe Alexandra (11), Wimbledon
Edgar Awaritefe: Local

Wembley versus Walthamstow

(Est. 1900) WALTHAMSTOW AVENUE (Nickname. The Avenue)

President: V. Ercolani
Chairman: J. Thompson
Manager/Coach: Trevor Harvey
Ass. Man: Tom Fearey
Physiotherapist: Ken Davey

Secretary: N. R. J. Moss
Address & Tel. No: 39 Royston Avenue, Chingford, E4 9DE. Tel. (01) 531 0468 (H&B)
Commercial Manager: L. Bater
Press Officer: Tel. (01) 529 8810

Ground Address & Tel. No: Green Pond Road, Hicham Hill Road, Walthamstow E17. Tel. (01) 527 1130/2759
Capacity: 9,500 **Covered accommodation:** 6000 **Seating:** 900 **Floodlights:** Yes
Simple ground directions: Victoria Line (Underground) to Blackhorse Road, 123 bus to Lord Palmerston.
Clubhouse details: Open 7 days a week. Refreshment bar. Various sporting sections:- Darts, pool, angling, pigeons, etc.
Programme details: 16 page 30p **Editor:** Norman Moss **Club metal badges:** Yes (Supporters Club)
Local Newspaper(s): Guardian/Gazette. Tel. (01) 531 4141

Club Colours: Light & dark Blue hoops
Midweek match day: Monday
Change colours: Red/White
Previous Leagues: Athenian & Spartan
Record transfer fee paid:
Record transfer fee received: £13,000 D. Crown (Brentford)
Record attendance: 12,500 v Stockport City, F.A. Cup 1939
Senior honours/best performance: F.A. Amateur Cup (2), Essex Senior (12), London Senior (8), Isthmian League, F.A. Cup 5th Round, Draw. Drew at Manchester United, lost replay at Highbury 1953
Past players (who progressed to Football League): 27 players incl. D. Crown (Brentford) v Groves & L. Julians (Orient), D. Saunders (Chelsea), W. Walters & H. Gilberg (Spurs), W. Fielding (Everton), K. Facey (Otient), W. Shergold (Newport)

SEASON 1985/86
League posn: 6th**A.C. Delco Cup:** Lost 2nd Rd**County Cup:** Winners London Sen.**F.A. Trophy:** Lost 1st Q. Billericay (A)
F.A. Cup: Lost Dunstable (A) Replay 3rd Qual. Rd.
Club Captain:
Player of the Year: Billy Harrigan

Leading Goalscorers:	Hat-tricks:	Penalties:	Most appearances:
C. Zachhau 36	C Zachhau 1	N Wolstenholme 2	C. Zachhau 52
A. Hunter 13			W. Harrigan 51
D. Gayle 12			D. Root 50

Goalkeepers
David Root: Stansted, Barking, Launceston Town
Phil Jenkin: Local

Defenders
Billy Harrigan: Bishop's Stortford, Cambridge United
John Neighbour: Billericay Town
Simon Bumfrey: Local
Nicky Bissett: Hornchurch
Jesse Roast: Hornchurch, Walthamstow Avenue Dagenham, Brighton
Paul Shirt: Woodford Town, Barking

Midfield
Graham Stewart: Billericay Town, Hornchurch, Leytonstone & Ilford, Hendon
Glen Bickles: Orient
Steve Jones: Billericay Town, Dagenham, Charlton Athletic, Arsenal
Tim Sheringham: Barking
Tommy Williams: Orient
Chris Wright: Local

Forwards
Carl Zachhau: Rochdale, Hibernian F.C. (Malta)
Paul Turnpenny: Local
Alan Hunter: Harlow Town
Steve Wolsey: Maidstone United

Spectacular action from Walthamstow Avenue's F.A. Cup Tie at Wembley Photo: Peter Burrin

(Est. 1902) WINDSOR AND ETON F.C. LTD. (Nickname. The 'Royalists')

President: Sir David Hill Wood B.t
Chairman: Bill French
Manager: John Clements
Ass. Man/Coach: Keith Collins
Physiotherapist: Bryn Pippin

Secretary: To be appointed
Address & Tel. No:

Commercial Manager: Not as yet
Press Officer:

Ground Address & Tel. No: Stag Meadow, St. Leonards Road, Windsor. Tel. 860656
Capacity: 4,500 **Covered accommodation:** 650 **Seating:** 350 **Floodlights:** Yes
Simple ground directions: 1 mile from town centre on St. Leonards Road.
Clubhouse details: Open six days a week and Sunday lunchtimes 7.30-11.00pm. Dart boards and pool table. Availaible for private hire.
Programme details: 28 page 30p **Editor:** Sean Hoskin. W:854986 **Club metal badges:** Yes available from club shop 60p each
Local Newspaper(s): Windsor and Eton Express, Windsor and East Berks Observer, Evening Post.

Club Colours: Red shirts/shorts, White socks
Midweek match day: Tuesday

Change colours: White shirts/socks, Black shorts
Previous Leagues: Great Western Combination, Spartan, Metropolitan
Official Club Sponsors: Eton Travel Agency

Record transfer fee paid: None
Record transfer fee received: £2,000
Record attendance: 1,305
Senior honours/best performance: Athenian League Champions 1979-80, 1980-81. Athenian League Cup Winners 1979-80, Finalists 1980-81. Berks and Bucks Sinior Cup 1910-11, 1936-37, 1937-38, 1940-41, 1942-43, 1943-44, 1944-45, 1961-62. Delphian League Division 1 Runners-up 1962-63. F.A. Cup 1st Round 1925-26 1980-81, 1982-83, 1984-85. F.A. Cup 2nd Round 1983-84. F.A. Vase Semi-Final 1980-81. Isthmian League Division 2 Runners-up 1982-83. Isthmian League Division 1 Champions 1983-84. metropolitan Leaheu Cup Winners 1952-53. Metropolitan League Runners-up 1952-53. / F.A. Cup 1983-84 2nd Round v Bournemouth, Athenian. F.A. Trophy 1983-84, 1985-86 2nd Round Proper, Corinthian. F.A. Vase 1980-81 Semi-Final v Whickham, Delphian.
Past players (who progressed to Football League): Vic Woodley (Chelsea and England), Billy Coward (Q.P.R., Wallsall), Ken Groves (Preston, North End), Jack Dare (Southampton, Exeter City)

SEASON 1985/86
League posn: 11th **A.C. Delco Cup:** 1st Rd. **County Cup:** Q/Final **F.A. Trophy:** 2nd Rd.
F.A. Cup: 1st Rd Proper, H v Torquay Utd 1-1, A v Torquay 0-3
Club Captain: Jimmey Walsh **Player of the Year:** John Mitchell

Leading Goalscorers:	**Hat-tricks:**	**Penalties:**	**Most appearances:**
Chris Yates 20	Mark Davis 1	Jimmy Walsh 3	Chris Yates 51
Mark Davis 16		Chris Yates 1	Kevin Mitchell 50
Mark Franks 9			Mark Davis 50

Goalkeepers
Kevin Mitchell: Slough Town, Leatherhead, Woking, Windsor & Eton, Egham Town, Reading

Defenders
Mark Woods: Addlestone, Q.P.R.
Gary Woodcraft: Reading
John Mitchell: Woking, Windsor & Eton, Hayes, Windsor & Eton, Egham Town
Jimmy Walsh: Slough Town, Frickley Athletic, York City (99-2). Watford (65)
Martin Snow: Walton & Hersham, Chesham United, Staines Town

Midfield
Floyd Dennis: Slough Town
Jeff Chapman: Woking, Windsor & Eton, Slough Town, Egham Town, Hayes
Tony O'Driscoll: Chesham United
Kevin Hill: Slough Town, Woking, Windsor & Eton, Arcadia Shepherds (S.A.), Wealdstone, Amersham Town
Trevor Baron: Slough Town, Windsor & Eton, Chertsey, Burnham, Marlow
Richard Hill: Farnborough Town, Dorchester Town, Basingstoke Town, Southampton

Forwards
Mark Davis: Maidenhead United, Molesey, Woking, Windsor & Eton, Hampton
Mark Franks: Maidenhead United, Woking, Windsor & Eton, Harrow Borough, Guildford
Gary Huxley: Farnborough Town, Windsor & Eton, Chesham United, Staines Town, Hayes, Dartford, Aylesbury United, Weymouth, Hillingdon, Brentford
Keith Morris: Farnborough Town, Maidenhead United, Hayes, Addlestone, Hayes, Yeading

Front Row: (L-R) Kenny Jamieson, John Mitchell, Jimmy Walsh, Colin Smith, Mark Franks, Gary Woodcraft. Back Row: (L-R) Bill Stoves (Coach), Mark Woods, Bob King, Chris Yates, Kevin Mitchell, Jeff Chapman, Mark Davis, Bryn Pippin (Physiotherapist), Laurie Craker (Manager).

WOKINGHAM TOWN (Nickname. The Town)

President: D. Langley
Chairman: C. P. Gale
Manager: R. A. B. Merryweather
Coach: Ernie Howe
Physiotherapist: Andy Widdop
Secretary: J. White
Address & Tel. No: 36 Malvern Close, Woodley, Reading. Tel. 692661 (H), 780253 (B)
Commercial Manager: R. A. B. Merryweather
Press Officer: John Ansell
Ground Address & Tel. No: Finchamsetead Road, WoKingham. Tel. 780253
Capacity: 4,000 **Covered accommodation:** Yes **Seating:** 100 **Floodlights:** Yes
Simple ground directions: Half mile from town centre.
Clubhouse details: Open for Lunches. Wippet racing May to October.
Programme details: **Editor:** Anne Gale **Club metal badges:** Yes
Local Newspaper(s): Wokingham Times. Tel. 782000, Wokingham News. Tel. Bracknell 20363, Reading Evening Post Rgd. Tel. 55857

Club Colours: Amber/Black
Midweek match day: Tuesday
Change colours: Red/White
Previous Leagues: Corinthian, Athenian
Record transfer fee paid: 1,500 Derek Cottrell from Woking
Record transfer fee received: £2,000 Phil Alesander (Norwich)
Record attendance: 3,473 v Norton Woodseats F.A. Amateur Cup 1957-58
Senior honours/best performance: F.A. Cup 1982-83 v Cardiff 1st Round Proper, F.A. Trophy 1984-85 v Boston 3rd Round Proper
Past players (who progressed to Football League): Kirk Corbin (Cambridge), Steve Burler (Brentford), Phil Alexander (Norwich), George Torrace (Brentford)
SEASON 1985/86
League posn: 10th **A.C. Delco Cup:** 1st Rd. **County Cup:** S/Final 33F.A. Trophy: 1st Rd Proper **F.A. Cup:**
Club Captain: David Cox
Player of the Year: David Cox

Leading Goalscorers:	**Hat-tricks:**	**Penalties:**	**Most appearances:**
Wayne Wanklyn		Wayne Wanklyn 3	David Cox

Goalkeepers
Frank Parsons: Carshalton Athletic, Slough Town, Woking, Staines Town, Reading (1), Cardiff City (17), Crystal Palace (4)
Colin Caulfield: Wimbledon, Addlestone

Defenders
Kirk Corbin: Cambridge United (3), Wokingham Town
Micky Noad: Addlestone, Hounslow, Walton & Hersham, Hounslow
Roy Atkin: Local
Bobby Purser: Local
David Cox: Local
Gary Stroud: Local
Graham Harvey: Addlestone, Wokingham Town

Midfield
Micky Spencer: Local
Derek Cottrell: Woking, Wycombe Wanderers
Nicky Collier: Burnham
Gerry Crawford: Local
Paul White: Reading
Wayne Wanklyn: Wycombe Wanderers, Farnborough Town, Maidenhead United, Leatherhead, Basingstoke Town, Aldershot (18-2), Reading (54-3)

Forwards
Mark Matthews: Reading (8-1)
Micky Tune: Reading
Richard Evans: Local
Steve Aries: I.F. Nornan (Swe), Oxford United
Henry Pacquette: Tooting & Mitcham, Wycombe Wanderers, Slough Town, Wembley, Boreham Wood, Hendon, Harrow Borough

We did'nt recieive a photo this year but perhaps this one from 1957-8 will be of interest. It was published with this caption in the club's centenary brochure in 1975.
A team picture taken during season 1957-58 when Wokingham reached the quarter finals of the FA Amateur Cup. Seated on the extreme left is Mike Ashford — or Ray Hancox as he really was. He was a professional with Crystal Palace and Southend, but in order to play in amateur football he changed his name to Mike Ashford. Among those also shown are the Cox brothers, Bryan (next to Hancox) and Harold (third from right in the front row). Mr Charles Chipp, now a life member, is standing on the extreme right.

(Est. 1886) WORTHING (Nickname. The Rebels)

President: E. T. Ryan
Joint Chairmen: M. L. Hollis & A. J. W. Lander
Manager: Keith Rowley
Ass. Man/Coach: Gerry Offen
Physiotherapist:
Secretary: S. A. Rooke
Address & Tel. No: 168 Tarring Road, Worthing, West Sussex BN11 4HG. Tel. Worthing 201322 (H), 680188 (O)
Commercial Manager:
Press Officer: S. A. Rooke
Ground Address & Tel. No: Woodside Road, Worthing. Tel. Worthing 39575 (O), 39417 (C).
Capacity: 4,500 **Covered accommodation:** 400 **Seating:** 100 **Floodlights:** Yes
Simple ground directions: A24, A27, into Worthing.
Clubhouse details: Open to members every day including lunchtimes.
Programme details: 24 pages 30p **Editor:** Quentin Grimley **Club metal badges:** No
Local Newspaper(s): Evening Argus, Worthing Gazette & Herald

Club Colours: All Red
Change colours: All Blue
Midweek match day: Tuesday
Previous Leagues: Sussex County,Corinthian, Athenian
Record transfer fee paid: None
Record transfer fee received: £4,000 Richard Tiltman to Maidstone 1985
Record attendance: 5,000 F.A. Amateur Cup Quarter-Final 1907-08
Senior honours/best performance: Isthmian League Premier Division Runners-up 1984-85, F.A. Cup 2nd Round 1982-83, Winners Sussex Senior Cup 21 times, (not since 1978)
Past players (who progressed to Football League): None
SEASON 1985/86
League posn: 14th **A.C. Delco Cup:** 1st Rd. **County Cup:** S/Final **F.A. Trophy:** 3rd Rd. **F.A. Cup:** 4th Qual Rd.
Club Captain: Geoff Raynsford
Player of the Year: Martin Cox

Leading Goalscorers:	**Hat-tricks:**	**Penalties:**	**Most appearances:**
Mick Edmonds 40		2 Taking Worthing F.C. record to 242 Goals in 286 appearances	
Trevor Dove 10			Trevor Dove 55
			Kevin Foreman 55
			Simon Steele 53

Goalkeepers
Simon Steele: Scunthorpe United (5), Brighton (1), Everton

Defenders
Martin Cox: Brighton
Geoff Raynsford: Lewes, Horsham, Worthing
Peter Norlund: Local
Adrian Rowe: Burgess Hill Town
Tony Vessey: Steyning Town, Vasalund (Swe), Brighton (1)

Midfield
Andy Taylor: Local
Trevor Dove: Burgess Hill Town, Lewes, Haywards Heath
Peter O'Sullivan: Crawley Town, Maidstone United, Aldershot (14), Fulham (46-1), Brighton (24-2), San Diego Sockers (USA), Brighton (411-36), Manchester United
Gary Young: Local
Russell Saunders: Steyning Town, Eastbourne United, Hastings Town
Chris Punter: Local
Paul Lelliott: Local

Forwards
Mick Edmonds: Southwick
Kevin Foreman: Eastbourne United, Horsham, Dover, Worthing
Richard Rogerson: Local
Simon Drummer: Midhurst & Eastbourne United

Micky Edmonds who has totalled 242 goals in six seasons with Worthing scores from the penalty spot in a friendly against Chelmsford City
Photo: The Beckett Group of Newspapers

(Est. 1884) WYCOMBE WANDERERS (Nickname 'The Blues')

President: M. E. Seymour, MPS
Chairman: B. R. Lee

Secretary: J Goldsworthy
Address & Tel. No: 35 West Drive, High Wycombe, Bucks HP13 6JT. Tel. 38042

Manager: Alan Gane
Ass. Man/Coach: John Maskell
Commercial Manager: Paul Birdseye
Physiotherapist: David Springell **Press Officer:** Paul Lewis. Tel. 024026 2244 **Club Shop:** Yes
Ground Address & Tel. No: Loakes Park, High Wycombe. Tel. 0494 26567. information line High Wycombe 446763
Capacity: 12,000 **Covered accommodation:** 4,000 **Seating:** 1,000 **Floodlights:** Yes
Simple ground directions: One mile from High Wycombe Railway Station or M40 (interchange 4), adjacent to Hospital.

Clubhouse details: Match days. Steward: Dave Hutton. Naphill 5329
Programme details: 25 pages 30p **Editors:** Philip Ball and Paul Lewis **Club metal badges:** Yes
Local Newspaper(s): Bucks Free Press 0494 21212 **Club Sponsors:** Trend Communications

Club colours: Cambridge Blue and Oxford Blue **Change colours:** All Yellow
Midweek match day: Tuesday **Previous Leagues:** Southern Great Western Suburban, Spartan, Gola, Isthmian
Record transfer fee paid: £2,000 George Borg 1980
Record transfer fee received: £10,000 Ian Pearson, Millwall
Record attendance: 16,000 (1950) v St. Albans (see Directory).
Senior honours/best performance: Istmian League Champions (7), F.A. Amateur Cup Winner and Runners-up, Berks & Bucks Senior Cup (21), F.A. cup 3rd Round (2), F.A. Trophy Seni-Final (1)

Past players (who progressed to Football League): P. Suddaby, V. Busby, K. Swain, S. Perrin, I. Pearson, J.Delaney, M. Mellows, K. Abbis, S. Hyde, R. Rafferty, G. Truett, J. Tratt, P. fuschillo, A. Gane, D. Edwards, L. Worley

SEASON 1985/86
League posn: 20th **Bob Lord Trophy:** 1st Rd. **B & B. S.C.:** Losing finalists **F.A. Trophy:** Qt. Final **F.A. Cup:** 3rd Rd. Proper
Club Captain: Anton Vircavs **Player of the Year:** Gary Lester

Leading Goalscorers:	Hat-tricks:	Penalties:	Most appearances:
Simon Read 29			Anton Vircavs 69
Mark West 28			Mark West 66 + 5
Declan Linc 24			Gary Lester 66

Goalkeepers
Gary Lester: Chalfont St Peter

Defenders
Dave Burgess: Oxford City, Banbury United, Kidlington
Steve Toll: Flackwell Heath, Wycombe Wanderers
Anton Vircavs: Pressed Steel
Kevin Collins: Staines Town, Port Hacking (Aus), Staines Town, Slough Town, Wimbledon
Neil Price: Blackpool (13), Swansea City (10), Watford (8)
Graham Pearce: Local
Tony Riley: Local

Midfield
Bob Dell: Local
Graham Bressington: Local
Joe Blochel: Karlstad (Swe), R.S. Southampton, IFK Arvika (Swe), Southampton
Andy Harman: Local
Des McMahon: Wokingham Town, Reading (2), Wokingham Town, Hungerford Town, Hackley

Forwards
Simon Read: Staines Town
Neal Stanley: Wokingham Town
Roy Fairchild: Flackwell Heath
Mark West: Reading, West Ham United

Back Row (left to right): Neal Stanley, Dave Burgess, Gary Lester, Simon Read, Andy Harman, Sean Price, Dave Springell (Physio). Front Row: Anthony Riley, Mark West, Bob Dell, Anton Vircavs (captain), Kevin Collins, Des McMahon, Declan Link.
Jeff Holmes

YEOVIL TOWN

President: S.N. Burfield, J.P., M.B.E.
Chairman: G.A. Lock
Manager: Gerry Gold
Asst. Manager: P. Hillard
Player/Coach: Tom Ritchie
Physiotherapist: T. Rafferty
Press Officer & Tel. No. Gerry Gow

Secretary: Mrs Masters
Address & Tel. No. Yeovil Town F.C., Huish, Yeovil. Yeovil 23662
Commercial Manager: Alan Skirton
Address & Tel. No.

Address and Tel. No. of ground: Huish, Yeovil, Somerset BA20 1AZ
Simple ground directions: 400 yards from town centre
No. of seats: 1,625 **Covered accommodation:** 8,000 **Capacity:** 14,300
Year formed: **Nickname:** Glovers

Club shop:
Floodlights: Yes
Club sponsor:

Previous names:
Previous grounds:
Day for midweek home matches: Wednesday
Record attendance: 17,501
Best performance in: F.A. Cup:
F.A. Trophy:

Club colours: Green/white
Change colours: Yellow/blue
Club metal badges: Yes

Previous Leagues: Gola, Southern
Clubhouse details: Open every lunchtime and evenings and after matches. Meals available
Present players with Football League experience:
Past players who progressed into the Football League:
Record transfer fee paid: £7,500
Record transfer fee received: £8,000
Programme details: 28 pages, 30p
Programme editor:

Club Captain (1985-86): T. Ricketts
Player of the Year (1985-86): Phil James

Local newspapers & Tel. No. Western Gazette, Western Daily Press
Major Honours: South League (3), F.A. Cup 3rd Rd (9), F.A. Trophy semi-final 1970-1, 1971-2, V.O. League Runners-up

League 2nd **F.A. Trophy** 1st Rd **F.A. Cup** 1st Rd **A.C. Delco Cup** 1st Rd
County Cup Runners-up

Goalkeepers
David Walter: Torrington
Tim Bintley: Matlock Town

Defenders
David Linney: Oxford United (34), Birmingham City (1)
Neil Coates: AFC Bournemouth, Watford
David Craig: Weston Super Mare
Malcolm Gold: Salisbury
Gary Kember: Local
Forbes Phillipson-Masters: Bristol City (94-4), Plymouth Argyle (119), Southampton (9)
Tony Ricketts: Bath City, Clandown

Midfield
Gerry Gow: Burnley (9), Rotherham United (58-4), Manchester City (28-3), Bristol City (375-47)
Tom Ritchie: Bristol City (95-30), Sunderland (35-8), Bristol City (321-77)
Andy Pardew: Dulwich Hamlet, Corinthian Casuals, Whyteleafe, Corinthian Casuals, Epsom & Ewell, Whyteleafe
Paul Muir: Local
Andy Dymond: Forest Green Rovers, Clevedon Town

Forwards
Phil James: Keinton Mandeville
John McGinlay: Nairn County
Dave Spencer: Local
Paul Randall: Bristol Rovers (177-63), Stoke City (46-7), Bristol Rovers (52-33), Frome Town
Martin Tooze: Local
Gerry Pearson: Weymouth, Maidstone United, Weymouth, Bideford, Barnstaple Town, Sheffield United

Yeovil Town 1985/86

THE VAUXHALL-OPEL FOOTBALL LEAGUE SEASON 1985-86
DIVISION 1

LEAGUE TABLE

	Pl	W	D	L	Gf	Ga	Pts
St. Albans City	42	23	11	8	92	61	80
Bromley	42	24	8	10	68	41	80
Wembley	42	22	12	8	59	30	78
Oxford City	42	22	11	9	75	51	77
Hampton	42	21	11	10	63	45	74
Leyton Wingate	42	21	10	11	77	56	73
Uxbridge	42	20	8	14	64	49	68
Staines Town	42	18	10	14	69	66	64
Boreham Wood	42	15	16	11	62	54	61
Walton & Hersham	42	16	10	16	68	71	58
Lewes	42	16	8	18	61	75	56
Leytonstone Ilford	42	13	15	14	57	67	54
Finchley	42	12	17	13	61	59	53
Grays Athletic	42	13	11	18	69	75	50
Leatherhead	42	14	8	20	62	68	50
Tilbury	42	13	11	18	60	66	50
Maidenhead United	42	13	7	22	61	67	46
Basildon United	42	12	9	21	52	72	45
Hornchurch	42	11	11	20	44	59	44
Chesham United	42	12	6	24	51	87	42
Harlow Town	42	8	14	20	53	70	38
Aveley	42	8	6	28	59	98	30

RESULTS

RESULTS	Aveley	Basildon	Boreham	Bromley	Chesham	Finchley	Grays	Hampton	Harlow	Hornchurch	Leatherhead	Lewes	Leyton	Leytonstone	Maidenhead	Oxford	St Albans	Staines	Tilbury	Uxbridge	Walton	Wembley
Aveley		2-0	0-3	0-3	1-2	2-2	1-3	1-1	0-2	1-2	0-1	1-4	3-4	2-3	2-1	1-3	2-3	3-3	0-3	0-1	2-1	0-2
Basildon United	3-4		3-1	1-2	4-0	1-1	1-2	1-2	2-1	1-1	1-0	1-2	0-1	0-2	3-1	2-2	3-1	1-0	1-1	1-3	0-3	1-1
Boreham Wood	1-1	2-0		0-0	2-0	0-0	1-1	2-0	2-2	2-1	2-1	0-2	2-1	1-1	2-1	2-3	1-1	3-5	0-0	3-1	1-1	1-4
Bromley	5-1	1-1	1-1		1-0	0-1	0-0	1-0	2-1	1-0	4-2	1-1	2-1	3-0	2-0	1-2	1-0	2-0	1-0	1-0	1-0	1-0
Chesham United	1-4	2-3	2-1	2-4		1-0	1-4	1-1	0-1	0-2	1-0	2-1	0-3	4-1	2-2	0-4	1-4	0-1	3-0	3-1	0-2	2-2
Finchley	3-1	2-2	1-1	3-2	4-1		5-2	1-2	2-0	1-1	4-1	2-2	0-3	2-0	0-1	1-1	0-2	1-2	3-0	1-1	2-0	1-1
Grays Athletic	43	0-2	1-1	1-4	2-0	2-2		2-3	0-1	3-0	3-0	0-1	1-3	2-3	2-1	3-0	3-3	2-3	2-3	1-2	1-1	1-0
Hampton	2-0	2-1	3-2	2-1	1-1	2-0	2-2		2-3	2-0	1-2	2-0	3-1	1-1	1-0	0-1	3-3	0-2	4-2	0-1	2-0	1-1
Harlow Town	2-3	4-1	1-1	0-1	2-3	0-0	1-1	1-2		1-1	1-1	2-2	2-5	1-3	4-3	2-3	2-2	0-0	1-2	1-1	2-2	0-2
Hornchurch	0-0	3-1	2-2	1-3	1-2	4-2	1-4	1-1	1-1		0-1	4-1	0-0	1-0	0-1	0-2	1-1	1-0	2-0	1-2	3-0	0-1
Leatherhead	2-0	1-3	0-1	3-2	1-1	4-2	5-1	0-1	1-1	2-0		6-1	1-2	1-1	0-3	1-0	1-2	4-0	0-1	1-0	4-1	0-2
Lewes	2-0	3-1	0-1	0-2	2-3	1-1	1-5	0-3	2-0	0-0	1-0		3-1	2-1	2-1	3-2	1-7	1-1	0-4	2-0	4-1	1-3
Leyton-Wingate	2-1	3-0	3-3	3-2	2-0	0-0	1-0	2-1	3-0	2-1	2-2	2-0		1-2	1-1	0-2	0-3	2-0	3-2	2-4	1-1	1-4
Leytonstone Ilford	0-2	1-1	1-1	3-0	3-1	1-1	1-1	1-1	1-3	1-1	4-1	0-3	1-5		2-1	1-1	0-2	0-3	4-0	1-1	2-2	2-1
Maidenhead United	2-2	4-0	1-2	0-2	3-1	3-0	3-0	0-1	1-1	1-2	3-4	2-0	0-3	2-2		2-3	1-2	3-3	2-1	1-0	2-1	0-2
Oxford City	3-1	1-2	1-0	2-2	1-2	1-1	1-1	0-1	2-1	2-0	2-1	0-0	1-1	4-0	2-0		3-1	4-2	5-3	2-1	3-0	0-2
St. Albans City	3-2	3-1	1-3	2-1	2-1	2-0	2-0	2-2	3-2	4-2	6-2	3-3	1-1	4-1	3-1	0-3		1-1	3-0	2-1	1-1	0-1
Staines Town	5-2	2-1	0-4	2-2	1-1	1-2	2-1	0-2	2-0	2-0	2-0	2-1	1-1	2-1	1-2	3-0	4-0		3-2	0-3	3-2	1-1
Tilbury	2-4	0-0	2-1	1-1	4-0	2-2	1-2	0-1	1-2	1-0	2-2	3-2	0-2	2-2	3-2	0-0	0-0	4-1		2-1	5-1	0-0
Uxbridge	4-1	3-0	2-3	1-0	3-1	1-4	1-1	1-0	2-1	5-1	1-1	1-0	3-1	0-2	1-0	4-0	1-3	1-1	1-0		1-2	0-0
Walton & Hersham	3-2	1-0	1-0	2-0	3-1	4-1	5-1	4-2	1-0	2-1	3-2	1-3	1-0	0-0	1-1	2-2	2-4	4-2	1-1	2-3		1-2
Wembley	2-1	0-1	2-0	1-2	3-2	1-0	3-1	0-0	1-0	0-1	0-0	3-1	2-2	0-1	1-2	1-1	2-0	1-0	1-0	0-0	3-1	

Oxford City versus Hampton

(Est. 1963) BASILDON UNITED (Nickname 'The Bees')

President: Michael Roffey
Chairman: Ron Hill
Secretary: Terry Woolton
Address & Tel. No: 17 Viking Way, Wickford, Essex. 03744 61558 (H), 0268 3040 X 421 (B)

Manager: Ron Hanley
Ass. Man/Coach: D. Guiver / R. Page
Commercial Manager: None
Physiotherapist:
Press Officer: Robin Marshall
Ground Address & Tel. No: Basildon Stadium, Gardiner Close, Gardiners Lane South, Basildon, Essex. Tel. Basildon 20268 (Club), 282175 (Boardroom)
Capacity: 4,000 **Covered accommodation:** 3 stands **Seating:** 400 **Floodlights:** Yes
Simple ground directions: Take A176 off Soutyhend Arterial Road (A127), then left into Cranes Farm Road, proceed to end of dual carriageway, Gardiners Close is first on left.
Clubhouse details: Open every lunchtime and evening
Programme details: 24 pages **Editors:** Robin Marshall **Club metal badges:** Yes
Local Newspaper(s): Evening Echo, Yellow Advertiser
Club colours: Amber & Black stripes, Black **Change colours:** Blue & White Stripes, Blue shorts
Midweek match day: Tuesday **Previous Leagues:** Essex Senior, Athenian
Record attendance: 4,000 v West Ham Utd. (1963)
Senior honours/best performance: Essex Senior League (4), Essex Senior Trophy, Essex Senior League Cup, Isthmian League Division 2 Champions 1983-84
Past players (who progressed to Football League): Jeff Hull (Colchester Utd.)

BILLERICAY TOWN

President: Vacant
Chairman: J.R. Stacey
Manager: Peter Burton
Asst. Manager: Brian Moffatt
Physiotherapist: Brian King
Press Officer & Tel. No. L.S. Dewson
Secretary: L.S. Dewson
Address & Tel. No. 14 Graham Close, Billericay, Essex CM12 OQW. 027 74 22375 (H), 01 446 8351 (B) ext. 215
Commercial Manager: None
Address and Tel. No. of ground: New Lodge, Blunts Wall Rd., Billericay, Essex. Club Billericay 52188. Boardroom Ansaphone & Information Billericay 55177
Simple ground directions: From Shenfield (A129) turn right at first traffic lights, then first road on right. From Basildon (A129) proceed over first traffic lights in the town, then left at 2nd trafic lights and first road on the right
No. of seats: 250 **Covered accommodation:** 1,000 **Capacity:** 2,750 **Floodlights:** Yes
Year formed: **Nickname:** Town **Club sponsor:**
Previous names: **Club colours:** Shirts blue, shorts white, socks blue
Previous grounds: **Change colours:** Yellow
Day for midweek home matches: Tuesday **Club metal badges:** Yes, 80p
Record attendance: 3,641 v West Ham United, inaugural floodlight match in 1977
Previous Leagues: Romford & District, Mid Essex, Essex Olympian, Essex Senior, Athenian
Clubhouse details: Open each evening (except Monday) and Saturday & Sunday lunchtimes. Discos, live entertainment, bar snacks etc. Alcoves on ground floor. Glass fronted viewing gallery first floor
Present players with Football League experience:
Past players who progressed into the Football League: Danny Westwood (QPR, Gillingham), Terry Baker (Colchester United)
Programme details: 28 pages, 25p **Club Captain (1985-86):**
Programme editor: Len Dewson **Player of the Year (1985-86):** Alan Hull
Local newspapers & Tel. No. Billericay Gazette, Chelmsford 62421; Billericay Recorder, Basildon 22651; Evening Echo, Basildon 22791
Major Honours: F.A. Vase (3), Essex Senior League (3), Cup (4), Athenian (2), Isthmian Div 2, Runners-up Div 1, Rothmans Football Yearbook Award, Essex Senior Cup, Essex Senior Trophy (2)

Alan Hull left (Billericay's Player of the Season) and John Tone (Walthamstow Avenue), Vauxhall-Opel League (Premier Division)

(Est. 1948) BOREHAM WOOD (Nickname 'The Wood')

President: H. E. S. Payne
Chairman: W. F. O'Neill

Manager: John Drabwell
Ass. Man/Coach: Dave Wood / Les Baker
Physiotherapist: Alan Moore

Secretary: W. F. O'Neill
Address & Tel. No: 85 Cowley Hill, Boreham Wood, Herts WD6 SNA. Tel. (01) 953 3891

Commercial Manager: Bob Taylor. Tel. (01) 953 5097.
Press Officer: Johm Gill. Tel. (01) 904 1244

Ground Address & Tel. No: Broughinge Road, Boreham Wood, Herts. Tel. (01) 953 5097 (club)
Capacity: 2,500 **Covered accommodation:** 1,500 **Seating:** 250 **Floodlights:** Yes
Simple ground directions: Elstree & Boreham Wood Station, buses 292 & 107.

Clubhouse details: Full facilities for 250 people, club bar. Hall available for private hire, open market every Thursday
Programme details: 20 pages 25p **Editors:** John Gill **Club metal badges:** No
Local Newspaper(s): Boreham Wood Post, Herts Advertiser, Barnet Press Barnet & District Local Advertiser

Club colours: Black & White
Change colours: Red & White
Midweek match day: Tuesday
Previous Leagues: London Spartan, Surrey Senior
Record transfer fee paid: £1,000
Record transfer fee received:
Record attendance: 2,500 St. Albans
Senior honours/best performance: F.A. Cup 1973/74 1977/78 1st Round Proper. 1979/80 3rd Qualifying F.A. Trophy Istmian League Div 1 Championship 1976/77.

Past players (who progressed to Football League): Colin Franks

(Est. 1896) BRACKNELL TOWN (Nickname 'Town')

President: Ian McGregor
Chairman: A. McCowan

Manager: S. McClurg
Ass. Man/Coach: B. Mason / R. Haider
Physiotherapist: K. Creaser

Secretary: Mrs J. Bradley
Address & Tel. No: 7 Furzemoors, Bracknell, Berks RG121 4H7. Tel. 427304

Commercial Manager:
Press Officer: O. Ridge

Ground Address & Tel. No: Larges Lane, Bracknell 423255
Capacity: 3,000 **Covered accommodation:** 190 **Seating:** 90 **Floodlights:** Yes
Simple ground directions: Come off A329 at Met Office roundabout, Turn left at Tyre Co., ground about 100 yards on right.

Clubhouse details: 1 Bar open 7 nights & Saturday & Sunday lunchtime
Programme details: 12 pages **Editors:** O. Ridge **Club metal badges:** No
Local Newspaper(s): Bracknell News, Bracknell Times, Evening Post

Club colours: Red/White trim/Red/Red
Change colours: White/Red/Black
Midweek match day: Tuesday
Previous Leagues: London Spartan, Surrey Senior

EPSOM & EWELL

President: V. Barrett
Chairman: D. Ellins
Manager: Alan Webb
Asst. Manager: Ricky Kidd
Coach: Ricky Kidd
Physiotherapist: Kevin McIlroy
Press Officer & Tel. No. Mrs S Lamont

Secretary: Dave Wilson
Address & Tel. No. 33 Delaporte Close, Epsom KT17 4AF. Epsom 29817
Commercial Manager: I.E. Smith
Address & Tel. No.

Address and Tel. No. of ground: West Street, Ewell, Surrey. 01 393 7077
Simple ground directions: British Rail to Ewell West (10 mins). West St in Ewell village off A24 Epsom Rd**Club shop:**
No. of seats: 250 **Covered accommodation:** 250 **Capacity:** 4,750 **Floodlights:** Yes
Year formed: 1917 **Nickname:** E's **Club sponsor:**
Previous names:
Club colours: Royal blue
Previous grounds:
Change colours: Yellow
Day for midweek home matches: Tuesday
Club metal badges:
Record attendance: 1,604 F.A. Vase semi-final v Stamford 22.3.75
Best performance in: **F.A. Cup:** 1933-34 1st Rd
F.A. Trophy: 1981-82 2nd Rd
Previous Leagues: South Suburban, Surrey Senior, London League, Corinthian, Athenian
Clubhouse details: Open Mon to Sat evenings, Wed to Sun lunchtimes
Past players who progressed into the Football League: Phil Walker (Millway & Charlton), Trevor Lee (Millwall, Colchester, Bournemouth, Cardiff, Gillingham, Orient, Fulham), Mick Leonard (Halifax, Notts Co.), John Leedham (Millwall)
Record transfer fee paid:
Record transfer fee received:
Programme details: 25p (20 or 24 pages)
Club Captain (1985-86):
Programme editors: Dave Wilson, Stella Lamont
Player of the Year (1985-86):
Local newspapers & Tel. No. Epsom Advertiser, Epsom & Ewell Herald, Surrey Comet

FINCHLEY

President: W.R. Hunt
Chairman: A.S. Layson
Manager: Ted Goldney
Asst. Manager: Ray Kirstensen
Secretary: A.S. Layson
Address & Tel. No. 43 Ashurst Road, Cockfosters, Herts EN4 9LE.
Coach: Ray Kirstensen
Address and Tel. No. of ground: Summers Lane, North Finchley, London N12. 01 445 1400
Simple ground directions: via East Finchley (Northern Line), thence by bus direct to Summers Lane **Club shop:**
No. of seats: 650 **Covered accommodation:** 2,000 **Capacity:** 8,650 **Floodlights:** Yes
Year formed: 1874 **Nickname:** The Finches **Club sponsor:**
Day for midweek home matches: Tuesday
Record attendance: 10,000 v Bishop Auckland
Local newspapers Barnet Press, Finchley Times
Club colours: White/blue/white
Change colours: All blue or all yellow
Club metal badges: Yes
Previous Leagues: North London, Spartan, London, Athenian, Isthmian
Clubhouse details: Large hall, 2 bars, open every weekday and Sunday mornings
Past players who progressed into the Football League: George Robb (Tottenham), Eddis Baily (Tottenham), Tommy Harmer (Tottenham), Charlie Withers (Tottenham), John Westwood (Tottenham), H. Woodward (Tottenham), Arthur Willis (Tottenham), J. Ireland (Tottenham), Bob Brocklebank (Plymouth), Jack Chisholm (Plymouth), K. Tucker (West Ham), F. Lock (Charlton), J. Mullen (Fulham), S. Hall (Clapton Orient), W. Sperrin (Brentford), Peter Shreeve (Charlton), D. Uphill (Watford), P. Crossley (Manchester City)

GRAYS ATHLETIC

Patron: R.J. Billings
President: B.S. Coker
Chairman: Jim Myers
Twin Managers: Jeff & Fred Saxton
Coach: Peter Carey
Physiotherapist: Dave Lawson
Secretary: J.G. Saxton
Address & Tel. No. 2 Cotswold Gardens, Newbury Park, Ilford, Essex. 01 554 3920 (H), 01 592 0671 (B)
Commercial Manager: G.R. Jarvis
Address & Tel. No. 8 Pargetters Hyam, Hockley, Essex. 0702 546366
General Manager & Press Officer & Tel. No. Gordon Norman, 243b Wingletye Lane, Hornchurch. 04024 51733
Address and Tel. No. of ground: Recreation Ground, Bridge Road, Grays, Essex. 0375 377753
Simple ground directions: British Rail to Grays Stn (7 mins walk). A13 towards Southend, turn right at traffic lights, ½ mile turn left into Bridge Rd **Club shop:**
No. of seats: 200 **Covered accommodation:** 3,000 **Capacity:** 6,000 **Floodlights:** Yes
Year formed: 1890 **Nickname:** The Blues **Club sponsor:** The Boys from Rathbone Street
Previous names:
Previous grounds:
Day for midweek home matches: Tuesday
Club colours: Sky blue/sky blue/black
Change colours: Silver grey
Club metal badges: £1, **Car badges:** £3.50, **Key rings:** £1.20
Record attendance: 9,500 v Chelmsford City **Year:** 1959
Previous Leagues: Athenian, Corinthian, London
Clubhouse details: Bar, pool, indoor sports hall
Present players with Football League experience: Tony Mahoaney (Fulham, Brentford, Crystal Palace), Micky Welch (Wimbledon, Southend)
Past players who progressed into the Football League: Johnny Jordan (Spurs, Juventus), Neil Banfield (Orient), Bary Silkman (Orient), Dave Crown (Brentford, Portsmouth, Cambridge United), Gary O'Reilly (Spurs, Brighton), Micky Welch (Wimbledon, Southend)
Record transfer fee paid:
Record transfer fee received: £6,500 50% of £13,000 for D. Crown (Brentford), shared with Walthamstow Avenue
Programme details: 12 pages, 25p
Programme editors: Gordon Norman and Graham Deats
Club Captain (1985-86): Phil Whettell
Player of the Year (1985-86): Ian Cowell
Local newspapers & Tel. No. Thurrock Gazette, 0375 372293

An attractive view of the Grays Athletic v Bromley match Photo: Gordon Norman

HAMPTON

President: Alan Simpson
Chairman: Peter Turner
Manager: Steve Rogers
Asst. Manager: Dave Lucas
Coach: Bobby Green
Physiotherapist: Brian Lowe
Secretary: John Fuller
Address & Tel. No. 66 Green Lanes, West Ewell, Epsom, Surrey KT19 9UL. 01 393 2197 (H), 01 788 8165 (B) ext. 48
General Manager: Bob Read
Address & Tel. No.
Address and Tel. No. of ground: Beveree Stadium, Beaver Close, off Station Road, Hampton, Middlx TW12 2BX. 01 979 2456 (Club), 01 941 4936 (Boardroom)
Simple ground directions: Five minutes walk from Hampton Station along Station Road
No. of seats: 187 **Covered accommodation:** 2,000 **Capacity:** 3,500 **Floodlights:** Yes
Year formed: 1920 **Nickname:** The Beavers **Club sponsor:**
Previous names:
Club colours: White/black/black & white
Previous grounds:
Change colours: Red/red/red & black
Day for midweek home matches: Tuesday
Club metal badges: Yes
Previous Leagues: Kingston & District, South West Middlesex, Surrey Senior, Athenian & Isthmian
Clubhouse details: Open match days and training nights, along with Sunday lunchtimes. Hall available for hire
Past players who progressed into the Football League: Andy Rogers (Southampton, Plymouth Argyle, Reading)
Record transfer fee paid: Peter Shodeinde (Hendon) £400 November 1981
Record transfer fee received: Peter Shodeinde (Leatherhead) £400 December 1983
Programme details: 30p
Programme editor: Adrian Mann
Club Captain (1985-86):
Player of the Year (1985-86):
Local newspapers & Tel. No. Middlesex Chronicle, Surrey Comet, Richmond & Twickenham Times, The Informer, Richmond & Twickenham Guardian

KINGSBURY TOWN

President:
Chairman: Mark Hart
Manager: Terry Dyson
Asst. Manager: Ray Brandon
Coach: Ray Brandon
Physiotherapist: Judy Montieth
Secretary: Daniel Donald
Address & Tel. No. 135 Dryfield Road, Burnt Oak, Edgware, Middlx. 01 906 3387
Commercial Manager: Pat McCardle
Address & Tel. No.
Address and Tel. No. of ground: Silver Jubilee Park, Townsend Lane, Kingsbury, London NW9
Simple ground directions: Kingsbury (LT) then 183 to Townsend Lane on right **Club shop:** Yes
No. of seats: 100 **Covered accommodation:** 150 **Capacity:** 4,000 **Floodlights:** Yes
Year formed: **Nickname:** Town **Club sponsor:**
Previous names:
Club colours: Yellow/red/yellow
Previous grounds:
Change colours: All blue
Day for midweek home matches: Tuesday
Club metal badges: Not yet
Record attendance: 1,112
Previous Leagues: Partheon, Spartan, Isthmian (now Vauxhall-Opel Div 1
Clubhouse details: Open evenings and weekends
Past players who progressed into the Football League: Billy Dare, John Meadows, David Underwood
Record transfer fee paid: £500
Record transfer fee received: £600
Programme details: Yes
Programme editor: Mark Hart
Club Captain (1985-86):
Player of the Year (1985-86):
Local newspapers & Tel. No. Edgware and Finchley, Hendon Times
Major Honours: Promotion from Div 2 North to Div 1 Vauxhall-Opel 1985/6, F.A. Vase 4th Rd 1974/75

LEATHERHEAD

President: T. Dixon
Chairman: G. Darby
Manager: K. Oram
Asst. Manager: R. Wilson
Coach: R. Wilson
Physiotherapist: C. Arnold
Secretary: Jeff Morrell
Address & Tel. No. 4 Windsor Court, Anlaby Rd., Teddington TW11 OPE
Commercial Manager: Jeff Morrell
Address & Tel. No. As above
Address and Tel. No. of ground: Fetcham Grove, Leatherhead, Surrey. 0372 372634
Simple ground directions: Follow signs Leatherhead Leisure Centre. Ground is adjacent **Club shop:**
No. of seats: 406 **Covered accommodation:** 2,000 **Capacity:** 7,500 **Floodlights:** Yes
Year formed: **Nickname:** The Tanners **Club sponsor:**
Previous names:
Club colours: Green
Previous grounds:
Change colours: Blue
Day for midweek home matches: Tuesday
Club metal badges:
Record attendance: 32,000 v Leicester F.A. Cup 1975, game played at Filbert St
Previous Leagues: Surrey Senior, Corinthian, Athenian
Clubhouse details: 2 bars, hard court available for hire. Contact J. Morrell
Present players with Football League experience:
Past players who progressed into the Football League: C. Kelly (Millwall), B. Friend (Fulham), L. Harwood (P. Vale), W. Smith (Wimbledon)
Record transfer fee paid: £1500 B. Salkeld from Croydon
Record transfer fee received: £1500 B. Salkeld to Croydon
Programme details: 20 pages, 25p
Programme editor: Tim Edwards
Club Captain (1985-86):
Player of the Year (1985-86):
Local newspapers & Tel. No. Leath Advertiser, Surrey Advertiser
Major Honours:

LEYTON WINGATE

President: L. Aldridge
Chairman: G. Cross
Manager: G. Wakeling
Asst. Manager: K. Harris
Coach: K. Harris
Physiotherapist: Andy Taylor
Press Officer & Tel. No. George Cross
Secretary: Derek Dignum
Address & Tel. No. 37 Wyllen Close, Cleveland Way, London E1 4HQ. 01 790 4480
Commercial Manager: Alan Jackson
Address & Tel. No. 319 0482
Address and Tel. No. of ground: Wingate Leyton Stadium, 282 Lea Bridge Road, Leyton E10 7LD. 01 539 5405
Simple ground directions: Leyton Central line Clapton (BR), Blackhorse Rd (Vic Line) then bus 48, 55, 58 or 230 to Lea Bridge Rd
Club shop:
No. of seats: 80 **Covered accommodation:** Yes **Capacity:** 3,000 **Floodlights:** Yes
Year formed: 1868 **Nickname:** **Club sponsor:**
Previous names:
Previous grounds:
Day for midweek home matches: Tuesday
Club colours: Blue/white/blue
Change colours: White/blue/white
Club metal badges: Yes
Record attendance: 500 v Whickham 6th Rd F.A. Vase 1983-4
Previous Leagues: Athenian
Clubhouse details: Open 7 days a week
Programme details: 16 pages, 25p
Programme editor: G. Cross
Club Captain (1985-86):
Player of the Year (1985-86):
Local newspapers & Tel. No. Waltham Forset Guardian
Major Honours: 1st Rd F.A. Cup away to Swansea City, lost 2-0, 1986

Hampton's John Hales in a aerobatical action against Leatherhead at Fetcham Grove. Photo: Andrew Eggleton

LEWES

President: W.D. Carr
Chairman: D. Quinn
Manager: Team B. Jones, **General** D. Southouse
Res. Manager: J. Jefferson
Coach:
Physiotherapist: N. Strong
Press Officer & Tel. No. M.J. Webster
Secretary: M.J. Webster
Address & Tel. No. 2 Station Road, Seaford, Sussex. 0323 891890 (H & B)
Commercial Manager:
Address & Tel. No.
Address and Tel. No. of ground: The Dripping Pan, Lewes. Lewes 472100 (Clubhouse), Lewes 472574 (Boardroom)
Simple ground directions: Left from Lewes Station, left into Mountfield Rd, ground 100 yards on right
Club shop:
No. of seats: 400 **Covered accommodation:** 400 **Capacity:** 5,000 **Floodlights:** Yes
Year formed: 1885 **Nickname:** The Rooks **Club sponsor:**
Previous names:
Previous grounds:
Day for midweek home matches: Tuesday
Club colours: Red shirts, black shorts
Change colours: Yellow shirts, black shorts
Club metal badges: Yes
Record attendance: 2,500 v Newhaven **Year:** 1947
Previous Leagues: Sussex County, Athenian
Clubhouse details: Bar, tea bar, pool, table tennis
Present players with Football League experience:
Past players who progressed into the Football League: G. Elphick and S. Ford (Stoke City), G. Geard (Brighton), J. Hammond (Fulham)
Record transfer fee paid: None
Record transfer fee received: £2,000 from Stoke City for Steve Ford
Programme details: 36 pages, 25p
Programme editor: C. Francis
Club Captain (1985-86):
Player of the Year (1985-86):
Local newspapers & Tel. No. Sussex Express, Lewes 476363; Evening Argus, Brighton 606799; Kent and Sussex Courier Tunbridge Wells 26262
Major Honours: Sussex Senior Cup Winners (3), Athenian League Div 1 and Div 2 Winners, Berger Isthmian League Div 2 Runners-up, Gilbert Rice Floodlight Cup Winners

LEYTONSTONE/ILFORD

President:
Chairman: D.J. Andrews
Manager: J. Still
Asst. Manager: G. Dudley
Coach: G. Dudley
Physiotherapist: J. Payne
Secretary: K.H. Mizen
Address & Tel. No. 47 Rutland Drive, Hornchurch, Essex. Hornchurch 55103
Commercial Manager: L. Llewellyn
Address & Tel. No.
Press Officer & Tel. No. Steve Warren. Hornchurch 58294
Address and Tel. No. of ground: Green Pond Road, Walthamstow, E.17. (Ground sharing with Walthamstow Avenue)
Simple ground directions: **Club shop:**
No. of seats: 250 **Covered accommodation:** Yes **Capacity:** 8,500 **Floodlights:** Yes
Year formed: **Nickname:** The Stones **Club sponsor:**
Previous names:
Previous grounds:
Day for midweek home matches: Tuesday
Club colours: Red shirts, blue shorts
Change colours: All blue
Club metal badges: Yes, £1
Record attendance: 8,000 at Granleigh Road, Leytonstone
Past players who progressed into the Football League: Terry Hurlock, Trevor Morgan, (Brentford & Bournemouth)
Record transfer fee paid: £3,500 Steve Robinson from Dartford
Record transfer fee received: Undisclosed, Terry Hurlock to Brentford
Programme details: 12 pages, 20p
Programme editor: Len Llewellyn
Club Captain (1985-86):
Player of the Year (1985-86):
Local newspapers & Tel. No. Waltham Forest Guardian, Ilford Recorder
Major Honours: Isthmian League, Hitachi Cup, London Senior Cup, Essex Senior Cup, Isthmian Div 1

MAIDENHEAD UNITED

President: C.L. West
Chairman: R. Cross
Manager: Tim Smith
Secretary:
Address & Tel. No.
Commercial Manager: Brian Knights
Address & Tel. No. 0494 41849 (H), 0628 24739 (B)
Press Officer & Tel. No. Jon Swan (0628 781048/75911)
Address and Tel. No. of ground: York Road, Maidenhead, Berkshire
Simple ground directions: Ground in centre of town, 800 yards from BR station, 400 yards from coach/bus station
No. of seats: 400 **Covered accommodation:** 1,800 **Capacity:** 4,500 **Floodlights:** Yes
Year formed: **Nickname:** **Club sponsor:**
Previous names:
Previous grounds:
Day for midweek home matches: Tuesday
Club colours: Black and white stripes/black
Change colours: Yellow and blue
Club metal badges: Yes
Record attendance: 7,911
Previous Leagues: Southern, Great Western, Spartan, Corinthian, Athenian, Isthmian
Clubhouse details: Social club open every night
Present players with Football League experience:
Past players who progressed into the Football League: Paul Priddy, Laurie Sanchez (Wimbledon), Roy Davies (Reading), Alan Cordice (Norwich), David Kemp (Crystal Palace), E. Kelsey, J. Palethorpe
Record transfer fee paid: £1,000
Record transfer fee received: £5,000
Programme details: 20 pages, 25p
Programme editor: Jon Swan
Club Captain (1985-86):
Player of the Year (1985-86):
Local newspapers & Tel. No. Maidenhead Advertiser, Reading Evening Post
Major Honours: Spartan League Champions, Corinthian League Champions (2), Corinthian Shield Winners, Berks & Bucks Cup Winners (15), Mithras Cup Winners

OXFORD CITY

President: P.J. Tompkins
Chairman: L.T. Goodchild
Manager: I. Rundle
Asst. Manager: A. Lyne
Secretary: J. Shepperd
Address & Tel. No. Wheatley 2181 (H), Oxford 248391 (B)
Commercial Manager: E.J. Colliers
Address and Tel. No. of ground: White House Ground, White House Road, Oxford OX1 4PB. Oxford 24839
Simple ground directions: One mile south of city centre **Club shop:**
No. of seats: 800 **Covered accommodation:** 1,200 **Capacity:** 9,000 **Floodlights:** Yes
Physiotherapist: A. Glass & G. Bowerman
Press Officer & Tel. No. R. Collett
Day for midweek home matches: Tuesday
Club colours: Blue and white hoops shirts, white shorts & socks
Change colours: All white or all red
Club metal badges:
Record attendance: 9,500 v Leytonstone, Amateur Cup 1950
Clubhouse details: Open daily for beverages and food
Present players with Football League experience:
Past players who progressed into the Football League: C. Holton, K. Savin, F. Willcox, R. Adams, A. Jefferies, A. Blakeman, D. Gordon, V. Mobley, J. Varney, P. James, P. Lee, H. Poole, G. Parker, G. McKeown
Record transfer fee paid: £3,000 S. Adams from Woking
Record transfer fee received: £2,000 P. Dallaway to Witney Town
Programme details: Average 28 pages
Programme editor: R. Collett
Club Captain (1985-86):
Player of the Year (1985-86):
Local newspapers & Tel. No. Oxford Mail & Times, Oxford 244988
Major Honours: F.A. Amateur Cup Winners, Finalists (2)

SOUTHWICK

President:
Chairman: Terry Tribe
Manager: Alan Pook
Asst. Manager:
Coach: Graham Marchant
Physiotherapists: 'Max' Bland, Errol Keating

Secretary: Terry Grasty
Address & Tel. No. Timberleys, West Drive, Elmer Beach, Bognor Regis, West Sussex. 024369 3248 (H), 0243 777829 (B)
Commercial Manager:
Address & Tel. No.

Address and Tel. No. of ground: Old Bam Way, off Manor Hall Road, Southwick, West Sussex. 0273 591744
Simple ground directions: BR (Southern Region) to Fishersgate or Southwick station. Ground 10 minutes walk. By road, from Brighton on A27 Old Shorcham Road into Southwick, south into Hadrian Avenue, at end turn left into Manor Hall Rd, Old Barn Way 2nd on right (signs to Southwick Leisure centre) **Club shop:** No
No. of seats: 200 **Covered accommodation:** 800 **Capacity:** 3,500 **Floodlights:** Yes
Year formed: 1882 **Nickname:** The Wickers **Club sponsors:** Frosts Garage, Harrisons Racing, Poulter & Sons
Previous names: None
Club colours: Red & black striped shirts, black shorts & socks
Previous grounds: Southwick Recreation Ground
Change colours: Yellow & blue hooped shirts, blue shorts & socks
Day for midweek home matches: Tuesday
Club metal badges: No
Record attendance: 3,500 Charity match v Showbiz XI **Year:** 1971
Best performance in: **F.A. Cup:** 1974-5 1st Rd proper v Bournemouth (A) 0-5
F.A. Vase: 1979-80 + 1985-86 3rd Rd
Previous Leagues: Sussex County, Metropoliton, Combined Counties
Clubhouse details: Club open every evening, Sat, Sun lunchtimes. Licensed bar, members bar + VIP lounge. Snacks available on match days. Games machines, pool & darts. Available for private hire
Present players with Football League experience: Glen Geard
Programme details: 24 pages, 20p
Programme editor: Dave Bull
Club Captain (1985-86): Micky Farmer
Player of the Year (1985-86): Lee Cox
Local newspapers & Tel. No. Brighton Evening Argus, 0273 606799. Adur Gazette & Herald, 0273 455104
Major Honours: Sussex County League (6), Sussex Senior Cup (7), R.U.R. Charity Cup (6), Sussex League Challenge Cup (2), Vauxhall-Opel League Division 2 (South) 1985-86

Southwick celebrates a goal, a victory and the championship of Division Two South.

STAINES

President: A. Brown
Chairman: M. O'Shaughnessy
Manager: B. Butler

Secretary: J.D. Horne
Address & Tel. No. 49 Evelyn Close, Whitton, Twickenham, Middlesex TW2 7BL. 01 898 3581 (H & B)

Address and Tel. No. of ground: Wheatsheaf Lane, Staines, Middlesex. Staines 55988
Simple ground directions: From Staines (BR) turn right along Gresham Rd to 'T' junction, left into Laleham Rd (B376), Wheatsheaf Lane one mile on right, ground 100 yards on left. Bus No. 218 passes Wheatsheaf Lane
No. of seats: 400 **Covered accommodation:** 2,000 **Capacity:** 2,500 **Floodlights:** Yes
Year formed: 1892 **Nickname:** Swans **Club sponsor:**
Programme details: 16 pages, 25p
Programme editors: Steve Parsons & Colin Simpson
Club colours: Old gold/blue/blue
Change colours: Light blue & white stripes/white/white
Day for midweek home matches: Tuesday
Club metal badges: Yes
Record attendance: 2,750 v Banco de Ruma (Barassi Cup) 1975
Best performance in: **F.A. Cup:** 1st Rd 1984-85
F.A. Trophy: 2nd Rd 2nd replay 1976-7
Previous Leagues: West London Alliance, West London, West Middlesex, Great Western Suburban, Munitions Works, London Works, Spartan, Middlesex Senior (Parthenon), Hellenic, Athenian
Clubhouse details: Fully furnished clubhouse and function hall 7-11 pm
Present players with Football League experience:
Past players who progressed into the Football League: John Love (Crystal Palace), Peter Shaw (Charlton Athletic), Eric Young (Brighton), Bobby Bennett (Southend), Gordon Hill (Millwall, Man. Utd., Derby Co., England)
Record transfer fee paid: £1,750 to Slough for Richard Teale
Record transfer fee received: £10,000 from Charlton Athletic for Peter Shaw

STEVENAGE BOROUGH

President: A.A. Soul
Chairman: A.W.E. Rayner
Manager: Frank Cornwell
Secretary: Keith Berners
Address & Tel. No. 12 Wisden Road, Stevenage, Herts SG1 5HZ. 0438 724137 (H & B)
Press Officer & Tel. No. Phil Ravitz, 0438 351292 (H), Hitchin 31666 (B)
Address and Tel. No. of ground: Broadhall Way, Stevenage, Herts. 0438 367059
Simple ground directions: From A1 (M) take Stevenage south exit B197 (Broadhall Way). At second roundabout ground on right
Club shop:
No. of seats: 500 **Covered accommodation:** 700 **Capacity:** 6,000 **Floodlights:** Yes
Year formed: 1976 **Nickname:** The Boro **Club sponsor:**
Previous names:
Previous grounds:
Day for midweek home matches: Monday
Club colours: Red & white
Change colours: Blue & white
Club metal badges: No
Record attendance: 3,000 v All Star XI 1980
Previous Leagues: United Counties
Clubhouse details: 200 capacity. Open 7 nights, Sat & Sun lunchtimes during winter. Closed Mondays summer
Programme details: Approx. 25 pages, 20p
Programme editor: Phil Ravitz
Club Captain (1985-86):
Player of the Year (1985-86):
Local newspapers & Tel. No. Stevenage Comet, Hitchin 31666; Stevenage Gazette, Hitchin 59651
Major Honours: UCL Div 1 Champions 1980/1, UCL Div 1 Cup Winners 1980/1, Vauxhall-Opel Div 2 (N) Champions 1985/6

TILBURY

President: W. Goodrum
Chairman: J.B. Wilson
Manager: Martin Binks
Secretary: C.J. Beven
Address & Tel. No. 8 Milton Gardens, Tilbury. 03752 76360
Press Officer & Tel. No. L. Brown. 0375 77427
Address and Tel. No. of ground: St Chads Road, Tilbury, Essex. 03752 3093
Simple ground directions: 15 mins walk Tilbury Town (BR). Buses 370, 371, 377, 378
Club shop:
No. of seats: 250 **Covered accommodation:** 2,500 **Capacity:** 9,750 **Floodlights:** Yes
Year formed: 1900 **Nickname:** The Dockers **Club sponsor:**
Previous names:
Previous grounds:
Day for midweek home matches: Tuesday
Club colours: White/black/white
Change colours: All red
Club metal badges: No
Record attendance: 5,500 v Edrleston F.A. Cup 1949/50
Previous Leagues: Kent, London, Corinthian, Delphian, Athenian
Clubhouse details: Open every evening & weekend lunchtimes. Pool, darts, discos & live bands
Present players with Football League experience:
Past players who progressed into the Football League: J. Evans (Charlton, Liverpool), T. Scannell, T. Oakley (both Southend)
Programme details: 16 pages, 20p
Programme editor: L. Brown
Club Captain (1985-86):
Player of the Year (1985-86):
Local newspapers & Tel. No. Thurrock Gazette
Major Honours: Essex Senior Cup (5), London League (4), London League Cup (2), Mithras Cup, Isthmian League Cup, Essex Professional Cup, Hitachi Cup (1), F.A. Cup 3rd Rd v Stoke City 1977-78

UXBRIDGE

President: T.H. Try
Chairman: T.H. Barnard
Manager: R. Clack
Asst. Manager: P. Marshall
Coach: P. Marshall
Physiotherapist: E. Kempster
Secretary: D.L. Tucker
Address & Tel. No. 0895 832921 (H), 01 626 4588 (B)
Commercial Manager: None
Address & Tel. No.
Press Officer & Tel. No. G. Trimby, 01 848 8453 (H)
Address and Tel. No. of ground: Honeycroft, Horton Road, West Drayton, Middlesex. 0895 443557
Simple ground directions: From West Drayton (BR) station turn right, then 1st right into Horton Road, ground 1 mile down on left
Club shop:
No. of seats: 180 **Covered accommodation:** 480 **Capacity:** 5,000 **Floodlights:** Yes
Year formed: 1871 **Nickname:** Reds **Club sponsor:**
Previous names:
Previous grounds:
Day for midweek home matches: Tuesday
Club colours: Red/white/red
Change colours: Sky blue
Club metal badges: Yes, £1.40
Record attendance: 1,000 v Arsenal, Floodlight opening 1981
Previous Leagues: Corinthian, Athenian
Clubhouse details: Large clubhouse with bar and dance hall. Open every evening except Monday
Present players with Football League experience:
Past players who progressed into the Football League: Gary Churchouse
Programme details: 12 pages, 20p
Programme editor:
Club Captain (1985-86):
Player of the Year (1985-86):
Local newspapers & Tel. No. Middlesex Gazette, 0895 37161
Major Honours: F.A. Amateur Cup Runners-up 1897-8; Middlesex Senior Cup Winners 1893-4, 1895-6, 1950-1; Middlesex Senior Charity Cup Winners 1907-8, 1912-13, 1935-6, 1981-2, Runners-up 1982-3; Athenian League Cup Runners-up 1981-2; Corinthian League Champions 1959-60, Runners-up 1949-50; Servowarm Isthmian League Division 2 South Runners-up 1984-5, A.C. Delco Cup Runners-up 1985-6

WALTON & HERSHAM

President: Sir Stanley Matthews
Chairman: W.M. Bigmore
Manager: W. Millar
Asst. Manager: D. Collyer
Coach: D. Collyer
Physiotherapist: B. Mullett
Press Officer & Tel. No. B. Freeman
Secretary: Graham Pouncey
Address & Tel. No. 8 Heathlands, Queens Road, Weybridge, Surrey. 0932 53946
Commercial Director: A.H. Galustian
Address & Tel. No.
Address and Tel. No. of ground: Stompond Lane Sports Ground, Hersham Road, Walton on Thames, Surrey. 09322 45263
Simple ground directions: Bus 218, 10 minutes walk from BR southern region station, Walton on Thames **Club shop:**
No. of seats: 500 **Covered accommodation:** 2,500 **Capacity:** 6,500 **Floodlights:** Yes
Year formed: 1896 **Nickname:** Swans **Club sponsor:**N.B.S. Ltd
Previous names:
Previous grounds:
Club colours: Red shirts, white sleeves, red shorts, red socks
Change colours: Blue shirts, white sleeves, blue shorts, blue socks
Day for midweek home matches: Tuesday
Club metal badges:
Record attendance: 6,500 v Brighton F.A. Cup 1973-74
Best performance in: **F.A. Cup:** 2nd Rd proper 1972-3, 1973-4
F.A. Trophy: 4th Qual Rd 1983-4
Previous Leagues: Corinthian, Surrey Senior, Athenian
Clubhouse details: Open most nights. Bar, TV, darts, pool and refreshment bar open on match days
Present players with Football League experience:
Past players who progressed into the Football League: A. McCulloch (QPR), R. Teale (QPR), S. Parsons (Wimbledon)
Programme details: 32 pages, 30p
Programme editor:
Club Captain (1985-86): N. Jennings
Player of the Year (1985-86): S. Clifford
Major Honours: F.A. Amateur Cup Winners, Isthmian League Runners-up, Barassi Cup Winners, Surrey Senior Cup Winners (7), Athenian League Champions and Corinthian League Champions (3)

WEMBLEY

President: J.E. Bryan B.E.M.
Chairman: E.G. Stringer
Manager: Alan Dafforn
Asst. Manager:
Coach: Ernie Ford
Physiotherapist: Alan King
Secretary: Roy Calmels
Address & Tel. No. 01 902 4646
Treasurer: Cyril Farmer
Address & Tel. No. 01 902 4821
Press Officer & Tel. No. Pete Burrin. 01 328 0414 (H), 01 928 2345 ext. 675 (B)
Address and Tel. No. of ground: Vale Farm, Watford Road, Sudbury, Middlesex. 01 904 8169
Simple ground directions: Sudbury Town or North Wembley Underground **Club shop:**
No. of seats: 250 **Covered accommodation:** 1,000 **Capacity:** 3,000 **Floodlights:** Yes
Year formed: 1946 **Nickname:** The Lions **Club sponsor:** Sports Programmes
Previous names: None
Previous grounds: None
Day for midweek home matches: Tuesday
Club colours: Red/white/black
Change colours: All white
Club metal badges:
Record attendance: 2,000 v Hendon, M.G. Cup **Year:** 1959-60
Best performance in: **F.A. Cup:** 1980-1 1st Rd
F.A. Trophy: 1978-9 1st Rd
Previous Leagues: Middlesex, Spartan, Delphian, Corinthian, Athenian
Clubhouse details: Open nightly, large bar, usual club facilities
Present players with Football League experience: None
Past players who progressed into the Football League: G. Roberts, K. Coote (Brentford), K. Cassels (Watford), C. Johnson (Fulham), M. O'Donaguoe (Southampton), A. McGonigle (Olympiakos), R. Cadette (Orient)
Record transfer fee paid: None
Record transfer fee received: £10,000 from Brentford for Gary Roberts
Programme details: 32 pages, 20p **Programme editor:** Peter Burrin
Local newspapers & Tel. No. Wembley & Harrow Observer
Major Honours: Middlesex Senior Cup (1983-4), Middlx Charity Cup Winners (1982-3)

VAUXHALL-OPEL LEAGUE
DIVISION 2 NORTH
SEASON 1985-86

	1	2	3	4	5	6	7	8	9	10	11	12	13	14	15	16	17	18	19	20
1 Barton Rovers		0-1	0-3	3-2	1-1	1-1	2-1	1-2	1-2	3-1	1-2	2-1	0-1	1-3	5-1	0-2	2-1	3-0	0-2	0-3
2 Berkhamsted Town	0-0		0-1	1-1	1-0	1-1	2-0	2-1	2-2	2-0	0-1	0-1	2-3	1-2	3-4	1-0	2-0	3-1	0-5	0-0
3 Chalfont St Peter	1-1	3-3		0-1	1-2	1-2	1-1	2-1	5-2	0-0	1-4	2-1	2-0	2-2	1-3	0-2	1-0	1-1	2-0	0-0
4 Chestnut	1-2	1-0	0-0		1-1	1-2	0-1	2-0	1-1	0-1	1-2	4-0	6-1	3-1	3-0	0-3	1-0	2-1	1-0	2-1
5 Clapton	3-2	3-0	2-5	0-6		4-2	1-1	0-0	0-3	2-5	0-3	0-2	2-0	0-2	1-2	0-3	3-2	0-3	4-1	1-0
6 Harefield United	1-1	1-2	0-3	0-1	6-1		0-2	1-1	1-3	3-3	0-3	3-3	3-6	1-1	1-1	0-0	0-1	2-1	4-1	2-2
7 Haringey Borough	1-2	2-1	0-1	3-0	1-1	0-3		1-2	2-0	2-1	1-4	1-0	0-1	0-1	1-1	0-1	2-1	2-2	1-0	1-1
8 Hemel Hempstead	2-2	0-1	1-1	2-2	4-2	2-1	2-0		3-2	0-1	0-4	1-2	2-1	1-1	1-2	1-2	1-1	1-3	4-3	1-0
9 Hertford Town	2-1	4-0	0-1	1-1	0-4	2-0	1-2	2-1		0-0	0-4	1-0	7-1	3-0	3-0	2-1	3-4	2-1	0-0	1-0
10 Heybridge Swifts	2-1	0-1	3-0	0-1	3-0	4-2	2-1	2-1	1-3		4-2	0-0	1-2	2-1	0-0	1-2	2-0	2-1	3-0	1-1
11 Kingsbury Town	0-1	3-2	1-1	3-2	3-1	1-1	1-0	1-1	1-0	2-2		1-0	3-0	2-1	1-1	1-1	2-0	2-3	2-0	4-0
12 Letchworth Garden C.	0-2	3-1	3-0	2-1	2-2	1-0	0-2	3-1	0-0	0-1	0-0		3-5	0-0	2-2	1-0	1-2	3-2	0-4	0-1
13 Rainham Town	3-2	0-3	1-3	0-0	3-1	1-2	0-4	4-1	3-2	3-1	0-5	0-4		1-1	0-0	1-3	2-1	1-0	0-3	1-1
14 Royston Town	1-2	4-2	2-2	0-1	2-0	3-1	3-2	0-0	0-2	2-4	2-4	2-1	2-1		1-1	0-1	3-3	0-0	1-1	2-1
15 Saffron Walden Town	2-1	2-1	1-2	1-1	2-0	5-1	1-2	2-4	4-2	2-3	2-3	0-3	3-1	0-4		0-1	1-1	1-1	2-1	2-2
16 Stevenage Borough	4-1	1-2	3-0	1-2	3-4	3-0	4-1	2-0	1-0	3-1	2-1	1-0	6-1	3-3	2-0		0-0	3-0	0-0	1-0
17 Tring Town	1-1	0-0	3-1	1-1	2-0	3-0	3-1	2-0	0-1	1-1	2-2	2-1	5-0	2-2	1-3	0-0		0-1	3-1	4-1
18 Vauxhall Motors	2-0	1-0	0-1	3-3	3-0	1-3	1-4	6-1	1-1	1-3	1-0	5-1	4-1	1-2	0-3	0-2	2-2		4-4	0-2
19 Ware	2-1	0-0	1-0	1-2	5-5	2-2	3-2	1-2	2-0	0-1	0-3	1-1	3-2	3-1	2-1	0-1	1-1	1-1		0-2
20 Wolverton Town	2-1	1-2	2-3	1-2	5-0	0-3	1-1	1-2	1-0	1-3	1-3	0-1	0-3	2-1	3-3	0-3	1-2	0-0	2-2	

DIVISION TWO NORTH

	Pl	W	D	L	Gf	Ga	Pts
Stevenage Borough	38	26	6	6	71	24	84
Kingsbury Town	38	25	8	5	84	35	83
Heybridge Swifts	38	20	8	10	65	46	68
Cheshunt	38	18	10	10	60	40	64
Hertford Town	38	17	7	14	60	50	58
Chalfont St. Peter	38	15	11	12	53	50	56
Tring Town	38	14	13	11	58	46	55
Royston Town	38	13	13	12	59	57	52
Saffron Walden Town	38	13	12	13	61	65	51
Berkhamsted Town	38	14	8	16	45	52	50
Haringey Borough	38	14	7	17	49	51	49
Letchworth Garden C.	38	13	8	17	46	52	47
Rainham Town	38	14	4	20	54	91	46
Hemel Hempstead	38	12	9	17	50	66	45
Ware	38	11	11	16	56	61	44
Vuaxhall Motors	38	11	10	17	58	62	43
Barton Rovers	38	12	7	19	50	60	43
Harefield Utd.	38	9	12	17	56	72	39
Clapton	38	10	7	21	51	90	37
Wolverton Town	38	8	11	19	42	58	35

Stevenage Borough

Back Row (L-R): P. Gittings, D. Watkins, G. Simpson (now St Albans), D. Gallagher, R. Marshall, T. Ball, G. Cox (now Baldock), A. English (physio), F. Cornwell (manager)   Front Row (L-R): D. Tyler (captain), G. Harding (now Baldock), M. Gittings, D. Pirie, C. Myers, Steve Cornwell (mascot)

AVELEY

President: K. Clay
Chairman: A. Wallace
Manager: Terry. Matthews
Secretary: Ken Sutliff
Address & Tel. No. 9 Westlyn Close, Rainham, Essex. Rainham 55271
Address and Tel. No. of ground: Mill Field, Mill Road, Aveley, Essex.
Simple ground directions: ¼ mile off A13, Rainham Station and 375 bus
No. of seats: 500 **Covered accommodation:** 500 **Capacity:** 10,000
Year formed: 1927 **Nickname:** The Blues **Floodlights:** Yes
Club colours: Royal blue, white **Change colours:** Red, white
Day for midweek home matches: Tuesday **Club metal badges:** Yes
Previous Leagues: London Delphian, Athenian
Clubhouse details: Keep fit, darts, bingo and dancing, open lunchtimes and evenings
Past players who progressed into the Football League: Keith Day (Colchester United)
Programme details: 48 pages, 25p **Programme editor:** Steve
Local newspapers & Tel. No. Thurrock Gazette
Major Honours: London League Premier, Athenian League Div 2

BARTON ROVERS

President: T.W. Bailey
Chairman: F.S. Osborne
Managers: J. Burr & M. Huckle
Secretary: V.E. Evans
Address & Tel. No. 31 Sharpenhoe Road, Barton-le-Clay, Beds. Luton 882866 (H), Dunstable 603600
Address and Tel. No. of ground: Sharpenhoe Road, Barton-le-Clay. Luton 881075
Simple ground directions: M1 junction, take A5120 (Bedford), 2nd right through Harlington & Sharpenhoe, ground on right
No. of seats: 120 **Covered accommodation:** 1,000 **Capacity:** 4,000
Year formed: 1898 **Nickname:** Rovers **Floodlights:** Yes
Club colours: White/blue/white **Change colours:** Yellow/blue/yellow
Day for midweek home matches: Tuesday **Club metal badges:** Yes
Previous Leagues: Luton & District, South Midlands
Clubhouse details: Two bars, open match days and every evening. Light meals available weekends, snacks always
Past players who progressed into the Football League: None
Programme details: 20 pages, 20p **Programme editor:** O. Clark
Local newspapers & Tel. No. Luton News, Herald
Major Honours: F.A. Cup 1981 1st Rd v Torquay lost 2-0; F.A. Vase 1978 Final v Blue Star lost 2-1; Beds Senior Cup Winners 4 times

BERKHAMSTED TOWN

President: D. Mortimer
Chairman: Vacant
Manager: D. Jones
Secretary: S.G. Hastie
Address & Tel. No.
Address and Tel. No. of ground: Broadwater, Lower Kings Road, Berkhamsted, Herts. 04427 2815
Simple ground directions: Adjoins Berkhamsted station (line from Euston), A41 to Berkhamsted town centre traffic lights, turn into Lower Kings Road
No. of seats: 65 **Covered accommodation:** 300 **Capacity:** 2,000
Year formed: 1895 **Nickname:** Lillywhites **Floodlights:**
Club colours: All sky blue **Change colours:** White shirts, black shorts
Day for midweek home matches: Tuesday **Club metal badges:** Yes
Previous Leagues: Athenian 1983-4, London Spartan 1975-83, Spartan 1966-75, Athenian 1963-66, Delphian 1951-63, Spartan 1922-51, Herts Co. & West Herts 1895-1922
Clubhouse details: Open 7 days a week
Past players who progressed into the Football League: Frank Broome (Aston Villa & England), Maurice Coote (Watford & Fulham)
Programme details: 24 pages, 20p **Programme editor:** Bob Sear
Local newspapers & Tel. No. The Herald (Berkhamsted edition), Berkhamsted Gazette, Berkhamsted Mail
Major Honours: Winners of Herts Sen Cup 1952-3, London Spartan League Premier Div 1979-80, Spartan Div 2 1926-7, Herts Charity Shield 4 times

CHESHAM UNITED

President: None
Chairman: A. Warboys
Manager: D. Russell
Secretary: S. McDonnell
Address & Tel. No.
Address and Tel. No. of ground: The Meadow, Amersham Rd, Chesham, Bucks. Chesham 783964 (ground & clubhouse), 782456 (match information service)
Simple ground directions: Off A416, foot of Amersham Hill. 10 mins walk from Chesham station (Metropolitan Line)
No. of seats: 200 **Covered accommodation:** Both sides **Capacity:** 5,000
Year formed: 1917 **Nickname:** United **Floodlights:** Yes
Club colours: Claret& blue/white/blue **Change colours:** White/claret/claret
Day for midweek home matches: Tuesday **Club metal badges:** Yes
Previous Leagues: Spartan, Corinthian, Athenian
Clubhouse details: Open each night and lunchtimes, bar, snacks. Also available for private hire
Past players who progressed into the Football League: Stewart Scullion (Charlton Athletic, Watford, Sheffield United), Bill Shipwright (Watford), Kerry Dixon (Chelsea)
Programme details: 24/28 pages, 30p (plus Meadow Monthly 24 pages, 30p) **Programme editor:**
Local newspapers & Tel. No. Bucks Examiner, Chesham 4591; Bucks Advertiser
Major Honours: Berks & Bucks Senior Cup (9), Spartan League Div 1 (3), Prem Div, F.A. Amateur Cup Finalists

CHESHUNT

President: Roy Bailey
Secretary: F.C. Beer
Chairman: J. Rea
Address & Tel. No. Lea Valley 761138
Manager: David Bidwell
Address and Tel. No. of ground: The Stadium, Theobalds Lane, Cheshunt, Herts. Waltham Cross 26752
Simple ground directions: Ground on right, four miles after Enfield on London-Cambridge Rd (A11) or one mile from M25 orbital motorway
No. of seats: 300 **Covered accommodation:** 400 **Capacity:** 4,000
Year formed: 1946 **Nickname:** None **Floodlights:** Yes
Club colours: Yellow/blue/yellow **Change colours:** Red/black/red
Day for midweek home matches: Tuesday **Club metal badges:**
Previous Leagues: London, Delphian, Athenian, Spartan
Clubhouse details: Two bars open nightly
Past players who progressed into the Football League: Eddie Jones (Tottenham, Millwall)
Programme details: 12 pages, 20p **Programme editor:** Roger Carter
Local newspapers & Tel. No. Cheshunt-Waltham Telegraph, Enfield Advertiser
Major Honours:

CLAPTON

President: E.M. Gliksten
Secretary: Martin McShea
Chairman: M.E. Fogg
Address & Tel. No. 208 Portway, London E15 3QY
Manager: Michael Connelly
Address and Tel. No. of ground: The Old Spotted God Ground, Upton Lane, Forest Gate, London E7 9NP. 01 472 1655
Simple ground directions: Nearest BR station Forest Gate. Tube Plaistow. Bus 278 passes ground
No. of seats: 100 **Covered accommodation:** Two stands **Capacity:** 5,500
Year formed: 1878 **Nickname:** The Tons **Floodlights:** Yes
Club colours: Red & white stripes/black/red **Change colours:** Yellow/yellow/yellow
Day for midweek home matches: Tuesday **Club metal badges:** Yes
Previous Leagues: London, Southern (founder members)
Clubhouse details: Open all hours, basic, but friendly
Past players who progressed into the Football League: Harry Earle (Notts C), Stanley Earle (West Ham), Viv Gibbons (West Ham), Bill Bryant (Millwall), George Male (Arsenal)
Programme details: 18 pages, 15p **Programme editor:** Andy Barr. 01 449 4360
Local newspapers & Tel. No. Newham Recorder. 01 478 4444
Major Honours: F.A. Amateur Cup (5), Isthmian League (2), London Senior Cup, Essex Senior Cup, Middlesex Senior Cup, London Chaity Cup, Isthmian League Div 2, Essex Thameside Trophy. First English team to play on continent in 1890

COLLIER ROW

President:
Secretary: P. Sammons
Chairman: R. Walker
Manager: A. Marson
Address & Tel No of ground: Collier Row Road, Romford (078-22766)
Capacity: 1,000 **Covered accommodation:** None **Seating:** None **Floodlights:** Yes
Simple ground directions: A12 from London, left at Moby Dick (Public House) Traffic lights to next roundabout, right hand exit. Ground 200 yards on right.
Clubhouse details: Two bars, large hall, members bar, open 7 days and lunchtimes at weekends.
Programme details: **Editor:** **Club metal badges:**
Local Newspaper(s):
Club colours: Red/Black/Black **Change colours:** Silver Grey/White/White
Record Attendance: **Midweek match day:**
Previous Leagues: Essex Olympian
Senior Honours:/Best Performance:
Past players (who progressed to Football League):

HARINGEY BOROUGH

President: R. White
Secretary: M. O'Halloran
Chairman: M. Jaynoy
Address & Tel. No.
Manager: R. Richards
Address and Tel. No. of ground: Coles Playing Fields, White Hart Lane, Wood Green, London N17. 01 888 4586
Simple ground directions: Wood Green (Piccadilly Line), BR (ER) to White Hart Lane

No. of seats: 220 **Covered accommodation:** Yes **Capacity:** 2,500
Year formed: 1907 **Nickname:** Borough **Floodlights:** Yes
Club colours: Amber and black **Change colours:** Green and white
Day for midweek home matches: **Club metal badges:**
Previous Leagues: Isthmian, Delphian
Clubhouse details: Bar and social club
Past players who progressed into the Football League:

Programme details: Yes **Programme editor:**
Local newspapers & Tel. No.
Major Honours:

HARLOW

President: None
Chairman: P. Williams
Manager: Dave Edwards
Secretary: Graeme Auger
Address & Tel. No.
Address and Tel. No. of ground: Sportcentre, Hammarskjold Road, Harlow
Simple ground directions: BR to Harlow Town station, ground 10 mins walk
No. of seats: 450 **Covered accommodation:** 450 **Capacity:** 15,000
Year formed: 1879 **Nickname:** The Owls **Floodlights:** Yes
Club colours: All red **Change colours:** All yellow
Day for midweek home matches: Tuesday **Club metal badges:** No
Previous Leagues: Spartan, London, Delphian, Athenian
Clubhouse details: Darts, pool, usual opening hours
Past players who progressed into the Football League: Jeff Wood (Charlton), Neil Prosser (Bournemouth)
Programme details: 14 pages, 20p **Programme editor:** Phil Tuson
Local newspapers & Tel. No. Harlow Gazette, Harlow Star
Major Honours: Spartan League Cup, London League Cup, Athenian League Div 1 Champions, Isthmian League Div 1 Champions, F.A. Cup 4th Rd 1979-80

HEMEL HEMPSTEAD

President: R. Doyle
Chairman: S. Miller
Manager: A. Horsfall
Secretary: W.J. McGrae
Address & Tel. No.
Address and Tel. No. of ground: Vauxhall Road, Hemel Hempstead, Herts.
Simple ground directions: M1 motorway junction 8. Euston-Hemel Hempstead rail

No. of seats: 100 **Covered accommodation:** 500 **Capacity:** 3,000
Year formed: 1885 **Nickname:** Hemel **Floodlights:** Yes
Club colours: All red **Change colours:** All sky blue
Day for midweek home matches: Tuesday **Club metal badges:** No
Previous Leagues: Athenian, Delphian, Spartan
Clubhouse details: 650. Large bar, saloon bar
Past players who progressed into the Football League: C. Bateman, E. Bateman (Watford)

Programme details: 16 pages, 25p **Programme editor:** W.J. McGrae
Local newspapers & Tel. No. Hemel Hempstead Gazette, Hemel Herald, Hemel Mail
Major Honours: Herts Senior Cup Winners

HERTFORD TOWN

President: R. Dye
Chairman: A. Coker
Manager: T.G. Woodrow
Secretary: R.J. Brooke
Address & Tel. No.
Address and Tel. No. of ground: Hertingfordbury Park, West Street, Hertford, Herts. 0992 53716
Simple ground directions: By train Moorgate-Hertford North; Liverpool Street-Hertford East, both 15 mins walk. Bus Green Line-town centre, 10 minutes walk. By road, off bypass heading east, turn at Trimogo garage
No. of seats: 400 **Covered accommodation:** 3,000 **Capacity:** 6,500
Year formed: 1908 **Nickname:** The Blues **Floodlights:** Yes
Club colours: Blue **Change colours:** Red
Day for midweek home matches: Tuesday **Club metal badges:**
Previous Leagues: Spartan, Delphian, Athenian, Eastern Counties
Clubhouse details: Open every evening, Sat & Sun lunchtime
Past players who progressed into the Football League: G. Mazzon (Aldershot)

Programme details: With entrance fee **Programme editor:** L. Glabych
Local newspapers & Tel. No. Mercury
Major Honours: Herts Charity Cup, Herts Senior Cup, Eastern Counties Cup, East Anglia Cup, Milthras Cup

HEYBRIDGE SWIFTS

Patron: C. Gill
President: J. Knight
Chairman: M. Gibson
Manager: Ken Varney
Secretary: D. Fenn
Address & Tel. No.
Address and Tel. No. of ground: Scraley Road, Heybridge, Maldon, Essex. Maldon (0621) 52978
Simple ground directions: Leave Maldon on main road to Colchester, through village of Heybridge, then turn right following sign to Tolleshunt D'Arcy (Scraley Rd). Ground on right
No. of seats: 200 **Covered accommodation:** 200 **Capacity:** 5,000
Year formed: 1882 **Nickname:** Swifts/Blacks and Whites **Floodlights:** Yes
Club colours: Black and white stripes/black/white **Change colours:** Red/white/white
Day for midweek home matches: Tuesday **Club metal badges:**
Previous Leagues: Essex and Suffolk Border, Essex Senior
Clubhouse details: Two bars open every night, games room, boardroom, kitchen (matchdays only)
Past players who progressed into the Football League:
Programme details: 32 pages, 20p **Programme editor:** Chris Daines
Local newspapers & Tel. No.
Major Honours: Essex Senior League Champions (3), Essex Senior Trophy Winners and Finalists, Essex Senior League Cup Winners

HORNCHURCH

President: E.A. Prior
Chairman: J.A. Bradshaw
Manager: K. Goodwin
Secretary: E.W. Harris
Address & Tel. No. Upminstger 27891 (H)
Address and Tel. No. of ground: The Stadium, Bridge Avenue, Upminster, Essex. Upminster 20080
Simple ground directions: Fenchurch St to Upminster (BR), 10 mins Upminster station. LT to Upminster Bridge (District Line). Turn right outside station, ground 5 minutes away, 2nd turning right-Bridge Avenue
No. of seats: 300 **Covered accommodation:** Yes **Capacity:** 4,100
Year formed: 1923 **Nickname:** Urchins **Floodlights:** Yes
Club colours: White, red trim, white shorts and socks **Change colours:** Green and yellow stripes, green shorts
Day for midweek home matches: Tuesday **Club metal badges:** Yes
Previous Leagues: Romford, Corinthian, Athenian
Clubhouse details: Open 7.30 p.m. daily
Past players who progressed into the Football League: D. Armstrong (Millwall), R. Lee (Charlton A.)

Programme details: 10 pages, 15p **Programme editor:** R. Monger
Local newspapers & Tel. No. Romford Recorder, 66044
Major Honours: Romford League (2), Essex Junior Cup, Essex Thameside Trophy, Isthmian Youth Cup

LETCHWORTH GARDEN CITY

President: None
Chairman: Ken Fenemore
Manager:
Secretary: Jane Bygrave
Address & Tel. No. 0462 670471
Address and Tel. No. of ground: Baldock Road, Letchworth, Herts SG6 2GN. Letchworth 4691
Simple ground directions: Letchworth exit off A1, to A505, turn right, ground on right 150 yards in Baldock direction
No. of seats: 250 **Covered accommodation:** 550 **Capacity:** 3,000
Year formed: 1906 **Nickname:** Bluebirds **Floodlights:** Yes
Club colours: Blue/white/white/white **Change colours:** All red
Day for midweek home matches: Tuesday **Club metal badges:** No
Previous Leagues: Athenian
Clubhouse details: Capacity 200. Two bars, stage and dressing rooms, upstairs (40 people), downstairs hall (160 people approx.)
Past players who progressed into the Football League: Imré Varadi, Keith Larner
Programme details: 20 pages, 15p **Programme editors:** Ken Fenemore/Jane Bygrave
Local newspapers & Tel. No. Comet/Citizen Gazette
Major Honours: Herts Senior Cup (3), Athenian Premier Champions 1974-75

RAINHAM TOWN

President: H.G. Stoneham
Chairman: G.W. Burrell
Manager: Mike Acland
Secretary: T.M. King
Address & Tel. No.
Address and Tel. No. of ground: Deri Park, Wennington Rd., Rainham, Essex. Rainham 24857/58830
Simple ground directions: Along A13 turn into B1335 past Rainham station, 400 yards on right

No. of seats: 600 **Covered accommodation:** 1,500 **Capacity:** 4,000
Year formed: 1945 **Nickname:** The Reds **Floodlights:** Yes
Club colours: All red **Change colours:** White & black
Day for midweek home matches: Tuesday **Club metal badges:** Yes
Previous Leagues: South Essex, London, Delphian, Metropolitan, Athenian
Clubhouse details: Open 7 days, snacks available
Past players who progressed into the Football League: None

Programme details: 16 pages, 20p **Programme editors:** T. King/S. Acland
Local newspapers & Tel. No. Romford Recorder, Romford 66044
Major Honours: None

ROYSTON TOWN

President: H. Sermonds
Chairman: Fred Bradley
Manager: John Bailey
Secretary: T. Glasscock
Address & Tel. No. 9 Honey Way, Royston, Herts. Royston (0763) 44580 (H), 71611 ext 5093 (B)
Address and Tel. No. of ground: Garden Walk, Royston, Herts. 0763 41204
Simple ground directions: From Baldock take A595, to Town Hall roundabout, then A10 to Cambridge, first turn on right is Garden Walk, ground 100 metres on left
No. of seats: 40 **Covered accommodation:** 300 **Capacity:** 4,000
Year formed: 1875 **Nickname:** The Crows **Floodlights:** Yes
Club colours: White/black **Change colours:** Red/white
Day for midweek home matches: Monday **Club metal badges:** Yes
Previous Leagues: Herts County, South Midlands
Clubhouse details: Open every evening, large clubroom for darts and pool
Past players who progressed into the Football League: John Smith (Tottenham Hotspur)
Programme details: 16 pages, 20p **Programme editor:** Andy Clarke
Local newspapers & Tel. No. Royston Chronicle, Cambridge Evening News
Major Honours: Herts County Premier, Div 1 (2), S. Mid Div 1

SAFFRON WALDON TOWN

President: Mick Cashman
Chairman: Harold Clayden
Manager: John Ryan
Secretary: David Simper
Address & Tel. No. The Copses, Wixoe, Halstead, Essex CO9 4AS
Address and Tel. No. of ground: Catons Lane, S.W. 0799 22789

Simple ground directions: 250 yards north of common on B1052. Take old A11 from M11

No. of seats: 300
Covered accommodation: 500
Capacity: 1,200
Year formed:
Nickname: The Bloods
Floodlights: Yes
Club colours: Red and black
Change colours: Yellow
Day for midweek home matches: Tuesday
Club metal badges: Yes
Previous Leagues: Essex Senior, Eastern Counties, Herts County, Spartan
Clubhouse details: Hall and lounge, both with bars. Open most evenings
Past players who progressed into the Football League: None

Programme details: 8 pages, 20p
Programme editor: M. Franklin
Local newspapers & Tel. No. Saffron Walden Weekly News, Saffron Walden Reporter, Herts & Essex Observer
Major Honours: Essex Senior League, Eastern Counties League, Spartan League, Essex Senior Trophy (3) Div 2

TRING TOWN

President:
Chairman:
Manager: Roy Butler
Secretary: D.G. Bradding
Address & Tel. No.
Address and Tel. No. of ground: Pendley Sports Centre, Cow Lane, Tring. Tring 3075
Simple ground directions: One mile from centre of Tring on A41, turn right just after start of A41 (M) into Cow Lane
No. of seats: 200
Covered accommodation: 200
Capacity: 4,000
Year formed: 1904
Nickname:
Floodlights: Yes
Club colours: White/red/red
Change colours: All blue
Day for midweek home matches: Wednesday
Club metal badges: Yes
Previous Leagues: Gt Western Comb., Spartan, Athenian
Clubhouse details: Large all-in lounge with boardroom, bar, tea bar. Open every evening except Monday
Past players who progressed into the Football League: None
Programme details: 25p
Programme editor: Ray Pearson
Local newspapers & Tel. No. Bucks Herald, Tring Gazette, Aylesbury Plus, Hemel Mail, Chiltern Radio
Major Honours: Spartan League Champions 1967-8, Runners-up 1953-4, 1968-9

VAUXHALL MOTORS

President: N. Reilly
Chairman: G. Ions
Manager: Paul Peterson
Secretary: Vince Weatherhead
Address & Tel. No. 5 Plumpton Close, Luton, Beds LU2 8JU. 0582 414945 (H), 0582 21122 ext. 6591 (B)
Address and Tel. No. of ground: Brache Estate, Park Street, Luton. Luton 23061
Simple ground directions: Through Luton entering Park Street or M1 ext 10 Cuttenhoe Rd

No. of seats: Yes
Covered accommodation: Yes
Capacity: 2,000
Year formed:
Nickname:
Floodlights: Yes
Club colours: Yellow shirts, blue shorts, yellow socks
Change colours: All blue
Day for midweek home matches: Monday
Club metal badges: No
Previous Leagues: Spartan, United Counties, South Midlands
Clubhouse details: Bar and clubhouse
Past players who progressed into the Football League:

Programme details: Yes, with admission
Programme editor: Tony Talbot
Local newspapers & Tel. No. Luton News
Major Honours: F.A. Cup 1st Rd lost 1-0 at Luton Town ground, attend. 22,000

WARE

President:
Chairman: C.T. Hudson
Manager: John Godleman
Secretary: C.J. Dance
Address & Tel. No. 18 Salwey Crescent, Broxbourne, Herts EN10 7NJ. Hoddesdon 461177 (H)
Address and Tel. No. of ground: Buryfield, Park Road, Ware, Herts. Ware 3247

Simple ground directions: A10 off at junction with A602 & B1001, signposted behind Rank Radio factory

No. of seats: 250
Covered accommodation: 500
Capacity: 4,500
Year formed: 1892
Nickname: The Blues
Floodlights: Yes
Club colours: Blue/white stripe, blue, red
Change colours: Yellow/black
Day for midweek home matches: Tuesday
Club metal badges: No
Previous Leagues: Herts County, Spartan, Delphian, Athenian
Clubhouse details: Fully licensed, open most nights
Past players who progressed into the Football League: Derek Saunders (Chelsea), Ken Humphrey (QPR)

Programme details: 12 pages, 15p
Programme editor: C.J. Dance
Local newspapers & Tel. No. Hertfordshire Mercury, Hertfod 56401
Major Honours: Herts Senior Cup (5), Herts Charity Shield (5), Spartan League, Spartan League Div 1

WIVENHOE TOWN

President:
Chairman: Dave Whymark
Manager: Mick Loughton
Secretary: Roger Cordey
Address & Tel. No. 21 Keable Road, Marks Tey, Colchester, Essex. 0206 210505
Address and Tel. No. of ground: Broad Lane, Elmstead Road, Wivenhoe, Essex. 0206 225380

Simple ground directions: Coming out of Colchester towards Clacton, first turning right towards Wivenhoe, ground is clearly visible on left turning left towards Clacton (B1027)
No. of seats: 250 **Covered accommodation:** 250 **Capacity:**
Year formed: 1927 **Nickname:** Town **Floodlights:** Yes
Club colours: White and blue stripes **Change colours:** Green
Day for midweek home matches: Wednesday **Club metal badges:**
Previous Leagues: Essex & Suffolk Border, Colchester & East Essex, Essex Senior
Clubhouse details: Open 7 evenings
Past players who progressed into the Football League:

Programme details: 16 pages, 15p **Programme editor:** N. Andrews, 0255 420414
Local newspapers & Tel. No.
Major Honours: Worthington Evans Cup, Coggleshall Brotherhood Cup, Essex & Suffolk Border League, Harry Fisher Memorial Cup, F.A. Vase 5th Rd 1982-3

WOLVERTON TOWN

President: M. Cole
Chairman: S. Ridley
Manager: Roger Ashby
Secretary: Bob Swann
Address & Tel. No. 36 Bedford Street, Wolverton MK12 5HR. 0908 313374
Address and Tel. No. of ground: The Park, Old Wolverton. 0908 312264
Simple ground directions: M1 junction 14, A5 Bedford junction, adjacent to Wolverton Station

No. of seats: 500 **Covered accommodation:** 600 **Capacity:** 4,000
Year formed: 1887 **Nickname:** The Wolves **Floodlights:** Yes
Club colours: Old gold and black **Change colours:** White and black
Day for midweek home matches: Tuesday **Club metal badges:**
Previous Leagues: Spartan League, United Counties, London Spartan, Athenian
Clubhouse details: Club room with bar, separate function room also with bar
Past players who progressed into the Football League:

Programme details: With admission **Programme editor:** Peter Mumford
Local newspapers & Tel. No. Milton Keynes Mirror, Gazette, Citizen and Standard, Chronicle & Echo
Major Honours:

Harlow Town (above) Royston Town (below)

Clapton (above) Letchworth Garden City (below)

Hungerford Town (above) Southall after First Leg Semi-Finals FA Vase v. Wisbech (below)

VAUXHALL-OPEL LEAGUE
DIVISION 2 SOUTH
SEASON 1985/86

	1	2	3	4	5	6	7	8	9	10	11	12	13	14	15	16	17	18	19	20
1 Banstead Athletic...		0-5	2-1	0-1	4-0	1-0	3-2	2-0	2-1	3-3	2-0	0-2	1-2	1-2	2-1	1-1	2-2	1-3	0-3	4-2
2 Bracknell Town	2-1		4-1	3-0	2-0	4-0	1-0	2-0	2-0	6-0	3-1	1-1	2-0	1-1	3-0	1-0	0-1	1-2	6-0	2-0
3 Camberley Town ...	2-3	0-2		2-3	1-1	3-0	1-2	0-2	1-1	0-0	2-4	2-0	0-1	0-2	2-3	1-2	2-2	1-3	0-2	2-3
4 Dorking	2-1	1-1	3-2		2-0	3-0	1-1	3-1	4-1	0-2	4-1	2-0	1-0	2-1	0-0	1-1	1-1	0-3	0-1	1-2
5 Eastbourne Utd	0-2	0-1	1-4	1-3		1-2	1-6	1-0	1-1	4-1	7-3	2-2	0-0	3-2	3-1	0-0	1-2	1-3	3-0	1-5
6 Egham Town	3-1	0-2	0-6	1-1	3-1		1-2	1-2	1-2	3-4	1-1	2-0	1-6	3-2	0-2	3-3	1-3	0-0	0-4	2-2
7 Feltham	4-2	2-1	1-0	0-1	7-0	1-0		2-3	0-0	1-5	2-1	4-2	0-2	0-0	2-2	5-2	1-1	0-1	0-4	1-1
8 Flackwell Heath	1-1	2-1	0-1	2-8	0-0	1-2	2-5		0-2	3-1	5-1	3-0	0-2	2-3	0-3	2-0	2-0	2-2	0-0	0-4
9 Horsham	0-1	0-4	1-3	1-1	0-3	2-1	1-2	0-3		1-2	3-1	1-3	1-3	1-3	1-3	1-1	2-1	1-1	0-0	1-5
10 Hungerford Town ..	2-2	3-4	1-3	2-4	3-0	3-2	0-2	0-0	3-1		2-1	1-3	1-4	1-4	0-1	2-1	1-2	0-1	2-0	1-1
11 Marlow	1-4	1-3	1-1	1-1	0-3	1-2	2-1	4-2	1-1	1-0		0-3	1-3	1-4	0-1	3-1	2-4	1-2	1-2	1-8
12 Metropolitan Police.	2-1	0-0	2-1	4-3	4-0	3-0	5-2	3-0	0-2	1-0	3-0		3-0	2-3	4-0	4-0	4-1	1-1	1-1	0-2
13 Molesey	0-1	0-1	2-0	2-2	2-1	1-1	2-1	3-1	1-1	2-1	0-2	1-0		2-1	1-0	2-1	2-2	0-0	2-2	3-2
14 Newbury Town	2-2	1-1	2-0	6-1	2-2	3-1	1-2	1-0	1-0	0-3	5-0	5-1	0-1		4-3	2-1	3-2	4-2	0-0	3-3
15 Petersfield Utd	5-1	1-1	1-1	0-2	3-1	1-0	1-2	2-2	2-0	2-2	4-4	2-3	2-3	0-5		2-1	3-3	2-4	0-2	1-2
16 Ruislip Manor	0-0	2-2	1-3	3-3	2-2	0-0	1-1	0-3	3-0	3-1	4-2	1-2	0-1	0-2	1-5		0-5	0-6	1-1	3-0
17 Southall	0-1	0-5	1-1	2-3	3-1	2-1	2-0	1-0	4-0	2-1	5-1	0-3	2-1	1-2	3-0	6-3		2-1	3-0	1-2
18 Southwick	2-1	0-0	3-1	2-0	2-1	5-0	2-1	6-0	2-0	2-0	3-0	2-0	2-2	2-3	1-0	8-1	2-1		2-2	3-2
19 Whyteleafe	5-2	2-0	1-2	2-1	1-3	3-2	1-0	3-0	1-1	3-2	3-1	1-1	1-0	1-0	2-1	2-0	2-1	1-0		2-2
20 Woking	2-2	0-0	1-0	4-1	2-1	1-1	4-0	2-0	4-1	5-1	4-0	1-0	1-0	5-1	3-3	4-0	1-2	1-0	1-0	

DIVISION TWO SOUTH

	Pl	W	D	L	Gf	Ga	Pts
Southwick	38	25	8	5	86	34	83
Bracknell Town	38	24	9	5	80	23	81
Woking	38	23	9	6	94	45	78
Newbury Town	38	22	7	9	86	53	73
Whyteleafe	38	21	10	7	61	41	73
Molesey..............	38	21	8	9	59	39	71
Metropolitan Police ...	38	20	6	12	72	48	66
Southall	38	19	7	12	77	59	64
Dorking	38	18	10	10	70	57	64
Feltham	38	16	7	15	65	60	55
Banstead Athletic	38	15	8	15	60	66	53
Petersfield Utd.	38	12	9	17	61	71	45
Hungerford Town	38	11	6	21	57	78	39
Flackwell Heath	38	11	6	21	46	72	39
Eastbourne Utd.	38	9	8	21	51	81	35
Camberley Town	38	9	7	22	53	64	34
Egham Town	38	7	8	23	41	83	29
Horsham.............	38	6	10	22	33	74	28
Ruislip Manor	38	5	12	21	44	87	27
Marlow	38	6	5	27	47	108	23

The victorious Southwick F.C. with the Division 2 (South) trophy. Back Row (L-R); Alan Pook (Manager), Richard Cheal, Graham Marchant (Asst. Manager), Lee Cox, Kevin Crooks, Graham Farmer, Keith Cheal, Kevin Hotston, Alan Ingledew, Geoff Pook, 'Max' Bland and Errol Keating (Physios). Front Row (L-R); Terry Parris, Brian Jones, Micky Farmer (Captain) and Paul Thomsett. Photo: M. Southern.

Feltham's Mick Strazadala gets the tight marking treatment from two Met Police defenders much the interest of the Feltham ball boy!

Hungerford Town's Shane Chandler, who sadly broke a leg later in the season, celebrates a goal against Eastbourne United. Photo: Newbury Weekly News

BANSTEAD ATHLETIC

President:
Secretary: G.A. Taylor
Chairman: R.C. Everard J.P.
Address & Tel. No.
Manager: Colin Turner
Address and Tel. No. of ground: Merland Rise, Tadworth, Surrey. 07373 50982
Simple ground directions: Follow signs to Tattenham Corner (Epsom racecourse) then to Banstead swimming baths. Ground is next to pool. 15 mins from Tattenham Corner (BR)
No. of seats: 250 **Covered accommodation:** 250 **Capacity:** 3,000
Year formed: 1944 **Nickname:** The A's **Floodlights:** Yes
Club colours: Amber and black **Change colours:** Red and white
Day for midweek home matches: Tuesday **Club metal badges:** Yes
Previous Leagues: Surrey Senior, London Spartan, Athenian
Clubhouse details: 2 bars, dance hall, boardroom, kitchen
Past players who progressed into the Football League: Wally Chesney (Crystal Palace)
Programme details: 24-28 pages, 20p **Programme editor:** G.A. Taylor, 01 641 2957
Local newspapers & Tel. No. Banstead Advertiser
Major Honours: Surrey Senior League (6), League Cup (2), League Charity Cup (2), Surrey County Senior Shield (1), Athenian League Cup (2), Gilbert Rice Cup (1)

Back Row (L to R): R. Hayward (physio), R. A. Bartlett (com.), G. Foss (vice chairman), K. McGill, K. Dupree, J. Moynihan, A. Turner, G. Price, J. Hollis (team manager), R. Calver (gen. manager), R. Wakeman (chairman). Front Row (L to R): T. Calver, D. Hutton, D. Steele, P. Caulfield, S. Atkins, T. Copp, S. Kerbey.

CAMBERLEY TOWN

President: Ian Over
Secretary: Roy Calver
Chairman: Rick Wakeman
Address & Tel. No. 4 Lincoln Close, Camberley, Surrey GU15 1EN. Camberley 21287
Manager: John Hollis
Address and Tel. No. of ground: Krooner Park, Krooner Road, off Frimley Road, Camberley, Surrey. Camberley 65392
Simple ground directions: Halfway between A30 and Frimley on A321 or M3 (exit 4) bear left and follow A321 to shops, Krooner Road on left past mini roundabout
No. of seats: 250 **Covered accommodation:** 250 **Capacity:** 3,500
Year formed: 1896 **Nickname:** Town **Floodlights:** Yes
Club colours: Red/white **Change colours:** Sky blue
Day for midweek home matches: Tuesday **Club metal badges:** 1987
Previous Leagues: Surrey Senior, Spartan, Athenian, Isthmian
Clubhouse details: Large bar open most evenings
Past players who progressed into the Football League:
Programme details: 14 pages, 20p **Programme editor:** Roy Calver
Local newspapers & Tel. No. Camberley News
Major Honours: Surrey Senior Cup Winners 1979, F.A. Vase 6th Rd 1985-6

CHALFONT ST PETER

President:
Secretary: C.E.R. Franks
Chairman: D.N. Pembroke
Address & Tel. No. Gerrards Cross 884514
Manager: L. Craker, **Asst. Manager:** G. Bree
Address and Tel. No. of ground: The Playing Fields, Amersham Road, Chalfont St Peter, Bucks. Gerrads Cross 885797
Simple ground directions: Take A413 from Uxbridge (London) to Chalfont. Turn left at second major roundabout
No. of seats: 220 **Covered accommodation:** 200 **Capacity:** 4,000
Year formed: 1926 **Nickname:** The Saints **Floodlights:** Yes
Club colours: White/green/white **Change colours:** All yellow
Day for midweek home matches: Tuesday **Club metal badges:**
Previous Leagues: Great Western Combination, Spartan, Athenian
Clubhouse details: Open every evening, Saturday afternoons and Sunday lunchtime
Past players who progressed into the Football League:
Programme details: Yes **Programme editor:**
Local newspapers & Tel. No. Bucks Advertiser, Gerrards Cross 888333; Bucks Examiner, Bucks Free Press & Midweek
Major Honours:

CHERTSEY TOWN

President:
Chairman: Tony Gibbon
Manager: Derek Belsey
Secretary: Chris Gay
Address & Tel. No. 23 Richmond Close, Frimley, Camberley, Surrey. Camberley 20745
Address and Tel. No. of ground: Alwyns Lane, Chertsey, Surrey. Chrtsey 61774
Simple ground directions: BR (SR) to Chertsey, 10 minute walk, or buses 459 from Feltham, 436 or 462 from Staines

No. of seats: 200 **Covered accommodation:** 500 **Capacity:** 3,000
Year formed: 1898 **Nickname:** Curfews **Floodlights:** Yes
Club colours: Blue and white **Change colours:** Red and black
Day for midweek home matches: **Club metal badges:**
Previous Leagues: Surrey Junior, Surrey Senior, Metropolitan, Greater London, Spazrtan, London, Spartan, Athenian
Clubhouse details: Open match days and mosts evenings
Past players who progressed into the Football League:

Programme details: Yes **Programme editor:**
Local newspapers & Tel. No. Chertsey & Addlestone Herald (Surrey Herald Series)
Major Honours:

DORKING

President: Ingram Whittingham
Chairman: Tom Howes
Manager: Martin Collins
Secretary: Roger Young
Address & Tel. No.
Address and Tel. No. of ground: Meadowbank Ground, Mill Lane, Dorking, Surrey. 0306 884112
Simple ground directions: Mill Lane is a turning opposite the White Horse in Dorking High Street. Fork right in Mill Lane, past The Malthouse straight into ground
No. of seats: 100 **Covered accommodation:** 200 **Capacity:** 6,500
Year formed: 1977 **Nickname:** The Chicks **Floodlights:** Yes
Club colours: Green/white/red **Change colours:** White/black/white
Day for midweek home matches: Tuesday **Club metal badges:** No
Previous Leagues: Surrey Senior, Athenian
Clubhouse details: Small friendly clubhouse (to be extended). Open every evening and Sunday morning
Past players who progressed into the Football League: None, but Steven Scrivens played for Fulham first team 5-6 years ago. Still at Dorking
Programme details: 12 pages, 20p **Programme editor:** Paul McGuinness
Local newspapers & Tel. No. Dorking Advertiser, Surrey Advertiser
Major Honours: Joint Winners Michaels Plaice Cup 1985, 3rd Rd A.L. Delco Cup 1985-6, beat Billericay Town (Premier Div) in 2nd Rd

EASTBOURNE UNITED

President:
Chairman: K.R. Tocher
Manager: B. Donnelly
Secretary: J. Gregory
Address & Tel. No.
Address and Tel. No. of ground: The Oval, Channel View Road, Eastbourne BN23 7JP. 0323 26989
Simple ground directions: A22 to seafront, left to Princes Park, left into Channel View Road, first turn on right into ground
No. of seats: 250 **Covered accommodation:** 1,000 **Capacity:** 7,000
Year formed: 1894 **Nickname:** The U's **Floodlights:** Yes
Club colours: White shirts, black shorts/socks **Change colours:** Red shirts, white shorts/socks
Day for midweek home matches: Tuesday **Club metal badges:**
Previous Leagues: Athenian, Metropolitan, Sussex County
Clubhouse details: Large clubhouse, Scottish & Newcastle ales
Past players who progressed into the Football League: B. Salvage, T. Funnell, M. French
Programme details: 20p **Programme editor:** T. Horsman
Local newspapers & Tel. No. Eastbourne Gazette & Herald, Evening Argos
Major Honours: Sussex Senor Cup Winners 1960-1, 1962-3, 1963-4, 1964-5, 1966-7, 1968-9

EGHAM TOWN

President: J. Ward
Chairman: R. Selby
Manager: D. Brown
Secretary: L.D. Brown
Address & Tel. No. 0784 38755
Address and Tel. No. of ground: Tempest Road, Egham, Surrey. Egham 35226
Simple ground directions: Leave M25 at Staines exit, Victoria roundabout left at Police Station, over railway crossing, left at next road junction, past Prince Alfred pub, 1st road left
No. of seats: 250 **Covered accommodation:** 400 **Capacity:** 3,000
Year formed: 1963 **Nickname:** Town **Floodlights:** Yes
Club colours: Blue and gold **Change colours:** All yellow
Day for midweek home matches: Tuesday **Club metal badges:** No
Previous Leagues: Parthenon
Clubhouse details: Main hall and bar-lounge bar, games room, boardroom
Past players who progressed into the Football League: John Dempsey, Graham Wilkins (coach)
Programme details: 16 pages, 25p **Programme editor:** M. Ferguson
Local newspapers & Tel. No. Staines & Egham News
Major Honours: F.A. Cup 3rd Qual Rd., F.A. Case 4th Rd 1984

FELTHAM

President: E.J. Pawling, M.B.E., J.P.
Chairman: D.G.P. Neal
Manager: Brian Laing
Secretary: S. Payne
Address & Tel. No.
Address and Tel. No. of ground: Feltham Arena, Shakespeare Avenue, Feltham, Middlx.
Simple ground directions: From Feltham (SR) five minutes walk through Glebelands Park. By car M3/M4/A312 to Hanworth Road West, turn into Burns Avenue
No. of seats: 1,600 **Covered accommodation:** 2,500 **Capacity:** 12,000
Year formed: 1946 **Nickname:** The Blues **Floodlights:** Yes
Club colours: Blue/white hoops **Change colours:** Red
Day for midweek home matches: Wednesday **Club metal badges:** No
Previous Leagues: Surrey Senior, Spartan, Athenian
Clubhouse details: 3 bars, open lunchtimes and evenings, 7 days
Past players who progressed into the Football League: Rachid Harkouk (Crystal Palace, Q.P.R., Notts Co.), Andy Pape (Q.P.R.)
Programme details: 16 pages, 20p **Programme editor:** Richard Seuke
Local newspapers & Tel. No. Middlesex Chronicle, 01 572 0016, Recorder 01 577 7777
Major Honours: Surrey Senior League Charity Cup (2), Surrey Senior Legaue Cup, Isthmian League Division 2 Champions

FLACKWELL HEATH

President: W. Dean
Chairman: T. Corrick
Manager: T. Anning
Secretary: C.H. Robinson
Address & Tel. No. 5 Chapman Lane, Flackwell Heath, High Wycombe HP10 9AL. 06285 26204
Address and Tel. No. of ground: Tel. 23892, club hours only
Simple ground directions:
No. of seats: New stand proposed (150) **Covered accommodation:** **Capacity:**
Year formed: **Nickname:** **Floodlights:** Yes
Club colours: **Change colours:**
Day for midweek home matches: Tuesday **Club metal badges:**
Previous Leagues: Wycombe District Hellenic Athenian
Clubhouse details:
Past players who progressed into the Football League:
Programme details: **Programme editor:**
Local newspapers & Tel. No.
Major Honours: Berks & Bucks Cup semi-final 1985-6

HAREFIELD UNITED

President: G. Preston, Jnr
Chairman: L Wiggins
Manager: G. Talbot
Secretary: Terry Devereux
Address & Tel. No. 132 Organ Hall Road, Borehamwood, Herts WD6 4TL
Address and Tel. No. of ground: Preston Park, Breakspeare Road North. 089582 3474
Simple ground directions: M25 junction 16, bus 347, train S.R. to Denham
No. of seats: 200 **Covered accommodation:** 200 **Capacity:** 4,000
Year formed: 1868 **Nickname:** **Floodlights:** Yes
Club colours: Red and black **Change colours:** White
Day for midweek home matches: Tuesday **Club metal badges:**
Previous Leagues: Uxbridge & District, Parthenon, Middlesex, Spartan, Athenian
Clubhouse details: Two bars, café, pool, darts, bingo etc.
Past players who progressed into the Football League:
Programme details: 20p **Programme editor:** D. Carpenter
Local newspapers & Tel. No. Uxbridge Gazette, Watford Observer
Major Honours: Middlesex Premier Cup 1986, Athenian League Cup 1984, F.A. Vase 3rd Rd 1980-1

HORSHAM

President: G.G. Holtom
Chairman: John Isaacs
Manager: Ray McCarthy
Secretary: Jeff Barrett
Address & Tel. No.
Address and Tel. No. of ground: Queen Street, Horsham, West Sussex. 0403 52310
Simple ground directions: From Horsham Station, along North Street, past Arts Centre, fork left, turn left at traffic lights. Ground is opposite Queens Head public house (120 yards past bridge)
No. of seats: 300 **Covered accommodation:** 3 sides of ground **Capacity:** 3,000
Year formed: 1885 **Nickname:** **Floodlights:** Yes
Club colours: 12 pages, 25p **Change colours:** All white
Day for midweek home matches: Wednesday **Club metal badges:** No
Previous Leagues: West Sussex Senior, Sussex County, Metropolitan, Corinthian, Athenian
Clubhouse details: Members Club, open most evenings and Saturday afternoons
Past players who progressed into the Football League: None
Programme details: 12 pages, 25p **Programme editor:** Jeff Barrett
Local newspapers & Tel. No. West Sussex County Times, Market Square, Horsham. 0403 53371
Major Honours: Sussex Senior Cup (7), Sussex County League (5), Metropolitan League, Athenian League Div 2 & Div 2, F.A. Cup 1st Rd proper 1947 (1-9 Notts Co.), 1966 (0-3 Swindon Town)

HUNGERFORD TOWN

President: Sir Seton Wills, B.T.
Chairman: Ron Tarry
Manager: David Jones
Secretary: Keith Lovitt
Address & Tel. No.
Address and Tel. No. of ground: Bulpit Lane. 0488 82939
Simple ground directions: M4 junction 14 to A4, turn right, left at Bear Hotel through town on A338, turn left Prior Road, left Bulpit Lane
No. of seats: 100 **Covered accommodation:** 500 **Capacity:** 3,000
Year formed: 1886 **Nickname:** Crusaders **Floodlights:** Yes
Club colours: All red **Change colours:** All white
Day for midweek home matches: Tuesday **Club metal badges:** Yes
Previous Leagues: Newbury, Swindon, Hellenic
Clubhouse details: Two bars, stage, television & video. Open every evening lunchtime, weekends. Associated Darts section
Past players who progressed into the Football League: Steve Hetzke (Reading, Blackpool, Sunderland), Bruce Walker (Swindon, Bradford), Des McMahon (Reading), Brian Mundee (Bournemouth, Northampton)
Programme details: 12-16 pages **Programme editor:** Mike Hall
Local newspapers & Tel. No. Newbury Weekly News, Reading Evening Post, Marlborough Times
Major Honours: F.A. Cup 1st Rd 1979-80, F.A. Vase semi-final 1977-8, 1979-80, Berks & Bucks Senior Cup Winners, Runners-up 3 times

MARLOW

President: H.W. Swadling
Chairman: G.R. Thomson
Manager: Mike Keen
Secretary: P.C. Burdell
Address & Tel. No.
Address and Tel. No. of ground: Alfred Davis Memorial Ground, Oaktree Road, Marlow. 06284 3970
Simple ground directions: From M4 or M40 take A404 to Marlow then A4135 towards town centre. Turn right into Maple Rise (by Esso garage) ground in road opposite
No. of seats: 300 **Covered accommodation:** 300 **Capacity:** 8,000
Year formed: 1870 **Nickname:** The Blues **Floodlights:** Yes
Club colours: Royal blue, white trim **Change colours:** Orange, black
Day for midweek home matches: Tuesday **Club metal badges:** Yes
Previous Leagues: Southern, Spartan, Athenian
Clubhouse details: Open most nights and Sunday lunchtime
Past players who progressed into the Football League: L. Markham (Watford)
Programme details: 8 pages **Programme editor:** Paul Burdell
Local newspapers & Tel. No. Marlow Free Press, Maidenhead Advertiser
Major Honours: F.A. Cup 1881-2 semi finals, F.A. Vase 1974-5 5th Rd

METROPOLITAN POLICE

President: Sir Kenneth Newman
Chairman: G.D. McLean
Manager: Vic Rouse
Secretary: D.J.F. Alldridge, M.B.E.
Address & Tel. No. Woodbeck, 3 Elmshorn, Epsom Downs, Surrey. Burgh Heath 50527 (H), 01 230 2736 or 3518 (B)
Address and Tel. No. of ground: Police Sports Ground, Imber Court, East Molesey, Surrey. 01 398 1267
Simple ground directions: A3 then A308 to Scilly Isles roundabout, right into Hampton Court Way, left at roundabout into Embercourt Road and ground faces in 200 yds
No. of seats: 600 **Covered accommodation:** 1,000 **Capacity:** 5,000
Year formed: 1919 **Nickname:** The Blues **Floodlights:** Yes
Club colours: All blue **Change colours:** Red or yellow
Day for midweek home matches: Tuesday **Club metal badges:** No
Previous Leagues: Spartan, Metropolitan, Southern
Clubhouse details: Cafeteria, dining and dance hall with four bars
Past players who progressed into the Football League: None
Programme details: 8 pages, 10p **Programme editor:** Cyril Davis
Local newspapers & Tel. No. Surrey Comet
Major Honours: Spartan League (8), Middlesex Senior Cup, Surrey Senior Cup, Metropolitan League Cup

MOLESEY

President:
Chairman: Graham Pearce
Manager: D. Vaughan
Secretary: Kevin Wilkins
Address & Tel. No. 15 Berkeley Drive, West Molesey, Surrey. 01 979 4073
Address and Tel. No. of ground: Walton Road, West Molesey, Surrey. 01 979 4823
Simple ground directions: From Hampton Court take Esher Road, turn right to West Molesey, ground 1 mile on left
No. of seats: 400 **Covered accommodation:** 500 **Capacity:** 4,000
Year formed: 1950 **Nickname:** The Moles or Whites **Floodlights:** Yes
Club colours: White/black/black **Change colours:** Blue/sky blue/sky blue
Day for midweek home matches: Tuesday **Club metal badges:** No
Previous Leagues: Surrey, Spartan, Athenian
Clubhouse details: Open every night. Two bars, Saturday disco, live artists on occasional Saturday nights, bar nights, darts eight ball pool, bingo. Steward: T. Kavanagh
Past players who progressed into the Football League: Cyrille Regis (W.B.A. via Hayes)
Programme details: 12 pages, 20p **Programme editor:** Graham Pearce
Local newspapers & Tel. No. Surrey Herald, Surrey Comet, Molesey News and Mail
Major Honours: Surrey Senior League Charity Cup, Surrey Senior League, Spartan League Runners-up, Senior Challenge Cup Runners-up, Spartan League Challenge Cup & Runners-up, Surrey Senior Shield Runners-up

NEWBURY TOWN

President:
Chairman: David Griffiths
Manager: Ian Crossley
Secretary: David Brown
Address & Tel. No.
Address and Tel. No. of ground: Town Ground, Faraday Road, Newbury, Berks RG13 2AD. 0635 40048
Simple ground directions: Proceed to A34 Robin Hood roundabout, take A4 turn towards Reading, about 100 yards turn right into Faraday Road, ground is at far end
No. of seats: 100 **Covered accommodation:** 200 **Capacity:** 2,500
Year formed: **Nickname:** **Floodlights:** Yes
Club colours: Amber/amber **Change colours:** Red
Day for midweek home matches: Tuesday **Club metal badges:** Yes
Previous Leagues: Great Western, Suburban, Hampshire, Reading & District, Metropolitan, Hellenic, Athenian
Clubhouse details: Two bars with large dance hall and large kitchen
Past players who progressed into the Football League: D. McCartney (W.B.A.), D. Angell, B. Angell (Portsmouth)
Programme details: 20 pages, 30p **Programme editor:** Mrs S. Carr
Local newspapers & Tel. No. Newbury Weekly News, 0635 47000; Reading Evening Post, 0734 55833
Major Honours: Berks & Bucks Senior Cup 1898, Hellenic League

PETERSFIELD UNITED

President: To be elected
Chairman: John Stimpson
Manager: John Robson
Secretary: John Norris
Address & Tel. No. 0730 65276
Address and Tel. No. of ground: Love Lane, Petersfield, Hants. 0730 65252
Simple ground directions: 10 minutes' walk from railway station, heading towards London. From London on A3 circulatory system, Love Lane first left
No. of seats: 135 **Covered accommodation:** 250 **Capacity:** 4,000
Year formed: 1946 **Nickname:** United/Reds **Floodlights:** Yes
Club colours: Red and black stripes/black/black **Change colours:** White/red/red or black
Day for midweek home matches: Wednesday **Club metal badges:** No
Previous Leagues: Portsmouth, Hampshire
Clubhouse details: Bar, boardroom, showers, dressing rooms
Past players who progressed into the Football League: None
Programme details: 16 pages, 20p **Programme editor:** John Norris
Local newspapers & Tel. No. East Hants Post, The News (Portsmouth)
Major Honours: Hants League Div 2 Championship 1982; Aldershot Senior Cup Winners 1982, 1983; Portsmouth Senior Cup

RUISLIP MANOR

President: J. Barnett
Chairman: Ray Farrell
General Manager: Roger Goodhind
Physiotherapist: R. Moran
Secretary: C. Pacey
Address & Tel No: 12 Mapesbury Road, London NW2. 01-459 8102 (H), 01-458 9337 (B)
Address & Tel No of ground: Grosvenor Vale, Ruislip, Middlesex (Ruislip 37487)
Simple ground directions: Ruislip Manor Station, turn left, first right into Shenley Avenue then third left Cranley Drive to ground
No of seats: 160 **Covered accommodation:** 175 **Capacity:** 6,000 **Floodlights:** Yes
Year formed: 1938 **Nickname:** Manor **Club sponsors:** J. F. Containers Ltd (Ruislip 31838)
Club colours: White/Black/White **Change colours:** Red
Previous Leagues: Middlesex Senior, London, Spartan, Athenian
Programme: 32 pages, 25p **Programme Editor:** H. Klarfield
Mid-week evening matches: Wednesday
Record attendance: 2,000 v Tooting & Mitcham, FA Cup **Year: 1962**
Past player progressed Football League: Ray Knowles
Clubhouse details: Open every evening and lunchtime. Refreshments available, 3 bars, social functions, pool table, darts
Best Year in F.A. Vase: 1977-78 1980-81 1981-82 3rd Round
Local Newspapers: Ruislip Northwood Gazette
Club Captain (1984-85): C. Balls **Player of the Year (1984-85):** C. Balls

SOUTHALL

President: R.F. Fowler
Chairman: J. Davis
Manager:
Secretary: A.J. Brown
Address & Tel. No.
Address and Tel. No. of ground: Western Road, Southall. 01 574 1084
Simple ground directions: Turn left out of Southall station, 3rd right Western Road. From Southall (BR), buses 105, 195, 232 to ground
No. of seats: 250 **Covered accommodation:** 500 **Capacity:** 10,000
Year formed: 1871 **Nickname:** The Fowlers **Floodlights:** Yes
Club colours: Red/white stripes, red shorts/socks **Change colours:** All white
Day for midweek home matches: Tuesday **Club metal badges:** Yes, £1
Previous Leagues: Southern, London, Great Western Suburban, Athenian, Herts & Middx
Clubhouse details: Open every night and Sunday lunchtime
Past players who progressed into the Football League: Alan Devonshire (West Ham), Gordon Hill (Millwall, Manchester Utd), Chris Hutchings (Chelsea, Brighton), Roger Joseph (Brentford)
Programme details: 28 pages, 25p **Programme editor:** Alan Evans
Local newspapers & Tel. No. Ealing Gazette, Middlesex Chronicle
Major Honours: F.A. Vase Final, Amateur Cup Final, Athenian League Champions, Middlesex Senior Cup Winners (12 times)

WHYTELEAFE

President: E.H. Robinson
Chairman: F.E. Ovenden
Manager: Roy Burton
Secretary: S.M.J. Maddex
Address & Tel. No. 27 Orchard Avenue, Mitcham Junction, Surrey. 01 640 0703 (H), 01 648 3471 ext 345 (B)
Address and Tel. No. of ground: Church Road, Whyteleafe, Surrey. 01 660 5491
Simple ground directions: BR (SR) to Whyteleafe. By road on A22 to Whyteleafe, then up Whyteleafe Hill, Church Road 200 yards on left. 197 bus to Whyteleafe Tavern
No. of seats: 200 **Covered accommodation:** 200 **Capacity:** 5,000
Year formed: 1946 **Nickname:** Leafe **Floodlights:** Yes
Club colours: White/green/white
Change colours: Yellow/black/yellow
Day for midweek home matches: Tuesday
Club metal badges: Yes
Previous Leagues: Surrey Senior, London Spartan
Clubhouse details: Open every lunchtime and evening
Past players who progressed into the Football League:
Programme details: Yes
Programme editor:
Local newspapers & Tel. No.
Major Honours:

WOKING

President: L.A. Gosden, M.B.E.
Chairman: T.G. Spong
Manager: G. Chappell
Secretary: P.J. Ledger, J.P.
Address & Tel. No. Working 61971 (B)
Address and Tel. No. of ground: Kingsfield Sports Ground, Woking. Working 72470
Simple ground directions: Off M25 either 10 or 11 junction. Follow signs for Woking. Ground 1 mile from station, taxi and bus service available
No. of seats: 750 **Covered accommodation:** 750 **Capacity:** 6,000
Year formed: 1889 **Nickname:** Cardinals **Floodlights:** Yes
Club colours: Red shirts with white trim/red/red
Change colours: All yellow
Day for midweek home matches: Tuesday
Club metal badges: Yes
Previous Leagues: West Surrey
Clubhouse details: Members bar and separate function hall
Past players who progressed into the Football League:
Programme details: 16 pages, 25p
Programme editor: J. Woozley, L. Swan
Local newspapers & Tel. No. Woking News-Mail, Woking 61581; Surrey Advertiser, Guildford 571234
Major Honours: F.A. Amateur Cup, Surrey Senior Cup (5), Surrey Senior Shield (9), Surrey Invitation Cup, Guernsey Victory Cup (2), London Senior Cup Runners-up

Petersfield United: *Back Row (L to R): Robert Carter, Mark Wood, Steve Penny, Michael Clifford, Martin Gillard, Neil Darnley, Nicky Sillence, Paul Harris, Eddie Bentley, Owen McCartney. Front Row (L to R): Roger Buckland, Ian Watts, Bavva Biller, Bruce Kendall, Neil Hider, Mark Burton, Joe Laidlaw* Photo: Eric Marsh

Combined Counties Football League

President: N. E. McLellan
Chairman: W. E. J. Lale
General Secretary: J. J. Whitefoot
8 Compton Road, Church Crookham, Aldershot Hants. Tel: Fleet (02514) 7851

Successful Cup Season for Member Clubs

Once again a period of bad weather occuring in mid-season caused fixture congestion during April and May. However, the League Championship was settled with B.Ae (Weybridge) winning both Divisions. Chertsey Town ending as Runners-Up in the Premier and Malden Vale finishing similarly in the Reserve Division.

The Challenge Cup Finals resulted in Chertsey Town winning the Concours Motors Trophy by beating Malden Vale and Cobham overcoming Godalming Town in the Reserve Final. The Concours Final was again played at Woking Town FCs ground and was watched by a crowd in excess of 500 spectators. We are indebted to the Directors of The Concours Motor Company Ltd. of Haslemere for their continued sponsorship of this competition. The Reserve Final took place at Chertsey Town FCs ground and the generosity of the club ensured that the event was a financial success for the first time.

For the second successive year the club finishing in second spot in the League Championship have been promoted to the Vauxhall-Opel FL. This year it is Chertsey Town and we wish them every success with their future efforts. At the other end of the League Fleet Town have been have been relegated to the Surrey County Premier League. They will be replaced by Chipstead FC who, by finishing in second place in that league and having the necessary Senior Status, have now qualified for promotion in accordance with our arrangement with the Surrey County FA. They are the second club to achieve this, following in the path of Farleigh Rovers who were promoted some two seasons ago.

It has been a very successful season for clubs competing in the F. A. Vase and the County F. A. Senior Cups. Chertsey Town reached the final of the Allders Surrey County Senior Cup and lost to Vauxhall-Opel FL club Sutton United; Hartley Wintney reached the 4th Round of the Hampshire County FA Senior Cup before losing to Southern League side RS Southampton after extra-time in a replay. Finally, Cobham must be congratulated for progressing further in the FA Vase than any other CCFL club has done so previously.

The campaign by the Surrey County FA to improve standards throughout the County continues with a deadline of August 1987 by which time clubs must qualify. This therefore, is the critical close season for those who still have to achieve the 'C' grading (116 marks) for Senior Status. It cannot be stressed too much how important this is both for the clubs future and that of the Leagues' existence as a viable Senior competition. Currently there are only six clubs with confirmed 'C' grades. Together with two clubs from Hampshire that leaves us far short of what would be considered a minimum number for the League to continue. Several clubs are making efforts towards their gradings and it is hoped that enough will be achieved to satisfy Ground Inspectors.

HONOURS LIST

SURREY COUNTY SENIOR CUP: Runners-up – Chertsey Town
CONCOURS CHALLENGE TROPHY: Champions – Chertsey Town
Runners-up – Malden Vale
PREMIER DIVISION: Champions – British Aerospace (Weybridge)
Runners-up – Chertsey Town
RESERVE SECTION CHALLENGE CUP: Champions – Cobham
Runners-up – Godalming Town
RESERVE SECTION: Champions – British Aerospace (Weybridge)
Runners-up – Malden Vale

COMBINED COUNTIES LEAGUE—RECENT CHAMPIONS

Max Pts	Season	1st	2nd	3rd	4th
56	1979/80	51 Guildford & W	45 Ash U.	42 Malden T	41 BAe Wey.
72	1980/81	55 Malden T*	55 Hartley Wtny	54 Westfield	53 Farnham T
60E	1981/82	52 Malden T	42 Lingfield	31 Westfield*	31 BAe Wey.
60W		47 Ash U.	39 Alton T	35 Farnham T	31 Hartley Wtny
102	1982/83	75 Hartley Wtny	74 Ash U.	68 Godalming T	59 Chobham
96	1983/84	70 Godalming T	67 Malden T	60 Ash U.	57 Chobham
108	1984/85	82 Malden Vale	80 Southwick	75 Merstham	70 BAe Wey.
108	1985/86	84 BAe Wey.	81 Chertsey T.	78 Ash U.	69 Malden Vale

* goal average/difference
E = East
W = West

CLUB FORM 1979-86

No. of clubs competing	15	19	11 11	E W	18	17	19	19
Season	79-80	80-81	81-82		82-83	83-84	84-85	85-86
1 Ash. U	2	6	1	W	2	3	5	3
2 BAe Weybridge	4	9	4	E	7	11	4	1
3 Chessington U	5	5	9	E	6	17	—	—
4 Clarion	15	19	10	E	—	—	—	—
5 Cobham	7	11	5	E	9	10	17	8
6 Godalming T	9	10	6	E	3	1	9	10
7 Guildford & Worp.	1	7	5	W	12	7	—	—
8 Hartley Wintney	10	2	4	W	1	5	16	11
9 Lightwater	11	18	9	W	—	—	—	—
10 Lion Sports	8	8	——		—	—	—	—
11 Malden T	3	1	1	E	10	2	6	6
12 Sheerwater	12	15	11	E	—	—	—	—
13 Virginia Water	14	12	7	E	14	9	7	14
14 Westfield	6	3	3	E	16	6	8	9
15 Yateley T	13	17	11	W	17	14	—	—
16 Cranleigh	—	14	8	E	13	15	12	17
17 Farnham T	—	4	3	W	15	8	10	5
18 Lingfield	—	16	2	E	18	—	—	—
19 Wrecclesham	—	13	10	W	—	—	—	—
20 Alton T	—	—	2	W	11	16	—	—
21 Chobham	—	—	6	W	4	4	13	12
22 Cove	—	—	8	W	5	13	18	13
23 Frimley Green	—	—	7	W	8	12	14	18
24 Farleigh R	—	—	——		—	—	11	15
25 Fleet T	—	—	——		—	—	19	19
26 Horley T	—	—	——		—	—	15	16
27 Malden Vale	—	—	——		—	—	1	4
28 Merstham	—	—	——		—	—	3	7
29 Southwick	—	—	——		—	—	2	—
30 Chertsey T	—	—	——		—	—	—	2

ASH UNITED

President: **Chairman:** Jack Muir **Manager:**
Secretary: J. Muir, 86 Manor Road, Ash, Aldershot, Hants
Address and Tel. No. of ground: Shawfield Road, Ash, Aldershot. 0252 20385
Simple ground directions: Shawfield Road from A323 (Aldershot-Guildford Rd) at Greyhound PH roundabout, Ash
No. of seats: **Covered accommodation:** **Capacity:**
Year formed: 1911 **Nickname:** **Floodlights:**
Club colours: Green **Change colours:** Blue
Day for midweek matches: **Previous Leagues:** Surrey Senior, Aldershot Senior

BAe WEYBRIDGE

President: L. Hazeldene **Chairman:** J. Quantrell **Manager:** M. Slater
Secretary: J.E. Ashcroft, 149 Rydens Road, Walton-on-Thames, Surrey. WoT 22309, Ashford 48585
Address and Tel. No. of ground: BAe, Kings Head Lane. Byfleet 43601
Simple ground directions: Byfleet-New-Hall BRS, first right
No. of seats: 100 **Covered accommodation:** Excellent **Capacity:** 2,000
Year formed: 1909 **Nickname:** Planemen **Floodlights:** No
Club colours: Blue **Change colours:** Red
Day for midweek matches: **Previous Leagues:** Metropolitan, Surrey Senior

CHIPSTEAD

President: **Chairman:** **Manager:**
Secretary: M.E. Cook, 82 Meadway, Coulsdon, Surrey
Address and Tel. No. of ground: High Road, Chipstead. Downland 53250
Simple ground directions:
No. of seats: None **Covered accommodation:** No **Capacity:**
Year formed: **Nickname:** **Floodlights:** No
Club colours: Green/black **Change colours:** Yellow/black
Day for midweek matches: **Previous Leagues:** Surrey County Premier

CHOBHAM

President: Mr Unice **Chairman:** B. Osgood **Manager:** J. Adams
Secretary: Mrs D. Walley, 8 Brook Green, Chertsey Rd., Chobham, Surrey GU24 8PN. Chobham 8039
Address and Tel. No. of ground: Recreation Ground, Station Road, Chobham, Surrey. Chobham 7876
Simple ground directions: Railway Station Woking. Bus, Alder Valley 255 and 256
No. of seats: **Covered accommodation:** 600 **Capacity:**
Year formed: 1905 **Nickname:** **Floodlights:** No
Club colours: Two-tone blue/dark blue/dark blue **Change colours:** White/black/black
Day for midweek matches: **Previous Leagues:** Spartan

COBHAM

President: Vacant **Chairman:** B.C. Harlow **Manager:**
Secretary: B.C. Harlow, 15 Harecroft, Great Bookham, Nr Leatherhead, Surrey. Bookham 56811 (H), 01 997 8484 (B)
Address and Tel. No. of ground: Leg O'Mutton Field, Downside Bridge Rd, Cobham, Surrey. Cobham 65959
Simple ground directions: From London turn off AA3 at Cobham, proceed down hill, right into Between Streets
No. of seats: None **Covered accommodation:** **Capacity:**
Year formed: 1892 **Nickname:** Hammers **Floodlights:** No
Club colours: Red/navy/red **Change colours:** All navy strip with red & white trim
Day for midweek matches: **Previous Leagues:** Surrey Senior

COVE

President: C. Mortimore **Chairman:** R. Clarke **Manager:** J. Goode
Secretary: P. O'Brien, Camb. 33435
Address and Tel. No. of ground: Oak Farm Fields, off Romayne Close, Cove, Farnborough, Hants. F'boro 543615
Simple ground directions: Farnborough Main Station
No. of seats: **Covered accommodation:** **Capacity:**
Year formed: 1897 **Nickname:** **Floodlights:** No
Club colours: Amber/black **Change colours:** Blue/white
Day for midweek matches: **Previous Leagues:** Surrey Senior, Hants

CRANLEIGH

President: J.R. Wiskar **Chairman:** P. Ford **Manager:** B. Newman
Secretary: P. Auzins, 81 Glebe Road, Cranleigh GU6 7AJ. Cranleigh 275969 & Godalming 28585
Address and Tel. No. of ground: Snoxhall Fields, Knowle Lane, Cranleigh
Simple ground directions: A281 from Guildford, 300 yards off High Street on left
No. of seats: **Covered accommodation:** **Capacity:**
Year formed: 1893 **Nickname:** **Floodlights:**
Club colours: Blue **Change colours:** White
Day for midweek matches: **Previous Leagues:**

FARLEIGH ROVERS

President: C.D. Scott **Chairman:** R.B. Peters **Manager:** Mike McCue
Secretary: M. McCue, 8 Forge Croft, Edenbridge, Kent TN8 5BW. Edenbridge 0732 863645 (H), 0206 579555 (B)
Address and Tel. No. of ground: Parsonage Field, Harrow Road, Warlingham, Surrey. 08832 6483
Simple ground directions: Upper Warlingham (BR). B269, left Chelsham Rd, 1 mile left Harrow Rd. Bus 403
No. of seats: None **Covered accommodation:** **Capacity:** 2,000
Year formed: 1922 **Nickname:** None **Floodlights:** No
Club colours: Red/black/black **Change colours:** White/white/red
Day for midweek matches: **Previous Leagues:** Surrey Premier

FARNHAM TOWN

President: J.H. Winslade **Chairman:** J. Butters **Manager:** A. Varcoe
Secretary: S.W. Meaker, 55 Green Lane, Farnham, Surrey
Address and Tel. No. of ground: Memorial Ground, West St., Farnham, Surrey. Farnham 715305
Simple ground directions: Last roundabout Farnham Bypass, 3rd exit town centre into West St, approx. 500 yds right
No. of seats: None **Covered accommodation:** **Capacity:** 2,000
Year formed: 1921 **Nickname:** Town **Floodlights:** None
Club colours: Claret and blue **Change colours:** Yellow
Day for midweek matches: **Previous Leagues:** Surrey Intermediate, Surrey Senior, Spartan, London Spartan

FRIMLEY GREEN

President: B. Potter **Chairman:** K. Crease **Manager:** M. Carroll
Secretary: S.J. Varcoe, 8 The Ridings, Frimley, Surrey GU16 5RA
Address and Tel. No. of ground: Recreation Ground, Frimley Green
Simple ground directions:
No. of seats: None **Covered accommodation:** Yes **Capacity:**
Year formed: 1919 **Nickname:** **Floodlights:** No
Club colours: Grey/maroon **Change colours:** Light/dark blue
Day for midweek matches: **Previous Leagues:** Spartan

GODALMING TOWN

President: **Chairman:** **Manager:**
Secretary: Mrs J Phillips, 135 Manor Rd., Stoughton, Guildford, Surrey
Address and Tel. No. of ground: Weycourt, Meadrow, Godalming. Godalming 7520
Simple ground directions:
No. of seats: None **Covered accommodation:** None **Capacity:**
Year formed: **Nickname:** **Floodlights:** No
Club colours: Yellow/green **Change colours:** All green
Day for midweek matches: **Previous Leagues:** Surrey County Senior

HARTLEY WINTNEY

President: D. Gorsky **Chairman:** W. Mitchell **Manager:** I. Bedford
Secretary: D. Burgess, 2 Sherwood Cottages, West Green, Hartley Wintney, Hants. H.W. 2928
Address and Tel. No. of ground: Memorial Ground, Green Lane, Hartley Wintney, Hants. H.W. 3586
Simple ground directions: From village on A30, into Fleet Rd, cross right into Green Lane, ground 400 yards
No. of seats: **Covered accommodation:** **Capacity:**
Year formed: 1897 **Nickname:** The Row **Floodlights:**
Club colours: Tangerine/black **Change colours:** White/blue
Day for midweek matches: **Previous Leagues:** Basingstoke, Aldershot

HORLEY TOWN

President: B.T. Sired **Chairman:** J. Ansell **Manager:** L. Devine
Secretary: S.K. Osborne, 57 Silverlea Gardens, Horley, Surrey. Horley 782986
Address and Tel. No. of ground: The Defence, Smallfield Rd, Horley, Surrey. Horley 786075
Simple ground directions: British Rail to Horley Station
No. of seats: **Covered accommodation:** 2,000 **Capacity:** 2,000
Year formed: 1898 **Nickname:** **Floodlights:** Yes
Club colours: Claret and blue **Change colours:** Green and yellow
Day for midweek matches: **Previous Leagues:** Surrey Senior, Spartan, Athenian

MALDEN TOWN

President: **Chairman:** **Manager:**
Secretary: A.H. Dibble, 25 Woodcote Hurst, Epsom, Surrey
Address and Tel. No. of ground: Manor Park, Malden Road, New Malden
Simple ground directions:
No. of seats: Yes **Covered accommodation:** Yes **Capacity:**
Year formed: **Nickname:** **Floodlights:** No
Club colours: All red **Change colours:** All white
Day for midweek matches: **Previous Leagues:** Surrey County Senior

MALDEN VALE

President: G.J. Sladden **Chairman:** M.I. Webb **Manager:** R. Kingdon
Secretary: S.A. Pearce, 4 Raleigh Drive, Tolworth. 01 337 4302 (H & B)
Address and Tel. No. of ground: Grand Drive, Raynes Park. 01 542 2193
Simple ground directions:
No. of seats: 20 **Covered accommodation:** Small stand **Capacity:** 2,000
Year formed: 1967 **Nickname:** **Floodlights:** No
Club colours: Navy blue **Change colours:** Yellow
Day for midweek matches: **Previous Leagues:** London Spartan

MERSTHAM

President: F. Fox **Chairman:** S. Baker **Manager:** C. Humphreys
Secretary: F. Fox, 153 Albury Road, Merstham, Surrey RH1 3LW. Merstham 3279/4046
Address and Tel. No. of ground: Albury Road, Merstham
Simple ground directions: Leave A23 at Merstham, School Hill, Weldon Way
No. of seats: 100 **Covered accommodation:** 2,000 **Capacity:** 2,100
Year formed: 1892 **Nickname:** **Floodlights:** No
Club colours: Amber and black **Change colours:** White/black
Day for midweek matches: **Previous Leagues:** Surrey Senior, Combined Counties, London Spartan

VIRGINIA WATER

President: P. Gostage **Chairman:** R.T. Fisher **Manager:** M. Gowan
Secretary: Mrs J. Gostage, 23 Brookside, Chertsey, Surrey
Address and Tel. No. of ground: The Timbers, Crown Road, Virginia Water. Wentworth 3811
Simple ground directions:
No. of seats: **Covered accommodation:** **Capacity:**
Year formed: **Nickname:** **Floodlights:**
Club colours: Green/red **Change colours:** Maroon
Day for midweek matches: **Previous Leagues:** London Spartan

WESTFIELD

President: **Chairman:** **Manager:**
Secretary: R. Hill, 16 Westfield Avenue, Woking, Surrey. Woking 67144
Address and Tel. No. of ground: Woking Park, Kingfield
Simple ground directions:
No. of seats: None **Covered accommodation:** None **Capacity:**
Year formed: **Nickname:** **Floodlights:** No
Club colours: Royal blue **Change colours:** Yellow
Day for midweek matches: **Previous Leagues:** Surey County Senior

Twins Ivan (left) of Farnham Town and David Muir (Ash United) played against each other last season. Photo Eric Marsh.

Seven Brentwood defenders keep out a Burnham Ramblers attack and the system seems to work as the visitors win 1-0. Photo Chris Hussey.

Essex Senior Football League

President: D. Pond, F.C.A.
Hon. Secretary: H. Gordon King

REVIEW OF SEASON 1985/86

"WITHAM TOWN'S TROPHY AND CHAMPIONSHIP TRIUMPH"

WITHAM TOWN, so close to honours last season, made no mistake this term and deservedly won the Championship in fine style from Wivenhoe Town who had led the table from August to May. Witham's superb season also brought reward in the form of the Essex Senior Trophy – a great honour for the League which ses them enter the F. A. Cup for the first time in 86/7. The Senior Section's top goalscorer was their centre-forward Colin Mitchel with 26.

The season started with an additional club in the Senior section Burnham Ramblers, and two Junior clubs, Purfleet and Southend Manor together with one Intermediate, Stambridge, in Division One. Last season's Reserve League Champions, Loughton Athletic changed their name and ground but not their form and virtually the same 'eleven' took the double of league and Cup as Woodford Town Reserves at the expense, on both occasions of Southend Manor who, nevertheless inflicted the only defeat in two seasons on the Champions and produced the Leagues top scorer in David Hughes, with 31 goals.

The Challenge Cup threw up the one shock of the season with little Coggeshall Town winning 4 ties on their way to the final despite being able to win only 4 league matches in two seasons. They even scored in the final but it was in their own net and Ford United won their first piece of silverware since joining the League. Consolation came for Coggeshall when they retained the Sportsmanship Shield – proof of their 'never say die' attitude both on and off the field. The Harry Fisher Cup Final brought together the League's top two clubs in Witham and Wivenhoe and the Champions went one up before half time but Wivenhoe battled on for victory at Manorway, East Ham on Bank Holiday Monday. Two attendances of note were, over 400 at Wivenhoe Town for a League match on a Friday night and 225 at a Division One match in Southend between Manor and Stambridge. Season 1986/87 Purfleet elevated to the Senior section and the Competition will be known as the ESSEX LEAGUE. We welcome Earls Colne FC and St. Osyth FC into Division One which will be split between North and South of County for easier administration.

Robert Herrington *Publicity Officer*

Ford United Essex Senior League Challenge Cup Winners 1985 – 86
Picture by David Kilburn
Team: C. Night, J. Massey, D. Matthews, T. Luscombe, A. Jackson, A. Rowe, S. Munday, S. Hawkins, R. Jackson, K. Finucane, T. Lawrence, A. Tickner (sub), Don Wiltshire (Manager), Peter Brabrook (Coach) (ex Chelsea with England)
Coggeshall 1-0, Attendence 400.

ESSEX SENIOR FOOTBALL LEAGUE

SENIOR DIVISION

		P	W	D	L	F	A	Pts
1	Witham Town	32	24	5	3	73	23	77
2	Wivenhoe Town	32	19	5	8	82	47	62
3	Ford United	32	19	4	9	65	41	61
4	Maldon Town	32	17	9	6	48	24	60
5	East Thurrock United	32	16	9	7	64	41	57
6	Brentwood	32	18	0	14	71	47	54
7	Chelmsford	32	15	7	10	48	38	52
8	Bowers United	32	13	7	12	54	49	46
9	Canvey Island	32	10	11	11	53	45	41
10	Eton Manor	32	11	6	15	52	80	39
11	Brightlingsea United	32	10	8	14	46	52	38
12	Burnham Ramblers	32	10	7	15	45	54	37
13	Standted	32	10	4	18	37	51	34
14	Sawbridgeworth Town	32	9	6	17	53	72	
15	Halstead Town	32	8	6	18	47	67	30
16	East Ham United	32	7	9	16	41	74	30
17	Coggeshall Town	32	2	5	25	31	105	11

ESSEX SENIOR LEAGUE CUP RESULTS SENIOR CHALLENGE CUP

PRELIMINARY ROUND

Maldon Town	2	Witham Town	1

FIRST ROUND

Canvey Island	5	Sawbridgeworth Town	0
Coggeshall Town	2	Brightlingsea United	1
East Thurrock	1	Brentwood	1 (2-1)(aet)
Eton Manor	3	Halstead Town	1
Ford United	5	Burnham Ramblers	1
Maldon Town		Wivenhoe Town	1
Stansted	0	Bowers United	4
Chelmsford	2	East Ham United	0

ROUND TWO

Canvey Island	1	Coggeshall Town	2
Chelmsford	1	East Thurrock United	4
Eton Manor	2	Bowers United	0
Maldon Town	0	Ford United	0 (1-2)

SEMI-FINAL

Coggeshall Town	1	East Thurrock	0 1st leg
East Thurrock	3	Coggeshall Town	4 2nd leg
Ford United	2	Eton Manor	2 1st leg
Eton Manor	1	Ford United	5 2nd leg

FINAL

Coggeshall Town	0	Ford United	1

(Own goal—18 mins) H/T 0-1 at Rosemary Lane, Halstead. Saturday, May 17th 1985. Attendance 400.
Teams:
Coggeshall Town: R. Redding, T. French, D. Russell, T. Robson, C. Howitt, J. Blackwell, G. Bailey, C. Mayes, S. Whitelaw, M. Simmons, N. Haythorne.
Ford United: C. Tight, J. Massey, D. Matthews, T. Luscombe, A. Jackson, A. Rowe, S. Munday, S. Hawkins, R. Jackson, K. Finucane, T. Lawrence.
·*Sub.* A. Tickner.

THE HARRY FISHER MEMORIAL CUP 1985-86

PRELIMINARY ROUND

Burnham Ramblers	6	Stansted	0

FIRST ROUND

Burnham Ramblers	0	Brentwood	3
East Ham United	3	Brightlingsea United	5(aet)
Sawbridgeworth	1	Witham Town	3
Wivenhoe Town	2	Halsted Town	1

SEMI-FINALS

Brentwood	1	Witham Town	3
Wivenhoe Town	4	Brightlingsea	2

FINAL

Witham Town	1	Wivenhoe Town	2

at *East Ham United FC* Monday May 5th: Attendance 85
Scorers: Witham: Scofield (5m) H/T 1-0
Wivenhoe: D. Jarvis (57m), P. Harrison (74m)

LEADING GOALSCORERS 1985-86
Senior Section
(League, League Cup and Harry Fisher Cup only)
Qualification.....8 goals

26 — Colin Mitchell (Witham)
24 — Robert Jackson (Ford United)
22 — Steve Tilson (Bowers Utd.)
20 — Mark Keen (Witham)
19 — Jefferies (Brightlingsea), Mitch Springett (Wivenhoe)
18 — Lawrence (Ford United)
17 — Dean Coney (Eton Manor)
16 — Clayden (13 Etu; 3 Wivenhoe), (East Thurrock United), Danny Greaves (Maldon Town)
14 — Stittle (Brentwood), Gallagher (Brentwood), Bailey (Coggeshall), Milburn (Wivenhoe)
13 — A. Burrows (Sawbridgeworth)
12 — Johnson (Canvey), Hindley (Eton Manor)
11 — Hatcher (Burnham), Cutmore (Halstead)
10 — Chapman (Burnham), Pike & Cook (Brentwood)
9 — Butcher (Brentwood), Carter (Brightlingsea), D. Woolley (Bowers), Farthing (Wivenhoe)
8 — Birleston (East Ham Utd), Britnell (4 Can. 4 Chelm.), (Chelmsford), Burns (Sawbridgeworth), Dave Green (Stansted), Hawkins (Ford United)

Representative Matches:

Herts Senior County League 2, Essex League 0
Played at Witham Town FC March 25th 1986.
Team: Eddie Coe (Stansted), Allan Pitts (Maldon), Kevin Gildea (Brentwood), Mick Packer (Wivenhoe), Alan Moody (Maldon), Craig Coney (Eton Manor), Alex Gallagher (Brentwood) & Mark Farthing (Wivenhoe), Jim Hallybone (East Thurrock), Ian Fowlie (Brentwood), Nigel Theobald (Wivenhoe).
Sub: Danny Dreaves (Maldon) 65 mins.
Scorer: Alex Gallagher 22m:75m. *Manager:* Derek Stittle (Brentwood).

		1	2	3	4	5	6	7	8	9	10	11	12	13	14	15	16	17
1	Bowers		2-3	0-1	3-1	1-3	1-1	1-1	4-2	3-2	1-2	3-1	2-0	1-3	2-2	1-0	1-2	4-3
2	Brentwood	4-0		3-0	2-0	3-1	4-1	5-0	3-0	0-1	3-1	1-2	1-0	2-1	2-1	0-1	3-4	5-1
3	Brightlingsea	1-3	2-0		5-2	3-0	2-0	5-2	4-1	2-4	1-1	3-2	2-2	1-1	0-2	1-1	0-4	1-4
4	Burnham Ramb.	1-1	1-3	2-0		0-0	2-0	0-3	4-1	1-1	1-2	1-3	1-0	0-0	3-5	1-0	2-0	2-3
5	Canvey Island	2-2	2-3	3-1	2-0		1-1	7-1	1-1	2-1	3-0	2-2	5-1	0-1	0-1	0-0	0-1	4-4
6	Chelmsford	0-1	0-2	0-0	3-2	4-1		2-1	0-1	2-1	2-0	2-1	5-0	2-1	3-2	0-1	0-0	1-2
7	Coggeshall	1-2	1-6	0-3	1-5	1-2	1-4		1-1	2-5	2-3	1-4	0-5	2-2	3-1	1-3	0-4	1-8
8	East Ham Utd.	1-1	4-3	1-0	1-1	2-1	1-2	1-0		1-1	1-0	1-3	0-1	0-0	0-3	3-1	1-1	2-7
9	East Thurrock	1-0	1-0	3-1	5-1	2-1	1-1	0-0	1-1		3-1	3-1	1-1	3-3	5-1	5-0	1-1	2-1
10	Eton Manor	4-3	2-1	2-2	1-4	2-2	2-2	2-1	4-2	0-3		2-2	3-3	0-5	2-1	3-1	1-9	0-3
11	Ford United	2-1	4-2	2-1	1-0	3-1	0-3	3-0	4-1	2-0	4-1		3-0	0-1	5-1	3-1	0-1	1-0
12	Halstead Town	0-1	6-2	0-2	2-3	2-2	1-2	3-3	5-1	2-1	2-4	0-3		0-1	5-2	1-2	0-5	1-3
13	Maldon Town	1-0	1-0	1-1	0-0	0-0	1-0	1-0	3-1	0-1	2-1	3-0	4-0		3-1	2-0	0-1	3-1
14	Sawbridgeworth	0-4	2-1	3-0	1-3	0-1	2-3	3-0	4-4	2-2	2-0	1-1	0-1	0-0		2-3	0-1	4-2
15	Stansted	1-4	0-1	2-1	1-1	0-3	0-1	3-0	3-1	2-0	4-2	0-1	1-2	2-3	2-2		1-2	0-1
16	Witham Town	2-0	3-2	1-0	1-0	1-1	1-1	4-0	2-1	5-2	3-1	2-0	1-0	2-0	6-1	2-1		0-1
17	Wivenhoe Town	1-1	2-1	0-0	3-0	1-0	2-0	7-1	6-2	1-2	2-3	2-2	1-1	2-1	5-1	1-0	2-1	

BOWERS UNITED (1946)

Manager: J. Wilson
Chairman: C. Wiggins
Secretary: M. Carter 75 Winifred Road, Pitsea. Tel: 0268 554650
Address & Tel. No. of ground: Crown Avenue, Off Kenneth Road, Pitsea, Basildon. Tel: 0268 555583
Simple ground directions: Turn into Rectory Road from Pitsea Broadway, turn into Kenneth Road, right turn at top into Crown Avenue, off Old London Road (A13)
Clubhouse: Yes
Club colours: Red, Black **Change colours:** All White
Programme: Yes
Previous Leagues: Thurrock Thameside Combination : Olympian. ESL Champions 1980-81

BRENTWOOD

Chairman: **Manager:** D. Stittle
Secretary: D.F. Douglas, 74 Clifton Avenue, South Benfleet, Essex. Tel: S.B. 51026
Simple ground directions: "LaRKINS" Ongar Road, Brentwood. Tel: 210464
Address & Tel. No of ground: ¾ mile North of Brentwood Town Centre on Ongar Road, on left hand side.
Year formed: 1955
Capacity: **Covered accommodation:** Yes **Seating:** None **Floodlights:** None
Clubhouse: Yes
Colours: All Blue **Change Colours:** White, Red & Blue **Programme:** With Admission
Honours:/Previous Leagues: Essex Olympian. ESL Op Winners 1978-79

BRIGHTLINGSEA UNITED

Chairman: J. Couzens **Manager:** T. Jenkinson
Secretary: H. Beere
Address & Tel. No of ground: Tel. 4199
simple ground directions: Top of town, turn left into north Road, Ground at top end. Bus EN78 from Colchester.
No. of seats: **Ground accommodation:** 1500 **Floodlights:** No
Year formed: 1902
Club colours: Red & White **Change colours:** Blue & White
Clubhouse details: 7 days per week - excluding Sunday evening.

BURNHAM RAMBLERS

Chairman: J.R. Richardson
Secretary: Gordon Brasted
Address & Tel. No: 4 Riverside Road, Burnham-on-Crouch
Manager: D.G. Tyrell
Physiotherapist: D. Aitken
Address & Tel. No. of ground: Wick Road, Burnham-on-Crouch. Tel. No: Maldon 784383
Simple ground directions: Bottom of town turn left into Silver Road, ground ahead. Burnham (BR) 10 mins
No. of seats: None **Covered accommodation:** 200 **Capacity:** 5,000 **Floodlights:** No
Year formed: 1900 **Nickname:** Ramblers **Midweek Games:** Tuesday
Club colours: Royal Blue **Change colours:** Red
Previous Names: None **Previous Grounds:** None
Record attendance: 1,500
Previous Leagues: Essex Olympian, Mid Essex, North Essex
Programme: 12 pages, 50p with entrance
Clubhouse details: Evenings & weekend

CANVEY ISLAND FOOTBALL CLUB

Chairman: Paul Norton-Ashley
Secretary: John Wellmen
127 Church Parade, Canvey Island, Essex SS8 9RD
Manager: Ben Embery
Physiotherapist: Steve Jackson
Address & Tel. No of ground: Park Lane, Canvey Island. Tel. No.: 0268 682991
Simple ground directions: Take A130 from A13 or A127 (A12) from London or A130 from Chelmsford. Follow signs for Town centre, at one-way system turn left into High St., past Old Eastern Bus Garage (now Bus Museum) and Park Lane is first on right past the garage. By train to Benfleet (from Fenchurch St.), Bus No. 3 or 151 to stop after Admiral Jellicoe (Public House).
Club colours: Yellow shirts, Royal Blue Shorts & Socks **Change colours:** Blue White & White
Year formed: 1926 Floodlights: No
Nickname: Gulls **Programme:** 20p 24 or 28 pages
Record attendance: v Tottenham Hotspur XI 1964 v Billericay Feb. 1980 (Est.)
Previous Grounds: King Heorges Playing Fields, Paddocks and Furtherwick School
Previous Leagues: Greater London, Metropolitan, Parthenon, Thurrock & Thameside Combination, South East Essex.
Programme Editor: Currently Secretary. Tel. 697657
Senior Honours: G.L.L. Championship 1967/68 : 1968/69. G.L.L. Cup 1968/69, Sportsmanship Award 1983/84
Clubhouse: Tuesday, Thursday, Friday, Sat. evenings. Sunday lunchtimes.

COGGESHALL TOWN

Chairman:
Manager: M. Rayner
Secretary: I. Kitchener
Address & Tel. No. 20 Hawkes Road, Coggeshall CO6 1QP
Address & Tel. No of grounds: West Street, Coggeshall, Essex
Simple ground directions: ½ mile West of Town Centre on South side of West Street. 70 Bus from Marsten (BR).
Capacity: **Covered accommodation:** Yes **Seating:** **Floodlights:** No
Year formed: 1878
Programme: Yes
Colours: White & Black
Change colours: Red
Honours:/Previous Leagues: Essex & Suffolk Border League Champions 1968/69. ESL Sportsmanship Award 1985/86, 1984/85

EAST HAM UNITED

Chairman: E.S. Whatmough
Secretary: Reuben Gane
108 Beccles Drive, Barking, Esstex
Manager: Reuben Gane
Physiotherapist: Phil Smith
Address & Tel. No of ground: Manorway Ground, East Ham Manorway, London E6. Tel. No. 01-476 5514
Simple ground directions: 101 Bus from East Ham (Tube station).
Year formed: 1933
Programme: 10p 4 pages
Club colours: Green-White-Gold
Change colours: Red & Black
Capacity: 2,500 **Stand:** 200 Yes
Nickname: The Hammers
Record Attendance: 4,250 at Terrance McMillan Stadium, February 15th 1976, East Ham United (incl. George Best) v West Ham United XI (Friendly). 2,400 1953 v Sutton United FA Amateur Cup
Previous Grounds: Tillets Farm, London E6
Manor Honours: Met/London Cup Winners, Quarter Finalists. F.A. Vase

EATON MANOR

Chairman:
Secretary: J. Rose:
117 Somerville Road, Chadwell Heath RM6 5AX. Tel. No. 01-590 2209
Address & Tel. No of ground: Roding Lane, Buckhurst Hill. Tel. No. 01-504 9937
Capacity: **Covered accommodation:** **No. of seats:** None **Floodlights:** No.
Simple ground directions: Buckhurst Hill LT.Station. Ground just east of same.
Club colours: Light Blue/Dark Blue
Change colours: White/Blue
Clubhouse: Yes
Programme: Yes
Previous Leagues: London Lge, Metropolitan Lge, Senior Trophy Finalists 1938/39

EAST THURROCK UNITED

Chairman: Mr. B. Grover
Secretary: Mr. M. Harris
Manager: Mr. R. Bond
14 Colne Valley, Upminster, Essex RM14 1QA.
Address & Tel. No. of ground: Rookery Hill, Corringham, Essex. Tel. No. Stanford-le-Hope 644166
Simple ground directions: A13 London-Southend. Tal 1014 at Stanford-le-Hope. Follow A1014 for 2½ miles. Ground on left. Nearest station - Stanford-le-Hope.
Club colours: Amber/Black
Change colours: Blue
No. of seats: None **Capacity:** 2,000 **Floodlights:** Planned for 1987
Stand: Planned for 1987. Temporary stand at moment.
Year formed: 1969
Programme: 24 pages. 25p
Previous Leagues: Greater London, Metropolitan-London and London Spartan.
Midweek games: Tuesday
Programme Editor: Mr. T. Keating. Tel. No. 0375 644166 or 641009
Nickname: Rocks
Major Honours: Metropolotian London League, Division Two Champions 1972/73
Previous Grounds: Bullet Ground, Grays F.C. Tilbury F.C. New Thames Club
Clubhouse: 7 days a week - All day

FORD UNITED

Chairman: L.H.R. Constable
Secretary: K.D. Dobson
Manager: D. Wiltshire
16 Tenby Court, Walthamstow E17 7AT
Address & Tel. No of ground: Ford Sports Club, Rush Green Road, Romford, Essex. Tel. No 0708-45678
Simple ground directions: On the A124 (Rush Green Road) on the left hand side going towards Hornchurch.
No. of seats: 800 **Capacity:** 2,500 **Floodlights:** No
Club colours: Royal Blue & White
Change colours: All Red
Programme: 16 pages, 10p
Midweek games: Tuesday/Wednesday
Year formed: 1933 (Briggs Sports FC) Almagated 1958
Nickname: Motormen
Previous Grounds: Victoria Road (Now Dagenham FC)
Major Honours: FA Amaetur Cup Semi-Finalists 1954. London Senior Cup 55/6, 56/7. Essex Senior Cup 39/40, 49/50, 50/51, 51/52. Spartan Lge 49/50, 50/51, 55/6, 56/7, 57/8, London Lge 36/37, 38/39, Essex Elizabethan 59/60, 60/61. 70/71. Greater London Lge 70/71. Essex Sen. Lge Cup. 85/86. Essex Sen. Lge Sportsmanship Trophy 77/78, 79/80, 80/81.
Clubhouse details: Every evening. Mid-day at weekends also.

HALSTEAD TOWN

Chairman:
Manager: Barry Archer
Secretary: Mrs. C. White
44 Beridge Road, Halstead. Tel. No. 0787 475037
Address & Tel. No of ground: Rosemary Lane, Halstead. Tel. No. 0787 472082
Simple ground directions: A131 from South into Halstead. Rosemary Lane is left turning at bottom of hill entering town. 311 Bus from Braintree (BR)
Capacity: 2,500 **Covered accommodation:** Yes **Seating:** 500 **Floodlights:** No
Clubhouse: Yes **Programme:** Yes
Club colours: Green & Black **Change colours:** White
Previous Leagues: Essex and Suffolk Border

MALDON TOWN

Chairman:
Secretary: J.C. Spence
66 Gloucester Avenue, Maldon, Essex CM9 6LA
Tel: 0621 54543
Address & Tel No of grounds: Fombridge Road, Maldon. Tel. No. 0621 53762
Simple ground directions: ½ mile South of Town on East side of Fombridge Road.
Capacity: **Covered accommodation:** Yes **Seating:** Yes Floodlights: No
Colour colours: Blue & White Hoops **Change colours:** Yellow & Emerald
Clubhouse: Yes **Programme:** Yes
Honours/Previous Leagues: Essex & Suffolk Border. Eastern Counties.

PURFLEET

Chairman: H. South
Manager: Tommy South
Secretary: Norman Posner
1 Chase House Gardens, Hornchurch.
Tel. No. Hornchurch 58301
Address & Tel. No of grounds: Essex Sports Leisure Centre, Ship Lane, Aveley. Tel. No. Purfleet 868901
Simple ground directions: M25 or A13 to Dartford Tunnel Roundabout. Ground is 50 yds on right down Ship Lane.
Capacity: 1,500 **Stand:** No **Midweek Games:** Tuesday **Floodlights:** No
Club colours: Green with Yellow trim **Change colours:** Blue with Yellow trim
Record Attendance: 49 **Programme:** 12 pages. incl. with Admission
Programme Editor: Bob Andrews. Tel. No. Grays Thurrock 376602
Clubhouse: Yes. 7 days a week

SAWBRIDGEWORTH TOWN

Chairman: Mike Lennard
Manager: Barry Crouch
Secretary: David Pask
16 Gilders, Sawbridgeworth, Herts, CM21 0EF
Address & Tel. No. of grounds: Crofters End, West Road, Sawbridgeworth. Tel. No. 0279 722039
Simple ground directions: ¾ mile from Station. Up Station Road then West Road.
Club colours: All Red **Change colours:** Blue
Capacity: **Stand:** Yes **Floodlights:** No
Year formed: 1890 **Midweek Games:** Tuesday
Programme: 15 pages inclusive admission **Programme Editor:** Ron Alder Tel. No. 0279 722360
Nickname: Robins **Previous Leagues:** Essex Olympian League
Previous Grounds: Hyde Hall, Pishiobury, Hand & Crown
Clubhouse details: Tuesday/Thursday evenings

SOUTHEND MANOR

Chairman: Malcolm Frost
Manager: John Welbourn
Physiotherapist: Colin Lee
Secretary: Lester Medcalf
30 Mallard Place, East Grinstead
Address & Tel. No of grounds: Southchurch Park Arena, Lifstan Way, Southend-on-Sea. Tel. No. 0702 610111. *The Ground is also the home of Southend Athletic Club and the park containing the ground is where Essex play Championship Cricket in Southend.*
Simple ground directions: A127, then A1159, turn left at first roundabout and keep going for ¾ mile, ground on left near sea front.
Capacity: Approx. 2,000 **Stand:** About 500 **Floodlights:** Yes
Club colours: Yellow Shirts, Black Shorts & Socks **Change colours:** All Blue
Year formed: 1955 **Record attendance:** 225 (v Stambridge)
Midweek games: Wednesday **Programme:** 40-45 pages: 50p (also incl. admission)
Programme Editor: Margaret Errington Tel. No. 0702 613713
Nickname: The Manor **Senior Honours:** Not a Senior Club
Previous grounds: Victory Sports Ground
Previous Leagues: Southend Borough Combination and Southend & District Alliance

STAMBRIDGE

Chairman:
Secretary: A. Hines
62 Earlshall Avenue, Prittlewell, Southend-on-Sea
Tel. No. 0702 330534
Address & Tel. No of grounds: Memorial Ground, Rochford Road, Great Stambridge.
Simple ground directions: 3 miles from Rochford BR Station. Buses 10, 12 & 13 from Southend and Rochford.
Capacity: – **Covered accommodation:** – **Seating:** – **Floodlights:** No
Clubhouse: Yes Programme: Yes
Club colours: Gold & Black **Change colours:** Red
Previous Leagues: Southern Alliance. Southend & District

STANSTEAD

Chairman: T. Shoebridge
Manager: Keith Woods
Physiotherapist: Peter Fox
Secretary: P.A.G. Heal
28 Mountfitchey Road, Stansted, Essex
Address & Tel. No of grounds: Hargrave Sports Ground. Tel. No. 0279 812053
Simple ground directions: B1383 3 miles North of Bishops Stortford, Cambridge Road.
Capacity: 2,000 **Stand:** 200 **Floodlights:** Yes
Club colours: Royal Blue Shirts, White Shorts **Change colours:** Red or White Shirts
Year formed: 1900 **Nickname:** None
Programme: 8 pages, 20p **Clubhouse details:** 1980
Programme Editor: Ken Turner. 0279 812170
Previous Grounds: Greens Meadow, Chapel Hill, Stansted
Previous Leagues: Spartan League, London League, Herts County League.
Major Honours: F.A. Vase Winners 1983/84. Essex Senior League Cup 1983/84, East Anglian Cup 1983/84. Courage Eastern Floodlight Comp. 1983/84. Harry Fisher Cup 1982/83, 1984/85.

WITHAM TOWN

Chairman: S. Kelly
Manager: A. Wenborn
Physiotherapist: A. McCulloch
Secretary: A. Dowdall
19 Cross Road, Witham.
Address & Tel. No of grounds: Spa Road, Witham. Tel. No. 515945
Simple ground directions: From Witham Station (BR) walk through Public House Car Park. Follow road marked Faulkbourne. At mini roundabout turn left, Ground is on right hand side.
Capacity: 2,000 **Stand:** 100 **Floodlights:** Yes
Club colours: Red & Black **Change colours:** Blue
Programme: 12 pages. 20p. **Programme Editor:** R. Thompson. Tel. 0621 58303
Year formed: 1947 Nickname: The Town
Previous grounds: The Rank, Maldon Road, Witham **Midweek games:** Tuesday
Clubhouse details: 7 days a week, 7-11 p.m. and Sat. & Sun. Lunchtimes 12-2 p.m.
Major Honours: Essex Senior League Champions. Essex Senior Trophy Winners 1985/86. Essex Senior League Champions 1971/72.
Previous Leagues: Mid Essex. Essex & Suffolk Border.

ESSEX SENIOR LEAGUE – PAST CHAMPIONS

Max Pts	Season	1st	2nd	3rd	4th
32	1971/72	25 Witham T.	24 Billericay T.	21 Pagasus Ath.	19 Teptree Utd.
36	1972/73	31 Billaricay	26 Basildon Utd.	21 Stanstead	20 Brightlingsea Utd
36	1973/74	31 Saffran Walden T.	29 Billericay T.	27 Coggeshall T.	24 Tiptree Und
56	1974/75	45 Billericay T.	39 Basildon Utd.	37 Coggeshall T.	35 Bowers Und.
64	1976/77	55 Basildon Utd.	53 Brentwood	51 Billericay T.	44 Brightlingsea Utd.
60	1977/78	54 Basildon Utd.	49 Tiptree Utd.	39 Ford Utd.	36 Brentwood*
64	1978/79	57 Basildon Utd.	52 Canvey Is.	44 Eton Manor	43 Heybridge Sw.
60	1979/80	53 Basildon Utd.	41 Wivenhoe T	39 Canvey Is.	38 Witham T.
64	1980/81	52 Bowers Utd.	47 Heybridge Sw.	45 Wevenhoe T.	41 Canvey Is.
64	1981/82	56 Heybridge Sw.	44 Wivenhoe T.	43 Brentwood	40 Bowers Utd.
64	1982/83	53 Heybridge Sw.	51 Stansted	50 Halstead T.	42 Bowers Utd.
64	1983/84	57 Heybridge Sw	44 Bowers Utd.	42 Witham T.	40 Stansted
90	1984/85	64 Maldon T.*	64 Witham T.	62 Stansted	58 Wivenhoe T.
96	1985/86	77 Witham T.	62 Wivenhoe T.	61 Ford Utd.	60 Maldon T.

*Goal average 1 difference

LONDON SPARTAN FOOTBALL LEAGUE

Chairman: B. Stallard, Esq. L.F.A.

Hon. Secretary: D. Cordell, 44 Greenleas, Waltham Abbey, Essex EN9 1SZ

Tel: Lea Valley (0992) 712428

COLLIER ROW MOVE UP A LEAGUE

The London Spartan Leagues 90th Season came to a close with Collier Row winning the League Championship in the most closely fought contest for many years. Only one point finally separated them from Yeading with Redhill in third place.

The prize for the champions was a place in the Vauxhall Opel League Division Two North, only a few years ago Collier Row were playing intermediate football in the league. Since then they have slowly moved up the divisions, had two successful seasons in the F.A. Vase, were League Champions in 1983/4, Runners-up in 1984/85. They have been good ambasadors for the League and the League wish them well.

Yeading nevertheless won the League Cup beating Waltham Abbey in the final. No doubt Yeading will feel sorry in not clinching the top spot after being leaders for so long. Yeading like Collier Row have progressed from intermediate football to the part of the League in a short period and will be pressing for the top spot again next season.

A couple of seasons ago the League accepted Corinthian Casuals into the Premier Division when they suddenly found themselves no longer members of the Isthmian League. Unfortunately they were relegated last season but this coming season they will be back in the Premier Division. In becoming Champions of Division One it is believed that broke a record that had stood for 104 years, they had never won a Championship before!

The runners up in Division Two was yet another club who only just received senior status, Southgate Athletic. The League can rightly be proud of its record of encouraging so many intermediate clubs in gaining senior status. The list is quite impressive with Welling United being the latest club to go forward from this League and after a few years in the Southern League now move on to the Alliance League.

The reorganisation of Division One has come about by the expansion of the Vauxhall Opel League coupled with the fact that intermediate clubs obtaining senior status have not kept pace with the movements out of the League. In this respect the League has to report the loss of Thatcham Town to the newly formed Wessex League which is not within the Pyramid System. Thatcham Town had applied to the Vauxhall Opel League for consideration under the Pyramid System but on finding that they would not finish in the top three decided that the Pyramid was not for them. Further down the League the three lower divisions have also been reorganised this time into two divisions. There will be more league matches which will eliminate the use of subsidiary competitions which often meant teams playing each other too many times.

B. Stallard

PAST CHAMPIONS

Max Pts	Season	1st	2nd	3rd	4th
60	1975/76	49 Farnborough T*	49 Bracknell T	46 Alma Swanley	40 Swanley T.
60	1976/77	49 Cray W	45 Alma Swanley	38 East Ham U.	37 Chingford
60	1977/78	47 Cray W.	44 Banstead Ath.	41 Alma Swanley	38 East Ham U.
68	1978/79	55 Swanley	47 Fisher Ath.	44 Merstham*	44 Bracknall T.
60	1979/80	45 Berkhamstd T	44 Amersham T	43 Merstham	38 Malden Vale
60	1980/81	47 Fisher Ath.	43 Malden Vale	40 Whyteleafe	36 Greenwch B
52	1981/82	41 Fisher Ath.	35 Bracknell T.	32 Merstham*	32 Malden Vale
48	1982/83	40 Bracknell T.	35 Swanley T*	35 Greenwch B	32 Malden Vale
56	1983/84	46 Collier Row	43 Malden Vale*	43 Brimsdwn R.	37 Bracknell T
60	1985/86	51 Collier Row	50 Yeading	49 Redhill	41 Thatcham T

PREMIER DIVISION

	P	W	D	L	F	A	Pt
1 Collier Row	30	24	3	3	79	27	51
2 Yeading	30	24	2	4	80	16	50
3 Redhill	29	22	3	4	57	19	*49
4 Thatcham Town	30	18	5	7	57	36	41
5 Brimsdown Rov	30	15	6	9	56	38	36
6 Beaconsfield	30	13	6	11	45	44	32
7 Edgware	29	11	6	12	40	37	28
8 Northwood	30	9	10	11	42	44	28
9 Hanwell Town	30	10	6	14	44	50	26
10 Waltham Abbey	30	9	7	14	44	44	25
11 Crown & Manor	30	8	9	13	40	53	25
12 Danson	30	8	7	15	42	53	23
13 Beckton Utd.	30	7	7	16	28	52	21
14 Pennant	30	8	3	19	30	66	19
15 Amersham Town	30	4	7	19	29	85	15
16 Swanley Town	30	2	7	21	31	90	11

*Two points awarded in unplayed match v Edgware.

SENIOR DIVISION

1Cor Casuals	24	17	4	3	45	26	38
2 Southgate Ath	24	14	5	5	50	27	33
3 Brob Barnet	24	11	8	5	43	24	30
4 Catford Wands	24	12	6	6	36	24	30
5 Barkingside	24	11	6	7	39	26	28
6 Penhill Stand	24	10	7	7	43	37	27
7 Wandsworth	24	10	6	8	50	33	26
8 Ulysses	24	12	2	10	52	41	26
9 Nrt Greenford	24	8	6	10	41	37	22
10 Southwark Spt	24	9	2	13	34	47	20
11 Brent	24	4	8	12	29	48	16
12 Chingford	24	4	7	13	37	50	15
13 Royal Arsenal	24	0	1	23	13	92	1

PREMIER DIVISION 1985/86

	1	2	3	4	5	6	7	8	9	10	11	12	13	14	15	16
1 Amersham Town	–	0-4	0-1	1-1	1-2	2-2	0-0	0-3	4-2	1-4	2-3	0-3	1-1	1-3	0-0	0-7
2 Beaconsfield Und.	0-1	–	1-0	2-2	1-2	0-3	0-0	0-0	1-3	1-1	2-1	0-1	6-2	2-1	2-1	1-0
3 Beckton Und.	4-2	0-2	–	0-3	1-3	1-1	1-1	1-0	1-2	1-1	1-0	0-3	1-1	0-4	2-0	0-2
4 Brimsdown Rov.	4-2	1-2	2-0	–	1-2	1-0	2-1	0-2	2-2	3-0	3-1	2-0	6-2	0-0	3-1	0-3
5 Collier Row	5-1	0-1	3-1	4-2	–	2-1	3-0	1-0	3-0	4-1	6-0	2-1	1-1	2-0	5-0	3-1
6 Crown & Manor	4-0	0-0	2-2	1-4	0-3	–	1-2	2-1	2-0	1-4	1-1	0-1	0-0	1-0	0-0	2-3
7 Danson	4-2	3-2	2-0	0-1	1-2	7-3	–	1-1	1-1	4-4	1-0	1-2	2-0	1-3	0-2	0-1
8 Edgware	5-1	1-2	0-1	0-2	0-4	2-1	2-0	–	1-1	1-1	2-0	0-2	2-1	1-1	2-1	4-2
9 Hanwell Town	3-1	1-2	1-2	2-1	3-1	1-1	2-3	1-3	–	2-0	3-0	0-1	2-1	0-1	5-1	0-3
10 Northwood	1-2	2-1	2-2	0-0	1-3	0-1	3-2	2-4	2-0	–	0-0	0-1	6-0	0-5	1-0	0-1
11 Pennant	1-2	2-1	1-0	1-1	2-4	3-1	2-1	3-4	2-0	0-2	–	0-2	1-0	2-4	1-2	0-1
12 Redhill	0-0	7-0	3-0	3-2	1-0	3-2	1-0	*	1-1	1-0	3-0	–	5-1	1-2	2-1	1-0
13 Swanley Town	1-1	2-6	2-2	2-4	2-3	1-2	2-1	2-0	1-4	2-2	0-2	1-5	–	1-4	0-2	1-2
14 Thatcham Town	5-0	1-0	3-2	2-1	0-3	0-2	4-2	2-1	3-1	0-0	5-1	1-1	7-0	–	1-0	1-5
15 Waltham Abbey	6-0	2-2	2-1	1-2	0-2	1-1	6-1	1-1	1-1	1-1	2-0	1-2	6-1	3-2	–	0-1
16 Yeading	6-1	4-1	3-0	1-0	1-1	8-2	0-0	1-0	4-0	0-1	7-0	2-0	4-0	2-0	2-0	–

*Match awarded to Redhill

LEAGUE CUP 1985/86

1st Round

Waltham Abbey	(bye)		
Chingford	2	Beckton Utd	0
Cor Casuals	3	Penhill Stand	0
South Wark Spts	0	Beaconsfield	4
Thatcham Town	(Bye)		
Royal Arsenal	0	Collier Row	5
Barkingside	0, 0,	Hanwell Town	0, 3
Danson	1	Dennant	2
Edgware	(Bye)		
North Greenford	6	Amersham Town	0
Wandsworth	0	Catford Wands	3
Northwood	1	Brob Barnet	0
Ulysses	3	Swanley Town	1
Southgate Atu	2	Brent	1
Brimsdown Row	1	Redhill	2
Crown Manor	1	Yeading +	3

+ Home Team * After extra time

2nd Round

Waltham Abbey	1	Chingford +	0
Cor Casuals	2	Beaconsfield	1
Thatcham Town	1	Collier Row	3
Hanwell Town	3	Pennant	0
Edgware	0*, 2	North Greenford	0*, 1
Catford Wands	3	Northwood	5
Ulysses	0	Southgate Ath	2
Redhill	1	Yeading	2

3rd Round

Waltham Abbey	2	Cor Casuals	1
Collier Row	6	Hanwell Town	1
Edgware	0*	Northwood	1*
Southgate Ath	2*, 0	Yeading	2*, 3

Semi Finals

Waltham Abbey	0*, 2	Collier Row	0*, 1
Northwood	1	Yeading	6

Final

Waltham Abbey	2*	Yeading	3*

(At Redhill F.C.)

HARRY SUNDERLAND SHIELD SEASON 1985/86

	P	W	D	L	F	A	Pts
Group B							
1 N. Greenford	4	4	0	0	17	2	8
2 Southgate	4	1	1	2	5	4	3
3 Royal Arsenal	4	0	1	3	1	17	1
Group D							
1 Brob Barnet	4	3	1	0	9	2	7
2 Chingford	4	1	1	2	4	6	3
3 Catford	4	1	0	3	5	10	2
Group C							
1 Barkingside	4	1	3	0	5	4	5
2 Penhill	4	1	2	1	4	4	4
3 Cor Casuals	4	1	1	2	4	5	3
Group A							
1 Brent	4	2	1	1	8	6	5
2 Southwark	4	2	0	2	7	8	4
3 Wandsworth	4	1	1	2	4	5	3

Semi Finals

North Greenford	7	Brob Barnet	0
Barkingside	0*	Brent	0*

(Brent won 10-9 on Pens)

Final

North Greenford	2	Brent	0

(At Hanwell Town F.C.)

AMERSHAM TOWN

Chairman: H. King **Manager:** D. Holland **Asst. Manager:** G. Inks
Secretary: R. K. Leigh, 17 Piggotts End, Amersham, Bucks HP7 0JF. (7579 (H), 21905 (B))
Ground Address & Tel No: Spratley's Meadow, School Lane, Amersham. (7428)
Directions to Ground: A413 to B oadway, right into Church Street, first left into School Lane; ground situated on left 200 y rds past school.
Previous Leagues: Hellenic **Colours:** Black & White Stripes/Black **Change colours:** Tang./Black
Clubhouse: Clubroom, players lounge, bar kitchen, boardroom **Floodlights:** Yes **Seating:** 150

BARKINGSIDE

Chairman: J. F. Hooper **Manager:** R. Barnaby **Asst. Manager:** L. Nunn
Secretary: N. A. Ingram, 45 Cheneys Road, Leytonstone, London E11 3LL (01-455 1447 (H) 01-247 5422 (B)
Ground Address & Tel No: Oakside, Station Road, Barkingside, Ilford, Essex (01-550 3611)
Directions to Ground: From London A12 to Green Gate, left into Hurnes Road, Barkingside; right into Craven Gardens; right again into Carlton Drive leading to Station Road
Previous Leagues: Ilford & District, Metropolitan, Greater London
Colours: Sky Blue with Dark Blue Strip/Navy/Sky blue **Change colours:** Red/Navy/Red
Clubhouse: Open matches, Functions, Training nights **Floodlights:** No **Seating: 50** **Capacity:** 2,500

BEACONSFIELD UNITED

Chairman: D. J. Piercy **Manager:** Ian Bradley **Asst. Manager:** Brian Blackburn
Secretary: 37 Malthouse Square, Beaconsfield, Bucks HP9 2LE. (04946 71507 (H))
Ground Address & Tel No: Hollowways Park, Slough Road, Beaconsfield. (04946 6868)
Directions to Ground: M40 (Jn 2), 1st exit to A355, Club 100 yds on right
Previous Leagues: Wycombe & District
Colours: Royal Blue/White/Blue **Change colours:** Orange/Black/Orange
Clubhouse: Bar, Committee Room, Hall, Kitchen, Changing Room **Floodlights:** No **Capacity:** 2,000

BRIMSDOWN ROVERS

Chairman: G. Dodd **Manager:** P. Anglis **Asst. Manager:** P. Maybury
Secretary: G. Dodd, 57 Roundmoor Drive, Cheshunt, Herts EN8 9HU. (0992 26820 (H), 01-529 7041 (B)
Ground Address & Tel No: Brimsdown Sports & Social Club, Golddown Road, Enfield, Middlesex. (01-804 5491)
Direction to Ground: BR from Liverpool Street. By road off Green Street, itself off Hertford Road
Previous Leagues: Northern Suburban
Colours: Black & White Stripes/Black/Black **Change colours:** All yellow
Clubhouse: Large lounge and main clubroom, games room & stage with 3 bars (300 capacity) **Floodlights:** No **Capacity:** 50

CHINGFORD

Chairman: J. Hobley **Manager:** C. Davis **Asst. Manager:** M. Stannard
Secretary: W. W. Forbes, 12 Durbin House, 440 Fore Street, London N9 (01-807 3467 (H))
Ground Address & Tel No: Chingdale Road, Chingford Hatch (01-529 0485)
Directions to Ground: Turn into Chingford Lane from A11; ground at bottom of hill, turn into Chingford Mount Road from A406, Ground at Chingford Hatch
Previous Leagues: None **Colours:** All Red **Change colours:** All Blue
Clubhouse: Bar, Canteen, accommodation for 120 **Floodlights:** No **Seating:** 18 **Capacity:** 5,000

CORINTHIAN CASUALS

President: Sir Maurice Coop
Chairman: G. D. Harvey **Manager:** J. Langford **Asst. Manager:** R. Langford
Secretary (General): B. Neenan, 77 Somerset Avenue, Chessington, Surrey. (01-3975995)
Ground Address & Tel No: Wimbledon Park Stadium, Wimbledon Park Road, Wimbledon, London SW 19
Directions to Ground: 5 minutes walk from Southfields Tube Station
Previous League: Isthmian **Colours:** White/Navy/White **Change colours:** All Yellow
Clubhouse: None **Floodlights:** No **Seating:** 500 **Capacity:** 4,500

CROWN & MANOR

Chairman: H. Morris **Manager:** J. Collins **Asst. Manager:** D. Tekell
Secretary: W. J. Vincent, 38 Windsor House, Wenlock Road, London N1 (01-253 1659 (H))
Ground Address & Tel No: Turkey Street, Enfield
Directions to Ground: North Circular Road to Gt. Cambridge Street, pass Enfield Crematorium; 1st left Turkey Street
Previous Leagues: Parthenon **Colours:** Red & Black **Change colours:** Blue
Clubhouse: **Floodlights:** No **Seating:** **Capacity:**

DANSON (Bexley Borough)

President: E. G. White
Manager: J. C. Challow
Secretary: A. H. Nicholls, 16 Blackthorn Grove, Bexleyheath, Kent. (01-304 3121 (H), 01-640 0101 (B)
Ground Address & Tel No: Crook Log, Brampton Road, Bexleyheath, Kent. (01-303 6052)
Directions to Ground: None listed
Previous Leagues: S.E. London Amateur
Colours: Sky Blue & Black/Sky Blue/Sky Blue **Change colours:** All Red
Clubhouse: Tea bar, games room **Floodlights:** No **Seating:** 80 **Capacity:** 3,000

EDGWARE

Chairman: J. E. Cook **Manager:** B. Rider
Secretary: T. J. Higgins, 34 Francis Road, Harrow, Middlesex HA1 2QX (01-863 4022 (H))
Ground Address & Tel No: White Lion Ground, High Street, Edgware, Middx. (01-952 6799)
Directions to Ground: Edgware Station (LT) turn left to traffic lights, left again, ground on right hand side
Previous Leagues: Athenian, Corinthian **Colours:** Green/Black/Green **Change colours:** Green/Black/Black
Clubhouse: Dance hall, back bar, pool, darts, etc. **Floodlights:** Yes **Seating:** 250 **Capacity:** 3,000

HANWELL TOWN

Chairman: P. S. Kelso **Manager:** D. Finn **Asst. Manager:** R. Nairn
Secretary: R. Walker, 3 Dryden Avenue, Hanwell, London W7. (01-567 8487 (H)
Ground Address & Tel No: Reynolds Field, Perivale Lane, Perivale, Greenford, Middx
Directions to Ground: On South side of Western Avenue (A20) past Hoover Factory
Previous Leagues: Middx League, Middx County **Colours:** White/Blue trim
Change colours: All Blue/White trim **Floodlights:** No **Capacity:** Not listed
Clubhouse: Clubroom, bar, dressing rooms, toilets, etc.

NORTHWOOD

Chairman: A. Johnson **Manager:** P. M. Coburn
Secretary: Mrs. B. Walley, 8 Chamberlain Lane, Pinner, Middx. (01-866 2649)
Ground Address & Tel No: Chestnut Avenue, Northwood (0927-427148)
Directions to Ground: A404 (Pinner—Rickmansworth). Chestnut Avenue on left before large bridge ¼ mile beyond Northwood Hills roundabout
Previous Leagues: Harrow & Wembley, Middlesex, Hellenic **Colours:** All Red **Change colours:** All White
Clubhouse: Being rebuilt after fire at cost of £170,000, Ready Oct. 1985
Floodlights: Yes **Seating:** 30 **Capacity:** 1,500

PENHILL STANDARD

Chairman: A. Chambers **Manager:** R. Williams **Asst. Manager:** V. Williams
Secretary: E. Batty, 11 Dunstable Court, St. John's Park, Blackheath, London SE13 7TN
Ground Address & Tel No: Rochester Way Sports Ground, Eltham, London SE9 (01-858 9492 (H))
Directions to Ground: Near 'Dover Patrol' Public House, Rochester Way, Eltham
Previous Leagues: Metropolitan Sunday
Colours: Sky-Blue & White Stripes/Black/Black **Change colours:** Yellow/Sky Blue/White
Clubhouse: No **Floodlights:** No **Seating:** **Capacity:**

REDHILL

Chairman: J. Denham **Manager:** Martin Eede **Asst. Manager:** J. Corner
Secretary: Dr. B. S. Thomas, Surrey View, The Green, Godstone, Surrey RH9 8DY. (0883-842502 (H))
Ground Address & Tel No: Kilnbrow, Three Arch Road, Redhill Surrey (01-242 0200 (W)) (Redhill 62926)
Directions to Ground: Off A23 Brighton Road south side of Redhill Station, buses 405, 411, 435 pass ground
Previous Leagues: Athenian **Colours:** All Red **Change colours:** All Yellow
Clubhouse: Temporary Portacabin **Floodlights:** Yes **Seating:** 100 **Capacity:** 3,000

SOUTHGATE ATHLETIC

Chairman: B. Nicholls **Manager:** A. Field **Asst. Manager:** R. Keough
Secretary: K. P. Cullen, 39 Hill Rise, Potters Bar (0707 56136 & 0279 26862)
Ground Address & Tel No: Tottenhall Road Sports Ground, Tottenhall Road, Palmers Green, London N13 (01-888 1542)
Directions to Ground: Off North Circular Road going West into Chequers Way by Metal Box Factory. Proceed to top of Road. Ground entrance is by junction with Tottenhall Road
Previous Leagues: Northern Suburban **Colours:** Amber/Black **Change colours:** All Navy
Clubhouse: Club Room & Licenced Bar **Floodlights:** No **Seating:** No **Capacity:** Not Known

ULYSSES

Chairman: A. McTaggart **Manager:** **Asst. Manager:**
Secretary: P. A. Bailes, 33 Kenley Road, Merton Park
Ground Address & Tel No: University of London SW19 3JJ (01-542 4333 & 581 6905), London Athletic, Motspur Park, New Malden, Surrey (01-942 1161)
Directions to Ground: A3 Kingston By-Pass to Malden roundabout underpass, left into Malden Road, after 400 metres left into Motspur Park Road
Previous Leagues: None
Colours: Purple/White/Purple **Change colours:** Red or Yellow or White or Light Blue/White/Purple or White
Clubhouse: None **Floodlights:** No **Seating:** 250 **Capacity:** 250

YEADING

Chairman: P. Spurden **Manager:** R. Gritt
Secretary: P. Bickers, 120 Cranbourne Way, Hayes, Middlesex (01-8480669)
Ground Address & Tel No: Beaconsfield Road, Hayes, Middx. (01-848 7362)
Directions to Ground: Uxbridge Road, seek Hayes Gatehouse near Southall Tax Office Beaconsfield Road
Previous Leagues: SW Middlesex, Middlesex **Colours:** Red/Black **Change colours:** White/Black
Clubhouse: Yes, good **Floodlights:** Yes **Seating:** 100 **Capacity:** Not listed

Alan Whittle (ex Everton and Crystal Palace) scores for Corinthian Casuals in a London Spartan League Cup tie.
Photo: D. West

The impressive Pavilion/Stand is in the background as Hanwell attack during their 2-0 home victory over Northwood.

BENSKINS SOUTH MIDLANDS FOOTBALL LEAGUE

Hon Secretary and Treasurer: Clive Moyse, 33 Markham Crescent, Dunstable, Beds LU5 4SS. Tel: 0582 64682

REVIEW OF SEASON 1985-86

"A very competitive Premier Division campaign culminated in Selby winning the title for the first time after a hectic final run-in. They just edged out Welwyn Garden City with Leighton Town finishing in third place. It was a tremendous season for St. Albans-based Selby who, as well as clinching the Premier title also won the Herts. Senior Centenary Trophy defeating league rivals Hoddesdon Town in the final at Ware. Selby and Hoddesdon also met in the two legged Challenge Trophy final. Selby won the first leg 3-1 but Hoddesdon levelled matters with a victory by the same scoreline at home. In an eventful replay at Welwyn Garden City Hoddesdon deprived Selby of a treble by winning 3-1 for their first trophy win in the Benskins South Midlands League. Newcomers Cranfield Utd., Langford and Milton Keynes Borough all struggled to hold on to their Premier status and Langford in fact only escaped relegation because only one team qualified for promotion from Division One. Cranfield did better in the Cove Windows trophy by reaching the final but lost after a replay to Eaton Bray who thus redeemed a mediocre Season by their recent standards.

Newcomers Buckingham Athletic were the champions of Division One but were unable to take their place in the top flight as their facilities are not yet of an acceptable standard. In second place were Totternhoe who will be promoted back to the Premier Division where they last competed in Season 1974/75. Harpenden Town and Pitstone & Ivinghoe enjoyed better form and will be looking to be among the honours next Season. In the O'Brien Trophy Ickleford earned the distinction of reaching the final despite having to apply for re-election to the League. In the Final at Langford Welwyn Garden United just edged the game by winning 2-1.

The Second year of Benskins sponsorship has now been completed and the regular monthly award winners were pleased to receive their various prizes. Cove Windows and O'Brien Butchers are continuing to sponsor their respective Cup Competitions and Charlie O'Brien is also sponsoring a League Review to be published in August by Paul Gardner.

Next Season three more Clubs will be joining Hoddesdon Town by having the use of floodlights and two more are hopeful of joining them during the Season.

As part of the Isthmian Pyramid the League is hoping to play its part in enabling the movement of Clubs to be undertaken in an orderly fashion and the future is looked forward to with optimism.

PREMIER DIVISION	P	W	D	L	F	A	Pts
Selby	30	18	7	5	59	25	61
Welwyn Garden City	30	16	9	5	47	24	57
Leighton Town	30	16	5	9	39	28	53
The 61 FC (Luton)	30	14	10	6	44	31	52
Shefford Town	30	12	12	6	47	31	48
Knebworth	30	12	12	6	38	29	48
New Bradwell St. Peter	30	11	10	9	35	29	43
Eaton Bray United	30	10	11	9	44	35	41
Hoddesdon Town	30	11	7	12	34	37	40
Milton Keynes Borough	30	9	8	13	42	50	35
Pirton	30	8	10	12	43	41	34
Winslow United	30	9	7	14	34	52	34
Shillington	30	6	12	12	37	38	30
Cranfield United	30	7	7	16	41	61	28
Langford	30	8	4	18	30	66	28
Ashcroft Co-op.	30	5	5	20	29	66	20

DIVISION ONE	P	W	D	L	F	A	Pts
Buckingham Athletic	22	14	5	3	53	20	47
Totternhoe	22	14	5	3	44	21	47
Electrolux	22	11	8	3	58	23	41
Harpenden Town	22	12	2	8	44	36	38
Pitstone & Ivinghoe	22	10	7	5	41	20	37
Welwyn Garden United	22	8	9	5	31	28	33
Walden Rangers	22	6	7	9	31	38	25
Biggleswade Town	22	6	4	12	23	44	22
Brache Sparta	22	5	6	11	19	34	21
Sandy Albion	22	5	4	13	24	40	19
Ickleford	22	4	5	13	21	40	17
MK United	22	4	4	14	18	63	16

PREMIER DIVISION

Ashcroft Co- op		2-3	3-1	3-0	0-3	0-1	0-0	2-1	2-1	0-4	0-1	1-4	1-1	0-2	2-2	0-4
Cranfield Utd.	0-0		2-3	0-5	0-1	1-3	0-2	3-4	2-3	1-0	0-1	1-3	0-0	0-1	2-1	1-2
Eaton Bray Utd.	2-2	2-1		2-0	3-1	7-0	1-2	4-0	1-0	3-0	1-5	0-0	3-0	0-2	1-1	0-1
Hoddesdon Town	1-0	1-1	0-0		1-1	3-0	0-2	1-1	2-1	1-2	1-0	1-1	2-0	0-2	1-1	3-1
Knebworth	2-0	2-2	1-0	3-1		1-1	1-1	1-0	1-0	4-1	2-2	0-2	1-1	0-2	0-1	2-1
Langford	4-1	1-3	0-2	0-1	1-1		1-2	1-1	2-1	2-2	1-5	2-4	1-4	2-0	0-2	1-3
Leighton Town	3-1	1-2	2-0	0-1	1-2	2-0		1-0	0-0	2-1	2-1	2-1	1-0	0-1	0-0	0-1
Milton Keynes Bor.	2-0	3-1	1-1	0-1	1-1	2-0	2-0		1-1	2-6	1-2	1-0	4-1	1-1	4-2	1-2
New Bradwell St. Peter	1-0	3-2	1-1	0-0	0-0	3-0	2-3	2-0		2-1	0-0	0-2	1-1	0-1	4-0	2-2
Pirton	1-4	3-3	0-0	6-2	2-0	3-0	0-1	0-1	2-0		1-2	1-0	1-1	0-2	1-1	1-1
Selby	7-1	5-0	2-2	2-1	0-0	3-0	0-0	3-1	1-2	1-1		4-0	1-0	0-0	3-1	2-4
Shefford Town	5-2	2-2	2-2	1-0	1-1	1-2	2-1	3-1	0-0	0-0	0-1		3-2	0-0	5-1	0-0
Shillington	3-0	3-0	1-1	0-1	1-2	0-1	5-0	3-1	1-1	3-2	0-1	1-1		1-1	2-2	0-0
Welwyn Garden City	3-2	1-2	3-0	3-1	1-1	5-0	1-3	3-3	0-1	1-1	1-2	1-1	2-0		3-1	1-0
Winslow United	1-0	1-4	2-1	3-1	0-3	2-3	0-4	2-0	0-1	0-0	0-1	0-2	2-1	1-2		1-0
61 FC (Luton)	3-0	2-2	0-0	2-1	2-1	1-0	2-1	2-2	1-2	1-0	2-1	1-1	1-1	1-1	1-3	

1985-86 CHALLENGER TROPHY

FIRST ROUND

Electrolux v Leighton Town....................1-3
Ickleford v 61 FC (Luton)....................0-3
Ashcroft Co'Op v Agt. New Bradwell............2-1
Pitstone & Ivinghoe v Langford 3-1
Hoddesdon Town v MK United....................7-1
Welwyn GC v AET Shillington (Ineligible player)..2-1
Replay: Shillington v Welwyn GC...............0-3
Selby v Pirton................................3-1
Knebworth v Sandy Albion......................3-3
Replay: Sandy Albion v Knebworth..............0-3
Shefford Town v Walden Rgrs...................1-0
Brache Sparta v Harpenden Town................2-1
Winslow Utd v Biggleswade Town................4-0
M.K. Borough v Eaton bray..................... 3-4
Byes: Totternhoe, Cranfield Utd, Buckingham Ath & Welywyn Gdn Utd.

SECOND ROUND

Barche Sparta v Welwyn GC.....................0-3
Hoddesdon Town v Buckingham Ath...............4-0
Knebworth v Selby.............................0-1
Totternhoe v AET Ashcroft Co'Op...............0-0
Ashcroft Co'Op v Totternhoe...................0-4
Welwyn Gdn Utd v Shefford Town................2-4
61 FC (Luton) v Pitstone & Ivinghoe...........1-0
Leighton Town v Cranfield UTD.................2-3
Winslow Utd v Eaton Bray Utd..................2-3

THIRD ROUND

Hoddesdon Town v Welwyn GC....................2-1
Selby v AET Cranfield Utd.....................1-0
Totternhoe v 61 FC (Luton)....................2-1
Eaton Bray Utd v Shefford Town................0-1

SEMI FINALS

Totternhoe v Selby............................0-1
Hoddesdon v AET Shefford Town.................1-0

FINALS

1st Leg. Shelby v Hoddesdon Town..............3-1
2nd Leg. Hoddesdon Town v Selby...............3-1
Replay: Hoddesdon Town v Selby................3-1
(at Welwyn Garden City)

C & V E WINDOWS SML TROPHY 1985/86

FIRST ROUND

	1st Leg	2nd Leg	Age
61 FC v Pirton	3-0	0-0	3-2
Eaton Bray v Mk Borough	0-0	4-2	4-2
Ashcroft Co'Op v Cranfield	1-0	0-2	1-2
Winslow Utd v Shefford	0-2	0-3	0-5
Welwyn GC v Hoddesdon	3-0	0-0	3-0
Leighton v Langford	2-1	2-0	4-1
New Bradwell v Selby	0-0	0-1	0-1
Knebworth v Shilling	3-1	3-1	6-2

SECOND ROUND

Cranfield Utd v Knebworth.....................1-0
Eaton Bray Utd v Welwyn GC....................2-1
Leighton Town v AET Selby.....................3-4
Shefford Town v 61 FC (Luton).................2-1

SEMI FINALS

Cranfield Utd v Shefford Town.................1-0
Selby v Eaton Bray Utd........................0-3

FINAL

Cranfield Utd v AET Eaton Bray Utd............0-0
Replay:
Eaton Bray Utd v Cranfield Utd................1-0
(Both played at Leighton Town)

O'BRIEN BUTCHERS SML TROPHY

Group A
Winners Buckingham Athletic
Runners up Electrolux
Group B
Winners Ickleford
Runners up Welwyn Garden Utd
Semi Finals
Buckingham Ath 0 Welwyn Garden Utd 2
Ickleford 2 Electrolux 1 (AET
Final (At Langford)
Ickleford 1 Welwyn Garden United 2

Leading Goalscorers Season 1985-1986 (Lge Games only)

PREMIER DIVISION

D. Drewe (Milton Keynes Borough) 16, R. Vale (Langford) 16, P. Robinson (Selby) 14, S. McMellon (The 61 FC Luton) 13, T. Metcalfe (Pirton) 13, S. Lerwill (Selby) 12, A. Wood (New Bradwell St. Peter) 11, K. Stapleton (Cranfield United) 11, J. Balach (Winslow United) 11

DIVISION ONE

R. Singfield (Electrolux) 20, D. Rowe (Buckingham Ath.) 16, M. East (Buckingham Ath.) 10, C. Vinent (Sandy Albion) 10, V. Justin (Harpenden Town) 9, T. Stevens (Ickleford) 9, M. Southon (Pitstone & Ivinghoe) 9, D. Ewington (Walden Rangers) 9.

Main stand at Biggleswade Town F.C.

CRANFIELD UNITED

Chairman: M. Sadler **Manager:** M. Johnson
Secretary: T.E.L. Corkrey, 7 Plough Close, Cranfield, Beds. Tel: Bedford 750317 (H)
Ground Address & Tel. No: Crawley Road, Cranfield. Tel: 0582-85 2481 (B)
Directions to Ground: From M1 Juntion 13 through village towards North Crawley (and Newport Pagnell). Ground after last house on way from village.
Previous Leagues: Bedford & District **Colours:** Yellow/Black **Change colours: Sky Blue/Black**
Clubhouse: No details given **Floodlights:** No

EATON BRAY UNITED (1946)

Chairman: A. Fieldhouse **Manager:** J. Rogers
Secretary: Frank Ashton, 17 Tottenhoe Road, Eaton Bray, Dunstable, Beds. Tel: Eaton Bray 220132
Ground Address & Tel No: The Rye, Eaton Bray. Eaton Bray 221443
Directions to Ground: Leave Dunstable on Aylesbury road, turn right towards Totternhoe, follow signs to Eaton Bray
Previous Leagues: Luton & South Beds **Colours:** White/Blue/Red **Change colours:** All Blue
Programmes: 30 pages, 25p **Clubhouse:** Yes (Main bar, Snug bar, Kitchen, Dressing room) **Floodlights:** No **Seating:** 25

HODDESDON TOWN (1879)

Chairman: Elmer Elliott **Manager:** Terry Scales
Secretary: Dave Smith, 19 Nursery Gardens, Enfield, Middx. Tel. No. 01-804 3608
Address & Tel No. of ground: Lowfield, Parkview, Hoddesdon, Herts.
Simple ground directions: Broxbourne or Rye House Station, 392 bus to Hoddesdon High Street, 5 minute walk.
No. of seats: 250 **Floodlights:** Yes **Programme:** 24 pages, 15p
Club colours: White/Black. **Change colours:** All Yellow
Previous Leagues: East Herts, Herts County, Spartan, London Spartan, Athenian.
Clubhouse details: Open match days, training nights, and other functions

---

KNEBWORTH (1901)

Chairman: M.R. Thody **Manager:** Bob Boyden
Secretary: John Stevens, 12 Olden Mead, Letchworth, Herts. Tel: Letchworth 73735 (H) Hemel Hempstead 42281 x 66941 (B)
Ground Address & Tel. No: Old Knebworth Lane, Stevenage 313863
Directions to Ground: B197 to Roebuck Motel, Stevenage, Old Knebworth Lane opposite Motel. Ground entrance 150 yards on left
Previous Leagues: Herts County, North Herts **Colours:** Tangerine/Black **Change colours:** Sky Blue
Programmes: 4 pages, free **Clubhouse:** (Clubroom, bar, catering for 100+, Pool, Darts, TV) **Floodlights:** No
Seating: Yes

LANGFORD FOOTBALL CLUB

Chairman: E. Rutt **Secretary:** F.A. Woodward
Address & Tel. No. of Ground: Forde Park, Langford Road, Henlow. Tel. No. 0462 816106
Simple ground directions: On main A6001 Road between Langford and Henlow.
Capacity: 4,000 **Covered accommodation:** 150 **Seating:** 25
Floodlights: For 1986/87 season **Club colours:** All Red **Change colours:** All Blue
Clubhouse: Yes. Open Tues-Thurs-Sat-Sun. Extension planned for 1986/87.
Programme: 8 pages (inc. with admission)
Honours/Previous Leagues: S.M.L. Challenge Cup Winners 1973)74, 75/76. O'Brien S.M.L. Trophy Winners 1985/86. Bedford League. Beds Int. Cup Winners, North Beds Charity Cup Winners 69-70, 74/75. Hinchingbrooke Cup Winners (1)

LEIGHTON TOWN

Chairman: Mr. Bruce Warner **Secretary:** Mr. John Williams:
Address & Tel. No of grounds: Bell Close, Lake Street, Leighton Buzzard, Beds.
Capacity: 4,000 **Covered accommodation:** Yes **Seating:** Yes **Floodlights:** Yes
Simple ground directions: From Dunstable turn left off A5 to Stanbridge. Through Stanbridge to L. Buzzard. Ground behind Camden Motors.
Clubhouse: Yes **Club colours:** Red White Stripes, Red Shorts **Change colours:** Blue
Programme: Yes **Previous Leagues:** Beds Senior Cup 1966/7/8/9

MILTON KEYNES BOROUGH F.C. (1966)

Chairman: D. Hamilton **Manager:** E. Byrne
Secretary: A. Bond **Address & Tel No.** 89 Buckingham Road, Bletchley, Milton Keynes MK3 5HW. Milton Keynes 78398 (H) 0908 74811 (B)
Address & Tel. No of ground: Manor Fields, Bletchley, Mitlon Keynes.
Simple ground directions: On Watling Street (old A5), Fenny Stratford.
No. of seats: 200 **Floodlights:** Yes
Club colours: Sky Blue/Dark Blue Change colours: Green & Yellow stripes/Green/Yellow
Previous Leagues: United Counties, Hellenic. Programme: For special matches.
Clubhouse details: Bar open daily. Hall for club or private functions.

NEW BRADWELL ST. PETER (1902)

Chairman: G. Hall **Manager:** M. Burridge
Secretary: D. Ferguson, 178 Church Street, Wolverton, Milton Keynes MK12 5 JS. Tel: 0908 318009
Ground Address & Tel. No. Recreation Ground, Bradwell Road, New Bradwell, Milton Keynes 0908 313835
Directions to Ground: M1, Junction 14, go towards Newport Pagnell, left at 1st roundabout onto H3-A422 Monks Way, go 6 roundabouts, turn right onto V6 Grafton Street, 1st right then left, ground ½ mile on left.
Previous Leagues: North Bucks **Colours:** Claret & Blue/Sky Blue/Sky Blue **Change colours:** White/Black/White
Programmes: 12 pages, 25p **Clubhouse:** Yes **Floodlights:** No **Seating:** Yes

---

PIRTON

Chairman: Brian Britnell **Manager:** Tony Martin
Secretary: Bob Castle, 26 Crab Tree Lane, Pirton, Hitchin, Herts. **Asst. Manager:** S. Crosby
Ground Address & Tel. No: Walnut Tree Road, Pirton, Hitchin. 712531
Directions to Ground: From A6, through Barton and Shillington, from Hitchin, first right off Luton Road (A505)
Previous Leagues: North Herts, Herts Co. **Colours:** Yellow/Royal Blue/Royal Blue **Change colours:** All Red
Programmes: **Clubhouse:** Yes **Floodlights:** No **Capacity:** 1,000

SELBY

Chairman: K. O'Gorman **Manager:** G. Ellis
Secretary: R. Gwynn, 22 College Place, St. Albans. Tel: (38554)
Ground Address & Tel No: Toulmin Drive, New Greens Estate, St. Albans. St. Albans 52401
Directions to Ground: From A5 or A6 enter Batchwood Drive, enter Green Lane, first left into Toulmin Drive. Ground at end of Toulmin Drive (near Batchwood Golf Club)
Previous Leagues: Mid Herts, St. Albans **Colours:** Red/White/Red **Change colours:** Blue/White/Blue
Programmes: with admission, 50p **Clubhouse:** No **Floodlights:** No
Seating: 50 **Capacity:** 2,000

SHEFFORD TOWN (1948)

Chairman: C. Rockall **Manager:** R. Legate
Secretary: P. Ward, 7 George Street, Shefford SG17 5BP
Ground Address & Tel. No: Ivel Road, Shefford, Beds. Hitchin 813487
Directions to Ground: From Hitchin, turn left into Ivel Road at fire station. From Bedford, first right after traffic lights.
Previous Leagues: Parthenon, United Counties **Colours:** Sky Blue **Change colours:** Claret
Programmes: 8 pages, 20p **Clubhouse:** Yes **Floodlights:** No **Seating:** No

---

SHILLINGTON

Chairman: Stan Burgoine **Secretary:** Aubrey Cole
Address & Tel No. of ground: Playing Field, Greenfields, Shillington, Hitchin, Herts SG5 3NX. Hitchin 711757
Capacity: 800 **Covered accommodation:** Yes **Seating:** Yes **Floodlights:** No
Simple ground directions: Turn off A6 at Barton-Le-Clay. From Bedford or Hitchin turn off R.A.F. Henlow Camp.
Clubhouse: Yes **Club colours:** White **Change colours:** Red
Programme: Yes

TOTTERNHOE

Chairman: Mr. M.S. Stewart **Secretary:** Mr. J.D. Basterfield
Address & Tel. No. of ground: Totternhoe Recreation Ground.
Capacity: 1,000 **Covered accommodation:** 200 **Seating:** 30 **Floodlights:** No
Simple ground directions: Two miles west of Dunstable
Clubhouse: Situated adjacent to ground **Programme:** Yes
Club colours: Red Shirts, Shorts, Socks **Change colours:** Light blue shirts, Royal Blue Shorts & Socks
Previous Leagues: Luton & District League 1957/58 Winners, South Midlands League Division 1 Winners 1961/2, Runners Up 1968/9 & 1985/6. Beds Senior Cup Finalists 1969/70, Beds Intermediate Cup Winners 1977/8

WELWYN GARDEN CITY

Chairman: Mr. Dave Williams
Secretary: R.J. Dunning. Tel. 334536
Address & Tel. No of ground: Herns Lane, Welwyn Garden City, Herts. Tel. 328470
Capacity: 1,500 **Covered accommodation:** 120 **Seating:** 40 **Floodlights:** No
Simple ground directions: Club off B1000 Hertford to Welwyn Road. Adjacent to Panshanger Golf Course.
Clubhouse: Yes **Club colours:** All Maroon **Change colours:** Sky Blue **Programme:** Yes 16 pages
Major Honours: Herts Charity Shield 1927/28. Herts Senior Trophy 1984/85. South Midlands Premier 1973/74. South Midlands Div. 1 1981/82.
Previous Leagues: Spartan, Metropolitan, Greater London.

WINSLOW UNITED (1891)

Chairman: **Manager:** Dermot Callaghan
Secretary: C. Spencer, 4 Western Lane, Winslow, Buckingham (Winslow 4690)
Ground Address & Tel. No: Recreation Ground, Elmfields Gate. Winslow 3057.
Directions to Ground: Ground off High Street, turn right after pelican crossing from Aylesbury, turn left before pelican crossing from Buckingham.
Previous Leagues: North Bucks **Colours:** Yellow/Blue/Blue **Change colours:** Red/Black/Black
Programmes: 16 pages, 20p. **Clubhouse:** Bar open most evenings and Saturday and Sunday lunchtimes
Floodlights: No **Seating:** 25

THE 61 F.C. (LUTON)

Chairman: C. Everitt
Secretary: R. Everitt, 11 Chiltern Gardens, Luton. Tel. 508112
Ground Address & Tel. No.: Kingsway, Beverley Road, Luton. Tel. 582965
Capacity: — **Covered accommodation:** Yes **Seating:** 25 **Floodlights:** —
Simple ground directions: Situated on A5050 Luton, Dunstable Road. approx. 1½ miles from M1 Junction II.
Clubhouse: Yes, open 7 nights and Sat. & Sun lunchtime. **Programme:** Yes, 8 pages 20p
Club colours: Sky/Royal Blue. **Change colours:** Red/Black
Honours/Previous Leagues. Beds Senior Cup Winners 1984. Luton League. Hellenic League.
Metal Badge: Yes

A REVIEW OF NON-LEAGUE FOOTBALL IN HERTS

1986/87

(SIXTH EDITION)

ONLY

£1.00

INC P&P

Discounts on five or more copies

The book comprehensively covers football at all levels throughout the County and contains approx. 200 pages.

Now available from:—
Derek Fieldsend.
42 Rodney Crescent,
Hoddesdon,
Herts.
(0992) 443308

COPIES OF PREVIOUS EDITIONS ALSO AVAILABLE

HERTS SENIOR COUNTY LEAGUE

Founded 1898

Hon. General Secretary: Mr. E.H. Dear. Tel: Welwyn 5415
48 Wilshere Road, Welwyn, Herts AL6 9PX

SENIOR SECTION

Premier Division	P	W	D	L	F	A	Pts
1. Bedmond Special.	30	19	8	3	59	29	46
2. London Colney...	30	19	7	4	57	22	45
3. Wingate.........	30	20	2	8	71	39	42
4. Cockfosters......	30	16	5	9	46	32	37
5. Mount Grace Potters Bar........	30	13	9	8	45	32	35
6. St. Margaretsbury.	30	13	8	9	40	26	34
7. Sandridge Rovers.	30	15	4	11	52	42	34
8. Potters Bar Crusaders.........	30	13	6	11	48	37	42
9. Rolls Royce Engines	30	12	7	11	49	27	31
10. Bovingdon.......	30	10	8	12	35	38	28
11. Leavesden Hospital	30	11	4	15	42	53	26
12. Sun Sports.......	30	10	6	14	35	46	26
13. Leverstock Green.	30	8	7	15	39	53	23
14. B.A.C. Stevenage.	30	7	7	16	47	70	21
15. Oxhey Jets.......	30	5	4	21	27	78	14
16. Evergreen........	30	2	2	26	17	85	6

Division One	P	W	D	L	F	A	Pts
1. J & M Sports....	30	21	7	2	78	32	49
2. Park Street.......	30	18	4	8	83	48	40
3. Colney Heath....	30	18	4	8	70	43	40
4. Tudor Corinthians	30	14	8	8	58	44	36
5. Elliott Star.......	30	13	7	10	57	48	33
6. Welwyn.........	30	13	7	10	61	59	33
7. Walkern.........	30	12	9	9	58	56	33
8. Wormley Rovers..	30	14	4	12	57	43	32
9. Kings Langley....	30	10	10	10	49	39	30
10. Hatfield United...	30	12	6	12	58	57	30
11. Cuffley..........	30	9	9	12	50	55	27
12. Wellcome........	30	11	4	15	51	60	26
13. Sarratt..........	30	8	10	12	44	65	26
14. St. Ippolyts......	30	8	7	15	44	65	23
15. Harpenden Rovers	30	5	4	21	44	89	14
16. Chipperfield......	30	2	4	24	30	89	8

Division Two	P	W	D	L	F	A	Pts
1. Lucas Sports.....	26	19	4	3	79	31	42
2. Little Heath.....	26	15	8	3	61	30	38
3. I.C.L. Letchworth	26	16	3	7	54	30	35
4. Birtono Little Gaddesden...	26	12	7	7	61	45	31
5. DeHavilland Hatfield...........	26	14	3	9	44	31	31
6. Allenburys Sports.	26	12	6	8	37	28	30
7. Kimpton Rovers..	26	8	10	32	39	26	
8. Bushey Rangers...	26	9	7	10	39	36	25
9. Dynamic Hatfield	27	11	3	12	44	52	25
10. Welham Albion...	26	8	8	10	39	48	24
11. Rank Xerox......	26	7	10	9	38	49	24
12. Hemel Hempstead Rovers............	26	6	4	16	39	67	16
13. Radlett..........	26	4	2	20	35	71	10
14. Biggleswade Utd..	26	2	3	21	24	67	7

Heartiest congratulations are extended to the following clubs for their achievements:

Herts Senior County League Honours:

	Champions	Runners-Up
Senior Section		
Premier Division	Bedmond	London Colney
Division 1	J & M Sports	Park Street
Division 2	Lucas Sports	Little Heath
Reserve Section		
Division 1	Sandridge Rovers	Bedmond
Division 2	Elliott Star	Leavesden Hospital
Division 3	St. Ippolyts	Sarratt
Aubrey Cup Winners	Wingate	St. Margaretsbury
Reserve Cup Winners	Bedmond	Leavesden Hospital
Herts Intermediate Cup Winners	Tudor Corinthians	

B.A.C. (STEVENAGE)
Secretary: M. R. Swain, 12 Chiltern Place, Henlow, Beds. Tel: Hitchin 812840
Ground: Bragbury End, Stevenage, Herts. Tel: Stevenage 812985
Colours: Yellow/Green/Black **Change Colours:** Royal Blue

BEDMOND SOCIAL
Secretary: Mrs C. M. Sims, 18 Chiltern Avenue, Berkhamsted
Ground: Toms Lane, Bedmond, Herts. Tel: Kings Langley 67991
Colours: Red/Green **Change Colours:**

BOVINGDON
Secretary: R. Carter, 254 Galley Hall, Gadebridge, Hemel Hempstead HP1 3LP
Ground: Green Lane, Bovingdon, Herts. Hemel Hempstead 832 628
Colours: Green and White stripes/White/Green **Change Colours:** All Yellow

COCKFOSTERS
Secretary: R. Board, 6 Trent Gardens, Southgate, London N14 4PV. Tel: 01-440 8011
Ground: Dacre Field, Chalk Lane, Cockfosters. Tel: 01-449 5833
Colours: Red shirts, Red shorts **Change Colours:** White

LEAVESDEN HOSPITAL
Secretary: V. J. Collier, 177 Boundary Way, Watford, Herts. Tel: 0923 661293
Ground: Leavesden Hospital, Woodside Road, Garston
Colours: Black & White stripes/Black/Black **Change Colours:** Sky Blue

LEVERSTOCK GREEN
Secretary: K. Osbourne, 206 Windmill Road, Hemel Hempstead, Herts. Tel: Hemel Hempstead 57456
Ground: Pancake Lane, Leverstock Green
Colours: White shirts with Green trim/White/White **Change Colours:**

LONDON COLNEY
Secretary: Mrs E. J. A. Runchman, 95 White Horse Lane, London Colney. Tel: Bowmansgreen 22817
Ground: Cotlardswick, London Colney. Tel: Bowmansgreen 22132
Colours: Royal Blue shirts and shorts **Change Colours:**

MOUNT GRACE OLD SCHOLARS
Secretary: P. Waller, 26 Queen Annes Grove, Enfield, Middx. Tel: 01-360 7859
Ground: Parkfield, The Walk, Potters Bar, Herts
Colours: Blue & Scarlet stripes/Blue/Blue **Change Colours:** Yellow

OXHEY JETS
Secretary: D. G. Fuller, 41 Herons Lea, Watford WD2 6PN. Tel: Garston 679494
Ground: Sth Oxhey Community Assoc. Building, Chilwell Gardens, Sth Oxhey, Herts. Tel: 01-428 0235
Colours: Royal Blue shirts & shorts **Change Colours:** Red shirts & shorts

POTTERS BAR CRUSADERS
Secretary: M. Meadows, 25 Queens Avenue, Whetstone, London N20 0HZ Tel: 01-445 7206
Ground: King George V Playing Fields, Mutton Lane, Potters Bar. Tel: Potters Bar 50764
Colours: All Blue with White pinstripe **Change Colours:** Red/ White/Red

ROLLS ROYCE ENGINES
Secretary: W. M. Williamson, 12 Hivings Park, Chesham, Bucks HP5 2LG. Tel: Chesham 782197
Ground: Rolls Royce Sports Club, South Way, Leavesden Aerodrome. Tel: Garston 73676
Colours: Amber/Black/Black **Change Colours:** Blue/Black/Black

ST MARGARETSBURY
Secretary: A. J. Grossfield, 37 Eversley Lodge, Park View, Hoddesdon EN11 8PH. Tel: Hodd. 461826
Ground: St. Margaretsbury Rec. Ground, Stanstead Abotts. Tel: Ware 870473
Colours: Red with Black pinstripes short/Black shorts **Change Colours:**

SANDRIDGE ROVERS
Secretary: G. C. Hardwick, 21 Woodcock Hill, Sandridge, St. Albans. Tel: St. Albans 55334
Ground: Recreation Ground, Sandridge, Herts. Tel: St Albans 55159
Colours: All Red **Change Colours:** Blue or Yellow

SUN SPORTS
Secretary: M. J. Jeffs, 35 Eastfield Avenue, Watford. Tel: 29938
Ground: Bellmont Wood Avenue, Watford Tel: Watford 27453
Colours: Yellow/Blue/Gold **Change Colours:**

TUDOR CORINTHIANS
Secretary: A. J. Smith, 32 Oaklands Avenue, Oxhey, Watford WD1 4LW. Tel: Watford 31218
Ground: Barton Way Playing Fields, Croxley Green
Colours: Red/Black/Red **Change Colours:**

WINGATE
Secretary: W. Orkin, 41 Highview Avenue, Edgware, Middx HA8 9TY. Tel: 01 958 5145
Ground: Brickfield Lane, off Barnet Road, Arkley. Tel: 01-441 5332
Colours: All Royal Blue **Change Colours:**

VERCO CHILTONIAN FOOTBALL LEAGUE

Formed in 1984

Patron: Mr. R.F.S. Vere
Chairman: Mr. D. Newell (Tel: 02406) 3186)
Secretary: Mr. C. Williams (Tel: 0753 35074)
6 Cippenham Lane, Slough, Berkshire

The Verco Chiltonian Football League are now at the end of a second successful campaign and is maintaining its progress towards becoming a feeder League and a major force in the Chiltern and Thames Valley region.

The league continues with its expansion and after attracting four new members last term another four newcomers including Maidenhead Town from the Hellenic League Premier Division who also play in the F.A. Vase and the others are Denham United previously in the Slough & Windsor District Premier Division and Two clubs from the Wycombe Ercol Senior League namely Seer Green, who were runners up in this years Berks & Bucks Intermediate Cup, along with Stokenchurch who were also once in the Hellenic. With this continual influx of new blood to expand the competition the founder members are realising they must continue improving facilities, not only to keep up with their fellow clubs but to help the Chiltonian in its progress towards joining the pyramid system.

Finally the Chiltonian League are indebted to William Vere Limited the High Wycombe based Office furniture manufacturers - known throughout as VERCO for their continual sponsoring of the League which we are certain will prove to be of mutual benefit to both sides.

Division 1	P	W	D	L	F	A	Pts
Holmer Green	18	5	1	2	56	21	46
St. Johns Hospital	18	13	3	2	32	16	42
Coopers Payen	18	11	4	3	40	13	37
Soldiers Return	18	7	4	7	31	27	25
Prestwood	18	7	2	9	26	36	23
Penn & Tylers Green	18	6	1	11	24	41	19
Sandhurst Town	18	5	3	10	31	34	18
Bromley Park Rgers	18	5	3	10	26	33	18
Chalfont Wasps	18	4	5	9	20	27	17
Wooburn Athletic	18	3	2	13	25	63	11

Division 1	P	W	D	L	F	A	Pts
Drayton Wanderers	16	12	2	2	34	16	38
Martin Baker Sports	16	11	2	3	48	19	35
Chinnor	16	10	1	5	35	18	31
Brill United	16	9	3	4	36	25	30
Molins Sports	16	7	3	6	27	27	24
Broomwade Sports	16	5	2	9	29	38	17
Haddenham United	16	4	4	8	34	42	16
Henley Town	16	3	0	13	15	43	9
Hambleden	16	2	1	13	17	47	7

Holmer Green — Verco Chiltonian Champions 1985/85 Photo by courtesy The Bucks Free Press

VERCO CHILTONIAN FOOTBALL LEAGUE DIVISION ONE CLUBS 1986

BROMLEY PARK RANGERS **(1964): Ground:** Coney Green, Uxbridge Road, Hillingdon. (Uxbridge 38130). **Seats:** No. **Programme:** No.
Secretary: J.C. Whitehead (Uxbridge 21012). **Colours:** Green/Black. **Clubhouse:** Yes
Secretary: D. Czerwinski, 10 Beech Road, Chinnor, Oxford (Kingston Blount 51945) **Colours:** Blue/White

CHINNOR **(1884) Ground:** Sports Field, Station Road, Chinnor. (Kingston Blount 52579) **Seats:** No **Programme:** Yes
Secretary: D.J. Rick, 77 Grange Way, West Square, Iver, Bucks. (0753 652780). **Colours:** Red/Black. **Clubhouse:** Yes

COOPERS PAYEN **(1983) Ground:** The Pavillion, Farnham Park, Farnham Royal, Slough (Farnham Royal 3629). **Programme:** No
Secretary: R.J. Ash, 28 Newham Avenue, Eastcote, Middx MA4 9RN (01-868 5761) **Colours:** Black/White **Clubhouse:** No

DRAYTON WANDERERS **(1964) Ground:** Cowley Recreation Ground, High Road, Cowley, Middx. **Programme:** Yes
Secretary:C. Buckle, 10 Rookery Meadow, Holmer Green, Bucks (0494 713717) **Colours:** Green **Clubhouse:** Yes

HOLMER GREEN (1908) Ground: Holmer Green Sports Club, Watchet Lane, Holmer Green, Bucks (0494 711485) **Programme:** Yes
Secretary: D. Jenkins, Woodfell, Mossy Vale, Maidenhead (27239) **Colours:** Blue/White **Clubhouse:** Yes

MAIDENHEAD TOWN (1956) Ground: Braywick Sports Centre, Windsor Road (22340) **Seats:** No **Programme:** Yes
Secretary: J. Walford, 18 Tilehouse Way, Denham, Uxbridge, Middx. (0895 834641) **Colours:** White with Blue Stripes/Blue **Clubhouse:** Yes

MARTIN BAKER SPORTS **(1961) Ground:** Martins Field, Tilehouse Lane, Denham, Uxbridge, Middx (0895 833077). **Programme:** Yes
Secretary: D. Raleigh, 50 Carver Hill Road, High Wycombe (M.W. 445533) **Colours:** Grey/Maroon **Clubhouse:** Yes

PENN & TYLERS GREEN F.C. **(1905) Ground:** French School Meadow, Elm Road, Penn (Penn 5346) **Programme:** No
Secretary: B. Parsons, Chomsee, New Road, Prestwood, Bucks (02406 4720) **Colours:** Claret/Sky Blue **Clubhouse:** Yes

PRESTWOOD **(1934) Ground:** Sports Centre, Honor End Lane, Prestwood, Bucks (02406 5946) **Seats:** No **Programme:** Yes
Secretary: J. Parker, 24 Florence Road, College Town, Camberley, Surrey (Camberley 32308) **Colours:** Red/Black **Clubhouse:** Yes

SANDHURST TOWN **(1910) Ground:** Memorial Ground, Yorktown Road, Sandhurst, Berks (N/A) **Seats:** No **Programme:** Yes for 1986/87
Secretary: M. Davis, 451 Abbey Road, Popley Abeeys, Basingstoke (0256 468873) **Colours:** Red **Clubhouse:** Yes

SOLDIERS RETURN **(1971) Ground:** Whiteditch, Sherbourne Road, Basingstoke, Hants **Seats:** No **Programme:** Yes
Secretary: J.P. Blackburn, 22 rowland Way, Aylesbury, Bucks (0296 20279) **Colours:** Red/Black **Clubhouse:** Yes

ST. JOHNS HOSPITAL **(1970) Ground:** St. Johns Hospital, Stone, Nr. Aylesbury, Bucks (0296 748787) **Programme:** No

ESSEX THAMES-SIDE CHALLENGE TROPHY

(Affiliated to Essex County F.A.)

President: M. S. Jeffers, ECFA
Chairman: J. J. A. Bays, ECFA
Chairman: N. Posner

WALTHAMSTOW AVENUE'S GALLEON

The Essex Thames-side Challenge Trophy was formed in 1945, the season when football started up again at the end of the war. A year later, Mr. Latilla — the President of Walthamstow Avenue Football Club at that time presented the competition with the magnificent silver galleon that is now the competition's proud "Trophy'. Walthamstow Avenue have won the trophy no less than five times over the years since then and 1985-86 saw them bring it back home again to roost in one of the best competitions ever staged.

Early in September, East Thurrock United met Orient at home and pulled off one of the major giant killing efforts in beating them by 2 goals to 1. Ford United then beat Leytonstone-Ilford, Barkingside beat Rainham and Collier Row disposed of Hornchurch; all wins by lesser league clubs against opposition from the Vauxhall Opel league. East Thurrock United continued their successful run by defeating Tilbury but then succumbed to Walthamstow in the quarter-finals.

Chelmsford City suffered from a crippling backlog of fixtures and in a busy week in March lost at home to Southend United while Billericay Town re-entering the competition this season, after a few years break, looked favourites for a place in the final as they disposed of Barkingside 5-0 and Clapton 2-1 but, after establishing a 2-0 lead through Keith Pope, and then a 3-1 lead shortly into the second half, crashed out in the Semi Final against Grays Athletic losing by 3 goals to 4. Despite their earlier goals advantage, one always had the feeling that Grays would win. The Billericay defence played very square and being slow on the turn were caught out time and again by the fast Grays forwards. The footwork and saves by the Vauxhall-Opel League representatives' goalkeeper helped Billericay hold out until a last minute goal took Grays into the Final.

Southend United were visitors to Walthamstow Avenue in the other semi-final and paid them the honour of fielding their full first team. A close game ensued indicative by the result that took Walthamstow into a home final match by the solitary goal scored.

Within the first ten minutes of the Final, Walthamstow Avenue served notice on Grays Athletic that the trophy belonged at Walthamstow by jumping into a two goal lead. Lesser teams might have capitulated, but Grays profiting from a defensive error clawed back one goal. Walthamstow undaunted by this effort again restored their two goal lead, only for Grays to narrow the gap within minutes. From then on until the final whistle, end-to-end football ensued in no way affected by the very wet pitch caused by a pre-match cloud burst. 3-2 was the score at the end when Maurice Jeffers, President of the competition presented the trophy to Walthamstow Avenue.

Preliminary Round

Hornchurch	0	Collier Row	1
Ford United	2	Leytonstone/Ilford	0
(played at Leytonstone)			
East Thurrock United	2	Orient	1
Rainham T. (3 penalties)		Barkingside (4 penalties)	
(After a 2-2 draw after extra time)			

First Round

Barkingside	0	Billericay Town	5
(played at Billericay)			
Clapton walkover owing to Epping's withdrawal			
Tilbury	1	East Thurrock United	2
Southend United	2	Ford United	0
Aveley	1	Grays Athletic	2
Woodford Town	0	Chelmsford City	1
Barking	1	Leyton-Wingate	0
Collier Row	1	Walthamstow Avenue	2

Second Round

Billericay Town	2	Clapton	1
Grays Athletic	2	Barking	1
Chelmsford City	1	Southend United	2
Walthamstow Avenue	4	East Thurrock United	1

Semi-Finals

Walthamstow Avenue	1	Southend United	0
Billericay	3	Grays Athletic	4

Final

Walthamstow Avenue	3	Grays Athletic	2

HOME COUNTIES RESERVE TEAM COMPETITIONS

SUBURBAN LEAGUE

North

	P	W	D	L	F	A	Pts
1. Wembley	34	24	5	5	99	31	53
2. Staines Town	34	21	7	6	60	27	49
3. Wokingham Town	34	20	8	6	84	37	48
4. Hendon	34	19	8	7	70	38	46
5. Farnborough Town	34	16	4	14	63	55	·36
6. Harrow Borough	34	15	5	14	77	64	35
7. Camberley Town	34	14	7	13	41	41	35
8. Chesham United	34	13	8	13	58	69	34
9. Woking	34	13	6	15	55	47	32
10. Edgeware	34	11	10	13	55	60	32
11. Hounslow	34	11	10	13	46	54	32
12. Uxbridge	34	11	8	15	33	43	30
13. Maidenhead Utd.	34	9	12	13	35	50	30
14. Southall	34	10	7	17	40	56	27
15. Slough Town	34	9	9	16	43	73	27
16. Feltham	34	9	8	17	45	79	26
17. Chertsey Town	34	6	10	18	29	70	22
18. Egham Town	34	5	8	21	36	75	18

South

	P	W	D	L	F	A	Pts
1. Sutton United	34	28	3	3	86	22	59
2. Hampton	34	24	6	4	62	21	54
3. Dorking	34	21	5	8	75	45	47
4. Dulwich Hamlet	34	18	6	10	73	45	42
5. Leatherhead	34	15	10	9	59	45	40
6. Croydon	34	15	9	10	58	37	39
7. Walton Casuals	34	14	11	9	53	46	39
8. Metropolitan Police	34	13	7	14	46	52	33
9. Banstead Athletic	34	13	7	14	46	52	33
10. Tooting & Mitcham United	34	12	7	15	47	50	31
11. Epsom & Ewell	34	11	6	17	47	52	28
12. Carshalton Athletic	34	9	8	17	38	55	26
13. Molesey	34	9	8	17	43	66	26
14. Bromley	34	9	7	18	43	60	25
15. Walton & Hersham	34	9	7	18	39	82	25
16. Kingstonian	34	8	7	19	41	70	23
17. Whyteleafe	34	8	6	20	45	67	22
18. Redhill	34	6	6	22	30	77	18

Roll of Honour Season 1985/86

North Division:
Wembley Winners. Staines Town Runners Up

South Division:
Sutton United Winners. Hampton Runners Up

League Challenge Cup:
Hampton Winners. Metropolitan Police Runners Up

Surrey Premier Cup:
Sutton United Runners Up

Middlesex Premier Cup:
Hampton Runners Up

Kent Intermediate Cup:
Bromley Winners

B & W CHAMPIONS' CUP

Sponsored by:
B & W Darts & Trophies Ltd., Wellington Works, Wellington Road, Walthamstow, London E17.
Secretary: B.W. Hitchings, 18 Tany's Dell, Harlow, Essex CM20 2LJ. Harlow (0279) 39757

Semi-Finals:

Basildon United (EHBC) 2 Wokingham town (SFL) 1
Wokingham Town 4 Basildon United 0
(Wokingham won 5-2 on aggregate)

Chalfont St Peter (MBL) 0 Wokingham Town 0
Wokingham Town 3 Chalfont St Peter 3
(Chalfont St Peter won on "away" goals)

Final

Chalfont St Peter 0 Wokingham Town 0
Wokingham Town 3 Chalfont St Peter 3
(Chalfont St Peter won on "away" goals)

DRAW FOR SEASON 1986-87

Semi-Finals

Aylesbury United (MBL) v Basildon United (EHBC)
Sutton United (SFL) v Banbury United (WSCL)

ESSEX & HERTS BORDER COMBINATION

Secretary: D.F. Jenkins, 8 Duxford Close, Hornchurch, Essex RM12 5PS
Rainham (04027) 55320

Eastern Division	P	W	D	L	F	A	Pts
Basildon United	22	13	5	4	51	29	44
Heybridge Swifts	22	12	6	4	40	23	42
Maidstone United	22	12	3	7	50	38	39
Welling United	22	12	3	7	46	36	39
Billericay Town	22	10	6	6	42	30	36
Barking	22	11	3	8	49	39	36
Rainham Town	22	9	3	10	36	33	30
Tilbury	22	8	5	9	25	31	29
Hornchurch	22	7	5	10	31	39	26
Grays Athletic	22	6	3	13	33	45	21
Ford United	22	4	6	12	18	47	18
Corinthian	22	3	2	17	25	56	11

Western Division	P	W	D	L	F	A	Pts
Walthamstow Avenue	24	18	0	6	71	36	54
Leyton-Wingate	24	16	4	4	56	27	52
Enfield	24	13	6	5	86	36	45
Haringey Borough	24	14	3	7	44	35	45
Harlow Town	24	12	5	7	52	36	41
Cambridge City	24	11	8	5	48	34	41
Collier Row	24	10	4	10	45	56	34
Kingsbury Town	24	8	6	10	31	38	30
Clapton	24	7	7	10	29	46	28
Saffron Walden Town	24	6	5	13	32	53	23
Ware	24	4	7	13	25	34	19
Hoddesdon Town	24	2	7	15	23	51	13
Hertford Town	24	3	2	19	22	82	11

Championship Play-Off:
Walthamstow Avenue 0 Basildon United 2 aet

Combination Cup Final
Heybridge Swifts 3 Enfield 2

Fred Budden Trophy Final
Heybridge Swifts 3 Welling United 2

MIDDLESEX BORDER LEAGUE

Secretary: M.D. Collas, 8 Wiltshire Gardens, Whitton, Twickenham, Middlesex TW2 6ND
Telephone: 01-894 6759

	P	W	D	L	F	A	Pts
Aylesbury United	30	23	2	5	92	31	48
Harefield United	30	20	7	3	53	23	47
Yeading	30	20	5	5	73	31	45
Chalfont St Peter	30	18	9	3	65	27	45
Bracknell Town	30	17	4	9	61	36	38
Thatcham Town	30	15	2	13	44	49	32
Berkhamsted Town	30	14	3	13	53	37	31
Dunstable	30	13	5	12	42	43	31
Newbury Town	30	12	6	12	58	55	30
Ruislip Manor	30	12	3	15	38	56	27
Burnham & Hillingdon	30	9	5	16	42	62	23
Flackwell Heath	30	10	2	18	47	64	22
Marlow	30	7	4	19	29	69	18
Beaconsfield United	30	6	4	20	41	70	16
Hemel Hempstead	30	4	6	20	36	62	14
Amersham Town	30	6	1	23	38	97	13

WALLSPAN SOUTHERN COMBINATION

Secretary: Ken Thornton, 42 Carrington Road, Aylesbury, Bucks HP21 3JE. Aylesbury (0296) 86644

	P	W	D	L	Pts
Banbury United	22	15	4	3	49
Oxford City	22	14	3	5	45
Witney Town	22	10	7	5	37
Hitchin Town	22	11	2	9	35
Vauxhall Motors	22	10	3	9	33
St Albans City	22	8	7	7	31
Stevenage Borough	22	9	4	9	29
Baldock Town	22	8	4	10	28
Royston Town	22	5	9	8	24
Barton Rovers	22	5	9	8	24
Wolverton Town	22	1	10	11	13
Letchworth Gdn City	22	3	3	16	12

Wallspan Cup Final
Witney Town 2 Oxford City 1

MIDDLESEX COUNTY FOOTBALL LEAGUE

DIVISION ONE

	P	W	D	L	F	A	Pts
Mill End Sports	28	19	4	5	60	26	61
Lucas CAV	28	16	9	3	62	23	57
Ruislip	28	15	5	8	56	45	50
Evershed Social	28	15	3	10	62	48	48
Harrow St. Mary's	28	14	5	9	49	48	47
Conatantine United	28	13	6	9	60	44	45
Brook House	28	10	10	8	56	40	40
Chorleywood Com.	28	9	10	9	47	51	37
Croxley Guild	28	9	7	12	51	64	34
Hanwell Town	28	7	11	10	46	52	32
North Greenfold Utd	28	9	5	14	55	64	32
Technicolor Sports	28	8	6	14	45	66	30
Pitshanger Dynamo	28	8	5	15	37	52	29
Hanworth Villa	28	5	11	12	32	46	26
Northwood	28	1	7	20	22	71	10

DIVISION TWO

	P	W	D	L	F	A	Pts
Harrow St. Mary's	18	14	1	3	47	28	43
Constantine United	18	12	1	5	49	28	37
Brook House	18	10	6	2	41	22	36
Evershed Social	18	9	4	5	58	32	31
Mill End Sports	18	8	3	7	40	36	27
North Greenford Utd.	18	7	1	10	48	44	22
Pitshanger Dynamo	18	6	4	8	23	35	22
Croxley Guild	18	5	0	13	30	48	15
Technicolor Sports	18	3	4	11	23	59	13
Hanwell Town	18	3	2	13	31	58	11

D.R.G. WEST HERTS SATURDAY LEAGUE SEASON 1985/1986

PREMIER DIVISION

	P	W	D	L	F	A	Pts
Kodak	20	18	1	1	73	19	37
Royal Oak	20	15	3	2	70	28	33
Northchurch	20	13	3	4	49	27	29
Springwell Athletic	20	8	3	9	46	38	19
Aldbury Sports	20	7	4	9	42	41	18
Brother	20	8	2	10	42	42	18
Emeralds	20	8	1	11	39	51	17
D & B Builders	20	7	2	11	39	51	16
Oxhey	20	4	6	10	32	52	14
Chorleywood C. Res.	20	3	6	11	31	47	12
Antilles Sports	20	2	3	15	22	79	7

FA CHALLENGE CUP COMPETITION - SEASON 1986-1987

PRELIMINARY ROUND - 30TH AUGUST 1986

1 Alnwick Town v Guisborough Town
2 Consett v Annfield Plain
3 Ferryhill Athletic v Darlington Clevedon Bridge
4 Ashington v Seaham CW Red Star
5 Bridlington Town v Murton
6 North Shields v Denaby United
7 Norton & Stockton Ancients v Newcastle Blue Star
8 Ryhope Community Association v Farsley Celtic
9 Durham City v Shildon
10 Fleetwood Town v Clitheroe
11 Northallerton Town v Guiseley
12 Darwen v West Auckland Town
13 Langley Park Welfare v Evenwood Town
14 Thackley v Netherfield
15 Ashton United v Ossett Albion
16 Curzon Ashton v Armthorpe Welfare
17 Penrith v Glossop
18 Accrington Stanley v Lancaster City
19 Chadderton v Irlam Town
20 Ilkeston Town v Emley
21 Bootle v Belper Town
22 Burscough v Kirkby Town
23 Formby v Droylsden
24 Colwyn Bay v Rossendale United
25 Congleton Town v Bridgnorth Town
26 Radcliffe Borough v Eastwood Hanley
27 Sutton Town v Stalybridge Celtic
28 Walsall-Wood v Skelmersdale United
29 Bilston Town v Lye Town
30 Brigg Town v Arnold
31 Leicester United v Friar Lane OB
32 Rothwell Town v Tividale
33 Oldswinford v Boldmere St Michaels
34 Wellingborough Town v Sutton Coldfield Town
35 Coventry Sporting v Racing Club Warwick
36 Highgate United v Banbury United
37 Mile Oak Rovers & Youth v Leamington
38 Bourne Town v Tamworth
39 Gresley Rovers v Wolverton Town
40 Rushall Olympic v Moor Green
41 Spalding United v Rushden Town
42 Stevenage Borough v Milton Keynes Borough
43 Barton Rovers v Saffron Walden Town
44 Hemel Hempstead v Baldock Town
45 March Town United v Histon
46 Berkhamsted Town v Tiptree United
47 Felixstowe Town v Ely City
48 Royston Town v Finchley
49 Aveley v Hornchurch
50 Basildon United v Potton United
51 Hoddesdon Town v Great Yarmouth Town
52 Cheshunt v Rainham Town
53 Sudbury Town v Gorleston
54 Billericay Town v Stowmarket Town
55 Harwich & Parkeston v Collier Row
56 Soham Town Rangers v Hertford Town
57 Boreham Wood v Egham Town
58 Burnham & Hillingdon v Rayners Lane
59 Edgware v Corinthian-Casuals
60 Chesham United v Metropolitan Police
61 Crockenhill v Feltham
62 Kingsbury Town v Erith & Belvedere
63 Alma Swanley v Southall
64 Clapton v Yeading
65 Desborough Town v Flackwell Heath
66 Merstham v Leytonstone/Ilford
67 Tring Town v Chertsey Town
68 Burgess Hill Town v Staines Town
69 Chatham Town v Vauxhall Motors
70 Sittingbourne v Dorking
71 Epsom & Ewell v Three Bridges
72 Horsham YMCA v Haringey Borough
73 Redhill v Maidenhead United
74 Dover Athletic v Tunbridge Wells
75 Molesey v Wick
76 Leatherhead v Eastbourne Town
77 Arundel v Ringmer
78 Camberley Town v Shoreham
79 Tonbridge AFC v Haywards Heath
80 Horndean v Woking
81 Lancing v Peacehaven & Telscombe
82 Thanet United v Lewes
83 Ashford Town v Steyning Town
84 Eastbourne United v Portfield
85 Sheppey United v Chichester City
86 Andover v Sholing Sports
87 Devizes Town v Farnham Town
88 Petersfield United v Hailsham Town
89 Havant Town v Radstock Town
90 Brockenhurst v Westbury United
91 Clandown v Abingdon Town
92 Shortwood United v Melksham Town
93 Trowbridge Town v Hungerford Town
94 Clevedon Town v Paulton Rovers
95 Bristol Manor Farm v Evesham United
96 Maesteg Park v Llanelli
97 Ottery St Mary v Merthyr Tydfil
98 Saltash United v Gloucester City
99 Welton Rovers v Taunton Town
100 Weston-super-Mare v Torrington

FA CHALLENGE CUP COMPETITION - SEASON 1986-1987

FIRST ROUND QUALIFYING - 13TH SEPTEMBER 1986

1 Bedlington Terriers v Chester-le-Street Town
2 Harrogate Town v Ferryhill Athletic or Darlington Clevedon Bridge
3 Barrow v Easington Colliery
4 Consett or Annfield Plain v Alnwick Town or Guisborough Town
5 Bishop Auckland v Gateshead
6 Whitley Bay v North Shields or Denaby United
7 Morecambe v Esh Winning
8 Bridlington Town or Murton v Ashington or Seaham CW Red Star
9 Eppleton Colliery Welfare v Brandon United
10 Workington v Billingham Synthonia
11 South Bank v Billingham Town
12 Ryhope CA or Farsley Celtic v Norton & Stockton Anc or Newcastle Blue Star
13 Blyth Spartans v Crook Town
14 Yorkshire Amateur v Northallerton Town or Guiseley
15 Gretna v Horden Colliery Welfare
16 Fleetwood Town or Clitheroe v Durham City or Shildon
17 Bridlington Trinity v Peterlee Newtown
18 Wren Rovers v Thackley or Netherfield
19 Tow Law Town v Spennymoor United
20 Langley Park Welfare or Evenwood Town v Darwen or West Auckland Town
21 Chorley v Horwich RMI
22 Warrington Town v Penrith or Glossop
23 St Helens Town v Heanor Town
24 Curzon Ashton or Armthorpe Welfare v Ashton United or Ossett Albion
25 Hyde United v Rhyl
26 Leyland Motors v Ilkeston Town or Emley
27 Southport v Garforth Town
28 Chadderton or Irlam Town v Accrington Stanley or Lancaster City
29 Caernarfon Town v Marine

30 Winsford United v Formby or Droylsden
31 Mossley v Eastwood Town
32 Burscough or Kirkby Town v Bootle or Belper Town
33 Buxton v Leek Town
34 Oldbury United v Radcliffe Borough or Eastwood Hanley
35 Oswestry Town v Prescot Cables
36 Congleton Town or Bridgnorth Town v Colwyn Bay or Rossendale United
37 Long Eaton United v Northwich Victoria
38 Worksop Town v Armitage
39 Witton Albion v Hednesford Town
40 Walsall-Wood or Skelmersdale United v Sutton Town or Stalybridge Celtic
41 Goole Town v Scarborough
42 North Ferriby United v Leicester United or Friar Lane OB
43 South Liverpool v GKN Sankey
44 Brigg Town or Arnold v Bilston Town or Lye Town
45 Alfreton Town v Gainsborough Trinity
46 Wisbech Town v Wellingborough Town or Sutton Coldfield Town
47 Grantham v Wednesfield Social
48 Oldswinford or Boldmere St Michaels v Rothwell Town or Tividale
49 Hinckley Athletic v Kidderminster Harriers
50 Wigston Fields v Mile Oak Rovers & Youth or Leamington
51 Matlock Town v Malvern Town
52 Highgate United or Banbury United v Coventry Sporting or Racing Club Warwick
53 Shepshed Charterhouse v Stafford Rangers
54 Atherstone United v Rushall Olympic or Moor Green
55 Willenhall Town v Paget Rangers
56 Gresley Rovers or Wolverton Town v Bourne Town or Tamworth
57 Letchworth Garden City v Burton Albion
58 Halesowen Town v Ampthill Town
59 Dudley Town v Arlesey Town
60 Stevenage Borough or Milton Keynes Borough v Spalding United or Rushden Town
61 Alvechurch v Bedworth United
62 Wootton Blue Cross v March Town United or Histon
63 Bromsgrove Rovers v Holbeach United
64 Hemel Hempstead or Baldock Town v Barton Rovers or Saffron Walden Town
65 Corby Town v Irthlingborough Diamonds
66 Ware v Royston Town or Finchley
67 Kettering Town v Lowestoft Town
68 Felixstowe Town or Ely City v Berkhamsted Town or Tiptree United
69 Braintree Town v Cambridge City
70 Newmarket Town v Hoddesdon Town or Great Yarmouth Town
71 Kings Lynn v Haverhill Rovers
72 Basildon United or Potton United v Aveley or Hornchurch
73 Chatteris Town v Harlow Town
74 Tilbury v Witham Town
75 Stamford v Bury Town
76 Sudbury Town or Gorleston v Cheshunt or Rainham Town
77 Grays Athletic v Hitchin Town
78 Woodford Town v Soham Town Rangers or Hertford Town
79 Walthamstow Avenue v Heybridge Swifts
80 Harwich & Parkeston or Collier Row v Billericay Town or Stowmarket Town
81 Aylesbury united v Barking
82 Harefield United v Edgware or Corinthian-Casuals
83 Kingstonian v Cray Wanderers
84 Burnham & Hillingdon or Rayners Lane v Boreham Wood or Egham Town
85 Fisher Athletic v Harrow Borough
86 Walton & Hersham v Kingsbury Town or Erith & Belvedere
87 Tooting & Mitcham United v Hampton
88 Crockenhill or Feltham v Chesham United or Metropolitan Police
89 Chalfont St Peter v Hayes
90 Uxbridge v Desborough Town or Flackwell Heath
91 Sutton United v Hounslow
92 Clapton or Yeading v Alma Swanley or Southall
93 Bracknell Town v Croydon
94 Welling United v Darenth Heathside
95 Hendon v Banstead Athletic
96 Tring Town or Chertsey Town v Merstham or Leytonstone/Ilford
97 Barnet v Dulwich Hamlet
98 Wembley v Sittingbourne or Dorking
99 St Albans City v Ruislip Manor
100 Chatham Town or Vauxhall Motors v Burgess Hill Town or Staines Town
101 Buckingham Town v Dunstable
102 Whyteleafe v Redhill or Maidenhead United
103 Wokingham Town v Marlow
104 Horsham YMCA or Haringey Borough v Epsom & Ewell or Three Bridges
105 Bromley v Carshalton Athletic
106 Whitehawk v Leatherhead or Eastbourne Town
107 Leyton-Wingate v Faversham Town
108 Molesey or Wick v Dover Athletic or Tunbridge Wells
109 Canterbury City v Folkestone
110 Whitstable Town v Tonbridge AFC or Haywards Heath
111 Worthing v Herne Bay
112 Camberley Town or Shoreham v Arundel or Ringmer
113 Crawley Town v Gravesend & Northfleet
114 Eastleigh v Thanet United or Lewes
115 Hastings Town v Horsham
116 Lancing or Peacehaven & Telscombe v Horndean or Woking
117 Gosport Borough v Newport IOW
118 Waterlooville v Sheppey United or Chichester City
119 Southwick v Hythe Town
120 Eastbourne United or Portfield v Ashford Town or Steyning Town
121 Fareham Town v Oxford City
122 Newbury Town v Petersfield United or Hailsham Town
123 Road-Sea(Southampton) v Littlehampton Town
124 Devizes Town or Farnham Town v Andover or Sholing Sports

125 Chippenham Town v Poole Town
126 Wimborne Town v Clandown or Abingdon Town
127 Totton AFC v Calne Town
128 Brockenhurst or Westbury United v Havant Town or Radstock Town
129 Frome Town v Redditch United
130 Stourbridge v Abingdon United
131 Salisbury v Bridgend Town
132 Trowbridge Town or Hungerford Town v Shortwood United or Melksham Town
133 Basingstoke Town v Ton Pentre
134 Sharpness v Maesteg Park or Llanelli
135 Witney Town v Mangotsfield United
136 Bristol Manor Farm or Evesham United v Clevedon Town or Paulton Rovers
137 Dorchester Town v Barry Town
138 Forest Green Rovers v Yate Town
139 Cheltenham Town v Bideford
140 Saltash United or Gloucester City v Ottery St Mary or Merthyr Tydfil
141 St Blazey v Barnstaple Town
142 Minehead v Tiverton Town
143 Exmouth Town v Glastonbury
144 Weston-super-Mare or Torrington v Welton Rovers or Taunton Town

Non-Football League Clubs Exempt

First Round Proper

Altrincham
Frickley Athletic
Runcorn
Telford United

Fourth Round Qualifying

Bath City
Bishops Stortford
Bognor Regis Town
Boston United
Chelmsford City
Dagenham
Dartford
Enfield
Farnborough Town
Macclesfield Town
Maidstone United
Nuneaton Borough
Slough Town
V.S Rugby
Wealdstone
Weymouth
Whitby Town
Windsor & Eton
Wycombe Wanderers
Yeovil Town

FA CHALLENGE CUP COMPETITION - SEASON 1986-1987

SECOND ROUND QUALIFYING - 27TH SEPTEMBER 1986

1	2	v	1	25	50	v	49	49	98	v	97
2	4	v	3	26	52	v	51	50	100	v	99
3	6	v	5	27	54	v	53	51	102	v	101
4	8	v	7	28	56	v	55	52	104	v	103
5	10	v	9	29	58	v	57	53	106	v	105
6	12	v	11	30	60	v	59	54	108	v	107
7	14	v	13	31	62	v	61	55	110	v	109
8	16	v	15	32	64	v	63	56	112	v	111
9	18	v	17	33	66	v	65	57	114	v	113
10	20	v	19	34	68	v	67	58	116	v	115
11	22	v	21	35	70	v	69	59	118	v	117
12	24	v	23	36	72	v	71	60	120	v	119
13	26	v	25	37	74	v	73	61	122	v	121
14	28	v	27	38	76	v	75	62	124	v	123
15	30	v	29	39	78	v	77	63	126	v	125
16	32	v	31	40	80	v	79	64	128	v	127
17	34	v	33	41	82	v	81	65	130	v	129
18	36	v	35	42	84	v	83	66	132	v	131
19	38	v	37	43	86	v	85	67	134	v	133
20	40	v	39	44	88	v	87	68	136	v	135
21	42	v	41	45	90	v	89	69	138	v	137
22	44	v	43	46	92	v	91	70	140	v	139
23	46	v	45	47	94	v	93	71	142	v	141
24	48	v	47	48	96	v	95	72	144	v	143

FA CHALLENGE CUP COMPETITION - SEASON 1986-1987

THIRD ROUND QUALIFYING - 11TH OCTOBER 1986

1	2	v	1	13	26	v	25	25	50	v	49
2	4	v	3	14	28	v	27	26	52	v	51
3	6	v	5	15	30	v	29	27	54	v	53
4	8	v	7	16	32	v	31	28	56	v	55
5	10	v	9	17	34	v	33	29	58	v	57
6	12	v	11	18	36	v	35	30	60	v	59
7	14	v	13	19	38	v	37	31	62	v	61
8	16	v	15	20	40	v	39	32	64	v	63
9	18	v	17	21	42	v	41	33	66	v	65
10	20	v	19	22	44	v	43	34	68	v	67
11	22	v	21	23	46	v	45	35	70	v	69
12	24	v	23	24	48	v	47	36	72	v	71

THE SOUTHERN FOOTBALL LEAGUE

President: G. E. Templeman *Chairman:* H. J. Eastment
Secretary: D. J. Strudwick, 11 Welland Close, Darrington, Worthing BN13 3NR.
Telephone: 0903 67788

SECRETARY'S REPORT

Yet another highly competitive season in the Southern Football League reached its peak in the final week, when six of the ten Promotion/Relegation issues were still to be decided. And none worked out to be closer than Salisbury's promotion from the Southern Division to the Premier.

Being a point in arrears but with an identical goal difference to Hastings Town, Salisbury went into their last game on the final day of the season against Woodford Town knowing that only a win would decisively earn the runners-up spot behind Cambridge City. The point from a 0-0 or 1-1 draw would bring the Cathedral City level with Hastings but the seasiders would go up by virtue of having scored more goals. A 2-2 draw would mean a tie and a play-off. A 3-3 draw would swing the balance in Salisbury's favour by having scored more than Hastings. On a sunny Bank Holiday afternoon at Woodford, Salisbury looked certainties at half-time with a 3-0 lead. Despite being reduced to ten men throughout the second period Woodford did everything possible and reduced the arrears to 3-2 before time ran out.

By a quirk of fate, Hastings Town heard of their destiny whilst playing simultaneously in the Sussex Senior Cup final at Brighton. The unfortunate decision to make the announcement at full-time may have affected Hastings' extra time performance and they eventually lost 1-0 to Steyning Town.

Back on the League scene, there was no disputing the Champions. Welling United made certain of the Premier Division title with three weeks and four matches to spare. Welling scored as many goals and conceded as few goals as any other team in the League. They won as many games as any other Club and lost only three matches which was three fewer than anyone else. Their twenty three point margin over eventual runners-up Chelmsford City, reflects their supremacy of the Division. Congratulations Welling United. I feel totally confident that you will maintain the good and successful name of the Southern League when on your new 'pastures green' in the Gola League next year. Good Luck!

Bromsgrove Rovers led almost a similar charge towards their quest for the Midland Division title and won the Bill Dellow Challenge Cup on the way. In a two-legged final against Trowbridge Town, the first final contested without a Premier Division Club, Bromsgrove won by an aggregate score of 4-3 in front of over 3,500 people.

Bromsgrove's closest rivals in the League, and indeed nearest neighbours, Redditch United appeared to do everything possible to surrender a comfortable second position. Only nine wins in their final twenty games allowed Merthyr Tydfil who won their last eight fixtures, to catch and pass Redditch during the penultimate week of the season. Redditch's last day 1-0 win over Gloucester finally clinched the runners-up spot in a breathtaking climax.

The Southern Division proved to be the most open race for years. Any one of five teams could have won the Championship during the final month. Cambridge City, having taken some valuable points off their nearest challengers during the 'run-in' eventually took the title in a photo-finish with Salisbury, Hastings Town and Dover Athletic.

Relegation battles proved to be equally as close. Gravesend and Northfleet were relegated to the Southern Division by Fareham Town's Houdini escape. Fareham's defeat of Worcester City 1-0 in their last fixture was enough to leapfrog the Kent club at the bottom of the Division.

A final run-in of nine consecutive defeats plummeted Oldbury United into bottom spot of the Midland Division. Their companions in the relegation zone, however, were not known until the final day when Moor Green (third from bottom) and Leamington (second from bottom) were scheduled to play one another. Moor Green won 2-0 and the positions remained unchanged.

A wretched season for Dorchester Town possibly the worst in the Club's history, seldom saw the Dorset outfit out of the bottom place in the League. Their companions for most of the season, Andover, were finally sunk by a one win in ten games run, despite having six successes in eight games during mid season.

In a year when the League's Clubs has a considerable amount of County Cup success, Dover Athletic, Hastings Town, Aylesbury United, Chelmsford City, Dudley Town, Willenhall Town, Corby Town and Bromsgrove Rovers were a few who made final appearances it would be difficult not to recall the season without mentioning the weather. The winter produced some of the wettest and coldest weather for many years bringing its familiar spate of postponements. And matters were made worse by the prolonged nature of the spell. Matches were still being postponed up to and including the penultimate week of the season. Clubs are to be congratulated therefore, on their tremendous efforts to complete the season on time.

Some postponements were, of course, caused by success in Cup Competitions. Apart from the County F.A. successes listed above, Aylesbury United, Chelmsford City, Fareham Town and V.S. Rugby are all to be congratulated for having reached the First Round Proper of the F.A. Cup. Fareham were then beaten by Maidstone United, Orient and Slough Town required replays to overcome W.S. Rugby and Aylesbury respectively while Chelmsford defeated Weymouth but lost in the Second Round against Wycombe Wanderers.

Chelmsford also made fine progress in the F.A. Trophy. Again they were the last Southern League survivor. This time the eventaul Champions of the Gola League, Enfield, ended City's run 5-3 in the Third Round. Corby Town, Bromsgrove Rovers and Crawley Town all reached the Second Round Proper.

Once again, though, results in the F.A. Vase were very disappointing from the League's point of view. Newcomers Bilston Town flew the Banner the longest, into the Fourth Round Proper. The Competition was eventually won for the second successive year by Halesowen Town. And this, of course, brings me on to the Clubs making application to join the league for the 1986-87 season.

There has been a good deal of interest from potential Members this year, which is a sign of the bouyancy of the liaison with the Feeders Leagues in our part of the Pyramid structure. On behalf of all concerned with the League I extend a warm welcome to Buckingham Town and Halesowen Town. We wish you a long and successful association with the 'Southern' and congratulate you on your promotion. In extending metaphoric bouquets to these and the promoted Clubs within our League, commiserations are also sent to Clubs who did not do quite so well. Better luck next year.

The League will have a slightly different shape next year. It was decided at a meeting of Club Chairmen to relegate only two Clubs from the Premier Division (one of whom would be R.S. Southampton who had given notice of withdrawal from the League) for one year only in order to make a complement of 22 Clubs in the top flight. The Regional divisions would be re-instated to 20 teams notwithstanding the promotion/relegation agreement with the Feeder Leagues. It was further decided, that a future objective of the League would be to install 22 Clubs into each of the Regional First Divisions.

DENNIS STRUDWICK

HONOURS LIST

Championship Match
League Winners 1984-85 v.
Challenge Cup Winners 1984-85
Winners: CHELTENHAM TOWN

Bill Dellow Cup
Winners: BROMSGROVE ROVERS
Runner-up: TROWBRIDGE TOWN

Premier Division
Winners: WELLING UNITED
Runner-up: CHELMSFORD CITY

Midland Division
Winners: BROMSGROVE ROVERS
Runner-up: REDDITCH UNITED

Southern Division
Winners: CAMBRIDGE CITY
Runner-up: SALISBURY

Merit Cup
Joint Winners: BROMSGROVE ROVERS
& WELLING UNITED

MACKENZIE'S MANAGER OF THE MONTH AWARDS

August
Graham Hobbins (Welling United)

October
Philip Emblem (Tonbridge A.F.C.)

November
Bernard Clarke (Redditch United)

December
Bobby Hope (Bromsgrove Rovers)

January
Bernard Clarke (Redditch United)

February/March
Graham Hobbins (Welling United)

April
Lyn Jones (Merthyr Tydfil)

May *(Manager of the Season)*
Graham Hobbins (Welling United)

BILL DELLOW CHALLENGE CUP 1985-86

Second Round

Bromsgrove Rovers v. Bedworth United 2-0
Alvechurch v. Worcester City 4-2
Aylesbury United v. V.S. Rugby 1-1, 1-0
Willenhall Town v. Dudley Town 3-5
Folkestone v. Chelmsford City 1-4
Crawley Town v. Welling United 3-0
Fisher Athletic v. Tonbridge A.F.C. 0-3, 0-2
Salisbury v. Trowbridge Town 0-1, 1-4

Third Round

Bromsgrove Rovers v. Alvechurch 1-0
Aylesbury United v. Dudley Town 1-0
Chelmsford City v. Crawley Town 2-1
Fisher Athletic v. Trowbridge Town 1-3

Semi-Finals (over two legs)

Bromsgrove Rovers v. Aylesbury United 2-2, 3-1
(first game at Bromsgrove)

Chelmsford City v. Trowbridge Town 1-0, 1-3
(first game at Chelmsford)

Cup Final (over two legs)

Bromsgrove Rovers 2-1, 2-2
(first game at Bromsgrove—attendance 2,129
second game at Trowbridge—attendance 1324)

LEADING GOALSCORERS BY DIVISIONS

Premier Division:	J. Bartley	Welling United	48
	T. Robbins	Crawley Town	38
	C. Cotton	Alvechurch	32
	L. Ebrey	Worcester City	26
	J. Wood	Crawley Town	21
	J. Muir	Worcester City	20
	P. Taylor	Chelmsford City	20
	P. Earles	R.S. Southampton	18
	A. King	Willenhall Town	18
	G. Stevens	Willenhall Town	18
Midland Division:	C. Hanks	Bromsgrove Rovers	31
	S. Norris	V.S. Rugby	26
	A. Ricketts	Wellingborough Town	23
	M. Cummingham	Bilston Town	20
	P. Mullen	Bromsgrove Rovers	20
	C. Rossi	Sutton Coldfield Town	20
	M. Dunkley	Bromsgrove Rovers	19
	M. Whitehouse	Redditch United	19
	D. Webley	Merthyr Tydfil	18
	D. Westerberg	Merthyr Tydfil	18
Southern Division:	F. Ovard	Dover Athletic	31
	T. Funnell	Poole Town	30
	R. Nelson	Ruislip	25
	K. Dawtrey	Salisbury	24
	G. Grogan	Cambridge City	24
	T. Patterson	Salisbury	24
	D. Arter	Ashford Town	23
	L. Ryan	Dunstable	22
	G. Daniels	Cambridge City	20
	P. Heritage	Hastings Town	20
	K. Todd	Waterlooville	20
	D. White	Hastings Town	20

THE SOUTHERN FOOTBALL LEAGUE
PREMIER DIVISION 1985-86

LEAGUE TABLE

	P	W	D	L	F	A	Pts
Welling United	38	29	6	3	95	31	93
Chelmsford City	38	20	10	8	68	41	70
Fisher Athletic	38	20	7	11	67	45	67
Alvechurch	38	19	9	10	71	56	66
Worcester City	38	19	9	10	64	50	66
Crawley Town	38	18	5	15	76	59	59
Shepshed Charterhouse	38	19	1	18	51	52	58
Aylesbury United	38	14	10	14	52	49	52
Folkestone	38	14	10	14	56	56	52
Bedworth United	38	14	8	16	44	49	50
Willenhall Town	38	12	13	13	51	44	49
Dudley Town	38	15	4	19	58	62	49
Corby Town	38	14	7	17	61	67	49
King's Lynn	38	12	10	16	39	42	46
Basingstoke Town	38	13	4	21	36	67	43
R.S. Southampton	38	11	9	18	44	61	42
Witney Town	38	11	6	21	44	74	39
Gosport Borough	38	10	8	20	42	66	38
Fareham Town	38	8	13	17	40	62	37
Gravesend & Northfleet	38	9	9	20	29	55	36

PREMIER DIVISION 1985-86	Alvechurch	Aylesbury United	Basingstoke Town	Bedworth United	Chelmsford City	Corby Town	Crawley Town	Dudley Town	Fareham Town	Fisher Athletic	Folkestone	Gosport Borough	Gravesend & N.	King's Lynn	R.S. Southampton	Shepshed C.	Welling United	Willenhall Town	Witney Town	Worcester City
Alvechurch	—	0-0	1-1	0-0	4-2	4-1	2-4	5-2	1-1	1-1	1-0	4-1	3-1	3-2	3-0	4-1	0-3	1-0	2-1	1-0
Aylesbury United	5-0	—	0-1	2-0	0-1	1-2	1-0	2-1	2-4	4-1	0-2	2-0	1-0	1-0	1-1	3-1	1-3	3-2	0-2	1-1
Basingstoke Town	0-2	0-1	—	0-3	1-0	0-4	2-1	2-4	2-0	1-1	2-1	2-1	1-1	0-3	2-4	3-2	0-1	2-1	2-0	0-0
Bedworth United	0-3	1-2	0-1	—	0-3	2-2	2-1	2-1	1-1	2-2	2-1	0-1	2-0	2-1	4-1	1-2	0-0	0-1	1-1	2-1
Chelmsford City	1-2	5-2	3-1	5-1	—	4-1	2-3	0-3	1-1	2-1	2-1	3-3	1-1	0-1	1-0	1-0	2-0	4-1	3-1	5-1
Corby Town	2-2	3-0	2-1	1-3	1-3	—	4-1	1-0	6-1	2-1	3-2	1-1	1-2	2-2	2-4	2-1	1-3	2-1	0-1	2-3
Crawley Town	5-2	3-2	4-0	1-0	3-0	2-2	—	3-1	1-0	1-0	1-1	3-0	3-0	2-1	0-0	6-2	3-3	2-2	4-1	1-3
Dudley Town	1-4	1-3	2-0	1-0	0-0	4-0	3-1	—	4-1	3-2	1-1	1-0	2-0	0-0	0-1	2-0	0-3	3-1	3-4	1-4
Fareham Town	3-3	2-2	3-1	0-1	0-0	0-2	0-2	0-2	—	1-2	1-1	4-2	0-0	0-0	0-0	0-1	1-4	2-0	1-0	1-0
Fisher Athletic	1-1	3-1	3-0	1-0	0-0	3-0	1-0	2-0	4-0	—	4-2	4-2	3-0	2-1	2-3	2-1	1-3	0-1	2-3	1-0
Folkestone	1-3	0-0	1-0	1-3	1-2	2-0	1-0	1-0	2-2	1-4	—	1-0	2-1	2-1	3-1	0-1	1-4	1-1	3-3	3-3
Gosport Borough	1-1	0-3	3-2	3-0	0-0	1-0	2-1	1-2	1-4	0-2	1-3	—	1-0	5-4	3-0	1-2	0-1	0-0	0-2	3-1
Gravesend & N.	1-0	0-0	0-1	0-1	1-1	2-1	0-6	4-1	1-2	1-1	1-1	4-0	—	1-0	1-0	0-2	0-3	1-0	0-3	0-1
King's Lynn	0-2	2-1	1-1	0-1	1-2	0-1	2-0	1-0	1-0	2-0	2-1	0-0	2-0	—	2-0	1-3	0-0	1-1	1-0	0-0
R.S. Southampton	0-2	0-0	2-1	2-2	0-0	0-4	2-0	3-1	3-0	2-4	1-2	2-1	0-2	0-0	—	0-1	1-3	1-1	4-0	1-1
Shepshed C.	2-0	1-0	2-0	0-1	1-2	0-0	4-1	2-1	2-1	0-1	0-2	2-1	3-1	0-1	2-1	—	1-3	2-0	4-1	0-1
Welling United	3-1	2-2	5-0	2-1	3-0	5-1	2-1	2-1	3-0	2-0	4-2	3-0	2-1	3-0	4-0	1-0	—	0-0	6-1	1-2
Willenhall Town	4-0	1-1	1-2	2-1	0-3	2-0	5-2	4-1	1-1	1-1	0-0	1-1	1-1	2-0	1-2	4-0	1-1	—	3-0	1-0
Witney Town	2-1	2-1	0-1	1-1	0-3	1-1	1-2	0-3	3-2	0-2	0-2	1-1	0-0	2-1	2-1	0-2	2-3	0-2	—	1-3
Worcester City	3-2	1-1	3-0	2-1	1-1	2-1	3-2	2-2	0-0	1-2	1-4	0-1	3-0	2-2	3-1	3-1	3-1	2-1	3-2	—

PREMIER DIVISION

ALVECHURCH

President: Alan D. Wiseman
Chairman: Don Pedley
Manager: Chris Wright
Asst. Manager/Coach: Reg Brassington
Physiotherapist: Alan Johnson
Secretary: Brian Nevett
Address & Tel. No.: 4 Verbena Close, Stoke Prior, Bromsgrove. 0527 36684
Commercial Manager: Roy Yardley
Press Officer: Dick Arney
Address & Tel. No. of ground: Lye Meadow, Redditch Road, Alvechurch. 021 445 2929
Simple ground directions: Situated on the Birmingham to Redditch Road, 10 miles Birmingham, 3 miles Redditch.
No. of seats: 350 **Covered accommodation:** Seated and Standing **Capacity:** 7,500 **Floodlights:** Yes
Year formed: 1929 **Nickname:** The Church **Club Sponsors:** British Alcan Tubes Ltd.
Previous names: none
Club Colours: Amber/Black
Previous grounds: 'The Meadows'
Change colours: All White
Day for midweek home matches: Wednesday
Previous Leagues: Midland Combination, West Midland
Record attendance: 13,500 v. Enfield Amateur Cup **Year 1964**
Best performance in: F.A. Cup: 1973-4 v. Bradford 3rd Round
F.A. Trophy: 1980-81 Last 16
Club metal badges: Yes
Clubhouse details: Function Room for 200. Separate Lounge, open seven nights, Sunday lunchtime and match days
Past players who progressed to Football League: Ron Green (Bristol Rovers), Sean O'Driscoll (Bourenmouth), Richard O'Kelly (Walsall), David Kelly (Walsall), Alan Smith (Leicester), Colin Brazier (Walsall).
Programme Editor: Dick Arney
Programme details: 36 pages, 30p
Record transfer fee paid: £2,000
Local Newspapers: Redditch Indicator, Bromsgrove Messenger
Record transfer fee received: £25,000
Leading Goalscorers: Chris Cotton (32), **Hat-tricks:** Melvyn Langford, **Most appearances:** Nigel Green
Club captain (1985-86): Kevin Collins
Player of the year (1985-86): Chris Cotton

Goalkeepers
Dave Lawrence: Coleshill Town, W.B.A.
Derek Allen: Bromsgrove Rovers

Defenders
Nigel Connif: Redditch United, Shifnal Town, Oldswinford, Walsall, W.B.A.
Nigel Green: Oldbury United
Kevin Collins: Shrewsbury Town (1), Boldmere, Causeway Green
Mark Owen: Malvern Town
Malcolm Goodman: Halifax Town (88-3), Bromsgrove Rovers

Midfield
Kevin Byrne: Moor Green, Bromsgrove Rovers, Brookfield, Paget Rangers
Paul Shipley: Gloucester City, Aston Villa
Ian Pinner: Moor Green
Royston Richardson: Moor Green

Forwards
Melvyn Langford: Gloucester City, Bromsgrove Rovers, Astwood Bank
Chris Cotton: Moor Green, Redditch United, Bromsgrove Rovers
Tony Donnelly: Moor Green, Highgate United

Alvechurch defending during their visit to Gravesend. Photo David Hills

AYLESBURY UNITED

President: N. P. Ramsden
Chairman: C. Doherty
Manager: Trevor Gould
Physiotherapist: P. Smith
Secretary: Tony Graham
Address & Tel. No.: 8 Windsor Road, Aylesbury, Bucks. HP 21 7JG. 0296 88178 (H) 0844 291881 Ex. 562 (B)
Press Officer: Tony Graham
Address & Tel. No. of ground: The Stadium, Buckingham Road, Aylesbury, Bucks. 0296 20044
Simple ground directions: Follows ring road to A413 exit in direction Buckingham. Ground 100 yards on right.
No. of seats: 400 **Covered accommodation:** 1,000 **Capacity:** 5,000 **Floodlights:** Yes
Year formed: 1897 **Nickname:** The Ducks **Club Sponsors:** Aylesbuyr Plus
Previous names: none
Previous grounds:
Club Colours: All Green
Change colours: All Red
Day for midweek home matches: Tuesday
Previous Leagues: Athenian Delphian, Spartan
Record attendance: 7,440 v. Watford **Year 1951-2**
Best performance in: F.A. Cup: 1951-52 v. Watford 1st Round
1985-86 v. Slough Town
F.A. Trophy: 1980-81 v. Sutton United Quarter Finals
Berks & Bucks Senior Cup: 1985-86 Winners
Club metal badges: Yes
Clubhouse details: Part newly developed ground in its first season. Open every evening.
Past players who progressed to Football League: R. Mabbutt (Bristol Rovers), P. Barber (Crystal Palace)
Programme Editor: Derek Plater
Programme details: 24 pages, 25p
Local Newspapers: Bucks Herald, Bucks Advertiser Aylesbury Plus
Record transfer fee paid: £2,000 for Steve Brinkman (Barnet)
Record transfer fee received: £75,000 for Phil Barber (Crystal Palace)
Senior Honours: County Cup
Leading Goalscorers: David Botterill (24), Cliff Hercules (23), Cliff Campbell (17), **Penalties:** David Botterill (12),
Most appearances: Keith Baker (63), Kevin James (63)
Club captain (1985-86): Peter Mead **Player of the year (1985-86):** Cliff Hercules

Goalkeepers
Keith Baker: Witney Town, Grimsby Town, Millwall, Oxford United

Defenders
Peter Mead: Northampton Town (77-4), Luton Town
Gordon Kelly: Rushden Town
Paul Saunders: Northampton Town (141-5), Watford
Kevin James: Rushden Town, Hitchin Town, Bedford Town
Gary Tipping: Local
Mick Martin: Chesham United, Aylesbury United

Midfield
Paul Hackett: Banbury United, Oxford City, Morris Motors
Chris Williams: Local
Peter Coffill: Northampton Town (83-5), Torquay United (133-11), Watford (70-7), Westham United
Dave Botterill: Rushden Town, Northampton Spencer
Neil Pronger: Local

Forwards
Cliff Campbell: AP Leamington, Bedford Town, Nuneaton Borough, Banbury United
Cliff Hercules: Local
Tony McGuiness: Local

It's no wonder the lads look thrilled, Aylesbury United have just beaten Wycombe Wanderers to win the Berks & Bucks Cup. Photo Bucks Herald.

BASINGSTOKE TOWN

President: C. Foyle
Chairman: Gordon A. Hill
Manager: Goff White
Coach: Ray Dobson
Physiotherapist: Harry Wildish
Secretary: Bryan Banning
Address & Tel. No.: 52 Lordsfield Gardens, Overton, Hants. RG25 3EW. 0256 770077 (H), 0256 21234 (B)
Commercial Manager: none
Press Officer: Bryan Banning
Address & Tel. No. of ground: Camrose Ground, Western Way, Basingstoke, Hants
Simple ground directions: 2 miles Bus and Rail Station. Ring road West old A30. Exit 6 off M3
No. of seats: 840 **Covered accommodation:** 1,000 **Capacity:** 6,000 **Floodlights:** Yes
Year formed: 1896 **Nickname:** Stoke **Club Sponsors:** Basingstoke Press Ltd.
Previous names: none
Club Colours: All Blue
Previous grounds: Castle Field
Change colours: White Shirts & Socks, Black Shorts
Day for midweek home matches: Tuesday **Previous Leagues:** Hampshire
Record attendance: 4,000 v. Northampton F.A. Cup **Year** 1971-72
Best performance in: F.A. Cup: 1971-2 v. Northampton 1st Round
F.A. Trophy: 1984-5 Qualifying **Club metal badges:** Yes
Clubhouse details: 1,500 members. Open seven days a week and lunchtimes
Past players who progressed to Football League: Tony Godfrey (Southampton), Mick Doherty (Reading)
Programme Editor: Neil Tysoe/Dave Partridge **Local Newspapers:** Basingstoke Gazette 0256 461131
Programme details: 20 pages, 25p
Record transfer fee paid: £500 for Alan Tyler (Guildford) **Club Shop:** Yes
Record transfer fee received: £2,000 for Mick Doherty (Reading)
Leading Goalscorers: Dave Eddie (14), **Penalties:** (2), **Most appearances:** Tommy Clegg (14)

Goalkeepers
Keith Champ: Fleet Town, Malshanger, Epsom & Ewell, Tooting & Mitcham

Defenders
Gary Kingston: Swansea City
Steve Mellor: Mexborough Town Athletic
Dave Dodd: Hampton
Tommy Clegg: Fleet Town, Overton United, Farnborough Town, Aldershot
Terry Davies: Portals Athletic, Farnborough Town, Basingstoke Town, Guildford City, Basingstoke Town, Reading

Midfield
Billy Coombs: Newbury Town, Basingstoke Town, Fleet Town, Basingstoke Town,
Wally Cameron: Portals Athletic
George McElhinney: Local
Mark Davies: Portsmouth
Murray Brodie: Aldershot (511-93), Leicester City (3-2), Cumbernauld United

Forwards
Dave Eddie: Fleet Town, Basingstoke Town
Alan Flaherty: Skelmersdale United
Brian Lucas: Farnborough Town, Aldershot (125-19)
Declan Elward: Local
Goff White: Waterlooville, Fareham Town, Gosport Borough, Waterlooville, Havant, Ryde, Gosport Borough, Portsmouth, AFC Bournemouth

A view from the main stand at Basingstoke

BEDWORTH UNITED

President: Alan Robinson
Chairman: H. Jones
Manager: John Brady
Physiotherapist: John Roberts
Secretary: Dennis Grimes
Address & Tel. No.: c/o Bedworth United
Coach: Roger Mason
Press Officer: Chairman 0203 334746
Address & Tel. No. of ground: The Oval, Miners Welfare Park, Bedworth 0203 314302/314752 **Club Shop:** Yes
Simple ground directions: On main Coventry to Bedworth Road, near town centre, ½ mile from M6 junction 3 (A444) next to swimming baths
No. of seats: 300 **Covered accommodation:** 1,000 **Capacity:** 10,000 **Floodlights:** Yes
Year formed: 1968 **Nickname:** Greenbacks **Club Sponsors:** Harry Shaw Travel
Previous names: Bedworth Town
Previous grounds: none
Club Colours: Green/White pinstripes, White Shorts
Change colours: Yellow, Green Shorts
Day for midweek home matches: Tuesday
Previous Leagues: Birmingham Combination, West Midlands
Record attendance: 5,127 v. Nuneaton B (S. League) **Year 1982**
Best performance in: F.A. Cup: 1975 3rd Qualifying Round
F.A. Trophy: 1980-81 2nd Round
Club metal badges: Yes
Clubhouse details: Social club. Normal evening opening times and Saturday, Sunday mid-day
Past players who progressed to Football League: Ray Train
Programme Editor: Chairman
Programme details: 20 pages, 25p
Record transfer fee paid: £500 for Ian Crawley
Record transfer fee received: N/A
Local Newspapers: Nuneaton Tribune. Nuneaton 382251
Bedworth Echo
Coventry Evening Telegraph
Senior Honours: Birmingham Senior Challenge Cup (2), Midland Floodlight Cup
Club captain: M. Martin
Player of the year (1985-86): S. Jackson

Goalkeepers
Mick Martin: Hinckley Athletic, Leicester City

Defenders
Gary Shaw: Coventry City
Martin Smith: Coventry Sporting
Steve Jackson: Local
Mick Howarth: Local
Neil Humphrey: Racing Club Warwick

Midfield
Steve Ross: AP Leamington, Long Buckby
Malcolm Randle: Local
Graham Fearn: Shepshed Charterhouse, Burton Albion, Derby County
Mark Thomas: Shepshed Charterhouse, Chesterfield, Notts County
Owen Wright: Local

Forwards
Chris Downes: V.S. Rugby, AP Leamington, Bedworth United, Coventry Sporting, Lincoln City
Philmore George: Coventry Sporting
Paul Thomas: Local
Pantelis Varnava: New Salamis (Cyprus)
Mark Charnley: Hurley Daw Mill, Atherstone, Bedworth United
Gerard O'Neill: Coventry Sporting, V.S. Rugby, Bedworth United, Long Buckby

Bedworth United *Back Row (L-R): J. Roberts (Physio), J. Taylor, D. Taylor, J. Boneham, M. Howarth, M. Martin, G. Fearn, S. Jackson, M. Haycock (Coach), J. Hanna (Manager). Front Row (L-R): P. Thomas, M. Charnley, P. George, M. Smith, M. Randle (Capt), S. Ross, J. Coyle, K. Trickett.*

BROMSGROVE ROVERS

President: C. W. Poole
Chairman: Jack Sharkey
Manager: Bobbie Hope
Coach: Doug Griffiths
Physiotherapist: P. O'Connell
Secretary: B. A. Hewings
Address & Tel. No.: 21 Carol Avenue, Bromsgrove, Worcs; B61 8RN. 0527 31182 (H)
Commercial Manager: B. H. Evans. 0562 3760
Press Officer: Brian Evans. 0562 3760
Address & Tel. No. of ground: Victoria Ground, 33 Birmingham Road, Bromsgrove, Worcs. 0527 78260
Simple ground directions: A38 twixt Midland Red bus garage/Victoria Road, Birmingham side town centre. opposite petrol station
No. of seats: 375 **Covered accommodation:** 5,700 **Capacity:** 6,500 **Floodlights:** Yes
Year formed: 1885 **Nickname:** The Greens or Rovers **Club Sponsors:** G.L.P. Glazing Ltd.
Previous names: none
Club Colours: Green/White/Green
Previous grounds: Well Lane
Change colours: White
Day for midweek home matches: Tuesday
Previous Leagues: Birmingham Combination
West Midland (Regional)
Club Shop: Yes
Record attendance: 7,563 v. Worc. City Birmingham Senior Cup **Year 1957-8**
Best performance in: F.A. Cup: 1st Round 4 times
F.A. Trophy: 1975-6 Quarter Finals **Club metal badges:** Yes
Clubhouse details: Open 7 nights per week and match afternoons Monday to Saturday. Licensed. Television and Pool Table
Past players who progressed to Football League: S. Smith, B. McGarry, T. Smith, G. Hackett
Senior Honours: Southern League Midland Div Championship 1985-6, Bill Dellow Cup Winners 1985-6
Programme Editor: M. Davies. 0527 77388
Local Newspapers: Bromsgrove Messenger 72254
Bromsgrove Advertiser
Programme details: 20 pages, 20p
Record transfer fee paid: Not available **Record transfer fee received:** £10,000 for Steve Smith from Walsall
Leading Goalscorers: C. Hanks (40), P. Mullen (23), M. Dunkley (22), **Hat-tricks:** C. Hanks, P. Mullen, **Penalties:** A. Kurila (5), S. Omeara (3), **Most appearances:** B. McLaren (66), P. Cooper (66), R. Shilvock (63)
Club captain: M. O'Connell **Player of the year (1985-86):** C. Hanks

Goalkeepers
Bruce Maclaren: Oldbury United

Defenders
Maurice O'Connel: Sutton Coldfield, Northfield Town
Jimmy Skelding: Walsall
Alan Kurila: Bedford Town, Birmingham City
Paul Cooper: Oldbury United, AP Leamington, Nuneaton Borough, Grimsby Town (3), Huddersfield Town (2)
Paul Baker: Local
Robert Shilvock: Halesowen Town

Midfield
Shaun O'Meara: Alvechurch, Stourbridge, Bromsgrove Rovers
Andy Chappell: Willenhall Town
Peter Allbutt: Highgate United
Steve Stott: Local
Simon Moverley: Worcester City, Evesham United, Worcester City

Forwards
Chris Hanks: Studley
Malcolm Dunkley: Local
Colin Coppin: Luton Town
Stan Jones: Oldbury United, Burton Albion, Oldbury United
Phil Mullen: Moor Green, Alvechurch, Kidderminster Harriers, Bromsgrove Rovers, Moor Green, Cinderford Town

Bromsgrove Rovers Back Row *(L-R): A. Tettsall (Asst. Trainer), P. O'Connell (Physio), D. Griffiths (Coach), P. Cooker, P. Baker, S. Stott, B. Maclaren, M. Dunkley, R. Shilvock, J. Skelding, A. Chappell, M. Hart, S. Pinfield (Trainer), B . Hewings (Sec)*
Front Row *(L-R) D. Fearon, M. Langford, P. Allbutt, M O'Connell (Capt) B. Hope (Manager), A. Kurka, C. Hanks, S. Omeara, P. Mullen. Mascot S. Lacy*

CAMBRIDGE CITY

Chairman: D. Few
Manager: W. E. Leivers
Asst. Manager: P. Martin
Physiotherapist: Secretary
Commercial Manager: J. Mills 0233 357973
Secretary: P. Woolson
Address & Tel. No.: 9 Armitage Way, Cambridge CB4 2UE. 314632 (H), 357973 (Club)
Press Officer: As Secretary
Address & Tel. No. of ground: City Ground, Milton Road, Cambridge CB4 1UY. Cambridge 357973 **Club Shop:** Yes
Simple ground directions: 50 yards on left from the beginning of A10, Cambridge to Ely Road
No. of seats: 400 **Covered accommodation:** 3,000 **Capacity:** 3,400 **Floodlights:** Yes
Year formed: 1908 **Nickname:** City Devils **Club Sponsors:** none
Previous names: Cambridge Town
Previous grounds: none
Club Colours: White/Black
Change colours: All Sky Blue
Day for midweek home matches: Wednesday
Previous Leagues: Southern Amateur Spartan Athenian
Record attendance: 22,000 v. Walthamstow Avenue **Year:** 1950
Best performance in: F.A. Cup: 1965 1st Round proper
F.A. Trophy: 1978 1st Round proper
Clubhouse details: Open every night. Bingo, dances, darts, pool, stag nights
Present players with Football League experience: Keith Pointer, Peter Martin
Past players who progressed to Football League: Tommy Carroll (Ipswich)
Programme Editor: D. Crane
Programme details: 16 pages, 20p
Local Newspapers: Cambridge Evening News 35877
Record transfer fee paid: £500 for Dave Hickson
Record transfer fee received: £1,500 Tommy Carrol to Ipswich
Senior Honours: County Cup, Southern Premier Champions
Club captain (1985-86): Keith Pointer
Player of the year (1985-86): Gary Grogan

Goalkeepers
Ian Ladley: Local
Mick Tonner

Defenders
John Cowan: Local
Karl Simper: Local
Keith Moore: Saffron Walden Town
Phil Hubbard: Burwell Swifts, Soham Town
Colin Jobling: Local
Geoff Hancocks: Local
Steve Roach: Local

Midfield
Keith Pointer: Thanet United, Folkestone Town Cambridge United, West Ham United
Steve Gawthrop: Local
Terry Milbourne: Harlow Town
Peter Lindsay: Local
Peter Martin: Bedford Town, Cambridge City, Chelmsford City, Cambridge City, Barnsley, Hull City
Steve Carey: Local

Forwards
Garry Grogan: Ely City, Barnstaple Town
Kevin Parish: Local
Mario Ippolito: Rushden Town, Stamford, King's Lynn, Peterborough (8-3)
Graham Daniels: Cambridge United, (39-4), Cardiff Corinthians
Colin Lennihan: Epping Town

Ruislip v. Cambridge City. *(White shirts) Ruislip press home an attack in this their first ever home Southern League (Southern Section) match at Breakspear Road in September 1985, the result was 1-0 to the City*

CHELMSFORD CITY

Chairman: B. T. Reeve
Manager: Joe Sullivan
Asst. Manager/Coach: D. O'Leary
Physiotherapist:
Secretary/Gen. Manager: V. A. W. Keeble
Address & Tel. No.: 13 Station Road, Earls Colne. 2978
Press Officer: As Secretary
Address & Tel. No. of ground: The Stadium, New Writtle Street, Chelmsford. 353052
Simple ground directions: 5 minutes walk from Railway Station. 2 minutes off A12
No. of seats: 1,500 **Covered accommodation:** 12,500 **Capacity:** 16,000 **Floodlights:** Yes
Year formed: 1980 **Nickname:** City **Club Sponsors:** none
Previous names: Chelmsford City (1938)
Club Colours: White Shirts, Claret Trim, Maroon Shorts, White Socks
Club shop: yes
Previous grounds: none
Change colours: Gold Shirts, Black Shorts, Gold Socks
Day for midweek home matches: Monday **Previous Leagues:** none
Record attendance: 15,557 v. Ipswich TownF.A. Cup 3rd Round **Year** 1973
Best performance in: F.A. Cup: 1938-9 v. Birmingham 4th Round
F.A. Trophy: 1969-70 Semi-final v. Telford **Club metal badges:** Yes
Clubhouse details: Available for private hire. Open every evening. Social events. Snacks
Past players who progressed to Football League: Peter Collins (Spurs), Nigel Spink (Aston Villa), M. Dziadulowicz (Wimbledon)
Programme Editor: Secretary
Local Newspapers: Essex Chronical
Programme details: 20 pages, 30p
Record transfer fee paid: none
Record transfer fee received: £4,000—Nigel Spink (Aston Villa), Mark Dziadulowicz (Wimbledon)
Leading Goalscorers: Peter Taylor, Phil Thrift, Ron Pountney. **Hat-tricks:** Ron Pountney (1), T. Glynn (1). **Penalties:** P Taylor (7). **Most appearances:** Peter Taylor, John Kooley, Colin Johnson
Club captain (1985-86): Bob Makin **Player of the year (1985-86):** Peter Taylor

Goalkeepers
John Keeley: Maldon Town, Southend United (63)

Defenders
Colin Johnson: Hounslow, Wealdstone, Dartford, Orient
Steve Dixson: Gravesend, Bromley, Dartford, Leatherhead, Crystal Palace
Steve Oliver: Dagenham, Enfield, Barnet, Barking, Tottenham Hotspur
Bob Makin: Dartford, Dagenham, Barking
Mark Entwistle: Local
Kevin Lee: Heybridge Swifts

Midfield
Adrian Owers: Southend United (27)
Dave Spittle: Charlton Athletic
Adrian Foley: Welling United, Sutton United, Maidstone United, Gravesend, Dartford
Neil Banfield: Woodford Town, Dagenham, Orient (31), Adelaide City (Aus), Crystal Palace (3)
Mark Simpson: Crawley Town, Maidstone United, Charlton Athletic

Forwards
Paul Lazarus: TPS Turn (Fin), Maidstone United, Dartford, Dagenham, Wimbledon (18-6), Charlton Athletic (2-1)
Ron Pountney: Southend United (348-26), Bilston, Port Vale, Walsall
John Herbert: Local
Ken Taylor: Bishop's Stortford, Chatham Town
Phil Thrift: New Writtle

Back Row:— Joe Sullivan (Manager, Paul Marlow, Steve Oliver, John Devine, Dennis Longhorn, Kevin Foster, John Keeley, Terry Warren, Bob Makin, Dave Grrom, Danny O'Leary (Coach), Don Walker (Trainer) Front Row:— Colin Johnson, Adrian Owers, Steve Kilbey, Phil Thrift, Terry Glynn, Peter Taylor, Ron Pountney, Adrian Foley, Kevin Lee.

CORBY TOWN

President: H. Hetterley
Chairman: J. Bowman
Manager: Colin Foster
General Manager: Harry Fallon
Secretary: John Wiseman
Address & Tel. No.: 19 Fineshade Grove, Corby, Northants NN17 1HR. 0536 68144 (H)
Club Shop: Yes
Address & Tel. No. of ground: Rockingham Triangle, Corby, Northants. 0536 63610
Simple ground directions: On northern outskirts of town. At intersection of A6116 and A6003 roads above village of Rockingham (opposite Rockingham Castle grounds)
No. of seats: 1,150 **Covered accommodation:** 1,150 **Capacity:** 3,000 **Floodlights:** Yes
Year formed: 1948 **Nickname:** The Steelmen **Club Sponsors:** Graham Holmes Plastics (Astraseal)
Previous names: Stewarts & Lloyds
Previous grounds: none
Day for midweek home matches: Monday
Club metal badges: Yes
Club Colours: White Shirts, Black Shorts
Change colours: All Yellow
Previous Leagues: United Counties Midland Leagues
Record attendance: 863 v. Kidderminster Harriers F.A. Trophy 2nd Round proper **Year 1986**
Best performance in: F.A. Cup: 1965-6 v. Plymouth Argyll 3rd Round
F.A. Trophy: 1969-70, 1975-6 2nd Round
Clubhouse details: Open 7 days a week, usual club facilities
Past players who progressed to Football League: D. Dall (Scunthorpe), P. Bannon (Carlisle), D. McNeil (Wrexham), G. Reilly (Cambridge, Watford), V. Overson (Burnley), Phil Chard (Peterborough), Len Chalmers (Leicester), Andy McGowan (Northampton Town), Andy McCabe (Chesterfield), Peter Kearns (Aldershot)
Programme Editor:
Programme details:
Local Newspapers: Northamptonshire Evening Telegraph 0536 81111
Record transfer fee paid: £2,700 for Elwyn Roberts (Barnet)
Record transfer fee received: £10,200 Trevor Morley (Nuneaton)
Senior Honours: V.C.L. League Championship (2), Southern League Merit Cup, County Senior Cup (2)
Leading goalscorers: David Hofbauer (27), Derek Walker (18), Elwyn Roberts (14). **Hat-tricks:** David Hofbauer (1) also 4 goals in one match. **Penalties:** Derek Walker (5), John Lane (1). **Most appearances:** John Timlin (54), Jem Palmer (51), David Hofbauer (50), Tony Ferns (50)
Club captain (1985-86): Gordon Hall **Player of the year (1985-86):** John Lane

Goalkeepers
Steve Parkin: Northampton Town
Dick Dighton: Stewarts & Lloyds, Stamford, Irthlingborough, Rushden Town, Kettering Town, Peterborough United, Coventry City, Corby Town

Defenders
John Timlin: Rushden Town
Jem Palmer: Kettering Town, Desborough Town
Callum Morrison: Stewarts & Lloyds, Rothwell Town, Desborough Town
John Lane: Shepshed Charterhouse, Worcester City, Corby Town, Wigston Fields, Leicester United, Leicester City
Colin Foster: Rushden Town, Shepshed Charterhouse, King's Lynn, Grantham, Peterborough United (71-4), Mansfield Town (205-17)

Midfield
Elwyn Roberts: Kidderminster Harriers, Corby Town, Barnet, Apia (Aus), Bedford Town, Corby Town, Nottingham Forest
Derek Walker: Nuneaton Borough, Corby Town, Kettering Town
Kevin Byrne: Stewarts & Lloyds, Desborough Town
Tim Gale: Wisbech Town, King's Lynn, Peterborough United

Forwards
Roy Clayton: Irthlingborough, Corby Town, Nun-eaton Borough, Barnet, Kettering Town, Oxford United, Warley Borough
David Hofbauer: Kettering Town, Corby Town
Paul Murphy: Cottingham
Shaun Diver: Kettering Town
Mick Keall: Rothwell Town, Desborough Town

An inpromptu tactics talk in front of Corby Town's imposing new grandstand during the opening game at their £800,000 Rockingham Triangle Sports Ground.

(picture by courtesy of Northamptonshire Evening Telegraph)

CRAWLEY TOWN

Chairman: K. N. Symons
Team Manager: J. W. Maggs
Coach: J. W. Maggs
Secretary/Gen. Manager: S. H. Markham
Address & Tel. No.: 105 Winchester Road, Crawley 22371 (H), 029331133 x329 (B)
Commercial Manager: F. Pitts. Crawley 37190
Physiotherapist: D. Haining
Press Officer: J. Green (Dennis Lovell 0293 37427)
Address & Tel. No. of ground: 'Town Mead', Ifield Avenue, West Green, Crawley, Sussex 21800 **Club shop:** Yes
Simple ground directions: Crawley BR S.R. 10 min. walk 'thru High Street. Ground next to Fire Station in Ifield Avenue
No. of seats: 250 **Covered accommodation:** 4,750 **Capacity:** 5,000 **Floodlights:** Yes
Year formed: 1896 **Nickname:** The Reds **Club Sponsors:**
Previous names: none
Club Colours: All Red
Previous grounds: none
Change colours: All Blue
Day for midweek home matches: Tuesday
Previous Leagues: Sussex County Metropolitan
Record attendance: 3,250 v. Wimbledon F.A. Cup replay **Year** 1969
Best performance in: F.A. Cup: 1970 v. Chelmsford City, 1971 v. Exeter City 1st Round
F.A. Trophy: Never beyond 3rd Qualifying Round
Club metal badges: Yes
Clubhouse details: Daily except Tuesday, lunchtime; Saturday evening 4.45-6.30 p.m.
Past players who progressed to Football League: none
Programme Editor: Dennis Lovell
Local Newspapers: Crawley Observer. 29551 Crawley News. 510148
Programme details: 16 pages, 25p
Record transfer fee paid: none
Record transfer fee received: £2,250 for Trevor Smith to Gravesend
Leading goalscorers: Terry Robbins, Jeff Wood. **Hat-tricks:** 2. **Penalties:** 1. **Most appearances:** Bob Glozier (57/58), Terry Robbins (56/58), Jeff Wood (56/58)
Club captain (1985-86): Steve Breach
Player of the year (1985-86): Terry Robbins

Goalkeepers
Gary Moseley: Dartford, Crawley Town, Dover, West Ham United, Tonbridge
Trevor Inch: Brentford, Portsmouth

Defenders
Alan Lester: Fulham
Steve Breach: Dover, Thanet United, Brighton, Arsenal
Bob Glozier: Hastings United, Gravesend, Maidstone United, Dover, Dartford, Guildford City, Torquay United, West Ham United
Andy Coghill: Walton & Hersham, Carshalton Athletic, Thanet United, Folkestone Town, Gravesend
Malcolm McKinnon: Local
Phil Keeping: Chelmsford City, Dartford, Chelmsford City, Southend United

Midfield
Cliff Cant: Carshalton Athletic, Fulham, Arsenal
David Myers: Chatham Town, Gravesend, Dartford, Canterbury City, Tonbridge
Marcus Cook: Local
Gary Richards: Local
Giles Stille: Sutton United, Norrkoeping (Swe), Brighton (27-4), Kingstonian

Forwards
Gary Julians: Dover, Chelmsford City, Crawley Town, Gravesend, Welling United, Maidstone United, Dartford, Millwall
Terry Robbins: Maidstone United, Tottenham Hotspur
Jeff Wood: Greenwich Borough, West Ham United
Keith Browning: East Grinstead Athletic
Jimmy Sweetzer: Wokingham Town, Leatherhead, Dartford, Wealdstone, Millwall, Oxford United (11-2)

Crawley Town F.C. *Back Row (L-R): Trevor Inch, Stan Markham (Sec./Gen.Man), Bob Glozier, Andy Coghill, Neil Bryant, Alan Lester, Barry Morgan, David Myers, Jeff Wood, Dave Haining (Physio./Trainer), John Maggs (Team Man.) Front Row(L-R): Gary Julians, Terry Robbins, Steve Breach, Cliff Cant, Mark Simpson.*

DARTFORD

Chairman: Brian Alford
Manager: Peter Taylor
Asst. Manager/Coach: Terry Harris
Physiotherapist: J. Payne
Secretary: Dick Mace
Address & Tel. No.: 64 Brent Lane, Dartford, Kent 0322 22052
Commercial Manager: Kathy Tree c/o Dartford F.C.
Press Officer: Mike Brett-Smith 0322 77243 (H), 21266 (B)
Address & Tel. No. of ground: Watling Street, Dartford, Kent. 0322 73639 **Club shop:** Yes, open match days
Simple ground directions: From town centre/B.R. Station proceed up East Hill, take third turning on right into Watling Street from Dartford Tunnel. A2 turn off. Floodlights visible from Princes Hotel roundabout.
No. of seats: 898 **Covered accommodation:** 3,000 **Capacity:** 8,500 **Floodlights:** Yes
Year formed: 1888, reformed 1921 **Nickname:** The Darts **Club Sponsors:** Daniel Homes Ltd.
Previous names: none
Previous grounds: Lowfield Street
Club Colours: White/Black/Black
Change colours: All Yellow
Day for midweek home matches: Tuesday
Record attendance: 11,004 v. Leyton Orient F.A. Cup 1st Round **Year** 1948-9
Best performance in: F.A. Cup: 1935-6 v. Derby C. 3rd Round proper
1936-7 v. Darlington 3rd Round proper
F.A. Trophy: 1973-4 Finalists, 1980-1 Semi-Finalists
Previous Leagues:
Kent
Southern
Alliance Premier/Gola
Clubhouse details: Players Bar open match days. Snooker Club (members only) open 7 days a week
Past players who progressed to Football League: Idris Hodkins (Brentford, Wales), Fred Dell (West Ham U), Riley Cullum & Fred Alexander (Charlton), Derek Hales (Luton Town), Trevor Morgan (Bournemouth)
Programme Editor: Mike Brett-Smith
Local Newspapers: Dartford Times, Dartford Reporter Kent Evening Post
Programme details: 24 pages, 30p
Club metal badges: Yes
Record transfer fee paid: £3,000 Micky Dingwall (Maidstone United) 1984
Record transfer fee received: £4,000 Gay Julians (Maidstone United)
Senior Honours: Southern League Premier Division (2), Southern League (2), Southern League Southern Section (1), Southern League Cup Winners (1), Runners up (2), Southern League Challenge Match Winners (1), F.A. Trophy Final (1), Kent Senior Cup (7), Inter-League Challenge Match Winners 1974
Leading Goalscorers: Tony Barman (17), Micky Dingwall (9) **Hat-tricks:** Tony Burman (1).
Penalties: Jon Gille (2). **Most appearances: David Jacques (53), Tony Burman (51), Francis Cowley (40)**
Club captain (1985-86):
Player of the year (1985-86): David Jacques

Goalkeepers
Terry Jessop: Welling United, Hastings United, Maidstone United
Mark Poultney: Enfield, Tottenham Hotspur

Defenders
David Jacques: Leytonstone & Ilford
Tony Pamphlett: Cray Wanderers
Tony Isaacs: Arsenal
Martin McCayna: Leytonstone & Ilford, Aveley, Southend United
John Reeves: Aveney, Maidstone United, Barking, Dagenham, Billericay Town, Basildon United

Midfield
Francis Cowley: Tooting & Mitcham, Wimbledon (8), Derby County, Chelsea

Forwards
Terry Lee: Gravesend, H.J.K. Helsinki (Fin), Arsenal
Gary Campbell: Finchley, Arsenal
Tony Burman: Charlton Athletic (19-3), Q.P.R.
Nicky Crown: Barking, Grays Athletic, Epping Town
Tony Rogers: Tilbury, Basildon United, Leystonstone & Ilford
Dave Wadhams: Sheppey United
Malcolm Stewart: Maidstone United, Dagenham, Hoddesdon Town
Paul Blade: Erith & Belvedere, Southend United, Crystal Palace, Charlton Athletic
Mark Gerbaldi: Charlton Athletic, Arsenal
Peter Taylor, Chelmsford City, Heybridge Swifts, Maidstone United, Exeter City (6), Maidstone United, Orient (62-11), Tottenham Hotspur (140-33), Crystal Palace (144-38), Southend United (78-13)

Standing: D. Letchford (Director), John Still (Manager), Tony Rogers, Micky Dingwall, Steve Robinson, Dave Mallett, Paul Powell, Tony Pamphlett, Marting McCayna, George Dudley (Asst. Manager), Alan Carrington (Coach)
Kneeling: Jimmy Paine(Physio), John Sille, Tony Burman, Francis Cowley, Malcolm Stewart, Nicky Crown
Photo: Reporter Newspapers Ltd

DUDLEY TOWN

President: none
Chairman: N. D. Jeynes
Manager: Graham Smith
Asst. Manager/Coach: Lionel Martin
Physiotherapist: E. Mordan
Secretary: A. J. Turpin
Address & Tel. No.: 24 Andrew Drive, Short Heath, Willenhall, West Midlands 0922 475541 (H)
Commercial Manager: J. T. Edwards
Press Officer: Secretary
Address & Tel. No. of ground: Round Oak Stadium, John Street, Brierley Hill, Dudley, West Midlands
Year formed: 1893 **Nickname:** The Robins **Club Sponsors:** Bronx Engineering
Previous names: none
Club Colours: Red Shirts, White Shorts
Previous grounds: Shavers End
Change colours: Yellow Shirts and Shorts
Day for midweek home matches: Tuesday **Previous Leagues:** West Midlands (Regional)
Record attendance: 8,200 v. Worcester City F.A. Cup **Year 1964**
Best performance in: F.A. Cup: 1976-6 1st Round Proper **Club metal badges:** Yes
F.A. Trophy: 1984-5 2nd Round Proper **Club shop:** No
Clubhouse details: Dudley Town Sports & Social Club, John Street, Brierley Hill
Past players who progressed to Football League: Joe Mayo, Ken Price
Programme Editor: J. T. Edwards
Local Newspapers: Express and Star, Dudley Evening Mail
Programme details: 24 pages, 20p
Record transfer fee received: £1,000 for Ken Price (Southend)
Senior Honours: Southern League Midland Division Champions 1984-5, Birmingham Senior Cup Winners 1985-6
Leading Goalscorers: Russell Gordon (22), Malcolm Hazelwood (2), Mark Stanton (20). **Penalties:** 5.
Most appearances: Ben Brown (58), Andy Foote (55), Mick Rich (55)
Club captain (1985-6): Benny Brown
Players of the year (1985-6): David Shelton/Russell Gordon

Goalkeepers
Steve Pomroy: Brereton Social, Bromsgrove Rovers, Nuneaton Borough, Walsall, Shrewsbury Town
Steve Johnson: Local

Defenders
Danny McCormack: Sutton Coldfield, Aston Villa
Benny Brown: Hendesford Town, Bilston Town, Brierley Hill, Hednesford Town
Andy Foote: Coleshill Town, Banbury United, Shrewsbury Town, Luton Town
Steve Morrall: Local
Dave Francis: Blackenall, Dudley Town, Bromsgrove Rovers, Worcester City, Dudley Town
Dave Shelton: Local

Midfield
Malcolm Hazlewood: Halesowen Town, Walsall
John Loveridge: Alvechurch, Walsall (26-2), W.B.A.
Stuart Penrose: Local
Micky Rich: Stafford Rangers, Stourbridge, Brierly Hill, Tividale, Swansea City
Peter Duckett: Local

Forwards
Brendan Drummond: Stafford Rangers, Stourbridge, Oldswinford, Dudley Town, Gornal Athletic
Micky James: Armitage, Sutton Coldfield, Rushall Olympic, Burton Albion, Walsall
Mark Stanton: Local
John Wesson: Oldswinford
Russell Gordon: Banbury United, Nuneaton Borough, Coventry City

Dudley Town *Back Row (L-R): Lionel Martin (Asst. Man.), John Wesson, Malcolm Hazlewood, Russell Gordon, Steve Morrall, Steve Pomroy, Andy Foote, Dave Shelton, Dave Francis, Ernie Mordan (Physio.)*
Front Row: (L-R): Danny McCormack, John Loveridge, Brendan Drummond, Graham Smith (Man.), Benny Brown (Capt.), Micky Rich, Mark Stanton, Micky James

FAREHAM TOWN

President: L. E. Abraham
Chairman: R. A. Grant
Manager: Trevor Parker
Asst. Manager/Coach: R. Gill/T. Williams
Physiotherapist: G. Buckner
Club shop: Yes
Secretary: K. F. Atkins
Address & Tel. No.: 4 Cedar Close, Elson, Gosport Hants. PO12 4AT. 0705 583049
Commercial Manager:
Press Officer: M. Willis Waterlooville 28163
Address & Tel. No. of ground: Cams Alders, Highfield Avenue, Fareham, Hants. 0329 231151
Simple ground directions: From Fareham railway station follow A27 towards Southampton take second turning left into Redlands Lane, right at Redlands Inn and then left into Highfield Avenue
No. of seats: 450 **Covered accommodation:** 500 **Capacity:** 5,500 **Floodlights:** Yes
Year formed: 1947 **Nickname:** The Town **Club Sponsors:** Hellyers Travel
Previous names: none
Previous grounds: Bath Lane, Fareham
Day for midweek home matches: Wednesday
Record attendance: 2,650 v. Wimbledon F.A. Cup **Year** 1965
Club Colours: Red/White/Red
Change colours: White/Black/White
Previous Leagues: Hampshire Portsmouth
Best performance in: F.A. Cup: 1979-80 1st Round
F.A. Trophy: 1975-6, 1983-4 1st Round Proper
Club metal badges: No
Clubhouse details: Open each evening except Sunday
Past players who progressed to Football League: Ray Hiron, John Hold, Steve Claridge and Dave Leworthy
Programme Editor: Roy Grant
Programme details: 20 pages, 30p
Local Newspapers: Evening News Portsmouth Evening Echo Southampton
Record transfer fee paid: £1,000 P. Baxter (Poole Town)
Record transfer fee received: £43,000 David Leworthy (Tottenham Hotspur)
Senior Honours: Hants Senior Cup (3), Hants County League (8). F.A. Sunday Cup, S.W. Counties Cup (2)
Club captain (1985-86):
Player of the year (1985-86):

Goalkeepers
Paul Grant: Local

Defenders
Russell Davies: Andover, Gosport Borough
Trevor Smith: Andover, Basingstoke Town, Andover, Salisbury, Aldershot
Shaun North: East Cowes Vics
Andy Bye: Gosport Borough
Steve Watt: Waterlooville, Fareham Town, Newport I.o.W., Havant Town

Midfield
Stuart McIntyre: Havant Town
Nigel Long: Macclesfield Town, Burton Albion, Frickley Athletic, Doncaster Rovers
Malcolm Wilkes: Newport I.o.W., Fareham Town, Waterlooville
Sandy Baird: Horndean
Barry Andrews: Andover, Basingstoke Town, Salisbury, Andover, Aldershot
Peter Tindall: Bognor Regis Town, Salisbury, Yeovil Town, Portsmouth
Alan Hallett: Local

Forwards
Kevin Bartlett: Portsmouth (3)
Kim Hopcroft: East Cowes Vics
Darren Brown: Local
Derek Barnes: Local

A great save from the Fareham goalkeeper while under pressure from the Gravesend attack. Photo David Hills

FISHER ATHLETIC

President: Lord Mellish of Bermondsey
Chairman: T. McCarthy
Manager: D. Arif
Asst. Manager/Coach: Steve Bowtell
Physiotherapist: Pat "The Fizz"
Secretary: Les Rowe
Address & Tel. No.: c/o The ground
Commercial Manager: Tony Incenzo
Press Officers: Tony Incenzo/Geoff Coe
Address & Tel. No. of ground: Surrey Docks Stadium, Salter Road, London SE16 **Club Shop:** Yes
Simple ground directions: Head for southern entrance to Rotherhithe Tunnel, turn into Brunel Road, continue on into Salter Road. Ground on right. Stations Rotherhithe (Metropolitan Line) 10 minutes walk London Bridge (B.R.) two miles
No. of seats: 400 **Covered accommodation:** Being Built **Capacity:** 5,000 **Floodlights:** Yes
Year formed: 1908 **Nickname:** The Club **Club Sponsors:** Master Mail
Previous names: none **Club Colours:** Black & White Stripes
Previous grounds: Mitcham **Change colours:** All Red
Day for midweek home matches: Tuesday
Record attendance: 2,000 v. Bristol City F.A.C. 1st Round **Year** 1984-5
Best performance in: F.A. Cup: 1984-5 1st Round
F.A. Trophy: 1983-4, 1984-5 3rd Round
Previous Leagues: Kent Amateur, London Spartan
Club metal badges: No
Clubhouse details: Bar and light refreshments. Open lunchtimes and evenings. Not Mondays.
Past players who progressed to Football League: Paul Shinners (Gillingham, Orient), T. Aylott (Chelsea, Barnsley, Luton)
Programme Editors: Tony Incenzo/Geoff Coe
Programme details: 24 pages, 30p
Record transfer fee paid: none
Record transfer fee received: none
Local Newspapers: South London Press, Kentish Mercury, Downtown Review
Senior Honours: Kent Senior Trophy, Kent Senior Cup, London Spartan Premier/Senior Division, Southern League Div. 1(3), Champions (1983), Southern League Premier Division Runners-up 1984, Bill Dellow Southern League Cup 1985, London Senior Cup 1985, F.A.C. 1st Round 1984
Leading goalscorers: C. Lewington, T. Dark, P. Wilkins. **Hat-tricks:** W. O'Sullivan, T. Dark, P. Wilkins. **Penalties:** M. Dennehy, T. Dark
Club captain (1985-86): Dennis Sharp **Player of the year (1985-86):** T. Dark

---

Goalkeepers
Engin Salih: Bromley, Dulwich Hamlet, Millwall
Steve Bowtell: Woking, Dulwich Hamlet, Thanet United, Orient

Defenders
Bert Davis: Finchley, Fisher Athletic, Cardiff City
Chris Hiscock: Epsom & Ewell, Beckenham Town, Dartford, Millwall
Dennis Sharp: Local
Bobby Shinners: Derby County
Paul Collins: Millwall
Ray Shinners: Croydon

Midfield
Trevor Dark: Carshalton Athletic, Hendon, Birmingham City (5-1)
Chris Lewington: Carshalton Athletic, Dulwich Hamlet, Wimbledon, Crystal Palace, Q.P.R., Chelsea
Alan Hodges: Local
Willie O'Sullivan: Gravesend, Dartford, Charlton Athletic (2)
Mark Hobbs: Charlton Athletic, Chelsea

Forwards
Leroy Ambrose: Esbjerg (Den), Kolding (Den), Hvidovre (Den), Charlton Athletic (34-1), Croydon
Paul Wilkins: Walthamstow Avenue, Preston N.E., (6-2), Crystal Palace (13-3), Tottenham Hotspur
Mark Dennehy: Dagenham, Kuopio Elo (Fin), Millwall
Godfrey Jacobs: Local
David Regis: Dunstable
Paul Rulton: Dulwich Hamlet, Corinthian Casuals, Hampton, Croydon, Crystal Palace

Fisher Athletic Photo: Eric Marsh

FOLKESTONE TOWN

President: W. Armory
Chairman: G. W. Rutherford (Acting)
Manager: Allan Jones
Asst. Manager/Coach: Keith Lissenden
Physiotherapist: Keith Lissenden
Secretary: G. W. Rutherford
Address & Tel. No.: "Sheridan", Alkham Valley Road, Alkham Nr. Dover, Kent 0304 823993
Commercial Manager: Alvin Marshallsey
Press Officer: Mike Stone
Address & Tel. No. of ground: Cheriton Road, Folkestone, Kent. 0303 51374 **Club shop:** Yes
Simple ground directions: On the A20 behind Presto Stores, midway between Folkestone Central and West Stations
No. of seats: 900 **Covered accommodation:** 7,100 **Capacity:** 8,000 **Floodlights:** Yes
Year formed: 1884 **Nickname:** The Town **Club Sponsors:** Vista Windows
Previous names: Folkestone & Shepway,
Club Colours: Amber/Black/Amber
Change colours: All Red
Day for midweek home matches: Tuesday **Previous Leagues:** Kent
Record attendance: 7,801 v. Margate, Kent Senior Cup **Year** 1958
Best performance in: F.A. Cup: 1932-3, 1965-6 3rd Round
F.A. Trophy: 1979-80 3rd Qualifying Round **Club metal badges:** No
Clubhouse details: Open every day. Normal opening hours. Pool, Darts, etc.
Past players who progressed to Football League: P. Hilton, T. Pearce, G. Towse, J. Hill, M. Barham, J. Goss
Programme Editor: Neil Pilcher
Programme details: 24 pages, 25p
Local Newspapers: Folkestone Herald & Gazette 0303 41411
Record transfer fee paid: £1,500 N. Fusco (Maidstone United)
Record transfer fee received: £5,000 F. Ovard (Maidstone)
Senior Honours: Kent Senior Cup (5), Kent Senior Shield (7), F.A. Cup 1932-3, 1965-6 3rd Round F.A. Trophy, 1979-80 3rd Qualifying Round
Leading goalscorers: Terry Holley (17), Lee Welsh (14), Pat Hilton (11). **Most appearances:** Maurice Munden (51), Kevin Smart (49), Ricky Fusco (49)
Club captain (1985-86): Kenny Hill **Player of the year (1985-86):** Maurice Munden

Goalkeepers
Maurice Munden: Charlton Athletic

Defenders
Kevin Smart: Wigan Athletic (49-1), Plymouth Argyle (32)
Terry Norton: Thanet United, Dover, Thanet United, Brighton
Kenny Hill: Maidstone United, Washington Diplomats (USA), Baltimore Comets (USA), Lincoln City (1), Gillingham (125-7)
Terry Martin: Faversham Town
Colin Binder: Local

Midfield
Chris Hamshare: Hastings United, Dover, Gillingham
Terry Collins: Thanet United, Hythe Town, Folkestone
Terry Jolley: Gravesend, Dover, Gillingham (21-5), West Ham United
Ricky Fusco: Dover, Thanet United, Maidstone United, Ramsgate
David Bean: Dover, Gravesend

Forwards
Micky Heynes: Hythe Town
Lee Welsh: Canterbury City, Dover
Andy Allon: Dover, Folkestone
Pat Hilton: Dover, Folkestone, Southport (27-5), Gillingham (26-1), Blackburn Rovers (16-2), W.B.A., Brighton (20-1), Canterbury City, Folkestone
Martin Stevens: Local

Folkestone F.C.

GOSPORT BOROUGH

President: F. G. Schomberg
Chairman: G. R. Barratt
Manager: A. J. Brickwood/P. Edgar
Physiotherapist: R. J. Hollyer
Secretary: W. J. Adams
Address & Tel. No.: "Clapper Oaks", 13 Bentham Road, Alverstoke, Gosport PO12 2HN. 0705 581604
Press Officer: Paul Campbell
Address & Tel. No. of ground: Privett Park, Privett Road, Gosport. 0705 583986 **Club shop:** Yes
Simple ground directions: A32 from Fareham 3 miles. Follow signs from Fort Brockhurst to Privett Road
No. of seats: 500 **Covered accommodation:** 500 **Capacity:** 5,000 **Floodlights:** Yes
Year formed: 1944 **Nickname:** The Borough **Club Sponsors:** M. D. Weston & Co. (Builders)
Previous names: Gosport Borough Athletic
Previous grounds: none
Day for midweek home matches: Tuesday
Club Colours: Blue & Gold
Change colours: Silver and Maroon
Previous Leagues: Hampshire
Record attendance: 3,500
Best performance in: F.A. Cup: 1980-1 v. Windsor & Eton 4th Qual. Round
F.A. Vase: 1976-7 v. Barton R. 6th Round
F.A. Trophy: 1980-1 v. Aylesbury 3rd Qual. Round
Clubhouse details: Bar facilities **Club metal badges:** No
Past players who progressed to Football League: Peter Harris (Portsmouth & England), Jimmy Scoular (Portsmouth, Newcastle & Scotland), Albert Mundy (Portsmouth), Ronnie Blackman (Reading), Gary Juryeff (Portsmouth), B. Sherwood, D. Dimmer, S. Berry
Programme Editors: P. Campbell & P. Francis
Programme details: 20 pages, 20p
Record transfer fee paid: nil
Local Newspapers: Portsmouth News, Southampton Echo
Record transfer fee received: £5,000
Senior Honours: Hampshire League (3), S.W. Counties Pratten Cup
Club captain (1985-86):
Player of the year (1985-86):

Goalkeepers
Tony Stares: Havant Town, Southampton

Defenders
Gary Juryeff: Portsmouth, Gosport Borough
Tim Coak: Waterlooville, Salisbury, Southampton (4)
Steve Ingman: Local
Mark Foster: Waterlooville, Gosport Borough
Tony Mahoney: Brockenhurst
Martin Winning: Fareham Town, Havant Town, Bognor Regis Town, Gosport Borough

Midfield
Paul Wiltshire: Waterlooville, Chelsea, Southampton
Ken Finlay: Waterlooville, Portsmouth
Tony Callahan: Fareham Town, Waterlooville, Gosport Borough
Graham Wake: Local
David Lappage: Portsmouth

Forwards
Simon Pope: Havant Town, Fareham Town
Ally Unitt: Waterlooville, Bognor Regis Town, Banbury United, Oxford United, Derby County
Andy Lowman: Local
John Hawes: Trowbridge Town, Gosport Borough, Alton Town, Gosport Borough, Plymouth Argyle

Action from the Gosport's visit to Gravesend. Photo David Hills

KING'S LYNN

President: Len Rush
Chairman: Brian Rawlinson
Manager: Fred Easthall
Asst. Manager/Coach:
Physiotherapist: Mrs. Packer
Secretary: Graham Mussett
Address & Tel. No.: 13 Coronation Road, Clenchwarton, King's Lynn. 0553 763962
Commercial Manager: David Renn
Press Officer: Peter Osborne
Address & Tel. No. of ground: The Walks Stadium, Tennyson Road, King's Lynn. 0553 760060 **Club shop:** Yes
Simple ground directions: Junction of A47 and A17 on south side of town
No. of seats: 1,200 **Covered accommodation:** 5,000 **Capacity:** 8,200 **Floodlights:** Yes
Year formed: 1879 **Nickname:** The Linnets **Club Sponsors:** Skoda
Previous names: Lynn Town
Previous grounds: none
Club Colours: Yellow/Blue/Blue
Change colours: White/Black/Red
Day for midweek home matches: Wednesday
Record attendance: 13,500 v. Exeter City F.A. Cup 1st Round **Year** 1951
Best performance in: F.A. Cup: 1961-2 v. Everton 3rd Round
F.A. Trophy: 1978-9 2nd Round
Previous Leagues:
Eastern Counties
Midland League
Club metal badges: No
Clubhouse details: Normal licensing hours plus extension for match days
Past players who progressed to Football League: John Neal (Swindon, Aston Villa), John Stevens (Swindon), George Catleugh (Watford), Wayne Biggins (Burnley, Norwhich C.)
Programme Editor: Bryn Brothers
Programme details: 16 pages, 30p
Local Newspapers: Lynn News & Advertiser. 0553 761188
Eastern Daily Press. 0603 628311
Record transfer fee paid: none
Record transfer fee received: £1,00 from Kettering for Fred Easthall
Senior Honours: Eastern Counties League & League Cup 1953-4, Norfolk Senior Cup 18 times, East Anglian Cup 4 times, 1961-2 F.A. Cup Coventry (A) won 2-1, lost at Everton 4-0 same season (F.A. Cup)
Leading Goalscorers: Kevin Ready (11). **Hat-tricks:** Paul Hooton (1). **Penalties:** Kevin Ready (4).
Most appearances: Chris Watts (51)
Club captain (1985-86): Clive Adams **Player of the year (1985-86):** Steve Mercer

Goalkeepers
Andy Claxton: Local
Brian Benefer: Local

Defenders
Freddie Eastall: Kettering Town, King's Lynn, Norwich City
Steve Mercer: Peterborough United (3), Cambridge United
Colin Hipkin: Local
Chris Watts: Wisbech Town, Gorleston, King's Lynn, Norwich City
Clive Adams: March Town United, King's Lynn, Wisbech Town, King's Lynn
Tim Warner: Local
Steve Bunting: Local

Midfield
Martin Boyers: Grantham, Boston F.C. Skegness Town, Gainsborough Trinity, Grantham, Bridlington Trinity, Louth United, Grimsby Town
Neil Fryatt: Local
Darren Gray: Local
Richard Lant: Local

Forwards
Marc Smelt: Gravesend
Mark Howard: Local
Dave Massingham: Local
Paul Hooton: Local
Dave Osborn: Local

Kings Lynn F.C. Photo: Lynn News & Advertiser

REDDITCH UNITED

President: Bob Edwards
Chairman: R. T. Berry
Manager: B. J. Clark
Asst. Manager: A. Wood
Physiotherapist: J. Haywood
Secretary: M. A. Langfield
Address & Tel. No.: 174 Harport Road, Redditch
Redditch 26603 (H), 63646 (B)
Commercial Manager: Dave Roberts
Press Officer: A. Kings. Redditch 67450
Address & Tel. No. of ground: Valley Stadium, Bromsgrove Road, Redditch 62540 **Club shop:** Yes
Simple ground directions: Ground located near town centre on Bromsgrove side of Redditch—on Bromsgrove Road
No. of seats: 600 **Covered accommodation:** 8,900 **Capacity:** 9,500 **Floodlights:** Yes
Year formed: 1900 **Nickname:** Reds **Club Sponsors:** J. T. Edwards & Phoenix Building Supplies
Previous names: Redditch Town
Previous grounds: Millsborough Road & HDA
Club Colours: Red & White Stripes, White, Red
Change colours: Yellow & Black
Day for midweek home matches: Tuesday
Record attendance: 5,300 v. Bromsgrove **Year** 1955
Best performance in: F.A. Cup: 1971-2 v. Peterborough 1st Round replay
F.A. Trophy: 1978-9 v. King's Lynn 1st Round
Previous Leagues:
West Midland (Regional)
Founder member of
Alliance Premier
Clubhouse details: Large club room and lounge board room. Room holds 150 people and is open most nights
Present players with Football League experience: Phil Parker (Wolves)
Past players who progressed to Football League: Micky Tuohy (Southend, now with Kiddermister Harriers)
Programme Editor: Dave Cooke. 65813
Programme details: 8 pages, 30p
Local Newspapers: Redditch Indicator. 63611
Redditch Advertiser, Birmingham Evening Mail
Record transfer fee paid: £1,500 Eddie Hogan (Burton A)
Record transfer fee received: £7,500 for Mick Tuohy (Southend United)
Senior Honours: Birmingham Senior Cup (4), Runners-up (3), Worcs. Senior Cup (4), Runners-up (3), Southern League Div. 1 (N) Champions
Leading Goalscorers: Mark Whitehouse (26), Gary Wright (12), Steve Ferguson (10). **Most appearances:** Steve Ferguson (51), Mark Whitehouse (45), Phil Parkes (43)
Club captain (1985-86): Dave Round
Player of the year (1985-86): Ronnie Skinner

Goalkeepers
Phil Parkes: Stourbridge, Toronto Blizzard (Can), Oklahoma City (USA), Worcester City, Chicago Sting (USA), Vancouver Whitecaps (Can), Wolves (313)

Defenders
Jerry Brosnan: Moor Green, Bromsgrove Rovers
Dave Round: Stourbridge, Swindon Town
Joe Chaney: Oldbury United, Moor Green, Cradley Town, Coleshill Town, Bromsgrove Rovers, Worcester City, W.B.A.
Tony Billingham: Worcester City
Ron Skinner: Moor Green, Kidderminster Harriers, Bromsgrove Rovers, Redditch United, Paget Rangers
Mark Chambers: Malvern Town, Worcester City, Hereford United
Malcolm Phelps: Worcester City, Nuneaton Borough, Alvechurch

Midfield
Steve Ferguson: Alvechurch, Redditch United, Forest Green Rovers, Moor Green, Redditch United, Bromsgrove Rovers
Ian Hendry: Worcester City, Nuneaton Borough, Hibernian, Aston Villa
Colin Caddick: Worcester City, Walsall
Dave Daniels: Worcester City
Micky Brennan: Alvechurch, Worcester City, Kidderminster Harriers, Telford United, Redditch United

Forwards
Mirek Kalewski: Alvechurch, Gloucester City, Bromsgrove Rovers, Ledbury Town, Swindon Town
Gary Wright: Alvechurch, Worcester City, Alvechurch, Worcester City, Moor Green
Steve Rhodes: Oldbury United, Redditch United, AP Leamington, Tamworth, Sutton Coldfield, Boldmere
Mark Whitehouse: Tamworth, Oldbury United, Moor Green

Last season's leading scorer Mark Whitehouse (No. 9) gets a hand-up from team mate Norman Pemberton during a game at the Valley Stadium — or is he trying to fly?

SALISBURY

President: L. Whitmarsh
Chairman: Ray McEnhill
Manager: G. Butler
Asst. Manager/Coach: E. Lisle
Physiotherapist: D. Barnes
Secretary: Derek F. Sharp
Address & Tel. No.: 21 Melvin Close, Laverstock, Salisbury SP1 1PG. 0722 27248
Commercial Manager: G. Butler. 0722 26454
Press Officer: none
Address & Tel. No. of ground: Victoria Park, Castle Road, Salisbury. 0722 336689 **Club shop:** Yes
Simple ground directions: On A345 North of City Centre to Amesbury/Stonehenge 800 yards from ring road
No. of seats: 300 **Covered accommodation:** 1,000 **Capacity:** 8,000 **Floodlights:** Yes
Year formed: 1947 **Nickname:** none **Club Sponsors:** Churchfields Dairies
Previous names: none
Previous grounds: none
Club Colours: White/Black
Change colours: Red/White
Day for midweek home matches: Monday **Previous Leagues:** Western League
Record attendance: 8,900 v. Weymouth Western League**Year 1948**
Best performance in: F.A. Cup: 1959-60 v. 2nd Round
F.A. Trophy: 3rd Qualifying Round on 5 occasions **Club metal badges:** Yes
Clubhouse details: Open 7 nights. Saturday and Sunday lunch time. Lounge Bar and Function Room.
Past players who progressed to Football League: Jan Thompson (Bournemouth)
Programme Editor: Secretary
Programme details: 28 pages, 20p
Local Newspapers: Salisbury Journal Southern Daily Echo
Record transfer fee paid: £1,750 for Richard Haysom
Record transfer fee received: £18,000 for Jan Thompson (Bournemouth)
Senior Honours: Runners-up Southern League (South), 1985/6, 1st Round F.A. Trophy 1985-6, F.A. Cup 1959-60 2nd Round, 1979-80 1st Round
Club captain (1985-86):
Player of the year (1985-86):

Goalkeepers
Dave Hookway: AFC Totton, Salisbury
Iain Watson: AFC Totton, Woking, AFC Totton

Defenders
Bob Diaper: Swindon Town, Oxford United
Terry Smith: AFC Totton
Barry Cranmer: Andover
Ricky Haysom: Andover, B.A.T.
Bob French: Sholing Sports, Netley
Mark Bailey: Andover, Basingstoke Town, B.A.T., Portsmouth

Midfield
Sean Newark: Local
Kevin Dawtry: RS Southampton, AFC Bournemouth (27-5), Reading (4), AFC Bournemouth (44-6), Crystal Palace, Southampton (1)
Pat Russell: Army, Andover
Andy Groves: Pirelli General
Brian Chambers: Poole Town, Halifax Town (10-1), AFC Bournemouth (42-7), Millwall (59-9), Luton Town (76-9), Arsenal (1), Sunderland (63-5)
Dave Stanbrook: Pirelli General

Forwards
Peter Johnson: Dorchester Town, Weymouth, Barnet, Weymouth, AFC Bournemouth (107-11), Crystal Palace (7), Orient (3)
Steve Slade: RS Southampton, Andover, AFC Totton
Tommy Patterson: Dorchester Town, Poole Town, Weymouth, Darlington (7-2), AFC Bournemouth (57-10), Middlesbrough (1)
Mark Barber: Sholing Sports
Grant Orchard: Poole Town, Andover, Baskingstoke Town, Andover, Farnborough Town, Reading, Aldershot, Swindon Town
Derek Courtney: Poole Town, Weymouth, Wareham Rangers

Back row: Eric Lisle (assistant Manager), Dave Barnes (Trainer), Pat Russell, Bob French, Iain Watson, Dave Hookway, Barry Cranmer, Ricky Haysom, Mark Barker, Bob Diaper, Geoff Butler, (manager).
Front row: Andy Groves, Pete Johnson, Calvin Cranmer, Terry Smith, Tommy Paterson, Kevin Dawtry, Grant Orchard, Sean Newark.
Photo Courtesy of The Salisbury Journal

SHEPSHED CHARTERHOUSE

President:
Chairman: Maurice F. Clayton
Manager: Evan Sutherland
Asst. Manager/Coach: Steve Powell
Physiotherapist: Paul Stanton
Secretary: Brian Edwards
Address & Tel. No.: 27 Warwick Avenue, Quorn Leicestershire. 0509 413311 (H) 236561 (B)
Commercial Manager: Steve Lodge
Press Officer: Maurice Brindley
Address & Tel. No. of ground: The Dovecote, Butthole Lane, Shepshed, Leic. 0509 502684 **Club shop:** No
Simple ground directions: M1 Junction 23, A512 to Ashby, right at traffic lights, right at garage into Forest Street, right into Butthole Lane opposite Black Swan P.H.
No. of seats: 45 **Covered accommodation:** 1,000 **Capacity:** 5,000 **Floodlights:** Yes
Year formed: 1891 **Nickname:** none **Club Sponsors:** Charterhouse Textiles
Previous names: Shepshed Albion
Previous grounds: none
Club Colours: White/Black & Black
Change colours: All Red
Day for midweek home matches: Wednesday
Record attendance: 1,250
Best performance in: F.A. Cup: 1981-2 1st Round Proper
F.A. Vase: 1978-9 Semi-Finalists
Previous Leagues: Southern, Midland Div., North East Counties
Club metal badges: Yes
Clubhouse details: Brick Built, accommodates 120 in main room, 50 in others.
Past players who progressed to Football League: Neil Grencock, Mark Smith
Programme Editor: Jim Lodge
Programme details: 16 pages, 25p
Local Newspapers: Loughborough Echo Leicester Mercury, Notts Post
Leading Goalscorers: J. Lissman. **Most appearances:** J. Lissman
Club captain (1985-86): Jeff Lissman
Player of the year (1985-86): Gil Scoular

Goalkeepers
Nicky Goodwin: Kettering Town, Graham St. Prims

Defenders
Mark Kendrick: Leicester City
Stuart Franklyn: Grantham, Belper Town, Alfreton Town
Steve Yates: Doncaster Rovers (44-1), Southend United (224-8), Leicester City (19)
Austin Straker: Local
Keith Dakin:
Steve Cam: Matlock Town, Norton Woodseats
Paul Mitchell: Local

Midfield
Wayne Oxley: Burton Albion, Buxton, Hallam
Andy Cale: Local
Gilbert Scoular: Leicester United, Bedworth United, Shepshed Charterhouse
John Humphreys:
Jeff Lissaman: Markfield Rovers, Peterborough United
Chris Gaffney: Spalding United, Goole Town, Worksop Town

Forwards
Colin Blackburn: Bishop Auckland, Nuneaton Borough, Middlesbrough (1)
Martin Twigger: King's Lynn, Arnold
Larry Burrell: Local
Eddie Mighton: Local

Shepshed Charterhouse F.C.

WILLENHALL TOWN

President:
Chairman: J. Williams
Manager: Graham Newton
Physiotherapist:

Secretary: J. J. D. Davenport
Address & Tel. No.: 130 Silverton Way, Wednesfield, Wolverhampton. Willenhall 632505 (H), Wolverhampton 731271 (B)
Commercial Manager: V. Parker

Press Officers: J. J. Davenport/T. Wilkins
Address & Tel. No. of ground: Noose Lane, Willenhall. Willenhall 65132 (Club) 636586 (Office) **Club shop:** Yes
Simple ground directions: Noose Lane is off the main Walsall to Wolverhampton road 3 miles from Junction 10 of M6
No. of seats: 220 **Covered accommodation:** 500 **Capacity:** 4,000 **Floodlights:** Yes
Year formed: 1953 **Nickname:** The Reds **Club Sponsors:**
Previous names: none **Club Colours:** All Red
Previous grounds: Memorial Park, Willenhall **Change colours:** White/Blue
Day for midweek home matches: Tuesday
Record attendance: 3,454 v. Crew Alexandria F.A. Cup 1st Round **Year** 1981
Best performance in: F.A. Cup: 1981-2 v. 1st Round Proper
F.A. Trophy: 1st Qual. Round
F.A. Vase: 1980-81 Finalist

Previous Leagues:
Wolverhampton Amateur
Staffs County (South)
W. Midlands (Regional)
Club metal badges: Yes

Clubhouse details: Bar, Lounge, V.I.P. Lounge, Boardroom. Open lunch time and evening. Food, entertainment, room hire available. Stewardess: Mrs. Maureen Mills
Past players who progressed to Football League: Sean O'Driscoll (Fulham, Bournemouth), Joe Jackson (Wolves), Stuart Watkiss (Wolves), Tony Moore (Sheffield United)
Programme Editor: Terry Wilkins. 0902 734283 **Local Newspapers:** Express & Star
Programme details: 24 pages, 20p Wolverhampton Chronicle, Walsall Observer
Record transfer fee paid: £2,000
Senior Honours: Staffs County (South) League & Cup, West Midlands League Div. 1/Premier/Premier Cup, Southern League Midland Div. Championship & Merit Cup, Birmingham County F.A. Senior Cup Finalists, F.A. Vase Finalists, Staffordshire Senior Cup Finalists, F.A. Cup 1st Round Proper, F.A. Trophy 1st Round Proper
Leading Goalscorers: Archie King (23),Garry Stevens (29), Tony Smith (10. **Hat-tricks:** Archie King 1 + 1 (4 goals), Garry Stevens (2). **Penalties:** Garry Stevens (2), **Most appearances:** Jim Skidmore (62), Allan Dulleston (60), Chris Birch (53), Kevin Foster (53)
Club captain (1985-86): Chris Birch **Player of the year (1985-86):** Kevin Foster

Goalkeepers
Allan Dulleston: Kidderminster Harriers, Nuneaton Borough, AP Leamington, Bilston

Defenders
Mark Prescott: Worcester City, Evesham United
Chris Birch: Alvechurch, Hednesford Town
Kevin Ash: Stourbridge
Paul Brown: Alvechurch, Stourbridge, Nuneaton Borough, Leicester City, Aston Villa
John Williams: Local
Russell Walton: Hednesford Town, Stourbridge, Telford United, W.B.A.

Midfield
Steve Bowater: Alvechurch, Kidderminster Harriers, Alvechurch, Worcester City, Walsall, Wolves
Garry Stevens: Cheltenham Town, Worcester City, Alvechurch, Bilston, Darlaston, Willenhall Town
Andy Walsh: Hednesford Town
Mark Unitt: Hednesford Town, Willenhall Town, Blakenall, Armitage
Kevin Foster: Hednesford Town
Dave Liggins: Blakenall, Rushall Olympic, Willenhall Town

Forwards
Tommy Smith: Northwich Victoria, Altrincham, Witton Albion, Emley, Huddersfield Town (4-1), Sheffield United
Archie King: Hednesford Town, Stourbridge, Hednesford Town, Darlaston
Carl Page: Walsall
Jim Skidmore: Sutton Coldfield, Tividale, Bilston, Redditch United, Tividale

Back row (L to R): Archie King, Tom Smith, Russell Walton, Steve Bowater, Allan Dulleston, Andy Walsh, Jim Skidmore, Mark Unitt, Ray Taylor, Barry Young.
Front row (L to R): Kevin Foster, John Williams, Stuart Edwards, Chris Birch (Capt.), Kevin Ash, Paul Brown, Brian Forsbrook (Coach).

WITNEY TOWN

President: T. D. Gittins
Chairman: A. N. Oakey
Manager: Dick Lucas
Asst. Manager/Coach: Jimmy Light
Physiotherapist: To be appointed
Secretary: C. F. J. Miles
Address & Tel. No.: 50 The Crofts, Witney, Oxon. OX8 7AE. Witney 3592
Commercial Manager: To be appointed
Press Officer: To be appointed
Address & Tel. No. of ground: Marriott's Close, Welch Way, Witney, Oxon. 2549 & 5930 **Club shop:** Yes
Simple ground directions: Near centre of the Town, adjacent to main public car park
No. of seats: 150 **Covered accommodation:** 1,500 **Capacity:** 3,500 **Floodlights:** Yes
Year formed: 1885 **Nickname:** none **Club Sponsors:** Charles Early & Co.
Previous names: Witney
Previous grounds: none
Club Colours: Yellow & Royal Blue
Change colours: White
Day for midweek home matches: Tuesday
Record attendance: 3,500 WBA v. Notts Forest. Trevor Stokes benefit match 1965
Best performance in: F.A. Cup: 1971-2 1st Round
F.A. Trophy: 1978-9 2nd Rounds
Previous Leagues: Hellenic League, Oxfordshire Senior
Club metal badges: Yes
Clubhouse details: Open every evening (except Christmas Day), also lunchtime on Saturdays, Sundays and Bank Holidays. Four bars including clubroom, lounge, and 2 function rooms. Entertainment 5-6 nights each week. Basket meals and snacks
Past players who progressed to Football League: H. Smith, F. Clack, A. Hall, J. Newman, D. Moss
Programme Editor: R. H. G. Basson
Programme details: 24 pages, 20p
Local Newspapers: Witney Gazette, Oxford Mail, Oxford Times
Record transfer fee paid: £3,000 Peter Dallaway (Oxford City)
Record transfer fee received: £3,000 John Bailey (Aylesbury United)
Senior Honours: Southern League Div. 1 North Champions 1977-8, Winners Oxon Senior Cup (9), Hellenic League Premier (8)
Club captain (1985-86): M. McIntosh **Player of the year (1985-86):** K. Drackett

---

Goalkeepers
Nick Taylor: Local

Defenders
Jimmy Light: Oxford United (64)
David Ebsworth: Local
Kent Drackett: Headington Amateurs
Malcolm McIntosh: Abingdon Town, Banbury United, Oxford United (2), Kettering Town, Oxford United (63)
Paul Townsend: Local
Paul Lewis: Local
David Cook: Local
Malcolm Young: Oxford United

Midfield
Bob Prately: Oxford City, Abingdon United
Mark Gee: Banbury United, Oxford United
Chris Panter: Local
John Thorne: Oxford City, Banbury United, Witney Town
David Groves: Local

Forwards
John Davie: Banbury United, Aylesbury United, Banbury United, Oxford City, Witney Town, Chester-le-Street
Wayne Tutty: Reading (13-4), Banbury United
Bruce McCrae: Banbury United, Oxford City, Chipping Norton Town
Paul Berry: Oxford United (110-20)
Russell Wilton: Gloucester City, Cheltenham Town

No picture supplied by club for current season

WORCESTER CITY

Chairman: G. W. Turner
Manager: John Jones
Player/Coach: Phil Neale
Physiotherapist: Tom Bradley
Press Officer: Secretary

Secretary: Mrs. D. G. Fulbrook
Address & Tel. No.: 15 Upper Ferry Lane, Callow End, Worcester. 830549
Commercial Manager: Dick Rummery. Worcester 612231

Address & Tel. No. of ground: St. George's Lane, Worcester. 23003 **Club shop:** Yes
Simple ground directions: From M5 Junction 5 follow A38 through Droitwich into Worcester. Ground is 500 yards from first set of traffic lights on left. From M5 Junction 7 follow A44 into Worcester go past racecourse follow A38 Bromsgrove. Ground on right
No. of seats: 2,500 **Covered accommodation:** 5,000 **Capacity:** 15,000 **Floodlights:** Yes
Year formed: 1908 **Nickname:** The City **Club Sponsors:** Christian Salvesen
Previous names: none
Previous grounds: none
Club Colours: Blue & White Stripes/White/White
Change colours: All Red
Day for midweek home matches: Monday
Record attendance: 17,042 v. Sheffield United F.A. Cup **Year** 1958-9
Previous Leagues: Gola
Best performance in: F.A. Cup: 1958-9 4th Round. After beating Liverpool 2-1 at home lost 2-0 to Sheffield Utd. (h)
F.A. Trophy: 1969-70, 1973-4, 1981-2 Quarter-Finals
Clubhouse details: Two Social Clubs, V.I.P. Lounge, Bar, etc.
Past players who progressed to Football League: John Barton (Everton), Jimmy Williams (Walsall), Neil Merrick (Bournemouth), John Fairbrother (Peterborough), Keith Ball (Walsall)
Programme Editor: Under Review
Programme details: 20 pages, 25p
Local Newspapers: Worcester Evening News, Worcester Source
Record transfer fee paid: £8,500 for Jimmy Williams (Walsall)
Record transfer fee received: £27,000 for John Barton (Everton) **Club metal badges:** Yes
Senior Honours: F.A. Cup 1958-9
Leading Goalscorers: Les Ebrey (31), John Muir (22). **Hat-tricks:** Les Ebrey (3), Joun Muir (2). **Most appearances:** Paul Hayward (52), John Wootton (51)
Club captain (1985-86): Tony Larkin **Player of the year (1985-86):** Mark Shail

Goalkeepers
Paul Hayward: Paget Rangers

Defenders
John McGrath: Shrewsbury Town
David Hughes: Lincoln City, Scunthorpe United (21), Lincoln City (62-1), Aston Villa (4-1)
John Wootton: Moor Green, Sutton Coldfield, Blakenall, Sutton Coldield
Tony Larkin: Hereford United (35-2), Carlisle United (49-2), Shrewsbury Town (55), Wrexham

Midfield
Neil Mason: Bilston Town, Willenhall Town, Sutton Coldfield, Walsall, Aston Villa
Mark Shail: Local
Mark Prescott: Alvechurch, Worcester City
Andy Preece: Local
Clive Bullock: Local
John Jones: Willenhall Town, Sutton Coldfield, Nuneaton Borough, Telford United, Kettering Town, Redditch United, Kidderminster Harriers, Darlaston

Forwards
John Muir: Willenhall Town, Gornal Athletic
Les Ebrey: Coventry Sporting, Bedworth United, Hinckley Athletic, Coventry Sporting
Paul Moss: Scunthorpe United (42-7), Hull City (54-7), Wolves
John Dale: Local
Chris Hyde: Pegasus Juniors
Bobby Evans: Blakenall, Tividale, Stourbridge, Shifnal Town, Everton

Worcester City
Back Row (L-R): Tony Larkin, John McGrath, Les Cartwright, Bobby Evans, Paul Hayward, Mark Shail, Les Ebrey, John Wootton   Front Row (L-R): Paul Moss, John Muir, Neil Mason, Bryan Mogford, Graham Selby

DIVISION ONE MIDLAND

LEAGUE TABLE 1985-86

	P	W	D	L	FA	Pts	
Bromsgrove Rovers	40	29	5	6	95	44	92
Redditch United	40	23	6	11	70	42	75
Merthyr Tydfil	40	21	10	9	60	40	73
V.S. Rugby	40	17	14	9	41	31	65
Stourbridge	40	15	14	11	62	49	59
Rushden Town	40	17	7	16	69	74	58
Bilston Town	40	15	12	13	60	48	57
Bridgnorth Town	40	13	18	9	56	45	57
Gloucester City	40	15	12	13	61	57	57
Grantham	40	16	7	17	46	59	55
Wellingborough Town	40	15	9	16	56	56	54
Sutton Coldfield Town	40	13	14	13	60	45	53
Hednesford Town	40	14	9	17	67	70	51
Forest Green Rovers	40	14	9	17	52	56	51
Mile Oak Rovers	40	14	8	18	56	73	50
Leicester United	40	13	10	17	41	48	49
Banbury United	40	13	8	19	38	55	47
Coventry Sporting	40	10	15	15	42	48	45
Moor Green	40	12	6	22	63	91	42
Leamington	40	10	6	24	40	77	36
Oldbury United	40	8	7	25	50	87	31

MIDLAND DIVISION 1985-86

	A.P. Leamington	Banbury United	Bilston Town	Bridgnorth Town	Bromsgrove Rovers	Coventry Sporting	Forest Green R	Gloucester City	Grantham	Hednesford Town	Leicester United	Merthyr Tydfil	Mile Oak Rovers	Moor Green	Oldbury United	Redditch United	Rushden Town	Stourbrige	Sutton Coldfield T.	V.S. Rugby	Wellingborough T.
A.P. Leamington	—	0-1	2-1	0-1	0-1	0-0	3-1	2-1	0-2	4-1	1-0	0-2	1-2	1-5	2-1	0-3	3-2	1-1	0-3	0-1	2-0
Banbury United	2-1	—	0-2	0-2	1-3	2-0	1-0	0-2	0-1	0-2	1-0	0-0	2-0	3-0	3-1	1-5	0-1	1-3	2-1	0-1	4-3
Bilston Town	2-0	1-0	—	0-1	0-1	2-2	0-0	3-0	3-0	3-0	1-0	2-0	5-2	4-1	0-0	3-2	3-3	0-1	1-0	0-0	1-2
Bridgnorth Town	6-0	0-0	2-2	—	2-0	1-1	1-1	3-3	1-1	4-2	3-2	1-1	0-0	4-2	0-3	0-1	0-2	1-3	0-1	0-3	1-1
Bromsgrove Rovers	2-0	3-1	6-2	3-2	—	2-1	1-0	3-0	1-2	2-1	1-0	1-1	4-1	2-1	5-2	2-0	4-1	2-1	1-0	1-1	3-0
Coventry Sporting	2-2	0-0	3-1	1-1	3-2	—	1-0	3-0	2-0	2-2	0-2	3-0	0-1	4-1	0-1	0-1	0-2	2-2	2-0	0-0	01
Forest Green R.	3-0	1-1	1-1	1-1	4-3	3-0	—	2-4	1-2	3-0	4-2	2-1	1-3	1-3	2-0	0-2	2-2	2-0	1-0	0-2	2-0
Gloucester City	2-3	5-1	0-3	1-2	2-2	1-1	0-1	—	0-2	1-0	1-3	2-2	0-0	4-1	1-0	2-2	4-0	1-1	1-1	0-0	1-1
Grantham	5-2	1-0	1-1	0-2	2-2	0-0	3-2	1-1	—	2-1	0-2	2-3	1-0	1-2	0-1	1-0	1-2	2-0	2-0	0-0	2-0
Hednesford Town	3-1	2-1	2-1	1-1	3-2	3-0	1-5	3-2	1-0	—	0-3	1-2	4-1	4-0	5-2	1-3	0-1	2-3	1-1	0-0	3-2
Leicester United	0-0	0-3	0-1	0-0	0-3	2-0	0-0	1-2	1-2	1-1	—	4-1	2-0	0-3	1-0	0-3	1-1	0-4	0-0	0-1	3-2
Merthyr Tydfil	3-0	1-1	1-0	1-0	3-2	2-0	2-3	3-1	2-0	1-0	0-0	—	3-1	2-0	3-1	3-0	2-1	0-0	1-3	3-0	0-0
Mile Oak Rovers	0-2	0-2	2-1	0-0	2-2	2-1	1-1	0-1	4-0	1-5	1-1	0-1	—	4-0	4-1	2-3	1-4	1-3	0-6	2-1	4-2
Moor Green	2-0	1-1	1-0	1-0	0-3	1-2	7-0	1-5	2-1	2-2	1-3	0-0	1-3	—	6-2	1-2	2-2	0-3	0-5	2-3	3-1
Oldbury United	3-3	4-0	1-2	3-3	3-8	0-2	0-0	0-1	2-1	2-2	2-3	0-4	0-1	2-4	—	1-3	3-2	1-2	0-1	2-1	3-1
Redditch United	1-1	2-0	2-1	1-2	0-2	0-0	2-0	1-0	4-0	2-1	0-1	0-3	0-2	1-1	1-0	—	6-2	1-0	0-0	2-1	2-3
Rushden Town	1-0	3-0	2-2	1-3	0-2	2-0	1-0	1-2	1-1	0-0	2-0	4-1	2-3	6-4	3-1	1-6	—	0-3	4-1	1-0	1-4
Stourbrige	4-2	0-0	1-1	1-1	0-1	2-2	0-1	1-2	4-0	1-1	0-1	3-0	3-3	3-0	1-1	1-2	3-0	—	1-1	0-1	0-1
Sutton Coldfield T.	2-1	1-1	3-3	1-1	3-4	1-1	2-0	1-1	5-1	1-3	1-0	0-0	1-0	5-0	5-1	0-2	1-3	1-1	—	2-2	0-0
V.S. Rugby	1-0	1-0	0-0	0-3	0-1	2-0	1-0	0-1	3-1	4-1	1-1	2-1	1-1	1-1	0-0	2-1	3-2	0-0	1-0	—	0-0
Wellingborough T.	4-0	1-2	3-1	0-0	0-2	1-1	2-1	2-3	1-2	3-2	1-1	0-1	5-2	1-0	1-0	1-1	2-0	0-2	2-0	2-0	—

MIDLAND DIVISION

BANBURY UNITED

Chairman: B. R. Stone
Manager: P. Lines
Asst. Manaer/Coach: B. Robinson
Secretary: D. K. Jesson
Address & Tel. No.: "Wychwood", 9 Willoughby Road, Banbury, Oxon. 0295 57262 (H), 0295 4433 (B)
Address & Tel. No. of ground: The Stadium, Off Station Road, Banbury, Oxon. Banbury 3354 **Club shop:** No
Simple ground directions: Right turn before entering station forecourt at eastern end of town
No. of seats: 400 **Covered accommodation:** 2,500 **Capacity:** 6,500 **Floodlights:** Yes
Year formed: 1965 **Nickname:** none **Club Sponsors:** Everstone Cladding Ltd.
Previous names: Banbury Spencer
Club Colours: White
Day for midweek home matches: Tuesday
Change colours: Blue
Record attendance: 7,000 F.A. Cup Qualifying Round v. Oxford City **Year 1947**
Best performance in: F.A. Cup: 1947, 1960, 1973 1st Round Proper Replay
F.A. Trophy: 1973-4 3rd Round Proper
Previous Leagues:
West Midlands
Birmingham Combination
Clubhouse details: Open match days and at week-ends. Mid-weekdays on hire
Present players with Football League experience: R. Pratley (Derby County). D. Bristow (Swindon Town)
Past players who progressed to Football League: O. Kearns (Reading), K. Wilson (Derby County, Ipswich Town), M. Singleton (Coventry)
Programme Editor: Norman Matthews
Programme details: 12 pages, 25p
Club metal badges: No
Local Newspapers: Banbury Guardian, Banbury 4321 Oxford Mail, Oxford 44988, Banbury Focus Banbury 51011, Banbury Cake, Banbury 56111/5
Record transfer fee paid: £2,000 P. Emsden (Oxford United)
Record transfer fee received: £20,000 K. Wilson (Derby)
Club captain (1985-86): M. Allen
Player of the year (1985-86): D. Matthews

BILSTON TOWN

President: J. K. Taylor
Chairman: Tony Tomlinson
Manager: Derek Preston
Press Officer: Alan Owen
Secretary: Morris Baker
Address & Tel. No.: 27 Wimborne Road, Fallings Park, Wolverhampton WV10 ON15. 0902 733703 (H)
Commercial Manager: Graham Morgan 0902 62530
Address & Tel. No. of ground: Queen Street, Bilston. 0902 41498 **Club shop:** No
Simple ground directions: M6 Junction 10, A454 Wolverhampton, pick up A463 Bilston after approximately 1¼ miles turning left Beckett Street
No. of seats: 400 **Covered accommodation:** 600 **Capacity:** 7,000 **Floodlights:** Yes
Year formed: 1895 **Nickname:** Steelmen **Club Sponsors:** Maddison Travel
Club Colours: Tangerine Shirts
Change colours: All White
Day for midweek home matches: Tuesday
Record attendance: 7,000 v. Halifax Town
Previous Leagues:
West Midland
Best performance in: F.A. Cup: 1st Round proper v. Halifax
Clubhouse details: Bilston Town Football & Social Club, Queen Street, Bilston. Licensed premises and dancing
Past players who progressed into the Football League: R. Ellows (Birmingham City), S. Crowther (Aston Villa), R. Pountney (Southend), K. Price (Gillingham)
Programme Editor: Alan Owen
Local Newspapers: Express & Star
Programme details: 20p
Senior Honours: Staff Senior Cup Winners (4)
Club metal badges: Yes
Club captain (1985-86):
Player of the year (1985-86):

BRIDGNORTH TOWN

President: Mike Spilebury
Chairman: Pat Fellows
Manager: Ken Jones
Asst. Manager/Coach: Dave Edge
Physiotherapist: Wilf Preece
Secretary: Gordon Thomas
Address & Tel. No.: 7 Meadow Close, Oldbury Wells, Bridgnorth. 07462 5178
Commercial Manager: Stan Johnson
Press Officer: Gordon Thomas
Address & Tel. No. of ground: Crown Meadow, Innage Lane, Bridgnorth. 07462 2747
Simple ground directions: From High Street ½ mile
No. of seats: 50 **Covered accommodation:** 400 **Capacity:** 1,600 **Floodlights:** Yes
Year formed: 1946 **Nickname:** The Town **Club Sponsors:** Tatung UK Ltd.
Previous names: none
Club Colours: Blue/White
Day for midweek home matches: Tuesday
Change colours: Red/White
Record attendance: 1,600 v. South Shields F.A. Vase **Year** 1975-6
Best performance in: F.A. Cup: 1984-5 3rd Qualifying Round
F.A. Vase: 1975-6 6th Round
Previous Leagues:
Midland Combination
Kidderminster League
Clubhouse details: Open 7 nights and week-end lunchtime. Separate function room
Past players who progressed to Football League: Roger Davies (Derby County)
Programme Editor: John Bray
Programme details: 14 pages, 20p
Club metal badges: Yes £1 each
Local Newspapers: Shropshire Star Bridgnorth Journal
Senior Honours: Welsh Amateur Cup, Shropshire Senior Cup, Shropshire Challenge Cup (5), Shropshire Junior Cup, Midland Combination (2), Midland Combination League Cup (1)
Club captain (1985-86):
Player of the year (1985-86):

BUCKINGHAM TOWN

President: Robin B. Taylor
Chairman: C. D. Lawrance
Manager: Gary Knibbs
Asst. Manager: Frank Holman
Physiotherapist: Willie Holman
Secretary: P. G. Holman
Address & Tel. No.: 18 Downer Close, Lindon Villas, Buckingham. 812787 (H)
Commercial Manager: C. D. Lawrence
Address & Tel. No: "Newlands", Leckhampstead Road, Akeley, Buckingham. Lillingstone Dayrell 318
Press Officer & Tel. No.: D. A. Hacker, 7 Clynswood Road, Buckingham 812176
Address & Tel. No. of ground: Ford Meadow, Ford Street, Buckingham 816257 **Club shop:**
Simple ground directions: 400 yards from town centre, off Buckingham to Aylesbury road
No. of seats: 100 **Covered accommodation:** Yes **Capacity: 4,000Floodlights:** Yes
Year formed: 1883 **Nickname:** Robins **Club Sponsors:** Taylors Estate Agents
Club Colours: All Red, White trim **Change colours:** All White, Red trim
Day for midweek home matches: Tuesday
Record attendance: 2,451 v. Orient, F.A. Cup **Year** 1984-5
Best performance in: F.A. Cup: 1984-5 1st Round Proper
F.A. Vase: Last 16
Previous Leagues: Hellenic, South Midlands, North Bucks, Aylesbury & District
Clubhouse details: Open 7 days a week and Friday, Saturday, Sunday lunchtimes. Concert room with stage for hire, capacity 240. Bingo, domino, ladies and mens darts teams
Programme Editor: Secretary **Club metal badges: Yes**
Programme details: 16 pages, 10p
Senior Honours: 1983-4 Centenary Season, Berks & Bucks Senior Cup Winners, Premier Division UCI Champions, League Knock-out Cup Winners, Buckingham Senior Charity Cup Winners
Club captain (1985-86): **Player of the year (1985-86):**

COVENTRY SPORTING

Chairman: Burt Craddock**Secretary:** George Calcott
Manager: David Kite
Address & Tel. No.: 103 Eastcotes, Tile Hill, Coventry CV4 9AW
0203 461664 (H), 0203 464547 (B)
Physiotherapist: Paul Nicholson
Address & Tel. No. of ground: Kirby Corner Road, Canley, Coventry CV4 8GL
Simple ground directions: Take A5 from Birmingham, at first roundabout in city boundary turn right. Then proceed over traffic lights, turn first right into Kirby Corner Road. ½ mile on left-hand side is ground. Next to Warwick University
No. of seats: 100 **Covered accommodation:** Yes **Capacity:** 5,000 **Floodlights:** Yes
Year formed: 1946 **Nickname:** none **Club Sponsors:** Henlys
Club Colours: All Red**Change colours: All Gold**
Day for midweek home matches: Tuesday Previous Leagues:
Record attendance: 8,500 v. Peterborough (Played at Highfield Road) **Year** 1975
Previous Leagues: Central Amateurs, Warwickshire Combination, West Midlands (Regional)
Clubhouse details: Open 7 days a week. Facilities for all types of functions private and public, also nightclub and restaurant
Past players who progressed to Football League: Paul Sugrue
Programme Editor: Rob Kane **Local Newspapers:** Coventry Evening Telegraph
Programme details: 20 pages, 25p **Club metal badges:** No
Club captain (1985-86): **Player of the year (1985-86):**

FOREST GREEN

President: G. C. Mills
Chairman: John Duff
Manager: Steve Millard
Asst. Manager/Coach: Peter Higgins
Secretary: Martin Morgan
Address & Tel. No.: 10 Badgers Way, Forest Green, Nailsworth. 4639
Club Shop: Yes
Address & Tel. No. of ground: The Lawn, Nympsfield Road, Forest Green, Nailsworth, Glos. Nailsworth 4860
Simple ground directions: Nailsworth is on the A46 (Bath, Stroud) 4 miles south Stroud. From town centre proceed up Spring Hill for 1 mile ground is on left.
No. of seats: 131 **Covered accommodation:** Grandstand/Standing **Capacity:** 4,500 **Floodlights:** Yes
Year formed: 1898 **Nickname:** Rovers **Club Sponsors:** Various
Club Colours: White/Black **Change colours:** All Green
Day for midweek home matches: Tuesday
Record attendance: 2,200 v. Wolverhampton Wanders **Year:** 1981
Best performance in: F.A. Cup: 1979-80 2nd Round Qualifying
F.A. Vase: Winners of F.A. Vase 1982
Previous Leagues: Hellenic, Premier Glos. County League
Clubhouse details: Bar, lounge open every night
Past players who progressed into the Football League: Kenny Gill (Newport County), Mike England (Bristol Rovers)
Programme Editor: Brian Cook. Stonehouse 3281 **Local Newspapers:** Stroud Journal, Glos. Citizen
Programme details: 20 pages, 20p
Senior Honours: 1981-2 F.A. Vase Winners, Hellenic Premier League Winners 1981-2, Glos. Senior Professional Cup Winners 1984-5, 1985-6
Club metal badges: Yes
Club captain (1985-86): **Player of the year (1985-86):**

GLOUCESTER CITY

Chairman: G. K. Hester
Manager: Steve Scarrott
Asst. Manager/Coach: Tim Harris
Commercial Manager: David Stallworthy
Secretary: Brian Hobbs
Address & Tel. No.: 8 Chantry Road, Thornbury, Bristol BS12 1ER 0454 412201 (H)
Club shop: Yes
Address & Tel. No. of ground: Meadow Park, Sudmeadow Road, Gloucester. 0452 421400
Simple ground directions: Take A40 into city centre towards dock area then Severn Road into Hempstead Lane, into Sudmeadow Road
No. of seats: 512 **Covered accommodation:** 2,000 **Capacity:** 7,000 **Floodlights:** Yes
Year formed: 1980 (1889) **Nickname:** The Tigers **Club Sponsors:** Westbury Homes
Previous names: Gloucester City (1889)
Club Colours: Yellow, Black, Black
Previous grounds: Longlevens
Change colours: White, Red, Red
Day for midweek home matches: Tuesday
Club metal badges: Yes
Previous Leagues: Western, North Gloucester, Gloucester Northern Senior, Birmingham Combination
Record attendance: 4,000 v. Tottenham Hotspurs (Friendly) 1952
Best performance in: F.A. Cup: 1948, 49, 50, 52, 55 1st Round Proper
F.A. Trophy: 1980-1, 1983-4, Gola 1st Round Proper
Clubhouse details: Open every day
Past players who progressed into the Football League: Bob Etheridge, Alan Grubb, Gordon Boseley
Programme Editor: B. E. Howe
Programme details: 4 pages, 10p
Local Newspapers: Gloucester Citizen, Gloucester Express Western Daily Press
Senior Honours: Southern League Cup Winners 1955-6, Runners-up 1981-2
Club captain (1985-86):
Player of the year (1985-86):

GRANTHAM F.C.

President: P.M. The Rt. Hon. Mrs. Margaret Thatcher
Chairman: John Moore
Manager: Barry Shaw
Secretary: G. Howard Kilbourn
Address & Tel. No.: 35 Cliff Road, Carlton, Nottingham NG4 1BS. 0602 876463 (H) 0602 623892 (B)
Asst. Manager/Coach: Phil Boyer
Address & Tel. No. of ground: London Road, Grantham, Lincs. 0476 62011
Club shop: Yes
Simple ground directions: 200 years from town centre
No. of seats: 250 **Covered accommodation:** On two sides **Capacity:** 7,500 **Floodlights:** Yes
Year formed: 1876 **Nickname:** The Gingerbreads **Club Sponsors:** Capitol Batteries, Yale Lift Trucks, Spittalgate Motors
Previous names: Grantham Town
Club Colours: Black & White, Black, Black
Previous grounds: none
Change colours: Blue/Gold, Gold, Blue
Day for midweek home matches: Tuesday
Record attendance: 6,578 v. Middlesborough F.A. Cup 3rd Round **Year** 1974
Best performance in: F.A. Cup: 1974 v. Middlesborough 3rd Round
F.A. Trophy: 1971-2 v. Yeovil Quarter Final. Lost 1-0
Previous Leagues: Northern Premier, Midland League, Central Alliance
Clubhouse details: Open 7 days a week. Licence on match day afternoons to 6.00 p.m. Re-open 7.00-11.00 p.m.
Past players who progressed to Football League: Archie Burgin (Tottenham Hotspur), Colin Thompson (Peterborough), Jimmy Rayner (Notts County), David Dall (Scunthrope), Robbie Cooke (Peterborough), Nicky Jarvis (Scunthorpe)
Programme Editor: M. Koranski. 0476 62104
Local Newspapers: Grantham Journal, Evening Post 0476 63232, 0476 6229
Programme details: 28 pages, 25p
Club metal badges: Yes £1 each
Record transfer fee paid: £2,500 David Leadbeater (Bridlington Trinity)
Record transfer fee received: £12,000 by Peterborough United for Robbie Cooke
Senior Honours: F.A. Cup 1974 v. Middlesborough
Club captain (1985-86):
Player of the year (1985-86):

HALESOWEN TOWN F.C.

President: N. Siviter
Chairman: C. Murphy
Manager: P. Page
Asst. Manager/Coach: H. Crampton
Trainer: F. Birch
Physiotherapist: B. Wyle
Secretary: H. Rudge, JP
Address & Tel. No.: 19 Carol Crescent, Halesowen, West Midlands 021 550 1456 (All correspondence to the Secretary)
Commercial Managers: R. Pepper. 0384 635580 R. Moseley 021 550 4310
Address & Tel. No. of ground: Grove Recreation Ground, Old Hawne Lane, Halesowen 021 550 2179
Simple ground directions: From M5; Leave at Junction 3, follow sign A456 to 1st roundabout (turn right), at second roundabout (turn left) A458, next roundabout, Ground on right approximately 500 yards.
No. of seats: 250 **Covered accommodation:** 800 **Capacity:** 6,000 **Floodlights:** Yes
Year formed: 1873 **Nickname:** The Yeltz **Club Sponsors:** Hardanger Properties plc
Previous names: None
Previous grounds: None
Club Colours: Royal Blue/White
Change colours: Red and Black/White
Record attendance: 5,000 v. Hendon F.A. Cup 1st Round **Year:** 1955
18,324 F.A. Vase Final (Wembley) Year: 1985
Previous Leagues: Birmingham Combination prior to 1946, Birmingham League, West Midlands (Regional) League
Club metal badges: Yes **Club shop:** Yes **Programme:** 28 pages, 20p
Clubhouse details: Yes, open 7 nights + match days 021 550 8907 **Day for midweek matches:** Tuesday/Thursday
Senior Honours: Birmingham League 1946-7. Worcs. Senior Cup 1951-2, 1961-2. F.A. Cup 1st Round Proper 1955-6. W. Midlands League 1982-3, 1983-4, 1984-5, 1985-6. Thorn EMI Floodlighting Competition 1982-3. Birmingham Senior Cup 1984. F.A. Vase winners 1985, 1986, runners-up 1983
Club captain (1985-86): J. Woodhouse
Player of the year (1985-86): A. Pemberton

HEDNESFORD TOWN

President: Ron Gray
Chairman: Mike Smith
Manager: Bob Wickett
Asst. Manager/Coach: Kevin Lane
Physiotherapist: Trevor Saunders
Secretary: Tim Craner
Address & Tel. No.: 15 Goldthorn Avenue, Cannock, Staffs. Cannock 70095
Commercial Manager: Terry Brumpton
Press Officer: Craig Ingram
Address & Tel. No. of ground: Cross Keys Ground, Hill St., Hednesford, Staffs. Hednesford 2870 **Club shop:**
Simple ground directions: Leave M6 Junction 11. Take A460 to Cannock then Hednesford, turn right opposite Globe P.H. into Lower Road, turn right at end of Lower Road—ground is 25 yards on right
No. of seats: 350 **Covered accommodation:** 1,500 **Capacity:** 7,000 **Floodlights:** Yes
Year formed: 1880 **Nickname:** The Pitmen **Club Sponsors:**
Previous names: The Colliers, The Lilywhites
Club Colours: White/Black/Black
Previous grounds: Anglesey Ground (The Tins)
Change colours: Blue/White/Blue
Day for midweek home matches: Monday
Record attendance: 10,000 v. Walsall **Year** 1922
Best performance in: F.A. Cup: 1919-20 1st Round Proper
F.A. Trophy: 1977-8 3rd Round Proper
Previous Leagues: Walsall & District, Birmingham Combination, Birmingham, West Midlands, Midlands
Clubhouse details: Open 7 days a week and match day extension
Present players with Football League experience: Joe Jackson (Wolves), Kevin Lane (Torquay Utd.)
Past players who progressed to Football League: V. Allatt (Crewe), S. Biggins (Oxford Utd., Derby Co.), B. Horton (Hull City)
Programme Editor: Terry Brumpton
Programme details: 20 pages, 20p
Local Newspapers: Express & Star. W'hampton 22351
Club metal badges: Yes
Record transfer fee paid: £500 Andy Allen (Kidderminster)
Club captain (1985-86):
Player of the year (1985-86):

LEAMINGTON F.C.

Chairman: M. Brady
Manager: John Hanna
Asst. Manager/Coach: Pat Brady
Commercial Director/Press Oficer: Bill Branston 0926 26039 (24 hr Ansaphone)
Secretary: Martin Higgins
Address & Tel. No.: 12 Scott Road, Leamington Spa 0926 23732 (H)
Physiotherapist: To be appointed
Club shop: Yes
Address & Tel. No. of ground: 'The Windmill', Tachbrook Road, Leamington Spa, Warwicks. 0926 26039
Simple ground directions: Leave A41 at Bishops Tachbrook turning, 2 miles into Leamington Spa, Ground on right hand side
No. of seats: 440 **Covered accommodation:** 1,600 **Capacity:** 5,000 **Floodlights:** Yes
Year formed: 1945 **Nickname:** The Brakes **Club Sponsors:** 3D Wyndows
Previous names: Lockheed Leamington
Club Colours: Gold, Black
Previous grounds: none
Change colours: All White, Blue Trim
Day for midweek home matches: Tuesday
Record attendance: 3,200 v. Staffprd Rangers F.A. Cup 1975
Best performance in: F.A. Cup: 1978 2nd Round
F.A. Trophy: 1983-4 Quarter Finals
Previous Leagues: Midland, Southern, Alliance Premier (as A.P. Leamington)
Clubhouse details: Open to non members match days (before and after) snacks available
Past players who progressed into the Football League: Roger Brown (Bournemouth, Norwich, Fulham), Vince O'Keefe (Exeter, Torquay), Errington Kelly (Bristol Rovers, Peterborough), Maurice Muir (Northampton), Mark Buckland (Wolves)
Programme Editor: M. Berry
Programme details: 24 pages, 25p
Local Newspapers: Leamington Morning News, Leamington Courier, Coventry Telegraph
Record transfer fee paid: Various
Record transfer fee received: for Roger Brown from Bournemouth
Senior Honours: Birmingham Senior Cup (3), Southern Leaue Cup (2), Southern League Premiership Trophy, Southern League Champions, 2nd Round F.A. Cup 1978, Quarter Final F.A. Trophy 1984
Club captain (1985-86):
Player of the year (1985-86):

LEICESTER UNITED

President: Arthur Capers
Chairman: George Smith
Manager: John Perkins
Asst. Manager/Coach: Peter DowSing
Physiotherapist: John Goodman
Secretary: Garry C. Glover
Address & Tel. No.: 16 Rawson Street, Enderby, Leicester 0533 862358 (H). 0533 888961 extn 232 (B)
Commercial Manager: Alan Foreman
Press Officer: Joe Taylor
Address & Tel. No. of ground: United Park, Winchester Road, Blaby, Leicester. 0533 771366 **Club shop:** Yes
Simple ground directions: 2 miles from Junction 21 M1 and M69. Leave Motorway take B4 — — 4 to Narborough then B582 to Blaby
No. of seats: 500 **Covered accommodation:** Not yet known **Capacity:** 8,000 approx. **Floodlights:** Yes
Year formed: 1900 **Nickname:** none **Club Sponsors:** Casepack (Midlands) Ltd.
Previous names: Enderby Town
Club Colours: Red & White/White/Black
Previous grounds: George Street
Change colours: White/Black/Red
Day for midweek home matches: Wednesday
Record attendance: 6,000 Schoolboy England v. Wales **Year** 1978
Best performance in: F.A. Cup: 1977-8 1st Round
F.A. Trophy: 1978-9 3rd Round
Previous Leagues: Leicestershire Senior, East Midland (Regional)
Clubhouse details: Open every evening—meals, etc.
Club metal badge: No
Past players who progressed to Football League: Robert Atkins (Sheffield United)
Programme Editor: Alan Headley
Programme details: 10 pages, 20p
Local Newspapers: Leicester Mercury
Record transfer fee paid: £1,000
Record transfer fee received: £1,500
Senior Honours: F.A. Cup 1st Round 1977-8, F.A. Trophy 3rd Round 1978-9
Club captain (1985-86):
Player of the year (1985-86):

MERTHYR TYDFIL

President: Eddie Thomas
Chairman: John Eastment
Manager: Lyn Jones
Secretary: Ken Tucker
Address & Tel. No.: 16 The Parade, Merthyr Tydfil 3884
Commercial Manager: Roy Jenkins
Address & Tel. No. of ground: Penydarren Park, Merthyr Tydfil. 75125 (match days only), 71395
Club shop: No
Simple ground directions: Situated in the town a few hundred yards from the Railway Station
No. of seats: 300 **Covered accommodation:** 3,300 **Capacity:** 8,000 **Floodlights:** Yes
Year formed: 1945 **Nickname:** The Martyrs **Club Sponsors:** T.S.B.
Previous names: Merthyr Town
Club Colours: White Shirts, Black Shorts
Previous grounds: none
Change colours: Blue Shirts, Maroon Shorts
Day for midweek home matches: Tuesday
Previous Leagues: Welsh League
Record attendance: 21,000 v. Reading F.A. Cup **Year** 1949
Best performance in: F.A. Cup: 3 x 2nd Round 1979-80 lost 3-1 home Chesham United
F.A. Trophy: 1978-9 Quarter Finals
Clubhouse details: On ground, open every evening and match days
Past players who progressed to Football League: Syd Howarth, Cyril Beech, Gilbert Beech, Bill Hullett, Ken Tucker, Nick Peacy, Gordon Davies, Ray Pratt
Programme Editor: Ken Tucker
Programme details: 8 pages, 20p
Local Newspapers: Merthyr Express, South Wales Echo
Record transfer fee received: £12,000 by Exeter for Ray Pratt
Club metal badges: Yes
Senior Honours: Southern League (5), Southern League Cup (2), Welsh Cup (2)
Club captain (1985-86):
Player of the year (1985-86):

MILE OAK ROVERS & YOUTH F.C.

President: Horace Thomas
Chairman: Albert Wright
Manager: Mr. R. J. Bott
Asst. Man/Coach: M. Hawkins
Physiotherapist: A. Gee
Secretary: Paul Blood
Address & Tel. No.: 61 Parkfield Crescent, Two Gates, Tamworth, Staffs, B77 1HB 0827 250116
Commercial Manager: Mr. Colin Burton
Press Officer: Mr. J. Woodall
Address & Tel. No. of ground: Recreation Ground, Price Ave., Mile Oak, Tamworth, Staffs.
Simple ground directions: Situated on the A5, from Mile Oak Hotel travel south take third turning right, ground is 200 yards on the right hand side
No. of seats: 60 **Covered accommodation:** 300 **Capacity:** 2,500 **Floodlights:** Yes
Year formed: 1958
Previous names:
Club colours: All Blue
Previous grounds: None
Change Colours: All Yellow
Day for midweek home matches: Wednesday
Record attendance: 380
Previous Leagues: Trent Valley, Mercian, Midland Combination
Best performance: Midland Comination Premier Division Champions (1984-85)
Clubhouse details: Large bar with separate lounge facilities open every lunch time and night
Past players who progressed into the Football League: Tony Coton (Birmingham City), Colin Robinson (Shrewsbury), Keith Downing (Notts. Co.)
Record transfer fee paid: Nil
Record transfer fee received: £10,000
Programme details: 20 pages, 20p
Programme Editor: Paul Draper
Local newspaper & Tel. No.: Tamworth Herald
Club metal badges: No
Senior Honours: Midland Combination Premier Division Champions (1984-85)

MOOR GREEN

President: Geoff Hood
Chairman: John Mowl
Manager: Bob Faulkner
Asst. Manager: Ray Monnington
Press Officer: Peter Clynes 021 444 7903
Secretary: Brian Smith
Address & Tel. No: 15 Bowen Court, Wake Green Park, Moseley, Birmingham B13 9XP 021 449 8738 (H) 021 777 1990 (B)
Club shop: Yes
Address & Tel. No. of ground: The Moorlands, Sherwood Road, Hall Green, Birmingham B28 0EX
Simple ground directions: A34 Birmingham to Stratford Road—5 miles city centre Highfield Road, Sherwood Road 2nd right
No. of seats: 300 **Covered accommodation:** 600 **Capacity:** 3,000 **Floodlights:** Yes
Year formed: 1901 **Nickname:** The Moors **Club Sponsors:** T.S.B.
Previous grounds: Moor Green Lane, Windermere Road
Club Colours: Dark/Light Blue stripes
Change colours: All Yellow
Day for midweek home matches: Tuesday
Record attendance: 5,000 v Romford, F.A. Amateur Cup **Year:** 1951
Best performance in F.A. Cup: 1979-80, v Stafford Rangers, 1st Round Proper
F.A. Trophy: 2nd Qualifying
Previous Leagues: Central Amateur, Birmingham Combination, West Midland, Midland Combination
Club metal badges: Yes
Clubhouse details: Open evenings (except Mondays); plus Saturday/Sunday Lunch, two bars, one with dance floor, many functions
Past players who progressed into the Football League: Ken Barnes (Manchester City), Brian Mack West Bromich Albion), Steve Cooper (Birmingham City & Plymouth A), Herbie Smith (Villa)
Record transfer fee paid: £1,000 for Adrian O'Dowd from Alvechurch
Record transfer fee received: £1,000 Adrian O'Dowd from Kidderminster Harriers
Programme Editor: Peter Clynes
Programme details: 1st Team games, 25p
Local newspapers & Tel. No.: Solihull News, Daily Times, Birmingham Post & Mail, Daily News
Senior Honours: Midland Combination League and Cup 1980-81, Birmingham Senior Cup 1957

Gloucester City A.F.C.

Players only—Middle row (L-R): Steve Johnson, Robert Simpson, Gary Goodwin, Steve Scarrott (Player/Manager), Bernie Wright, Mario Waite, Martin Lander
Front Row—Tim Harris, Nigel Smith, Ken Norman, Neil Goff, Stewart Martyn, Kevin Trusswell
Photo: courtesy of Gloucester Citizen

Southern League Midland Division—Bilston Town 0 Bromsgrove 1. Bilston on attack Photo: David Shute

Merthyr Tydfil F.C. Ground Pennydarren Park Photo: Alan Bunce

RUSHDEN TOWN

Chairman: D. Atlee
Manager: C. Corby
Asst. Manager/Coach: I. Jenkins
Physiotherapists: D. Atlee & T. Graham
Press Officer: Secretary
Secretary: B. Lake
Address & Tel. No.: 30 Balham Close, Rushden 0933 57968 or 0933 312568 (messages only)
Commercial Manager: T. Graham
Address & Tel. No. of ground: Hayden Road, Rushden. 093353575
Club shop: Yes
Simple ground directions: A6 turn left into Newton Road third left into Cromwell Road, straight into Hayden Road. From Junction 15 or 16 M1 Motorway follow signs A45 to Rushden
No. of seats: 300 **Covered accommodation:** 500 **Capacity:** 6,000 **Floodlights:** Yes
Year formed: Reformed 1919 **Nickname:** Russians **Club Sponsors:** Totectors Footwear
Club Colours: Red, Black, Blue **Change colours:** Black, All Blue
Day for midweek home matches: Tuesday
Record attendance: 5,600 v. Kettering 1948-9
Best performance in: F.A. Cup: 4th Qualifying Round
Previous Leagues: Newe Group, United Counties
Clubhouse details: 1968 present Clubhouse erected, extended 1973 to include lounge, office, etc.
Past players who progressed into the Football League: G. W. Inwood (W.B.A.) 1948-9
Programme Editor: Secretary
Programme details: 12-16 pages, 20p
Local Newspapers: Evening Telegraph, Chronicle & Echo, Northants Post
Senior Honours: F.A. Cup 4th Qualifying Round, County Senior Cup Winners
Club metal badges: No

STOURBRIDGE

President: J. L. Guest
Chariman: Geoff Taylor
Manager: Malcolm Lycett
Physiotherapist: Colin Saunders
Press Officer: Hugh Clark
Secretary: Hugh Clark
Address & Tel. No.: 10 Burnt Oak Drive, Stourbridge, DY8 1HL. 0384 392975
Commercial Manager: Andrew Hill
Club shop: Yes
Address & Tel. No. of ground: War Memorial Athletic Ground, High Street, Amblecote. 6384 394040
Simple ground directions: 200 yards from Stourbridge Ring Road on A491 to Wolverhampton—opposite The Royal Oak P.H.
No. of seats: 460 **Covered accommodation:** 2,000 **Capacity:** 6,000 **Floodlights:** Yes
Year formed: 1876 **Nickname:** The Glassboys
Club Colours: Red, White & Black
Change colours: All White
Day for midweek home matches: Tuesday
Record attendance: 5,726 v. Cardiff City, Welsh Cup Final, 1979
Best performance in: F.A. Cup: 1967-8 v. Arnold 4th Qualifying Round
F.A. Trophy: 1970-1 v. Yeovil Quarter Final
Previous Leagues: West Midlands (Regional), Birmingham, Birmingham Combination
Clubhouse details: Open every evening from 8.00 p.m. and on Sunday lunchtimes. Regular entertainment
Past players who progressed into the Football League: T. Cunningham, S. Cooper, L. Lawrence, P. Bates, R. Haywood, P. Freeman, C. Taylor, G. Pulley, A. Rowley
Record transfer fee received: £20,000 for Tony Cunningham (Lincoln City) 1979
Programme Editor: Hugh Clark
Programme details: 20 pages, 25p
Local Newspapers: Stourbridge News & County Express, Express & Star, Dudley Evening Mail
Senior Honours: Birmingham Senior Cup & Worcs. Senior Cup several times, 4th qualifiers FA Cup (3), F.A. Trophy: Quarter Finalists 1970/71
Club metal badges: Football Club and Supporters' Club badges on sale in Club Shop

SUTTON COLDFIELD TOWN

Chairman: R. S. Timmings
Manager: Alan Parsons
Asst. Manager/Coach: David Seddon
Physiotherapist: Tom Slater
Secretary: Derek S. Garratt
Address & Tel. No.: 47 Elms Road, Sutton Coldfield, West Midlands B72 1JE. 021 354 9292 (H). 021 236 7742 (B)
Press Officer: Peter Bundock. 021 588 7014 (AnsaPhone Service)
Address & Tel. No. of ground: Central Ground, Coles Lane, Sutton Coldfield, W. Midlands B72 1NL. 021 354 2997, 021 355 5475
Club shop: Yes
Simple ground directions: Ten minutes walk from Sutton Coldfield main shopping centre
No. of seats: 250 **Covered accommodation:** 300 **Capacity:** 4,500 **Floodlights:** Yes
Year formed: 1879 **Nickname:** None **Club Sponsors:** Home Brewery
Club Colours: Royal Blue Shirts & Socks/White Shorts
Change colours: All White
Day for midweek home matches: Wednesday
Record attendance: 2,000 v. Doncaster Rovers, F.A. Cup 1st Round Proper **Year** 1980-1
Previous Leagues: Midland Combination, West Midlands (Regional)
Best performance in: F.A. Cup: 1980-1 1st Round Proper
F.A. Trophy: 1980-1, 1981-2 3rd Round Qualifying
Club metal badges: No
Clubhouse details: Brick built, Lounge and Concert Room, fully carpeted and expensively decorated
Past players who progressed to Football League: Paul Cooper, Barry Cowdrill, Noel Blake, Stephen Cooper
Programme Editor: Ian Price
Programme details: 16 pages, 25p
Local Newspapers: Sutton Coldfield News, Sutton Observer
Record transfer fee paid: £1,000
Record transfer fee received: £5,000
Senior Honours: Midland Football Combination Div. 1 (twice), West Midland (Regional) League Premier Div. & Cup (twice), Walsall Senior Cup (3)

V.S. RUGBY

Chairman: Roy Gallimore
Managing Director: Michael Vousden
Manager: Jimmy Knox
Asst. Manager: Bob Ward
Coach/Physiotherapist: Barrie Fergusson
Press Officer: Doug Hughes. Leamington 0926 316261
Secretary: Keith Coughlan
Address & Tel. No.: 3 Evans Road, Rugby, Warw. CV22 7HT. 0788 814746 (H) 0203 554247 (B)
Commercial Director: Tony Hearn
Address & Tel. No: Leamington 0926 29152
Club shop: Yes
Address & Tel. No. of ground: Butlin Road, Rugby, Warwickshire CV21 3ST. Rugby 0788 3692
Simple ground directions: Butlin Road is off Clifton Road, Rugby which is B5414 near to Rugby Golf Club within walking distance of Rugby Midland Station—exactly 1 mile
No. of seats: 200 **Covered accommodation:** 250 **Capacity:** 5,000 **Floodlights:** Yes
Year formed: 1956 **Nickname:** The Valley **Club sponsors:** Byfield Builders
Previous names: Valley Sports and Valley Sports Rugby
Club Colours: Sky Blue/Navy and White
Previous grounds: Thornfield
Change colours: Green
Day for midweek home matches: Wednesday
Record attendance: 3,961 v. Northampton Town, F.A. Cup Round and Replay **Year** 1984
Best performance in: F.A. Cup: 1984-5 Round One Replay
F.A. Vase: 1983 Winners
Clubhouse details: Top class facilities open 7 nights per week plus Saturday lunch and after match and Sunday lunch. Top local groups featured every Saturday evening, disco night on last Friday of month. Darts, pool and skittles teams in local leagues
Past players who progressed into the Football League: S. Bicknell (Leicester), S. Storer (Birmingham)
Record transfer fee received: S. McGinty to Telford United, 1985
Programme Editor: Doug Hughes
Programme details: 38 pages, 20p
Club Captain:
Club metal badges: Yes
Club shop: Yes
Player of the Year (1985-6):

WELLINGBOROUGH TOWN

President: B. Abbott
Chairman: M. McNamee
Manager: B. Knight
Asst. Manager/Coach: D. Bartram
Physiotherapist: P. Brown
Secretary: M. Walden
Address & Tel. No.: 5 Fernie Way, Wellingborough, Northants 0933 79561
Commercial Manager: V. Edwards
Address & Tel. No. of ground: London Road, Wellingborough. 0933 223536 **Club shop:** Yes
Simple ground directions: 200 yards off A45 by-pass
No. of seats: 300 **Covered accommodation:** 500 **Capacity:** 5,000 **Floodlights:** Yes
Year formed: 1867 **Nickname:** Doughboys **Club Sponsors:** Astraseal
Club Colours: All Blue **Change colours:** All Red
Day for midweek home matches: Wednesday
Record attendance: 4,013 v. Kettering
Best performance in: F.A. Cup: 1965 v. Aldershot 1st Round
F.A. Trophy: 1973 1st Round
Previous Leagues: West Midland Metropolitan & United Counties
Clubhouse details: On ground with full facilities
Past players who progressed to Football League: Phil Neal
Club metal badges: No
Programme Editor: D. Joyce
Programme details: 20p
Local Newspapers: Northants Evening Telegraph Northampton Chronicle & Echo
Senior Honours: Northants Senior Cup Winners, F.A. Cup 1st Round v. Aldershot 1965
Club Captain (1985-6):
Player of the Year (1985-6):

Stourbridge: *Standing: A. Webb (Trainer), A. Reece, B. Williams, K. Tudor, N. Jewes, P. Fitzpatrick, V. Sharrard, P. Nicholls, G. Matthews, N. Morgan.*
Seated: A. Forrester, R. Dams, P. Stringer, G. Newton (Manager), R. White, P. Rose, W. Carr, R. Peck

Folkestone's Maurice Mundon stops this penalty from Ernie Batten of Gravesend Photo: David Hills

The Thanet United defenders can only stand and watch as John Griffiths has the simple task of scoring the only goal of the Southern League match for Burnham & Hillingdon

Photo: Maidenhead Advertiser

Steve Kirby heads home for Gravesend's second against Corby Town. Gravesend won 1-2 Photo: David Hills

THE SOUTHERN FOOTBALL LEAGUE
SOUTHERN DIVISION 1985-86

LEAGUE TABLE

	P	W	D	L	F	A	Pts
Cambridge City	40	23	11	6	87	41	80
Salisbury	40	24	8	8	84	51	80
Hastings Town	40	23	9	8	83	51	78
Dover Athletic	40	23	6	11	89	53	75
Corinthian	40	20	9	11	78	45	69
Tonbridge A.F.C.	40	17	13	10	65	51	64
Dunstable	40	17	11	12	70	61	62
Ruislip	40	17	6	17	67	66	57
Erith & Belvedere	40	14	12	14	35	40	54
Waterlooville	40	16	6	18	52	58	54
Burnham & Hillingdon	40	16	6	18	44	59	54
Canterbury City	40	13	13	14	58	58	52
Trowbridge Town	40	13	13	14	57	63	52
Sheppey United	40	14	10	16	43	53	52
Thanet United	40	13	7	20	58	63	46
Woodford Town	40	12	10	18	49	62	46
Poole Town	40	12	7	21	55	63	43
Ashford Town	40	10	12	18	45	65	42
Chatham Town	40	8	15	17	53	70	39
Andover	40	10	8	22	52	92	38
Dorchester Town	40	5	8	27	35	94	23

SOUTHERN DIVISION 1985-86	Andover	Ashford Town	Burnham & H.	Cambridge City	Canterbury City	Chatham Town	Corinthian	Dorchester Town	Dover Athletic	Dunstable	Erith & Belvedere	Hastings Town	Poole Town	Ruislip	Salisbury	Sheppey United	Thanet United	Tonbridge A.F.C.	Trowbridge T.	Waterlooville	Woodford Town
Andover	—	2-0	1-2	1-5	3-2	5-3	0-3	2-0	2-4	3-2	1-0	0-3	0-1	1-1	1-2	2-1	3-1	2-7	2-2	1-2	3-1
Ashford Town	2-1	—	2-0	1-1	1-1	3-2	0-4	3-0	1-2	1-1	2-1	0-1	1-0	1-2	2-3	1-1	1-0	2-2	0-1	1-1	1-1
Burnham & H.	2-2	2-3	—	2-5	1-0	0-0	0-2	1-2	1-0	1-0	1-0	0-1	3-1	0-4	2-0	1-0	1-0	0-1	1-1	2-0	1-1
Cambridge City	6-1	1-1	1-0	—	4-3	4-0	2-2	3-0	0-1	6-3	1-0	0-2	2-2	2-0	0-0	0-0	6-0	2-0	4-1	4-1	0-1
Canterbury City	0-0	1-0	3-1	2-2	—	1-1	3-0	3-1	2-1	4-3	1-1	3-0	2-1	1-0	2-2	1-1	0-2	4-4	1-2	1-2	2-4
Chatham Town	1-1	2-0	1-1	2-1	0-0	—	1-1	2-0	2-2	3-3	1-2	1-3	1-1	0-3	1-3	3-1	2-1	0-1	3-1	0-0	0-0
Corinthian	8-1	1-0	2-0	0-1	1-0	2-2	—	3-1	1-3	0-0	3-0	4-1	1-1	4-0	2-1	6-1	0-0	0-1	1-2	3-0	2-0
Dorchester Town	2-1	2-2	1-2	2-3	0-3	3-1	0-3	—	4-3	0-0	0-2	3-3	0-5	0-4	0-2	0-1	2-2	0-2	2-2	1-3	0-1
Dover Athletic	3-1	6-1	2-1	0-0	1-2	2-2	1-1	2-1	—	1-2	2-0	3-1	6-1	1-0	2-3	2-0	0-1	3-0	2-0	4-1	3-1
Dunstable	4-1	3-2	2-0	3-2	1-1	0-1	2-2	1-0	4-4	—	1-0	3-1	2-0	2-4	3-1	3-0	0-2	2-2	1-0	4-2	20
Erith & Belvedere	2-1	2-0	1-0	1-2	2-1	1-0	2-0	0-2	0-2	1-1	—	0-2	0-0	2-1	0-0	0-0	2-1	1-1	1-0	2-0	3-2
Hastings Town	1-1	1-1	6-0	2-3	2-0	3-0	2-1	3-3	3-1	2-2	0-0	—	2-1	3-0	5-3	4-0	2-1	2-0	3-0	2-1	2-0
Poole Town	4-0	1-0	0-1	3-0	3-0	2-4	1-2	2-0	2-2	1-0	1-2	0-2	—	2-0	2-1	1-3	3-1	1-3	0-1	2-3	1-3
Ruislip	1-3	4-3	3-5	0-1	1-1	2-2	4-1	4-1	1-4	2-2	2-0	2-3	2-2	—	1-2	3-3	2-1	0-1	3-1	3-0	0-2
Salisbury	1-1	2-0	2-0	0-2	3-1	2-1	4-2	3-0	3-2	3-1	1-1	3-3	2-0	5-1	—	4-0	4-0	4-1	2-2	2-0	3-0
Sheppey United	3-0	3-0	0-2	0-0	1-1	2-1	2-1	3-0	0-5	0-1	3-0	2-0	2-1	0-1	2-0	—	2-0	1-1	1-3	1-0	1-0
Thanet United	3-0	2-3	2-3	1-2	0-2	3-1	1-1	5-0	1-3	3-2	0-0	2-0	0-1	0-1	1-2	1-1	—	3-1	2-2	3-1	2-1
Tonbridge A.F.C.	1-1	4-1	3-0	0-3	3-0	4-2	3-1	1-1	0-2	1-1	1-1	1-1	3-1	0-1	4-1	0-0	1-1	—	2-1	1-1	2-0
Trowbridge T.	1-0	0-1	1-1	3-6	2-2	2-1	1-4	3-0	1-1	4-0	1-1	3-2	1-1	0-1	1-1	1-0	1-4	2-1	—	1-2	4-1
Waterlooville	3-1	1-1	0-1	0-0	0-1	1-0	1-2	4-0	1-2	2-1	1-0	1-2	3-2	3-1	0-1	1-0	1-3	2-0	1-1	—	4-0
Woodford Town	2-0	0-0	2-2	0-0	1-0	3-3	0-1	1-1	5-1	0-2	1-1	2-2	2-1	1-2	2-3	2-1	3-2	0-1	1-1	1-2	—

ANDOVER

President: J. S. Monro
Chairman: A. F. Baker
Asst. Manaer/Coach: Brian Hunt
Physiotherapist: Terry Carr
Secretary: Robin L. Adcock
Address & Tel. No.: 2 Bridge House, 154 Junction Road, Andover, Hants. SP10 3JF
0264 55120 (H). 0264 65951 (B)
Press Officer: Secretary
Address & Tel. No. of ground: The Walled Meadow, London Road, Andover. 0264 23152 **Club shop:** Yes
Simple ground directions: Head for the town centre, the ground is approximately ½ mile east of the town in London Road
No. of seats: 300 **Covered accommodation:** 1,300 **Capacity:** 6,800 **Floodlights:** Yes
Year formed: 1883 **Nickname:** The Lions **Club Sponsors:** Doves Andover
Previous names: Andover Town
Club Colours: Red/Black broad stripe shirts, Black/Red
Previous grounds: Weyhill Road, Andover
Change colours: Tangerine/White/Tangerine
Day for midweek home matches: Tuesday
Previous Leagues: Salisbury District, May, Hampshire, Western
Record attendance: 3,484 v. Gillingham F.A. Cup 1st Round Proper **Year** 1962-3
Best performance in: F.A. Cup: 1962-3 v. Gillingham 1st Round
F.A. Trophy: 3rd Qualifying Round
Clubhouse details: Dance Hall, bars, etc., as pubs
Past players who progressed to Football League: A. Kingston (Southampton), P. Brown (Southampton, Walsall), N. Spackman (Bournemouth, Chelsea), M. Nwajiobi (Luton Town)
Programme Editor: c/o Meadow Club
Programme details: 12-24 pages, 25p
Local Newspapers: Andover Advertiser. 62600
Southern Evening Echo
Club metal badges: Yes
Record transfer fee paid: £1,200 to Salisbury for Alan Green
Record transfer fee received: £1,750 from Salisbury for Ricky Haysom
Senior Honours: Western League Runners-up (2), Hants League (7), Hants Senior Cup (4), Russell Cotes Cup (8)
Club captain (1985-86):
Player of the year (1985-86):

BURNHAM & HILLINGDON

President: Dr. Maxwell Summers, DSO, OBE
Chairman: Malcolm Higton
Manager: Mick Jones
Asst. Manager/Coach: Jackie Graham
Physiotherapist: Brian Burke
Secretary: Dave Eavis
Address & Tel. No.: 32 Peel Close, Windsor, Berks. SL4 3NP
Commercial Manager: Jimmy Thomas
Press Officer: Michael Boxall
Address & Tel. No. of ground: Wymers Wood Road, Burnham, Slough SL1 8JG. Burnham 2467 & 2697
Simple ground directions: 2 miles from M4 (Junction 7) and 5 miles from M40 (Junction 2)
No. of seats: 200 **Covered accommodation:** 200 **Capacity:** 2,500 **Floodlights:** Yes
Year formed: 1878 Burnham **1872 Hillingdon— merger 1985** **Nickname:** The Blues **Club Sponsors:** A.C. Frost & Co. (Estate Agents)
Club shop: No
Club Colours: Blue & White Quarters **Change colours:** Red
Day for midweek home matches: Tuesday **Club metal badges:** No
Previous Leagues: Windsor, Slough & District, Great Western Combination, Wycombe Combination, Reading Combination, Hellenic, Athenian, London Spartan
Record attendance: 2,400 v. Halesowen Town F.A. Vase **Year** 1983 (Burnham F.C.)
Best performance in: F.A. Vase: 1982-3 Semi-Final
Clubhouse details: Two bars, catering, live entertainment. Open every lunchtime and evening
Programme Editor: Michael Boxall
Programme details: 20 pages, 20p
Local Newspapers: Slough Observer, South Bucks Express
Maidenhead Advertiser, Bucks Free Press
Club metal badge: No
Senior Honours: (Burnham F.C.) Hellenic League Winners 1975-6, London Spartan League Winners 1984-5, F.A. Vase Semi-Finalists 1982-3
Leading Goalscorers: Ray Knowles (12) Selwin Cambell (11)
Most appearances: Peter Lammin (39), Selwin Campbell (37), Derek Payne (35)
Club captain (1985-86):
Player of the year (1985-86): Peter Lammin

ASHFORD TOWN

President: J. Skinner, M.B.E.
Chairman: D. S. R. Gillard
Manager: Peter Sillett
Asst. Manager/Coach: Nicky Sparks
Physiotherapist: George Sergeant
Press Officer: Secretary
Secretary: Alan G. Lancaster
Address & Tel. No.: 128 Kingsnorth Road, Ashford, Kent TN23 2HY
Commercial Manager: Ernie Warren
8 Hawks Way, Ashford, Kent
Address & Tel. No. of ground: Essella Park, Essella Road, Ashford, Kent. 0233 20528 **Club shop:** Yes
Simple ground directions: Leave inner ring road in town at the Folkestone junction. Proceed down Mace Lane across round-about in 400 yards turn right and then sharp left at Fina Filling Station
No. of seats: 200 **Covered accommodation:** 2,000 **Capacity:** 5,500 **Floodlights:** Yes
Year formed: 1930 **Nickname:** Nuts & Bolts **Club Sponsors:** Korker Sausages (1st team)
Club Colours: All Green **Change colours:** All Yellow
Day for midweek home matches: Tuesday
Previous Leagues: Kent League
Record attendance: 6,525 v. Crystal Palace F.A. Cup 1st Round **Year** 1959
Best performance in: F.A. Cup: 1961-2 v. QPR (H) lost 3-0, 1966-7 v. Swindon (a) lost 5-0 2nd Round
F.A. Trophy: 1972-3 v. Scarborough at Peterborough, Semi-Final, lost 1-0
Clubhouse details: Small single room clubroom with licensed bar which opens on match days only
Past players who progressed into the Football League: Tony Godden (Goal) to W.B.A.
Programme Editor: Ernie Warren
Programme details: 16 pages, 20p
Local Newspapers: Kentish Express. 0233 23232
Ashford Advertiser
Club metal badge: No
Record transfer fee received: £2,500 for Alan Morton from Maidstone United
Senior Honours: F.A. Cup 1961-2 1st Round, 1966-7 2nd round, Kent Senior Cup Winners (2), Semi-Finalist of F.A. Trophy 1972-3

CANTERBURY CITY F.C.

President: F. Wood
Chairman: K. T. Longley
Manager: Carl Gilbert
Asst. Manager/Coach: Phil Nash
Physiotherapist: none
Secretary: V. H. Heslop
Address & Tel. No.: 119 Tennyson Avenue, Canterbury, Kent CT1 1ER. 68555
Commercial Manager: D. J. Owen
Press Officer: Keith Smith. 456116
Address & Tel. No. of ground: Kingsmead Stadium, Kingsmead Road, Canterbury, Kent. 464732
Club shop: Yes
Simple ground directions: A28 signposted
No. of seats: 600 **Covered accommodation:** 1,500 **Capacity:** 10,000 **Floodlights:** Yes
Year formed: 1947 **Nickname:** The City **Club Sponsors:** Three Way School of Motoring
Previous name: Canterbury Waverley
Club Colours: Green Shirts, Black Shorts
Previous grounds: Bretts Corner
Change colours: All Blue
Day for midweek home matches: Tuesday
Previous Leagues: Kent, Metropolitan
Record attendance: 3,001 v. Torquay United, F.A. Cup 1st Round **Year** 1964
Best performance in: F.A. Cup: 1964 v. Torquay, 1968 v. Swindon 1st Round
F.A. Trophy: 1974-5 v. Dagenham 2nd Round
Clubhouse details: Bar open match days
Programme Editor: Keith Smith
Programme details: 8 pages
Local Newspapers: Kentish Gazette. 68181, Adscene. 454545
Club metal badge: Yes
Record transfer fee paid: £2,000 for Graham Knight (Maidstone United)
Record transfer fee received: £2,000 for Dave Wiltshire (Gillingham)
Senior Honours: Kent league Cup, Kent Messenger Trophy, Kent Senior Cup, Kent Senior Trophy, F.A. Cup 1st Round Proper in 1964 v. Torquay United and 1968 v. Swindon Town
Past players who progressed to Football League: Pat Hilton (Brighton), Tommy Horsfall (Cambridge United), Terry Norton (Brighton), Mark Weatherly (Gillingham), Dave Wiltshire (Gillingham)
Club captain (1985-86):
Player of the year (1985-86):

CHATHAM TOWN

President: The Mayor, Rochester upon Medway
Chairman: G. Swayland
Manager: D. McLachlan
Asst. Manager/Coach: D. Richardson
Secretary: D. T. Terry
Address & Tel. No.: 15 Reculver Walk, Senacre, Maidstone Kent. ME15 8QE. Maid 0622 63908
Physiotherapist: J. Whitely
Address & Tel. No. of ground: Maidstone Road Sports Ground, Maidstone Road, Chatham. Kent. Medway 43678
Simple ground directions: M2 A229 Chatham turn off, follow signs to Chatham, ground approximately 1½ miles on right opposite garage
No. of seats: 500 **Covered accommodation:** 1,000 **Capacity:** 5,000 **Floodlights:** Yes
Year formed: 1882 **Nickname:** Chats **Club Sponsors:** Discount Windows Ltd/Kingsferry Candies Ltd.
Club Colours: Red, White, Red & White hooped **Change colours:** All White
Day for midweek home matches: Tuesday **Club metal badges:** No
Previous Leagues: Metropolitan, Aetolian, Kent, Southern
Record attendance: 5,500 v. Gillingham **Year** 1980
Best performance in: F.A. Cup: 1889 beat Notts Forest 2-0, reched Quarter Final
F.A. Trophy: 1970-1 last 16
Clubhouse details: Open Tuesday and Thursday evenings and match days. Medway 43678
Programme Editor: D. T. Terry **Local Newspapers:** Chatham News
Programme details: 18 pages, 25p
Senior Honours: Kent League Championship (4), Runners-up (3), Kent League Cup Winners (2), Runners-up (3), in F.A. Cup 1889 beat Notts Forest 2-0 reached Quarter Finals, F.A. Trophy 1970-1 last 16.
Club captain (1985-86): D. Richardson **Player of the year (1985-86):** G. Milne

CORINTHIAN F.C.

President: R. Shaw
Manager: A. Sitford
Secretary: R. J. Billings
Address & Tel. No.: Gay Dawn Farm, Pennis Lane, Fawkham, Dartford, Kent. Longfield 2335 (H), Gravesend 66765 (B)
Address & Tel. No. of ground: Gay Dawn, Pennis Lane, Dartford, Kent. Longfield 2335 **Club shop:** No
Simple ground directions: A2 off Longfield take Fawkham Road 300 yards past church turn left. Or A20 to Fawkham Green, Valley Road to Longfield turn on right well singposted
No. of seats: 75 **Capacity:** 2,000 **Floodlights:** Yes
Year formed: 1971-72 **Nickname:** none **Club Sponsors:** none
Club Colours: Green/White hooped Shirts, White Shorts **Change colours:** Red/Black
Record attendance: 480 v. Tottenham Hotspur **Year** 1979
Clubhouse details: Bar, kitchen, large lounge
Programme Editor: none **Programme details:** none
Senior Honours: Essex F.A. Senior Cup, Kent Senior Cup, Fort Lauderdale (USA) Amateur International Tournament
Club captain (1985-86): **Player of the year (1985-86):**

DORCHESTER TOWN

President: J. Pitfield
Chairman: P. J. Aiken
Manager: Keith Miller
Physiotherapist: Bill Hall
Secretary: A. E. Miller
Address & Tel. No.: 29 Shaston Crescent, Dorchester 0305 64843
Press Officer: S. L. Legge
Commercial Manager: J. Jewer
Address & Tel. No. of ground: Avenue Grround, Dorchester. 0305 62451. **Club shop:** Yes
Simple ground directions: On Weymouth Road, A354, out of town ½ mile
No. of seats: 300 **Covered accommodation:** 3,000 **Capacity:** 5,250 **Floodlights:** Yes
Year formed: 1880 **Nickname:** The Magpies **Club Sponsors:** Old's Motor Group
Club Colours: Black & White Stripes **Change colours:** Red
Day for midweek home matches: Tuesday
Record attendance: 5,250 v. Bournemouth F.A. Cup **Year** 1962-3
Best performance in: F.A. Cup: 1954-5, 1957-8, 1981-2 2nd Round Proper
F.A. Trophy: 1971-2 3rd Round
Previous Leagues: Western, Dorset
Clubhouse details: Magpie Social Club and Vice-Presidents Club within the ground. Open every evening and Sunday lunchtimes. Dance hall, skittle alley, etc.
Past players who progressed to Football League: R. Gundry (Portsmouth), L. Drake (Bristol Rovers) M. Turner (Swindon Town), D. Noake (Luton Town), T. Senior (Portsmouth), D. West (Liverpool)
Programme Editor: S. L. Legge. 0305 63799
Programme details: 20 pages, free with admission
Local Newspapers: Dorset Evening Echo, Western Gazette, Western Daily Press
Club metal badges: Yes
Record transfer fee paid: £1,500 to Yeovil for Kevin Leigh
Record transfer fee received: £35,000 from Portsmouth for Trevor Senior
Senior Honours: Southern League Div 1 (South), Mark Frowde Cup (3), Western League
Club captain (1985-86): **Player of the year (1985-86):**

DOVER ATHLETIC

Chairman: J. Husk
Manager: C. Kinnear
Physiotherapist: R. Jennings
Secretary: J. B. L. McManus
Address & Tel. No.: 131 St. Francis Close, Deal, Kent Deal 368212 (H) St. Marys R.C.P. School, Deal 375046 (B)
Press Officer/Commercial Manager: Secretary
Address & Tel. No. of ground: Crabble Athletic Ground, Lewisham Road, River, Dover. 822373 **Club shop:** Yes
Simple ground directions: Main A2 from Canterbury to Hammonds roundabout, follow directions to town centre, left at mini-roundabout, right at traffic lights where ground is signposted
No. of seats: 1,500 **Covered accommodation:** 4,000 **Capacity:** 7,500 **Floodlights:** Yes
Year formed: 1983 **Nickname:** Lillywhites **Club Sponsors:** Sealink
Previous names: Dover United, Dover
Previous grounds: none
Club metal badge: No
Club Colours: White/Black shirts, Black shorts & socks
Change colours: All Red
Day for midweek home matches: Tuesday
Record attendance: 6,900 v. Folkestone F.A. Cup **Year** 1951-2
Best performance in: F.A. Cup: 1975-6 lost to Southend 2nd round
F.A. Trophy: 1970-1 last 16
Previous Leagues: Kent
Clubhouse details: Social Club open 7 days per week, meals available
Past players who progressed into the Football League: P. Broadbent (Wolves), A. Knight (Brighton), T. Horsfall (Southend), G. Pugh (Bournemouth)
Programme Editor: C. Collings
Programme details: 16 pages, 20p
Local Newspapers: Dover Express, East Kent Mercury
Record transfer fee received: £4.000 for T. Jolley to Gillingham
Record transfer fee received: £12,00 from Brighton
Senior Honours: Kent Senior Cup (7), Kent Senior Sheild, Southern League Div. 1 (as Dover F.C.)
Club captain (1985-86): **Player of the year (1985-86):**

DUNSTABLE

President: G. Fox
Chairman: D. Agutter
Manager: P. Morrissey
Asst. Manager/Coach: A. Easterbrook
Club shop: Yes
Secretary: J. Crumley
Address & Tel. No.: 10 Olma Road, Dunstable, Beds. 0582 67638 (H), 0582 62559 (B)
Press Officer: D. Simpson
Physiotherapist: B. Lay
Address & Tel. No. of ground: Creasey Park, Brewers Hill Road, Dunstable. 0582 606691. Clubroom 0582 63800
Simple ground directions: Brewers Hill Road runs west from A505 at the north end of Dunstable at large traffic island. Turn right 150 yards
No. of seats: 500 **Covered accommodation:** 750 **Capacity:** 10,000 **Floodlights:** Yes
Year formed: 1895 **Nickname:** The Blues **Club Sponsors:** none
Previous names: Dunstable Town
Previous grounds: Kingsway, Dunstable
Club Colours: Royal Blue
Change colours: Red
Day for midweek home matches: Wednesday
Record attendance: 6,000 v. Manchester United **Year** 1974
Best performance in: F.A. Cup: 1956 1st Round
F.A. Trophy: 1971-2, 1975-6 3rd Qualifying Round
Previous Leagues: Metropolitan, Hellenic, United Counties
Clubhouse details: Large Clubroom and Bar
Past players who progressed to Football League: Kerry Dixon, Bill Garner (Southend, Chelsea)
Programme Editor: John Crumley
Programme details: 16 pages, 20p incl. adverts.
Local Newspapers: Dunstable Gazette, Herald
Club metal badges: Yes
Record transfer fee paid: £1,500 to Wycombe 1979 for Stuart Atkins
Record transfer fee received: £20,000 from Reading for Kerry Dixon
Senior Honours: Bedfordshire Senior Cup (6) including 1985-6, Bedfordshire Premier Cup (twice)

ERITH & BELVEDERE

President: L. O'Connell
Acting Chairman: C. Sims
Manager: Peter Peters
Asst. Manager/Coach: Tommy Sampson
Physiotherapist: Ron Bates
Secretary: Leslie G. Meakins
Address & Tel. No.: 23 Windermere Close, Dartford, Kent DA1 2TX. 0322 29406
Commercial Manager:
Press Officer: Secretary
Address & Tel. No. of ground: Park View, Lower Road, Belvedere, Kent. 01 311 4444 **Club shop:** No
Simple ground directions: Adjoining Belvedere (S.R.) Station
No. of seats: 820 **Covered accommodation:** 2,000 **Capacity:** 6,000 **Floodlights:** Yes
Year formed: 1922 **Nickname:** Deres **Club Sponsors:** Gentry's Sports
Club Colours: Blue White **Change colours:** Red
Day for midweek home matches: Tuesday
Record attendance: 8,000 v. Coventry F.A. Cup **Year** 1932
Best performance in: F.A. Cup: 1st Round (twice)
F.A. Vase: 1981 2nd Round
Previous Leagues: Kent, Corinthian Athenian, Metropolitan
Clubhouse details: Licensed Social Club with separate Tea Bar
Past players who progressed into the Football League: none
Programme Editor: Secretary
Programme details: Free with admission
Local Newspapers: Kentish Times, Kentish Independent
Club metal badge: No
Senior Honours: F.A. Amateur Cup Finalists (2), Kent League Champions, Kent Amateur Cup
Club captain (1985-86): **Player of the year (1985-86):**

GRAVESEND & NORTHFLEET

Chairman: David Hockley
Manager: Eddie Presland
Asst. Manager/Coach: Dennis Moore
Physiotherapist: Geoff Brittain
Club shop: Yes
Secretary: Daryl Lucas
Address & Tel. No.: 16 Woodfield Avenue, Gravesend, Kent DA11 7QG. 0474 323778
Commercial Manager: Carol Sidwell
Address & Tel. No. of ground: Stonebridge Road, Northfleet, Gravesend, Kent DA11 9BA. 0474 533796 Club 0474 534404 (Social)
Simple ground directions: From A2 trunk road take B262 Northfleet turn off, then B2175 to T junction with A226. Turn left continue to bottom of hill—ground is on right. 5 minutes walk Northfleet station (B.R.)
No. of seats: 1,300 **Covered accommodation:** 5,000 **Capacity:** 12,500 **Floodlights:** Yes
Year formed: 1946 **Nickname:** The Fleet **Club Sponsors:** Batt Cables
Previous names: Northfleet Utd & Gravesend Utd
Club Colours: Red/White/White
Previous grounds: none
Change colours: Blue/White/Black/Blue
Day for midweek home matches: Tuesday
Record attendance: 12,032 v. Sunderland F.A. Cup 4th Round **Year** 1963
Best performance in: F.A. Cup: 1962-3 v. Gillingham 1st Round
F.A. Trophy: 1969-70, 1977-8 2nd Round Proper
Previous Leagues: Southern Premier Hampshire, Western Alliance Premier
Clubhouse details: Bar open match days, Tuesday, Thursday, Friday, Saturday evenings, Sunday
Past players who progressed to Football League: Lee Smelt (Nottingham Forestm Cardiff, Peterborough, Halifax)
Programme Editor: Paul Harrison
Programme details: 32 pages, 30p
Local Newspapers: Gravesend & Dartford Reporter Kent Evening Post
Club metal badges: Yes
Record transfer fee paid: £3,500 to Barrow for Dave Busby
Record transfer fee received: £15,000 from Nottingham Forest for Lee Smelt
Senior Honours: Southern League, Southern League Div. 1 South & Runners-up, Southern League Cup & Runners-up, Southern League Championship Cup, Kent Senior Cup (3), & Runners-up (2), Kent Floodlight Cup & Runners-up
Club captain (1985-86): **Player of the year (1985-86):**

HASTINGS TOWN

President: Vic Wisden
Chairman: Peter Eastman
Manager: Joe White
Asst. Manager/Coach: Jack Dalton
Physiotherapist: Chris Emary
Secretary: R. A. Cosens
Address & Tel. No.: 22 Baldslow Road, Hastings, Sussex 0424 427867 (H), 436868 (B)
Commercial Manager: Joe Taliana
Press Officer: Tony Cosens
Club shop: Yes
Address & Tel. No. of ground: The Firs, Elphinstone Road, Hastings. 0424 444635 or 434755
Simple ground directions: From town centre take Queens Road (A2101), turn right at traffic lights into Elphinstone Road. Ground 1 mile on the right
No. of seats: 1,300 **Covered accommodation:** 2,800 **Capacity:** 10,000 **Floodlights:** Yes
Year formed: 1948 **Nickname:** The U **Club Sponsors:** D. L. Coleman Soft Drinks
Club Colours: All White with red trim **Change colours:** All blue with yellow hoops
Day for midweek home matches: Tuesday
Record attendance: 844 v. Cambridge City S.L. Match **Year:** 1986
Best performance in: F.A. Cup: 1953-4, 1954-5 3rd Round
F.A. Trophy: 1979-80, 1980-1 3rd Round
Previous Leagues: Sussex County
Clubhouse details: Social Club open every night plus Saturday & Sunday lunchtimes. Additional bar open on match days
Programme Editor: Tony Cosens
Programme details: 32 pages, 30p
Local Newspapers: Hastings News, Hastings Observer Evening Argus
Club metal badge: Yes, 50p
Senior Honours: Sussex Senior Cup Winners 1938, losing finalists 1986
Club captain (1985-86): **Player of the year (1985-86):**

POOLE TOWN

Chairman: Derek Block
Manager: Neil Merrick
Asst. Manager/Coach: Ian Hickson
Physiotherapist: Kim Sturgess
Club shop: Yes
Secretary: M. P. Smith
Address & Tel. No.: 49 Sopers Lane, Poole, Dorset 0202 696276
Commercial manager: Tonny Funnel
Press Officer: Tony Harvey 0202 676162
Address & Tel. No. of ground: Poole Stadium, Wimborne Road, Poole, Dorset BH15 2BP. 0202 670909/676162
Simple ground directions: Centre of Poole, behind fire station
No. of seats: 1,500 **Covered accommodation:** 9,000 **Capacity:** 10,500 **Floodlights:** Yes
Year formed: 1880 **Nickname:** The Dolphins **Club Sponsors:**
Club Colours: Blue & Yellow shirts, Blue shorts, Yellow socks **Change colours:** All White with Blue trim
Day for midweek home matches: Monday or Wednesday
Previous Leagues: Western
Record attendance: 11,155 v. Watford F.A. Cup **Year** 1962-3
Best performance in: F.A. Cup: 1926-7 3rd Round Newport County
F.A. Trophy: 1969-70, 1970-1, 1974-5 1st Round Proper
Clubhouse details: Open every evening and lunchtime
Past players who progressed to Football League: Bob Iles (Chelsea), P. Ferns jnr. (Bournemouth), D. Lyon (Southport)
Present players with Football League experience: N. Merrick, B. Elliott, T. Funnell
Programme Editor: T.B.A.
Programme details: New one being launched
Local Newspapers: Evening Echo, Gazette
Club metal badges: Yes
Record transfer fee paid: £1,500 for Derek Courtney
Record transfer fee received: £3,000 for Paul Morrell
Senior Honours: Western League Champions, Western Counties Cup (2), Anglo-Italian Cup Runners-up
Club captain (1985-86):
Player of the year (1985-86):

RUISLIP

President: F. Deanus
Chairman: R. Woodward
Manager: C. Barnes
Asst. Manager/Coach: P. Ryan
Physiotherapist: R. Clark
Secretary: J. Schrijver
Address & Tel. No.: 47 Myrtle Avenue, Ruislip, Middx. HA4 8SA. 01886 5713 (H)
Press Officer: S. Grimwood
Address & Tel. No. of ground: Breakspear Road, Ruislip. Ruislip 39544
Simple ground directions: Bottom High Street, Ruislip, left turn mini round about, turn left at Breakspear Road, 100 yards past Crematorium
No. of seats: 50 **Covered accommodation:** Yes **Capacity:** 2,000 **Floodlights:** Yes
Year formed: 1980 **Club sponsors:** Yes **Club metal badges:** No
Club Colours: Yellow shirts, Green sleves, Green shorts **Change colours:** Lt.Blue shirts, Black shorts, Black socks
Day for midweek home matches: Tuesday
Previous Leagues: Middlesex
Record attendance: 1,850
Clubhouse details: Yes
Programme Editor: C. Barnes
Programme details: 8 pages, 25p
Local Newspapers: Ruislip Northwood Gazette
Club captain (1985-86):
Player of the year (1985-86):

SHEPPEY UNITED

Chairman: V. E. Ward
Manager: Malcolm Ainsley
Secretary: G. E. Carpenter
Address & Tel. No.: 53 Cecil Avenue, Sheerness, Kent. ME12 1OX. 0795 662013
Press Officer: D. Harvey, 2 Linden Drive, Sheerness ME12 1LG. 0795 666039
Address & Tel. No. of ground: Botany Road, St. George's Avenue, Sheerness, Kent. 0795 665299
Simple ground directions: 200 yards from main shopping area of Sheerness, turn by Castle pub
No. of seats: 150 **Covered accommodation:** 4,000 **Capacity:** 7,000 **Floodlights:** Yes
Year formed: 1890 **Nickname:** Islanders or Ites **Club Sponsors:** Sealink Shipping Company
Previous names: Sheppey Athletic
Previous grounds: none
Day for midweek home matches: Tuesday
Club Colours: Red & White shirts, Black shorts
Change colours: All Light Blue
Clubhouse details: Open match days
Previous Leagues: Southern League, founder members, 1894, Kent, Aetolian, Greater London, Metropolitan
Record attendance: 4,000+ v. Sittingbourne **Year** 1927
Best performance in: F.A. Cup: 1919-20 v. Thornecroft 6th Qualifying Round
F.A. Trophy: 1969-70 v. Dover 3rd Qualifying Round
Past players who progressed to Football League: E. C. Harper (England International, Blackburn R., Tottenham H., Preston N.E.)
Programme Editor: D. Harvey
Programme details: 8 pages, 20p
Local Newspapers: Sheerness Times, Guardian
Senior Honours: F.A. Cup 1919-20 6th Qual. Round, F.A. Trophy 1985-6 1st Round Proper, Kent Amateur Cup (2), Kent Senior Shield, Kent Senior Cup Finalists (3), Kent League Champions (6), Kent League Cup (2), Greater London League Champions
Club captain (1985-86):
Player of the year (1985-86):

Minehead F.C. Photo: David Wells

Ruslip versus Cambridge City

Canterbury City *Back Row (L-R): John Brooks, John Lineham, Dave Linstrem, Dave Huddart, Tommy Sloan, Billy Fogarty, Ian Cook*
Front Row (L-R): Simon Bryant, Peter Venn, Graham Knight, Mark Harrop.

Photo: Trevor Jeal

THANET UNITED

President: R. W. Griffiths
Chairman:
Manager: John Wickens
Coach: Phil Winfield
Physiotherapist: Dave Garrod
Secretary: D. Bennett
Address & Tel. No.: "Beachcomber" 103 Beacon Road, Broadstairs, Kent
Commercial Manager/Press Officer: D. Bennett
Club shop: Yes
Address & Tel. No. of ground: Hartsdown Park, Hartsdown Road, Margate, Thanet, Kent. 0843 221769
Simple ground directions: Hartsdown Park is 5 minutes walk from Margate railway station (Southern Region). By road take main A28 towards Margate turn right opposite Westbrook Day Hospital into George V Avenue, follow road round and at 'T' junction turn right into Hartsdown Road. Ground on left.
No. of seats: 600 **Covered accommodation:** All 4 sides **Capacity:** 8,500 **Floodlights:** Yes
Year formed: 1880 as Thanet F.C. became Margate F.C. in 1896. Reformed as Thanet United in 1981
Nickname: The Islanders **Club Sponsors:** Various **Club metal badges:** Yes
Club Colours: White/Blue/Red **Change colours:** Red & White or All White
Day for midweek home matches: Tuesday
Record attendance: 8,500 v. Tottenham Hotspur F.A. Cup 3rd Round **Year** 1973
Previous Leagues: Kent League
Best performance in: F.A. Cup: 1936-7 3rd Round v. Blackpool (a), 1972-3 v. Spurs (h)
F.A. Trophy: 1978-9 3rd Round Replay v. Runcorn (h)
Clubhouse details: Luxurious Club open on match days, and by arrangement. Available for private hire
Past players who progressed into the Football League: D. Carr (Luton, Lincoln), T. Jenkins (Reading, Southampton, Swindon), R. Flannigan (Reading), B. Gregory (Luton), J. O'Mara (Aldershot), L. Smelt (Nottingham Forest)
Programme Editor: Ray Hopper
Programme details: 16 pages, 20p
Club metal badge: Yes
Record transfer fee paid: £3,750 for Neil Cugley
Record transfer fee received: £2.500
Local Newspapers: Isle of Thanet Gazette Thanet Times 0843 221313, Thanet Extra, Adscene
Senior Honours: Southern League (2), Southern Leage Div. 1 (2), Southern League Cup Finalists (2), Southern League Merit Cup (3), Kent Senior Cup (2), Kent Floodlight Cup (3), Eastern Floodlight Competition Finalists

TONBRIDGE A.F.C.

Chairman: F. Davis**Secretary:** Pat Westguard
Manager: P. Emblen
Physiotherpist: C. Gower
Address & Tel. No.: 7 Baltic Road, Tonbridge, Kent 0732 358492 (H), 352417 (B)
Commercial Manager: G. Dunster. Maidstone 41579
Press Officer: Kevan Martin 0622 51511 (H), 679532 (B) **Club shop:** Yes
Address & Tel. No. of ground: Longmead Stadium, Darenth Avenue, Tonbridge, Kent. 0732 352417
Simple ground directions: From Tonbridge station through High Street, up Shipbourne Road to Pinnacles pub, Darenth Avenue immediately left, then straight on down for Longmead Stadium,. approximately 2 miles
No. of seats: none **Covered accommodation:** Standing on side **Capacity:** 5,000 **Floodlights:** Yes
Year formed: 1948. New company 1976 **Nickname:** The Angels **Club Sponsors:** Cannon Lane Timbers
Previous names: Tonbridge F.C. **Club Colours:** Blue/Navy/Navy
Previous grounds: The Angel until 1950 **Change colours:** Yellow/White/White
Day for midweek home matches: Tuesday
Record attendance: 8,236 v. Aldershot F.A. Cup 1st Round **Year** 1951
Previous Leagues: none
Best performance in: F.A. Cup: 1951-2, 1952-3, 1967-8, 1972-3 1st Round Proper
F.A. Trophy: 1970-1, 1971-2 1st Round Proper
Clubhouse details: Licensed bar, tea bar. Open match days, Tuesdays, Thursdays and Sunday lunchtimes. Also hired out for parties, etc.
Past players who progressed to Football League: R. Saunders, M. MacDonald, T. Burns, I. Seymour, G. Moseley, T. Morgan
Programme Editors: Tom Spence/Kevan Martin
Club metal badges: Yes
Record transfer fee paid: £1,200 to Salisbury for Alan Green
Local Newspapers: Kent & Sussex Courier T.W. 26262, Kent Messenger Maid. 77880 News Revies T.W. 46577
Senior Honours: Southern League Cup Runners-up (2), Kent Senior Cup (2), Runners-up (2), Kent Senior Shield (4)

TROWBRIDGE

President: D. C. Hurst
Chairman: L. M. Doel
Physiotherapist: N. Basson, MSRE
Secretary: G. Bolton
Address & Tel. No.: c/o Club. 02214 3403
Address & Tel. No. of ground: Frome Road, Trowbridge. 2076 **Club shop:** Yes
Simple ground directions: Entrance 100 yards from traffic lights in Frome Road (100 yards from Ship Inn)
No. of seats: 450 **Covered accommodation:** 8,000 **Capacity:** 8,500 **Floodlights:** Yes
Year formed: 1880 **Nickname:** none **Club Sponsors:** none
Previous names: Trowbridge FC **Club Colours:** Old Gold/Black
Previous grounds: Old Flower Show Ground **Change colours:** Red & White
Day for midweek home matches: Tuesday **Club metal badges:** Yes
Record attendance: 9,009 v. Weymouth F.A. Cup 4th Qual. Round **Year** 1949-50
Previous Leagues: Somerset Senior, Trowbridge & District, Wiltshire, Western, Southern, Alliance
Best performance in: F.A. Cup: 1947-8 v. Brighton 1st Round Replay 1963-4 v. Coventry C. 1st Round
F.A. Trophy: 1970 v. Leytonstone & Ilford 1st Round Replay
Clubhouse details: Refreshments available before and after matches. Steward, M. Davenport. Trowbridge 2600
Present players with Football League experience: D. Bartley
Past players who progressed into the Football League: Paul Compton (Bournemouth), John Smeulders (Bournemouth), Andy Feeley
Programme Editor: S. H. White 02214 5752
Programme details: 24 pages, 20p
Club metal badge: Yes
Record transfer fee paid: £5,000 for John Smeulders
Local Newspapers: Wiltshire Times, Trow. 2532. Bath Evening Chronicle, 0225 63052. Western Daily Press, Evening Post 0272 20080
Record transfer fee received: £10,000 for Paul Compton

WATERLOOVILLE F.C.

President: M. Hibberd
Chairman: F. P. Faulkner
Manager: Ernie Bradwell
Physiotherapist: Len Slaughter
Secretary: M. Richards
Address & Tel. No.: 124 Highbury Grove, Cosham, Portsmouth. 0705 388119
Commercial Manager: Ray Stainton
Address & Tel. No. of ground: Jubilee Park, Aston Road, Waterlooville, Hants. 0705 263867 (Office) 0705 255333 (Commercial Dept.)
Simple ground directions: Easily located near town centre
No. of seats: 560 **Covered accommodation:** 1,500 **Capacity:** 6,000 **Floodlights:** Yes
Year formed: 1910 **Nickname:** The Ville **Club Sponsors:** H. Standley & Sons and Toyota GB Ltd.
Previous names: none
Previous grounds: Rowlands Avenue (Rec)
Colours: White with Blue trim
Day for midweek home matches: Tuesday
Change colours: All Yellow
Previous Leagues: Waterlooville & District, Portsmouth, Hampshire **Club shop:** Yes
Record attendance: 4,500 v. Wycombe Wanderers F.A. Cup 1st Round Proper **Year** 1976-7
Best performance in: F.A. Cup: 1983-4 v. Northampton Town 1st Round Proper & Replay
F.A. Trophy: 1976-77 v. Hendon 2nd Round Proper
Clubhouse details: The Jubilee Club. One of the finest social clubs in non-league football
Present players with Football League experience: Kenny Todd (Wolves, Port Vale & Portsmouth)
Past players who progressed to Football League: Paul Hardyman (Portsmouth & England U-21's), Campbell Chapman (Wolves), Phil Figgins (Portsmouth), John Robson (St. Johnstone, Scotland)
Programme Editor: Andy Stonebridge
Local Newspapers: The News & Sports Mail. 0705 664488
Programme details: 16 pages, 25p
Club metal badges: Yes
Record transfer fee received: £800 from Salisbury for Colin White
Record transfer fee paid: £500 to Salisbury for Colin White (3 months later)
Senior Honours: Southern League Div 1 South 1971-2 and Hampshire Senior Cup on three occasions
Leading Goalscorers: Kenny Todd (21), Ricky Burnside (16), Colin White (9). **Hat-tricks:** Calvin Hore. **Penalties:** Dave Maskell (5). **Most appearances:** Kenny Todd (52), Calvin Hore (49), Ian Turner (48)
Club captain (1985-86): Kenny Todd **Player of the year (1985-86):** Billy Cole

WOODFORD TOWN

President: J. Burton
Chairman: F. Sinclair
Manager: Keith Elley
Asst. Manager/Coach: Lyndon Lynch
Physiotherapist: Dave Dickens
Secretary: V. J. Hammerton
Address & Tel. No.: 202 Stanstead Road, Bishops Stortford, Hearts. CM23 2AR. 0297 52821 (H) Club (B)
Press Officer: Richard Adler, 32 Sweetmead Road, Saffron Walden, Essex. 0297 36750 (H), 01 283 2081 x 2512 (B)
Address & Tel. No. of ground: 265 Snakes Lane East, Woodford Green, Essex. 01 504 0831 **Club shop:** Yes
Simple ground directions: Woodford station (Central Line) 5 minues walk to ground
No. of seats: 300 **Covered accommodation:** 500 **Capacity:** 6,000 **Floodlights:** Yes
Year formed: 1937 **Nickname:** The Town **Club Sponsors:** P. J. Weller & Son Ltd.
Previous names: none
Club Colours: Blue/White/Blue/Blue
Previous grounds: Woodford Wells
Change colours: Red, White/White/Red
Day for midweek home matches: Wednesday
Previous Leagues: Metropolitan, Athenian
Record attendance: v. Colchester United F.A. Cup **Year** 1952-3
Best performance in: F.A. Cup: 1951-2, 1958-9 4th Qual. Round
F.A. Vase: 1981-2 3rd Round
Clubhouse details: Woodys Club, luxuriously appointed
Past players who progressed into the Football League: C. Flatt (Orient, Southend), D. Hyde (Cambridge United), P. Fishenden (Norwich City)
Programme Editor: R. Adler
Local Newspapers: Ilford Recorder. 478 4444 Redbridge Guardian 531 4141
Programme details: 12 pages, 10p
Record transfer fee received: £10,000 from Norwich for Peter Fishenden
Senior Honours: F.A. Vase 1981-2 3rd Round, F.A. Cup 1951-2, 1958-9 4th Qual. Round.
Club captain (1985-86):
Player of the year (1985-86):

Tonbridge win at home against Corinthian (3-1) and Dixon lashes home the second goal on 24.4.86.
Photo: David Schute

Gravesend give Gosport Borough a drubbing (4-0) at home and Steve Kirby here is seen shouting for goal.
Photo: David Mills

Burnham & Millingdon turn back Poole Town's challenge in the Southern League (3-1) Conley Hall fires in a strong shot.
Photo: Slough Observer

Hastings Town F.C.:— Back-row (l to r): M. Streeter, W. Peacock, P. Heritage, D. Winterton, T. White, P. Barnett, P. Hopkinson. Front-row (l to r): K. Burgess, J. Newton, M Harrision, C. Spray, P. Petkovic.

BUILDING SCENE EASTERN FOOTBALL LEAGUE

President: A.E. Westwood, J.P.
Secretary: Bruce Badcock, 12 Dolphin Close, Linton, Cambridge CB1 6XA

Review of Season 1985-86

A successful and enjoyable season on the field of play was overshadowed by the death on 7th April of the League's President and Patron, Arthur Rudd.

Actively involved in the League for its fifty-one years of existance, Arthur had been secretary for thirty-seven years from 1946 to 1983 and then President from 1985. It was his efforts that first saw the formation of the League back in 1935, and then later move through an era that saw the 'A' teams of the likes of Arsenal, Tottenham Hotspur, Chelsea and West Ham United bring to East Anglia a level of football never before experienced in this part of the country.

His firmness guided the League through a long period of its development, but always fair with people, Arthur will be greatly missed by the League.

On the field of play, Sudbury Town won the League and Tiptree United retained the League Cup, known for the season as the Bulldog Petroleum Cup.

The race for the League title lasted until the final weekend of the season, and with two matches left, it was still possible for Sudbury, Great Yarmouth Town or Colchester United Reserves to carry off the title. However, by the end of May Day Bank Holiday Monday Sudbury had won the race, and were creditable champions of the Building Scene Eastern League.

Tiptree United won the Cup by beating March Town United with the only goal of the match played at Newmarket Town Football Club. March had had their chances, including a penalty kick, but were unable to take the Cup away from their Essex rivals.

Braintree Town made the furthest progress in the F.A. Cup, eventually going out one round away from joining the Football League clubs to two late goals at Halesowen after leading for most of the match.

In the F.A. Vase a number of unfortunate pairings in the early rounds of the competition matched the leading teams in the League together. Wisbech reached the semi-finals for the second year running, but after gaining an excellent draw at Southall in the first leg, a disappointing result at home in the second leg saw them throw away the chance of reaching Wembley.

The League celebrated its first fifty years by playing a representative match against the Essex and Suffolk Border League (who were celebrating 75 years) at Sudbury—a game which they won by five goals to three.

Despite the problems of the winter, the clubs reaped the benefits of extensive floodlighting facilities, and the League programme was virtually completed by the 5th May. Next season Ely City move to new facilities in their city, which will see them have floodlights from September, whilst Felixstowe are hard on their heels hoping to have their lights working during the season. That only leaves three clubs without these facilities to play evening matches throughout the League, and these all have plans to follow suit.

Next season Watton United will join the League from the Anglian Combination League. One of the most progressive clubs outside the Building Scene Eastern League, they already have full floodlighting facilities on their rapidly developing ground. They certainly show to other towns of their size in the Eastern Counties what can be achieved as the League looks towards its eventual ambition of two divisions and its continuance as the East of England's premier League.

EASTERN COUNTIES FOOTBALL LEAGUE CUP

FIRST ROUND

Chatteris v Wisbech 1-3
Colchester Utd Res v Newmarket 4-3
Ely City v March Town 1-2
Soham Town v Lowestoft 1-0
Thetford v Great Yarmouth 1-2
Tiptree v Bury Town 1-0

SECOND ROUND

Brantham v Tiptree 2-4
Clacton v March Town 0-2
Felixstowe v Histon 1-0
Gorleston v Braintree 1-3
Harwich & P'ston v Wisbech 1-2
Haverhill v Great Yarmouth 0-1
Stowmarket v Soham Town 3-1
Sudbury v Colchester Utd Res 1-2

THIRD ROUND

Colchester Utd Res v March Town 1-2
Stowmarket v Felixstowe 1-1
Tiptree v Great Yarmouth 3-1
Wisbech v Braintree 0-2
Replay
Felixstowe v Stowmarket 2-0

SEMI-FINALS

Felixstowe v March Town 0-4
Tiptree v Braintree 2-1

FINAL

(Played at Newmarket Town F.C.)
March Town v Tiptree 0-1

FINAL LEAGUE TABLE 1985/86

	P	W	D	L	F	A	Pts
Sudbury Town	42	30	6	6	107	45	66
Colchester United Res	42	29	6	7	109	49	64
Great Yarmouth Town	42	29	5	8	95	46	63
Bury Town	42	23	10	9	93	54	56
Tiptree United	42	24	7	11	78	54	55
Braintree Town	42	22	11	9	91	53	53*
March Town United	42	22	8	12	74	62	52
Stowmarket Town	42	19	13	10	79	62	51
Wisbech Town	42	22	5	15	79	55	49
Histon	42	20	7	15	75	58	47
Lowestoft Town	42	16	12	14	75	50	44
Felixstowe Town	42	19	6	17	62	54	44
Gorleston	42	15	9	18	74	64	39
Haverhill Rovers	42	16	6	20	61	59	38
Thetford Town	42	10	10	22	48	87	30
Brantham Athletic	42	13	4	25	57	108	30
Harwich & Parkeston	42	10	9	23	52	72	29
Soham Town Rangers	42	11	7	24	55	92	29
Chatteris Town	42	10	6	26	37	79	26
Ely City	42	8	9	25	46	82	25
Newmarket Town	42	9	5	28	59	119	23
Clacton Town	42	2	5	35	28	130	9

* Two points deducted for ineligible player

LEADING GOALSCORERS

D. Hubbick (Colchester) 32
M. Goldspink (Gorleston) 31
A. Hall (Bury/Harwich) 28
P. Smith (Sudbury) 28
R. Irving (Colchester) 27
M. Money (Lowestoft) 27
C. Guy (Braintree) 26
S. Kearns (Newmarket) 22
P. Harvey (Bury) 21
R. Sainty (March) 21
A. Pearson (Soham) 20
J. Tippett (Histon) 20
G. Powell (Tiptree) 19
N. Relizani (Histon) 18
J. Scase (Wisbech) 18
L. Steward (Great Yarmouth) 18
J. Taylor (Sudbury) 18
G. Plumb (March) 16
D. Davis (Sudbury) 15
M. Woolsey (Great Yarmouth) 15
R. Atterton (Lowestoft) 14
T. Bryson (Tiptree) 14
L. Newman (Felixstowe) 14
C. Oldfield (Stowmarket/Bury) 14
G. Chalmers (Haverhill) 13
P. Grimsey (Stowmarket) 13
G. Harvey (Tiptree) 13
G. Rider (Wisbech) 13
J. Wallace (Bury) 13
N. Barton (Stowmarket) 12
T. English (Colchester) 12
M. Lomas (Brantham) 12
R. Wilkins (Haverhill) 12
W. Woodhouse (Braintree) 12

EASTERN COUNTIES LEAGUE 1985/86	Braintree	Brantham	Bury	Chatteris	Clacton	Colchester	Ely	Felixstowe	Gorleston	Gt Yarmouth	Harwich & P	Haverhill	Histon	Lowestoft	March	Newmarket	Soham	Stowmarket	Sudbury	Thetford	Tiptree	Wisbech
Braintree		7-3	1-1	8-2	4-0	3-1	3-1	2-3	2-1	0-3	2-3	1-2	1-0	1-0	2-2	2-2	6-3	4-1	1-2	1-1	1-2	4-0
Brantham	1-3		1-2	1-0	2-1	1-5	4-1	0-3	2-3	0-3	1-4	4-3	1-2	2-4	1-2	1-2	4-2	1-1	0-4	1-1	0-4	3-2
Bury	1-3	7-1		5-0	8-0	3-1	3-1	2-0	1-0	2-4	3-0	0-0	3-1	4-0	3-3	4-2	3-1	0-0	3-1	0-0	3-2	2-3
Chatteris	0-0	0-3	0-1		3-1	1-4	0-2	0-1	2-1	1-4	0-1	3-0	2-1	1-1	1-1	2-0	2-3	0-1	0-2	0-1	1-2	0-3
Clacton	0-2	0-3	0-1	2-1		0-6	0-1	1-2	0-5	1-5	2-2	0-1	0-1	2-5	1-3	2-1	0-1	1-1	0-5	1-2	1-1	0-5
Colchester	3-1	3-0	3-2	1-1	4-0		3-0	1-0	2-1	2-2	4-1	1-0	2-0	1-1	1-0	3-3	2-1	1-4	2-0	2-2	2-0	3-0
Ely	1-1	0-1	0-0	1-0	6-1	2-5		2-3	0-2	0-2	1-2	0-2	3-2	0-0	0-1	2-1	1-2	0-1	0-0	1-1	0-0	1-0
Felixstowe	0-3	3-0	2-4	0-1	4-0	1-2	4-0		1-0	1-1	2-0	2-1	0-2	1-0	2-1	3-1	5-5	0-0	0-1	3-0	1-1	2-0
Gorleston	1-1	8-0	1-1	3-0	2-0	0-3	4-0	1-1		0-1	2-1	2-1	1-1	1-1	2-2	4-1	3-1	2-3	3-1	4-2	0-1	0-1
Gt. Yarmouth	2-4	5-0	2-1	2-0	2-1	2-1	2-2	1-0	3-2		2-0	2-1	4-2	2-1	2-0	2-1	3-0	1-0	0-1	3-1	1-0	3-1
H'wich & P'ston	0-1	1-2	0-2	0-1	2-2	1-2	2-1	1-2	1-1	1-0		1-2	3-1	1-2	1-1	2-0	0-0	0-1	2-3	1-2	0-1	1-0
Haverhill	0-1	1-1	0-3	1-2	5-1	0-1	5-3	2-1	2-1	1-1	1-1		3-0	1-3	0-3	2-5	1-3	1-3	0-1	0-1	6-0	2-0
Histon	0-3	3-1	4-0	2-2	3-1	2-4	4-1	3-2	3-1	3-1	3-1	1-0		1-0	0-1	4-0	1-1	1-1	1-2	3-1	1-2	3-0
Lowestoft	3-0	0-0	0-0	2-0	4-0	2-5	5-1	5-1	4-2	0-0	1-1	2-0	1-1		0-1	6-1	0-1	3-1	2-3	3-1	0-0	1-3
March	1-1	1-2	1-4	2-1	5-2	1-0	3-2	2-0	3-0	3-2	2-0	1-4	5-3	1-0		3-1	1-2	1-2	2-4	4-0	1-0	2-2
Newmarket	0-1	0-2	2-2	0-1	2-0	1-7	1-3	1-2	4-1	0-4	2-1	0-2	1-6	1-7	1-2		1-0	0-2	2-4	1-2	0-0	2-1
Soham	1-0	1-3	0-3	1-1	1-1	2-4	2-1	0-2	1-1	1-2	2-1	1-3	2-1	1-4	2-3	3-1		3-4	0-1	1-1	1-4	2-5
Stowmarket	1-1	4-1	4-1	5-2	3-1	0-6	3-3	0-0	1-2	1-3	4-4	0-0	0-1	1-1	2-0	4-5	3-0		0-3	7-2	5-3	1-0
Sudbury	2-2	3-0	5-0	1-0	10-0	3-2	1-1	3-2	3-1	4-1	3-2	0-1	1-1	2-1	0-0	6-2	4-1	1-1		2-0	3-5	1-0
Thetford	1-2	3-2	1-1	1-2	3-1	0-3	2-0	1-0	1-3	0-6	2-2	1-3	0-2	2-2	0-2	3-4	2-0	1-1	1-4		1-4	1-2
Tiptree	1-4	1-0	1-3	5-0	2-1	1-1	2-0	1-0	4-1	3-2	1-3	2-1	0-0	1-0	3-1	8-1	3-0	1-0	0-5	2-0		3-1
Wisbech	1-1	5-1	3-1	3-1	1-0	6-0	2-1	2-0	1-1	3-2	5-1	0-0	0-1	1-0	6-0	3-3	1-0	1-2	3-2	1-0	2-1	

BRAINTREE TOWN F.C.

Back Row (L-R): Gary Nash, John Bibby (captain), Kevin Ketley, Dave Harrington, Shaun Gascoyne, Ian Smith Front Row (L-R): Trevor Goldsmith, Chris Guy, Nicky Lee, Gary Hollocks, Ivan Gooday, James Greenyer Photo: Jon Weaver

BUILDING SCENE EASTERN COUNTIES CLUBS BEST CUP PERFORMANCES

Braintree — ECo 70-, Met 66-70
C. 4Q 69/70, 85-86
V. 2(2) 74/75 & 83/84

Brantham Athletic — ECo 78-
V. 5 82/83

Bury Town — ECo 76-, Sth 71-76, Met 64-71, Met 64-71, ECo 35-64
C. 1 68/69
T. 2 70/71
T. 2 70/71
V. Extra Prel (2) 81/82 & 83/84

Chatteris Town — ECo 66-
C. 3Q 72/73
V. 1(5) 77/78, 79/80, 80/81, 82/83 & 83/84

Clacton Town — ECo 64-, Sth 58-64, ECo 38-58
C. 1 60/61
T. 1Q(2) 69/70 & 78/79
V. 4 74/75

Colchester United Reserves — ECo 76-

Ely City — ECo 60-
C. 1 56/57
T. 2Q 73/74
V. 2(2) 76/77 & 79/80

Felixstowe Town — ECo 76-
C. 2Q(2) 79/80 & 83/84
V. 3(2) 78/79 & 80/81

Gorleston — ECo 69-
C. 1(2) 51/52 & 57/58
T. 1Q(2) 76/77 & 77/78
V. 4(2) 79/80 & 81/82

Gt Yarmouth Town — ECo 35-
C. 2(2) 52/53 & 53/54
T. 3Q 69/70
V. 5F 82/83

Haverhill Rovers — ECo 64-
C. 2Q 79/80
T. 2Q 69/70
V. 2(3) 79/80, 82/83, 83/84

Histon — ECo 65-, Ath 63-65, Delph 60-63, Spart 48-60, ECo 35-
C. 3Q 73/74
T. 2Q 72/73
V. 3 78/79

Lowestoft Town
C. 1(5) 26/27, 38/39, 66/67 67/68 & 77/78
T. 2 71/72

March Town United — ECo 54-, Utd Co. 48-54
C. 1(2) 55/56 & 78/79
T. 2Q(2) 70/71 & 72/73
V. 3 75/76

Newmarket Town — ECo 59-
C. 3Q 69/70
T. 2Q 69/70
V.1 83/84

Saffron Walden Town — ECo 74-, Essex 71-74
C. 2Q(2) 46/47 & 83/84
V. 3 83/84

Soham Town Rangers — ECo 63-
C. 3Q 70/71
T. 1Q(5) 69/70-72/73 & 74/75
V. 4/78/79

Stowmarket Town — ECo 52-
C. 2Q 80/81
T. 1Q(2) 74/75 & 77/78
V. 4 82/83

Sudbury Town — ECo 55-
C. 4Q
T. 3Q 74/75

Thetford Town — ECo 63-
C. 2Q(5) 70/71-73/74 & 75/76
T. 1Q(2) 70/71 & 71/72
V. 1 83/84

Tiptree United — ECo 79-, Essex 71-79
C. 1Q (2) 80/81 & 82/83
V. 3(2) 81/82 & 83/84

Wisbech Town — ECo 70-, Sth 58-70, Mid Co 52-58, ECo 50-52, Utd Co 35-50
C. 2 57/58
T. 2Q(4) 70/71-72/73 & 75/76
V. SF(2) 84-85, 85-86

EASTERN COUNTIES CLUB RECORDS

No. of clubs competing	21	21	22	22	22	22	22	22	22	22
Season	76/77	77/78	78/79	79/80	80/81	81/82	82/83	83/84	84/85	85/86
1 Braintree Town	14	13	8	22	17	19	18	1	1	6
2 Brantham Athletic	—	—	10	6	14	8	4	11	16	16
3 Bury Town	17	3	4	5	9	18	12	13	9	4
4 Cambridge United Res	—	—	12	—	—	—	—	—	—	—
5 Chatteris Town	20	19	21	21	21	9	16	10	15	19
6 Clacton Town	12	9	20	14	15	20	20	21	17	22
7 Colchester United Res	13	8	18	16	13	10	6	3	7	2
8 Ely City	8	11	6	12	4	15	22	20	18	20
9 Felixstowe Town	19	17	17	18	16	14	8	14	14	12
10 Gorleston	3	4	7	1	1	3	2	7	11	13
11 Gothic	18	18	—	—	—	—	—	—	—	—
12 Great Yarmouth Town	5	2	2	9	5	4	3	9	3	3
13 Harwick & Parkeston	—	—	—	—	—	—	—	—	21	17
14 Haverhill Rovers	10	7	1	17	20	11	15	17	20	14
15 Histon	9	15	15	13	22	16	19	16	8	10
16 Lowestoft Town	6	1	3	7	8	13	7	4	4	11
17 March Town United	21	16	11	15	6	12	11	15	6	7
18 Newmarket Town	15	20	22	8	10	7	10	12	19	1
19 Saffron Walden Town	4	10	16	20	7	6	1	6	—	—
20 Soham Town Rangers	16	21	13	10	18	21	17	18	12	18
21 Stowmarket Town	11	14	19	19	12	22	14	19	10	8
22 Sudbury Town	2	12	5	4	2	2	5	5	2	1
23 Thetford Town	7	6	14	11	19	17	21	22	22	15
24 Tiptree United	—	—	—	2	3	1	13	8	13	5
25 Wisbech Town	1	5	9	3	11	5	9	2	5	9

BRAINTREE TOWN

President:
Chairman: A. Stewart
Manager: C.J. Symes
Secretary: T.A. Woodley
Address & Tel. No. 19a Bailey Bridge Road, Braintree. Braintee 26234
Address and Tel. No. of ground: Cressing Road, Braintree. 0376 45617
Simple ground directions: 1 mile from town centre on B1018 to Witham

No. of seats: 400
Covered accommodation:
Capacity: 4,000
Year formed: 1894
Nickname: The Iron
Floodlights: Yes
Club colours: Yellow/blue/yellow
Change colours: Blue/blue/white
Day for midweek home matches: Tuesday
Club metal badges:
Previous Leagues: London, Metropolitan, Spartan
Clubhouse details: Bar open evenings and weekends; darts, pool etc.
Past players who progressed into the Football League: J. Dick (West Ham)
Programme details: 20 pages, 20p
Programme editor:
Local newspapers & Tel. No. Braintree & Witham Times
Major Honours: Eastern Counties League Champions (3), East Anglian Cup Winners (2), Metropolitan League Cup Winners

BRANTHAM ATHLETIC

President: T. Ingram
Chairman: D. White
Manager: J. Barker
Secretary: J. Newton
Address & Tel. No. Gurdons, Sturton Road, Brantham, Manningtree, Essex CO11 1PW. 0473 328821
Address and Tel. No. of ground: B.A.S. Club, New Village, Brantham, Manningtree, Essex. 0206 392506
Simple ground directions: Leave A12 at B1070 junction (sign post Manningtree), ground just off A137

No. of seats: 100
Covered accommodation: 100
Capacity: 1,500
Year formed: 1887
Nickname: Blue Imps
Floodlights: None
Club colours: White-blue & red piping/blue/white
Change colours: Blue/white/blue
Day for midweek home matches: Tuesday
Club metal badges: None
Previous Leagues: Essex & Suffolk Border League
Clubhouse details: Open each day during licensing hours, two floors, two bars, dancing, snooker, pool, refreshments
Past players who progressed into the Football League:
Programme details: 6 pages, 10p
Programme editor: J. Newton
Local newspapers & Tel. No. East Anglian
Major Honours: Suffolk Senior Cup 1926/7, Essex Border League (4), E & S Border League Cup 1975-6, 1976-7, Suffolk Premier Cup 1983/4

BURY TOWN

President: C.G. Elsey
Chairman: R. Ingay
Manager: M. Spore
Secretary: Eric F. Barbrooke
Address & Tel. No. 9 West Road, Bury St Edmonds. Bury St Edmonds 4115 (H)
Address and Tel. No. of ground: Ram Meadow, Cotton Lane
Simple ground directions: Just off centre of town, on main car park off the Angel Hill

No. of seats: 200
Covered accommodation: 2,000
Capacity: 5,000
Year formed: 1872
Nickname: The Blues
Floodlights: Yes
Club colours: Blue/black stripes
Change colours: Red
Day for midweek home matches: Wednesday
Club metal badges: Supporters Club only
Previous Leagues: Southern Metropolitan
Clubhouse details: Darts, crib, discos, pool
Past players who progressed into the Football League: Larry Carberry (Ipswich & England), Gary Stevens (Spurs & England)
Programme details: 20 pages, 20p
Programme editor: Tony Hall
Local newspapers & Tel. No. Bury Free Press, East Anglian Daily Times
Major Honours: F.A. Cup 1st Rd 1968 v Bournemouth, lost 3-0 after 0-0 draw

CHATTERIS TOWN

President: A. Munns
Chairman: D. Green
Manager: D. Eldred
Secretary: R.W. Salisbury
Address & Tel. No. 16 Westbourne Road, Chatteris, Cambs. Chatteris 2144
Address and Tel. No. of ground: West Street, Chatteris. Chatteris 2139
Simple ground directions: Enter Chatteris on A141 from Huntingdon, turn right into West Street after going round bypass roundabout

No. of seats: 250
Covered accommodation: 100
Capacity: 2,000
Year formed: 1920
Nickname: The Lillies
Floodlights: Yes
Club colours: White shirts, blue shorts
Change colours: Red shirts, black shorts
Day for midweek home matches: Wednesday
Club metal badges: No
Previous Leagues: Peterborough League
Clubhouse details: Bar & tea, kitchen
Past players who progressed into the Football League: Andy Rogers (Reading), Dave Gregory (Wrexham)
Programme details: 12 pages
Programme editor: S. Snell
Local newspapers & Tel. No. Cambridgeshire Times
Major Honours: Peterborough League (3), Hinchingbrooke Cup (7)

The main stand at Old Road, Clacton Town Photo: David Shute

CLACTON TOWN

President: None
Chairman: P.G. Ingham
Manager: F. Thompson
Secretary: A.R. Harvey
Address & Tel. No. 4 Fairlop Close, Clacton-on-Sea. 0255 420219
Address and Tel. No. of ground: Old Road Stadium, Old Road, Clacton-on-Sea. Clacton 432590
Simple ground directions: Follow signs to Council coach park, Old Road

No. of seats: 750
Covered accommodation: Yes
Capacity: 2,500
Year formed: 1892
Nickname: Seasiders
Floodlights: No
Club colours: White/blue/blue
Change colours: All red
Day for midweek home matches: Wednesday
Club metal badges: No
Previous Leagues: Southern League
Clubhouse details: Supporters Social Club, holds 120
Past players who progressed into the Football League: Mick Everitt (Arsenal, Northampton)

Programme details: 6 pages, 10p
Programme editor: L. Chandler
Local newspapers & Tel. No. Clacton Herald, East Essex Gazette
Major Honours: Southern League Div 1 Champions 1959-60

COLCHESTER UNITED RESERVES

President: W.J. Osborne
Chairman: M.J. Cadman
Manager: Mike Walker
Secretary: Martin R. Bennett
Address & Tel. No. Colchester 574042 (B)
Address and Tel. No. of ground: Layer Road Ground, Colchester CO2 7JJ. Colchester (0206) 574042
Simple ground directions: 1½ miles south west of town centre on road to Layer (B1026)

No. of seats: 1,200
Covered accommodation: 1,500
Capacity: 4,900
Year formed: 1937
Nickname: The U's
Floodlights: Yes
Club colours: Royal blue and white
Change colours: Red and black
Day for midweek home matches: Tuesday
Club metal badges: £1.20 (incl. p & p)
Previous Leagues: —
Clubhouse details: Supporters Club open for one hour after match, pay bar in operation
Past players who progressed into the Football League: n/a

Programme details: On application
Programme editor: Secretary
Local newspapers & Tel. No. Colchester Evening Gazette, East Anglian Daily Times, Essex County Standard (Weekly)
Major Honours: League Winners 1938-9, 1956-7, 1958-9; League Runners-up 1951-2, 1954-5, 1985-6

ELY CITY

President: D. Unwin
Chairman: T. Chapman
Manager: R. Crane
Secretary: G.W. Gillett
Address & Tel. No.
Address and Tel. No. of ground: Downham Road, Ely. Ely 2035
Simple ground directions: Downham-A.W. bypass, lt Downham

No. of seats:
Covered accommodation:
Capacity:
Year formed: 1885
Nickname: The Robins
Floodlights: Yes
Club colours: Red
Change colours: White
Day for midweek home matches: Friday
Club metal badges:
Previous Leagues:
Clubhouse details:
Past players who progressed into the Football League:

Programme details: Yes
Programme editor:
Local newspapers & Tel. No. Ely Standard
Major Honours:

FELIXSTOWE TOWN

President: Jack Nicholls
Chairman: Dave Ashford
Manager: Paul Adams
Secretary: Steve Page
Address & Tel. No. 11a Lonsdale Close, Ipswich. Ipswich 712613 (H), 687181 (B)
Address and Tel. No. of ground: Dellwood Avenue, Felixstowe. Felixstowe 282917
Simple ground directions: A45 into Felixstowe, 5 mins BR station and town centre

No. of seats: 200
Covered accommodation: 200
Capacity: 1,800
Year formed: 1890
Nickname: Seasiders
Floodlights: No, planned for 1987-8
Club colours: Red/black
Change colours: White/black
Day for midweek home matches: Wednesday
Club metal badges: No
Previous Leagues: Essex and Suffolk Border League, Ipswich & District League
Clubhouse details: Bar/snack bar/TV/darts/pool table
Past players who progressed into the Football League:
Programme details:
Programme editor: Paul Griffiths
Local newspapers & Tel. No. E.A.D.T.
Major Honours: Suffolk Senior Cup Winners 1967, 1975

Braintree's Chris Guy shoots for goal in one of the last matches to be played at Ely's Paradise ground
Photo: Jon Weaver

GORLESTON

President: J.J. Jones
Chairman: R. Carter
Manager: T. Harrison
Secretary: E.W.H. Proudfoot
Address & Tel. No. Lowestoft 730952
Address and Tel. No. of ground: Woodfarm Lane, Gorleston, Great Yarmouth. 602802
Simple ground directions: 50 yards from Gorleston Church

No. of seats: 400
Covered accommodation: 5,000
Capacity: 5,000
Year formed: 1908
Nickname: The Greens
Floodlights: Yes
Club colours: All green
Change colours: All white
Day for midweek home matches: Tuesday
Club metal badges:
Previous Leagues: Eastern Counties, Norfolk & Suffolk, Anglian Combination
Clubhouse details: Bar, colour TV, pool table, darts, snacks, canteen
Past players who progressed into the Football League: Billy Bailey (Wolves), D. Stringer (Norwich), R. Carter (Aston Villa), D. Carter (Man City), S. Morgan (Cambridge)
Programme details: Match programme
Programme editor: A. Jones
Local newspapers & Tel. No. Yarmouth Mercury
Major Honours: Senior Cup Winners (13), Finalists (24)

GREAT YARMOUTH TOWN

President: Derek Needham
Chairman: John Baldry
Manager: Bill Punton
Secretary: Jack A. Pegg
Address & Tel. No. 66 Louise Close, Gt Yarmouth N30 3RF. 842652
Address and Tel. No. of ground: Wellesley Recreation Ground, Wellesley Road, Great Yarmouth. (0493) 842936 ground, 843373 clubhouse
Simple ground directions: Just off Marine Parade, north of Britannia Pier
No. of seats: 600
Covered accommodation: 2,100
Capacity: 5,000
Year formed: 1897
Nickname: Bloaters
Floodlights: Yes
Club colours: Amber & black/black
Change colours: Black/white stripes
Day for midweek home matches: Tuesday
Club metal badges: Yes
Previous Leagues: Norfolk & Suffolk
Clubhouse details: Built 1980. Bar, colour TV, pool table, darts, snacks, open weekday evenings and on match days, regular functions, capacity 80
Past players who progressed into the Football League: Mel Blyth and Nolan Keeley (Scunthorpe), Gary Butcher (Blackburn), Steve Davey, Kevin Ready
Programme details: 8 pages, 5p
Programme editor:
Local newspapers & Tel. No. Yarmouth Mercury 844201, Eastern Football News, Norwich 28311
Major Honours: East Counties League, East Anglian Cup, Eastern Counties League Cup (3), Norfolk Senior Cup (12)

HARWICH & PARKESTON

President: J. Whitmore
Chairman: A.C. Lowe
Managers: A. Armstrong, M. Payne, E. Keegan
Secretary: G. Firth
Address & Tel. No. 24 Glebe Close, WIX. Tel. 805
Address and Tel. No. of ground: Royal Oak, Main Road, Dovercourt, Harwich. 503649
Simple ground directions: Main road into Dovercourt

No. of seats: 650
Covered accommodation: 1,000
Capacity: 5,000
Year formed: 1877
Nickname: Shrimpers
Floodlights: Yes
Club colours: White with black hoop, white shorts, blue socks
Change colours: All blue
Day for midweek home matches: Tuesday
Club metal badges: No
Previous Leagues: Athenian
Clubhouse details: Open 7 days, dances, bingo, darts, pool, function room
Past players who progressed into the Football League: G. Waites, K. Sanderson
Programme details: 28 pages
Programme editor: M. Payne
Local newspapers & Tel. No. Harwich & Manningtree Standard
Major Honours: Essex Senior Cup (2), Amateur Cup Finalists (2)

HAVERHILL

President: R.C. Carter
Chairman: R. Harding
Manager: P. Dyer
Secretary: C. Davies
Address & Tel. No.
Address and Tel. No. of ground: Hamlet Croft. 0440 702137
Simple ground directions: Centre of Haverhill

No. of seats: 200
Covered accommodation: 200
Capacity: 3,000
Year formed:
Nickname:
Floodlights: Yes
Club colours: Red
Change colours: Light blue
Day for midweek home matches: Tuesday
Club metal badges: No
Previous Leagues: Essex & Suffolk Border League
Clubhouse details: Open match days and organised functions. Country & Western every Sunday
Past players who progressed into the Football League: None
Programme details: 4 pages, 10p
Programme editor: Secretary
Local newspapers & Tel. No. Haverhill Echo
Major Honours: E.S.B.L. Winners 1962-3, 1963-4, E.C.L. Cup Winners 1964-5, E.C.L. Winners 1978-9

HISTON

President: G.P. Muncey
Chairman: R. Hands
Manager: Alan Doyle
Secretary: N. Haylock
Address & Tel. No. 28 Byron Square, Trumpington, Cambridge CB2 2JL. Camb. 841803 (H), 62561 (B)
Address and Tel. No. of ground: Bridge Road, Impington, Cambridge. Histon 2301
Simple ground directions: Situated on B1049 Cambridge-Cottenham Road, approx. ¼ mile from junction with A45

No. of seats: 100
Covered accommodation: 200
Capacity: 2,000
Year formed: 1904
Nickname: None
Floodlights: Yes
Club colours: Red and navy
Change colours: White
Day for midweek home matches: Tuesday
Club metal badges: None
Previous Leagues: Spartan, Delphian, Corinthian
Clubhouse details: Bar/lounge open Tuesdays to Sundays, evenings and Sunday lunchtime, plus matchdays
Past players who progressed into the Football League: None
Programme details:
Programme editor:
Local newspapers & Tel. No. Cambridge Evening News
Major Honours: Cambridge Invitation Cup (3)

LOWESTOFT TOWN

President: R. Harrod
Chairman: A. Peck
Manager: P. Chick
Secretary: P. Atkins
Address & Tel. No. 15 Oxford Road, Lowestoft. 0502 88866
Address and Tel. No. of ground: Crown Meadow, Lowestoft. 0502 3818
Simple ground directions: 10 mins walk from railway station

No. of seats: 400
Covered accommodation: 500
Capacity: 5,000
Year formed: 1890
Nickname: Blues
Floodlights: Yes
Club colours: Blue and white
Change colours: Yellow
Day for midweek home matches: Tuesday
Club metal badges: No
Previous Leagues: Norfolk & Suffolk
Clubhouse details: Pub hours
Past players who progressed into the Football League:
Programme details: 16 pages, 15p
Programme editor: Secretary & Treasurer
Local newspapers & Tel. No. Lowestoft Journal
Major Honours: Eastern League (10), League Cup (8), Suffolk Premier (6), East Anglian Cup (5), F.A. Amateur Cup Runners-up 1900, F.A. Cup 1st Rd (5)

MARCH TOWN UNITED

President: D. Wilkinson
Chairman: D.J. Warrington
Manager: M. Simmons
Secretary: C.R.W. Woodcock
Address & Tel. No. 59 Russell Avenue, March. 54817
Address and Tel. No. of ground: GER Ground, Robin Goodfellow's Lane, March. 53073
Simple ground directions: 5 mins from town centre, 15 mins from BR station

No. of seats: 500
Covered accommodation: Main stand
Capacity: 3,000
Year formed: 1889
Nickname: Hares
Floodlights: Yes
Club colours: Yellow and navy blue
Change colours: White and red
Day for midweek home matches: Tuesday
Club metal badges: No
Previous Leagues: United Counties, Peterborough League, Isle of Ely League
Clubhouse details: On ground, bar and small room. Seat approx. 100
Past players who progressed into the Football League: None
Programme details: To be produced by
Programme editor: Anglia Sporting Promotions
Local newspapers & Tel. No. Cambridgeshire Times, Fenland Advertiser, Peterborough Evening Telegraph
Major Honours: Eastern Counties League Cup 1960-1, Cambridgeshire Invitation Cup 1954-5, United Counties League Champions 1953-54, F.A. Cup 1st Rd proper v Brentford 1953-4, v Swindon 1977-8

NEWMARKET TOWN

President: A.C. Warren
Chairman: F. Trowsdale
Manager: G. Johnson
Secretary: D. Sadler
Address & Tel. No. 22 Windsor Road, Newmarket CB8 OPY. (0638) 663920
Address and Tel. No. of ground: Cricketfield Road, New Cheveley Road, Newmarket. (0638) 663637
Simple ground directions: From station turn right into Green Road, then right at crossroads, follow road round into New Cheveley Rd. Ground is at top of the hill on left

No. of seats: 300
Covered accommodation: 150
Capacity: 3,000
Year formed: 1888
Nickname: The Jockeys
Floodlights: Yes
Club colours: Yellow shirts, navy shorts, yellow socks
Change colours: White/royal/royal
Day for midweek home matches: Tuesday
Club metal badges: No
Previous Leagues: Peterborough, Bury Leagues, Essex Border Leagues, Bury Thursday League
Clubhouse details: Open matchdays only
Past players who progressed into the Football League: Mick Lambert (Ipswich Town), Dave Sexton, John Gavin (Norwich)
Programme details: 16 pages, 20p
Programme editor: D. Sadler
Local newspapers & Tel. No. Newmarket Journal
Major Honours: Suffolk Senior Cup Winners 1935, Cambs Invitation Cup 1959

SOHAM

President: B.E. Owers
Chairman: K. Barber
Manager: J. Fretwell
Secretary: P. Claringbold
Address & Tel. No.
Address and Tel. No. of ground: Julius Martins Lane, Soham, Cambridgeshire. Ely 720732

Simple ground directions: A142 between Newmarket and Ely—Julius Martin Lane
No. of seats: 200
Covered accommodation: Part
Capacity: 2,000
Year formed:
Nickname:
Floodlights: Yes
Club colours: Emerald Green/white/emerald green
Change colours: Red/white/white
Day for midweek home matches: Wednesday
Club metal badges: No
Previous Leagues: Peterborough League, C.F.A., Premier Division
Clubhouse details: General bar, stud bar, lounge bar
Past players who progressed into the Football League: None
Programme details: Emerald Green 10p
Programme editor: Club secretary
Local newspapers & Tel. No. Ely Standard, NKT Journal, Camb. Evening News
Major Honours: 6-0 defeat of Pegasus; Peterborough League Champions (3)

STOWMARKET TOWN

President: D. Hopgood
Chairman: Vacant
Manager: Don James
Secretary: John Doward
Address & Tel. No. Deepland House, Stowupland, Stowmarket, Suffolk IP14 4DE. 0449 612003 (H), 55811 (B)
Address and Tel. No. of ground: Greens Meadow Stadium, Bury Road, Stowmarket. 0449 612533
Simple ground directions: Taffic lights town centre, leave by Bury Street, continue to roundabout. Ground on right hand side
No. of seats: 300
Covered accommodation: 200
Capacity: 2,000
Year formed: 1878
Nickname:
Floodlights: Yes
Club colours: Gold and black
Change colours: Red
Day for midweek home matches: Wednesday
Club metal badges: No
Previous Leagues: Essex & Suffolk, Border League
Clubhouse details: Licensed bar, various meeting rooms, kitchen, entertainments Saturdays, bar, snooker etc.
Past players who progressed into the Football League:
Programme details: 20 pages, 20p
Programme editor: Paddy Lillistone (676734)
Local newspapers & Tel. No. East Anglian-Bury Free Press
Major Honours: Suffolk Premier Cup (3), Current holders Suffolk Senior Cup (10), Suffolk Junior Cup (1)

Action during Gorleston's 2-1 victory at Stowmarket Photo: David Shute

SUDBURY TOWN

President: H.D.J. Yallop
Chairman: R.A.F. Ashdown
Manager: M.S. Mackenzie
Secretary: L.A. Baldry
Address & Tel. No.
Address and Tel. No. of ground: Priory Stadium, Priory Walk, Friars Street, Sudbury, Suffolk. Sudbury (0787) 79095
Simple ground directions: Turn off Friars Street at the Ship & Star public house

No. of seats: 300
Covered accommodation: 1,200
Capacity: 6,000
Year formed: 1898
Nickname: The Borough
Floodlights: Yes
Club colours: Yellow/yellow/yellow
Change colours: White/white/white
Day for midweek home matches: Tuesday
Club metal badges: No
Previous Leagues: Essex & Suffolk Border League
Clubhouse details: Pool, darts. Open match days and for other functions
Past players who progressed into the Football League: Dickie Dowsett (Bournemouth)
Programme details: 16 pages
Programme editor: A. Simpson
Local newspapers & Tel. No. Suffolk Free Press, East Anglian Daily Times
Major Honours: Winners Building Scene Eastern League 1973-4, 1974-5, 1975-6, 1985-6, (Runners-up in 6 other seasons), Winners of Eastern Counties League Cup 1969-70, 1976-7, 1982-3, Winners of East Anglian Cup 1985-6, reached last 8 in F.A. Vase 1984-5, last 16 1985-6

THETFORD TOWN

President: F. Huson
Chairman: M. Burgess
Manager: Dave Pinkowski
Secretary: John Wordley
Address & Tel. No. 0842 62530 (H), 3353 (B)
Address and Tel. No. of ground: Mundford Road, Thetford. (no telephone)
Simple ground directions: On Mundford Road, signposted via Lynn, Downham Market on A143 off A11

No. of seats: 400
Covered accommodation: 400
Capacity: 2,000
Year formed: 1882
Nickname: The Town
Floodlights: No
Club colours: Claret/blue
Change colours: All yellow
Day for midweek home matches: Wednesday
Club metal badges: No
Previous Leagues: Norfolk & Suffolk
Clubhouse details: Bar, teas, refreshments, light meals
Past players who progressed into the Football League: Dick Scott (Norwich, Cardiff), Kevin Seggie (Leeds)
Programme details: 28 pages, 10p
Programme editor:
Local newspapers & Tel. No. Thetford & Watton Times, Bury Free Press
Major Honours:

TIPTREE UNITED

President: L. Foakes
Chairman: M. Hunt
Manager: R. Powling
Secretary: K.G. Pullon
Address & Tel. No. 37 Blue Road, Tiptree. 0621 817610 (H), 0245 353221 x4576 (B)
Address and Tel. No. of ground: Chapel Road, Tiptree. 0621 815213
Simple ground directions: Enter Tiptree on B1023, at 2nd crossroads turn left into Chapel Road
No. of seats: 100 **Covered accommodation:** 250 **Capacity:** 2,500
Year formed: 1933 **Nickname:** Jammakers **Floodlights:** Yes
Club colours: Red shirts and shorts **Change colours:** Blue
Day for midweek home matches: Tuesday **Club metal badges:** No
Previous Leagues: Essex Senior League
Clubhouse details: Sports hall and licensed bar, snooker, pool, darts, badminton, open every evening and weekends
Past players who progressed into the Football League:
Programme details: 30 pages, 15p **Programme editor:** Secretary
Local newspapers & Tel. No. Colchester Evening Gazette, Essex County Standard
Major Honours: Eastern Counties League Champions 1981-2, Cup Winners 1981-2, 1984-5, 1985-6, Essex Senior Trophy 1980-1

WATTON

President: Jim Tooke
Chairman: Phil Scott
Manager: Mick Wright
Secretary: Rick Neave
Address & Tel. No.
Address and Tel. No. of ground: Dereham Road, Watton. 881281
Simple ground directions: On A1075 towards Dereham, approx. ½ mile from junction with B1108
No. of seats: None **Covered accommodation:** 150 **Capacity:** 2,000
Year formed: 1888 **Nickname:** The Brecklanders **Floodlights:** Yes
Club colours: Green shirts/black shorts **Change colours:** All white
Day for midweek home matches: **Club metal badges:**
Previous Leagues: East Anglian League, Anglian Combination Football League
Clubhouse details: Watton 881281
Past players who progressed into the Football League: Chris Watts (Norwich City)

Programme details: (0760) 440239 **Programme editor:** Phil Scott
Local newspapers & Tel. No. E.D.P. & Thetford
Major Honours: 1985-6 League + Cup double, 1969-70 League Cup, 1967-8 League, 1966-7 League + Cup double

Clacton Town (in white) lose (1-2) at home to Thetford Photo: David Shute

Wisbech Town before the F.A. Vase semi-final first leg at Southall Photo: Eric Marsh

WISBECH TOWN

President: A. Harrold
Chairman:
Manager: R. McManus
Secretary: M.E. Davis
Address & Tel. No. Ely House, 158 Lynn Road, Wisbech. 583567
Address and Tel. No. of ground: Fenland Park, Lerowe Road, Wisbech
Simple ground directions: From Freedom Bridge roundabout (junction A47 & A1101) take A47 direction King's Lynn, approx. ¾ mile, turn right into Lerowe Road, ground 300 yards on right
No. of seats: 350 **Covered accommodation:** 3,000 **Capacity:** 7,500
Year formed: 1920 **Nickname:** Fenmen **Floodlights:** Yes
Club colours: All red **Change colours:** All blue
Day for midweek home matches: Tuesday **Club metal badges:** Yes £1.20 + pennants £1.50
Previous Leagues: Peterborough, United Counties, Midland, Southern
Clubhouse details: Open 7 days a week
Past players who progressed into the Football League: B. Harvey (Newcastle), T. Marshall (Newcastle), J. Gallagher ('Posh'), P. Scott (Blackpool), C. Coates ('Posh')
Programme details: 20 pages, 20p **Programme editor:** Secretary
Local newspapers & Tel. No. Wisbech Standard, Fenland Advertiser, Peterborough Evening Tel
Major Honours: F.A. Cup 2nd Rd proper (1), 1st Rd proper (5), CIC Winners (7), United Counties League Winners (4) and Runners-up, K.O. Cup Winners, Southern League Div 1 Winners, Midland League Runners-up, Eastern Counties League Winners (3), Runners-up (3), League Cup Winners (3), F.A. Vase Semi-finalists 1984-5, 1985-6

WINSTONLEAD KENT LEAGUE

Chairman: P. Wager. **Secretary:** D.D. Baker, 17 Sterling Road, Sittingbourne, Kent ME10 1SJ

DIVISION ONE

	P	W	D	L	F	A	Pts
1 Alma Swanley	34	22	9	3	78	—39	75
2 Sittingbourne	34	21	7	6	76	—37	70
3 Crockenhill	34	21	5	8	68	—33	68
4 Darenth Heathside	34	17	11	6	57	—32	62
5 Tunbridge Wells	34	15	13	6	99	—58	58
6 Faversham	34	16	6	12	53	—50	54
7 Greenwich Boro'	34	13	10	11	—	54	49
8 Ramsgate	34	12	8	14	50	—53	44
9 Kent Police	34	12	7	15	53	—61	43
10 Thames Polytechnic	34	11	9	14	36	—49	42
11 Herne Bay	34	12	6	16	34	—52	42
12 Hythe Town	34	11	7	16	50	—59	40
13 Met. Police (4 area)	34	12	4	18	54	—63	40
14 Cray Wanderers	34	9	12	13	34	—51	39
15 Beckenham Town	34	10	7	17	43	—64	37
16 Whitstable Town	34	9	9	16	37	—52	36
17 Slade Green	34	5	10	19	14	—42	25
18 Deal Town	34	6	4	24	36	—74	22

DIVISION TWO

	P	W	D	L	F	A	Pts
1 Fisher Athletic	34	25	5	4	95	—34	80
2 Sheppey United	34	25	5	4	76	—30	80
3 Sittingbourne	34	20	7	7	75	—38	67
4 Ashford	34	19	5	10	53	—44	62
5 Faversham	34	16	7	11	67	—52	55
6 Thames Polytechnic	34	15	7	12	58	—55	52
7 Snowdown C.W.	34	15	5	14	51	—45	50
8 Folkestone	34	13	9	12	49	—48	48
9 Darenth Heathside	34	12	11	11	63	—54	47
10 Thanet United	34	13	8	13	54	—54	47
11 Erith & Belvedere	34	13	7	14	58	—52	46
12 Dover Athletic	34	14	4	16	58	—56	46
13 Hythe Town	34	14	4	16	63	—61	46
14 Deal Town	34	8	11	15	42	—61	35
15 Canterbury City	34	9	7	18	49	—71	34
16 Herne Bay	34	6	8	20	33	—67	26
17 Whitstable Town	34	5	8	21	32	—86	23
18 Chatham Town	34	4	2	28	39	—107	14

BECKENHAM TOWN

President: F. Starmer
Chairman: G. L. Ward
Manager: R. Chilvers
Asst. Man Coach: G. Shepherd
Physiotherapist: F. Wray
Secretary: H. D. Smith
Address & Tel No: 85 Eden Park Avenue, Beckenham, Kent. 01-650 3667 (H)
Commercial Manager:
Press Officer & Tel No: G. L. Ward. 01-777 0125
Address & Tel No of ground: Eden Park Avenue, Beckenham, Kent. (01-650 1066)
Simple ground directions: 1 mile west of town, off A214, 2 minutes walk from Eden Park Station
No. of seats: 60 **Ground accommodation:** 2,000 **Capacity:** **Floodlights:** Yes
Year formed: (Present club) 1971 **Nickname:** Town **Club sponsors:** Charringtons
Club colours: All red **Change colours:** All Blue
Previous Names: None **Previous Grounds:** Stanhope Grove, Beckenham
Record attendance: 692 v Fisher **Year:** 1982 **Programme:** 4 pages, 10p
Previous Leagues: London Spartan 1975–82, London 1971–75 **Programme Editor:** G. L. Ward
Clubhouse details: Open 7 days a week, bar, dance area
Senior Honours: Spartan League Cup Finalists 1977–78, 1978–79, Kent Senior Trophy Finalists 1981–82
Club Captain (1984–85): P. Wellman

CRAY WANDERERS FC

President: None
Chairman: B. W. Faulkner
Manager: Alan Payne
Asst. Man/Coach: Alan Dickie
Physiotherapist: Tim Holt
Secretary: P. McCarthy
Address & Tel No: 23 Bostall Road, St. Pauls Cray, Kent. 01-309 0854 (H)
Commercial Manager: B. W. Faulkner 01-300 3421
Press Officer & Tel No: Gerry Dowlin. 0689 25326
Address & Tel No of ground: Oxford Road, Sidcup, Kent. 01-300 9201
Simple ground directions: Between Sidcup High St. and Footcary High St.
No of seats: 20 **Ground accommodation:** 3,000 **Capacity:** 3,000 **Floodlights:** No
Year formed: 1860 **Nickname:** The Wands **Club sponsors:** Capp Walker Builders Merchants
Club colours: Amber/Black **Change colours:** White
Previous Names: None **Previous Grounds:** Grassmeade, St. Mary's Cray
Record attendance: 1,500 v Stamford F.C. 6th Round F.A. Vase **Year:** 1979–80
Previous Leagues: Greater London, London, London Spartan, Aetolian, London Met.
Clubhouse details: Open match days and Tues. and Thurs. evenings **Programmes:** 8 pages, by donation
Club Honours: Kent League (2), London League (2) & League Cup, Aetolian League & League Cup, Greater London League & League Cup (2), Metropolitan London League & League Cup, London Spartan (2), Kent Amateur Cup (4), Kent League Div 1 Cup Winners 1983–84
Club Captain (1984–85): T. French

CROCKENHILL F.C.

President: H. Miller
Chairman: A. Powell
Manager: R. Dowling
Coach: None
Physiotherapist: None
Secretary: C. J. A. Nicholls
Address & Tel No: 97 West View, Crockenhill, Swanley, Kent. 0322 62719
Commercial Manager: None
Press Officer & Tel No: None
Address & Tel No of ground: 'Wested', Eynesford Road, Crockenhill, Swanley, Kent. 0322 62097
Simple ground directions: Off main Swanley Road, Station—Swanley Junction. Bus 477 route
No of seats: 100 **Covered accommodation:** **Capacity:** 1,500 **Floodlights:** No
Year formed: 1946 **Nickname:** Crocks **Club sponsors:** Eastwoods Metals
Club colours: Red & White stripes, Black shorts **Change colours:** All Blue
Previous Names: None **Previous Grounds:** None
Record attendance: 800 v Maidstone K.A.C. **Year:** 1948 **Programmes:** 4 pages, 10p
Previous Leagues: Kent Amateur, Aetolian, Greater London **Programme Editor:** Secretary
Clubhouse details: E ery Friday night, Saturday night and match days, on ground licenced bar
Club Honours: Sevenoaks Charity Cup, West Kent Senior Cup, Kent Amateur Cup Finalists, Kent Senior Trophy

DARENTH HEATHSIDE F.C.

President: None
Chairman: B. W. Smith
Manager: David Munn
Coach: Jimmy Coyne
Secretary: P. R. Thompson
Address & Tel No: 168 Claremont Road, Hextable, Kent Swanley 68832 (H)
Commercial Manager: None
Physiotherapist: H. Peploe
Press Officer & Tel No: M. S. Wiseman (Orpington 33083) (Programme Editor)
Address & Tel No of ground: Heathside Club, Horton Road, South Darenth, Dartford, Kent (0689 863554)
Simple ground directions: A2 or A20 hence A225 and turn off at Farningham Road Station, ground opposite 'The Sun' public house next brick viaduct
No of seats: 140 **Covered accommodation:** **Capacity:** 2,000 **Floodlights:** No
Year formed: 1951 **Nickname:** None **Club sponsors:** None
Club colours: All Blue **Change colours:** All Red
Previous Names: Heathside Sports F.C. **Previous Grounds:** None
Record attendance: Approx 900 Silver Jubilee Match v Internationals XI. **Year:** 1976
Previous Leagues: Metropolitan 1971–75, Greater London 1968–71, London Spartan 1975–78, Dartford
Clubhouse details: Open for match days and other events **Programme:** 4 pages, included in admission
Club Honours: Kent Intermediate Cup Finalists 1974–75, Kent League Div II Cup Finalists 1978–79, 1983–84, Kent League Div I Cup Finalists 1980–81
Club Captain (1984–85): Colin Turner

Whitstable Town entertain Alma Swanley. (Photo: David Shute)

Crockenhall's second goal in their (6-0) home victory over Herne Bay Photo: David Shute

FAVERSHAM TOWN

President: R. Neame
Chairman: F. W. White
Manager: D. McFall
Asst. Man/Coach: R. Heward
Secretary: Wendy Woolhouse
Address & Tel No: BT. London Road, Faversham, Kent. 0795 532790 (H)
Physiotherapist: R. Heward
Address & Tel No of ground: Salters Lane, Faversham. 0795 532738
Simple ground directions: On A2. Just west of town (Canterbury Road)
No of seats: 200 **Ground accommodation:** 2,000 **Capacity:** 2,000 **Floodlights:** Yes
Year formed: 1901 **Nickname:** Town **Club sponsors:** Owen Doran/Abbeywood Double Glazing
Club colours: White/Black/Black **Change colours:** Blue/White
Previous Names: None **Previous Grounds:** Gordon Square
Midweek match evening: Tuesday
Record attendance: 1,400 v Sheppey **Year:** 1979 **Programme Editor:** E. Glover (Fav. 534436)
Previous Leagues: Metropolitan, Athenian **Programme:** 10 pages, 15p
Clubhouse details: Tues. & Thurs. evenings and Match Days plus special events
Club Honours: Kent Amateur Cup Winners 1957, 1959, 1972, 1973, 1974; Kent League Champions 1970, 1971, 1978, Kent League Cup Div I Winners 1971; Kent Senior Trophy Winners 1977, 1978
Club Captain (1984–85): Bob Mason

DEAL TOWN

President: None
Chairman: R. Dixon
Secretary: V. Medus (Programme Editor)
Address & Tel No: 22 Marlborough Road, Margate, Kent. 0843 291829
Manager: W. Herron
Asst. Man/Coach: G. Connelly
Physiotherapist: W. Summersgill
Commercial Manager: None
Press Officer & Tel No: None
Address & Tel No of ground: Charles Sports Ground, Mill Road, Deal, Kent. 03047 375623
Simple ground directions: Follow A258 through Walmer, left into Cornwall Road, into Hamilton Road, into Manor Road, right into St. Leonards Road
No of seats: 500 **Ground accommodation:** 1,500 **Capacity:** 2,000 **Floodlights:** Yes
Year formed: 1908 **Nickname:** Town **Club sponsors:** Southern Stock-taking Services Ltd
Club colours: Black & White stripes/Black/Black **Change colours:** Yellow/Blue/Blue
Previous Names: None **Previous Grounds:** None
Record attendance: 4,000 v Billy Wright Showbiz XI **Year:** 1961
Previous Leagues: Southern, Greater London, Aetolian **Programme:** 4 pages, 10p
Clubhouse details: Open match days and for functions. Supporters club, bar, pool, darts, etc.
Club Honours: Kent League Champions 1952–53, Kent League Div I Cup Winners 1955–56, 1981–82, Greater London Cup Winners 1967–68, Kent Senior Trophy Finalists 1982–83
Club Captain (1984–85): Fred Doncaster

GREENWICH BOROUGH

President: T. H. M. Edwards
Chairman: E. T. Moore
Manager: W. J. Wakefield
Asst. Man/Coach: F. W. Sells
Physiotherapist: L. T. Cole
Secretary: M. P. Redmond
Address & Tel No: 92 Dunvegan Road, Eltham London SE9 1SB. 01-859 4127 (H), 01-318 7625 (B)
Commercial Manager: W. D. Kinsey
Address & Tel No: 01-318 0551 (H)
Address & Tel No of ground: Harrow Meadow, Eltham Green Road, Eltham, London SE9. 01-850 3098
Simple ground direction: South Circular Road (A205) to 'Yorkshire Grey' (public house) ground opposite
No of seats: 50 **Covered accommodation:** **Capacity:** 5,000 **Floodlights:** Yes
Year formed: 1928 **Nickname:** Boro' **Club sponsors:** Crabtree Electrical Industries
Club colours: Red/White **Change colours:** Yellow/Blue/Yellow
Previous Names: None **Previous Grounds:** None
Midweek match evening: Tuesday
Record attendance: 2,000 v Charlton Athletic (opening of new floodlights) **Year:** 1978
Previous Leagues: South London Alliance, London Spartan
Best performance in F.A. Vase: 4th Round 1981–82
Clubhouse details: Large pavilion, 2 bars, cafe **Programme Editor:** Secretary
Major Honours: Kent Senior Trophy, Kent League Cup (1984–85), Spartan League Div I Senior Cup
Club Captain (1984–85): T. O'Brien

Alma Swanley on the attack during their (5-1) win at Hythe Town. Photo: Leo Hoenig

Deal Town who finished at the foot of the League battle for a (0-0) draw at home to Hythe Town.
Photo: David Shute

HERNE BAY

esident: None
ıairman: J. Brownett
ınager: G. Burden
ıach: F. Saker
ıysiotherapist: J. Hodgkinson
Secretary: Miss G. Carter
Address & Tel No: 17 Oxenden Park Drive, Herne Bay, Kent. 0227 372934
Commercial Manager: None
Press Officer & Tel No: None
ldress & Tel No of ground: Winch's Field, Herne Bay, Kent. 0227 374156
mple ground directions: Leave A299 at Herne Bay Roundabout second turning on left
› of seats: 250 (Directors 40) **Covered accommodation:** 4,000 **Capacity:** 4,290 **Floodlights:** No
:ar formed: 1886 **Nickname:** The Bay **Club sponsors:** None
lub colours: All Blue
Change colours: All Red
revious Names: Herne Bay United
Previous Grounds: None
.id-week match evening: Tuesday
ecord attendance: 3,000 v Margate F.C. **Year:** 1970
Programme Editor: H. Hardy
revious Leagues: Athenian
Programme: 4 pages, 10p
lubhouse details: Match Days and Functions
:lub Honours: Athenian League Cup Winners 1966–67; Kent Senior Cup Semi-finalists 1970; Athenian League Champions 1970–71; Kent Senior Trophy Winners 1979–80; Kent League Cup Finalists 1978–79
:lub Captain (1984–85): P. Sullivan

HYTHE TOWN

President: E. Whittlesea-Webster
Chairman: M. J. Leach
Manager: G. Demsey
Asst. Man Coach: D. Williams
Physiotherapist: F. Barham
Secretary: A. J. Maycock
Address & Tel No: 14, Crofters Close, Hythe, Kent.
Commercial Manager: None
Press Officer & Tel No: None
Address & Tel No of ground: Reachfields, Fort Road, Hythe, Kent. 0303 65658
Simple ground directions: A259 road from London to Folkestone, Dymchurch Road $\frac{1}{4}$ mile out of town, close to Light Railway Station
No of seats: 200 **Ground accommodation:** 2,000 **Capacity:** 2,000 **Floodlights:** No
Year formed: 1922 **Nickname:** None **Club sponsors:** Burlington Insurance
Club colours: White shirts Black shorts
Change colours: Blue & White stripes White shorts
Previous Names: None
Previous Grounds: None
Mid-week match evening: Wednesday
Record attendance: 300
Programme Editor: Secretary
Previous Leagues: Kent Amateur
Programme: 4 pages, 10p
Clubhouse details: Match Days and every evening, two bars, one dance hall
Club Honours: Kent League Div I Runners-up 1978–79, 1982–83
Club Captain (1984–85): T. Hunter

KENT POLICE

President: F. Jordan, Chief Constable
Chairman: E. Cren, Asst. Chief Constable
Manager: P. Spittles
Asst. Man Coach: D. Tank
Physiotherapist: None
Secretary: R. M. Jones
Address & Tel No: 1 Coverdale Avenue, Maidstone, Kent ME15 9DR. 0622 681740 (H)
Commercial Manager:
Press Officer & Tel No: None
Address & Tel No of ground: Police H.Q., Sutton Road, Maidstone, Kent. 0622 65432
Simple ground directions: Leave Maidstone on Hastings Road, then on to A274 to Rye Road
No of seats: 40 **Ground accommodation:** 60 **Capacity:** 3,000 **Floodlights:** No
Year formed: 1951 **Nickname:** None **Club sponsors:** None
Club colours: Royal Blue White
Change colours: White Red
Previous Names: None
Previous Grounds: None
Record attendance: Not known **Year:**
Mid-week match evening: Tuesday
Previous Leagues: Kent Amateur
Programme: None
Clubhouse details: Use HQ Bar on Match Days
Club Honours: Kent League Cup Div I Winners 1969–70; Kent League Div I Runner-up 1969–70

MET. POLICE HAYES (KENT)

President: D. A. C. R. Hunt
Chairman:
Manager: E. Holbrook
Secretary: A. T. Austridge
Address & Tel No: 4 Wood Road, Biggin Hill, TN16 3RN.
0959 75532 (H), 01-407 8044 x227 (B)
Press Officer & Tel No: I. Munro. 01-641 4564
Address & Tel No of ground: 'The Warren' Croydon Road, Hayes, Kent. 01-462 1266
Simple ground directions: On A232 between Orpington and Croydon just south of Bromley and Hayes
No of seats: None **Covered accommodation:** **Capacity:** 1,000 **Floodlights:** No
Year formed: 1979 **Nickname:** None **Club sponsors:** None
Club colours: Blue Black Black **Change colours:** All White
Midweek match evening: Tuesday
Record attendance: Approx 200 v Crystal Palace Select **Year:** 1.5.1984
Previous Leagues: Beckeham & District, Kent Amateur
Clubhouse details: Two storeyed ground floor—10 changing rooms (8 with showers); first floor—bar, tea bar, hall
Programme: 8 pages, 10p **Programme Editor:** Press Officer
Club Captain (1984–85): P. Hardy

RAMSGATE F.C.

President: A. Blatley
Chairman: M. Mitchell
Manager: L. Smith
Coach: S. Frampton
Physiotherapist: D. Beagley
Secretary: C. West
Address & Tel No: 44 Elmley Way, Margate, Kent. 227900
Commercial Manager:
Press Officer & Tel No: C. Hill (33879)
Address & Tel No of ground: Southwood Football Ground, Prices Avenue, Ramsgate. 591662
Simple ground directions: Coming from London A299 joining the A253 which takes you into Ramsgate
No of seats: 500 **Covered accommodation:** 1,000 **Capacity:** 5,000 **Floodlights:** Yes
Year formed: 1946 **Nickname:** Rams **Club sponsors:** Stelrad
Club colours: All Red **Change colours:** All Yellow
Previous Names: Ramsgate Athletic **Previous Grounds:** None
Mid-week match evening: Tues Wed
Record attendance: 5,200 v Margate F.C. **Year:** 1956–57 **Programme Editor:** I. Thomas
Previous Leagues: Southern 1959–75 **Programme:** Free
Clubhouse details: Match days an functions, 2 bars, 2 pool tables, darts, table tennis
Club Honours: Kent League 1949–50, 1955–56, 1956–57; League Cup 1948–49; Kent Intermediate Cup 1954–55; Kent Senior Cup 1963–64; Thames Medway Cup 1960–61; Kent Senior Shield 1960–61; Kent Floodlight Trophy 1969–70
Club Captain (1984–85): R. King

SITTINGBOURNE F.C.

President: D. Roberton
Chairman: J. Jarrett
Manager: A. Ervin
Coach: B. Watkins
Physiotherapist: None
Secretary: L. Davies
Address & Tel No: 41 Murston Road, Sittingbourne, Kent
0795 25441
Commercial Manager: None
Press Officer & Tel No: Secretary
Address & Tel No of ground: Bull Ground, Roman Road, Sittingbourne, Kent. 0795 72528
Simple ground directions: Rear of High Street, Sittingbourne
No of seats: 500 **Covered accommodation:** 5,000 **Capacity:** 5,500 **Floodlights:** Yes
Year formed: 1881 **Nickname:** Brickies **Club sponsors:** None
Club colours: Red & Black stripes Black shorts **Change colours:** All White
Previous Names: None **Previous Grounds:** None
Record attendance: 5,583 v Gravesend F.A.C. **Year:** 1961 **Mid-week match evening:** Tuesday
Previous Leagues: Southern, Thames & Medway, Kent **Programme:** None
Clubhouse details: New Club House open every day, bar, dining room
Club Honours: Kent League 1902–03, 1957–58, 1958–59, 1975–76, 1983–84; Kent League Cup 1954–55, 1980–81; Kent Senior Cup 1901–02, 1928–29, 1929–30, 1957–58; Kent Senior Shield 1926–27, 1927–28, 1953–54; Thames-Medway Cup 1955–56, 1958–59
Club Captain (1984–85): W. Finch

SLADE GREEN F.C.

President: W. Dudley
Chairman: B. Smith

Manager: K. Gurr
Coach: M. Springer
Physiotherapist:

Secretary: B. W. Smith
Address & Tel No: 15 Gumping Road, Orpington, Kent.
Farnborough 58782 (H), 01-353 3030 x271 (B)
Commercial Manager:
Press Officer & Tel No: None

Address & Tel No of ground: The Glen, 35 Moat Lane, Slade Green, Erith, Kent. 03224 38381
Simple ground directions: Slade Green Station 300 yards from Ground
No of seats: 20 **Covered accommodatin:** 200 **Capacity:** 2,000 **Floodlights:** To be erected
Year formed: 1946 **Nickname:** The Green **Club sponsors:** Russell Stoneham Estates
Club colours: Green/Black stripes
Change colours: Yellow/Blue
Previous Names: None
Previous Grounds: None
Record attendance: Not Known
Previous Leagues: London, Kent Amateur, Dartford
Programme: 12 pages, 60p, included in admission
Clubhouse details: Every evening and match days
Club Honours: Kent League Cup Winners 1983
Club Captain (1984–85): Denis Harbert

TUNBRIDGE WELLS F.C.

President: None
Chairman: F. J. Oakley

Manager: M. Higgs
Coach: P. Littlechild
Physiotherapist: G. Piper

Secretary: P. C. Wager (Programme Editor)
Address & Tel No: 46 Mereworth Road, Tunbridge Wells, Kent TN4 9PL. 0892 24182

Commercial Manager:
Press Officer & Tel No: R. Bonny. 0892 31898

Address & Tel No of ground: Culverden Stadium, Culverden Down, Tunbridge Wells, 0892 20517
Simple ground directions: Leaving town on main Tonbridge Road turn left opposite Red Lion pub
No of seats: 200 **Covered accommodation:** 700 **Capacity:** 5,000 **Floodlights:** No
Year formed: 1967 **Nickname:** Wells **Club sponsors:** None
Club colours: Red & White
Change colours: All Blue
Previous Names: None
Previous Ground: None
Record attendance: 967 v Maidstone **Year:** 1969
Previous Leagues: None
Programmes: 8 pages, 15p
Clubhouse details: Match days and functions
Mid-week match evening: Wednesday
Club Honours: Kent League Cup Winners 1974–75, 1977–78, 1984–85, Kent League Cup (2)
Club Captain (1984–85): T. Atkins

WHITSTABLE TOWN

President: Cllr. L. R. Bennett
Chairman: Cllr. P. Burke
Manager: J. Newman
Coach: None
Physiotherapist: B. Smith

Secretary: R. F. Simmons
Address & Tel No: 15 Paradise Row, Sandwich, Kent (H), 3 Queen Street, Deal, Kent (B)
Commercial Manager: None
Press Officer & Tel No: None

Address & Tel No of ground: Belmont Road, Belmont, Whitstable. 0227 266012
Simple ground directions: From Thanet Way (A299) down Millstrood Road, ground at bottom. By train, 400 yards from station
No of seats: 300 **Ground accommodation:** 1,500 **Capacity:** 1,800 **Floodlights:** No
Year formed: 1885 **Nickname:** The Oystermen, The Reds **Club sponsors:**
Club colours: Red White Red
Change colours: All White
Previous Names: Whitstable F.C.
Previous Grounds: None
Record attendance:
Programme: None
Clubhouse details: Used for social and recreative purposes, bar
Club Honours: Kent League Div II Champions 1927–28, 1933–34, 1949–50; Kent League Premier Division 1960–61; Kent Amateur Cup Winners 1928–29; Kent League Cup Winners 1979–80; Kent Senior Trophy Finalists 1978–79
Cup Captain (1984–85): G. Mitchell

SUSSEX COUNTY FOOTBALL LEAGUE

Patron: Dr John O'Hara
Chairman and Hon. Fixtures Secretary: P.R. Bentley
199 Chanctonbury Road, Burgess Hill, RH15 9HF. Tel: Burgess Hill 3181
Hon. Secretary: D.D. Welsh, 301 Hangleton Rd, Hove BN3 7LR. Tel: Brighton 732160

STEYNING'S GREAT SEASON

Events off the field during the close eason had led to Hastings Town being accepted into the Southern League Southern Division replacing Hastings United who had ceased activities. It was decided not to relegate Midhurst from Division One, nor Newhaven from Division Two, while the A.G.M. voted in favour of Hailsham's retention in Division One, although at the due date their facilities had not reached the required standard, but would be by the season's start.

The 6-A-Side Tournament was held in July at Peacehaven where the winners were Whitehawk who defeated the host club in the final by 2 goals to 1.

Steyning Town achieved the most difficult task of retaining the League championship, having fought off determined challenges from Three Bridges and Eastbourne Town. They also lifted the County F.A. Senior Cup, in the final defeating Hastings Town who had become strong promotion contenders in the Southern League and having in the semi-final disposed of Vauxhall-Opel Premier side Worthing, both matches going to extra time. In doing so, Steyning became the first County League side to lift the trophy since Ringmer won it in 1972-73. Steynings season comprised some 51 matches.

The League Cup Final staged at Wick and Sponsored by host Chairman Barry Wadsworth and his Vice-Chairman Tom Stabler, required a replay. Steyning gained their third trophy in defeating Arundel 3-1, after a remarkable 4-4 draw, which had seen Arundel take a 3-0 lead, trail 3-4, before netting a late equaliser. Both semi-finals were for the first time on neutral grounds.

In March, in the first Senior Final of the season, the R.U.R. Charity Cup of the County F.A. was won by Eastbourne Town defeating Steyning at Lancing by 3-0, thereby preventing their opponents gaining the full house of trophies. This defeat, however, should not detract from the overall tremendous season experienced by Steyning in only their eighth season in Division One.

The 5-A-Side at the Brighton Centre was won by Littlehampton defeating near neighbours Wick 3-0 in the Annual tournament in February.

At the lower end of Division One, a three way contest was carried on until very late in the season before Midhurst did what has become their annual 'Houdini' act in escaping from the bottom, leaving Horsham YMCA and Ringmer occupying those places. This was especially disappointing for Horsham YMCA in a season when they had switched on their floodlights for the first time in entertaining a County League Representative side. It is only proper that this and a number of other improvements made by clubs should be acknowledged, allied to their plans for the future.

Equally at the top end of Division Two, the promotion race went literally to the last minute of the last match, when at Pagham in front of a crowd of just under 500, the home side obtained a 1-1 draw with Wick. This result meant that Wick were the champions with 72 points, promoted after only one season following relegation last term and remaining undefeated from 4th January. Haywards Heath with 71 points were runners-up, returning to the first division after six seasons just pipping Pagham who were two points behind at 69. In many seasons the team with this number could well have been promoted as champions. In the Division Two Cup Final staged by Horsham YMCA, Pagham had earlier defeated Haywards Heath 3-0. At the lower end, Selsey had for a long time looked relegation certainties, but rallied to escape leaving Franklands Village and Lingfield in the bottom two spots. A special word for two teams in this division in the Senior Cup, Bosham and Storrington. The former, new to senior football following their promotion from Division Three, took Vauxhall-Opel League side Eastbourne United to a replay before losing 2-1, while Storrington took Brighton and Hove Albion from the Combination League to a replay before losing at the Goldstone.

Despite some good early results by Littlehampton, Pagham and Ringmer in the F.A. Cup and Burgess Hill, Eastbourne Town, Haywards Heath, Pagham, Ringmer, Shoreham, Whitehawk and Wick in the F.A. Vase, no club progressed as far as was hoped. Steyning looked to improve on last season's achievement but were elminated in the third round of the Vase by Whyteleafe.

In other competitions Wick won the Brighton Charity Cup, Midway reached the Final of the Vernon Wentworth Cup where they lost to Mile Oak, an unsuccessful Division 3 applicant, in a replayed Final, while Langney Sports won the Eastbourne Challenge Cup defeating another unsuccessful applicant, Dental Estimates Board, by 3-2 in the Final. However, a pride of place in other competitions must surely go to Hassocks Reserves who won the AFA Intermediate Cup defeating a number of good sides on the way to the Final where they overcame National Westminster Bank 2-0.

The P.G. Cunningham Sportsmanship Trophy was won by Albion United, while the top five places in the Merit Table were occupied by Wick as winners, Haywards Heath second, Steyning third, Three Bridges fourth and Pagham fifth. Haywards Heath emulated East Grinstead's record of last year in not recording a caution or send-off in their league matches.

The leading goalscorers were John Kemp of Eastbourne Town in Division One, Micky Dillon of Bosham and Wick in Division Two and Steven Lane of Westdene in Division Three, while Club Linesman of the Year went to Tim Willows of Steyning. Manager of the Month Awards presented at the Annual Dinner held at the Brighton Centre went to Steve Piper (Pagham), Norman Cairns (Wick), Dave John (Haywards Heath), Alan Knight (Three Bridges), Fred Stenning (Peacehaven), Ian Cunningham (Littlehampton), Bob Collyer (Bosham) and Barry Youell (Steyning) with Barry Youell receiving the Manager of the Season Award for the second successive season.

LEAGUE CHALLENGE CUP
1985-86

Bosham	v	Littlehampton	0-2
Ferring	v	Arundel	0-4
Franklands Village	v	Steyning	0-7
Horsham YMCA	v	Wigmore	2-0*
Lingfield	v	Burgess Hill	1-4
Midhurst	v	Storrington	3-2
Newhaven	v	Hailsham	1-4
Oakwood	v	Eastbourne Town	1-2
Pagham	v	Lancing	2-3
Peacehaven	v	Hassocks	3-2
Portfield	v	East Grinstead	2-1
Ringmer	v	Albion United	3-1
Selsey	v	Chichester	0-2
Shoreham	v	Sidley	2-3*
Three Bridges	v	Haywards Heath	1-1*
Whitehawk	v	Wick	3-0

Replay

Haywards Heath	v	Three Bridges at Three Bridges	1-2*

Second Round

Arundel	v	Sidley	2-0
Chichester	v	Peacehaven	0-1
Horsham YMCA	V	Eastbourne Town	3-1
Littlehampton	v	Hailsham	2-0
Portfield	v	Ringmer	4-1*
Steyning	v	Burgess Hill	3-0
Three Bridges	v	Midhurst	4-2
Whitehawk	v	Landing	3-1

Third Round

Arundel	v	Peacehaven	3-0*
Portfield	v	Horsham YMCA	4-3
Steyning	v	Whitehawk	3-0
Three Bridges	v	Littlehampton	1-0

Semi-finals

Arundel	v	Portfield at Wick	4-0
Steyning	v	Three Bridges at Horsham YMCA	3-3

Replay

Steyning	v	Three Bridges at Burgess Hill	3-0

Final

Arundel	v	Steyning at Wick	4-4*

Replay

Steyning	v	Arundel at Wick	3-1*

DIVISION ONE

	P	W	D	L	F	A	Pts
Steyning Town	30	22	6	2	61	16	72
Three Bridges	30	19	6	5	58	24	63
Eastbourne Town	30	18	7	5	71	23	61
Whitehawk	30	13	11	6	46	30	50
Peacehaven & Tels	30	15	4	11	55	44	49
Littlehampton Town .	30	13	7	10	44	29	46
Burgess Hill Town	30	13	6	11	47	41	45
Portfield	30	13	6	11	40	48	45
Arundel	30	12	8	10	55	37	44
Lancing	30	11	7	12	42	52	40
Hailsham Town	30	9	7	14	45	49	34
Shoreham	30	10	4	16	42	57	34
Chichester City	30	7	6	17	35	64	27
Midhurst & Easebne .	30	5	7	18	33	65	22
Horsham YMCA	30	5	4	21	33	90	19
Ringmer	30	4	6	20	19	57	18

DIVISION TWO

	P	W	D	L	F	A	Pts
Wick	30	22	6	2	94	35	72
Pagham	30	22	5	3	70	18	71
Haywards Heath	30	22	5	3	72	26	71
Sidley United	30	15	8	7	52	36	53
East Grinstead	30	15	5	10	44	30	50
Albion United	30	13	6	11	49	48	45
Bosham	30	12	7	11	56	53	43
Ferring	30	12	6	12	47	51	42
Storrington	30	10	10	10	48	41	40
Oakwood	30	10	7	13	31	50	37
Hassocks	30	8	9	13	38	38	33
Newhaven	30	8	5	17	32	57	29
Selsey	30	7	5	18	35	67	26
Wigmore Athletic	30	7	2	21	44	71	23
Franklands Village	30	6	4	20	36	74	22
Lingfield	30	5	2	23	35	88	17

DIVISION THREE CHALLENGE CUP 1985-86

First Round

APV Athletic	v	Eastbourne Rangers	2-1
Broadbridge Heath	v	Midway	1-1★
Cooksbridge	v	Bexhill	3-3*
Crowborough	v	Saltdean	1-4
East Preston	v	Leftovers SC	3-1
Ifield	v	Westdene at Westdene	0-1
Seaford	v	Hurstpierpoint	0-0§

Replays

Bexhill	v	Cooksbridge	4-1
Hurstpierpoint	v	Seaford	0-4
Midway	v	Broadbridge Heath	1-0

Second Round

Bexhill	v	Midway	3-0
Saltdean	v	APV Athletic	1-0
Seaford	v	East Preston	1-1*
Westdene	v	Langney Sports	2-1

Replay

East Preston	v	Seaford	3-4*

Semi-finals

Saltdean	v	Westdene	3-2
Seaford	v	Bexhill	3-0

Final
(at Peacehaven)

Saltdean	v	Seaford	1-2

★ Abandoned 112 minutes
* After extra time
§ Abandoned in extra time

DIVISION THREE

	P	W	D	L	F	A	Pts
Seaford Town	28	18	5	5	64	31	59
Bexhill Town	28	17	7	4	72	31	58
East Preston	28	15	5	8	54	32	50
Langney Sports	28	14	4	10	53	39	46
Saltdean United	28	13	6	9	58	41	45
Ifield	28	13	3	12	56	66	42
APV Athletic	28	12	5	11	50	72	41
Eastbourne Rangers ..	28	11	6	11	55	63	39
Crowborough Ath	28	10	6	12	49	56	36
Westdene	28	9	7	12	44	49	34
Hurstpierpoint	28	8	8	12	43	56	32
Midway	28	6	9	13	44	51	27
Cooksbridge	28	6	8	14	50	57	26
Broadbridge Health ..	28	5	10	13	35	50	25
Leftovers S C	28	6	5	17	33	66	23

R.U.R. CHARITY CUP 1985-86

First Round

Albion United	v	Burgess Hill	1-2
Ferring	v	Horsham YMCA	2-0
Hailsham	v	Sidley	4-0
Haywards Heath	v	Three Bridges	4-1
Lancing	v	Midhurst	1-1*
Littlehampton	v	Wigmore	3-1
Newhaven	v	East Grinstead	0-3
Oakwood	v	Ringmer	2-0
Pagham	v	Wick	0-1
Portfield	v	Shoreham	0-2
Selsey	v	Bosham	2-4*
Storringtin	v	Arundel	1-3
Whitehawk	v	Franklands Village	5-0

Replay

Midhurst	v	Landing	3-0

Second Round

Bosham	v	Steyning	0-5
East Grinstead	v	Burgess Hill	0-0★
Eastbourne Town	v	Oakwood	3-0
Ferring	v	Arundel	1-4
Hailsham	v	Haywards Heath	2-1
Littlehampton	v	Wick	5-1
Shoreham	v	Midhurst	2-3
Whitehawk	v	Peacehaven	2-4

Replay

Arundel	v	Steyning	0-0*
Eastbourne Town	v	Burgess Hll	2-0
Midhurst	v	Hailsham	2-3
Peacehaven	v	Littlehampton	3-2

Replay

Steyning	v	Arundel	1-0

Semi-finals

Eastbourne Town	v	Peacehaven	3-1
Steyning	v	Hailsham	8-1

Final
(at Lancing)

Eastbourne Town	v	Steyning	3-0

* After extra time
★ Abandoned in extra time

SUSSEX COUNTY FOOTBALL LEAGUE
MERIT TABLE
SEASON 1985-86

	Games Played	Win Points	Draw Points	Goal Points	Clean Game Points	Dismissals	TOTAL POINTS
Wick	30	110	12	94	280		496
Haywards Heath	30	110	10	72	300		492
Steyning Town	30	110	12	61	270		453
Three Bridges	30	95	12	58	280		445
Pagham	30	105	12	72	250		439
Whitehawk	30	65	22	46	270	–10	393
Portfield	30	65	12	40	270		387
East Grinstead	30	75	10	44	250		379
Peacehaven & T.	30	75	8	55	240		378
Albion United	30	65	12	49	250		376
Eastbourne T.	30	90	14	71	220	–20	375
Arundel	30	50	16	55	240		371
Storrington	30	50	20	48	250		368
Oakwood	30	50	14	31	270		365
Ferring	30	60	12	47	250	–10	359
Wigmore Ath.	30	35	6	46	270		357
Burgess Hill T.	30	65	12	47	240	–10	354
Lancing	30	55	14	42	240		351
Littlehampton T.	30	65	14	44	240	–20	343
Bosham	30	60	14	56	220	–10	340
Hailsham Town	30	45	14	45	240	–10	334
Sidley United	30	75	16	52	200	–20	323
Ringmer	30	20	12	19	270		321
Midhurst & E.	30	25	14	33	250	–10	312
Franklands Vill.	30	30	8	36	230		304
Shoreham	30	50	8	42	220	–20	300
Hassocks	30	40	18	38	200		296
Selsey	30	35	10	35	230	–20	290
Horsham YMCA	30	25	8	33	230	–10	286
Chichester City	30	35	12	35	210	–10	282
Lingfield	30	25	4	35	220	–10	274
Newhaven	30	40	10	32	180	–10	252

5 points for a win, 2 points for a draw and 1 point for each goal scored. 10 points for a clean game, 10 points deducted for a player dismissed.

DIVISION 2 CHALLENGE CUP
1985-86

First Round

Albion United	v	Franklands Village	0-2
Ferring	v	East Grinstead	0-3
Newhaven	v	Bosham	3-1
Oakwood	v	Haywards Heath	1-3
Selsey	v	Pagham	1-1
Storrington	v	Lingfield	1-3
Wick	v	Sidley	0-3
Wigmore	v	Hassocks	0-2

Replay

Pagham	v	Selsey	3-0

Second Round

Hassocks	v	Lingfield	3-1
Haywards Heath	v	Sidley	0-0*
Newhaven	v	Franklands Village	2-2*
Pagham	v	East Grinstead	2-2*

Replays

East Grinstead	v	Pagham	0-4
Franklands Village	v	Newhaven	4-1
Sidley	v	Haywards Heath	0-4

Semi-finals

Franklands Village	v	Pagham	0-3
Haywards Heath	v	Hassocks	2-1

Final

Haywards Heath	v	Pagham at Horsham YMCA	0-3*

* After extra time

DIVISION ONE SEASON 1985-86

	Arundel	Burgess Hill Town	Chichester City	Eastbourne Town	Halisham Town	Horsham YMCA	Lancing	Littlehampton Town	Midhurst & Easebourne	Peacehaven & Telscombe	Portfield	Ringmer	Shoreham	Steyning Town	Three Bridges	Whitehawk
Arundel		1-2	2-1	0-4	3-1	13-0	1-2	0-0	1-1	2-1	1-1	2-2	1-0	1-3	1-0	2-1
Burgess Hill Town	2-1		2-0	2-1	1-2	0-2	2-1	2-1	3-1	2-3	4-1	4-0	2-3	L/W	1-2	0-0
Chichester City	0-2	1-1		1-1	4-2	2-1	4-1	3-1	1-1	2-1	0-0	1-0	1-1	1-3	0-4	1-1
Eastbourne Town	2-1	2-0	5-0		2-0	4-0	3-0	3-2	3-0	5-0	4-0	3-0	3-1	2-2	3-1	0-0
Hailsham Town	1-2	1-1	3-1	2-2		3-0	1-3	0-1	2-0	2-2	0-2	2-0	3-1	0-2	2-2	2-4
Horsham YMCA	2-2	1-3	2-5	0-4	1-5		0-2	3-3	0-4	0-3	2-3	2-1	4-2	0-0	0-2	1-3
Lancing	0-5	3-1	2-0	1-1	2-1	3-2		1-2	5-0	2-1	1-2	1-0	2-2	0-5	0-0	2-2
Littlehampton T.	1-1	2-1	3-0	2-2	0-0	2-0	6-1		2-0	0-1	2-0	3-0	2-0	0-1	1-0	0-0
Midhurst & E.	0-0	1-2	3-2	1-2	1-1	3-4	1-0	1-1		2-4	0-2	1-0	3-2	0-4	0-3	1-2
Peacehaven & T.	1-4	4-2	4-1	1-0	1-1	1-1	3-4	1-0	6-1		6-0	2-1	0-2	0-0	2-0	1-0
Portfield	3-2	2-2	3-0	0-2	1-3	2-1	0-0	0-2	1-0	1-0*		5-2	4-1	1-0	1-3	0-0
Ringmer	2-1	0-1	2-0	2-1	1-3	1-0	0-0	1-4	1-1	0-1	0-0		0-6	2-2	0-0	0-1
Shoreham	1-0	1-2	3-2	0-6	1-0	1-2	2-1	2-1	3-1	0-3	1-3	1-0		1-2	2-2	0-2
Steyning Town	2-1	1-1	3-0	1-0	1-0	7-0	2-0	1-0	2-0	3-0	2-0	3-1	3-1		1-1	4-1
Three Bridges	1-1	3-1	6-1	2-0	4-1	W/L	1-0	2-0	3-2	3-1	3-1	5-0	1-0	2-0		1-0
Whitehawk	0-1	0-0	1-0	1-1	3-1	6-2	2-2	2-0	3-3	3-1	4-1	1-0	1-1	0-1	2-1	

* The match Portfield v Peacehaven was replayed resulting in 1-0, the original result was 3-1

DIVISION TWO 1985-86

	Albion United	Bosham	East Grinstead	Ferring	Franklands Village	Hassocks	Haywards Heath	Lingfield	Newhaven	Oakwood	Pagham	Selsey	Sidley United	Storrington	Wick	Wigmore Athletic
Albion United		2-2	2-0	1-4	2-0	1-1	2-2	4-0	3-0	1-1	1-4	2-1	0-1	0-3	1-3	5-0
Bosham	2-1		2-0	3-1	4-1	1-3	1-4	2-2	5-2	1-1	0-1	2-2	1-3	3-1	1-3	3-1
East Grinstead	2-1	3-1		1-1	3-0	0-0	0-1	1-3	2-1	2-0	0-2	2-2	1-0	1-1	0-1	3-0
Ferring	0-3	2-1	0-3		1-0	2-4	2-3	2-6	1-1	0-0	0-2	2-0	1-0	1-1	2-3	2-0
Franklands Village	0-1	0-2	4-3	4-2		2-0	1-2	1-2	2-3	2-1	0-0	1-3	1-1	0-2	2-2	0-3
Hassocks	0-2	1-2	0-3	0-2	0-1		L/W	3-1	4-0	1-0	0-0	1-3	1-1	4-0	1-3	2-2
Haywards Heath	6-1	1-0	1-0	4-2	4-2	1-1		6-0	1-1	3-0	0-2	2-0	3-0	2-0	1-2	4-0
Lingfield	2-3	0-2	1-1	0-3	1-4	1-2	0-3		2-1	1-4	1-3	1-4	0-1	3-9	0-5	0-4
Newhaven	1-1	1-1	1-2	0-1	3-1	2-0	1-2	3-2		1-3	2-0	0-1	0-2	1-4	0-1	2-1
Oakwood	2-1	2-0	0-1	1-1	3-1	2-1	0-5	1-0	0-0		0-1	2-1	1-1	2-0	0-5	3-2
Pagham	0-0	7-2	2-1	5-1	6-1	1-0	1-2	3-0	3-0	5-0		5-0	4-0	0-2	1-1	3-0
Selsey	1-2	1-2	1-3	1-5	2-1	2-2	0-0	0-2	0-2	2-0	1-3		1-5	0-2	0-3	4-3
Sidley United	3-0	2-2	2-0	0-2	4-1	2-2	3-0	4-1	2-1	1-0	1-3	3-0		1-1	3-3	3-2
Storrington	1-2	1-1	0-1	2-2	1-1	0-0	0-3	2-1	1-2	0-0	0-1	1-1	3-1		0-2	4-0
Wick	5-0	2-1	0-3	2-1	8-1	1-0	3-3	5-1	6-0	7-1	2-2	6-1	1-2	2-2		4-3
Wigmore Athletic	1-4	2-6	0-2	0-1	5-1	0-4	1-3	2-1	2-0	3-0	2-2	2-0	0-0	3-4	2-3	

DIVISION THREE 1985-86

	APV Athletic	Bexhill Town	Broadbridge Heath	Cooksbridge	Crowborough Athletic	East Preston	Eastbourne Rangers	Hurstpierpoint	Ifield	Langney Sports	Leftovers SC	Midway	Saltdean United	Seaford Town	Westdene
APV Athletic		2-1	4-1	3-2	1-6	1-0	4-3	4-3	0-3	3-1	2-2	2-2	2-6	1-2	3-1
Bexhill Town	4-0		1-2	2-0	4-0	1-1	5-1	2-0	2-1	5-0	7-0	4-1	1-0	2-0	1-1
Broadbridge Heath	0-3	2-3		2-2	0-0	2-1	0-0	1-1	3-4	0-2	2-2	1-3	0-0	1-4	1-3
Cooksbridge	1-2	4-3	2-7		2-4	3-3	3-3	0-2	7-0	1-3	5-1	2-4	1-1	3-1	1-2
Crowborough Athletic	2-3	0-3	2-1	1-0		3-2	3-4	2-3	5-1	1-1	0-2	3-1	3-2	1-2	0-3
East Preston	5-0	2-2	2-0	1-2	2-2		5-0	1-1	3-1	2-1	1-0	3-1	0-1	0-2	3-0
Eastbourne Rangers	6-1	1-1	2-2	2-1	2-3	3-2		0-3	5-2	0-1	3-2	1-1	4-1	0-6	3-1
Hurstpierpoint	2-4	2-2	2-0	2-2	3-3	0-2	4-3		1-4	1-3	0-0	2-1	0-4	0-3	1-1
Ifield	4-0	3-2	2-3	0-0	1-0	2-1	2-1	3-2		0-2	2-3	2-5	3-2	1-2	2-2
Langney Sports	4-1	1-1	1-1	3-1	3-0	0-1	0-1	3-1	4-0		4-1	2-0	2-3	2-3	0-2
Leftovers SC	0-0	1-4	2-1	1-0	2-4	0-2	3-3	0-1	2-4	3-1		2-1	1-3	1-4	0-2
Midway	3-0	1-1	0-0	1-1	0-0	1-2	1-2	2-4	1-3	2-2	5-1		0-2	1-2	3-1
Saltdean United	1-1	2-3	0-2	2-1	5-0	0-1	4-1	1-1	0-0	3-1	2-1	4-1		2-3	6-4
Seaford Town	2-2	2-3	2-0	1-1	1-1	2-3	2-0	3-0	6-2	0-1	1-0	1-1	3-0		1-1
Westdene	5-1	1-2	0-0	0-2	2-0	1-3	0-1	2-1	2-4	2-5	2-0	1-1	1-1	1-3	

Patcham (1903) commenced the season in this division, but withdrew after a few matches and so their record was deleted.

Goalmouth action at Arundel as Lancing's Dave Menzies takes a tumble under pressure from Nigel Huddlestone (7). Also in the picture are Richard Styles, Arundel Striker Paul Bennett and (right) Kevin Keehan. Photo: Worthing Gazette and Herald.

Lancing Player-Manager Kevin Keehan (left) wins a midfield tussle with Shoreham's Paul Bibby. Photo: Worthing Gazette and Herald.

SUSSEX COUNTY LEAGUE
LEADING GOALSCORERS
1985-86

DIVISION 1

Club	10 or club highest
Arundel	- Keith Kirkham 17, Paul J. Bennett 15
Burgess Hill Town	- Mark Davis (incl. 3 for Three Bridges), Sean Guirey, both 8
Chichester City	- Stephen White 11
Eastbourne Town	- John Kemp 19, Derrick Smith 13, Neil Ivemy 10
Hailsham Town	- Greg Osborne 11
Horsham YMCA	- Lee Mobsby 7 (incl. 1 for Oakwood)
Lancing	- Kevin Keehan 9
Littlehampton Town	- Andy Horn 11, Herbie Smith 10
Midhurst & Easeb.	- Simon Dummer 9
Peacehaven & Tels.	- Peter Edwards 16, Robin Brady 13
Portfield	- Robin Sopp 9
Ringmer	- David Stevens 11 (incl. 7 for Whitehawk)
Shoreham	- David Smith 13
Steyning Town	- Danny Deans 14, Lee King 11 (incl. 6 for Lancing)
Three Bridges	- Gary Brooker, David Gates both 12
Whitehawk	- Phil Somers 11

Leading goalscorers:

John Kemp (Eastbourne)	19
Keith Kirkham (Arundel)	17
Peter Edwards (Peacehaven & Tels.)	16

DIVISION 2

Albion United	- Nigel Hole 23, Terry Button 10
Bosham	- Richard Hatton 10
East Grinstead	- Steven Norris 12
Ferring	- Kevin Bennett 11
Franklands Village	- Lee Berry 10
Hassocks	- Nigel Carr 16
Haywards Heath	- Stephen Hards 18, Simon Hall & Ian Rogers both 12
Lingfield	- Bobby North 8
Newhaven	- William Collinson 10
Oakwood	- John Smith 7
Pagham	- Adrian Skeites 16, Tony McVey 11, Ian Cole 10
Selsey	- Stuart O'Connell 7
Sidley United	- Guy Bentley, Mark Stevens both 7
Storrington	- Chris Searle 13
Wick	- Michael Dillon (incl. 16 for Bosham) 24, Steven Guille 19, Terry Withers 19, Ron Wood 16, Alan Herbert 11
Wigmore Athletic	- Mark Searle (incl. 1 for Arundel) 11

Leading goalscorers:

Michael Dillon (Wick)	24
Nigel Hole (Albion U)	23
Steven Guille (Wick)	19
Terry Withers (Wick)	19

DIVISION 3

APV Athletic	- Mark Russell 10
Bexhill Town	- Paul Saxby 15, Kevin Bevis 14, Richard Bexhall 12
Broadbridge Heath	- Neil Adams 10
Cooksbridge	- Terry Cornwell 9
Crowborough Athletic	- Rod Harman 10
Eastbourne Rangers	- Carl Schaaf 16
East Preston	- Tony Harvey 15
Hurstpierpoint	- Nigel Brockes 9
Ifield	- Gary Chandler 20, John Wort 11
Langney Sports	- Tim Williams 16, Lee Whittall 11
Leftovers SC	- Richard Stow 9
Midway	- Mark Hardwick, Ian Storrie both 9
Saltdean United	- Russell Grant 18, David Powell 13, John Buttress 11
Seaford	- Nigel Parks 18, Alan Russell 12, Doug Melville 11, Richard Melville 10
Westdene	- Stephen Lane 28

Leading goalscorers:

Stephen Lane (Westdene)	28
Gary Chandler (Ifield)	20
Russell Grant (Saltdean U)	18
Nigel Parks (Seaford)	18

Chichester City F.C. 1985/86. Back Row. N. McDonald (Trainer), M. Wiseman, C. Puttock, D. Barnes, R. Keates (Capt.), R. Hawes, A. Parrott, N. Hillier (Manager). Front Row. G. Ashton, S. White, A. Campbell, N. Drinkwater, N. Spurway, P. Stares, R. Crosby.

Haywards Heath

ARUNDEL

President: Brigadier R.H.E. Robinson, C.B.E.
Chairman: M. Monk
Manager: Michael Peters
Secretary: Peter Wells
Address & Tel. No: 0903 771146
Address and Tel. No. of ground: Mill Road, Arundel. 882548
Simple ground directions: Follow road into centre of town, over the bridge, turn right for 50 yards, into Mill Road car park, ground at rear
No. of seats: None **Covered accommodation:** 450 **Capacity:** 2,200
Year formed: 1889 **Nickname:** The Mullets **Floodlights:** None
Clubhouse details: 2 bars, 1 function room, pool, darts, music, toilets, telephone
Club colours: Red shirts, white shorts **Change colours:** Blue
Day for midweek matches: — **Previous Leagues:** West Sussex
Programme details: 4 pages **Programme editor:** The Secretary
Local newspapers & Tel. No. Arun Gazette, Evening Argus
Senior Honours: S.C.F.L. Winners 1957-8, 1958-9, Sussex R.V.R. Cup Winners 1969, 1973, 1979, 1980

BURGESS HILL TOWN

President: A.G. Lake
Chairman: D. Wingfield
Manager: F. Croney
Secretary: R. Puttick
Address & Tel. No: 04446 43080
Address and Tel. No. of ground: New Pavillion, Leylands Park. Tel. 42429
Simple ground directions: Wivelsfield Station, turn right, first left, ground on right

No. of seats: **Covered accommodation:** Yes **Capacity:** 4,000
Year formed: **Nickname:** **Floodlights:** Yes
Clubhouse details: Bar open 7 nights a week, Saturday and Sunday lunchtimes
Club colours: Yellow, green **Change colours:** White and black
Day for midweek matches: Tuesday **Previous Leagues:** Mid-Sussex League
Programme details: **Programme editor:** L. Parsons
Local newspapers & Tel. No. Mid-Sussex Times
Senior Honours:

CHICHESTER CITY

President:
Chairman: J. Burnett
Manager: N. Hillier
Secretary: J.F. Hutter
Address & Tel. No: Chichester 785839
Address and Tel. No. of ground: Oaklands Park, Chichester. 785978
Simple ground directions: ½ mile north of city centre, adjacent to Festival Theatre, turn into Oaklands car park and entrance to ground is next to Tennis Club. Nearest BR station, Chichester
No. of seats: None **Covered accommodation:** 500 **Capacity:** 2,500
Year formed: 1873 **Nickname:** **Floodlights:** No
Clubhouse details: Licensed, open matchdays and some evenings
Club colours: White/black/red **Change colours:** Red/white/white
Day for midweek matches: Tuesday**Previous Leagues:** Founder member Sussex County League, West Sussex League
Programme details: 16 pages, 20p **Programme editor:** T. Wallis
Local newspapers & Tel. No. Chichester Observer, Portsmouth Evening News, Brighton Evening Argus
Senior Honours: Susex County League (5), Sussex Senior Cup 1926, RUR Cup (2), League Cup (4), Division 2 Cup (1)

EASTBOURNE TOWN

President: Mrs B. Stone
Chairman: Roland Hutchinson
Manager: Trevor Wood
Secretary: Mrs Kim Prior
Address & Tel. No: Polegate 6594
Address and Tel. No. of ground: The Saffrons, Compton Place Road, Eastbourne, East Sussex. 0323 23724
Simple ground directions: Turn south west from A22 into Grove Road (opposite railway station) and ground is ¼ mile on the right
No. of seats: Yes **Covered accommodation:** Yes **Capacity:** 5,000
Year formed: 1882 **Nickname:** The Town **Floodlights:** No
Clubhouse details: Bar and refreshment facilities
Club colours: Yellow shirts, blue shorts, yellow socks **Change colours:** Royal blue shirts and shorts, red socks
Day for midweek matches: Tuesday **Previous Leagues:** Corinthian, Athenian, Sussex County
Programme details: Weekly **Programme editor:** Roland Hutchinson
Local newspapers & Tel. No. Eastbourne Gazette & Herald
Senior Honours:

HAILSHAM TOWN

President: J. Langford
Chairman: R. Soan
Manager: S. Courtney
Secretary: D. Murray
Address & Tel. No: 316 Lion House Park, Mill Road, Hailsham BN27 2SE. Hailsham 848006
Address and Tel. No. of ground: Western Recreation Ground. Hailsham 840446
Simple ground directions: Access via Diplock Road, off South Road
No. of seats: No **Covered accommodation:** Yes **Capacity:**
Year formed: 1885 **Nickname:** **Floodlights:** Yes
Clubhouse details: Bar, lounge, pool tables
Club colours: Yellow/green **Change colours:** Royal blue
Day for midweek matches: Tuesday **Previous Leagues:** Sussex Combination
Programme details: 12 pages **Programme editor:** Mrs J. Pacham
Local newspapers & Tel. No. Sussex Express
Senior Honours: Hasting Senior Cup, Southern Combination Cup

HAYWARDS HEATH

President: Martin Hilton
Chairman: Frank Hall
Manager: Dave John
Secretary: Pat Bucknell
Address & Tel. No: Haywards Heath 457726
Address and Tel. No. of ground: Hanbury Park Stadium, Allen Road, Haywards Heath. 412837
Simple ground directions: One mile, east from railway station
No. of seats: 700 **Covered accommodation:** 700 **Capacity:** 5,000
Year formed: **Nickname:** **Floodlights:** No
Clubhouse details: Bar, small dance floor
Club colours: Blue **Change colours:** Red
Day for midweek matches: Wednesday **Previous Leagues:** Mid-Sussex, Metropolitan
Programme details: 20p **Programme editor:** Linda Chambers
Local newspapers & Tel. No. Mid-Sussex Times
Senior Honours: Sussex City League Champions 1949-50, 1950-51, 1969-70; Sussex Senior Cup Winners 1957-58; R.V.R. Cup 1943-44, 1966-67, 1974-75

HORSHAM Y.M.C.A.

President: S. Knight
Chairman: G. Head
Managers: R. Moulding and J. Laker
Secretary: C. James
Address & Tel. No: 21 Lynwood Court, Rushams Road, Horsham RH12 2QA. Horsham 51818
Address and Tel. No. of ground: Gorings Mead. Horsham 52689
Simple ground directions: A281 off Brighton Road, Horsham
No. of seats: 60 **Covered accommodation:** Yes **Capacity:** 2,000
Year formed: 1898 **Nickname:** **Floodlights:** Yes
Clubhouse details: Bar and lounge, stage and dance floor, committee room, billiard room
Club colours: Red/black **Change colours:** White
Day for midweek matches: Wednesday **Previous Leagues:** Horsham & District, Brighton, Mid-Sussex
Programme details: 12 pages **Programme editor:** R. Rashbrook
Local newspapers & Tel. No. West Sussex County Times
Senior Honours:

LANCING

President: R.S. Steele
Chairman: John Brown
Manager: Kevin Keehan
Secretary: John Chisnall
Address & Tel. No: 15 Orchard Way, Lancing. (0903) 763048
Address and Tel. No. of ground: Culver Road. Lancing 764398
Simple ground directions: 200 yards north of Lancing railway station
No. of seats: 400 **Covered accommodation:** Yes **Capacity:** 3,500
Year formed: 1941 **Nickname:** **Floodlights:** Yes
Clubhouse details: Open match days and training nights
Club colours: Yellow shirts, blue shorts **Change colours:** All red
Day for midweek matches: Wednesday **Previous Leagues:** Brighton League
Programme details: 32 pages, 10p **Programme editor:** Peter Butcher. (0903) 34853
Local newspapers & Tel. No.
Senior Honours: Sussex County League Runners-up 1949-50, 1964-5; Division 2 Champions 1957-8, 1969-70, Runners-up 1982-3; Division 2 Cup Winners 1981-2, Sussex RVR Cup Winners 1965-6

LITTLEHAMPTON TOWN

President: A.W. Welch
Chairman: A.J. Randall
Manager: I. Cunningham
Secretary: A.C. Wickens
Address & Tel. No: Rustington 774807
Address and Tel. No. of ground: The Sportsfield, Littlehampton. Littlehampton 713944
Simple ground directions: A259 from Bognor and Worthing, A284 from Bognor, Littlehampton railway station 10 minutes walk
No. of seats: 200 **Covered accommodation:** Yes **Capacity:** 3,000
Year formed: 1896 **Nickname:** **Floodlights:** No
Clubhouse details: The Sportsman Club
Club colours: Yellow shirts, black shorts, black socks **Change colours:** White shirts, blue shorts, white socks
Day for midweek matches: Tuesday or Wednesday **Previous Leagues:** West Sussex League (Reserves)
Programme details: 15p **Programme editor:** A.W. Welch
Local newspapers & Tel. No. Arun Gazette
Senior Honours: Sussex Senior Cup 1948-9, 1969-70

MIDHURST & EASEBOURNE UNITED

President: Hugh Carter
Chairman: Robert Boxall
Managers: Bernie May and Colin Thiselton
Secretary: E.S. Dummer
Address & Tel. No: Midhurst 3887
Address and Tel. No. of ground: Rotherfield

Simple ground directions: ¼ mile from River Bridge in Midhurst on A286, road to Haselmere. Opposite BP garage
No. of seats: 60 **Covered accommodation:** 200 **Capacity:** 2,000
Year formed: 1946 **Nickname:** **Floodlights:** No
Clubhouse details: Clubhouse with canteen and bar
Club colours: Royal blue **Change colours:** Red
Day for midweek matches: **Previous Leagues:** West Sussex
Programme details: Free **Programme editor:** E.S. Dummer
Local newspapers & Tel. No. Midhurst & Petworth Observer, West Sussex Gazette
Senior Honours:

PEACEHAVEN & TELSCOMBE

President: W. Parris
Chairman: J. Edwards
Managers: Allan Solomon & Terry Stanley
Secretary: Mrs P. Solomon
Address & Tel. No: Peacehaven 5773
Address and Tel. No. of ground: Piddinghoe Avenue, Peacehaven. Tel. 2471

Simple ground directions: A259 coast road from Brighton to Newhaven, Piddinghoe Avenue is about 1 mile past roundabout, leading to Meridian Centre
No. of seats: 50 **Covered accommodation:** Yes **Capacity:** 3,000
Year formed: **Nickname:** The Haven or The Tye **Floodlights:** n/a
Clubhouse details: Licensed bar, catering facilities
Club colours: White, black trim shirts, black shorts and socks **Change colours:** Light blue
Day for midweek matches: n/a **Previous Leagues:** Brighton
Programme details: 20 pages, 15p **Programme editor:** J. Godden, F. Parris
Local newspapers & Tel. No. Sussex Express, Evening Argus
Senior Honours: Divions 1 Champions 1978-9, 1982-2, 1982-3; Senior Cup Runners-up 1981-2; RVR Cup 1977-8, 1981-2

PORTFIELD

President: E. White
Chairman: J. Dowling
Manager: J. Kew
Secretary: J. Dowling
Address & Tel. No: 36 St James Square, Chichester PO19 4HZ. Chichester 779044
Address and Tel. No. of ground: Church Road, Portfield. Chichester 779875
Simple ground directions: One mile east of city centre on A27
No. of seats: 50 **Covered accommodation:** 200 **Capacity:** 250
Year formed: 1896 **Nickname:** Field **Floodlights:** No
Clubhouse details: Bar and lounge, pool tables, dance floor and stage
Club colours: Black/amber **Change colours:** White
Day for midweek matches: Tuesday **Previous Leagues:** West Sussex
Programme details: 16 pages **Programme editor:**
Local newspapers & Tel. No. West Sussex Gazette
Senior Honours: Sussex County Football League Division 2 Champions

SHOREHAM

President:
Chairman: G. Croydon
Manager: J. Thompson
Secretary: T. Parker
Address & Tel. No: 13 Wyck Court, Fishergate West Sussex. Brighton 417205
Address and Tel. No. of ground: Middle Road, Shoreham. Shoreham 454261

Simple ground directions: Follow A27 to Shoreham. At Southlands hospital turn left along Hammy Lane
No. of seats: No **Covered accommodation:** Yes **Capacity:** 2,000
Year formed: 1895 **Nickname:** **Floodlights:** No
Clubhouse details: Bar and lounge
Club colours: Royal blue **Change colours:** White
Day for midweek matches: Wednesday **Previous Leagues:** West Sussex
Programme details: 8 pages **Programme editor:**
Local newspapers & Tel. No. Brighton Gazette
Senior Honours: Division 1 Winners 1978; Division 2 1978 and 1985; Division 2 Cup Winners 1975, 1983

Three Bridges. Back Row (L-R) B. Nash (Coach), D. Gates, S. Welch, D. Palmer, B. Norris, J. Malthouse, T. Williamson, A. Knight (Manager), G. MacConnell (Phsio). Front Row, D. Easton, T. Martin, G. Brooker, R. Martin, E. Joselyn, S. Thomas, M. Davis (now with Burgess Hill)

THREE BRIDGES

President:
Chairman: C.J. Steele
Manager: A. Knight
Secretary: W.M. Day
Address & Tel. No: 23 Oakfields, Worth, Crawley RH10 4FN. Crawley 883658
Address and Tel. No. of ground: Jubilee Field, Three Bridges. Crawley 30540
Simple ground directions: 200 yards from BR station-Three Bridges
No. of seats: No **Covered accommodation:** 350 **Capacity:** 2,500
Year formed: 1901 **Nickname:** The Bridges **Floodlights:** Yes
Clubhouse details: Bar, lounge, pool tables
Club colours: Amber/black **Change colours:** Red/white
Day for midweek matches: Wednesday **Previous Leagues:** Mid-Sussex
Programme details: 24 pages **Programme editor:**
Local newspapers & Tel. No. Crawley Observer
Senior Honours: Sussex RVR Charity Cup 1983; Sussex County League Invitation Cup 1971

WHITEHAWK

President:
Chairman: Ken Powell
Manager: Tony (Butch) Reeves
Secretary: John Rosenblatt
Address & Tel. No: Brighton 680322
Address and Tel. No. of ground: East Brighton Park. Brighton 609736

Simple ground directions: North of Brighton Marina
No. of seats: **Covered accommodation:** 500 **Capacity:** 5,000
Year formed: **Nickname:** **Floodlights:**
Clubhouse details: Licensed bar, 200 capacity. Open all week
Club colours: Red/white **Change colours:** Blue
Day for midweek matches: **Previous Leagues:** Brighton & Hove District
Programme details: 14 pages **Programme editor:** Mrs S Moore
Local newspapers & Tel. No. Evening Argus
Senior Honours: Sussex Senior Cup 1951, 1962, Sussex County League 1962, 1964, 1984

WICK

President: M. Hood
Chairman: B. Wadsworth
Manager: N. Cairns
Secretary: M. Short
Address & Tel. No: Littlehampton 724111. **Match Secretary:** T. Davies, Littlehampton 721887
Address and Tel. No. of ground: Crabtree Park, Coomes Way, Wick, Littlehampton
Simple ground directions: A27 to Crossbush, turn left at Howards Hotel after 1 mile, over level crossing, first left by Locomotive pub. Ground at end of road
No. of seats: 60 **Covered accommodation:** 300 **Capacity:** 3,000
Year formed: 1892 **Nickname:** **Floodlights:** Yes
Clubhouse details: Two storey building, clubhouse opened 1970. P.A. system, bar, changing rooms, showers, toilets, kitchen, stage, dance floor, beer cellar, pool table, darts, TV.
Club colours: Red, white, blue. Hoopey shirts, white shorts, white socks **Change colours: All yellow**
Day for midweek matches: Tuesday or Wednesday **Previous Leagues:** West Sussex
Programme details: 16 pages **Programme editor:** Secretary, Match Secretary & L. Hawkins

Local newspapers & Tel. No. Arun Gazette
Senior Honours: Winners of County League Div 2 (2), Merit Table Winners 1981-2, 1985-6; Brighton Charity Cup Winners 1985-6

Wick F.C. 1985/86. Back Row (L-r) T. Stabler (Vice-Chairman), A. Clayton, D. Skinner, P. Croft, R. Hooper, G. Chitty, T. Still, Barry Wadsworth (Chairman, Norman Cairns (Manager). Front Row. P. Matthew, M. King, S. Guille, A. Herbert, R. Wood, T. Withers, G. Tompsett. Right at front, Stuart Davies (Mascot).

BEXHILL TOWN

President:
Chairman: A. Hammond
Manager:
Secretary: R. Foster
Address & Tel. No: 9 Willowbed Walk, Hastings TV34 2QL. Hastings 432065
Address and Tel. No. of ground: The Polegrove, Brockley Road, Bexhill. Bexhill 220732
Simple ground directions: Turn right to town centre from traffic lights to Lond Road from A27
No. of seats: 100 **Covered accommodation:** Yes **Capacity:** 400
Year formed: **Nickname:** **Floodlights:** No
Clubhouse details: Yes, bar and lounge
Club colours: Green/white **Change colours:** Yellow
Day for midweek matches: **Previous Leagues:**
Programme details: 8 pages **Programme editor:**
Local newspapers & Tel. No.
Senior Honours: Sussex County League Champions 1956-7, 1965-6, 1966-7; Sussex RVR Charity Cup Winners 1958, 1974

BOSHAM

President:
Chairman: Don Fowler
General Manager: Bob Collyer
Secretary: Bob Probee
Address & Tel. No: c/o 39 Arnold Way, Bosham, Chichester PO18 8NJ. 029 383 244 (B)
Address and Tel. No. of ground: Walton Lane, Bosham, Chichester PO18 8QF. 0243 574011
Simple ground directions: South off A27 at roundabout 3 miles west of Chichester. Left at T junction. Entrance 50 yards on left
No. of seats: None **Covered accommodation:** None **Capacity:** 2,000 approx.
Year formed: **Nickname:** **Floodlights:**
Clubhouse details: Open every evening, weekend lunchtimes and after matches. Food available on match days
Club colours: Red shirts, white shorts, red socks **Change colours:** White shirts, black shorts, white socks
Day for midweek matches: **Previous Leagues:** Chichester & District League, West Sussex League
Programme details: 16 pages, 25p **Programme editor:**
Local newspapers & Tel. No.
Senior Honours:

EAST GRINSTEAD

President:
Chairman: P. Cadman
Manager: M,. Arnold. Tel. 314638
Secretary: G.E. Tizzard
Address & Tel. No: 22167
Address and Tel. No. of ground: East Court, East Grinstead. 25885
Simple ground directions: Turn east from A22 into Moat Road. Continue to junction with Holtye Road (A264) roadway to ground (signposted) opposite entrance road to council and police offices
No. of seats: None **Covered accommodation:** 600 standing **Capacity:** 2,500
Year formed: **Nickname:** **Floodlights:** No
Clubhouse details: Yes, licensed bar
Club colours: Amber/black **Change colours:** All red
Day for midweek matches: **Previous Leagues:** Mid Sussex, Southern Amateur
Programme details: Yes **Programme editor:**
Local newspapers & Tel. No.
Senior Honours:

FERRING

President:
Chairman: H.W. McIlwain
Manager:
Secretary: S.H. Blake
Address & Tel. No: 9 Fernhurst Drive, Goring, W. Sussex
Address and Tel. No. of ground: Glebelands, Greystoke Road, Ferring, W. Sussex. Worthing 43618
Simple ground directions: Take Ferring Lane off A259 in Ferring, continue into Ferring Street, left to Rife Way, left to Greystoke Road
No. of seats: None **Covered accommodation:** Yes **Capacity:**
Year formed: **Nickname:** **Floodlights:** No
Clubhouse details:
Club colours: Royal blue **Change colours:** Yellow/green
Day for midweek matches: **Previous Leagues:**
Programme details: Yes **Programme editor:**
Local newspapers & Tel. No.
Senior Honours:

FRANKLANDS VILLAGE

President:
Chairman: Paul Field
Manager:
Secretary: David Worsfold
Address & Tel. No: 151a Franklands Village, RH16 3RF. Haywards Heath 416475
Address and Tel. No. of ground: Hardy Memorial Playing Field, Franklands Village, Haywards Heath. 412435
Simple ground directions: A272 Haywards Heath-Uckfield Road. Turn left at Birch S/St which leads to the village
No. of seats: **Covered accommodation:** 200 **Capacity:** 1,500
Year formed: **Nickname:** **Floodlights:** No
Clubhouse details: Yes
Club colours: All blue **Change colours:** Yellow and red
Day for midweek matches: **Previous Leagues:** Mid-Sussex, Crawley, Brighton, Southern Counties Combination
Programme details: 20 pages, (10 editorial) **Programme editor:**
Local newspapers & Tel. No.
Senior Honours: S.C.F.L. Div 3 Ruppers-up; Brighton League Champions (2); Southern Counties Combination Champions; M.S.F.A. Cup Winners (3)

Bosham F.C. Div. 2

Franklands Village

HASSOCKS

President:
Chairman: M.A. Boxall
Manager:
Secretary: R. Ward
Address & Tel. No: 3 Bishops Close, Hurstpierpoint, BN6 9XO. Hurst 832036
Address and Tel. No. of ground: Adastra Park, Hassocks. 2668
Simple ground directions: Located off B2117 between Hassocks and Ditchling
No. of seats: None **Covered accommodation:** 200 **Capacity:** 500
Year formed: **Nickname:** **Floodlights:** No
Clubhouse details: Adastra Park, Hassocks
Club colours: Red shirts and socks, black shorts **Change colours:** All blue
Day for midweek matches: **Previous Leagues:**
Programme details: Yes **Programme editor:**
Local newspapers & Tel. No.
Senior Honours: Southern Counties Combination League Champions 1977; Southern Counties Combination Cup Winners 1980; Sussex Intermediate Cup Winners 1975; Brighton League Champions 1972; A.F.A Intermediate Cup Winners 1986

LITTLE COMMON ALBION

President:
Chairman: K.E. Cherry
Manager:
Secretary: M Cherry
Address & Tel. No: 3 Lewes Close, Bexhill TN39 WDQ. Bexhill 217191
Address and Tel. No. of ground: Little Common Rec, Pear Tree Lane, Little Common
Simple ground directions: Main A27 road to Hastings
No. of seats: **Covered accommodation:** 200 **Capacity:**
Year formed: **Nickname:** **Floodlights:**
Clubhouse details: Yes
Club colours: Claret/blue **Change colours:** White
Day for midweek matches: **Previous Leagues:**
Programme details: Yes **Programme editor:**
Local newspapers & Tel. No.
Senior Honours:

NEWHAVEN

President:
Chairman: M. Godden
Manager:
Secretary: F.D. Dixon
Address & Tel. No: 33 Friars Bay, Peacehaven BN9 8UR. Peacehaven 5514
Address and Tel. No. of ground: Fort Road, Newhaven
Simple ground directions: A275 from Lewes or A259 coast road to Newhaven, one way system
No. of seats: 200 **Covered accommodation:** 3,000 **Capacity:**
Year formed: **Nickname:** **Floodlights:** Part for training
Clubhouse details: Yes
Club colours: Red, white trim **Change colours:** Blue
Day for midweek matches: **Previous Leagues:**
Programme details: Yes **Programme editor:**
Local newspapers & Tel. No.
Senior Honours: Sussex RVR Cup 1904-5; Sussex County League Champions 1953-4, 1973-4; Division 2 Champions 1971-2; Invitation Cup Winners 1948-9

OAKWOOD

President:
Chairman: A.T. Bridges
Manager:
Secretary: G. Martin
Address & Tel. No: Singlegate, Tinsley Green, RH10 3NS. Crawley 882400
Address and Tel. No. of ground: Tinsley Lane, Three Bridges, Crawley, Sussex.
Simple ground directions: From A23 to Gatwick, take first set of traffic lights into Manor Royal, pass next set of traffic lights, over roundabout to warehouse marked Canon. Turn right signposted Oakwood. Last Clubhouse down lane
No. of seats: 60 **Covered accommodation:** 150 **Capacity:**
Year formed: **Nickname:** **Floodlights:** No
Clubhouse details: Yes
Club colours: Red shirts, black shorts **Change colours:** Blue shirts/shorts
Day for midweek matches: **Previous Leagues:**
Programme details: **Programme editor:**
Local newspapers & Tel. No.
Senior Honours: Southern Counties League/Cup Winners

PAGHAM

President:
Chairman: I. Baker
Manager:
Secretary: P. Cambell
Address & Tel. No: No. 4, 136 Aldwick Road, Bognor Regis, PO21 2PA. (0243) 820557
Address and Tel. No. of ground: Nyetimber Lane, Pagham. (0243) 26612
Simple ground directions: A27 Chichester bypass, turn off to Pagham, Nyetimber Lane 2 miles
No. of seats: 50 **Covered accommodation:** Yes **Capacity:** 2,000
Year formed: **Nickname:** **Floodlights:** No
Clubhouse details: New members and players' bar open match days and Sundays
Club colours: White/black **Change colours:** Red
Day for midweek matches: **Previous Leagues:** West Sussex Football League
Programme details: 12 pages **Programme editor:**
Local newspapers & Tel. No.
Senior Honours: Sussex County League Champions, Runners-up; Division 2 Cup Winners; F.A. Vase 4th Round

Hassocks

Oakwood F.C.

RINGMER

President:
Chairman: D.M. Jeary
Manager:
Secretary: Mrs J.M. Feltham
Address & Tel. No: 11 The Martlets, Lewes BN7 2HR
Address and Tel. No. of ground: Caburn Anchor Field, Ringmer. Ringmer 424854
Simple ground directions: From Lewes Road, turn into Springett Avenue, 1st left into Anchor Field
No. of seats: No **Covered accommodation:** Yes **Capacity:** 400
Year formed: **Nickname:** **Floodlights:** No
Clubhouse details:
Club colours: Light and dark blue **Change colours:** Red
Day for midweek matches: **Previous Leagues:**
Programme details: 12 pages **Programme editor:**
Local newspapers & Tel. No.
Senior Honours: Sussex County League Champions 1970-1; F.A. Cup 1st Round 1970-1; Sussex Senior Cup Winners 1972-3; Sussex Senior Cup Finalists 1980-1

SEAFORD TOWN

President:
Chairman: J. Garred
Manager:
Secretary: Mrs M Stone
Address & Tel. No: 49 Saltwood Road, Seaford BN25 3SR. Seaford 894631
Address and Tel. No. of ground: Crouch Gardens, East Street, Seaford. 892221

Simple ground directions: After passing railway station, 3rd right, then 3rd left
No. of seats: None **Covered accommodation:** Yes **Capacity:**
Year formed: **Nickname:** **Floodlights:** No
Clubhouse details: Yes
Club colours: All red **Change colours:** Yellow
Day for midweek matches: **Previous Leagues:**
Programme details: Yes **Programme editor:**
Local newspapers & Tel. No.
Senior Honours: Sussex County League Div 3 Champions; Division 3 Cup Winners 1985-6

Seaford Town

SELSEY

President:
Chairman: Derek Longworth
Manager:
Secretary: Denny Lee
Address & Tel. No: 7 Elm Tree Close, Selsey, Sussex PO20 OSQ. Selsey 605961
Address and Tel. No. of ground: The High Street Ground, Selsey. 6093420
Simple ground directions: Turn right into car park alongside fire station. Ground is in southern corner
No. of seats: 100 **Covered accommodation:** 200 **Capacity:** 2,000
Year formed: **Nickname:** **Floodlights:** None
Clubhouse details: Yes
Club colours: Blue **Change colours:** Red
Day for midweek matches: **Previous Leagues:** Chichester & District, West Sussex
Programme details: Yes **Programme editor:**
Local newspapers & Tel. No.
Senior Honours: Malcolm Simmonds Cup 1955-6, 1956-7, 1957-8, 1958-9; League Winners 1954-5, 1956-7, 1957-8, 1958-9, 1960-1

Selsey

Sidley Utd.

SIDLEY UNITED

President:
Chairman: Denis R. Scotcher
Manager:
Secretary: Judy Scotcher
Address & Tel. No: 311 London Road, Bexhill TN39 4AJ. Bexhill 223402
Address and Tel. No. of ground: Gullivers, North Road, Sidley. 217078
Simple ground directions: :

No. of seats: None
Covered accommodation: None
Capacity:
Year formed:
Nickname:
Floodlights: None
Clubhouse details: Yes
Club colours: Light blue/dark blue
Change colours: All red
Day for midweek matches:
Previous Leagues:
Programme details: Yes
Programme editor:
Local newspapers & Tel. No.
Senior Honours: Division 2 1958-9, 1964-5; Invitation Cup 1957-8

STORRINGTON

President:
Chairman: Alan Pockett. Tel. Storrington 2197
Manager:
Secretary: Robin S. Bishop
Address & Tel. No: 50 Timbermill Court, Haslemere, Surrey. Haslemere 56842
Address and Tel. No. of ground: Recreation Ground, Pulborough Road, Storrington. Storrington 5860
Simple ground directions: On A283 west of Storrington village centre, opposite pond
No. of seats: None
Covered accommodation: 50
Capacity: 1,000+
Year formed:
Nickname:
Floodlights: None
Clubhouse details: Yes
Club colours: Royal blue
Change colours: White shirts, navy blue shorts and socks
Day for midweek matches:
Previous Leagues:
Programme details: Yes
Programme editor:
Local newspapers & Tel. No.
Senior Honours: Division 2 S.C.F.L. Cup Winners

WIGMORE

President:
Chairman: W. Edwards
Manager:
Secretary: E.A. Graveson, 42 Raleigh Crescent, Goring by Sea, Worthing, W. Sussex BN12 6EE.
Address & Tel. No: Beeches Avenue, Worthing. Worthing 34466
Address and Tel. No. of ground: Beeches Avenue, Worthing. Worthing 34466
Simple ground directions: From west on A27 Beeches Avenue is 4th left past Phill Barn roundabout. From east 2nd right past the traffic lights between PDH garage and Downlands Hotel
No. of seats: 50
Covered accommodation: Yes
Capacity: 5,000
Year formed:
Nickname:
Floodlights: No
Clubhouse details: Yes
Club colours: All red
Change colours: All white
Day for midweek matches:
Previous Leagues:
Programme details: Yes
Programme editor:
Local newspapers & Tel. No.
Senior Honours: Sussex County League Div 2 Champions 1952-3, 1973-4; Invitation Cup Winners 1959-60; Division 2 Invitation Cup 1967-8; Sussex Junior Cup 1949-50

Broadbridges Heath

Eastbourne Rangers

Langney Sports F.C. 1985/86

Saltdean United F.C.

A.P.V. ATHLETIC

President:
Chairman: M. Wragg
Manager:
Secretary: M. Robbins
Address & Tel. No: 38 Clive Way, Poundhill, Crawley
Address and Tel. No. of ground: Jordans, London Road, Crawley. 0293 30700
Simple ground directions: Take A23 from South Ground, 150 yards before traffic lights to industrial estate

No. of seats: No
Covered accommodation: No
Capacity:
Year formed:
Nickname:
Floodlights: No
Clubhouse details:
Club colours: Maroon
Change colours: Blue/yellow

BROADBRIDGE HEATH

President:
Chairman: J. Martin
Manager:
Secretary: G. Manktelow
Address & Tel. No: 110 Clarence Road, Horsham RH13 5SG. Horsham 53297
Address and Tel. No. of ground: Woodstock Close, Horsham. Horsham 64871
Simple ground directions: Off Wimblehurst Road, Hersham

No. of seats: No
Covered accommodation: No
Capacity:
Year formed:
Nickname:
Floodlights: No
Clubhouse details: Yes
Club colours: Royal blue
Change colours: Red
Day for midweek matches:
Previous Leagues: Southern Counties Combination

COOKSBRIDGE

President:
Chairman: J. Mander
Manager:
Secretary: P. Barker
Address & Tel. No: 14 Caburn Crescent, Lewes, Sussex. Lewes 476784
Address and Tel. No. of ground: Cooksbridge Recreation Ground, Beechwood Lane. Cooksbridge 476277
Simple ground directions: 150 yards from Lewes side of railway crossing, signposted to East Chiltington

No. of seats:
Covered accommodation:
Capacity:
Year formed:
Nickname:
Floodlights:
Clubhouse details: Yes
Club colours: Green/white
Change colours: Yellow/black

CROWBOROUGH ATHLETIC

President:
Chairman: B.J. Sykes
Manager:
Secretary: H.J. Collick
Address & Tel. No: Oaklands, Oakhurst Drive, Crowborough TN6 2TA. Crowborough 5565
Address and Tel. No. of ground: Alderbrook Recreation Ground. Crowborough 61893
Simple ground directions: From Crowborough Cross through High Street, Croft Road and Whitehill Road into Fermor Road, then second right
No. of seats: No
Covered accommodation: Yes
Capacity:
Year formed:
Nickname:
Floodlights: No
Clubhouse details: Yes
Club colours: White/navy blue
Change colours: Blue/white/blue

EASTBOURNE RANGERS

President:
Chairman: Byran Wiggins
Manager:
Secretary: Mrs Glynis Mockett
Address & Tel. No: 15 Orchid Close, Langney, Eastbourne. Eastbourne 766903
Address and Tel. No. of ground: Old Town Recreation Ground, Longland Road, Old Town, Eastbourne, Sussex.
Simple ground directions: From Brighton enter Eastbourne on A259, second left into Longland Road, ground 300 yards on left
Year formed:
Nickname:
Floodlights:
Clubhouse details:
Club colours: Gold shirts and socks, black shorts
Change colours: Blue shirts and shorts, white socks
Day for midweek matches:
Previous Leagues: Eastbourne & Hastings

EAST PRESTON

President:
Chairman: D. Cooper
Manager:
Secretary: I. Long
Address & Tel. No: 60 Roundstone Drive, East Preston BN16 1EP. Rustington 774179
Address and Tel. No. of ground: Roundstone Drive Recreation Ground. Rustington 776026
Simple ground directions: Off A259 at Roundstone Hotel, over the level crossing, turn left and first right
No. of seats:
Covered accommodation: None
Capacity:
Year formed:
Nickname:
Floodlights: No
Clubhouse details: Yes
Club colours: White/black
Change colours: Red/white

HURSTPIERPOINT

President:
Chairman: W. Marchant
Manager:
Secretary: P.A. John
Address & Tel. No: 16 Chuch Close, Burgess Hill, West Sussex. Burgess Hill 47183
Address and Tel. No. of ground: Fairfield Rec, Cuckfield Road
Simple ground directions: Between numbers 158 and 160 Cuckfield Road
Club colours: Blue and white
Change colours: Red and black
Day for midweek matches:
Previous Leagues: Mid Sussex, Brighton

IFIELD

President:
Chairman: H. Izan
Manager:
Secretary: S. Corbett
Address & Tel. No: 29 Romain Road, Hove BN3 4LB. Brighton 414699
Address and Tel. No. of ground: Ifield Green
Simple ground directions: From A23 Crawley bypass, turn left at roundabout, signposted Charlwood. 3rd left into Ifield Green
No. of seats: **Covered accommodation:** No **Capacity:**
Year formed: **Nickname:** **Floodlights:** No
Clubhouse details: Yes
Club colours: White/red **Change colours:**

LANGNEY SPORTS

President:
Chairman: C. Field
Manager:
Secretary: Mrs J. Field
Address & Tel. No: 17 Montague Way, Westham, Sussex. Eastbourne 765859

Address and Tel. No. of ground: Langley Sports Club, Priory Lane, Eastbourne
Simple ground directions: From north on A22 to Polegate, turn left on A27 to Stone Cross. Turn right at B2104 past Langley shopping centre. Turn left at B2191 past crematorium. First right into Priory Road, first left into Priory Lane
No. of seats: Yes **Covered accommodation:** Yes **Capacity:** Not known
Year formed: **Nickname:** **Floodlights:** No
Clubhouse details: Yes
Club colours: Red/black **Change colours:** Blue

LEFT OVERS SPORTS CLUB

President:
Chairman: D. Turnham
Manager:
Secretary: Kevin Bottle
Address & Tel. No: Ferndale, Nursery Lane, Nutley, Sussex. Nutley 2280
Address and Tel. No. of ground: Kings Sports Centre, Moat Road, East Grinstead, Sussex
Simple ground directions: Turn east from A22 into Moat Road, 500 yards on right
Clubhouse details: Yes
Club colours: Red shirts/black shorts **Change colours:**

LINGFIELD

President:
Chairman: M. Tomsett
Manager:
Secretary: J. Thomas
Address & Tel. No: 24 Gun Pit Road, Lingfield, Surrey. Lingfield 832223
Address and Tel. No. of ground: Godstone Road, Lingfield, Surrey. Lingfield 834269
Simple ground directions: Godstone Road ¼ mile outside village
No. of seats: **Covered accommodation:** Yes **Capacity:** 1,000
Year formed: **Nickname:** **Floodlights:** Yes
Clubhouse details: Yes
Club colours: Scarlet/amber stripe **Change colours:** White

MIDWAY

President:
Chairman: J. Lambert
Manager:
Secretary: M.E. Neal
Address & Tel. No: 214 Upper Shoreham Road, Shoreham BN4 6BG. Brighton 453857
Address and Tel. No. of ground: Southwick Rec., Leisure Centre, Old Barn Way, Southwick. Brighton 593202
Simple ground directions: A27 from Brighton left into Hadrians Avenue, left at bottom, 2nd turning on right
No. of seats: None **Covered accommodation:** None **Capacity:** Open ground
Year formed: **Nickname:** **Floodlights:** No
Clubhouse details: Leisure Centre
Club colours: Claret/blue trim **Change colours:** White

SALTDEAN UNITED

President:
Chairman: R. Wedge
Manager:
Secretary: M. Walker
Address & Tel. No: 8 Greenbank Avenue, Saltdean BN2 8AS. Brighton 36026
Address and Tel. No. of ground: Hill Park, off Coombe Vale, Saltdean, Brighton, E. Sussex. Brighton 309898
Simple ground directions: A259 to Saltdean Lido, then Arundel Drive West and Saltdean Vale to bridlepath sign at beginning of Coombe Vale. Club 200 yards along track
No. of seats: None **Covered accommodation:** Yes **Capacity:** 2,500
Year formed: **Nickname:** **Floodlights:** No
Clubhouse details: Yes
Club colours: Red and black stripes **Change colours:** Light blue

WESTDENE

President:
Chairman: M. Plumstead
Manager:
Secretary: Mrs B. Plumstead
Address & Tel. No: 87 Applesham Way, Portslade BN4 2LN. Brighton 416890
Address and Tel. No. of ground: Blackstone Playing Field, Woodmancote

No. of seats: **Covered accommodation:** None **Capacity:**
Year formed: **Nickname:** **Floodlights:** No
Clubhouse details: No
Club colours: Red/black **Change colours:**

GREAT MILLS WESTERN LEAGUE

President: L.G. Webb *Chairman:* S.G. Priddle

Secretary: M.E. Washer, 126, Chessel Street, Bristol BS3 3DQ

WESTERN LEAGUE PREMIER LEAGUE

	P	W	D	L	F	A	Pts
Exmouth	42	30	9	3	95	31	69
Liskeard	42	31	6	5	103	34	68
Bideford	42	27	8	7	97	27	62
Saltash	42	21	13	8	81	44	55
Chippenham	42	21	10	11	60	44	52
Mangotsfield	42	18	13	11	86	58	49
Taunton	42	19	9	14	59	54	47
*Dawlish	42	19	8	15	53	49	45
Bristol C	42	18	6	18	74	61	42
Clevedon	42	12	18	12	55	47	42
Bristol MF	42	16	9	17	71	72	41
Minehead	42	16	9	17	55	70	41
*Frome	42	14	12	16	49	62	39
Clandown	42	15	8	19	46	57	38
Torrington	42	13	11	18	51	62	37
Melksham	42	11	13	18	50	77	35
Barnstaple	42	13	7	22	46	68	33
Weston	42	12	8	22	69	93	32
Paulton	42	9	12	21	50	82	30
Plymouth	42	9	11	22	60	67	29
Chard	42	8	4	30	33	112	20
Shepton Mlt*	42	4	8	30	36	110	15

* One point deducted for playing an ineligable player

DIVISION ONE

	P	W	D	L	F	A	Pts
Portway Br	42	27	9	6	100	42	63
Radstock	42	26	9	7	116	54	61
*Yeovil	45	25	7	10	79	36	56
Wimborne	42	18	13	11	77	51	49
Larkhall	42	18	11	13	72	56	47
Backwell	42	19	9	14	63	47	47
Ottery	42	18	11	13	61	60	47
Swanage	42	18	9	15	91	79	45
Weymouth	42	18	8	16	84	78	44
Heavitree	42	17	10	15	60	69	44
Bath	42	16	10	16	74	69	42
Wellington	42	14	12	16	70	70	40
Tiverton	42	16	7	19	68	74	39
Devizes	42	10	18	14	43	58	38
Elmore	42	12	13	17	56	78	37
Keynsham	42	9	8	15	37	53	36
Welton	42	13	9	20	61	84	35
Glastonbury	42	12	11	19	52	79	35
Ilfracombe	42	10	14	18	55	69	34
Westbury	42	10	10	22	55	82	30
Odd Down	42	9	12	21	57	90	30
Warminster	42	9	6	27	40	93	24

*One point deducted for playing an ineligable player

WESTERN LEAGUE PREMIER DIVISION 1985-6	Barnstaple Town	Bideford	Bristol City	Bristol Manor Farm	Chard Town	Chippenham Town	Clandown	Clevedon Town	Dawlish Town	Exmouth Town	Frome Town	Liskeard Athletic	Mangotsfield United	Melksham Town	Minehead	Paulton Rovers	Plymouth A	Saltash United	Shepton Mallet	Taunton Town	Torrington	Weston Super Mare
Barnstaple Town		0-1	2-0	0-3	3-0	2-1	2-0	1-1	1-0	1-2	2-0	1-2	0-3	3-0	3-1	4-2	1-1	1-1	2-1	0-1	2-1	0-0
Bideford	0-0		4-1	0-0	3-0	4-1	5-0	1-1	2-0	0-1	0-1	0-2	5-0	4-0	2-1	7-2	1-0	2-0	7-0	1-0	4-0	2-0
Bristol City	0-1	2-1		0-2	4-1	1-2	4-0	1-1	2-2	0-3	4-1	1-2	3-3	1-4	3-0	4-2	3-2	1-4	5-0	0-5	6-0	1-1
Bristol Manor Farm	4-1	1-3	1-3		3-1	2-2	1-1	0-2	0-2	1-3	1-1	2-0	1-2	4-2	1-1	4-1	2-5	1-2	4-1	2-0	1-0	3-1
Chard Town	2-1	0-2	0-6	1-1		0-2	2-1	2-0	0-2	0-6	0-4	0-6	0-3	1-1	1-3	1-1	1-4	1-4	2-1	0-3	2-1	3-2
Chippenham Town	3-0	1-0	1-0	1-0	4-0		2-1	2-1	1-0	1-1	0-0	0-1	3-2	1-1	1-1	4-1	1-1	1-3	2-0	1-2	1-1	2-0
Clandown	1-0	1-1	0-0	2-1	1-0	2-1		2-0	3-2	1-2	0-3	1-0	0-1	0-1	1-2	2-1	3-1	0-0	4-0	2-3	0-1	3-3
Clevedon Town	4-1	1-1	0-2	1-2	4-0	2-2	0-1		2-2	1-4	0-0	3-2	0-1	1-0	0-0	2-1	0-0	1-1	6-0	0-0	0-1	4-1
Dawlish Town	2-0	0-3	1-0	1-0	2-1	2-1	2-1	1-0		0-1	4-0	1-4	0-0	2-2	0-1	4-0	3-1	1-0	0-1	0-1	3-1	2-1
Exmouth Town	1-0	0-0	2-0	8-1	2-0	4-1	2-0	0-0	2-0		1-1	1-3	5-0	1-1	1-1	2-1	4-0	4-3	2-1	4-0	2-1	6-1
Frome Town	4-1	1-1	0-1	3-2	4-1	0-2	0-3	1-1	2-0	1-3		0-3	2-2	0-3	2-0	0-0	1-0	1-0	2-1	1-1	2-0	4-1
Liskeard Athletic	4-1	0-3	3-1	1-0	2-0	3-0	4-0	3-2	6-0	1-1	2-1		3-1	4-0	2-0	2-1	3-0	3-1	0-0	2-0	1-1	5-0
Mangotsfield United	0-0	2-4	1-3	3-2	5-1	0-1	0-1	1-2	2-0	3-0	2-0	3-3		5-0	4-0	3-1	1-1	3-3	2-0	1-2	1-1	5-0
Melksham Town	1-1	0-4	0-2	1-4	3-2	2-0	0-0	2-2	0-2	0-1	2-0	1-1	1-1		2-0	0-0	4-2	0-2	0-0	1-1	0-1	0-2
Minehead	4-3	0-3	1-0	1-1	1-2	1-5	1-0	3-3	0-1	2-2	2-0	1-2	0-0	1-2		2-1	2-0	1-5	3-0	1-0	2-0	2-2
Paulton Rovers	1-0	0-1	1-0	2-3	1-0	0-0	2-0	0-0	0-0	0-2	6-0	0-2	1-1	2-1	2-5		1-1	0-1	4-1	1-1	1-1	1-1
Plymouth A	5-0	2-1	0-1	4-2	2-2	0-0	0-1	0-1	1-2	0-1	7-1	0-6	1-2	0-1	0-1	8-0		1-1	0-0	0-2	2-0	1-0
Saltash United	3-0	0-4	2-0	3-0	1-2	1-1	2-1	0-0	1-1	1-0	1-1	0-2	2-3	5-3	2-1	7-0	1-1		0-0	2-0	3-0	1-1
Shepton Mallet	1-4	3-2	0-4	2-4	1-2	1-2	1-3	0-2	0-0	1-2	0-0	2-5	0-6	6-4	0-1	0-4	1-1	0-2		3-1	1-1	1-2
Taunton Town	2-1	1-1	0-0	3-1	3-1	0-1	2-2	3-0	0-3	1-2	0-3	1-2	2-2	1-1	2-1	2-1	2-1	2-4	5-2		1-0	1-0
Torrington	1-0	2-3	4-1	1-1	3-0	2-1	1-0	1-1	1-1	1-1	2-1	1-1	2-1	1-2	1-2	2-2	4-2	0-0	3-2	0-1		1-3
Weston Super Mare	4-0	0-4	1-3	1-2	3-0	0-1	1-1	1-3	4-1	0-3	0-0	2-0	2-6	6-1	8-2	1-2	3-2	1-3	5-1	3-1	1-6	

Exmouth Town: *Back Row: (L-R) Peter Amos, Jerry Sharland, Mark Gennard, Tony Stuart, Mike Lawson, Mike Barrett, Graham Weeks, Jeff Weeks, Paul Gidley, Steve Hynds, Keith Sprague, Lionel Thomas, Lenny Jones, Alan Hooker, Robbie Hook, Bill Potter. Front Row: (L-R) Ian Hill, Bob Davis, Wally Maggs, Ray Clements, Rod Webber, Geoff Morris, Tony White, Mike Blackstone, Paul Dixon, Mel Pym.*

WESTERN LEAGUE FIRST DIVISION 1985-86

	Blackwell United	Bath City	Devizes Town	Elmore	Glastonbury	Heavitree United	Ilfracombe Town	Keynsham Town	Larkhall Athletic	Odd Down	Ottery St Mary	Portway Bristol	Radstock Town	Swanage & H	Tiverton Town	Warminster Town	Wellington Town	Welton Rovers	Westbury United	Weymouth	Wimbourne	Yeovil Town
Backwell United		0-1	2-0	2-0	1-1	5-1	2-0	1-2	2-1	2-0	3-0	2-1	0-3	2-1	1-1	2-0	3-2	2-0	3-0	3-0	0-1	0-1
Bath City	1-1		6-0	4-0	2-2	1-1	2-2	2-0	0-1	1-1	0-1	1-1	1-1	4-1	1-2	4-2	4-0	3-0	3-1	1-0	1-5	1-1
Devizes Town	1-1	1-0		0-0	1-2	1-1	1-1	0-3	2-2	0-2	0-1	1-1	1-1	2-1	4-2	2-2	2-3	0-0	3-1	1-0	1-0	0-2
Elmore	1-0	2-1	1-1		2-2	1-0	1-1	2-0	1-5	5-1	6-0	1-2	2-5	2-2	1-0	1-1	4-2	1-3	2-2	2-1	1-1	3-2
Glastonbury	0-2	1-3	0-2	4-1		2-1	1-1	1-2	2-0	1-1	0-2	2-7	0-2	2-3	3-3	1-0	1-0	1-0	1-0	2-2	2-0	1-2
Heavitree United	2-0	1-5	2-2	5-0	4-1		2-1	1-1	1-0	2-1	2-2	0-3	2-6	0-2	2-0	3-0	1-3	2-2	0-3	1-1	0-4	1-0
Ilfracombe Town	0-0	1-1	1-1	0-1	1-0	0-3		3-1	0-0	2-1	5-1	2-2	2-2	2-2	1-2	5-2	2-4	2-0	2-0	2-1	0-2	1-1
Keynsham Town	0-0	0-2	0-0	1-1	2-1	2-1	2-0		0-3	2-0	0-0	1-4	0-2	0-4	1-1	3-1	0-0	0-0	3-1	0-1	1-1	0-1
Larkhall Athletic	0-0	2-1	0-0	0-0	1-1	1-2	1-4	0-0		1-0	3-0	1-1	1-6	0-1	3-2	8-0	0-0	2-1	4-0	3-5	4-1	2-1
Odd Down	0-1	3-3	2-0	3-0	1-1	0-0	1-0	4-1	1-1		0-0	3-5	1-4	2-2	3-0	1-0	1-5	1-4	2-2	4-4	4-1	0-2
Ottery St Mary	3-1	4-0	0-1	1-5	1-1	0-1	2-0	1-0	2-1	3-1		2-3	2-0	3-0	2-2	3-0	2-1	5-1	1-1	2-2	0-0	1-0
Portway Bristol	4-2	0-2	4-0	2-1	4-0	0-1	0-0	2-1	1-4	2-1	3-1		0-1	4-1	6-3	7-0	4-0	0-2	2-1	4-1	0-0	1-1
Radstock Town	0-5	7-2	2-2	5-1	3-1	3-2	6-0	5-3	4-1	6-1	2-2	0-1		2-1	2-1	2-0	3-2	4-0	3-3	2-0	2-2	0-2
Swanage & H	0-1	3-2	0-3	6-2	5-0	0-1	2-1	3-1	2-1	8-2	5-1	3-2	1-1		3-1	1-3	2-2	3-1	3-1	1-1	1-0	1-1
Tiverton Town	3-1	2-0	3-2	0-0	2-2	1-2	1-0	0-1	0-1	3-0	0-2	0-2	0-3	1-2		3-0	3-0	3-1	5-1	2-3	1-5	2-1
Warminster Town	0-3	1-0	1-0	1-0	1-2	4-0	1-3	0-0	2-3	2-2	0-1	0-2	2-1	2-3	0-1		1-1	1-1	1-0	1-0	1-4	0-4
Wellington Town	3-2	1-2	2-2	2-0	0-2	2-2	2-1	1-1	0-4	3-0	1-1	0-1	0-2	4-0	4-1	1-0		2-1	5-0	3-3	1-1	1-0
Welton Rovers	1-1	4-1	1-2	3-1	3-2	0-3	4-3	1-1	0-1	3-0	0-2	0-5	1-1	8-5	1-2	0-1	2-2		1-4	1-5	3-2	0-0
Westbury United	1-2	4-1	2-2	2-0	2-0	0-1	2-1	0-0	3-4	2-2	2-2	0-1	0-5	3-1	1-3	3-2	2-1	1-3		0-1	1-0	2-0
Weymouth	3-1	4-1	2-1	4-0	1-2	5-2	3-0	1-0	3-0	2-3	1-4	1-2	0-5	4-3	1-3	4-2	4-2	3-1	3-0		3-0	0-2
Wimborne	1-0	3-0	3-0	3-0	3-0	1-1	4-0	2-2	2-2	2-1	2-0	1-1	2-3	2-2	0-3	5-2	1-1	3-1	2-0	5-1		0-0
Yeovil Town	6-3	2-3	2-0	0-0	5-1	3-0	2-2	0-0	2-0	2-0	3-0	0-4	3-0	2-1	2-0	2-0	1-0	1-2	4-1	4-0	3-1	

Bath City Reserves win (2-0) at Portway Bristol Photo: Mike Brown

Gospel Borough on this attack against Bristol Manor Farms Photo: Eric Marsh

BARNSTAPLE TOWN

President: J. Symons
Chairman: V. Hamilton-Philip
Manager: David Baglow
Secretary: Alan Sampson
Address & Tel. No. 10 Harman Walk, Barnstaple, Devon EX32 8AL. 0271 77818
Address and Tel. No. of ground: Mill Road, Barnstaple. 0271 43469
Simple ground directions: Follow A361 Ilfracombe signs, turn left after Rolle Quay

No. of seats: 400 **Covered accommodation:** 1,000 **Capacity:** 5,000
Year formed: 1895 **Nickname:** Barum **Floodlights:** 1986
Club colours: Red/black/red **Change colours:** All white
Day for midweek home matches: Wednesday **Club metal badges:**
Previous Leagues: North Devon, Exeter, Plymouth, South Western
Clubhouse details: Open weekday evenings, Saturday midday and evenings
Past players who progressed into the Football League: F.L Scott, P. Ewings, L. Pickard, B. Vassallo, I. Doyle, J. Neale
Programme details: 28 pages, 20p **Programme editor:** A. Sampson
Local newspapers & Tel. No. North Devon Journal Herald
Major Honours: Western League Champions, Western League Merit Cup, Devon Professional Cup, Devon League Champions

BIDEFORD

President: Ernie Hopkins
Chairman: Michael Evans
Manager: Keith Bowker
Secretary: John Wenham
Address & Tel. No. 48 Broadlands, Bideford, Devon EX39 4QL. 02372 77269
Address and Tel. No. of ground: Sports Ground, Kingsley Road, Bideford. 02372 74974
Simple ground directions: On entering town follow signs towards Westward Ho and Northam, ground ½ mile on left

No. of seats: 300 **Covered accommodation:** 3,000 **Capacity:** 6,000
Year formed: 1946 **Nickname:** Robins **Floodlights:** Yes
Club colours: All red **Change colours:** All blue
Day for midweek home matches: Wednesday **Club metal badges:**
Previous Leagues: Southern League
Clubhouse details: Open lunch times and evenings
Past players who progressed into the Football League: P. Griffiths

Programme details: 20 pages, 20p **Programme editor:** P. Day
Local newspapers & Tel. No. Bideford Gazette, North Devon Journal
Major Honours: Western League, Devon Cup, Western League Cup, Western League Merit Cup, F.A. Cup first round proper

BRISTOL CITY RESERVES

President:
Chairman: D.J. Williams
Manager: Terry Cooper
Secretary: Miss Jean Harrison
Address & Tel. No. Bistol City F.C., Ashton Gate, Bristol BS3 2EJ. 0272 622929
Address and Tel. No. of ground: Ashton Gate, Bristol. 0272 632812
Simple ground directions: City Centre, Hotwell Road-Cumberland Basin (A370), left into Winterstoke Road

No. of seats: 7,500 **Covered accommodation:** 16,000 **Capacity:** 30,000
Year formed: 1894 **Nickname:** Robins **Floodlights:** Yes
Club colours: Red/white **Change colours:** Sky blue
Day for midweek home matches: Tuesday **Club metal badges:**
Previous Leagues: Football Combination
Clubhouse details: Supporters Club/Kickers Club
Past players who progressed into the Football League:

Programme details: Team sheet, 5p **Programme editor:** J. Cox
Local newspapers & Tel. No. Bristol Evening Post, Western Daily Press
Major Honours: Western League

BRISTOL MANOR FARM

President: Colin Howlett
Chairman: Alex Thomas
Manager: Mike Fisher
Secretary: Iain Anderson
Address & Tel. No. 182 Forest Road, Kingswood, Bristol BS15 2EN. 0272 616426
Address and Tel. No. of ground: The Creek, Portway, Sea Mills, Bristol. 0272 683571
Simple ground directions: Leave motorway at Junction 18 (Avonmouth Bridge) signs for Bristol at first roundabout leads into Portway
No. of seats: None **Covered accommodation:** 150 **Capacity:** 2,500
Year formed: 1964 **Nickname:** The Farm **Floodlights:** Yes
Club colours: Red/black/white **Change colours:** White
Day for midweek home matches: Tuesday **Club metal badges:**
Previous Leagues: Somerset Senior League
Clubhouse details: Lounge bar, entertainments, skittle alley, bar meals Thursday-Saturday. Open every evening, open lunch time Saturday and Sunday
Past players who progressed into the Football League:
Programme details: 20 pages with admission **Programme editor:** Alex Thomas
Local newspapers & Tel. No. Bristol Evening Post, Western Daily Press
Major Honours: Somerset Senior League Div 2, League Cup, Somerset Senior League Div 1, Western League Div 1

CHARD TOWN

President: F. Wilson
Chairman: B.D. Beer
Manager: Ray Pratt
Secretary: Colin Dunford
Address & Tel. No. c/o Sherton Mill Feeds, East Farm, Bradford Abbas, Sherborne, Dorset DT9 6JN. 0935 23165
Address and Tel. No. of ground: Dening Sports Field, Zembard Lane, Chard. 0460 61402
Simple ground directions: 150 yards from town centre
No. of seats: None **Covered accommodation:** 200 **Capacity:** 2,000
Year formed: 1920 **Nickname:** Robins **Floodlights:** Yes
Club colours: White/maroon **Change colours:** Maroon/sky blue
Day for midweek home matches: Tuesday **Club metal badges:**
Previous Leagues: Perry Street, Somerset Senior
Clubhouse details: Open every night except Sunday. 12-2 on match days, usual hot meals service
Past players who progressed into the Football League: M. Thresher

Programme details: 16 pages, 15p **Programme editor:** Commercial Dept.
Local newspapers & Tel. No. Pullmans Weekly News, Chard and Ilminster News
Major Honours: Western League Runners-up, Somerset Senior League, Somerset Cup

CHIPPENHAM TOWN

President: John Northover
Chairman: D.S. Webb
Manager: K.J. Owens
Secretary: Arthur Wimble
Address & Tel. No. 31 Southmead, Chippenham, Wilts SN14 ORT. 0249 655461
Address and Tel. No. of ground: Hardenhuish Park, Bristol Road, Chippenham. 0249 650400
Simple ground directions: 5 minutes walk from railway station on main A420 Bristol Road

No. of seats: 100 **Covered accommodation:** 300 **Capacity:** 4,000
Year formed: 1873 **Nickname:** Bluebirds **Floodlights:** Yes
Club colours: Royal blue **Change colours:** White
Day for midweek home matches: Wednesday **Club metal badges:**
Previous Leagues: Hellenic, Wiltshire Senior, Wiltshire Premier
Clubhouse details: On ground above Stand, with bar, skittles etc.
Past players who progressed into the Football League:
Programme details: 16 pages, 10p **Programme editor:**
Local newspapers & Tel. No. Chippenham News, Wiltshire Gazette
Major Honours: F.A. Cup 1st Rd proper, Western League Div 1 and 2, Wiltshire Shield, Wiltshire Senior Cup, Wiltshire Senior League

CLANDOWN

President: L. Ricketts
Chairman: T. Gillard
Manager: A. Pensford
Secretary: John E. Pool
Address & Tel. No. 111 Charlton Park, Midsomer Norton, Avon BA3 4BP. 0761 415190
Address and Tel. No. of ground: Thyne Field, Clandown. Radstock 34274
Simple ground directions: Leave Bath on A367, follow signs to Radstock, turn right into Clandown village, ground 500 yards on top of hill
No. of seats: 150 **Covered accommodation:** 150 **Capacity:** 2,000
Year formed: 1875 **Nickname:** The Dons **Floodlights:** Yes
Club colours: Black/white stripes **Change colours:** Light blue
Day for midweek home matches: Tuesday **Club metal badges:**
Previous Leagues: Wiltshire Premier, Somerset Senior
Clubhouse details: Full social facilities, skittles, function room
Past players who progressed into the Football League: None

Programme details: 24 pages, 10p **Programme editor:** C. Herrow
Local newspapers & Tel. No. Western Daily Press, Bristol Evening Post, Somerset Guardian
Major Honours: Senior Cup, Western League Div 1 and Runners-up

CLEVEDON TOWN

President: D. Hand
Chairman: B. Baker
Manager: To be appointed
Secretary: Tom Oliver
Address & Tel. No. 24 Metherways, Yeo Park, Clevedon, Avon BS21 7YU. 0272 871617
Address and Tel. No. of ground: Teignmouth Road, Clevedon. 0272 871636
Simple ground directions: 2 minutes from M5 motorway, junction 20

No. of seats: 24 **Covered accommodation:** 800 **Capacity:** 2,500
Year formed: 1880 **Nickname:** Seasiders **Floodlights:** Yes
Club colours: White shirts, green collars and cuffs **Change colours:** Tangerine
Day for midweek home matches: Tuesday **Club metal badges:**
Previous Leagues: Somerset Senior, Bristol Charity
Clubhouse details: Open every midday and evening, separate skittle alley on ground
Past players who progressed into the Football League: None

Programme details: 20 pages, 20p **Programme editor:** Nick Ball
Local newspapers & Tel. No. South Avon Mercury
Major Honours: F.A. 1st Rd proper, F.A. Amateur Cup 3rd Rd., Bristol Charity League

DAWLISH TOWN

President: M. Swift
Chairman: R. Webster
Manager: A. Chown
Secretary: Gerry R. Turner
Address & Tel. No. 43 Exeter Road, Dawlish, Devon EX7 OAB. 0626 862438
Address and Tel. No. of ground: Playing fields, Exeter Road, Dawlish. 0626 863110
Simple ground directions: Approx. 1 mile from the centre of town, off main Exeter Road (A379)

No. of seats: 200 **Covered accommodation:** 200 **Capacity:** 2,000
Year formed: 1889 **Nickname:** Seasiders **Floodlights:** 1986
Club colours: Green/white **Change colours:** Blue
Day for midweek home matches: Tuesday **Club metal badges:**
Previous Leagues: Devon and Exeter
Clubhouse details: Open every night. Situated in car park opposite ground
Past players who progressed into the Football League: S. Harrower

Programme details: 16 pages, 10p **Programme editor:** R. Bolt
Local newspapers & Tel. No. Express and Echo, Dawlish Gazette
Major Honours: Western League Challenge Cup, Devon Premier Cup

EXMOUTH TOWN

President: David Scott
Chairman: Rod Webber
Manager: Bob Davis
Secretary: Geoff Morris
Address & Tel. No. 34 Salterton Road, Exmouth, Devon EX8 2EF. 0395 272141
Address and Tel. No. of ground: Southern Road, Exmouth. 0395 263348
Simple ground directions: On right side of main Exeter to Exmouth Road (town bypass)

No. of seats: 150 **Covered accommodation:** 300 **Capacity:** 2,500
Year formed: 1933 **Nickname:** Town **Floodlights:** Yes
Club colours: Blue and white **Change colours:** Red/black
Day for midweek home matches: Wednesday **Club metal badges:**
Previous Leagues: Devon and Exeter
Clubhouse details: Skittles, darts, pool, open every night
Past players who progressed into the Football League: G. Lear

Programme details: 40 pages, free with admission **Programme editor:** Mike Blackstone
Local newspapers & Tel. No. Exmouth Journal, Exmouth Herald, Express and Echo
Major Honours: Devon County Cup, Western League, F.A. Vase semi-final

FROME TOWN

President: E.G. Berry
Chairman: E.G. Berry
Manager: To be appointed
Secretary: Peter M. Bishop
Address & Tel. No. 10 Stevens Lane, Frome, Somerset BA11 4AY. 0373 61794
Address and Tel. No. of ground: Badgers Hill, Berkeley Road, Frome. 0373 64087
Simple ground directions: Locate Vine Tree Inn (Bath Road), ground 100 yards from Inn

No. of seats: 250 **Covered accommodation:** 800 **Capacity:** 5,000
Year formed: 1904 **Nickname:** Robins **Floodlights:** Yes
Club colours: Red **Change colours:** Yellow
Day for midweek home matches: Wednesday **Club metal badges:**
Previous Leagues: Wiltshire Premier
Clubhouse details: Modern Ballroom holds 400. Open everyday, two skittle alleys, 3 bars
Past players who progressed into the Football League: P. Randall, G. Smith, D. Wiffil
Programme details: 12 pages, 15p **Programme editors:** P.M. Bishop & S. Pearce
Local newspapers & Tel. No. Western Daily Press
Major Honours: Western League, Alan Young Cup, Western League Cup, Somerset Professional Cup, Wilts Premier League, Western League Subsidiary Cup, Western Counties Floodlight Cup

LISKEARD ATHLETIC

President: E.K. Brown
Chairman: A. Wilton
Manager: B. Hodge
Secretary: Albert James
Address & Tel. No. 59 Higher Lux Street, Liskeard, Cornwall PL14 3JY. 0579 43862
Address and Tel. No. of ground: Lux Park, Liskeard. 0579 42665
Simple ground directions: Take Tavistock Road (A390) from town centre, after ½ mile turn left on St Cleer Road, and the ground is 200 yards on left
No. of seats: 200 **Covered accommodation:** 750 **Capacity:** 3,500
Year formed: 1889 **Nickname:** The Blues **Floodlights:** Yes
Club colours: Blue/white **Change colours:** White/blue/white
Day for midweek home matches: Tuesday **Club metal badges:**
Previous Leagues: East Cornwall, Plymouth and District, South Western
Clubhouse details: Dancing, food. Open everyday
Past players who progressed into the Football League: B. Swiggs
Programme details: 16 pages, 10p **Programme editor:** E.K. Brown
Local newspapers & Tel. No. The Cornish Times
Major Honours: South Western League, Charity Cup, South Western League Cup, Pratten Cup, Western League Merit Cup, Cornwall Senior Cup

Liskeard Athletic keeper Steve Note saves bravely from Bristol Manor Farm's Paul Williams but was unable to prevent the home side winning (2-0) Photo: Mike Brown

Mark John scores Bristol Manor Farms' last goal in their (4-1) home victory over Shepton Mallet Town. Photo: Mike Brown

MANGOTSFIELD UNITED

President: A.H. Hill
Chairman: B. Tilling
Manager: R. Miller
Secretary: Paul Britton
Address & Tel. No. 41 South Road, Kingswood, Bristol BS15 2JL. 0272 676229
Address and Tel. No. of ground: Cosham Street, Mangotsfield. 0272 560119
Simple ground directions: From M32 through Downend to Mangotsfield. From M4 follow A4174 to Mangotsfield, turn left by village church, ground on right
No. of seats: 200 **Covered accommodation:** 1,000 **Capacity:** 2,500
Year formed: 1950 **Nickname:** The Field **Floodlights:** Yes
Club colours: Sky blue/claret pinstripe **Change colours:** White/claret
Day for midweek home matches: Wednesday **Club metal badges:**
Previous Leagues: Bristol and District, Avon Combination
Clubhouse details: Large function room with separate lounge and kitchen facilities. Lounge bar for official functions etc
Past players who progressed into the Football League: G. Megson, S. White, C. Prentice, P. Purnell
Programme details: 24 pages, 20p **Programme editor:** Barry Tilling
Local newspapers & Tel. No. Bristol Evening Post, Western Daily Press
Major Honours: Gloucester Senior Cup, Avon Combination Winners, Hungerford Cup Winners

MELKSHAM TOWN

President: L.A.W. Crook
Chairman: H.J. Goodenough
Manager: M. Gingell
Secretary: Mike J. Perrin
Address & Tel. No. 26 Carisbrooke Road, Melksham, Wilts SN12 6BS. 0225 704523
Address and Tel. No. of ground: The Conigre, Melksham. 0225 702843
Simple ground directions: Turn into car park in the town marketplace, then left into Melksham House grounds, proceed up drive, ground is on left
No. of seats: 500 **Covered accommodation:** 1,500 **Capacity:** 3,000
Year formed: 1876 **Nickname:** Town **Floodlights:** 1986
Club colours: Gold/black **Change colours:** Blue/white/blue
Day for midweek home matches: Tuesday **Club metal badges:**
Previous Leagues: Wiltshire County
Clubhouse details: Open every night of week and Saturday and Sunday lunchtimes
Past players who progressed into the Football League: A. Stephens, S. Panes
Programme details: 28 pages, 10p **Programme editor:** Dave Phillips
Local newspapers & Tel. No. Wiltshire Times, Bath Evening News
Major Honours: Wiltshire League, Wiltshire Senior Cup, Wiltshire Professional Shield, Western League Div 1, Wiltshire Subsidiary Cup, Wiltshire Combination

MINEHEAD

President: A.C. Copp
Chairman: N. Elston
Manager: Harry Thomas
Secretary: T.M. Smith
Address & Tel. No. 4 Mocin T, Royal Weirfield Road, Minehead 5QF 8EF. 0643 3698
Address and Tel. No. of ground: The Recreation Ground, Irnham Road, Minehead. 0643 4989
Simple ground directions: Follow Town Road, look for signs Coach Park/Car Park pointing to left, this will lead you into car park at the entrance to the ground
No. of seats: 250 **Covered accommodation:** 700 **Capacity:** 3,500
Year formed: 1889 **Nickname:** The Blues **Floodlights:** Yes
Club colours: Blue **Change colours:** Yellow
Day for midweek home matches: Wednesday **Club metal badges:**
Previous Leagues: Somerset Senior, Southern League
Clubhouse details: Open everyday, skittle, bingo, darts, pool, discos on Fridays, dances on Saturday
Past players who progressed into the Football League:
Programme details: 20 pages, 10p **Programme editor:** Secretary
Local newspapers & Tel. No. West Somerset Free Press, County Gazette
Major Honours: South League Div 1 (South), Southern League Premier, Southern League Merit, Somerset Professional Cup, Western Counties Floodlight Cup

PAULTON ROVERS

President: R. Carter
Chairman: F.B. Lewis
Manager: Kim Book
Secretary: Keith Simmons
Address & Tel. No. 1 Underhill Lane, Midsomer Norton, Avon BA3 2RT. 0761 418030
Address and Tel. No. of ground: Athletic Field, Winterfield Road, Paulton. 0761 412907
Simple ground directions: From Bristol approx. 15 miles south towards Wells. From Bath via Radstock and Midsomer Norton, approx. 10 miles south towards Wells into Village, hospitals on both sides. Ground ¼ mile down road on right
No. of seats: None **Covered accommodation:** 200 **Capacity:** 4,000
Year formed: 1881 **Nickname:** Rovers **Floodlights:** Yes
Club colours: Maroon/white **Change colours:** Yellow with red trim
Day for midweek home matches: Tuesday **Club metal badges:**
Previous Leagues: Somerset Senior
Clubhouse details: Bar, lounge, skittle alley. Dance hall for 400
Past players who progressed into the Football League:

Programme details: 16 pages, with admission **Programme editor:** Secretary
Local newspapers & Tel. No. Bath Evening Chronicle, Bristol Evening Post, Western Daily Press
Major Honours: Somerset Senior Cup, Somerset Senior League

PLYMOUTH ARGYLE RESERVES

President: G.H. Gillan
Chairman: S.W. Dawe
Manager: Dave B.Smith
Secretary: Graham Little
Address & Tel. No. Plymouth Argyle F.C., Home Park, Plymouth, Devon PL2 3DQ. 0752 702951
Address and Tel. No. of ground: Home Park, Plymouth. 0752 52561/2/3
Simple ground directions: From city centre to railway station, ground at top of hill behind station

No. of seats: 4,000 **Covered accommodation:** 20,000 **Capacity:** 35,000
Year formed: 1886 **Nickname:** Pilgrims **Floodlights:** Yes
Club colours: Green/black/white **Change colours:** Yellow
Day for midweek home matches: Tuesday **Club metal badges:**
Previous Leagues: Plymouth and District
Clubhouse details: V.P. Club
Past players who progressed into the Football League:

Programme details: Team sheet, 5p **Programme editor:** Secretary
Local newspapers & Tel. No. Western Morning News, Western Evening Herald
Major Honours: Western League

RADSTOCK TOWN

President:
Chairman: L. Salter
Manager: S. Gay
Secretary: James Mitchard
Address & Tel. No. 6 Lime Terrace, Radstock, Avon BA3 3TF. 0761 35097
Address and Tel. No. of ground: Southfields, Frome Hill, Radstock. 0761 35004
Simple ground directions: A362 from A39 Glastonbury & M5 junction 23, enter Radstock along Sommerville Road, junction with A367 from Bath, turn into Frome Road A362, approx. 1 mile turn right before Frome Inn to ground
No. of seats: 150 **Covered accommodation:** 150 **Capacity:** 2,000
Year formed: 1895 **Nickname:** Town or Reds **Floodlights:** Yes
Club colours: Red/black stripes **Change colours:** Blue
Day for midweek home matches: Wednesday **Club metal badges:**
Previous Leagues: Somerset Senior League, Wiltshire County
Clubhouse details: 2 bars, skittle alley and darts
Past players who progressed into the Football League:

Programme details: 20 pages, 10p **Programme editor:** Secretary
Local newspapers & Tel. No. Western Daily Press, Bristol Evening Post, Somerset Guardian
Major Honours: Somerset Senior League, Wiltshire County

SALTASH UNITED

President: P. Skinnard
Chairman: M. Howard
Manager: Peter Darke
Secretary: Julian Chenery
Address & Tel. No: 28 Home Park Road, Saltash, Cornwall PL12 6BH. 07555 3959
Address and Tel. No. of ground: Kimberley Stadium, Callington Road, Satlash. 07555 5746
Simple ground directions: Via Tamar Bridge. Along main street approx. ½ mile from town centre

No. of seats: 250 **Covered accommodation:** 250 **Capacity:** 3,000
Year formed: 1947 **Nickname:** Ashes **Floodlights:** Yes
Club colours: Red/white stripes **Change colours:** Blue/white stripes
Day for midweek home matches: Wednesday **Club metal badges:**
Previous Leagues: East Cornwall, South Western
Clubhouse details: Club attached to Stand. Caters for dancing and club activities
Past players who progressed into the Football League: None

Programme details: 16 pages, 20p **Programme editor:** J. Chennery
Local newspapers & Tel. No. Western Evening Herald, The Cornish Times
Major Honours: Western League, South Western League, South Western League Cup

TAUNTON TOWN

President: Rt. Hon. Edward Du Cann
Chairman: T.F. Harris
Manager: Sammy Kingdom
Secretary: Mrs Joan Ellis
Address & Tel. No Taunton Town F.C., Wordsworth Drive, Taunton, Somerset TA1 2HG. 0823 412423
Address and Tel. No. of ground: Wordsworth Drive, Taunton. 0823 78191
Simple ground directions: Leave M5 junction 24, ground ½ mile from junction on main road leading to town centre

No. of seats: 250 **Covered accommodation:** 1,000 **Capacity:** 4,000
Year formed: 1947 **Nickname:** The Peacocks **Floodlights:** Yes
Club colours: Sky blue/claret, claret shorts **Change colours:** Yellow/blue
Day for midweek home matches: Monday **Club metal badges:**
Previous Leagues: Southern, Somerset Senior League
Clubhouse details: Social club to accommodate 300, full bar facilities, separate bar and hall for private functions
Past players who progressed into the Football League: C. Rutter, S. Brace, P. Rogers, J. Sherwood
Programme details: 28 pages, 20p **Programme editor:** Secretary
Local newspapers & Tel. No. Somerset County Gazette, Western Daily Press
Major Honours: Western League, Alan Young Cup, Charity Challenge Cup, Somerset Senior League, Somerset Premier Cup finalist

TORRINGTON

President: C. Quick
Chairman: C. Slade
Manager: John Hore
Secretary: Keith Franks
Address & Tel. No. 10 Potacre Street, Great Torrington, Devon EX38 7BH. 0805 23952
Address and Tel. No. of ground: Vicarage Field, School Lane, Great Torrington. 0805 22853
Simple ground directions: Town centre by church

No. of seats: None
Covered accommodation: 2,000
Capacity: 4,000
Year formed: 1908
Nickname: Super Greens
Floodlights: No
Club colours: Green/white
Change colours: Blue/black/white
Day for midweek home matches: Wednesday
Club metal badges:
Previous Leagues: South Western, North Devon, Devon and Exeter
Clubhouse details: 2 bars, committee room, kitchen
Past players who progressed into the Football League:

Programme details: 16 pages, 20p
Programme editor: Bob Dymond
Local newspapers & Tel. No. North Devon Journal, Bideford Gazette
Major Honours: South Western League, Devon Cup

WESTON SUPER MARE

President: D. Usher
Chairman: K. Refault
Manager: Harry Thomas
Secretary: Brian White
Address & Tel. No. 100 Walliscote Road, Weston Super Mare BS23 1EF. 0934 31974
Address and Tel. No. of ground: Woodspring Park, Winterstoke Road, Weston Super Mare. 0934 21618
Simple ground directions: From M5 southbound, 1st set of traffic lights, turn left, proceed half a mile. From M5 northbound proceed along Bristol route, over 1st bridge, last turning on roundabout, proceed ¼ mile
No. of seats: None
Covered accommodation: 400
Capacity: 4,000
Year formed: 1948
Nickname: Seasiders
Floodlights: None
Club colours: Royal blue
Change colours: Red/black/red
Day for midweek home matches: Tuesday
Club metal badges:
Previous Leagues: None
Clubhouse details: Open every night, social activities, refreshments, 2 skittle alleys, 3 bars
Past players who progressed into the Football League: I. Maine, J. Palmer

Programme details: 16 pages, 20p
Programme editor: W. Hill
Local newspapers & Tel. No. Bristol Evening Post, Western Daily Press
Major Honours: League K.O. Cup, Somerset Senior Cup, Western League Cup, Merit Cup

Farewell to Shepton Mallet Town who have now left the Western League. Photo: Leo Hoenig

BACKWELL UNITED

President: C. W. Jones
Chairman: J. Walmsley
Manager: J. Southern
Secretary: William G. Coggins,
Address & Tel. no: 027583 3424
Address and Tel. No. of ground: Recreation Ground, Backwell, Avon. 027583 2612
Simple ground directions: A370 Bristol to Weston Super Mare, 8 miles on right
No. of seats: None **Covered accommodation:** 150 **Capacity:** 1,000
Year formed: 1911 **Nickname:** Reds **Floodlights:** None
Club colours: All red **Change colours:** All sky blue
Day for midweek matches: Tuesday **Previous Leagues:** Bristol Leagues, Somerset Senior
Senior Honours: Somerset Senior Champions, Somerset Challenge and League Cup Winners

CALNE TOWN

President: Local Council Mayor on election each year
Chairman:
Manager:
Secretary: A.J. Brewer
Address & Tel. No: 9 Fitzmuarice Square, Calne SN11 8NL. 0249 815744
Address and Tel. No. of ground: Lickhill Road, North End, Calne. 0249 816716
Simple ground directions: From centre of town take Swindon Road
No. of seats: None **Covered accommodation:** 200 **Capacity:** 2,000
Year formed: **Nickname:** **Floodlights:** None
Club colours: Black/white pin stripes **Change colours:** Red/black
Day for midweek matches: Wednesday **Previous Leagues:** Wiltshire County
Senior Honours: Wiltshire Senior Ghia Cup, Wiltshire Senior Cup, Wiltshire Div 2 Cup

DEVIZES TOWN

President:
Chairman: B. Collins
Manager: A. Stevens
Secretary: Derek Neale
Address & Tel. No: 0380 71472
Address and Tel. No. of Ground: Nursteed Road, Devizes. 0380 2817
Simple ground directions: On entering Devizes turn into Sidmouth Road, then right into Nursteed Road. Ground on right
No. of seats: 370 **Covered accommodation:** 400 **Capacity:** 2,500
Year formed: 1883 **Nickname:** Town **Floodlights:** None
Club colours: Red/white stripes, black shorts **Change colours:** All blue
Day for midweek matches: Wednesday **Previous Leagues:** Wiltshire Combination, Wiltshire Premier
Senior Honours: Western League

ELMORE

President: Bill Jones
Chairman: L.M.V. Jones
Manager: M. Howe
Secretary: M.A. Howe
Address & Tel. No: 0884 254268
Address and Tel. No. of Ground: Horsdon Park, Tiverton. 0884 252341
Simple ground directions: Leave M5 at Junction 27, A373 to Tiverton
No. of seats: 150 **Covered accommodation:** 150 **Capacity:** 1,000
Year formed: 1947 **Nickname:** Eagles **Floodlights:** None
Club colours: All green **Change colours:** Red/black
Day for midweek matches: Wednesday **Previous Leagues:** Exeter and District, Devon and Exeter, South Western
Senior Honours: Devon Senior Cup, East Devon Senior Cup

GLASTONBURY

President:
Chairman: R. Wilcox
Manager: S. Dovey
Secretary: Leslie Heal
Address & Tel. No: 0458 32037
Address and Tel. No. of Ground: Abbey Moor Stadium, Godney Rd., Glastonbury. 0458 31460
Simple ground directions: From marketplace take Northland St., turn right (first) over railway bridge
No. of seats: None **Covered accommodation:** 200 **Capacity:** 1,500
Year formed: 1890 **Nickname:** None **Floodlights:** Yes
Club colours: Tangerine/black **Change colours:** White/blue trim
Day for midweek matches: Monday or Wednesday **Previous Leagues:** Bristol and District, Bristol Suburban
Senior Honours: Western League, Western League Cup, Somerset Professional Cup

HEAVITREE UNITED

President: E. Drew
Chairman: F. Toze
Manager: To be appointed
Secretary: David Richardson
Address & Tel. No: Exeter 67496
Address and Tel. No. of Ground: Wingfield Park, East Wonford Hill, Exeter. 0392 73020
Simple ground directions: Leave M5, take second turn off second roundabout, turn sharp left at top of first hill on entering Exeter
No. of seats: 150 **Covered accommodation:** 150 **Capacity:** 2,500
Year formed: 1886 **Nickname:** The Heavies **Floodlights:** None
Club colours: White shirts, blue collars/cuffs **Change colours:** Yellow/green/yellow
Day for midweek matches: Tuesday **Previous Leagues:** Devon and Exeter
Senior Honours: Devon and Exeter Premier Div, Devon Senior Cup, East Devon Senior Cup

ILFRACOMBE TOWN

President: Mike Edmunds
Chairman: J.G. Grafton
Manager: L. Percival
Secretary: Jean Lawson
Address & Tel. No: 0271 62686
Address and Tel. No. of Ground: Marlborough Road, Ilfrcombe. 0271 65939
Simple ground directions: A361 into Ilfracombe, pass the first set of traffic lights right on brow of hill into Marlborough Road, ground on left approx. ½ mile
No. of seats: 20 **Covered accommodation:** 200 **Capacity:** 4,500
Year formed: 1902 **Nickname:** Bluebirds **Floodlights:** None
Club colours: Blue with white pinstripes/white/blue **Change colours:** White with blue pinstripe/blue/white
Day for midweek matches: Wednesday **Previous Leagues:** East Devon, North Devon, South Western League
Senior Honours: East Devon Premier, North Devon Senior, North Devon Premier

Welcome to Calne Town who join the Western League from the Wiltshire League. Photo: Leo Hoenig

Keynsham go close with a header during their (1-1) home draw with Wimborne (white) Photo: David Shute

KEYNSHAM TOWN

President:
Secretary: Roy Neal
Chairman: K. Dowling
Address & Tel. No: 02756 2143
Manager: R. Stone
Address and Tel. No. of ground: Crown Field, Bristol Road, Keynsham. 02756 5876
Simple ground directions: A4 from Bristol to Bath
No. of seats: None **Covered accommodation:** 200 **Capacity:** 2,000
Year formed: 1896 **Nickname:** Canaries **Floodlights:** None
Club colours: White/black **Change colours:** All red
Day for midweek matches: Wednesday **Previous Leagues:** Bristol District, Avon Premier Combination, Somerset Senior
Senior Honours: Somerset Senior Cup, Somerset Premier Cup

LARKHALL ATHLETIC

President: A.J. Rhymes
Secretary: Mervyn Liles
Chairman: A.J. Grace
Address & Tel. No: 0225 319427
Manager: C. Jeffrey
Address and Tel. No. of ground: Plain Ham, Charlcombe Lane, Larkhall, Bath. 0225 334952
Simple ground directions: Leave A4 (to Chippenham), 1 mile from centre, to Larkhall Square, up Charlcombe Lane for 1 mile, ground on right as lane narrows
No. of seats: None **Covered accommodation:** 50 **Capacity:** 1,000
Year formed: 1914 **Nickname:** The Larks **Floodlights:**
Club colours: Royal blue **Change colours:** Red
Day for midweek matches: Tuesday **Previous Leagues:** Somerset Senior
Senior Honours: Som'set Senior Cup, Som'set Senior League, Western League Merit Cup, Western League Div 1 Merit Cup

ODD DOWN

President:
Secretary: M. Mancini
Chairman: P. Hill
Address & Tel. No: 0225 23293
Manager: S. Gower
Address and Tel. No. of ground: Combe Hay Lane, Odd Down, Bath. 0225 832491
Simple ground directions: On main Bath/Exeter and Wells Road
No. of seats: None **Covered accommodation:** 50 **Capacity:** 1,000
Year formed: 1901 **Nickname:** The Down **Floodlights:** None
Club colours: Red/black/red **Change colours:** Yellow with blue trim
Day for midweek matches: Tuesday **Previous Leagues:** Wilts County Premier, Bath and District, Somerset Senior
Senior Honours: Western League Cup Semi-finals

OTTERY ST MARY

President: H.F. Pinney
Secretary: B. Doutch
Chairman: D. Bluck
Address & Tel. No: Sidmouth 2563
Manager: Bryn Jones
Address and Tel. No. of ground: Washbrook Meadows, Butts Road, Ottery St Mary. Ottery St Mary 3539
Simple ground directions: Main square, turn left, following road round church, 2nd on the right into Butts Road
No. of seats: 120 **Covered accommodation:** 120 **Capacity:** 2,000
Year formed: 1911 **Nickname:** The Otters **Floodlights:** Yes
Club colours: Royal blue **Change colours:** All red
Day for midweek matches: Wednesday **Previous Leagues:** Devon and Exeter Premier, South Western
Senior Honours: East Devon Senior Cup, Devon and Exeter Premier

PORTWAY BRISTOL

President:
Secretary: George Balsdon
Chairman: J. Cummings
Address & Tel. No: 0272 824266
Manager: D. Stone
Address and Tel. No. of ground: Penpole Lane, Shirehampton, Bristol. 0272 825691
Simple ground directions: M5 Avonmouth Junction to Shirehampton
No. of seats: 40 **Covered accommodation:** 100 **Capacity:** 1,000
Year formed: 1955 **Nickname:** None **Floodlights:** None
Club colours: Red **Change colours:** Blue
Day for midweek matches: Wednesday **Previous Leagues:** Bristol and Suburban
Senior Honours: Western League Div 1 Champions

SWANAGE AND HERSTON

President:
Secretary: H.F. Stillwell
Chairman: N. Hayward
Address & Tel. No: 0929 425302
Manager: Ian Cunningham
Address and Tel. No. of ground: Day's Park Swanage. 0929 424673
Simple ground directions: North end of town, adjacent to north beach car park
No. of seats: 150 **Covered accommodation:** 150 **Capacity:** 1,500
Year formed: **Nickname:** The Swans **Floodlights:** Yes
Club colours: White/black **Change colours:** Orange/blue
Day for midweek matches: Tuesday **Previous Leagues:** Dorset League, Dorset Combination
Senior Honours: Western League Merit Cup, Dorset Combination

TIVERTON TOWN

President: Dan McCauley
Secretary: Alan Disney
Chairman: Derek Long
Address & Tel. No: 0884 253829
Manager: John Owen
Address and Tel. No. of ground: Ladysmead, Bolham Road, Tiverton. 0884 256243
Simple ground directions: Leave M5 at Junction 27, ground on A396 ¼ mile from town centre
No. of seats: 300 **Covered accommodation:** 300 **Capacity:** 2,000
Year formed: 1920 **Nickname:** Tivvy **Floodlights:** Yes
Club colours: Amber/black **Change colours:** All blue
Day for midweek matches: Wednesday **Previous Leagues:** Devon and Exeter
Senior Honours: Devon County Senior Cup

A different view of a penalty from the visitors during Portway, Bristol's (6-3) home victory over Tiverton Town.
Mike Brown

A close range header from Welton Rovers' Shaun Parker gives the visitors the lead at Portway Bristol where they won (2 0)
Photo: Mike Brown

WARMINSTER TOWN

President:
Secretary: Alistair Lawrie
Chairman: N. Warr
Address & Tel. No: 0985 218265
Manager: T. Welffe
Address and Tel. No. of ground: Weymouth Street, Warminster. 0985 217828
Simple ground directions: Take A36, traffic lights in town left
No. of seats: 200 **Covered accommodation:** 200 **Capacity:** 2,000
Year formed: 1882 **Nickname:** Town **Floodlights:** None
Club colours: Red/black **Change colours:** All yellow
Day for midweek matches: Wednesday **Previous Leagues:** Wiltshire
Senior Honours: None

WELLINGTON TOWN

President: Alan Baker
Secretary: Tony Brown
Chairman: D. Northam
Address & Tel. No: 082347 2920
Manager:
Address and Tel. No. of ground: Wellington playing field, North Road, Wellington. 082347 4810
Simple ground directions: Turn right at town centre traffic lights into North Street and first left by Fire Station
No. of seats: None **Covered accommodation:** 200 **Capacity:** 3,000
Year formed: 1892 **Nickname:** Town **Floodlights:** 1986
Club colours: Tangerine/black **Change colours:** All blue
Day for midweek matches: Tuesday **Previous Leagues:** Taunton Saturday, Somerset Senior
Senior Honours: Somerset Senior League Div 1, Western League Div 1 Runners-up, Rowbarton & Seward Cup

WELTON ROVERS

President:
Secretary: Tony Salvage
Chairman: J.C. Anderson
Address & Tel. No: 0761 413330
Manager: J. Elliott
Address and Tel. No. of ground: West Clewes, North Road, Midsomer Norton. 0761 412097
Simple ground directions: A367 Bath/Radstock-A362 Radstock/Midsomer Norton
No. of seats: 350 **Covered accommodation:** 350 **Capacity:** 2,000
Year formed: 1887 **Nickname:** Rovers **Floodlights:** None
Club colours: Green and white stripes **Change colours:** Royal blue
Day for midweek matches: Wednesday **Previous Leagues:** None
Senior Honours: Western League Champions, Alan Young Cup, Somerset Senior Cup

WESTBURY UNITED

President:
Secretary: E.L. Barber
Chairman: E. Manasseh
Address & Tel. No: 0373 822117
Manager: B. Neate
Address and Tel. No. of ground: Meadow Lane, Westbury. 0373 823409
Simple ground directions: 10 minutes walk from railway station, turn right into Meadow Lane
No. of seats: 150 **Covered accommodation:** 350 **Capacity:** 2,000
Year formed: 1921 **Nickname:** The White Horse Men **Floodlights:** None
Club colours: Green/white **Change colours:** Yellow/white
Day for midweek matches: Tuesday **Previous Leagues:** Wiltshire County, Wiltshire Combination
Senior Honours: Wiltshire Senior Cup, Wiltshire Combination

WIMBORNE TOWN

President:
Secretary: Geoffrey Theobald
Chairman: B. Medler
Address & Tel. No: 0202 697994
Manager: C. Croad
Address and Tel. No. of ground: Cuthbury, Cowgrove Road, Wimborne. 0202 884821
Simple ground directions: Wimborne-Blandford Road, behind Victoria Hospital
No. of seats: None **Covered accommodation:** 300 **Capacity:** 3,000
Year formed: 1878 **Nickname:** The Magpies **Floodlights:** Yes
Club colours: White/black **Change colours:** Yellow/blue
Day for midweek matches: Tuesday **Previous Leagues:** Dorset County, Dorset Combination
Senior Honours: Dorset County, Dorset Senior Amateur Cup

THE JEWSON SOUTH-WESTERN LEAGUE

President: G.H. Gillin *Chairman:* T.H. Scott
Secretary: R. Lowe, Panorama, Lamerton, Tavistock, Devon PL19 8SD
Tel: Tavistock 3516

THE BAYLY BARTLETT SOUTH-WESTERN FOOTBALL LEAGUE

	P	W	D	L	F	A	Pts
Falmouth Town	38	27	6	5	113	42	60
Newquay	38	24	7	7	94	55	55
Millbrook	38	23	7	8	88	41	53
Bodmin Town	38	25	3	10	84	44	53
Bugle	38	19	11	8	71	40	49
Truro City	38	21	5	12	85	64	47
Wadebridge Town	38	19	7	12	77	47	45
St. Austell	38	19	7	12	74	63	45
St. Blazey	38	14	13	11	77	47	41
Newton Abbot	38	14	13	11	58	54	41
Clyst Rovers	38	14	8	16	74	89	36
Torpoint Athletic	38	12	11	15	71	93	35
Torquay Utd Res	38	12	7	19	69	80	31
Appledore/Bid AAC	38	11	8	19	52	71	30
Penryn Athletic	38	11	6	21	66	97	28
Tavistock	38	12	3	23	54	91	27
Penzance	38	8	9	21	51	96	25
Teignmouth	38	9	6	23	46	67	24
Launceston	38	7	10	21	49	85	24
Holsworthy	38	4	3	31	41	128	11

APPLEDORE AND B.A.A.C.

Secretary: E.G. Nichols, 30 Stucley Road, Bideford EX39 3EG. (02372 75493)
Ground: Marshford **Colours:** Yellow-blue trim shirts, blue shorts

BODMIN TOWN

Secretary: R. Clark, 21 St Nicholas Street, Bodmin. (0208 2774)
Ground: Priory Park, Bodmin **Colours:** Amber and black shirts, black shorts

BUGLE

Secretary: A. Pearce, 14 Symons Close, Boscoppa, St Austell. (0726 67985)
Ground: Molinnis **Colours:** Black and white shirts, black shorts

CLYST ROVERS

Secretary: B. Harvey, Sapele House Farthing Down, Holywell Luke, Nr. Wellington.(0823 672483)
Ground: Waterslade Park, Clyst Honiton **Colours:** All blue

FALMOUTH TOWN

Secretary: M.J. Rowe, 9 Treverbyn Parc, Budock Water, Falmouth. (0326 73017)
Ground: Bickland Park (0326 75156) **Colours:** Black and amber

HOLSWORTHY

Secretary: M. Goodenough, Rose Cottage, Horrelsford, Milton Damerel, Holsworthy. (040926 402)
Ground: Upcott Field **Colours:** Black and white stripes, black shorts

LAUNCESTON

Secretary: C. Bradshaw, 4 Poltamar, Tavistock Road, Launceston. (0566 4355)
Ground: Pennygillam (0566 3279) **Colours:** Claret and blue

MILLBROOK

Secretary: B. Harvey, 27 Hounster Drive, Millbrook. (0752 822066)
Ground: 0752 822113 **Colours:** Black and white striped shirts, black shorts

NEWQUAY

Secretary: B.A. Biggin, 8 Mitchell Avenue, Newquay. (06373 5623)
Ground: Mount Wise, Newquay. (06373 2935) **Colours:** Red and white stripes, black shorts

NEWTON ABBOT

Secretary: R. Perkins, 21 Prospect Terrace, Newton Abbot. (0626 61596)
Ground: Centrax Sports Field **Colours:** All red

PENRYN ATHLETIC

Secretary: M.A. Young, Trewindle, 90 Helston Road, Penryn. (0326 74098)
Ground: Kernick **Colours:** Red and black striped shirts, black shorts

Bodmin Town F.C. The main stand at Priory Park before the match with Torpoint Athletic

St Blazey F.C. Photo Leo Hoenig.

PENZANCE
Secretary: D.R. Ferris, 96 Polmor Road, Crowlas, Penzance. (0736 740585)
Ground: Penlee Park. (0736 61964) **Colours:** Black and white striped shirts, black shorts

ST AUSTELL
Secretary: P. Beard, 24 Alexandra Road, St Austell. (0726 64138)
Ground: Poltair, St Austell. (0726 66099) **Colours:** White shirts, black shorts

ST BLAZEY
Secretary: B. Saunders, 67 Tywurdreath Highway, St Blazey, Par. (072681 4510)
Ground: Station Road, St Blazey **Colours:** Green and black shirts, green shorts

TAVISTOCK
Secretary: R. Lowe, 'Panorama', Lamerton, Tavistock. (0822 3516)
Ground: Langsford Park, Tavistock. (0822 4447) **Colours:** Red shirts, black shorts

TEIGNMOUTH
Secretary: W. Parker, 23 Higher Coombe Drive, Teignmouth. (06267 4277)
Ground: Coombe Valley **Colours:** White shirts, black shorts

TORPOINT ATHLETIC
Secretary: J. Millward, 92 Woodland Way, Torpoint. (0752 813447)
Ground: The Mill Field, Torpoint **Colours:** Royal blue shirts, white shorts

TORQUAY UNITED
Secretary: D.J. Easton, Plainmoor, Torquay. (0803 38666/7)
Ground: Plainmoor **Colours:** Blue shirts, blue shorts

TRURO CITY
Secretary: A. Rowe, 5 Lander Court, Truro. (0872 77577)
Ground: Treyew Road. (0872 78853) **Colours:** Red shirts, black shorts

WADEBRIDGE TOWN
Secretary: L. George, 32 Wellington Place, Wadebridge. (020881 2503)
Ground: Bodieve Park, Wadebridge **Colours:** Red shirts, red shorts

A rare Tavistock attack during their 0-6 home defeat by Teignmouth. Photo Leo Hoenig.

Gloucestershire County League — Recent Champions

Max Pts.	Season	1st	2nd	3rd	4th
64	1978/79	49 Almondsbury Gr.	48 Hambrook	43 Worrell Hill	42 Port of Bristol
68	1979/80	53 Almondsbury Gr.	46 Shortwood U.	41 Sharpness	40* Matson Ath.
68	1980/81	58 Almondsbury Gr.	49 Shortwood U.	48 Wilton R.	43 Port of Bristol
64	1981/82	50 Shortwood U.	49 Almondsbury Gr.	45 Lydbrook Ath.	42 Wilton R.
64	1982/83	55 Old Georgians	47 Port of Bristol	42* Laurence W.H.	42 Hanham Ath.
68	1983/84	62 Sharpness	55 Old Geogians	43 Bristol St. George	39 Port of Bristol
72	1984/85	56 Old Georgians	50 Port of Bristol	46 Hanham. Ath.	45 Ludbrook Ath
72	1985/86	59 Patchway	53 Old Georgians	50 Ellwood	47 Brimscombe & Thrupp

* goal average/difference

GLOUCESTERSHIRE COUNTY

	P	W	D	L	F	A	Pts
Patchway	36	27	5	4	80	20	59
Old Georgians	36	22	9	5	80	25	53
Ellwood	36	21	8	7	78	45	50
Brims. & Thrupp	36	19	9	8	54	45	47
Wootton Rovers	36	17	11	8	53	42	45
Cinderford Town	36	16	10	10	52	37	42
Lydbrook Ath.	36	17	7	12	66	47	41
Port of Bristol	36	14	12	10	59	46	40
Bristol St. George	36	17	4	15	57	52	38
Harrow Hill	36	14	10	12	66	64	38
Hanham Ath.	36	11	10	15	49	61	32
Avon St. Philip	36	11	8	17	54	66	30
Cad. Heath St. Josephs	36	12	5	19	54	69	29
Law. Weston Hallen	36	8	9	19	44	62	25
Hambrook	36	8	9	19	31	58	25
Stonehouse	36	8	9	19	41	69	25
Frampton Utd.	36	8	8	20	38	59	24
Newent Town	36	7	10	19	39	71	24
Oldland Decora	36	3	11	22	42	99	17

GLOUCESTER NORTHERN SENIOR LEAGUE

Division One

	p	w	d	l	f	a	Pts
ICI Fibres	30	19	9	2	64	17	47
Wilton Rovers	30	19	8	3	74	25	46
Bymacks	30	17	8	5	78	33	42
St. Marks	30	17	4	9	51	30	38
Viney St Swithins	30	14	10	6	49	31	38
Shortwood Utd Res	30	15	7	8	57	36	37
Longlevens	30	13	7	10	47	35	33
Tuffley Rovers	30	13	5	12	42	41	31
Sharpness Res	30	10	9	11	50	52	29
Berkeley Town	30	10	6	14	45	47	26
Dursley Town	30	10	6	14	48	56	26
Frampton Utd Res	30	9	6	15	41	52	24
Broadwell	30	8	7	15	51	58	23
Lydney Town	30	7	8	15	34	47	22
Coleford United	30	2	5	23	15	98	9
Newent Town Res	30	3	3	24	28	116	9

Division Two

	P	W	D	L	F	A	Pts
Smiths Athletic	30	21	6	3	71	15	48
Kings Stanley	30	18	9	3	68	28	45
Mitcheldean	30	15	9	6	67	32	39
Harrow Hill Res	30	13	10	7	49	32	36
Hardwicke	30	14	6	10	49	32	34
Charfield	30	13	8	9	36	34	34
Whiteshill United	30	13	6	11	46	38	32
Cinderford Town Res	30	11	8	11	54	57	30
Cope Chat	30	12	4	14	52	56	28
Bibury	30	10	7	13	52	46	27
Huntley	30	9	8	13	37	50	26
Hilldene Athletic	30	9	7	14	40	58	25
Lydbrook Ath Res	30	11	3	16	42	69	25
Cam Bulldogs	30	9	4	17	39	68	22
Chalford	30	6	5	19	32	81	17
Minchinhampton	30	5	4	21	34	73	14

THE WILTSHIRE COUNTY FOOTBALL LEAGUE

Division 1

Final League Table

Season 1985§86	Pld	W	D	L	F	A	Pts
Purton	26	20	4	2	82	30	44
Bemerton Athletic	26	20	3	3	97	25	43
Calne Town	26	18	6	2	69	23	42
Park	26	15	7	4	66	29	37
Chipp'nham Town Res	26	12	6	8	43	28	30
Wooton Bassett Town	26	10	6	10	44	44	26
Pinehurst	26	10	2	14	53	78	22
Aldbourne	26	8	6	12	48	57	21*
Sanford	26	8	5	13	37	62	21
Wroughton	26	9	2	15	41	76	20
Pewsey Vale	26	8	3	15	41	62	19
Wills	26	3	10	13	31	51	16
Amesbury Town	26	4	4	18	30	63	12
Melksham Town Res	26	4	2	20	40	94	10

***one point deducted*

THE WILTSHIRE COUNTY FOOTBALL LEAGUE

Division 2

Final League Table

Season 1985§86	P	W	D	L	F	A	Pts
Ferndale Athletic	28	19	7	2	69	21	45
Old Manor	28	18	7	3	70	33	43
Plessey Sports	28	18	5	5	90	35	41
Corsham Town	28	16	7	5	79	31	39
Allied Dunbar	28	17	4	7	72	47	38
Laberstock & Ford	28	17	3	8	62	35	37
Blundson United	28	11	7	10	52	53	29
Shrewton United	28	10	7	11	46	49	27
Dorcan	28	10	5	13	38	47	25
Westbury United Res	28	9	4	15	39	56	22
Burmah House	28	6	8	14	35	48	20
Devizes Town Res	28	7	5	16	31	61	19
Marlborough Town	28	5	8	15	38	64	18
Avebury	28	5	2	21	31	89	12
Warminster Town Res	28	2	1	25	27	110	5

SOMERSET SENIOR LEAGUE
Premier Division

	P	W	D	L	F	A	Pts
Robinsons	34	28	4	2	94	24	60
East Worle	34	23	6	5	75	27	52
Hengrove	34	22	8	4	67	37	52
Long Sutton	34	18	10	6	76	44	46
Avon Police	34	19	5	10	60	48	43
Peasedown	34	18	4	12	74	58	40
Brislington	34	14	9	11	56	53	37
Clevedon	34	16	4	14	58	49	36
Bristol MF	34	13	10	11	46	46	36
Longwell Grn	34	10	7	17	55	65	27
Bishops Stn	34	10	7	17	49	62	27
Portishead	34	9	9	16	38	60	27
Castle Cary	34	10	7	17	45	56	25
Watchet	34	8	9	17	43	61	25
Burnham	34	8	7	19	39	72	23
Redwood	34	6	7	21	39	69	19
Nailsea	34	7	5	22	33	76	19
Imperial	34	6	4	24	47	87	16

SOMERSET SENIOR LEAGUE
Division One

	P	W	D	L	F	A	Pts
Imperial	34	22	7	5	83	33	51
Westland	34	21	5	8	75	30	47
Mangotsfield	34	19	8	7	62	44	46
Robinsons Rs	34	21	3	10	77	63	45
Clandown	34	19	5	10	55	38	43
Ilminster	34	17	6	11	73	52	40
St. George	34	15	7	12	78	67	37
Larkhall	34	15	7	12	63	49	35
Bishops Hsp	34	15	5	14	57	61	35
Timsbury	34	12	9	13	54	62	33
Harptree	34	12	6	16	66	71	30
Shirehampton	34	9	12	13	53	59	30
Tunley	34	10	10	14	43	52	30
Brislington	34	12	5	17	59	74	29
Wells City	34	9	8	17	35	54	26
Bath Univ	34	7	8	19	43	70	22
Imperial Res	34	8	5	21	42	70	19
Wellington	34	2	6	26	28	97	10

SOMERSET SENIOR LEAGUE
Division Two

	P	W	D	L	F	A	Pts
Clevedon	38	29	8	1	116	20	66
Weston	38	28	5	5	110	39	61
Bridgwater	38	28	6	4	97	28	60
Street	38	26	4	8	89	47	56
Taunton	38	24	3	11	90	52	51
Hengrove Rs	38	20	10	8	72	47	50
Backwell	38	21	7	10	87	51	49
Dundry 82	38	15	10	13	61	54	40
Keynsham	38	15	6	17	70	71	36
Temple Cloud	38	14	3	21	97	101	31
Yatton	38	9	12	17	60	72	30
Chard	38	9	11	18	64	85	29
Saltford	38	10	9	19	60	95	29
Odd Down	38	11	7	20	59	94	29
Shepton Mlt	38	10	9	19	54	94	29
Weston St J	38	11	5	22	62	78	27
Winscombe	38	7	11	20	45	92	25
Glastonbury	38	7	10	21	48	97	24
Nailsea	38	5	7	26	45	105	17
Congresbury	38	9	1	28	51	115	17

SOMERSET SENIOR LEAGUE
Division Three

	P	W	D	L	F	A	Pts
Frome Tn	38	27	8	3	127	45	60
Long Ashton	38	25	7	6	120	52	57
Welton Rvr	38	23	4	11	92	62	50
Cheddar	38	21	7	10	113	64	49
Wrington	38	22	5	11	93	48	47
Banwell	38	19	8	11	94	61	46
Avon Pl Rs	38	20	6	12	81	82	46
Clutton	38	15	11	12	78	72	41
Keynsham	38	17	7	14	76	72	41
Mendip Hosp	38	15	9	14	73	61	39
Portishead	38	13	11	14	57	48	37
Westland Rs	38	13	11	14	78	75	37
Worle	38	16	4	18	82	81	34
Paulton	38	13	9	16	61	61	33
Harptree Rs	38	12	9	17	68	71	31
Clevedon Rs	38	12	6	20	52	80	30
Redwood Rs	38	12	6	20	77	125	26
Yatton Rs	38	7	5	26	53	104	19
Tunley Rs	38	5	3	30	48	137	11
Wells Rs	38	4	2	32	42	164	10

COUNTY OF AVON PREMIER COMBINATION
Division One

Season 1985/86	P	W	D	L	F	A	Pts
Stapleton Manulife	34	21	10	3	84	33	52
Wick	34	22	5	7	92	43	49
Bristol Spartak	34	18	11	5	76	34	47
Hillfields Park	34	18	11	5	78	46	47
Lawrence Rovers	34	19	8	7	75	42	46
Highbridge United	34	17	8	9	90	53	42
Winterbourne United	34	16	9	9	62	43	41
Bishops SB Rovers	34	13	9	12	62	60	35
Nicholas Wanderers	34	13	9	12	51	49	35
Lawrence WH Res	34	11	10	13	51	64	32
Manor Farm BC	34	13	5	16	51	77	31
Victoria Park	34	13	2	19	55	67	28
Shaftesbury Crusade	34	11	6	17	42	69	28
Staple Hill	34	7	12	15	56	65	26
Bitton	34	10	4	20	55	76	24
Made For Ever	34	11	1	22	59	74	23
Soundwell	34	5	7	22	39	105	17
Sea Mills Park	34	2	5	27	39	118	9

COUNTY OF AVON PREMIER COMBINATION

	P	W	D	L	F	A	Pts
Henbury OB	30	25	5	0	97	15	55
Pucklechurch Sports	30	20	5	5	71	62	34
Eden Grove	30	16	6	8	63	41	38
Iron Acton	30	14	8	8	52	46	36
R W P	30	12	8	10	34	33	32
Thornbury Town	30	12	7	11	49	56	31
Bristol Union	30	13	4	13	60	57	30
Filton Town	30	13	4	13	53	55	30
Hillfields OB	30	12	5	13	50	57	29
St. Philips MAS	30	10	9	11	48	56	29
Frampton Athletic	30	8	12	10	61	63	28
Barr United	30	10	7	13	47	44	27
Sun Life	30	10	6	14	49	55	26
Frys	30	7	12	11	32	49	26
Bristol University	30	5	6	19	63	82	16
Hambrook Res	30	0	2	28	19	104	2

DIVISION 1 (Top 2)	P	W	D	L	F	A	Pts
Stapleton Manulife	34	21	10	3	84	33	52
Wick	34	22	5	7	92	43	49

DEVON & EXETER LEAGUE

Premier Division

	P	W	D	L	F	A	Pts
Exeter City 'A'	30	23	5	2	102	24	51
Alphington	30	18	5	7	75	48	41
Budleigh Salterton	30	18	3	9	75	74	39
Exmouth Town Res	30	17	3	10	86	61	37
Chelston	30	16	5	7	52	55	34
Cullompton Rangers	30	12	10	8	52	55	34
Bideford Res	30	11	11	8	51	38	33
Dawlish Res	30	11	9	10	60	48	31
Crediton United	30	12	6	12	45	46	30
Exeter Arms	30	11	7	12	47	58	29
Exeter Civil Service	30	10	6	14	48	55	26
Clyst Valley	30	9	5	16	39	59	23
Topsham Town	30	7	5	18	38	65	19
Honiton Town	30	6	6	18	31	60	18
Ottery St Mary Res	30	6	5	19	33	60	17
Sidmouth Town	30	6	3	21	43	88	15

DIVISION 1 (Top 2)	P	W	D	L	F	A	Pts
Newton St Cyres	28	23	3	2	111	23	49
Exeter University	28	19	6	3	96	28	42

COUNTY OF AVON PREMIER COMBINATION

Premier Division

Season 1985/86	P	W	D	L	F	A	Pts
Henbury Old Boys	30	25	5	0	97	15	55
Pucklechurch Sports	30	20	5	5	71	32	45
Eden Grove	30	16	6	8	63	41	38
Iron Acton	30	14	8	8	52	46	36
R W P	30	12	8	10	34	33	32
Thornbury Town	30	12	7	11	49	56	31
Bristol Union	30	13	4	13	60	57	30
Filton Town	30	13	4	13	53	55	30
Hillfields Old Boys	30	12	5	13	50	57	29
St Philips Marsh A.S	30	10	9	11	48	56	29
Frampton Athletic	30	8	12	10	61	63	28
Barr United	30	10	7	13	47	44	27
Sun Life	30	10	6	14	49	55	26
Frys	30	7	12	11	32	49	26
Bristol University	30	5	6	19	63	82	16
Hambrook Reserves	30	0	2	28	19	104	2

BRISTOL & DISTRICT LEAGUE

Senior Division

Season 1985/86	P	W	D	L	F	A	Pts
Henbury Old Boys Res	32	25	5	2	90	25	55
Hanham Mount	32	23	5	4	122	34	51
Patchway Res	32	22	4	6	106	46	48
Frampton Athletic Res	32	19	3	10	70	48	41
Hanham Athletic Res	32	17	6	9	68	56	40
Puck'church Sport Rs	32	18	3	11	72	57	39
Kingsway United	32	16	5	11	56	44	37
Filton Town Res	32	13	9	10	64	58	35
Olveston United	32	13	6	13	76	70	32
Westerleigh Sports	32	13	5	14	58	57	31
South Bristol Central	32	9	8	15	54	76	26
idland Decora Res	32	9	4	19	47	75	22
House of Faith	32	8	3	21	56	97	19
Parnalls Fishponds	32	6	7	19	41	90	19
Chipping Sodbury	32	7	4	21	42	84	18
Gardiner Erickson	32	6	5	21	40	87	17
Avon St Phillips Res	32	6	2	24	41	99	14

BRISTOL & DISTRICT LEAGUE

Premier Division One

Season 1985/86	P	W	D	L	F	A	Pts
Stockwood Green	34	30	2	2	94	27	62
Totterdown Athletic	34	24	4	6	85	41	52
Wessex Glass	34	23	6	5	100	49	52
The Mill YC	34	22	7	5	101	41	51
Plough & W'mill Utd	34	17	8	9	56	44	42
Avonmouth	34	15	9	10	57	43	39
Broad Plain House	34	15	8	11	79	58	38
Lockleaze C.A	34	14	7	13	92	70	35
St Aldhelms	34	13	8	13	60	64	34
Yate Town Res	34	10	10	14	55	63	30
Teylant Athletic	34	8	11	15	60	73	27
Bristol St Andrews	34	7	13	14	36	57	27
De Veys	34	9	18	17	48	76	26
Exeter United	34	8	7	19	41	63	23
St Andrews YC	34	9	5	20	47	93	23
Avon Fire Brigade	34	6	10	19	34	70	22
Port of Bristol Res	34	5	7	22	36	91	17
Dynamo	34	2	8	24	38	98	12

A save from St. Blazey's Gary Rowden (stripped shirt). (Photo: Leo Hoenig)

BANK'S BREWERY WEST MIDLANDS (REGIONAL) LEAGUE

President: R. H. Juggins
Secretary: K. H. Goodfellow
43 Yardley Green, Bordesley Green, Birmingham B9 5PU. Tel: 021- 772 0375

Final League Tables — Season 1985/86

Premier Division

	P	W	D	L	F	A	Pts
Halesowen Town	38	31	4	3	108	28	66
Gresley Rovers	38	25	9	4	91	29	59
Atherstone United	38	26	7	5	90	48	59
Harrisons	38	22	9	7	82	40	53
Wednesfield Social	38	21	7	10	88	48	49
Lye Town	38	18	11	9	54	39	47
GKN Sankey	38	15	12	11	59	64	42
Hinckley Athletic	38	15	11	12	60	50	41
Tamworth	38	15	8	15	68	52	38
Brereton Social	38	13	11	14	58	54	37
Rushall Olympic	38	14	9	15	63	65	37
Malvern Town	38	13	10	15	51	61	36
Shifnal Town	38	9	10	19	38	76	28
Oldswinford	38	9	9	20	46	68	27
Blakenall	38	9	8	21	38	61	26
Tividale	38	8	10	20	51	83	26
Chasetown	38	7	10	21	40	74	24
Wolverhampton Utd.	38	8	8	22	31	66	24
Tipton Town	38	8	8	22	43	79	24
Armitage	38	7	3	28	44	118	17

FA Challenge Vase:
Halesowen Town 3 Southall 0
League Cup:
Atherstone Utd. 1 Tamworth 2

Division 1

	P	W	D	L	F	A	Pts
Halesowen Harriers	34	24	7	3	108	26	55
Wolverhampton Cas.	34	21	5	8	62	33	47
Westfields	34	19	7	8	67	32	45
Ettingshall H.T.	34	17	9	8	69	39	43
Newport Town	34	16	9	9	68	46	41
Halesowen Town Res.	34	14	9	11	50	43	37
Pelsall Villa	34	15	7	12	43	42	37
Great Wyrley	34	13	10	11	61	52	36
Nuneaton Bgh. Res.	34	13	8	13	46	56	34
Cradley Town	34	12	9	13	48	62	33
Brewood	34	13	6	15	60	65	32
Darlaston	34	11	9	14	51	58	31
Bilston United	34	10	10	14	52	61	30
Gornal Athletic	34	9	8	17	43	53	26
Ludlow Town	34	8	9	17	51	64	25
Northpark United	34	9	6	19	43	84	24
Lichfield	34	9	2	23	34	81	20
Shirley Town	34	4	8	22	35	94	16

Shropshire County F.A. Cup: Mewport Town 2 Morda o
Kingston Challenge Cup: Westfields 2, Presteigne 0
Hereford County F.A. Cup: Westfield 1 Hintons 0
League Cup: Ettingshall HT 1 Wolverhampton Casuals 2

Division 2

	P	W	D	L	F	A	Pts
Springvale-Tranco	34	25	5	4	80	27	55
Metal Box Sports	34	23	6	5	66	32	52
Broseley Athletic	34	20	8	6	72	32	48
Stourport Swifts	34	16	12	6	60	36	44
Aero Lucas	34	18	6	10	66	45	42
Millfields	34	15	7	12	48	41	37
Atherstone Utd. Res.	34	15	6	13	80	63	36
Donnington Wood	34	14	8	12	62	59	36
Bloxwich Town	34	12	10	12	49	54	34
Jamaica City	34	13	7	14	64	55	33
Chasetown Reserves	34	12	9	13	58	55	33
Harrisons Reserves	34	12	6	16	61	67	30
Albright & Wilson	34	11	5	18	58	63	27
Wednesbury Town	34	8	8	18	52	73	24
Dowty Ashchurch	34	10	4	20	29	63	24
Oldswinford Res.	34	7	8	19	32	76	22
Clancey Halestown	34	8	4	22	40	92	20

West Midlands (Regional) League — Recent Champions

Max Pts.	Season	1st	2nd	3rd	4th
84	1979/80	*67 Sutton Coldfield	67 Lye T.	57 Willenhall T.	54 Hednesford T.
84	1980/81	69 Shifnal T.	63 Lye T.	61 Willenhall T.	52 Brereton Social
84	1981/82	63 Shifnal T.	61 Sutton Coldfield	56 Halesowen T.	54 Bilston T.
76	1982/83	62 Halesowen T.	55 Hinkley Ath.	48 Hednesford T.	*47 Shifnal T.
76	1983/84	67 Halesowen T.	56 Hednesford T.	45 Atherstone U.	43 Gresley R.

* goal average/difference

Gresley Rovers before their final match against Tipton Town — May 6th 1986. Back-row (L to R): S. Dolby, K. Banton, R. Priest, M. Bromley, K. Austin, J. Branch, G. West. Front-row (L to R): J. Laws, R. Philpot, C. Arthur, D. King (capt.), I. Earley, B. Beresford. (Photo Derrick Kinsey).

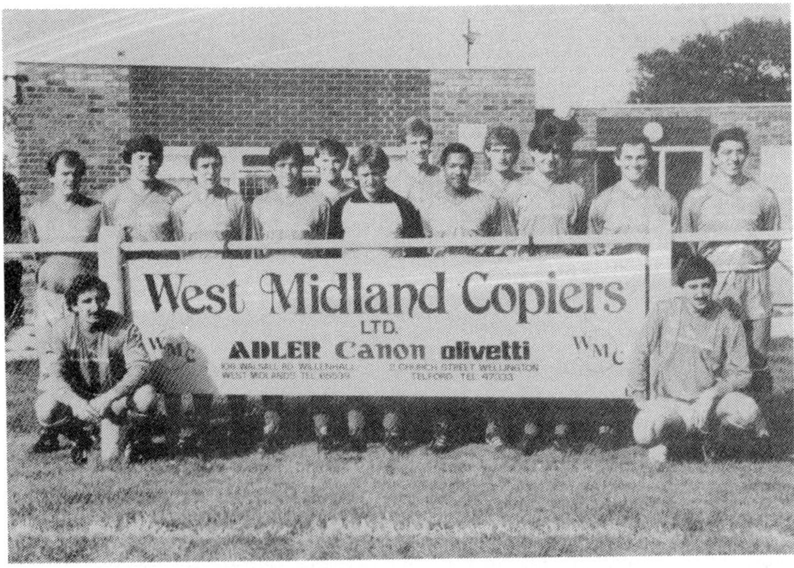

Wolverhampton Casuals — 1985-86. Back-Row (L to R): M. Czyzyk, M. Drury, N. Loftus, S. Ingleby, G. Jackson, G. Kitson, T. Hadfield, M. Lawrence, D. Stait, M. Russell, J. Lees, P. Butters. Kneeling: P. Tonks, M. Hill.

ARMITAGE

President: D. Morris
Chairman: H. R. Bailey
Manager: R. Edwards
Asst. Man Coach: D. Devin
Physiotherapist: K. Davies
Secretary: Ken Conway
Address & Tel No: 17 Riskworth Avenue, Rugeley, Staffs 08894 5746 (H), Armitage 0543 490253 (B)
Commercial Manager: C. W. Wood (Yoxall 472114)
Press Officer & Tel No: Secretary
Address & Tel No of ground: Kings Bromle Road, Handsacre, Rugeley, Staffs. (0543 491077)
Simple ground directions: Situated on A513 between Handsacre and Kings Bromley
No of seats: 52 **Floodlights:** Yes **Club sponsors:** Anderson Envreeland
Mid-week match evening: Tuesday
Best performance in: F.A. Cup: 3rd Qualifying
F.A. Trophy: 1976–77 1st Round Qualifying
F.A. Vase: 2nd Round twice
Previous Leagues: Staff County
Clubhouse: Bar, catering for 100
Programme Editor: C. W. Wood
Club colours: All Royal Blue
Change colours: Red
Programme: 12 pages, 15p
Major honours: W. Midlands Div 1, Walsall Senior Cup

ATHERSTONE UNITED

President: Mrs. Evans
Chairman: P. L. Barber
Manager: Ron Bradbury
Secretary: Alan Kendall
Address & Tel No: 109 Green Lane, Nuneaton, Warwicks CV10 9EQ. 0203 394492 (H), 0827 893267 (B)
Coach: J. Peacock
Physiotherapist: M. Toff
Address & Tel No of ground: Sheepy Road, Atherstone, Warwicks,. (08277 67829)
Simple ground directions: ½ mile north of town centre on B4416 Tycross—Ashby road. Atherstone is bypassed by main A5 trunk road
No of seats: 500 **Ground accommodation:** 7,500 **Capacity:** 10,000 **Floodlights:** Yes
Year formed: 1979 **Nickname:** The Adders **Club sponsors:** Crompton & Rathbone Tools
Club colours: Red & White Red Red & Black **Change colours:** Yellow
Record attendance: 740 v Tamworth **Year:** 1984–85
Best performance in: F.A. Vase: 1984–85, 1985–86 5th Round
Previous Leagues: None **Programme Editor:** Brian Wills (08277 4560)
Present player with Football League experience: P. Summerill
Programme: 12 pages, 15p **Local newspapers & Tel No:**
Major Honours: Division 1 West Midland League Champions 1981–82, League Cup Winners 1981–82, Walsall Senior Cup
Club Captain (1985–86): G. Bradder **Player of the Year (1985–86):** Bobby Parker

BLAKENALL F.C.

President: F. Rowley
Chairman: S. Lyons
Manager: P. Whitehouse
Asst Man Coach: C. Till
Physiotherapist: J. Ruddell
Secretary: W. E . Roberts
Address & Tel No: 115 Somerfield Road, Bloxwich (0384 404074)
Commercial Manager: J. Ruddell
Address & Tel No: 0384 36471
Press Officer & Tel No: F. Rowley
Secretary's Office: (0384 400600)
Address & Tel No of ground: Somerfield Road, Bloxwich. (0922 405835)
Simple ground directions: Half mile from A34 in centre of Bloxwich
No of seats: 25 **Covered accommodation:** 300 **Capacity:** 4,000 **Floodlights:** No, plans passed
Year formed: 1946 **Nickname:** The 'Nall' **Club sponsors:** J. L. S. Heating
Club colours: All White **Change colours:** Claret & Blue
Previous Names: **Previous Grounds:**
Record attendance:
Previous Leagues: Bloxwich Combination, Staffs County, Midlands Combination **Programme:** None
Clubhouse details: Members lounge
Major Honours: Midland Combination 1977, Walsall Senior Cup (6)
Club Captain (1985–86): K. Harding
Player of the Year (1985–86): P. Hollingsworth

BRERETON SOCIAL

President: J. Healey
Chairman: W. Bott
Manager: Mick Morris
Secretary: George Burton
Address & Tel No: Lea Hall Lane, Brereton, Rugeley, Staffs.
Address & Tel No of ground: Red Lion Ground, Armitage Lane, Brereton, Rugeley, Staffs. 08894 5526
No of seats: 100 **Ground accommodation:** 2,000 **Floodlights:** Yes
Club colours: All Red **Change colours:** All Blue
Previous Leagues: Staffs County **Programme:** 14–18 pages, 20p
Clubhouse details: Bar, stage, dance floor, changing rooms, pool table & T.V.
Club Captain (1985–86): Dean Page
Local Newspapers: Rugeley Newsletter, Rugeley Mercury

CHASETOWN

Chairman: A. Scorey
Manager: Paul Darby
Secretary: Brian Simpson
Address & Tel No: 23 Freeth Road, Brownhills, Walsall, West Midlands W58 6JG. (0543 373 889)
Asst. Man/Coach: M. Rowe
Physiotherapist: E. Highfield
Press Officer:
Address & Tel No of ground: "The Scholars", The Church Street, Chasetown. 05436 2222
Club colours: Blue with White pinstripes/Blue/Blue
Change colours: Red with Blue & White trim/Red/Red
Programme: 10 pages, 15p
Programme Editor: M. Joiner (Cannock 2358)
Mid-week match evening: Tuesday or Thursday
Previous Leagues: Staffs County
Clubhouse details: Own clubhouse, bar, kitchen
Major Honours: W. Midlands Div 1
Club Captain (1985–86): R. Sheppard
Player of the Year (1985–86): A. Cox

GKN SANKEY

Chairman: B. Parr
Manager: K. Howells
Secretary: T. R. Booth
Address & Tel No: 16 Johnstone Close, Wroulwardine Wood, Telford. Telford 0952 615036 (H), 44321 x2398 (B)
Coach: B. Clark
Physiotherapist: R. Roberts
Commercial Manager: None
Press Officer: None
Address & Tel No of ground: Sankey Stadium, Castle Street, Hadley, Telford. (0952 3411)
No of seats: 500 **Covered accommodation:** Yes **Capacity:** 5,000 **Floodlights:** No
Year formed: 1910
Nickname: 'Blues'
Club colours: All Blue
Change colours: All Yellow
Previous Names: None
Record attendance: 1,500 **Year:** 1960
Mid-week match evening: Tuesday, Thursday
Previous Leagues: Shropshire County, Cheshire
Clubhouse details: Capacity of 100
Programme Editor: P. J. Evedon (55634)
Programme details: 8 pages, 10p
Major Honours: Shropshire FA County Cup Winners 1966–67, 1968–69, 1982–83, West Midlands Div II Champions 1981–82, Shropshire Senior Cup 1961–62
Club Captain (1985–86): W. Lochrie
Player of the Year (1985–86): W. Lochrie

GRESLEY ROVERS

President: G. Duggins
Chairman: D. Nish
Manager: F. Northwood
Physiotherapists: None
Treasurer: P. Jenkinson
Address & Tel No: 30 Chatsworth Road, Newhall, Burton-on-Trent DE110JA. 0283 214358 (H)
Press Officer: None
Address & Tel No of ground: Moat Street, Church Gresley (Burton 216315)
Simple ground directions: Off A514 or A444 near Swadlincote **No of seats:** 100
Covered accommodation: 150 **Capacity:** 2,000 **Seated:** 120 **Floodlights:** Yes
Year formed: 1882 **Nickname:** 'Moatmen' **Club sponsors:** Bass Worthington
Club colours: White/Red/Red
Change colours: Sky-blue
Previous names: None
Previous grounds: Mushroom Lane, Albert Village
Record attendance: 3,950 v Burton Albion **Year:** 1957
Previous Leagues: Birmingham Combination, Midland, Leics Senior, East Midlands **Programme:** Yes
Clubhouse details: Social club on ground open Mon–Thurs evenings and Saturday (match day).
Present players with Football League experience: None
Past players who progressed into the Football League: G. Duggins
Programme Editors: Brian Spare/Derek Kinsey **Programme:** 8–10 pages, 15p
Club Captain (1985–86): D. King (left) **Player of Year (1985–86):** S. Dolby
Secretary: M. J. Eaton, 29 Goseley Avenue, 0283 213450 (H) Hartshorne, Nr Burton-on-Trent

HALESOWEN HARRIERS

Chairman: R. Rudge **Manager:** D. Beasley **Asst. Manager:** D. Kettle
Secretary: R. P. Beasley, 90 Haden H Road, Halesowen. Tel. 021-550 1721 (H), 359 3666 (22652)
Ground Address & Tel No: Harriers Sports Complex, Park Road, Halesowen. (Lye 6748)
Simple Directions to Ground:
Previous Leagues: No Saturday League **Colours:** Sky Blue **Change colours:** White
Clubhouse: None, only tearoom **Floodlights:** No **Seats:** None listed **Capacity:** 5,000

HARRISONS

Chairman: B. Malpass **Manager:** B. Williams **Asst. Manager:** B. Fisher
Secretary: M. Gibbins, 1 Weston Drive, Cheslyn Bay. Tel. 0922 417321
Ground Address & Tel No: Hazel Lane, Great Wyrley. (410073)
Simple Directions to Ground:
Previous Leagues: Staffs County South **Colours:** Blue/White **Change colours:** Orange/Black
Clubhouse: Clubroom and bar **Floodlights:** No **Seats:** 100 **Ground Accommodation:** 200

HINCKLEY ATHLETIC

Chairman: D. W. Loakes
Manager: B. Vincent
Coach:
Physiotherapist: A. Sanders

Secretary: J. Colver
Tel No: (H) Hinckley 30263, (B) Hinckley 636361
Commercial Manager:
Tel No:
Press Officer:

Address & Tel No of g ound: Middlefield Lane, Hinckley (0455) 613553
Simple ground direction Off A447 through town centre, follow signs to public weighbridge
No of seats: 300 **Ground accommodation:** 1,000 **Capacity:** 5,000 **Floodlights:** Yes
Year formed: 1879 **Nickname:** Robins **Club sonsors:** Couture
Club colours: All Red **Change colours:** White/Black/Black
Previous Names: Hinckley, Hinckley Town, Hinckley United
Previous Grounds: Holywell, London Road, Hinckley
Record attendance: 5,410 v Nuneaton Borough **Year:** 1949

Previous Leagues: Nuneaton Comb, Birmingham League, Southern League
Present players with Football League experience: John Allen (Port Vale)
Past players who progressed into the Football League: John Allen (Port Vale)
Clubhouse details: New Social Club with lounge, games room and concert room. Open eac evening, Sunday lunch and match days (Hinckley 615012)
Major Honours: Birmingham Comb. champions 1923–24, 1926–27; Leicestershire Senior League champions 1897–98, 1899–1900, 1908–09, 1913–14; Birmingham Senior Cup joint winners 1954–55; Leicestshire Senior Cup winners 1899–1900, 1900–01, 1909–10, 1982–83; Leicestershire Challenge Cup winners 1957–58, 1958–59, 1959–60, 1960–61, 1961–62,1964–65, 1967–68
Best performance in F.A. Cup: 2nd Round Proper 1954–55, 1962–63
F.A. Trophy: 1st Qualifying Round 1969–70, 1972–73, 1973–74
F.A. Vase: 4th Round Proper 1976–77, 1977–78, 1978–79, 1985–86
Programme: 24 pages, 25p **Programme Editor:** Alan Mason (Leicester 891899)
Club metal badges: No **Club shop:** No
Club Captain (1985–86): M. Haskins **Players of the Year (1985–86):** David Tedds

OLDBURY UNITED

President: S. Warren
Chairman: S. Warren
Manager: R. Smart
Ass. Man/Coach: G. Clarke
Physiotherapist: F. Anson

Secretary: J. Hall
Address & Tel No: 48 Pottery Road, Oldbury, Warley West Mids. B68 GE2 021-421-7182
Commercial Manager:
Press Officer: M. Scott

Ground Address & Tel. No: "The Cricketers" York Road, Warley, West Mids. 021-559-5564
Capacity: 6,000 **Covered accommodation:** 500 **Seating:** 100 **Floodlights:** Yes
Simple ground directions: M5 Junction 2 onto Halesowen, 1st left at traffic lights, then 1st right.
Clubhouse details: Members club & bar facilities, 021-559-3528
Programme details: 20p, 12 pages **Editor:** F. Johnson **Club metal badges:** Yes £1
Local newspaper(s): Birmingham Mail, Express & Star
Club colours: Blue & White Stripe **Change colours:** White
Midweek match day: Tuesday **Previous Leagues:** Midland Combination, Southern League
Record transfer fee paid: None
Record transfer fee received: £1,000
Record attendance: 2,200 v Walsall Wood 1982
Senior honours/best performance: Walsall Senior Cup Winners, Birmingham Amateur Cup
Past players (who progressed to Football League): C. Gordon, L. Conoway, J. Scott, R. O'Kelly, Nardiello, Dakin, T. Reece.

OLDSWINFORD

President:
Chairman: H. C. Hackett
Managers: M. Woodhouse & E. Edwards
Coach:
Physiotherapist: G. Thompson

Secretary: D. G. Dew
Address & Tel No: 148 King William Street, Amblecote, Stourbridge 0384 376902 (H)
Commercial Manager:
Press Officer & Tel No: Secretary

Address & Tel No of ground: The Dell, Sports Stadium, Bryce Road, Pensnett, Brierley Hill, West Midlands. (0384 77289)
Simple ground directions: $1\frac{1}{4}$ miles from Brierley Hill town centre on Pensnett Road
No of seats: 300 **Covered accommodation:** 300 **Capacity:** 5,000 **Floodlights:** No
Year formed: 1955 **Nickname:** Swinford **Club sponsors:** Several
Club colours: Royal Blue & Sky Blue **Change colours:** Claret/Yellow/Red
Previous Names: None **Previous Grounds:** Cottage Street, Brierley Hill, South Road, Stourbridge
Record attendance: Not known
Previous Leagues: Staffs County, Kidderminster
Clubhouse details: Open nightly, licensed bar, open Monday, Wednesday and match days
Programme: 15 pages, 20p **Local newspapers & Tel No:**
Programme Editor: Secretary
Major Honours: West Midlands Div 1, West Midlands League Cup Div 1 Winners

Derek Kinsey catches Gresley Rovers as they press against Halesowen at the Moat Ground on Easter Saturday. The visiting goalkeeper clears off the head of Glen West.

Lee Hoenig catches a siege of the Halesowen goal by Harrisions in the West Midlands (Regional) League. All to no avail! Visiting Halesowen score the game's only goal.

RUSHALL OLYMPIC

President: J. Arris
Chairman: B. W. Greenwood
Manager: Joe Owen
Coach: None
Physiotherapist: B. Coyne
Secretary: J. Burks
Address & Tel No: 4 Bush Grove, Heath End, Pelsall Pelsall (0922) 684519
Commercial Manager: None
Press Officer: D. Sedgwick (Walsall 935636)
Address & Tel No of ground: Dale's Lane, off Daw End Lane, Rushall, nr Walsall, Staff (Walsall 641021)
Simple ground directions: Daw End Lane off Walsall-Lichfield (A461) main road, ground 500 yards on right (on B4154) 1 mile from Rushall Centre
No of seats: 175 **Covered accommodation:** 100 **Capacity:** 5,000 **Floodlights:** Yes
Year formed: 1951 **Nickname:** The Pics **Club sponsors:** Goodfellows Garage Kennings
Club colours: Old Gold/Black/Black **Change colours:** White/Red/Red
P evious Names: None **Previous Grounds:** Rushall Recreational
Record attendance: 2,400 v Leeds XI (charity game) **Year:** 1977 **Programme:** 10 pages, 10p
Mid-week match evening: Tues/Thurs days **Programme Editor:** David Sedgwick
Previous Leagues: Walsall Amateur League, Staffs County League
Clubhouse details: Excellent bar-lounge, kitchen, adjoining large refreshment facilities
Present players with Football League experience: J. Ray, M. Bowater, J. Owen
Past players to progress to Football League: L. Sinnott (Watford), L. Palin (Aston Villa, Nottm. Forrest)
Club Captain (1985–86): John Ray **Players of the Year:**

TAMWORTH

Chairman: John Bayliss
Managers: Roger Smith & Barry Meads
Physiotherapist: R. Sims
Secretary: L. A. Greenfield
Address & Tel No: 5 Mercia Close, Coton Green, Tamworth, Staffs. Tamworth 61019 (H)
Commercial Manager: P. Young (Tamworth 53194)
Address & Tel No of ground: The Lamb Ground, Kettlebrook, Tamworth, Staffs, Tamworth 65798
Club shop: Yes
Simple ground directions: From town centre follow one-way road marked 'South' into Kettlebrook Road, ground is on right, opposite Railway Arches. From A5 to Two Gates traffic lights, left into Tamworth Road, one mile to 'Lamb Inn', then left into Ground car park
No of seats: **Ground accommodation:** 4,500 **Capacity:** 5,000 **Floodlights:** Yes
Year formed: 1933 **Nickname:** The Lambs **Club sponsors:** J. C. Bailey Construction Ltd
Previous names: None **Club colours:** Red/White
Previous grounds: None **Change colours:** All Yellow
Mid-week match evening: Tuesday
Record attendance: 5,000 v Torquay **Year:** 1969–70 **Previous Leagues:** Birmingham, Southern, Northern Premier
Best performance in: F.A. Cup: 1969–70 2nd Round
F.A. Trophy: 1970–71 Quarter Final
Clubhouse: On ground, registered club
Present players with Football League experience: M. Kendall, C. Lockett, D. Hugh, B. Livingstone
Past players who progressed into the Football League: P. Wier (Cardiff C), S.Fox (Wrexham, Birmingham C)
Record transfer fee paid: None **Record transfer fee received:** None
Programme Editor: Rod Hadley Tel. Tamworth 66786
Programme details: 8 pages, 20p **Local newspapers:** Tamworth Herald, Tamworth Trader
Senior Honours: Birmingham Senior Cup (3), Staffordshire Senior Cup (3) West Mid. Lge (3) West Mid. L. Cup (4)
Club metal badges: No
Club Captain (1985–86): Gary Brown **Player of the Year (1984–85):** Corrigan Lockett

TIPTON TOWN F.C.

Chairman: D. Powell
Manager: R. Corbett
Asst. Man/Coach: G. Andrews 021-556 3566
Secretary: John A. Cross
Address & Tel No: 1 Moreton Close, Tipton DY4 0DG
Presss Officer: J. A. Cross **General Manager:** G. Bunch (Sedgley 70445)
Address & Tel No of ground: Tipton Sports Union Stadium, Wednesbury Oak Road, Tipton. (021-556 3566)
Simple ground direction: Ground lies mid-way between Dudley and Wednesbury on 245 bus route connecting two towns. Ground by large Asda superstore in Tipton
Stand: 100 **Floodlights:** No
Year formed: 1948 **Nickname:** None **Capacity:** 1,000
Club colours: Black & White stripes/Black/Red **Change colours:** All Blue
Mid-week match evening: Wednesday
Record attendance: 486 v Halesowen **Year:** 1985
Programme Editor: Secretary **Programme details:** 12 pages, 20p
Clubhouse details: Bar, lounge, large concert room
Major Honours: West Midland Div 1, W. Midlands Div 1 Cup
Club Captain (1985–86): P. Marsh **Player of the Year (1985–86):** Eric Smith

TIVIDALE

President: P. Archer, MP
Chairman: D. McDonald
Manager: E. Woodbine
Coach: T. Edge/G. Thompson
Asst.Manager: K. Hughes
Physiotherapist: G. Bennett
Football Secretary: R. Hyde
Address & Tel No: 30 St. Andrews Close, Lower Gornal, Dudley, West Midlands. Sedgley 09073 77305 (H), Dudley 0384 52322 (B)
Commercial Manager: Vacant
Press Officer & Tel No: Secretary
Address & Tel No of ground: The Beeches, Packwood Road, Tividale, Warley, West Midlands (Dudley 211743)
Simple ground directions: Dudley Port Station to Burnt Tree, left towards B'ham ground 1 mile on right or M5 to Junction 2 (Oldbury Junction) right towards Wolverhampton ground, approx. 2 miles on left
No of seats: 200 **Covered accommodation:** Stand, one side of ground **Capacity:** 3,000 **Floodlights:** No
Year formed: 1957 **Nickname:** The Dale **Club sponsors:** J. B. Services
Club colours: Yellow **Change colours:** Sky Blue
Previous Names: None **Previous Grounds:** City Road, Tividale
Mid-week match evening: Tuesday & Thursday
Record attendance: 2,500 (approx) v Telford, F.A. Cup **Programme Editor:** R. Hyde
Previous Leagues: **Programme:** 10 pages, 10p
Clubhouse details: Clubhouse and ground combined, open 7 nights weekly and Saturday/Sunday lunchtimes
Past players who progressed into the Football League: G. Hughes
Major Honours: West Midland League Cup Winners (19), West Midland League Division One Winners

BREWOOD

Chairman: A. Worton **Manager:** T. Wharton **Asst. Manager:** P. Embrey
Secretary: B. Charlesworth, 28 Brook House Close, Featherstone. Tel: Wolverhampton 0902 730249 (H), 734516 (B)
Ground Address & Tel No: Engleton Lane, Brewood, Staffs. (0902 850395)
Simple Directions to Ground: M6 to Gailey Island, A5 left, 1 mile to Ground
Previous Leagues: Wolverhampton Amateur **Colours:** Blue/White **Change colours:** White/Black
Clubhouse: Bar and lounge **Floodlights:** No **Capacity:** Not listed

CRADLEY TOWN

Chairman: R. Hutt **Manager:** G. Grosvenor
Asst. Manager: R. Bingham
Secretary: N. Turner. Tel. Stourbridge 396006 (H), 021773 8361 (B)
Ground Address & Tel No: Beeches View Avenue, Cradley, Halesowen. (Cradley Heath 69904)
Simple Directions to Ground: Halesowen–Stourbridge Road, left at 'Round of Beef', right at 'Smith's Arms', end of road left and 300 yards on right
Previous Leagues: Kidderminster, West Midlands Metropolitan, Midland Combination
Clubhouse: Bar and other facilities **Colours:** Red/Green/Green **Change colours:** All Yellow
Floodlights: No **Capacity:** 4,000 **Seating:** 100 **Ground Accommodation:** 2,000

DARLASTON

Chairman: G. H rtland **Manager:** D. Davies **Asst. Manager:**
Secretary: N. Chambers, 3 Wrexham Avenue, Bentley, Walsall. Tel 0922 32141 (H)
Ground Address & Tel No: The City Ground, Waverley Road, Darlaston
Simple Directions to Ground: 5 minutes from Junction 9 & 10 of M6 Motorway
Previous Leagues: Birmingham Combination
Colours: Blue & White stripes/White/Blue **Change colours:** Yellow/Blue/Red
Clubhouse: Bar and clubhouse (capacity of 150), small private committee room
Floodlights: No **Seats:** 300 **Capacity:** 2,500

GORNAL ATHLETIC

Chairman: K. Taylor **Managers:** R. Green
Secretary: V. Burns, 65 Grafton Road, Oldbury, Warley, West Midlands B68 8BJ. Tel. 021-559 1992 & 021-233 2001
Ground Address & Tel No: Garden Walk Stadium, Lower Gornal, Dudley, W. Midlands
Simple Directions to Ground: Central Drive off Himley Road, 1st left off Central Drive
Previous Leagues: Birmingham, Worcester Combination, Wolverhampton Amateur
Colours: Yellow & Green **Change colours:** Sky blue
Clubhouse: Bar, committee room, lounge **Floodlights:** No **Capacity:** 1,200

LICHFIELD

President: Ken Hughes
Chairman: Ron Walters
Manager: Brian Sawyer
Secretary: Brian Smith
Address & Tel No: Beech Gardens, Lichfield, Staffs. 05432 57855
Address of ground: Shortbutts Lane, Lichfield
Simple ground directions: London/Coventry/Warwick road out of Lichfield (via Upper St. John Street), in ½ mile turn right at lights at London Road Garage into Shortbutts Lane. Ground 200 yards on right
Year formed: 1966 **Club colours:** All Royal Blue **Change colours:** All Red
Previous Leagues: Staff County Premier Div. (South)
Programme: 16 pages, 15p **Programme Editor:** Brian Smith
Major Honours: Walsall Challenge Cup 1967, Lichfield Charity Cup (3)
Club Captain (1984–85): Richard Baker

LUDLOW TOWN

Chairman: A. Cade **Manager:** D. Mulliner
Secretary: M. Geary. Tel. Ludlow 3395 (H), 2381 x38 (B)
Ground Address & Tel No: Riddings Park, Riddings Road, Ludlow (5103)
Simple Directions to Ground: From Clee-Hill Island on By-pass, take Henley road into Ludlow, second left into Sandpits Road, follow for 1 mile, first right after chip shop
Previous Leagues: Kidderminster **Colours:** Red/Black/Black **Change colours:** All Blue
Clubhouse: Bar seating 50, three changing rooms, hot drinks and food served at matches
Floodlights: No **Seating:** 6 **Capacity:** Not certain

NORTHPARK UNITED

Chairman: J. McMahon **Manager:** A. Morris **Asst. Manager:** P. Richards
Secretary: T. Connolly, 14 Kerridge Close, Pendeford, Wolverhampton. Tel. 788266
Ground Address & Tel No: Claregate Boys Club, Aldersley Road, Claregate. (W'ton 756961)
Simple Directions to Ground: Wolverhampton—Stafford Road, Oxley More Road, Aldersley Road
Previous Leagues: Staffs County South **Colours:** Blue/Yellow **Change colours:** White
Clubhouse: No details given **Floodlights:** No **Seats:** None **Capacity:** 1,000

PELSALL VILLA

Chairman: V. Dolphin **Manager:** B. Hill
Secretary: R. White, 10 Smithfield Road, Blakehall. Tel. Bloxwich 75857
Ground Address & Tel No: Walsall Road, Pelsall. (682018)
Simple Directions to Ground: Walsall Road (Pelsall) next to 'Bush' public house at side of Cricket Club next door
Previous Leagues: Staffs County
Colours: Red & Black stripes/Black/Red & Black **Change colours:** All Blue
Clubhouse: At next door Cricket Club **Floodlights:** No **Capacity:**

WESTFIELDS F.C.

President: Ken Morris
Chairman: Robert Doddy
Manager: Phil Hallett
Coach: Jim Greenly
Physiotherapist: Peter Isaac
Secretary: Andy Morris
Address & Tel No: 17 Fair Oaks Green, Kings Acre, Hereford. 0432 266775
Commercial Manager: Stuart Davies
Address & Tel No: 61 Cotterell St. Hereford (268114)
Press Officer: Andy Morris
Address & Tel No of ground: Thorn Lighting, Holme Lacy Road, Rotherwas, Hereford. 0432 268131 Ground, 266670 Club
Simple ground directions: Proceed 1 mile south of Hereford, turn left into Holme Lacy Road, proceed 1 mile to Thorn Lighting Rotherwas, ground on right
Floodlights: No **Year formed:** 1966 **Nickname:** The Fields
Club sponsors: Stoke Hill & Co (Estate Agents)
Club colours: Sky Blue/Maroon **Change colours:** White **Programme:** Yes
Previous Names: None **Previous Grounds:** Widemarsh Common **Programme Editor:** Andy Morris
Clubhouse details: "Thorn Lighting" on ground

WOLVERHAMPTON CASUALS

President: Clive Hammond
Chairman: G. Jones **Manager:** S. Plant **Asst. Manager:** M. Gunter
Secretary: D. Parker, 38 Wolverley Avenue, Wollaston, Stourbridge, W. Mid DY8 3RJ. Tel. 0384 371402
Ground Address & Tel No: Brinsford Lane, Coven, Wolverhampton WV10 7PR. (0902 783214)
Simple Direction to Ground: M6 Junction 10A—M54 Junction 2—A449 right towards Stafford, after 500 yards first right, Ground on left 100 yards **Club sponsors:** Hammond Heat Treatment/West Midland Copiers
Year formed: 1896 **No of seats:** None **Capacity:** 2,000 **Floodlights:** No **Nickname:** The Casuals
Previous Leagues: Birmingham A.F.A., Wolverhampton Amateur
Colours: All Green (shadow stripes) **Change colours:** All red
Clubhouse: Bar and snacks, open Tues, Wed, Thurs, Sat, Sun & alternate Mon
Programme: 24 pages, 20p **Programme Editor:** Nick Loftus
Club Captain (1985–86): Tim Hadfield

Westfield F.C.

GKN Sankey's main stand is not over-populated during the home team's draw with Oldswinford (2-2). Leo Hoenig records the scene.

HALLS BREWERY HELLENIC LEAGUE

President: C.J. Green Esq (1963)
Chairman: N.A.S. Matthews (1953), Cedar Court, Steeple Aston, Oxford.
Tel. Steeple Aston (0869) 40347
Hon. Secretary and Premier Division Hon. Match Secretary: D.A.G. Harrison (1959), 107 Thame Road, Haddenham, Aylesbury, Bucks.
Tel: Haddenham (0844) 290590
Hon. Treasurer & Assistant Secretary: R.D. Darvill (1966), 4 Chapel Lane, Enstone, Oxford.
Tel: Enstone (060872) 260

THRILLING SEASON SEES SHARPNESS TRIUMPH

The strength and competitive nature of HALLS BREWERY Hellenic League football has never been more clearly illustrated or dramatically demonstrated than in the closing stages of the season's quest for Premier Division Championship honours. Hounslow Town, Shortwood Utd., Supermarine, Sharpness, Abingdon Town and Abingdon Utd. were all involved in an exciting and nail-bitting finish. Hounslow faltered in the final run-in while the challenges of Shortwood Utd. and Sharpness gathered momentum, with Supermarine and the two Abingdon Clubs fading, Shortwood Utd. became favourites for the title but Sharpness were a constant threat. They needed to win their last nine matches — a daunting challenge but one that they accepted with determination. And win them they did, although Shortwood were surprisingly defeated on their own ground by the unpredictable Moreton Town in their final match, thus conceding the Championship to Sharpness and making their visit to Morris Motors a formality in which they confirmed their championship form by the only goal and deservedly took the honours, Their achievement was quite remarkable and they are worthy Champions. Shortwood Utd., the 1985 Champions, finished as runners-up.

Bicester Town were the surprise winners of the SKOL Premier Division Challenge Cup when they defeated Thame Utd. by three goals to two after extra time in a most exciting Final. Although Bicester are founder members of the League, it is the first time they have won this trophy and the match was a personal success for their Captain, Andrew Truby, who scored all their three goals.

The success of Viking Sports in becoming Division 1 Champions was well merited and throughly deserved. They took over the leadership in the early stages and enjoyed a commanding lead as the New Year approached. However, newcomers to the League, Penhill, were always in contention and did, in fact, narrow the gap but were unable to catch the Middlesex Club. Their achievement in finishing as runners-up, and therefore gaining promotion at the first time of asking is indicative of their playing strength and both promoted Clubs are capable of providing formidable opposition for Premier Division Clubs next season. The Hounslow Town v Viking Sports fixtures will be most interesting encounters with Father and Son in opposition. Roy Bartlett is the founder and President of Viking Sports while his son, Gordon is the Manager of Hounslow.

Clanfield and Didcot Town provided good entertainment in the Final Tie of the SKOL Division 1 Challenge Cup and excitement mounted in the scond half. With the score standing at 1 — 1, both teams adopted all-out attack but were unable to break down well organised defences. It was not until the closing minutes that Clanfield scored the all important decider.

Moreton Town can never be denied success and they are the holders of the Gloucestershire Senior Trophy, having defeated Old Georgians by two goals to nil in the Final Tie of that Competition.

The Wiltshire Senior Cup Final was all Hellenic. Supermarine became the holders of the trophy by defeating Penhill from Division 1 by two goals to nil.

Pegasus Juniors were most impressive in the Final Tie of the Worcestershire Senior Urn and throughly deserved their 2 — 1 win over the West Midlands Police.

The success of Sharpness adds yet another interesting feature. Prior to 1982, the Premier Division Championship had been dominated by Oxfordshire and Berks and Bucks Clubs, but since that year the honours have gone to Gloucestershire based Clubs, so balance of power is now in the West Country, but could next season change the swing of the pendulum? With Hounslow Town strengthening their challenge under their new Manager Gordon Bartlett, who took Southall to the F.A. Vase Final last season, with Rayners Lane always serious contenders and with the newly promoted Viking Sports adding their challenge, next season could well see the Middlesex based Clubs to the forefront of Hellenic League activities.

Hounslow Town, having finished the season in third place in the Premier Division, qualified for promotion to the Southern League within the Pyramid System, but their application was surprisingly rejected as their ground and facilities did not reach the required standards, so they remain in membership of the League for next season.

At the other end of the Premier Division League Table, Almondsbury Greenway are relegated to Division 1, but Maidenhead Town, unable to overcome their ground problems to the satisfaction of the Hellenic League, have left the League to join the Chiltonian League.

For next season, the League's Division 1 welcomes the return of Chipping Norton Town, together with Purton from Wiltshire County League, Cheltenham Town Reserves from the Midland Combination, Cheltenham Saracens and Carterton Town.

An outstanding feature of last season was the success of the Sponsorship of the League by HALLS OXFORD & WEST BREWERY COMPANY LIMITED, and the Sponsorship of the League's Challenge Cup Competitions by SKOL. Not only did the joint sponsorship provide member Clubs with finanial incentives but they gave a new impetus to the League as a whole and the League wishes to place on record its appreciation and gratitude for all that has been achieved as a result of the backing, interest and support so readily given by the Sponsors. Particular mention must be made of the HALLS BREWERY HELLENIC FOOTBALL LEAGUE WEEKLY BULLETIN which has proved to be such an outstanding and popular publication. Circulation increased throughout the season and with Clubs reproducing it in their match programmes, it now has over 1,000 readers spread over more than six counties. This is a classic example of what can be achieved through sponsorship, especially when the Sponsor is as enthusiastic as HALLS BREWERY have been. The partnership has been an enormous success and the League is delighted to announce its continuance next season.

Norman Matthews

Season 1985-86
HONOURS

Halls Brewery Premier Division Champions	—	Sharpness F.C.
Halls Brewery Premier Divison Runners-up	—	Shortwood Utd. F.C.
Premier Division Skol Challenge Cup Winners	—	Bicester Town F.C.
Premier Division Skol Challenge Cup Finalists	—	Thame Utd. F.C.
Halls Brewery Division 1 Champions	—	Viking Sports F.C.
Halls Brewery Division 1 Runners-up	—	Penhill F.C.
Division 1 Skol Challenge Cup Winners	—	Clanfield F.C.
Division 1 Skol Challenge Cup Runners-up	—	Didcot Town F.C.
Halls Brewery Reserve Section Champions	—	Viking Sports F.C.
Halls Brewery Reserve Section Runners-up	—	Pressed Steel F.C.
Reserve Section Skol Challenge Cup Winners	—	Abingdon Town F.C.
Reserve Section Skol Challenge Cup Finalists	—	Viking Sports F.C.
Gloucestershire Senior Trophy Winners	—	Moreton Town F.C.
Wiltshire Senior Cup Winners	—	Supermarine F.C.
Wiltshire Senior Cup Finalists	—	Penhill F.C.
Worcestershire Senior Urn Winners	—	Pegasus Juniors F.C.
Berks & Bucks Intermediate Cup Winners	—	Didcot Town Res. F.C.
Gloucestershire Senior Amateur Cup Winners	—	Shortwood Utd, Res. F.C.
Gloucestershire Junior Challenge Cup Finalists	—	Bishops Cleeve Res. F.C.
Middlesex Intermediate Cup Finalists	—	Viking Sports Res. F.C.

Sharpness — League Champions. Back-Row (L to R): P. Casey (Manager), A. Kerr, R. Breedon, S. Billett, P. Mason, T. Haile, D. Foxwell, P. Hayden, R. Powell (Trainer). Front-Row (L to R): A. Bathe, J. Rigg, J. Turner, M. Williams, G. Marsh.

PREMIER DIVISION

	P	W	D	L	F	A	Pts
1 Sharpness	34	24	4	6	88	41	76
2 Shortwood Utd.	34	23	2	9	79	43	71
3 Hounslow	34	20	6	8	83	44	66
4 Abingdon Town	34	19	8	7	60	36	65
5 Supermarine	34	21	2	11	56	48	65
6 Rayners Lane	34	18	7	9	65	48	*60
7 Abingdon Utd.	34	17	8	9	46	33	59
8 Yate Town	34	15	8	11	57	44	53
9 Moreton Town	34	15	8	11	51	40	53
10 Thame Utd.	34	13	8	13	51	54	47
11 Pegasus Juniors	34	13	5	16	56	64	44
12 Wallingford Town	34	12	5	17	45	56	41
13 Fairford Town	34	8	8	18	39	49	32
14 Morris Motors	34	7	10	17	30	44	31
15 Bicester Town	34	9	3	22	46	79	30
16 Wantage Town	34	7	6	21	40	65	27
17 Almondsb'y G'way	34	7	3	24	34	82	24
18 Maidenhead Town	34	5	5	24	34	90	20

*1 point deducted

DIVISION 1

	P	W	D	L	F	A	Pts
1 Viking Sports	30	22	5	3	100	37	71
2 Penhill	30	22	4	4	78	24	70
3 Bishops Cleeve	30	17	6	7	72	45	57
4 Didcot Town	30	16	7	7	78	42	55
5 Highworth Town	30	15	6	9	61	38	51
6 Kidlington	30	13	8	9	52	48	47
7 Clanfield	30	11	8	11	53	56	41
8 Hazells	30	8	12	10	38	46	36
9 Badminton	30	8	10	12	39	62	34
10 Lambourne Sports	30	8	9	13	43	56	33
11 Pressed Steel	30	9	6	15	44	62	33
12 Cirencester Town	30	8	8	14	52	54	32
13 Avon Bradford	30	6	13	11	38	62	31
14 Easington Sports	30	8	4	18	50	81	28
15 Kintbury Rangers	30	4	10	16	38	67	22
16 AFC Aldermaston	30	5	4	21	39	95	19

ABINGDON TOWN

President: R.F. Cox
Chairman: A.R. Bricknell
Manager: Paul Lee
Coach: R. Nicholas
Physiotherapist: B. Knapp
Secretary: B.M. Crook
Address & Tel. No. 41 Radley Rd, Abingdon, Oxon OX14 3PL. 0235 24461
Commercial Manager: E.J. Quail
Address & Tel. No. 0635 68967
Press Officer & Tel. No. A. Worgan, Abingdon 812781
Address and Tel. No. of ground: Culham Road, Abingdon 0235 21684
Simple ground directions: A415 Abingdon — Dorchester Road, ½ mile from town centre
No. of seats: none **Covered accommodation:** 200 **Capacity:** 2,000 **Floodlights:** No
Year formed: 1880 **Nickname: The Town** **Club sponsor:**
Previous names:
Club colours: Green /Yellow
Previous Leagues: Reading & District
Change colours: Blue
Clubhouse details: Social Club opens 7 days a week
Programme details: Free with Ground Admission
Club Captain (1985-86): John Harvey Lynch
Programme editor: A. Worgan
Player of the Year (1985-86): John Harvey Lynch
Major Honours: Berks & Bucks Senior Cup 1958-59, Hellenic League Winners 1956-57, 1958-59, 1959-60, Cup 1957-58, 1970-71, 1981-82

ABINGDON UNITED

President: R.H. Barlow
Chairman: A. White
Manager: Nick Brown
Coach: Martin Presscot
Physiotherapist: I. McKay
Secretary: Terry Hutchinson, 14 Glyme, Close, Abingdon
Address & Tel. No. 0235 23017
Commercial Manager:
Address & Tel. No.
Press Officer & Tel. No.
Address and Tel. No. of ground: Northcourt Road, Abingdon. 0235 20255
Simple ground directions: A4183 Abingdon, Oxford. Ground approx 1 mile north of town centre.
No. of seats: None **Covered accommodation:** None **Capacity:** 2,000 **Floodlights:** Yes
Year formed: 1946 **Nickname:** **Club sponsor:** Glasurit Beck
Previous names:
Club colours: Yellow shirts, Blue shorts
Previous Leagues:
Change colours: White shirts, Blue shorts
Clubhouse details: Small club house, 2 bars, membership 350. Open normal hours.
Programme details: 15p
Club Captain (1985-86): Neil Taylor
Programme editor: William Fletcher
Player of the Year (1985-86): N. Cattell
Major Honours:

BICESTER TOWN

President: G. Titchener, Esq.
Chairman: D. Waller
Manager: Trevor Cuss
Coach: As above
Physiotherapist: None
Secretary: C. H. Rawlings
Address & Tel. No. Bicester 241085
Commercial Manager: As above
Address & Tel. No. As above
Press Officer & Tel. No. As above
Address and Tel. No. of ground: Sports Ground, Oxford Road, Bicester
Simple ground directions: Outskirts of town on the Oxford Road
No. of seats: 250 **Covered accommodation:** 250 **Capacity:** Plenty **Floodlights:** No
Year formed: 1873 **Nickname:** Foxhunters **Club sponsor:** Bicester Roofing Co.
Previous names: None
Club colours: Red shirts, Black shorts
Previous Leagues: Oxon Senior
Change colours: Light Blue stripes
Clubhouse details: Bar separate from hall (alterations now taking place for a lounge, clubhouse on the ground itself)
Programme details: None
Club Captain (1985-86):
Programme editor: D. Waller
Player of the Year (1985-86):
Major Honours: Hellenic Champions 1960-61, 1977-78, Reserve Champions same year after winning Hellenic Div 1 1976-77 and gaining promotion

FAIRFORD TOWN

President: A.E. Smith
Chairman: M.B. Tanner
Manager: S. Crowley
Coach: G. Fell
Physiotherapist: T. Williams
Secretary: M.J. Cook
Address & Tel. No. "Bow Wow", Down Ampney, Cirencester, Glos. Tel: (H) Swindon 751240 (B) Cirencester 5995
Commercial Manager: E. Howard
Press Officer & Tel. No. As Secretary
Address and Tel. No. of ground: Cinder Lane, Fairford (Cirencester 712071)
Simple ground directions: Entering Fairford from Lechlade turn left down Cinder Lane opposite petrol filling Station on right.
No. of seats: None **Covered accommodation:** 2,000 **Capacity:** 2,000 **Floodlights:** No
Year formed: 1891 **Nickname: Town** **Club sponsor:** Jewson
Previous names:
Previous Leagues: Cirencester and District, Swindon and District
Club colours: Red Shirts, White Shorts **Change colours:** Yellow/Green
Clubhouse details: Open every evening and Saturday, Sunday and Bank Holiday Lunchtimes
Major Honours: Gloucester Challenge Trophy Winners 1979-80, Runners-Up 1982-83

HOUNSLOW TOWN F.C.

President: Stuart Das
Chairman: Jeff Brewster
Manager: Gordon Bartlett
Coach: Leo Morris
Physiotherapist:
Secretary: Barry Sutherns
Address & Tel. No. 01-898 8230
Commercial Manager:
Address & Tel. No.
Press Officer & Tel. No. As Secretary
Address and Tel. No. of ground: Denbigh Road, Hounslow
Simple ground directions: Off Kingsley Rd. Hounslow
No. of seats: 500 **Covered accommodation:** 2,000 **Capacity:** 5,000 **Floodlights:** Yes
Year formed: 1884 **Nickname:** The Town **Club sponsor:**
Previous names:
Previous Leagues: Spartan, Corinthian, Athenian, Southern
Club colours: Red and Black
Change colours: Yellow and Red
Clubhouse details: Open every day. Lunchtime and Evenings.
Programme details: 16 pages. 20p
Programme editor: Barry Sutherns
Club Captain (1985-86): Danny Pipe
Player of the Year (1985-86):
Major Honours: F.A. Amateur Cup R/U 1962

MORETON TOWN

President: Lord Dulverton
Chairman: C. Miles. Tel. 50653/50452
Manager: C. Shepherd
Coach: J. Hooke
Physiotherapist: M. Pugh
Secretary: H.J. Eldridge
Address & Tel. No. 40 Stockwells, Moreton-in-Marsh Tel. 51133
Commercial Manager:
Address & Tel. No.
Press Officer & Tel. No. Secretary
Address and Tel. No. of ground: London Road, Moreton-in-Marsh. Tel. 50861
Simple ground directions: On main Oxford — Worcester Road
No. of seats: None **Covered accommodation:** Yes **Capacity:** 3,000 **Floodlights:** Yes
Year formed: Pre-1908 **Nickname:** Lilywhites **Club sponsor:**Cotswold Casement Co.
Previous names: None
Club colours: White/Blue White
Previous Leagues: Cheltenham, Mid Cotswold
Change colours: Red/White Red
Clubhouse details: Open every night except Monday
Programme details:
Major Honours: Biggart Cup Winners 1969-70, League Champions 1973-74, 1975-76, Glos County Cup Winners 1973-74, Champions (3), League Cup Winners 1982-83, Gloucester Challenge Trophy (4)

MORRIS MOTORS F.C.

President:
Chairman: E. Whitworth
Manager: P. Buck
Coach: K. Norton
Physiotherapist:
Secretary: S.P. Giles
Address & Tel. No. 60 Glebelands, Headington, Oxford OX3 7EN Tel. 0865 60810
Commercial Manager:
Address & Tel. No.
Press Officer & Tel. No.
Address and Tel. No. of ground: The Barracks, Holloway, Cowley Oxford (0865) 776890
Simple ground directions: Turn right off South by-pass at Pressed Steel roundabout into Horsepath road and right again at traffic lights. Ground on right hand side approx. 200 yards up road.
No. of seats: **Covered accommodation:** **Capacity:** **Floodlights:** No
Year formed: 1920 **Nickname:** Motors **Club sponsor:**
Previous names:
Club colours: All Blue
Previous Leagues: Oxford Senior league
Change colours: All White
Clubhouse details: Morris Motors Athletic and Social Club, Crescent Road, Cowley, Oxford. Tel 0865-778476
Programme details:
Programme editor:
Club Captain (1985-86): Paul Baker
Player of the Year (1985-86): Kevin Dempsey
Major Honours: Oxon Senior Cup Winners; 1921, 1964, 1985, Hellenic League Div. 1 Winners 1983/84 Runners up. 1962/63, 1974/75 Hellenic League Premier Cup Winners 1979/80. Hellenic League Div. 1 Cup Winners 1962/63.

PEGASUS JUNIORS

President: D.S. Hill
Chairman: R.W. Pasley
Manager: D. Llewellyn
Coach: M. Williams
Physiotherapist: Greyfriars Physio
Secretary: R.J. Perks
Address & Tel. No. 46, Foley Street, Hereford. (0432) 272524
Commercial Manager:
Address & Tel. No.
Press Officer & Tel. No. As Secretary
Address and Tel. No. of ground:
Simple ground directions:
No. of seats: 4,000 **Covered accommodation:** 765 **Capacity:** 15,000 **Floodlights:** Yes
Year formed: 1955 **Nickname: The Reds** **Club sponsor:**
Previous names:
Club colours: Red
Previous Leagues: Hereford/Worcester
Change colours: White
Clubhouse details: 48 Stowens Street
Programme details: 20p
Programme editor:
Club Captain (1985-86): Dave Jones
Player of the Year (1985-86): Bill Fraser
Major Honours: H.F.A. County Cup 1972, 1982/83/85. W.F.A. Senior Urn 1986. Hellenic League Div One. 1985.

PENHILL

President: B. Little
Chairman: A. Garland
Manager: A. Dyton
Secretary:
Address & Tel. No.
Address and Tel. No. of ground: Southbrook Recreation Ground, Pinehurst Road, Swindon, Wilts. (0793) 611171
Simple ground directions: Cricklade Rd, Ferndale Rd, St. Mary's Grove, Pinehurst Rd., Ground on right 400yds.
No. of seats: **Covered accommodation:** **Capacity:** **Floodlights:** No
Year formed: 1970 **Nickname:** PYC **Club sponsors:** James Davis (Timber)
Previous names:
Club colours: Amber/White
Previous Leagues: Wilts County, Swindon & District
Change colours: Blue/White
Clubhouse details:
Major Honours: Wilts Senior Cup (1), Wilts County Champions (2)

RAYNERS LANE

President:
Chairman: Tom Lynn
Manager: Don Durkin
Coach: Don Durkin
Physiotherapist:
Secretary: Tony Pratt
Address & Tel. No. 4 Stirling Close, Cowley, Uxbridge, Middlesex UB8 2BA (0895) 33853 (H) 01-848 2203 (B)
Commercial Manager: T. Lynn
Address & Tel. No. 01-868 4761 (H) 01-866 7089 (B)
Press Officer & Tel. No. D. Durkin (0753 889502 (H) 01-879 1760 (B)
Address and Tel. No. of ground: 51 Rayners Lane, Harrow, Middlesex 01-866 9659
Simple ground directions: Turn right from Rayners Lane LT Station, take 2nd turning left (Rayners Lane), ground on right after garage on corner and following road to junction.
No. of seats: **Covered accommodation:** Yes **Capacity:** 1,000 **Floodlights:** No
Year formed: 1933 **Nickname:** The Lane **Club sponsor:** A & J Bull Ltd
Previous names:
Club colours: Yellow & Green stripes/Green
Previous Leagues: Parthenon, Spartan, Middlesex
Change colours: Blue & White/Blue
Clubhouse details: 2 bars, entertainment hall, separate dressing rooms
Programme details: 4-8 pages, 20p
Club Captain (1985-86):
Programme editor: T. Lynn
Player of the Year (1985-86):
Major Honours: Middlesex League Cup 1971-72, Hellenic Div 1 Cup 1980-81, Champions 1982-83, Middlesex Premier Cup Winners 1983-84.

SHARPNESS A.F.C.

President: A. Aldridge
Chairman: D. Thomas
Manager: P. Casey
Coach: G. Marsh
Physiotherapist: R. Powell
Secretary: R.W. Sherman
Address & Tel. No. 9 Severn Road, Sharpness Nr. Berkely. Gloucester GL13 9UF (0453) 811616
Commercial Manager: To be appointed
Address & Tel. No.
Press Officer & Tel. No. Secretary
Address and Tel. No. of ground: "The Port", The Docks, Sharpness, Gloucester. 0453 810659
Simple ground directions: Leave M5 at Junction 13 or 14, A38 to B 4066 Sharpness (Signposted) Ground within Docks Confines
No. of seats: 250 **Covered accommodation:** Yes **Capacity:** 3,000 **Floodlights:** No
Year formed: 1900 **Nickname:** **Club sponsors:** J.C. Aldridge & Son. Newport Towers Motel (Kit)
Previous names:
Club colours: Red/White/Red
Previous Leagues: Glos. North. Senior, Glos. County
Change colours: All Blue
Clubhouse details: Bar, Skittle Alley and Function Room. Open every evening and Match Days
Programme details: 16 Pages, 20p.
Club Captain (1985-86): John Turner
Programme editor: K. Coughlin
Player of the Year (1985-86): Doug Foxwell
Major Honours: Glos. County League Winners 1983/84. Hellenic League Premier Division Winners 1985/86

SHORTWOOD UNITED

President: J. Claridge
Chairman: I. Martin
Manager: M. Carroll
Coach: A. Townsend
Physiotherapist:
Press Officer & Tel. No.
Secretary: P.J. Grant
Address & Tel. No. 2 Green View, Shortwood, Nailsworth, Glos GL6 0SE. Nailsworth 2577
Commercial Manager: R.C. Webb
Address & Tel. No. 11 Kings Road., Rodborough, Stroud, Glos, Stroud 79494
Address and Tel. No. of ground: "Meadow Bank", Shortwood, Nailsworth, Glos. Tel: Nailsworth 3936
Simple ground directions: ¼ mile from Nailsworth, keep left past "Britannia"
No. of seats: **Covered accommodation:** Granstand Standing **Capacity:** 5,000 **Floodlights:** No
Year formed: 1900 **Nickname:** The Wood **Club sponsor:** Astro Vision & Video Libraries, Stroud & Gloucester
Previous names:
Club colours: Red/White stripes
Previous Leagues: Gloucester County
Change colours: White/Blue stripes
Clubhouse details: Sports and social club on ground open after matches at 4.00pm
Programme details: Free with Ad charge to ground (12 pages) **Programme editor:** Richard Webb
Club Captain (1985-86):
Player of the Year (1985-86):
Major Honours: Glos County League 1981-82, Glos F.A. Trophy 1983-84, Hellenic League Division One Cup 1983-84

SUPERMARINE

President: A. Cox
Chairman: C. Humphreys
Manager: A.J. Belcher
Coach: D. Firman
Physiotherapist: Kevin Retter
Secretary: E. Stott
Address & Tel. No. 43 Stanier Street, Swindon SN1 5QU. Swindon 21301
Commercial Manager:
Address and Tel. No. of ground: Supermarine Sports & Social Club, Hunts Copse, Highworth Road, South Marston, Swindon. 0973 824828
Simple ground directions: Highworth Road (A361) north of Swindon, via Stratton. St Margaret
No. of seats: **Covered accommodation:** North Stand **Capacity:** Approx 100 **Floodlights:** No
Year formed: 1947 (as Vickers) **Nickname:** **Club sponsors:** Allen Coin
Previous names: Vickers
Previous Leagues: Wilts
Programme details: 1st Team match days
Programme editor: George Ransom (0793 782808)
Club colours: Blue & White
Change colours: Red & White
Club Captain (1985-86):
Player of the Year (1985-86):
Major Honours: Wilts Senior Cup R-Up 1974-75, Wilts Comb. League Senior Winners 1975-76, Dr Elliott Cup Winners 1974-75, 1977-78, 1978-79, 1979-80, 1980-81, Farn'don Thurs. Mem.l Cup Winners 1973-74, 1974-75, 1978-79, Hellenic League Div. League Div. One R-Up 1982-83, Hellenic Reserve Section Cup Winners 1983-84.

THAME UNITED

President: M. Matthews
Chairman: R.T. Elee
Manager: Hughie Curran
Coach: Peter Arch
Secretary: D.W. Blake
Address & Tel. No. 4 Sun Crescent, Oakley, Bucks HP18 9RF 0844 237573
Press Officer S. Summersbee, 65 Chinnor Rd
Address and Tel. No. of ground: Windmill Road, Thame
Simple ground directions: Market Square, into Nelson Street
No. of seats: 200 **Covered accommodation:** Yes **Capacity:** 3000 **Floodlights:** Yes
Year formed: 1883 **Nickname:** United **Club sponsors:** McVities
Previous names:
Previous Leagues: Oxon Senior League
Clubhouse details: Catering and Bar Facilities
Programme details: Price 50p including admission
Programme editor: D.W. Blake
Record Attendance: 2,000
Club colours: Red
Change colours: Blue
Club Captain (1985-86): Simon Dexter
Player of the Year (1985-86): Neil Edwards
Major Honours: Oxon Senior Cup Winners 1906, 1909, 1910, 1976, 1981. Oxon Charity Cup Winners 1911, 1912, 1913, 1957. Oxon Senior League Winners 1907, 1908, 1909, 1930, 1931, 1955, 1956, 1957. Hellenic Premier Division Winners 1961, 1962, 1969, 1970. Hellenic Premier Cup Winners 1960, 1961, 1962, 1963, 1967, 1968, 1976, 1977

VIKING SPORTS

President: R. Bartlett
Chairman: R. Bartlett
Manager: Roy Ruffell
Coach: Ted Dale
Physiotherapist: E.G. Neil
Secretary: J.D. Bennett
Address & Tel. No. 6 Bridge House, Boston Manor Road, Brentford TW8 9LH 01-568-9047
Commercial Manager: B. Dusgate
Address & Tel. No. 6 Barbican Road, Greenford. 01-578-9645
Press Officer & Tel. No. H.E. Rose. 47 Newdene, Northolt Middlesex. 01-845-5837
Address and Tel. No. of ground: Avenue Park, Western Avenue, Greenford, Middlesex. 01-578-2706
Simple ground directions: On London bound carriageway of A40, 300 yards before Greenford Flyover
No. of seats: 20 **Covered accommodation:** 40 **Capacity:** 400 **Floodlights:** No
Year formed: 1945 **Nickname:** Vikings **Club sponsors:** Northoly Glass
Previous names:
Previous Leagues: Middlesex
Clubhouse details: Open every night in season except Sundays
Programme details: Admission 50p including programme
Programme editor: S. Baxter
Club colours: Tangerine
Change colours: Blue
Club Captain (1985-86): Peter Caryer
Player of the Year (1985-86): Jim Davey
Major Honours: Champions Halls Brewery Hellenic League 1985-86

WALLINGFORD TOWN

President: A. Hume
Chairman: A. Miles
Manager: S. Melledew
Coach: M. Hunt
Physiotherapist: W. Revell, BEM
Secretary: Alan Brannan
Address & Tel. No. 1 St. Georges Green, Wallingford, Oxon. OX10.OPD (h) 0691 35757
Commercial Manager:
Address & Tel. No.
Press Officer & Tel. No.
Address and Tel. No. of ground: The Hithercroft Sports Complex, Wallingford Oxon, Wallingford 35044.
Simple ground directions: St Johns Rd and follow signs marked Industrial Estate, Ground 200 yds on right past Habitat Showrooms.
No. of seats: **Covered accommodation:** **Capacity:** 1,200 **Floodlights:** No
Year formed: 1992 **Nickname:** The Town **Club sponsors:** Polar Homes
Previous names:
Previous Leagues: Reading and District
Clubhouse details: Bar and Members Lounge, club house open every night
Programme details: 16 Pages
Programme editor: S. Hardy (0233 815572)
Club colours: Red/Black
Change colours: Blue
Club Captain (1985-86):
Player of the Year (1985-86):
Past player to progress to Football League: J. Dreyer (Oxford 4th)
Major Honours: Hellenic League Premier 1969

WANTAGE TOWN

President:
Chairman: E. Smart
Manager: Clive Corrigan
Coach: Clive Corrigan
Physiotherapist: Jim Potter
Secretary: Mr J.K. Thomas
Address & Tel. No. Rose Cottage, Main Street, Grove, Wantage, Oxon OX12 7JT. Wantage 68556
Commercial Manager: John Russell
Address & Tel. No.
Press Officer & Tel. No. Geoff Smith
Address and Tel. No. of ground: Alfredian Park, Wantage, Oxon. 4781
Simple ground directions: Take Hungerford Road from Wantage, ground on right opposite recreation ground
No. of seats: 50 **Covered accommodation:** 300 **Capacity:** 5,000 **Floodlights:** Yes
Year formed: 1892 **Nickname:** **Club sponsors:** National Bus Co., Normans Cash & Carry, Bear Hotel Wantage
Previous names:
Club colours: Green/White
Previous Leagues: Swindon & District
Change colours: White
Clubhouse details: Bar open evenings, Tuesday, Wednesday, Thursday, Friday, Saturday
Record attendance: 1,800
Club Captain (1985-86):
Programme editor: Geoff Smith
Player of the Year (1985-86):
Major Honours: Hellenic Division Champions 1981, Premier Runners-Up 1982, Senior Cup Winners 1983

YATE TOWN

President: R. Hewetson
Chairman: R.G. Hawkins
Manager: P. Jackson
Coach:
Physiotherapist: R. Jordan
Secretary: T. Tansley
Address & Tel. No. 57 Prestbury, Yate, Bristol BS17 4LD. 0454 313607 (H) 0272 854041 (B)
Commercial Manager: R. Hawkins
Address & Tel. No. 0454 311029
Press Officer & Tel. No. R. Seymour (0454 318632)
Address and Tel. No. of ground: Lodge Road, Yate, Chipping Sodbury (0454) 228103
Simple ground directions: A432 to Yate, turn into North Road at top of railway bridge, first left past traffic lights.
No. of seats: **Covered accommodation:** **Capacity:** 2,000 **Floodlights:** No
Year formed: **Nickname:** Whites **Club sponsors:** Bath Reclamation Ltd
Previous names:
Club colours: White shirts, Navy shorts
Previous Leagues: Gloucestershire County
Change colours: Sky Blue shirts, Black shorts
Clubhouse details: On ground bar facilities, car park.
Mid-week match evening: Wednesday
Programme details:
Club Captain (1985-86):
Programme editor: E. Seymour
Player of the Year (1985-86):
Major Honours: G.F.A. Senior Amateur Cup Winners 1977-78, G.F.A. Challenge Trophy Runners-Up 1978-79 Hellenic Div 1 R.V. 1984-85

Viking Sports — 1986-86. Back-Row (L to R): R. Ruffell (Manager), T. Farrell,, B. Callaghan, P. Buckland, T. Cross, P. Carter, J. Davey, E. Dale (Coach). Front-Row (L to R): F. Healy, M. Howe, P. Davey, E. Dale, K. Lawton. The team were Champions of Halls Brewery Hellenic League Division One.

ALMONDSBURY GREENWAY

Chairman: Dr. B.G.H. Levers
Manager: D. Wookey
Coach: J. Higgs
Physiotherapist: J. Higgs
Secretary: D.W. Winston
Address & Tel. No. 4 St. Michael's Close, Winterbourne BS17 1NS (0454 773771) (H) 0272 823681 (B)
Address and Tel. No. of ground: Oaklands Park, Almondsbury, Bristol. Almondsbury (0454 612240)
Simple ground directions: From M4 West leave at junction 20 to M5 (South West). Leave immediately at junction 16 (A38), turn right onto A38 — 7 miles north of Bristol on A38
No. of seats: None **Covered accommodation:** **Capacity:** 2,000 **Floodlights:** No
Year formed: 1897 **Nickname:** The Almonds
Previous names: Almondsbury, Greenway Sports
Previous Leagues: Bristol Weslyan early 1900s. Bristol Suburban League 1949-1973. Bristol Premier Combination 1968-1975. Gloucestershire County League 1975-1982.
Club colours: Blue/White **Change colours:** All White
Clubhouse details: Open 7 days (evenings, lunchtimes). All sport catered for, refreshments, entertainment, function rooms, hockey, tennis, skittles and cricket
Programme details: 32 pages, 50p, including admission **Club Captain (1985-86):** J. Saunders
Major Honours: Glos County League Champions 1976-77, 1977-78, 1978-79, 1979-80, 1980-81, Runners-Up 1975-76, 1981-82, GFA Challenge Trophy Winners 1978-79, Runners-Up 1980-81, FA Vase Wembley Finalists 1978-79, Semi-finalists 1977-78, Avon Premier Combination Champions 1974-75. (NB Honours relate to Almondsbury Greenway from 1974), Hellenic League Premier Division: Runners-Up 1982-83, Champions 1983-84, Premier Division Challenge Cup: Winners 1983-84.

AVON (BRADFORD) F.C.

President: Mr B. Carter
Chairman: Mr Terry Byrne
Manager: Mr Andy O'Pray
Coach: Mr Alan MacFarlane
Physiotherapist:
Secretary: Mr Colin Lewis
Address & Tel. No. 43 Tudor Drive, Trowbridge. Trowbridge 67425
Commercial Manager:
Address & Tel. No.
Address and Tel. No. of ground: Avon Sports and Social Club, Trowbridge Road, Bradford-on-Avon (02216) 6649
Simple ground directions: ½ mile from Town Centre on Trowbridge Road
No. of seats: **Covered accommodation:** Tiny stand **Capacity:** 3,000 **Floodlights:** No
Year formed: 1920 **Nickname:** The Firm **Club sponsor:** Terry Byrne Dairies
Previous names:
Club colours: Green/White Hoops, Green
Previous Leagues: Western, Wilts County League
Change colours: Yellow — White
Clubhouse details: Bar with Lounge, Dance Floor, Skittle Alley, Pool Table, Dart Board etc.
Programme details: Free with Admission
Club Captain (1985-86): Colin Trott
Programme editor: Andy O'Pray
Player of the Year (1985-86): Andy Beaven
Major Honours: Halls Brewery Hellenic League, Division One Cup Winners 1985

BADMINTON PICKSONS F.C.

President: His Grace The Duke of Beaufort
Chairman: C.A. Pick
Manager: B. Tufton
Treasurer: A. England
Physiotherapist:
Secretary: S.J. Martin
Address & Tel. No. 8 Stadium Road, Westbury Park, Bristol. BS6 7YE. Bristol (0272) 43329
Commercial Manager:
Address & Tel. No.
Address and Tel. No. of ground: Badminton Sports Field. (045 421) 493 — Match days only
Simple ground directions: Situated approx. 4 miles N.E. of No. 18 Tomarton Interchange M4 Motorway in the centre of the village.
No. of seats: **Covered accommodation:** **Capacity:** **Floodlights:** Yes
Year formed: 1880/90s **Nickname:** **Club sponsor:** Picksons Parts Distribution Ltd.
Club colours: Sky Blue Shirts, White Shorts with Blue Black Trim
Previous Leagues: Stroud and District League
Change colours: Red Shirts, White Shorts with Blue Black trim
Clubhouse details:
Programme details: 25p
Club Captain (1985-86): D. Richards
Programme editor: C.A. Pick
Player of the Year (1985-86): D. Richards
Major Honours: Glos. Senior Cup Winners 1981/2, Glos. Minor Cup Winners 1957/58, 1981/82, Berkeley Hospital Cup Winners 1979/80, 1982/83, Cossham Hospital Cup Winners 1978/79, Stroud Charity Cup Winners 1980/81, Stroud League Div. 1 Champions 1980/81, Div. 2 Champions 1979/80.

BISHOPS CLEEVE

President: Mr A. Davies
Chairman: Mr D. Billingham
Manager: Mr D. Walker
Coach: Mr D. Goring
Physiotherapist: Mr D. Goring
Secretary: Mr D. Walker
Address & Tel. No.
Commercial Manager:
Address & Tel. No.
Press Officer & Tel. No.
Address and Tel. No. of ground: Stoke Road, Bishops Cleeve. Bishops Cleeve 6752
Simple ground directions: 3 Miles North. Cheltenham
No. of seats: **Covered accommodation:** **Capacity:** **Floodlights:** No
Year formed: 1936 **Nickname:** **Club sponsor:**
Previous names:
Club colours: Green/ Black and Red
Previous Leagues: Cheltenham, North Gloucester
Change colours: White
Clubhouse details: Full facilities, Bar, Dance Area.
Club Captain (1985-86): T. Bayliffe
Player of the Year (1985-86): T. Bayliffe

CARTERTON TOWN F.C.

President: G. Fox
Chairman: D. Thompson
Manager: G. Amer
Coach: J. Andrews
Physiotherapist: B. Bowles
Secretary: B.A. Hathaway
Address & Tel. No. 4 Minty Close, Carterton OX8 3LL, 0993 842578
Commercial Manager: See Secretary
Address & Tel. No.
Press Officer & Tel. No. A. Matthews
Address and Tel. No. of ground: Kilkenny Lane. 0993 842410
Simple ground directions: Through Swinbrook Road
No. of seats: **Covered accommodation:** **Capacity:** **Floodlights:** No
Year formed: 1983 **Nickname:** **Club sponsor:** Starr Computer Printers
Previous names:
Club colours: Blue Shirts with Yellow Trim Blue Shorts
Previous Leagues: Witney & District
Change colours: All Yellow Blue Trim
Clubhouse details: Lounge & Full Licensed Bar Facilities
Programme details:
Club Captain (1985-86): Nigel Montague
Programme editor:
Player of the Year (1985-86): Kevin Rose
Major Honours: Oxfordshire Junior Shield 85/86. Witney & District F.A. Division 1 Winners 84/85, 76/77 Premier Division Winners 65/66.

CHELTENHAM TOWN RESERVES

For details see GM Vauxhall Conference Section

CHELTENHAM SARACENS F.C.

President: P. Tarling
Chairman: L. Finch
Manager: A. Davis
Coach:
Physiotherapist:
Secretary: R. Attwood
Address & Tel. No. 179 Arle Road, Cheltenham 0242 515855
Commercial Manager:
Address & Tel. No.
Press Officer & Tel. No. T. Coates, 2 Riverland Road, Swindon Village, Cheltenham 520499
Address and Tel. No. of ground: Tewkesbury Road
Simple ground directions: On A38 Cheltenham-Tewksbury
No. of seats: **Covered accommodation:** Yes **Capacity:** 500 **Floodlights:** No
Year formed: 1964 **Nickname:** Saras **Club sponsor:**
Previous names:
Club colours: Blue
Previous Leagues: Cheltenham
Change colours: Yellow
Clubhouse details:
Programme details:
Club Captain (1985-86): T. Castleton
Programme editor:
Player of the Year (1985-86):
Major Honours:

CHIPPING NORTON

President: Mr David Mason
Chairman: Mr Brian Caswell
Manager: Mr Percy Hickman
Coach: Mr Paul Smith
Physiotherapist:
Secretary: Mr Robert James Tanner
Address & Tel. No. 3 Cotswold Terrace, Chipping Norton. Chipping Norton 41490
Match Secretary: Mr A. Smith
Address & Tel. No. 155 Cornish Road, Chipping Norton, Oxon. Chipping Norton 3787
Press Officer & Tel. No.
Address and Tel. No. of ground: Hailey Road
Simple ground directions: On Junction of Hailey Road and Walterbush Road
No. of seats: **Covered accommodation:** 300 **Capacity:** 1000 **Floodlights:** Yes
Year formed: 1893 **Nickname:** Magpies **Club sponsor:** Murphy's Crisps
Previous names:
Previous Leagues: Midland Combination and Oxford Senior
Club colours: Black and White Vertical Stripes **Change colours:** All Blue
Clubhouse details: Well Furnished Bar and Hall with own Bar
Programme details: Adverts and Fill-in page 10p **Club Captain (1985-86):** Mr Paul Souch
Programme editor: Mr Robert James Tanner **Player of the Year (1985-86):** Mr Paul Snell
Major Honours: Oxon Junior Shield 1899, Oxon Senior League 1950/51. Oxon Charity Cup 1949. Oxon Benevolent Cup 1950, Oxon Senior Cup 1977/78, Hellenic League Premier 1978, Div. 1. 1961, Cold Shield Cup 1979. Midland Football Combination Premier 1981.

CIRENCESTER TOWN F.C.

President: Alec Hibberd
Chairman: Ron Swatton
Manager: Brian Horne
Coach:
Commercial Manager: Ron Swatton
Secretary: M.A. Hall
Address & Tel. No. Winterwell Cottage, Barnsley Road, Near Cirencester. 0825 3618
Address and Tel. No. of ground: Tetbury Road Ground (Ciren 4783)
Simple ground directions: Follow by-pass towards Bristol. The ground is on left hand side approx ¼ mile from town centre; sign showing turning to ground has been erected.
No. of seats: **Covered accommodation:** Yes **Capacity:** 150 **Floodlights:** No
Year formed: 1870 **Nickname:** The Town **Club sponsors:** Gardiner Home Improvement Centre
Previous names:
Previous Leagues:
Club colours: Red and Black Stripes Black/Black
Change colours: Yellow/Blue/Yellow
Clubhouse details: Open 7 nights
Major Honours: G.F.A. Senior Amateur Cup Winners 1980, Hellenic League Division One Champions 1973-74.

CLANFIELD F.C.

President: H. Wallis
Chairman: J. Paris
Manager: P. Bridgewater
Coach: P. Bridgewater
Physiotherapist: S. Neenan
Secretary: J.M. Osborne
Address & Tel. No. Witney 71631
Commercial Manager:
Address & Tel. No.
Press Officer & Tel. No. L. Tooley, Witney 71817
Address and Tel. No. of ground: Radcot Road. 036 781314
Simple ground directions: A 4095. 8 miles West of Witney
No. of seats: **Covered accommodation:** Yes **Capacity:** 2,000 **Floodlights:** No
Year formed: 1890 **Nickname:** Robins **Club sponsor:** Country Style Blinds
Previous names:
Previous Leagues: Witney and District
Club colours: All Red
Change colours: Blue, White, Blue
Clubhouse details: Open every evening plus Saturday and Sunday Lunchtime.
Programme details:
Programme editor:
Club Captain (1985-86): Gary Lock
Player of the Year (1985-86):
Major Honours: Oxon Junior Shield 1933, Oxon Intermediate Cup 1968, Witney Div 2 64-65 Witney Div 1 65-66 Witney Press 66-67, Hellenic Div 1 and Cup 69-70, Hellenic Premier Cup 73.

DIDCOT TOWN

President: John Merrifield
Chairman: Peter Robinson
Manager: L. Hill
Coach: K. Rees
Secretary: Ken Coles
Address & Tel. No. 8, Lockinge House 0235 818008
Press Officer & Tel. No. K. Coles, 8 Lockings House, Didcot (818008)
Address and Tel. No. of ground: 58 Station Road, Didcot. 813212
Simple ground directions: Midway down Station Road, Didcot, situated on right, ¼ mile from Railway Station towards town centre.
No. of seats: **Covered accommodation:** Yes **Capacity:** 500 **Floodlights:** No
Year formed: 1907 **Nickname: Railway Men** **Club sponsors:** Express Dairies
Previous names:
Previous Leagues: Metropolitan
Club colours: Red/White
Change colours: White/Red
Clubhouse details: Daily evenings and Sunday lunchtimes
Programme details: 10p
Programme editor: S. Culliford (Didcot 818601)
Major Honours: Hellenic Premier 1953-54, Premier Cup 1965-66, 1966-67, Hellenic Div. 1 1976-77, Div. 1 Cup 1976-77.

EASINGTON SPORTS F.C.

President: Vacant
Chairman: Terry Horley
Manager: George Veitch
Secretary: B. Cogbill
Address & Tel. No. 30 Addison Road, Banbury, Oxon.
Coach: T. Davies
Address and Tel. No. of ground: Addison Rd. Easington Estate, Banbury Oxon
Simple ground directions: From Oxford A423. After passing under flyover on the outskirts take the first turning left into Grange Rd, then third turning right into Addison Rd. (a cul-de-sac).
No. of seats: 50 **Covered accommodation:** Yes **Capacity:** 500 **Floodlights:** No
Year formed: 1945 **Nickname:** **Club sponsor:**
Previous names:
Previous Leagues: Banbury Junior, Oxen Senior, Warwick Combination
Club colours: Red/Black/Red
Change colours: Amber
Clubhouse details: Changing Rooms and showers, Bar facilities and food available.
Programme details: Yes
Programme editor: D. Foreman
Programmme editor: D. Foreman
Major Honours: Oxon Senior Cup Finalists, Oxon Intermediate League & Cup Winners, Oxon Senior League

HAZELLS CLUB

President: M.A. Pegge
Chairman: K. Downham
Manager: T. Craker
Coach:
Physiotherapist:

Secretary: C.M. Plumb
Address & Tel. No. Hazell, Watson & Viney Ltd. Tring Road, Aylesbury (Bus. Hours): 0296 82345 Ext. 4520
Commercial Manager:
Address & Tel. No.
Press Officer & Tel. No.

Address and Tel. No. of ground: Victoria Park, Oakfield Road, Aylesbury. Aylesbury 0296 82868
Simple ground directions: Oakfield Road is just off the A41 Tring Road, by Adams Garage Roundabout.
No. of seats: **Covered accommodation:** **Capacity:** 2,000 **Floodlights:** No
Year formed: 1886 **Nickname:** The Printers **Club sponsors:** M & O Electrical
Previous names:
Previous Leagues: Spartan League, Great Western League
Club colours: White Shirts with Red and Black Trim, Black shorts
Change colours: Red Shirts, Red Shorts
Clubhouse details: Large Brick Building with 3 bars, games rooms and large multi-purpose hall.
Programme details:
Programme editor:
Club Captain (1985-86):
Player of the Year (1985-86):
Major Honours: 1935/36 Winners Spartan League Div. 2 Western Section, 1959/60 Winners Hellenic League Div. 1, 1979/80 Winners Hellenic League Div. 1, 1965/66 Runners Up Berks and Bucks Senior Cup, 1966/67 Runners Up Hellenic League Prem. Div. 1967/68 Winners Hellenic League Prem. Div 1980/81 Winners Hellenic League Prem. Div. Cup.

HIGHWORTH TOWN

President: Alan Vockins
Chairman: Rob Haines
Manager: Peter Webb
Coach:
Physiotherapist:

Secretary: Ken Loveday
Address & Tel. No. 3 Roman Way, Highworth, Wilts SN6 7BU (0793) 762446
Commercial Manager:
Address & Tel. No.
Press Officer & Tel. No. David Haines (0793) 762446

Address and Tel. No. of ground:
Simple ground directions: Enter town on A361, turn left into the Green by Veterinary Surgery — Ground and Car park 200 yds on left
No. of seats: **Covered accommodation:** **Capacity:** **Floodlights:** Yes
Year formed: 1904 **Nickname:** **Club sponsor:**
Previous names:
Previous Leagues: Wiltshire League /Swindon and District
Club colours: Red Shirts/Black Shorts
Change colours: Blue Shirts/Black Shorts
Clubhouse details: Bar Facilities etc
Programme details: Yes
Programme editor:
Club Captain (1985-86):
Player of the Year (1985-86):
Major Honours: County Senior Cup twice

KIDLINGTON F.C.

President: H. Blake
Chairman: A.F. Grose
Manager: Andy Sinnott
Coach: Matt Hunt
Physiotherapist: David Jones

Secretary: M.W.J. Claridge
Address & Tel. No. 76 Queens Ave, Kidlington, Oxford OX5 2JJ. Kid. 2680
Commercial Manager: P.J. Garrett
Address & Tel. No. 15 Meadow Way, Yarnton Oxford OX5 1TA Kid. 5128

Press Officer & Tel. No. A.R. Sinnott, 6 The Moorlands, Kidlington Oxford OX5 2XX Kid. 6561
Address and Tel No. of ground: Yarnton Road, Kidlington, Oxford
Simple ground directions: From the Kidlington roundabout travel north on A423 towards Kidlington; after first set of traffic lights take second turning on left (Yarnton Rd) and ground 200 yds along on left.
No. of seats: **Covered accommodation:** **Capacity:** **Floodlights:** No
Year formed: 1920 **Nickname:** **Club sponsors:** Newman Insulations Ltd
Previous names:
Previous Leagues: Oxfordshire Senior League
Club colours: Light Blue Shirts Shorts & Socks
Change colours: Yellow Shirts Green Shorts, Yellow or Green Socks
Clubhouse details: Two bars open after matches
Programme details: 12 pages, 20p
Programme editor: M.A. Canning
Club Captain (1985-86): Phil Ellis
Player of the Year (1985-86): Phil Ellis
Major Honours: Joined Oxfordshire Senior League 1947/48; Runners-up same season; Champions 1953/54. Joined Hellenic League 1954/55, one year after its inception. Runners-up Hellenic League Division One 1963/64 and 1978/79; Winners Hellenic League Division One Challenge Cup 1974/75 and Finalists 1963/64 and 1983/84. Winners Oxfordshire Intermediate Cup 1952/53 and 1984/85; Finalists 1968/69, 1973/74 and 1974/75. F.A. Vase — reached last sixteen in 1976/77.

Clanfield F.C. Winners Hellenic Division One Skol Cup 85-86. Photo Leo Hoenig

Leigh James scores the last minute winner to knock Sharpness out of the Hellenic Premier League Cup. Wallingford 2 Sharpness 1. Photo: Leo Hoenig.

4-1 victory in a top of the table Hellenic League match for Pinhall v Viking Sports. Chris Joyce (7) scores for Penhill.

Kintbury v Lambourn, Berks and Bucks Cup Tie.

KINTBURY RANGERS

President: P. Adamson
Chairman:
Manager: B. Walker
Coach:
Physiotherapist:
Secretary: A.K. Plank
Address & Tel. No. 26 Kennet Road, Kintbury, Newbury, Berks. RG15 0XW. Kintbury 58460
Commercial Manager:
Address & Tel. No.
Press Officer & Tel. No. As secretary
Address and Tel. No. of ground: Recreation Ground, Inkpen Road, Kintbury
Simple ground directions: Turn off A4 between Newbury/Hungerford. 2nd left into Inkpen Rd. 200 yards on right by Jubilee Centre
No. of seats: **Covered accommodation:** **Capacity:** **Floodlights:** No
Year formed: 1943 **Nickname:** Rangers
Club sponsors: Highcross Group and Dundas Arms
Previous names:
Club colours: Amber Shirts Black Shorts
Previous Leagues: Newbury District, North Berks
Change colours: White Shirts Blue Shorts
Clubhouse details: Open every night except Wednesdays
Programme details:
Club Captain (1985-86): Nigel Thorne
Programme editor:
Player of the Year (1985-86):
Major Honours: North Berks Winners 1977/78, 1981/82

LAMBOURN SPORTS F.C.

President: N.L. Fraser
Chairman: A.E. Cripps
Manager: N. Matthews
Coach: C. Moyle
Physiotherapist:
Secretary: C.G. Bettison
Address & Tel. No. Carabey House, Newbury Road, Lambourn, Berks. RG16 7LL. (0488) 71834
Commercial Manager:
Press Officer & Tel. No. As Secretary
Address and Tel. No. of ground: Lambourn Sports Club, Bockhampton Road, Lambourn, Berks., (0488) 71335
Simple ground directions: From Lambourn Church, takey Newbury St., then 1st right into Station Rd., then left at 'T' junction into Bockhampton Rd., Ground on left
No. of seats: **Covered accommodation:** 150 **Capacity:** 2,000 **Floodlights:** No
Year formed: 1889 **Nickname:** **Club sponsor:**
Previous names:
Previous Leagues: Newbury and District 1911/51, Swindon and District 1951/61, North Berks 1972/77, Hellenic 1961/72 and 1977 to date.
Club colours: Red/White Stripes
Change colours: Blue
Clubhouse details: Bars, Lounge, Dance Hall, Billiard room, Kitchen, etc. Open 7 nights, Saturday match-days from 4pm
Programme details: 12 pages
Club Captain (1985-86): G. Smith
Programme editor:
Player of the Year (1985-86): A. Andrews
Major Honours: Berks and Bucks County Cup: 1961/62 and 1979/80, Hellenic Div. 1 Cup: 1961/62 and 1979/80, Hellenic Div. 1 Champions 1981/82, Runners Up: 1961/62

PURTON F.C.

President: Graham Price
Chairman: Alan Eastwood
Manager: Tony Brown
Secretary: Alan Eastwood
Address & Tel. No. 36 Portal Road, Swindon SW21 1PY (0793) 6940361
Press Officer & Tel. No. Alan Eastwood
Address and Tel. No. of ground: Red House, Purton (0793) 770262
Simple ground directions: On B4041 Wibarratt — Cricklade
No. of seats: **Covered accommodation:** **Capacity:** **Floodlights:** No
Reformed: 1923 **Nickname:** **Club sponsor:** Compton Welding
Club colours: Red Shirts, White Shorts, Black/Red Socks
Change colours: Black/White Stripes, Black Shorts Red Socks
Clubhouse details: Red House Club from 4.30 — 6pm match Saturdays and after early midweek matches
Programme details: 4 or 6 page. No charge.
Club Captain (1985-86): Steve Paish
Programme editor: Alan Eastwood
Player of the Year (1985-86): Steve Paish
Major Honours: Wilts Div. 2 Champions 1983/84, Wilts Div. 1 Champions 1985/86. Senior Cup Winners 1938/39, 1950/51 Wilts County Winners 1946/47, 1948/49, 1949/50.

PRESSED STEEL

President:
Chairman: R. Boulter
Manager: T. Bishop
Coach: Colin Maskery
Physiotherapist:
Secretary: B. Barr
Address & Tel. No. 7B Farm Close Road, Wheatley, Oxon. Wheatley 2508
Commercial Manager: T. Bishop
Address & Tel. No. 51 Delbush Avenue, Sandhills, Oxford. Oxford 61778
Address and Tel. No. of ground: Roman Way, Cowley, Oxford. Oxford 770163
Simple ground directions: Turn off Oxford Ring Road as signposted for Cowley. Turn off at roundabout to Horspath. Proceed 300 yds, turn right, ground on left.
No. of seats: 250 **Covered accommodation:** Yes **Capacity:** **Floodlights:** No
Year formed: 1927 **Nickname:** The Steelmen **Club sponsors:** Hartwells (Oxford) Ltd
Previous names:
Club colours: Green with Blue Trim
Previous Leagues: Oxfordshire Senior
Change colours: White
Clubhouse details: 50 yards from ground. 4 Bars, 2 dance halls, lounge.
Programme details:
Club Captain (1985-86):
Programme editor:
Player of the Year (1985-86):
Major Honours:

MIDLAND FOOTBALL COMBINATION

Chairman: P. Fellows

Hon. Gen. Secretary/Treasurer: L.W. James JP, 175 Barnett Lane, Kingswinford, Brierley Hill, West Midlands DY6 9QA. Tel: Kingswinford 3459

PREMIER DIVISION

	P	W	D	L	F	A	Pts
1 Boldmere St. Michaels	38	25	10	3	72	24	60
2 Paget Rangers	38	24	9	5	94	31	57
3 West Midlands Police	38	23	8	7	65	41	54
4 Northfield Town	38	18	12	8	74	50	48
5 Bloxwich A.F.C.	38	18	11	9	77	50	47
6 Stratford Town	38	17	12	9	53	32	46
7 Solihull Borough	38	18	7	13	62	45	43
8 Walsall Borough	38	15	13	10	52	37	43
9 Polesworth North Warwick	38	16	10	12	52	46	42
10 Racing Club Warwick	38	13	15	10	52	50	41
11 Coleshill Town	38	14	13	11	54	54	41
12 Highgate Utd	38	16	8	14	56	55	40
13 Evesham Utd	38	12	9	17	62	80	33
14 Hurley Daw Mill	38	12	8	18	44	59	32
15 New World	38	9	7	22	46	73	25
16 Knowle North Star	38	8	9	21	35	63	25
17 Southam Utd	38	6	12	20	52	90	24
18 Studley Sporting	38	7	8	23	43	75	22
19 Smethwick Highfield	38	5	11	22	31	75	21
20 Kings Heath	38	5	6	27	24	70	16

CONSTITUTION OF DIVISION 1

Alcester Town	Chelmsley Town	Coleshill Town Reserves
Dudley Sports	Enville Athletic	Henley Forest of Arden
Highgate United Reserves	Kingsbury United	Kings Heath
Kings Norton Old Boys	Shelfield United	Shifnal W.U.
Shirley Town	Solihull Borough Reserves	Triplex
West Heath United	Wilmcote	Wythall

Horley Daw Mill 0, Stratford Town 3. Steve Johnson (7) scores one of his two first half goals in this Midland Combination. Premier Division Match. Photo Leo Hoenig.

ASHTREE HIGHFIELD

President: L.A. Key
Chairman: R. Unitt
Manager: D. Garratt
Secretary: K.R. Edwards
Address & Tel. No. 021 557 5575
Address and Tel. No. of ground: Oldbury Sports Centre, Newbury Lane, Oldbury. 021 552 1795
Simple ground directions: Birmingham A-Z ref P60, A1

No. of seats: 200
Covered accommodation: 600
Capacity: 3,000
Year formed: 1918
Nickname: The Stags
Floodlights: Yes
Club colours: White and black
Change colours: Amber and black
Day for midweek home matches: Wednesday
Club metal badges: No
Previous Leagues: Birmingham Alliance
Clubhouse details: Licensed bar overlooking pitch. Open Monday-Sundays
Past players who progressed into the Football League:
Programme details: 12 pages, 20p
Programme editor: J. Unitt
Local newspapers & Tel. No. Sandwell Evening Mail
Major Honours: Birmingham Junior Cup, Presidents Cup

BLOXWICH

President: M. Ross
Chairman: K. Moseley
Manager: P. Bradburn
Secretary: S. Duncombe
Address & Tel. No. 0902 633111
Address and Tel. No. of ground: Abbey Park, Glastonbury Crescent, Bloxwich. 77640
Simple ground directions: From Bloxwich to Wolverhampton on Lichfield Road, turn right on Mosseley Estate before Youth Club into Glastonbury Crescent, ½ mile left of Abbey School

No. of seats: None
Covered accommodation: 200
Capacity: 500
Year formed: 1977
Nickname: The Kestrels
Floodlights: No
Club colours: White and navy
Change colours: Yellow and navy
Day for midweek home matches: Tuesday/Thursday
Club metal badges: No
Previous Leagues: Bloxwich Comb, Staffs County
Clubhouse details: No clubhouse
Past players who progressed into the Football League: None
Programme details: 10/12 pages
Programme editor: G. Carter
Local newspapers & Tel. No. Walsall Observer
Major Honours: Staffs Co. Div 1, Bloxwich Comb Div 1 (2), Alan Peck Cup (3)

BOLDMERE ST MICHAELS

President:
Chairman: H. Peakman
Manager: J. Morris
Secretary: John Shaw
Address & Tel. No. 021 350 5869
Address and Tel. No. of ground: Church Road, Boldmere, Sutton Coldfield. 021 373 4435
Simple ground directions: A38 from Birmingham to Yenton lights, turn left on Chester Road, then 5th right into Church Road

No. of seats: 80
Covered accommodation: Yes
Capacity: 2,500
Year formed: 1883
Nickname: The Mikes
Floodlights: No
Club colours: White and black
Change colours: Sky blue/dark blue/gold
Day for midweek home matches: Tuesday/Thursday
Club metal badges: No
Previous Leagues: Birmingham League, Worcestershire Combination
Clubhouse details: Bar and lounge, open 7 nights and 4 lunchtimes
Past players who progressed into the Football League:
Programme details: 8 pages, 15p
Programme editor: Mrs Hilary Shaw
Local newspapers & Tel. No. Sutton Coldfield News
Major Honours: Midland Combination Champions 1985-6, Midland Combination Challenge Cup Winners 1977-8, F.A. Amateur Cup Semi-finalists

BOLEHALL SWIFTS

President: J. Hill
Chairman: M. Hill
Managers: C. Lyons/P. Garnell
Secretary: M. Tooley
Address & Tel. No. Tamworth 895972
Address and Tel. No. of ground: Rene Road, Bolehall, Tamworth. Tamworth 62637
Simple ground directions: Follow Amington signs from Tamworth

No. of seats: No
Covered accommodation: 50
Capacity: 2,000
Year formed: 1953
Nickname: Swifts
Floodlights: No
Club colours: Yellow and green
Change colours: Red and black
Day for midweek home matches: Tuesday
Club metal badges: Yes
Previous Leagues: Staffs County League
Clubhouse details: Every evening and lunchtime
Past players who progressed into the Football League:

Programme details: 8 pages, 25p
Programme editor: W. Gould
Local newspapers & Tel. No. Tamworth Herald
Major Honours:

COLESHILL TOWN

President: J. Wright
Chairman: H. Davies
Manager: K. Shrimpton
Secretary: Sheila Davies
Address & Tel. No. Coleshill 65486
Address and Tel. No. of ground: Park Meadow, Packington Lane, Coleshill. Coleshill 63259
Simple ground directions: Exit junction 4 M6-Coleshill (A446), right hand lane cross dual carriageway. Ground 400 yds on right

No. of seats: None **Covered accommodation:** 250 **Capacity:** 3,000
Year formed: 1894 **Nickname:** The Colemen **Floodlights:** No
Club colours: Green and black **Change colours:** White and black
Day for midweek home matches: Tuesday/Thursday **Club metal badges:** No
Previous Leagues: Sutton Coldfield
Clubhouse details: Bar open 7 nights per week, bar manager lives in cottage on ground
Past players who progressed into the Football League: Gary Shaw (Aston Villa)
Programme details: None **Programme editor:**
Local newspapers & Tel. No. Coleshill Herald
Major Honours: Walsall Senior Cup 1983, Midland Comb. Runners-up 1983-4

EVESHAM

President:
Chairman: M. Davis
Manager: T. Freely
Secretary: R. Porter
Address & Tel. No. 0386 47438
Address and Tel. No. of ground: Common Road, Evesham, Worcs. 0386 2303
Simple ground directions: From Birmingham, turn left into Swan Lane, then Common Road
No. of seats: 400 **Covered accommodation:** 400 **Capacity:** 4,000
Year formed: 1945 **Nickname:** Robins **Floodlights:** Soon
Club colours: All red **Change colours:** All white/black
Day for midweek home matches: Tuesday **Club metal badges:** Yes
Previous Leagues: Worcester League
Clubhouse details: Open Monday to Thursday evenings, Sat & Sun (matchdays)
Past players who progressed into the Football League: Bill Tucker (Hereford, Bury, Swindon), Gary Stevens (Cardiff, Shrewsbury, Brentford)
Programme details: 16 pages (incl. admission) **Programme editor:** Nigel Howe
Local newspapers & Tel. No. Evesham Journal, Evesham Admag, Worcester Evening News, Radio Wyvern
Major Honours: Midland Combination Champions 1952-3, 1954-5, 1965-6, 1967-8, 1968-9; Worcs Senior Urn 1976-7, 1977-8

HIGHGATE UNITED

President:
Chairman: N. Smith
Manager: B. Francis
Secretary: G. Woolley
Address & Tel. No.
Address and Tel. No. of ground: The Coppice, Tythe Barn Lane, Shirley, Solihull. 021 744 4194
Simple ground directions: Off main Stratford Road, south end of Shirley out of Birmingham. Turn right George and Dragon
No. of seats: 250 **Covered accommodation:** 750 **Capacity:** 5,000
Year formed: 1947 **Nickname:** The Gate **Floodlights:** No
Club colours: All red **Change colours:** All white
Day for midweek home matches: Tuesday **Club metal badges:** No
Previous Leagues: Worcs Comb., W. Midlands Alliance, S. Birmingham League, S. Birmingham Combination
Clubhouse details: Members club, open Tuesday, Wednesday, Thursday and Saturday
Past players who progressed into the Football League: Keith Leonard (Aston Villa), Geoff Scott (Stoke, Birmingham, Leicester)
Programme details: 40 pages, 20p **Programme editor:** Terry Bishop
Local newspapers & Tel. No. Solihull News
Major Honours: F.A. Amateur Cup Semi-finalists 1972-3, Quarter Finalists 1967-8, 1971-2; Birmingham Senior Cup Winners 1973-4, Finalists 1971-2; B'Ham Senior Amateur Cup Finalists 1972-3; Mid Comb. Champions 1972-3, 1973-4, 1974-5; Mid Comb. Challenge Cup Winners 1972-3, 1973-4, 1975-6, 1976-7, 1984-5

KINGS HEATH

President: G. Walsh
Chairman: R.S. Kite
Manager: M. Sutton
Secretary: D. Ellis
Address & Tel. No. 021 459 7444
Address and Tel. No. of ground: The Glen, Tilehouse Lane, Shirley, Solihull
Simple ground directions: Stratford Road, turn right Haslucks Green Road, follow to end, left into Tilehouse Lane
No. of seats: None **Covered accommodation:** 100 **Capacity:** 3,000
Year formed: 1964 **Nickname:** The Kings **Floodlights:** No
Club colours: Gold shadow stripes/black **Change colours:** All red
Day for midweek home matches: Tuesday/Thursday **Club metal badges:** No
Previous Leagues: Mercian AFA, South Birmingham
Clubhouse details: Matchdays, training nights
Past players who progressed into the Football League: Geoff Scott (Birmingham, Stoke, Leicester)
Programme details: 12 pages **Programme editor:** R.S. Kite
Local newspapers & Tel. No. Solihull News
Major Honours:

KNOWLE

President:
Secretary: R. Gardner
Chairman: J. Dean
Address & Tel. No. 021 770 9273
Manager: R. Mason
Address and Tel. No. of ground: Hampton Road, Knowle, Solihull. Knowle 79807
Simple ground directions: Main Warwick Road (A41) to Knowle from Birmingham, turn left at Wilsons pub, 200 yards on right
No. of seats: 50 **Covered accommodation:** 200 **Capacity:** 3,000
Year formed: 1926 **Nickname:** None **Floodlights:** No
Club colours: Yellow and black **Change colours:** Blue
Day for midweek home matches: Wednesday **Club metal badges:** No
Previous Leagues: Birmingham Youth and Old Boys, Birmingham Alliance
Clubhouse details: Seating for 60, tea bar
Past players who progressed into the Football League:
Programme details: Planned 1986-7 **Programme editor:**
Local newspapers & Tel. No. Solihull News
Major Honours: 1971 Finalists Birmingham County Junior Cup

NORTHFIELD TOWN

President: D. Caney
Secretary: D. Hale
Chairman: E. Rough
Address & Tel. No.
Manager: B. Pedley
Address and Tel. No. of ground: Shenley Lane, Birmingham B29. 021 475 5009
Simple ground directions: A38 (Bristol Road) into Northfield, then turn into Shenley Lane

No. of seats: None **Covered accommodation:** Yes **Capacity:** 3,500
Year formed: 1966 **Nickname:** The Cross **Floodlights:** No
Club colours: Yellow and blue **Change colours:** Blue and yellow
Day for midweek home matches: Tuesday/Thursday **Club metal badges:** No
Previous Leagues: Worcester Combination
Clubhouse details: Brick-built new club
Past players who progressed into the Football League: C. Palmer (WBA), C.Whitehead (Bristol City, WBA), M. Rees (Walsall), C. Brazier (Wolves, Birmingham City)
Programme details: 24 pages, 15p **Programme editor:** Norman Harrison
Local newspapers & Tel. No. Evening Mail
Major Honours: Birmingham Senior Amateur Cup 1974-5, Midland Combination Champions 1975-6, Challenge Cup Winners 1983-4, Presidents Cup Winners 1980-1, Birmingham County Youth Cup 1970, 1971, 1972 Worcester Youth Cup 4 times Winners

PAGET RANGERS

President: E. Angelides
Secretary: R. Broadfield
Chairman: N.J. Hunt
Address & Tel. No.
Manager: E. Caulfield
Address and Tel. No. of ground: Springfield Road, Walmley, Sutton Coldfield. 021 351 1563
Simple ground directions: 114 bus from Birmingham city centre to ground. From Sutton town centre take Walmley Road end, turn right into Springfield Road
No. of seats: 250 **Covered accommodation:** 250 **Capacity:** 3,500
Year formed: 1938 **Nickname:** The P's **Floodlights:** Yes
Club colours: Gold and black **Change colours:** Red and black
Day for midweek home matches: Wednesday **Club metal badges:** No
Previous Leagues: Worcestershire Combination
Clubhouse details: Licensed clubhouse with full social facilities. Open six evenings, Saturday & Sunday lunchtime
Past players who progressed into the Football League: L. Canning, R. Brown, V. O'Keefe, B. Wright, J. Gittens
Programme details: 16 pages, 20p **Programme editor:**
Local newspapers & Tel. No. Sutton Coldfield News
Major Honours: Midland Combination Champions 1959-60, 1960-61, 1969-70, 1970-71, Midland Combination Challenge Cup Winners 1959-60, 1966-67, 1970-71, 1982-83

POLESWORTH NORTH WARWICK

President: A.T. Bass
Secretary: E. Guild
Chairman: E. Harris
Address & Tel. No. 0827 893690
Manager: F. Gilmore
Address and Tel. No. of ground: Tamworth Road, Polesworth, Tamworth. 892482
Simple ground directions: B5000 from Tamworth
No. of seats: 50 **Covered accommodation:** Yes **Capacity:** 1,000
Year formed: 1966 **Nickname:** None **Floodlights:** No
Club colours: Green and yellow **Change colours:** Tangerine and black
Day for midweek home matches: Tuesday/Thursday **Club metal badges:** No
Previous Leagues: Mercian A.F.A.
Clubhouse details: Licensed bar, tea bar and refreshments
Past players who progressed into the Football League: D. Tunnicliffe (Birmingham City)
Programme details: 8 pages **Programme editor:** B. Woodhouse
Local newspapers & Tel. No. Tamworth Herald
Major Honours: Midland Combination Presidents Cup 1982-3; Midland Combination Challenge Cup and Presidents Cup 1983-4; Birmingham Junior Cup 1983-4

PRINCES END UNITED

President:
Secretary: K. Jones
Chairman: K. Jones
Managers:
Capacity: 1,000 **Covered Accommodation:** Yes **Seating:** 50 **Floodlights:** Not yet
Address and Tel No. of ground: Newey Sports, Sedgely Road, Tipton, West Midlands DY4 9NN
Clubhouse Details: Newey Sports
Year formed: 1970
Local newspapers:
Club Colours: All White
Change Colours: All Red
Midweek Match Day:
Record Attendance:
Previous Leagues:
Senior Honours/Best Performance:

RACING CLUB WARWICK

President: J. Fenton
Secretary: P.J. Murphy
Chairman: E. Haines
Address & Tel. No. 0926 612675
Manager: J. Bettles
Address and Tel. No. of ground: Hampton Road, Warwick. Warwick (0926) 493622
Simple ground directions: Situated on B4095 Warwick to Redditch Road, follow signs for Warwick race course

No. of seats: 50 **Covered accommodation:** 150 **Capacity:** 750
Year formed: 1919 **Nickname:** Racing **Floodlights:** No
Club colours: Gold and black **Change colours:** White and black
Day for midweek home matches: Tuesday **Club metal badges:** No
Previous Leagues: West Midlands Regional League, Warwickshire Combination
Clubhouse details: Open every night, plus Saturday, Sunday, Monday & Friday lunchtimes
Past players who progressed into the Football League: None known
Programme details: No **Programme editor:**
Local newspapers & Tel. No. Warwick Advertiser, Leamington Courier, Coventry Evening Telegraph
Major Honours:

SOLIHULL BOROUGH

President: J. McGorian
Secretary: H. Cherry
Chairman: J. Hewitson
Address & Tel. No. 021 707 4285
Manager: T. Stevens
Address and Tel. No. of ground: Widney Lane, Solihull, W. Midlands. 021 705 3169
Simple ground directions: From Solihull town centre, follow Blossomfield Road for 2 miles, turn left at traffic lights into Widney Lane. Ground is one mile on right
No. of seats: 60 **Covered accommodation:** 200 **Capacity:** 1,500
Year formed: 1951 **Nickname:** The Borough **Floodlights:** No
Club colours: All blue **Change colours:** Yellow and blue
Day for midweek home matches: Tuesday **Club metal badges:** No
Previous Leagues: Mercian F.A.
Clubhouse details: Clubhouse and bar on ground
Past players who progressed into the Football League: Andy Williams (Coventry City), Geoff Scott (Leicester, Birmingham, Stoke)
Programme details: Sometimes **Programme editor:**
Local newspapers & Tel. No. Solihull News
Major Honours: F.A. Vase 5th Rd

SOUTHAM UNITED

President: J. Greenway
Secretary: R.J. Hancocks
Chairman: R. Greenway
Address & Tel. No. Southam 3483
Manager: A. Flear
Address and Tel. No. of ground: Banbury Road, Southam. Southam 2091
Simple ground directions: Follow Coventry Road through Southam on A423, ground on right going towards Banbury

No. of seats: 50 **Covered accommodation:** 200 **Capacity:** 2,000
Year formed: 1905 **Nickname:** The Saints **Floodlights:** No
Club colours: All red **Change colours:** Yellow/black
Day for midweek home matches: Tuesday/Thursday **Club metal badges:** No
Previous Leagues: Coventry and N. Warwicks
Clubhouse details: Open
Past players who progressed into the Football League:

Programme details: Yes **Programme editor:** R.J. Hancocks
Local newspapers & Tel. No. Leamington Courier, Coventry Evening Telegraph, Rugby Advertiser
Major Honours: Midland Combination Div 3 Winners 1980-81

STRATFORD TOWN

President: B. Wheeler
Chairman: G. Cutler
Manager: B. Lynch
Secretary: P. Gardner
Address & Tel. No. Stratford on Avon 68432
Address and Tel. No. of ground: Masons Road, off Alcester Road, Stratford on Avon. 297479
Simple ground directions: Follow Worcester signs when in Stratford, Masons Road 1st right turn after passing railway bridge

No. of seats: 200 **Covered accommodation:** 250 **Capacity:** 4,000
Year formed: 1944 **Nickname:** The Town **Floodlights:** No
Club colours: Tangerine and black **Change colours:** Silver and black
Day for midweek home matches: Tuesday/Thursday **Club metal badges:** No
Previous Leagues: West Midlands League, Hellenic League
Clubhouse details: Open 7 nights and Sunday lunchtime
Past players who progressed into the Football League: M. Hicks (Charlton, Reading)
Programme details: None in 1985-6 **Programme editor:**
Local newspapers & Tel. No. Stratford Herald, Coventry Evening Telegraph
Major Honours: Midland Combination Champions 1956-7, Birmingham Senior Cup Winners

STUDLEY SPORTING

President: H. Whitehouse
Chairman: T. Heath
Manager: J. Adams
Secretary: V.F. Smith
Address & Tel. No. 0527 85 3417
Address and Tel. No. of ground: N.I. Sports Ground, Eldorado Close, High Street, Studley. 052 785 2671
Simple ground directions: In the centre of the village

No. of seats: No **Covered accommodation:** 100 **Capacity:** 1,000
Year formed: 1920 **Nickname:** The Needles **Floodlights:** No
Club colours: Red and blue **Change colours:** Sky blue and royal blue
Day for midweek home matches: Tuesday/Thursday **Club metal badges:** No
Previous Leagues: Since reformed in 1970: Stratford Alliance, N. Worcester League, Mercian A.F.C.
Clubhouse details: Open every evening, lunchtimes at weekend
Past players who progressed into the Football League: None
Programme details: 12 pages, 20p **Programme editor:** V.F. Smith
Local newspapers & Tel. No. Redditch Indicator and Advertiser
Major Honours: Midland Combination Division 2 Champions 1982-3, Premier Division Champions 1983-4

WALSALL WOOD

President:
Chairman: D. Preston
Manager: B. Holden
Secretary: C. Mycock
Address & Tel. No. 0543 372278
Address and Tel. No. of ground: Oak Park, Lichfield Road, Walsall Wood, Brownhills. Brownhills 2223
Simple ground directions: From M6 to centre of Walsall, take A461 and go through Rushall, Shelfield, Walsall Wood, ground on left at corner of Oak Park

No. of seats: 200 **Covered accommodation:** Yes **Capacity:** 3,000
Year formed: 1982 **Nickname:** None **Floodlights:** Yes
Club colours: Red and white **Change colours:** Yellow and blue
Day for midweek home matches: Tuesday **Club metal badges:** No
Previous Leagues: None
Clubhouse details: Two clubrooms, open seven nights a week
Past players who progressed into the Football League:
Programme details: None **Programme editor:**
Local newspapers & Tel. No. Walsall Observer, Walsall Post, Walsall Advertiser
Major Honours: Midland Combination Challenge, Cup Winners 1954-5, 1960-61

WEST MIDLANDS POLICE

President: Chief Constable G. Dear
Chairman: Dep. Chief Constable L Sharp
Manager: C. Brookes
Secretary: B. Pigott
Address & Tel. No. 021 382 3958
Address and Tel. No. of ground: W.M. Police Sports Ground, 'Tally Ho', Pershore Road, Edgbaston, Birmingham. 021 472 2944
Simple ground directions: Pershore Road (A441) 200 yards on left hand side, past junction with Edgbaston Road, travelling out of city
No. of seats: 200 **Covered accommodation:** 200 **Capacity:** 1,000
Year formed: 1974 **Nickname:** None **Floodlights:** No
Club colours: Red and black **Change colours:** White and green
Day for midweek home matches: Tuesday/Thursday **Club metal badges:** No
Previous Leagues: Birmingham Works League, Birmingham Youth and Old Boys
Clubhouse details: Complex of three bars, snooker room, ballroom and large kitchen
Past players who progressed into the Football League:
Programme details: 8 pages **Programme editor:** B. Pigott
Local newspapers & Tel. No. Sutton Coldfield News, Solihull News
Major Honours: Midland Combination Challenge Cup Winners 1974-5, Finalists 1985-6, Worcestershire Senior Urn Finalists 1981-2, 1985-6, National Police (B. Isles) Champions numerous occasions

LEICESTERSHIRE SENIOR LEAGUE 1985-86

President: L. T. Shipman CBE, MBE

Secretary: P. Henwood, 450 London Road, Leicester LE2 2PP

Tel: Leicester 704121

THRINGSTONE TRIUMPH IN EXCITING FINISH

The Challenge for the championship of the Premier Division was a very hard fought battle throughout the season, but they were always under pressure from several clubs including Birstall United, Narborough, Thringstone, Wigston Town and Holwell Works.

Eventually Thringstone emerged from the pack, having occupied second spot for most of the season and won their last games to take over the leadership of the League on the 21st April. At this stage, however, Anstey Nomads were three games in hand and required 5 points to clinch the title, but they only managed to make a draw in each of these games and had to be content with the runners-up position. This meant that Thringstone took the title for the second season running, again a fine tribute to their consistent all-round team work and also their very competent, enthusiastic and industrious Manager, Barry Hartley.

Wigston Town, too, had a very good season. After losing 3 of their first four League games, they then went twenty-one League games without defeat before going down to Thringstone by 2-1. Their run took them from the 26th August until 5th April. Unfortunately, they lost 3 of their last 4 games, otherwise they could have challenged for the top position. They did have some consolation, however, by defeating Narborough 2-1 in the final of the Leicestershire Senior Cup, this being the first time they had won this Trophy.

Holwell works did well in their first season in the Premier Division (having been Division 1 champions the previous season) finishing sixth having at one time headed the League.

The disappointment of the season was Friar Lane O.B., whose poor showing meant that they only dodged the relegation spot by securing a point from Anstey Nomads in the last game of the season.

In Division 1 there was very little dividing the top six teams for most of the season. Harborough Town occupied the top spot for at least half of the season, but towards the latter end both Syston St. Peters and Kirkby Muxloe exerted considerable pressure and, in fact, Syston won their last 9 League games, and with both Harborough and Kirkby Muxloe faltering at the last hurdles they managed to clinch the title by one point from Harborough Town — only 3 points separated the top 4 teams.

The final of the Tebbutt-Brown Trophy won by Narborough (Premier Division) by five goals to one over Rolls Royce (Division 1), but only after extra time.

This was some consolation to Narborough after losing the Leicestershire Senior Cup Final.

PREMIER DIVISION

	P	W	D	L	F	A	Pts
Thringstone	30	21	2	7	62	32	44
Anstey Nomads	30	17	8	5	69	21	42
Narborough & Littlethorpe	30	17	8	5	63	32	42
Birstall United	30	17	6	7	53	35	40
Wigston Town	30	14	10	6	47	29	38
Holwell Works	30	15	7	8	69	43	37
Wigston Fields	30	13	8	9	64	40	34
Stapenhill	30	14	6	10	54	39	34
Hinckley Town	30	12	7	11	46	43	31
Newfoundpool WMC	30	9	9	12	47	58	27
Oadby Town	30	9	7	14	33	43	25
Lutterworth Town	30	8	8	14	51	53	24
Hillcroft	30	7	4	19	27	67	18
Friar Lane O.B.	30	7	3	20	38	63	17
Desford Colliery	30	8	1	21	37	96	17
Earl Shilton Albion	30	3	4	23	38	104	10

DIVISION ONE

	P	W	D	L	F	A	Pts
Syston St. Peters	30	18	7	5	55	34	43
Harborough Town	30	17	8	5	54	31	42
Kirby Muxloe	30	17	7	6	60	29	41
Sileby Town	30	16	8	6	54	38	40
Leicester United Res.	30	16	6	8	55	29	36*
Houghton Rangers	30	15	6	9	51	40	36
Barrow Town	30	14	4	12	52	48	32
Rolls Royce	30	10	11	9	39	31	31
Barwell Athletic	30	10	11	9	38	34	31
St. Andrews S.C.	30	11	5	14	51	56	27
Anstey Town	30	9	8	13	35	48	26
Whetstone Athletic	30	9	6	15	38	44	24
Barlestone St. Giles	30	8	6	16	39	50	22
Quorn	30	8	6	16	39	56	22
Thurmaston Town	30	7	5	18	29	63	19
Leicester Y.M.C.A.	30	1	4	25	15	73	6

Leading Scorers

Premier Division

McManus (Narborough & Littlethorpe)	25
Jarram (Anstey Nomads)	20
Kempin (Holwell Works)	19
Freestone (Desford Colliery)	18
Birkenhead (Stapenhill)	18
Massey (Thringstone)	17

Division One

Humter (Barrow Town)	36
Carr (Sileby Town)	19
Payne (Whetstone Ath.)	18
Sanderson (Rolls Royce)	16
Kee (Syston St. Peters)	15

LEICESTERSHIRE SENIOR LEAGUE
Recent Champions

Max Pts	Season	1st		2nd		3rd		4th	
60	1972/73	52	Oadby T.	49	Newfoundpool WMC	44	Friar Lane O.B.	42	Thringstone
60	1973/74	48	Friar Lane O.B.	47	Oadby T.	44	Newfoundpool WMC	42	Earl Shilton Alb.
60	1974/75	52	Friar Lane O.B.	44*	Jones & Shipman	44	Oadby T.	43	Newfoundpool WMC
60	1975/76	44	Friar Lane O.B.	42	Jones & Shipman	41	Thringstone	38	Oadby T.
56	1976/77	46	Friar Lane O.B.	43*	Oadby T.	43	Wigston Fields	38*	Jones & Shipman
60	1977/78	53	Friar Lane O.B.	43	Oadby T.	41	Newfoundpool WMC	38	Jones & Shipman
60	1978/79	47	Shepshed Ch.	43	Anstey Nomads	40	Friar Lane O.B.	39	Oadby T.
60	1979/80	51	Shepshed Ch.	47	Anstey Nomads	42	Oadby T.	41	Birstall U.
60	1980/81	49	Shepshed Ch.	47*	Anstey Nomads	47	Wigston Fields	39	Birstall U.
60	1981/82	49	Anstey Nomads	44	Birstall U.	42	Leicester U. Res.	38	Stapenhill
60	1982/83	47	Anstey Nomads	46	Wigston Fields	38*	Friar Lane O.B.	38	Wigston T.
60	1983/84	50	Melton T.	41	Narborough & L.	40	Anstey Nomads	39	Birstall U.
60	1984/85	51	Thringstone	48	Wigston Fields	39	Anstey Nomads	34	Friar Lane O.B.
60	1985/86	44	Thringstone	42*	Anstey Nomads	42	Narborough & L.	40	Birstall U.

* goal average/difference

LEICESTERSHIRE SENIOR FOOTBALL LEAGUE 1985-86 PREMIER DIVISION

	1	2	3	4	5	6	7	8	9	10	11	12	13	14	15	16
1 Anstey Nom.		1-2	5-1	7-0	4-0	2-0	2-3	1-1	2-1	3-0	2-1	0-1	4-0	2-1	0-0	2-2
2 Birstall	0-0		4-0	4-3	3-2	2-0	2-0	0-1	1-0	1-0	1-2	2-0	1-0	4-1	3-5	2-0
3 Desford Coll	0-5	4-1		2-0	2-0	1-1	0-2	4-3	0-5	1-3	1-3	4-1	0-5	3-1	0-5	0-1
4 Earl Shilton	1-4	1-3	2-3		4-3	2-3	1-2	1-7	1-4	2-2	1-5	2-1	0-7	0-5	0-3	0-4
5 Friar Lane	0-0	2-0	9-1	2-1		1-2	2-0	2-6	4-2	1-2	0-0	2-3	0-2	0-3	0-2	0-1
6 Hillcroft	0-4	0-0	3-2	0-2	0-2		1-1	0-2	2-1	0-8	2-3	1-1	0-2	0-1	0-3	2-4
7 Hinckley T.	0-3	1-2	1-3	1-1	3-0	3-1		3-1	1-4	0-0	1-1	5-1	1-1	5-1	0-2	1-1
8 Holwell W.	1-0	3-1	7-1	4-1	3-1	1-3	2-1		2-2	0-3	6-2	3-0	2-0	2-0	2-1	1-1
9 Lutterworth	0-3	1-4	5-2	2-2	6-2	0-1	0-1	3-1		1-3	1-1	1-1	0-0	0-3	0-1	1-1
10 Narborugh	1-1	1-1	6-1	3-2	3-0	2-1	3-0	2-0	1-1		2-0	1-0	1-0	3-4	4-2	1-1
11 Newfoundpool	0-6	1-3	5-0	2-2	0-0	2-0	0-2	2-1	3-3	1-2		0-2	4-2	1-3	2-2	1-1
12 Ordby T.	0-0	1-0	4-1	3-0	2-1	4-1	1-0	1-1	2-3	1-1	1-1		0-2	1-2	1-1	0-1
13 Stapenhill	2-2	1-2	1-0	4-3	4-0	0-2	1-3	1-1	1-0	2-0	5-1	2-0		1-0	6-4	0-0
14 Thringstone	3-1	0-0	3-0	7-1	2-0	2-1	3-1	2-2	2-1	2-1	1-0	1-0	4-0		1-0	0-1
15 Wigston Field	0-2	3-3	3-0	5-2	0-1	6-0	2-2	2-1	2-3	1-1	3-0	3-0	1-1	0-2		2-2
16 Wigston Town	0-1	1-1	2-0	2-0	2-1	3-0	1-2	2-2	3-0	2-3	2-3	1-0	3-1	1-2	1-0	

LEICESTERSHIRE SENIOR FOOTBALL LEAGUE 1985-86 DIVISION ONE

	1	2	3	4	5	6	7	8	9	10	11	12	13	14	15	16
1 Anstey Town		1-0	0-0	0-3	1-3	2-1	1-2	1-2	1-0	3-3	0-3	0-0	0-1	2-1	2-2	2-0
2 Barlestone	0-1		3-4	5-1	0-3	1-2	1-2	0-0	1-0	1-2	3-2	3-1	3-0	0-1	1-1	1-0
3 Barrow	4-1	2-1		2-3	1-2	1-2	0-3	3-0	7-0	0-2	2-0	1-3	1-1	2-2	3-0	1-0
4 Barwell	3-0	0-1	0-1		0-1	0-2	1-0	0-2	1-1	1-1	3-1	1-1	2-3	1-1	3-0	1-1
5 Harborough	3-0	2-2	1-0	1-1		2-2	0-0	1-2	2-0	2-0	2-1	1-2	0-0	0-1	2-1	2-0
6 Houghton	0-0	1-1	3-1	1-0	2-1		3-3	3-1	5-0	1-0	1-0	6-0	0-0	1-2	4-3	0-3
7 Kirkby Muxloe	4-1	1-1	3-1	1-1	1-2	2-0		2-1	3-0	3-1	0-0	4-2	0-2	4-1	1-2	1-0
8 Leic. Utd. Rgs.	4-2	3-0	7-0	0-1	2-3	4-0	1-1		1-0	2-0	1-1	2-0	1-4	1-1	2-0	2-0
9 Leics YMCA	1-1	0-2	1-2	1-1	0-2	1-1	1-4	0-2		1-3	0-1	0-2	2-4	0-1	0-2	1-3
10 Quorn	1-5	3-2	3-2	1-2	0-1	1-2	1-2	0-5	1-4		0-2	2-2	2-1	2-2	0-0	4-3
11 Rolls Royce	1-1	0-0	0-3	2-2	2-2	3-1	1-0	1-1	5-0	1-1		0-0	1-2	0-1	5-1	1-1
12 St Andrews	2-2	4-2	2-3	0-2	0-2	2-1	0-2	2-3	5-0	3-1	0-1		5-1	4-1	2-1	0-2
13 Sileby Town	0-2	6-1	3-1	2-1	4-4	1-0	2-2	1-0	3-0	1-0	1-1	5-3		0-2	1-0	2-0
14 Syston St. Peters	1-2	2-1	1-1	1-1	3-2	3-2	2-1	1-1	4-1	1-0	1-2	4-0	2-1		4-0	2-0
15 Thurmaston Town	1-0	2-0	0-1	0-1	1-3	1-2	1-6	2-1	1-0	0-4	0-1	3-2	0-0	1-4		0-0
16 Whetstone	2-1	3-2	1-2	1-1	2-2	1-2	0-3	0-2	2-0	1-0	1-0	0-2	2-2	1-2	8-3	

ANSTEY NOMADS
Secretary: T.W. French, 6 James Street, Anstey, Leicester. Tel: 0533 362838
Ground: Gropston Road, Anstey. Tel: 0533 364868
Colours: All Red **Change Colours:** All White

BIRSTALL UNITED
Secretary: S. Fisher, 24 Iris Avenue, Birstall Tel: 677422
Ground: Meadow Lane, Birstall. Tel: 671230
Colours: White/Navy **Change Colours:** All Blue

FRIAR LANE O.B.
Secretary: T.J. Knibbs, 75 Brighton Avenue, Wigston Fields, Leics.LE8 1JB. Tel: 0533 888928 (H)
Ground: Knighton Lane East, Leicester 0533 833629
Colours: Black & White Stripes/Black/Black **Change Colours:** Red with White Pinstripe/White/Red

HINCKLEY TOWN
Secretary: Mrs. E. Dyer, 117 Roston Drive, Hinckley, Leics. LE10 0UQ. Tel: 0455 38628 (H)
Ground: Hinkley Sports Club, Leicester Road, Hinkley, Leics. Tel: 0455 615062
Colours: Claret & Blue **Change Colours:** White

MARBOROUGH & LITTLETHORP
Secretary: Peter Jackson, 93 Cleveleys Avenue, Braunston, Leicester.
Ground: The Recreation Ground, Leicester Road Narborough, Leicester
Colours: Blue & White Stripes/Blue/Red **Change Colours:** White

NEWFOUNDPOOL WMC
Secretary: L. Wilson, 23 Tilton Drive, Oadby, Leics. Tel: 0533 715892
Ground: Blenheim Road, Birstall, Leicester.
Colours: Green & Amber Pinstripe/Green/Green **Change Colours:** Red & White Vertical Stripe/Black/Redd

OADBY TOWN
Secretary: S.D. Young, 21 Orange Street, South Wigston, Leicester. Tel: 0533 783300
Ground: Wigston Road, Oadby, Leicester. Tel: 0533 715728
Colours: All Red **Change Colours:** Sky Blue/Navy/Navy & Sky Blue

STAPENHILL
Secretary: E.A. Sleigh, 48 Long Street, Stapenhill, Burton-on-Trent, Staffs. Tel: 0283 65957 (H) 42145 (W)
Ground: Edge Hill, Maple Grove, Stapenhill, Burton-on-Trent, Staffs. Tel: 0283 62471
Colours: Red/White/Red **Change Colours:** Blue/White/Blue

THRINGSTONE
Secretary: P. Allgood, 61 Swallowdale, Thringstone, Coalville. Tel: 0530 22817
Ground: Homestead Road, Thringstone
Colours: All Yellow **Change Colours:** All Blue

WIGSTONE FIELDS
Secretary: N. Jelley, 35 Copinger Road, Aylestone Park, Leicester LE2 6LF. Tel: 0533 838475
Ground: Windsor Avenue, Glen Parva, Leics. Tel: 0533 771039
Colours: All Red **Change Colours:** All Yellow

WIGSTON TOWN
Secretary: D.A. Young, 10 Willowpark Drive, Wigston, Leics
Ground: Holmes Park, Dog & Gun Lane, Whetstone, Leics. Tel: 0533 861521
Colours: Red **Change Colours:** White

TEBBUTT — BROWN CUP 1985/86

Round 1
Desford Coll 1, Anstey 0
Earl Shilton A. 0, Wigston T. 2
Friar Lane 4, Lutterworth 1 (aet)
Holwell 3, Birstall 0
Narborough 2, Wigston F. 1
Newfoundpool 1, Thringstone 5
Oadby 2, Hillcroft 0
Stapenhill 2, Hinckley T. 0
Barwell 0, Leicester Utd Res 4
Houghton 6, Thurmaston 1
Leic. YMCA 0, Kirby Muxloe 2
Rolls Royce 4, Anstey T. 1 (aet)
St. Andrews 1, Barrow T. 3
Sileby T. 1, Quorn 2
Syston St. P 2, Harborough 0
Barlestone 2, Whetstone 0 (aet)

Round 2
Desford Coll 3, Stapenhill 0 (aet)
Frair Lane 0. Wigston T. 3
Thringstone 3, Holwell 2 (aet)
Oadby 0, Narborough 2
Barrow T. 3, Quorn 1 (aet)
Kirby Muxloe 0, Leic. Utd Res 1
Houghton 4, Syston St. P 1
Rolls Royce 2, Barlestone 0

Round 3
Narborough 2, Wigston T. 0
Desford Coll 1, Barrow T. 0
Thringstone 2, Leic. Utd Res 1
Rolls Royce 2, Houghton 1

SEMI FINALS
Narborough 4, Desford Coll 3
Rolls Royce 4, Thringstone 2

FINAL
Narborough 5, Rolls Royce 1 (aet)

NENE GROUP UNITED COUNTIES LEAGUE
REVIEW OF SEASON 1985-86

Chairman: T.N. Bates

Secretary/Treasurer: M.J. Wall

17 Mendip Road, Northampton. Telephone: 0604 57239

With Nene Group UCL clubs experiencing a disappointing season in outside competitions for the most part, attention was directed to domestic football and in particular the intriguing championship race between two clubs of vastly differing resources, former champions Buckingham Town and surprise package Stewart & Lloyds.

The early season favourites, Buckingham nevertheless struggled for form in the early weeks of the campaign. St. Neots, champions Arlesey, Long Buckby, Stewart & Lloyds and Raunds all topped the table before the Robins took over at the start of November. Stewart & Lloyds matched their form and regained the lead in December. In mid season, though, around half the division could still consider themselves realistic contenders with Arlesey and Irthlingborough looking likely stayers.

For the latter two there were severe midwinter blows. Arlesey were hit badly with injuries, rarely fielded their strongest line up after the turn of the year and slid slowly into a mid table position. Irthlingborough were rocked by the resignation of popular and successful manager Roger Ashby and thereafter lacked the consistency needed to win titles.

The big freeze hindered many clubs with eyes on the crown - but Buckingham saw more regular action than any of their rivals and had built up an eight point lead by the time part two of the season started in earnest. A run of 25 games without defeat in the league had virtually guaranteed them the crown by the middle of April when they were beaten at Stamford - only their second defeat and their first away from Ford Meadow.

Buckingham's last eight games brought them only seven points and they had to wait until the 39th game before a draw at Holbeach assured them of the top spot. Stewart & Lloyds, perhaps the only completely amateur side in the division, surprised a few pundits by finishing second - and but for a few poor results against lowly opposition they might have been champions themselves. Nevertheless, a magnificent season for the Corby outfit, with essentially the same squad as that which finished mid table a year earlier, and what a first season in charge for NGUCL Manager of the Year Jackie Phillips. In third place were Baldock, who collected just seven points from the first ten games, in contrast to 51 from the last 30 matches. They finished as the highest scorers and would surely have collected some silverware had not their cup season been decimated by expulsions from three competitions after it transpired that goalkeeper Shaun Wilkinson had played while under suspension from another club, unbeknown to Norton Road officials.

At the foot of the table Newport Pagnell, as always looked in trouble at Christmas. This time they couldn't produce their customary spring revival and eventually finished six points adrift at the bottom. Next season they will be playing in Division 1 after a four year spell in the Premier. Eynesbury displayed good form in the last two months of the season to pull away after looking favourites for the drop for some months.

In Division One Lou Adams assembled a side of vast experience at Kempston to launch an assault on the championship. It worked as the Rovers were unbeaten in their first 25 games - and despite a few late stutters they held on to top place and will commence their career on their new ground as a Premier side once again. Second place went to Towcester Town for the second season in a row after another excellent season that saw them regain the Northants Junior Cup. The other main contenders for honours were two of the new recruits from the Peterborough League, Baker Perkins and Ramsey.

Both produced some sparkling football but finished just short of a promotion place. Baker Perkins were slow starters and came off second best against the clubs ahead of them; neighbours Ramsey started with a goal rush but never looked quite the same side after their player-coach Chris Turner joined Cambridge United as manager. There was some consolation for Ramsey with success in the Huntingdonshire Senior Cup.

At the foot of the table Ford Sports had a traumatic season, winning just three times and suffering some heavy defeats. They were joined in making application for re-election by newcomers Cogenhoe, who have not quite got the team yet to go with their excellent facilities. Both clubs were re-elected, and under new management, both should look forward to better campaigns next time round. Olney displayed good end of season form to pull clear, while Burton Park Wanderers, who rarely found their best form after their exciting league cup run ended, also narrowly edged their way to safety.

The League Knockout Cup was won in some style by Stamford, 7-0 aggregate victors over holders London Nuckby,; a very creditable achievement by the Daniels' boss Paul Brackwell who virtually had to build a team from scratch in the close season. Another feature of the cup competition was the number of giant-killing acts by Division One clubs. Mirrlees Blackstone, despite finishing mid table, equalled the best ever performance by a Division One club in reaching the last four. Burton Park Wanderers, Cottingham, Ramsey and Towcester all joined them in beating Premier opposition.

Buckingham were the only club to survive in the Vase as far as the Near Year. After a number of postponements they were surprisingly beaten on an icy Ford Meadow by Havant at the fifth round stage, eliminated not for the first time by unfancied opponents.

In the FA Cup the league's last representatives were Irthlingborough and Stamford, both reaching the 3rd Round Qualifying.

Buckingham Town are leaving the league having obtained promotion to the Southern League through the non-league 'pyramid' and we wish them success in the future. The League also welcomes back Spalding United from the Northern Counties East League, after an eight year absence.

Jeremy Biggs

Constitution of Divisions 1986-87

Premier Divison (21): Ampthill Town, Arlesey Town, Baldock Town, Bourne Town, Brackley Town, Desborough Town, Eynesbury Rovers, Holbeach United, Irthlingborough Diamonds, Kempston Rovers, Long Buckby, Northampton Spencer, Potton United, Raunds Town, Rothwell Town, St Neots Town, Spalding United, Stamford, Stewart & Lloyds, Stotfold, Wootton Blue Cross.

Division One (19): Baker Perkins, British Timken Athletic, British Timken Duston, Burton Park Wanders, Cogenhoe United, Cottingham, Ford Sports, Higham Town, Irchester Eastfield, Mirrlees Blackstone, Newport Pagnell Town, O.N. Chenecks, Olney Town, Ramsey Town, St Ives Town, Sharnbrook, Thrapston Venturas, Towcester Town, Whitworths.

Kemston Rovers: *Back row: (L-R) Tony Albone (Secretary), Lou Adams (Manager), Paul Spencer (Linesman) Graham Vail, Doug Jack (Committee), Colin Williams, Curt Davenport, Steve Byrne, Bobby Folds, Ronnie Simons, Stuart Panter (Committee), Dave Earl (Captain). Richard Hirst (Trainer), Bob Lambert (Committee). Front row: (L-R) Steve Cox, Dave Liddle, Ian Tomlin, Mick Handy, Mark Collier.*

NENE GROUP UNITED COUNTIES LEAGUE HONOURS LIST 1985-86

Premier Division
Champions - Buckingham Town
Runners-Up - Stewart & Lloyds Corby
Division One
Champions - Kempston Rovers
Runners-Up - Towcester Town
Reserve Division One
Champions - Irthlingborough Diamonds
Runners-Up - Stewart & Lloyds Corby
Reserve Division Two
Champions - Wootton Blue Cross
Runners-Up - Holbeach United
Premier/One Knockout Cup
Winners - Stamford
Runners-Up - Long Buckby
Reserve Knockout Cup
Winners - Rushden Town
Runners-Up - Stotford
FA Vase - best performance
Buckingham Town (5th Round)
FA Cup - best performance
Irthlingborough Diamonds and Stamford
(3rd Round Qualifying)
Huntingdonshire Senior Cup
Winners - Ramsey Town
Northamptonshire Junior Cup
Winners - Towcester Town
Hinchingbrooke Cup
Winners - Irthlingborough Diamonds
Runners-Up - St. Ives Town

MANAGER OF THE MONTH AWARD WINNERS

	Premier	Division 1
September	Jackie Phillips (S&L Corby)	Geoff Manning (Ramsey)
October	Alan Day (Holbeach)	John Mayes (Irchester)
November	Roger Ashby (Irthlingborough)	Bev Ironmonger (Cottingham)
December	Gary Knibbs (Buckingham)	Lou Adamds (Kempston)
January	Brian Williams (Baldock)	Ian Day (Baker Perkins)
February	No awards made due to weather	
March	Paul Brackwell (Stamford)	Peter Robinson (st Ives)
April	Brian Abraham (Eynesbury)	Tony McPhillips (B. Timken Ath.)
May	Jackie Phillips (S&L Corby)	Bev Harrison (Thrapston)

Manager of the Year - Jackie Phillips (S & L Corby)

Premier Division							Home	GoalsAway			Goals	
	P	W	D	L	F	A	W	D	L	F	A	Pts
Buckingham Town	40	15	4	1	51	14	10	6	4	27	17	16
Stewart & Lloyds Corby	40	12	5	3	47	17	12	6	2	38	15	59
Baldock Town	40	12	4	4	47	25	14	2	4	44	18	58
Irthlingborough Diam.....40	12	2	6	37	24	10	6	4	32	21	52	
Stamford	40	11	4	5	34	21	11	2	7	37	31	50
Long Buckby	40	9	5	6	38	27	9	5	6	37	27	46
Potton United	40	11	3	6	42	28	9	3	8	27	25	46
Wootton Blue Cross	40	9	5	6	38	33	7	6	7	25	25	43
Arlesey Town	40	8	3	9	37	27	8	6	6	26	30	41
Holbeach United	40	8	5	7	34	30	8	3	9	32	45	40
Northampton Spencer	40	6	7	7	32	36	9	3	8	32	38	40
Rothwell Town	40	11	4	5	30	19	6	1	13	30	43	39
Raunds Town	40	8	6	6	35	36	8	1	11	26	38	39
Ampthill Town	40	10	5	5	32	21	3	5	12	23	47	36
Desborough Town	40	5	5	10	38	40	6	4	10	32	49	31
Brackley Town	40	7	5	8	30	30	3	5	12	22	40	30
Bourne Town	40	6	6	8	20	24	3	6	11	23	47	30
St. Neots Town	40	6	4	10	33	3	5	12	26	41	27	
Stotfold	40	9	0	11	29	36	1	7	12	14	41	27
Eynesbury Rovers	40	4	7	9	24	42	3	5	12	21	44	26
Newport Pagnell Town	40	3	5	12	22	32	1	7	12	21	45	20

Division One	P	W	D	L	F	A	W	D	L	F	A	Pts
Kempston Rovers........36		3	2	39	16	12	4	2	15	16	57	
Towcester Town............	36	14	2	2	42	10	10	5	3	32	15	55
Baker Perkins..............	36	12	5	1	58	16	11	2	5	29	20	53
Ramsey Town..............	36	13	2	3	60	22	9	4	5	34	20	50
Cottingham................	36	10	5	3	37	19	9	5	4	32	29	48
Thrapston Venturas.........	36	11	3	4	50	17	7	3	8	27	28	42
St. Ives Town.............	36	12	1	5	49	22	7	8	21	29	42	
Higham Town.............	36	6	4	8	27	34	9	5	4	32	31	39
Irchester Eastfield..........	36	10	3	5	32	24	7	1	10	38	36	38
Whitworths	36	8	5	5	36	30	6	3	9	37	36	36
Mirrlees Blackstone.........	36	8	3	7	31	35	6	4	8	29	31	35
Birtish Timken Athletic.....	36	7	6	5	34	23	2	6	10	28	35	30
Sharnbrook................	36	7	6	5	27	25	4	1	13	17	38	29
British Timken Dunston....	36	6	1	11	27	39	7	2	9	27	44	29
On Chenecks..............	36	5	5	8	24	38	5	3	10	15	39	28
Burton Park Wanderers.....	36	3	4	11	15	32	2	6	109	19	41	20
Olney Town...............	36	4	3	11	14	31	3	3	12	21	51	20
Cogenhoe United...........	36	4	2	12	15	33	3	1	14	20	40	17
Ford Sports...............	36	3	4	11	19	53	0	6	12	11	57	16

Corby Gainsborough withdrew during the season and all matches involving them were deleted from the table. At the time of withdrawal their record was:
15 1 2 5 7 21 0 1 7 6 27 4

SEASON 1985/86 PREMIER DIVISION	Ampthill	Arlesey	Baldock	Bourne	Brackley	Buckingham	Desborough	Eynesbury	Holbeach	Irthlingborough	Long Buckby	Newport Pagnell	N'tham Spencer	Potton	Raunds	Rothwell	St. Neots	Stamford	Stewart & Lloyds	Stotfold	Wootton
Ampthill		2-1	3-1	5-1	5-1	0-1	1-1	2-2	0-2	1-0	3-3	0-0	2-3	2-0	0-2	1-0	2-1	1-0	0-0	2-1	0-1
Arlesey	2-0		0-3	1-2	2-2	1-2	6-1	1-1	4-0	1-2	0-2	3-1	4-2	0-3	0-1	4-0	6-2	2-1	0-1	0-1	0-0
Baldock..........	2-1	2-1		0-1	3-2	1-1	3-4	5-1	5-0	2-2	2-0	4-2	1-2	1-2	3-0	2-1	2-1	3-1	0-0	3-0	3-3
Bourne	4-1	1-2	0-5		2-0	1-1	1-2	1-0	0-2	0-1	1-1	0-0	1-1	3-0	1-2	1-0	2-1	0-1	0-3	1-1	0-0
Brackley	5-1	0-0	0-5	3-0		0-3	1-2	1-2	3-2	2-2	1-2	1-1	1-2	1-2	2-1	3-2	1-1	0-1	0-0	3-0	2-1
Buckingham......	2-1	4-1	1-1	2-0	2-0		4-0	1-0	0-2	3-2	1-1	3-0	3-0	5-1	5-0	5-1	0-0	4-2	2-2	1-0	3-0
Desborough......	3-1	3-4	1-3	2-2	3-4	0-2		5-0	1-2	2-2	2-4	3-3	0-2	1-1	1-0	2-1	1-2	3-4	1-1	3-0	1-2
Eynesbury	2-2	0-0	2-6	1-1	1-1	2-0	2-2		1-3	1-3	0-3	2-1	0-3	0-5	1-1	0-3	3-1	3-1	1-2	0-0	2-4
Holbeach	2-0	0-1	1-2	3-3	2-1	1-1	4-1	1-0		2-0	1-0	2-2	1-2	1-2	2-0	2-4	3-0	1-3	0-5	4-0	1-1
Irthlingborough...	6-0	2-0	1-1	1-1	0-1	1-0	1-4	3-1	2-1		2-0	2-1	0-1	3-2	5-2	1-3	2-0	1-2	0-2	2-1	2-1
Long Buckby....	4-1	2-3	2-4	2-0	2-0	0-2	1-1	2-2	4-1	1-1		4-3	2-1	0-1	0-1	2-0	2-1	1-1	2-3	5-1	0-0
Newport Pagnell.	0-1	0-0	0-1	0-1	1-1	0-1	2-3	2-3	1-1	0-0	1-3		2-5	3-0	2-0	2-3	4-0	0-3	1-3	1-1	0-2
Northampton S	1-1	1-2	0-2	1-1	4-3	1-1	3-1	0-1	2-2	1-1	2-5	1-1		0-2	3-1	3-2	2-2	1-2	2-4	2-1	2-1
Potton	3-2	4-0	0-2	2-2	0-2	2-3	2-1	2-0	4-2	1-0	3-2	6-1	4-1		1-4	3-0	3-3	0-1	1-2	0-0	1-0
Raunds	1-3	3-3	0-2	2-1	3-0	2-1	4-4	1-1	5-3	1-3	0-0	3-1	1-1	1-0		1-4	0-3	4-3	1-2	1-1	1-0
Rothwell.........	2-0	1-2	2-0	2-0	2-1	1-1	2-0	2-1	2-1	0-1	4-2	3-0	1-0	0-0	3-1		0-0	0-1	0-4	2-2	1-2
St. Neots.......	1-1	1-1	0-1	7-1	3-0	0-1	2-1	2-2	2-3	1-4	0-3	2-1	0-2	0-2	1-4	3-1		0-2	0-0	4-1	1-2
Stamford........	3-0	3-0	0-1	3-1	0-0	2-1	2-0	3-2	1-1	0-1	1-3	3-0	1-1	0-0	1-2	3-1	2-1		0-4	3-0	3-2
Stewart & Lloyds	2-0	0-1	2-1	3-1	1-0	1-1	0-1	5-0	7-0	1-2	2-2	2-1	8-1	2-0	3-1	1-1	3-1	2-1		1-1	1-1
Stotfold.........	0-3	1-4	0-1	4-2	2-1	1-3	5-1	2-1	0-2	0-2	1-0	0-1	3-0	1-0	1-2	3-1	1-6	2-4	1-0		1-2
Wootton	2-2	0-0	3-2	3-2	2-2	0-1	3-2	3-1	1-2	1-3	0-1	11-1	3-2	1-4	3-1	1-2	2-0	3-3	3-0	3-2	

SEASON 1985/6 DIVISION ONE	Baker Perkins	B. Timken Ath.	B. Timken Duston	Burton PW	Cogenhoe	cottingham	Ford Sports	Higham	Irchester	Kempston	M. Blackstone	ON Chenecks	Olney	Ramsey	St Ives	Sharnbrook	Thrapston	Towcester	Whitworths
Baker Perkins		4-2	4-1	6-0	5-0	1-1	9-1	1-3	7-0	0-0	5-2	3-0	2-2	1-1	4-0	2-1	2-1	0-0	2-1
B. Timken Athletics...	2-6		5-0	3-0	1-0	2-3	4-0	0-0	4-0	0-0	3-3	1-1	3-0	0-0	1-2	1-4	1-1	1-2	2-1
B. Timken Dunston...	0-3	1-0		6-4	2-1	1-4	2-2	1-2	0-2	1-2	1-3	1-2	1-3	0-3	1-2	1-0	3-0	3-5	2-1
Burton PW..........	0-1	2-2	1-3		0-2	1-3	1-1	1-1	2-2	0-3	0-4	1-0	0-1	1-2	0-1	2-0	0-4	0-2	3-0
Cogenhoe	0-1	1-2	0-1	0-0		1-4	2-1	2-3	3-0	0-2	0-4	0-1	0-2	0-3	0-0	3-2	1-3	0-3	2-1
Cottingham...........	3-1	3-0	1-0	1-1	1-0		3-0	2-2	1-5	0-3	6-1	5-1	3-1	1-0	4-0	0-1	1-1	0-0	2-2
Ford Sports..........	0-2	1-9	1-3	1-1	1-4	2-1		2-2	1-6	0-6	1-0	0-1	3-3	0-3	0-2	2-0	0-3	0-3	4-4
Highham............	1-2	2-0	3-3	0-2	3-2	1-2	0-0		1-0	2-5	1-0	3-2	1-1	2-5	0-1	2-4	1-0	1-2	3-3
Irchester	0-2	2-2	0-1	3-1	3-1	3-0	1-0	5-0		1-1	2-1	3-1	3-2	0-3	1-0	1-1	2-3	0-4	2-1
Kempston............	3-1	1-1	5-2	2-3	3-2	4-0	2-0	2-1	2-0		0-0	3-1	1-0	3-2	2-0	3-0	1-0	0-0	2-3
M Blackstone.........	1-1	1-0	0-2	4-2	2-2	1-2	1-1	1-4	1-5	1-6		6-1	3-2	0-3	2-0	2-0	1-2	1-0	3-2
ON Chenecks.........	1-3	2-2	1-4	2-2	1-0	0-1	2-0	2-3	1-8	0-6	0-0		4-0	1-1	1-1	2-0	2-0	1-3	1-4
Olney	0-1	1-1	0-2	2-0	0-3	1-3	1-1	1-3	0-5	0-2	1-1	3-0		0-1	0-3	2-1	1-0	0-2	1-2
Ramsey.............	0-1	3-1	6-0	4-1	4-1	3-3	4-1	1-1	3-1	2-3	4-2	2-0	8-1		2-0	5-0	6-2	1-0	2-4
St. Ives.............	3-1	3-2	3-3	2-0	5-0	5-1	3-1	1-3	2-1	4-1	0-1	7-0	3-0	1-0		5-1	0-1	1-2	1-4
Sharnbrook...........	1-0	2-1	3-0	0-0	3-1	2-2	3-0	1-2	1-0	2-2	2-3	1-1	1-0	2-5	1-1		0-2	1-1	1-4
Thrapston............	0-1	1-0	3-1	2-0	3-1	0-0	4-1	3-0	5-1	0-5	1-2	0-1	7-1	1-1	3-0	4-0		2-2	1-0
Towcester............	3-0	3-1	6-0	2-1	2-0	0-0	1-1	5-1	2-0	1-2	1-0	0-2	4-1	4-0	3-1	1-0	2-0		2-0
Whitworths	2-2	2-2	2-1	1-1	1-0	1-2	4-0	0-1	0-2	2-1	3-2	0-0	4-1	3-1	4-7	0-2	4-4	3-1	

Knockout Cup Winners Stamford. *Back Row: (L-R) Paul Brackwell (Manager) Ross McKinnon, Jimmy Rogers, John Mackin, Andy Tillson, Les Thurbon, Andy Redding, John Watson (Physio). Front Row: (L-R) Stuart Hodson, Graham Leech, Robbie Gutteridge, Mick Emms, (Captain), Giovanni Nespoli, Danny Reilly.*

Knockout Cup Runners-Up Long Buckby. *Back Row: (L-R) Greg Harrison, Des Waldock, Craig Everiss, Andy Lay, Gary Wall, Simon Barfoot. Front Row: (L-R) Richard Green, Russ Ashenden, Peter Peach, Rob McKay, Kevin Simmonds, Paddy Walls.*

NENE GROUP UNITED COUNTIES LEAGUE KNOCKOUT CUP

Preliminary Round
Holbeach United 2 (Cole, Kirby) Ramsey Town 5 (Cozens 3, Maison 2)
Buckingham Town 1 (Roberts) Irthlingborough Diamonds 2 (Atkinson 2)
Kempston Rovers 4 (Williams, Earl, Handy, Cox) Ford Sports 0
Newport Pagnell Town 3 (Howe 2, P. Large) Thrapston Venturas 0
Sharnbrook 2 (Guerin, Miles) Brackley Town 2 (Allen, Turvey) a.e.t.
Replay: Brackley Town 1 (Allen) Sharnbrook 1 (oogstraten) a.e.t.
Brackley won 5-4 on penalties
Timken Athletic 2 (Haynes, og) O.N. Chenecks 3 (Francis, I. Gray, Leslie)
St Ives Town 2 (Brown 2) Olney Town 2 (Peters, Wilson) a.e.t.
Replay: Olney Town 2 (Abbott 2) St Ives Town 0
Northampton Spencer 2 (Vaughn, Lambert) Arlesey Town 0
Stotfold O Wootton Blue Cross 1 (Thompson)

First Round
Baldock Town 5 (Iddenden, Cox, Corney, Donnelly, Harvey) Eynesbury Rovers 0
Match ordered to be replayed - Baldock fielded suspended player:
Baldock Town 4 (R. O'Keefe, Cox, Donnelly 2) Eynesbury Rovers 1 (Marino)
Kempston Rovers 0 Raunds Town 1 (Walters)
Northampton Spencer 1 (Jelley) Irthlingborough Diamonds 3 (Atkinson 3)
Stewart & Lloyds 1 (P.J. Hamill) St Neots Town 2 (Humphrey, Seaton)
Wootton Blue Cross 2 (K. Remblance, Fay) Timken Duston 1 (Williams)
Ramsey Town 2 (Hollis 2) O.N. Chenecks 0
Bourne Town 2 (Bemrose, Bloodworth) Ampthill Town 0
Rothwell Town 3 (Hunter, Stewart, Bones) Whitworths 1 (Hanger)
Baker Perkins 1 (Bonner) Mirrlees Blackstone 2 (Pemberton, Richardson)
Irchester Eastfield 1 (Hollis) Long Buckby 4 (Harrison, Peach, Worthington, og) a.e.t.
Towcester Town 3 (Green, Westland, McAuley) Potton United 0
Brackley Town 5 (McDowell 2, Warrington, Raybould, Jarvis) Higham Town 2 (Newton, Dyte)
Cogenhoe United 1 (Fieldwick) Stamford 2 (Hodson, Redding7
Olney Town 3 (Abbot 2, Williams) Burton Park Wanderers 3 (Middleton, Tressler, Evans)
a.e.t. Olney postponed replay - tie awarded to Burton Park Wanderers
Newport Pagnell Town walkover. Corby Gainsborough withdrew
Desborough Town 0 Cottingham 2 (Murphy, Toseland)

Second Round
Stamford 2 (Hodson, Redding) St Neots Town 1 (Hill)
Irthlingborough Diamonds 4 (Head, Atkinson, Sargent, Hamilton) Rothwell Town 1 (Crabb)
Cottingham 0 Raunds Town 2 (James, Walpole)
Bourne Town 0 Burton Park Wanderers 0 a.e.t.
Replay: Burton Park Wanderers 3 (Tressler 3) Bourne Town 1 (Addison)
Ramsey Town 0 Mirrlees Blackstone 1 (Flynn)
Baldock Town 1 (Sayer) Wootton Blue Cross 0
Long Buckby 7 (Pearson 2, Peach 2, Barfoot, Harrison, og) Towcester Town 1 (English)
Newport Pagnell Town 4 (Bailey 2, Richardson, Morgan) Brackley Town 1 (Eyles7

Third Round
Raunds Town 0 Long Buckby 2 (Ashenden, Pearson)
Baldock Town 3 (M. Allinson, Wright, Corney) Burton Park Wanderers 1 (I. Clarke)
Stamford 3 (Seconde, Reilly 2) Newport Pagnell Town 0
M. Blackstone 3 (Halliday, Flynn, Grose) Irthlingborough Diamonds 1 (Geeves)

Semi-Finals
Mirrlees Blackstone 1 (Hand) Stamford 2 (Hodson, Rogers)
Long Buckby 2 (Pearson 2) Baldock Town 1 (Cox)

Final
1st Leg - May 12
Long Buckby (0)0 Stamford (1) 2 (Gutteridge, McKinnon)
Long Buckby: Russell, Wall, Green (Sub: Peach), Waldock, Simmonds, Ashenden, Walle, Pearson, Barfoot, Harrison, McKay.
Stamford: Thurbon, Emms, Leech, Tillson, Mackin, Gutteridge, Hodson, Rogers, Nespoli, McKinnon, Hardy. (Sub: Grys) (Not used).

2nd Leg - May 19
Stamford (1)5 (Rogers 3, Tillson, Reilly) London Buckby (0)0
Stamford: Thurbon, Emms, Leech, Tillson, Mackin, Gutteridge, Hodson, Rogers, Nespoli (Sub: Redding), Reilly, McKinnon.
Long Buckby: Lay, Wall, Green, Waldock, Simmonds, Everiss, Harrison, Peach, Barfoot (Sub: Walle), Ashenden, McKay.
Referee: G. Abbott (both matches)
Stamford won 7-0 on aggregate

NENE GROUP UNITED COUNTIES LEAGUE —LEADING GOALSCORERS 1985-86

Ampthill	Paul Targett 16	Pete Fossey 9	Tyrone Clarke 8
Arlesey Town	Boyd Skeggs 8	Steve Taverner 8	Trevor Carter 6
			Alan Holt 6
			Mike Tizzard 6
Baldock Town	Graham cox 19	Ian Donnelly 13	Snowy Wright 11
Bourne Town	Darren Bloodworth 9	Mark Bemrose 8	Laurence Pask 6
Brackley Town	Paul Warrington 12	Wayne McDowell 11	Andy Cullinane 6
			Dick Turvey 6
Buckingham Town	Wayne Larkins 16	Peter Robinson 11	John Frost 7
			Steve Hodge 7
Desborough Town	Joey Martin 14	Shaun Diver 9	Paul Murphy 8
Eynesbury Rovers	Ray Skonnell	Ray Seekings 7	Dave Albone 5
Holbeach United	Jerry Lowery 15	Paul Langford 13	John Wilson 13
Irthlingborough Diam.	Gary Sargent 26	Derek Atkinson 21	David Harris 6
			Paul York 6
Long buckby	Tom Pearson 30	Peter Peach 12	Greg Harrison 11
Newport Pagnell Town	Phil Bone 7	Martin Howe 5	Greg Brown 4
			Alan Byron 4
			Clive Reson 4
Northampton Spencer	Tony Lambert 10	Freddie Vaughn 10	Steve Jelley 7
Potton United	Billy Horn 25	Steve Cran 10	Ian Jarrett 10
Raunds Town	Gabby Arraia 11	Mark James 10	Mick Walpole 8
Rothwell Town	Ian Hunter 12	Les Watson 9	Graham Stewart 8
St Neots Town	Steve Kuhne 17	Val Simpson 9	Mark Humphrey 7
Stamford	Jimmy Rogers 19	Danny Reilly 11	Andy Redding 10
Stewart & Lloyds	John Hamill 2	Alec Djeneralovic 13	Kevin McGuire 12
Stotfold	Mick Frost 6	Glen Bambrick 4	Roy Boon 4
		Colin Geddis 4	John Philbin 4
Wootton Blue Cross	Paul Fossey 15	John Carmichael 14	Derek Fay 10
			Phil Silvestri 10

NENE GROUP UNITED COUNTIES LEAGUE LEADING APPEARANCES 1985-86

Premier Division			
Ampthill town	Les Caves 41	Paul Targett 39	Richard Acton 36
Arlesey Town	Bill Goodyear 40	Alan Holt 33	Steve Taverner 31
Baldock Town	Martin Allinson 45	Keith Stanton 43	Ian Donnelly 36
			Alan Iddenden 36
			Steven Corney 36
Bourne Town	Charlie Marr 43	Darren Bloodworth 39	Jimmy Jackson 36
Brackley Town	Paul Jones 44	Aiden Kearns 41	Tony Rose 36
			Paul Warrington 36
Buckingham Town	Trevor Hopps 41	Kevin Heap 41	Ian Russell 41
			Peter Robinson 41
Desborough town	Pat Coe 35	Gary wood 28	Shaun Diver 25
Eynesbury Rovers	Lenny Morris 42	Paul McInnes 38	Dave Albone 37
Holbeach United	Paul Kirby 39	Jerry Lowery 38	John Hines 34
			Dave Whisker 34
Irthlingborough Diam.	Gary Sargent 44	Paul York 44	Dave Harris 42
Long Buckby	Gary Wall 45	Greg Harrison 43	Des Waldock 42
Newport Pagnell Town	Danny Janes 38	Clive Resch 38	Greg Brown 37
Northampton Spencer	Steve Jelley 29	Freddie Vaughn 29	Pete Gammons 27
Potton United	Andy Lloyd 41	Dick Newman 38	Billy Horn 37
			Steve Cran 37
Raunds Town	Chris Hullett 43	Gavin Duffett 40	Richard norris 34
Rothwell Town	Dave Chandler 42	Ian Hunter 36	Graham Brown 33
St Neots Town	Mark Humphrey 42	Steve Kuhne 40	Alan Bareham 39
Stamford	Nick Emms 43	Jimmy Rogers 42	Andy Tillson 42
Stewart & Lloyds	John Hamill 41	Jimmy Lamond 40	Mick Bihanycz 38
Stotfold	Francis Graves 39	Terry Kitchener 38	Dave Chellew 35
Wootton Blue Cross	John Carmichael 41	George Cleary 41	Russell Shreeves 40

Long Buckby Keeper Andy Russell saves bravely from Stamford's Danny Reilly. Giovanni Nespoli races in. Photo Mark Cotton.

NENE GROUP UNITED COUNTIES LEAGUE SEQUENCES 1985-86

Premier Division

Longest run without defeat	Buckingham Town 24 games
Longest run without a win	St Neots Town 14 games
Most consecutive wins	Buckingham Town & Raunds Town 8 games
Most consecutive draws	Stewart & Lloyds 5 games
Most consecutive defeats	Stotfold 7 games
Most consecutive games scoring	Buckingham Town 20 games
Most consecutive games without scoring	Brackley Town, Potton United & St Neots Town 4 games
Most consecutive games conceding	Eynesbury Rovers 24 games
Most consecutive games without conceding	Buckingham Town 7 games

Division One

Longest run without defeat	Kempston Rovers 25 games
Longest run without a win	Olney Town 15 games
Most consecutive wins	Irchester Eastfield, Kempston Rovers, St Ives Town, Towcester Town 6 games
Most consecutive draws	Burton Park Wanderers, Cottingham, British Timken Athletic, Higham Town 3 games
Most consecutive defeats	Olney Town 8 games
Most consecutive games scoring	Ramsey Town 19 games
Most consecutive games without scoring	Burton Park Wanderers, Cogenhoe United, Ford Sports, Thrapston Venturas 4 games
Most consecutive games conceding	Ford Sports 22 games
Most consecutive games without conceding	Baker Perkins, Kempston Rovers (twice), St Ives Town, Thrapston Venturas, Towcester Town (twice) 4 games)

HIGHEST WINS & HIGHEST SCORING MATCHES

Premier Division

Biggest home wins:	Stewart & Lloyds 8 Northampton Spencer 1 17.4.86
	Stewart & Lloyds 7 Holbeach United 0 11.1.86
Biggest away wins:	Stotfold 1 St Neots Town 6 23.11.85
	Eynesbury Rovers 0 Potton United 5 7.12.85
	Brackley Town 0 Baldock Town 5 11.1.86
	Holbeach United 0 Stewart & Lloyds 5 28.4.86
	Bourne Town 0 Baldock Town 5 17.5.86
Highest scoring draw	Raunds Town 4 Desborough Town 4 15.3.86
Highest aggregate	Stewart & Lloyds 8 Northampton Spencer 1 17.4.86

Division One

Biggest home win	Thrapston Venturas 14 Ford Sports 1 24.4.86
Biggest away win	Ford Sports 1 British Timken Athletic 9 21.4.86
Highest scoring draw	Ford Sports 4 Whitworths 4 17.8.85
	Whitworths 4 Thrapston Venturas 4 1.2.86
Highest aggregate	Thrapston Venturas 14 Ford Sports 1 24.4.86

NENE GROUP UNITED COUNTIES LEAGUE HAT TRICKS 1985-86

Premier Division
4 goals
P. Targett (Ampthill) v Bourne 21.5.86

3 goals
S. Kuhne (St Neots) v Raunds 24.8.85
J. Martin (Desborough) v Brackley 12.10.85
K. Horn (Potton) v N. Spencer 2.11.85
T. Carter (Arlesey) v St Neots 30.11.85
I. Jarrett (Potton) v Newport P. 14.12.85
M. James (Raunds) v Brackley 21.2.85
J. Middleton (S&L) v Holbeach 11.1.86
R. O'Keefe (Baldock) v Brackley 11.1.86
P. Fossey (Ampthill) v Brackley 18.1.86
G. Sargent (Irthlingboro) v Raunds 18.1.86
S. Wright (Baldock) v Eynesbury 18.1.86
A. Holt (Arlesey) v Desborough 25.1.86
G. Sargent (Irthlingboro) v Potton 28.1.86
G. Sargent (Irthlingboro) v St. Neots 29.3.86
S. Marlow (Desborough) v Newport P. 9.4.86
V. Simpson (St Neots) v Potton 23.4.86
R. Ashenden (L. Buckby) v Holbeach 4.5.86
T. Pearson (L. Buckby) v Ampthill 5.5.86
P. Targett (Ampthill) v L. Buckby 5.5.86
L. Pask (Bourne) v Ampthill 19.5.86
R. Seekings (Baldock) v Holbeach 20.5.86

Knockout Cup
3 goals
J. Cozens (Ramsey) v Holbeach 7.9.85
D. Atkinson (Irthlingboro) v N. Spencer 9.11.85
G. Tressler (Burton PW) v Bourne 22.3.86
J. Rogers (Stamford) v L. Buckby 19.5.86

DIVISION ONE
5 goals
M. Cuthbert (ST Ives) v Cogenhoe 29.3.86

4 goals
J. Cozens (Ramsey) v Thrapston 4.9.85
J. Peevor (Thrapston) v Sharnbrook 7.12.85
J. Peevor (Thrapston) v Olney 19.4.86
S. Welch (Thrapston) v Ford 24.4.86

3 goals
A. Brown (St. Ives) v ON Chenecks 17.8.85
J. English (Towcester) v Timken Ath. 20.8.85
M. Furness (Ramsey) v Blackstone 20.8.85
T. O'Keefe (Irchester) v ON Chenecks 20.8.85
A. Franklin (Baker P) v Timken Ath. 21.9.85
M. Furness (Ramsey) v Olney 26.10.85
A. Hollis (Ramsey) v Olney 26.10.85
N. Grose (M. Blackstone) v ON Chenecks 2.11.85
I. Richardson (M. Black) v ON Chen. 2.11.85
T. O'Keefe (Irchester) v Olney 2.11.85
D. Holis (Higham) v ON Chenecks 9.11.85
J. Peevor (Thrapston) v Higham 23.11.85
N. Bird (Baker P.) v Timken D. 21.12.85
S. Freeman (Higham) v Olney 21.12.85
K. Hanger (Whitworths) v ON Chenecks 21.12.85
M. Newell (Towcester) v Timken D. 26.12.85
G. Scotcher (Baker P) v Irchester 4.1.86
N. Bird (Baker P.) v Ford 18.1.86
D. Bonner (Baker P.) v Ford 18.1.86
M. Handy (Kempston) v ON Chenecks 1.2.86
D. Hollis (Higham) v Whitworths 29.3.86
M. Harvey (Ramsey) v Timken Ath. 5.4.86
P. Currier (Timken A) v olney 12.4.86
D. Eaton (Cottingham) v M. Blackstone 17.4.85
C. Ford (Timken A) v Ford 21.4.86
K. Bettles (Thrapston) v Ford 24.4.86
J. Peevor (Thrapston) v Ford 24.4.86
J. English (Towcester) v Ramsey 27.4.86
A. Hollis (Ramsey) v Sharnbrook 1.5.86
I. Tomlin (Kempston) v Ford 7.5.86

United Counties League Div. One. Ramsey Town 2, St. Ives Town 0. Ramsey clear their lines in this hard fought New Years Day Derby. Photo: Derek Shute.

AMPTHILL TOWN

President: H.E Hoskins
Chairman: K. Brown
Secretary: C. Batchelor, 2 Brinsmade Rd, Ampthill Tel. 402349
Ground Address & Tel. No: Ampthill Park, Woburn Road. Tel: (0525) 404440.
Capacity: 3000 **Covered accommodation:** 500 **Seating:** 100 **Floodlights:** No
Simple ground directions: A418 Ampthill to Woburn Road.
Clubhouse details: Comfortable brick built
Programme details: 16 pages, 10p
Editor: E. Turner (0625) 403128
Year formed: 1887
Club colours: White
Change colours: Yellow & Red
Local newspapers: Bedfordshire Times, Ampthill Times, Luton News, Evening Post
Midweek matchdays: Tuesday/Wednesday
Record attendance: 1250 v St. Neots 1959
Previous Leagues: South Midlands
Senior Honours/Best Performance: South Midlands League, South Midlands League Championship Shield (2).

ARLESEY TOWN

President: Derek Larman
Chairman: Maurice Crouch
Manager: Lou Adams
Secretary: John Albon
13 St. Johns Road, Arlesey. Tel. (0462) 731318
Ground Address & Tel. No: Lamb Meadow, Hitchin Road, Arlesey. Tel. (0462) 731448
Capacity: 4,000 **Covered accommodation:** 200 **Seating:** 200 **Floodlights:** Yes
Simple ground directions: Enter village from Hitchin, 200 yards past Biggs Wall on left hand side.'
Clubhouse details: Open Eves. & L/times. Members Bar
Programme details: 24 pages, Free
Editor: Tony Smith (0462) 54328
Local Newspaper: Biggleswade Chronicle, Hitchin Gazette
Club colours: Light Blue
Change colours: Red&White
Year formed: 1891
Nickname: The Blues
Midweek matchday: Tuesday
Record attendance: 2000 v Luton Town Res. 1096
Previous Leagues: Biggleswade & District, Beds County, South Midlands, Parthenon, London.
Senior Honours/Best Performance: United Counties League Premier Division, South Midlands League, Premier Divison (2), South Midlands League Challenge Trophy; Bedfordshire Senior Cup (2)
Past players: Roland Legate, Pat Kruse

BALDOCK TOWN

President: T. Pu!
Chairman: Ray Chuuerstone
Manager: Brian Williams
Secretary: Bob Brown
6 Anchor Road, Baldock (0462) 895355
Ground Address & Tel. No: Norton Road, Baldock. (0462) 895449
Simple ground directions: A505 Hitchin to Baldock, turn left into Norton Road. From railway station, west down Icknield Way, right at gasometer into Norton Road and under railway bridge.
Capacity: 5,000 **Covered accommodation:** 100 **Seating:** 100 **Floodlights:** Yes
Clubhouse details: New clubhouse, capacity 300, open lunchtimes & evenings.
Programme details: 20 pages, 20p
Editor: Bob Brown
Local newspaper: Gazette, Comet
Midweek matchday: Tuesday
Club colours: All Red
Change colours: All White (floodlight) All Blue
Record attendance: 1250 v Arsenal 6.3.84
Previous Leagues: South Midlands, Parthenon, London
Senior Honours/Best Performance: South Midlands League (3), Beds County League, SML Championship Shield (2), Herts Charity Shield

BOURNE TOWN

President: E.C. Moody
Chairman: Chris Notley
Secretary: Peter Dowse,
Address & Tel. No: 10 Dovecote Estate, Rippingale-bourne, Lincs. (09785 305)
Ground Address & Tel. No: Abbey Lawn, Abbey Road, Bourne. (0778) 422292
Capacity: 3000 **Covered accommodation:** 750 **Seating:** 300 **Floodlights:** No
Simple ground directions: In Market Place, take Spalding Road. Ground 500 yards on right
Clubhouse details: Small - Open Matchdays and specific events
Programme details: 8 pages, 10p
Editor: Peter Dowse
Local newspapers: Stamford Mercury, Lincs. Free Press, Evening Telegraph
Club colours: Red/Blue Striped Shirts, Blue Short
Change colours: All Yellow
Year formed: 1883
Nickname: The Wakes
Midweek matchdays: Tuesday/Wednesday
Previous Leagues: Peterborough, Central Alliance, Midland Counties
Record attendance: 3,000 vs Chelmsford City, FA Trophy, 1970
Senior Honours/Best Performance: United Counties League (3), UCL Knockout Cup, Lincs Senior Cup 'A', Central Alliance Division 1 South
Past players: Peter Grummutt (Notts. Forest), Shaun Cunnington (Wrexham)

BRACKLEY TOWN

President: Miss C. Billingham
Chairman: N. Howard
Secretary: T.N. Howard
Address & Tel. No: 63 Pavillons Way, Brackley. (0280) 704416
Manager: Wally Hastie
Ground Address 8 Tel. No: St. James Park, Churchill Way, Brackley. (0280) 704077
Capacity: 3,500 **Covered accommodation:** 400 **Seating:** 50 **Floodlights:** No
Simple ground directions: Churchill Way, East off A3, south end of town
Clubhouse details: Lounge & main hall. Open all week
Programme details: 16-20 pages with admission
Year formed: 1890
Nickname: Saints
Local newspaper: Banbury Guardian
Midweek matchday: Tuesday or Wednesday
Record attendance: 357 v Buckingham 1984
Club colours: Blue/White
Change colours: White/Black Stiped
Previous Leagues: Banbury & District, North Bucks, Hellenic
Senior Honours/Best Performance: United Counties League Division 1, Buckingham Charity Cup

DESBOROUGH TOWN

President: John Marlow
Chairman: E. Parsons
Secretary: Ray Coe
Address 8 Tel. No: 5 Hilltop Close, Desborough. (0536) 760386
Manager: John Marlow
Ground Address 8 Tel. No: Waterworks Field, Braybridge Road, Desborough. Tel: (0536) 761350
Capacity: 8000 **Covered accommodation:** 500 **Seating:** 250 **Floodlights:** Yes
Simple ground directions: Half mile west of A6
Clubhouse details: 2 lounges, bar, games room. Open 7 nights a week, Sat & Sun Lunchtimes.
Local newspapers: Evening Telegraph, Northants Post, Chronicle & Echo, Harborough Mail
Programme details: 12 pages, free
Editor: John Lee (0536) 760002
Club colours: All Blue
Change colours: All Yellow
Midweek matchday: Tuesday. Res. Thursday
Record attendance: 8000 v Kettering
Previous Leagues: None
Senior Honours/Best Performance: United Counties League (2); UCL Knockout Cup, Northants League (7), Northants Senior Cup (4)
Past players: Wakeley Bage (Peterborough), Jon Purdie and Campbell Chapman (Wolves. Wand.)

EYNESBURY ROVERS

President: W.A. Stephenson
Chairman: John Pinkney
Secretary: Deryck Irons,
Address 8 Tel. no: 12 Hadleigh Close, Bedford. (0234) 68111
Manager: Neil King
Ground Address 8 Tel. No: Hall Road, Eynesbury, St. Neots, Cambs. (0480) 74041
Capacity: 3,000 **Covered accommodation:** 270 **Seating:** 270 **Floodlights:** Yes
simple ground directions: Approx 2 miles from A1 on south side of St Neots urban area. Near Ernolf School.
Clubhouse details: capacity 150
Year formed: 1897
Nickname: Rovers
Programme details: 8 pages, 10p
Editor: Patrick Worrall
Local Newspapers: Hunts Post, Cambridge Evening News
Club colours: Royal Blue/White
Change colours: Yellow & Green
Midweek matchday: Wednesday
Record attendance: v Charlton 1953, 5000
Previous Leagues: South Midlands, Eastern Counties
Senior Honours/Best Performance: United Counties League Division 1, Hunts Senior Cup (9), Hinchingbrooke Cup
Past players: Chris Turner (Peterborough, Luton, Cambridge), Denis Emery (Peterborough).

HOLBEACH UNITED

President: Dr. J.C. Hunter
Chairman: B. Paul
Secretary: Bryan Stamp
Address & Tel. No: 6 Tolls Lane, Holbeach, Spalding, Lincs. (0406) 22930
Manager: Alan Day
Ground Address & Tel. No: Carters Park, Park Road, Holbeach. Tel. (0406) 22381
Capacity: 4000 **Covered accommodation:** 150 **Seating:** 150 **Floodlights:** No
Simple ground directions: Second left at traffic lights in town centre, 200 yds down road on left. From Kings Lynn sharp right at traffic lights
Clubhouse details: Clubhouse large enough to hold dances. Lounge & Kitchen
Local newspaper: Lincs Free Press, Spalding Guardian, Evening Telegraph.
Club colours: Amber/Black
Change colours: Green/Black
Midweek matchdays: Wednesday
Year formed: 1929
Nickname: The Tigers
Previous Leagues: Peterborough, Eastern Counties, Midland
Record attendance: 4094 v Wisbech 1951-52
Senior Honours/Best Performance: UCL Knockout Cup, Lincolnshire Senior Cup 'A' (2), Lincs Senior Cup 'B'

IRTHLINGBOROUGH DIAMONDS

President: C.M. Jones
Chairman: A.C. Jones
Secretary: George Whiting
Address 8 Tel. No: 5 Clare Walk, Higham Ferrers. (0933) 56717
Manager: Chris Smith
Ground Address & Tel. No: Nene Park, Station Road, Irthlingborough. (0933) 650345
Capacity: 3000 **Covered accommodation:** 650 **Seating:** 300 **Floodlights:** Yes
Simple ground directions: Alongside A6
Clubhouse details: Open Evenings & Sun. L/time
Programme details: 12 pages, 10p
Editor: G. Whiting
Year formed: 1946
Nickname: Diamonds
Midweek matchday: Tuesday
Club colours: Red/Blue
Change colours: All White (floodlight), All Blue
Record Attendance: 2470 v Dagenham FA Cup 1978
Previous Leagues: Rushden Youth, Rushden & District, Kettering Amateur
Senior Honours/Best Performance: United Counties League (4), UCL Knockout Cup (2), Northants Senior Club.
Past players: Scott Endersby (Ipswich, Tranmere, Swindon).

KEMPSTON ROVERS

President: B. Wake
Chairman: P. burrage
Secretary: T. Albone
Address 8 Tel. No: 98 Winifred Road, Bedford. (0234) 43784
Manager: Bobby Folds
Ground Address 8 Tel. No: Hillgrounds Road, Kempston. (0234) 852346
Capacity: 1000 **Covered accommodation:** 150 **Seating:** 50 **Floodlights:** No
Simple ground directions: M1 Junction 13 to Bedford, opposite Sainsburys in Kempston
Clubhouse details: New ground & clubhouse 1986
Year formed: 1884
Nickname: The Walnut Boys
Programme details: 4 pages
Editor: T. Albone
Local newspapers: Beds times
Club colours: Red & White
Midweek matchday: Tuesday
Record attendance: Unknown
Previous Leagues: South Midlands
Senior Honours/Best Performance: United Counties League Premier Div (1), UCL Division 1 (1), UCL KO Cup (4), Bedfordshire Senior Cup (2).

LONG BUCKBY

President: Tim Pearson
Chairman: A. Bruce
Secretary: E.M. Thresher
Address 8 Tel. No: 19a Church Street, Long Buckby (0327) 842959
Manager: Mick Worthington
Ground Address 8 Tel. No: Station Road, Long Buckby. (0327) 842682
Capacity: 1000 **Covered accommodation:** 150 **Seating:** 50 **Floodlights:** No
Simple ground directions: Situated on Daventry - Long Buckby Road, 400 yards from Main Rugby to Northampton Railway.
Clubhouse details: Bar & Concert room
Programme details: 8 pages, 20p
Editor: R. Pryor
Year formed: 1945
Nickname: The Bucks
Midweek matchdays: Tuesday
Record attendance: unknown
Club colours: Sky Blue & Navy
Change colours: Red & White
Previous Leagues: Rugby & District, Central Northants Combination
Senior Honours/Best Performance: United Counties League KO Cup; UCL Division 2(2) UCL Division 3
Past players: Gary Mills (Nott. Foredst), Alan Kurica (Birmingham), Vince Overson (Burnley), Des Waldock (Northampton)

NORTHAMPTON SPENCER

President: B.S. Rumford
Secretary: M.J. Tyrer
Chairman: G.T. Wrighting
Manager: John Petts
Ground Address & Tel. No: Kingsthorpe Mill, Studland Road, Northampton. 0604 718898
Capacity: 2000 **Covered accommodation:** 150 **Seating:** 50 **Floodlights:** No
Simple ground directions: Turn off Kingsthorpe Road at traffic lights into Thornton Road, 1st right into Studland Road, ground at end.
Clubhouse details: Large lounge & Bar
Year formed: 1936
Programme details: 8 pages, free
Editor: A. Goldsmith (0604) 412382
Local newspaper: Chronicle & Echo
Midweek matchday: Tuesday
Club colours: Yellow & Green
Change colours: White
Previous Leagues: Northampton Town League
Senior Honours/Best Performance: United Counties League Division 1
Past players: Paul Stratford (N/pton Town), Wakeley Gage N/pton Town, Chester city, P'boro. Utd

POTTON UNITED

President: P. Hutchinson
Chairman: A. Hutchinson
Secretary: D.F. Inskip
Manager: Terry King
Ground Address & Tel. No: The Hollow, Biggleswade Road, Potton (0767) 261100
Capacity: 2000 **Covered accommodation:** 150 **Seating:** 100 **Floodlights:** Yes
Simple ground directions: Outskirts of Potton on Biggleswade Road
Clubhouse details: Large, capacity for 100. Opened 1985
Editor: D.F. Inskip
Club colours: All Blue
Midweek matchday: Tuesday
Previous Leagues: South Midland, Central Allia.
Programme details: 8 pages, 5p
Local newspapers: Biggleswade Chronicle
Change colours: Red & Black
Record attendance: v Bedford Town
Year formed: 1943
Senior Honours/Best Performance: United Counties League KO Cup (1), Bedfordshire Senior Cup (5)

RAUNDS TOWN

President: Reg Harris
Chairman: Barry Burridge
Secretary: Frank Matson
Address 8 Tel. No: 15 St. Chads Close, Kettering. (0536) 517055
Manager: Alan Wright
Ground Address & Tel. No: Berristers Place, Raunds. (0933) 623351
Capacity: 2000 **Covered accommodation:** 200 **Seating:** 50 **Floodlights:** Applied for
Simple ground directions: Entering Raunds on A6, travel through town over pelican crossing, 1st turn right, 1st left, road finishes on ground
Clubhouse details: On ground
Programme details: 12 pages, 10p
Local newspapers: Evening Telegraph
Change colours: All Yellow
Nickname: Shopmates
Editor: Ian Brown
Club colours: Red & Black
Midweek matchday: Tuesday
Record attendance: Not known
Previous Leagues: Rushden District, Northants Combination
Senior Honours/Best Performance: United Counties League Division 1, Northants Junior Cup
Past players: Greg Downs to Norwich City

ROTHWELL TOWN

President: J. Covington
Chairman: Stuart Andrews
Secretary: Bill Park
Address & Tel. No: 223 Rockingham Road, Kettering. 0536 82809
Manager: Dennis Walker
Ground Address & Tel. No: Cecil Street, Rothwell (0536) 710694
Capacity: 3000 **Covered accommodation:** 460 **Seating:** 460 **Floodlights:** Yes
Simple ground directions: Enter Rothwell on A6, turn into George Street at Midland Bank, turn at 3rd left (Tresham St.) + Ground is at top
Clubhouse details: Large Sportsmans Bar, Top of the Town Ballroom & Lounge for 200
Programme details: 24 pages, 10p
Editor: Bill Parker
Local newspapers: Evening Telegraph, Chronicle 8 Echo
Year formed: 1896
Nickname: Bones
Club colours: All Red
Change colours: Yellow & blue
Midweek matchday: Tuesday or Wednesday
Record Attendance: 2100 v Irthlingborough 1971
Previous Leagues: Kettering Amateur, Leicestershire Senior, Central Alliance;
Senior Honours/Best Performance: UCL Division 1 KO Cup (5) UCL Division 2 (2) UCL Division 2 KO Cup (2), Northants Senior Cup (2)

ST NEOTS TOWN

President: J. Wright
Chairman: P. McCreanor
Secretary: John Delaney,
Address & Tel. No: 28 Sandwich Road, St. Neots. (0480) 218096
Manager: Mick Kemp
Ground Address & Tel. No: Shortsands, Cambridge St. St. Neots. (0480) 72457
Capacity: 200 **Covered accommodation:** 2 sides **Seating:** 150 **Floodlights:** No
Simple grounds directions: On A45 eastbound towards Cambridge. Entrance in Cambridge St. between 'Bull' and 'Queen Victoria' Public Houses.
Clubhouse details: As dressing room. Cap. 120
Nickname: Saints
Editor: J. Walker
Midweek matchday: Tuesday
Club colours: All Blue
Year formed: 1879
Programme details: 8 pages, free
Local newspapers: Hunts Post
Record Attendance: 2000 v Wisbech 1966
Change colours: Orange & White
Previous Leagues: South Midlands, Central Alliance, Metropolitan, Eastern Counties.
Senior Honours/Best Performance: United Counties League (1), UCL Knockout Cup (2); South Midlands League (1), Metropolitan League (1), Met. League Cup (1), Met. League Professional Cup (1); Hunts Senior Cup (33)

SPALDING UNITED

Chairman: Vacant
Manager: Bob Duncan
Secretary: R. Luxford
Address & Tel. No: 31 Odecroft, Ravensthorpe, Peterborough. 0733-260344
Ground Address & Tel. No: Sir Halley Stewart Field, Winnrey Avenue, Spalding. (0775) 4957
Capacity: 7000 **Covered accommodation:** 2500 **Seating:** 350 **Floodlights:** Yes
Simple ground directions: Town Centre off A16. Adjacent Bus Station
Clubhouse details: Open matchdays **Programme details:** 16 pages, 15p
Local newspapers: Lincs Free Press, Spalding Guardian, Evening Telegraph
Club colours: White/Claret/White **Change colours:** Yellow/Green/Yellow
Midweek matchday: Tuesday **Record attendance:** 6972 v Peterborough FA Cup 1952
Previous Leagues: Eastern Counties, Central Alliance, Midland, Northern Counties East.
Senior Honours/Best Performance: United Counties League (2), UCL Knockout Cup (1), Northern Co. East League, Lincs Senior Cup (1), Lincs Senior Cup 'B' (17
Past players: Carl Shutt (Sheffield Wednesday)

STAMFORD

Chairman: Vacancy
Manager: Paul Blackwell
Secretary: R.W. Aldridge
Address & Tel. No: (0780) 51584
Ground Address & Tel. No: Lothorpe Rd, Stamford. (0780) 63079
Capacity: 5000 **Covered accommodation:** 1250 **Seating:** 250 **Floodlights:** Yes
Simple ground directions: Off A43 Kettering Road, 1 mile east of A1. Railway Station 200 yards.
Clubhouse details: Matches, Functions, Training Nights
Year formed: 1896 **Nickname:** The Daniels
Programme details: 28 pages, 20p **Editor:** A. Eason
Club colours: Red & Blue **Change colours:** All White
Midweek matchday: Tuesday **Record attendance:** 4200 v Kettering 1953
Previous Leagues: Northants, Peterborough, Central Alliance, Midland.
Senior Honours/Best Performance: FA Vase Winners, Runners Up (2), UCL Premier Division (5), UCL Knockout Cup (5), Northants League, Lincs Senior Cup 'A' (2), Lincs Senior Cup 'B' (2)
Past players: Alan Birchenall (Chelsea, C. Palace, Leic.), Gerry Fell (Southend, Brighton, Torquay, York), Campbell Chapman (Wolves), Brian Stubbs (Notts county), Steve Collins (Peterboro., Lincoln)

STEWARTS & LLOYDS

Chairman: C. Balway
Manager: Jackie Phillips
Secretary: Phil Mackay
Address & Tel. No:115 Federation Avenue, Desborough. (0536) 761041
Ground Address & Tel. No: Recreation Ground, Occupation Road, Corby. (05363) 3231
Covered accommodation: 400 **Seating:** 100 **Floodlights:** No
Simple ground directions: Adjacent to Old Corby Town FC Ground.
Clubhouse details: Licensed Bar **Year formed:** 1935
Club colours: All Yellow **Change colours:** Silver Grey
Previous Leagues: Kettering Amateur
Senior Honours/Best Performance: United Counties League Division 1 (2)
Past players: Andy McGowan (Northampton), Willie Graham (Brentford)

STOTFOLD

President: B.A. Clark
Chairman: T.R. Talbot
Secretary: W. Clegg
Address & Tel. No: 12 Common Road, Stotford, Hitchin. (0462) 73042
Manager: Roland Legate
Ground Address & Tel. No: Roiler Park, The Green, Stotfold. (0462) 730421
Capacity: 5000 **Covered accommodation:** Yes **Seating:** 50 **Floodlights:** Yes
Simple ground directions: A507 from A1. Turn right at traffic lights, right at T-Junction, A507 from Bedford, via Shefford left at lights right at T-Junction.
Year formed: 1904 Reformed 1945 **Nickname:** Eagles
Clubhouse details: Clubroom, bar, dressing rooms, physio room
Programme details: 20 pages **Editor:** Miss J. Longhurst
Club colours: Amber/Black **Change colours:** White
Local newspapers: Hitchin Gazette, Biggleswade Chronicle
Midweek matchday: Tuesday
Previous Leagues: Biggleswade, North Herts, South Midland
Senior Honours/Best Performance: South Midlands League (1), SML Challenge Trophy (1), Beds Senior Cup (1)

WOOTTON BLUE CROSS

President: G. Robinson
Chairman: A. Brittain
Secretary: W.D. Watt
Address 8 Tel. No: 7 Lorraine Road, Wootton, Bedford. (0234) 767855
Manager: Dave Skinn
Ground Address & Tel. No: Weston Park, Bedford Road, Wootton. (0234) 767662
Capacity: 2000 **Covered accommodation:** 250 **Seating:** 50 **Floodlights:** No
Simple ground directions: 4 miles south of Bedford, on main road through village at rear of post office.
Year formed: 1887 **Nickname:** Blue Cross
Clubhouse details: Open every night, Sat. & Sun Lunchtime. Main Hall, Bar, Bingo, Darts, Pool.
Programme details: 12 pages. **Editor:** R. Howe (234) 852218
Local newspapers: Bedfordshire times, Bedford Journal, Bedford Express
Club colours: All Blue **Change colours:** All Yellow or All White
Midweek matchday: Tuesday
Record attendance: 243 v Burton Albion 1984
Previous Leagues: Bedford & District, South Midlands
Senior Honours/Best Performance: UCL Division 2(2), UCL Division 2 KO Cup(1), South Midlands League (1), Bedfordshire Senior cup (1). Hinchingbrooke Cup
Past players: A. Biggs (Arsenal)

Long Buckley 2, Baldock Town 1. United Counties League Cup Semi-Final. Long Buckby on the attack. Photo: Leo Hoenig.

Hinchingbrooke Cup Semi-Final St. Ives Town (white) 4, Potton Utd 2. St. Ives open the scoring in their surprise win over premier division opponents.

BAKER PERKINS

Chairman: D. Gibson **Manager:** Ian Day
Secretary: R.J. Brudnell. 18 Ascot Drive, Garden End road, Peterborough. Tel. 0733 51944
Ground Address & Tel. No: Alma Road, Peterborough. (0733) 54002/46601
Capacity: 3000 **Covered accommodation:** Yes **Seating:** Yes **Floodlights:** No
Clubhouse: Yes, Two bars, dance hall, bar and lounge, snooker & pool facilities.
Programme: Yes **Club colours:** Red/Navy
Change colours: Blue/Blue Yellow Socks
Previous League: Peterborough League

BRITISH TIMKEN ATHLETIC

Chairman: S. Aitken **Manager:** Tony McPhillips
Secretary: A.J. Agius, 17 Holden Grove, Daventry. Tel. 0327 703552
Ground Address 8 Tel. No: Braunston Road, Daventry. Tel. 03272 52311 Ex. 4296
Capacity: 2,5000 **Covered accommodation:** Yes **Seating:** 150 **Floodlights:** No
Simple ground directions: Follow A45 from Northampton to outskirts of Daventry, works entrance top of Braunston Road.
Clubhouse: Yes **Programme:** Yes
Club colours: Tangerine/Black **Change colours:** Silver Grey
Previous League: Rugby & District

BRITISH TIMKEN DUSTON

Chairman: A. Watts **Manager:** Mr. Don Mason
Secretary: Mr. R.J.N. Marriott, 211 Ryeland road, Duston, Northampton NN5 6XF. 0604 57389
Ground Address 8 Tel. No: Cotswold Avenue, Duston, Northampton. Tel. 0604 52311. Ext 3612
Capacity: 8,000 **Covered accommodation:** Yes **Seating:** 320 **Floodlights:** Yes
Simple ground directions: A428 Rugby Road, leaving Northampton, 1st left Cotswold Avenue.
Clubhouse: Large, including changing facilities, sports centre.
Programme: No
Club colours: Tangerine/Black **Change colours:** Green/Black

BURTON PARK WANDERERS

Chairman: R. Patrick **Manager:** Dave Haynes/Ian Clarke
Secretary: L.A. Litchfield, 176 St. Johns Road, Kettering. Tel: 0536 518469
Ground Address 8 Tel. No: Latimer Park, Folwell Road, Burton Latimer. Tel. 053672 3639
Capacity: Unknown **Covered accommodation:** No **Seating:** No **Floodlights:** No
Simple ground directions: On Entering Burton Latimer turn into Station Road and right into Folwell Lane and the ground is on the right.
Clubhouse: Yes **Programme:** No
Club colours: Blue/White **Change colours:** Red/White
Previous League: Kettering Amateur

COGENHOE UNITED

Chairman: Brian Foley **Manager:** Dave Conlon
Secretary: R.M. Marriott, 14 Corn Kiln Close, Cogenhoe, Northants. (0604) 890043
Ground Address & Tel. No: New Ground, Brafield Road, Cogenhoe. (0604) 890521

Capacity: 5000 **Covered accommodation:** Yes **Seating:** No **Floodlights:** No
Simple ground directions: Turn off A428 at Brafield-on-the-Green, first right, turn to Cogenhoe or turn off A45 to Billing Aquadrome. Carry on, take second Cogenhoe turn on left.
Clubhouse: All week **Programme:** 28 pages
Club colours: White/Navy **Change colours:** All Sky Blue
Previous Leagues: Central Northants Combination

COTTINGHAM

Chairman: M. Beadswoth **Manager:** Ben Ironmonger
Secretary: J. Tilley, 7 Berryfield Road, Cottingham, Market Harborough. Tel. 0536 771015
Ground Address & Tel. No: Berryfield Road
Covered accommodation: Yes **Seating:** No **Floodlights:** No (Possibly installed Season 1986/87)
Clubhouse: No (Possible 1986/87 season) & Changing Rooms
Club colours: Amber/Blue **Change colours:** Green
Previous Leagues: East midlands Alliance, Kettering Amateur, Mkt Harborough

FORD SPORTS (DAVENTRY) FC

Chairman: Mr. David Taylor **Manager:** Brian Dominy
Secretary: D.A. Kendrick, 9 Grenadier Road, Cherry Orchard, Daventry. Tel: 03272 78808
Ground Address 8 Tel. No: Royal Oak Way, Daventry. Tel. 03272 71111 Ext. 2219
Capacity: Not known **Covered accommodation:** Yes **Seating:** No **Floodlights:** No
Simple ground directions: Come in on either A45 or A361 and follow directions fro Royal Oak Way.
Clubhouse: Yes **Programme:** Yes
Club colours: Red/Black **Change colours:** Blue/Black
Previous League: Central Northants Combination

HIGHAM TOWN

Chairman: C. Britchford **Manager:** Mick Dyke
Secretary: C.B. ruff, 23 Queensway, Higham Ferrers. Tel. 0933 58862
Ground Address 8 Tel. No: Vine Hill Drive, Higham Ferrers. Tel. 0933 53751
Capacity: 1,000 **Covered accommodation:** 100 **Seating:** No **Floodlights:** No
Simple ground directions: From Kettering 1st right on A6 after A45 Junction to St. Neots. From Bedford 3rd left after A45 Junction to Northampton'
Clubhouse: Yes **Programme:** Yes
Chahge colours: Green & Yellow **colours:** All Blue
Previous League: Rushden & District

IRCHESTER EASTFIELD

Manager: Howard Reid
Secretary: M.G. Leach, 32 Gilutts Road, Wellingborough. Tel. 0933 74239
Ground Address & Tel. No: Alfred Street. Tel. 0933 312877
Covered accommodation: Yes **Seating:** No **Floodlights:** No
Simple ground directions: Off Rushden to Woolaston Road. Next to recreation ground.
Clubhouse: Yes **Programme:** No
Club colours: All Red **Change colours:** Green/White
Previous Leagues: Rushden & District

MURRLEES BLACKSTONE

Chairman: Mr. T.A. Atkin **Manager:** Ian Jarvie
Secretary: I. MacGillivary, 20 New road, Ryhall, Stamford, Lincs. (0780) 62263
Ground Address & Tel. No: Lincoln road, Stamford.
Capacity: 5000 **Covered accommodation:** Yes **Seating:** Yes **Floodlights:** No
Simple ground directions: A6121 to Bourne, out of Stamford. 2nd road on left past M.B. works.
Clubhouse: Open after matches **Programme:** 8 pages
Club colours: Silver Grey/Maroon **Change colours:**
Previous Leagues: Peterborough & District

NEWPORT PAGNELL TOWN

Chairman: P. Rose **Manager:** Terry Ashton
Secretary: J. Anderson, 6 Waterlow Close, Newport Pagnell. (0908) 610453
Ground Address & Tel. No: Willen Road. (0908) 611993
Capacity: 2000 **Covered accommodation:2 300** **Seating:** 30 **Floodlights:** No
Simple ground directions: Adjacent to A442 N.P. by-pass
Clubhouse: Open 7 days a week. Lunchtime & Evenings **Programme:** Yes
Club colours: Green & White **Change colours:** Black
Previous Leagues: UCL Division One

O.N. CHENECKS

Chairman: E. Sunn
Secretary: J. Going, 5 Parklands Crescent, Parklands, Northampton. (0604) 44830
Ground Address & Tel. No: Billing Road, Northampton (0604) 34045.
Capacity: 350 **Covered accommodation:** None **Seating:** None **Programme:** Yes
Simple ground directions: South ring road, exit A43 Kettering, left a traffic lights top of hill. Ground on right 200 yards.
Clubhouse: Yes
Club colours: White/Blue **Change Colours:** Red/Black
Previous League: Northampton Town

OLNEY TOWN

Secretary: A. Baldwin, 49 Midland Road, Olney, Bucks. Tel. 0234 711071
Ground Address & Tel. No: East Street. Tel. 0234 712227
Capacity: 2000 **Covered accommodation:** Yes **Seating:** No **Floodlights:** No
Clubhouse: Yes **Programme:** Yes
Club colours: Green **Change colours:** Yellow
Previous League: North Bucks

RAMSEY TOWN

Chairman: W.B. Hibbins **Manager:**Lloyds Smith
Secretary: M.B. Avery, 127a Great Whyte, Ramsey, Huntingdon, Cambs. Tel. 0487 813134
Covered accommodation: Yes **Seating:** No **Floodlights:** No
Simple ground directions: Huntingdon (South Trans), Peterborough (North)
Clubhouse: Yes **Programme:** Yes
Club colours: Amber/Black **Change colours:** White/Red/Blue
Previous League: Peterborough

SHARNBROOK

Chairman: R. Pacey

Secretary: D. Martin, 1 Dychurch Lane, botsat, Wellingborough, Northants. Tel. 0933 664827
Ground Address 8 Tel. No: Lodge Road, Sharnbrook, Beds.
Covered accommodation: Yes **Seating:** No **Floodlights:** No
Clubhouse: Yes **Programme:** Yes
Club colours: Yellow/Navy **Change colours:** Blue/Red

THRAPSTON VENTURAS

Chairman: N. Webster **Manager:** Bev Harrison
Secretary: D. Bailey, 20 Fair Lane, Thrapston, Kettering. Tel. 08012 2604
Ground Address 8 Tel. No: Chancery Lane.
Capacity: Not know **Covered accommodation:** No **Seating:** No **Floodlights:** No
Simple ground directions: Chancery Lane, off A605 in town centre.
Clubhouse: Yes **Programme:** No
Club colours: All Blue **Change colours:** All Red

ST IVES TOWN

Chairman: K. Booth

Secretary: D.J. Bull, 47 Hurstingstone, St Ives, Cambs. Tel. 0480 62203
Ground Address & Tel. No: Westwood Road. Tel. 0480 63207
Capacity: 5000 **Covered accommodation:** Yes **Seating:** No **Floodlights:** No
Simple ground directions: Near golf course and St Ivo recreation centre.
Clubhouse: Yes, Bar & Entertainment Room **Programme:** Yes
Club colours: White/Black Change colours: Blue/Blue Shorts

TOWCESTER TOWN

Chairman: A. Lovell **Manager:** Dave Tarbuck
Secretary: E. Burley **Ground Address & Tel. No:** Castle Park
Capacity: 150 **Covered accommodation:** Yes **Seating:** No **Floodlights:** No
Simple ground directions: Ground by A5
Clubhouse: Yes **Programme:** Yes
Club colours: White/Blue **Change colours:** Tangerine/Black
Previous League: South Midlands

WHITWORTHS

Chairman: R. Stratton **Manager:** Ian Young
Secretary: R. Edwards, 15 James road, Wellingborough. Tel. 0933 227765
Ground Address & Tel. No: London Road, Wellingborough. Tel. 0933 227324
Capacity: 700 **Covered accommodation:** Yes5**Seating:** No **Floodlights:** No
Simple ground directions: Off London Road at Dog & Duck Public House
Clubhouse: Yes **Programme:** Yes
Club colours: Yellow Black **Change colours:** Claret
Previous Leagues: Rushden & District, East Midlands Alliance

HAMPSHIRE FOOTBALL ASSOCIATION

The Constitution for the Wessex and Hampshire Leagues for 1986/87 has been agreed as follows:

Wessex League:
A.F.C. Totton; Bashley; Bournemouth; Brockenhurst; Eastleigh; Havant Town; Horndean; Lymington; Newport; Portals Athletic; Portsmouth R.N.; Romsey Town; R.S. Southampton; Sholing Sports; Thatcham Town; Wellworthy Athletic.

Hampshire League Division One:
Awbridge; Bass (Alton); B.A.T.; Blackfield & Langley; Brading Town; Christchurch; Colden Common; Downton; East Cowes Vics; Folland Sports; Locksheath; Malshanger; Netley Central Sports; New Street; Overton United; Pirelli General; Ringwood Town; Winchester Castle

Hampshire League Division Two:
A.C. Delco; Alton Town; Basing Rovers; Bishops Waltham; Braishfield; Compton; Cowes Sports; Hampshire Police; I.S.L. Midanbury; Liphook; McMurdo; New Milton; Ryde Sports; Sway; Warsash; West Wight; Whitchurch United; Winchester City

Hampshire League Combination:
A.F.C. Totton Res.; Andover Res.; Bashley Res.; Basingstoke Town Res.; Bass (Alton) Res.; Bournemouth Res.; Brockenhurst Res.; Eastleigh Res.; Fareham Town Res.; Folland Sports Res.; Havant Town Res.; Horndean Res.; Lymington Res.; Netley Central Sports Res.; Petersfield United Res.; Pirelli General Res.; Portals Athletic Res.; Ringwood Town Res.; Romsey Town Res.; Sholing Sports Res.; Waterlooville Res.; Wellworthy Athletic Res.

HAMPSHIRE LEAGUE FINAL TABLES

DIVISION ONE

	P	W	D	L	F	A	Pts
East Cowes Vics	38	31	7	0	97	24	60
AFC Totton	38	23	9	6	71	26	55
Horndean	38	29	9	6	90	55	51
Havant Town	38	20	9	9	80	47	49
Eastleigh	38	20	9	9	69	45	49
Sholing Sports	38	20	6	12	67	42	46
Newport IOW	38	17	9	12	75	65	43
Portals Athletic	38	16	10	12	62	55	42
Pirelli General	38	16	9	13	58	47	41
Blackfield & L	38	15	11	12	60	51	41
Lock's Heath	38	17	2	19	79	67	36
Lymington	38	16	4	18	52	61	36
Portsmouth RN	38	13	9	16	49	60	35
Fareham Town Res	38	11	10	17	55	70	32
Romsey Town	38	10	10	18	55	78	30
Brading Town	38	9	11	18	45	71	29
Bass Alton	38	7	9	22	51	79	23
Netley Central	38	6	10	22	47	94	22
Brockenhurst	38	6	8	25	30	79	20
Downton	38	1	9	28	24	91	11

DIVISION TWO

	P	W	D	L	F	A	Pts
Christchurch	34	23	6	5	68	30	52
Folland Sports	34	21	8	5	66	32	50
Ringwood Town	34	21	7	6	70	37	49
Bashley	34	19	9	6	72	33	47
Overton United	34	19	4	11	50	33	42
Awbridge −1	34	17	7	10	58	42	40
Coldon Common	34	17	4	13	66	49	38
Eastleigh Res	34	15	8	11	46	44	38
BAT	34	11	12	11	48	44	34
AFC Totton Res	34	12	7	15	57	59	31
Winchester Castle	34	12	7	15	49	55	31
New Street	34	13	4	17	52	59	30
Malshanger	34	10	10	14	49	56	30
Cowes Sports	34	7	9	18	35	58	23
Sholing Sporta Res	34	6	8	20	41	77	20
Sway	34	8	4	22	47	87	20
Warsash	34	5	8	21	47	79	18
Brockenhurst Res	34	7	4	23	39	95	18

DIVISION THREE

	P	W	D	L	F	A	Pts
Liphook	34	27	3	4	97	44	57
Wellworthy	34	26	2	6	104	43	4
AC Delco	34	18	10	6	63	33	46
Basing Rovers	34	20	6	8	61	39	46
West Wight	34	17	4	13	67	53	38
McMurdo	34	15	7	12	59	56	37
Pirelli Gen. Res.	34	11	12	11	55	55	34
Folland Sp. Res.	34	13	7	14	65	57	33
Winchester City	34	13	6	15	62	61	32
Ryde Sports	34	10	10	14	62	56	30
Ryde Sports	34	11	8	15	69	66	30
Petersfield Utd. Res.	34	11	6	17	71	73	28
Whitchurch Utd.	34	12	3	19	71	81	27
New Milton	34	11	6	17	71	73	28
Andover Res.	34	12	3	19	71	81	27
Netley Cen. Res.	34	12	3	19	49	68	27
Bournemouth	34	10	6	18	44	55	26
Romsey Town Res.	34	10	3	21	35	93	23
Alton Town	34	2	3	29	27	128	7

WELCOME TO THE WESSEX LEAGUE

Under the jurisdiction of the Hampshire F.A. an exciting new competition has been introduced for the ambitious clubs in this area.

'The Wessex Football League' will give clubs developing good facilities a chance to prepare together for possible promotion to the Southern League and we wish all founder member clubs and the Hampshire Football Association good luck in their inaugural year.

BASHLEY **President:** David Jose **Chairman:** Trevor Adams
Secretary: Mr. Hurlock, 14 Wheaton Road, Folkestone, Bournemouth 620280
Ground Address & Tel. No: Bashley Village Ground, Bash Common Road, New Milton, Hants Yes
Directions to Ground: Off A35 to B3050, follow Bashley In Road
Clubhouse: Yes **Programme:** Yes, free with 50p admission
Local Newspapers: Southern Echo, The New Milton Advertiser
Colours: Yellow/Black stripes/Black/Black Change colours: Blue/White stripes/Navy shorts/White **Midweek Match** days: Tues/Wed/Thurs
Senior Honours: Won Hants III, Hants Interim Cup 84/85, IV Div. IIe won Russel Coates Cup, Bournemouth Senior Cup,¼ finals Senior Cup 85/86
Floodlights: Yes

BOURNEMOUTH
Secretary: W.G. Johnston, 425 Kinson Road, Bournemouth BH10 5HG (0202 570377 (h) 36318 (b))
Ground Address & Tel. No.: Victoria Park, Winton, Bournemouth (0202515123)
Colours: Red, White sleeves/White/Red **Change colours:** All Yellow

BROCKENHURST (1898) **Chairman:** Mr. Lewis Manager: Mr. Brown
Secretary: D. Chandler, 300 Salisbury Road, Totton, Southampton 862957
Ground Address & Tel. No: Grigg Lane, Brickenhurst, Hants. Tel: Lymington 22504
Directions to Ground: ¼ mile from Brockenhurst Railway Station (SR) just off main shopping centre
Previous Leagues: New Forest, Bournemouth **Colours:** White/Red trim
Change colours: Yellow **Local Newspapers:** Lym Times, South Echo
Midweek match day: Wednesday **Programmes:** 8 pages, 10p
Clubhouse: open every day and after every game **Floodlights:** Yes **Seating:** 250 seat stand

Eastleigh F.C. Back row:— C. Webb, M. Falla, M. Bevis, G. Prior, S. Blaxall, B. Joslin (capt.), P. Barney (Trainer). Front row:— M. Allen, R. Sheean, I. Knight, M. Cole, K. McCann.

EASTLEIGH **President:** MA. Poore **Chairman:** J.C. Samson
Secretary: D.H. Brooks, 50 Forest Hills Drive, Townhill Park, Southampton. 557147
Manager: Dick Donohoe **Coaches:** Dave Sanders, Mick Lagdon, Pete Young
Ground Address & Tel. No: Ten Acres, Stoneham Lane, North Stoneham, Eastleigh, Hants. (Eastleigh 0703 613361)
Directions to Ground: Road - M27 to Junction 5 (S.P. Eastleigh) to roundabout, exit marked Stoneham Lane, ground on left, but carry on to roundabout and come back down Stoneham Lane and turn right opposite Concord Club. Ground 400 yards on left. Rail - B.R. Eastleigh (SR) then bus to North Stoneham Church or B.R. Swaythling (SR) and bus as above or 20 minutes walk
No. of Seats: 110 **Covered Accommodation:** 210 **Capacity:** 3,000 **Floodlights:** Yes
Year formed: 1946 **Club Sponsors:** B&Q and Fullbrooks
Previous Names: Swaythling Athletic (1946-73) and Swaythling (1973-80)
Colours: Sky Blue (Navy trim) **Change colours:** White
Midweek Day: Tuesdays **Previous Leagues:** Southampton Juniors (1946-48), Southampton Senior (1948-50), Hampshire (1950-86)
Record Attendance: 2,500 v Southampton (first floodlit game) 30.9.75
Best Performance: FA Cup, 3rd Qualifying Round, 1980-81; FA Amateur Cup, 4th Qualifying Round 1970-71; FA Vase, 4th Round, 1982-83
Clubhouse: Yes **Programme:** Free with admission. **Editor:** Gary Day

HAVANT TOWN (1958) **Chairman:** P. Wilson **Manager:** D. Pope
President: R. Jones **Secretary:** T.V. Ashman, 3 Woodcot Crescent, West Leigh, Havant, Hants PO9 5LD. Tel: Havant 484871
Ground Address & Tel. No: West Leigh Park, Martins Road, West Leigh, Havant, Hants. 455465
Directions to Ground: From London A3 to Petersfield. From West M27 from Southampton
Previous Leagues: Portsmouth **Colours:** Gold/Black/Gold **Change colours:** All White
Programmes: 4 pages, 10p **Clubhouse:** New extension. Normal pub hours
Floodlights: No. **Seating:** No **Covered accommodation:** 108/(Seating)
Senior Honours: Quarter final F.A. Vase **Record attendance:** 3000

Havant Town (Hants Div 1) reached Quarter Final F.A. Vase.

HORNDEAN F.C.

President: Ted Heath **Chairman:** George Cable
Secretary: Trevor Brock, 2 Betula Close, Waterlooville, Hants. 0705 267276 (h)
Manager: Dave Reid **Coach:** Pete Langrish, John Knight **Physiotherapist:** Mick Oliver
Ground Address & Tel. No: Five Heads Park, Five Heads Road, Horndean, Hants 0705 591363
Directions to Ground: A3 from Portsmouth (8 miles), left into Five Heads Road. Ground ½ mile on left
Seating: 50 **Covered Accommodation:** 150 **Capacity:** 3,200
Year Formed: 1887 **Nickname:** The Deans **Floodlights:** Yes
Sponsors: Whitbread Wessex Ltd. **Colours:** Red shirts, Black shorts
Change colours: Yellow shirts, green shorts **Midweek Home Night:** Tuesday
Previous Ground: Horndean Recreation Ground (pre-1970)
Record Attendance: 1,560 v Waterlooville , Victory Cup, 1971
Previous Leagues: Waterlooville & District, 1926-39; Portsmouth League, 1946-69; Hampshire League, 1970-86; Wessex League, 1986 -
Honours: 1980 Champions, Hants Div. 2; Winners Portsmouth Senior Cup, 1980, 1975; 1976 Champions, Hants Div. 3; 1975 Champions, Hants Div. 4

LYMINGTON TOWN

Secretary: E. Drake, 28 Southampton Road, Lymington, Hants SO41 9GG. 0590 75647 (h)
Ground Address & Tel. No.: Lymington Sports Ground, Southampton Road, Lymington
Clubhouse: 400 metres from ground **Seating:** 150 **Floodlights:** Yes
Colours: Red with White pinstripes/Red/Red **Change colours:** White with Black trim
Previous Leagues: Hants II & III **Programme:** Yes

NEWPORT I.O.W.

Secretary: C.R. Cheverton, 289 Upton Road, Ryde, Isle of Wight PO33 3HP (0983 67355 (h) & 63732 (b))
Ground Address & Tel. No.: Church Litten, Newport, I.O.W. (0983 525027)
Directions to Ground: Church Litten is 100 metres South-East of the bus station and clearly visible from there.
Colours: Yellow with Blue sleeve **Change colours:** Blue/White/Red **Programme:** Yes
Seating: 350 **Floodlights:** Yes
Previous Leagues: Hampshire, Isle of Wight

PORTALS

Secretary: C.J. Phillimore, 1 Crossways, Station Road, Whitchurch, Hants (025 682 3480 (h) 0256 471060 (b))
Ground Address & Tel. No.: Batts Meadow, Laverstone, Whitchurch, Hants (025682 2316)
Colours: Royal Blue/Royal Blue/Yellow **Change colours:** Red/Black/Red

PORTSMOUTH ROYAL NAVY

Chairman: Captain A. Wheatley, RN **Manager:** Lieutenant J.H. Millington, RN
Secretary: Lt. D.W. Bridger, RN, 2 Orion Close, Stubbington, Hants. Tel: Stubbington 667274
Ground Address & Tel. No: Royal Navy Stadium, Burnaby Road West, Portsmouth 822351 ext 24527
Directions to Ground: From Portsmouth Harbour Station, drive towards Southsea along "The Hard" Pass under the rail bridge, road is now St. Georges Road, Ground and entrance on left
Colours: Blue/White/Blue **Change colours:** All Red
Programmes: No **Clubhouse:** being built in 1986 **Floodlights:** Yes **Seating:** 500
Local Newspaper: Southern Evening Echo, The News
Senior Honours: Basingstoke II, Hants III, II, I, Wessex
Midweek match day: Thursday night occasionally

ROMSEY TOWN (1885) **Chairman:** Derek Edwards **Manager:** Raymond Hillier

Secretary: F.J. Matthews, 14 Eight Acres, Hillside Gardens, Romsey, Hants. Tel: Romsey: (0794) 513825)
Ground Address & Tel. No: The By-Pass Ground, Romsey. 0749 512003
Directions to Ground: On A27 through Romsey at Southampton end of Romsey Bypass, adjacent to large roundabout
Previous Leagues: Southampton Premier, Hants Div 4, 3, 2, 1
Colours: Yellow & Blue **Change colours:** All Red
Programmes: 16 pages, 10p **Clubhouse:** Yes **Floodlights:** Yes **Seating:** No
Local Newspaper: Romsey Advertiser

ROAD-SEA SOUTHAMPTON **President:** P. Price **Chairman:** J.W. Brett

Secretary: S.A. Farmery, Road-Sea House, 18 Canute Road, Southampton SO1 1FJ 0703 30656 (b), 0329 662499 (h) **Manager:** P. Price
Ground Address & Tel. No: Road-Sea Park, Long Lane, Marchwood, nr Southampton 0703 869010
Directions to Ground: A35 out of Southampton to Bournemouth, at Totton A326 to Fawley, 2nd left off A326 into Staplewood Lane
Capacity: 4,000 **Seating:** 300 **Covered Accommodation:** 500 **Floodlights:** Yes
Clubhouse: Yes, open on matchdays **Programme:** 16 pages - 25p **Editor:** J. Gorman
Local Newspapers: Southampton Evening Echo, Sports Echo (Saturday)
Colours: Red shirts/Black trim, Black shorts and socks with Red trim
Change colours: All White, Red trim Record Attendance: 350 v AFC Totton, 7.5.1984
Previous Leagues: City of Southampton Sunday Afternoon League; Southern Football League
Senior Honours: Southern League - Southern Division champions, 1983-84
Russel Cotes Cup winners, 1983-84; Sutton Transformer Vase winners, 1983-84; Anglo-Italian Trophy, 1984-85; Pratton Cup winners, 1979-80
Best Performance: F.A. Cup: 3rd Qual. Round replay v Ton Pentre, 1985-86 (h)
F.A. Trophy: 2nd Qual. Round replay v Bridgend Town, 1985-86 (a);
Senior Cup: Semi-Final v Farnborough Town, 1985-86 (n)
Past Players (who progressed to Football League: Dean Mooney (Torquay United); Kevin Maddock (Willem II Tilburg, Netherlands)

SHOLING SPORTS (1914)ChairmanG. DunnJoint Managers: Len Wolfe/Tony Noble

Secretary: Steve Smith, 21 Whites Road, Bitterne, Southampton S)2 7NP. Tel: 0703 440345 (H), 738181 (B)
Ground Address & Tel. No: Birch Lawn, Northeast Road, Sholing, Southampton 0703 449381
Directions to Ground: M27 Junc 8 (Southampton East) follow A3024 towards Southampton, take 6th left into North East Road, Ground ¼ mile on right
Previous Leagues: Southampton Senior **Coach:** A. Long
Colours: Black & White stripes/Black/White **Change colours:** Red & Black stripes/Black/Black
Programmes: 24 pages, free with admission **Clubhouse:** Yes **Floodlights:** Yes
Seating: 100 **Local Newspaper:** Southern Evening Echo
Senior Honours: 83/84 Won Hants League 1, Hants Senior Cup, Russel Coates Cup

Thatcham Town F.C. From Hellenic League to Athenian League to Spartan League to new Wessex League. Left to right, back row: Brian Laurence (manager), Clive Upton (trainer), Lee Tillen, Dave Mooney, Charlie Penny, George Martin, Freddie Stephens, Nigel Cook, Nigen Warrick, Arthur Milne. Front: Graeme Gourlay, Paul Upton, Chris Chard, Mark Meagrow, Colin Upton, Kevin Davies.

THATCHAM TOWN **Chairman:** David Ware **Manager:** Brian Laurence
Secretary: R.G. Taylor, 16 Lancaster Close, Thatcham, Berks RG13 4DD. (0635) 62686 (h)
Ground Address & Tel. No.: Lancaster Close, Thatcham. (0635) 62016.
Directions to Ground: Leave A4 on road from Thatcham to Newbury turning right at traffic lights by Northfield Row. Turn right after shops and then first right into Lancaster Close.
Clubhouse: Two bars and dance hall **Programme:** 8 pages - 10p **Editor:** Secretary
Local Newspaper: Newbury Weekly News **Colours:** Blue & White stripes
Senior Honours: Last sixteen in F.A. Vase - 1985-86
Seating: 50 **Floodlights:** Yes **Capacity:** 3000

TOTTON A.F.C. **Chairman:** A. Peckham **Manager:** Don Gowans
Secretary: R.G. Kearslake, 10 Binsey Close, Millbrook, Southampton. 0703 779545
Ground Address & Tel. No: Testwood Park, Testwood Place, Totton, Southampton 0703 868981
Directions to Ground: Five minutes from Totton Station turn off roundabout in centre of town
Colours: Blue & White stripes, Blue shorts **Change colours:** All Red
Clubhouse: with bar, open matchdays, training nights and Sunday lunchtimes
Seating: for 200, Covered standing room for 150, **Day for midweek matches:** Wednesdays
Local Newspapers: Southampton Sports Echo, Portsmouth Sports Mail
Senior Honours: Hants Division I Champions 1982, 1985

WELLWORTHY ATHLETIC
Secretary: J. Minns, 2 Clausen Way, Pennington, Lymington, Hants (0590 75084(h))
Ground Address & Tel. No.: Wellworthy Works, Lymington, Hants
Colours: Silver Grey/Black/Silver Grey **Change colours:** Royal Blue & Amber/Royal Blue/Amber & Royal Blue

Brockenhurst F.C. Ground

Downton v Eastleigh.

DORSET FOOTBALL COMBINATION LEAGUE SEASON 1985-86 FINAL LEAGUE TABLE

	P	W	D	L	F	A	Pts
Bridport	34	26	5	3	112	25	57
Parley Sports	34	25	4	5	112	42	54
Poole Town Res.	34	23	4	7	86	38	50
Flight Refuelling	34	18	8	8	71	47	44
Sherborne Town	34	20	3	11	75	47	43
Sturminster Newton	34	16	8	10	87	48	40
Westland Sports	34	15	8	11	85	50	38
Hamworthy United	34	17	4	13	64	51	38
Shaftesbury	34	16	4	14	75	56	36
Blandford United	34	13	6	15	60	60	32
Bournem'th Water Co.	34	12	4	18	49	75	28
Wareham Rangers	34	10	7	17	54	102	27
Portland Utd.	34	10	6	18	46	74	26
Wimborne Town Res.	34	9	5	20	50	82	23
Dorchester Town Res.	34	9	4	21	44	94	22
Gilling'm Town	34	8	4	22	46	79	20
Holt Utd.	34	8	4	22	51	139	20
Swan. T. & Her. Res.	34	5	4	25	48	106	14

SOUTHAMPTON SENIOR LEAGUE

Premier Division

	P	W	D	L	F	A	Pts
Bishops Waltham Tn	26	21	2	3	77	25	44
Braishfield	26	16	3	7	61	39	35
Eastleigh Boys Cl	25	15	2	8	63	39	32
Midanbury Nth End	24	13	4	7	51	34	30
West End	26	13	3	10	56	53	29
Hedge End	26	12	3	11	57	49	25
Ordinance Survey	26	11	3	12	40	50	25
Simmarians	25	10	5	10	38	49	25
North End	26	7	10	9	43	43	24
Cadnam United	26	9	6	11	43	52	24
North Baddersley	26	9	1	16	48	61	19
Vospers Thorneycroft	26	7	4	15	29	44	18
Brendon	26	5	7	14	32	57	17
Swanmore	26	3	5	18	36	79	11

DIVISION 1 (Top 2)	P	W	D	L	F	A	Pts
Millbrook	26	19	3	4	94	35	41
Fair Oak	26	14	7	5	59	30	35

Hampshire League — Recent Champions

Max Pts.	Season	1st	2nd	3rd	4th
60	1978/79	51 Newport (I.O.W.)	43 Fareham T.	37 Brockenhurst	36 Waterlooeville Res.
60	1979/80	52 Newport (I.O.W.)	48 Brockenhurst	38 Sholing Sports	37 Romsey T.
76	1980/81	63 Newport (I.O.W.)	51 AFC Totton	51 Sholing Sports	50 Southampton 'A'
76	1981/82	55 AFC Totton	52 Sholing Sports	49 Newport (I.O.W.)	46 Eastleigh
76	1982/83	68 Sholing Sports	58 AFC Totton	48 Havant T.	46 Newport (I.O.W.)
76	1983/84	64 Sholing Sports	62 AFC Totton	48 Pirelli General	46 Eastleigh
76	1984/85	64 AFC Totton	63 Sholing Sports	*47 Havant T.	47 Eastleigh
76	1985/86	69 East Cowes Vics.	55 AFC Totton	51 Horndean	49* Havant T.

* goal average/difference

Pegasus Juniors' goalkeeper Gary Morgan advances to save as Abingdon Town (the visitors) press hard. Is that snow behind the goal?

THE MULTIPART LEAGUE

President: N. White, Esq.
Chairman: K. Marsden, Esq.
Vice Chairman: K. F. Brown, Esq.
Secretary: R. D. Bayley, Esq., 22 Woburn Drive, Hale, Altrincham, Cheshire WA15 8LZ.
Tel.: 061-980 7007 (Home), 061-834 8600 (Business).

League Championship

Gateshead finally clinched the championship from under the noses of Merseysiders, Marine, following a maximum point double-header away from home. A Friday night only goal victory at Oswestry Town corresponded with Marine's 2–0 success at Buxton, leaving the Mariners one point ahead with their games completed and a next day trip to Rhyl as helpless bystanders to see if they could retain top spot. This was not to be, with the North Easterners winning more comfortably than the 3–2 scoreline may suggest.

Now, Gateshead, after one year back in the Multipart League, will return to the Gola League where they will be joined by the respective champions of the Southern and Vauxhall-Opel Leagues—Welling United and Sutton United. The relegated Gola League club to come back to the Multipart League after a two year absence is Barrow, ironically now managed by Ray Wilkie who only six weeks ago was Chairman and Manager at Gateshead. One could understand if Ray was a little confused, particularly as he was known to be a strong admirer of the Gola League. He has, however, already strengthened his backroom staff at Holker Street in preparation for next season with the appointment of Chorley based Les Rigby as his assistant.

At the other end of the table Chorley's last day 2–2 draw at Mossley gave them the point they needed to go above Matlock Town on goal difference, leaving the Derbyshire Club to apply for re-election, along with Goole Town.

Sponsorship

The League are pleased to announce that their sponsorship agreement with Multipart has been extended for another season on slightly more beneficial terms. 1985–86's end of season benefactors to receive their awards at the Annual Dinner on 14th June are top three, Gateshead (£1,000), Marine (£650) and Morecambe (£350)—leading goalscorers, Gateshead (£500), Southport (£300) and Macclesfield Town (£200). The awards for the best disciplinary records have yet to be finalised.

Manager of the Month—Sponsored by P. MacKenzie & Co Distillers Ltd.

The winner of the MacKenzie Manager of the Month Award for April was Marine's Roley Howard which must be some consolation for just losing out in the championship race. Six wins and only one defeat—that to Hyde United in the League Challenge Cup Final—made Roley the out and out winner and he will receive his one gallon bottle of the Real MacKenzie Scotch Whisky at the Annual Dinner.

SEASON 1985-86 HONOURS

League Champions: Gateshead	**League Runners-Up:** Marine
League Challenge Cup Winners: Hyde United	**League Challenge Cup Finalists:** Marine
President's Cup Winners: Worksop Town	**President's Cup Finalists:** Burton Albion
Derbyshire Senior Cup Winners: Buxton	
Lancashire Challenge Trophy Winners: Morecambe	**Lancashire Challenge Trophy Finalists:** Chorley
Liverpool Senior Cup Final Winners: South Liverpool	**Finalists:** Southport
Shropshire Senior Cup Final: Bridgenorth Town	**Finalists:** Oswestry Town

MULTIPART LEAGUE (Final Table 1985–86)

		Home					Away					
	P	W	D	L	F	A	W	D	L	F	A	Pts
GATESHEAD	42	15	4	2	49	21	9	6	6	36	30	82
Marine	42	13	1	7	40	23	10	10	1	23	12	80
Morecambe	42	10	9	2	32	15	7	8	6	27	24	68
Gainsborough T	42	14	4	3	48	23	4	10	7	18	29	68
Burton Albion	42	11	5	5	32	22	7	7	7	32	25	66
Southport	42	7	7	7	30	29	10	4	7	40	37	62
Worksop Town	42	9	6	6	28	22	8	4	9	23	26	61
*Workington	42	6	10	5	26	23	8	8	5	28	23	59
Macclesfield T	42	8	5	8	38	28	9	3	9	29	37	59
Hyde United	42	9	7	5	32	27	5	8	8	31	35	57
*Witton Albion	42	8	7	6	30	28	7	6	8	26	31	57
Mossley	42	6	10	5	32	30	7	6	8	24	30	55
Bangor City	42	9	6	6	28	22	4	9	8	23	29	54
Rhyl	42	7	5	9	33	34	7	5	9	32	37	52
South Liverpool	42	5	8	8	20	23	6	9	6	23	21	50
*Horwich R.M.I.	42	10	3	8	30	28	5	3	13	23	35	50
Caernarfon T	42	8	10	3	32	31	3	7	11	19	32	50
Oswestry T	42	6	9	6	23	20	6	4	11	28	40	49
Buxton	42	9	5	7	33	33	2	7	12	22	43	45
Chorley	42	6	7	8	23	33	3	8	10	33	31	42
Matlock T	42	7	9	5	34	32	2	6	13	25	43	42
*Goole T	42	4	6	11	19	37	3	5	13	18	41	31

*One point deducted for breach of rule.
Total goals scored: 1,275 in 462 matches (average 2.759).

LEADING GOALSCORERS 1985–96

	League	*Lge & Pres. Cup*	*Total*
Bob Gauden (Gainsborough Trinity)	22	4	26
Keith McNall (Gateshead)	23	—	23
Carl Dale (Rhyl)	19	1	20
Gary Stewart (Mossley)	19	—	19
Tibo Szabo (Morecambe)	19	—	19
	(7 with Mossley & Goole Town)		
Billy Gilmour (Workington)	17	2	19
Steve Burr (Macclesfield Town)	16	3	19
Bryan Davies (Bangor City)	16	3	19
			(11 with Rhyl)
John Coleman (Southport)	16	1	17
			(1 with Marine)
Mark Edwards (Chorley)	16	1	17
John Timmons (Hyde United)	14	3	17
Jeff Cook (Worksop Town)	16	—	16
Jimmy Snee (Gainsborough Trinity)	16	—	16
Paul Moss (Horwich)	15	1	16

LEAGUE CHALLENGE CUP 1985-86

First round

	1 2 (agg)
Caernarfon Town v Morecambe	2-2, 0-2 (2-4)
Chorley v Gateshead	2-1, 3-1 (5-2)
Gainsborough Trinity v Buxton	2-4, 2-0 (4-4)
	Buxton won on away goals
Mossley v Matlock Town	2-1, 4-3 (6-4)
South Liverpool v Oswestry Town	1-1, 0-3 (1-4)
Southport v Rhyl	4-0, 2-3 (6-3)

Second Round

Bangor City v Burton Albion 1-1
(Replay 2-2, Bangor City won 6-4 on pens.)
Goole Town v Southport 0-3
Horwich v Workington 0-2
Hyde United v Worksop Town 4-2
Macclesfield Town v Oswestry Town 2-1
Marine v Buxton 1-0
Morecambe v Chorley 1-0
Mossley v Witton Albion 0-0
(Replay 1-2)

Third Round

Macclesfield Town v Workington 1-0
Marine v Morecambe 2-1
Southport v Bangor City 0-1
Witton Albion v Hyde United 1-2

Semi-Finals

	1 2 (agg)
Bangor City v Marine	3-1, 0-3 (3-4)
Macclesfield Town v Hyde United	0-0, 1-4 (1-4)

Cup Final (at Manchester City)

Hyde United v Marine 1-0

PRESIDENT'S CUP

First Round

	1 2 (agg)
Burton Albion v Workington	3-1, 2-1 (5-2)
Macclesfield Town v Hyde United	4-2, 1-0 (5-2)
Witton Albion v Horwich	0-1, 1-1, (1-2)
Worksop Town v Marine	1-0, 1-0 (2-0)

Semi-Finals

Horwich v Worksop Town	2-2, 1-2 (3-4)
Macclesfield Town v Burton Albion	2-2, 0.1 (2-3)

Cup Final

Burton Albion v Worksop Town 2-0, 0-3 (2-3)
After extra time.

LEAGUE CHALLENGE SHIELD

Stafford Rangers 3 Marine 2

	Bangor City	Burton Albion	Buxton	Caernarfon Town	Chorley	Gainsborough Trinity	Gateshead	Goole Town	Horwich	Hyde United	Macclesfield Town	Marine	Matlock Town	Morecambe	Mossley	Oswestry Town	Rhyl	South Liverpool	Southport	Witton Albion	Workington	Worksop Town
Bangor City		2-2	1-0	0-1	1-1	3-1	0-2	1-3	3-1	0-1	0-0	1-2	3-2	0-0	1-0	4-0	1-1	2-1	2-3	1-0	1-1	1-0
Burton Albion	0-0		2-0	1-0	2-1	1-0	1-3	5-1	3-0	0-0	1-2	1-1	2-1	1-1	2-2	0-3	2-1	1-0	2-3	3-2	2-0	0.1
Buxton	2-0	1-0		1-3	1-0	0-0	1-5	2-2	1-0	3-2	1-2	0-2	6-2	2-4	0-3	4-2	2-0	0-0	3-2	1-2	1-1	1-1
Caernarfon Town	1-3	0-0	1-1		1-9	0-0	2-2	1-0	2-0	2-1	1-2	3-1	1-0	3-3	2-1	5-2	1-1	0-0	3-2	0-0	2-2	1-1
Chorley	0-4	0-5	0-0	1-1		0-2	1-1	4-0	1-3	2-2	1-4	0-1	1-1	0-2	0-1	3-1	2-1	2-1	1-1	0-0	2-0	2-1
Gainsborough Trinity	2-0	0-1	4-1	1-0	2-1		2-2	2-1	0-3	2-1	3-1	1-1	4-3	3-0	3-0	2-0	6-2	2-3	5-0	1-1	2-2	1-0
Gateshead	3-0	2-0	5-0	3-2	1-0	4-0		2-0	3-1	1-1	1-3	1-1	2-2	4-2	2-0	2-2	5-4	1-0	3-1	2-0	0-2	2-0
Goole Town	1-1	1-5	2-1	0-1	0-4	1-2	0-2		1-1	1-3	0-0	0-0	2-0	1-2	20	2-1	0-3	1-1	1-5	1-1	0-1	2-3
Horwich	1-2	2-1	2-2	1-0	0-0	2-1	2-1	4-0		1-4	2-0	2-3	3-1	2-1	0-1	2-1	2-1	0-1	1-1	0-1	0-3	1-3
Hyde United	0-4	0-0	2-1	2-0	2-1	2-2	3-3	3-2	1-0		0-1	1-3	2-0	0-0	2-0	0-1	3-0	2-2	0-2	2-2	2-2	3-1
Macclesfield Town	4-0	2-1	2-1	7-2	1-1	0-1	1-0	2-1	7-2	2-3		0-1	3-2	0-2	0-1	2-3	0-0	2-2	0-1	1-1	1-1	1-2
Marine	1-1	1-3	2-3	3-1	3-1	3-0	3-1	1-0	1-0	3-0	4-0		1-3	1-0	2-0	2-0	2-3	0-1	2-3	3-1	1-0	1-2
MatlockTown	2-2	0-2	3-2	1-1	2-2	1-1	1-1	3-0	1-3	1-1	0-2	0-0		1-0	4-4	2-3	1-1	2-1	2-1	1-2	2-1	4-2
Morecambe	1-0	1-0	4-1	1-1	1-1	1-1	2-0	2-0	1-1	1-1	5-1	0-0	0-1		0-2	2-0	2-2	1-1	2-1	4-1	0-0	1-0
Mossley	0-0	3-3	2-1	1-0	2-2	2-2	9-9	1-1	3-2	2-2	5-1	1-1	2-2	1-1		1-0	1-3	0-2	1-2	0-2	1-2	3-1
Oswestry Town	0-0	3-1	0-0	0-0	2-0	1-1	0-1	0-1	1-0	2-2	2-4	0-0	3-0	0-0	0-0		2-3	2-1	2-4	2-0	0-1	1-1
Rhyl	3-1	1-0	3-0	3-2	4-1	0-0	2-3	1-1	0-1	3-3	1-0	0-2	2-2	4-2	0-2	1-2		1-1	1-3	2-4	1-3	0-1
South Liverpool	1-1	2-2	1-2	1-0	2-1	1-1	1-2	2-2	1-0	0-1	0-0	1-2	1-0	0-0	2-2	0-0	1-2		1-2	2-0	0-1	0-2
Southport	3-1	1-2	2-2	3-3	3-1	2-0	3-1	3-1	2-0	2-0	0-2	0-0	2-2	0-3	1-1	0-3	0-1	1-2		1-2	2-2	0-0
Witton Albion	1-1	1-1	1-1	1-1	0-3	1-2	0-2	1-0	1-4	3-2	3-2	0-1	1-1	1-2	5-1	3-1	2-0	1-1	1-1		2-1	1-0
Workington	2-1	1-2	2-1	0-0	1-1	1-1	4-2	1-1	0-0	3-1	3-0	0-0	1-0	0-0	1-2	3-3	0-2	0-0	2-2	1-3		0-1
Worksop	1-1	1-1	2-2	1-0	2-2	3-0	1-2	0-1	2-1	1-0	4-2	0-1	1-0	0-2	1-1	0-0	2-1	0-2	2-0	3-1	1-2	

BANGOR CITY

President: Lady Janet Douglas-Pennant
Chairman: Eddie Dogan
Manager: John Mahoney
Coach: John Roberts
Physiotherapist: Len Davies
Secretary: Michael Jones
Address & Tel. No: 6 Ffriddoedd Road, Bangor. Tel. Bangor 364424
Commercial Manager: Eddie Dowson
Press Officer & Tel. No: Keith Evans (0248-712464)
Address & Tel. No of ground: Farrar Road, Bangor. Tel. Bangor 351716
Simple ground directions: To centre of Town, on left by Station (BR)
Club shop: Yes
No of seats: 900 **Covered accommodation:** 2,000 **Capacity:** 10,000
Floodlights: Yes
Year formed: 1876 **Nickname:** Citizens
Club sponsors:
Previous names: None
Club colours: All Blue
Change colours: All Red
Day for midweek home matches: Wednesday
Record attendance: 10,000 v Wrexham **Year:** 1978-79
Previous Leagues: Birmingham, Lancashire Combination. Cheshire County, Alliance Premier.
Best performance in: F.A. Cup: 1st round
F.A. Trophy: 2nd round
Clubhouse details: Open seven nights & days. Live entertainment three nights.
Present players with Football League experience:
Past players who progressed into the Football League: John McClelland (Northern Ireland & Watford), Neville Southall (Wales & Everton)
Record transfer fee paid: Mark Carter (S. Liverpool)
Record transfer fee received: John McClelland (Mansfield)
Programme details: 12 pages, 25p
Programme Editor: Keith Evans
Local newspapers & Tel No: Daily Post (712464), Chronicle (352051), Weekly News (362747)
Club metal badges: Yes
Senior Honours: Reached 2nd round of European Cup Winners Cup 1985-86
Club Captain (1985-86): Phil Lunn **Player of the Year (1985-86):** Les Armour

BANGOR CITY
Goalkeepers
Dai Davies: Tranmere Rovers (42), Swansea City (71), Wrexham (144), Everton (82), Swansea City (9), Ammanford Town
Tony Walsh: Local

Defenders
Terry Banks: Caernarfon Town
Mark Cartweright: Portmadog, Oswestry Town, Wrexham
Gary Evans: Oswestry Town, Wrexham, Liverpool
Phil Lunn: Chester City, Bangor City
Tony Gunns: Local

Midfield
Neville Powell: Tranmere Rovers (86-4)
Bruce Urquhart: Wrexham
Les Armor: Rhyl, Colwyn Bay
Paul Whelan: Local
Ian McMullen: Tranmere Rovers (2)
Wayne Aspinall: Northwich Victoria, Barrow, Wigan (8)

Forwards
Viv Williams: Llanerchymedd
Brian Davies: Rhyl, Winsford United, St. Helens Town
Reg McGuire: Local
Everton Williams: Chester City, Wrexham
John Aspinall: Altrincham, Tranmere Rovers (107-25)

Bangor City on the attack in the first round of The European Cup Winners Cup. Photo: Eric Marsh

BARROW

President: Sir Leonard Redshaw
Chairman: W. A. McCullough
Manager: Ray Wilkie
Commercial Manager: D. McGerty
Press Officer & Tel. No: Phil Yelland, 031332 6411
Coach: Bernard Taylor
Physiotherapist: Mal Richmond
Secretary: Phil Cowing
Address & Tel. No: 18 Meamess Drive, Ulverston, Cumbria
Tel 0229 55309 (H) 33271 (W)
Address & Tel. No of ground: Holker Strteet, Barrow-in-Furness, Cumbria. Tel. 0229 20346
Simple ground directions: M6 to Junction36; A590 to Barrow, Turn right 4th set of lights (at station) **Club shop:** Yes
No of seats: 1,250 **Covered accommodation:** All **Capacity:** 9,000 **Floodlights:** Yes
Year formed: 1901 **Nickname:** Bluebirds **Club sponsors:** Various
Previous names: None
Club colours: Blue/White/White
Change colours: Yellow
Day for midweek home matches: Tuesday
Record attendance: 16,840 F.A. Cup v Swansea Town **Year:** 1954
Previous Leagues:
Football League,
Northern Premier League
Alliance Premier League
(Gola League)
Best performance in: F.A. Cup: 1st qualifying round
F.A. Trophy: 1st round
Clubhouse details: Bluebird Club, Holker Street. Seats 250. Tel. 0229-25346
Present players with Football League experience:
Past players who progressed into the Football League: Ian McDonald, Neil McDonald, Steve Brooks, Nigel Keen, Barry Diamond, Frank Gamble, Barry Knowles
Record transfer fee paid:
Record transfer fee received: Over £20,000 from Derby County for Glen Skivington
Programme details: 16 pages, 30p
Programme Editor: Secretary
Local newspapers & Tel No: N/W Evening Mail
0229 21835
Club metal badges: Yes
Senior Honours: NPL Winners 1983-84, NPL Shield Winners 1984-85; Cumbrian Cup Winners 1982-83, 1983-84, Runners Up 1984-85; Lancashire Junior Cup Winners 1980-81, Runners Up 1981-82, 1985-85; F.A. Cup 3rd Round several times; F.A. Trophy Quarter-final 1979-80
Club Captain (1985-86): Glen Skivington
Player of the Year (1985-86):

Goalkeepers
Lee Copeland: Vickers S.C.
Keven Brockbank: Local

Defenders
Glen Skivington: Southend United (15-2), Derby County (54-3), Barrow
Jamie Frankland: Crooklands Casuals
Jim Capstick: Dalton United, Vickers S.C.
Andy Wright: Local
Brian Kettle: Runcorn, Burscough, Wigan Athletic (14-1), Houston Hurricane (USA), Liverpool (3)
Peter Nicholson: Lytham, Chorley, Lytham, Carlisle United (1), Bolton W. (318-12), Blackpool (6)

Midfield
Paul Lodge: Bolton W. (4), Preston N.E. (38), Everton (24)
Kevin Proctor: Dalton United, Barrow
Andy Forbes: Local
George Armes: Local
Colin Moore: Vickers S.C.
Walter Nesbitt: Wythenshawe Amateurs, Mossley
Stuart Parker: Runcorn, Witton Albion, Stockport County (1), Drogheda (Eire), Blackpool, Chester City (9-5), Preston N.E., Mechelen (Bel), Bury (34-9), Sparta Rotterdam (Holl), Blackburn Rovers (9-1), Chesterfield (34-8), Southend United (64-23), Blackpool (16-2)

Forwards
David Johnson: Preston N.E. (24-3), Manchester City (6-1), Everton (40-4), Liverpool (149-55), Ipswich Town (137-35), Everton (50-11)
Ronnie Goodlass: Tranmere Rovers (21), Happy Valley (H.K.), Scunthorpe United (9), Fulham (22-2), Den Haag (Hol), NEC Breda (Hol), Everton (35-2)
Eddie Kennedy: Local
Colin Cowperthwaite: Netherfield, Nilnthorpe
Mark Hetherington: Local

Back (l to r): Stuart Parker (now Runcorn), David Johnson (no longer with the club), Brian Kettle (now South Liverpool), George Armes, Lee Copeland, Kevin Proctor, Peter Nicholson (no longer with the club). Front (l to r) Paul Lodge (no longer with the club), Walter Nesbitt, Dave Conlin, Glen Skivington, Colin Cowperthwaite.

BURTON ALBION

President: T. Bradbury
Chairman: Dave Mellor
Manager: Brian Fidler
Commercial Manager: J. Kield
Physiotherapist: Joe Mulholland
Secretary: Stan King
Address & Tel. No: 204 Newton Road, Burton on Trent Staffs DE15 0TU Tel. 0283 44303 (H)
Tel No: 0283 65939 **Press Officer & Tel. No:** J. Kield
Address & Tel. No of ground: Eton Park, Princess Way, Burton-on-Trent, DE14 2RU. Tel. 0283 65938
Simple ground directions: From A50 take 1st left (Shakespeare Rd) after passing under by-pass bridge. From A38 take A5121 turn right at island, ground 250yds on left. **Club shop:** Yes
No of seats: 286 **Covered accommodation:** 5,000 **Capacity:** 10,000 **Floodlights:** Yes
Year formed: 1950 **Nickname:** The Brewers **Club sponsors:** Ind Coope Brewery, Burton
Previous names:
Club colours: Yellow/Black/Yellow
Change Colours: White/Red/Red
Day for midweek home matches: Wednesday
Record attendance: 5,860 v Weymouth **Year:** 1964
Previous Leagues: Birmingham, Southern
Best performance in: F.A. Cup: 4th round
F.A. Trophy: 3rd round
Clubhouse details: Open to all on match days.
Present players with Football League experience:
Past players who progressed into the Football League: Richie Barker, Alan Buckley, Corrigan, Pollock, Potter, Swan, Jobson, Bailey and Peter Ward
Record transfer fee paid: £2,250 for Carl Swan from Buxton
Record transfer fee received: £15,000 for Richard Jobson to Watford
Programme details: 20 pages, 25p
Programme Editor: Rex Page
Local newspapers & Tel No: Burton Daily Mail (0283 43311)
Club metal badges: Yes
Senior Honours: Southern League Cup 1964, Bass Charity Vase, 1981, Birmingham Sen. Cup, Staffordshire Sen. Cup, Bass Challenge Cup & 3rd Round F.A. Cup 1985, (Leicester City)
Club Captain (1985-86): David Vaughan **Player of the Year (1985-86):** Alan Icamara

Goalkeepers
Martin New: Nuneaton Borough, Barnsley (24), Mansfield Town (21), Arsenal
Dave Buxton: Local

Defenders
Les McJannet: King's Lynn, Mansfield Town (74)
Alan Kamara: Retford Town, York R.I., Darlington (144-1), York City (10), Kiveton Park
David Vaughan: Mossley, Boston F.C.
Steve Dolby: Local
Steve Essex: Gresley Rovers

Midfield
David Pugh: Goole Town, Doncaster Rovers (6), York City (77-2), Rotherham United (58), Halifax Town (96-3), Chesterfield (213-12), Newport County (78-9)
Gary Clayton: Gainsborough Trinity, Spalding United, Rotherham United
Nigel Simms: Local
Guy Hall: Local
Phil Saunders: Arnold, Mansfield Town
Ian Heap: Local
John Bottomley: Local

Forwards
Stewart Mell: Halifax Town (30-8), Doncaster Rovers (76-14), Appleby Frodingham
David Staniforth: Halifax Town (69-21), Bradford City (115-25), Bristol Rovers (153-31), Sheffield United (21-3)
Tim Graham: Local
Colin Kersley: Macclesfield Town, Stafford Rangers, Leek Town
Neal Dorsett: Borrowash Victoria
Paul Edmunds: Grantham, Bentley Victoria, A.F.C. Bournemouth (14-2), Leicester City (8-2)

Back row (l to r): Gary Clayton, Colin Kersley, S. Essex, M. New, G. Hall, P. Saunders, G. Hand, N. Simms.
Front row (l to r): N. Dorsett, S. Mell, D. Vaughan (Captain), D. Mellor (Chairman), B. Fidler (Manager); L. McJannett, A. Kamara.

BUXTON

President: E. Lampard
Chairman: A. Brailsford
Manager: Bob Murphy
Coach: E. Bryne
Trainer: K. Perrin
Physiotherapist: None
Secretary: Ronald A. Malpass
Address & Tel. No: 20 Alport Avenue, Fairfield, Buxton SK17 7TH. Tel. (0298) 3443 (H)
Commercial Manager: None
Address & Tel. No of ground: The Silverlands, Buxton, Derbyshire. Tel. (0298) 4733
Simple ground directions: From Buxton Market Place opposite the County Police HQ and TA Drill Hall **Club shop:** No
No of seats: 654 **Covered accommodation:** 2,500 **Capacity:** 6,500 **Floodlights:** Yes
Year formed: 1877 **Nickname:** The Bucks **Club sponsors:** None
Previous names: None
Club colours: White shirts/socks, Blue shorts
Change colours: All Yellow
Day for midweek home matches: Tuesday
Record attendance: 6,000× v Barrow F.A. Cup 1st Round **Year:** 1962-3
Previous Leagues: Combination, North Derbyshire, East Cheshire, Manchester, Chester C.
Best performance in: F.A. Cup: 151-2 v Doncaster R. 3rd Round
F.A. Trophy: 1970-1, 1971-2 Quarter-Finals
Clubhouse details: Marstons beers, all spirits, bingo, darts and dominoes. Every night, Sunday morning. Run by committee. Two tea bars. Tel. 0298 3197
Present players with Football League experience: None
Past players who progressed into the Football League: Tony Parkes, John Froggart, Jack Gaskell, Billy Haydock
Record transfer fee paid: £2,000 by Manchester City for Bily Haydock
Record transfer fee received: £3,250 for Tony Parkes to Blackburn Rovers
Programme details: 8 pages, 20p
Local newspapers & Tel No: Buxton Advertiser, (0298) 2118/2119. Matlock Mercury (Matlock 2432/3)
Club metal badges: Yes, scarves and pennants
Senior Honours: Manchester League Champions (2), Cheshire League Champions 1972/73, Derbyshire Senior Cup Winners (6), The Presidents Cup 1981/82, Cheshire League Cup Winners (3)
Club Captain (1985-86): K. Gorman **Player of the Year (1985-86):** A. Rodwell

Goalkeepers
Gary Weighill: Staveley Works, Worksop Town, Heanor Town, Chesterfield
Defenders
Steve Jackson: Southport, Ellesmere Port & Neston
David Vaughan: Newcastle KB (Aus), Bootle, Barrow
Steve Allcock: Crewe Alexandra
Nigel Phillips: Narwich & Parkeston, Chelmsford City, Colchester United
Vinroy Panton: Local
David Bainbridge: Local
Midfield
Kevin Gorman: Barrow, Southport, Hyde United, Mossley, Droylsden, Bacup Borough, Barrow
Kenny Hulme: Barrow, Southport, Ellesmere Port & Neston, Formby
Mike Halliday: Stalybridge Celtic, Mossley, Irlam Town, Prestwich Heys, Witton Albion, Stockport County, Manchester United
Lenny Yates: Matlock Town, Buxton, Worksop Town, Sheffield United
Tony Rodwell: Southport
John White: Macclesfield Town, Witton Albion

Forwards
Les Harris: Burton Albion, Gainsborough Trinity, Buxton, Barnsley (26-2)
Gary Hodgkinson: Local
Malcolm Hill: West Ham United
Kevin Keelan: Barrow, Stalybridge Celtic, Macclesfield Town, Mossley, Newcastle KB (Aus), Stalybridge Celtic, Buxton

Buxton F.C. Photo: Rod Leach

CAERNARFON TOWN

President: H. Jones
Chairman: R. A. Roberts
Manager: J. King
Coach: G. Griffiths
Physiotherapist: I. Humphreys
Secretary: H. H. Williams
Address & Tel. No: 36 High Street, Caernarfon
Simple ground directions: A55 coast road to new A487 Bypass to Caernarfon, Inner relief road, over flyover, follow Beddgelent sign, 2nd right after 300 yds, ground facing.
Club shop: Yes
No of seats: 250 **Covered accommodation:** 1,200 **Capacity:** 10,000 **Floodlights:** Yes
Year formed: 0000 **Nickname:** Canaries **Club sponsors:** None
Previous names: None
Club colours: Yellow, Green, Yellow
Change colours: Red, White, Red
Day for midweek home matches: Wednesday
Record attendance: 6,000 v Bournemouth F.A. Cup 2nd Round **Year:** 1929
Previous Leagues: Welsh
Lancashire Comb. N.W. Counties
Best performance in: **F.A. Cup:** 4th Qual Round, 1981-2
F.A. Trophy: 3rd Qual Round 1981-2
Clubhouse details: On the ground
Present players with Football League experience: None
Past players who progressed into the Football League: Ernie Walley, Tom Walley, Wyn Davies
Record transfer fee paid: None
Record transfer fee received: £1,000
Programme details: 24 pages, 25p
Programme Editor: R, Morris Jones
Local newspapers & Tel No: Caernarfon & Denbigh Herald,
Liverpool Daily Post
Club metal badges: No
Senior Honours: Lancs Competition Cup and League Champions, North West Counties runner up. 2nd Round FA Cup 1928
Club Captain (1985-86): Phil Wilson **Player of the Year (1985-86):** Ken Jones

Goalkeepers
Neil McAdam: Oswestry Town, Port Vale (2), Northwich Victoria, Airdrie

Defenders
Ken Jones: Northwich Victoria, Ellesmere Port, W.B.A.
Mal Bailey: Hyde United, Telford United, Altrincham, Runcorn, Northwich Victoria, Port Vale
Mark Dean: Northwich Victoria, Chester City
Huw Williams: Wrexham
Robin Jones: Local

Midfield
Gareth Pritchard: Cardiff City
Dave Wignall: Rhyl, Gainsborough Trinity, Colchester United, Doncaster Rovers (41-1), Preston N.E.
Steve Craven: Northwich Victoria, Bangor City, Altrincham, Northwich Victoria, Crewe Alexandra (29-3), Tranmere Rovers (114-17)
Paul Wilson: Northwich Victoria, Mossley, Runcorn, Tranmere Rovers, Blackburn Rovers

Forwards
Austin Salmon: Witton Albion, Winsford United, Witton Albion, Whitchurch Alport, Nantwich Town
Ian Cockbain: Local
Melir Owen: Pwllheli, Bangor City, Caernarfon Town

Back Row (l to r): H.H. Williams (General Secretary), I. Humphreys (Physio), I. Cockbain, H. Williams, A. Salmon, N. McAdam, S. Craven, D. Wignall, D. Martindale, R. A. Roberts (Chairman)
Front Row (l to r): S. Clynch, R. Woods, P. Wilson (Capt), K. Jones, R. Jones, M. Dean, J. King (Manager)

CHORLEY

President: Dr. P. J. Wren
Chairman: W. Conway
Manager: Ken Wright
Coach: Phil Parry
Physiotherapist: None
Secretary: M. Wearmouth
Address & Tel. No: 6 Avondale Road, Chorley. Tel 02572-63406 (B)
Address & Tel. No of ground: Victory Park, Duke Street, Chorley, PR7 3DU. 02572 63406
Simple ground directions: A6 Manchester to Preston, Duke Street is off the A6 (Bolton Street), half a mile south of Chorley town centre (behind Plaza cinema)
Club shop: Yes
No of seats: 700 **Covered accommodation:** 4,000 **Capacity:** 9,900 **Floodlights:** Yes
Year formed: 1883 **Nickname:** Magpies **Club sponsors:** None
Previous names: None
Club colours: Black/White Stripes, Black, Black
Change colours: Red, White, Red
Day for midweek home matches: Tuesday
Record attendance: 9,679 v Darwen **Years:** 1931/2
Best performance in: **F.A. Cup:** 1st Round Proper
F.A. Trophy: 3rd Qual Round
Previous Leagues:
Cheshire League, Lancashire Combination, Lancashire League, Lancashire Alliance
Clubhouse details: Open every evening, snacks available, entertainment at weekends. Tel. 02572 75662
Present players with Football League experience: None
Past players who progressed into the Football League: Teddy Hodgson (Burnley), Roger Heywood (Leicester), Arthur Cunliffe (Blackburn, England), Charlie Ashcroft (Liverpool, England 'B'), Derek Hogg (Leicester), Paul Mariner (Plymouth, Ipswich, Arsenal, England), Steve Galliers (Wimbledon, Crystal Palace), Geoff Twentyman (Prseton N.E.), Peter Devine (Bristol City, Blackburn, Burnley, Vancouver Whitecaps)
Record transfer fee paid: £900 to Formby for Geoff Twentyman
Record transfer fee received: £22,500 from Plymouth Argyle for Paul Mariner
Programme details: 24 pages, 25p
Programme Editor: Colin White
Local newspapers & Tel No: Chorley Guardian, 02572 67859, Lancashire Evening Post 0772 54841
Club metal badges: Yes
Senior Honours: Champions: Lancashire Alliance, Lancshire League, Lancashire Combination (Division 1 and 2). Runners-up: Lancashire Alliance, Lancashire Combination, Cheshire League. Winners: ATS Lancashire F.A. Challenge Trophy (14) Lancashire Combination Cup, Lancashire F.A. Flootlit Trophy.
Club Captain (1985-86): Simon Westwell **Player of the Year (1985-86):** John Hughes

Goalkeepers
Gary Pierce: Blackpool (27), Barnsley (81), Wolves (98), Huddersfield Town (23), Mossley
Ian Senior: Southport, Leek Town, Witton Albion, Altrincham, Manchester City, Ashton United, Horwich R.M.I., Bury, Rossendale United, Mossley, Horwich R.M.I., Rochdale, Radcliffe Borough, Bolton Wanderers, Mossley, Oldham Athletic, Stalybridge Celtic, Prestwich Heys
Defenders
Simon Westwell: Preston N.E. (74-1)
Paul Gardner: Bury (90), Blackpool (152-1)
Dave Serella: Altrincham, Blackpool (55-4), Walsall (305-13), Nottingham Forest (78)
Steve Waywell:
Hyde Unitewd, Horwich R.M.I., Chorley, Darwen, Stalybridge Celtic
Roy Silous: Horwich R.M.I., Macclesfield Town, Horwich R.M.I., Bedford Town

Midfield
John Hughes: Witton Albion, Bury (1)
John Butler: Barrow, Yeovil Town, Runcorn, Blackpool (8)
Royston Taylor: Morecambe, Barrow, Blackburn Rovers (3-1), Sunderland (3)
Geoff Gay: Mossley, Macclesfield Town, Bangor City, Southport, Wigan Athletic (1), Southport (40-5), Macclesfield Town, Bolton W.
Garath Webster: Bolton S.T.
Dennis Haslam: Horwich R.M.I.

Forwards
Mark Edwards: St. Helens Town, Horwich R.M.I.
Mark Barrow: Leyland Motors
Dave Liptrot: Horwich R.M.I., Stockport County
Neil McLachlan: Norwich R.M.I., Morecambe

Standing (l to r): Phil Parry (Assistant Manager), Bill Conway (Chairman), Steve Waywell, Charlie Cooper, Gary Pierce, Neil McLachlan, Dave Liptrot, Ian Seddon, Bob Lancaster, Ray Silous, Ken Wright (Manager).
Seated (l to r): Dennis Haslam, Simon Westwell, John Hughes, Mark Edwards, Geoff Gray, Gary Lowe.

GAINSBOROUGH TRINITY

President: None
Chairman: J.M. Davis
Team Manager: P. Buckley
Chief Coach: C. Stanley
Commercial Manager: R. Hearn
Address & Tel. No. Gainsborough 4307 or 3295
Press Officer & Tel. No. As Secretary
Secretary/Director: K. Marsden
Address & Tel. No. 22, Cavendish Drive, Lea, Gainsborough, Gainsborough (0427) 2577 (H)
Address and Tel. No. of ground: The Northolme, Gainsborough, Lincs (0427 3295) **Club shop:** No
Simple ground directions: From town centre to General Post Office, Ground in North St 300yds form Post Office
No. of seats: 350 **Covered accommodation:** 6,000 **Capacity:** 10,000 **Floodlights:** Yes
Year formed: 1873 **Nickname:** The Blues **Club sponsor:** Crown Wallpaper
Previous names: None
Club colours: Royal Blue/White/Royal Blue **Change colours:** Red/Black/Red
Previous grounds: None **Day for midweek home matches:** Tuesday
Record attendance: 9,760 v Scunthorpe Utd
Best performance in: F.A. Cup: 1959-60, 1st Round Replay v Doncaster 1983-84, Blackpool 1st Rd.
F.A. Trophy: 1975-6 2nd Round Replay
Previous Leagues: Football League
Clubhouse details: Midland Counties
Present players with Football League experience: A. Lodge
Past players who progressed into the Football League: A. Morton, S. Foxall (both West Ham), N. Curtis (Sheffield Wed), S. Evans (Sheffield Utd), J. Cockcroft (West Ham)
Record transfer fee paid: 1,500 to Matlock for R. Barrett
Record transfer fee received: £6,000 from Sheffield Utd for S. Evans
Programme editor: Roy Hearn (0427 4307 **Club Captain (1985-86):** Andy Lodge (1985-86)
Player of the Year (1985-86): Jimmy Smee (1985-86)
Local newspapers & Tel. No. Gainsborough News, Lincolnshire Echo
Senior Honours: Midland Counties League Champions & Cup Winners, Lincolnshire Senior Cup

GAINSBOROUGH TRINITY
Goalkeepers
Paul Evans: Burton Albion, Macclesfield Town, Worksop Town, Mansfield Town (6), Worksop Town, Kiveton Park

Defenders
Mark Burrell: Retford Town
Richard Warburton: Matlock Town, Buxton
Andy Lodge: Blackburn Rovers, Ashby Town
Gary Elliman: Long Eaton United, Grantham, Burton Albion, Buxton, Skegness Town, Boston F.C., Sunderland

Midfield
Gary Brattan: Goole Town, Hall Road Rangers, Bridlington Trinity, Hull City
Steve Lee: Local
Andy O'Dell: Rotherham United (18), Grimsby Town (20)
Ashley Taylor: Rotherham United (23)

Forwards
Gary Mozley: Retford Town
Bob Gauden: Burton Albion, Scarborough, Buxton
Jimmy Snee: Appleby Frodingham, Gainsborough Trinity
Paul Froggatt: Burton Albion, Worksop Town, Sheffield Wednesday, Manchester City
Dave Hoyland: Frickley Athletic, Worksop Town, Canberra City (Aus), Doncaster Rovers, Grimsby Town

Unfortunately we didn't receive a photograph from Gainsborough Trinity

An anxious moment for the Chorlwy Defence as Mike Farrelly challenges for Altrincham in the first round of the F.A. Cup. Photo: John Rooney.

GOOLE TOWN

President: E. K. Holt
Chairman: S. R. Ullathorne
Manager: M. E. Bullock
Coach: None
Physiotherapist: Colin Naylor
Secretary: H. Harrison
Address & Tel. No: 8 Devonshire Drive, Goole DN14 6PJ.
Tel. 0405 4172 (H), 0405 5141 ext. 271 (W)
Commercial Manager: C. J. Raywood
Tel No: Goole 0405
Press Officer & Tel. No: As Secretary
Address & Tel. No of ground: Victoria Pleasure Ground, Carter Street, Goole. Tel. Goole 2794 **Club Shop:** Yes
Simple ground directions: Entering Goole from M62 turn right at 2nd set of traffic lights. Carter Street is 6th street on the right
No of seats: 200 **Covered accommodation:** 4,000 **Capacity:** 8,500 **Floodlights:** Yes
Year formed: 1900 **Nickname:** Town **Club sponsors:** Autotrams (Renault), Phoenix Engineering
Previous names: None
Club colours: Yellow/Black/Yellow
Change colours: All Red
Day for midweek home matches: Tuesday
Record attendance: 8,700 v Scunthorpe **Year:** 1950
Previous League: Yorkshire League
Best performance in: **F.A. Cup:** 1957 3rd Round Proper v Nottm Forest (A)
F.A. Trophy: 1978 Quarter-Final
Clubhouse details: None
Present players with Football League experience: None
Past players who progressed into the Football League: I. Pearson (Plymouth), J. Kaye (Scunthorpe), T. Galvin (Tottenham)
Record transfer fee paid: None
Record transfer fee received: £10,000 from Tottenham for T. Galvin
Programme details: 4 pages, 15p
Programme Editor: Secretary
Local newspapers & Tel No: Goole Times, 3391; Hull Mail, 2647
Club metal badges: No
Senior Honours: West Riding Cup (10), Yorkshire Cup (4), Yorkshire League (5)
Club Captain (1985-86): John Overton **Player of the Year (1985-86):** Mark Worton

Goalkeepers
Paul Blackburn: Gainsborough Trinity, Goole Town, Gainsborough Trinity, Bridlington Trinity

Defenders
Tony Moore: Gainsborough Trinity, Worksop Town, Sheffield F.C., Sheffield United (29), Burton Albion
Mark Worton: Local
Steve Rogers: Bridlington Trinity
Peter Heaney: Local
Paul Stanley: Mansfield Town, Buxton, Scunthorpe United
Carl Swan: Belper Town, Buxton, Mossley, Goole Town, Chesterfield, Doncaster Rovers (17-1), Burton Albion, Worksop Town, Matlock Town, Buxton

Midfield
John Overton: Frickley Athletic, Gillingham (178-3), Aston Villa (3)
Ian Thompson: Worksop Town, Goole Town, Worksop Town, Gainsborough Trinity, Huddersfield Town
John Black: Stop Out Wellington (N.Z.), Scarborough, Hereford United (5), Bradford City (60-15), Wolves (6)
Andy Brolly: Burton Albion, Gainsborough Trinity, Frecheville Community, Bristol Rovers, Rotherham United
Dave Stewart: Grantham, Goole Town, Kanberra Denmark (Den), Scunthorpe United (97-19), Chelsea, Hull City (51-7)
Ken Harrison: Hull City

Forwards
Tibor Szabo: Mossley, Gainsborough Trinity, Mossley, Macclesfield Town, Bradford City (13-1)
Mark Downing: Armthorpe Welfare, Grantham, Armthorpe Welfare
Mark Hamilton: Leeds Ashley Road
Peter Camm: Armthorpe Welfare, Grantham, Goole Town, Armthorpe Welfare

Unfortunately we didn't receive a photograph from Goole Town

Oswestry Town players line up behind the club's £20,000 appeal banner. Good luck to them!
(Photo: Shropshire Star)

HORWICH R.M.I.

President: G.H. Fisher
Chairman: C.J. Healey
Manager: A. Webber
Coach: J. Cavanagh
Commercial Manager: Secretary
Address & Tel. No. As Secretary
Press Officer & Tel. No. As Secretary

Secretary: H. Taylor
Address & Tel. No. 194, Victoria Road, Horwich Bolton, Lancs, BL6 5AB (0204) 691589

Address and Tel. No. of ground: Victoria Road, Horwich, Tel: 66908 **Club shop:** No
Simple ground directions: Ground at side of Horwich Leisure Centre
No. of seats: 500 **Covered accommodation:** 3 sides **Capacity:** 5,000 **Floodlights:** Yes
Year formed: 1896 **Nickname:** Railwaymen **Club sponsor:** Clousaw
Previous names: None
Club colours: Royal Blue/White/Royal Blue **Change colours:** All Yellow
Previous grounds: None **Day for midweek home matches:** Monday
Record attendance: Not known
Best performance in: **F.A. Cup:** 1928, 1983, 1st Round Proper.
F.A. Trophy: 1978-79 1st Round Proper
Previous Leagues: Lancashire Combination, Cheshire County, North West Counties
Clubhouse details: Open each evening
Present players with Football League experience: S. Thompson, B. Hart
Past players who progressed into the Football League: Frank Wignell (Everton, Nottm. Forest, Derby C., England), Tony Caldwell (Bolton Wanderers)
Record transfer fee paid: Not known
Record transfer fee received: £2,000 from Bolton Wanderers for Tony Caldwell in 1983
Programme editor: C.J. Healey **Club Captain (1985-86):** Brian Hart
Player of the Year (1985-86): Brian Hart
Local newspapers & Tel. No. Bolton Evening News, Bolton 22345
Senior Honours: Lancashire Combination, Cheshire County League, Lancashire Junior Cup

Goalkeepers
Geoff Foster: Rochdale, Horwich R.M.I.
Mike Allison: Local

Defenders
Nick Jones: Darwen, Southport
Joe Nicholl: Irlam Town
Allan Froggatt: Bolton Wanderers
Charlie Pawsey: Hyde United, Irlam Town
John Fielding: Chorley
Brian Hart: Mossley, Hyde United, Barrow, Southport, Horwich R.M.I., Bangor City, Glossop, Northwich Victoria, Rochdale (78), Bolton Wanderers
Neil Peters: Irlam Town

Midfield
Wayne Lancaster: Irlam Town, Chorley
Tony Ellis: Local
Paul Jones: Glossop
Dave Sheridan: Local
Mark Russell: Leeds United
Mike Kolojeski: Local

Forwards
Andy Stafford: Chorley, Mossley, Rochdale, Stockport County (25-1), Halifax Town (41-1)
Paul Moss: Winsford United, Stalybridge Celtic, Darwen
Charlie Cooper: Chorley, Huddersfield Town
Billy McGivern: Local
Bobby Grimshaw: Morecambe, Stalybridge Celtic, Horwich R.M.I., Rossendale United, Darwen

Unfortunately we didn't receive a photograph from Horwich R.M.I.

Hyde United with the Mulipart League Challenge Cup. Photo: John Rooney

HYDE UNITED

President: Fred Pye
Chairman: Bill Patterson
Manager: Peter O'Brien
Coach: None
Physiotherapist: C. I. Wych
Press Officer & Tel. No: Secretary
Secretary: David Goodwin
Address & Tel. No: 3 Everest Close, Hyde, Cheshire SK14 4DY Tel. 061-368 6689
Commercial Manager: Syd Hampton
Address & Tel. No of ground: Ewen Fields, Miles Street, Hyde, Cheshire SK14 2SB. Tel. 061-368 1031
Simple ground directions: From Hyde Town centre take A57 (Sheffield & Barnsley) through 2 sets of lights, turn right Bankfield Hotel into Grange Road, first right Miles Street, ground and car park at end of street
Club shop: Yes
No of seats: 600 **Covered accommodation:** 3,500 **Capacity:** 6,000 **Floodlights:** Yes
Year formed: 1919 **Nickname:** Tigers **Club sponsors:** None
Previous names: None
Club colours: All Red
Change colours: White Shirts, Black Shorts and socks
Day for midweek home matches: Monday
Previous League: Cheshire
Record attendance: 9,500 **Year:** 1952
Best performance in: **F.A. Cup:** 1st Round Proper Burnley 1983
F.A. Trophy: 2nd round 1981-2
Clubhouse details: Open most nights, full facilities, seats 150
Present players with Football League experience: None
Past players who progressed into the Football League: D. Constantine (Bury), D. Graham (Bury), G. Oghani (Bolton), K. Glendon (Burnley), P. Coyne (Swindon)
Record transfer fee paid: £600 Paul Knight
Record transfer fee received: £5,000 for David Constantine and G. Oghani
Programme details: 20 pages, 25p
Programme Editor: Milan Pavasovic, 061-330 7864
Local newspapers & Tel No: North Cheshire Herald & Hyde Reporter 061-368 3595; Advertiser,. 061-308 2621
Club metal badges: Yes
Senior Honours: Cheshire League, Cheshire League Cup, Cheshire League Shield, Cheshire Senior Cup
Club Captain (1985-86): Glyn Chamberlain **Player of the Year (1985-86):** Colin Jackson

Goalkeepers
Colin Darcy: Altrincham, Bury (6), Everton

Defenders
David Lees: Chorley, Ashton United, Stoke City
Colin Jackson: Chorley, Glossop, Everton
Paul Knight: Chorley, Stalybridge Celtic
Wayne Roberts: Stalybridge Celtic, Southport, Mossley, Workington, Droylsden
Glyn Chamberlain: Buxton, Kettering Town, Halifax Town (35), Chesterfield (18), Burnley

Midfield
Terry Cook: Chorley, Stalybridge Celtic, Leek Town, Mossley, Stockport County
Steve Johnson: Stockport County, Manchester City
Jimmy Curran: Nottingham Forest, Hyde United, Mossley
Phil Marsden: Macclesfield Town, Stafford Rangers, Prestwich Heys, Bolton W.
David Betts: Local

Forwards
Malcolm O'Connor: Curzon Ashton, Rochdale (16-3), Curzon Ashton
John Timmons: Maine Road
Steve Curley: Local
Ian Rogers: Buxton, Boston F.C., Worksop Town

End of File B—Disc 19

Hyde United, jublilant after winning the N.P.L. Cup
Back row (L to R): Steve Curley, John Timmons, Wayne Roberts, Jim Curran, Steve Johnson, Ian rogers, Mark Molyneaux, Colin Jackson, Eric Campbell.
Front row (L to R): Graham Holder, Steve Saunders, Colin Darey, Pete O'Brien, Glyn Chamberlain, Malcolm O'Connor, Terry Cook, Dave Lees, Phil Marsden. Photo: Carl Royle

MACCLESFIELD

Chairman: A. Brocklehurst
Manager: P. Wragg
Coach: None
Physiotherapist: M. Whiteside (club doctor)
Press Officer & Tel. No: None
Secretary: R. Campbell
Address & Tel. No: 16 Malvern Close, West Heath, Congieton, Cheshire CW12 4PD
Commercial Manager: None
Address & Tel. No of ground: Moss Rose, London Road, Macclesfield. Tel. 0625 24324
Simple ground directions: Situated at south end of town on main road to Leek (A523)
Club shop: Yes
No of seats: 600 **Covered accommodation:** 2,000 **Capacity:** 10,000
Floodlights: Yes
Year formed: 1875 **Nickname:** Silkmen
Club sponsors: None
Previous names: None
Club colours: Royal Blue and White
Change colours: All Yellow
Day for midweek home matches: Tuesday
Record attendance: 8,900 v Stockport County, F.A. Cup 2nd round **Years:** 1968/69
Previous League: Cheshire County
Best performance in: **F.A. Cup:** 3rd Round v Fulham 1968/69
F.A. Trophy: Trophy Winners 1969/70
Clubhouse details: Open match days
Present players with Football League experience: None
Past players who progressed into the Football League: I. Elsby (Port Vale), S. Waddington (Stoke City), S. Hanlon (Crewe Alexandra)
Record transfer fee paid: £2,000 to Crewe for P. Connelly
Record transfer fee received: £4,000 for G. Collier from Notts County
Programme details: None
Programme Editor: C. Westbury
Local newspapers & Tel No: Macclesfield Express (24445)
Club metal badges: No
Senior Honours: F.A. Trophy 1970, Cheshire League (6), NPL (2), Cheshire Senior Cup (15)
Club Captain (1985-86): Mark Fielding **Player of the Year (1985-86):** Nigel Shaw

MACCLESFIELD TOWN
Goalkeepers
Alan Zelem: Skelmersdale United, Winsford United, Bolton Wanderers

Defenders
Neil Fairclough: Stalybridge Celtic
Mark Fielding: Runcorn, Witton Albion, Preston N.E., Witton Albion
Mike Hardman: Altrincham, South Liverpool, Runcorn, Warrington Town, Runcorn, Warrington Town
Martyn Smith: Port Vale (13-1)
Ian Elsby: Port Vale (43-1)
Graham Tobin: Altrincham, Burscough

Midfield
Nigel Shaw: Congleton Town
Steve Hanlon: Oswestry Town, Yaro (Fin), Nantwich Town, Crewe Alexandra (18)
Steve Waddington: Chesterfield (18-1), Port Vale (1), Walsall (130-14), Stoke City (52-5)
Dave Goodwin: Witton Albion, Macclesfield Town, Stafford Rangers, Crewe Alexandra (7), Mansfield Town (46-5), Stoke City (26-3)

Forwards
Bob Askey: Port Vale
Steve Burr: Stafford Rangers, Lichfield, Atherstone
John Askey: Milton
Dave Esser: Witton Albion, Northwich Victoria, Witton Albion, Altrincham, Hyde United, Karlskrona (Swe), Rochdale (180-24), Everton

Unfortunately we didn't receive a photograph from Macclesfield

Bangor City celebrate after their First Round Victory in the European Cup Winners Cup. Photo: Eric Marsh

MARINE

President: G. R. Baker
Chairman: P. T. Culshaw
Manager: Roley Howard
Coach: Roger Patience
Physiotherapist: Jimmy Graham
Press Officer & Tel. No: John Wildman
Secretary: W. Reid
Address & Tel. No: 76 Sunnyside Road, Liverpool L23 3AZ. Tel. 051-924 8469 (H), 051-207 3388 (B)
Commercial Manager: None
Address & Tel. No of ground: Rossett Park, College Road, Crosby, Liverpool 23. Tel. 051-924 4046
Simple ground directions: Mersey Rail Nth Line, Blundellsands/Crosby (10min walk)
Club shop: Yes
No of seats: 4000 **Covered accommodation:** 2,500 **Capacity:** 4,000 **Floodlights:** Yes
Year formed: 1894 **Nickname:** Mariners **Club sponsors:** Brosley Homes
Previous names: None
Club colours: White Shirts, Black Shorts/Socks
Change colours: Yellow Shirts/Socks, White Shorts
Day for midweek home matches: Tuesday
Record attendance: 4,000 v Nigeria **Year:** 1947
Previous Leagues:
I. Zingari, Liverpool Combination, Lancashire Combination and Cheshire
Best performance in: **F.A. Cup:** 1975-6v Hartlepool 2nd Round
F.A. Trophy: 1983-84 Semi-Final
Clubhouse details: Open all week. Concert hall 250 seats (fore hire), Lounge 150 seats. Snooker Room with Bar
Present players with Football League experience: Tony Quinn (Wigan), Paul Meachin (Southport)
Past players who progressed into the Football League: Mark Kearney (Mansfield Town), John Lacy (Fulham and Tottenham Hotspur)
Record transfer fee paid: None
Record transfer fee received: £10,000 for Mark Kearney from Everton
Programme details: 12 pages, 30p
Programme Editor: John Wildman
Local newspapers & Tel No: Crosby Herald, 71 36655; Liverpool Echo, Daily Post, 051-227 2000
Club metal badges: Yes
Senior Honours: F.A. Amateur Cup Finalists, Lancashire Junior Cup, Cheshire County League Champions (3), Liverpool Senior Cup, Lancashire Combination Cup (3)
Club Captain (1985-86): Peter Smith **Player of the Year (1985-86):** Paul Edwards

Goalkeepers
Kevin O'Brien: South Liverpool, Runcorn, Chorley, Oswestry Town, Burscough, Rhyl, New Brighton, Maghull, Everton
Brian Parkinson: South Liverpool, Marine, Los Angeles Aztecs (USA), Witton Albion, Winsford United

Defenders
Paul Dawson: Winsford United
Paul Edwards: Local
Peter Smith: Los Angeles Aztecs (USA), Marine, Wrexham
Keith Johnson: Prescot Cables
Jonathan Gautrey: Southport, Bolton Wanderers

Midfield
Tony Edwards: Witton Albion, Skelmersdale United, Liverpool
Paul Proctor: Tranmere Rovers
Glenn Walker: Horwich R.M.I., Crewe Alexandra (2)
John Smith: Workington, Halifax Town (28-6), Preston N.E. (91-4)

Forwards
Derek McClatchey: Barrow, Liverpool
Jimmy Williams: Witton Albion, Oswestry Town, Liverpool
Darrell McCarty: Bolton Wanderers, Leyland Motors, Horwich R.M.I., Chorley
Steve Haw: Kirkby Town, South Liverpool
Paul Meachin: New Brighton, Southport (3)

Back Row (l to r): Jimmy Graham (Physio), Paul Dawson, John Gautry, John Smith, Kevin O'Brien, Glen Walker, Keith Johnson, Paul Meachin, Roger Patience (Assistant Manager).
Front Row (l to r): Paul Edwards, Derek McClatchey, Peter Smith (Capt), Roley Howard (Manager), Tony Edwards, Jimmy Williams.

MATLOCK TOWN F.C.

President: D. T. Carr
Chairman: C. Britland
Manager: E. Oliver
Coach: D. Pugh
Physiotherapist: T. McDonald
Press Officer & Tel. No: G. M. Tomlinson, 0629 3763
Secretary: K. F. Brown
Address & Tel. No: 'Janeith', 6 Malvern Gardens, Matlock, Derbyshire. Tel. 0629 4321 (H), 033-525 301 (W)
Commercial Manager: Mrs S. Tomlinson
Address & Tel. No of ground: Causeway Lane, Matlock, Derbyshire. Tel. 0629 55362
Simple ground directions: 500 yards from town centre on A615
Club shop: Yes
No of seats: 240 **Covered accommodation:** 2,000 **Capacity:** 7,500 **Floodlights:** Yes
Year formed: 1885/86 **Nickname:** The Gladiators **Club sponsors:** None
Previous names: None
Club colours: Royal Blue Shirts/Socks, White Shorts
Change colours: All Yellow
Day for midweek home matches: Tuesday
Record attendance: 5,123 v Burton Albion, Semi-Final F.A. Trophy **Year:** 1975
Previous League:
Matlock & District, Central Alliance, Midland League
Best performance in: **F.A. Cup:** 3rd Round Proper 1976/77
F.A. Trophy: Winners 1974/75
Clubhouse details: Gladiators Social Club situated on ground, open 6 nights a week
Present players with Football League experience:
Past players who progressed into the Football League: Wayne Biggins (Burnley, Norwich)
Record transfer fee paid: £300 to Grantham for Mick Chambers
Record transfer fee received: £7,500 for Wayne Biggins from Burnley
Programme details: 12 pages, 15p
Programme Editor: D. Phillips, 0629 55035
Local newspapers & Tel No: Matlock Mercury, Derbyshire Times
Club metal badges: Yes
Senior Honours: Northern Premier League: Runners Up, League Cup Winners, Challenge Shield Winners; Derbyshire Senior Cup: Winners (5)
Club Captain (1985-86): Alan Lukasik **Player of the Year (1985-86):** Ian Travis

Goalkeepers
Stewart Wilson: Dronfield United, Horden C.W.

Defenders
Mark Fletcher: Bradford City (6), Barnsley (1)
Ian Travis: Heanor Town, Matlock Town, Lincoln City
Andy Bircumshaw: Burton Albion, Matlock Town, King's Lynn, Mansfield Town
Alan Lukasik: Oxley Park, Matlock Town
Steve Myles: Frickley Athletic, Worksop Town, Sheffield Wednesday

Midfield
Ian Smith: Frickley Athletic, Scarborough, Mossley
Steve Hirst: Buxton, Boston United, Ilkeston Town, Long Eaton United
Del Chambers: Sheffield United
Mark Frid: Spalding United, Woolley M.W., Worsbrough Bridge M.W.
Nick Fenoughty: Buxton, Stafford Rangers, Matlock Town, St. Georges Budapest (Aus), Matlock Town
Mark Rhodes: Rotherham United (258-13)

Forwards
Steve Shutt: Goole Town, Scunthorpe United (2-1), Goole Town, Barnsley (1)
Allan Semley: Barnsley (4)
Ian Helliwell: Chesterfield
Graham Hoyland: Worksop Town

Unfortunately we didn't receive a photograph from Matlock Town

Action from the St. Helens v Morecambe F.A. Cup Replay. Photo: Eric Marsh.

MORECAMBE

President: G. Newsham
Chairman: E. Weldrake
Manager: J. Wojciechowicz
Coach: R. Lockwood
Physiotherapist: W. C. Carleton
Press Officer & Tel. No: L. Taylor. Tel. 0524 52593
Secretary: K. D. Ormrod
Address & Tel. No: 16 Battismore Road, Morecambe LA4 4QG. Tel. 0524 415324 (H), 0524 55611 ext. 211 (W)
Commercial Manager: None
Address & Tel. No of ground: Christie Park, Lancaster Road, Morecambe LA4 5TJ. Tel. 0524 411797/417849
Simple ground directions: Main Town Centre Road
Club shop: Yes
No of seats: 1,250 **Covered accommodation:** 3 sides **Capacity:** 9,750 **Floodlights:** Yes
Year formed: 1920 **Nickname:** Shrimps **Club sponsors:** Carleton Caterers
Previous names: Seasiders (nickname)
Club colours: Red with White Sleeves, White Shorts, Red Socks
Change colours: White/White/Red
Day for midweek home matches: Tuesday
Record attendance: 12,000 F.A. Cup 3rd Round v Weymouth **Year:** 1962
Previous League:
Lancashire Combination
Best performance in: **F.A. Cup:** 1962 3rd Round v Weymouth
F.A. Trophy: 1974 Winners
Clubhouse details: World Cup Bar
Present players with Football League experience:
Past players who progressed into the Football League: R. Charnley (Blackpool, England), A. Taylor (Rochdale, West Ham, Burnley), R. Mitchell (Leeds United)
Record transfer fee paid: £400 for K. Galley (Netherfield) and N. Halsall (Chorley)
Record transfer fee received: £2,500 for Alan Taylor from Rochdale
Programme details: 20 pages, 30p
Programme Editor: L. Taylor, K. Ormrod, M. Hoyle
Local newspapers & Tel No: Morecambe Visitor, Tel. 9524 414531
Club metal badges: Yes
Senior Honours: F.A. Trophy, Lancs Comb. (5), Lancs Junior Cup (4), Lancs Senior Cup, Lancs Comb. Cup (3)
Club Captain (1985-86): K. Kennedy **Player of the Year (1985-86):** K. Galley

Goalkeepers
Peter McDonnell: Barrow, Hong Kong Rangers, Oldham Athletic (137), Liverpool, Bury (1), Netherfield

Defenders
Graham Jones: Gainsborough Trinity, Bradford City (4)
Keith Kennedy: Barrow, Mansfield Town (35), Bury (405-4), Newcastle United (1)
David Large: Barrow
Kenny Gordon: Barrow
Steve Brooks: Halifax Town (16), Barrow, Hartlepool (63-2), Southport (65-3), Marine

Midfield
Jon Balm: Barrow, Everton
Mark Walsh: Preston N.E. (62-2)
Graham Gill: Workington, K.T.V. Kokkola (Fin), Lancast
City, Netherfield, Leyland Motors
Dave Woodburn: Barrow
David Wynn: Local

Forwards
Keith Galley: Netherfield, Morecambe, Southport (60-11
Rochdale, Telford United, Morecambe
Jimmy Thornton: Marine, South Liverpool
Peter Sayer: Chester City (36-6), Preston N.E. (45-6), Bright
(55-6), Cardiff City (82-14)
David McNiven: Halifax Town (12-4), Blackpool (49-1
Bradford City (212-64), Leeds United (22-6)

Back Row (l to r): R. Lockwood (Coach), K. Gordon, M. Walsh, P. McDonnell, G. Gill, S. Brooks, J. Balm, K. Galley, J. Wojciechowicz (Manager).
Front row (l to r): P. Sayer, G. Jones, K. Kennedy, J. Thornton, D. Wynn.

MOSSLEY

President: John Heap
Chairman: Jim Wharmby
Manager: Jimmy O'Connor
Coach: Paul Webb
Physiotherapist: Peter Ward

Press Officer & Tel. No: As Secretary
Secretary: Brian Cowburn
Address & Tel. No: 11 Windsor Road, Hyde, Cheshire SK14 5JB. Tel. 061-368 21256 (H), 061-320 4806 (B) **Commercial Manager:** Brian Gesty, C/O Mossley A.F.C.

Address & Tel. No of ground: Seel Park, Market Street, Mossley, Ashton-Under-Lyne, Lancs. Tel. 04575 2369
Simple ground directions: Off M62 from West via Oldham, From East via Saddleworth. From Manchester via Ashton-Under-Lyne
Club shop: Yes
No of seats: 250 **Covered accommodation:** 1,450 **Capacity:** 4,000 **Floodlights:** Yes
Year formed: 1909 **Nickname:** Lilywhites **Club sponsors:** Service Print
Previous names: None
Club colours: All White

Record attendance: 7,000 v Stalybridge Celtic **Year:** 1950
Previous Leagues:
Ashton, S.E. Lancs, Manchester AM, Cheshire County
Best performance in: **F.A. Cup:** 2nd Round 1980
F.A. Trophy: Finalists 1980
Clubhouse details: Open nights and matchdays
Present players with Football League experience:
Past players who progressed into the Football League: A. Tyrer (Leeds), P. Tilley (Arsenal, Bury), Don Megson (Sheff. Wed.), Harvey McReadie (Hibs), Alan Roberts (Bradford), Gary Pierce (Wolves, Hudd Town), Eamon O'Keefe (Everton), David Young (Wigan)
Record transfer fee paid: £2,300 for Phil Wilson
Record transfer fee received: £25,000 for Eamon O'Keefe
Programme details: Every match
Programme Editor: Mike Smith
Local newspapers & Tel No: Oldham Evening Chronicle; Saddleworth & Mossley Reporter
Club metal badges: No
Senior Honours: N.P.L. Champions 1978-79, 1979-80, Runners up (3), N.P.L. Cup Winner, Runners up (2)
Club Captain (1985-86): Jim Connor **Player of the Year (1985-86):** Jim Connor

MOSSLEY
Goalkeepers
Roger Lewis: Bolton St., Winsford United, Rossendale United
Phil Pritchard: Stafford Rangers, Stoke City

Defenders
David Fretwell: Northwich Victoria, Wigan Athletic (112), Carolina Lightning (USA), Bradford City (253-5)
Craig Wardle: Macclesfield Town, Bolton W.
Dave McDougall: Highfield United
Mike Grech: Local
Jim Connor: Dunedin City (N.Z.), Burscough
Gary Devany: Rossendale United

Midfield
Jimmy O'Connor: Droylsden, Runcorn, Macclesfield Town, Mossley, Bury
Kevin Glendon: Witton Albion, Burnley (4), Hyde United, Crewe Alexandra (4), Manchester City
Jimmy Golder: Northwich Victoria, Hyde United, Witton Albion, New Mills, Stalybridge Celtic, Stockport County
Gary Stewart: Irlam Town
Peter Beaumont: Radcliffe Borough, Accrington Stanley

Forwards
Martin Farnworth: Rossendale United, Accrington Stanley
Gary Dunford: Accrington Stanley
Martin Forry: Highfield United, Rossendale United, Winsford United
Joe Connor: Hyde United, Stockport County, Stalybridge Celtic

Mossley F.C.

OSWESTRY TOWN

President: Ted Williams
Chairman: Tony Jones
Manager: Trevor Storton
Coach: Trevor Phillips
Physiotherapist: Colin Storton

Press Officer & Tel. No: Secretary
Secretary: James Bond
Address & Tel. No: 86 Upper Church Street, Oswestry, Shropshire SY11 2AF
Commercial Manager: Carleton Leonard

Address & Tel. No of ground: Victoria Road, Oswestry, Shropshire. Tel. 0691 653800
Simple ground directions: From north M56 (M53 from Merseyside) and Chester by-pass to Wrexham and Oswestry (A483/A5) into town centre turn left at light, ground ¼ on right. From Potteries, through Whitchurch and follow A495 to Oswestry towne centre, then as above. From South, A6 then A4083 to Oswestry, fork left after hump-back bridge for ground
Club shop: Yes
No of seats: 350 **Covered accommodation:** 1,500 **Capacity:** 5,000 **Floodlights:** Yes
Year formed: 1860 **Nickname:** Blues **Club sponsors:**
Previous names:
Club colours: Blue Shirts with White Sleeves, White Shorts/socks
Change colours: All Yellow
Day for midweek home matches: Wednesday
Record attendance: 5,500 v Hereford United **Year:** 1950
Previous League:
Various local leagues, then Lancashire Combination, Welsh League, Birmingham League, Cheshire League, Southern League

Programme details: 12 pages, 20p
Programme Editor: Mike Clarke, 50 Langland Rod, Oswestry. Tel. 0691 661985
Local newspapers & Tel No: North Shropshire News Agency, Tel. 0691 650501; Shropshire Star, Tel. 0691 654251; Shropshire Radio Sport. Tel. 0743 248484
Club metal badges: Yes

Best performance in: **F.A. Cup:** 1st round proper 1927 v Stockport
F.A. Trophy: 2nd round proper 1979
Clubhouse details: Oswestrian Sports and Social Club, open most days, and for functions
Present players with Football League experience:
Past players who progressed into the Football League: G. Williams, E. Potts, S. Sharratt, H. Roberts, G. Antonio, G. Pulley, K. Thomas, N. Hobson, W. Shadbolt, C. Sear, F. Morris, P. Bebbington, I. Hughes, J. Quinn, E. Rogers, G. Davies, S. Roberts. Alan Ball (Senior) went into Football League management after managing Oswestry
Record transfer fee paid: £2,000 for Jim Smith from Stafford Rangers)
Record transfer fee received: £5,000 from Sheffield Wednesday for Billy Shadbolt
Senior Honours: Welsh Cup Winners (3), Shropshire Cup Winners (11).
Club Captain (1985-86): Derek Goulding **Player of the Year (1985-86):** Phil McFerran

Goalkeepers
Steve Ellison: Local

Defenders
Derek Goulding: Stafford Rangers, Bangor City, Altrincham, Prescot Cables
Steve Guest: Netherfield
Trevor Storton: Chester City (396-17), Liverpool (5), Tranmere Rovers (118-9)
Paul Needham: Chester City (60-1)
Alan Roberts: Cammell Lairds
Peter Donnelly: Chester City (1)
Midfield
Bryn Jones: Witton Albion, Oswestry Town, Bangor City, Scarborough, Chester City (162-17)
Danny Nield: Local
Phil McFerran: South Liverpool, Bootle, Burscough, South Liverpool, Macclesfield Town, Witton Albion, Marine
Steve Lampkin: Bradford City (7-1)
Dave Barbour: Local
Trevor Phillips: Chester City (10-2), Oswestry Town, Stockport County (54-5), Chester City (66-11), Hull City (24-3), Rotherham United (363-92)

Forwards
Phil Williams: Crewe Alexandra (20-3), Wigan Athletic (3), Crewe Alexandra (39-3), Blackpool, Arsenal
Chris Camden: Chester City (9-2), Tranmere Rovers
Peter Henderson: Winsford United, Witton Albion, Macclesfield Town, Runcorn, Telford United, Chester City (28-5), Gillingham (7-3), Chester City (64-10), Witton Albion
Adrian Jones: Local
Owen Brown: Hyde United, Chester City (10-3), Tranmere Rovers (56-12), Crewe Alexandra (1), Tranmere Rovers (37-8), Carlisle United (4-2), Liverpool

Oswestry Town's 'Player of The Year' Phil McFerron (left) and top scorer Bryn Jones receive their trophies from Club officials Mel Holgate (Far Left) and Mike Clarke.
Photo: Star Journal

RHYL F.C.

Chairman: M. Georgieff-Jones
Manager: PEter Owen
Coach:
Physiotherapist: R. Davison
Press Officer & Tel. No: P. Espin. Tel. 53704
Secretary: John B. Williams
Address & Tel. No: 7 Parc Esmor, Rhyl, Clwyd. Tel. 50566
Commercial Manager: None
Tel No:
Address & Tel. No of ground: Belle Vue
Simple ground directions: Opposite Rhyl Sports Centre (follow signs)
Club shop: Yes
No of seats: 200 **Covered accommodation:** 1,000 **Capacity:** 6,200 **Floodlights:** Yes
Year formed: 1928 **Nickname:** Lilywhites **Club sponsors:**
Previous names:
Club colours: White/Blue/White
Change colours: All Red
Day for midweek home matches: Wednesday
Record attendance: 10,000 v Cardiff City, Welsh Cup **Year:** 1953
Previous League:
Cheshire County (N. West Counties)
Best performance in: **F.A. Cup:** 4th Round
F.A. Trophy: 1st Round Proper
Clubhouse details: Fully equipped social club
Present players with Football League experience:
Past players who progressed into the Football League: Ian Edwards, Grenville Millington, Brian Lloyd, Andy Holden, Barry Horne and Andy Jones
Record transfer fee paid:
Record transfer fee received: £3,000 from Port Vale for Andy Jones
Programme details: 24 pages, 25p
Programme Editor: W. H. Prandle. Tel. 37409
Local newspapers & Tel No: Rhyl Journal, Rhyl and Prestatyn Visitor
Club metal badges: No
Senior Honours:
Club Captain (1985-86): Terry Nugent
Player of the Year (1985-86): Terry Nugent

Goalkeepers
Gareth Hughes: Bangor City

Defenders
Peter Newey: Worksop Town
Dean Martin: Local
Paul Harrison: Local
Alan Morris: Bangor City, Chester City (1), Bangor City, Caernarfon Town
Terry Nugent: Local
Mark Joseph: Oswestry Town, Wrexham
Micky Kilduff: Witton Albion, Runcorn, Oswestry Town, Marine, Telford United, Oswestry Town, Bangor City, Coventry City

Midfield
Paul Blackwell: Chester City (94-3)
Kevin Rogers: Wrexham (35-3), Birmingham City (98-1), Aston Villa
Mark Palios: Southport, Bangor City, Tranmere Rovers (59-7), Crewe Alexandra (118-23), Tranmere Rovers (190-25)
Allan Bickerstaff: Local
Andy Puddle: Bangor City
Tim Williams: Local

Forwards
John Allen: Bangor City, Mansfield Town (2), Chester City (79-5)
Carl Dale: Conwy United
Selwyn Morris: Local
Steve Fox: Tamworth, Chester City (32-4), Port Vale (74-6), Wrexham (142-10), Birmingham City (29-1), Tamworth
Adrian Nixon: Local
Geraint Davies: Local

Top Row: Gerrant Davies, Barry Roberts, Gareth Hughes, Brian Davies (moved to Bangor City), Mark Joseph, Adrian Nixon, Russell Davison (Physiotherapist) Darren Johnson. Bottom Row: Terry Nugent, Allan Bickerstaff, Dean Martin, Kevin Warner, Tim Williams, Bobby Woods, Kenny Pollard.

SOUTH LIVERPOOL

President: J. E. Hesketh
Chairman: J. B. Smith
Manager: C. M. Roberts
Coach: B. Whitbread
Physiotherapist: J. Bakstad
Press Officer & Tel. No: D. McCormick. Tel. 051-428 1946
Secretary: J. C. Stanway
Address & Tel. No: 10 Olive Vale, Wavertree, Liverpool L15 8JH. Tel. 051-733 1286 (H), 051-709 0150 (B)
Commercial Manager: c/o Manager

Address & Tel. No of ground: Holly Park, Garston, Liverpool L19 5NQ. Tel. 051-427 7372
Simple ground directions: M62, left Queens Drive, left Allerton Road, right Mather Avenue, adj. Allerton stn. Also follow signs for Garston, M56, follow signs for Liverpool Airport, turn right after Speke Road Gardens
Club shop: Yes
No of seats: 500 **Covered accommodation:** 2,000 **Capacity:** 6,000 **Floodlights:** Yes
Year formed: 1934 **Nickname:** South **Club sponsors:** MSS
Previous names: None
Club colours: White Shirts, Black Shorts, Red/Black Socks
Change colours: Various
Day for midweek home matches: Wednesay
Record attendance: 13,000 v Nigerian XI**Year:** 1949
Previous League:
Lancashire Combination, Cheshire League
Best performance in: **F.A. Cup:** 1937-7 v QPR, 1937-8 v Brighton, 1964-5 v Workington, 2nd Round
F.A. Trophy: Goole Town, 2nd Round 1974
Clubhouse details: To be open July 1986. Seven nights a week, Saturday and Sunday lunchtime
Present players with Football League experience:
Past players who progressed into the Football League: Billy Jones (Bolton), Jimmy Case (Liverpool), Joe Hinnigan (Wigan), Peter Houghton (Wigan), John Aldridge (Newport), Peter Billinge (Everton)
Record transfer fee paid: None
Record transfer fee received: From Everton for Peter Billinge
Programme details: 16 pages, 20p
Programme Editor: R. Ruddock
Local newspapers & Tel No: Liverpool Daily Post & Echo, Liverpool Star, Merseymart
Club metal badges: Yes
Senior Honours: Lancashire Combination Winners 1937, 1938, 1939, 1966; Lancashire Challenge Trophy Winners 1937, 1938, 1939, 1984; Liverpool Senior Cup Winners 1984, 1986; N.P. League Cup Winners 1984
Club Captain (1985-86): John Carroll **Player of the Year (1985-86):** Dave Thompson

Goalkeepers
Dick Johnson: Burscough, Altrincham, Tranmere Rovers (355)
Russ Hughes: Local

Defenders
Lawrence Iro: Altrincham, Southport, Wigan Athletic, Liverpool
Dave Higgins: Tranmere Rovers (28), Eagle
Dave Thompson: Cammell Lairds, Poulton Vics, Hoylake, Oswestry Town
John Carroll: Local
Peter Billing: Local
Tim Rutter: Witton Albion, Telford United, Runcorn

Midfield
Ian Baker: Altrincham, South Liverpool
Dave Anderson: Caernarfon Town, South Liverpool, Runcorn
Jimmy Blackhurst: Marine, Formby
John McInnes: Southport, Liverpool
Kevin Harrison: St. Dominics
Ronnie Kilshaw: Southport, Prescot Cables, Runcorn, Tranmere Rovers, Liverpool

Forwards
Barry Whitbread: Runcorn, Lancaster City, Marine, Altrincham, Runcorn, Northwich Victoria, Macclesfield Town
Mick Thomas: Local
Gary Wade: Local
Steve Whittingham: Southport, Tranmere Rovers (2)
Steve Jones: Heswall

Back row (l to r): Jim Bakstad (Trainer), Stuart Parker, Lawrence Iro, Ian Baker, Derek Brownbill, Kevin Harrison, John Carroll (Capt), Steve Skeete, Colin Ridler, Steve Whittingham, Barry Whitbread (Assistant Manager).
Front row (l to r); John McInnes, Jimmy Blackhurst, Cliff Roberts (Manager), Peter Withers, Dave Thompson.

SOUTHPORT

President: None
Chairman: C. Clapham
Manager: Bryan Griffiths
Commercial Manager: Charlie Clapham
Press Officer & Tel. No. Peter Williams
Secretary: Peter Williams
Address & Tel. No. 3, Sunnyside, Southport, Merseyside PR8 2EE (0704) 66646
Tel. No. 0704 44170 (H), 051 486 6101 (B)
Address and Tel. No. of ground: Haig Avenue, Southport. Tel: 0704 33422. Social Club 0704 30930**Club shop:** Yes
Simple ground directions: Signposted on all roads into Southport
No. of seats: 1,576 **Covered accommodation:** Three sides **Capacity:** 15,000 **Floodlights:** Yes
Year formed: 1881 **Nickname:** The Sandgrounders **Club sponsors:** None
Previous names: Southport Vulcan, Southport Central
Club colours: Old Gold and Black
Change colours: Blue/White Trim
Previous grounds: Ash Lane
Day for midweek home matches: Tuesday
Record attendance: 20,000 v Newcastle United, F.A. Cup 1932
Best performance in: **F.A. Cup:** 1930, 6th Round as Football League Club.
F.A. Trophy: 1985-86 Last sixteen
Previous Leagues: Football League
Clubhouse details: Directors' Ladies, VIP Lounges. Club on ground (0704 30930)
Present players with Football League experience: Paul Lodge, Peter King, Brian Jackson
Past players who progressed into the Football League: Numerous
Record transfer fee paid: 6,000 for Malcolm
Record transfer fee received: £16,000 for Tony Field
Programme editor: Simon Williams
Club Metal Badges: Yes £1 including postage
Local newspapers & Tel. No. Southport Visitor (0704 36655), Southport Star (0704 34237)
Senior Honours: Divison Four Champions & Runners-Up

SOUTHPORT
Goalkeepers
Paul Evans: Blackpool
Glen Campbell: Preston N.E. (18)

Defenders
George Carr: Heswall, Macclesfield Town
Ronnie Naden: South Liverpool
Shaun Teale: Ellesmere Port & Neston, Burscough, Huddersfield Town, Everton
Andy Reid: Witton Albion, Worksop Town
Rob Sturgeon: Formby, Coventry City
Ray Mawson: Marine, Southport, Dingle Rail
Kenny Tym: Chorley, Morecambe, Marine, St. Helens Town

Midfield
Mick Fagan: Altrincham, Burscough, Runcorn, Macclesfield Town
Chris Hunter: Chorley, Preston N.E. (5), Chorley, Preston N.E. (1)
David Bleasdale: Altrincham, Preston N.E. (5), Liverpool
Peter King: Crewe Alexandra (64-5), Liverpool
Graham Rowlands: Preston N.E.

Forwards
Tony Quinn: Marine, H.J.K. Helsingfors (Fin), Morecambe, Witton Albion, Wigan Athletic (43-4)
John Brady: Altrincham, Southport, Burscough
Kevin McCormack: Local
John Coleman: Marine, Burscough

Unfortunately we didn't receive a photograph from Southport

A view of the Main Stand at Workington

WITTON ALBION

President: P. Lynch
Chairman: P. Broadhurst
Manager: J. C. Rogers
Coach: G. Heathcote
Physiotherapist: C. Dutton
Press Officer & Tel. No: V. Conneeley
Secretary: D. M. Leather
Address & Tel. No: 34 Grosvenor Avenue, Hartford, Northwich, Cheshire. Tel. 76488
Commercial Manager: J. O'Brien
Address & Tel. No of ground: Central Ground, Albion Way, Northwich. Tel. 3493
Simple ground directions: M6 junction 19, follow A556 into Northwich, 1st right after roundabout, down by side of 'Shell' garage and first left after 50 yds
Club shop: Yes
No of seats: 600 **Covered accommodation:** 1,500 **Capacity:** 8,500 **Floodlights:** Yes
Year formed: 1890 **Nickname:** Albion **Club sponsors:** County Glass
Previous names: None
Club colours: Red/WhiteStripes, Red Socks
Change colours: Amber/White/Amber
Day for midweek home matches: Tuesday
Record attendance: 10,000 v Northwich Victoria**Year:** 1948
Previous League:
Cheshire County League (Now North West Counties League)
Programme details: Albion Review
Programme Editor: P. Chadwick
Local newspapers & Tel No: Northwich Chronicle, Northwich Guardian
Club metal badges: Yes
Best performance in: **F.A. Cup:** 1951-2 v Workington 2nd Round Proper
F.A. Trophy: 1978-9. 1081-2 3rd Round Proper
Clubhouse details: Conert Room, Lounge, open 7 nights per week
Present players with Football League experience:
Past players who progressed into the Football League: Peter Henderson to Chester, Chris Nicholl (now Southampton Manager), Peter Mellor, Dave Carrick
Record transfer fee paid: £800 to Oswestry Town for M. Brennan
Record transfer fee received: £10,500 from Chester City for P. Henderson
Senior Honours: Cheshire County League (3), Cheshire County F.A. Senior Cup (5)
Club Captain (1985-86): Dave Pennell **Player of the Year (1985-86):** Noel Bradley

Goalkeepers
Mike Sherlock: Macclesfield Town, Mossley, Macclesfield Town, Rochdale

Defenders
Trevor Brissett: Stafford Rangers, Darlington (12), Port Vale (55), Stoke City
Russ Hooton: Droylsden, Mossley, South Liverpool, Stockport County
Noel Bradley: Mossley, Chester City (35), Bury (28-1), Manchester City
Dave Pennell: Southport, Burscough, Runcorn
Benny Phillips: Barrow, Witton Albion, Mossley, Stalybridge Celtic, Bury (14), Crewe Alexandra
Dave Constantine: Winsford United, Altrincham, Bury (70-2), Hyde United

Midfield
Graham Heathcote: Altrincham, Northwich Victori: Altrincham
Paul Cross: South Liverpool
Terry Megram: Curzon Ashton, Northwich Victoria
Keven Hawkins: South Liverpool, Altrincham
Steve Phillips: Horwich R.M.I., Irlam Town

Forwards
Bob Horton: Leek Town, Northwich Victoria, Leek Town
Barry Howard: Hyde United, Altrincham, Stockport County Runcorn, Hyde United
Terry Farrell: Chester City, Caernarfon Town, Oswestry Town Stafford Rangers, Oswestry Town, Whitchurch Alport
Malcolm Wagstaffe: Winsford United, Urmston Town, Wittor Albion, Mossley, Marine, Irlam Town
Kevin Scarborough: Prestwich Heys, Mossley, Stalybridge Celtic, Hyde United, Witton Albion

Buch row (l to r): C. Dutton, D. Goodwin, E. Blore, A. Salmon, M. Kilduff, M. Sherlock, T. Brissett, N. Bradley, B. Hughes, K. Scarborough, D. Brownbill.
Front row (l to r): T. Farrell, T. Megram, D. Esser, B. Phillps, L. Sutton, B. Howard, D. Garner, T. Rutter, G. Heathcote.
(Photo: Northwich Guardian)

WORKINGTON

President: E. D. Smith
Chairman:
Manager: W. Harrison
Coach:
Physiotherapist: I. Hodgson
Press Officer & Tel. No: Secretary

Secretary: Colin W. Doorbar
Address & Tel. No: Hartside, 87D Main Road, High Harrington, Workington, Cumbria CA14 4LH. Tel. 0900 3332 (D), 0946 830832 (E)
Commercial Manager: Grant Payne

Address & Tel. No of ground: 0900 2871
Simple ground directions: On entering Workington to T Junction turn right to Maryport under bridge 20 yds turn right, stadium 150 yds on left
Club shop: Yes
No of seats: 400 **Covered accommodation:** 1,200 **Capacity:** 10,000 **Floodlights:** Yes
Year formed: 1884 **Nickname:** The Reds **Club sponsors:** None
Previous names: None
Club colours: Red/Red

Record attendance: 21,000 v Manchester United **Year:** 1958
Previous League:
Football League
Best performance in: **F.A. Cup:** 1934 4th Round
F.A. Trophy: 1977-8
Clubhouse details: Bar open match days, voluntary staff
Present players with Football League experience:
Past players who progressed into the Football League:
Record transfer fee paid: B. Donaghy from W.B.A.
Record transfer fee received: I. McDonald to Liverpool
Programme details: 16 pages, 20p
Programme Editor: Steve Durham
Local newspapers & Tel No: Evening News, Times and Star.
Tel. John Walsh 0900 5801
Club metal badges: Yes
Senior Honours: Promotion from Division Four, Cumberland Cup Winners
Club Captain (1985-86): Martin Gaffney **Player of the Year (1985-86):** Billy Gilmour

Goalkeepers
Keith Hunton: Local
Mike McMullen: Penrith, Birmingham City

Defenders
Martin Gaffney: Carlisle City, Bury, Workington, Hartlepool
Tony Chilton: Hartlepool, Burnley (1), Sunderland
Ian Johnston: Local (49)
Keith Rowntree: Local
Chris Collins: Local

Midfield
Alan Carruthers: Penrith, Netherfield, Carlisle Spartans, Coventry City
Mark Dobie: Carlisle City
John George: Local
Kenny Wallace: Penrith, Workington (6)
Wayne Harrison: Barrow, Workington, Blackpool (86-6), Sheffield Wednesday, Workington (4), Everton
Gary Messenger: Local

Forwards
Billy Gilmour: Gretna, Penrith
Jimmy Irvin: Local
Martin Harris: Scarborough, Morecambe, Burton Albion, Hartlepool (1), Workington (106-13), Grimsby Town
Peter McClachlan: Carlisle City, Netherfield, Carlisle United
Tony Stones: Cleator United

Back row (l to r): Paul Tynan (now Ipswich), Tony Stones, Gary Messenger, Ian Johnston, Andy Horne (now left club), Keith Hunton, Keith Sawyers, Martin Gaffney, Eric Snookes (left the club), coach Ron Lewin (sadly deceased).
Front row (l to r): Mark Dobie, Graham Emerson, Manager Wayne Harrison, Tony Chilton, Kevin Rowntree, Martin Harris, Alan Carruthers.

WORKSOP TOWN

President:
Chairman: J. Saunders
Manager: T. Spencer
Coach: J. Scott
Physiotherapist:

Press Officer & Tel. No: A. A. Ridsdale
Secretary: A. A. Ridsdale
Address & Tel. No: Tigers Club, Netherholme Precinct, Worksop. Tel. 0909 475008 (H), 0909 480784 (B)
Commercial Manager: None

Address & Tel. No of ground: Central Avenue, Worksop. Tel. 0909 480784
Simple ground directions: Town centre to rear of Netherholme Shopping Precinct, M1 Junction 30 (South) Junction 31 (North)
Club shop: Yes
No of seats: 300 **Covered accommodation:** 2,000 **Capacity:** 6,000 **Floodlights:** Yes
Year formed: 1861 **Nickname:** Tigers **Club sponsors:**
Previous names:
Club colours: Amber/Black/Black
Day for midweek home matches: Wednesday
Record attendance: 8,171 v Chestefield F.A. Cup **Year:** 1925
Previous League:
Midland Counties
Best performance in: **F.A. Cup:** Last 64
F.A. Trophy:
Clubhouse details: The Tigers offers bar snacks, disco, parties catered for
Present players with Football League experience:
Past players who progressed into the Football League: Bert Bowery (Notts Forest), Jack Brown (Sheffield Wed, England), Alan Hodgkinson (Sheffield Utd, England)
Record transfer fee paid: None
Record transfer fee received: £2,000 from Nottingham Forest for Bert Bowery
Programme details: 12 pages, 25p
Programme Editor: A. A. Ridsdale
Local newspapers & Tel No: Worksop Guardian, 474747; Worksop Star, 486335; Nottingham Football Post, 0602 475221
Club metal badges: Yes
Senior Honours: N.P.L. Presidents Cup (1), Midland League Champions (3), Mansfield Charity Cup Winners (1), Sheffield Senior Cup Winners (7)
Club Captain (1985-86): Phil Annable **Player of the Year (1985-86):** Trevor Thompson, Phil Annable

Goalkeepers
Eddie Green: Retford Town, Grantham, Stamford, Grantham

Defenders
Phil Annable: Grantham, Burton Albion, Boston United, Burton Albion, Mansfield Town
Ian Vaughan: Gainsborough Trinity, Burton Albion, Rotherham United (6-1)
Russell Richardson: Scunthorpe United (2)
Trevor Thompson: Gainsborough Trinity, Lincoln City (80-1), Newport County (35-2), W.B.A. (20)
Kevin Woods: Matlock Town, Worksop Town, Tulsa Roughnecks (USA), Chesterfield

Midfield
Martin Hardy: Notts County
Gary Marrow: Burton Albion, Worksop Town, Kuuysi Lahti (Fin), Sheffield United
Steve Adams: Rotherham United
Graham Gladwin: Harworth Colliery, Sutton Town, Long Eaton United, Belper Town, Gainsborough Trinity, Notts County
Brian Strutt: Sheffield Wednesday

Forwards
Rob Haddrell: Spalding United, Worksop Town, Maltby Miners Welfare
Jeff Cook: Halifax Town (56-9), Plymouth Argyle (55-21), Stoke City (30-5), Hellenic (S.A.)
Paul Fisher; Gainsborough Trinity, Stafford Rangers, Burton Albion, Macclesfield Town, Worksop Town
Paul Cavell: Local

Back row (l to r): Paul Cavell, Brian Strutt, Martin Hardy, Gil Hopkinson, Phil Annable, Tim Wragg, Steve Adams.
Front row (l to r): Russell Richardson, John Stokes, Trevor Thompson, Jeff Cook, Craig Thompson, Gary Marrow.
(Before NPL President's Cup Final)

Leek 2 Macclesfield 1. F.A. Trophy 2nd. Round.

Leek Town. Back Row: Martin Parr (Phsio), N. Baker (asst. Manager), C. McMullen, F. Sromek, M. Brindley, M. Deville, S. Goldstraw, B. Mellor, K. Lewis (Manager). Front Row. T. Griffiths, C. France, A. Morgan, T. Robson, D. Mallaburn, G. Stribling, G. Pearce.

Kirkham Town (West Lancs).

THE BASS NORTH WEST COUNTIES FOOTBALL LEAGUE

President: Canon J. R. Smith, M.A.

Secretary: Fred Hunter, 53 Darby Road Liverpool L19 9BP. Tel. 051 427 1719 (H), 051 227 3911 ext. 785 (B)

In the closest finish yet to a N.W.C.F.L. season, the championship was only clinched by Clitheroe when they drew their last match of the programme at Irlam Town, thus winning the title on goal difference over runners-up Congleton Town. Clitheroe have therefore won the three divisions in consecutive seasons. For the last few weeks of the campaign most people assumed that Stalybridge Celtic would accumulate sufficient points from their games in hand to take the First Division crown; however, defeats at Netherfield, Leek and Clitheroe, in their last three games put an end to Stalybridge's dreams, and also their chance to again apply for Multipart League membership.

Kirkby Town romped away with the Second Division championship, leaving Rossendale United in their wake by seven points at the finish. Kirkby will now be aiming to 'do a Clitheroe' by topping the three divisions in three years.

In the Third Division, Blackpool Mechanics, despite losing two points for an infringement of rules early in the season, had the title sewn up by the end of March. Oldham Town, much publicised during the year for the television filming at their ground of popular childrens' programme 'Jossy's Giants', took runners-up position.

The Reserve Divisions, proving ever more popular, saw Chadderton emerge as Division I champions with St. Helen's Town second on goal difference, and Great Harwood Town winners of Division II followed a mere one point behind by Atherton L.R.

For the first time in four years of the N.W.C.F.L. the League Challenge Cup Final produced a result without the need for extra time, replay, or penalty shoot-out. Warrington of the Second Divison coming through as victors over Clitheroe by 2-0. This is the third time in four years that a Second Division outfit has reached the Final, and the second time that one has proved victorious. As always the match was staged at Bury's first class Gigg Lane ground.

In the annual match between League Champions and League Challenge Cup Winners, Warrington again came out on top by beating Clitheroe on their own Shawbridge ground by 3-1 on penalties after ninety minutes had proved goalless.

There being only fifteen clubs in the Third Division, a new trophy was competed for to make up a sufficient number of fixtures. This was the 'LUXOR' Trophy, sponsored by Swedish T.V. company Luxor. Atherton Collieries won a two-legged Final against Newton by an aggregate score of 5-2.

The Reserve Division Cup Final saw Irlam Town defeat near neighbours Curzon Ashton by 1-0. This match was kindly staged by Ashton United.

A successful season was enjoyed in National and County Competitions: the good progress made by several clubs causing the Fixture Secretary many headaches. St. Helen's Town reached the Fourth Qualifying Round of the F.A. Challenge Cup, losing 0-1 in a home replay versus Morecambe after drawing 1-1 at Christie Park. Leek Town carried the League banner in the F.A. Challenge Trophy, finally being put out 1-0 by Wycombe Wanderers in a third replay of the Third Round Proper, having earlier drawn 2-2, 5-5, and 1-1. In the F.A. Vase, Warrington Town strove hard to emulate Fleetwood Town's performance of last year, but unfortunately they were ousted in the semi-finals by Vase specialists Halesowen Town. This tie also went to a replay, at Telford, where Warrington lost 3-6 having drawn 1-1 and 3-3 in the original two legs.

Maghull won the Liverpool Challenge Cup by defeating Waterloo Dock 3-1; Curzon Ashton took home the Manchester Premier Cup after beating Irlam Town 1-0: and Eastwood (Hanley) ensured that the Staffordshire Senior Cup would be on show at the Annual Presentation in Blackpool by seeing off Bilston Town of the Southern League in a two-legged Final by 5-1 on aggregate.

In other County Competitions Member Clubs reached the semi- final stages of the Senior Cups of Cheshire, Cumberland, Lancashire and Liverpool. All-in-all a very good effort by everyone concerned.

The League enjoyed its first sponsorships during the season: A Manager-of-the-Month/Year Competition was sponsored by leading double-glazing company ASTRASEAL; leading sportswear manufacturers NIKE ran a Player-of-the-Month/Year Competition; as stated previously LUXOR sponsored the Third Division Cup Competition; and for the first time the League Challenge Cup Final was sponsored, this most generous boost being provided by L. A. McDONALD & SON (North-West) Limited of Ashton-Under-Lyne.

Now for 1986/87: From the commencement of the new season the League Championship will be known as THE BASS NORTH WEST COUNTIES FOOTBALL LEAGUE, being sponsored by famous brewers BASS. This arrangement is firm for three years, and it is hoped that it will continue long after this initial period. The Manager-of-the-Month will also be BASS sponsored in future.

The League is greatly indebted to all its sponsors, whose interest and financial help is much appreciated by Management and Member Clubs alike.

A new Secretary and an Assistant Secretary will be taking over for the new season, as I am retiring from Office having served ten years as Secretary, firstly with the Cheshire County League, and for the past four years the North West Counties.

May I close by wishing Fred Hunter (ex-Liverpool County Combination), the new Secretary, and John Deal his assistant, all the very best in their positions with the League. Also, many thanks and good wishes to all those connected with Non-League football with whom I have had meetings and dealings over the years.

Chris Mahood

Steven Norris (Captain of Eastwood Hanley F.C.) lifts The Staffordshire F.A. Senior Cup for the first time in the clubs history with Staffs F.A. President Len Hickman on his left and Chairman Bob Heath to the right.

First Division

	P	W	D	L	F	A	Pts	G.D.
Clitheroe	38	20	14	4	61	30	54	+31
Congleton Town	38	22	10	6	51	29	54	+22
Eastwood Hanley	38	22	9	7	68	45	53	+23
Stalybridge Celtic	38	21	10	7	62	39	52	+23
Fleetwood Town	38	21	10	7	70	34	*50	+36
Irlam Town	38	16	14	8	66	45	46	+21
Leek Town	38	20	6	12	64	44	46	+20
Curzon Ashton	38	18	9	11	52	50	45	+2
Burscough	38	15	10	13	45	35	40	+10
St. Helens Town	38	15	8	15	65	55	38	+10
Accrington Stanley	38	13	11	14	62	60	37	+2
Leyland Motors	38	13	8	17	62	67	34	—5
Winsford United	38	14	6	18	55	68	34	—13
Radcliffe Borough	38	12	9	17	48	49	33	—1
Bootle	38	11	7	20	46	54	29	—8
Penrith	38	9	8	21	46	63	26	—17
Netherfield	38	8	10	20	38	76	26	—38
Glossop	38	7	10	21	37	69	24	—32
Prescot Cables	38	5	9	24	33	68	19	—35
Formby	38	5	8	25	35	86	18	—51

FIRST DIVISION RESULTS — SEASON 1985/86

	1	2	3	4	5	6	7	8	9	10	11	12	13	14	15	16	17	18	19	20
1 Accrington Stanley		2-1	0-1	0-1	1-0	0-1	1-2	2-2	1-1	3-3	1-2	3-0	1-2	3-0	1-0	2-0	2-1	3-1	2-3	2-1
2 Bootle	2-1		0-0	0-1	1-2	1-0	1-1	1-3	1-1	9-1	3-1	0-1	2-1	0-2	2-1	1-0	2-1	0-1	0-1	1-2
3 Burscough	0-0	0-1		0-0	1-2	2-0	2-1	0-4	0-0	1-0	1-2	2-0	0-2	0-1	0-0	3-0	0-2	3-1	1-1	6-0
4 Clitheroe	4-3	4-2	1-1		0-0	2-0	0-0	1-1	3-1	2-0	0-0	2-0	2-1	4-0	3-2	2-2	1-1	3-1	1-0	3-1
5 Congleton Town	0-0	1-1	2-1	0-0		2-0	2-0	1-3	3-0	3-0	0-2	0-0	1-3	1-0	1-0	2-1	1-0	0-3	1-1	2-1
6 Curzon Ashton	0-2	3-2	0-1	1-0	3-2		2-2	1-1	3-2	3-2	1-0	3-1	1-1	0-1	3-1	2-0	1-1	3-1	3-0	2-4
7 Eastwood Hanley	3-3	0-0	0-1	1-0	1-2	6-1		2-2	1-0	2-1	5-3	3-1	2-1	2-1	4-2	2-0	2-1	3-2	1-3	1-0
8 Fleetwood Town	2-1	1-1	1-2	3-2	0-0	0-1	3-0		2-0	4-0	1-1	0-2	3-0	1-0	2-1	6-0	3-1	0-0	0-1	3-2
9 Formby	3-3	4-0	0-4	2-3	3-5	0-1	0-3	0-0		0-2	0-10	1-3	4-2	2-2	0-3	1-1	1-0	1-5	0-1	2-1
10 Glossop	1-3	2-0	1-3	0-1	0-0	1-1	1-2	0-1	1-1		1-3	1-3	1-1	0-0	2-0	1-1	0-3	0-2	1-2	2-2
11 Irlam Town	0-0	0-2	2-1	1-1	1-1	2-2	2-0	0-2	1-0	2-0		0-2	5-1	2-2	3-2	3-0	1-2	2-1	2-1	1-1
12 Leek Town	1-1	2-1	2-0	1-1	0-3	2-3	1-1	1-0	2-0	3-0	1-1		3-0	4-0	2-0	4-1	2-2	2-3	1-0	4-0
13 Leyland Motors	2-2	2-1	2-0	1-2	1-2	1-2	1-2	2-4	2-0	1-3	0-0	2-0		4-1	1-2	0-0	4-2	1-5	1-1	0-2
14 Netherfield	1-2	2-1	0-2	1-4	1-3	0-0	0-2	1-3	4-1	0-2	2-2	0-3	1-4		3-1	2-2	3-2	1-3	2-1	1-5
15 Penrith	4-2	1-1	1-3	1-1	0-1	1-1	0-1	1-3	3-1	1-1	1-1	0-1	0-2	1-1		2-1	3-0	1-4	0-2	3-3
16 Prescot Cables	1-4	1-2	2-0	0-4	0-0	0-0	1-2	1-2	2-0	0-1	0-1	1-3	1-1	0-0	2-3		0-1	2-3	1-2	3-1
17 Radcliffe Borough	2-0	3-1	0-0	0-1	0-1	3-0	0-3	1-1	3-0	0-1	1-1	1-3	4-1	0-0	2-0	1-3		1-1	1-1	2-0
18 St. Helens Town	2-2	2-1	1-1	1-1	0-1	0-1	1-2	2-0	3-1	1-1	2-4	2-1	1-3	1-1	0-2	0-2	3-2		0-1	5-0
19 Stalybridge Celtic	7-1	2-1	2-2	0-0	0-2	2-0	1-1	0-2	2-1	3-2	1-1	3-2	2-2	3-0	2-1	2-1	2-0	2-1		1-1
20 Winsford United	3-2	1-0	1-0	1-0	0-1	1-3	2-2	2-1	0-1	2-1	3-1	3-0	2-6	5-1	0-1	2-0	0-1	0-0	0-3	

ACRRINGTON STANLEY

President: J.C. Prescott
Chairman: J.S. Alty
Secretary: John Walker
Address & Tel. No: 12 Owen Street, Accrington. 0254 393273
Physiotherapist: A.A. Clements
Commercial Manager: Alan Harker
Ground Address & Tel. No: Crown Ground, Livingstone Rd, Accrington 383235
Simple ground directions: M66 to A680 to Accrington Ground on A680. Thro town centre, behind Crown pub.
Capacity: 3,000 **Covered accommodation:** 1,000 **Seating:** 80 **Floodlights:** By Oct 1985
Club colours: All Red
Change colours: Yellow/Green Stripes
Programme details: 32 pages/25p. **Editor:** J.S. Alty **Club metal badges:** Yes
Clubhouse details: Open two nights and match days
Nickname: Stanley or The Reds
Midweek match day: Wednesday
Previous Leagues: Cheshire County/Lancs. Comb
Record transfer fee received: £1000 for D. Hargreaves to Blackburn Rovers
Senior honours:/best performance: Cheshire League Div 2, Lancashire Comb. (2)
Record attendance: 1200 v Blackburn Rovers in 1987
Past players: D. Hargreaves

BOOTLE

President: A. Roberts MP
Chairman: John Doran
Manager: A. McCumiskey
Ass. Man/Coach: T. Kidman
Secretary: Edward Lyons
Address & Tel. No: 26 Dooley Drive, Netherton, Bootle L30 8RS (051 531 6021)
Press Officer: P. Carr
Ground Address & Tel. No: Buck's Park, Northern Perimeter Rd, Netherton (051-526 1850)
Capacity: 6,000 **Covered accommodation:** 500 **Floodlights:** No
Programme Editor: Paul Carr **Club metal badges:** No **Local newspaper:** Bottle Times
Club colours: Blue
Changer colours: Amber/Black/Amber
Nickname: The Bucks
Midweek matchdays: Wednesday
Previous Leagues: Liverpool County Club, Liverpool Shipping
Record attendance: 750 v Carshalton **Player of the Year 1985/86:** G. Redder

BURSCOUGH

President: John Maudsley
Chairman: Frank Parr
Manager: Ray Coleman
Physiotherapist: George Ford
Secretary: Ken Hilton
Address & Tel No: 58 Higgins Lane, Burscough, Ormskirk, Lancs. 0704 8945094 (H) 0704 840775 (B)
Press Officer: L.J. Richards
Ground Address & Tel. No: Victoria Park, Mart Lane, Burscough. 0704 893237
Simple ground directions: 300 yards from main Liverpool Preston Road (A59), 3 miles north of Ormskirk.
Year Established: 1946
Nickname: The Linnets
Capacity: 3,500 **Covered accommodation:** Main Stand & One End **Seating:** 400 **Floodlights:** Yes
Club colours: Yellow/Green/Green
Change colours: All Blue
Programme details: 12 pages 20p **Editor:** Mark Parr (0704 24667 **Club metal badges:** Yes
Local Newspapers: Ormskirk Advertiser, Liverpool Daily Post & Echo, Ormskirk Star
Midweek matchday: Tuesday
Previous Leagues: Liverpool County Combination, Lancashire Combination.
Senior honours/best performance: F.A. Cup 1st Round, 1959, 1977, 1979, 1980. F.A. Trophy 2nd Rd, 1974/75. Cheshire County League Cup, Cheshire County League Cup Runners Up, Liverpool Senior Cup, Lancashire Comb. (2), Lancashire Junior Cup (3), North West Counties Div. One
Record attendance: 3,500 v Crewe Alexander F.A.P. Cuper 1st Rd, Cheshire County.
Past players Frank Gamble (Derby County), Bobby Langton (Blackburn Rovers & England), Matt Woods (Blackburn Rovers

CLITHEROE

President: J.E.R. Aspinall
Chairman: C.H. Whiteside
Manager: D. O'Neill
Secretary: Stuart Ellison
Address & Tel. No: 37 Pothouse Lane, Darwen, Lancs. 71758
Physiotherapist: K. Lord
Ground Address & Tel. No: Shawbridge 23344
Simple ground directions: Off A59, 1 mile down Pendle Road
Capacity: 4,200 **Seating:** 200 **Floodlights:** No
Clubhouse details: Open Match days Mon-Fri nights
Midweek matchdays: Tuesday
Club colours: All Blue
Change colours: All Red
Local Newspaper: Clitheroe Advertiser
Previous Leagues: Lancashire Combination
Record Attendance: 1,350 v Atherstone Utd. F.A. Vase 1982-83
Senior honours: 1979-80 Lancs. Comb. 1983-84 3rd Div. Champions N.W.C. F.L., 1984-85 2nd Div. Champions N.W.C.F.L., 1984-85 L.A. Trophy Winners, 1985-86 1st Div. Champions. N.W.C.F.L.
Past Players: Ray Woods (Leeds Utd), Chris Sims (Blackburn Rovers)

CONGLETON TOWN

President: Mr. Clifford Cresswell
Chairman: Mr. Mark Williamson
Manager: Mr. Colin Moss
Assistant Manager: Mr. Martin Scholes
Reserve Team Manager: Mr. Dave Nixon
Secretary: Mr. John Pullen, 70 Belgrave Avenue, Congleton, Cheshire. Tel. (0260) 277128
Address & Tel. No. of Ground: Booth Street Ground, Off Crescent Road, Congleton, Cheshire. Tel. (0260) 274460
Commercial Manager/Press Officer: As Secretary
Club Sponsors: Dave Moss Promotions **Year Formed:** 1901
Ground Capacity: 5000 **Covered accommodation:** 1100 (3 stands) **Seats:** 250
Floodlights: Yes **Club Shop:** Yes **Nicknames:** The Bears/The Humbugs **Midweek matchday:** Tuesday
Club colours: Black/White Striped Shirts, Black Shorts Black socks
Change colours: Gold Shirts, White Shorts, Gold Socks
Clubhouse details: Open 7 days a week & on matchdays
Record attendance: 7000 v Macclesfield Town 1953-54
Best performance: FA Cup : 2nd qualifying round. FA Vase, 5th round 1980-81
Record transfer fee received: £5000 for D. Frost from Leeds Utd
Present players with Football League experience: Martin Scholes, Craig Moores
Past Players: L. Hamlet, D. Frost (Leeds Utd), J. Quinn (Blackburn & N. Ireland), I. Brightwell (Man. City)
Programme details: 1st Team, 25p, 32 pages **Reserve team:** 25p, 24 pages
Programme Editor: Mr. Andrew Warren, Tel. Congleton (0260) 275994
Previous Leagues: Crewe and District League, North Staffordshire League, Macclesfield District League, Mid-Chesire League, Cheshire County League
Honours: Crewe and District League Champions (3), Crewe F.A. Cup Winners (2), Cheshire Amateur Cup Winners (2), North Staffordshire League Champions, Cheshire Senior Cup Winners (2), Mid Cheshire League Champions (3), Mid-Cheshire League Cup Winners (2), Cheshire Saturday Cup Winners, Cheshire League Div. Two Champions, North West Counties Foot. League Runners-Up.
Local Newspapers: The Congleton Chronicle, The Staffordshire Evening Sentinel

CURZON ASHTON

President: M. Rubin
Chairman: H. Tawmley
Manager: Peter Mayo
Ass. Manager: Brian Needham
Secretary: I. Seymour
Address 8 Tel. No: 131 Burlington St., Ashton-U-Lyne Lancs. 061-339 5987
Physiotherapist: Chris Wych
Ground Address & Tel. No: National Park, Katherine St. Ashton-U-Lyne. 061 330 6033
Capacity:8000 **Covered accommodation:** 350 **Seating:** 350 **Floodlights:** Yes
Simple ground directions: Behind Ashton Police Station
Clubhouse details: Open Tue-Thur, M/days, Soc. Events
Club colours: Blue/White/Blue
Nicknames: Curzon
Midweek matchdays: Monday
Record transfer fee: £2000 Steve Wigley (Notts For.)
Record attendance: 1,826 v Stamford 1980
Programme: 8 pages, 20p
Change colours: White/Blue/Red
Local newspapers: Ashton Reporter, Ashton Advertiser
Previous Leagues: Manchester Amateur, Manchester Cheshire County
Senior honours/best performance: Manchester Premier Cup Winners, Cheshire Lge Div. 2 Runners Up. FA Vase Semi-Final
Past players: Gordon Taylor (Bolton), Steve Wigley (Notts For.), E. Nixon (Man. City)

EASTWOOD HANLEY FOOTBALL CLUB

President: Mr. P. Goel
Chairman: A.P. Key
Manager: Kevin Roche
Ass. Man./Coach: Alan Kelly
Physiotherapist: Graham Plant
Secretary: G. Eccleston
Address & Tel. No: 20 Redcar Road, Trentham, **Stoke on Trent. Staff. 0782 633063**
Commercial Manager: G. Eccleston
Press Officer: G. Eccleston
Ground Address & Tel. No: Trentmill Road, Hanley, Stoke on Trent. 0782 29174
Capacity: 5000 **Covered accommodation:** 1000 **Seating:** 200 **Floodlights:** Yes
Simple ground directions: M6 to A500 (Junction 16) via Stoke Road, Cauldon Road and Leek Road.
Clubhouse details: Large Bar. Games Room, Priv. Bar
Editor: G. Eccleston
Established: 1946
Club colours: All Blue
Midweek matchday: Tuesday
Programme details: 32 pages 20p.
Nickname: The Blues
Local newspaper: Staffordshire Evening Sentinel
Change colours: All Red
Previous Leagues: Mid Cheshire, Manchester. West Midlands Premier, Cheshire County
Record attendance: 5000 v Stoke City, Bros. Testimonial 1978
Senior honours/best performance: Staff Senior Cup Winners 1985/86. Staffs F.A. Vase
Past players: Melia Alecksic (Spurs)
Player of the Year 1985/86: M. Cartwright
Secretarys Bus. Tel. No: 0782 47187
Club Captain: S. Norris
Club Sponsors: F.W.B. Products Ltd

FLEETWOOD TOWN

Chairman: F. Whelan
Manager: A. Tinsley
Secretary: R.G. Atkinson
Address & Tel. No: 42 Warren Ave North, Fleetwood, Lancs, FY7 7BB. Tel. 03917 70810 (H) (0253) 891009 Ex. 66 (B)
Ass. Man/Coach: R. Dobson
Commercial Manager: R. Dobson
Physiotherapist: A. Tuson
Press Officer: S. Presnall. Tel. (03917) 79948
Ground Address & Tel. No: Highbury Stadium, Park Ave, Fleetwood. Tel. 30917 6443
Capacity: 9,500 **Covered accommodation:** 1,200 **Seating:** 300 **Floodlights:** Yes
Simple ground directions: M6 to Broughton (Junction 32), M55 to Kirkham (Junction 3) via A585 to Fleetwood - Ground behind fire station.
Clubhouse details: Open normal licensing hours
Programme details: 20p. - 20 pages
Editor: S. Presnall
Local newspapers: West Lancs Evening Gazette, Fleetwood Weekly News
Club colours: Red & White/Black/Black
Change colours: White/White/White
Midweek matchday: Wednesday
Previous Leagues: Local, Cheshire County, Lancs Combination Northern Premier
Record attendance: 3,000 v Exmouth Town. F.A. Vase Semi-Final 1985
Senior honours/best performance: N.W. Counties League Division 2 Champions 1983/84, F.A. Vase Finalists 1984/85
Past players: P. Sanderson (Manchester City, Chester, Halifax)

GLOSSOP A.F.C. LTD

President: T. Boak
Chairman: P. Hammond (acting)
Secretary: P. Hammond
Address & Tel. No: 15 Longmoor Road, Simmondley, Glossop, Derbyshire, SK13 9NH. Glo. 63852
Manager: David Yarwood
Ass. Man/Coach: Neil Wilson
Ground Address & Tel. No: Surrey Street. Glossop 5469
Capacity: 2000 **Covered accommodation:** Yes **Seating:** 250 **Floodlights:** No
Simple ground directions: Quarter mile from town centre, just off main A57 road.
Clubhouse details: Licensed. Open 6 days a week
Programme details: 8 pages. 20p
Editor: Frank Wood
Local newspapers: Glossop and High Peak Chronicle
Club colours: Royal Blue, White trim
Change colours: Yellow, Blue trim
Nickname: The Hillsmen
Midweek matchdays: Tuesday
Previous Leagues: Football League (Div. 1 & 2), North Cheshire League, Manchester League, Lancashire Combination, Cheshire County
Senior honours/best performance: Cheshire League Division 2 Runners Up 1981, Football League Divison 2 Runners up 1897/98. F.A. Cup Quarter Final 1909 (Lost to Bristol City)
Past Players: Ray Redshaw (Wigan)

IRLAM TOWN

President: J. Sanderson
Chairman: W. Veldhoven
Secretary: D.W. Murray
Address & Tel. No: 8 Marston Drive, Irlam, Manchester 061-775 7509
Manager: I. Thompson
Press Officer: D.W. Murray
Ass. Man/Coach: D. Miggs
Ground Address 8 Tel. No: Silver St, Irlam. 061-775 5599
Capacity: 3000 **Covered accommodation:** 800 **Seating:** 250 **Floodlights:** Yes
Simple ground directions: Junction 21 on M6, 5½ miles to ground. Junction 2 on M63, 2½ miles to ground
Clubhouse details: Lounge, Vault, Kitchen, Dressing Rooms, Ref. Room, Committee Room
Programme details: 24 pages, 25p
Editor: D.W. Murray
Midweek matchday: Tuesday
Club colours: All Royal Blue
Change colours: Red/White
Previous Leagues: Manchester, Cheshire
Past Players: T. Caldwell (Bolton)
Senior honours/Best performance: Manchester Premier Cup 1985

KIRKBY TOWN

President: The Mayor of Knowsley
Chairman: Paul G. Orr
Manager: Paul J. Orr
Senior Coach: Peter Campbell
Press Officer: Hal Kerr
Secretary: Hyder Jawad
Address 8 Tel. No: 22 Stratford Rd, Aigburth, Liverpool LL9 3RF
Commercial Manager: Ged Comerford
Club Shop: Certain games only
Address & Tel. No. of ground: Kirkby Sports Centre, Whitefield Road, Kirkby
Simple ground directions: One mile from Town Centre. Ten minute walk from Kirkby Station
Capacity: 25,000 **Covered accommodation:** 3000 **Seating:** 500 **Floodlights:** Under construction
Year formed: 1984
Midweek matchdays: Wednesday
Club colours: All White
Change colours: All red
Previous grounds: Simonswood Lane
Record attendance: 900 v Everton, Liverpool Senior Cup. 1984/85
Best performance: F.A. Vase 2nd round, 1985-86
Clubhouse details: Bar facilities at home games
Programme details: 20 pages, 20p
Programme Editor: Hyder Jawad
Local newspapers: Liverpool Echo, Liverpool Daily Post, Liverpool Star
Senior honours: N.W.C.L. Div. 3 Champions 1984-85, N.W.C.L. Div. 2 Champions 1985-86
Club Captain: Mick Quinn
Player of the year: Such awards against club policy.

LEEK TOWN

President: B. Joyce
Chairman: Godfrey Heath
Secretary: John Reid
Address & Tel. No: 2 Northam Road, Sneyd Green, Stoke-on-Trent ST1 6OA. S-O-T 279062
Manager: Neil Baker
Press Officer: John Reid
Ground Address & Tel. No.: Hamil Park, Macclesfield Road, Leek, Staffs. Leek 383734
Capacity: 4,500 **Covered accommodation:** 1,000 **Seating:** 200 **Floodlights:** Yes
Simple ground directions: Main Leek—Macclesfield Road (A523)
Clubhouse details: Open Every Night plus weekend dinnertime
Programme details: 10 pages 20p
Editor: J.L. Reid
Club metal badges: Yes. £1.20 + post
Local newspapers: Leek Post & times, Evening Sentinel
Club colours: Blue and White
Change colours: Yellow
Midweek matchday: Tuesday
Previous Leagues: Staffs County, Birmingham, Manchester, Cheshire
Record transfer fee paid: £200 to Macclesfield S. Nelson
Record transfer fee received: £2.500 from Telford Tony Griffiths
Record attendance: 3,500 v Macclesfield 1973
Senior honours/best performance: Cheshire League Champions, N.W.C.L. Cup Winners 1984-85 + Challenge Shield (84-85). Reach last 16 of FA Trophy (1985-86) only N.W.C. Club to ever reach this stage.
Past Players: Bill Summerscales (Port Vale)

LEYLAND MOTORS

President: L. Southworth
Chairman: W. Kirby
Secretary: J.A. Hickson
Address & Tel. No: 395 Leyland Lane, Leyland, Preston PR5 3AA. 0772 431066
Manager: B. Lamb
Commercial Manager: C. Pass
Ass. Man./Coach: D. Haslam
Press Officer: W. Kirby
Ground Address 8 Tel. No: 0772 422400 (Office hours)
Capacity: 5,000 **Covered accommodation:** 500 **Seating:** 200 **Floodlights:** Yes
Simple ground directions: M6 Exit 28. Follow road into centre of Leyland (3 mins from motorway)
Clubhouse details: Large Clubhouse offering weekend entertainment, 3 bars, catering facilities.
Programme details: 20 pages, 10p
Editor: J. Hickson
Local newspapers: Lancs Evening Post, Leyland & Chorley Guardian
Chahge colours: Red/White/White **colours:** Amber/Navy/Amber
Midweek matchday: Wednesday
Previous Leagues: West Lancashire, Lancs Combination, Cheshire County
Record transfer fee received: 8,200
Record attendance: 4,000 v Man City 1981
Senior honours/best performance: Lancashire Combination Cup, F.A. Cup 2nd Qual. Rd. F.A. Trophy 3rd Qualifying Rd.
Player of Year: Alan Heaton

NETHERFIELD

President: J.R. Peat
Secretary: Mrs Pauline A. Bainbridge
Address & Tel No.: 2 Howgill Close, Burnside, Cumbria LA9 6QJ. (0539 217238 H) (0539 20028 W)
Managers: Malcolm Burgess
Chairman: G. Inchmore
Ground Address & Tel. No: Parkside Road, Kendal, Cumbria (0539 22469)
Capacity: 6,000 **Covered Accommodation:** 2,000 **Seating:** 300 **Floodlights:** Yes
Simple Ground directions: Parkside Road adjacent to "K" Shoe Factory, Kendal
Clubhouse Details: Daily 1300-1700, 1900-2300
Year formed: 1920
Programme details: 20 pages 20p
Editor: Tristan Savage
Local newspapers: Westmoreland Gazette (0539 20555)
Club Colours: White, thin black stipe/Black/Red
Change Colours: Tangerine/Emerald/Emerald
Midweek Match Day: Tuesday
Record Attendance: 2,500 for T. Brown Lee (Bradford City)
Previous Leagues: Westmoreland West Lancashire. Lancashire Combination, N.P.L.
Senior Honours/Best Performance: Lancashire Combination (2)
Past Players who have progressed to Football League: M. Graham (Bolton), J. Wright (Wigan), J. Simpson (Gillingham), P. McDonnell (Oldham).

PENRITH

Chairman: D. Johnson
Manager: W. Armstrong
Secretary: L.N. Bailey
Address & Tel. No: 20 Broughham St, Penrith, Cumbria. P.64664 (H), Hacathorpe 333 (B)
Ass. Man/Coach: W. Gill
Press Officer: Club Secretary
Physiotherapist: J. Balmer
Capacity: 4,000 **Covered accommodation:** 1,000 **Seating:** 250 **Floodlights:** Yes
Simple ground directions: Turn off M6 at junction 40, onto dual carriageway to Appleby & Scotch Corner, then turn off at next roundabout, approx. ½ mile, into Penrish, follow A6 into town taking 1st left for ground.
Clubhouse details: Open all matchdays, evenings & weekends. Tel. P. 632121
Programme details: 20 pages, 10p. **Editor:** D. Johnson
Local newspapers: Cumb & Westmorland Herald, Cumberland News
Club colours: Blue shirts/White shorts/Blue (S) **Change colours:** White shirts/Blue shorts/White (S)
Midweek matchday: Wednesday **Previous Leagues:** Northern (Dryboroughs)
Nickname: The Blues
Record transfer fee paid: A. Carruthers from Netherfield.
Record transfer fee received: B. Brown, Q. of the South
Record attendance: 4,000 West Auckland
Senior honours/best performance: Runners Up in N.W.C.F.L. Season 83/84 to Staleybridge.
Past players: K. Sawyers, G. Fell, G. Mossop (All Carlisle)

RADCLIFFE BOROUGH F.C. (1980)

President: A.A. Warbrick
Chairman: R. McLaughlin
Secretary: G.E. Fielding
Address & Tel. No: 93 Callender St, Ramsbottom, Bury, Lancs. BL0 9DU. Rams. 5299
Manager: D. Morris
Commercial Manager: S. Baculey (061-724 0343)
Ass. Man./Coach: F. O'Kane
Physiotherapist: K. Bridge
Ground Address & Tel. No: Stainton Park, Pilkington Road, Radcliffe, Lancs. M26 0PE.
Capacity: 5,000 **Covered accommodation:** 1,000 **Seating:** 200 **Floodlights:** Yes
Simple ground directions: M62 Junction 17. Follow signs for Whitefield and Radcliffe.
Clubhouse details: The Footballers, Public House on ground
Programme details: 20 pages. 25p. **Editor:** Miss F. Carr
Local newspapers: Radcliffe Times & Bury Times
Club colours: All Blue **Change colours:** All Yellow
Midweek matchday: Wednesday **Nicknames: Boro'**
Previous Leagues: S.E. Lancs, Lancs. Combination & Cheshire County
Record transfer fee received: £1,5000 John Denham to **Northwich Victoria 1980**
Record attendance: 1,465 v Caernarfon Town 1983
Senior honours/best performance: N.W. Counties - Div 1. Champions 1984/85

ROSSENDALE UTD

President: C. Barcroft J.P.
Chairman: D. Hutchinson
Secretary: D.A. Rogan
Address & Tel. No: 7 East St, Rawtenstall, Lancs. (0706) 218341
Manager: Dave O'Neill
Ass. Man/Coach: Steve Connaghan
Ground Address 8 Tel. No: Dark Lane, Newchurch, Rawtenstall, Rossendale, Lancs. (0706) 213296
Capacity: 5,000 **Covered accommodation:** 650 **Seating:** 400 **Floodlights:** No
Simple ground directions: Newchurch Road, onto Staghills Rd, 1¼ miles from Rawtenstall Centre.
Clubhouse details: Open Every Night Saturday and Sunday Lunchtimes
Programme details: 10 pages 20p. **Editor:** D. Howorth
Local newspapers: Rossendale Free Press, Lancs Evening Telegraph.
Club colours: Blue and White **Change colours:** All Yellow
Midweek matchday: Tuesday **Previous Leagues:** Lancs Comb. Cheshire Lge
Record transfer fee recieved: £1,000 from Huddersfield T. for Dave O'Neill 1974
Record attendance: 12,100 v Bolton FA Cup 2nd Rnd 1971. FA Cup 2nd Rnd 1971-72, FA Trophy 2nd Rnd 1981-82.
Senior honours/best performance: Lancs Comb Champions (1), Cup Winners (1), Cheshire Lge Champions (1), Runners up (2), Cup Winners (1), Lancs Junior Cup Winners (2), N.W.C.F.L. Div. 2. Runners up (1)
Present players: Paul Round (Blackburn), M. Higgins (Blkburn & Workington), S. Metcalfe (Blkburn & Carlisle), D. Bradford (Blkburn, Sheff. Utd. & Peterborough), P. Ashworth (Blkburn, Southport, Bournemouth, Portsmouth, Scunthorpe), G. Kennan (Bury, Port Vale)

ST HELENS TOWN

President: Joe Jones
Chairman: Joe Roscoe
Secretary: Bill Burrows
Address & Tel. No: 48 Fisher St. Sutton, St. Helens, Merseyside WA9 3PU. 0744 811856
Manager: Alan Wellens
Press Officer: Jim Barrett 0744 35703
Ground Address & Tel. No: Hoghton Rd, Sutton, St. Helens. 0744 812721 S/C 817225. Sels. Office
Capacity: 10,000 **Covered accommodation:** 800 **Seating:** 200 **Floodlights:** No
Simple ground directions: 20 yards, St. Helens Junction Station.
Clubhouse details: Seats 700 Bingo, Artistes, Dancing, Darts, Dominoes, Snooker
Programme details: 10 pages **Editor:** Jim Barrett 0744 35703
Club colours: Blue/White/Blue **Change colours:** All Yellow
Local newspapers: Reporter, Star, Leader, Liverpool Post, Echo
Midweek matchdays: Tuesday **Record attendance:** 4,000
Previous Leagues: Liverpool Combination, Lancashire Combination, Cheshire League.
Senior honours/best performance: FA Cup 75/76, Lancashire Combination League Winners 71/72, Bass Charrington Cup 71/72.

STALYBRIDGE CELTIC

President: J. Knott
Chairman: R. Conner

Vice Chairman: J. Hammersley
Coach: W. Dodd

Physiotherapist: L. Brown

Secretary: J. Dillon
Address & Tel. No: 12 Moorland Road, Carr Brook, Stalybridge, Cheshire 04575 2593 (H) 061-368 1961 (B)
Commercial Manager: J.M. Hall
Address 8 Tel. No: 39 Bardsley Gate Avenue, Stalybridge, Cheshire. Mottram 65634
Press Officer & Tel. No: J.M. Hall (0457 65634)
Address & Tel. No of ground: Bower Fold, Mottram Road, Stalybridge, Cheshire. Tel: 061-338 2828.
Club Shop: Yes
Simple ground directions: On A6108 Ashton to Glossop Road. Nearest rail station, Stalybridge (1 mile away). Bus 236 from Stalybridge bus station stops at ground (service every ½ hour)
No. of seats: 500 **Covered accommodation:** 4,000 **Capacity:** 7,500 **Floodlights:** Yes
Year formed: 1909 **Nickname:** Celtic **Club sponsors:** Barcrest & Longdendale Mastiffs, Pioneer Concrete
Previous names: None
Previous grounds: None
Club colours: All Blue
Change colours: All Red
Day for midweek home matches: Tuesday
Record attendance: 13,000 v Dick Kerr's Ladies XI
Best performance: in F.A. Cup: 1923 v WBA, 1st Round, lost replay 0-2. F.A. Trophy: 1979-80 v Dagenham, 2nd Round, lost 0-5, 1982-83 v Scarborough, 2nd Round, lost 3-1.
Previous Leagues: Football League Div. 3, Central, Lancashire Combination, Southern, Lancashire & Cheshire, Manchester Amaetur
Clubhouse details: Bistroteque on ground, 8pm-2am Wed, Thur, Fri & Sat. Converted railway carriage with licenced bar open on match days for spectators. Three refreshment kiosks on ground
Present players with Football League experience: R. Simpson (Stockport Co), P., Morgan (Manchester City), D. Lutevitch (Blackburn R.), V. Garmory (Manchester City), G. Butterworth (Rochdale), A. Morley (Blackburn R.)
Past players: E. O'Keefe (Everton), J. Anderson (Everton & Chester), E. Kerfoot (Leeds U), Jack Gaskell, John Johnston.

Record transfer fee paid: £500 each for N. Nicklin (Droylesden), D. Bourne (Leek Town)
Programme details: 24 pages, 20p **Local newspapers & Tel. No:** Report 061-330 5311, Advertiser 061 339 7611
Club metal badges: Yes
Senior Honours: Cheshire League & Shield, Cheshire Senior Cup, N.W. League Div. 1 & Trophy Winners (all once each)
Club Captain (1984-85): P. Brown **Player of the Year (1984-85):** P. Brown

WINSFORD UNITED

President: J. Deans
Chairman: N. Abberley
Manager: T. Woods
Physiotherapist: P. Lee

Secretary: P. Warburton
Address & Tel. No: 3 Massey Avenue, Wharton
Ass. Man./Coach: M. Sidebottam

Ground Address & Tel. No: Barton Stadium, Winsford, Cheshire. 060-593021
Capacity: 8,000 **Covered accommodation:** 2,500 **Seating:** 300 **Floodlights:** Yes
Simple ground directions: From North: Junction 19 (M6) tgake A533 thru' Davenham. From South: Junction 18, take A54 for Middlewich. Barton Stadium is less than ¼ off these main roads in the Wharton Area of Winsford
Clubhouse details: Open every night. **Programme details:** 20 pages. 20p
Editor: A.J. Maylor (0606 594681
Local Newspapers: Winsford Chronicle, Winsford Garduain
Club colours: Navy/White/Navy **Change colours:** Red/Blue/Red
Midweek matchday: Wednesday
Record transfer fee received: £6,000 for N. Southall from Bury. **Record attendance:** 7000 v Witton Alb. 1947
Past players who progressed into the Football League: W. Hughes, J. Richardson (Sheff Utd), R. Walters (Shrewsbury), N. Southall (Bury), B. Sutton (West Ham)
Senior Honours: Cheshire County League Champions 1976-77, Runners-Up 1979-80, Challenge Cup Winners 1949-50, 1955-56, 1959-60, 1976-77, 1978-79, 1979-80, 1980-81

Darwen v Chadderton N.W.C.L. Chadderton attacking.

Blackpool Mechanics F.C. who have had a successful season in N.W. Counties Division 3. Photo: Leo Hoenig

THE NORTH WEST COUNTIES FOOTBALL LEAGUE SEASON 1985/86
THIRD DIVISION

LEAGUE TABLE

	P	W	D	L	F	A	Pts	G.D.
Kirkby Town	34	24	7	3	85	30	55	55
Rossendale United	34	20	8	6	81	36	48	45
Wren Rovers	34	18	8	8	60	46	44	14
Warrington Town	34	17	9	8	62	48	43	14
Colwyn Bay	34	17	8	9	74	53	42	21
Chadderton	34	15	12	7	66	48	42	18
Colne Dynamoes	34	15	9	10	59	43	39	16
Great Harwood Town	34	13	10	11	38	45	36	−7
Skelmersdale United	34	14	5	15	58	53	33	5
Droylsden	34	13	7	14	48	56	33	−8
Atherton L.R.	34	12	6	16	49	61	30	−12
Lancaster City	34	10	9	15	57	66	29	−9
Ellesmere Port & N.	34	9	9	16	45	61	27	−16
Ashton United	34	11	5	18	46	64	*25	−18
Darwen	34	8	8	18	48	57	24	−9
Salford	34	9	4	21	38	72	22	−34
Ford Motors	34	5	10	19	36	64	20	−28
Nantwich Town	34	5	8	21	31	78	18	−47

RESULTS

Ashton United		2-3	1-1	1-1	0-4	1-0	1-0	2-2	3-1	2-1	1-4	3-3	5-0	1-2	2-1	1-4	1-2	0-1
Atherton L.R.	2-0		2-2	1-1	3-1	0-2	1-1	2-0	4-1	3-0	1-2	1-1	1-0	0-4	4-0	0-0	1-3	2-1
Chadderton	1-3	3-1		4-4	5-1	1-0	0-0	2-2	3-0	1-1	1-1	5-2	4-0	2-2	1-0	3-1	5-3	1-2
Colne Dynamoes	3-2	3-1	2-1		0-2	3-0	2-0	4-1	4-2	0-0	2-1	1-0	3-0	2-3	3-0	1-2	3-2	0-1
Colwyn Bay	4-1	5-1	1-1	1-0		2-2	4-4	1-2	1-2	0-1	1-4	1-0	3-1	1-3	4-0	3-0	1-3	3-0
Darwen	1-0	2-3	1-2	1-1	2-3		0-1	5-0	3-0	0-1	1-1	2-4	4-0	0-4	1-3	0-0	0-1	1-1
Droylsden	3-0	2-1	0-4	1-3	0-1	3-1		3-2	1-4	6-0	1-1	0-1	2-2	1-4	2-1	1-0	0-3	3-0
Ellesmere Port & Neston	2-3	1-0	2-0	1-5	1-1	1-2	1-2		1-1	0-0	0-2	1-1	6-1	0-0	0-3	2-0	0-5	1-3
Ford Motors	0-1	2-1	1-2	2-2	0-2	2-4	0-1	0-3		0-1	0-1	5-3	3-3	2-3	0-1	1-3	0-0	1-4
Great Harwood Town	2-1	3-0	1-2	0-0	3-3	3-2	3-0	1-0	0-0		1-3	3-1	3-0	0-7	0-2	2-0	0-2	2-1
Kirkby Town	2-0	4-0	2-2	0-2	1-2	2-2	3-2	3-2	1-1	2-0		0-0	5-1	3-1	5-1	3-2	4-1	3-0
Lancaster City	3-0	2-3	0-0	4-3	1-2	3-0	3-2	3-3	1-1	0-0	1-4		0-1	2-2	3-1	3-7	1-2	1-3
Nantwich Town	3-1	0-1	1-2	2-0	5-2	2-2	0-0	0-2	0-1	0-0	0-5	1-3		2-2	0-1	1-5	0-1	0-1
Rossendale United	1-2	4-1	3-0	0-0	3-3	2-1	3-0	1-0	1-1	3-1	0-1	1-2	2-2		2-0	2-1	3-1	1-0
Salford	2-3	3-2	2-2	1-1	0-3	1-0	1-1	0-1	1-1	1-3	1-3	2-1	1-2	0-7		1-2	2-3	1-5
Skelmersdale United	2-0	2-2	4-1	1-0	0-4	2-3	1-3	1-2	3-0	1-0	0-3	1-2	4-0	2-1	2-1		1-2	1-1
Warrington Town	2-1	3-1	0-2	3-0	3-3	1-1	1-2	1-1	0-0	1-1	0-1	2-1	1-1	0-3	2-1	2-1		3-3
Wren Rovers	1-1	1-0	2-0	2-0	1-1	3-2	4-0	3-2	2-1	1-1	0-5	3-1	2-0	2-1	1-2	2-2	3-3	

Warrington Town. Back Row (L-r) N. Williams, N. Cook, R. Mather, I. Kinsey, F. Dolan, C. Hope and J. King. Middle Row (L-r) E. Shaw (Physio), I. Reid, S. Hughes, K. Gratton, G. Cuneely, G. Hunter (Capt), J. Wilbraham, D. Reid, P. Copeland, I. Vernon and R. Harvey. Front Row (L-R) A. Gibson (Coach), P. Hornby, P. Gannon, J. Bremend, D. Taylor (Manager), S. Allcock, P. Warrilow and D. Ward. Colours: Yellow/Blue/Yellow.

ASHTON UNITED

President: Mr. D. Wallwork
Secretary: K. Wickham
Chairman: Mr. C.H. Buxton
Manager: A. Pike
Ground Address & Tel. No: Hurst Cross, Ashton-U-Lyne. 061 339 4158
Capacity: 7,000 **Covered accommodation:** 3,500 **Seating:** 350 **Floodlights:** Yes
Simple ground directions: From town centre, up Mossley Road, left at 1st lights, up Queens Rd. Next lights turn left, ground on right.
Clubhouse details: Open 6 nights a week, matchdays
Programme details: 24 pages, 15p.
Editor: Malcolm Smart
Club colours: Red/Black/Red
Change colours: Blue/White/Blue
Local newspapers: Ashton Report, Advertiser
Midweek matchday: Monday
Record attendance: 11,500 v Halifax (FA Cup, 1st Round Replay 1953)
Previous Leagues: Cheshire, Manchester, Midland, Lancs. Comb
Senior Honours/Best Performance: Manchester Senior Cup, Manchester Premier, Lancs Comb Div. 2 Chapions, Man. League Champions.
Past players: Alfa Arrowsmith, Barney Daniels, Alan Ball, John Mahoney, John Platt
Year form: 1878

ATHERTON L.R.

President: J. Sumner
Secretary: Brian Seddon
Chairman: A. Grundy
Manager: Harold Crilly
Ground Address & Tel. No: Crilly Park. 883950
Simple ground directions: A579 to Central Station from Bolton, left at Upton Road, left Springfield Road, left Hillside, follow road to ground.
Capacity: 3,000 **Covered accommodation:** 100 **Seating:** 60 **Floodlights:** No
Clubhouse details: Bar facilities
Programme details: 16 pages 20p
Editor: David Jackson
Local newspaper: Bolton Evening News
Club colours: Yellow
Change colours: Blue
Midweek matchday: Wednesday
Previous Leagues: Bolton Comb. Cheshire League
Senior Honours/Best Performance: Runner Up Second Division Reserve League 1985/86
Past players: K. Stott, W. Aspinall, B. Butler

BLACKPOOL MECHANICS

Chairman: P. Sutton
Secretary: W. Singleton, 12 Morley Road, Blackpool, Lancashire FY4 4EP.
Telephone: (0253) 68105
Ground Address and Telephone No: Common Edge Road, South Shore, Blackpool, Lancashire
Telephone: (0253) 61721
Colours: Yellow Shirts, Green Shirts, Yellow stockings
Change Colours: Red Shirts, Blue Shorts, Blue Stockings

CHADDERTON

President: D. Glynn
Secretary: John Regan, 3 Hill Top, Healds Green, Chadderton, Oldham OL1 2SB. 061 624 3307 (H), 061 834 4079 (B)
Chairman: N.H. McDonald
Manager: Roya Ashton
Ground Address 8 Tel. No: Andrew St, Chandderton. 061 624 9733, 061 330 6108
Capacity: 2000 **Seating:** 200 **Floodlights:** No
Simple ground directions: M62 Junction 20, A627 (M) Left at first lights, then first left.
Clubhouse details: Players lounge, refreshment bar, licensed bar, toilets
Programme details: 20 pages. 10p
Editor: D. Ball
Local newspaper: Oldham Evening Chronicle
Club colours: Red/Navy/Red
Change colours: All Blue
Midweek matchday: Wednesday
Record Attendance: 1500
Previous Leagues: Oldham Amateur, South East Lancs, Manchester Amateur, Manchester, Lancs Comb.
Senior Honours/Best Performance: Manchester League Gilgryst Cup
Past players: Graham Bell (Oldham, Preston, Carlisle, Bolton), Paul Hilton (Bury, West Ham Utd), Ian Johnson (Rochdale), Dave Platt (Man. Utd. Crewe), John Pemberton (Rochdale, Crewe), Brian Marriott (Oldham Ath.)

COLNE DYNAMOES

President: P. Parry
Chairman: H. Pickup
Secretary: P. Terry, 8 Princess Street, Colne, Lancs
Address & Tel. No: Colne (0282) 866768 (H); 865777 (W)
Manager: G.L. White
Coach: W. Gaskell
Commercial Manager: As above
Physiotherapist: S. Parkinson
Press Officer: As above
Address & Tel. No of ground: Holt House, Colne (0282) 862335
Club Shop: No
Simple ground directions: Go to top of Harrison Drive, Colne, ground on right.
Seating: 50 **Covered accommodation:** 200 **Capacity:** 2,.000 **Floodlights:** August 1985
Year formed: 1963 **Nickname:** Dynamoes **Club sponsors:** Riddiough's Timber (Raab Marcher) Colne
Previous names: None
Club colours: All Red
Previous grounds: None
Change colours: All Sky Blue
Midweek matchday: Wednesday
Record attendance: 1,500. 1964
Previous Leagues: Lancs Combination, West Lancs, Burnley Comb, Nelson & Colne Prem.
Clubhouse details: None
Present players with Football League experience:
None
Past players who progressed into the Football League: Kevin Hird (Blackburn, Leeds, Burnley), Peter Bourne (Burnley)
Record transfer fee paid: None
Record transfer fee received: None
Local newspapers: Nelson Leader/Colne Times, Nelson 62561
Senior Honours: NW Counties Div 3 Champions 1982-83, Lancashire Combination Runners-Up 1980-81, 1981-82, Lancashire Amateur League 1972-73
Club Captain (9184-85: Andrew Samuels
Player of the Year: Dave Stobbs

COLWYN BAY

President: Mr. R. Griffith
Secretary: Mr. A.J. Banks
Chairman: Mr. G. Owens
Manager: Mr. Bryn Jones
Ground Address & Tel. No: Llanelian Rd, Old Colwyn, Clwyd. Tel. 0492 514581
Capacity: 4,000 **Covered accommodation:** 400 **Seating:** 200 **Floodlights:** Possibly this season
Simple ground directions: 1st exit off by-pass (signposted Old Colwyn), straight on at mini roundabout into Llanelian Rd. Ground ½ mile on right.
Clubhouse details: K.L. Club. After matches only
Programme details: 16 pages, 20p
Editor: Mr. N. Jones
Club metal badges: No
Local newspapers: North Wales Weekly News. Tel. Abergele 825512. North Wales Pioneer
Club colours: Sky Blue/Maroon/Sky Blue
Change colours: Maroon/Sky Blue/Maroon
Midweek matchday: Tuesday
Record Attendance: 5,000 (on previous ground)
Previous Leagues: Welsh League (North
Senior Honours/Best Performance: Welsh Champions, N.W. Coast Challenge Cup. Various Local Cups. S/F Welsh Cup 82-83. 2-2 at Swansea City
Past players: Gareth Davies (Wrexham), Peter Suddaby (Blackpool)

DARWEN

President: J. Haworth
Chairman: J.D. Jepson
Secretary: R.D. Norton
Address & Tel. No: 43 Thorncliffe Drive, Darwen, Lancs
BB3 3QA. Darwen 774851 (H), Blackburn 53938 (B)
Manager: D.G. Entwistle
Coach: D. Bell
Commercial Manager: D.B. Bent
Physiotherapist: A. Raw
Address & Tel. No: 0254 59847
Address 8 Tel. No. of ground: Anchor Ground, Anchor Road, Darwen, Lancs. BB3 0BB. (Darwen 75627)
Club shop: Yes
Simple ground directions: Just off the main A666 twixt Bolton/Blackburn, approx 1 mile north of Darwen town centre
No of seats: 80 approx. **Covered accommodation:** 4,500 **Capacity:** 9,000 **Floodlights:** No
Year formed: 1875 **Nickname:** The Salmoners **Club sponsors:** Senator
Previous names: None
Club colours: Maroon/Sky Blue
Previous grounds: Barley Bank
Change colours: Navy/White Stripes
Midweek matchdays: Tuesday
Record attendance: 9,000 v Luton, FA Cup. 1909
Previous Leagues: Football Alliance, Football League Div. 1, Div. 2, Lancashire Combination, Cheshire County
Best performance in: 1881 Semi-Final, 1932 3rd Round, FA Trophy: 1978-9, 2nd Qualifying Round
Clubhouse details: Light refreshments available matchdays
Present players with Football League experience: Norman Bell (Wolves, Blackburn Rovers)
Past Players who progressed into the Football League: S. Mullen (Bury), A. Whitehead (Brentford), P. Devine (Burnley), J. Waddington (Blackburn Rovers), R. Jackson (Bury), H. Jackson (Burnley), T. Prest (Burnley), T. Haslam (Manchester U)
Record transfer fee received: £3,000 for S. Mullen
Programme details: 8 pages 10p
Programme Editor: Secretary
Local newspapers & Tel. No: Darwen Advertiser & News, Lancashire Evening Telegraph
Senior Honours: Lancashire Combination (4), NW Counties, Cup Winners
Club Captain: G. Dickenson
Player of the Year: G. Dickenson

DROYLSDEN

President: W.J. Mercer
Secretary: A.S. Fenna, 277 Manchester Road, Audenshaw, Manchester M34 5QS
Chairman: D. Sterling
Manager: M. Fallon
Capacity: 3,500 (reduced 1982) **Covered accommodation:** 1000 **Seating:** 200 **Floodlights:** Yes
Simple ground directions: 4 miles east of Manchester via A662 Ashton New Road. Ground is directly behind Butchers Arms Hotel in Droylsden town centre.
Clubhouse details: Open six evenings a week and Saturday afternoon match days. Bingo Wednesday, Friday, Saturday, Sunday. Entertainment Saturday, Sunday. Bars in Lounge and Games Room.
Programme details: Not known at time of going to press
Club metal badges: Yes
Local newspaper: Reporter 061-3031910
Club colours: RED/RED/RED
Change colours: White/Black/White
Midweek matchday: Tuesday
Year formed: 1866
Record attendance: 4,250 v Grimsby Town, F.A. Cup First Round. 1976
Previous Leagues: Lancashire Combination, Manchester, Cheshire County
Senior Honours/Best Performance: Cheshire County League Runners-Up (2), Cheshire County League Challenge Cup Winners & Runners-Up, Manchester Senior Cup Winners (3), Runners-Up (3), Manchester Challenge Shield Winners (2) & Runners-Up, Manchester Intermediate Cup Winners (3), Manchester Premier Cup Winners & Runners-Up.

ELLESMERE PORT & NESTON

President: J.F. Price
Secretary: L. Jones, 15 Ure Court, Overpool, Ellesmere Port, South Wirral. Tel. 051 356 2308
Chairman: H. Thelwell
Ground Address & Tel. No: Thornton Road Stadium, Thornton Road, Ellesmere Port, Wirral 355 7475
Capacity: 8,450 **Covered accommodation:** 2,500 Seating: 450 **Floodlights:** Yes
Simple ground directions: Junction 10 M53, left, then first right follow signs for stadium (approx 2 miles).
Clubhouse details: Next to ground
Programme details: 8 pages 20p
Editor: Secretary
Club metal badges: None
Local newspapers: Pioneer, Liverpool Echo
Year formed: 1979
Club colours: All Green
Change colours: All Yellow
Midweek matchday: Wednesday
Previous Leagues: Clwyd
Senior Honours/Best Performance: North West Counties Challenge Cup Winners 1983/84

FORMBY F.C.

President:
Secretary: Ray Roberts
Chairman: Chris Welsh
Manager: Vic Manning
Ground Address & Tel. No: Brows Lane, Formby. Tel. Formy 72603
Capacity: 2,000 **Covered accommodation:** 300 **Seating:** 200 **Floodlights:** No
Simple ground directions: A565 Formby Village Centre.
Clubhouse details: Tues, Thurs, Sat, Sun
Programme details: 6 pages 15p
Editor: D. Griffiths
Club metal badges: Pennants
Local Newspapers: Formby Times 72237
Year formed: 1920
Club colours: Yellow/Yellow/Blue
Change colours: Blues Stripes/Blue
Midweek matchdays: Tuesday
Previous Leagues: Cheshire League
Record attendance: 2,500 v Oldham Ath. F.A. Cup 1973
Senior Honours/Best Performance: Liverpool Senior Cup Winners.
Past players: Geoff Twentman, Paul Welsh

GREAT HARWOOD TOWN

President: None
Secretary: None at present
Chairman: T.E. Edwardson
Address & Tel. No.:
Manager: R.H. Grogan
Coach: H.J. Martin
Commercial Manager: B. Marsden
Physiotherapist: None
Press Officer & Tel. No: Dave Holden (Gt. Harwood 884255)
Address & Tel. No of ground: Cloggers S.C., Showground, Wood Street, Great Harwood, Blackburn, Lancs. (Gt. Harwood 888103)
Simple ground directions: Look for gas holder, ground 100 yds away.
Seating: 220 **Covered accommodation:** 1,000 **Capacity:** 4,000 **Floodlights:** Yes
Year formed: 1966 **Nickname:** Arrad **Club sponsors:** Blackburn Fork Lifts Ltd.
Previous names: Great Harwood Wellington
Club colours: All Red
Previous grounds: Memorial Park, Gt Harwood
Change colours: All Blue
Midweek matchday: Wednesday
Record attendance: 550 v Clitheroe (League). 1984-85
Previous Leagues: Blackburn Comb, West Lancashire, Lancs Comb.
Best performance: FA Cup. Not entered. FA Vase: 1981-2 2nd Qualifying Round
Clubhouse details: Cloggers Social Club, licensed bar and refreshments
Programme Editor: Dave Holden (G.H. 884255)
Programme details: 20 pages, 10p
Senior Honours: Lancashire Combination Cup
Club Captain 1984-85: B. Moran
Player of the Year 1984-85: H.J. Martin

LANCASTER CITY

President: M. Woodhouse
Chairman: J. Bagguely
Secretary: B. Roberts
Address & Tel. No: 231 Bowerham Rd, Newlands, Lancaster. 0524 67654 (H) 0524 65222 (B)
Manager: R. Danson
Ground Address & Tel. No: Giant Axe, West Road, Lancaster 0524 382238
Capacity: 5,000 **Covered accommodation:** 1,000 **Seating:** 350 **Floodlights:** Yes
Simple ground directions: M6 Junction 34. Follow signs to Lancaster, past University, through roundabout, through two sets of pedestrian lights. Left at traffic lights, first right over railway bridge, left at end of road. Ground on right at bottom of hill.
Programme details: 24 pages, 20p **Editor:** Avenue Prog. J. Downham
Year formed: 1902 **Nicknames:** Dolly Blues
Local newspapers: Lancaster Guardian/Morecombe Visitor/Lancs Evening Post
Club colours: Blue/White/Blue **Change colours:** Yellow/Red/Red
Midweek matchday: Wednesday **Record attendance:** 7500 v Carlisle 1936
Previous Leagues: Lancs Combination, Northern Premier League
Senior Honours/Best Performance: Lancs Trophy 5 times, FA Cup 2nd Round 3 times, (Last 1972-3 v Notts Co.), FA Trophy 3rd Round twice.
Past players: Alan Taylor, Brendan O'Callaghan

OLDHAM TOWN

President: L. Charnock **Secretary:** R. Manton
Chairman: J. Stanley **Manager:** K. Hughies
Ground Address & Tel. No: Nordens Road, Chadderton. Oldham. (061 624 0914)
Capacity: 600 **Covered accommodation:** Yes **Seating:** Yes **Floodlights:** No
Simple ground directions: From Manchester. Oldham Rd to Broadway. Proceed along Broadway to Middleton Rd, turn left. Proceed along Middleton Road to Norden Road on right. Along to ground.
Clubhouse details: None at present **Year formed:** 1985
Programme details: None at present **Midweek matchday:** Tues/Thurs.
Club colours: White/Blue/White **Record attendance:** 354
Previous Leagues: Manchester Amateur/Lancashire Combination/NWC
Senior Honours/Best Performance: Runners Up Third Division North West counties 1985/86. Pettit Cup Winners 1975/76, Cosling Cup Winners 1979/80.
Past players: G. Walker (Stockport County)

PRESCOT CABLES

President: B.F. Taylor **Secretary:** Non known yet
Chairman: G. Johnson **Manager:** Bill Hennesey
Ground Address & Tel. No: Hope Street, Prescot, Merseyside. 051-426 1286
Simple ground directions: M6-M62 junction 7, A57 Prescot
Capacity: 10,000 **Covered accommodation:** 4,000 **Seating:** 600 **Floodlights:** No
Club colours: Yellow/Black **Change colours:** All Red
Programme details: 16 pages, 20p **Editor:** J. Richards
Midweek matchday: Wednesdays
Previous Leagues: Lancashire Comb, Mid-Cheshire, Cheshire County
Record attendance: 8,122. 1932
Senior Honours: Lancs Comb Cup, Lancs Comb League, Liverpool Senior Non-League Cup (4), Liverpool Challenge Cup (6)

SALFORD

President:
Chairman: Harold Brearley
Manager: David Enwhistle
Asst. Manager/Coach: Eric Haslam
Physiotherapist: Alan Raw
Secretary: Frank McCawley
Address & Tel. No: 22 Beverley Road, Pendlebury Swinton M27 1HY. 061-736 0021 (H) 061 736 4117 (B)
Commercial Manager: P. Fitzhugh 061-775 8313 (B)
Trainer: David Bell
Address & Tel. No. of ground: Moor Lane Ground, Nevile Road, Kersal, Salford 7. 061-792 6287
Simple ground directions: Take Bury road out of Manchester (Bury New Road), Moor Lane 3 miles from Cathedral (Deansgate), Nevile Road first left
No. of seat: 200 **Covered accommodation:** 600 **Capacity:** 8,000 **Floodlights:** No
Year formed: 1937 **Nickname:** Ammies **Club sponsors:** None
Club colours: Amber/Amber/Blue **Change colours:** Tangerine/Black/Black
Record attendance: 3,000 v Whickham, F.A. Vase. Year: 1981
Best performance: F.A. Vase 1981 Last 16
Present players with Football League experience: A. Dean (Rochdale), M. Ennis (Rochdale)
Previous Leagues: Manchester **Programme:** 12 pages, 10p
Clubhouse details: None **Programme Editor:** Secretary
Major Honours: Lancashire Amateur Cup 1973, 1975, 1977, Manchester Premier Cup (Senior) 1973, 1974, 1976, Manchester County Champion of Champions 1975, Manchester League Champions 1975, 1976, 1977, 1979, Runners-Up 1971, 1973, 1978, First Division & Cup Winners 1969

SKELMERSDALE UNITED

President: R. Glover
Secretary: T. Rogers
Chairman: K. Houghton
Manager: Russ Perkins
Ground Address & Tel. No: White Moss Park, White Moss Road, Skelmersdale. (22123)
Capacity: 10,250 **Covered accommodation:** 2,000 **Seating:** 250 **Floodlights:** Yes
Simple ground directions: M6 to Junc 26. M58 to Junc. 3. Right at roundabout, 100 yds to next roundabout. Turn right and follow road ¾ mile to ground.
Programme details: 12 pages
Editor: K. Houghton
Local newspapers: Ormskirk & Skelmsdale Advertiser
Club colours: All Blue
Change colours: All Yellow
Midweek matchday: Wednesday
Record attendance: 7,500 v Slough, FA Amateur Cup 1967
Previous Leagues: Liverpool County Comb. Lancs. Comb. Northern Prem. Cheshire County
Senior Honours/Best Performance: FA Cup 1st Round. FA Amateur Cup - 1971 Winners. 1967 Runners-Up.
Past players: Steve Heighway, Mickey Burns, Alan Mansley, Alan Birmingham, Peter Southerby, Peter Hardcastle, Dave Moorcroft

WARRINGTON TOWN

President: J. Drinkwater
Secretary: C. Hope
Chairman: R. Smith
Manager: D. Taylor
Ground Address & Tel. No: Common Lane, off Loushers Lane, Latchford, Warrington, Cheshire 31932
Simple ground directions: From Warrington via A49, turn left into Loushers Lane, 2 miles from town centre
Capacity: 3,000 **Covered accommodation:** 1,000 **Seating:** 200 **Floodlights:** No
Clubhouse details: Excellent clubhouse with 2 bars, concert room and players lounge
Programme details: 10 pages, 20p
Editor: M. Lappin
Club colours: Yellow/Blue/Yellow
Change colours: Blue/Blue/White
Record attendance: 2,200 v Halesowen FA Vase Semi. 1st Leg
Previous Leagues: Mid Cheshire, Cheshire
Midweek matchday:
Senior Honours/Best Performance: North West Counties League Cup Winners, Winners of Champion of Champions League Winners Div 1. J. League Cup Winners 85/86. Semi-Finalist, FA Vase 85/86
Past players: Roger Hunt, John Richards, John Bramhall

WREN ROVERS SPORTS CLUB

President: J.P. Sutton
Secretary: P. Kimberley
Chairman: B. Cartmel
Address 8 Tel. No. 34 Priory Gate, Blackpool FY4 2QE. 0253 49853 (H) 0253 737464 (B)
Manager: Mike Emery
Coach: Dave Furnival
Physiotherapist: J. McMillan
Address & Tel. No of ground: School Road, Marton, Blackpool 68425
Simple ground directions: Follow 'Airport' signs from M55 or A583 to South Shore, Ground on right 1½ miles
No of seats: 200 **Covered accommodation:** 400 **Capacity:** 4,000 **Floodlights:** No
Year formed: 1931 **Nickname:** Wrens **Club sponsors:** Many
Midweek matchdays: Tuesday
Previous Leagues: Blackpool Amateur, West Lancashire
Club colours: Red/White
Change colours: Blue/White
Clubhouse details: Members lounge bar, visiting officals lounge
Present players with Football League experience: Rob Thomas, John Armfield, John Butler
Past players who progressed into the Football League: Mark Lawrenson (Liverpool)
Programme details: 8 pages
Programme editor: Paul Kimberley
Local newspapers & Tel. No: Black Evening Gazette
Senior Honours: Lancashire Combination League (2), Lancashire F.A. Challenge Shield Winners (2), Lancashire Combination Cup (1) (League and Cup Double 1979)
Club Captain: Kevin Royston
Player of the Year: Ian Stewart

THE NORTH WEST COUNTIES FOOTBALL LEAGUE SEASON 1985/86
THIRD DIVISION

LEAGUE TABLE

	P	W	D	L	F	A	Pts	G.G.
Blackpool Mechanics	28	22	2	4	77	33	*44	44
Oldham Town	28	14	9	5	56	29	37	27
Maghull	28	15	6	7	62	36	36	26
Daisy Hill	28	13	7	8	62	45	33	17
Atherton Collieries	28	13	7	8	48	37	33	11
Bolton S.T.	28	12	7	9	42	34	*29	8
Cheadle Town	28	9	10	9	42	26	28	16
Bacup Borough	28	10	36	40	28	−4		
Padiham	28	8	10	10	44	45	26	−1
Prestwich Heys	28	10	6	12	53	66	26	−13
Newton	28	7	10	11	43	48	24	−5
Whitworth Valley	28	7	8	13	42	48	22	−6
Huyton Town	28	7	7	14	41	71	21	−30
Nelson	28	7	7	14	36	65	*19	−29
Ashton Athletic	28	1	6	21	24	85	8	−61

RESULTS

	Ashton Athletic	Atherton Collieries	Bacup Borough	Blackpool Mechanics	Bolton S.T.	Cheadle Town	Daisy Hill	Huyton Town	Maghull	Nelson	Newton	Oldham Town	Padiham	Prestwich Heys	Whitworth Valley
Ashton Athletic		1-1	0-0	1-3	0-1	0-3	2-5	1-4	3-1	1-2	1-1	2-4	1-3	0-4	2-2
Atherton Collieries	2-1		4-1	2-3	0-1	1-3	2-4	3-1	2-1	3-1	1-1	1-1	1-0	2-0	4-0
Bacup Borough	1-0	0-0		0-1	1-0	0-0	0-2	9-0	1-1	2-1	3-1	0-3	3-2	3-0	1-0
Blackpool Mechanics	6-0	4-0	1-0		2-0	1-0	3-0	4-3	4-2	3-0	3-1	1-0	6-0	7-1	1-3
Bolton S.T.	5-0	1-3	0-2	2-4		0-0	1-1	4-2	0-1	3-0	4-1	2-2	1-0	5-2	1-0
Cheadle Town	1-1	1-1	3-0	0-1	2-0		1-1	6-0	0-1	0-1	1-1	0-3	1-1	1-2	0-1
Daisy Hill	4-2	2-1	4-1	0-1	3-1	2-2		1-1	2-4	4-0	2-2	2-3	0-0	4-5	0-0
Huyton Town	1-1	2-2	0-0	2-1	2-2	0-1	3-2		1-4	2-1	1-1	1-0	4-2	3-3	2-3
Maghull	4-0	1-0	5-0	3-2	0-1	2-1	0-3	2-0		3-1	1-2	2-0	2-2	3-3	3-0
Nelson	3-1	0-2	3-1	1-4	1-1	0-6	3-2	2-1	2-2		1-1	1-2	0-6	2-2	2-2
Newton	5-1	2-2	4-1	2-2	1-2	1-4	3-0	1-2	1-0	3-0		1-2	2-2	2-3	0-0
Oldham Town	7-0	1-2	2-2	4-1	0-0	1-1	0-1	1-0	2-2	4-1	4-0		1-1	2-2	3-1
Padiham	4-0	2-0	0-0	2-2	1-1	2-2	1-2	4-0	0-6	1-4	1-0	2-3		0-1	0-0
Prestwich Heys	4-1	2-4	2-3	1-2	0-1	2-1	2-6	4-2	1-4	1-1	1-2	0-0	0-2		2-1
Whitworth Valley	4-1	0-2	1-1	3-4	3-2	0-1	1-3	6-1	2-2	2-2	3-1	0-1	2-3	2-3	

Nelson F.C. 1985-6. Back Row (L-R) G. Sowerbutts, G. Taylor, A. Livesey, D. Gregory, J. Omerod, P. Marshall, P. Snape, B. Redhead. Front Row (L-R) A. Dildes, P. Wharton, M. Thompson, G. Woodall, G. McMillan, A. Cocaran.

NORTH WEST COUNTIES — DIVISION THREE

ASHTON TOWN
Secretary: E.J. Williams. Tel: 0942 57543
Ground: Edge Green Street, Stubsman Cross, Ashton-in-Makerfield. Tel: 0942 57543
Colours: All Red **Change Colours:** Yellow & Green Stripes/Green/Green

ATHERTON COLLERIES
Secretary: Christine Howell. Tel: 0942 879767
Ground: Alder House, Alder Street, Atherton, Lancashire. Tel: 0942 879209
Colours: White with Black pinstripe/Black/Black **Change Colours:** Yellow with red pinstripe/Yellow/Yellow

BACUP BOROUGH
Secretary: S. Lloyd. Tel: 070 685 3508
Ground: West View, Cowfoot Lane, Blackthorn, Bacup, Lancs
Colours: Black — Black & White stripes Black/Black **Change Colours:** Blue/Blue/Red

CHEADLE TOWN
Secretary: G.J. Furness. Tel: 061 428 7468
Ground: Park Road Stadium, Park Road, Cheadle, Cheshire. Tel: 061 428 2510
Colours: All White **Change Colours:** Green & Black Stripes Black/Black

DAISY HILL
Secretary: R. Naylor. Tel: 0942 813720
Ground: New Sirs, St. James Street, West Houghton, Bolton, Lancs. Tel: 0942 818544
Colours: All Royal Blue **Change Colours:** Red/Navy Blue/Red

FLIXTON
Secretary: J. Fitzpatrick. Tel: 061 865 9215
Ground: Valley Road, Flixton, Manchester
Colours: Blue & White Stripes/Black/Blue **Change Colours:** Red & Black Stripes/Black/Black

FORD MOTORS
Secretary: J. Pilkington. Tel: 051 226 9435
Ground: Ford Sports & Social Club, Cronton Lane, Widnes, Cheshire. Tel: 051 424 7078 or 4615
Colours: All Sky Blue **Change Colours:** White/Red/Red

MAGHULL
Secretary: D. Sherlock. Tel: 051 526 2306
Ground: Old Hall Field, Hall Lane, Maghull, Merseyside. Tel: 051 526 7320
Colours: All Blue **Change Colours:** Red/Black/Black

NANTWICH TOWN
Secretary: J.F. Lindop. Tel: 0270 626458
Ground: Jackson Avenue, London Road, Nantwich, Cheshire. Tel: 0270 624098
Colours: Green/White/Green/White **Change Colours:** Yellow/White/Yellow & White

NELSON
Secretary: R. Codd. Tel: 0282 37667
Ground: Victoria Park, Lomeshaye Way, Nelson, Lancs. 0282 63820
Colours: Blue/White/White **Change Colours:** White/Red/White

NEWTON
Secretary: A.K. Crook. Tel: 0204 693421
Ground: Vista Park, Vista Road, Newton-le-Willos, Merseysude. Tel: 092 52 29893
Colours: Navy Blue/White/Red **Change Colours:** Yellow/Black/Black

PADIHAM
Secretary: T. Opacic. Tel: 0282 31770
Ground: The Arbories Memorial Ground, Well Street, Padiham, Lancs. Tel: 0282 73742
Colours: Navy Blue/White/Red **Change Colours:** Yellow/Black/Black

WHITWORTH VALLEY
Secretary: A. Hampton. Tel: 070 685 3237
Ground: Rawstron Street, Whitworth, Rochdale, Lancashire
Colours: Blue/Navy/Blue/Blue **Change Colours:** Yellow/Yellow/Black

THE WEST LANCASHIRE FOOTBALL LEAGUE

BAC Preston are Champions at last

The season's fixture programme was devastated by the appalling weather conditions. From quite early on games were postponed due to rain. As time progressed the wet turned to frost and back again to wet. Some clubs did not play more than four games in three months.

This was not the case though, for BAC Preston. Their well maintained pitch saw them playing and more importantly winning games when other teams were idle.

The points accrued from these games put their opponents under pressure to win the games in hand that they had over the Preston team.

Longridge United were amongst the early leaders. It was not until February that they suffered their first defeat. This was at the hands of Squires Gate. Lady luck had certainly played a big part in this run of Longridge.

Holker Old Boys from Barrow-in-Furness were surprise contenders. They had been i the shadows of both Dalton United and Vickers S.C. for a long time. This season they reached their highest position ever by taking second place. Their last two games involved travelling to both Longridge United and Colne Dynamoes Reserves. Two hard trips. Holker won the first but lost the second at Colne. This last game needed to be won by a rugby score for them to pip BAC.

After the disappointment of missing out last season BAC Preston were in no mood to allow it to happen again. The lads from Preston were not only winning games but also scoring goals, on six occasions they scored five or more. However, it was not unknown for the odd hiccup to happen. After putting six past College they ost to the same team only forty eight hours later. This defeat shook the team into action for their derby game at Freckleton which was won handsomely by four goals. The championship was finally secured in the last game at Vickers. It certainly was not a classic but BAC will not be too worried about that.

At the other end of the table Feniscowles pulled off their 'Houdini' trick again by staving off relegation. The two teams from the Lancaster area, Lansil and Middleton face second division football next season.

The Richardson Cup provided quite a few shocks. All three teams from Barrow were soon eliminated. At the semi final stage Burnley United and Colne Dynamoes faced each other with BAC Preston and Wigan College contending the other. On paper the first named clubs should have come out on top. This was not to be so. Both games were dull affairs. The final was played at Deepdale with Wigan College proving too strong for Colne Dynamoes.

The race for promotion from division two was just as exciting and wide open. The main contenders were Blackpool Rangers, BAe Warton, ICI Thornton, Colne British Legion, Stanley United, Kirkham Town and Mill Hill St. Peters. The lead kept changing hands but then Blackpool Rangers were dealt a fair but hard blow. Due to a serious offence they had two points deducted.

The weather and county cup competitions were taking their toll on fixtures, especially those of Kirkham Town and Mill Hill St. Peters. Towards the end of March neither side had played more than half their fixtures. Meanwhile ICI Thornton were maintaining some sort of continuity of games. Unfortunately they were not putting the points in the bag. The Thornton team could only watch their lead eroding away and then look on as other teams passed them by.

The Kirkham team must be congratulated on their magnificence of the past season. The team won a county cup competition. In doing so their league programme was affected to such an extent that they finished up playing four night games a week. Despite the Carnforth Rangers and Lucas S.C. were two teams who showed a lot of enterprise and could be contenders next season. Colne British Legion, Stanley United and Wigan Roves all fell by the wayside when the going got tough.

If Kirkham's fixture congestion had not been bad enough with league commitments it was certainly aggravated by their cup win. They went from the preliminary round right through to the final. Their opponents were Blackpool Rangers. The opening twenty five minutes were very much like a chess game and it was not until the Kirkham 'keeper made a bad mistake that a goal was scored. From there on it was Blackpool's game. Squires Gate retained the Reserve Division North/West Championship although it did take until their last game to secure it. Kirkham Town ran them a close second. In the South/East division Burnley United emerged as the top team. Vernon Carus, after many years in the doldrums took second place.

The Houston Cup was played on a group basis with the top team of the four groups meeting in te semi finals. The South/East teams dominated this competition by providing three teams. Longridge United needed extra time to see off Squires Gate whilst Burnley United after trailing three-nil at half time scored five in the second half. In the Final Longridge proved too strong for Burnley.

Once again the high standard of football was shown throughout. The honours were not decided until the last games of the season. Despite the weather the league programme was completed only a few days late.

FINAL LEAGUE TABLES:
SEASON 85-86 — DIVISION 1

	P	W	D	L	F	A	Pts
BAC Preston	34	24	5	5	87	30	53
Holker OB	34	22	7	5	73	35	51
Longridge United	34	20	7	7	62	37	47
Freckleton	34	17	8	9	54	42	42
Haslingden	34	17	7	10	83	60	41
Poulton	34	17	6	11	72	53	40
Burnley United	34	16	7	11	61	47	39
Wigan College	34	14	9	11	74	62	37
Dalton United	34	14	8	12	53	54	36
College	34	13	6	15	58	60	32
Colne Dyn. Res	34	12	6	16	60	68	30
Squires Gate	34	9	12	13	54	67	30
Anchor Cables	34	11	7	16	62	81	29
Crown Paints	34	11	6	17	59	68	28
Vickers SC	34	9	9	16	49	54	27
Feniscowles	34	6	9	19	56	81	21
*Middleton	34	5	6	23	45	87	14
*Lansil	34	5	6	23	45	87	14

*2 Points deducted.

LEADING GOALSCORERS

SEASON 1985/86 — DIVISION 1

J. Wylie	Haslingden	35
G. Collier	Poulton	23
P. Jackson	Feniscowles	19
G. Moss	BAC (Preston)	19
S. Donaghey	College	17
K. Farnworth	Wigan College	17
P. Swarbrick	Holker O. B.	16
M. Ballantyne	Holker O. B.	15
A. Dilworth	BAC (Preston)	15
D. Johnson	Dalton United	15
A. Butterworth	Longridge United	14
C. Jones	Dalton United	14
M. Kayley	Haslingden	14
P. Stanley	BAC (Preston)	14

Division 1

ANCHOR CABLES: Etherstone St. Leigh
Colours: All sky blue. Change White/sky blue/sky blue.
Secretary: E. Baguley 0942-674801.

BAC PRESTON: Riverside Sports Ground, South Meadow Lane, Preston.
Colours: Black/and white striped shirts, white shorts, black socks. Change: Red/white/white.
Secretary: P. Ardern, 46 Garstone Croft, Preston. 0772-719391.

BURNLEY UNITED: Bardon Sports Ground, Barden Lane, Burnley.
Colours: All blue. Change: All yellow.
Secretary: J. Britton, 1 Bulcock St., Burnley. 0282-31870.

COLNE DYNAMOES RESERVES: Holt House, Colne.
Colours: Red/red/black. Change: All sky blue.
Secretary: P. Terry, 8 Princess St., Colne. 0282-866768.

COLLEGE: College of Further Education, Lancaster Rd., Morecombe.
Colours: Gold/black/black. Change: All blue.
Secretary: W. Theobold, 2 Barbon Place, Lancaster. 0524-60448.

CROWN PAINTS F.C.: Oakenhurst, Anchor Rd., Darwen.
Colours: All red. Change: Blue and white stripes.
Secretary: S. Lawrenson, 11 Feniscliffe Dr., Blackburn. 0254-22086.

DALTON UNITED: Railway Meadow, Beckside Rd., Dalton-in-Furness.
Colours: Scarlet and blue stripes/scarlet/scarlet and blue hoops.
Secretary: D. R. Lacy, 12 Brent Ave., Dalton-on-Furness. 0229-64202.

FENISCOWLES: Recreation Ground, Livesey Branch Rd., Feniscowles, Blackburn.
Colours: Blue and white stripes/navy/navy. Change: All red.
Secretary: R. Tomlinson, 12 Fielding St., Rishton, nr Blackburn. 0254-886699.

FRECKLETON: Hodgson Memorial Ground, Bush Lane, Freckleton, nr Preston.
Colours: Yellow/red/red. Change: Orange/green/green.
Secretary: Mrs. C. Bell, 27 Ribble Ave., Freckleton, nr Preston 0772-632036.

HASLINGDEN: Ewood Bridge, Rossendale.
Colours: All green. Change: Tangerine/black/tangerine.
Secretary: J. Taylor, 88 Burnley Rd., Edenfield, Ramsbottom. 0706-822994.

HOLKER OLD BOYS: Rakesmoor Lane, Barrow-in-Furness.
Colours: White and green stripes/green/green. Change: Blue/white.
Secretary: R. Nelson, 39 Dunmail Raise, Barrow-in-Furness. 0229-26858.

LANSIL: Lansil Sports Ground, Caton Rd., Lancaster.
Colours: All sky blue. Change: Red and Black stripes/black/black.
Secretary: M. Miller, 81 Coniston Rd., Lancaster. 0524-33962.

LONGRIDGE UNITED: Recreation Ground, Barclay Rd., Longridge.
Colours: Blue and white. Change: Red and yellow stripes/black/red.
Secretary: A. Wilson, 30 Wyresdale Cres., Preston. 0772-798256.

MIDDLETON: Middleton Playing Fields, Middleton. nr Morecombe.
Colours: All blue. Change: All yellow.
Secretary: P. Oldrieve, 13 Longlands Ave., Heysham. 0524-53561.

POULTON: Cottam Hall Playing Fields, Blackpool Old Rd., Poulton-le-Fylde.
Colours: All blue. Change: Gold and black/black/amber.
Secretary: D. Sponder, 11 Fairfield Ave., Poulton-le-Fylde. 0253-890284.

SQUIRES GATE: School Rd., Marton, Blackpool.
Colours: All blue. Change: All yellow.
Secretary: W. Carr, 60 Selby Ave., Blackpool. 0253-48450.

VICKERS S.C.: Hawcoat Park, Barrow-in-Furness.
Colours: Maroon/white/white. Change: All white.
Secretary: L. Ferguson, 23 Dundee St., Barrow-in-Furness.

WIGAN COLLEGE: Christopher Park, Standish.
Colours: White/black white.
Secretary: P. McAllister, 20 Loxton Cres., Hawkley Hall, Wigan. 0942-30943.

SPEEDWELL RICHARDSON CUP

Preliminary
Vickers 0, College 1
Holker OB 2, Anchor Cables

1st Round
Crown Paints 0, Wigan College 1
College 4-0, Longridge United 4-2
BAC Preston 4,Squires Gate 0
Haslingden 4, Dalton United 1
Freckleton 4, Anchor Cables 0
Poulton 0, Burnley United 4
Lansil 0, Feniscowles 3
Middleton 3, Colne Dynamoes 5

2nd Round
Longridge United 1, Wigan College 2
BAC Preston 2-3, Haslingden 2-0
Burnley United 5, Freckleton 1
Feniscowles 0, Colne Dynamoes 1

Semi Final
Wigan College 1, BAC Preston 0
Burnley United 1, Colne Dynamoes 2

Final
Wigan College 2, Colne Dynamoes 1

Sponsors:
League Competition: Ismail Tea and Coffee Co.
Richardson Cup: Speedwell Tool Co Preston
Presidents Cup: British Nuclear Fuels
Hourlon Cup: G. Bamber Esq.
Secretary of the Year: H. Johnstone Esq.
Referee of the Year: C. Barwise Esq.

NU-FRONTS WEST CHESHIRE A.F. LEAGUE

FINAL LEAGUE TABLES
DIVISION ONE

	P	W	D	L	F	A	Pts
Vauxhall	30	23	2	5	91	33	48
Mersey Royal	30	22	2	6	64	19	46
Poulton Victoria	30	19	7	4	61	19	45
General Chemicals	30	17	8	5	55	37	42
Hoylake	30	17	6	7	75	61	40
West Kirby	30	16	3	11	73	55	35
Heswall	30	13	9	8	59	43	35
Cammell Laird	30	15	4	11	64	48	34
Ashville	30	9	8	13	35	50	26
Christleton	30	10	5	15	44	58	25
Willaston	30	8	7	15	46	58	23
Bromborough Pool	30	7	6	17	40	66	20
Moreton	30	7	5	18	29	48	19
Stork	30	5	5	20	38	87	15
Cadbury	30	5	4	21	26	71	14
Newton	30	5	3	22	32	79	13

DIVISION TWO

	P	W	D	L	F	A	Pts
Merseyside Police	34	29	3	22	134	30	61
Poulton Victoria	34	27	4	3	107	34	58
Upton AA	34	24	5	5	95	50	53
Vauxhall Res	34	16	10	8	86	50	42
Shell	34	17	6	11	89	62	40
Rivacre Sports	34	16	7	11	86	60	39
Cammell Laird Res	34	15	9	10	74	61	39
HR Bebington	34	15	7	12	66	53	37
Heswall Res	34	14	7	13	72	60	35
Mond Rangers	34	13	9	12	73	71	35
Christleton Res	34	12	6	16	74	74	30
Ashville Res	34	12	5	17	65	84	29
Blacon Youth Club	34	10	5	19	68	65	25
West Kirby Res	34	8	7	19	53	91	23
Chester College	34	10	1	23	70	151	21
Stork Res	34	9	0	25	60	134	18
Cadbury Res	34	5	8	21	39	78	16
Brom. Pool Res	34	3	3	28	29	132	9

LANCASHIRE AMATEUR LEAGUE
FINAL LEAGUE TABLES SEASON 1985-1986

PREMIER DIVISION

	P	W	D	L	F	A	Pts
Old Boltonians	26	18	5	3	61	26	41
Fulwood Amateurs ...	26	13	8	5	49	31	34
Broughton Amateurs .	26	12	8	6	48	30	32
Burnley Belvedere	26	10	9	7	63	46	29
Old Mostonians	26	12	5	9	53	52	29
Bury Amateurs	26	11	6	9	43	33	28
Southport Amateurs .	26	12	4	10	48	42	28
Old Gregorians	26	12	3	11	57	41	27
Burnley GSOB	26	12	3	11	51	38	27
Rochdale St Clem.	26	9	6	11	48	54	24
Old Blackburnians	26	9	2	15	42	65	20
Hesketh Casuals	26	4	10	12	32	59	18
Old Rivingtonians	26	4	6	16	36	71	14
Rossendale Amateurs	26	5	3	18	36	79	13

DIVISION ONE

	P	W	D	L	F	A	Pts
Lymm OB	26	18	2	6	68	35	38
Bury GSOB	26	17	3	6	55	38	37
Preston GSA	26	14	6	6	55	38	37
Old Chaddertonians ..	26	12	6	8	47	41	30
Chorley Amateurs	26	13	3	10	65	58	29
Ashton GSOB	26	10	7	9	47	32	27
Newman College	26	9	7	10	47	44	25
Old Chorltonians	26	8	8	10	41	41	24
Little Lever SC	26	10	4	12	44	63	24
Walshaw SC	26	9	5	12	46	44	23
Oldham Hulmeians ...	26	10	3	13	47	63	23
Old Sladians	26	8	5	13	32	40	21
Bolton County	26	6	5	15	48	70	17
Hayward	26	3	6	17	31	70	12

DIVISION TWO

	P	W	D	L	F	A	Pts
Ainsdale United	26	21	1	4	94	36	43
Bolton Wyresdale	26	18	2	6	64	41	38
Middleton	26	16	2	8	74	39	34
Leigh Athletic Am. ...	26	14	6	6	59	36	34
Hathershaw SOB	26	14	4	8	64	57	32
Burnage HSOR	26	12	6	8	60	43	30
Old Smithillians	26	10	6	10	48	44	26
Old Salfordians	26	9	5	12	45	48	23
Accrington Amaeurs .	26	8	7	11	52	62	23
Thornleigh COB	26	8	6	12	46	53	22
Old Mancunians	26	9	4	13	51	59	22
North Man. HSOB ...	26	7	3	16	29	63	17
Manchester YMCA ...	26	3	6	17	32	79	12
Radcliffe Amateurs ...	26	1	6	19	19	77	8

STAFFORDSHIRE SENIOR LEAGUE

	P	W	D	L	F	A	Pts
Rochester	28	22	5	1	66	18	49
Eastwood	28	15	8	4	57	28	38
Eccleshall	28	15	7	6	66	26	37
Knypersley Vic	28	16	5	7	55	33	37
Hanford	28	14	7	7	41	23	35
Milton Utd	28	13	7	8	45	31	33
Stafd'shire Plc	28	13	3	12	44	38	29
Meir K.A.	28	10	7	11	43	49	27
Redgate Utd	28	10	6	12	45	53	26
Goldenhill Wandrs	28	8	7	13	32	51	23
Staffordshire Town	28	6	8	14	41	50	20
Leek CSOB	28	6	6	16	36	70	18
Ball Haye Green	28	3	11	14	25	59	17
H & R Johnson	28	3	10	15	25	49	16
Hednesfd Prog	28	4	7	17	29	71	15

LIVERPOOL COUNTY COMBINATION

Division One

	P	W	D	L	F	A	Pts
St Dominics	30	22	6	2	118	49	50
Waterloo Dock	30	21	3	6	82	33	45
Earle	30	19	6	5	79	42	44
Speke BCOB	30	18	6	6	104	47	42
BRNESC	30	18	5	7	98	42	41
Kirkby Town Res	30	15	6	9	62	44	36
Littlewoods Ath	30	13	9	8	69	51	35
UNIASCO	30	16	3	11	69	60	35
Ayone—2	30	9	11	10	60	55	27
Cheshire Lines	30	11	4	15	56	77	26
Royal Seaforth	30	9	6	15	47	57	24
A C Sparks	30	8	7	15	68	91	23
Plessey FC	30	9	4	17	52	68	22
Crawfords U B	30	5	5	20	43	91	15
L M T	30	3	6	21	48	130	12
Garswood United	30	0	1	29	29	147	1

Division Two

	P	W	D	L	F	A	Pts
Avon Athletic	30	24	3	3	103	34	51
Evans	30	21	4	5	79	41	46
Dunlop Speke	30	19	6	5	87	44	44
Yorks Imperial	30	18	5	7	70	52	41
Plessey FC Res	30	15	8	7	69	47	38
Fleetwood Hesketh	30	16	3	11	87	56	35
Kraft	30	14	6	10	85	70	24
Lucas Sports	30	14	2	14	52	43	30
Beesix—2	30	13	4	13	74	77	28
BRNESC Res	30	8	7	15	61	74	23
Ward Blenkinsop	30	8	4	18	41	61	20
I C I Widnes	30	8	4	18	54	77	20
Bootle Reserves	30	8	4	18	52	78	20
Crawfords U B Res	30	7	6	17	45	88	20
Liverpool Transport	30	8	1	21	59	101	17
Garswood Utd Res	30	3	5	22	43	118	11

MANCHESTER LEAGUE

Premier Division

	P	W	D	L	F	A	Pts
Maine Road	34	26	3	5	88	29	55
Flixton	34	24	5	5	79	25	53
East Manchester	34	19	11	4	64	37	49
Little Hulton	34	19	8	7	84	52	46
Wythenshawe Amt	34	18	7	9	49	28	43
Milton	34	14	9	11	58	54	37
Abbey Hey	34	14	7	13	50	51	35
Mount Pleasant	34	13	6	15	39	59	32
Dukinfield Town	34	10	11	13	50	40	31
Highfield Utd	34	10	11	13	50	57	31
Moravian	34	11	8	15	41	63	30
Glossopians	34	10	8	16	59	74	28
North Withington	34	9	10	15	41	63	28
Waterloo	34	9	8	17	47	63	26
Shell	34	7	12	15	38	55	26
Coldhurst Utd	34	10	5	19	55	72	25
Walkden Town	34	6	8	20	44	69	20

Division One

	P	W	D	L	F	A	Pts
Adswood Amateurs	30	26	3	1	115	21	55
Glossop Hillmen	30	23	2	5	78	36	48
Kendal Sports	30	21	4	5	75	34	46
Monton Amateurs	30	16	6	8	62	55	38
O. Altrinchamians	30	15	6	9	59	48	36
Ashton Town	30	14	6	10	70	57	34
Urmston Town	30	14	5	11	70	54	33
Atherton Town	30	12	6	12	55	62	30
Eccles Town	30	9	8	13	44	54	26
Urmstonians	30	10	5	15	56	64	25
R S H 85	30	9	5	16	58	69	23
Castleton Gabriel	30	9	3	18	60	92	21
Pennington	30	6	8	16	48	78	20
Hollinwood	30	5	7	18	46	92	17
M/C University	30	5	6	19	35	71	16
Clifton	30	3	6	21	38	82	12

NORTHERN COUNTIES (EAST) FOOTBALL LEAGUE

Chairman: Cliff Morris
General Secretary: B. Wood, 6 Restmore Ave, Guiseley, Leeds LS20 9DG.
Tel: 0943 74558

GENERAL SECRETARY'S REPORT

As is usual on these occasions the first part of my report deals with our clubs' progress in our various competitions.

Having taken some time to agree on the exact constitution of the divisions at the AGM and at a specially convened Meeting the divisions had to be revised at a late stage because of the withdrawal of Retford Town and negotiations have been proceeding with the Notts FA to have the club and its players and officials barred from football until their club's debts are paid. It has been learned recently that no affiliation will be accepted by Notts FA until the debts are discharged. Taking advantage of Retford Town's withdrawal were North Ferriby who moved up to Div. 1 and Kiveton Park who were allotted a place in Div. 2. The League's Div. 3 therefore operated with 15 clubs.

With a full complement of 20 teams in the Premier Division it was 'relative newcomers' Pontefract Colls. who took an early lead in the Division which they were able to maintain until mid-December. With cup matches and then later postponements taking their toll of League matches to was difficult to forecast a likely winner for any of a dozen clubs had a realistic chance of the championship at one stage. As the year progressed, however, the dual challenge of Emley and Arnold (not necessarily in that order) emerged and it was left to the other clubs to chase the leaders. Weather interference caused a preponderence of matches for certain clubs but at the end it was Arnold who held off Emley's challenge to take the Prem. Div. Championship by 2 pts. Late efforts by Guiseley and Sutton Town left those clubs in 3rd. and 4th. positions.

Division 1 was dominated by North Ferriby who never left top position since the first League Table was produced. Having entered the Division at a late stage because of Retford Town's withdrawal their success was all the more creditable and the only question remained as to who would be the Runners-up. The very last match of the season gave Sheffield that honour in front of Harrogate Town and Rowntree Mackintosh.

The race in Division 2 was particularly intriguing centred round Staveley, Lincoln United and Garforth Town. Leadership of the Division did fluctuate but the honours were always going to be contested by these three clubs. At the end Lincoln United won by a single point from Garforth Town with Staveley and York RI having to settle for 3rd. and 4th positions.

Collingham over the years have not been among the leading contenders for honours but last season was certainly a vintage one for the club. Although challenged by Worsbrough Bridge MW throughout the season it was the north Leeds club who took the lead in November and never let their grasp on the championship slip away. With a final tally of 55pts. they finished a good 8 pts. ahead of Worsbrough Bridge with Eccleshill United and Glasshoughton Welf. (both new clubs to the League) finishing in 3rd. and 4th. positions. Unhappily, this Division was affected by the decision of Blidworth MW not to play their final two away matches at Wombwell SA and Worsbrough Bridge because of events associated with their League Cup-tie at Grimethorpe MW earlier in the season and, as their fixtures were not completed, under Rule 25 the match results of the club were expunged from the record of that Division.

When reviewing the fortunes of clubs in the main Divisions of the League it is usual to mention those who did not do so well, particularly where relegation is involved, but as we are faced yet again with a revision of the Divisions suffice to say that the 'drop' has been avoided as relegation does not apply at the end of this season.

Our League Cup Competition was very fortunate in obtaining the sponsorship of the Yorkshire Charities & Sport Association and Mr Dennis Barnes of the organisation has been thanked by the Treasurer in his report for his £1,500 made available for the purchase of trophies and as prizes to the clubs reaching the later stages of the competition. For the clubs outside the Premier Division this was a vintage competition with Bradley Rgrs. carrying the honours from Div. 1 into the final at Denaby United to do battle with Sutton Town who featured at Shepshed in the very first League Cup Final. After a 1-1 draw in the first match where tension perhaps got the better of good football the replay really did produce a good match with Sutton Town only narrowly taking the cup and the cheque for £375 by a single goal. With a cheque for £225 in their pockets Bradley Rangers could be proud of their own contribution to the Final.

In National Comps. our progress was again not of the best—FA CUP – Bridlington Trinity and Alfreton Town reached the 3rd. Qual. Round; FA TROPHY – Alfreton Town reached the 3rd. Qual. Round; FA VASE – Sheffield and North Ferriby reached the 4th. Round.

We did a little better in County Cup competitions this season with the following winners—LINCS CITY CUP – Lincoln Utd. WEST RIDING CITY CUP – Harrogate Town. EAST RIDING INTERMEDIATE CUP – Hall Road Rgrs. Res. I need hardly add that there is considerable room for improvement in National and County competitions.

In the second part of my report I wish to link my remarks to those of the Chairman. I do not propose to dwell at great length on those clubs who have decided to leave us – merely to point out that the facts as we saw them associated with any exodus of clubs and the dangers involved for them have been somewhat borne out by recent events in the 'south'. We wish them well in the future but we will now turn our attention to progress without them. As a result of clubs leaving the N.C.E. League – a decision must be reached by clubs at the A.G.M. as to the exact members in each Division though it is obvious that it will no longer be necessary to operate a Div. 3.

I would like to mention the work of our new Publicity & Promotions Officer, Terry Bradley, whose enthusiasm has been reflected in his visits to many grounds and the collating of information for the League's News Letter. Another area where we enjoy an excellent relationship is with our sister League – the North West Counties League. Although the Northern Premier League continue to show intransigence in their dealings with both Leagues our relationship with the North West continues to prosper and, indeed, we are hoping to continue this with talks on topics of mutual interest. A close and rewarding relationship has also continued with the Referees & Linesmens Association and we wish their inaugural Secretary, Graham Dove, our best wishes for the work he has put in for his Association. Graham is now stepping down after retiring from the League's Referees List.

BARRY WOOD

Sutton Town — winners of the Northern Counties East League Cup.

NORTHERN COUNTIES EAST – LEAGUE CUP 1985/86

ROUND 1

Sheffield v Pickering Town	6–3
Frecheville CA v Lincoln Utd.	0–1
Bridlington Town v Mexborough	2–3
York RI v Liversedge	2–0
Collingham v BSC (Parkgate)	1–2
Bradley Rangers v Yorkshire Main	4–0
Graham St Prims v Pilkington R.	7–4
Harrogate Railway v North Ferriby	2–1
Borrowash Vict. v Harrogate Tn.	1–0
Ossett Albion v Garforth Town	1–0
Kimberley Town v Harworth CI	1–2
Maltby MW v Arnold Kingswell	1–3
Grimethorpe MW v Blidworth Welf	4–2
Worsbrough Bridge v Rowntree Mack.	0–3
Eccleshill Utd. v Hatfield Main	2–5
Kiveton Park v Selby Town	2–1
Woolley MW v Oakham United	5–2
Thorne Colly. v Yorkshire Amat.	0–1
Stocksbridge Wks. v Tadcaster A.	0–2
Fryston CW v Hallam	2–4
Dronfield Utd. v Brigg Town	0–1
Glasshoughton W v Ossett Town	1–2
Hall Road Rangers v Staveley	2–0

Wombwell SA – Bye

Competition sponsored by
YORKSHIRE CHARITIES & SPORT ASSOC.

Losing Quarter Finalists each received
£75 Boston
Sheffield
Pontefract Colls.
Thackley

Losing Semi-Finalists each received
£150 Belper Town
Borrowash Vict.

Losing Finalist received £225
Bradley Rangers

Cup Winners received £375
Sutton Town

ROUND 2

Borrowash Vict. v Kiveton Park	4–0
BSC (Parkgate) v Tadcaster Alb.	3–1
Hatfield Main v Ossett Town	2–4
Arnold Kingswell v Hall Road R.	0–1, 0–0
Ossett Albion v Graham St Prims	2–1
Yorkshire Amat. v Bradley Rangers	0–3
Wombwell SA v Lincoln Utd.	1–4
Woolley MW v York RI	5–1
Rowntree Mack. v Hall Road Rgrs.	1–3
Sheffield v Harworth CI	3–0
Grimethorpe MW v Mexborough Tn.	0–3
Hallam v Brigg Town	4–2

ROUND 3

Armthorpe Welfare v Spalding United	0–1
Belper Town v Ossett Albion	2–1
Borrowash Vict. v Harrogate Railway	2–0
Boston v Hall Road Rangers	2–1
BSC (Parkgate) v Ilkeston Town	0–1
Denaby United v Alfreton Town	2–1
Emley v Bridlington Trinity	1–0
Long Eaton United v Appleby Frodingham	2–1
Pontefract Colls. v Eastwood Town	3–1
Lincoln United v Bradley Rangers	0–1
Sutton Town v Woolley MW	3–2
Ossett Town v Sheffield	1–4
Guiseley v Bentley VW	6–1
Farsley Celtic v Arnold +	1–3
+ Arnold disqualified.	
Mexborough Town v Thackley	1–2
Hallam v Heanor Town	2–1

ROUND 4

Long Eaton United v Bradley Rangers	0–2
Borrowash Vict. v Emley	2–1
Boston v Farsley Celtic	1–0
Denaby United v Belper Town	1–2
Guiseley v Sheffield	1–5, 3–3
Pontefract Colls. v Ilkeston Tn.	2–1
Spalding United v Thackley	1–3
Sutton Town v Hallam	3–2

ROUND 5

Bradley Rangers v Boston	2–0
Belper Town v Pontefract Colls.	2–0
Borrowash Vict. v Sheffield	3–2
Sutton Town v Thackley	2–1

SEMI-FINALS

Sutton Town v Belper Town	3–1
Borrowash Vict. v Bradley Rangers	1–2

FINAL

Bradley Rangers v Sutton Town	0–1, 1–1

NORTHERN COUNTIES EAST FOOTBALL LEAGUE
LEADING SCORERS – SEASON 1985/6

PREMIER DIVISION

30 gls.—D.A. Jenas (Arnold)
25—J.A. Francis (Emley)
24—G.N. Kemm (Eastwood Town)
21—D.M. Chapman (Long Eaton Utd), M. Coupe (Sutton Town)
20—W. Ingleson (Farsley Celtic)
19—M. Mattok (Guiseley), R.I. Wetton (Belper Town)
18—R.S. Farrow (Arnold), M. Richardson (Sutton Town)
17—R. Sacchetto (Thackley)
16—C. Townsend (Arnold), M.A. Wood (Guiseley)
15—P. Haycock (Heanor Town), A.J. Lambert (Long Eaton Utd)
14—G. Saxby (Sutton Town)
13—R.J. Downing (Belper Town), M.D. Jones (Alfreton Tn), D.C. Scotney (Boston)
12—R.V. Baker (Farsley Celtic), L. Burrows (Guiseley), M.T. Buxton (Eastwood Town), P. Doidge (Bentley VW), E. Jarrett (Farsley Celtic), P.A. Orton (Sutton Town), D. Penney (Pontefract Colls.)

DIVISION 1

28—T. Adams (Rowntree Mackintosh)
21—S. Lowe (Sheffield)
19—P.M. Acklam (Borrowash Vict.)
18—C. Kendrick (Woolley MW)
16—J.A. Dembickjy (Harrogate Town)
15—S.P. Brown (Bridlington Town)
14—D.R. Ballantyne (Harrogate Town), J. Balmer (Bradley Rgrs), R. Guest (Woolley MW), D.A. Ingham (Ossett Albion), J.T. Sheppard (Sheffield), D. Whiteman (Hatfield Main)
13—K. Miles (Mexborough Town), C.F. Teare (Rowntree Mackintosh)
12—S.R. Cant (Borrowash Vict.), H. Cardwell (North Ferriby)

DIVISION 2

27—K. Carter (Lincoln United)
18—V. Archer (Garforth Town)
16—G.D. White (Hallam)
15—M. Barnett (York RI), P. Brown (Lincoln United)
14—G.J. Betteridge (Garforth Town)
13—S. Payne (Arnold Kingswell), W.F. Rawlings (Arnold Kingswell), G. Rhodes (Staveley)

DIVISION 3

31—J.E. Dickson (Collingham)
19—I. Noteman (Yorkshire Amat.), W. Manning (Graham St Prims)
11—P.A. Ramsey (Wombwell SA), R. Taylor (Worsbrough Bridge MW)

RESERVE DIVISION

18—C.D. Helliwell (Emley)
13—K. Sanderson (Farsley Celtic)
12—R.V. Baker (Farsley Celtic), P. Haggerty (Thackley), J. Speak (Hall Road Rgrs), C.P. Stanley (Thackley), S.A. Stewart (Farsley Celtic)

B. WOOD
General Secretary

Northern3

SEASON 1985/6 N.C.E. LEAGUE PREMIER DIVISION Home Team	Alfreton Town	Appleby Frodingham	Armthorpe Welfare	Arnold	Belper Town	Bentley VW	Boston	Bridlington Trinity	Denaby United	Eastwood Town	Emley	Farsley Celtic	Guiseley	Heanor Town	Ilkeston Town	Long Eaton United	Pontefract Colls.	Spalding United	Sutton Town	Thackley
Alfreton Town		3-0	3-1	0-1	1-2	5-1	3-0	0-1	1-3	1-0	0-1	1-2	2-3	2-0	1-0	1-0	1-5	1-0	3-1	5-1
Appleby Frodingham	1-4		3-1	0-8	0-0	1-1	1-1	1-1	1-1	1-3	0-1	1-1	2-2	1-3	1-0	0-2	0-5	2-2	2-5	2-1
Amthorpe Welfare	2-1	3-0		0-0	2-1	3-4	1-0	3-0	2-4	5-0	0-2	2-3	1-1	3-2	3-1	1-1	1-1	0-0	2-4	4-0
Arnold	0-0	1-0	2-1		0-1	1-0	3-1	4-1	3-1	1-2	3-2	1-1	5-2	1-0	0-0	2-0	4-0	0-1	4-0	1-1
Belper Town	2-3	5-0	0-1	1-1		2-2	2-0	1-1	3-1	0-1	1-2	1-1	1-2	0-1	2-1	1-0	4-1	1-0	1-2	1-2
Bentley VW	2-4	3-1	1-2	0-3	4-1		2-2	7-0	1-5	2-2	3-1	2-1	2-1	1-1	0-0	0-2	1-1	3-1	0-3	1-1
Boston	1-0	4-2	3-1	1-3	0-2	0-1		5-1	1-2	1-1	0-5	2-1	0-2	1-0	2-1	0-5	0-1	1-1	0-5	2-1
Bridlington Trinity	4-3	1-0	0-1	0-3	0-3	1-0	1-3		0-0	0-2	2-4	2-2	0-5	1-1	1-1	1-3	2-2	3-3	0-2	1-2
Denaby United	1-0	2-2	3-0	0-1	3-3	2-2	1-0	2-1		1-3	1-2	2-0	1-1	2-3	1-1	3-3	3-1	2-2	1-1	2-3
Eastwood Town	1-2	0-2	2-1	3-2	0-2	1-4	2-1	3-0	2-1		1-1	3-2	6-3	2-1	8-1	1-1	1-0	1-3	2-2	6-2
Emley	0-2	4-2	0-0	3-3	3-1	3-1	0-0	2-2	2-0	3-0		2-2	2-2	5-1	3-2	1-1	1-0	3-3	2-1	2-0
Farsley Celtic	0-1	3-3	1-1	1-3	3-0	2-2	7-0	2-2	1-1	3-2	2-0		1-0	6-1	6-1	1-3	1-0	3-3	1-0	0-3
Guiseley	4-2	5-0	3-2	1-2	0-2	3-0	1-0	3-1	3-0	2-0	2-5	0-3		3-0	1-0	3-0	2-0	1-1	1-1	2-0
Heanor Town	0-1	2-1	1-0	2-5	1-1	0-2	1-3	4-1	1-1	3-4	6-1	0-2	1-2		3-0	2-2	2-2	0-1	5-0	1-1
Ilkeston Town	1-2	1-2	1-2	0-2	1-1	1-3	3-2	0-0	1-1	1-2	0-1	0-3	0-1	4-3		2-0	1-3	0-2	0-4	2-1
Long Eaton United	3-0	2-0	2-0	3-3	0-0	2-1	5-1	5-0	0-1	2-0	1-1	3-1	2-1	1-0	2-0		0-1	4-2	3-1	3-3
Pontefract Colls.	0-0	0-4	3-0	3-4	2-0	3-2	3-1	0-0	2-1	0-1	1-2	3-0	3-4	0-2	1-0	1-1		2-1	3-4	0-1
Spalding United	0-4	0-0	2-0	1-0	0-1	2-0	1-1	1-0	2-5	0-1	0-3	0-0	0-5	2-3	0-3	1-2	0-1		2-0	1-3
Sutton Town	2-3	1-1	0-1	3-2	3-2	1-0	5-1	1-1	0-1	1-2	1-2	2-1	3-0	2-2	1-0	1-0	2-0	3-0		0-3
Thackley	1-0	1-0	3-4	0-1	0-2	0-0	2-1	1-1	1-1	4-2	0-0	2-1	1-4	2-2	1-0	1-1	0-1	0-0	3-1	

NORTHERN COUNTIES EAST FOOTBALL LEAGUE
SEASON 1985–86
PREMIER DIVISION

LEAGUE TABLE	P	W	D	L	F	A	Pts
Arnold	38	24	8	6	83	36	79x
Emley	38	22	11	5	77	47	77
Guiseley	38	22	6	10	81	52	72
Long Eaton United	38	19	11	8	70	39	68
Eastwood Town	38	21	5	12	73	62	67x
Alfreton Town	38	21	2	15	66	47	65
Sutton Town	38	18	6	14	69	57	60
Farsley Celtic	38	14	12	12	71	55	54
Belper Town	38	15	9	14	54	45	54
Thackley	38	14	11	13	52	58	53
Denaby United	38	13	14	11	63	56	52x
Pontefract Colls.	38	15	7	16	55	54	52
Armthorpe Welfare	38	15	7	16	57	58	52
Bentley VW	38	12	11	15	61	65	47
Heanor Town	38	11	9	18	61	69	41x
Spalding United	38	9	12	17	41	62	39
Boston	38	10	6	22	42	79	36
Appleby Frodingham	38	6	12	20	40	83	30
Bridlington Trinity	38	4	14	20	34	85	26
Ilkeston Town	38	5	7	26	31	72	22

x denotes 1pt deducted for breach of rule

DIVISION ONE

LEAGUE TABLE	P	W	D	L	F	A	Pts
North Ferriby	30	18	5	7	54	31	59
Sheffield	30	16	8	6	54	39	56
Harrogate Town	30	16	6	8	65	42	54
Rowntree Mackintosh	30	16	5	9	67	45	53
Ossett Albion	30	13	11	6	54	39	50
Bridlington Town	30	11	13	6	49	41	46
Borrowash Vict.	30	12	10	8	53	48	46
Harworth CI	30	12	6	12	51	50	42
Woolley MW	30	12	7	11	59	59	42x
Bradley Rangers	30	12	4	14	51	51	40
Hatfield Main	30	8	13	9	57	43	37
Brigg Town	30	8	8	14	31	42	32
Mexborough Town	30	8	7	15	39	68	30x
Harrogate Railway	30	6	6	18	47	70	23x
Dronfield United	30	6	6	18	32	61	23x
Pilkington Recs.	30	4	9	17	32	66	21

x denotes 1pt deducted for breach of rule

RESULTS SEASON 1985/6 N.C.E. LEAGUE DIVISION 1

Home Team	Borrowash Vict.	Bradley Rangers	Bridlington Town	Brigg Town	Dronfield United	Harrogate Railway	Harrogate Town	Harworth CI	Hatfield Main	Mexborough Town	North Ferriby	Ossett Albion	Pilkington Recs.	Rowntree Mackintosh	Sheffield	Woolley MW
Borrowash Vict.		3-1	1-1	0-3	5-1	1-0	1-3	4-0	5-3	3-3	2-1	0-2	0-0	5-2	0-1	2-1
Bradley Rangers	2-2		1-2	2-1	3-1	4-1	1-0	1-1	0-1	3-0	0-2	1-2	1-0	2-0	5-1	1-4
Bridlington Town	1-1	4-2		2-0	3-1	3-0	2-2	2-1	2-2	2-0	1-0	3-3	4-0	1-1	0-1	0-0
Brigg Town	2-1	1-0	3-1		1-0	1-3	2-3	0-1	1-1	0-3	3-3	1-2	1-1	0-1	1-1	0-2
Dronfield United	1-3	2-2	0-0	2-0		1-1	1-1	2-3	0-3	1-4	0-2	3-0	0-0	4-2	0-2	1-3
Harrogate Railway	1-1	0-2	1-2	2-2	1-2		2-3	1-3	5-4	4-0	0-4	1-2	1-3	0-1	2-4	8-2
Harrogate Town	7-2	6-3	3-1	2-1	1-0	0-0		3-2	1-1	3-0	1-0	1-3	1-0	2-2	3-1	1-1
Harworth CI	0-0	4-1	0-1	2-0	3-0	0-0	2-1		2-2	4-3	0-2	1-2	5-2	4-1	0-2	1-3
Hatfield Main	2-2	0-2	3-3	0-0	0-0	5-0	1-0	2-2		8-0	1-2	0-1	3-0	1-2	4-1	2-1
Mexborough Town	0-1	3-1	2-2	0-0	1-2	2-5	2-1	3-1	0-0		0-1	3-2	0-0	0-7	1-1	0-3
North Ferriby	2-0	2-1	0-0	0-1	5-1	2-1	2-1	1-1	2-1	3-2		1-1	4-1	2-1	0-2	0-1
Ossett Albion	0-1	0-2	2-2	1-1	3-2	3-0	5-1	3-0	1-1	4-0	0-0		1-2	2-2	0-2	1-1
Pilkington Recs.	1-2	1-3	3-3	2-0	1-8	1-4	0-7	0-2	3-3	1-2	0-1	3-3		2-1	1-1	2-2
Rowntree Mackintosh	3-1	2-1	3-0	2-3	2-1	7-0	2-1	2-3	2-1	2-0	2-3	2-2	2-0		4-1	4-1
Sheffield	1-1	2-0	3-0	1-0	4-1	1-1	1-2	3-2	3-2	1-1	1-3	2-2	3-1	0-0		3-0
Woolley MW	3-3	3-3	2-1	1-2	2-0	4-2	1-4	3-1	0-0	2-4	5-4	0-1	4-1	2-3	2-4	

DIVISION TWO

LEAGUE TABLE	P	W	D	L	F	A	Pts
Lincoln United	30	20	5	5	73	29	65
Garforth Town	30	20	4	6	66	29	64
York RI	30	17	5	8	58	39	56
Staveley	30	17	4	9	52	33	55
Hallam	30	15	2	13	48	42	47
Maltby MW	30	12	7	11	44	48	43
Grimethorpe MW	30	12	7	11	50	48	40+
Kiveton Park	30	11	6	13	42	48	39
BSC (Parkgate)	30	11	7	12	43	50	39x
Liversedge	30	11	5	14	46	56	38
Frecheville CA	30	9	8	13	43	61	35
Arnold Kingswell	30	10	4	16	48	57	34
Yorkshire Main Coll.	30	10	5	15	38	53	34x
Ossett Town	30	8	7	15	40	53	31
Pickering Town	30	5	10	15	33	52	24x
Thorne Colliery	30	7	4	19	31	57	24x

x denotes 1pt deducted for breach of rule
+ denotes 3pts deducted for breach of rule

RESULTS SEASON 1985/6 N.C.E. LEAGUE DIVISION 2 Home Team	Arnold Kingswell	BSC (Parkgate)	Frecheville CA	Garforth Town	Grimethorpe MW	Hallam	Kiveton Park	Lincoln United	Liversedge	Maltby MW	Ossett Town	Pickering Town	Staveley	Thorne Colliery	York RI	Yorkshire Main Colly.
Arnold Kingswell ...		1-3	4-2	2-3	0-2	0-2	1-3	2-3	4-2	0-1	2-1	2-0	1-3	0-0	1-0	6-1
BSC (Parkgate)	2-4		1-0	0-6	2-2	3-1	1-1	2-0	1-3	4-1	1-2	1-0	2-1	0-1	1-1	1-3
Frecheville CA	3-3	0-3		1-2	1-1	0-3	2-2	1-4	2-3	1-0	1-0	2-1	1-4	1-1	1-1	1-1
Garforth Town	4-0	0-2	2-3		3-0	3-1	1-2	1-0	2-2	1-1	3-0	2-1	1-0	0-1	3-1	0-0
Grimethorpe MW ...	2-1	4-2	1-1	1-3		1-0	0-1	0-4	3-1	2-1	1-1	5-1	1-1	4-1	0-1	1-0
Hallam	0-3	3-2	0-1	1-2	1-4		3-2.	3-0	2-0	0-1	0-1	0-0	5-1	5-1	0-1	3-0
Kiveton Park	5-2	0-1	1-3	0-1	1-2	1-2		1-4	1-2	1-1	2-1	3-1	1-1	3-2	0-3	1-0
Lincoln United	2-1	4-0	3-0	4-1	2-2	6-0	3-0		2-0	3-3	1-1	1-0	4-1	5-1	6-1	2-1
Liversedge	1-0	3-0	4-3	1-0	2-0	0-3	0-0	1-2		1-3	2-2	1-4	2-1	2-0	1-2	4-0
Maltby MW	1-4	1-1	2-1	1-3	2-1	4-2	0-2	1-1	3-1		5-2	0-0	1-2	1-2	2-1	1-2
Ossett Town	2-2	2-1	1-4	1-3	1-1	2-4	3-2	0-1	2-2	5-0		0-1	0-1	2-0	0-3	2-3
Pickering Town	1-1	1-1	1-1	1-3	2-6	0-1	2-2	1-0	2-1	1-1	1-1		0-1	2-2	4-1	2-5
Staveley	3-0	1-0	7-0	1-2	1-0	1-1	3-0	0-2	3-0	1-2	2-1	2-1		2-0	1-3	2-0
Thorne Colliery	0-1	1-2	0-1	0-5	4-1	0-1	1-2	2-1	3-2	0-1	1-2	1-1	0-1		1-2	2-4
York RI	4-0	2-2	3-1	0-0	4-2	2-0	1-2	2-2	4-0	3-1	3-0	3-1	0-2	3-2		2-1
Yorkshire Main Colly	1-0	1-1	2-4	1-6	3-0	0-1	1-0	0-1	2-2	0-2	0-2	2-0	2-2	0-1	2-1	

Lincoln United skipper Allen Crombie gets in a shot at the Pickering goal in United's surprising 1-0 defeat in late April which threatened to ruin their Championship hopes. T. Sandell-Codd

Oakham United 2, Tadcaster Albion 1.

DIVISION THREE

LEAGUE TABLE	P	W	D	L	F	A	Pts
Collingham	26	16	7	3	66	23	55
Worsbrough Bridge	26	14	5	7	60	32	47
Eccleshill United	26	13	6	7	43	34	45
Glasshoughton Welf.	26	12	7	7	42	33	43
Yorkshire Amat.	26	11	10	5	38	29	42x
Hall Road Rangers	26	9	9	8	37	33	36
Oakham United	26	10	6	10	38	35	36
Graham St Prims	26	10	5	11	43	41	35
Tadcaster Albion	26	9	7	10	44	39	34
Stocksbridge Works	26	9	6	11	42	43	33
Selby Town	26	8	7	11	47	59	31
Fryston CW	26	5	6	15	32	72	21
Wombwell SA	26	6	5	15	28	49	20+
Kimberley Town	26	4	6	16	26	64	18

Blidworth Welf. competed in the Division but did not complete their fixtures.

x denotes 1pt deducted for breach of rule
+ denotes 3pts deducted for breach of rule

RESULTS SEASON 1985/6 N.C.E. LEAGUE DIVISION 3

Home Team	Collingham	Eccleshill United	Fryston CW	Glasshoughton Welf.	Graham St Prims	Hall Road Rangers	Kimberley Town	Oakham United	Selby Town	Stocksbridge Works	Tadcaster Albion	Wombwell SA	Worsbrough Bridge MW	Yorkshire Amat.
Collingham		1-1	3-0	3-3	5-0	2-0	5-2	3-0	0-2	3-1	2-2	0-2	2-0	1-1
Eccleshill United	1-2		3-0	1-1	0-2	2-3	3-0	3-0	3-1	3-1	2-1	2-0	2-1	2-0
Fryston CW	0-6	1-2		1-3	1-1	2-3	1-1	1-4	2-3	2-1	1-4	2-0	1-1	1-3
Glasshoughton Welf.	2-1	1-1	1-2		2-1	0-2	5-2	2-0	1-1	2-0	2-3	2-2	1-3	1-0
Graham St Prims	2-3	3-0	3-0	0-2		2-0	1-1	3-4	2-5	4-0	6-3	1-0	4-2	0-2
Hall Road Rangers	1-1	4-1	1-1	1-1	1-1		3-0	1-0	2-0	0-3	0-1	1-2	0-1	1-2
Kimberley Town	0-3	3-1	3-3	0-4	0-0	0-2		1-0	2-4	3-2	0-2	2-3	0-0	1-2
Oakham United	0-5	0-0	6-0	2-0	1-0	1-1	3-0		4-1	0-2	2-1	0-0	3-4	1-1
Selby Town	0-0	2-4	3-3	0-1	2-1	3-3	2-2	2-1		3-2	2-2	2-1	2-3	2-3
Stocksbridge Works	1-1	4-0	6-0	2-1	2-1	1-1	3-1	1-3	2-1		1-4	1-1	0-5	0-0
Tadcaster Albion	0-3	0-2	3-0	0-2	3-1	2-0	5-0	0-0	1-1	2-2		1-2	0-2	1-1
Wombwell SA	1-7	1-2	1-3	0-1	1-2	2-2	0-2	0-1	4-2	0-3	2-1		0-3	2-2
Worsbrough Bridge MW	1-2	1-1	3-4	5-1	1-2	1-1	4-0	1-0	8-0	1-0	1-1	3-1		3-1
Yorkshire Amat.	0-2	1-1	4-0	0-0	0-0	1-3	3-0	2-2	2-1	1-1	2-1	1-0	3-2	

Blidworth Welf. also competed in the Division but did not complete their fixtures

Belper Town striker Kevin Jackson (left) crashes a first time shot just past the post from a left wing cross by Carl Gregory.

Sutton Town F.C. 1985-86 *pictured before the League Cup Final against Bradley Rangers at Denaby. Back row (l to r):— K. Burton (Physio), J. Pearson, N. Lovell, P. Fisher, S. Chadbourne, P. Millns, P. Orton, M. Richardson, B. Chambers (Manager). Front row (l to r):— G. Saxby, S. Beaver, A. Kirk, S. Lamb, D. Burrows, N. Coups. Mascot: M. Butler.*

ALFRETON TOWN

President: Mr. C. Thornton
Chairman: G. Worth
Manager: S. Egan
Ass. Man/Coach: C. Prophett
Physiotherapist:
Secretary: T. McRoy
Address & Tel. No: 12 Alma Street, Alfreton, Derby DE5 7HX. Alfreton 834707
Commercial Manager: None
Press Officer:
Ground Address & Tel. No: North Street, Alfreton. 832819
Capacity: 6,000 **Covered accommodation:** 1,000 **Seating:** 110 **Floodlights:** Yes
Clubhouse details: Open 6.30 till 11pm. Sunday 7pm till 10.30pm. Midday Monday, Friday, Saturday and Sunday.
Programme details: Nightly 18 pages 15p **Editor:** W. Draper **Club metal badges:** No
Local Newspaper(s): Derbyshire Times, Derby Evening Telegraph, Nottingham Evening Post, Ripley and Heanor News.
Club colours: Red/White/Red and Black **Change colours:** All White
Midweek match day: Wednesday **Previous Leagues:** Midland Counties. Central Alliance.
Record transfer fee paid: £1,000 to Matlock for R. Mountain.
Record transfer fee received: £1,500 from Chesterfield for T. Henson.
Record attendance: 5,023. v Matlock Town, Central Alliance. 1960.
Senior honours/best performance: Champions Midland League 3 times. Winners Derbyshire Senior Cup 6 times. Midland League Cup 3 times. Northern Counties League Cup 1984 & 1985.
Past players (who progressed to Football League): A. Woodward, Grimsby. T. Henson, Chesterfield. R. Greenough, Chester.
Player of the Year: J. Shirt

ARMTHORPE WELFARE

President: Alan Bell
Chairman: Alan Bell
Manager: Joey Johnson
Ass. Man/Coach: John McKeowan
Physiotherapist: Ken Padgett
Secretary: Martin Kennedy
Address & Tel. No: 37 Charles Crescent, Armthorpe, Doncaster. 834116
Commercial Manager: Charlie Down 0302 834081
Press Officer:
Ground Address & Tel. No: Welfare House, Church St, Armthorpe 0302 831871.
Capacity: 3,000 **Covered accommodation:** 250 **Seating:** None **Floodlights:** Under Construction
Simple ground directions: MI – M18 – A630 into Armthorpe
Clubhouse details: Under construction.
Programme details: 20 pages 15p **Editor:** John Morgan **Club metal badges:** None
Local Newspaper(s): Doncaster Star. 0302 834475
Club colours: White/Navy. **Change colours:** Navy/White
Midweek match day: Wednesday **Previous Leagues:** Doncaster Senior
Record attendance:1,500
Senior honours/best performance: Club Captain Stephen Taylor. Player of Year Stephen Taylor. 2nd Team Player of Year Stuart Hall. Supporters Player of Year Gary Leighton.

BELPER TOWN

President: G. Glossop
Chairman: J. Greenham
Manager: M. Cheshire
Ass. Man/Coach: P. Baker
Physiotherapist:
Secretary: D.R. Laughlin
Address & Tel. No: Lorne Cottage, Fritchley, Derbyshire. 077385 6556 (H), 0332 363371 (B)
Commercial Manager: R. Kirkland. 077382 6090 (H)
Press Officer: S. Wilton 0332 880199 (H) 0332 47111 x3022 (B)
Ground Address & Tel. No: Christchurch Meadow, Bridge Street, Belper, Derbyshire. 077385 5549
Capacity: 6,000 **Covered accommodation:** 1,000 **Seating:** 200 **Floodlights:** Yes
Simple ground directions: Ground on A6 at Junction with A517.
Year formed: 1883
Clubhouse details: Open match days
Programme details: 24 pages 15p **Editor:** Stan Wilton **Club metal badges:**No **Club Shop:** Yes
Local Newspaper(s): Belper News, Derby Evening Telegraph
Club Sponsors: Ford & Taylor
Club colours: Old Gold Shirts, Black Shorts, Old Gold Socks **Change colours:** All White
Midweek match day: Tuesday **Previous Leagues:** Central Alliance, Midland Counties
Record transfer fee received: £700 for Brian Hall to Mansfield Town
Player of Year 85/86: Steve Mann
Record attendance: 3,600 v Ilkeston Town 1953
Senior honours/best performance: Midland League, Northern Counties East League Champions. Derbyshire Senior Cup Winners.
Past players (who progressed to Football League): Brian Hall (Mansfield), Andy Higgins (Rochdale).

BENTLEY VICTORIA WELFARE

President:
Chairman: G. Jennings
Manager: N. Brandon
Coach: M. Bates
Physiotherapist:
Secretary: Mrs. E. Follows
Address & Tel. No: 5 Cross Street, Bentley, Doncaster, S. Yorks DN5 0EN. Doncaster 873546
Commercial Manager: Bill Neville. Rotherham 94363407
Press Officer: None.
Ground Address & Tel. No: The Welfare Ground, The Avenue, Bentley, Doncaster.
Capacity: 8,000 **Covered accommodation:** Stand 200 **Seating:** None **Floodlights:**
Simple ground directions: A19, from Doncaster (2 miles& to bottom of High Street, right at Arksey Lane, first left to 'Avenue'
Clubhouse details: None
Programme details: 8 pages 15p **Editor:** G. Jennings **Club metal badges:** None
Local Newspaper(s): Doncaster Star
Club colours: White, White Shorts & Stocking **Change colours:** Red Shirts, Blue Shorts & Stockings
Midweek match day: Tuesday **Previous Leagues:** Yorkshire
Record transfer fee paid: None
Record transfer fee received: None
Record attendance: 900 v Emley Semi Final League Cup 1982
Senior honours/best performance: Yorks League Division 2 Runners up, Division 3 Champions
Past Players (who progressed to Football League): None

BOSTON

President: W. Jackson
Chairman: W.M. Stanwell
Manager: R.A. Gell
Ass. Man/Coach: M.A. Brittain
Physiotherapist: F. Traves
Secretary: B.N. Payne
Address & Tel. No: 51 Kings Crescent, Boston (0205) 649955 (None)
Commercial Manager: None
Press Officer: Secretary
Ground Address & Tel. No: Tattershall Road, Boston (0205) 65470
Capacity: 7,050 **Covered accommodation:** 600 **Seating:** 450 **Floodlights:** None
Simple ground directions: From the inner relief road take the Horncastle Road (B1183), turn first left and at the sluice bridge turn right into Tattershall Road.
Clubhouse details: Open match days
Programme details: 12 pages, 20p **Editor:** S. Shipp **Club metal badges:** None
Local Newspaper(s): Lincolnshire Standard, Lincolnshire Echo, Boston Target
Club colours: White/Navy/White **Change colours:** All Red
Midweek match day: Tuesday
Previous Leagues: Lincolnshire, Central Alliance, Eastern Counties, Midland Counties
Record transfer fee paid: None
Record transfer fee received: £2,000 for Mark Cox from Boston United
Record attendance: 2,700 v Boston United, F.A. Cup, 1970.
Senior honours/best performance: Lincolnshire League, Central Alliance League, Lincolnshire Senior Cup (4), Midland Counties League (3), Midland Counties League Cup.
F.A. Cup: 1976-7 v Barnsley, 1st Round Proper, 1-3 (A). F.A. Trophy: 1979-80 v Mossley, 2nd Round Proper, 0-0, 3-6.
Past Players (who progressed to Football League): None.

BRIDLINGTON TOWN

President: K. Richinson
Chairman: J. Hornsby
Manager:
Ass. Man/Coach:
Physiotherapist: P. Johnson, D. Roberts
Secretary: J.A. Brunton
Address & Tel. No: 87 Sewerby Road, Bridlington. 0262 671570
Commercial Manager: C. Skinner
Press Officer:
Ground Address & Tel. No: Queensgate Football Ground
Capacity: 3,000 **Covered accommodation:** **Seating:** 250 **Floodlights:** No
Simple ground directions: A166 from Driffield to Bridlington
Clubhouse details: Hilderthorpe
Programme details: 4 pages, free press **Editor:** C. Kerfoot **Club metal badges:**
Club colours: White/Red/Red **Change colours:** Blue
Midweek match day: Tuesday **Previous Leagues:** Northern Counties East F.L.
Record transfer fee paid:
Record transfer fee received:
Record attendance: 2,102
Senior honours/best performance: Yorkshire League Cup
Past Players (who progressed to Football League): C. Fountain, J. Cotton, D. Roberts.

BRIDLINGTON TRINITY

President: Ian Brackenbury
Chairman: H.F. Catt
Manager: Colin McLocklan
Coach:
Physiotherapist: Sharon Williams
Secretary: Arthur W. Petch
Address & Tel. No: 18 Midway Avenue, Bridlington, E. Yorks YO16 4NU. 0262 670448
Commercial Manager: None
Address & Tel. No:
Club shop: No
Address & Tel. No. of ground: Queensgate Football Ground, Queensgate, Bridlington. 0262 603879 (match days only)
Simple ground directions: A166 to Bridlington, turn left at traffic lights, over railway bridge to next set of lights and turn right into Queensgate, Ground 400 yards on right.
No. of seats: 250 **Ground accommodation:** 750 **Capacity:** 3,000 **Floodlights:** No
Year formed: 1935 **Nickname:** Emerald Greens **Club sponsors:** Broader & Spencer
Previous names: None
Previous grounds: None
Club colours: Emerald/White
Change colours: Royal Blue
Day for midweek home matches: Wednesday
Best performance in: F.A. Cup: Unknown
F.A. Trophy: 1969-70, 1973-74 1st Round
Previous Leagues: East Riding Amateur, Yorkshire, Midland Counties
Clubhouse details: Blenheim Road, Bridlington. Open licence hours
Present players with Football League experience: None
Past players who progressed into the Football League: Paul Olberg (Scunthorpe)
Record transfer fee paid: None
Record transfer fee received: £2,500, David Leadbeater, Grantham
Programme details: 10 pages, 10p
Programme Editor: H.F. Catt (0262 673974)
Club metal badges: No
Local newspapers & Tel. No: Hull Daily Mail 0262 672327, Sports Mail 0482 27111, Bridlington Free Press 0262 677305
Senior Honours: Yorkshire League Div 1 (3), Midland Counties Cup, Midland Counties League Runners-up, East Riding Senior Cup & Runners-up
Club Captain (1984-85): P. Featherstone

BRIGG TOWN

President: B. Robins
Chairman: H. Williams
Manager: J. Wilkinson
Asst. Man/Coach: M. Hind
Physiotherapist: A. Ashton
Secretary: R.B. Taylor
Address & Tel. No: Highfield House, Barton Road, Wrawby, Brigg. Brigg 52284
Commercial Manager: H. Williams
Address & Tel. No: 53195
Address & Tel. No. of ground: The Hawthorns, Hawthorn Avenue, Brigg. 52767
Simple ground directions: A15/A18 to Brigg; through Brigg on Grimsby Road; turn left at Recreation Ground
No. of seats: 250 **Covered accommodation:** 2 Stands **Capacity:** 4,000 **Floodlights:** No
Year formed: 1864 **Nickname:** Zebras **Club sponsors:** Robert Clark (Roofing)
Club colours: Black/White stripes
Change colours: Orange shirts
Previous Names: None
Previous Grounds: Brocklesby Ox, Manor House Convent
Record attendance: 2,500 v Boston F.C. **Year:** 1953
Programme: 8 pages, 10p
Previous Leagues: Midland, Lincolnshire
Programme Editor: Secretary
Clubhouse details: Licensed social club open on match days
Club Captain (1984-85): S. Guilliatt
Player of the Season (1984-85): Dave Othen

DENABY UNITED

President: A. Wilson
Chairman: G. Whitewick
Manager: R. Evans
Ass. Man/Coach: G. Brackpool
Physiotherapist:
Secretary: A. Jones
Address & Tel. No: 23 Cornhill, Conisbrough, Doncaster. 0709 866316
Commercial Manager:
Press Officer:
Ground Address & Tel. No: Tickhill Square, Denaby Main, Doncaster. Tel. 0709 864042
Capacity: 6,000 **Covered accommodation:** 2 Stands **Seating:** 750 **Floodlights:** No
Simple ground directions: From Mexborough - Hill Top Road, Bolton Street, Wheatley Street. From Conisbrough - Wadworth Street
Clubhouse details:
Programme details: 20 pages, 15p **Editor:** D. Spooner **Club metal badges:**
Local Newspaper(s): S. Yorks Times, Doncaster Post.
Club colours: Red
Change colours: Green & Yellow
Midweek match day: Tuesday
Previous Leagues: Midland League, Yorkshire League
Record transfer fee paid:
Record transfer fee received: £2,500 A. Barnsley to Rotherham United
Record attendance: 3,801 v Oldham Ath. F.A. Cup 1st Round Proper. **Year:** 1958
Senior honours/best performance: Yorks. League Cup
Past players (who progressed to Football League): Numerous

EASTWOOD TOWN

President: Dennis Pettitt
Chairman: George Belshaw
Manager: Bill Jeffrey
Res. Team Man: Bill Fossey
Physiotherapist: Derek Myatt
Secretary:
Address & Tel. No:
Commercial Manager:
Press Officer:
Ground Address & Tel. No: Coronation Park. 0773 712301
Capacity: 6,600 **Covered accommodation:** 1,000 **Seating:** 200 **Floodlights:** Yes
Simple ground directions: M1 (Exit 27 North, 26 South) - ground behind fire station enter via Chewton Street
Clubhouse details: Daily 11-2.30pm, 7-10.30pm (Sat 5-11pm) Meals by arrangement - snacks always available
Programme details: **Editor:** **Club metal badges:**
Local Newspaper(s):
Club colours: **Change colours:** **Club sponsor:** Frank Groome (Nottm) Limited
Midweek match day: **Previous Leagues:**
Record transfer fee paid:
Record transfer fee received:
Record attendance:
Senior honours/best performance:
Past players (who progressed to Football League):

EMLEY

President: Peter Maude
Chairman: John D. Miller
Manager: Gerry Quinn
Ass. Man/Coach: Stephen Dyson/Daryl Brook
Physiotherapist: A. England
Secretary: Gordon Adamson
Address & Tel. No: 219 Rowley Lane, Lepton, Huddersfield HD8 0EH. 0484 602720
Commercial Manager:
Press Officer: None
Ground Address & Tel. No: Emley Welfare Sports Ground, Emley, Huddersfield. 0924 848398
Capacity: 5,000 **Covered accommodation:** 1,000 **Seating:** None **Floodlights:** Yes
Simple ground directions: M1 to Junction 38, follow Hudds. signs to roundabout, turn left onto A636 for approx. ¾ mile, then turn right 1 mile into Emley.
Clubhouse details: Open 7 days. Bingo, dancing, artists, food supplied.
Programme details: 10 pages, 15p **Editor:** D. Oates (0924 848084) **Club metal badges:** No
Local Newspaper(s): Huddersfield Examiner (0484 537444)
Club colours: Maroon/Sky Blue **Change colours:** Sky Blue/Maroon
Midweek match day: Tuesday **Previous Leagues:** Huddersfield League, Yorks. League
Record transfer fee paid: None
Record transfer fee received: None
Record attendance: 5,134 v Barking, FA Amateur Cup 1969
Senior honours/best performance: Yorkshire League Champions, Yorkshire League Cup Winners, Sheffield Senior Challenge Cup Winners, Best Performance, reached 1st Round Proper FA Trophy, lost 4-2 to Blythe Spartons after replay.
Past players (who progressed to Football League): Graham Cooper (Huddersfield Town)

FARSLEY CELTIC

President: G. Dunkerley
Chairman: J. Palmer
Manager: D. Metcalf
Ass. Man/Coach: R. Brown, J. Price
Physiotherapist: T. Gregg, P. Wigglesworth
Secretary: B. Falkingham
Address & Tel. No: 27 Rycroft Court, Swinnow, Leeds LS13 4PE (0532) 550749
Commercial Manager:
Press Officer: D. Martin
Ground Address & Tel. No: Throstle Nest, Newlands, Farsley, Pudsey, West Yorkshire. 0532 561517
Capacity: **Covered accommodation:** **Seating:** **Floodlights:** Due this summer
Simple ground directions: M62 Junction 28, turn right into Leeds Ring Road to A647, turn right at roundabout then left, down New Street to Newlands Ground at bottom of road
Clubhouse details: Luxury lounge, games room (for 350)
Programme details: 12 pages, 15p **Editor:** P. Bell **Club metal badges:** Yes
Local Newspaper(s): Yorkshire Evening Post, Pudsey Times
Club colours: Sky & Navy Stripes, Blue Shorts & Socks **Change colours:** Red & White or Red - Yellow
Midweek match day: Wednesday **Previous Leagues:** West Riding County Amateur, Leeds Red Triangle, Yorkshire League
Record transfer fee paid:
Record transfer fee received:
Record attendance:
Senior honours/best performance: W/R County Cup 5 times. last 32 vase 83/84. 1st Round Proper F.A. Cup 1973/74 lost 2-0 Tranmere
Past players (who progressed to Football League): Paul Madeley, Peter Hardcastle

GUISELEY

President: N. Threaplton
Chairman: P. Rogerson
Manager: M. Beck
Ass. Man/Coach:
Physiotherapist:
Secretary: A.G. Betts
Address & Tel. No: 4 Sleningford Road, Shipley BD18 4DL. Tel: 0274 598260 (H), 0274 307373 (B)
Commercial Manager: M. Schofield, Tel: 0943 79204
Press Officer: H. Pittendreigh, Tel: 0532 677207
Ground Address & Tel. No: Nethermoor Ground, Otley Road, Guiseley, Nr. Leeds. Tel: 0943 72872
Capacity: 4,000 **Covered accommodation:** 600 **Seating:** 400 **Floodlights:** No
Simple ground directions: A65 from Leeds direct to Ground - 10 miles from Leeds City Centre
Clubhouse details: Social Club open evenings and weekends
Programme details: 8 pages **Editor:** Mike Schofield **Club metal badges:**
Local Newspaper(s): Bradford Telegraph & Argus, Yorkshire Evening Post, Airedale & Wharfedale Observer
Club colours: White/Blue/Yellow
Change colours: Yellow/Yellow/Blue
Midweek match day: Wednesday
Previous Leagues: West Riding County Amateur, West Yorkshire F.L., Yorkshire League
Record transfer fee paid:
Record transfer fee received:
Record attendance: 2,000 v Willenhall Town FA Vase Quarter Final 1980/81
Senior honours/best performance: F.A. Cup - none, F.A. Vase 1980/1 6th Round. West Riding County Cup (4). Yorkshire League Cup. Yorkshire League Runners-up
Past Players (who progressed to Football League): K. Walwyn, York City.

HARROGATE TOWN

President: L. Margolis
Chairman: R. Cundall
Manager: Alan Smith 0423 521066 (B)
Ass. Man: Graham Shepherd
Physiotherapist: Miss B. Scatchard
Secretary: R. Dalby
Address & Tel. No: 123A Dene Park, Harrogate, N. Yorks HG1 4JX. 0423 67973 (H), 0423 702581 (B)
Commercial Manager:
Press Officer:
Ground Address & Tel. No: Wetherby Road, Harrogate. 0423 883671
Capacity: 5,000 **Covered accommodation:** 350 **Seating:** 350 **Floodlights:** Yes
Simple ground directions: From Leeds turn right at traffic lights (Appleyard's) into Hookstone Road, continue to Woodlands Hotel (traffic lights) turn left into Wetherby Road. The ground is on the right.
Clubhouse details: On ground (Tues, Wed, Thurs, Sat)
Programme details: 20 pages 20p **Editor:** K. Welford (0423 889186) **Club metal badges:** Yes
Local Newspaper(s): Yorkshire Post, Harrogate Herald Advertiser
Club colours: Amber & Black
Change colours: All Blue
Midweek match day: Tuesday
Previous Leagues: West Yorkshire, Yorkshire
Record transfer fee paid:
Record transfer fee received:
Record attendance: 3,208 v Starbeck LNER - Whitworth Cup Final 1948
Senior honours/best performance: Yorkshire League Div II 1981-82 - West Riding County Cup 1963, 1973, 1986.
Past players (who progressed to Football League): A. Ingham, Leeds United and Q.P.R.

Harrogate Town:— County Cup winners 1985-86. Back row (l to r):— Alan Smith (Manager), Deacey, Wilkings, Parker, Steel, Johnson, Wilson, Smith (J), A. Potter (Picture Secretary). Front row (l to r): Dembickjy, Ballantyne, King, Dawes, Donaldson (Captain), Swaine, Marshall, Notte, Passmore.

Denaby United repel the visiting Bridlington Trinity (2-1), although the visitors attack here.

North Feriby United F.C. 1985-86.

LONG EATON UNITED

President:
Chairman: D. Hampson
Manager: P. McGurk
Ass. Man/Coach: D. Anderson
Physiotherapist:
Secretary: G.W. Whitehead
Address & Tel. No: 16 Holly Avenue, Breaston, Derby, Draycott. 033 17 2849
Commercial Manager: Ivan Winup
Press Officer: G.W. Whitehead
Ground Address & Tel. No: Grange Park, Station Road, Long Eaton, Nottingham. 0602 735700
Capacity: 5,000 **Covered accommodation:** Yes **Seating:** No **Floodlights:** No
Simple ground directions: M1 exit 25. A52 Nottingham 1st roundabout turn right. To 'T' Junction turn right to Long Eaton. Left into Station Road. Ground on left.
Clubhouse details: Refreshments on match days
Programme details: 20 pages 20p **Editor:** G.W. Whitehead **Club metal badges:** No
Local Newspaper(s): Long Eaton Advertiser, Nottingham Evening Post, Derby Telegraph
Club colours: All Blue **Nickname:** The Blues **Change colours:** Yellow Shirts, Green Shorts
Midweek match day: Tuesday **Previous Leagues:** Central Alliance, Midland Counties
Record transfer fee paid: None
Record transfer fee received: £5,000 for Anton Lambert (Scunthorpe United), £3,000 Gary Birtles (Nottm Forest)
Record attendance: v Matlock Town (Derbyshire Senior Cup) 1977
Senior honours/best performance: Derbyshire Senior Cup Winners 1964/65 and 1975/76
Past Players (who progressed to Football League): Gary Birtles, Anton Lambert, Gerry Fell

NORTH FERRIBY UNITED

President: J.R. Bingham
Chairman: K.S. Alexander
Manager: John Thompson
Ass. Man/Coach: Chris Chilton
Physiotherapist: K. Foxon
Secretary: M.R. Wallis
Address & Tel. No: 60 Spring Gardens, Anlaby Common, Hull. 0482 55639 & 0482 24851
Commercial Manager: K. Dobbins
Press Officer: Roy Wallis
Ground Address & Tel. No: Church Road, North Ferriby, N. Humberside. 0482 634601
Capacity: 5,000 **Covered accommodation:** 2,000 **Seating:** 200 **Floodlights:** None
Simple ground directions: Ferriby 8 miles west of Hull on A63. Ground 100 yards past church.
Clubhouse details: Bar, lounge, T.V. pool - open nightly
Programme details: None **Editor:** **Club metal badges:**
Local Newspaper(s): Hull Daily Mail
Club colours: White/Green **Change colours:** All Red
Midweek match days: Tuesday **Previous Leagues:** Church, East Riding Amateur, Yorkshire
Record transfer fee paid:
Record transfer fee received:
Record attendance: 1,100 v Ashington Amateur Cup 1972-73
Senior honours/best performance: East Riding Senior Cup (4). Yorkshire League Cup 1974-75, Yorkshire League Div II Champions 1970-71, Northern Counties East Div I Champions 1985/86.
Past Players (who progressed to Football League):

PONTEFRACT COLLERIES

President: R. Blatherwick
Chairman: A. Dunwell
Manager: J. Brown
Ass. Man/Coach: A. Thaler
Physiotherapist: D. Sharp
Secretary: S. Mason
Address & Tel. No: 16 Harefield Road, Pontefract, West Yorkshire WF8 2HX. 0977 707756
Commercial Manager: Not yet appointed
Press Officer:
Ground Address & Tel. No: Skinner Lane, Pontefract. 0977 702180
Capacity: 400 **Covered accommodation:** Yes **Seating:** None **Floodlights:** No
Simple ground directions: Exit Junction 32 from M62. Left at 1st traffic lights to ground. Adjacent to Colliery and opposite Racecourse.
Clubhouse details: Bar. Open before & after match
Programme details: 16 pages, 20p **Editor:** A. Dean **Club metal badges:** No
Local Newspaper(s): Pontefract and Castleford Express
Club colours: All Blue **Nickname:** The Colls. Change colours: All Red
Midweek match day: Tuesday **Previous Leagues:** West Yorkshire League
Record transfer fee paid:
Record transfer fee received:
Record attendance: 500 v Winterton Rangers - Y.L. Cup Quarter Final 1981
Senior honours/best performance: N.C.E. League Division 1 Champions 1983/4
Past Players (who progressed to Football League): D. Penney to Derby County Sept. 1985.

SUTTON TOWN

President: Frank Haynes M.P.
Chairman: Steve Cook 0623 555512 (B)
Manager: Bryan Chambers
Ass. Man/Coach: Alan Humphries
Physiotherapist: Ken Burton

Secretary: Derek Skermer
Address & Tel. No: 7 Forest St, Annesley, Woodhouse, Kirkby-in-Ashfield, Notts. 0623 752798 (H) 0623 555000 (B)
Commercial Manager: Chairman
Press Officer: Steve Jarvis 0623 34466

Ground Address & Tel. No: Lowmoor Road, Kirkby-in-Ashfield, Notts. 0623 752181
Capacity: 8,000 **Covered accommodation:** 200 (reduced-safety) **Seating:** None **Floodlights:** Yes
Simple ground directions: M1 Junction 27 follow signs for Mansfield into Kirkby-in-Ashfield, 2nd left, straight across traffic lights into Lowmoor Road. Ground at rear of Lowmoor Inn.
Clubhouse details: None
Programme details: 24 pages, 20p **Editor:** Steve Jarvis 0623 34466 **Club metal badges:** Yes - new for 86/7
Local Newspaper(s): Notts Free Press, Sutton & Kirkby News
Club Shop: Yes, c/o 159 Sheepbridge Lane, Mansfield, Notts NG18 5DT
Club colours: Claret & Blue **Nickname:** Snipes **Change colours:** White/Black
Previous Leagues: Notts & District; Notts & Derbys; Midland Comb; Derbys Senior; Central Comb; Notts Alliance; Central Alliance; Midland League
Midweek match day: Tuesday
Record transfer fee paid: None
Record transfer fee received: £300 for Ivan Hollett (Mansfield Town)
Record attendance: 1,562 at Lowmoor Road (1980 v Leeds Fldlt Open); 6,000 at Priestsic Road v Peterboro' U (1958); 8,000 at The Avenue v Reading (FA Cup) 1933.
Senior honours/best performances: Winners Notts Senior Cup 17 times, Notts & Dist League (2), Derbyshire Senior League (3), Central Alliance (1), Northern Counties East League Cup 1985/6, FA Cup 2nd RP 1933-4.
Past Players (who progressed to Football League): Ivan Hollett (Mansfield), Colin Walker (Barnsley)

THACKLEY

President: P. Hockney
Chairman: D.W. Brayshaw
Manager: Jim Mackay
Ass. Man/Coach: Graham Smith
Physiotherapist: Maurice Atkinson

Secretary: S.L. Willingham
Address & Tel. No: 3 Kirklands Close, Baildon, Shipley, West Yorks. 0274 598589 (H), 0943 607550 (B)
Commercial Manager: S.L. Willingham
Press Officer: M. Green

Ground Address & Tel. No: 'Dennyfield', Ainsbury Avenue, Thackley, Bradford. Tel: 0274 615571
Capacity: 3,000 **Covered accommodation:** 300 **Seating:** 300 **Floodlights:** Yes
Simple ground directions: Off main Leed/Keighley Road (A657) to Thackley Road & Ainsbury Avenue
Clubhouse details: Open every night (except Monday)
Programme details: 8 pages, 15p **Editor:** S.L. Willingham **Club metal badges:** No
Local Newspaper(s): Bradford Telegraph & Argus
Club colours: Red/White/Black
Midweek match day: Tuesday
Record transfer fee paid: None
Record transfer fee received: None
Record attendance: 1,500 v Leeds United (1983)

Change colours: Blue
Previous Leagues: Bradford Amateur, West Riding County Amateur, West Yorkshire, Yorkshire.

Senior honours/best performance: West Riding County Cup (2), Yorkshire League Division 2, Bradford & District Cup (7)
Past Players (who progressed to Football League): Tony Brown (Leeds United & Doncaster Rovers), Ian Ormondroyd (Bradford City).

Lincoln United's top scorer Kevin Carter climbs high to head for goal during United's penultimate match of the season at Ossett Town. Photo: T. Sandell-Codd

Hallam on the defensive against Thorne Colliery in the Northern Counties (East) League

Hallam, here seen defending stoutly, lose at Kiveton Park 1-2.

Hallam, one of the oldest clubs in the country, lose on their Sandygate pitch, a mud bath in this game, to Maltby miners Welfare.

BRADLEY RANGERS

President: Richard Sullivan
Chairman: Gerard Murphy
Manager: Tony Pearce
Ass. Man/Coach:
Physiotherapist: David Shirtliffe
Secretary: David Platt
Address & Tel. No: 34 Thorpe Green Drive, Golcar, Huddersfield HD7 4QU
Commercial Manager: Keith Stocks
Press Officer: David Platt
Ground Address & Tel. No: Warrenside, Deighton, Hudds. 0484 542044
Capacity: 1,000 **Covered accommodation:** Nil **Seating:** Nil **Floodlights:** No
Simple ground directions: Leave M62 at junction 25 to Huddersfield (East), turn right at lights, then left on Keldregate to Warrenside road. Train to Deighton Station
Clubhouse details: Lounge, pool room, reception room for 100, committee room, sec office
Programme details: Weekly **Editor:** David Platt **Club metal badges:** No
Local Newspaper(s): Huddersfield Examiner, Yorks Post
Club colours: Black/White stripes **Nickname:** Rangers **Change colours:** Blue
Midweek match day: Wednesday
Record transfer fee paid: None
Record transfer fee received: None
Record attendance: 300
Previous Leagues: Huddersfield League, West Yorkshire League, Yorkshire League
Senior honours/best performance: Enclosed copy and N.G.C. League Cup Runners-up 1986
Past Players (who progressed to Football League): Ronnie Liversedge, Andrew Watson.

DRONFIELD UNITED

President: D. Dooley
Chairman: D. Dooley
Manager: D. Wickens
Asst. Man: F. Roe
Player Coach: G. Rowbotham
Hon. Secretary: David Taylor
Address & Tel. No: 1 Lowedges, Chesterfield Road South, Sheffield S8 8LW. 376121
Address & Tel. No. of ground: Coach & Horses, Stubley Hollow, Dronfield
Simple ground directions: Sheffield-Dronfield road (A61) behind "Coach & Horses"
No. of seats: None **Covered accommodation:** 200 **Capacity:** 1,500 **Floodlights:** No
Year formed: 1911 **Nickname:** None **Club sponsors:** None
Club colours: Amber/Black/Amber & Black **Change colours:** Blue
Previous Names: Norton Woodseats **Previous Grounds:** None
Record attendance: 4,800 v Enfield **Year:** 1947 **Programme Editor:** D. Wickens (Dronfield 414156)
Previous Leagues: None **Programme: Price/Pages** None
Clubhouse details: None
Club Captain (1984-85): David Gillott **Player of the Season (1984-85):** Andrew King

GARFORTH TOWN

President: K. Warner
Chairman: J. Hill
Manager:
Coach:
Physiotherapist: J. Garlick
Secretary: W.S. Hayle
Address & Tel. No: 17 Richmondfield Lane, Barwick-in-Elmet. Leeds 812548 (H), 704941 (B)
Commercial Manager: W.S. Hayle
Press Officer & Tel. No: J. Griffiths. Leeds 871702
Address & Tel. No. of ground: Brierlands Lane, Garforth, Leeds. (0532 864083)
Simple ground directions: Off Aberford Road (A642), Garforth
No. of seats: None **Ground accommodation:** 500 **Capacity:** 2,000 **Floodlights:** None
Year formed: 1964 **Nickname:** **Club sponsors:** Mike Dobson & Son
Club colours: Green shirts, Black shorts **Change colours:** Blue and White stripes
Previous Names: Miners Arms A.F.C., Garforth Miners **Previous Grounds:** None
Record attendance: Not known **Programme:** 24 pages, 10p
Previous Leagues: Leeds Sunday, West Yorkshire, Yorkshire **Programme Editor:** Secretary
Club Captain (1984-85): Tony Ward **Player of the Season (1984-85):** P. Matthews

GRIMETHORPE M.W.

President: J. Blundell
Chairman: K. Donkin
Manager: T. Stevenson
Coach:
Physiotherapist: None
Secretary: H. Livett
Address & Tel. No: 4A Beech Road, Shafton, Barnsley, S. Yorks S72 8QG. 0226 710774, 0924 370161
Commercial Manager: None
Press Officer & Tel No: None
Address & Tel. No of ground: Grimethorpe Miners Welfare, Cemetery Road, Grimethorpe (0226) 711544
Simple ground directions: From Barnsley A628 to Grimethorpe – A1 Pontefract (A628)
No. of seats: None **Covered accommodation:** 150 **Capacity:** 3,000 **Floodlights:** No
Year formed: 1972 **Nickname:** Colliers **Club sponsors:** Appleyards Bros
Club colours: Blue/White/White **Change colours:** Red
Previous Names: None **Previous Grounds:** None
Record attendance: 3,000 Leeds All Stars Charity Match **Year:** None
Previous Leagues: Barnsley & Doncaster Premier **Programme:** 16 pages, 10p
Clubhouse details: Tearoom **Programme Editor:** S. Nadin
Club Captain (1984-85): A. Reed **Player of the Year (1984-85):** A. Reed

HALLAM

President: T. Stones
Chairman: W. Powall
Manager: Jack Whitham
Coach: John Fantham
Asst. Manager: P. Ellis
Physiotherapist: John Beachall
Secretary: G.L. Holland
Address & Tel. No: 34 Standon Crescent, Sheffield S9 1PP. 0742 381899 (H), ditto (B)
Commercial Manager: None
Address & Tel. No:
Publicity Officer: M. Radford, 198 Spicey Avenue, Sheffield S5. Tel: 0742 389115
Address & Tel. No. of ground: Sandygate Road, Sheffield 10 (0742 301802)
Simple ground directions: Off A57 Crosspool, Sheffield 10
No. of seats: None **Covered accommodation:** 250 **Capacity:** 2,000 **Floodlights:** No
Year formed: 1862 **Nickname:** None **Club sponsors:** Hallamshire Inc Services
Club colours: All Blue
Change colours: All Red
Previous Names: None
Previous Grounds: None
Record attendance: 3,000 v Evenwood Town, Amateur Cup **Year:** 1959
Previous Leagues: None
Programme: 10 pages, 10p
Clubhouse details: None
Programme Editor: Barry Holmes (0742 6655011)
Club Captain (1984-85): Cliff Wilson
Player of the Season (1984-85): M. Higginbottom

HARROGATE RAILWAY ATHLETIC

President: J. Blakey
Chairman: D. Bentley
Manager: F. Cliffe
Coach: J. O'Byrne
Physiotherapist:
Secretary: S. Fountain
Address & Tel. No: Harrogate 62399 (H), 0274 722512 (B)
Commercial Manager: J. Render
Address & Tel. No: 0423 883467
Press Officer & Tel. No: J. Render (0423 883467)
Address & Tel. No. of ground: Station View, Starbeck, Harrogate, No. Yorks (0423-883104)
Simple ground directions: A59 Harrogate to Knaresboro Road at Starbeck Pelican crossing turn left
No. of seats: None **Covered accommodation:** 350 **Capacity:** 4,000 **Floodlights:** No
Year formed: 1935 **Nickname:** The 'Rail' **Club sponsors:** ANC & Robinson
Club colours: Red/Black with stripe
Change colours: Yellow with Red pinstripe/Yellow/Yellow
Previous Names: Starbeck L.N.E.R.
Previous Grounds: None
Record attendance: 4,000 v Penrith **Year:** 1952
Programme: 4 or 8 pages, 20p
Previous Leagues: W. Yorks, Harrogate District
Programme Editor: M. Johnson 886778 (H), 865641 (B)
Clubhouse details: Games, TV room & Lounge. Beers, spirits and snacks available, open regularly.

HATFIELD MAIN

President: V. Deeming
Chairman: D. Willis
Manager: J. Reed
Asst. Man/Coach: J. Kirk
Physiotherapist:
Secretary: W.A. Jones
Address & Tel. No: 26 Hampton Road, Broadway, Dunscroft, Doncaster. 0302 843388
Press Officer & Tel. No: As above
Address & Tel. No. of ground: Dunscroft Welfare Grounds, Dunscroft, Nr Doncaster
Simple ground directions: From Doncaster: A18 Scunthorpe Road, turn left at Flarepath Hotel in Dunsville. Ground half mile down Broadway on the right
No. of seats: None **Ground accommodation:** 300 **Capacity:** 4,000 **Floodlights:** No
Year formed: 1936 **Nickname:** None **Club sponsors:** K & S Motors, Doncaster
Club colours: All Yellow
Change colours: All White
Previous Names: None
Previous Grounds: None
Record attendance: 750 v Bishop Auckland (F.A. Trophy) **Year:** Not known
Previous Leagues: None
Programme: 10 pages, 10p
Clubhouse details: Open every evening
Club Captain (1984-85): I. Preston
Player of the Year (1984-85): W. Whiteman

KIVETON PARK

President: None
Chairman: E. Banks
Manager: John Warnock
Press Officer & Tel No:
Secretary: John Holden
Address & Tel. No: 184 Wales Road, Kiveton Park, Sheffield S31 8RE. Worksop 770558 (H), 0742 446934 (B)
Commercial Manager:
Address & Tel. No. of ground: Kiveton Park, Miners Welfare Ground, Hard Lane, Kiveton Park, Nr Sheffield
Simple ground directions: From north or south on the M1, Junction 31, signposted Worksop, after ¼ mile turn right down Goosecar Lane, through Todwick Village to Hard Lane Crossroad. Ground 200 yards on right.
No. of seats: 200 **Ground accommodation:** 2,000 **Capacity:** 2,000 **Floodlights:** No
Year formed: Early 1900 **Nickname:** Park **Club sponsors:**
Club colours: All Red
Change colours: All Blue
Previous Names: Kiveton Park Colliery United
Previous Grounds: None
Record attendance: None **Year:** None
Mid-week match evening: Wednesday
Previous Leagues: Yorkshire
Programme: 12 pages, free
Clubhouse details: None
Major Honours: Yorkshire League Division 2 Champions 1977-78
Club Captain (1984-85): R. Collins
Player of the Year (1984-85): I. Montisci

Harrogate Town press hard during their 6-3 home victory over Bradley Rangers.

A last gasp save by the Grimethorpe goalkeeper at the feet of Lincoln United's Paul Brown in September 1985.
Photo: T. Sandell-Codd

MALTBY M.W. F.C.

President: J. Layden
Chairman: H. Henson
Manager: R. Habbin
Physiotherapist:
Secretary: Peter Kenny
Address & Tel. No: Rotherham 813675
Commercial Manager:
Address & Tel. No:
Press Officer & Tel No: None
Address & Tel. No. of ground: Muglet Lane, Maltby
Simple ground directions: Situated on Muglet Lane opposite Maltby Miners Welfare Club
No. of seats: None **Ground accommodation:** 2,000 **Capacity:** 2,000 **Floodlights:** No
Year formed: 1970 **Nickname:** **Club sponsors:** Steelphalt Ltd
Club colours: White/Black/White
Change colours: Yellow/Blue/Yellow
Record attendance: 940 **Year:**
Programme: 20p
Previous Leagues: Yorkshire, Sheffield County Senior
Programme Editor: R. Habbin (Roth 541383)
Clubhouse details: None
Major Honours: County Senior Cup
Club Captain (1984-85): Richard Habbin
Player of the Season (1984-85): John Biggs

MEXBOROUGH TOWN ATHLETIC

President: Tony Sleight
Chairman: A. Severns
Manager: Steve Mellor
Secretary: D. Mower
Address & Tel. No: 60 Windmill Crescent, Mexborough, Yorks. S64 0EB. 0709 588360
Commercial Manager: W.G. Stones
Address & Tel No: 0709 586939
Address & Tel No. of ground: Hampden Road, Mexborough, South Yorkshire (0709) 586479/583426
Simple ground directions: Just off the A6023 (Conisbrough - Mexborough Road) **Club shop:** Yes
No. of seats: 250 **Covered accommodation:** Stand **Capacity:** 5,000 **Floodlights:** No
Year formed: 1962 **Nickname:** The Boro' **Club sponsors:** Tony Sleight Car Sales
Previous names: Mexborough Town
Club colours: Blue & White/Navy
Previous grounds: None
Change colours: Yellow/Black/Red
Day for midweek home matches: Tuesday
Record attendance: 1,800 v Scarborough, F.A. Trophy 3rd Round **Year:** 1972-3
Best performance in: F.A. Cup: 1975-6 4th Qualifying Round
F.A. Trophy: 1972-3 3rd Round Proper (last 16)
Previous Leagues: Yorkshire, Midland Counties
Clubhouse details: Mexborough Athletic Club & Miners' Welfare. Snooker room.
Present players with Football League experience: None
Past players who progressed into the Football League: Billy Whitehurst
Record transfer fee paid: Not disclosed by club
Record transfer fee received: £1,800 from Hull City for Billy Whitehurst
Programme details: 12 pages, 10p
Local newspapers & Tel. No: South Yorkshire Times, Sheffield "Green-un"
Programme Editor: Bill Stones
Club metal badges: No
Senior Honours: Yorkshire League Div 1, Yorkshire League Cup, Sheffield Senior Cup (8), Yorkshire League Double 1972-3
Player of the Year: (1984-85) M. Fletcher
Club Captain (1984-85): G. Paskin

OSSETT ALBION

President: J.B. Burrows
Chairman: N.A. Wigglesworth
Secretary: D.R. Chambers
Address & Tel. No: 109 South Parade, Ossett WF5 0EB. (0924) 276004 (H), (0924) 275421 (B)
Manager: J.P. Ogilvie
Coach: R. Radford
Physiotherapist: M. Osbourne
Press Officer & Tel No: Chairman (0924 275630)
Address & Tel. No. of ground: Queen's Terrace, Dimple Well Rd., Ossett. Wakefield (0924) 273618
Simple ground directions: Leave M1 at Junction 40, take Wakefield Road for 200 yards, turn right at the Post House Hotel, down Queens Drive to the end, turn right, then second left down Southdale Road, turn right at end, then first left down Dimple Wells Road.
No. of seats: 200 **Covered accommodation:** 200 **Capacity:** 2,000 **Floodlights:** No
Year formed: 1944 **Nickname:** Albion **Club sponsors:** Burmatex Ltd/Post House Hotel
Club colours: Old Gold/Black
Change colours: Blue/White
Record attendance: **Year:**
Local newspaper: Ossett Observer
Previous Leagues: Yorkshire
Programme: 12 pages, 20p
Programme Editor: S. Hanks (0924 276832)
Clubhouse details: Full bar facilities open 7 days and catering.
Major Honours: Yorkshire League Champions 1975, Yorkshire League Cup Winners 1976, 1977, Fletcher Motors Cup Winners 1984
Club Captain (1984-85): P. Eaton
Player of the Year (1984-85): D. Ingham

PARKGATE

President: M. Sharpe
Chairman: T. White
Manager: B. Tonks
Asst. Man/Coach: M. Horne
Physiotherapist: I. Hill
Secretary: R. Mortimer
Address & Tel. No: 10 Cardew Close, Rawmarsh, Rotherham, S. Yorks. Rotherham 523150
Commercial Manager: S. Bailey
Address & Tel. No: Rotherham 524031
Press Officer & Tel No: Secretary
Address & Tel. No. of ground: Green Lane, Rawmarsh, Rotherham (Rotherham 523471)
Simple ground directions: From Rotherham to Rawmarsh down Green Lane for 800 yards
No. of seats: None **Covered accommodation:** Yes **Capacity:** **Floodlights:** No
Year formed: 1969 **Nickname:** The Gate **Club sponsors:** Kitchen Gallery
Club colours: All Sky Blue **Change colours:** Yellow/Black
Previous Names: None **Mid-week match evening:** Tuesday
Record attendance: v Worksop **Year:** 1982 **Programme:** 12 pages, with entrance
Previous Leagues: Yorkshire **Programme Editor:** S. Bailey
Clubhouse details: Members bar, two lounges, including dance floor
Club Captain (1984-85): G. Cooke **Player of the Season (1984-85):** John Wheeler

PILKINGTON RECREATION

President: J. Denis
Chairman: P. Ostle
Manager: M. Hughes
Asst. Man/Coach: S. Brookes
Physiotherapist: Graham Brierley
Secretary: Brian Wood
Address & Tel. No: 1 St. Michael's Drive, Thorne. (B) 812001 (Thorne)
Commercial Manager:
Address & Tel. No:
Press Officer & Tel No:
Address & Tel. No. of ground: Moor Lane, Kirk Sandall, Doncaster. Doncaster 883391
Simple ground directions: Take A18 from Doncaster Town Centre. At Wheatley Hotel take left fork to Kirk Sandall, over railway bridge; left fork to Kirk Sandall. Ground on right.
No. of seats: None **Covered accommodation:** Stand **Capacity:** 300 **Floodlights:** No
Year formed: 1921 **Nickname:** Pilks **Club sponsors:** None
Club colours: Sky Blue **Change colours:** White, Red Trims
Previous Names: None **Previous Grounds:** None
Record attendance: 498 v Swinton Athletic **Year:** 1974/5 **Programme:** 50p (including admission)
Previous Leagues: Yorkshire, Sheffield County Senior **Programme Editor:** Manager
Clubhouse details: Lounge, dance room, pool room, darts room, licensed bar opens 2.00pm, match days until 11.00pm.

ROWNTREE MACKINTOSH (YORK)

President: Mr. K. Thompson
Chairman: Mr. G.B. Shaw
Manager: Mr. J. Collis
Ass. Man/Coach: M. Carter
Physiotherapist: G. Calpin
Secretary: M.E. Hodgson
Address & Tel. No: 139 Huntington Road, York. Tel. 0904 26519
Commercial Manager: G.B. Shaw
Press Officer: As Above
Ground Address & Tel. No: Mille Crux, Haxby Road. 23933
Capacity: 1,000 **Covered accommodation:** Nil **Seating:** Nil **Floodlights:** No
Simple ground directions: North side of the city, 1 mile from city centre. Ground on Haxby Road, 200 yards past the factory on right side.
Clubhouse details: Refreshments on ground. No licence.
Programme details: 10p **Editor:** G.B. Shaw **Club metal badges:**
Local Newspaper(s): Yorkshire Evening Press
Club colours: White/Blue White **Change colours:** Yellow/White Yellow
Midweek match day: Tuesday **Previous Leagues:** York & District
Record transfer fee paid: None
Record transfer fee received: None
Record attendance: 200
Senior honours/best performance: North Riding Senior Cup Finalist
Past Players (who progressed to Football League): Andy Leaning (Goalkeeper) to York City. 86.

SHEFFIELD

President: J.K. Healey
Chairman: J.K. Healey
Manager: R. Evans
Asst. Man./Coach: T. Dale
Physiotherapist: P. Foster
Secretary: W.E. Peace
Address & Tel. No: 72 Woodburn Drive, Chapeltown, Sheffield S30 4YT. 468160 (H)
Commercial Manager: A. Methley
Address & Tel No: Sheffield 884608
Press Officer & Tel. No: A. Methsey
Address & Tel. No. of ground: Abbeydale Park, Dore, Sheffield 17. (0742 362040)
Simple ground directions: 4½ miles from City Centre on A621 (Sheffield - Bakewell Rd). Sheffield Amateur Sports Club ground, on right after passing Abbeydale Gardεn Centre
No. of seats: 100 **Ground accommodation:** 4,000 **Floodlights:** No
Year formed: 1857 **Nickname:** None **Club sponsors:** N/A
Club colours: Red/Black **Change colours:** Blue/White
Previous Names: None **Previous Grounds:** None
Record attendance: 2,000 v Barton Rovers, FA Vase) **Year:** 1976/77
Previous Leagues: Yorkshire **Programme:** (whenever possible) 4 pages included with admission
Major Honors: Amateur Cup Winners 1903-04, F.A. Vase Finalists 1976-77
Player of the Year (1984-85): H. Millington

STAVELEY

President: A. Colleyshaw, BSc
Chairman: D. Howitt
Secretary: M.A. Wake
Address & Tel. No: Chesterfield 475994 (H) 77251 ext. 272 (B)
Manager: C. Millward
General Manager:
Coach:
Address & Tel. No:
Physiotherapist:
Press Officer & Tel No: D. Howitt (Sheffield 441724)
Address & Tel. No. of ground: Handley Wood Sports Ground, Barrow Hill. Chesterfield 472576
Simple ground directions: M1 North Junction 30. From South Junction 29, then A619 to Staveley, following signposts to "Staveley Works"
No. of seats: None **Covered accommodation:** Yes **Capacity:** 2,000 **Floodlights:** Yes
Year formed: 1968 **Nickname:** **Club sponsors:** Chesterfield Volvo Centre
Club colours: Red/Black **Change colours:** Blue/White
Record attendance: 850 **Year:** 1982-83 (FA Vase v. Rainworth MW)
Previous Leagues: Midlands Div 1, East Midland, Chesterfield **Programme:** 10 pages with admission.
Clubhouse details: Licensed social club. Open most nights. **Programme Editor:** Dave Howitt
Club Captain (1984-85): B. Hemstack **Player of the Season (1984-85):** M. Ryan

---

WOOLLEY MINERS WELFARE

President: G.C. Biggins
Chairman: J. Henderson
Manager: G. Bedford
Ass. Man/Coach: C. Chambers
Physiotherapist:
Secretary: G.A. Britton
Address & Tel. No: 17 Eastfield Crescent, Mapplewell, Barnsley, S. Yorks, S75 6DN. Barnsley (0226) 384277
Commercial Manager:
Press Officer: L. Dodd (0226) 387194
Ground Address & Tel. No: Colliery Road, Woolley Colliery
Capacity: 2,500 **Covered accommodation:** 200 **Seating:** 200 **Floodlights:** No
Simple ground directions: Exit 38 on M1 follow Woolley Colliery signs (not Woolley). Ground 2 miles from Exit 38.
Clubhouse details:
Programme details: 15 pages, 20p **Editor:** J.H. Howard **Club metal badges:**
Local Newspaper(s): Barnsley Chronicle
Club colours: Amber & Black **Nickname:** "The Colliers" **Change colours:** Blue & White
Midweek match day: **Previous Leagues:** Sheffield, Hallamshire County Senior
Record transfer fee paid:
Record transfer fee received:
Record attendance: 1,500 Emley v Frickley (Sheffield Senior Cup)
Senior honours/best performance: N.C.E. Division 2 1982-83
Past Players (who progressed to Football League): None

YORK RAILWAY INSTITUTE

President: None
Chairman: F. Webster
Secretary: G. Lewington
Address & Tel. No: 33, Wilton Rise, Holgate Road, York. 0904 58614
Manager: R. Mollatt
Commercial Manager: None
Asst. Man/Coach: B. Carreral
Address & Tel. No:
Physiotherapist: None
Press Officer & Tel. No: None
Address & Tel. No. of ground: Railway Institute Sports Ground, New Lane, Acomb Road, York. 0904 798930
Simple ground directions: N/A **Mid-week match evening:** Tuesday
No. of seats: None **Covered accommodation:** None **Capacity:** 1,500 **Floodlights:** None
Year formed: 1912 **Nickname:** None **Club sponsors:** TSB & York Builders
Club colours: White/Navy/Navy **Change colours:** Blue/White/White
Previous Names: None **Previous Grounds:** None
Record attendance: Not known **Programme:** 1/10, 30p (admission)
Previous Leagues: York & District **Programme Editor:** B. Carreral
Club Captain (1984-85): G. Green **Player of the Season (1984-85):** T. Metcalfe

Sutton Town go two up against Multipart League side Marine, but the visitors end the game all square in this F.A. Cup tie.

Marine fight back away to Sutton Town in the F.A. Cup to draw (2-2). Their first goal here sets them onto their recovery.

NORTHERN COUNTIES EAST DIVISION TWO 1986/87

COLLINGHAM
Secretary: J.A. Learoyd. Tel: 0532 713540 (H)
Ground: Harewood Road, Collingham. Tel: 0937 72207
Colours: All Sky Blue **Change Colours:** All White

ECCLESHILL UNITED
Secretary: G. Flynn. Tel: 0274 501287 (H)
Ground: Plumpton Park, Shipley, Bradford. Tel: 0274 615739
Colours: Blue/Blue **Change Colours:** All Yellow

FRENCHEVILLE COMMUNITY
Secretary: G.C. Warman. Tel: 0742 390728 (H) & 344204 (W)
Ground: Silkstone Road, Sheffield, 12. Tel: 0742 396395
Colours: Amber/Black **Change Colours:** Blue/White

FRYSTON COMMUNITY
Secretary: B. Bennett. Tel: 0977 558531 (H) & 556565 x2287 (W)
Ground: Fryston CW, Ferry Fryston, Castleford. Tel: 0977 553413
Colours: All Red with White Trim **Change Colours:** Yellow/Green/Yellow

GLASSHOUGHTON WELFARE
Secretary: E. Jones. Tel: 0977 556257 (H) & 514445 (W)
Ground: Glasshoughton Welfare, Leeds Road, Glasshoughton, Castleford.
Colours: All Blue **Change Colours:** All Green

HALL ROAD RANGERS
Secretary: E. Richardson. Tel: 0482 43782 (H) & 26104 (W)
Ground: Dene park, Dene Close, Dunswell, Near Hull. Tel: 0482 850101
Colours: Blue & White Hoops **Change Colours:** All Green

IMMINGHAM TOWN
Secretary: T. Paul. Tel: 0763 843654 (H) & 0724 842030 (W)
Ground: Woodlands Avenue, Immingham. Tel: 0469 75724
Colours: Maroon & Sky Trim/Sky Blue/Maroon **Change Colours:** White & Black pinstripe/Black/Black

LIVERSEDGE
Secretary: M. Balmforth. Tel: 0274 871426 (W) for messages
Ground: Glayborn, Quaker Lane, Hightown Road, Cleckheaton, West Yorks.
Colours: Royal Blue & White/Royal **Change Colours:** Red & Navy Blue

OSSETT TOWN
Secretary: F. Lloyd. Tel: 0226 382415 (H)
Ground: Ingfield, Ossett. Tel: 0924 272960
Colours: Red/White **Change Colours:** White/Navy

PICKERING TOWN
Secretary: D.L. Jemison. Tel: 0751 73210 (H) & 73568 (W)
Ground: Recreation Ground, Malton Road, Pickering. Tel: 0751 73317
Colours: Royal Blue/White **Change Colours:** Green & Black Stripes

SELBY TOWN A.F.C.
Secretary: M.D. Segass. Tel: 0757 638827 (H) & 682020 x247 (W)
Ground: Flaxley Ground, Selby N. Yorks
Colours: All Red **Change Colours:** All White

STOCKBRIDGE PARK STEELS
Secretary: M. Grimmer. Tel: 0742 886470 (H) & 888224 (W)
Ground: Bracken Moor Lane, Stocksbridge, Sheffield. Tel: 0742 882045
Colours: Yellow/Blue **Change Colours:** Red/Blue

TADCASTER ALBION
Secretary: L. West. Tel: 0937 832948 (H) & 0937 832225 x262 (W)
Ground: The Park, Ings Land, Tadcaster. Tel: 0937 834119
Colours: Royal Blue/White/Blue **Change Colours:** White/Black/Black

WINTERTON RANGERS
Secretary: G. Spencer. Tel: G. Spencer 0724 853117 (H) & 0724 853378 (W)
Ground: West Street, Winterton. Tel: 0724 732628
Colours: Sky Blue with Red trim/Maroon/Sky Blue **Change Colours:** Gold/Black/Gold

WOMBWELL S.A.
Secretary: P. Schofield. Tel: 0924 864719 (H)
Ground: The Stadium, Station Road Wombwell. Tel: 0226 752128
Colours: Black & White Stripes **Change Colours:** Blue/White/Blue

WORSBROUGH BRIDGE NW
Secretary: D. Smith. Tel: 0226 243418 (H) & 284452 (W)
Ground: Park Road, Worsbrough Bridge, Barnsley. Tel: 0226 284452
Colours: All Red **Change Colours:** Yellow & Blue

YORKSHIRE AMATEURS
Secretary: A. Wilkinson. Tel: 0532 402597 (H) & 48211 x200 (W)
Ground: 'Bracken Edge', Sycamore Avenue, Leeds LS7 4JF Tel: 0532 624093
Colours: White/Blue/Red **Change Colours:** Blue/White or Orange/Black/Black

YORKSHIRE MAIN
Secretary: A. Summers. Tel: 0302 834907
Ground: Yorkshire Main Miners Welfare, Edlington Lane, Edlington, Doncaster. Tel: 0709 864075
Colours: Red/Black **Change Colours:** White Black

Pontefract Collieries attack Armthorpe on their way to a conclusive triumph (3-0).

Dronfield United go down at home to North Ferriby United 0-2.

Lincoln United's Andy Wood taking on his Maltby defensive opponent in the October 3-3 draw at Ashby Avenue.
Photo: T. Sandell-Codd

Graham St. Prims, playing on the Derby County training ground ('The Ramarena') as usual, beat Eccleshill United 3-0.

CENTRAL MIDLANDS FOOTBALL LEAGUE

President: L. Nowicki (Esq.)
General Secretary: A.E. Goodacre (Tel: 672986)
6 Madison Avenue, Chaddesden, Derby DE2 6HZ

For the 6th season in a row the Premier Division has produced a League and Cup Double performance. On this occasion the victorious club are Stanton F.C. who carried off the Championship with a six point margin over Derby Carriage & Wagon with Mickleover R.B.L. a further two points adrift in 3rd place with Rolls Royce in 4th place, 1 point behind the "Legion".

In the Manns Premier Cup the top 3 League teams were in contention at the Semi Final stages. Carriage & Wagon fought through to the Final by beating Radford Olympic 2-1 in a replay following a 1-1 draw whilst 3rd place Mickleover met the Champions Stantion and in a superb match Stanton edged through with a 3-2 scoreline. In the Final, again played at the Baseball Ground by kind permission of Derby County F.C., it was Stantion who snatched the Double with a 2-0 victory. Carriage & Wagon can feel well pleased with the season despite finishing as "Bridesmain" twice. There was some consolation also to Mickleover as their second string finished Runners Up in the Senior Division.

The Central Division also produced a League "Cup Double" winner in Huthwaite F.C. who only joined the Central Midlands League this season. Secretary, Don Collins Manager, Trevor Wass and their Committee have transformed an ailing Club in 1980 to one we are all proud of. They have since 1980 achieved 4 Championships, 3 Cup Wins, 1 County Cup Win and 1 Cup Runner Up. A superb performance highlighted with their "Double" in the first season in the Central Midlands Football League. The Cup Final saw them 2-0 victors over another of our new Clubs, Thorntons F.C. who can also be pleased with their first season in the League. Beside reaching the Cup Final they finished a respectable 6th in the League (at one stage were title contenders:), and highlighted their season by winning the Derbyshire Copunty Cup (South). Theirs was one of 3 teams from the Central Midlands Football League to achieve County Cup victories. The others being Shirebrook Colliery who won the Derbyshire County Cup (North), and Retford Rail who won the Notts County Cup. Whilst Blackwell Miners Welfare had the misfortune to meet Shirebrook in the County Cup Final their also met Huthwaite in the League Cup Semi-Final and finished runners up in the Central Division. Still an extremely praiseworthy performance. Sandiacre Town came with a late run to snatch 3rd place from Rossington who were 2 points adrift.

Shirebrook Colliery in winning the Senior Division Title had the distinction of being the only Club to remain unbeaten in the entire season and in fact did not lose any games League or Cup. They achieved an incredible "Treble" in lifting the League, County Cup and finally the League Cup in which they beat Swanwick Reserves 6-0. Their hardest game came in the County Cup against Blackwell from our Central Division. With 10 minutes of play remaining Blackwell were coasting home at 2-1 when the Colliery hit them with 2 late goals. Mickleover Reserves finished League Runners Up with Castle Donington Town taking 3rd place on goal difference from Draycott F.C.

Division One was dominated by the top 3 teams and as in the Premier all 3 contested the League and Cup. Denby Drury Lowe Reserves clinched the League Title from Alvaston & Boulton Reserves with Slack & Parr Reserves in 3rd place. In the Cup Denby reached the Final by beating Draycott Reserves 3-1 in the Semi-Final. Alvaston met Slack & Parr in the other Semi-Final and Slack & Parr went through 5-4. In the Final Denby looked to provide the Leagues fourth "Double" but were caught out in the 89th minute by a Slack & Parr goal who took the Cup 1-0.

Premier One produced the closest finish with the Championship being decided by the final match of the season. Long Eaton United had led the table for some time and completed the season on 61 points, Lincoln United and Shepshed with games in hand closed the gap and they met at Shepshed and Lincoln won 2-1 to complete their fixtures on 62 points. This left Shepshed on 60 with 1 game to play and in a nail biting finish took the title by beating Worksop Town 4-0.

Shepshed failed in their efforts to retain the Manns Premier One Cup when they lost 0-1 to Burton Albion in the Semi-Final. In the other Semi-Final it took a replay to see Arnold F.C. into the Final at the expense of Eastwood Town.

The Final was played at the City Ground by kind permission of Nottingham Forest F.C. and an exciting game went in favour of Arnold with a 2-0 scoreline over the pre-match favourites.

The Central Midlands Football League are again indebted to our sponsors, Manns Brewery (Northampton), Leangate Welding Limited and B.E. Webbe (Removals) Limited for their support.

The B.E. Webbe Cup provided a second change for Shepshed to complete a League and Cup "Double". They had to overcome a spirited Belper Town before finally taking the Cup 4-1 on aggregate. The first leg at Belper ended 0-2 and the second leg 1-2 at Shepshed.

The Central Midlands Football League are fortunate to have the use of 2 Football League Grounds on which to play our major Finals and to the Directors and Staff of both Derby County F.C. and Nottingham Forest F.C. we pass our sincere thanks.

1986 concludes the Leagues 15th season but is also the birth of a new era in the Leagues progression. Following previous seasons attempts to form a League of Semi-Professional Standards, it is pleasing that the 1986-87 season will see the first stages put into operation as the League look to fill the void between the Northern Premier and the Southern League in the Midlands.

A New Supreme Division has been formed and the League have completely revised its structure to accomodate Clubs of the highest Semi-Professional Standards. Although the Division will start slightly under strength the League are confident that other Clubs will follow this seasons pioneers and join in future seasons. Indeed the League have already received firm commitment from 2 high quality clubs for next season.

In line with this "Professional" thinking the League have agreed to join forces with Nottingham Forest in a major joint fund raising scheme which commences this season and if clubs respond the first season could produce some £20,000 to be shared by the Clubs. We are delighted to be involved with the Midlands "Top" Football League Club and thank their Commercial Manager, Dave Pullan for his efforts on behalf of both parties.

Premier Division	P	W	D	L	F	A	Pts
Stanton FC	30	23	4	3	88	36	73
Carriage & Wagon	30	20	7	3	78	21	67
Mickleover RBL	30	19	8	3	70	31	65
Rolls Royce	30	19	7	4	80	38	64
Rossington Main	30	14	7	9	56	34	49
Radford Olympic	30	10	12	8	47	53	42
Denby Drury Lowe	30	11	8	11	55	58	41
Clay Cross Works	30	11	8	11	54	64	41
Retford Rail	30	11	6	13	50	55	39
Newhall United	30	11	3	16	58	58	36
Slack & Parr	30	9	6	15	48	66	33
Sutton Trinity	30	7	9	14	34	60	30
Swanwick Pentrich Road	30	8	5	17	35	61	29
Nuthall FC	30	5	5	20	36	80	20
Alvaston & Boulton	30	3	10	17	38	69	19
Holbrook Miners Welfare	30	4	5	21	34	77	17

Cental Division	P	W	D	L	F	A	Pts
Huthwaite FC	30	28	1	1	119	18	85
Blackwell Miners Welfare	30	12	4	5	83	40	67
Sandiacre Town	30	18	5	7	71	32	59
Rossington Main Res.	30	18	3	9	54	48	57
Carriage & Wagon Res	30	17	3	10	83	46	54
Thornton's FC	30	16	5	9	75	42	53
Brailsford FC	30	16	4	10	98	77	52
Thorpe Acre Hallam	30	15	6	9	83	57	51
Attenborough FC	30	15	3	12	71	51	48
Priory FC	30	14	2	14	51	64	44
Smalley Villa	30	6	6	18	39	85	24
Nuthall FC Res	30	6	5	19	48	79	23
Kilburn Miners Welfare	30	6	5	19	31	79	23
Ridding St. James	30	6	3	21	43	89	21
FC Ashbourne	30	5	3	22	34	114	18
Ibstock Penistone Robers	30	3	2	25	25	87	11

Leading Scorers

R. Smith, Thorpe Acre Hallam FC	32
N. Owers Rolls Royce FC	29
T. Bailey Brailsford FC	26
K. Young Thorpe Acre Hallam FC	25
S. Cooke Huthwaite FC	25
P. Ollernshaw Denby Drury Lowe Reserves	25
K. Bull Shirebrook Colliery	21
R. Hall Stanton FC	21
G. Millington Clay Cross Works	20
G. Edwards Carriage & Wagon	19
G. Henderson Rossington Main FC	19
M. Taplin Borrowash Victoria	19
K. Preston Shirebrook Colliery	19
M. Bailey Slack & Parr Reserves	19

CUP FINAL RESULTS 1986

PREMIER DIVISION
Carriage & Wagon v Stanton FC................0-2
at the Baseball Ground, Derby
by kind permission of Derby County FC

PREMIER ONE
Arnold FC v Burton Albion....................2-0
at the City Ground, Nottingham
by kind permission of Notts Forest FC

CENTRAL DIVISION
Huthwaite FC v Thornton FC 2-0
at Belper Town FC

SENIOR DIVISION
Shirebrook Colliery v Swanwick Pentrich Road....6-0
at Borrowash Victoria FC

DIVISION ONE
Denby Drury Low FC v Slack & Parr FC........0-1
at Borrowash Victoria FC

Lincoln United striker Paul Brown scores against Ossett Town at home in October 1985. Photo: T. Sandell-Codd

Lincoln United midfielder Tony Jeffrey foiled by the emerging bravery of the Yorkshire Main goalkeeper in March, 1986. Photo: T. Sandell-Codd

SEASON 1985/6
PREMIER DIVISION

	Carriage & Wagon	Alveston & Boulton	Clay Cross Works	Denby Drury Lowe	Holbrook M.W.	Mickleover R.B.L.	Newhall Utd	Nethall F.C.	Radford Olympic	Retford Rail	Rolls Royce	Rossington Main	Slack & Parr	Stanton FC	Sutton Trinity	Swanwick P.R.
Alvaston & Boulton		1-3	6-6	2-2	1-0	2-2	0-2	2-3	2-2	3-2	1-4	0-5	1-2	0-3	0-0	2-2
Carriage & Wagon	0-0		5-0	3-3	2-0	4-1	0-1	5-0	0-0	5-0	1-1	3-0	4-0	1-1	3-0	4-0
Claycross Works.............	0-0	1-3		0-2	4-1	1-1	1-0	6-4	2-2	2-2	1-4	2-2	1-0	0-1	5-1	2-0
Denby Drury Lowe..........	5-2	0-5	6-1		3-0	4-2	1-1	3-0	2-2	2-3	2-2	1-3	2-1	2-2	3-1	0-2
Holbrook Miners Welfare.....	3-3	0-5	3-6	0-0		2-1	2-2	2-1	0-1	0-3	1-4	0-5	1-0	1-3	2-3	1-2
Mickleover RBL.............	4-0	3-1	3-2	2-0	2-0		2-1	1-0	5-0	2-2	2-2	4-1	4-2	1-1	5-1	3-0
Newhall Utd................	2-0	1-2	4-1	2-0	4-1	0-3		5-0	3-0	1-2	5-5	2-3	4-5	3-1	2-3	5-0
Nuthall FC..................	2-1	1-1	0-3	1-2	2-3	0-0	2-1		4-3	2-3	0-2	0-3	0-2	2-3	0-2	3-1
Radford Olympic............	1-0	0-2	1-1	1-2	3-2	1-1	2-1	2-2		4-1	3-2	2-1	3-2	1-3	0-0	2-2
Retford BR.................	4-0	0-4	0-1	4-0	3-2	0-2	3-1	1-1	0-1		0-1	0-2	0-0	1-4	2-1	2-3
Rolls Royce.................	2-0	2-4	5-1	4-1	3-2	1-1	3-1	3-0	2-2	3-0		1-0	4-1	1-2	3-0	3-2
Rossington Main.............	2-0	0-1	0-1	3-0	0-0	1-3	4-0	3-1	3-0	0-0	1-1		4-1	2-3	1-1	1-0
Slack & Parr................	1-0	1-3	0-0	3-1	2-2	1-2	3-4	6-1	2-2	3-3	1-6	1-4		0-5	1-2	2-0
Stanton FC..................	3-2	3-1	7-1	4-1	3-2	1-4	4-0	5-1	3-1	3-2	3-0	4-0	1-2		1-1	5-0
Sutton Trinity..............	1-1	0-0	0-2	1-4	3-1	0-3	2-0	2-2	2-2	2-4	0-3	1-1	0-1	3-5		1-0
Swanwick Pentrich Rd........	1-6	1-3	1-0	1-1	3-0	0-1	3-0	4-1	1-3	0-3	0-3	1-1	2-2	0-1	3-0	

CENTRAL MIDLANDS FOOTBALL LEAGUE PROPOSED FORMATION 1986-87

SUPREME DIVISION

Team	Former League
Arnold FC (Notts)	Northern Counties East League
Borrowash Victoria (Derby)	Northern Counties East League
Crookes FC (Sheff)	Whitbread County Senior League
Gainsborough Town (Lincs)	Lincolnshire Premier League
Harworth CI (Sheff)	Northern Counties East League
Heanor Town (Derby)	Northern Counties East League
Hinckley FC (Leics)	
Hinckley Town (Leics)	Leicester Senior League
Ilkeston Town (Derby)	Northern Counties East League
Kettering FC (Northants)	
Kimberley Town (Notts)	Northern Counties East League
Lincoln United (Lincs)	Northern Counties East League
Oakham United (Notts)	Northern Counties East League
Retford FC 86 (Notts)	
Rossington Main FC (sheff)	Central Midlands Football League

PREMIER DIVISION

Arnold Kingswell (Notts)	Northern Counties East League
Blidworth Welfare (Notts)	Northern Counties East League
Clay Cross Works (Derby)	Central Midlands Football League
Denby Drury Lowe (Derby)	Central Midlands Football League
Derby Carriage & Wagon (Derby)	Central Midlands Football League
Graham St. Prims (Derby)	Northern Counties East League
Grantham F.C. (Linc.)	Midland Regional Alliance
Huthwaite FC (Notts)	Central Midlands Football League (Promoted)
Melton Town (Leics)	Leicestershire District
Mickleover RBL (Derby)	Central Midlands Football League
Newhall United (Derby)	Central Midlands Football League
Radford Olympic (Notts)	Central Midlands Football League
Retford Rail (Notts)	Central Midlands Football League
Rolls royce (Derby)	Central Midlands Football League
Slack & Parr(Leics)	Central Midlands Football League
Stanton FC (Derby)	Central Midlands Football League
Sutton Trinity (Notts)	Central Midlands Football League
Swanwick Pentrich Road (Derby)	Central Midlands Football League

Lincoln United: Back Row (L-R) Wilson, Crombie (capt), Walker, Cox, Brown (P), Carter. Front Row (L-R) Wood, Ellis, Jeffrey, Lowman, Crosby, Coultan Photo: T. Sandell-Codd

Aston-on-Trent F.C. 1985/86 Photo: Paul Neal

DIVISION ONE

Team	Former League
Alvaston & Boulton (Derby)	Central Midlands Football League (Relegated)
Aston on Trent (Derby)	Derby Senior League
Attenborough FC (Notts)	Central Midlands Football League
Blackwell MW (Derby)	Central Midlands Football League
Brailsford FC (Derby)	Central Midlands Football League
Holbrook MW (Leics))	Central Midlands Football League (Relegated)
Loughborough FC (Leics)	Central Midlands Football League
Nuthall FC (Notts)	Central Midlands Football League
Priory FC (Notts)	Central Midlands Football League
Sandiacre Town (Derby)	Central Midlands Football League
Shirebrook Colliery (Derby)	Central Midlands Football League
Shirebrook Construction (Derby)	Sutton & Skegby League
Station FC (Sheff/Hallam)	Doncaster Senior League
Thorntons FC (Derby)	Central Midlands Football League
West Hallam (Derby)	Midland Regional Alliance

DIVISION TWO

Team	Former League
Arcspeed Services (Derby)	Central Midlands Football League
Belper Athletic (Derby)	Central Midlands Football League
Castle Donington Town (Leics)	Central Midlands Football League
Draycott FC (Derby)	Central Midlands Football League
FC Ashbourne (Derby)	Central Midlands Football League
Kilburn MW (Derby)	Central Midlands Football League
Matlock United (Derby)	Hope Valley League
Pastures Hospital (Derby)	Derby Senior League
Ridding St James (Derby)	Central Midlands Football League
Selston FC (Notts)	Midland Regional Alliance
Shardlow St James (Derby)	Central Midlands Football League
Smalley Villa (Derby)	Central Midlands Football League
Teversal FC (Notts)	Sutton & Skegby League
Tradepart FC (Notts)	Nottinghamshire Sparton League

ARNOLD F.C.

President: Mr D. Elvin
Secretary:
Chairman: Mr W. Whittaker
Managers: Mr J. Harrison, Mr I. Hollett
Capacity: 3,500 **Covered Accommodation:** 700 **Seating:** 150 **Floodlights:** Yes
Simple Ground directions: 5 miles North of Nottingham ½ mile off A60 Mansfield Road
Clubhouse Details: 144 St. Albans Road, Arnold
Year formed: 1928
Local newspapers: Nottingham Football Post
Club Colours: Yellow Shirts, Maroon Shorts
Change Colours: Red Shirts, White Shorts
Midweek Match Day: Tuesday
Record Attendance: 3,390
Previous Leagues: Midland League, Northern Counties League
Senior Honours/Best Performance: 1st Rd, F.A. Cup. 1967 & 1977. Northern Counties, East Champions 1985-86

BORROWASH VICTORIA A.F.C.

President: I. Anderson
Secretary: W.I. Collins
Chairman: E. Fletcher
Manager: I. Anderson
Ground Address & Tel. No. Spondon Leisure Centre, Borrowash Road, Spondon, Derby 668656
Capacity: 5,000 **Covered Accommodation:** Yes **Seating:** No **Floodlights:** Yes
Simple Ground directions: Via M1 to Junction 25, then via A52 Derby Road. Take 3rd turning left to Borrowash Rd.
Programme details: 16 pages, 15p
Editor: K. Tyler
Local newspapers: Derby Evening Telegraph
Midweek Match Day: Tuesday
Club Colours: Red and White, Black Shorts
Change Colours: Yellow
Record Attendance: 2,000 against Nottingham Forest to open new dressing rooms and Floodlights
Previous Leagues: Northern Counties East League. **Senior Honours/Best Performance:** Northern Counties, East League Div. 1 South Winners 1983-84 League Champions 77-78, 80-81, 83-84 Runners-Up. 12 times since 1965-66

CROOKES F.C.

President: —
Secretary: G. Stirling
Chairman: D. Learad
Manager: D Hague **Comm. Manager:** M.J. Buckley
Ground Address & Tel. No. Aurora Sports Ground, Bantry Road, Brintsworth, Nr Rotherham
Capacity: 1,500 **Covered Accommodation:** 250 **Seating:** No **Floodlights:** No
Simple Ground directions: M1 to J34 take A631 towards Rotherham. Approx. 1 mile on right
Clubhouse Details: Social Club, Lounge overlooking pitch
Programme details: 8 pages
Editor: M. Buckley
Local newspapers: Sheffield Green-un
Club Colours: White, Navy Blue
Change Colours: Red, Red
Midweek Match Day: Mon/Wed
Record Attendance: 300
Previous Leagues: Whitbread County Senior League, Hatchard League,
Senior Honours/Best Performance: Sheffield Senior Cup Finalist 85/86 v Frickley Athletic (0-2), Hatchard Div. One winners 82/83, Whitbread County Senior League Div. One Winners 84/84, Whitbread Trophy Finalist 85-86, Sheffield/Hallamshire Senior cup Finalist 85-86

GAINSBOROUGH TOWN

President: F. Bailey
Chairman: C. Anyan
Ground Address & Tel. No: Northholme, Gainsborough. 0427 3295
Simple ground directions: Main Gainsborough to Scunthorpe Road.
Capacity: 5,250 **Covered accommodation:** 3,500 **Seating:** 282 **Floodlights:** Yes
Club colours: All Blue
Year formed: 1982
Previous Leagues: Linc. Premier
Secretary: F. Nicholason
Manager: B. Martin
Change colours: White
Midweek matchday: Wednesday
Record Attendance: 500

HARWORTH C.I. F.C.

President: A. Allsop
Chairman: L. Daniels
Secretary: A. Fullwood
Manager: I. Young
Ground Address & Tel. No: Scrooby Road, Bircotes.
Simple ground directions: Turn off A1 at Blyth Roundabout into Harworth. Then right and up on to Scrooby Road, ground is on right.
Capacity: 3,000 **Covered accommodation:** Being erected **Seating:** No **Floodlights:** No
Club colours: Red & White
Clubhouse details: On Ground
Programme details: 30p.
Previous Leagues: North East Counties
Senior Honours: Wharncliffe Cup Winners.
Past Players: B. Griffin, R. Lindsay
Change colours: Green & White
Midweek matchday: Tuesday
Editor: I. Young
Record Attendance: 500

HEANOR TOWN F.C.

President: Mr. H. Holmes
Chairman: Mr. E. Abbott
Ground Address & Tel. No.: Maxfield Avenue, Heanor. Tel. 0773 713742
Secretary: Mr. K. costello
Manager: Mr. G. Clarence
Capacity: 5,000 **Covered accommodation:** **Seating:** 200 **Floodlights:** Yes
Club colours: White Shirts, Black Shorts
Clubhouse details: Open 7.30-11 pm and after matches
Year formed: 1883
Programme details: 15p 8 pages
Previous Leagues: N. Counties East
Change colours: All Red or Yellow Shorts
Midweek matches: Wednesday
Record attendance: 6,411
Past players: Nigel Pearson, Shrewsbury, Adrian Thorpe, Bradford City, Nigel Clough, Notts Forest

HINCKLEY F.C.

Chairman: D.C. Curtis
Manager: R. Rogers
Secretary: Mrs. C. Goadby
Ground Address & Tel. No.: Middlefield Lane, Hinckley. (0455) 636361
Simple ground directions: A447 through town centre. Signs to public weighbridge.
Capacity: 5,000 **Covered accommodation:** 1,000 **Seating:** 100 **Floodlights:** Yes
Club colours: Yellow/Black
Programme details: 24 pages
Clubhouse details: Social Club Open Daily
Change colours: White/Black
Editor: A. Mason
Midweek matchdays: Wednesday

HINCKLEY TOWN F.C.

Manager: Mr. D. Grundy
Secretary: Mrs. E. Dyer
Ground Address & Tel. No.: Hinckley Town F.C. Leicester Road, Hinckley, Leics.
Simple ground directions: A47 between Hinckley and Earl Shilton
Capacity: 3,000 **Covered accommodation:** 200 **Seating:** N/A **Floodlights:** N/A
Club colours: Blue and Claret
Clubhouse details: Bar with facilities for functions
Programme details: Yes
Recordance attendance: 500
Change colours: Green and Black
Midweek matchdays: Tuesday & Thursday
Editor: R. King
Previous Leagues: Senior League
Senor Honours: Division Two Champions 1972/73. Division One Runners Up 1983/4

KETTERING F.C.

Chairman: Mr. C. Gingell
Manager: B. Jeffrey
Secretary: R. Abraham
Ground address & Tel. No. Rockingham Road, Kettering NN16 9AW
Simple ground directions: On A6003 Kettering to Oakham.
Capacity: 11,000 **Covered accommodation:** 7,000 **Seating:** 1,800 **Floodlights:** Yes
Year formed: 1986
Club colours: All Red
Programme details: 36 pages.
Midweek match days: Wednesday
Senior Honours: None
Clubhouse details: Small club outside ground.
Change colours: All Yellow
Editor: G. Ellitson **Club metal badges:** Yes
Previous Leagues: None

KIMBERLEY TOWN

President: R.J. Penney Esq.
Secretary: Mr. H. Hibbert (0602) 383382
Chairman: G. Giddens
Manager: Carl Francis
Ground Address & Tel. No: Stag Ground, Nottingham Road, Kinbermley. (0602) 382788.
Simple ground directions: M1 South and North Exit 26. Then via Nuthall B6010, 2 miles.
Capacity: 2,500 **Covered accommodation:** Yes **Seating:** Nil **Floodlights:** No
Club Colours: All Royal Blue
Change colours: Red/White
Programme details: 6 pages. No charge
Editor: Neil Hibbert
Year formed: 1948
Club metal bades: None
Clubhouse details: Open match days only. Light refreshments.
Previous Leagues: Midland League. Northern Counties East.
Past Players: Andy Hill, Carlisle United.

LINCOLN UNITED F.C.

President: A. Rylatt
Secretary: Steve Roberts
Chairman: Arthur Simpson
Manager: Fred Green
Simple ground directions: Ashby Avenue is off Skellingthorpe Road in the Hartsholme area of Southern Lincoln.
Capacity: Est. 2,500 **Covered accommodation:** Stand **Seating:** 150 **Floodlights:** Yes
Club colours: White with Red trim
Change colours: Yellow with Red Trim
Year formed: 1938
Programme details: 8 pages inc. Advert.
Editor: Miss V. MacPherson
Midweek match day: Tuesday
Record attendance: 2,000 v Crook Town 1968
Clubhouse details: Bar, Television, Video, Music, Pool, Space Invader, Food available on match days.
Previous Leagues: Northern Counties East, Yorkshire League, Lincolnshire League.
Best Performance: Yorkshire League 'Double' 1970-71.
Past Players: S. Hodson (now Lincoln ex. Notts County/Charlton), C. Goodyear (now Plymouth ex. Luton), D. Peacock (Doncaster ex Nott. Forest/Bolton), D. Crombie (Grimsby), S. Sims (Notts Co. ex. Leicester/Watford), P. Neale (Lincoln, Worcestershire CCC Captain), R. Greenough (Chester).

OAKHAM UNITED

President: J. Richardson
Secretary: S. Brown
Chairman: R. Barnes
Manager: G. Saxby
Ground Address & Tel. No: Hosiery Mills Sports Ground, Sutton in Ashfield. Tel. 552376
Simple ground directions: From M1 Junction 28. A38 for Mansfield, 1 mile thr Sutton town centre.
Capacity: 2,000 **Covered accommodation:** 200 **Seating:** — **Floodlights:** —
Club colours: White Shirts, Navy Shorts, White Socks
Change colours: All Yellow
Year formed: 1969
Midweek match day: Tuesday
Programme details: 18 pages.
Editor: J. Vazson
clubhouse details: Social Club open 7 days plus Match Day license.
Previous Leagues: Midland Counties League Division 1. Northern Counties East Division 1, 2, & 3.
Senior Honours: Midland Counties Div. 1 League Cup Winners 1979-80. Midland Counties Div. 1 League Runners Up 1979-80.

RETFORD F.C. (1986)

Chairman: J. Denman
Secretary: A. Roddis
Ground Address & Tel. No.: River Lane, Retford.
Simple ground directions: A638 from Doncaster or A1 onto A620 to Retford Roundabout. Ground signposted.
Capacity: 3,000 **Covered accommodation:** 500 **Seating:** 200 **Floodlights:** No
Change colours: White
colours: Green
Programme details: 8 pages 15p.
Editor: Secretary
Clubhouse details: None
Midweek matchday: Wednesday
Previous Leagues: Midland, NCEL, Deroys Premier

ROSSINGTON MAIN F.C.

Chairman: Roy Hinton
Secretary: Norman Peach
Ground Address & Tel. No: Welfare Ground, Rossington. Doncaster 865524
Simple ground directions: M1 to M18. Then A631 through Tickhill then B to Rossington.
Club colours: Green/Yellow Shirts & Green Shorts, Yellow Socks
Year formed: 1924
Change colours: Blue/White Stripes, Blue Shorts
Capacity: 1,350 **Covered accommodation:** Small Stand **Seating:** No **Floodlights:** Yes
Clubhouse details: Adjacent to ground
Programme details/Editor: N. Peach
Previous Leagues: C.M. F.L. Yorkshire League, Doncaster Senior League.
Honours/Best Performance: League & Cup Winners 1984/85 Premier Division C.M.F.L.

NOTTS FOOTBALL ALLIANCE

President: R.J. Leafe
Chairman: J.W. Stokeld
General Secretary Registrar: E.R. Rudd

SAVE & PROSPER NOTTS FOOTBALL ALLIANCE

Senior Division	P	W	D	L	F	A	Pts
John Players FC	30	20	6	4	66	36	46
Plessey FC	30	19	7	4	60	31	45
Keyworth United	30	16	8	6	48	30	40
Rainworth MW	30	16	7	7	51	26	39
Hucknall CW	30	16	5	9	65	30	37
Clipstone MW	30	15	7	8	53	46	37
Basford Utd	30	11	11	8	48	38	33
Southwell City	30	11	9	10	53	49	31
City Sher Hospitals	30	13	4	13	49	43	30
Dunkirk FC	30	10	8	12	44	41	28
Worthington Simpson	30	8	8	14	50	52	24
Boots Athletic	30	8	7	15	40	57	23
Clifton All Whites	30	8	7	15	47	64	23
Meadows Albion	30	6	8	16	27	63	20
Nott Academicals	30	4	5	21	28	78	13
Carlton Athletic	30	3	5	22	23	68	11

Division One	P	W	D	L	F	A	Pts
Notts Police	30	24	5	1	94	30	53
Greenwood FC	30	20	5	5	102	39	45
Bulwell F Villa	30	20	4	6	72	37	44
Sneinton FC	30	19	5	6	100	48	43
Rolls Royce Welf	30	19	5	6	82	39	43
Rainworth MW Res	30	16	7	7	84	49	39
British Rail	30	14	6	10	85	69	34
Hucknall CW Res	30	13	7	10	56	50	33
Keyworth Utd Res	30	14	2	14	69	70	30
Clipstone MW Res	30	11	7	12	60	51	29
John Players Res	30	8	6	16	54	80	22
Plessey FC Res	30	6	4	20	43	67	16
Meadows Alb Res	30	5	6	19	32	72	16
Gedling CW	30	6	2	22	45	99	14
Nottm Acads Res	30	4	4	22	32	117	12
Collingham FC	30	1	5	24	31	124	7

NOTTS SENIOR CUP WINNERS
Clipstone Miners Welfare
Finalists
Hucknall Colliery Welfare

NOTTS INTERMEDIATE CUP WINNERS
John Players Reserves

LEAGUE SENIOR CUP WINNERS
Plessey FC
Finalists
Notts Police

LEAGUE INTERMEDIATE CUP WINNERS
Ruddington FC
Finalists
Rainworth MW Reserves

SENIOR DIVISION CHAMPIONS
John Player FC
Runners Up
Plessey FC

DIVISION ONE CHAMPIONS
Notts Police
Runners Up
Greenwood FC

DIVISION TWO CHAMPIONS
Ruddington FC
Runners up
Balderton Wanderers

NOTTS ALLIANCE LEAGUE — RECENT CHAMPIONS

1st	2nd	3nd	4th
Max. Pts. 60. Season: 1979/80			
47* Rainworth M.W.	47 Thorseby C.W.	41 John Player	37 Plessey
Max. Pts. 60. Season 1980/81			
50 Rainworth M.W.	47 Thorseby C.W.	42 Hucknall C.W.	37 Keyworth U.
Max. Pts. 60. Season 1981/82			
46 Rainworth M.W.	44 Thorseby C.W.	42* City & Sher. Hosp.	42 Meadows Alb.
Max. Pts. 60. Season 1982/83			
45 Rainworth M.W.	44 Keyworth U.	36* Plessey	36 Worthington Simp.
Max. Pts. 60. Season 1983/84			
45 Meadows Albu.	44* Rainworth M.W.	44 Keyworth U.	37 City & Sher. Hosp;
Max. Pts. 56. Season 1984/85			
46 Keyworth U.	43 Rainworth M.W.	41 Clipstone M.W.	36 Meadows Alb.
Max. Pts. 60. Season 1985/86			
46 John Player	45 Plessey	40 Keyworth U.	39 Rainworth M.W.

**goal average 1 difference.*

BASFORD UNITED

Chairman: N. Sheldon **Secretary:** M. McGowan (Nottingham 782250) **Manager:** D. Webster
Ground Address & Tel. No: Mill St. Basford Nottingham. (702572)
Simple ground directions: From Nottingham Ring Road take A610 to Ripley. Turn right onto B6004. Bear left into Mill St.
Capacity: 5,000 **Covered accommodation:** 100 **Seating:** None **Floodlights:** No
Clubhouse: No **Club colours:** Yellow/Black/Yellow **Change colours:** All Red
Programme: Yes **Honours/Previous Leagues:** Notts Combination.

BOOTS ATHLETIC

Chairman: D. Kissman **Secretary:** K. Radford (Nottingham 787979)
Ground Address & Tel. No. Lady Bay, West Bridgford, Nottingham (822392).
Simple ground directions: Rear of Nottingham Forest F.C.
Capacity: 1,000 **Covered accommodation:** None **Seating:** None **Floodlights:** Training only
Club colours: Blue & White Stripes **Change colours:** Red **Programme:** No
Honours: League Cup

CITY & SHERWOOD HOSPITALS

Chairman: A. Kord **Secretary:** B. Richards (Nottingham 892661)
Ground Address & Tel. No.: C.O.D. Military Ground, Chilwell (Nottingham 254811)
Simple ground directions: Off A6005 Nottingham-Long Eaton Road.
Capacity: 1,000 **Covered accommodation:** Non3 **Seating:** None **Floodlights:** No
Clubhouse: No **Club colours:** Sky Blkue **Change colours:** Yellow
Programme: No **Honours/Previous Leagues:** Notts Alliance Div. 1 Championship.

CLIFTON ALL WHITES

Chairman: P. Brodie **Secretary:** K. Elliott (Nottingham 215401)
Manager: K. Elliott **Ground Address & Tel. No.:** Green Lane, Clifton Estate, (Nott. 844903)
Simple ground directions: From Nottingham Ring Road follow A453 (B'ham) to lights. Left thru' Farnborough Rd for mile. Left into Green Lane.
Capacity: 1,000 **Covered accommodation:** None **Seating:** 200 **Floodlights:** Training only
Clubhouse: Yes (Unlicensed) **Club colours:** All White (Black Pinstripe)
Change Colours: Red or Blue **Programme:** No
Honours/Previous Leagues: E. Midland League, Notts Alliance Div. 1

CLIPSTONE MINERS WELFARE

Chairman: J. Collier **Manager:** J. Wholey **Secretary:** P. Peat (Mansfield 653737)
Ground Address & Tel. No: Lido Ground, Clipstone. (Mansfield 22190).
Simple ground directions: B6030 from Mansfield, on left entering Clipstone.
Capacity: 2,500 **Covered accommodation:** Nil **Seating:** 250 **Floodlights:** No
Club colours: Yes (License applied for) **Change colours:** Royal Blue **Programme:** Yes
Honours: Notts Senior Cup 1986, Notts Alliance Lge Cup 'Double' 1973/4/5. Notts Intermediate Cup 1956.

DUNKIRK

Chairman: T. Buxton **Manager:** S. Throstle
Secretary: S. Harbottle (Nottingham 222380)
Ground Address & Tel. No: Trentside Farm, Lenton Lane, Nottingham.
Simple ground directions: Ring Road - Clifton Bridge (North End) - Industrial Estate, Lenton Lane.
Capacity: 1,000 **Covered accommodation:** None **Seating:** None **Floodlights:** No
Club colours: All Red **Change colours:** White and Blue **Programme:** No
Clubhouse: Under construction
Honours/Previous Leagues: 1983 Notts Alliance Div. 2 Champions, 1984 Notts Intermediate Cup Winners, 1985 Notts Alliance Div. 1 Champions & League Cup Finalists.

GREEN WOOD

Chairman: M. Bradley **Manager:** G. Hazeldine **Secretary:** K. Marshall (Nott. 271551)
Ground Address & Tel. No.: Standhill Road, Carthon
Simple ground directions: Off Carlton Road, Nottingham (A612) **Programme:** No
Capacity: 2000 **Covered accommodation:** None **Seating:** None **Floodlights:** No
Clubhouse: No **Club colours:** All white, red pinstripes **Change colours:** Green
Honours/Previous Leagues: 1986 Div. 1 Runners up.

HUCKNALL COLLIERY WELFARE

Chairman: P. Hurst **Manager:** Ted Mullane
Secretary: E. Jackson, 43 Florence Street, Hucknall. Nottingham 634321.
Ground Address & Tel. No: Watnall Road, Hucknall. **Programme:** No
Simple ground directions: On B6009, Hucknall, Watnall Road.
Capacity: 2000 **Covered accommodation:** 200 **Seating:** None **Floodlights:** No
Club colours: Yellow/Black/Yellow **Change colours:** All red
Honours/Previous Leagues: Notts Alliance Champions 1976, 1977. League Cup Winners 1978, 79. Notts Senior Cup Winners 1985, Finalists 1984, 86.

JOHN PLAYER

Chairman: G. Davis **Manager:** D. France, P. Harvey
Secretary: R.H. Walton, 6 Watson Avenue, Bakersfield, Nott. 504631 **Programme:** No
Ground Address & Tel. No.: Aspley Lane. Nott. 293213 (Groundsmans house).
Simple ground directions: Corner of Nottingham ring road. B690, turn towards City Centre.
Capacity: 1,500 **Covered accommodation:** None **Seating:** None **Floodlights:** No
Clubhouse: Yes **Programme:** No
Club colours: Green/Gold **Change colours:** Blue/Black.
Honours:/Previous Leagues: Notts Alliance Champions 1922/3/4/5/6/7/8, 1967/8/9/70, 1986.

KEYWORTH UNITED

Chairman: B. Baker **Manager:** A. Oldham
Secretary: M.G. Simpson, 30 Main St, Keyworth, Nott. (Plumtree 4689).
Ground Address 8 Tel. No.: Platt Lane, Keyworth (Plumtree 5998)
Simple ground directions: A606 Nott.-Melton Road to crossroads with Keyworth-Normanton Road. Turn towards Keyworth, ground on right just through railway bridge. **Programme:** Yes
Club colours: Green/Black **Change colours:** All white **Clubhouse:** Yes
Honours/Previous Leagues: Notts Intermediate Cup 1979. Notts Alliance Div. 2 1979, Div 1. 1980. Senior Div. Runners up 1983. Champions 1985.

MEADOW ALBION

Chairman: S. Anderson **Manager:** C. Johnson
Secretary: Bob Kew, 18 Tiptree Close, Kimberley, Nottingham. 384871.
Ground Address & Tel. No: Grove Farm, Lenton Lane, Nottingham.
Simple ground directions: Nottingham Ring Road. Clifton Bridge (North End). Industrial Estate. Lenton Lane to far end.
Capacity: 1000 **Covered accommodation:** None **Seating:** None **Floodlights:** None
Club colours: Pale Blue & White Stripes **Change colours:** Red/Blue/Red **Programme:** No
Clubhouse: No.
Honours/Previous Leagues: League Champion 1984, League Cup Winners 1985.

NOTTS POLICE

Chairman: Chief Superintendent Stapleford. **Manager:** Vacant
Secretary: R. Fawcett, 19 Bracken Hill, Mansfield 36911 (H) Nott. 269700 ex. 429 or 430 (B)
Ground Address & Tel. No.: Police Sports Ground, Mansfield Road, Carrington. Nott. 475544
Simple ground directions: On A60 Mansfield Rd, on right from City Centre (2 miles).
Capacity: 1,000 **Covered accommodation:** None **Seating:** None **Floodlights:** No
Clubhouse: No **Club colours:** Black & White stripes/Black Change colours: Green & Yellow Stripes
Programme: No
Honours/Previous Leagues: 1986 Alliance Div. 1 Champions & League Senior Cup Runners up. 1964 Police Athletic Association National Knock-Out Competition Winners.

PLESSEY (BEESTON)

Chairman: A. Brown **Manager:** T. Froggatt
General Secretary: R. Marshall, Football Secretary: D. Tindall. Sports Office, Plessey Co Ltd., Beeston, Nottingham 254831 ex 3669.
Ground Address & Tel. No: Trent Vale Road, Beeston, Nottingham. 254831 ex 5700 or 258320.
Simple ground directions: From Nottingham A6005, to Beeston, left into Station Rd, over bridge, right, left, right. (5 minutes walk from Beeston Station).
Capacity: 2500 **Covered accommodation:** 50 **Seating:** None **Floodlights:** None
Club colours: All Sky Blue **Change colours:** All Sky Blue **Programme:** No
Clubhouse: Yes (Pavillion on ground).
Honours/Previous Leagues: League Cup 1984, 86. League Runners-Up 1986.

RAINWORTH MINERS WELFARE

Chairman: Dennis Cope **Manager:** B. Philips
Secretary: A. Wright, 10 Fareclay Road, Mansfield. (24379) (H). 553237 (B) **Programme:** No
Ground Address & Tel. No: Kirklington Road, Rainworth, Mansfield.
Simple ground directions: On A617 Mansfield-Newark Road. **Clubhouse:** Yes
Club colours: All white blue trim **Change colours:** Sky blue or red
Honours/Previous Leagues: League Champions 1978/79/80/81/82/83. League Cup 1982. Notts Senior Cup 1981/82 (Runners Up 1983). FA Vase Finalists 1982. Thorn-EMI Finalists 1983/84/5

SOUTHWELL CITY

Chairman: J. Rushby **Manager:** R. Cottarm
Secretary: P.K. Johnson, 65 The Ropewalk, Southwell. 812594
Ground Address & Tel. No.: War Memorial Recreation Ground, Bishops Drive, Southwell.
Simple ground directions: A612 Westgate - Bishops Drive behind Minster. **Programme:** Yes
Capacity: 2000 **Covered accommodation:** None **Seating:** None **Floodlights:** No
Club colours: White & Black pinstripes. Black Shorts. **Change colours.** Red **Clubhouse:** Yes
Honours/Previous Leagues: Nottingham Alliance Div. 2 1961. Div. 1 1976, 1982.

WORTHINGTON-SIMPSON (SENIOR)

Chairman: K. Cowam **Manager:** M. Coote
Secretary: L. Colman, 26 Colman Avenue, New Balderton. Newark 78623
Ground Address & Tel. No: Lowfields, New Balderton. Newark 702672 **Programme:** No
Simple ground directions: From Newark Town Centre: A6065 to Newark Hospital (lights), right into Bowbridge Rd, continue for 1 mile left by timber yard, over bridge then right. From A1 (Newark by-pass south end) A6065 'Newark' to lights, ahead then left into Mawton Lane, left just before bridge.
Capacity: 1000 **Covered accommodation:** None **Seating:** 30 **Floodlights:** None
Club colours: Burgundy & Blue **Change colours:** White/Blue. **Programme:** No
Clubhouse: Yes
Honours/Previous Leagues: League Cup Winners

WHITBREAD COUNTY SENIOR LEAGUE

Chairman: Maurice Matthews
Secretary: R. A. Bowler, 144 Coniston Road, Dronfield Woodhouse, Sheffield, S18 5PZ

LEAGUE REVIEW

The 1985-86 season, which was devastated by the winter's worst conditions, built up to an exciting climax with vital issues not settled up until the last games.

The Premier Division was won by BSC Parkgate who also lifted the Whitbread Trophy. But Windsor who had never led the table, emerged with a tremendous late challenge for the championship and met Parkgate in the final game of the season for the showdown.

Both clubs were equal on points but Windsor needed to win having an inferior goal difference. Parkgate clinched the vital goal, however, for a 1-0 victory to complete their highly successful season.

At the foot of the table the struggling clubs were having an equally absorbing battle for survival.

Arthur Lee Sc, Trophy winners in 1984-85, were never out of a relegation position until their final games when a remarkable sequence of nine points out of ten pulled them clear.

Oughtibridge WMSc had games in hand to escape but some poor results left them as wooden-spoonists in a hectic run-in.

Ecclesfield Red Rose, champions the previous season, and Davy McKee hovered around the relegation zone all through but they had the comfort of two clubs below them.

But when Lees put together their run, they were both threatened. As Red Rose played their final game with Windsor they were equal on points and goal difference with Davy. But Windsor, needing a victory to maintain their title assault duly won 2-1 to relegate Ecclesfield Red Rose for the first time in 28 years.

In the First Division Sheffield had been the leaders for most of the season but were pipped for the title when Oxley Park won this final game 1-0 to edge them out on goal difference.

In the very last game played in the League on the morning of the F.A. Cup Final, Old Edwardians clinched promotion with a 2-1 win at Hallam, the winner arriving just moments before the final whistle.

Crookes grabbed all the headlines in mid-season as they were on the verge of a remarkable treble, the Premier Division, the Whitbread Trophy and the Sheffield Senior Cup.

But with a hectic end-of-season programme Crookes' hopes all went sour and they were left to reflect on the season that might have been.

They did reach the Final of the Sheffield Senior Cup after knocking out four sides from the Northern Counties East which was a great achievement.

Crookes put up a creditable performance against Frickley Athletic who were to finish runners-up in the Gola League before going down 2-0.

PREMIER DIVISION

	P	W	D	L	F	A	Pts
BSC Parkgate	26	17	7	2	69	28	41
Windsor	26	18	3	5	59	37	39
Crookes	26	15	6	5	54	29	36
Mexborough Main St.	26	12	4	10	47	38	28
Ash House	26	10	8	8	35	28	28
Swinton Athletic	26	10	7	9	42	40	27
Centralians	26	10	6	10	43	41	26
Treeton Welfare	26	10	6	10	38	42	26
Firparnians	26	8	6	12	42	58	22
Frenchville C.A.	26	7	6	13	37	55	20
Arthur Lees	26	6	7	13	41	63	19
Davy McKee	26	4	10	12	41	49	18
Ecclesfield Red Rose	26	7	4	15	46	55	18
Oughtibridge WMCS	26	4	8	14	39	70	16

DIVISION ONE

	P	W	D	L	F	A	Pts
Oxley Park	26	18	5	3	72	26	41
Sheffield	26	18	5	3	59	30	41
Old Edwardians	26	17	5	4	50	14	39
Brunsmeer Athletic	26	17	5	4	73	38	39
Dronfield United	26	13	3	10	52	42	29
Pilkington REC	26	11	6	9	40	36	28
Bankers	26	11	3	12	56	48	25
Hallam	26	9	5	12	44	44	23
Maltby MW	26	8	7	11	49	59	23
Woodsetts Welfare	26	8	3	15	47	43	19
East Dene SC	26	7	4	15	35	70	18
Kiveton Park	26	8	1	17	47	59	17
Forgemasters	26	6	3	17	35	80	15
Rotherham Club RM2	26	2	3	21	26	96	7

Leading Goalscorers (League only)

M. Ellison (Oxley Park) Div. 1 26
C. Beaumont (Brunsmeer Ath.) Div. 1 23
S. Cavill (Bradley) Div. 3 23
D. Lockwood (Oxspring Utd.) Div. 3 22
L. Robinson (Oxspring Utd.) Div. 3. 20

WHITBREAD TROPHY COMPETITION

SEMI-FINALS

BSC Parkgate	4	Hallam	0
(At Sheffield FC)			
Crookes	3	Old Edwardians	0
(At Davy McKee)			

FINAL

BSC Parkgate	2	Crookes	1

(At Silkstune Road, Sheffield – Wednesday 23rd April. Referee: M. Swift (Rotherham).

BSC Parkgate: M. Gee; W. Shepard, K. Brockley, V. Brady, A, Courts; R. Scott, A. Shenton, P. Kettleborough; L. Packer, K. Green, S. Lill.
Subs: P. Ward. B. Green.
Scorers: P. Ward, B. Green. **Crookes:** P. Fidler; P. Scothorne, A. Cooke, P. Mitchell, N. Pickering; M. Hannah, N. Callery, D. Staniforth; B. Saville, S. Marshall, A. Hughes.
Subs: A. Mazur, N. Windle.
Scorer: N. Windle.

WHITBREAD TROPHY FINALS

(1981/2)	Windsor v BSC River Don	5-1
(1982/3)	JFS v Ash House	3-2
(1983/4)	Swinton v Rotherham Club	3-1
(1984/5)	Arthur Lees v BSC Parkgate	3-2
(1985/6)	BSC Parkgate v Crookes	2-1

	Ash House (GC)	BSC Parkgate	Crookes	Davy McKees & SC	Ecclesfield RR	Firparnians	Frenchville Comm.	A. Lee SC	Mexborough Main St	Oughtbridge WMSC	Sheffield Centralians	Swinton Athletic	Treeton Welfare	Windsor
Ash House (GC)		0.0	0.4	2.1	1.1	1.2	1.1	4.1	1.2	1.1	2.0	6.0	1.1	1.2
BSC Parkgate	0.0		1.2	3.2	4.2	1.1	3.1	7.0	3.0	7.1	1.0	1.2	2.0	1.0
Crookes	2.0	1.2		3.1	3.0	4.0	4.0	2.0	2.0	2.1	2.1	3.2	4.3	0.2
Davy McKee & SC	3.2	1.3	0.0		4.0	3.3	2.2	2.2	2.1	1.2	3.3	1.1	1.1	2.4
Ecclesfield RR	0.1	0.3	0.1	1.1		2.4	2.3	4.4	1.2	5.2	4.0	1.2	3.1	1.2
Firparnians	2.2	1.7	2.2	1.1	3.0		1.3	0.2	3.5	1.2	3.0	1.1	4.1	2.1
Frenchville Comm.	0.1	0.1	0.2	3.2	0.3	2.3		0.0	2.1	3.2	1.4	3.2	2.4	1.4
A. Lee SC	1.2	1.2	6.5	2.1	1.5	3.0	1.1		2.1	2.2	2.3	3.3	2.0	3.3
Mexborough Main St.	0.0	2.2	2.1	0.2	2.0	4.1	2.0	3.0		5.5	2.1	3.2	6.0	0.1
Oughtbridge WMSC	1.2	3.3	2.2	1.1	1.5	0.2	2.2	1.0	1.1		0.1	1.3	2.6	1.5
Sheffield Centralians	1.0	2.2	1.1	2.1	3.1	4.0	2.1	5.2	0.1	5.1		0.1	1.1	3.3
Swinton Athletic	1.2	2.3	1.1	2.0	2.2	2.0	3.0	4.0	3.1	0.1	1.1		o.3	0.0
Treeton Welfare	0.2	2.2	0.0	2.1	0.1	3.1	1.1	1.0	1.0	2.1	1.0	3.1		0.2
Windsor	1.0	2.5	2.1	3.2	5.2	2.1	2.5	2.1	2.1	3.2	4.0	0.1	2.1	

CLUB DIRECTORY FOR THE WHITBREAD COUNTY SENIOR LEAGUE

Club	Ground	Capacity	Seats	Covered Accom	Clubhouse
Ash House	Meadowhead, Sheffield	700	Nil	Nil	Yes
Aurora United	Bawtry Road, Rotherham	800	Nil	200	Yes
Crosspool Sports	Springfield Close, Millhouses	400	Nil	100	No
Denaby & Cadeby MW	Tickhill Square, Denaby	6000	750	1250	Yes
Dronfield United	Coach & Horses, Dronfield	1500	20	200	No
Ecclesfield Red Ruse	Green Lane, Ecclesfield	1300	Nil	150	Yes
Elsecar Main	Armroyd Lane, Elsecar	1800	200	Seats only	Yes
Firparnians	Meadowhead, Sheffield	700	Nil	Nil	Yes
Frenchville CA	Silkstone Road, Sheffield	1500	Nil	200	Yes
Hallam	Sandygate Road, Sheffield	2000	Nil	250	Yes
Kiveton Park	Hard Lane, Kiveton	2000	200	Seats only	at Miners Welfare
Midland Bank	Hathersage Road, Dore	700	20	Seats only	Yes
Midland Bank	Hathersage Road, Dore	700	20	Seats only	Yes
Old Edwardian	Bawtry Road, Sheffield	800	Nil	150	No
Outhtibridge WMSC	Station Lane, Oughtibridge	800	Nil	Nil	Yes
Parkgate BSC	Green Lane, Rawmarsh	2000	Nil	200	Yes
Penistone Church	Memorial Ground, Penistone	1200	Nil	300	Yes
Sheffield	Abbeydale Park, Sheffield	1800	Nil	75	Yes
Sheffield Gas	MMalin Bridge, Sheffield	600	Nil	Nil	Yes
Swinton Athletic	Park Road, Swinton	1400	Nil	30	Yes
Windsor	Waverley Lane, Sheffield	700	Nil	Nil	Yes
Woodsetts Welfare	Recreation Ground, Woodsetts	700	Nil	Nil	Yes
Worsborough Bridge	Park Road, Worsborough Bridge	2000	200	Seats only	Yes
Staveley Works	Barrow Hill, Chesterfield	2000	Nil	200	Yes

(BSC) Parkgate issue programmes and Staveley have floodlights.

DRYBROUGHS NORTHERN LEAGUE

Chairman: A. Clark
Secretary: G. Nicholson, 99 Watling Road, Bishop Auckland, Co. Durham
Tel: 0388 602176

'BISHOPS CELEBRATE CENTENARY'

The increasing strength in depth of the Drybroughs Northern League produced a highly competitive season which saw one of the league's oldest clubs, Bishop Auckland, top the First Division, and one of the newest, Blue Star, run away with the championship of the Second Division.

The "Bishops" celebrated their centenary season by repeating their league championship and Durham Challenge Cup "double" of 1984/85. Once again this famous club had to clear a backlog of games and come from behind to win the league. Just one defeat in their last thirteen games brought them from sixth place to clinch the title by six points from Bedlington Terriers, who were the surprise team of the season. After winning promotion in 1985 the Terriers just missed out on a debut title win after proudly leading the First Division table for several weeks.

The Durham Challenge Cup final was a repeat of the previous season when Bishops beat near neighbours Spennymoor United after a replay. This time the Two Blues did it at the first attempt, beating the Moors 3–1 at Shildon's Dean Street ground. To round off a memorable 100th season for Bishop Auckland, ever-consistent sweeper Gary Lormor was voted the DNL's Player of the Year.

Newcomers Blue Star swept all before them in their first season in the DNL. Not only did Star win the Second Division title with 36 wins, one draw and just one defeat in 38 games—surely a record never to be equalled—they took the league cup and the Northumberland Senior Cup for good measure. Remarkably, the League Cup final at Spennymoor was contested by two second division clubs, Blue Star defeating Durham City 2–0 to deny the Citizens consolation for again missing out on promotion.

Star captured the Northumberland Senior Cup for the third time in four years, defeating Whitley Bay 3–2 in the final. In response to a request from the Northumberland FA that club names should identify their location, the Woolsington outfit now compete as Newcastle Blue Star.

DNL clubs almost always make an impact on the FA Cup. This time Whitby Town returned to the fore under a new player-manager, former Leeds United and Scotland goalkeeper David Harvey. Whitby made the second round proper for the second time in three years, losing 3–1 away to York City.

The FA Trophy and FA Vase have yet to provide a finalist from the DNL, a surprising fact in view of the league's proud history in the much-loved FA Amateur Cup. While Bishop Auckland, ten times the Amateur Cup winners, lost 1–0 away to eventual Trophy victors Altrincham at the third round stage, it was South Bank who carried the DNL flag into round four after a memorable 2–1 extra time victory over Trophy holders Wealdstone. The Normanby Road ground attracted 2,384 for the visit of Enfield who deservedly won 2–0. Bankers then showed their character with a 12-match unbeaten run in the league to take third spot for the second year in succession.

Blue Star, Vase winners in 1978, made the best progress from the DNL in their last season before switching to the Trophy. Their interest ended with a 1–0 defeat away to Hucknall CW in round five.

With Star making certain of one of the two second division promotion places, a fierce three-club tussle ended with Easington Colliery clinching th runners-up position over Guisborough Town and Durham City. Like Star, Easington topped 100 league goals for the season, and both look certain to make their mark in division one.

Making the opposite journey are the two Billingham clubs, Synthonia and Town, the latter after only one season in the top flight. Billingham Town have however given a vote of confidence to their manager Dave Buckle by immediately re-appointing him for another season. Peter Feenan was much in demand as a club manager. After being sacked by Blyth early in the season, he went on to Rhyope CA and guided them out of trouble before moving on to do the same at Gretna, winning "Team of the Month" awards at both clubs.

These monthly club awards are yet another new feature. League sponsors Drybroughs, the Edinburgh-based brewers, have added to their already large commitment to the league by providing £250 each month to be donated to the charity of the winning club's choice. The eight awards for 1985/86 were equally shared between the first and second divisions, with Blue Star the only club to win twice.

The past year saw the league lose three "stalwarts", management committee member Arthur Harrison, long connected with Evenwood Town, Alan Brown, general secretary and treasurer of Alnwick Town, and league press officer David Simon. The sudden death of David Simon at the age of 52 was particularly keenly felt throughout the league. A prolific football and cricket correspondent, David Simon was much involved in planning for the centenary of the league in 1989. Formed one year after the Football League, the Northern League is the second oldest soccer league in the world.

Due to the late decision of Darlington Reserves to switch from the DNL to the Central League, the Second Division will operate with 19 instead of 20 clubs. Esh Winning and Shildon were re-elected, but the application by Blackhall CW to join the league was rejected due to lack of facilities. CHRIS FOOTE WOOD

DRYBROUGHS NORTHERN LEAGUE AWARDS 1985–86

	Final League Placings	Goal Scoring Awards	Three Goal Wins	Total
Bedlington Terriers	1200	—	165	1365
Billingham Synthonia	—	—	110	110
Billingham Town	—	—	110	110
Bishop Auckland	1700	—	275	1975
Blyth Spartans	800	—	440	1240
Brandon United	—	650	110	760
Chester-Le-Street Town	—	—	220	220
Consett	—	—	110	110
Crook Town	—	800	220	1020
Ferryhill Athletic	—	—	55	55
Gretna	—	500	275	775
Hartlepool United Res.	—	—	110	110
North Shields	—	—	110	110
Peterlee Newtown	—	—	110	110
Ryhope Comm. Assoc.	—	—	110	110
South Bank	900	—	385	1285
Spennymoor United	—	—	220	220
Tow Law Town	—	650	275	925
Whitby Town	—	—	165	165
Whitley Bay	—	—	220	220
Alnwick Town	—	—	175	175
Ashington	—	500	140	640
Blue Star	1000	—	735	1735
Cleveland Bridge	—	—	105	105
Darlington Res.	—	—	35	35
Durham City	500	—	280	780
Easington C.W.	750	—	455	1206
Esh Winning	—	—	35	35
Evenwood Town	—	—	105	105
Guisborough Town	600	—	280	880
Horden C.W.	—	—	175	175
Langley Park Welf.	—	—	70	70
Northallerton Town	—	—	140	140
Norton & Stockton An.	—	400	210	610
Seaham C.W. R.S.	—	200	140	340
Shildon	—	—	105	105
Shotton Comrades	—	—	70	70
Stockton	—	—	105	105
West Auckland	—	300	35	335
Willington	—	—	175	175

DRYBROUGHS NORTHERN FOOTBALL LEAGUE
Season 1985–6
Final League Tables

FIRST DIVISION

	P	W	D	L	F	A	Pts
Bishop Auckland	38	21	10	7	79	45	73
Bedlington Terriers	38	19	10	9	65	44	67
South Bank	38	18	12	8	66	36	66
Blyth Spartans	38	19	9	10	79	52	66
Tow Law Town	38	18	10	10	72	47	64
Peterlee Newton	38	19	6	13	66	56	63
Chester-le-Street Town	38	18	7	13	62	53	61
Brendon United	38	16	10	12	72	68	58
Crook Town	38	15	8	15	73	70	53
Hartlepool United Res.	38	14	10	14	65	69	52
Gretna	38	13	11	14	70	69	50
North Shields	38	14	8	16	65	72	50
Consett	38	13	9	16	44	58	48
Spennymoor United	38	12	11	15	51	54	47
Ryhope Community	38	13	7	18	50	69	46
Whitby Town	38	12	9	17	59	74	45
Whitley Bay	38	11	8	19	65	73	41
Ferryhill Athletic	38	11	6	21	62	94	39
Billingham Synthonia	38	8	11	19	47	66	35
Billingham Town	38	6	8	24	46	89	26

SECOND DIVISION

	P	W	D	L	F	A	Pts
Blue Star	38	36	1	1	133	15	109
Easington Colliery	38	27	7	4	101	36	88
Guisborough Town	38	25	7	6	88	36	82
Durham City	38	22	9	7	89	48	75
West Auckland Town	38	19	7	12	64	61	64
Seaham Coll. Welf. RS	38	17	7	14	63	56	58
Stockton	38	15	9	14	62	56	54
Ashington	38	15	9	14	81	85	54
Norton & Stockton An.	38	16	5	17	67	72	53
Alnwick Town	38	13	12	13	62	56	51
Willington	38	15	5	18	53	65	50
Langley Park Welfare	38	11	11	16	43	57	44
Horden Colliery Welfare	38	12	8	18	54	85	44
Shotton Comrades	38	9	12	17	56	82	39
Darlington Reserves	38	9	9	20	45	86	36
Northallerton Town	38	10	5	23	54	83	35
Evenwood Town	38	9	7	22	51	79	34
Cleveland Bridge	38	10	4	24	55	89	34
Shildon	38	6	15	17	42	66	33
Esh Winning	38	5	9	24	49	99	24

League Cup Winners: Blue Star
League Cup Finalists: Durham City
J. R. Cleator Cup Winners: Whitby Town
Durham Challenge Cup Winners: Bishop Auckland
Northumberland Senior Cup Winners: Blue Star

INDIVIDUAL GOAL SCORING AWARDS

First Division—COLIN COWAN (Ryhope C.A.)—28 goals
Second Division—MARK DAVIS (Guisborough Town)—38 goals

DRYBROUGH CUP AWARDS 1985–86

Winners:—BLUE STAR—£300
Runners-up: DURHAM CITY—£200
In addition all 40 clubs received playing equipment from this sponsorship to the total value of £3,600

D.N.L. GOOD CONDUCT AWARDS 1985–86

NORTH SHIELDS, DURHAM CITY AND FERRYHILL ATHLETIC
All 3 clubs receive a complete set of shirts, shorts and stockings.

AWARDS, 1985/86 SEASON

Player of the Year:
1. Gary Lormor (Bishop Auckland)
2. Steve Dixon (Brandon United)
3. Colin Cowan (Ryhope CA)

Referee of the Year (Silver Whistle award):
Ken Lupton (Stockton)

Groundsman of the Year:
First Division, 1. Eddie Metcalfe (Whitby Town—third year running), 2. Justin Lane (Ferryhill Athletic). Second Division, 1. Joe Minter (Guisborough Town), 2. Bill Raine (Norton and Stockton Ancients).

Supporter of the Year:
1. Brain "Paddy" Spenceley (Whitby Town)
2. Herby Sparham (North Shields)
3. Mrs. Cissie Summers (West Auckland)

Special recognition:
Susan Doy (Spennymoor United), "Tot" Defty (Shotton Comrades)

Good Conduct award winners:
North Shields, Durham City, Ferryhill Athletic

"Team of the Month" awards:
September, Bedlington Terriers, October, Blue Star, November Ryhope CA, December, Ashington, January South Bank, February Gretna, March Blue Star, April Easington.

DRYBROUGHS NORTHERN LEAGUE CUP 1985/86

PRELIMINARY ROUND

Stockton v Chester-le-Street—aet	3—4
Seaham R.S. v Gretna	0—4
Whitley Bay v Bishop Auckland	2—0
Northallerton v Guisborough	0—5
West Auckland v Ferryhill—aet	2—3
Spennymoor v Ashington	6—3
Norton v Bedlington	0—3
Evenwood v Blyth Spartans	1—3

FIRST ROUND

Ryhope CA v Chester-le-Street	2—1
North Shields v Gretna	1—2
Easington v Whitley Bay—aet	4—2
Guisborough v Whitby Town	1—2
Ferryhill v Crook Town	4—3
Consett v Peterlee	0—3
Esh Winning v Tow Law	2—7
Blue Star v Langley Park	2—1
Brandon v Spennymoor—aet, pens 7—6	1—1
Willington v Darlington Res.	2—1
South Bank v Bedlington—aet, pens 6—7	1—1
Billingham T v Billingham Synth—aet	3—2
Shildon v Durham City	1—3
Alnwick v Horden CW—aet, pens 6—5	0—0
Hartlepool Res v Shotton	3—0
Blyth Spartans v Cleveland Br	5—0

SECOND ROUND

Ryhope CA v Gretna	2—1
Easington v Whitby T—aet	3—4
Ferryhill v Peterlee	1—3
Tow Law v Blue Star	0—1
Brandon v Willington	4—0
Bedlington v Billingham T	3—0
Durham City v Alnwick—aet	5—2
Hartlepool Res v Blyth Spartans	2—0

THIRD ROUND

Ryhope CA v Whitby Town	3—0
Peterless v Blue Star	0—2
Brandon v Bedlington	1—0
Durham C v Hartlepool Res	5—2

SEMI-FINALS

Ryhope CA v Blue Star	1—2
Brandon v Durham City—aet, pens 3—4	0—0

FINAL

Blue Star v Durham City	2—0

BEDLINGTON TERRIERS

"TERRIERS"

President: William Jordan
Chairman: Thomas Brash
Manager: Bobby Graham
Ass. Man/Coach: Colin Ayre
Physiotherapist: Terry Dobson

Secretary: Vince Donnelly
Address & Tel. No: 31 Doctor Terrace Bedlington 829464
Commercial Manager: Chris Sanderson & Roy Dobson
Press Officer: Manager

Ground Address & Tel. No: Dr Pit Welfare
Capacity: 3,000 **Covered accommodation:** Yes **Seating:** Yes **Floodlights:** No
Simple ground directions: Approx. ½ mile from Town Centre, opposite Bedlington Cricket Club ground
Clubhouse details: To be opened in near future
Programme details: Approx. 24 pages **Editor:** Chris Sanderson **Club metal badges:** None
Local Newspaper(s): Courier and Leader
Club colours: Red top/black shorts/black socks/red top
Change colours: Light blue shirt/dark blue shorts/light blue socks
Midweek match day: Wednesday **Previous Leagues:** Northern Alliance
Record transfer fee paid: None
Record transfer fee received: None
Record attendance: 1,300 v Blyth
Senior honours/best performance: DIV I & II Runners up
Past players (who progressed to Football League): None

BISHOP AUCKLAND

"THE BISHOPS"

President: W. B. Botcherby
Chairman: G. H. Metcalfe
Manager: Brian Newton
Ass. Man/Coach: J. Lee
Physiotherapist: —

Secretary: F. W. Jobson
Address & Tel. No: 20 Stanfield Road, Newton Aycliffe, Co Durham, (0325)313537
Commercial Manager: A. J. Russell
Press Officer: Secretary

Ground Address & Tel. No: 'Kingsway' Bishop Auckland, Co Durham. Tel: B. Auck (0388)603686
Capacity: 8,500 **Covered accommodation:** 1,000 **Seating:** 1,000 **Floodlights:** Yes
Simple ground directions: Town Centre—rear of Newgate Street, Bishop Auckland
Clubhouse details: Open daily—lunchtime & evenings
Programme details: 20p each **Editor:** Secretary **Club metal badges:** Yes. £1.50 each
Local Newspaper(s): Northern Echo
Club colours: Light/dark blue
Change colours: Red/white
Midweek match day: Wednesday **Previous Leagues:** Founder members—Drybroughs Northern League
Record transfer fee paid: None
Record transfer fee received: None
Record attendance: 6th Dec. 52, F.A. Cup 2nd Round—v Coventry City—approx. 17,000
Senior honours/best performance: FA Amateur Cup Winners—10 times, Beaten finalists—8 times. FA Cup 4th Round 1954–55. FA Trophy 1978–79—4th Round
Past players (who progressed to Football League): Many—last two: 'Nobbs' to Hartlepool, Toman to Lincoln City

BLYTH SPARTANS

President: J. E. T. Milburn
Chairman: J. A. Turney
Manager: J. Pearson
Ass. Man/Coach: D. L. Clarke
Physiotherapist: C. Tait

Secretary: G. Watson
Address & Tel. No: Not available
Commercial Manager: M. Turnbull
Press Officer: Secretary

Ground Address & Tel. No: Croft Park, Blyth. Office 352373, Club 354818
Capacity: 6,000 **Covered accommodation:** 2,500 **Seating:** 300 **Floodlights:** Yes
Simple ground directions: Near to Town Centre
Clubhouse details: Open every night, Sunday lunch, Saturday lunch, Match days
Programme details: 20 pages 15p **Editor:** R. R. Clark **Club metal badges:** Yes
Local Newspaper(s): Newcastle Journal & Evening Chronicle
Club colours: Green/white
Change colours: Yellow
Midweek match day: Tuesday **Previous Leagues:** North Eastern. Midland Northern Alliance
Record transfer fee paid: None
Record transfer fee received: £30,000 Hull City for Les Mutrie
Record attendance: 42,000 (at Newcastle) v Wrexham 1978
Senior honours/best performance: FA Cup 5th Round Proper Replay 1978. Northern League Champions (8). N.F.A. Senior Cup (19)
Past players (who progressed to Football League): Players to most league clubs

BRANDON UNITED

President: T. Gill
Chairman: N. Green
Manager: Ray Gowan
Ass. Man/Coach: Jock Thomson
Physiotherapist: Steve Jones
Secretary: Arthur Waggott
Address & Tel. No: 26 Grove Road, Brandon, Durham 781778
Commercial Manager: G. Williams
Press Officer: Secretary
Ground Address & Tel. No: Rear Commercial Street, Brandon 782957
Capacity: 3,000 **Covered accommodation:** 500 **Seating:** 50 **Floodlights:** Yes
Simple ground directions: A690—3 miles west of Durham City
Clubhouse details: Under construction
Programme details: Yes **Editor:** Secretary **Club metal badges:** No
Local Newspaper(s): Newcastle Journal—Northern Echo
Club colours: Blue shirts/blue shorts/blue socks
Change colours: Red/red/red
Midweek match day: Wednesday
Previous Leagues: Wearside League, Northern Alliance
Record transfer fee paid: None
Record transfer fee received: None
Record attendance: 1,500
Senior honours/best performance: Durham County Finalists—All England Sunday Cupwinners—1st Round Proper FA Cup
Past players (who progressed to Football League): B. Liddle (Hartlepool United)

CHESTER LE STREET

"CESTRIANS"

President: J. Lawrence
Chairman: R. Bell
Manager: M. Moore
Ass. Man/Coach: M. Mulvaney
Physiotherapist:—
Secretary: J. D. Burlison
Address & Tel. No: 4 Carrowmore Road, Chester le Street (0385)884607
Commercial Manager: P. Grieve
Press Officer: J. Thornback
Ground Address & Tel. No: Moor Park, Chester Moor, Chester le Street
Capacity: 3,000 approx. **Covered accommodation:** 500 **Seating:** 200 **Floodlights:** Yes
Simple ground directions: Approx. 2 miles south of Chester le Street on the A167
Clubhouse details: Open normal licencing hours
Programme details: 12 pages **Editor:** J. Thornback **Club metal badges:** None
Local Newspaper(s): Evening Chronicle, Journal, Northern Echo, Sunderland Echo
Club colours: Blue shirts/white shorts/blue hose
Change colours: All yellow
Midweek match day: Tuesday
Previous Leagues: Vaux Wearside League
Record transfer fee paid: £450
Record transfer fee received: £450
Record attendance: 3,000—Bradford City Appeal—Sunderland XI v Newcastle XI
Senior honours/best performance: Drybroughs Northern League Div. 2 Champions 1983–84, Vaux Wearside League Champions 1980–81
Past players (who progressed to Football League): Paul Atkinson (Junior player) Sunderland AFC, Anthony Gibson—Racing Jet (Belgium)

CONSETT

President: D. McVickers
Chairman: B. Suddes
Manager: G. Hindson
Ass. Man/Coach: —
Physiotherapist: G. McDonald
Secretary: —
Address & Tel. No: —
Commercial Manager: —
Press Officer: —
Ground Address & Tel. No: Belle Vue Park 503788
Capacity: 4,000 **Covered accommodation:** 1,000 **Seating:** 500 **Floodlights:** Yes
Simple ground directions: Follow signs for Sport Centre and Baths
Clubhouse details: Bar open matchdays
Programme details: Match programme **Editor:** C. Frend **Club metal badges:** No
Local Newspaper(s): —
Club colours: Red/white/red
Change colours: Sky blue/dark blue/sky
Midweek match day: Wednesday
Previous Leagues: North Eastern, North East Counties, Midland Lge
Record transfer fee paid: —
Record transfer fee received: —
Record attendance: —
Senior honours/best performance: —
Past players (who progressed to Football League):—

CROOK TOWN A.F.C.

President: Ramar Dresses Ltd
Chairman: Hurbert Hutchinson
Manager: Gary Moore
Ass. Man/Coach: Harry Wilson
Physiotherapist: John Lumley
Secretary: Eric Burton
Address & Tel. No: 12 West End Villas, Crook, Bp Auckland (0388)762026
Commercial Manager: None
Press Officer: Secretary
Ground Address & Tel. No: Millfield Ground, Crook (0388)762595
Capacity: 9,750 **Covered accommodation:** 600 **Seating:** 424 **Floodlights:** Yes
Simple ground directions: ¼ mile from Town Centre on Wolsingham Road
Clubhouse details: On Ground
Programme details: Every home game **Editor:** J. Pascoe **Club metal badges:** None
Local Newspaper(s): Northern Echo
Club colours: Black/amber
Change colours: White
Midweek match day: Wednesday **Previous Leagues:** North Eastern
Record transfer fee paid: —
Record transfer fee received: —
Record attendance: 17,250
Senior honours/best performance: 5 times Amateur Cup Winners
Past players (who progressed to Football League): Jimmy Goodfellow, Peter Garbutt, Mike Tracy, Frank Clark

EASINGTON COLLIERY

President: J. Oliver
Chairman: F. Wellburn
Manager: T. Dunster
Ass. Man/Coach: J. Ord
Physiotherapist: —
Secretary: D. Elliot
Address & Tel. No: 17 Cotswold Place, Peterleee, Co Durham 867581
Commercial Manager: —
Press Officer: Secretary
Ground Address & Tel. No: Welfare Park, Easington Colliery, Peterlee (0783)273047
Capacity: 2,000 **Covered accommodation:** 300 **Seating:** 50 **Floodlights:** No
Simple ground directions: Approx. 2 miles east of A19 trunk road, north of Peterlee. Take B1283 to Easington Village, continue to Easington Colliery, turning right after zebra crossing
Clubhouse details: Bar, seating 70, matchdays only
Programme details: 16 pages **Editor:** Secretary **Club metal badges:** No
Local Newspaper(s): Hartlepool Mail, Northern Echo, Journal
Club colours: Green/white stripes
Change colours: Tangerine black
Midweek match day: Wednesday **Previous Leagues:** Wearside
Record transfer fee paid: —
Record transfer fee received: —
Record attendance: 4,500 v Tranmere 1955–6
Senior honours/best performance: FA Cup 1st Round 1956, Wearside League Champions (6), Wearside League Cup (3), Monkwearmouth Cup (3), Shipowners Cup (2)
Past players (who progressed to Football League): —

FERRYHILL ATHLETIC

President: T. Southern
Chairman: J. Garnett
Manager: H. Nicholson
Ass. Man/Coach: —
Physiotherapist: T. Morris
Secretary: D. H. James
Address & Tel. No: 24 Windsor Avenue, Ferryhill 51177
Commercial Manager: —
Press Officer: D. H. James
Ground Address & Tel. No: Darlinton Road, Ferryhill 51937
Capacity: 6,000 **Covered accommodation:** 200 **Seating:** 400 **Floodlights:** No
Simple ground directions: —
Clubhouse details: Bar, lounge, planned extension
Programme details: — **Editor:** — **Club metal badges:** No
Local Newspaper(s): Northern Echo
Club colours: Amber & black shirts/black shorts/amber socks
Change colours: Red shirts/white shorts/black socks
Midweek match day: Wednesday **Previous Leagues:** —
Record transfer fee paid: —
Record transfer fee received: —
Record attendance: 13,000 Amateur Cup
Senior honours/best performance: Northern League Winners 1937–38, 1947–48, 1957–58
Past players (who progressed to Football League): —

GRETNA

"BLACK & WHITES"

President: I. Dalgliesh
Chairman: W. Kerr
Manager: P. Feenan
Ass. Man Coach: W. Gill
Physiotherapist: —
Secretary: K. Rhodes
Address & Tel. No: 8 Graitney, Gretna, Carlisle (0461)37447
Commercial Manager: F. Sheckley
Press Officer: Secretary
Ground Address & Tel. No: Raydale Park, Gretna (0461)37602
Capacity: 5,000 **Covered accommodation:** 1,000 **Seating:** 100 **Floodlights:** Yes
Simple ground directions: 8 miles north of Carlisle A74
Clubhouse details: 2,000 members entertainment w ends
Programme details: 6 page, free **Editor:** N. Hampson **Club metal badges:** No
Local Newspaper(s): Cumberland News
Club colours: White black black & white
Change colours: All green or all red
Midweek match day: Wednesday
Previous Leagues: Carlisle & District
Record transfer fee paid: £450
Record transfer fee received: £1,500
Record attendance: 1,500
Senior honours best performance: Last 16 FA Trophy 1985–86 season
Past players (who progressed to Football League): Russell Black & Donald Peattie

HARTLEPOOL UNITED RESERVES

"THE POOL"

President: E. Leadbitter (M.P.)
Chairman: J. W. Smart
Manager: W. Horner
Ass. Man/Coach: J. Bird
Physiotherapist: T. Johnson
Secretary: M. Kirby
Address & Tel. No: Victoria Ground, H/Pool, Cleveland 272584
Commercial Manager: A. Stephenson
Press Officer: —
Ground Address & Tel. No: Victoria Ground, Clarence Road H pool, Cleveland
Capacity: 3,300 **Covered accommodation:** 1,600 **Seating:** 1,600 **Floodlights:** Yes
Simple ground directions: 10 miles from bus and train station into centre of town
Clubhouse details: — **Editor:** A. Stevenson **Club metal badges:** Yes
Local Newspaper(s): H pool Mail, Northern Echo, Courier Scene
Club colours: Blue white stripe/blue/blue
Change colours: All red/all yellow
Midweek match day: —
Previous Leagues: —
Record transfer fee paid: £17,500
Record transfer fee received: £60,000
Record attendance: 17,500
Senior honours best performance: —
Past players (who progressed to Football League): —

NEWCASTLE BLUE STAR

President: R. F. S. Brown
Chairman: W. Dryden
Manager: C. Richardson
Ass. Man Coach: G. Defty W. Cruddas
Physiotherapist: W. Thompson D. Sayers
Secretary: R. Hunter
Address & Tel. No: 254A Baxterwood Court, Newcastle-upon-Tyne (091-2732655)
Commercial Manager: J. McKenna, R. Brownlees, K. Ellis, L. Hunter
Press Officer Programme editor: R. Barton
Ground Address & Tel. No: Wheatsheaf Sports Ground, Woolsington, Newcastle—up-upon-Tyne (091)2860425
Capacity: 2,500 **Covered accommodation:** 300 **Seating:** 300 **Floodlights:** —
Simple ground directions: 4 miles out of Newcastle on the Jedburgh (A696) Road, ½ mile before Newcastle Airport, turn left off road into Wheatsheaf car park
Clubhouse details: 80 seater lounge
Programme details: 16 pages information **Editor:** R. Barton **Club metal badges:** —
Local Newspaper(s): Newcastle Journal, Evening Chronicle, Sunday Sun, Northern Echo
Club colours: Blue strip blue shorts blue socks
Change colours: Red strip/white shorts white socks
Midweek match day: Monday
Previous Leagues: Newcastle Business Houses League, Tyneside Amateur League, Northern Combination League, Vaux Wearside League
Record transfer fee paid: —
Record transfer fee received: —
Record attendance: 1,800 (Almondsbury Greenway—FA Challenge Vase—Semi final
Senior honours best performance: FA Challenge Vase Winners 1977–78
Past players (who progressed to Football League): Barry Dunn (Sunderland), Peter Davidson (QPR & Berwick Rangers)

NORTH SHIELDS

"ROBINS"

President: Cllr G. M. M. Bilclough
Chairman: Len Murphy
Manager: Vic Hillier
Ass. Man Coach: Dave Robertson
Physiotherapist: Dave Robertson
Secretary: Peter Brown
Address & Tel. No: 48 Eleanor Street, Cullercoats, North Shields 0912524018(home), 0912575588(bus.)
Commercial Manager: —
Press Officer: Ken Green
Ground Address & Tel. No: Appleby Park, Hawkeys Lane, North Shields 0912570513 & 2570282
Capacity: 6,000 **Covered accommodation:** 3,000 **Seating:** 625 **Floodlights:** Yes
Simple ground directions: From N/S Metro proceed up Nile St into Albion Rd (left turn) along Albion Rd, pass Spring Gdns P.H. on right, then turn right into Hawkeys Lane—½ mile on left.
Clubhouse details: Open 7 days a week
Programme details: 20p **Editor:** Ken Green **Club metal badges:** No
Local Newspaper(s): Newcastle Journal & Evening Chronicle, Shields Weekly News
Club colours: All red
Change colours: All yellow
Midweek match day: Wednesday
Previous Leagues: North Eastern, Midland
Record transfer fee paid: —
Record transfer fee received: —
Record attendance: 12,500 v South Shields 1956
Senior honours/best performance: FA Amateur Cup Winners 1968–69
Past players (who progressed to Football League): —

PETERLEE NEWTOWN

"NEWTOWNERS"

President: D. J. B. Brown CBE FSIAD
Chairman: Brian Wall
Manager: Bobby Park
Ass. Man/Coach: Bobby Huntington
Physiotherapist: Stan Summerill
Secretary: Danny Cassidy
Address & Tel. No: 23 Melbury Street, Seaham, Co Durham (0783)814591
Commercial Manager: Len Richards
Press Officer: Secretary
Ground Address & Tel. No: "Eden Lane" (0783)863004
Capacity: 6,000 **Covered accommodation:** 200 **Seating:** 50 **Floodlights:** Yes
Simple ground directions: From Town Centre Fire Station, turn left into Edenhill Rd, then right into Robson Ave. Turn left at next junction—ground on right
Clubhouse details: Normal licencing hours
Programme details: Each match day **Editor:** Secretary **Club metal badges:** No
Local Newspaper(s): Hartlepool Mail, Sunderland Echo, N. Echo
Club colours: Sky blue/white/sky blue
Change colours: Yellow/black/yellow
Midweek match day: Wednesday
Previous Leagues: Northern Alliance 76–79, Wearside League 79–82, Northern League Div 2 82–83, Div 1 83–to date
Record transfer fee paid: £500
Record transfer fee received: £500
Record attendance: 1,750 v Nissan FC 1984
Senior honours/best performance: Northern League Div 2 Champions 1983, North Eastern Floodlit League Champions 1982, 4th Qual. Rnd. FA Cup 1985 (Replay lost 1-0 to Whitby)
Past players (who progressed to Football League): Brian Honour (Hartlepool), Keith Fairless (Belgium)

RYHOPE COMMUNITY

President: To be appointed
Chairman: T. Brace
Manager: Peter Quigley
Ass. Man/Coach: Gerry Davidson
Physiotherapist: To be appointed
Secretary: John Donoghue
Address & Tel. No: 40 Smith Street, Ryhope, Sunderland, Tyne & Wear (091)5236036
Commercial Manager: —
Press Officer: Norman Taylor
Ground Address & Tel. No: Meadow Park, Ryhope (091)5236555
Capacity: 4,200 **Covered accommodation:** 250 **Seating:** 200 **Floodlights:** Yes
Simple ground directions: Off A1018 at Junction to Ryhope Hospitals
Clubhouse details: Directors Lounge & refreshment area to seat 75
Programme details: Match programme **Editor:** Press Officer **Club metal badges:** Yes
Local Newspaper(s): Sunderland Echo, Sunderland Football Echo, The Journal, Northern Echo
Club colours: Royal blue
Change colours: All white
Midweek match day: Wednesday
Previous Leagues: Northern Alliance, Houghton and District
Record transfer fee paid: None
Record transfer fee received: £3,000
Record attendance: 1,200 v Newcastle
Senior honours/best performance: Northern Alliance League Cup Winners 1981, Runners-up Drybroughs Northern League 1983–4
Past players (who progressed to Football League): Kevin Todd (Newcastle), Neil Richardson Doncaster)

SOUTH BANK

"BANKERS"

President: C. Bugg
Chairman: M. Reid
Manager: T. Harrison
Ass. Man/Coach: B. Mulligan
Physiotherapist: B. O'Brien
Secretary: R. J. Kidd
Address & Tel. No: 8 Halton Court, Thorntree, Middlesbrough (0642)243412
Commercial Manager: D. Dale
Press Officer: Secretary
Ground Address & Tel. No: Normanby Rd, South Bank (0642)453193
Capacity: 8,000 **Covered accommodation:** 400 Tce **Seating:** 400 St **Floodlights:** Yes
Simple ground directions: Approaching S. Bank along Normanby Rd, on RHS, about 400yds from Bennets Corner lights
Clubhouse details: Open every evening & afternoon, Thurs & Sun concerts, Sat country & western
Programme details: 12 pages 20p **Editor:** D. Dale **Club metal badges:** Yes
Club colours: Red & white stripes/black shorts/red socks
Change colours: All white
Midweek match day: Wednesday **Previous Leagues:** None
Record transfer fee paid: None
Record transfer fee received: £1,000 Donation Rotherham
Record attendance: 10,000 Prewar
Senior honours/best performance: FA Amateur Cup Winners 1913
Past players (who progressed to Football League): G. Forrest (Southampton)

SPENNYMOOR UNITED

"THE MOORS"

President: K. G. Newell
Chairman: J. B. Hindmarch
Manager: W. M. Bell
Ass. Man Coach: T. Monkhouse
Physiotherapist: D. Lumley
Secretary: D. G. Makinson
Address & Tel. No: 4 Broadway Avenue, Trimdon, Co Durham (0429)880684
Commercial Manager: C. M. Whitehouse
Press Officer: Chairman
Ground Address & Tel. No: Durham Rd, Spennymoor 814100
Capacity: 7,000 **Covered accommodation:** 1,500 **Seating:** 320 **Floodlights:** Yes
Simple ground directions: Just off Town Centre
Clubhouse details: Bar & lounge
Programme details: 20p **Editor:** G. O. Smith **Club metal badges:** Yes
Local Newspaper(s): Northern Echo
Club colours: White black white
Change colours: All red
Midweek match day: Wednesday **Previous Leagues:** North Eastern League
Record transfer fee paid: —
Record transfer fee received: —
Record attendance: Not known
Senior honours best performance: Northern Lge Winners 1968, 1972, 1974, 1977, 1978, 1979
Past players (who progressed to Football League): —

TOW LAW TOWN

"LAWYERS"

President: John E. Wright
Chairman: Harry Hodgson
Manager: S. Leeming
Ass. Man/Coach: R. Carney
Physiotherapist: —
Secretary: B. D. Fairbairn
Address & Tel. No: 3 Coppice Walk, Mowden Park, Darlington
Commercial Manager: —
Press Officer: As above
Ground Address & Tel. No: Ironworks Rd, Tow Law (Bp Auckland)730247
Capacity: 5,000 **Covered accommodation:** 700 **Seating:** 300 **Floodlights:** None
Simple ground directions: Off High St, Tow Law
Programme details: None **Editor:** — **Club metal badges:** Yes
Local Newspaper(s): Northern Echo
Club colours: Black & white stripes
Change colours: Red
Midweek match day: Tuesday **Previous Leagues:** —
Record transfer fee paid: —
Record transfer fee received: —
Record attendance: 5,000 v Mansfield 1968
Senior honours/best performance: "Rothmans" National Cup Winners 1976–77
Past players (who progressed to Football League): Chris Waddell (Spurs)

WHITBY TOWN

"SEASIDERS"

President: Don Dunwell
Chairman: Ted Davis
Manager: David Harvey
Ass. Man/Coach: Garry Watson
Physiotherapist: —
Secretary: R. Scaife
Address & Tel. No: 17 White Leys Road, Whitby (0947)600776
Commercial Manager: —
Press Officer: Secretary
Ground Address & Tel. No: Turnbull Ground, Upgang Lane, Whitby (0947)604847
Capacity: 4,000 **Covered accommodation:** 500 **Seating:** 200 **Floodlights:** Yes
Simple ground directions: Take West Cliff signs when entering town—ground on main A174 road
Clubhouse details: Adjacent to Ground, open match days & every evening 7–11pm
Programme details: 10 page, 20p **Editor:** G. Trowsdale **Club metal badges:** Yes
Local Newspaper(s): Whitby Gazette (0947)602836
Club colours: All blue
Change colours: All white
Midweek match day: Wednesday
Previous Leagues: —
Record transfer fee paid: —
Record transfer fee received: —
Record attendance: 5,000
Senior honours/best performance: FA Cup 2nd Round 1983–84 v Wigan, 1985–86 v York, Amateur Cup Finalists 1964–65, FA Trophy quarter finals 1983–84, NL Cup—5 times, NL Runner-up—5 times, NR Senior Cup Winners 1964–65, 1967–68, 1982–83
Past players (who progressed to Football League): M. Poskett, M. Hine, D. Logan

WHITLEY BAY

"THE BAY"

President: C. E. Fuller MBE
Chairman: C. E. Fuller MBE
Manager: B. Dunn
Ass. Man/Coach: S. Bell
Physiotherapist: J. R. Jabs
Secretary: Robert Harding
Address & Tel. No: 24 Cambridge Avenue, Whitley Bay, Tyne & Wear 2515179
Commercial Manager: None
Press Officer: Chairman
Ground Address & Tel. No: Hillheads Park, Whitley Bay 2513680
Capacity: 4,500 **Covered accommodation:** 200 **Seating:** 450 **Floodlights:** Yes
Simple ground directions: 1 mile walk from local bus station. Leave St Paul's Church southward, turn right at roundabout, 3rd left, ground rear of Ice Rink
Clubhouse details: Attached to Ground (bar—concert room)
Programme details: — **Editor:** Len Bone **Club metal badges:** No
Local Newspaper(s): The News, Guardian
Club colours: Blue & white stripes/blue/blue
Change colours: All yellow
Midweek match day: Tuesday
Previous Leagues: North Eastern League
Record transfer fee paid: £250
Record transfer fee received: £350
Record attendance: 7,800
Senior honours/best performance: Semi-final (Amateur Cup), League (2) & Runners-up (4), League Cup (2) & Runners-up, Northumberland Senior Cup (9) & Runners-up (5)
Past players (who progressed to Football League): Gary Haire (Bradford), Tony Harrison (Southport), Mark Miller (Gillingham), John Richie (Port Vale)

Guisborough Town: *Back Row: R. Dewhurst (Asst. Manager), D. Jacques (Coach), M. Forster, S. Parkes, G. Shaw, P. Bates, B. Grainger, B. Crawley, V. Jackson, J. Lovatt (Captain), S. Roberts, M. Hodgson (Manager). Front Row: Jacques jun (Mascot), P. Roberts, G. Smith, R. Walker, N. Hodgson, M. Purvis, M. Davis, M. Hodgson (Mascot).*

SECOND DIVISION

ALNWICK TOWN

President: Hugh Philipson
Chairman: Graham Kent
Manager: Mike Daglass
Ass. Man Coach: Dave Cope
Physiotherapist: Malcolm Belisle Roger Howey
Secretary: Cyril Cox
Address & Tel. No: 19 Melness Road, Hazlerigg, Tyne & Wear (091)2366456
Commercial Manager: None
Press Officer: See Secretary
Ground Address & Tel. No: St James Park, Alnwick, Northumberland (0665)603162
Capacity: 1,500 **Covered accommodation:** 100 **Seating:** 100 **Floodlights:** No
Simple ground directions: 35 miles north of Newcastle on A1, take slip road off Alnwick By-pass into town, then 1st left up to roundabout, then 1st left to ground.
Clubhouse details: Full length panoramic view of pitch from clubhouse with bar & food sales, toilets & directors box
Programme details: Starting 86 87 10p **Editor:** C. Cox **Club metal badges:** No
Local Newspaper(s): Northumberland Gazette, Alnwick Advertiser
Club colours: Black & white shirts/black shorts/black socks
Change colours: All red
Midweek match day: Wed/Thur
Previous Leagues: Northern Alliance, Durham Central
Record transfer fee paid: —
Record transfer fee received: —
Record attendance: 600
Senior honours/best performance: 11–0 v Morpeth Town, N. Alliance 1971–72
Past players (who progressed to Football League): —

ASHINGTON

"COLLIERS"

President: —
Chairman: Andy Fairbairn
Manager: Tom Charlton
Ass. Man/Coach: Cecil Irwin
Physiotherapist: Mrs Grant
Secretary: Ron Talbot
Address & Tel. No: 38 Laburnum Terrace, Ashington (0670)818455
Commercial Manager: Chris Guthrie
Press Officer: Brian Bennett
Ground Address & Tel. No: Portland Place (0670)812240
Capacity: — **Covered accommodation:** 2 stands **Seating:** 200 **Floodlights:** Yes
Simple ground directions: North at traffic lights, Centre of Town
Clubhouse details: Bar and concert room
Programme details: — **Editor:** — **Club metal badges:** —
Local Newspaper(s): Leader & Courier
Club colours: Black & white striped shirts black shorts black & white socks
Change colours: All red
Midweek match day: Wednesday
Previous Leagues: North Eastern, Midland Wearside
Record transfer fee paid: —
Record transfer fee received: £3,500 Lowery W.B.A.
Record attendance: 9,500 Rochdale 1951
Senior honours best performance: English Amateur Cup Semi Finalists
Past players (who progressed to Football League): Humble (Mansfield), Milburn (Chesterfield, Leicester)

BILLINGHAM SYNTHONIA

"THE SYNNERS"

President: H. L. Davies MBE
Chairman: P. E. Lax
Manager: J. A. Lee
Ass. Man Coach: L. Gunn
Physiotherapist: R. Gomer
Secretary: J. K. Dunlop
Address & Tel. No: 21 Imperial Road, Billingham, Stockton 533008
Commercial Manager: P. Robinson
Press Officer: G. Craggs
Ground Address & Tel. No: The Stadium, Central Ave, Billingham, Cleveland (Stockton) 552358
Capacity: 6,000 **Covered accommodation:** 3,000 **Seating:** 300 **Floodlights:** Yes
Simple ground directions: From Railway Station ½ mile along Cowpen Lane
Clubhouse details: Restarted last season **Editor:** G. Craggs **Club metal badges:** No
Local Newspaper(s): M'Boro Evening Gazette
Club colours: Green & white stripes
Change colours: Blue
Midweek match day: Wednesday
Previous Leagues: Teesside League
Record transfer fee paid: £750
Record transfer fee received: £1,000
Record attendance: 4,000 v Bish p Auckland FC, 6th Sept 1958
Senior honours best performance: League Champions 1956–57. In season 1950–51 not conceding a goal at home: P-13, W-12, L-0, D-1, F-44, A-0, Pts-25
Past players (who progressed to Football League): Brian Clough

BILLINGHAM TOWN

President: Stan Linton
Chairman: Jef Nolan
Manager: Dave Buckle
Ass. Man Coach: John Madison
Physiotherapist: Dave Smith
Secretary: T. V. Donnelly
Address & Tel. No: 36 Cumberland Crescent, Billingham 555332
Commercial Manager: Dave Sparrow
Press Officer: Secretary
Ground Address & Tel. No: Bedford Terrace, Billingham, Cleveland (0642)560043
Capacity: 6,000 **Covered accommodation:** 2,500 **Seating:** 2,500 **Floodlights:** No
Simple ground directions: Leave A19 on 1027 towards Billingham over 2 roundabouts along Central Ave, turn left at next roundabout. 1st left, then 1st left again for ground
Clubhouse details: Members club
Programme details: Yes **Editor:** Jef Nolan **Club metal badges:** No
Local Newspaper(s): Northern Echo, Evening Gazette
Club colours: All royal blue
Change colours: All red
Midweek match day: Wednesday
Previous Leagues: Teesside League
Record transfer fee paid: £500
Record transfer fee received: £750
Record attendance: 2,000
Senior honours best performance: Durham Amateur Cup Winners 1977 and 1978
Past players (who progressed to Football League): Gerald Forrest (Southampton), Gary Pallister (Middlesbrough), Tony Barratt and Mark Hines (Grimsby Town)

CLEVELAND BRIDGE

"THE BRIDGE"

President: W. Tennet
Chairman: C. Bellwood
Manager: W. Shevels
Ass. Man Coach: —
Physiotherapist: R. Crust
Secretary: D. Shevels
Address & Tel. No: 202 North Road, Darlington 462753
Commercial Manager: —
Press Officer: Secretary
Ground Address & Tel. No: Neasham Rd, Darlington 469735
Capacity: 5,000 **Covered accommodation:** St. only **Seating:** 40 **Floodlights:** Yes
Simple ground directions: Neasham Rd, Darlington
Clubhouse details: Large clubhouse for spectators, players & officials on ground
Programme details: 4 pages **Editor:** Secretary **Club metal badges:** No
Local Newspaper(s): Northern Echo
Club colours: Yellow shirts black shorts black socks
Change colours: All white
Midweek match day: Tuesday
Previous Leagues: Darlington & District, Northern Alliance
Record transfer fee paid: None
Record transfer fee received: £400 for T. Swainston from Crook Town
Record attendance: 440 v Darlington Res
Senior honours best performance: Northern Alliance League Champions 1982–83
Past players (who progressed to Football League): Jeff Wealands (Manchester Utd)

DURHAM CITY

"CITIZENS"

President: N. Miller
Chairman: J. Lindsay
Manager: A. Hickman
Ass. Man Coach: D. Mason
Physiotherapist: —
Secretary: A. Young
Address & Tel. No: 21 Valley View, Ushaw Moor, Durham (0385)730727
Commercial Manager: N. Harrison, A. Thompson
Press Officer: Secretary
Ground Address & Tel. No: Ferens Park, The Sands, Durham (0385)69616
Capacity: 6,300 **Covered accommodation:** 300 **Seating:** 300 **Floodlights:** Yes
Simple ground directions: Down Ex-GPO Bank, along riverside, on right
Clubhouse details: Open week nights (ex Sun) and Matchdays
Programme details: 12 pages, 10p **Editor:** D. W. Asbery, A. Young **Club metal badges:** No
Local Newspaper(s): Northern Echo, Sunderland Echo
Club colours: Gold shirts blue shorts gold stockings
Change colours: All blue
Midweek match day: Tuesday
Previous Leagues: Wearside League
Record transfer fee paid: None
Record transfer fee received: None
Record attendance: 6,000 v Tranmere Rovers 1956 (FA Cup)
Senior honours best performance: Durham Benevolent Bowl 1955–56, Northern League Cup Runners-up 1976–77, 1985–86, Northern League Runners-up 1970–71, Durham Challenge Cup Runners-up 1971–72, 1973–74
Past players (who progressed to Football League): None

ESH WINNING

President: John Lumsden
Chairman: Charles Ryan
Manager: —
Ass. Man Coach: —
Physiotherapist: Fredrick Briggs
Secretary: Allan Morton
Address & Tel. No: 20 Durham Road, Esh Winning, Durham 733611
Commercial Manager: —
Press Officer: H. Wharton
Ground Address & Tel. No: West Terrace, Waterhouses, Durham 733872
Capacity: — **Covered accommodation:** 2 Stands **Seating:** 150 **Floodlights:** Yes
Simple ground directions: From Durham to Ushaw Moor, to Esh Winning—1 mile from Esh to Waterhouses
Clubhouse details: Seats 85
Programme details: — **Editor:** — **Club metal badges:** —
Local Newspaper(s): Northern Echo
Club colours: Green shirts yellow shorts
Change colours: Yellow shirts green shorts green socks
Midweek match day: Tuesday
Previous Leagues: Durham Sunday League, Northern Alliance
Record transfer fee paid: £250
Record transfer fee received: £300
Record attendance: 500—All England Sunday Cup v Liverpool Fantail 1980–81
Senior honours best performance: Sunday League Winners 1 Div 1978–79, 1979–80. Beaten Finalist County Sunday Cup Final 1978–79
Past players (who progressed to Football League): —

EVENWOOD TOWN

President: J. Hardesty
Chairman: R. Stelling
Manager: P. Cooke
Ass. Man Coach: D. Calland
Physiotherapist: B. Tray
Secretary: D. R. Reynolds
Address & Tel. No: 58 High Grange, Crook, Co Durham (0388)766332
Commercial Manager: —
Press Officer: R. Stelling
Ground Address & Tel. No: Welfare Ground
Capacity: 3,200 **Covered accommodation:** 200 **Seating:** 200 **Floodlights:** None
Simple ground directions: 1 mile north of Evenwood Gate off A688
Clubhouse details: None **Editor:** — **Club metal badges:** —
Local Newspaper(s): Northern Echo, Teesdale Mercury
Club colours: All blue
Change colours: Green shirts (yellow sleeves) green shorts green socks
Midweek match day: Wednesday
Previous Leagues: —
Record transfer fee paid: —
Record transfer fee received: —
Record attendance: 2,600
Senior honours best performance: Winners Durham CC 1969–70 Finalists 1970–71, Winners Northern League CC 1935–36, Winners Northern League 1948–49, 1969–70, 1970–71
Past players (who progressed to Football League): Gary Morgan (Darlington)

GUISBOROUGH TOWN

"PRIORYMEN"

President: Joe Morgan
Chairman: Sid Waller
Manager: Mike J. Hodgson
Ass. Man Coach: Bob Dewhurst Derek Jacques
Physiotherapist: Bob Cane
Secretary: Keith Smeltzer
Address & Tel. No: 55 Thames Avenue, Guisborough, Cleveland (0287)38993 (work 33551)
Commercial Manager: Dennis Wheeler
Press Officer: Mike Hodgson
Ground Address & Tel. No: King George V (0287)36925
Capacity: 5,000 **Covered accommodation:** 450 **Seating:** 35 **Floodlights:** Yes
Simple ground directions: —
Programme details: 25p: Team plus articles **Editor:** Joe Timney **Club metal badges:** No
Best prog. DNL 2nd Div 1985–86
Local Newspaper(s): M'Bro Evening Gazette, N'cstle Sunday Sun, Northern Echo, Journal
Club colours: Red & white stripe shirts black shorts
Change colours: All blue
Midweek match day: Wednesday
Previous Leagues: North East Counties
Record transfer fee paid: £750
Record transfer fee received: —
Record attendance: 3,112 v Hungerford—Semi final FA Vase 1980
Senior honours best performance: —
Past players (who progressed to Football League): —

HORDON COLLIERY WELFARE

President: A. Bamford
Chairman: E. Walker
Manager: R. Malone
Ass. Man/Coach: J. Cranson
Physiotherapist: S. Kirkup
Secretary: R. Matthews
Address & Tel. No: 16 Ninth Street, Horden, Peterlee, Co Durham (0783)870727
Commercial Manager: —
Press Officer: Secretary
Ground Address & Tel. No: Welfare Park Ground, Park Road, Horden (0783)861493
Capacity: 4,500 **Covered accommodation:** 400 **Seating:** 300 **Floodlights:** Yes
Simple ground directions: Off A19 signposted Horden
Clubhouse details: Open 7 nights per wk, Discos, Players functions, canteen facilities
Programme details: 12 pages, 20p **Editor:** A. Walker **Club metal badges:** No
Local Newspaper(s): Northern Echo, Hartlepool Mail
Club colours: Red & white shirts/black shorts/red & white socks
Change colours: Blue shirts/black shorts/blue socks
Midweek match day: Tuesday
Previous Leagues: Wearside, Midland, North Eastern
Record transfer fee paid: Not known
Record transfer fee received: Not known
Record attendance: 8,000 in 1937
Senior honours/best performance: Wearside League, Durham Challenge Cup
Past players (who progressed to Football League): Paul Dobson (Hartlepo l Utd), Robert Taylor (Leed Utd)

LANGLEY PARK WELFARE

"THE PARK"

President: Bobby Robson (Engld Manager)
Chairman: Brian Smart
Manager: Tommy Robinson
Ass. Man/Coach: —
Physiotherapist: Bill Richardson
Secretary: Jeff Dover
Address & Tel. No: 39 Quebec Street, Langley Park, Durham home—(0385)731381, bus—(091)4772125
Commercial Manager: —
Press Officer: Brian Smart
Ground Address & Tel. No: Low Moor Rd, Langley Park, Durham (0385)731526
Capacity: 3,500 **Covered accommodation:** 300 **Seating:** 40 **Floodlights:** No
Simple ground directions: —
Clubhouse details: Licenced lounge & concert room, capacity 80 & 200 respectively
Programme details: Home games **Editor:** Sec/Chair **Club metal badges:** No
Local Newspaper(s): Journal, Northern Echo, Sunday Sun
Club colours: Sky blue
Change colours: Yellow
Midweek match day: Wednesday
Previous Leagues: Durham & District
Record transfer fee paid: —
Record transfer fee received: —
Record attendance: 480
Senior honours/best performance: —
Past players (who progressed to Football League): —

NORTHALLERTON TOWN

President: J. Farndale
Chairman: R. Longstaff
Manager: C. Topping
Ass. Man/Coach: —
Physiotherapist: —
Secretary: P. Coulson
Address & Tel. No: 19 Ainderby Road, Romanby, Northallerton 779354
Commercial Manager: —
Press Officer: A. Barker
Ground Address & Tel. No: Ainderby Rd, Romanby, Northallerton 2418
Capacity: 2,200 **Covered accommodation:** Yes **Seating:** 300 **Floodlights:** Under construction
Simple ground directions: By road: A19 to Clack Lane Ends—6 miles Northallerton signposted. A1 to Leeming Motel—6 miles Northallerton signposted. By bus: 73 from Darlington. Local bus from Leeming Motel. By train: To Northallerton. Darlington–York line ¼ mile.
Clubhouse details: Bar/lounge—refreshments available on match days
Programme details: 20p **Editor:** A. Barker **Club metal badges:** No
Local Newspaper(s): Northern Echo, Darlington & Stockton Times, North Yorkshire News
Club colours: Amber shirts (black trim)/black shorts (amber trim)
Change colours: Red & white striped shirts/black shorts/red socks
Midweek match day: —
Previous Leagues: Allerton League, Darlington & District League, Claro League, Harrogate & District League to 82, Northern League Div 2 1982 to date
Record transfer fee paid: —
Record transfer fee received: —
Record attendance: 300 approx. v Leeds Utd 1983
Senior honours/best performance: Harrogate & District Champions, Richmond Cup Winners, Bedale Cup Winners, Millbank Cup Winners

NORTON & STOCKTON ANCIENTS

"ANCIENTS"

President: Wilf Lawson
Chairman: W.(Bill) H. Russell
Manager: Tony Screen
Ass. Man Coach: John Mernach
Physiotherapist: Brian Symons
Secretary: Richard Scott
Address & Tel. No: 3 Keld Grove, Fairfield, Stockton-on-Tess, Cleveland (0642)581360
Commercial Manager: —
Press Officer: —
Ground Address & Tel. No: Station Rd, Norton (0642)554031
Capacity: 2,000 **Covered accommodation:** Yes **Seating:** 200 **Floodlights:** No
Simple ground directions: Cleveland Transit to Junction Road, Norton (37, 39, 120 or 121)—2 miles from Stockton Town Centre
Clubhouse details: Full bar facilities—150 yds from ground
Programme details: Every home game **Editor:** R. Scott **Club metal badges:** No
Local Newspaper(s): Evening Gazette, Northern Echo
Club colours: Amber & black
Change colours: Blue
Midweek match day: Wednesday
Previous Leagues: Teesside League
Record transfer fee paid: —
Record transfer fee received: —
Record attendance: 400 (Blue Star)
Senior honours/best performance: Winners of Northern League Challenge Cup 1982–83
Past players (who progressed to Football League): None

SEAHAM CW RED STAR

"THE STAR"

President: Michael English
Chairman: Thomas English
Manager: Larry Phillips
Ass. Man Coach: Christopher Copeland Michael Harrison
Physiotherapist: Alan Black
Secretary: H. C. Hobson
Address & Tel. No: 43 General Graham Street, Sunderland 79472
Commercial Manager: H. C. Hobson
Press Officer: H. C. Hobson
Ground Address & Tel. No: Seaham CW, Stockton Rd 812540
Capacity: 2,000 **Covered accommodation:** 100 **Seating:** — **Floodlights:** Yes
Simple ground directions: From Tyne Tunnel take Teesside Rd (A19) for approx. 18 miles. Take B1404 (left) slip road (Seaham), turn left again off slip road at T-junction (Seaham), turn right at main road junction, first left into ground entrance
Clubhouse details: None
Programme details: 36 page edition **Editor:** D. Copeland **Club metal badges:** None
Local Newspaper(s): Sunderland Echo, Journal, Northern Echo, Football Echo, Washington Times
Club colours: White shirts (blue trim) blue shorts/blue socks
Change colours: Red shirts/white shorts/white socks
Midwee match day: Tuesday
Previous Leagues: Seaham & District, Northern Alliance, Wearside
Record attendance: 1,500
Senior honours best performance: Phillips Floodlit Trophy 1979, Durham Challenge Cup 1980, Wearside League Double 1982
Past players (who progressed to Football League): Bob Davison (Derby County, Huddersfield, Halifax), Nigel Greghorn (Ipswich Town)

SHILDON

"THE RAILWAYMEN"

President: C. Attwood
Chairman: W. Aisbitt
Manager: R. Heslington
Ass. Man Coach: M. Dawes
Physiotherapist: —
Secretary: J. M. Armitage
Address & Tel. No: 22 Hambleton Court, Byerley Park, Newton Aycliffe
Commercial Manager: —
Press Officer: Secretary
Ground Address & Tel. No: Dean Street, Shildon (Bishop Auckland) 773877
Capacity: 4,000 **Covered accommodation:** 1 stand **Seating:** 500 **Floodlights:** Being installed
Simple ground directions: Town Centre
Clubhouse details: Under grandstand, open 7.30–10.30 every night, 1.30–5.30 Sat. afternoons, 12.00–2.00 Sun. afternoons
Programme details: 8 pages, 10p **Editor:** — **Club metal badges:** None avail. at present
Local Newspaper(s): Northern Echo
Club colours: Red shirts/red shorts/white socks
Change colours: All white or sky blue
Midweek match day: Wednesday
Previous Leagues: North Eastern
Record transfer fee paid: —
Record transfer fee received: —
Record attendance: 13,000 Schoolboys match Leeholme v Perkinsville. Also 11,000 Shildon v Ferryhill (Durham Senior Cup 1922)
Senior honours/best performance: Northern League (5), Northern League Challenge Cup (6), Durham County Challenge Cup (3), Durham Benevolent Bowl (2)
Past players (who progressed to Football League): Kevin Stonehouse (Blackpool, Huddersfield & Blackburn Rovers), Andy Toman (Lincoln City)

Shildon F.C.

SHOTTON COMRADES

"THE COMRADES"

President: G. Robinson
Chairman: J. Scullion
Manager: W. Tuttle
Ass. Man/Coach: W. Banks
Physiotherapist: K. Price
Secretary: Paul Farn
Address & Tel. No: 17 Milton Lane, Easington, Co Durham (0783)272237
Commercial Manager: Secretary
Press Officer: Secretary
Ground Address & Tel. No: —
Capacity: 5,000 **Covered accommodation:** Yes **Seating:** Yes **Floodlights:** No
Simple ground directions: From A19 first left at Peterlee roundabout, ground on right hand side through village
Clubhouse details: —
Programme details: Yes **Editor:** Secretary **Club metal badges:** No
Local Newspaper(s): Durham Advertiser
Club colours: All blue
Change colours: Red shirts/white shorts/red socks
Midweek match day: Wednesday
Previous Leagues: Houghton & District, Northern Alliance
Record transfer fee paid: —
Record transfer fee received: —
Record attendance: 1,500
Senior honours/best performance: Houghton & District Lge Champions (3), Challenge Cup (2)
Past players (who progressed to Football League): —

STOCKTON

President: Keith Wren
Chairman: David Scott
Manager: Peter Mulcaster
Ass. Man/Coach: Alan Marples
Physiotherapist: Jeff Miller
Secretary: Glenn Youngman
Address & Tel. No: 10 Sadberge Grove, Fairfield, Stockton, Cleveland 587871
Commercial Manager: —
Press Officer: John Smith
Ground Address & Tel. No: Teesdale Park, Acklam Rd, Thornaby, Stockton-on-Tees, Cleveland (0642)606803
Capacity: 4,000 **Covered accommodation:** 1,000 **Seating:** 20 **Floodlights:** No
Simple ground directions: A19 to Thornaby, turn off—ground approx. ¾ mile on right hand side
Clubhouse details: Open Wed/Fri/Sat/Sun lunchtimes, every evening—membership 800
Programme details: 24 pages, 20p **Editor:** Allan Ruddy **Club metal badges:** No
Local Newspaper(s): Northern Echo, Evening Gazette
Club colours: Red & black striped shirts/black shorts/red socks
Change colours: All light blue
Midweek match day: Wednesday
Previous Leagues: Stockton & District Lge, Vaux Wearside Lge
Record transfer fee paid: —
Record transfer fee received: —
Record attendance: 1,000
Senior honours/best performance: FA Vase Round 2: 1981
Past players (who progressed to Football League): K. Smith (Darlington & Rotherham), S. Douglas (Darlington)

WEST AUCKLAND TOWN

President: R. Tomlinson
Chairman: L. Nevison
Manager: S. Alderson
Ass. Man Coach: S. Fellows
Physiotherapist: F. Patrick
Secretary: N. Ayon
Address & Tel. No: 3 Deerness Road, Bishop Auckland (0388)604375
Commercial Manager: G. Curtis
Press Officer: G. Curtis
Ground Address & Tel. No: Darlington Road
Capacity: 4,000 **Covered accommodation:** 300 **Seating:** 200 **Floodlights:** Yes
Simple ground directions: From Darlington motorway take A68 road turning on left entering village
Clubhouse details: At present refreshments and soft drinks only
Programme details: 15p **Editor:** P. Dedigote **Club metal badges:** None at present
Local Newspaper(s): Northern Echo
Club colours: All amber **Change colours:** All white
Midweek match day: Tuesday **Previous Leagues:** —
Record transfer fee paid: None
Record transfer fee received: None
Record attendance: 6,000
Senior honours best performance: Amateur Cup Finalists 1960–61, Semi-finalists 1961–62, Northern League Champions 1959–60 and 1960–61, Northern League Cup Winners 1958–59 and 1962–63, Durham Challenge Cup Winners 1965–66
Past players (who progressed to Football League): T. Blenkinsop (M'Bro), L. Dagger (Preston), W. Hopper (Halifax), J. Sproates & T. Atkinson (Darlington), Wilkinson (Burnley)

WILLINGTON

"BLUES"

President: Vacant
Chairman: D. Ayre
Manager: E. Kyle
Ass. Man Coach: A. Murray
Physiotherapist: —
Secretary: J. Nichol
Address & Tel. No: 36 High Croft, Middlestone Moor, Spennymoor 814720
Commercial Manager: —
Press Officer: Secretary
Ground Address & Tel. No: Hall Lane (0388)746221
Capacity: 5,000 **Covered accommodation:** Yes **Seating:** Yes **Floodlights:** Yes
Simple ground directions: Entering Willington from west or east, turn left or right at Black Horse Tavern, follow road for 100 yds, ground entrance on right
Clubhouse details: Social club
Programme details: Yes **Editor:** B. Nichol **Club metal badges:** No
Local Newspaper(s): Northern Echo
Club colours: Blue & white
Change colours: Yellow & green
Midweek match day: Wednesday **Previous Leagues:** Not known
Record transfer fee paid: None
Record transfer fee received: None
Record attendance: 11,000
Senior honours best performance: FA Amateur Cup Winners 1950, Losing Finalists 1939, Northern Lge Champions 1913–14, 1925–26, 1929–30, League Cup Winners 1924–25, 1925–26, 1927–28, 1930–31, 1931–32, 1948–49, 1956–57, 1974–75, Third Round Proper FA Trophy
Past players (who progressed to Football League): —

Winners of the North Riding F.A. County Cup Stockton. *Back Row (L-R): Woof, Wesson, Parry, Corner, Robson, Warriner, McQuade, Bell. Front Row: Hogg, Bartliff, Martin, Lockington, McGee.*

DIVISION ONE PLAYERS

BEDLINGTON TERRIERS
Goalkeepers
David Guthrie: Eppleton, Consett, Gateshead
Kevin Baldwin: Ponteland Utd., Berwick Rangers, Blue Star, North Shields

Defenders
Tony Gilmore: Eppleton, Durham City, Reyrolles
Bryan Turner: Ashington, Morpeth Town
Roy Peart: Ashington
Brian Penfold: Gateshead, Blyth Spartans, Whitley Bay, Morpeth Town
Jeff Peters: North Shields, Whitley Bay, Blyth Spartans, Middlesborough (16)

Midfield
Tony Burgess: Ashington RAOB Juniors
Colin Ayre: North Shields, Bishop Auckland, Ashington, Torquay Utd (2)
Colin Chambers: Durham Cith, Blyth Spartans, Alnwick Town, Seaham Red Star, Ashington, Bishop Auckland, Whitley Bay, Dudley Welfare

Forwards
David Willis: Alnwick Town, Newcastle United
Craig Mordue: Seaton Delaval Amateurs
Andy Rice: Alnwick Town, Forest Hall, Dudley Welfare, Gateshead
Ian Allison: Stobswood Welfare
Dave Dixon: Ashington, Blyth Spartans, Seaton Terracek Whitley Bay.
Jimmy Taylor: Ashington

BISHOPS AUCKLAND
Goalkeepers
Tony Harrison: Gateshead, Blue Star, North Shields, Carlisle Utd (8). Southport (48), Whitley Bay, Boldon
Phil Owers: Crook Town, Darlington (69), Gillingham (2), Darlington (45),

Defenders
Alan Barker: Hartlepool Utd (59-1), Bishop Auckland, Ferryhill, Gillingham (64-2), Newcastle United (21)
Malcolm Newton: Crook Town, Brandon Utd
Wilson Blair: Ferryhill, Brandon Utd, Ryhope C.A.
Gary Lormer: Horden C.W.
Paul Brown: Spennymoor Utd, Ferryhill, Brandon Utd, Willington

Midfield
David Varity: North Shields, Blyth Spartans, Whitley Bay
Mick Whitfield: Horden C.W., Hartlepool Utd (15), Sunderland (3)
Harry Dunn: Blyth Spartans, Scarborough, Bishop Auckland

Forwards
Colin Blackburn: Nuneaton Borough, Bishop Auckland
John Grady: Spennymoor Utd, Blue Star, Gateshead, Berwick Rangers
Phil Linacre: Hartlepool Utd (5-1), Whitby Town, Hartlepool utd (78-17)
David Newton: Blyth Spartans, Bishop Auckland, Crook Town, Willington
Warren Pearson: Tow Law
Mark Lawrence: Whitby Town, Port Vale (10), Hartlepool Utd (155-24)

BLUE STAR
Goalkeepers
Barry Goodwin: Whitley Bay, South Shields, Tow Law
David Lawson: Gateshead Tyne Sports

Defenders
Alan Scott; Whickham, Willington, Consett
Bryan Magee: Scarborough, Horden C.W.
John Swinburne: Consett
David Farrey: Whickham
Roger Wicks: Darlington (31-4), Netherfield

Midfield
John Reach: Workington, Durham Cith
John Carver: Cardiff City
Bobby Scaife: Blyth Spartans, South Bank, Whitby Town, Rochdale (95-19), Hartlepool Utd (77-10), Halifax Town (5-1)
Tony Robinson: Gateshead, Whitley Bay

Forwards
Kevin Todd: Darlington (56-17), Newcastle Utd (5-3), Ryhope C.A.
Alan Gates: Coundon T.T., Spennymoor Utd
Derek Hampton: Whitby Town, Hartlepool Utd (66-18), Whitby Town
Ian Crumplin: Bishop Auckland, Hartlepool Utd (25-5), Blue Star, North Shields, Ashington
Peter Bragan: Consett, Blyth Spartans, Consett
Leon Gill: Gateshead Tyne, Sports, Consett, Gateshead
Bob Arkless: Benwell Blues, Percy Main Amateurs

BLYTH SPARTANS
Goalkeepers
David Clarke: Gateshead, Gainsborough Trinity, Darlington (11), Doncaster Rovers (3), Newcastle Utd
Jimmy Mason; Gosforth St Nicholas, Ashington, High Pitt

Defenders
Alan Walker: Berwick Rangers, Ashington
Kevin Berry: Blue Star, Spennymoor Utd, Tow Law, Blyth Spartans
Jimmy Harmison: North Shields, Ashington, Yeovil Town, Ashington
Ronan Liddane: Alnwick Town, Dudley Welfare, Heaton Stannington
John Brownlie: Berwick Rangers, Hartlepool Utd (18-2), Middlesbrough (12) Newcastle Utd (124-2), Hibs

Midfield
Paul Walker: Horden C.W., Blue Star, Blyth Spartans, Scarborough, Hordeon C.W., Doncaster Rovers (4), Hull City
Peter Cartwright: Darlington (48-5), Scunthorpe Utd (2-2), Newcastle Utd (57-3), North Shields
Steve Baxter: Percy Main Amateurs
Tony Dawson: Whitley Bay

Forwards
David Buchannan: North Shields, Peterborough Utd (13-4), Northampton Town (3-2), Leicester City (24-7)
Tony McFadden: Darlington (44-10), Reyrolles, Tow Law, Spennymoor Utd
Michael Carroll: Kuysi Lahti (Fin), Blyth Spartans, North Shields, Blue Star, Chesterfield (5-1), Whickham

Defender
Chris Scott: North Shields, Whitley Bay, Cramlington

BRANDON UNITED
Goalkeepers
David Ramage: Evenwood
John Worrall: Bishop Auckland, West Auckland, Shildon, Willington

Defenders
Richard Cook: Langley Park
Keith Brown: Blyth Spartans, Bishop Auckland, Gateshead
Paul Stout: Grimsby Town
Gavin Liddle: Durham City, Seaham Red Star, Gateshead, Spennymoor Utd, Darlington (33-1)
Billy Park: Swalwell
John Thompson: Whitley Bay, Rossendale Utd, Bury, Newcastle United
Steve Dixon: Gateshead, Berwick Rangers, Blyth Spartans, Blue Star

Midfield
John McMahon: Guisborough Town, Darlington (4)
Martyn Angus: Middlesborough

Warren Teasdale: Morpeth Town
Willie Moat: Swalwell
Dean Gibb: Westerhope C.C. Juniors

Forwards
Neil Howie: Chester-Le-Street
Steve Herczeg: Murton C.W., Durham City, Whickham
Bryan Jennings: Whickham
Craig Gordon: Coundon T.T.
David Hawker: Bishop Auckland, Darlington (84-2), Hull City (33-2)

CHESTER-LE-STREET TOWN
Goalkeepers
John Lang: Annfield Plain, Willington, West Auckland, Tow Law, North Shields, Blyth Spartans

Defender
John Hall: Whitley Bay, Guisley
George Davison: North Shields, Murton C.W. Eppleton, Huddersfield Town
Shaun Myers: Ferryhill, West Auckland
Michael Farrey: Whickham
Billy Lisgo: North Shields, Wallsend Town
Jimmy Welch: High Pit, Chester-Le-Street, Town, Washington

Midfield
Brian Wray: Darlington
Dave Houlstone: Guiseley
Alan Hughes: Murton C.W., Blue Star, Spennymoor Utd, Blyth Spartans
Derek Ord: Blyth Spartans, Gateshead, North Shields, Crook Town

Forwards
Simon Docherty: Eppleton C.W.
Colin Howie: Gateshead
Ian Mutrie: North Shields, Blyth Spartans, Ashington, Blyth Spartans
Peter Ward: Local Football

CONSETT
Goalkeepers
Tony Morris: Unshaw Moor, Langley Park
Bobby Crooks: Prudhoe East End, Consett, Langley Park, Crook Town

Defenders
Ian Campbell: Gateshead, Evenwood
Stuart Bell: Annfield Plain
Tim Simpson: Annfield Plain
Gary Best: Local Football
Ian Robb: Local Football

Midfield
David Allen: Annfield Plain
Gary Butler: Annfield Plain
John Kerr: Local Football
Gerald McNamee: Hartlepool Utd (2-1)

Forwards
Gordon Hindson: Gateshead, Blyth Spartans, Consett, Evenwood, Workington, Blackburn Rovers (10), Carlisle Utd (1), Luton Town (63-3), Newcastle United (7-1)
Barry Hirst: Gateshead
Gary Bell: Annfield Plain
Brian Rutledge: Parsons Athletic, Crook Town, Bishop Auckland, Whitley Bay

CROOK TOWN
Goalkeepers
Kevin Youlden: Whitley Bay, Ferryhill
Chris McGuiness: S.C. Vaux

Defenders
Colin Barker: Ferryhill, Shildon, Tow Law
Peter Gardiner: Shildon, West Auckland
Harry Wilson: Hartlepool Utd (16), Darlington (82), Preston North End (36) Brighton (130-4), Burnley (10)
Steward Bainbridge: West Auckland, Evenwood
Kenny Hills: Bishop Auckland, Tow Law, Gateshead

Midfield
Gary Whetter: Teeside Polytechnic
Tony Swainston: Cleveland Bridge
Andy Fothergill: Torrington F.C.
Tony Metcalfe: Cleveland Bridge
Andy Johnson: Local Football

Forwards
Gerald Dobson: Ferryhill, Evenwood, West Auckland, Shildon
Tony Mason: Ferryhill
Steve Weldon: Evenwood, Willington, Shildon
Dennis Foster: Spennymoor Utd, Bishop Auckland, West Auckland

EASINGTON COLLIERY
Goalkeepers
Eddie Guy: Ryhope C.W.

Defenders
Alan Jones: Spennymoor Utd, South Bank, Whitby Town
Stephen Johnson: Peterlee, Durham City
Brian Pilkington: North Shields, Ashington, Blue Star
Trevor Beeston: Peterlee, Wingate, Horden C.W. Shotton Comrades
Alan Cowan: Shildon, Shotton Comrades

Midfield
Hugh Hutton: Colchester United
Les Tatum: South Shields
David Tate: Dawdon C.W., South Shields Boldon C.A.
John Bulley: Billingham Synthonia
Tony Maggiore: Chester-Le-Street, Blue Star, Workington, Hartlepool Utd (24)

Forwards
Chris Cain: Dawdon, C.W., Horden, C.W., Shotton Comrades
Paul O'Connor: South Shields
Paul Pitman: Billingham Town, Wingate
Gerry Hogan: Chester-Le-Street, Horden C.W., Blyth Spartans, Horden C.W.
David Howard: Crook Town, Hartlepool Utd (6-4), Newcastle Utd

FERRYHILL ATHLETIC
Goalkeepers
Ivan Wood: Willington, Durham City
Kevin Summer: S.C. Vaux, Durham, Ryhope C.W.

Defenders
Michael Vasey: Local football
Kevin Gillham: Ferryhill Juniors
Chris Sanders: Darlington (20)
Kenny Goodrick: Hartlepool BWOB
Colin Hallimond: Evenwood, Crook Town, Shildon, Brandon United, Evenwood

Midfield
Derek Aylesbury: Horden C.W. Durham City
Michael Seymour: Ferryhill Juniors
David Huntley: Wingate
Kevin Hallimond: Shildon Utd, Evenwood
Gary Cowell: Ferryhill Juniors

Forwards
Colin Marshall: Eppleton, Gateshead, Blyth Spartans, Durham City
Geoff Hart: Durham City, Blyth Spartans, Spennymoor Utd
Gary Markwell: Ferryhill Black/Decker
David Brand: Durham City
Lance Jopling: Gateshead, Reyrolles

GRETNA
Goalkeepers
Jonathon Rush: Workington, Carlisle Utd, Blackpool (11)
Bob Halbert: Ryhope C.A., Brandon Utd, Bedlington, Durham City, Blyth Spartans, Blue Star, Bishop Auckland.

Defenders
Ian Wilson: Workington, Penrith, Carlisle City
Gary Watson: Penrith, Carlisle City
Michael Currah: Evenwood, Penrith
Jeff Wright: Wark, Prudhoe East End, Wigan Athletic (139-19), Tow Law

Midfield
David Donaghue: Penrith, Carlisle City
David Taylor: Carslisle Cith, Penrith

Gerry Hogan slips the ball past visiting Cleveland Bridge keeper, to score Easington's fourth goal.

Gordon Dick: Penrith, Stirling Albion, Preston North End
Ian Potts: Blue Star, Peterlee, South Shields
Tony Monaghan: Carlisle City

Forwards
Ian Candlish: Wark, Prudhoe, Workington, Carlisle Utd.
Laurence Hardwick: Ponteland Utd.
Paul Heron: Hartlepool Utd, Whickham, Crook Town
Willie Armstrong: Penrith, Carlisle Utd
Geoff Simpson: Penrith, Carlisle City
Graham Mossop: Workington, Penrith, Carlisle Utd (2), Workington (1)

HARTLEPOOL UNITED (RESERVES)
Goalkeepers
Stuart Wilson: Horden C.W., Blue Star, Horden C.W.
Kenny Dodds: Gateshead

Defenders
Keith Nobbs: Bishop Auckland, Halifax Town (87-1), Middlesborough (1)
John Collogly: Whitby Town, Guisborough Town, Hartlepool Utd
Mark Taylor: Heary Smiths
David Linighan: Wingate
David Robinson: Local football

Midfield
Alan Little: Halifax Town (27-3), Torquay Utd (51-4), Doncaster Rov. (84-11), Barnsley (91-4), Southend (102-12), A. Villa (2)
Marty Hewitt: Junior football
Paul Proudlock: Junior football
Michael Smithies: Junior football

Forwards
Kevin Dixon: Darlington (loan), Carlisle Utd (5), Tow Law
Paul Dobson: Horden C.W., Hartlepool Utd (50-20)
John Borthwick: Owton MSC
Bob Newton: Chestefield (33-14), Port Vale (48-22), Hartlepool Utd (150-48), Huddersfield Town (37-7)

NORTH SHIELDS
Goalkeepers
David Burnett: Eppleton
Trevor Ramshaw: Gateshead, Durham, Blue Star, Hartlepool Utd

Defenders
Davie Steedman: Berwick Rangers, Stirling Albion, Hibs
Tim Gilbert: Darlington (62-3), Cardiff City (33-1), Sunderland (34-3)
John Robertson: Eppleton, Morpeth Town, Bishop Auckland, Percy Main
Dick Longstaffe: Whickham, Crook Town, Tow Law, Sunderland, Newcastle Utd
Paul Hedley: Blyth Spartans, South Shields, Whitley Bay, North Shields

Midfield
Dave Fairless: Consett, Tow Law
Ian Smith: Bishop Auckland
Dave Johnson: Chester-Le-Street, Bishop Auckland, Horden, C.W. North Shields, Annfield Plain
Martin Hamilton: Eppleton
Billy Johnson: Brandon United

Forwards
Micky Taylor: Blyth Spartans, South Shields, Whitley Bay
Keith Mills: Newcastle Turbinia F.C.
Kevin Blair: Tow Law, Bishop Auckland
Howard Smith: Ashington, High Pit, York R.I., Appleby Frodingham
Bobby Doig: South Shields, Percy Main, Blyth Spartans, Wallsend Town
Paul Robson: Percy Main, West Allotment Celtic, Bedlington Terriers, Whitley Bay, Percy Main
Steve McKenna: Alcan Lynemouth, Stobswood Welfare

PETERLEE NEWTOWN
Goalkeepers
Graeme Richardson: Easington, Hartlepool Utd (89)
Trevor Dixon-Cave: Consett, Spennymoor Utd, Horden C.W., Blue Star, Brandon Utd

Defenders
Graham Smith: Whitby Town, Shotton Comrades
Terry Bainbridge: Hartlepool Utd (34-1)
Carl Paylor: Shildon, Norton and Stockton Ancients, Guisborough Town
Darren Ellis: Local football
Gordon Huntingdon: Horden C.W., Seaham Red Star, Gateshead

Midfield
Paul McArdle: Spennymoor Utd, Consett, Evenwood
Kenny Charlton: South Bank, Shildon
Tony Lyons: Middlesbrough
Brian Lewins: Easington, Shotton Comrades
Dave Callaghan: Blue Star, Blyth Spartans, Blue Star, Spennymoor Utd

Forwards
Gordon Larkin; Blyth Spartans, Hartlepool Utd (5-1)
John Langridge: Hordon C.W., Easington, Blyth Spartans, Hartlepool Utd (5)
Ian Henderson; Seaham Red Star, Ferryhill, Durham City, Eppleton
Stephen Fairless: Horden C.W., Spennymoor Utd
Dave Evans: Blue Star, Horden C.W., Hartlepool Utd (2)

RYHOPE COMMUNITY ASSOCIATION
Goalkeepers
Rob Strong: Seaham Red Star

Defenders
John Burrell: Boldon C.A.
Jeff Wilson: Darlington (10)

Jimmy Usher: Ryhope C.W.
Stephen Moore: Seaham Red Star
Stephen Collins: Blyth Spartans

Midfield
Ray Banks: North Shields, South Shields
John Honour: Chester-Le-Street, Blue Star, Horden, C.W., Workington (38-1) West Bromwich Albion, Hartlepool Utd (107-8)
Geoff Langley: Gateshead, Bolton Wanderers (3)
Paul Carr: Sunderland Pyrex
Gary Cowley: Blyth Spartans

Forwards
Colin Cowan: Boldon C.A.
Peter Harding: Durham City
Jeff Simpson: Boldon C.A.
John Capewell: Reyrolles
Geoff Carver: Gateshead, NEI Parsons Athletic, Whitley Bay

SOUTH BANK
Goalkeepers
Maurice Gormley: St. George Budapest (Aust), Middlesbrough
Steve Toth: Whinney Banks

Defenders
Tony Lynch: Whinney Banks
Gerald Hartley: Stockton Town
Kevin Tayor: Whinney Banks
Ray Robinson: Billingham Town, South Bank, Guisborough Town, Whitby Town
Tony Escritt: Whitby Town, Guisborough Town

Midfield
Paul Burton: Shildon
Barney Malone: Whinney Banks, Guisborough Town
Martin McQuade: Stockton
Michael Howley: Peterlee Newtown, Billingham Synthonia, Guisborough Town
Neil Roberts: Billingham Town

Forwards
Geoff Lilley: Whitby Town, Nottingham Forest
Ronnie Sills: Whitby Town, Guisborough Town, South Bank, Whitby Town
Tommy Connor: Horden C.W.
Tony Boylan: Blyth Spartans, Scarborough, Bishop Auckland, Hartlepool Utd (11), Bishop Auckland
Mark Gatenby: Adelaide City (Aust), Stockton, Whitby Town
Charlie Butler: Stockton, Whitby Town

SPENNYMOOR UNITED
Goalkeepers
Kelvin Ross: Consett, Gateshead, Ferryhill, Grimsby Town
Damien Boyd: North Shields, Percy Main

Defenders:
Paul Gibbon: Peterlee Newtown, Brandon Utd
Marc Irwin: Gateshead
Robin Gill: West Auckland
Michael Heathcote: Middlesbrough
Garry Lowes: Junior football

Midfield
Tommy Mason: Berwick Rangers, Tow Law
Andy Walker: Junior Football
Steve Storey: Tow Law, North Shields
Ian Mohan: Ferryhill, Evenwood, Willington
Arthur Graham: Junior Football

Forwards
Barrie Fowler: Consett, Evenwood,
Paul Sheekey: Consett, Evenwood, Workington
Wayne Dobson: Gateshead
Paul Haley: Tow Law
Glen Dixon: Reserves

TOW LAW TOWN
Goalkeepers
Tony Gibson: Eppleton, Seaton Terrace, Dudley, Welfare

Defenders
Michael Haley: New Kyo
Peter Richardson: Wallsend Town
John Weatheritt: Gateshead
Steve Webb: Local football
John Housego; New Kyo

Midfield
Stefan Ross: Wallsend Town
Kenneth Carr: Heaton Stannington
Paul Bryson: Crook Town, Spennymoor Utd
Danny Wheatley: Whiley Bay, Blyth Spartans
Kevin Campbell: New Hartley Juniors

Forwards
Michael Dunleavy: Washington, Bishop Auckland
Kevin Gibson: Percy Main
Steve Turner: Marine Park
Steve Wright: South Shields, Alnwick Town, Whitley Bay, North Shields

WHITBY TOWN
Goalkeepers
David Harvey: Bradford City (6), Leeds United (73), Vancouver Whitecaps, Leeds United, Vancouver Wiltecaps, Leeds United (276)
Wayne Baker: Matlock Town, Halifax Town

Defenders
Peter Johnson: Chester City (8), Whitby Town, Darlington (89-2), Doncaster Rovers (12), Bristol City (20), Newcastle United (16), Middlesbrough (42)
Paul Dale: North Ormsby Institute
Gordon Rayner: Thackley, Otley Town
Graham Meggitt: Trinity Athletic (Bradford)
Les Scott: Shildon, Guisborough Town
Mick Sell: Stockton

Midfield
Garry Watson: Halifax Town (21), Doncaster Rovers (13), Bradford City (146-13)
Trevor Smith: Hartlepool Utd (30-2), Scarborough, Dartford, Hartlepool (27)
Simon McGovern: Farsley Celtic, Yorkshire Amateurs, Bradford City (1)
Mike Couzens: Pheonix Park, Thackerley

Forwards
Eddie Gray: Leeds United (439-52)
John Black: Goole Town, Scarborough, Bradford City (50-13), Hereford United (8), Wolves (5)
Paul Sharkey: Stockton
Steve Balcolmbe: Leeds United (1-1)
Paul Wellham: Fishburn Park

WHITLEY BAY
Goalkeepers
Kenny McDonald: Wallsend Town
David Marshall: West Allotment Celtic, Blyth Spartans, Whitley Bay

Defenders
Dean Walker: Alnwick Town, North Shields, Scunthorpe Utd (1)
Les Frizzell: Dunston Mechanics
Mark Cass: South Shields
Paul Manderson: Blyth Spartans
Gary Scullion Annfield Plain

Midfield
Alan Weir: Eppleton, Hartlepool Utd (9), Rochdale (96-3), Sunderland (1)
Barry Dunn: Annfield Plain, Seaham Red Star, Darlington (16-4), Preston North End (8-1), Sunderland (16-2), Blue Star, Tow Law
Robert Vincent: Orient (8), Sunderland (1)
Stewart Ferebee: Harrogate Town, Scarborough, York City (7)

Forwards
Bob McKenzie: Annfield Plain, Brandon, Whickham, Willington
Danny Olsen: Ipswich Town
Frank Deverdics: Whickham, Seaton Delaval, Percy Main
Ian Bensley: Local soccer
Paul Ross: Berwick Rangers, North Shields, Blyth Spartans, Dudley Welfar

Bishop Auckland win at Billingham Town (2-0). The home team's defence is under severe pressure. Photo: Leo Hoenig.

Shotton Comrades and Norton & Stockton Ancients draw in a tough F.A. Cup Preliminary Round replay (2-2). The ball seems to have gone into orbit! Photo: Leo Hoenig

Blue Star win at home against Shildon in a league match, the score 4-1. Blue Star's Kevin Todd passes as Gary Park and Graeme Joyce of Shildon look on. Photo: Leo Hoenig

The stand belongs to Billington Synthonia F.C. Photo: Leo Hoenig

VAUX WEARSIDE FOOTBALL LEAGUE

Secretary: M. G. Gordon, 9 Cliffe Park, Seaburn, Sunderland, Tyne & Wear ST6 9NS
Tel: 0783 490414

		P	W	D	F	A	Pts
1	Coundon	34	25	7	72	24	57
2	Murton	34	25	4	70	18	54
3	Wickham	34	22	7	68	23	51
4	Annfield Plain	34	17	9	71	49	43
5.	Sc Vaux	34	19	4	68	49	42
6.	Gateshead Res.	34	18	4	80	49	40
7.	Washington	34	16	8	54	44	40
8.	Marske Utd	34	18	3	70	44	39
9.	Wingate	34	15	8	55	49	38
10.	Eppleton CW	34	16	2	71	54	34
11.	Newton Aycliffe	34	12	5	46	67	29
12.	South Shields	34	9	8	46	60	26
13.	Reyrolles	34	10	6	51	76	26
14.	Roker	34	9	6	48	72	24
15.	Clarke Chapmans	34	7	8	39	62	22
16.	Boldon CA	34	8	5	34	67	21
16.	Dawdon CW	34	7	7	48	94	21
17.	Ryhope CW	34	1	3	21	111	5

As far as the season was concerned; Coundon took the title for the first time in only their fourth season in the League; with a run from the 1st April to the end of the season (six weeks); when they played 18 league games; two semi finals and two Cup Finals; and they completed a treble in winning both the Vaux League Challenge Cup (for the first time) and retained the Monkwearmouth Charity Cup. The fortunes of Murton FC have drastically changed in the past 18 months; after almost going out of existence; and they finished runners up in the League; three points adrift of Coundon. Whickham finished in third spot; and they lost in two Cup Finals to Coundon.

In the Shipowners Cup Final; Eppleton who had beaten both Coundon and Murton on their way to the Final; beat Annfield Plain at Hetton by 2-1 to lift the Cup for the first time since 1948. In the Monkwearmouth Cup Final Coundon travelled toWhickham and won 3-1; and the same two sides contested the Vaux League Cup Final at Coundon; where Coundon won 2-1 after extra time.

In the F.A. Vase Coundon were the Leagues main representative in losing at Tamworth by 4-0; in a replay when looking for a place in the last 16. In the Durham Challenge Cup.; Couldon who had won the trophy in 1984; lost in the semi finals to Spenymoor United from the Northern League by 2-1.

As far as the new season is concerned the League has a new vice-chairman in the form of Billy Gunn from Murton; who succeeds the late Billy Davison who died at the beginning of the year after being associated with the VWL for over 40 years as Club Secretary of Bolton CA.

Two new clubs were elected to the League for the coming season in the form of Hartlepool B.W.O.B. and Herrington CW; and the League will be at its full strength of 20 clubs.

VAUX LEAGUE CHALLENGE CUP

Preliminary Round: Reyrolles 2, Marske 0; Murton 1, Annfield Plain 0

1st Round: Boldon 2, SC Vaux 1; C. Chapmans 1, Dawdon 2; Eppleton 3, Wingate 1; Murton 0, Coundon 2; N. Aycliffe 1, Gateshead 0; Reyrollers 3, Ryhope 0; South Shields 1, Washington 2; Whickham 5, Roker 0.

2nd Round: Wickham 3, Reyrollers 0; Washington 4, Eppleton 3; Boldon 1, Dawdon 2; N. Aycliffe 0, Coundon 4.

Semi-Finals: Whickham 3, Washington 0; Coundon 5, Dawdon 0.

Cup Final: Coundon 2, Whickham 1 (after extra time).

SHIPOWNERS CUP

Preliminary Round: SC Vaux 3, Roker 1; S. Shields 0, Marske 1.

1st Round: Marske 0, Murton 3; C. Chapmans 3, Washington 2; Boldon 1, Dawdon 2; Ryhope 2, Wingate 1; Whickham 0, A. Plain 1; SC Vaux 2, Reyrollers 0; Eppleton 2, Coundon 1.

2nd Round: N. Aycliffe 0, Eppleton 1; C. Chapmans 3, Murton 4; A. Plain 3, SC Vaux 0; Ryhope 1, Dawdon 3.

Semi-Finals: Murton 0, Eppleton 2; Annfield Plain 2, Dawdon 1.

Cup Final: Eppleton 2, Annfield Plain 1 (after extra time)

MONKWEARMOUTH CHARITY CUP

Preliminary Round: Reyrollers 4, Roker 5; SC Vaux 1, Wingate 2.

1st Round: Marske 0, Coundon 2; Wingate 6, Boldon 1; Roker 0, Dawdon 2; Whickham 3, Washington 0; Ryhope 0, Gatehead 2; N. Acyliffe 1, Annfield Plain 4; Murton 3, Eppleton 1; S. Shields 2, C. Chapmans 1.

2nd Round: Coundon 4, Gatehead 3; Dawdon 3, Murton 2; Annfield Plain 1, S. Shields 2; Whickham 3, Wingate 2.

Semi-Finals: Coundon 2, Dawdon 1; Whickham 6, South Sheilds 2.

Cup Final: Whickham 1, Coundon 3.

VAUX WEARSIDE LEAGUE SPONSORSHIP AWARDS 1985-86

Club	Admin. Payt.	League Pl.	High Scorers	Sports mans	Goals Bon	VWL C.C.	Sub Total	+**	Less Cautions	Amount due
Annfield P.	50	85			75		210		19	£191
Boldon CA	50				15		65	+ 11	26	£50
C. Chaps.	50				30		80		19	£61
Coundon	50	400		120	105	100	775		5	£770
Dawdon	50				15	25	90		25	£65
Eppleton CW	50		60	60	90		260		8	£252
Gateshead	50		80		150		280		31	£249
Marske	50				135		185		29	£156
Murton	50	200			150		400		10	£390
N. Aycliffe	50				15		65	+ 18	33	£50
Reyrollers	50				45		95		10	£85
Roker	50				60		110		11	£99
Ryhope	50						50	+ 30	30	£50
S. Shields	50				45		95		16	£79
SC Vaux	50				135		185		11	£174
Washington	50				45	25	120		17	£103
Whickham	50	125			105	50	330		20	£310
Wingate	50			120	60		230		5	£225
Referee Awards	£110						110			£110
Totals	£1,010	£810	£140	£300	£1,275	£200	£3,735	£59	£325	£3,469

Balance to General Account £241

Received fron Vaux Breweries PLC £3,710

+** Adjustment to cautions total for Boldon; N. Aycliffe and Ryhope necessary for Minimum Payment of £50.

ANNFIELD PLAIN (1980)

President: D. Jackson
Secretary: M. H. Lawson
Chairman: J. Peadon
Address & Tel No:
Manager: K. Johnson
Coach: A. Harding
Address & Tel No of ground: Derwent Park, West Road, Annfield Plain
Simple ground directions: On A693 road to Consett, 200 yds west of junction with A6067
No of seats: 20 **Covered accommodation:** 200 **Capacity:** 6,000 **Floodlights:**
Club colours: Claret & Blue/Sky/Claret
Change colours: Sky/Navy/Sky
Previous Leagues: North Eastern
Midweek match day: Monday or Wednesday
Clubhouse details: Small Bar
Local Newspaper(s): Newcastle Journal **Editor:** **Club metal badges:**
Record attendance: 7,200 v Southport F.A. Cup 1st Round proper year 1928
Senior Honours:/Best Performance: Durham Challenge Cup (winners)
Past players (who progressed to Football League): A. Graver (Lincoln) N. Wilkinson (York City) K. Smith (Blackpool) J. Hather (Aberdeen)

COUNDON T.T. (1975)

President
Secretary: Maurice Flint
Chairman: Dennis Donohue
Address & Tel No: Bishop Auckland 601161
Manager: Paul Adams
Commercial Manager: None
Coach: Kevin Rielly
Address & Tel No:
Physiotherapist: J. Johnson
Press Officer & Tel No: Maurice Flint
Address & Tel No of ground: Leeholme School, Leeholme Road, Bishop Auckland
Simple ground directions: From Eden Arms, Rushyford, Bishop Auckland Road (A609), approx 2 miles pass crossroads, turn next right, then left at Welfare Hall about 300 yards behind Co-op
No of seats: None **Covered accommodation:** None **Capacity:** 2,000 **Floodlights:** No
Year formed: 1975 **Nickname:** None **Club sponsors:** None
Club colours: Red
Change colours: Blue
Previous Names: None
Previous Grounds: None
Record attendance: 800 **Year:**
Previous Leagues: Auckland District, Durham District
Programme: Price/Pages None
Clubhouse details: None
Major Honours: Auckland League 1977, 1978, 1979, 1980; Auckland Charity Winners 1979, 1981, 1982; Durham District 1981, 1982; (2), Durham Trophy Winners 1981, Durham Minor Cup 1979, Weardale Cup 1977, Durham Hospital 1979, 1982; Auckland League Cup 1978, 1979; Durham League Cup 1981, 1982; Brancepeth Cup 1979, 1980, 1981, 1982, Shipowners Cup 1984, Durham Challenge 1984, Monkwearmouth 1985
Club Captain (1984-85): John Wren
Player of the Year (1984-85): D. Wood

DAWDON C.W.F.C.

President:
Secretary: R. Pigg
Chairman: T. Dale
Address & Tel No:
Manager: J. Dixon
Coach: C. Cain
Commercial Manager:
Address & Tel No of ground: Dawdon, Seaham
Simple ground directions: Get on the A19 from either North or South, look for Seaham turn off, then head for Dawdon
No of seats: None **Covered accommodation:** 100 **Capacity:** 3,000 **Floodlights:** No
Local Newspaper(s): Sunderland Echo **Editor:** N. Kelly **Club metal badges:** None
Clubhouse details: None
Club colours: Claret/Blue, Claret shorts
Change colours: Yellow and Black shorts
Previous Leagues: Washington Savecentre, Houghton/District
Record attendance: 2,500 League Cup, Final v Eppleton 1984/85
Senior Honours:/Best Performance: Vaux League Cup Winners 1984/85. Reached semi finals in tree cups 1985/86 - Monkwearmouth Charity Shipowners Vaux League Cup
Past players (who progressed to Football League): None
Midweek match day: Monday/Wednesday

GATESHEAD CLARKE CHAPMAN

President: J. F. Howey
Secretary: G. T. Castlehow
Chairman: L. Crossley
Address & Tel No: 53 Burnhope Road, Barmston Village, Washington, Tyne & Wear NE38 8DZ. 091 4160106 (H), 091 2843191 (B)
Manager: J. Wales
Asst. Manager: W. Skelly
Physiotherapist: W. Thompson
Commercial Manager:
Address & Tel No of ground: Clarke Chapmans Sports Ground, Old Fold, Gateshead. (091 4782555/4781220)
Simple ground directions: A19/AIM take A6115 (Felling By-pass) towards Gateshead/Newcastle, turn left at traffic lights, next to International Stadium, Ground approx 100 yards on right
Year formed: 1949 **Nickname:** Clarkie's **Club sponsors:** NEI Clarke Chapman Ltd
Club colours: Red/Black/Red
Change colours: All Sky Blue
Previous Leagues: Northern Combination, Washington Amateur, Northern Amateur
Midweek match evening: Monday or Wednesday
Club metal badges: No
Clubhouse details: Run by NEI Clarke Chapman Sports & Social Club. Bar, lounge, games room, separate dance hall with bar.
Major Honours: Washington Amateur League, Gateshead Charity Cup (2), Heddon Homes Charity Cup
Club Captain (1984-85): M. Williamson
Player of the Year (1984-85): G. Reed

GATESHEAD RESERVES

Club details can be found in the GM Vauxhall Conference Section

HARTLEPOOL BWOB (1953)

President: Mr. E. Morley M.B.E.
Secretary: G. Henderson 0429 (264199)
Chairman: Mr. C. Bailey
Manager: B. Hall
Address & Tel No of ground: Grayfields
Capacity: 1500 **Covered accommodation:** No **Seating:** None **Floodlights:** None
Simple ground directions: Off A19 down A689, right at roundabout, right at Warren Service St., ground 100yds down on right.
Clubhouse details:
Programme details: **Editor:** **Club metal badges:**
Local Newspaper(s): Hartlepool Mail
Club Colours: White/Blue
Change colours: Red/White
Record attendance:
Midweek match day:
Previous Leagues: Hartlepool Church/Hartlepool District Teeside
Senior Honours:/Best Performance: F.A. Vase Round 3
Past players (who progressed to Football League): A. Walsh, Midd Darlington Bristol City current

HEBBURN REYROLLE

President: None
Chairman: J. Minto
Manager: Brian Hudson
Ass. Man/Coach: B. Errington
Physiotherapist: None
Secretary: J. Baker
Address & Tel No: 88 Cherwell, Washington, Tyne & Wear NE37 3LD. 832441 (H), 471033 (B)
Commercial Manager: None
Address & Tel No:
Press Officer & Tel No: Secretary
Address & Tel No of ground: Reyolle Sports Ground, Victoria Road West, Hebburn, Tyne & Wear
Simple ground directions: Next to the works on Victoria Road West, Hebburn
No of seats: 100 **Ground accommodations:** 2,000 **Capacity:** 2,000 **Floodlights:** No
Club colours: Blue & White stripes/Black/Blue
Change colours: Yellow
Previous Names: None
Previous Grounds: None
Record attendance: None
Previous Grounds: None
Record attendance: Not known
Mid-week match evening: Monday or Wednesday
Previous Leagues: Tyneside, Northern Combination, North Easton
Clubhouse details: None yet
Major Honours: Northern Combination, Wearside League, Monkwearmouth Charity Cup
Club Captain (1984-85): B. Hudson
Player of the Year (1984-85): K. Edgar

MARSKE UNITED (1956)

President: R. Jarvis
Secretary: G. J. Baldry
Chairman: J. M. Hodgson
Manager: D. Walker
Address & Tel No of ground:
Capacity: 1,000 **Covered accommodation:** None **Seating:** None **Floodlights:** None
Simple ground directions: A19 to Teesport, Redcar turn off, A174 to Marske.
Clubhouse details: Clubhouse with bar, lounge and full kitchen facilities.
Programme details: Every home game since '82' **Editor:** J. M. Hodgson **Club metal badges:**
Local Newspaper(s): Sunday Sun, Northern Echo, Middlesbrough Evening Gazette
Club colours: Yellow shirts, Blue Shorts, White socks
Change colours: All Red
Record Attendance: 600 approx.
Midweek match day: Wednesday
Previous Leagues: Cleveland League, South Bank & District, Teesside League
Senior Honours:/Best Performance: North Riding County Cup Winner 84-85
Best players (who progressed to Football League): Peter Beagrie (Middlesbrough), Dave Logan (Mansfield)

MURTON F.C.

President: J. Toft
Chairman: T. Torrence
Manager: R. Young
Asst. Man/Coach: F. Hissett
Physiotherapist: H. Robson
Managing Director: W. Harrison
Address & Tel No: 83 Toft Crescent, Murton, Seaham, Co. Durham (261891)
Address & Tel No of ground: Murton Park, Church Lane, Murton **Club Shop:** Yes
Simple ground directions: A19 to Murton
Capacity: 4,000
Programme Editor: A. Martin (265037)
Mid-week match evening: Wednesday
Club metl badges: No
Best performance in: F.A. Cup: 4th Qual Round
Record attendance: 5,000 v Sunderland, 1934
Sponsors:
Club colours: All White
Change colours: All Red
Previous League: North Eastern
Present players with Football League experience: R. Young
Past players who progressed into the Football League: 11
Clubhouse details: Murton Democratic Club. Bar, concert room, games room,
Club Captain (1984-85): D. Smith
Player of the Year (1984-85): I. Harrison

NEWTON AYCLIFFE

President:
Secretary: Arthur Crook
Chairman: Mike Fox
Address & Tel No:
Address & Tel No of ground: Vista Park, Vista Road, Newton Le Willows
Capacity: **Covered accommodation:** 300 **Seating:** 150 **Floodlights:** No
Simple ground directions: M6 Junction 23, A49 to Newton Le Willows
Clubhouse:
Club colours: Red Shirts/Black Shorts **Change colours:** Blue Shirts & Shorts
Programme: Yes
Honours:/Previous Leagues:

ROKER

President: Mr. M. Docherty
Secretary: D. R. Worthy
Chairman: T. Middlemist
Manager: L. Dodd
Address & Tel No of ground: Silksworth Recreation Park
Capacity: 2,000 **Covered accommodation:** None **Seating:** None **Floodlights:** Yes
Simple ground directions:
Clubhouse details:
Programme details: Match Day Publication **Editor:** J. Nicholson **Club metal badges:** No
Local Newspaper(s): Sunderland Echo
Club colours: Red White Stripes/Black Shorts **Change colours:** All Navy Blue
Record attendance: **Midweek match day:** Tuesday
Previous Leagues:
Senior Honours:/Best Performance:
Past players (who progressed to Football League): Paul Rutherford (Newcastle)

RYHOPE COLLIERY WELFARE

(Founded: 1956 as Ryhope Blue Star, also known as Ryhope Villa)

President: Russell Foster
Secretary: George Broadbent
Chairman: Peter Vincent
Manager: Paul Teasdale
Address & Tel No of ground: Ryhope Recreation Park, Ryhope, Sunderland. Wearside (091) 521 2843
Capacity: 2,000 **Covered accommodation:** None **Seating:** None **Floodlights:** Yes
Simple ground directions: By Road: On B1286 at Brick Row, Ryhope By Bus: 139, 140, 141, 142
Clubhouse details: Open every evening 7.00 p.m. until 10.30 p.m. Open Saturday midday to 3.00 p.m. and Sunday midday until 2.00 p.m.
Programme details: Programme free with entrance fee of 40p
Editor: Julie Errington **Club metal badges:** None
Local Newspaper(s): Sunderland Echo; Evening Chronicle; The Journal; Sunday Sun
Club colours: Amber/Black **Change colours:** Green/Amber
Record attendance: 1,600 vs Workington **Midweek match day:** Wednesday
Previous Leagues: Houghton and District League
Senior Honours/Best Performance: Wearside League Champions: 1962; 1963; 1964; 1966. Wearside League Cup Winners: 1964; 1978. Durham Challenge Cup Winners: 1978. Monkwearmouth Charity Cup Winners: 1966; 1967. Shipowners Cup Winners: 1962. Best F.A. Cup Performance: 1st round proper 1967/68. Best F.A. Vase Performance: 1st round proper 1981/82.
Past players (who progressed to Football League): Alan Harding — Lincoln City, Darlington, Hartlepool United. Kenny Ellis — Hartlepool, Darlington, Belguim Clubs. Kenny Mitchell — Professional Club in Iceland. Robert Malt — Leeds United. Brian Smiles — Chelsea.

SPORTING CLUB VAUX (1968)
(formerly Bishopwearmouth)

President: Frank Nicholson (Vaux Brewery)
Secretary: Trevor Whitehead 285366
Chairman: Robert Forster
Manager: Anthony Clark
Address & Tel No of ground: Glenesk Road 227750
Capacity: 1,000 **Covered accommodation:** None **Seating:** None **Floodlights:** None
Simple ground directions: From Sunderland Town centre, take A19 to Grangetown, turn right at Leechmere Road, ground two miles on right.
Clubhouse details: Bridge End Social Club
Programme details: 10 page programme 30p on entry **Editor:** George Hunter **Club metal badges:** None
Local Newspaper(s): Sunderland Echo
Club colours: All Red **Change colours:** All Yellow
Record attendance: 500 **Midweek match day:** Monday/Wednesday
Previous Leagues: North Eastern Amateur League
Senior Honours:/Best Performance: Champions & Cup Winners — Neal. Semi-final v Spennymoor (Ourham Challenge Cup)
Past players (who progressed to Football League): Nigel Saddington — Sunderland. Ronnie Robinson — Leeds Utd. (current)

SOUTH SHIELDS

President:
Secretary: Ian Joice (091) 2653567
Chairman: John Rundle
Manager: John Sayers
Address & Tel No of ground: Jack Clark Park, Horsley Hill Road, South Shields
Capacity: 2,000 **Covered accommodation:** None **Seating:** None **Floodlights:** No
Simple ground directions: Quarter mile east of Ingham Infirmary
Clubhouse details:
Programme details: Free 8 pages **Editor:** R. Butler **Club metal badges:** Yes
Local Newspaper(s): Shield Gazette, Newcastle Journal
Club colours: White/Black/Black **Change colours:** Orange/Black/Orange
Record attendance: 1,500 v Brigg Town 1976 **Midweek match day:** Monday/Wednesday
Previous Leagues:
Senior Honours:/Best Performance: Quarter Final F.A. Vase 1976. Champions Northern Football Alliance 1974-5, 75-6. Champions Vaux Wearside League 1976-77. Durham Challenge Cup Winners 1976-77.
Past players (who progressed to Football League):

President: R. Ducker
Secretary: G. W. Abbott
Manager: W. Blevins
Manager: T. Boylen
Address & Tel No of ground: Albany Park. Wash. 4177779
Capacity: 3,000 **Covered accommodation:** None **Seating:** None **Floodlights:** None
Simple ground directions:
Clubhouse details: Social Club within ground
Programme details: Six page weekly **Editor:** Secretary **Club metal badges:** None
Local Newspaper(s): S/land Echo. N/cle Chronicle
Club colours: Green/Yellow **Change colours:** Yellow/Green
Record attendance: 3,000 vs Bradford City **Midweek match day:** Monday/Wednesday
Previous Leagues: Northern Alliance. Wash. AM. League
Senior Honours:/Best Performance: Wash. League Winners eight times in succession. (Record)
Past players (who progressed to Football League): None

WHICKHAM

President:
Secretary: J. J. Gilbert
Chairman: A. Hutchinson
Manager: W. Hodgson
Address & Tel No of ground:
Capacity: 5,000 **Covered accommodation:** None **Seating:** None **Floodlights:** None
Simple ground directions: Bus from Marlbough Crescent Newcastle or Gateshead Metro Station to Rose & Crown Whickham Ground approx. 300 yds up Rectory Lane.
Clubhouse details: Glebe Sports Club
Programme details: Weekly **Editor:** G. Lamb **Club metal badges:** No
Local Newspaper(s): Newcastle Journal; Evening Chronicle; Gateshead Post
Club colours: Black & White Stripes **Change colours:** Red & White
Record attendance: 4,890 **Midweek match day:** Monday/Wednesday
Previous Leagues: Northern Combination
Senior Honours:/Best Performance: 1981 F.A. Vase Winners. Wembley losing 2-0 against Willenhall FC and Winning 3-2 at extra time.
Past players (who progresses to Football League): Fred Esle — Blackburn and Preston North End. Rocky Hudson, Newcastle Utd now playing in America. Nigel Walker, Newcastle utd now at Hartlepool Utd.

WINGATE

President: To be appointed
Secretary: Richard Hayes
Chairman: Tom Lenehan
Manager: John Hope
Address & Tel No of ground: Wingate Welfare Park, Wingate Co. Durham. Tel. Wellfield (0429) 838318 (clubhouse)
Capacity: 5,000 **Covered accommodation:** 250 **Seating:** None **Floodlights:** Yes
Simple ground directions: On B1280 turn at Queens Head Public House on Front Street, Wingate. Ground approx. 400 yds west, through housing estate.
Clubhouse details: Bar and lounge open evenings, Sat/Sun afternoons, Entertainment and Bar meals at weekends
Programme details: 16-20pps. 15p **Editor:** Secretary **Club metal badges:** No
Local Newspaper(s): Northern Echo, Hartlepool Mail, Sunderland Echo, Peterlee Times
Club colours: Silver Grey Shirts/Black Shorts **Change colours:** All Red
Record attendance: Not known **Midweek match day:** Wednesday
Previous Leagues: Hartlepool District
Senior Honours:/Best Performance: Monkwearmouth Charity Cup Winners 1978, 1984. Wearside League Runners Up 1979. Durham Challenge Cup Runners Up 1973
Past players (who progressed to Football League):

Two Washington defenders put their best foot forward to clear a Wingate attack. *Photo: Leo Hoenig*

Sporting Club Vaux

TEESIDE LEAGUE

	P	W	D	L	F	A	Pts
Hartlepool BWOB	34	30	3	1	100	31	63
Wolviston	34	20	8	6	77	44	48
Dormans Athletic	34	21	3	10	69	49	45
Tees Components	34	18	8	8	65	50	44
Cassel Works	34	16	9	9	69	46	41
I.C.I. Wilton	34	16	8	10	70	44	40
Hemlington S.C.	34	17	4	13	66	56	38
Scarborough Ath.	34	15	7	12	72	63	37
North Ormesby In. ...	34	14	6	14	64	62	34
Eastfield	34	14	5	15	70	74	33
Stockton Town	34	12	7	15	56	60	31
Smiths Dock	34	13	4	17	45	53	30
Teesside Poly.	34	10	9	15	44	55	29
Nunthorpe Ath.	34	9	10	15	38	45	28
Acklam Steelworks ...	34	8	6	20	50	80	22
Darlington Rail. Ath.	34	5	11	18	35	76	21
Fishburn Park	34	5	6	23	43	87	16
New Marske S.C.	34	2	8	24	37	95	12

Champions: Hartlepool B.W.O.B.
Runners-Up: Wolviston
Re-Election: Fishburn Park and New Marske S.C.
Macmillan Bowl Final:
I.C.I Wilton 2, Stockton Town 1
Scarborough Floodlit Trophy Final:
Fishburn Park 3, Filey Town 2

TEESIDE FOOTBALL LEAGUE CLUBS LEADING SCORERS - 1985/86

ACKLAM STEELWORKS J. Glence 22 (10 for Nunthorpe Ath), K. Mahoney 7, J. Woods 7.
CASSEL WORKS P. Lawrence 14, J. Hurren 13, C. Clare 8, C. Barnes 7.
DARLINGTON R.A. J. Robson 6, M. Ingleby 5.
DORMANS ATH: F. McGee 22, C. Bishop 17, D. McElvaney 9, P. Singh 8.
EASTFIELD J. Binnie 18 (8 for Scarborough Ath.), C. Salt 16, I. Hare 8, J. Jordon 7.
FISHBURN PARK S. Barron 6, I. Landers 5.
HARTLEPOOL B.W.O.B. K. Wright 34, S. Salvin 16, A. Hewitt 9, N. Lester 9.
HEMLINGTON S.C. R. Walker 14, D. Chisman 12, M. Gott 10, C. Graham 7.
I.C.I. WILTON P. Goldison 14, G. Briggs 9, R. Hadfield 8, G. Steel 7.
NEW MARSKE S.C. M. Peacock 8, B. Peacock 7, T. Bailey 5.
NORTH ORMESBY INSTITUTE B. Murgatroyd 7, G. Knight 6, G. Blyth 6.
NUNTHORPE ATH R. Thomas 9, S. Bivens 5.
SCARBOROUGH ATH S. French 18, S. Wood 10, G. Bowman 6, L. Cooper 6.
SMITHS DOCK T. Noteyoung 16, K. Robinson 6.
STOCKTON TOWN K. Whitehouse 14, V. Jaques 10, C. Abel 8 (5 for Cassel Works), P. Graham 8.
TEES COMPONENTS J. Hemlin 17, P. Kennedy 11, G. Playforth 8.
TEESSIDE POLYTECHNIC M. Riley 12, M. Najah 11.
WOLVISTON P. Simpson 21, B. Kleinee 16, J. Sutheran 9, K. Hamilton 8.

TRESSIDE LEAGUE
MACMILLAN BOWL
PRELIMINARY ROUND
Cassel Works 3 v 1 Fishburn Park (Whitby)
Dormans Athletic 4 v 3 Teesside Polytechnic

1st Round Cassel Works 3 v 0 Nunthorpe Athletic (A.E.T.)
Dormans Athletic 1 v 0 North Ormesby Institute
Eastfield (Scarborough) 2 v 1 Darlington R.A. (A.E.T.)
Hartlepool B.W.O.B. 0 v 1 I.C.I. Wilton
Hemlington S.C. 1 v 2 Stockton Town
Scarborough Athletic 6 v 1 Acklam Steelworks
Smiths Dock 2 v 0 New Marske S.C.
Wolviston 2 v 0 Tees Components

2nd Round Dormans Athletic 2 v 3 Smiths Dock (aet)
I.C.I. Wilton 1 v 0 Scarborough Athletic
Stockton Town 5 v 0 Eastfield
Wolviston 1 v 2 Cassel Works

Semi Finals Cassel Works 2 v 3 I.C.I. Wilton, Smiths Dock 1 v 2 Stockton Town.

Final I.C.I. Wilton 2 v 4 Stockton Town.

McEWANS NORTHERN ALLIANCE

	P	W	D	F	A	Pts
Gateshead Tyne	30	21	6	80	37	48
Prudhoe E. End	30	17	9	68	38	43
Morpeth Town	30	16	6	51	39	38
Ninlaton Qu. Head	30	12	11	53	40	35
West Allotment	30	12	8	48	36	32
Wigton	30	10	12	58	48	32
Seaton Terrace	30	11	9	56	54	31
Seaton Delaval	30	12	6	54	61	30
Carlisle City	30	13	3	50	56	29
Ponteland Utd	30	11	6	48	49	28
Dudley Welfare	30	11	6	52	57	28
Forest Hall	30	9	8	56	55	26
Percy Main	30	10	5	68	69	25
Gosforth St. Nich.	30	7	10	42	51	24
Wallsend Town	30	4	8	40	81	16
Stubswood Welfare	30	4	7	37	90	15

McEWANS NORTHERN COMBINATION LEAGUE

	P	W	D	L	F	A	Pts
Swalwell	26	22	1	3	88	21	45
Dunston Mechanics	26	17	7	2	66	32	41
Benwell Blues	26	16	7	3	70	27	39
Wark	26	14	7	5	51	41	35
N/c Turbinia	26	14	5	7	63	30	33
Haltwhistle C P	26	8	8	10	45	48	24
N/c University	26	10	4	12	41	47	24
Parsons Athletic	26	8	6	12	41	53	22
Northern SC	26	8	5	13	33	59	21
Winlaton Hallgarth	26	6	7	13	40	61	19
Wallsend Rising Sun	26	6	5	14	30	58	17
Ryton	26	7	3	16	44	74	17
Alcan Lynemouth	26	5	5	16	47	64	15
New York	26	2	8	16	29	73	12

McEWANS NORTHERN AMATEUR LEAGUE

	P	W	D	L	F	A	Pts
Heaton Stanngton	30	25	1	4	66	25	51
KOSA	30	18	7	5	78	32	45
Newbiggin CW	30	19	4	7	61	41	42
Lobley Hill	30	17	4	9	53	40	38
Belford	30	14	8	8	61	48	36
Longbenton LC	30	14	7	9	67	50	35
Leam Lane SC	30	16	2	12	75	70	34
NEERC	30	11	7	12	71	61	29
Gosforth Bohemians	30	11	7	12	57	52	29
Whitley Bay Res	30	11	3	16	52	64	25
Annitsford Welfare	30	9	6	15	47	65	24
Proctor & Gamble	30	9	6	15	45	65	24
Northern Co's OB	30	11	6	13	49	68	23
Ashington Buffs	30	9	3	18	69	78	20
Marden Athletic	30	5	7	18	42	73	14
Routefinder	30	5	3	22	45	103	13

COUNTY CUP COMPETITIONS 1985-86

This new County Cup Section should prove to be very popular indeed and my thanks go to Leo Hoenig who cheerfully took on the job of compilation with the help of the excellent 'Bureau of Non League Football'. In future years we may even extend this feature! T.W.

Introduction to County Cups Section

In order to improve readability, the County Cup results are now being given a section on their own, rather than being placed at the end of each of the regional league sections; County Cup formats, and their importance vary considerably from County to County, according to which teams enter the competition, and the level of importance they themselves place on the competitions - for many of the clubs in the major leagues, County Cups are a hinderence to a fixture list already complicated by National involvement in the FA Cup and Trophy, and their league cups. Some clubs, field weakened sides in the County Cups, but others (probably still a majority) still field their full first XIs in all matches, and hence maintain the importance and prestige of these often ancient competitions.

Some County's still insist that matches are played on Saturdays, even when both clubs in a match have floodlights, and would prefer to play the fixtures in mid-week; often mid-week matches for these comparitively local ties can attract crowds far larger than on a Saturday.

The results in this section may appear to be unevenly edited - this is not due to our own intention, but to the comparitive difficulties of obtaining and compiling the results. We must acknowledge the work done in this field by the Bureau of Non League Football, and where this magazine has been able to complile complete results of a competition, they are repeated here, hence if your areas cup has been missed out, the best solution would be to ensure that they are sent to the Bureau at 173, Leytonstone Road, London E15.

Leo Hoenig.

Bedfordshire Senior Cup

Preliminary Round	*Score*
Ampthill v Dunstable	0-2
Ashcroft Co-Op v Stotfold	1-0
Biggleswade T v Vauxhall M	0-0
Brache Sparta v Arlesey Town	0-4
Sandy Albion v Kempston Rvrs	0-2
Wootton Blue Cross v Leighton	2-2
Replays	
Biggleswade T v Vauxhall M	0-3
Wootton Blue Cross v Leighton	1-1
Second Replays	
Wootton Blue Cross v Leighton	1-2
First Round	
Barton Rovers v Kempston Rvrs	3-0
Eaton Bray Utd v Electrolux	2-3
Langford v Leighton Town	0-0
Shefford v Ashcroft Co-Op	3-0
Shillington v Vauxhall M	0-2
61 FC (Luton) v Cranford	2-0
Replays	
Langford v Leighton Town	2-4
Second Round	
Dunstable v Leighton	4-0
Vauxhall Motors v Barton Rvrs	3-2
Electrolux v Arlesey	2-3
61 FC (Luton) v Shefford Town	2-1
Semi-Finals	
61 FC (Luton) v Vauxhall M	2-3 aet
Arlesey T v Dunstable	1-5 aet

Final, at Barton Rovers FC

DUNSTABLE v VAUXHALL MOTORS 2-1 aet
(Southern S) (Vauxhall-Opel, 2N)

As Vauxhall Motors, like their oponents required extra time in the semi finals. It can be no surprise that an extra thirty minutes was also required in the final before Dunstable could claim the cup.

Berks & Bucks Senior Cup

Preliminary Round	
Beaconsfield Utd v Olney T	3-0
Marlow v Maidenhead Town	1-2
Burnham v Thatcham	0-2
First Round	
Abingdon Town v Aylesbury Utd	1-2
Amersham Town v Abingdon Utd	0-1
Beaconsfield U v Holmer Green	5-0
Thatcham Town v Newbury Town	2-0
Chalfont St Peter v Didcot T	3-1
Flackwell H v New Bradwell SP	2-2
Hazells (Aylesbury) v Bracknell	0-1
Hungerford v Milton Keynes	5-0
Maidenhead Utd v Maidenhead T	4-3
Newport Pagnell T v Wolverton T	1-1
Slough Town v Reading	2-1 aet
Wallingford T v Windsor	2-5 aet
Winslow Utd v Wantage T	3-2
Wycombe Wanderers v Buckingham T	2-1
Replays	
Flackwell H v New Bradwell	4-0
Newport Pagnell T v Wolverton T	0-1
Second Round	
Aylesbury v Thatcham	1-0 at Tring
Chesham Utd v Beaconsfield U	2-0
Flackwell Heath v Wolverton	1-0
Maidenhead U v Chalfont St P	7-4 aet
Winslow Utd v Abingdon Utd	0-1
Windsor & Eton v Slough Town	3-1
Wokingham T v Bracknell Town	1-0 aet
Wycombe Wand v Hungerford T	9-0
Third Round	
Abingdon Utd v Windsor	2-2
Aylesbury Utd v Chesham Utd	4-2
Flackwell Heath v Wokingham T	1-0
Wycombe Wanderers v Maidenhead U	3-1

Drawn Final! Simon Read (Wycombe Wanderers) scores against Aylesbury United at Slough Town's Wexham Park ground (12.4.86) in a draw (2-2). The nomadic Aylesbury score the only goal of the replay.

Replays

Abingdon Utd v Windsor 1-0

Semi Finals

Wycombe Wanderers v Flackwell H 3-0
Abingdon Utd v Aylesbury Utd 0-3

FINAL, at Slough Town FC, replay also at Slough

Aylesbury Utd v Wycombe Wanderers 2-2

Replay

Aylesbury Utd v Wycombe Wanderers 1-0
(Southern P) (Gola)

A replay was required to settle the final, and a 1-0 win did tremendous credit to an Aylesbury side who played the whole season without a ground

Birmingham Senior Cup

First Round

Boldmere St Micheals v Tividale 1-0
Darlaston v Bromsgrove Rovers 2-3
Mile OaK Rovers v Alcester T 0-1
Oldswinford v Lye Town 1-0
Tamworth v Wednesfield Social 1-0
Stourbridge v Halesowen Town 1-2
Racing Club (Warwick) v Sutton Coldfield 0-6
Cradley Town v Highgate United 0-0
Wolverhampton Utd v Malvern Town 0-1
Leamington v Stratford Town 2-1
Moor Green v Paget Rangers 2-4
Coventry Sporting v Northfield T 4-0
VS Rugby v Solihull Borough 1-0
Smethwick H v Banbury 0-0
Oldbury Utd v Redditch Utd 1-3

Replays

Cradley Town v Highgate United 0-6
Smethwick H v Banbury 1-2

Second Round

Banbury Utd v Evesham Utd 2-1
Tamworth v VS Rugby 1-0
Boldmere St M v Wolverhampton Wand 2-0
Halesowen Town v Atherstone 1-1
Bromsgrove Rvrs v Aston Villa 0-2
Nuneaton Borough v W Mids Police 3-0
Birmingham City v Dudley 2-3
Redditch United v Malvern Town 2-4
Sutton Coldfield T v Leamington 3-0
Highgate Utd v Bedworth Utd 1-0
West Brom Alb v Paget Rangers 2-3
Willenhall v Oldswinford 2-2
Hednesford Town v Coleshill T 2-1
Burton Albion v Coventry City 2-1
Alvechurch v Coventry Sporting 0-2
Hurley Daw Mill v Walsall 1-2

Replays

Halesowen Town v Atherstone 1-4
Willenhall v Oldswinford 1-1

Second Replays

Willenhall v Oldswinford 6-1

Third Round

Willenhall T v Walsall 5-0
Nuneaton Borough v Highgate 4-1
Boldmere St M v Hednesford 5-1
Tamworth v Aston Villa 2-1
Banbury Utd v Paget Rangers 2-1
Burton Albion v Sutton Coldfield 0-0
Dudley Town v Redditch Utd 4-3
Atherstone U v Coventry Sp 1-1

Replays

Burton Albion v Sutton Coldfield 2-0
Atherstone U v Coventry Sp 2-1

Fourth Round

Nuneaton Boro v Dudley 2-2
Boldmere St M v Burton Albion 0-1
Atherstone U v Banbury Utd 2-0
Tamworth v Willenhall Town 0-6

Replays

Nuneaton Boro v Dudley 0-1

Semi Finals

Dudley Town v Burton Albion 1-0
Willenhall Town v Atherstone 1-0

FINAL At West Bromich Albion FC.

Dudley Town v Willenhall T 4-2 aet

....612 witnessed one of the most exciting cup finals for many years, early goals by Gordon and Foote looked as if they put Dudley on the way to a famous victory, after a nomadic season, but in the last six minutes King and Skidmore brought the scores level. Willenhall's revival ended though with defender Chris Birch sent off in the last minute of normal time, and in extra time, Dudley took full advantage of the extra man, scoring through Gordon and Stanton. Like the Southern League rivals, Aylesbury who won the Berks & Bucks Cup, Dudleys win was a triumph over adversity, as they had to play the whole season away from home, after their Birmingham Road ground was closed due to subsidence.

Cheshire Senior Cup Results

First Qual Round

Barnton v General Chemicals	2-3
Cammell Laird v Dukinfield Town	5-1
Alsager T v Ellesmere Port	1-4
Bramhall v Cheadle Town	8-1
Vauxhall v Christleton	3-0
Warrington Town v Nantwich T	6-0
Knutsford v Poulton Vics	1-0

First Round

Altrincham v General Chemicals	4-0
Knutsford v Hyde Utd	0-4
Northwich Vics v Ellesmere Port	5-1 aet
Stalybridge Celtic v Congleton	0-2
Warrington Town v Runcorn	1-4
Macclesfield Town v Bramhall	1-0
Winsford Utd v Cammell L	1-1
Witton Albion v Vauxhall	3-1

Replays

Winsford Utd v Cammell	1-0

Second Round

Altrincham v Runcorn	2-2
Winsford Utd v Northwich Vics	0-2
Congleton Town v Macclesfield T	0-0
Witton Albion v Hyde Utd	3-0

Replays

Altrincham v Runcorn	0-1
Congleton Town v Macclesfield	1-0

Semi Finals (2 legs)

Witton Albion v Runcorn	0-1, 1-1
Congleton T v Northwich V	0-0, 0-0

FINAL at Altrincham FC, att 1044

Northwich Victoria (Gola) v Runcorn (Gola)	1-3

....two very close semi finals bought Gola League rivals Northwich and Runcorn together in the final, with Runcorn taking the cup in front of over 1000 spectators.

CAMBRIDGESHIRE Invitation Cup

Recent winners: '80 Histon (ECL), '81 Great Shelford (Cambs), '82 & '83 Wisbech T (ECL), '84 Cambridge C (South), '85 Histon (ECL)

Semi-Finals

Great Shelford v Soham Town Rangers	0-1
Cambridge C v Wisbech T	7-1

FINAL, at Soham Town Rangers FC

Cambridge City (Southern, South) v Soham Town Rangers (Eastern)	4-1

There is also a challenge cup normally won by teams from the Peterborough or Tyre Services Cambridge Leagues

CUMBERLAND

Recent winners: '80 Carlisle United Res, '81 Penrith (D Northern), '82 Haig Colliery (Carlisle), '83 & '84 Gretna (Dryborough Northern), '85 Haig Colliery (Carlisle)

FINAL, at Penrith FC

Gretna (Dryborough Northern) v Workington (Multipart)	4-6 aet

DORSET Senior Cup

First Round

Shaftesbury v Portland United	3-2

Second Round

Bridport v Wareham Rangers	4-0
Sherbourne T v Holt United	5-0
Swanage T & Herston v Bourn. Water Co.	3-1
Hamworthy United v Sturminster Newton	3-3
Gillingham T v Flight Ref	0-5
Parley Sports v Wimbourne Town	1-2
St Pauls (Jersey) v Weymouth	1-3
Shaftesbury v Blandford U	1-1

Replays

Hamworthy United v Sturminster Newton	0-5
Shaftesbury v Blandford U	1-2

Third Round

Swanage T & H v Wimbourne	1-2
Weymouth v Blandford United	7-0
Bridport v Sturminster Newton	2-3
Sherbourne T v Flight Ref	3-3

Replays

Sherbourne T v Flight Ref	0-3

Semi-Finals

Wimbourne T v Flight Refuelling	2-1
Sturminster Newton v Weymouth	0-2

FINAL at Swanage Town & Herston FC

Weymouth (Gola) v Wimbourne T. (Western 1)	8-0

Tamworth go two-up in the Birmingham Senior Cup Final (1.11.85) and hold out to win (2-1) against Aston Villa. Andy Maddocks is the scorer.

CORNWALL SENIOR CUP:

Liskeard 1, Bugle 0 (at Newquay)

DEVON ST. LUKE'S

Exmouth Town 0, Bideford 3
Plymouth Argyle 2, Ilfracombe Town 3
Bideford 4, Ilfracombe Town 0

Dorset Senior Trophy

First Round

Wool RBL v Britannia	4-3
Branksome Ath v Trinidad Jolliffe	1-3
Okeford United v Hamworthy FC	3-1
Verwood v Steering Wheel	2-2
Oakdale United v Royal Signals	1-1
Broadmayne v HMS Osprey	2-1
Replays	
Verwood v Steering Wheel	1-2
Oakdale United v Royal Signals	3-1
Second Round	
Broadmayne v Okeford United	0-1
Trinidad Jolliffe v Wool RBL	3-1
Oakdale United v Portesham	4-1
Steering Wheel v Puddletown	3-3
Replays	
Steering Wheel v Puddletown	0-3
Semi-Finals	
Okeford United v Trinidad Jolliffe	1-4
Oakdale U v Steering W	3-3
FINAL at Hamworthy United FC	
Trinidad Jolliffe (Bournemouth) v Steering Wheel (Dorset League 1)	1-2

DURHAM SENIOR CUP

First Qualifying Round

Darlington (Res) v Consett	3-3
Replays	
Darlington (Res) v Consett	0-5
Second Qual Round	
Norton & Stockton A v Darlington CB	1-2
Boldon Colliery v Billingham Syn	0-3
West Auckland T v Dawdon CW	5-3
Annfield Plain v Consett	2-0
Evenwood v Shildon United	0-0
Hartlepool BWOB v Hartlepool U (R)	3-1
Seaham CW Red Star v Shotton Com	2-0
Ferryhill John Dee v Ryhope CW	5-3
Willington v Durham City	5-1
Esh Winning v Swalwell	0-4
Clark Chapman v Reyrolle	2-1
Murton v Darlington RA	4-0
Eppleton CW v Langley Park W	1-2
Thornley WMC v Ryhope CA	0-1
Newton Aycliffe v South Shields	2-3
Dunston Mechs v Coundon FC	2-1
Replays	
Evenwood v Shildon United	6-0
First Round	
Annfield Plain v Washington	5-2
Billingham Syn v Stockton T	0-4
Chester-le-Street v W Auckland T	2-0
Dunston Mechs v Evenwood Town	3-1
Easington Coll v Coundon TT	1-2
Swallwell v Clarke Chapman	2-1
Ferryhill John Dee v Bishops Auck	0-11
Hartlepool BWOB v Murton	1-4
Langley Pk W v Sporting C Vaux	0-1
Ryhope CA v Peterlee Newton	2-3
Seaham CW RS v Darlington CB	2-1
South Shields v Brandon United	2-1
Spennymoor Utd v Ferryhill Ath	4-1
Whickham v Billingham Town	3-0
Willington v Crook Town	2-1 aet
Wingate v Shildon	3-1
Replays	
Langley Pk v Sporting C Vaux	0-1
Second Round	
Bishop Auckland v Stockton T	4-1
Chester-le-Street v Spennymoor	1-3
Seaham CW Red Star v Peterlee Newton	1-2 aet
South Shields v Sporting Club Vaux	2-0 aet
Willington v Dunston Mechanics	3-1
Wingate v Murton	6-2
Whickham v Annfield P	0-5
Swalwell v Coundon TT	1-3
Third Round	
Peterlee Newton v Annfield Plain	2-1
Willington v Bishop Auckland	0-3
Coundon TT v Wingate	2-0
Spennymoor United v South Shields	13-0
Semi-Finals	
Bishop Auckland v Peterlee Newton	3-1
Spennymoor U v Coundon TT	2-1
FINAL at Shildon FC	
Bishop Auckland (Dryborough Northern 1) v Spennymoor Utd (DNL 1)	3-1

A 3-1 victory over their old rivals means that the Bishop's retain both this Trophy and the Northern League Championship, a repeat of last seasons double achievement.

EAST ANGLIAN CUP

Group 1, Round 1	
Cambridge United v Bourne Town	3-0
Soham Town Rangers v Chatteris	2-1
Potton United v March Town Utd	3-2
Round 2	
Cambridge United v Eynesbury R	4-2
Soham Town v Histon	2-3
Kings Lynn v Cambridge City	1-0
Wisbech Town v Potton United	7-2
Semi-Finals	
Kings Lynn v Cambridge United	w/o
Wisbech Town v Histon	0-1
Group Final	
Kings Lynn v Histon	0-1
Group 2, Round 1	
Letchworth GC v Royston Town	2-1
Stofold v Hitchin Town	0-6
Round 2	
Baldock Town v Hoddeston T	3-0
Hitchin Town v Harlow Town	1-0
Hertford Town v Letchworth GC	1-0
Ware v Saffron Walden Town	1-2
Semi-Finals	
Hertford Town v Saffron Walden T	2-1
Hitchin Town v Baldock Town	2-0
Group Final	
Hertford Town v Baldock Town	1-2
Group 3, Round 1	
Stansted v Witham Town	0-5
Heybridge Swifts v E Thurrock U	4-1
Woodford Town v Billericay T	1-4
Round 2	
Braintree Town v Chelmsford C	2-1
Colchester Utd v Billericay	1-0
Clacton Town v Witham Town	0-5
Heybridge Swifts v Tiptree U	4-2
Semi-Finals	
Colchester Utd v Witham Town	2-1
Heybridge Swifts v Braintree T	1-3
Group Final	
Colchester United v Braintree	3-2 aet
Group 4, First Round	
Haughley United v Ransomes	3-2
Brantham Ath v Diss Town	2-1
Lowestoft v Westerfield	w/o
Round 2	
Brantham Ath v Sudbury	2-3
Westerfield v Watton Utd	2-2
Crane Sports v Gorleston	1-3
Stowmarket T v Haughley Utd	1-0

Semi-Finals

Sudbury Town v Gorleston	5-1
Watton United v Stowmarket	1-4

Group Final (ordered replayed)

Stowmarket T v Sudbury T	2-1

Replay

Stowmarket v Sudbury T	2-3

COMPETITION PROPER, SEMI-FINALS

Colchester United v Baldock Town	2-1
Sudbury Town v Histon	1-0

FINAL

Colchester United (Res) Eastern) v Sudbury Town (Eastern)	2-3

Summaries cont.
1... Kings Lynn, who had a semi final walkover; the Southern League side faired less well when having to play their match, giving Histon a notable scalp.
2... Hertford won to become the only non-Eastern League side to go through.
4... which Sudbury took full advantage of, winning 3-2. Histons run came to an end in the main semi-final, when they were away at Sudbury, and Sudbury then went to win the all Eastern League final by beating Colchester, who had knocked out Baldock in their semi.

Derbyshire Senior Cup
Recent winners: '80 Belper T (Mid Count), '81 Matlock Town (NPL), '82 Alfreton (Mid Count), '83 Ilkeston (NCE), '84 & '85 Matlock (NPL).
Results:

First Round

Staveley Works v Glossop	5-0
Borrowash Vics v Carriage & Wagon	4-0
Glossopians v Clay Cros Wks	2-3
Gresley Rovers v Mickleover RBL	3-1
Newhall United v Stanton	1-3
Heanor Town v Ilkeston T	4-2
Graham Street Prims v Stapenhill	0-1

Second Round

Heanor Town v Stapenhill	0-1
Borrowash Vics v Staveley Wks	0-0
Gresley Rovers v Buxton	0-0
Clay Cross Wks v Stanton	4-3

Replays

Borrowash Vics v Staveley Wks	0-3
Gresley Rovers v Buxton	3-6 aet

Third Round

Alfreton Town v Heanor Town	0-2
Belper Town v Clay Cross Wks	1-0
Staveley Wks v Long Eaton	0-1
Buxton v Matlock Town	4-3

Semi-Finals

Buxton v Heanor Town	1-1
Belper T v Long Eaton	3-1

Replays

Buxton v Heanor Town	4-2

FINAL, two legs

Buxton (Multipart) v Belper Town (NCE 1)	2-2, 1-0

Summary: North West Counties side Glossop suffered a 5-0 thrashing in the first round when they had to visit Northern Counties (East) side Staveley Works, while Stapenhill, who play in the Leicestershire Senior League won 1-0 at Graham St Prims. Buxton had a bye in the first round and needed a replay against Gresley in the second. Buxton took the lead three times in the first ninety minutes, each time Beresford pegged them back, but in extra time, Buxton built up an unassailable lead. Buxton then had to play Multipart League rivals in round 3, winning by 4-3. With the last Central Midlands League side, Clay Cross Works going down 1-0 at Belper, all the other three semi-finalists were from the Northern Counties (East) League. Buxton again needed a replay to go through against Heanor. The final was over two legs, and after finishing all square at Buxton, a single goal in the second leg gave the cup to the Multipart League club.

East Riding Senior Cup
Recent winners: '80 & '81 Hull City, '82 Bridlington Trinity, '83 Aero Albion, '84 Schultz YC, '85 Hull City

First Round

Kingburn v Bridlington Trinity	1-2
Wheeler White Star v Westella & W	2-1
Melton SC v Bridlington Town	1-3

Second Round

Astral Amateurs v Bridges Sports	4-3
Sculcoates Am v Sydney Smith YC	1-0
Greatfield OB v N Ferriby United	2-3 aet
Schultz YC (Am Lge) v Schultz YC (C. Lge)	1-3
Bridlington Town v Bridlington Trinity	2-2
Hull Old Gram's v Hall Road Rang	4-0
Wheeler White Star v Hull City	0-3
Wolfreton YC v Reckitts	8-0

Replays

Bridlington Town v Bridlington Trinity	3-1

Third Round

Astral Am v Schultz YC (Cty)	1-2
Hull City v Hull Old Gram's	3-3
Bridlington Town v N Ferriby Utd	1-0
Wolfreton YC v Sculcoates Am	2-3 aet

Semi-Finals

Sculcoates Am v Schultz YC	0-1
Bridlington Town v Hull City	2-1

FINAL

Bridlington T. (NCE 1) v Schultz YC (ER Cty)	1-2

Summary: I cannot say the exact status of this cup, but I believe that the Northern Counties East teams play their first XI's, whereas the Hull City side is their third or Junior XI. The other teams come from the county and Amateur Leagues, and confusion is aided by the fact that both of these leagues have a team called Schultz Youth Club, and these met in the second round, with the County League side going through. Bridlington also has two teams, both in the Northern Counties (East) League, and after each playing away in the first round, they met at their shared Queensgate home, and again for a replay before Town went through. Major shock was the defeat of Hall Road Rangers by Hull Old Gramarians. Bridlington Town beat North Ferriby, divisional champions of their own league and Hull City juniors to reach the final, but they were then beaten by the County League side, Schultz YC.

Essex Senior Trophy, First Round

Barkingside v E Thurrock Utd	0-2
Beckton United v Collier Row	0-2
Bowers United v Eton Manor	2-0
Braintree Town v Witham Town	1-2
Brightlingsea Utd v Woodford	1-1
Burnham Ramblers v Epping T	w/o
Clacton Town v Chingford	4-1
Clapton v Waltham Abbey	1-2
Wivenhoe Town v Brentwood	2-1
Ford United v Tiptree United	2-0
Halstead Town v Coggeshall	6-0
Harwich & Parkeston v Stanstead	2-1
Heybridge Swifts v Maldon Town	3-1
Rainham Town v Canvey Island	2-0
Saffron Walden Town v E Ham United	2-0
Pennant Sports	bye

Replays

Brightlingsea Utd v Woodford	1-3

Second Round

Bowers United v Clacton Town	3-2
Burnham Ramblers v Wivenhoe T	2-1
Heybridge Swifts v Collier Row	3-0
Rainham Town v Pennant Sports	1-2
Saffron Walden T v Harwich & P	1-2
Waltham Abbey v Halstead Town	3-0
Witham Town v Ford United	2-1
Woodford Town v East Thurrock U	2-1

Third Round

Woodford Town v Waltham Abbey	2-0
Pennant Sports v Witham Town	0-1
Bowers United v Harwich & P	2-1
Heybridge Swifts v Burnham Ramb	3-0

Semi-Finals

Bowers Utd v Heybridge Swifts	3-4 aet
Witham T v Woodford Town	1-1

Replays

Witham T v Woodford Town	2-0

FINAL, at Chelmsford City FC

Heybridge Swifts (Vauxhall Opes 2) v Witham Town (Essex)	2-3 aet

Braintree Town (Building Scene) 1, Witham Town (Essex Senior) 2. Braintree's Chris Guy (centre) slips past Witham's Graham Bird (right).

ESSEX Senior Cup

First Round

Hornchurch v Barking	3-3
Dagenham v Harlow Town	1-2
Southend Utd v Leytonstone-Ilford	4-0
Leyton-Wingate v Walthamstow Ave	0-3
Billericay Town v Basildon U	5-1
Grays Athletic v Chelmsford C	2-3
Replays	
Hornchurch v Barking	3-3
Second Replays	
Hornchurch v Barking	1-2
Second Round	
Walthamstow Ave v Chelmsford C	1-5
Billericay Town v Aveley	3-2
Barking v Harlow Town	1-0
Tilbury v Southend United	3-1
Semi-Finals	
Billericay Town v Tilbury	3-0
Chelmsford City v Barking	1-1
Replays	
Chelmsford City v Barking	3-0
FINAL, (2 legs)	
Chelmsford City (Southern Prem) v Billericay Town (Vauxhall Opel P)	2-0, 1-0

Thames-Side Trophy, Preliminary Round

E Thurrock United v Orient	2-1
Hornchurch v Collier Row	0-1
Ford United v Leytonstone I	2-0
Rainham v Barkingside	2-2 aet, 3-4 pens
First Round	
Aveley v Grays Athletic	1-2
Barking v Leyton Wingate	1-0
Barkingside v Billericay	0-5
Clapton v Epping Town	w/o
Collier Row v Walthamstow Ave	1-2
Southend United v Ford Utd	2-0
Tilbury v East Thurrock Utd	1-2
Woodford Town v Chelmsford City	0-1
Second Round	
Billericay Town v Clapton	2-1
Chelmsford City v Southend Utd	1-2
Grays Athletic v Barking	2-1
Walthamstow Ave v E Thurrock Utd	4-1
Semi-Finals	
Billericay v Grays A	3-4
Walthamstow v Southend U	1-0
FINAL, at Walthamstow Avenue FC	
Walthamstow Avenue (VOL-Prem) v Grays Athletic (VOL- 1)	2

GLOUCESTERSHIRE
Northern Senior Cup

Semi-Final

Cheltenham Town v Gloucester City	7-1
FINAL	
Cheltenham Town v Forest Green Rovers	1-1 aet, 3-4 pens

Senior Trophy, Preliminary Round

Yate Town v Mangotsfield U	3-0
First Round	
Wilton Rovers v Cinderford	2-0
Patchway v Bristol Manor Farm	1-2
Cheltenham Res v B St George	2-2
Avon St Phillips v Port of Bristol	3-3
Stonehouse v Longwell Green Abbotonians	3-2
Newent Town v Robinsons DRG	1-4
Campden Town v Hambrook	2-0
Harrow Hill v Cadbury Heath	1-3
Moreton Town v Brimscombe & Thrupp	5-1
Yate Town v Portway Bristol	0-1
Frampton United v Wotton Rovers	4-0
Almondsbury Greenway v Ellwood	2-0
Hanham Athletic v Shortwood U	0-6
Oldland v Old Georgians	2-5
Lawrence Weston H v Sharpness	1-4
Fairford T v Lydbrook A	4-3 aet
Replays	
Cheltenham Res v B St George	1-4
Avon St Phillips v Port of Bristol	5-4 inc pens
Second Round	
Fairford Town v Shortwood Utd	1-2
Moreton Town v Robinsons DRG	2-1 aet
Stonehouse v Almondsbury G	1-1
Wilton Rovers v Sharpness	1-4
Old Georgians v Campden Town	2-0
Bristol St George v Avon St Ph	0-1
B Manor Farm v Cadbury Heath	4-0
Portway Bristol v Frampton Utd	3-2
Replays	
Stonehouse v Almondsbury G	1-2
Third Round	
Almondsbury Greenway v Old Georgians	0-1
Bristol Manor Farm v Shortwood U	3-2
Sharpness v Portway Bristol	3-4 aet
Avon St Phillips v Moreton T	0-3
Semi-Finals	
Moreton Town v Bristol Manor Farm	1-0
Portway Bristol v Old Georgians	0-1
FINAL, at Forest Green Rovers FC	
Moreton Town (Hellenic Prem) v Old Georgians (Glos Cty)	2-0

.... both semi finals were close affairs with a single goal setting each one, Moreton Town, the only side to have won the trophy more than once scored a goal in each half to complete their third victory

Senior Amateur Cup (North), First Round

Whiteshill Utd v Newent T Res	3-1
Longlevens v Eagle Star	2-1
Bymacks v Viney St Swithens	4-1
Dowty Ashchurch v Lydbrook Res	3-0
College of St Paul v Cope Chat	3-1
Smiths Athletic v Mitcheldean	7-0
Cheltenham Saracens v Frampton U	7-6
ICI Fibres v Dursley Town	3-0
The Herd v Borough United	3-0
Berkeley Town v Tewkesbury YMCA	1-2
Huntley v Broadwell	1-6
Kings Stanley v Shipton Oliffe	0-0
Crescent Utd v Harrow Hill Res	3-1
Cinderford Res v Brockworth	2-1
Bibury v Coleford United	3-3
Bourton Rovers v Campden T Res	3-1
Badminton Picksons v Chalford	8-0

Replays

Kings Stanley v Shipton Oliffe	4-2
Bibury v Coleford United	1-3

Second Round

Dowty Ashchurch v Smiths Athletic	0-1
Coleford United v Charfield	0-1 aet
Whiteshill Utd v Cheltenham Saracens	2-0
Hardwicke v Tewkesbury YMCA	2-4
Dowty Dynamos v Kings Stanley	1-1
Minchinghampton v Gas Green	2-2
Crescent Utd v Badminton Picksons	1-3
Bourton Rovers v Bymacks	2-1
St Marks CA v Bishops Cleeve	0-2
Leckhampton v The Herd	1-2
Cinderford Res v Longlevens	1-0
ICI Fibres v Cirencester Town	1-2
Tuffley Rvrs v College of St P	3-1
Cam Bulldogs v Sharpness Res	3-1
Broadwell v Lydney Town	1-3
Shortwood U Res v Hilldene Ath	7-0

Replays

Dowty Dynamos v Kings Stanley	2-1
Minchinghampton v Gas Green	4-0

Third Round

Badminton Picksons v Bishops Cleeve	2-1
Cam Bulldogs v Smiths Ath	3-4 aet
Charfield v Minchinghampton	1-5
Cirencester Town v Tuffley Rovers	0-1
The Herd v Lydney Town	3-1
Shortwood Res v Dowty Dynamoes	1-0
Cinderford Res v Tewkesbury YMCA	0-1
Whiteshill Utd v Bourton Rvrs	6-1

Fourth Round

Minchinghampton v Shortwood Res	0-6
Tuffley Rovers v Badminton Pics	0-2
Whiteshill Utd v Smiths Ath	5-1
Tewkesbury YMCA v The Herd	3-2

Semi-Finals

Whiteshill Utd v Shortwood Res	2-3 aet
Tewkesbury YMCA v Badminton	1-0

FINAL, at Sharpness FC

Shortwood Utd Res (Glos NSL) v Tewkesbury YMCA (Worc & Dist)	4-2

Senior Amateur Cup (South) Preliminary Round

St Andrews YC v Fishponds OB	1-2
Frampton Ath v Hillfields OB	1-2
Port of Bristol Res v Hillfields Pk	1-3
Bitton v Cadbury Heath Res	1-0
Electricity Spts v Avonmouth	0-4
Robinsons Res v Sea Mills Park	4-2
Eden Grove v L Weson H res	3-0
Hartcliffe BC v Wanderers	3-1

First Round

The Mill v Bristol Union	2-2
Avonmouth v Saints	3-2
Filton Town v Bishop Rvrs	2-0
Thornbury Town v Pucklechurch	2-0
Fishponds v St Phillips MAS	2-3
Winterbourne U v Totterdown A	0-1
Frenchay v Manor Farm OB	7-1
Bristol Gen Hosp v Bucklers	2-3
Robinsons DRG Res v Hambrook Res	1-2
Eden Grove v Sun Life	2-0
Soundwell v Old Cots	3-2
P & W United v Iron Acton	1-1
Yate Town Res v Patchway OB	4-2
B Manor Farm Res v NSC	4-3
Staple Hill v St Vincents	1-1
Nicholsa Wand v Bitton	2-1
Victoria Park v Lockleaze	4-3
Nat West Court v Stockwood Green	0-1
Deveys v St Andrews YC	4-2
Hartclife BC v Stapleton	3-4
Longwell G A Res v Glenside St G	1-3
Old Georgians Res v Hillfields OB	1-3
Shaftesbury Crusade v Shirehampton	3-2
BCME v Southmead	2-0
Exeter United v Barr United	2-4
Made for Ever v RWP	0-2
Fishponds OB v Fire Brigade	2-3
Telephones v Hillfields Park	1-2
Cattybrook v Dynamo	1-1
Henbury OB v Teyfant	8-2
Lawrence Rovers v St Aldhelms	2-1
Wessex Glass v Wick	3-3

Replays

The Mill v Bristol Union	4-0
P & W United v Iron Acton	0-1
Staple Hill v St Vincents	2-4
Cattybrook v Dynamo	0-2
Wessex Glass v Wick	0-4

Second Round

St Phillips MAS v Nicholas Wand	3-2
Glenside St G v Shaftesbury Crus	3-1
Hillfields Park v Wick	1-2
Avonmouth v P & W Utd	0-2
Bucklers v Soundwell	6-0
Hambrook Res v Filton Town	3-2
Henbury OB v St Vincents	8-3 aet
RWP v Totterdown	4-2
Deveys v Lawrence Rovers	0-2
Casttybrook v Frenchay Hosp	2-0
Thornbury Town v Victoria Pk	2-1
Fire Brigade v BCME	2-2
Yate Town v Stapleton	1-3
B Manor Farm Res v Stockwood Gn	3-2
Barr United v Hillfields OB	0-2
Eden Grove v The Mill	1-1

Replays

Fire Brigade v BCME	1-3
Eden Grove v The Mill	3-0

Third Round

RWP v Ibstock Cattybrook	1-1
Stapleton v Thornbury T	0-3
Hambrook Res v St Phillips MAS	0-1
Eden Grove v Henbury OB	1-0
Hillfields OB v B Manor Farm Res	1-3
Glenside St G v Bucklers	3-1
P & W Utd v Lawrence Rovers	2-2
Wick v BCME	1-3

Replays

RWP v Ibstock Cattybrook	3-0
P & W Utd v Lawrence Rovers	0-3

Fourth Round

Glenside St G v St Phillips MAS	0-2
RWP v Eden Grove	3-0
Thornbury Town v BCME	1-0
Lawrence R v B Manor Farm Res	1-3

Semi-Finals

St Phillips MAS v RWP	0-2
Thornbury Town v B Manor Farm Res	3-2

FINAL, at Bristol Rovers FC

Thornbury Town (Avon Comb) v RWP (Avon Comb)	2-3

HAMPSHIRE Senior Cup

Sway v Downton	2-0
Ringwood Town v Hartley Wintney	0-2
Winchester Castle v Bashley	1-5
Locksheath v Brading Town	2-1
BAT v Overton United	1-3
Blackfield & Langley v Cove	7-1
Warsash v Christchurch	1-3
Netley Central Spts v Bass (Alton)	3-2
Fleet Town v Horndean	2-3
Portals Athletic v Follands Spts	4-2

First Round

Brockenhurst v Blackfield & L	1-2
Basingstoke T v Southampton Res	3-1
Romsey Town v Lymington	0-1
Andover v Pirelli General	2-1
Waterlooville v E Cowes Vics	4-3
Petersfield U v Portsmouth RN	4-1
Eastleigh v Fareham Town	0-2
Gosport Boro v Portals Ath	1-0
Sway v Newport IOW	1-4 aet
Bashley v AFC Totton	3-2
Locksheath v RS Southampton	0-4
Overton Utd v Netley Central S	3-2
Christchurch v Vale Rec (Geurnsey)	2-3
Horndean v Hartley Wintney	0-3
Havant Town v Farnborough T	0-5
Sholing S v First Tower (Jersey)	2-0

Second Round

Farnborough T v Waterlooville	2-0
Lymington v Andover	1-2
Fareham T v Vale Rec	3-3
Bashley v Basingstoke T	3-4
Overton Utd v RS Southampton	0-1
Hartley Wintney v Newport IOW	1-0
Sholing Spts v Gosport Boro	0-0
Petersfield Utd v Blackfield & L	7-2 aet

Replays

Fareham T v Vale Rec	2-0
Sholing Spts v Gosport Boro	1-3

Third Round

Petersfield U v Farnborough T	0-2
Hartley Wintney v RS Southampton	1-1
Basingstoke T v Andover	4-2
Fareham T v Gosport Boro	1-3

Replays

Hartley Wintney v RS Southampton	2-4

Semi-Finals

Farnborough T v RS Southampton	2-1
Basingstoke T v Gosport Boro	1-1

Replays

Basingstoke T v Gosport Boro	0-0, 5-4 pens

FINAL, at Southampton FC

Basingstoke T (Southern Prem) v Farnborough T (VOL- Prem)	0-2

....before going out 4-2. The local derby between Southern League rivals Fareham and Gosport was won 3-1 by Gosport, who then went on to play two matches against Basingstoke, both draws, before going out on penalties, but it was the Vauxhall Opel side Farnborough who went on to win the cup, after beating RS Southampton in the semis.

HEREFORDSHIRE

County Challenge Cup

Recent winners: '80 & '81 Ledbury Town (West Mid), '82 Pegasus (Worcester), '83 Pegasus (Hellenic), '84 Hinton YC (Worc), '85 Pegasus (Hellenic)

First Round

Pegasus Juniors v Sutton United	9-4
Hinton YC v Stoke Prior	6-0
Ewyas Harold v Bosbury	2-0
Leominster Utd v Westfields	0-2
Hfd Lads Club v Army	2-1
Ross United v Painters Ath	0-0
Fownhope v Wellington	1-3
Woofferton v Bromyard Town	2-1

Replays

Ross United v Painters Ath	2-0

Second Round

Pegasus Jnrs v Ross United	5-2
Hfd Lads Club v Ewyas Harold	1-0
Westfields v Woofferton	5-1 aet
Wellington v Hinton YC	2-2

Replays

Wellington v Hinton YC	1-4

Semi-Final

Hfd Lads Club v Westfields	1-5
Pegasus Jnrs v Hinton YC	0-1

FINAL

Westfields v Hinton YC	1-0

summary: the competition is competed for by a mixture of Herefordshire League, and Worcester & District League clubs, plus Hellenic Pegasus and Westfields of the West Midlands. As a rule the more succesful clubs around Hereford play in the Worcester & District, rather than the Hereford League, and both Pegasus and Westfields took this route before joining their present leagues. In fact the semi finals involved two teams from the Worcester & District League, Hereford Lads Club and Hinton Youth Club, with Pegasus and Westfields, and Hinton then produced the only minor shock with a victory over the Pegasus club.

Hertfordshire Senior Cup

First Round

Royston Town v Letchworth GC	1-0
Baldock Town v Hitchin Town	1-0
Berkhamsted T v Hemel Hempstead	0-0
Watford v Boreham Wood	6-0
Bishops Stortford v Ware	3-2
St Albans City v Hertford Town	2-0
Cheshunt v Stevenage Boro	2-4
Tring Town v Barnet	0-2

Replays

Berkhamsted T v Hemel Hempstead	1-2

Second Round

reinstated: Hitchin, Baldock played inelligible player

Stevenage Boro v Hemel Hempstead	1-1
Royston Town v Hitchin Town	1-4
Watford v Bishops Stortford	2-1
St Albans City v Barnet	0-1

Replays

Stevenage Boro v Hemel Hempstead	2-1

Semi-Finals

Stevenage Boro v Watford	2-0
Hitchin v Barnet	0-2

FINAL, at Bishops Stortford FC

Barnet (Gola) v Stevenage Borough (Vauxhall Opel, 2N)	4-0

Hertfordshire Senior Trophy

First Round

Knebworth v Potter Bar Crusaders	5-2
Welwyn Garden Utd v Wingate	2-1
Harpenden T v Evergren	2-1 aet
Hoddesdon Town v Mount Grace Potters Bar	3-1
Selby v BROB Barnet	4-1
St Margaretsbury v Sawbridgeworth	0-2
Leavesden Hosp v Leverstock Grn	3-2

Second Round

Harpendon Town v Selby	0-5
Welwyn Garden C v Knebworth	1-0
Rolls Royce v Bovington	1-2
London Colney v Leavesden Hosp	1-0
Sawbridgeworth v Hoddesdon	0-1
Sandridge Rvrs v Pirton	3-1
Welwyn Garden Utd v Sun Spts	2-0
Oxhey Jets v BAX Stevenage	1-3

Third Round

Welwyn Garden U v Hoddesdon	1-3
London Colney v BAC Stevenage	2-0
Welwyn Garden C v Bovington	1-1
Selby v Sandridge Rovers	2-1

Replays

Welwyn Garden C v Bovington	2-4

Semi-Finals

Bovington v Selby	0-4
Hoddesdon T v London Colney	3-2

FINAL, at Ware FC

Hoddesdon Town (S Mids) v Selby (S Mids)	1-2 aet

Hertfordshire Charity Cup

First Round

St Albans City v Hitchin Town	1-2
Berkhamsted Town v Boreham Wood	0-4
Hertford Town v Tring Town	1-0
Stevenage Borough v Bishops Stortford	2-1

Semi-Finals

Stevenage Borough v Boreham Wood	0-2
Hertford Town v Hitchin Town	1-3

FINAL, at Boreham Wood FC

Boreham Wood (VOL 1) v Hitchin Town (VOL-Prem)	1-1 aet, 4-3 pens

Willenhall 6, Oldswinford 1 (Birmingham Senior Cup). Arçhie King heads home Wilenhall's third.

Paul Kenny (Gravesend) tangles with a Welling defender as his team go down to Kent Senior Cup defeat (1-3).

Shepshed Charterhouse captain, Jeff Lissaman, celebrates with team-mates after the overwhelming (6-0) Leicestershire Challenge Cup success against Leicester United at Filbert Street.

Charity Shield

First Round

Welwyn Garden C v Royston T	0-1
Ware v Letchworth Garden	2-0
Baldock Town v Cheshunt	2-0
Pirton v Hemel Hempstead T	3-0

Semi-Finals

Pirton v Royston T	4-1
Ware v Baldock Town	2-4

Ware reinstated as Baldock had fielded and inelligible player

FINAL, at Stevenage Borough FC

Pirton v Ware	0-1

3Hertfordshire Summary

In the first round of the Senior Cup, Baldock of the United Counties League defeated Vauxhall Opel Premier side, Hitchin Town, unfortunately for them, they had fielded an inelligible player, and this resulted in the match being awarded the other way - the same fate overtook them in the FA Vase and Herts Charity Shield. Hitchin went through to the semis before bowing out to Gola League Barnet, while in the other semi, Stevenage Borough beat the strong Watford reserve team, bidding for a sixth successive win. They could not however hold the Gola Leaguers. Neither of the Herts County League sides that have opened the leagues account so well in the FA Vase could make an impression in the Senior Trophy, St Margaretsbury going out to Sawbridgeworth of the Essex League in the first round, and Leavesden to London Colney in the second. At the same stage South Midland League side Pirton lost 3-1 to Sandridge Rovers, while Welwyn Garden City fell to Bovington in a third round replay, but overall the South Midlands League sides had the edge over those for the County League, and they provided both finalists.

HINCHINBROOKE CUP

Probably the best of the independently run Senior Cups, and a bonus for groundhoppers, with non-floodlit teams often playing on Sundays.

First Round

Arlesey Town v Somersham Town	2-0
Sandy Albion v Wootton Blue Cross	2-5
Langford v St Ives Town	0-1
Chatteris Town v Huntingdon Utd	2-1
Eynesbury Rovers v Potton United	1-2
Irthlingborough D v Baldock	1-1
Pirton v Warboys Town	4-0
Royston Town v St Neots Town	2-1

Replays

Irthlingborough D v Baldock	2-0

Second Round

Royston Town v Irthlingborough	0-2
Wootton Blue Cross v Arlesey T	0-3
Potton United v Pirton	2-1
Chatteris Town v St Ives Town	0-3

Semi-Finals

Irthlingborough D v Arlesey Town	1-0
St Ives Town v Potton United	4-2

FINAL, at Eynesbury Rovers FC

Irthlingborough Diamonds (UCL Prem) v St Ives Town (UCL, 1)	3-1

HUNTINGDONSHIRE Senior Cup

Recent winners '80 & '81 St Neots T (UCL), '82 St Ives Town (Peterborough), '83 & '84 Yaxley (Peterborough, '85 Eynesbury Rovers (UCL)

First Round

Yaxley v Fletton	7-0
St Ives Town v Ortonians	1-2
Stilton v Ramsey Town	0-3
St Neots v Eynesbury Rov	1-1

Replays

St Neots v Eynesbury Rov	0-2

Second Round

Yaxley v Warboys	4-0
Somersham v Phorpres	3-1
Ramsey Town v Ortonians	2-1
Eynesbury Rov v Huntingdon Utd	1-2

Semi-Finals

Yaxley v Ramsey Town	0-2
Somersham T v Huntingdon Utd	1-1

Replays

Somersham T v Huntingdon Utd	0-2

FINAL, at Eynesbury Rovers FC

Ramsey Town (UCL, Div 1) v Huntingdon United (Peterborough)	1-0

Summary: The competition is played between teams form the Peterborough League and two from each division of the UCL. The two UCl Premier teams, local rivals St Neots Town and Eynesbury Rovers met in the First Round, with cup holders Eynesbury taking the honours in a replay, but Eynesbury failed to live up to expectations with a home defeat by Huntingdon. Ortonians knocked out one of the other UCL sides St Ives, but then came up against Ramsey Town. In a semi-final replay, Huntingdon beat Somersham, the other of last seasons finalists. Ramsey Town beat Yaxley in their semi, and a 1-0 win gave them the cup for the first time since 1910.

Kent Senior Trophy

First Round

Beckenham Town v Thames Poly	1-3
Cray Wanderers v Danson (Bexley Boro)	0-1
Herne Bay v West Wickham	0-1
Catford Wanderers v Met Police (4 Area)	0-2
Slade Green v Faversham T	0-3
Snowdown CW v Brent	2-2, 1-1, 2-4 pens
Royal Arsenal SRA v Swanley Town	0-1
Bexley v Corinthian	0-6
Hythe T v Kent Police	3-0
Ramsgate v Tunbridge Wells	2-5 aet 0-2
Crockenhill v Erith & Belvedere	2-1
Deal Town v Alma Swanley	1-0

Second Round Erith re-instated

Faversham Town v Brent	6-1
Hythe Town v Deal Town	1-0
Erith & Belvedere v Corinthian	1-3
Whitstable T v Swanley Town	5-0
Darenth Heathside v Danson	2-0
Tunbridge Wells v West Whickham	4-1
Penhill Standard v Greenwich B	0-2
Met Pol (4 Area) v Thames Poly	3-1

Third Round

Faversham T v Met Pol (4 Area)	0-1
Hythe Town v Corinthian	2-2, 1-0
Tunbridge Wells v Darenth H'side	2-2, 3-1
Greenwich Boro v Whitstable T	0-2

Semi-Finals

Met Pol (4 Area) v Hythe T	3-2
Tunbridge Wells v Whitstable	7-0

FINAL at Corinthian FC

Metropolitan Police (4 Area) (Kent Lge) v Tunbridge Wells (Kent)	2-1

Cup..... Bromley lost 2-0 at Gravesend in the second round, leaving only Dartford to challenge the Southern League clubs in the semis, but they disappointed their fans, going down to South division Dover Athletic, not suprisingly, Dover went down to Southern League champions Welling United in the final, who won the cup with four straight wins and only one goal conceded.

Trophy..... Only six days after they had lost 5-2 at home to the same team Met Police (4 Area) went through to the final with a 3-2 win over Hythe, and the Hayes based team went on to win the Trophy with a 2-1 win over League Cup winners Tunbridge Wells.

KENT Senior Cup

First Round

Maidstone United v Tonbridge AFC	1-2
Bromley v Chatham Town	2-0
Canterbury C v Welling United	0-1
Thanet United v Gravesend & Northfleet	0-2
Fisher Athletic v Sittingbourne	2-0
Dartford v Sheppey United	2-1
Dover Athletic v Ashford Town	1-0

Second Round

Gravesend & N v Bromley	2-0
Welling United v Fisher Athletic	2-0
Folkestone v Dover Athletic	0-1
Tonbridge AFC v Dartford	1-2

Semi-Finals

Dartford v Dover Athletic	0-2
Welling United v Gravesend & N	3-1

FINAL at Gillingham FC

Dover Athletic v Welling United	0-2

LANCASHIRE SATURDAY CUP RESULTS

First Round

Alsager Town v Ashville	3-1
Bollington v Cheadle Heath Nomads	6-4
Cheadle Heath v Mirrlees	6-2
Hazel Grove v Chester MANWEB	2-1
Hoylake Ath v Blacon YC	5-2
Knutsford v Styal	3-0
Lymm OB v Prestbury	8-1
Middlewich Ath v St Werberghs	2-5
Norwest Gas v Upton AA	1-7
Old Stopfordians v Trafford Sth	2-5
Poynton v Woodley SC	3-0
Newton v Stockport Georgians	2-0
Newton Ath v Chester College	1-2
Old Stoodonians v Higher Bebington	1-4
Moreton v Crewe Villa	5-4
Alderley St Phillips v Tattenhall	2-4

Second Round

Alsager College v Macclesfield ICI	8-1
Alsager Town v Newton	3-1
Bebington Hawks v Lymm OB	1-2
Bollington v Higher Bebington	2-1
Crewe LMR v Winnington Park	5-2
Crewe Rolls Royce v Cheadle Hulme	1-3
Chester College v Upton AA	0-4
Davenport v Chester Namads	4-2
General Chemicals v Rivacre	3-2
Knutsford v Hoylake Ath	2-5
Linotype v Moreton	3-1
Mond Rangers v Lostok Gralam	3-1
Poynton v Old Altrinchamians	2-4
St Wereburghs v Bromborough Pool	1-5
Tattenhill v Wythenshawe Am	4-1
Trafford South v Hazel Grove	3-3
Wilmslow Alb v Vauxhall	1-10
Willaston v Shell Carrington	3-0

Replays

Trafford South v Hazel Grove	0-0

Third Round

Adswood Ams v Christleton	3-2
Barnton v Lymm OB	4-1
Bramhall v Cadbury	2-0
Alsager Coll v Grove Utd	0-0A
Alsager Town v Linotype	0-1A
Mersey Royal v Bollington	6-2
Hoylake Ath v General Chem	3-2
Willaston v Upton AA	4-1
Bromborough Pool v West Kirby	2-5
Hazel Grove v Cheadle Hulme	1-5
Mond Rangers v Crewe LMR	2-1
Cammell Laird v Vauxhall	*3-2* aet
Davenport v Stork	2-3
Shell Carrington v Poulton Vics	1-5
Helsby BI v Heswall	1-6
Old Altrinchamians v Tattenhall	1-2

Replays

Alsager Coll v Grove Utd	1-4
Alsager Town v Linotype	0-1

Fourth Round

Mersey Royal v Barnton	3-1
Linotype v Cammell Laird	2-1
Bramhall v Cheadle Hulme	7-1
Heswall v Adswood Amateurs	1-3
Mond Rangers v Tattenhall	0-1
West Kirby v Willaston	1-0
Hoylake Ath v Grove Utd	
Poulton Vics v Stork	1-0

Fifth Round

Hoylake Athletic v Adswood Am	1-2
Linotype v Mersery Royal	2-1
Tattenhall v Poulton Vics	1-3
West Kirby v Bramhall	2-2

Replays

West Kirby v Bramhall	1-2

Semi Finals

Adswood Amateur v Linotype	0-1
Poulton Vics v Bramhall	3-0

FINAL at Nantwich Town FC

Linotype (Mid-Ches.) v Poulton Vics (W Ches.)	2-0

LANCASHIRE

ATS Lancashire Challenge Trophy

Recent winners: '80 Chorley (Ches CL), '81 Barrow (AFL), '82 Chorley (CCL), '83 Chorley (NPL), 'South Liverpool (NPL), '85 Clitheroe (NWC)

Results

First Round

Accrington Stanley v Fleetwood T	2-2
Blackpool Mechs v Lancaster C	1-1 abd
Darwen v Bacup Borough	2-2
Skelmersdale Utd v Nelson	1-0
Wren Rovers v Prestwich Heys	3-1
Morecombe v Atherton Coll	4-0
Netherfield v Radcliffe B	0-2
Rossendale Utd v Marine	0-0
Southport v Atherton LR	2-0

Replays

Accrington Stanley v Fleetwood T	1-2
Blackpool Mechs v Lancaster C	2-1
Darwen v Bacup Borough	1-3
Rossendale Utd v Marine	0-2

Second Round

Barrow v Radcliffe Borough	0-0
Clitheroe v Bacup Borough	4-1
Leyland Motors v Wren Rvrs	1-1
Morecambe v Burscough	1-1
Chorley v Fleetwood Town	0-0
Horwich RMI v Blackpool Mechs	0-2
Marine v S Liverpool	0-1 abd
Southport v Skelmersdale U	4-0

Replays

Barrow v Radclife Borough	3-1
Leyland Motors v Wren Rvrs	1-3
Morecombe v Burscough	4-0
Chorley v Fleetwood Town	3-2
Marine v S Liverpool	2-1

Third Round

Barrow v Morecambe	0-4
Marine v Southport	2-2
Chorley v Blackpool Mechs	4-0
Wren Rovers v Clitheroe	1-2

Replays

Marine v Southport	1-0

Semi-Finals

Clitheroe v Chorley	0-0
Morecambe v Marine	4-2

Replays

Clitheroe v Chorley	0-2

FINAL, at Preston North End FC

Chorley (Multipart) v Morecambe (Multipart)	2-3

The Multipart League sides came through the First Round unscathed, but a North West Counties Third Division side, Blackpool Mechanics won the second round honours with a 2-0 victory at Horwich RMI. They could not repeat this at Chorley in the quarter finals, when Gola League Barrow provided the biggest shock, in being thrashed 4-0 at home by Morecambe. No surprise in Clitheroe going through to provide the only challenge to the Multipart League in the semis, but although the holders held Chorley to a draw, they could not prevent them winning the replay and going into the final against Morecambe.

LEICESTERSHIRE Senior Cup

Semi Finals

Friar Lane OB v Narborough & Littlethorpe	0-3
Wigston Town v Anstey Nomads	1-0

FINAL at Holmes Park, Wigston Town FC

Wigston Town v Narborough & Littlethorpe	2-0

(This was not strictly a home match, as Holmes Park is the County FA ground, and as such is always used for the final)

Challenge Cup, First Round

Holwell Works v Shepshed Chart.	1-4
Friar Lane OB v Hinckley Ath	1-4
Thringstone MW v Leicester Utd	
Wigston Fields v Anstey Nomads	0-1

FINAL at Leicester City FC

Shepshed Charterhouse (Southern Prem) v Leicester Utd (South, Mid)	6-0

The challenge Cup is an invitation tournament for the two Southern League Clubs, Hinckley of the West Midlands League and invited Senior Leaguers, unlike the senior cup, the major teams put out full first teams in this contest.

LINCOLNSHIRE

Lincolnshire has the confusion of three senior competitions - the Senior Cup is as pre-season competition, between the three football league sides, and three Premier Non-league teams, Boston United, Gainsborough Trinity and Grantham - sadly even for this, fullstrength sides cannot be guaranteed. In the 1985 final, Boston United beat Lincoln City by four goals to nil. The Senior 'A' Cup had thirteen teams in 85-6, and includes all the Counties Northern Counties (East) and United Counties League sides, and the pick of the County League, while the rest of the County League sides and a few others play in the County 'B' Cup

Recent winners: 'A' '80 - '82 Boston FC (Mid Counties, then NC(E)), '83 Stamford (UCL), '84 & '85 Holbeach United (UCL)

Recent winners: 'B' [All Lincs League) '80 Drewery Sports, '81 Immingham, '82 Drewery Sports, '83 Ross Sp, '84 Lincoln Claytons, '85 Brigg T (NCE)

Results

'A' Cup, Preliminary Round

Spalding United v Brigg Town	2-1
Bourne Town v Skegness Town	0-1
Stamford v Appleby Frodingham	2-3
Barton Town v Lincoln United	0-2
Louth United v Ross Sports	1-2
First Round	
Immingham Town v Lincoln United	1-5
Boston FC v Holbeach Utd	1-1
Spalding Utd v Skegness T	0-0
Replays	
Boston FC v Holbeach Utd	0-1
Spalding Utd v Skegness T	3-1
Semi-Finals	
Spalding United v Ross Sports	1-0
Lincoln United v Holbeach Utd	4-2
FINAL	
Lincoln United (MCE, Div 2) v Spalding United (UCL, Prem)	4-1

'B' Cup, Preliminary Round

Cleethorpes CS v Ruston Spts	3-4
Mablethorpe Ath v Nettleham	1-0
Harrowby United v Messingham Trin	4-3
Saxilby Ath v Louth OB	2-3
First Round	
Crowle United v Gainsborough Town	1-2
Brigg White Horse v Bottesford	2-1
Ruston Spts v Sleaford Town	0-1
Cleethorpes Boro' v Louth OB	3-0
Market Rasen T v Grimsby SH FS	0-7
Mirrlees Blackstone v Lincoln Claytons	2-3
Harrowby Utd v Mablethorpe Ath	1-2
Grimsby Ams v Grantham United	3-2
Second Round	
Grimsby Amateurs v Grimsby SH FS	0-5
Lincoln Claytons v Sleaford T	2-4
Mablethorpe Ath v Cleethorpes B	3-0
Gainsborough Town v Brigg White Horse	3-0
Semi-Finals	
Gainsborough Town v Grimsby SH FS	1-1
Sleaford Town v Mablethorpe Athletic	4-0
Replays	
Gainsborough Town v Grimsby SH FS	0-0, 3-2 pens

FINAL, at Northolme (Gainsborough Trinity & Gainsborough Town FC)

Gainsborough Town (Lincs) v Sleaford Town (Lincs)	1-1, 4-5 pens

Barton Town, who played in the Preliminary Round, folded soon afterwards, to this one of the last games for the famous Lincolnshire side. Skegness exerted such a dominance over the early part of the season that their victory over Bourne Town was not really a surprise, but the 3-0 replay victory for Grimsby side Ross Sports against Appleby Frodingham must go down as a 'shock'. Ross lost 1-0 in the semi final to Spalding, thus ending any hopes of becomming only the second side form the County League to win the Cup (Brigg Town did it ten years ago), the Trophy going back into Northern Counties (East) hands when their second division champions, Lincoln won the final by 4-1.

LIVERPOOL

Senior Cup

Recent winners: '80 - '82 Liverpool Res (Central Lge), '83 Everton Res (Central), '84 S Liverpool (NPL), '85 Marine (NPL)

Results

First Round

Bootle v Formby	2-0
Kirkby Town v Marine	2-1
St Helens v South Liverpool	1-2
Burscough v Southport	2-2
Prescot Cables v Skelmersdale U	3-0
Replays	
Burscough v Southport	0-1
Second Round	
Kirkby Town v Bootle	2-1
South Liverpool v Everton Res	1-1
Tranmere Rovers Res v Prescot Cables	2-2
Southport v Liverpool Res	1-0
Replays	
South Liverpool v Everton Res	1-1
Tranmere Rovers Res v Prescot Cables	0-3
Second Replay	
South Liverpool v Everton Res	1-1
Third Replay	
South Liverpool v Everton Res	3-1
Semi-Finals	
Kirkby Town v South Liverpool	1-2
Southport v Prescot Cables	0-0
Replays	
Southport v Prescot Cables	4-0

FINAL, at South Liverpool FC

South Liverpool (Multipart) v Southport (Multipart)	2-1

North West Counties, div two side Kirkby Town provided the surprisen te irst round with a 2-1 win over Multipart League side Marine - the other two Premier sides went through, although Southport needed a replay against Busrcough. The three Football League reserve sides came in, and went out again at the second round stage, only Liverpool though, visiting Southport fell at the first attempt, Prescot needed a second match against Tranmere, while South Liverpool and Everton shared three one all draws before the Multipart side went through 3-1. With Kirkby beating Marine in the other match, both semi-finals were between Multipart and North West Counties teams. Although Southport needed a replay, both Multipart sides got through, and South Liverpool made best use of home advantage.

What a lovely day! Hendon (winners after extra-time - 2-0) contest the Middlesex Senior Cup Final with Southall at Griffin Park, Brentford.

London Senior Cup

First Qualifying Round

No matches

Second Qualifying Round

BROB Barnet v Southwark Sports	1-2
Barkingside v Ford United	2-0
Penhill Standard v Royal Arsenal SRA	0-2
Wandsworth v Southgate Ath	0-3
Danson (Bexley Boro) v Chingford	4-0
Hoddesdon v Pennant Sports	2-1
Eton Manor v Civil Service	1-0
Thames Poly v Hanwell Town	1-2

Third Qualifying Round

Edgeware v Corinthian Casuals	2-1 aet
Danson v Hanwell Town	1-2
Collier Row v Southgate Ath	2-1
East Ham Utd v Hoddesdon	1-1, 0-2
Southwark Sp v Crown & Manor	3-1
Beckton United v Brimsdown Rov.	0-1
Barkingside v Royal Arsenal SRA	7-0
Woking v Eton Manor	4-2 aet

First Round

kCollier Row v Fisher Athletic	3-1
Haringey Borough v Bromley	3-2
Welling United v Kingstonian	2-0
Walthamstow Ave v Southall	3-0
Barking v Woodford Town	0-1
Boreham Wood v Brimsdown Rovers	1-4
Carshalton Athletic v Clapton	7-1
Hampton v Woking	0-1
Barkingside v Croydon	1-0/
Hendon v Edgeware	3-1
Hoddesdon T v Leyton-Wingate	1-2
Leytonstone-Ilford v Cheshunt	2-0
Staines Town v Feltham	2-1
Houslow v Epsom & Ewell	0-2
Hanwell Town v Dulwich Hamlet	3-2
Southwark Sp v Finchley	1-2

Second Round

Epsom & Ewell v Hendon	H-w/o
Walthamstow Ave v Welling Utd	4-2
Woking v Leyton Wingate	4-0
Carshalton Ath v Barkingside	4-0
Finchley v Collier Row	2-0
Hanwell T v Leytonstone	HT-w/o
Saines Town v Brimsdown Rov	3-2
Woodford Town v Haringey Boro	2-3

London Senior Cup, Third Round

Carshalton Ath v Finchley	0-3
Haringey Boro v Woking	1-2
Staines Town v Hendon	1-2
Hanwell T v Walthamstow Ave	2-3

Semi-Finals

Walthamstow Avenue v Woking	3-0
Finchley v Hendon	2-0 aet

FINAL at Brentford FC

Finchley (VOL-1) v Walthamstow Avenue (VOL-Prem)	1-2

...and Epsom also failed to meet Hendon - other results give little indication of the strength of teams, but Welling's 4-2 defeat at Walthamstow causes, at least an eyebrow to be raised. After this the competition settled down, with Finchley scoring good wins over Carshalton and Hendon, both of whom narrowly avoided relegation from the Vauxhall Opel Premier Division, to reach the final at Griffin Park, where Walthamstow won by 2- 1.

MIDDLESEX Senior Cup Final, 1984-5 (held over), at Hendon FC

Enfield (Gola) v Wealdstone (Gola)	2-4

Senior Cup, 85-6

First Preliminary Round

Southgate Athletic v Hanwell T	0-3
N Greenford Utd v Rayners Lane	0-4
Northwood v Brimsdown Rovers	0-1
Harefield Utd v Hounslow	1-3

Second Preliminary Round

Crown & Manor v Rayners Lane	1-1
Kingsbury Town v Feltham	3-0
Brimsdown Rovers v Hounslow	2-3
Ruislip Manor v Edgeware	3-0
Southall v Hanwell Town	4-1
Yeading v Haringey Borough	0-4

Replays

Crown & Manor v Rayners Lane	2-4 aet

First Round

Finchley v Enfield	2-0
Harrow Borough v Uxbridge	2-1
Hayes v Hounslow	1-0
Hendon v Harrow Borough	1-0
Rusilip Manor v Staines Town	2-1
Southall v Rayners Lane	3-3
Wealdstone v Kinsbury Town	1-3
Wembley v Hampton	4-0

Replays

Southall v Rayners Lane	3-1

Second Round

Harrow Borough v Ruislip Manor	6-2
Hayes v Finchley	2-1
Wembley v Hendon	0-1
Southall v Kinsbury Town	3-0

Semi-Finals

Harrow Borough v Hendon	2-3
Southall v Hayes	1-0

FINAL, at Enfield FC

Hendon (VOL-Prem) v Southall (VOL-2S)	2-0 aet

....Unfortunately for the second division side, they could not hold out throughout the final, and after ninety scoreless minutes, two goals by Colin Tate gave the cup to Hendon in extra time

MANCHESTER Premier Cup

The Premier Cup was introduced in 1979-80, and has remained in the domain of what now constitutes the North West Counties League, and it's main predesessor the Cheshire County League.

Previous Winners: '80 Ashton United, '81 Droylesden, '82 Curzon Ashton, '83 Ashton United, '84 Curzon Ashton, '85 Irlam Town

Results

First Round

Chadderton v Irlam Town	1-5
Oldham v Droylesden	0-2
Mossley v Ashton United	3-2
Salford v Curzon Ashton	0-2

Second Round

Curzon Ashton v Mossley	1-0
Irlam Town v Droylesden	6-3

FINAL, at Oldham Athletic FC

Curzon Ashton (NWC, Div 1) v Irlam Town (NWC, Div 1)	1-0

The dominance of the North West Counties League is only really to be expected, as only one of the eight contestants comes from outside the League. That one, Multipart League Mossley, had to confine their attentions to Ashton-Under-Lyme, for after a 3-2 victory against United, they came up against Curzon in the semi-final, going down 1-0 in a dour affair. None of the other matches even went as far as producing a victory for lower division over higher division clubs, although Irlam, who won last season as a second division club, at least reached the final in some style, with 5-1 and 6-3 wins. The final though went more to Curzon's duller play, and the National Park club won 1-0, to put their name on the Trophy for the third time.

Middlesex Premier Cup

First Round

Ashford v Ruislip	2-5 aet
Harefield Res v Brimsdown Res	4-1
Haringey B Res v Enfield Res	0-5
Harrow St Mary's v Hanwell T Res	1-0
Southall Res v Harrow B Res	3-3
Replays	
Southall Res v Harrow B Res	2-8

Second Round

Constantine Utd v Cockfosters	2-3
Enfield Res v Uxbridge Res	1-0
Feltham Res v Bromley Prk Rangers	1-2
Hampton Res v Brook House	2-0
Hanworth Villa v Ruislip M Res	0-4
Harrow St Mary's v Ruislip	3-1
Lucas CAV v Harrow B Res	2-1
N Greenford Res v Edgeware Res	3-1
Pittshanger Dynamo v Staines R	2-1
Southgate Res v Hendon Res	2-4
Sunbury v Harefield Res	1-3
Technicolour Spts v Rayners L Res	3-2
Hounslow Res v Bedfont	1-2
Kingsbury Res v Borough Road	2-4
Viking Spts v Evershed Social	1-0
Yeading Res v Old Actonians	1-1
Replays	
Yeading Res v Old Actonians	6-2

Third Round

Bedfont v Lucas CAV	0-1
Borough Road v Harefield Res	0-2
Cockfosters v Ruislip M Res	3-0
Enfield Res v Viking Spts	2-1
Hampton Res v Yeading Res	2-0
Hendon Res v Bromley Pk Rang	2-0
Pittshanger Dynamo v Harrow St M	3-4
Technicolour S v N Greenford Res	0-4

Fourth Round

Cockfosters v Hampton Res	1-2
Harefield Res v Enfield Res	1-1
Hendon Res v N Greenford Res	1-2
Lucas CAV v Harrow St Mary's	1-0
Replays	
Harefield Res v Enfield Res	3-0

Semi-Finals

N Greenford Res v Harefield Res	1-1
Lucas CAV v Hampton Res	1-3
Replays	
N Greenford Res v Harefield Res	0-2

FINAL, at Staines Town FC

Hampton Res (Suburban) v Harefield Utd Res (Middx Border)	0-1

NORFOLK Senior Cup

Preliminary Round

Wells Town v Coltishall HV'85	0-1
Thetford Rovers v Proingland Utd	1-3

First Round

Overstrand v Bradenham	1-3
Wymondham Town v Dereham	3-1
St Andrews v Swaffham	1-0
Diss Town v C E Y M S	2-1
Downham Town v Poringland	1-5
Hempnall v Holt United	1-2
Blofield v Wroxham	1-3
Wymondham OB v Watton United	0-2
Reepham Town v Carrow	1-1
Lakeford v Kings Lynn Res	4-1
Coltishall HV'85 v Fakenham T	4-3
Harleston v Newton Flotman	1-0

Second Round

Grt Yarmouth v Wroxham	1-2
Holt United v Bradenham	2-4
Gorleston v Diss Town	3-0
Reepham Town v Norwich C Res	0-4
Watton United v St Andrews	3-0
Thetford TRown v Coltishall HV'85	2-4
Poringland v Wymondham T	3-1
Lakeford v Harleston	3-2

Third Round

Poringland v Wroxham	3-1
Lakeford v Gorleston	2-1
Watton United v Bradenham	2-2
Norwich Res v Coltishall HV'85	2-1
Replays	
Watton United v Bradenham	3-0

Semi-Finals

Lakeford Rangers v Poringland Utd	0-3
Watton Uniterd v Norwich C Res	0-3

FINAL, at Norwich City FC

Norwich City Res (F Comb) v Poringland United (Ang Comb)	4-1

NORTHAMPTONSHIRE Senior (Hillier) Cup

Since 1981, the Northamptonshire senior Cup has been known as the Hillier Cup, after a former secretary of the Northants FA

Recent Winners: '80 Kettering T (Gola), '81 Irthlingborough Diamonds (UCL), '82 Wellingborough T (Southern), '83 Corby Town (Southern), '84 & '85 Kettering Town (Gola)QLRound 1

Long Buckby v I'boro Diamonds	3-1
Rothwell Town v Brackley Town	1-2
Wellingborough T v Desborough Town	7-1
Northampton Spencer v Raunds Town	1-1
	4-2 replay
Rushden Town v Corby Stewarts & Lloyds	0-1

Round 2

Wellingborough T v N'ton Spencer	3-0
Corby Town v Corby Stewarts & Lloyd	4-1
Brackley Town v Long Buckby	1-2

Semi-Final

Corby Town v Long Buckby	5-4
Kettering Town v Wellingborough T	1-0

FINAL

Corby Town v Kettering Town	0-1

Hillier Cup summary

Corby Town had a bye to the second round, and holders Kettering to the semi final, this meant that two Southern League sides, and eight from the United Counties started in the first round, with Stewarts & Lloyds, from Corby winning 1-0 at Rushden, to set up a tie with their near neighbours Corby Town. Not quite as near as they used to be though, as Corby's old ground was adjacent to Stewarts & Lloyds in Occupation Road, but now they are two miles apart, and with the Southern League side winning 4-1, the only UCL side to make it into the semi-finals were Long Buckby, and they too fell to Corby Town, while still in keeping with the form book, two 1-0 wins gave Gola Leagues Kettering the Cup.

North Riding Senior Cup

Recent winners: '80 York City (FL), 81'& '82 Scarborough (Gola) '83 Whitby (Dryborough NL), '84 South Bank (Dryborough NL) '85 Scarborough (Gola)

Results : First Qualifying Round

York Railway Inst. v Nunthorpe Ath	4-2
Pickering T v Tees Components	2-0
New Marske SC v Acklam Steelworks	3-3
	3-2

Second Qualifying Round

Rowntree Mackingtosh v York RI	2-0
Pickering T v New Marske SC	4-1
Marske United v Wilton ICI	5-0
Northallerton v Stockton	1-2

Third Qualifying Round

Rowntree Mackingtosh v Marske Utd	1-1
	1-4
Stockton v Pickering T	2-1

First Round

Middlesborough v Scarborough	1-2
South Bank v Stockton	3-0
York City v Marske United	
Guisborough T v Whitby Town	0-1

Semi-Finals

Whitby Town v South Bank	4-2
Scarborough v York City	1-4

FINAL at Whitby Town FC

Whitby Town (Dryborough NL) v York City (Canon Lge)	0-1

Summary: The North Riding is the largest of the County FA's in terms of area, but not in number of clubs. The areas two football league clubs, Scarborough of the Gola League and three major Dryborough Northern League sides are exempt to the first round, leaving the others, from the Teeside, Wearside, Dryborough Northern and Northern Counties (East) leagues for two places. It was a poor season for the Teeside sides, with no winners, except when two of their own teams met, Marske United of the Wearside qualified with a replay win over Rowntree Mackintosh, and Dryborough Northern div 2 side Stockton also won through. Neither of these could beat exempt clubs in round one. Scarborough won 2-1 at Middlesborough, but then lost at home to York City, who have decided they like beating non-league opposition (4 in the FA Cup this season), and went on to win 1-0 at Whitby Town in the final.

NORTH RIDING
Saturday County Cup

Results

First Round

Dormans Athletic v Pickering Town	6-0
Scarborough Athletic v Eastfield	4-3
Acklam Steelworks v New Marske	2-3
Hemlington Soc v N Ormesby Inst	3-1

Second Round

Civil Service (York) v Nunthorpe Ath	1-2
Acklam Steelworks v Kirkby Moorside	2-2
Dormans Athletic v Smiths Dock	1-0
Marske United v Hemlington SC	4-0
Tees Components v ICI Wilton	1-3
Teeside Poly v Cayton Corinthians	4-2
Scarborough Ath v New Marske SC	7-2
Ryedale SC v Stockton FC	1-6

Replays

Acklam Steelworks v Kirkby Moorside	3-3

Second Replay

Acklam Steelworks v Kirkby Moorside	1-0

Third Round

Wilton ICI v Acklam Steelworks	1-0
Dormans Athletic v Nunthorpe Ath	5-1
Stockton FC v Scarborough Ath	8-0
Teeside Poly v Marske United	0-2

Semi-Finals

Stockton FC v Wilton ICI	4-1
Marske United v Dormans Ath	2-0

FINAL

Stockton FC (Teeside) v Marske United (Vaux Wearside)	2-1

NORTHUMBERLAND Senior Club

First Round

Blue Star v NEI Parson Ath	5-0
Ponteland Utd v Whitley Bay	2-3 at WB
Newcastle Utd v Stobswood Welfare	9-1
Ashington v Seaton Terrace	3-1

Second Round

Ashington v North Shields	0-3
Whitley Bay v Newcastle United	1-0
Blyth Spartans v Prudhoe East End	4-2 aet
Dudley Welfare v Blue Star	1-4

Semi-Finals

Blyth Spartans v Whitley Bay	1-2
North Shields v Blue Star	0-1 aet

FINAL at Newcastle United FC

Blue Star (DNL, 2) v Whitley Bay (DNL, 1)	3-2

Northumberland Senior Benevolent Bowl

Recent winners: '80 Prudhoe East End, '81 Cramlington High Pit SC '82 Ponteland United, '83 Dudley Welfare, '84 NEI Parsons Athletic '85 Stobswood Welfare (Nother FA, except Parsons Ath Northern Comb)

First Round

Newcastle University v Longbenton	1-0
Haltwhistle Crown Paints v Percy Main Amateurs	3-5
Gosforth St. Nicholas v Morpeth T	1-2
Forest Hall v Gosforth Bohemians	1-3
Bedlington Terriers v Annitsford Welfare	2-1
Wallsend T v Ashington Hirst Prog	1-3
W Allotment Celtic v Wark	3-2
Seaton Delaval Am v Alnwick T	2-1

Second Round

Morpeth T v Seaton Delaval Ams	3-2
Ashington Hirst Progressive v Newcastle University	2-3
Gosforth Bohemians v KWest Allotment Celtic	0-2

Semi-Finals

Morpeth T v Newcastle Univ.	4-2
W. Allotment Celtic v Bedlington T	1-0

FINAL at Whitley Bay FC

Morpeth Town (North FA ll) v West Allotment Celtic (North FA ll)	4-1

....Whitley Bay and Blue Star met in what turned out to be an exciting final - Blue Star took an early lead with a deflected shot from Pickford, and increased this before the break, again through Pickford, and again with a deflection. Two minutes into the second half, Todd put the Star into a seemingly unassailable 3-0 lead, especially when Todd missed a penalty chance to reduce the arrears, but then Ferebee pulled one back for the Seasiders, and Crumplin for Blue Star missed his chance with a penalty, Deverdics made the score 3-2, but despite pressure, Bay could not level the scores in the dying minutes. The Benevolent Bowl is mainly for clubs from the Northern Football Alliance, the Northern Combination and the Northern Amateur League, all of which are sponsored by McEwens Brewery. The exception is Bedlington Terriers from the First Division of the Dryborough Northern League, where they were runners up, so their semi-final defeat by West Allotment Celtic has to go down as the surprise result of the competition.

NOTTINGHAMSHIRE Senior Cup

First Round

Arnold Kingswell v John Player	1-0
Gedling CW v Keyworth Utd	0-6
Arnold v Meadows Albion	2-0
Clipstone Welfare v Southwell C	3-0
Dunkirk v Newstead MW	3-1
Sutton Town v Boots Athletic	2-0
Rolls Royce v Plessey	2-3
Rainworth MW v Radford Olympic	6-1
Cotgrave Utd v Carlton Athletic	3-4
City & Sherwood H v Sutton Trin	4-0
Hucknall CW v Eastwood Town	3-0
Kimberley T v Blidworth Welf	1-8
Nuthall v Basford United	0-2
British Rail v Oakham Utd	1-2
Clifton All Whites v Notts Accad	4-1
Attenborough v Worthington Simp	3-4

Second Round

Rainworth MW v Sutton Town	0-2
Worthington Simpsons v Dunkirk	2-1
Clifton All Whites v Arnold K	4-1
Basford United v Arnold	0-1
Chipstone Wel v City & Sgerwood H	1-0
Keyworth Utd v Blidworth Welf	2-1
Hucknall CW v Oakham United	3-2
Plessey v Carlton Athletic	5-3

Third Round

Clifton All Whites v Arnold	1-2
Clipstone Welf v Worthington Simps	2-1
Hucknall CW v Plessey	0-0 (Ab)
Sutton T v Keyworth U	5-5, 4-5 pens

Replays

Hucknall CW v Plessey	2-1

Semi-Finals

Clipstone Welfare v Arnold	4-1
Keyworth Utd v Hucknall CW	1-2

FINAL

Clipstone Welfare (Notts FA) v Hucknall CW (Notts FA)	1-0

....Arnold came unstuck in the semi-finals, going down 4-1 to Clipstone Welfare, who went on from this success to beat Hucknall and win the cup.

OXFORDSHIRE

Recent winners: '80 Peppard Sports (Reading), '81 Thame United (Hellenic), '82 Peppard (Reading), '83 & '84 Oxford City (Isthmian), '85 Morris Motors (Hellenic)

FINAL, at Banbury United FC

Oxford City (Vauxhall-Opel, 1) v Witney Town (Southern Prem)	2-1

Finally, thanks to Tony Williams for looking after Somerset, Devon and Cornwall, Paul Cowburn for Lancashire, Manchester and Liverpool, the County FA's for considerable help, and most of all the Bureau of Non-League football, without which, this section would have been impossible.

SHEFFIELD & HALLAMSHIRE Senior Cup

Recent Winners: '80 & '81 Emley (Yorks Lge), '82 Worksop (NPL), '83 Mexborough T (NCE), '84 Emley (NCE), '85 Worksop (NPL)

Preliminary Round

Jubilee Spts v Oughtibridge WMSC	5-3

First Round Qualifying

Tinsley Wire v Paramore Spts	1-0
Firparnians v Rotherham Club	1-2
Goldthorpe Coll v Oxley Pk Spts	2-1
Penistone Church v Dearne Comm MW	1-2
Abbeydale OB v Bethsda Methodist	0-6
Woodsetts Welf v Rossington Main	4-2
A Lee SC v Denaby & Cadeby MW	w/o
SKF & Dormer Spts v Ecclesfield	4-1
Stella v S Kirkby Town	6-1
Bradley v Oxspring United	5-0
Northgate WMC v Phoenix	4-0
Sheffield Bankers v Sheffield Centralians	1-2
Swinton Athletic v Jubilee Sports	2-1
Ash House GC v Mexborough Main St	3-2
East Dene Soc v Hickleton Main Wel	3-2
Midland Bank v Crosspool Sp	3-4
Aurora Utd v Record Ridgeway	3-2
BSC Tinsley v Rotherwood	3-3
Sheffield Gas v University	2-2, 6-8 pens
Old Edwardians v Windsor	0-3
Treeton Welf v Forgemasters	1-0
Houghton Main W v Brunsmeer Ath	1-2
Kilnhurst Coll v Crookes	0-4
Elescar Main Coll v Davy McKee	3-4

Replays

BSC Tinsley v Rotherwood	3-2

Second Round Qualifying

Windsor v Woodsetts Welf	6-1
Dearne Comm MW v Aurora Utd	6-0
Bathesda Methodist v Crosspool Sp	5-0
Denaby & Cadeby MW v Goldthorpe C	3-2
Ash House GC v Northgate WMC	0-1
East Dene Soc v SKF & Dormer S	2-6
Sheffield Centralians v Swinton A	1-0
Stella v Bradley	0-1
Treeton Welf v BSC Tinsley	3-0
Crookes v Davy McKee	2-0
University v Brunsmeer Athletic	4-2
Tinsley Wire v Rotherham Club	8-0

First Round

Maltby MW v Woolley MW	2-1
Sheffield University v Treeton W	1-2
Bentley VW v Denaby United	3-2
Dronfield United v BSC Parkgate	2-0
Sheffield v Frecheville Comm	2-1
Crookes v Worsborough Bridge	5-0
Yorkshire Main Coll v Kiveton P	0-1
Worksop Town v Harworth CI	2-1
Denaby & Cadeby MW v Stocksbridge W	2-3
Frickley A v S Centralians	5-1
Hallam v Tinsley Wire	6-3
Grimethorpe MW v SKF & Dormer	5-1
Northgate WMC v Bethesda Meth	3-2
Bradley v Wombwell SA	2-0
Emley v Dearne Comm MW	1-1
Mexborough T Ath v Windsor	2-0

Replays

Emley v Dearne Comm MW	1-2

Second Round

Dearne Comm MW v Frickley Ath	3-5
Crooke v Maltby MW	5-1
Bradley v Dronfield Utd	1-3
Northgate WMC v Treeton Wel	0-0
Hallam v Mexborough TA	2-2
Grimethorpe MW v Sheffield	0-1
Worksop T v Bentley Vic Wel	2-0
Kiveton Park v Stocksbridge W	1-0

Replays

Northgate WMC v Treeton Wel	0-3
Hallam v Mexborough TA	4-0

Third Round

Hallam v Kiveton Park	2-1
Dronfield United v Crookes	0-6
Worksop Town v Sheffield	6-2
Treeton Welfare v Frickley Ath	1-4

Semi-Finals

Crookes v Hallam	2-0
Frickley Athletic v Worksop T	3-0

FINAL, at Worksop Town FC

Frickley Ath (Gola) v Crookes (Whitbread County Lge)	2-0

Senior Cup - Summary

With many sides from local leagues in the competition, a Preliminary match and two qualifying rounds are played before the Northern Counties (East) teams, Frickley (Gola League) and Worksop (Multipart) join in. Probably the best known of those trying to quality are Central Midlands League side Rossington Main, who fell 4-2 to Woodsetts in the first qualifying round. In the First Round, Dearne Community MW scored a replay win over Emley FC, and they went on to score 3 goals against Frickley before going out 5-3. Bradley (not NCE side Bradley Rangers) scored a 2-0 win over Wombwell SA, but all honours go to Whitbread County League side Crookes, who conceded only one goal in moving from the first qualifying round to the final, this being during a 5-1 win over Maltby MW. Three other Northern Counties (East) clubs got the treatment, Worsborough Bridge 5-0, Dronfield United (who were drawn at home) 6-0, and Hallam by the lesser score, just 2-0 in the semi-final. Gola League Frickley beat Worksop (Multipart) 3-0 in the other semi. In the final, Crookes lived with their more esteemed rivals until half time, even hitting the bar, but not surprisingly, Frickley took control after the break, scoring two, missing a penalty and coming close on several other occasions.

Shropshire

There are two Cups in Shropshire, the Senior Cup is competed for only by four teams, Canon League Shrewsbury, Gola League Telford United, Southern League Bridgnorth and Multipart League Oswestry Town.

Recent winners : '80-'84 Shrewsbury T, '85 Oswestry Town.

The County Cup is competed for by 19 teams from West Midland, Mid Comb and County Leagues.

Recent winners : '80 Bridgnorth (Mid Comb), '81 Shifnal Town (W Mid) '82 Whitchurch Alport (Mid Ches), '83 GKN Sankey (W Mid), '84 Donnington Wood (W Mid), '85 GKN Sankey (W Mid).

Results:

Senior Cup, Semi-Finals

Shrewsbury Town v Bridgnorth Town	0-1
Telford United v Oswestry T	2-3

FINAL at Bridgnorth Town FC

Bridgnorth Town (Southern, Mid) v Oswentry Town (Multipart)	4-0

COUNTY CUP

Preliminary Round

Shifnal United v Wem Town	0-7
Donnington Wood v Snailbeach	3-1
GKN Sankey v Broseley Athletic	1-0

First Round

Wem Town v Morda	0-1
Madeley Court Centre v Oakengates	6-2
Sartofix v Shifnal Town	2-1
Highley Welfare v Admaston	5-2
Donnington Wood v Tibberton	3-2
GKN Sankey v Whitchurch Alport	3-1
Bridgnorth T res v Ludlow T	3-2
Newport Town v Wellington Ams	2-1

Second Round

Morda v Donnington Wood	3-1
Highley Welfare v Madeley Court Centre	0-3
Sartofix v Bridgnorth Town res	2-1
Newport Town v GKN Sankey	2-0

Semi-Finals

Newport Town v Madeley Court Centre	6-1
Morda v Sartofix	4-2

FINAL at Shrewsbury Town FC

Morda (Shropshire County Lge) v Newport Town (W Mids)	0-2

Sartofix, of the Shropshire County league made the early headlines with victories over W Midland Premier side Shifnal Town, and Mid Combination Bridgnorth Town reserves, but they were beaten by Morda, from the same League in the semis, Morda had previously beaten one West Midland League side in Donnington Wood, but could not stop Newport Town, who had beaten the holders GKN Sankey from winning the kcup, and keeping it within the West Midland League.

SOMERSET & AVON PREMIER CUP

Semi-Finals: Bath City 2, Taunton 0
Yeovil Town 4, Bristol City Reserves 2

Final: Bath City 1, Yeovil Town 0
Yeovil Town 0, Bath City 2
(Bath City win on aggregated 3-0)

SOMERSET & AVON SENIOR CUP

Final: Robinsons DRG 1, Brislington 0

SOUTH WESTERN COUNTIES SUTTON TRANSFORMER VASE

Previously known as the Pratten Cup - United only a few years ago this competition was considered as second only to the FA Vase for clubs in the region. However, many of the major teams that have entered have now withdrawn, others play substandard teams, and there are two Sunday teams, Clump Inn and North Stoneham, both from Southampton involved. Imperial Bristol are known to have fielded their reserve side this year. It is a rule that teams must play opposition from 'out of County' where possible, this makes for interesting ties, but does cause large travel bills, only partly offset by the sponsors.

First Round

North Stoneham v Wotton Rovers	2-0
P & W United v Congressbury	2-0
Clump Inn v Yate Town	1-1
	0-1
Imperial Bristol v Henbury OB	0-3
Portishead v Holsworthy	2-1
Bristol General Hosp v Bashley	1-2 aet
Kilkhampton v Locksheath	2-2

Second Round

Yate Town v Portishead	3-2
Pucklechurch v Locksheath	2-0
Bashley v Henbury OB	1-3
P & W United v North Stoneham	0-1

Semi-Finals (2 leagues)

Pucklechurch v N Stoneham	1-5 *
Yate Town v Henbury OB	1-1
	2-1

* Pucklechurch withdrew

FINAL (2 Leagues)

Yate Town (Hellenic Prem) v North Stoneham (Southampton Sun)	1-1
	4-0

STAFFORDSHIRE Senior Cup

Recent winners '80 Northwich Vics (APL), '81 Kidderminster (Southern), '82 Stoke C, '83-85 Kidderminster (Southern, then Gola.

Senior Cup Competition - Season 1985-86

First Round

Dudley Town v Tamworth	1-0
Hednesford Town v Halesowen Town	1-4
Oldbury United v Eastwood (Hanley)	0-3
Sutton Coldfield Town v Bilston Town	1-2

Second Round

Brereton Social v Malvern Town	4-1
Leek Town v Eastwood (Hanley)	1-2
Willenhall Town v Dudley Town	2-2
	replay2-2
second replay	*2-3*
Stafford Rangers v Port Vale	1-1
	replay 0-1
Rushall Olympic v Stoke City	*replay 2-3*
Alvechurch v Bilston Town	0-3
Halesowen Town v Stourbridge	3-2
Kidderminster Harriers v Armitage	6-0

Third Round

Bilston Town v Dudley Town	3-1
Halesowen Town v Port Vale	2-0
Eastwood (Hanley) v Brereton Social	4-2
Stoke City v Kidderminster Harrier	2-0

Semi Final Ties

Eastwood (Hanley) v Halesowen Town	1-0
Bilston Town v Stoke City	2-0

FINAL Tie

Eastwood (Hanley) v Bilston Town	5-1 (aggregate score)

Summary : Senior Cup - only nine of the twenty entries are affiliated to Staffs as their first County, most of the rest are from Birmingham, although Worcestershire is represented by Kidderminster and Stourbridge. Free scoring Kidderminster put six past hapless Armitage in the second round, but were slightly surprisingly beaten by Stoke City - the football league sides tending to play their reserves in this tournament. Dudley Town beat Tamworth 1-0 in the first round, and then met Willenhall for three of the seven matches between the two this season. Dudley won the second replay 3-2 (they also met in the Birmingham Senior Cup Final, and the Southern League Cup, with Dudley winning, plus twice in the league). Halesowen Town were naturally expected to do well, and looked the part with a convincing win at Hednesford, and a 3-2 victory against old rivals Stourbridge, followed by a good win over Port Vale. Bilston Town beat Dudley to reach the semis, and then accounted for Stoke, when Halesowen Town were beaten 1-0 by North West Counties League side Eastwood (Hanley). The final was played over two legs, with Bilston Town (Southern League, Midland Division) at home first 1-4 and Eastwood (Hanley) (North West Counties League Division One) winning the cup with a 1-0 home win.

The Senior Vase is competed for by sides from the Staff Senior League, and Staffordshire sides in W. Midlands and Mid Cheshire Leagues. Eastwood's side is the reserves from the Staffs League. W. Midland Premier side Harrisons were surprisingly beaten 2-1 at home by Knypersley in the first round, and in the second it was

Sussex R.U.R. Cup 1st Round. Storrington (all dark strip) 1, Arundel 3.

Midland Comb Premier sides' Bloxwich AFC time to go out, after a 2-2 draw, they lost 6-1 at Rocester. In the Quarter finals, there were still two survivors from the W Midlands League, but Premier Division Chasetown lost 2-1 at home to Eastwood (Hanley) res., while Wolves Casuals lost 2-0 at Eccleshall. Ecceshall then beat Eastwood in a replay, while Rocester won 4-1 against the only remaining non-Staffs League side, Kidsgrove, who compete in the Mid Cheshire League.

Staffordshire Vase Competition

First Round

Harrisons v Knypersley Vics	1-2
Eastwood (Hanley) v Goldenhill Wanderers	1-0
Penkridge Town v Lichfield	1-0
Hanley Town v Leek CSOB	2-2
	replay 2-0
Bloxwich Town v Kidsgrove Athletic	0-4
Brewood v Hanford	1-1
	replay 2-1
Bloxwich AFC v Staffordshire Police	3-2
Wolverhampton Casuals v Hednesford Progressive	6-0
Redgate United v Milton United	3-2
Chasetown v Paget Rangers	0-0
	replay 1-0
Great Wyrley v Newcastle Town	1-1
	replay 1-4
Rocester v Ball Haye Green	*2-0*
H & R Johnson v Meir KA	*2-3*

Second Round

Bilston United v Redgate United	0-3
Bloxwich AFC v Rocester	2-2
	replay 1-6
Eccleshall v Stafford Town	2-0
Chasetown v Penkridge	1-0
Newcastle Town v Brewood	4-0
Hanley Town v Eastwood (Hanley)	2-3
Knypersley Vics v Kidgrove AFC	0-1
Wolverhampton Casuals v Meir KA	1-1
replay 1-0	

Third Round

Chasetown v Eastwood (Hanley)	1-2
Eccleshall v Wolverhampton Casuals	2-0
Rocester v Newcastle Town	3-0
Kidsgrove AFC v Redgate United	1-1
replay 2-0	

Semi-Final Ties

Eastwood (Hanley) v Eccleshall	1-1
	replay 0-1
Kidsgrove AFC v Rocester	1-4

FINAL Tie

Rocester v Eccleshall	2-1

SUFFOLK

There are two cups, the Premier which involves major teams, mainly from the Eastern Counties League, and the Senior Cup, involves the reserves of the above teams, and teams from the Suffolk & Ipswich league.

Recent winners : Senior Cup '80 Nicholians Locomotive, '81 Ransomes, '82 Crane Sports, '83 Hadleigh, '84 Carne, '85 Bury Town res

Premier Cup : '80 Lowestoft, '81-3 Sudbury T, '84 Brantham '85 Sudbury.

Results : Senior Cup, First Round

Achilles v Bungay	3-1
Lakenheath v Coplestonians	1-0
Ipswich United v Lowestoft	2-0
Kirkley v BT Research	0-1
Long Melford v Haverhill	1-1
	replay 1-0
Oulton Broad v Sudbury	0-1
Whitton v Felixstowe	6-5
Leiston v Hadleigh	3-3
	replay 1-0
Crane Sports v Mildenhall	*0-3*
Bury T res v Ransomes	*1-2*
Sudbury Wanderers v Brantham	*3-1*
Willis Faber v Halesworth	*0-1*
Haughley v Old Newton	*2-0*
Grundisburgh v Beccles	*1-2*
Stowmarket v Stutton	*4-1*

Second Round

Sudbury Wanderers v Long Melford	2-4
Westerfield v Halesworth	3-0
Mildenhall v BT Research	3-3
	replay 3-1
Sudbury v Leiston	0-1
Haughley v Stowmarket	2-1
Whitton v Ransomes	2-4
Lakenheath v Ipswich Utd	1-2
Beccles Town v Achilles	3-2

Third Round

Long Melford v Westerfield	0-1
Haughley v Ransomes	0-0
	replay 2-1
Mildenhall v Leiston	2-3
Ipswich United v Beccles T	0-0
replay 2-1	

Semi-Finals

Westerfield v Ipswich United	4-2
Haughley v Leiston	1-1
replay ?-?	

FINAL at Ipswich Town FC

Leiston Town (Suffolk & Ips) v Westerfield United (Suffolk & Ips)	1-4

Premier Cup (Full results not available)

Semi Finals

Haverhill Rovers v Lowestoft	2-2
	replay 2-4
Stowmarket T v Felixstowe	*4-0*

FINAL at Sudbury Town FC

Stowmarket Town (Eastern) v Lowestoft Town (Eastern)	1-0

SURREY

First Qualifying Round : No matches

Second Qualifying Round

Chipstead v Chessington United	3-0
Egham Town v Shene Old Grammarians	3-0
Virginia Water v Carshalton FC	1-0
Cobham v Farnham Town	0-2
Horley Town v Frimley Green	3-2
Sheerwater v Chobham	0-3
Godalming Town v B Ae Weybridge	4-1

Third Qualifying Round

Corinthian Casuals v Egham Town	1-2
Malden Vale v Camberley Town	0-1
Chipstead v Farleigh Rovers	0-1
Chobham v Merstham	2-0
Godalming Town v Reigate Priory	7-0
Hartley Wintney v Virginia Water	3-1
Lingfield v Kew Association	1-2
Chertsey Town v Old Suttonians	2-1
Horley Town v Farnham Town	3-2
Westfield v Malden Town	3-2

Fourth Qualifying Round

Godalming Town v Farleigh Rovers	1-0
Horley Town v Camberley Town	2-3
Westfield v Chobham	0-2
Chertsey Town v Kew Association	5-0
Hartley Wintney v Egham Town	3-1

Fifth Qualifying Round

Woking v Camberley Town	1-2
Hartley Wintney v Banstead Ath	1-2
Ash United v Dorking	1-0
Chertsey Town v Godalming Town	2-1
Chobham v Molesey	1-3

First Round

Walton & Herstham v Banstead Ath	4-2
Redhill v Chertsey Town	1-3
Metropolitan Police v Ash United	3-1
Kingstonians v Epsom & Ewell	2-0
Tooting & Mitcham U v Molesey	1-0
Camberley Town v Leatherhead	2-4
Sutton United v Croydon	1-1
	replay 3-1
Carshalton Athletic v Whyteleafe	4-3

Second Round

Metrolpolitan Police v Chertsey T	1-2
Kingstonian v Tooting & Mitcham	2-0
Leatherhead v Walton & Herstham	1-0
Carshalton Ath v Sutton United	3-5

Semi Finals

Chertsey Town v Leatherhead	4-1
Kingstonian v Sutton United	1-4

FINAL at Kingstonian FC

Sutton United (VOL-Prem) v Chertsey Town (Comb Counties)	2-0

....Sutton completed their fourth successive win with two second half goals from Paul McKinnon and Mark Golley, hence claiming the record for successive victories.

RUR Charity Cup

First Round

Whitehawk v Franklands Village	5-0
Haywards Heath v Three Bridges	4-1
Hailsham Town v Sidley United	4-0
Oakwood v Ringmer	2-0
Newhaven v East Grinstead	0-3
Albion United v Burgess Hill T	1-2
Portfield v Shoreham	0-2
Storrington v Arundel	1-3
Lancing v Midhurst & Easeb'ne	1-1
Selsey v Bosham	2-4
Ferring v Horsham YMCA	2-0
Littlehampton T v Wigmore Ath	3-1
Pagham v E Wick	0-1

Replays

Lancing v Midhurst & Easeb'ne	0-3

Second Round

Whitehawk v Peacehaven & Tels	2-4
Eastbourne Town v Oakwood	3-0
Hailsham Town v Haywards Heath	2-1
East Grinstead v Burgess Hill T	0-0
Ferring v Aurndel	1-4
Shoreham v Midhurst & Easeb'ne	1-1
Bosham v Steyning Town	0-5
Littlehampton v Wick	5-1

Replays

East Grimstead v Burgess Hill T	2-6 aet
Shoreham v Midhurst & Easeb'ne	0-3

Third Round

Arundel v Steyning Town	0-0
Midhurst & Easebourne v Hailsham T	2-3
Eastbourne T v Burgess Hill T	2-0
Peacehaven & T v Littlehampton	3-2

Replays

Arundel v Steyning Town	0-1

Semi-Finals

Eastbourne Town v Peacehaven & Telscombe	3-1
Steyning Town v Hailsham Town	8-1

FINAL, at Lancing FC

Eastbourne Town v Steyning Town (both Sussex Cl)	3-0

...The semi-Finals were a disapointment to the Vauxhall Opel teams, with both defeated teams playing in their Premier section. An extra time goal gave Steyning, who had also won the County League and Cup double victory over Hastings Town, who narrowly missed promotion in their first season in the Southern League. This is the first time that a County League side has won the Cup since Ringmer in 1973.

Steyning also reached the final of the RUR Cup, but were surprisingly beaten 3-0 by Eastbourne Town in the match played at Lancing FC, which is in fact the County FA's ground.

SUSSEX Senior Cup

First Round

Bosham v Albion United	5-1
Storrington v Wigmore Athletic	3-0
Franklands Village v Newhaven	2-0
Chichester City v Pagham	1-4
Sidley United v Selsey	5-1
Hassocks v Haywards Heath	0-3
Wick v Ferring	4-0
Oakwood v East Grinstead	0-2

Second Round

Pagham v Hastings Town	0-5
Storrington v Brighton & Hove	2-2
	replay 0-4
Bognor Regis Town v Whitehawk	3-1
Sidley United v Peaceheaven & Telscombe	3-4
Bosham v Eastbourne Utd	3-3
	replay 1-2
Worthing v Crawley Town	3-2
Burgess Hill Town v Franklands Village	3-0
Shoreham v Southwick	0-5
Three Bridges v Horsham YMCA	2-2
	replay2-0
East Grinstead v Lewes	1-3
Steyning T v Midhurst & Easebourne	2-0
Wick v Littlehampton T	1-2
Hailsham Town v Portfield	5-1
Ringmer v Eastbourne Town	0-2
Haywards Heath v Arundel	2-2
	replay 2-3
Lancing v Hosham	0-1

Third Round

Southwick v Lewes	0-2
Brighton & Hove v Worthing	0-3
Hastings Town v Burgess Hill T	1-0
Littlehampton v Peacehaven & T	2-3
Hailsham Town v Steyning Town	2-4
Three Bridges v Eastbourne T	1-1
	replay 0-1
Eastbourne Utd v Arundel	3-3
	replay 2-0
Bognor Regis T v Lancing	3-1

Fourth Round

Bognor Regis Town v Eastbourne T	3-3
	replay 1-0
Lewes v Worthing	0-1
Eastbourne Utd v Hastings T	2-2
	replay 1-2
Peacehaven & Tels v Steyning T	0-1

Semi Final

Steyning Town v Worthing	1-0
Hastings Town v Bognor Regis	3-2

FINAL at Brighton & Hove Albion FC

Hastings Town (Southern, South) v Steyning Town (Sussex)	0-1 aet

Brighton & Hove Albion 0, Worthing 3 (Sussex Senior Cup 3rd Round). Martin Lambert (left) and Micky Edmonds hail their triumph.

WESTMORELAND Senior Cup

Recent winners: '80 Kendal County, '81 Burneside, '82 & '83 Kendal Cty, '84 Wetheriggs, '85 Shap

Results

First Round

Ambleside v Lunesdale United	3-1
Cartmell v Keswick	3-2
Burton Thistle v Burneside	0-2
Kendal United v Windermeere SC	1-6
Kent Victoria v Appleby	1-1
Esthwaite Vale v Coniston	2-4
Shap v Kirkoswald	5-2
Kendal County v Wetheriggs	0-0 abd
Kirkby Lonsdale v Penrith Utd	3-3
Corinthians v Sedburgh	3-2
Kirkby Stephen v Netherfield	1-1

Replays

Kent Victoria v Appleby	4-1
Kendal County v Wetheriggs	1-3
Kirkby Lonsdale v Penrith Utd	2-4
Kirkby Stephen v Netherfield	2-3

Second Round

Ibis v Endmoor KGR	5-0
Cartmel v Penrith United	2-0
Shap v Netherfield	3-1
Kent Victoria v Coniston	1-0
Burneside v Thurlemere	6-0
Wetheriggs v Corinthians	2-2
Windermere SC v Ullswater Utd	1-3
Ambleside v Staveley United	1-0

Replays

Wetheriggs v Corinthians	2-1

Third Round

Cartmel v Shap	2-0
Kent Victoria v Ibis	2-1
Ambleside v Ullswater Utd	1-0
Burneside v Wetheriggs	2-4

Semi-Finals

Cartmel v Kent Victoria	2-4
Wetheriggs v Ambleside	5-0

FINAL, at Netherfield FC

Kent Victoria (Westmorel Div 1) v Wetheriggs (Westmorel Div 1)	1-1

Replay

Kent Victoria v Wetheriggs	1-3

WEST RIDING

Recent winners: '80 & '81 GFuisley (Yorks), '82 Ossett Town (Yorks), '83 Guisley (NCE), '84 Farsley Celtic (NCE), '85 Goole Town (NPL)

FINAL

Goole Town (Multipart) v Harrogate Town (NCE, Div 1)	0-1

WILTSHIRE Senior Cup

Recent Winners, Senior Cup, (Wiltshire League unless stated)

'80 & '81 Downton (Hants), '82 Avebury, '83 Penhill, '84 Amesbury Town, '85 Calne Town

Results

First Round

Plessey Sports v Wroughton	4-1
Laverstock & Ford v Dorcan	4-1
Bemerton Athletic v Wootton Bassett	4-0
Corsham Town v Supermarine	0-4
Pewsey Vale v Avebury	3-1
Aldbourne v Penhill	0-2
Marlborough Town v Burmah Hse	6-5 pens
Ferndale Athletic v Purton	0-1
Pinehurst v Shrewton	w/o
Old Manor v Blunsdon United	3-0
Park v Downton	0-1

Second Round

Downton v Plessey Sports	6-3
Purton v Penhill	1-1
Sanford v Bemerton	2-5
Wills FC v Amesbury Town	1-0
Marlborough T v Supermarine	0-6
Pewsey Vale v Allied Dunbar	5-4
Laverstock & Ford v Old Manor	0-3
Pinehurst v Highworth	1-5

Replays

Purton v Penhill	0-1

Third Round

Penhill v Bemerton	2-1
Highworth Town v Wills FC	1-3
Pewsey Vale v Old Manor	1-4
Downton v Supermarine	1-3

Semi-Finals

Old Manor v Supermarine	0-1
Wills FC v Penhill	0-2

FINAL, at Swindon Town FC

Penhill (Hellenic Div 1) v Supermarine (Hellenic Prem)	0-2

There is also a Premier Cup, for more senior teams

First Round

Trowbridge Town v Devizes Town	1-0
Calne Town v Westbury United	3-0
Avon (Bradford) v Warminster T	1-0
Chippenham Town v Melksham Town	2-4

Semi-Finals

Melksham Town v Trowbridge	3-0
Avon (Bradford) v Calne Town	5-6 aet/pens

TEFINAL

Calne Town (Wiltshire) v Melksham Town (Western Prem)	0-2

WORCESTERSHIRE Senior Cup

Worcestershire also runs two cups - the senior cup is a floodlit tournament whereas the other cup is limited to major teams not in the senior cup - no Worcester League sides area entered

Recent winners, Senior Cup, (unless stated, Gola/APL) '80 Worcester C, '81 Stourbridge (Southern), '82 Worcester City, '83 Kidderminster H (Southern), '84 Worcester, '85 Kidderminster H

First Round

Malvern Town v Oldbury United	1-3
Alvechurch v Redditch Utd	2-2
Lye Town v Halesowen Town	0-1
Willenhall T v Stourbridge	3-1

Replays

Alvechurch v Redditch Utd	3-4

Second Round

Bromsgrove Rovers v Willenhall	2-0
Worcester City v Redditch United	3-1
Halesowen Town v Oldbury Utd	3-1
Kidderminster H v Dudley Town	3-0

Semi-Finals

Worcester C v Bromsgrove Rovers	0-0
Kidderminster v Halesowen	4-3

Replays

Worcester C v Bromsgrove Rovers	0-3

FINAL, 2 legs

Bromsgrove Rovers (Southern, Mid) v Kidderminster Harriers (Gola)	0-0, 2-3

...The Final must have been one of the most explosive finishes of the season. After a scoreless draw at Bromsgrove, The Southern League, Midland Division champions took a two goal lead early in the second half of the second leg, while Kidderminster Harriers had Adrian O'Dowd sent off with five minutes to go, Kidderminster Harriers pulled one back, and in the final minute, Man of the Season, Kim Casey struck...twice !

Senior Urn

Semi-Finals

Pegasus v Halesowen T Res	1-0
Evesham Utd v W Midlands Police	2-1

FINAL

Pegasus (Hellenic Premier) v W Midlands Police (Mid Comb)	2-1

WE WON THE CUP

Mid-Cheshire Senior Cup Final is won by Northwich Victoria against Winsford United of the North-West Counties League (2-0). Skipper Glyn Stephens (Northwich) waves the cup aloft.

SCOTTISH SENIOR SECTION REVIEW OF THE SEASON

North

The high standard of Football in the North was shown by the fact that the honours were well shared with Forres Mechanics the best team marginally over Elgin City, Peterhead and Caledonian, whose only success came in the McEwan's Lager North Cup against the improving Lossiemouth. Forres took the League title and the Inverness Cup with Keith (the League champions of the previous season) winning the Highland League Cup and Huntly in the absence of Aberdeen Reserves being successful in the Aberdeenshire Cup.

The Scottish Qualifying Cup (North) was won by Peterhead, who thrashed Buckie Thistle in the final, whilst in the Scottish Cup there was a fine 'giant-killing' act by Nairn County, who won a replay at Meadowbank before bowing out at home to Celtic by a score which need not be mentioned here.

East & South

Whitehill Welfare were the outstanding team in the East taking the League title yet again from the ever consistent Gala Fairydean. The margin was only two points. The roles were reversed in the South Qualifying Cup with the Border team winning the Final, but neither made any Scottish Cup progress nor did Hawick Royal Albert, who also qualified. In other competitions Whitehill also won the East qualifying Cup by beating Gala again in the Final, but the King Cup produced two different teams to contest the Final as Hawick R.A. lost to Vale of Leithen.

The East of Scotland Cup and Shield involve the Edinburgh Scottish League clubs and Hearts won the former against Hibernian, with Meadowbank Thistle taking the Cup against Whitehill in the Cup final.

Down in the South Dalbeattie Star were the outstanding side and their efforts won them the overall title. There were signs of a general improvement in standards after some poor seasons, although there were few indications that the East's monopoly in winning the Qualifying Cup would soon be ended.

The good news for the East of Scotland League was that three new teams will take part in the new season - Berwick Rangers Reserves, Selkirk (back again) and Pencaitland Athletic. This can only be good for the competition.

HIGHLAND LEAGUE

	P	W	D	L	F	A	P
Forres Mechanics	32	22	6	4	77	27	72
Elgin City	32	21	7	4	67	33	70
Peterhead	32	22	3	7	50	25	69
Caledonian	32	19	9	4	70	32	66
Keith	32	17	5	10	66	40	56
Huntly	32	15	8	9	58	45	53
Buckie Thistle	32	14	8	10	48	36	50
Inverness Thistle	32	12	9	11	56	53	45
Nairn County	32	11	6	15	47	60	39
Ross County	32	11	4	17	65	66	37
Rothes	32	9	8	15	51	62	35
Fort William	32	10	5	17	40	73	35
Clachnacuddin	32	8	7	17	43	72	31
Fraserburgh	32	8	6	18	40	60	30
Lossiemouth	32	6	8	18	38	63	26
Brora Rangers	32	6	5	21	39	74	23
Deveronvale	32	4	10	18	31	65	22

LEAGUE CHAMPIONS

Caledonian. 1976-77 1977-78
Keith 1978-79
Keith 1979-80
Keith 1980-81
Caledonian. 1981-82
Caledonian. 1982-83
Caledonian. 1983-84

SCOTTISH QUALIFYING CUP - NORTH SECTION

1st Round			
Aberdeen University	0	Deveronvale	5
Caledonian	3	Ross County	0
Fort William	1	Wick Academy	1
Inverness Thistle	4	Forres Mechanics	3
Replay			
Wick Academy	0	Fort William	1
2nd Round			
Caledonian	1	Deveronvale	0
Fort William	5	Lossiemouth	4
Inverness Thistle	0	Fraserburgh	0
Nairn County	1	Rothes	0
Keith	5	Golspie	0
Huntly	3	Brora	0
Elgin	2	Buckie	3
Peterhead	3	Clachnacuddin	0
Replay			
Fraserburgh	0	Inverness Thistle	1
3rd Round			
Buckie	2	Keith	1
Peterhead	2	Caledonian	1
Fort William	1	Inverness Thistle	0
Nairn County	1	Huntly	0
Semi Final			
Buckie	2	Fort William	0
Peterhead	1	Nairn County	1
Replay			
Nairn County	0	Peterhead	1
Final			
Buckie	1	Peterhead	5

SCOTTISH CUP

1st Round			
Queens Park	3	Buckie	0
Fort William, Peterhead and Nairn - Byes			
2nd Round			
Fort William	0	Stirling Albion	0
Nairn County	1	Meadowbank Thistle	1
Peterhead	1	Arbroath	2
Replay			
Meadowbank	1	Nairn County	2
2nd Round			
Nairn County	0	Dundee	7

SCOTTISH SENIOR SECTION

Aberdeen & District Cup

1st Round

Keith	5	Fraserburgh	1
Buckie Thistle	0	Nuntly	1
Peterhead	0	Deveronvale	0

Replay:

Deveronvale	2	Peterhead	1

Bye: Aberdeen University

Semi-Finals:

Huntly	1	Keith	1
Deveronvale	5	Aberdeen University	2

Replay:

Keith	1	Huntly	2

Final:

Huntly	4	Deveronvale	0

Inverness Cup

1st Round

Ross County	3	Nairn County	4
Caledonian	5	Clachnacuddin	1
Inverness Thistle	1	Forres Mechanics	2
Brora Rangers	6	Fort William	1

Semi Finals

Nairn County	2	Caledonian	1
Brora Rangers	1	Forres Mechanics	3

Final

Forres Mechanics	2	Nairn County	2

(Forres Mechanics won 5-4 on penalties)

McEwans Lager North Cup

1st Round

Rothes	1	Caledonian	5
Elgin City	3	Inverness Thistle	2
Fort William bye			
Golspie Sutherland	4	Wick Academy	1
Forres Mechanics bye			
Lossiemouth	2	Ross County	2
Brora Rangers	0	Clachnacuddin	1
Nairn County bye			

Replay

Ross County	0	Lossiemouth	3

2nd Round

Caledonian	3	Elgin City	1
Fort William	3	Golspie Sutherland	2
Forres Mechanics	1	Lossiemouth	1
Clachnacuddin	3	Nairn County	0

Replay

Lossiemouth	1	Forres Mechanics	1

(Lossiemouth won 5-4 on penalties)

Semi-Finals

Lossiemouth	3	Clachnacuddin	0
Fort William	0	Caledonian	3

Final

Caledonian	1	Lossiemouth	0

(at Forres)

Recent Finals

1977-78	Inverness Thistle beat Caledonian
1978-79	Rothes beat Inverness Thistle
1979-80	Clachnacuddin beat Elgin City
1980-81	Brora Rangers beat Inverness Thistle
1981-82	Caledonian beat Brora Rangers
1982-83	Elgin City beat Ross County
1983-84	Caledonian beat Inverness Thistle
1984-85	Inverness Thistle beat Caledonian

Highland League Cup
Winners: Keith

EAST OF SCOTLAND FOOTBALL LEAGUE

	P	W	D	L	F	A	P
Whitehill Welfare	28	21	5	2	85	23	47*
Gala Fairydean	28	20	5	3	59	28	45**
Postal United	28	17	6	5	56	30	40
Vale of Leithen	28	18	3	7	97	44	39
Kelso United	28	15	9	4	55	30	39
Peebles Rovers	28	11	8	9	43	36	30
Spartans	28	10	8	10	54	53	28
Hawick Royal Albert	28	10	5	13	54	53	25
Eyemouth United	28	7	9	12	56	71	23
Easthouses M.W.	28	8	6	14	34	43	22
Craig Royston	28	9	4	15	47	58	22
Civil Service Strollers	28	6	8	14	39	60	20
Coldstream	28	6	6	16	41	59	18
Heriot-Watt University	28	5	1	22	32	95	11
Edinburgh University	28	4	2	21	39	87	10

* Winners ** Runners up

Winners of Cochran Good Conduct Award - Coldstream

DETROIT TROPHY (OVERALL CHAMPIONSHIP)

	League	League Cup	Potts Cup	Chall Cup	Haig Gordon Cup	Tweedie Cup	Total
Threave Rovers	28	12	0	6	4	6	56
Newton Stewart	27	13	2	4	0	4	50
Dalbeattie St.	32	11	6	0	0	0	49
Annan Athletic	26	15	4	0	2	0	47
Wigtown & B.	16	9	0	0	0	2	27
Stranraer	13	7	0	0	6	0	26
Girvan	13	6	0	0	0	0	19
St. Cuthbert W.	14	3	0	0	2	0	19
Creetown	8	3	2	2	0	2	17
Tarff Rovers	3	1	0	0	0	0	4
Queen of South	0	0	0	2	0	0	2

KELVINATOR LEAGUE 1985-86

	Played	Won	Drawn	Lost	G/For	G/Ag	G/D	Pts
Dalbeattie St.	18	14	4	0	56	17	39	32
Threave Rovers	18	13	2	3	59	19	40	28
Newton Stewart	18	11	5	2	58	29	29	27
Annan Ath.	18	9	8	1	49	23	26	26
Wigtown & B.	18	6	4	8	54	44	10	16
St. Cuthberts W.	18	7	0	11	35	51	−16	14
Stranraer	18	5	3	10	39	35	4	13
Girvan	18	5	3	10	27	52	−25	13
Creetown	18	4	0	14	26	59	−33	8
Tarff Rovers	18	1	1	16	21	95	−74	3

LEAGUE CUP 1985-86

Section 1	Played	Won	Drawn	Lost	G/For	G/Ag	G/D	Pts
Annan Ath.	8	7	1	0	32	10	22	15
Threave Rovers	8	5	2	1	38	8	30	12
Wigtown & B.	8	4	1	3	24	19	5	9
Creetown	8	1	1	6	18	39	−21	3
Tarff Rovers	8	0	1	7	11	47	−36	1

Section 2	Played	Won	Drawn	Lost	G/For	G/Ag	G/D	Pts
Newton Stewart	8	6	1	1	26	17	9	13
Dalbeattie St.	8	4	3	1	34	18	16	11
Stranraer	8	3	1	4	25	19	6	7
Girvan	8	1	4	3	13	21	− 8	6
St. Cuthbert W.	8	0	3	5	14	37	−23	3

1st Leg	Annan Athletic 1	Newton Stewart 1
2nd Leg	Newton Stewart 2	Annan Athletic 2
Penalties	Newton Stewart 3	Annan Athletic 2
Aggregate	Newton Stewart 6	Annan Athletic 5

HONOURS LIST

The League Cup was won by Newton Stewart F.C. who defeated Annan Athletic F.C. in the final over two legs.

SOUTHERN COUNTIES ASSOCIATION

The Tweedie Cup was won by Threave Rovers F.C. who defeated Newton Stewart F.C. in the Final at Meadow Park Castle Douglas on March 15th 1986.

The Haig Gordon Cup was won by Stranraer F.C. who defeated Threave Rovers in the Final at Stair Park, Stranraer on 26 April 1986.

The Potts Cup was won by Dalbeattie Star F.C. who defeated Annan Athletic F.C. in the Final at Galabank, Annan on 28 April 1986.

The Challenge Cup was won by Threave Rovers F.C. who defeated Newton Stewart F.C. in the Final at Blairmount Park, Newton Stewart on 4 May, 1986.

The South of Scotland League, sponsored by Kelvinator Ltd. was won with 32 points by Dalbeittie Star F.C. for the second successive Season, completing the League programme undefeated. The runners up were Threave Rovers F.C. with 28 points. The Detroit Trophy (Overall Championship) was won by Threave Rovers F.C. with 56 points.

Pollok beat Shettleston away in the final of the Evening Times Cup Winners Cup. The crowd was 1,335. (Photo: Hoenig)

SCOTTISH JUNIOR CUP 1985 - 86

Third Round

Arnbank United v Beith	2 1
Bellshill Athletic v Jeanfield Swifts	1 0
Brechin Victoria v Armadale Thistle	2 0
Cambuslang Rangers v Stoneyburn United	3 3.2 1
Darvel v Blantyre Victoria	0 0.0.1
Fauldhouse United v Dunipace	1 2
Glenrothes v Sunnybank	1 0
Irvine Meadow v Kinnoull	4 1
Kilwinning Rangers v Glasgow Perthshire	1 2
Largs Thistle v Shotts Bon Accord	2 1
Leven v Lesmahagow	2 4
Lochee Harp v Pollok	1 5
New Elgin v Hill o' Beath Hawthorn	0 4
Oakley United v Kello Rovers	3 2
Stonehouse Violet v St. Andrews United	2 1
Tranent v Dunbar United	1 1.1 0
Whitletts Victoria v Kirrie Thistle	1 1.5 3
Balbeggie v Downfield	4 8
Bonnyrigg Rose Athletic v Neilston	0 0.2 2.2*2
(Bonnyrigg won on penalties)	
Dalkeith Thistle v Cumnock	0 0.0 6
Edinburgh United v Saltcoats Victoria	2 2.4 0
Glenafton Athletic v Kirkintillock Rob Roy	6 2
Hurlford United v Linlithgow Rose	1 4
Kilbirnie Ladeside v Sauchie	1 1.2 1
Lanark United v Forfar West End	5 1
Larkhall Thistle v Jubilee Athletic	6 2
Livingston United v Baillieston	1 0
Muirkirk v Thornton Hibs	2 1
Newtongrange Star v Auchinleck Talbot	1 2
Shettleston v Banks o' Dee	3 3.3 0
Thorniewood United v Ellon United	2 1
Whitburn v Inverurie	6 1

Fourth Round

Annbank United v Whitletts Victoria	0 0.2 1
Bonnyrigg Rose Athletic v Downfield	1 2
Glasgow Perthshire v Cambuslang Rangers	2 1
Hill o' Beath Hawthorn v Irvine Meadow	2 3
Largs Thistle v Glenrothes	1 2
Livingston United v Blantyre Victoria	1 4
Pollok v Brechin Victoria	8 0
Thorniewood United v Kilbirnie Ladeside	0 2
Auchinleck Talbot v Shettleston	5 0
Cumnock v Bellshill Athletic	4 0
Glenafton Athletic v Lesmahagow	2 3
Lanark United v Linlithgow Rose	1 0
Larkhall Thistle v Dunipace	2 1
Oakley United v Muirkirk	2 1
Stonehouse Violet v Edinburgh United	1 1.1 2
Tranent v Whitburn	1 2

Fifth Round

Arnbank United v Lesmahagow	1 0
Glasgow Perthshire v Oakley United	1 1.1 3
Irvine Meadow v Downfield	1 0
Lanark United v Pollok	0 3
Edinburgh United v Cumnock	0 2
Glenrothes v Auchinleck Talbot	1 2
Kilbirnie Ladeside v Whitburn	2 2.1 1.2 0
Larkhall Thistle v Blantyre Victoria	3 2

Sixth Round

Auchinleck Talbot v Irvine Meadow	1 1.0 0 4 1
Kilbirnie Ladeside v Larkhall Thistle	3 0
Cumnock v Oakley United	2
Pollok v Annbank United	2 1

Semi Finals

Pollok v Cumnock	2 1
(at Rugby Park, Kilmarnock)	
Auchinleck Talbot v Kilbirnie Ladeside	1 0
(at Somerset Park, Ayr)	

Final

Auchinleck Talbot v Pollok	3 2
(at Hampden Park, Glasgow)	

SCOTTISH JUNIOR CUP FINAL

(Hampden Park, Glasgow, Sunday, 18th May)

AUCHINLECK TALBOT 3 POLLOK 2

O'Donnell, McDonald 2 McCarthy, Marshall

H.T. 3-2 Attendance: 7,689

Teams:

Auchinleck Talbot: Wilson, Gemmell, Young, Findlay, McCulloch, McDonald, Ferguson, Patterson, McCool, McMillan, O'Donnell. Substitutes: Lennon, Dowdalls.

Pollok: Sammeroff, Marshall, Weir, McClurg, Fourna, Mullaney, Arnott, Wilson, Gordon, McGall, McCarthy. Substitutes: O'Brien, Rattray.

Referee: B. Gilgallon, Newton Mearns.

This was the hundredth Junior Cup Final and it was sad that this fact also coincided with the poorest attendance of all time, but it was also a very exciting match even though all the scoring came before the interval.

In fact, the final scoreline was reached as early as the thirty-first minute of the game after a real early goal-rush. Pollok, the holders, were two goals ahead in next to no time through McCarthy after Gordon had missed a cross from Weir and Marshall followed by scoring after a very classy and intricate move through the bewildered Ayrshire defence.

But then the wind played some tricks, Sameroff looked nervous and the Talbot fight-back achieved unexpected results. The first reward went to O'Donnell, who headed home a Ferguson centre which the Pollok keeper had missed. A collision between the Pollok defenders then left Marshall a clear chance which he happily accepted and then the Glasgow defence stood still for reasons best known to themselves so that Marshall was again able to net.

There the scoring - but not the excitement - ended and Pollok, the holders, lost their grip on the hard-won trophy, which went to Talbot for the first time in thirty-six years - and deservedly so.

	SCOTTISH JUNIOR CUP		FIFE & LOTHIANS CUP*	WEST OF SCOTLAND CUP**
	WINNERS	RUNNERS UP		
1968-69	Cambuslang R	Kirkintilloch R R	Linlithgow Rose	Petershill
1969-70	Blantyre Vics	Penicuik Ath	Whitburn	Irvine Meadow
1970-71	Cambuslang R	Newtongrange Star	Camelon	Irvine Meadow
1971-72	Cambuslang R	Bonnyrigg Rose	Glenrothes	Cambuslang R
1972-73	Irvine Meadow	Cambuslang R	Linlithgow Rose	Cambuslang R
1973-74	Cambuslang R	Linlithgow Rose	Linlithgow Rose	E Kilbride Th
1974-75	Glenrothes	Glencairn	Linlithgow Rose	Shettleston
1975-76	Bo'ness Utd	Darvel	Arniston R	Arthurlie
1976-77	Kilbirnie L	Kirkintilloch R R	Penicuik Ath	Lanark Utd
1977-78	Bonnyrigg Rose	Stonehouse V	Newtongrange St	Arthurlie
1978-79	Cumnock	Bo'ness Utd	Linlithgow Rose	Auchinleck T
1979-80	Baillieston	Benburb	Linlithgow Rose	Auchinleck T
1980-81	Pollok	Arthurlie	Penicuik Ath	Auchinleck T
1981-82	Blantyre Vics	Baillieston	Bonnyrigg Rose	Auchinleck T
1982-83	E Kilbride Th	Bo'ness Utd	Oakley Utd	Benburb
1983-84	Bo'ness Utd	Baillieston	Linlithgow Rose	Auchinleck T
1984-85	Pollok	Petershill	Linlithgow Rose	Auchinleck T
1985-86	Auchinleck T	Pollok	Linlithgow Rose	Auchinleck T

* Known now as 'Radio Forth Cup'. Competed for by members of East Fife Regions.

** Known now as 'Whyte & Mackay Cup'. Competed for by members of Central and Ayrshire Regions. **Note** achievement of Auchinleck Talbot 1978-86!

Auchinleck Talbot (stripes) draw at home in the Scottish Junior Cup 6th round against Irvine Meadow. Talbot eventually won the second replay — and even later — the Cup.
(Photo: Paul Crankshaw)

SCOTTISH JUNIOR FOOTBALL

The SJFA was formed in 1886 and celebrates its centenary in October 1986.

Its administration is totally independent of the Scottish Football Association (often referred to as 'Senior Football') to which the nonleague clubs of the Highland League, East of Scotland League and South of Scotland League are affiliated.

It is little appreciated outwith Scotland that the SJFA is more representative of non-league football in the country than the 'senior' non-league clubs. Junior football is dominant in the central industrial belt of Scotland where the vast majority of the population lives. Comparison of playing standards between the 'senior' non-league clubs and the SJFA clubs is difficult since they do not meet competitively, but it is accepted (and is borne out by the results of the occasional friendly matches) that the strongest Junior clubs are a match for the Highland League clubs and are superior to the majority of East of Scotland League clubs and all South of Scotland League clubs.

In 1968, as a result of the Chester Report, the large number of leagues dotted about the country were re-organised into 6 regional competitions. These 6 league competitions are :

North Regional League (34 clubs in 1985-86). Because this region covers such a large area it is sub-divided into an **East Section** (mainly Aberdeenshire) with 2 divisions of 10 clubs each, and a **North Section** (mainly Morayshire and Banffshire) with one division of 14 clubs.

Tayside Regional League (26 clubs). This covers the area around Dundee and Perth and consists of 2 divisions of 14 and 12 clubs.

Fife Regional League (18 clubs). One division.

East Regional League (27 clubs). This covers the area of Edinburgh and the Lothians. There are 2 divisions of 12 and 15 clubs.

Central Regional League (41 clubs). This league covers West Central Scotland, in particular Glasgow and Lanarkshire. There are 3 divisions of 14, 14 and 13 clubs.

Ayrshire Regional League (23 clubs). 2 divisions of 11 and 12 clubs.

In terms of playing strength Central, Ayrshire and East Region are the strongest, with the North Region the weakest.

The relatively small size of the divisions is partially explained by the fact that several cup competitions are played within each Region. In addition there are 2 national competitions: the Dryborough Cup and most importantly the Scottish Junior Cup.

The Dryborough Cup is a national knock-out competition for the 6 Regional Dryborough Cup winners, the holders of the National Dryborough Cup and the Scottish Junior Cup winners.

The Scottish Junior Cup is the most coveted trophy in Junior Football. From the first round the draw is made on a national basis and no clubs are exempted until later rounds. Crowds in the Scottish Junior Cup match sometimes exceed crowds in the equivalent round of the FA Trophy. The final is played at Hampden Park. For the past 10 years the Final has been televised live in Scotland (although moves are afoot to bring this to an end because of the alleged effect upon the size of the crowd).

Scottish Junior Cup 5th round action sees Annbank United win at home against Lesmahagow.
(Photo: Paul Crankshaw)

A Few Statistics

Since re-organisation in 1968 the Scottish Junior Cup has been won by clubs from :

Central Region	10 times
Ayrshire Region	4 times
East Region	3 times
Fife Region	1 time

The TREBLE of Scottish Junior Cup, League winner and Inter-League Cup winner has been achieved twice :

Cambuslang Rangers	1971-72
Auchinleck Talbot	1985-86

The DOUBLE of Scottish Junior Cup and League winner has been achieved (in addition to the two above) by the following :

Pollok	1980-81, 1984-85
Kilbirnie Ladeside	1976-77
Glenrothes	1974-75
Cambuslang Rangers	1973-74

REGIONAL LEAGUE WINNERS

	Central*	Ayrshire	East	Fife
1968-69	Petershill	Beith	Bo'ness Utd	Thornton Hibs
1969-70	Renfrew	Irvine Meadow	Arniston R	Glenrothes
1970-71	Cumbernauld U	Irvine Meadow	Musselburgh Ath	Glenrothes
1971-72	Cambuslang R	Cumnock	Arniston R	Oakley Utd
1972-73	Cambuslang R	Hurlford Utd	Broxburn Ath	Newburgh
1973-74	Cambuslang R	Cumnock	Broxburn Ath	Lochgelly Albert
1974-75	E Kilbride Th	Kello Rovers	Linlithgow Rose	Glenrothes
1975-76	E Kilbride Th	Kilbirnie L	Bonnyrigg Rose	Glenrothes
1976-77	Shettleston	Kilbirnie L	Bonnyrigg Rose	Newburgh
1977-78	Lesmahagow	Auchinleck T	Linlithgow Rose	Glenrothes
1978-79	Port Glasgow	Auchinleck T	Pennicuik Ath	Oakley Utd
1979-80	E Kilbride Th	Auchinleck T	Camelon	Oakley Utd
1980-81	Pollok	Cumnock	Penicuik Ath	Halbeath
1981-82	E Kilbride Th	Cumnock	Linlithgow Rose	Leven
1982-83	Petershill	Glenafton Ath	Fauldhouse Utd	Dundonald B
1983-84	Petershill	Cumnock	Linlithgow Rose	Glenrothes
1984-85	Pollok	Cumnock	Bonnyrigg Rose	Glenrothes
1985-86	Pollok	Auchinleck T	Whitburn	Oakley Utd

* Div A/Prem Div Winners. Until 1982 'Champions' were decided by play-off between winners of Divs A, B and C

	Tayside	North (East Sec)	North (North Sec)
1968-69		Banks o' Dee	Formartine Utd
1969-70	Blairgowrie	Banks o' Dee	Islavale
1971-72	Blairgowrie	Sunnybank	Forres Thistle
1972-73	Jeanfield Sw	Banks o' Dee	Burghead Thistle
1973-74	Kirrie Thistle	Parkvale	Burghead Thistle
1974-75	Blairgowrie	Sunnybank	Buckie Rovers
1975-76	Carnoustie	Sunnybank	Nairn St. Ninian's
1976-77	Carnoustie	Banks o' Dee	Burghead Thistle
1977-78	Carnoustie	A'deen East End	
1978-79	Carnoustie	Banks o' Dee	Nairn St. Ninian's
1979-80	Lochee Utd	Fraserburgh U	Forres Thistle
1980-81	Carnoustie	Banks o' Dee	Bishopmill Utd
1981-82	Lochee Utd	Banks o' Dee	Nairn St Ninian's
1982-83	Perth Kinnoull	Sunnybank	
1983-84	Perth Kinnoull	Banks o' Dee	Deveronside
1984-85	Lochee Harp	FC Stoneywood	Fochabers
1985-86	Lochee Harp	Banks o' Dee	Deveronside

NORTH REGIONAL JUNIOR F.A. NORTH SECTION

	P	W	D	L	F	A	P
Deveronside	26	19	4	3	78	33	42
Fochabers	26	15	4	7	81	47	34
Bishopmill United	26	14	6	6	68	46	34
Caberfeidh	26	12	5	9	65	54	29
New Elgin	26	11	5	10	53	50	27
R.A.F. Lossiemouth	26	12	3	11	57	65	27
Forres Thistle	26	10	6	10	57	52	26
Nairn St Ninian	26	9	7	10	62	59	25
Lossiemouth Utd.	26	9	5	12	49	50	23
R.A.F. Kinloss	26	8	7	11	39	45	23
Buckie Rovers	26	10	3	13	62	77	23
Rothes Decimals	26	8	4	14	43	57	20
Burghead Thistle	26	8	4	14	48	80	20
Islavale	26	4	3	19	33	80	11

Cup-Winners

Robertson	-	Deveronside
Connon	-	Rothes Decimals
Stewart	-	Caberfeidh
Matthew	-	Fochabers
Tom Gordon	-	Caberfeidh
Nicholson	-	Buckie Rovers
Gordon Williamson	-	Deveronside
Morayshire	-	Fochabers
Chisholm	-	Fochabers
White Horse	-	Deveronside
North of Scotland	-	Forres Thistle

ROSSLYN LEAGUE DIVISION I
(NORTH REGION - EAST SECTION)

	P	W	D	L	F	A	P
Banks o' Dee	27	19	5	3	84	21	43
Turriff Utd.	27	16	6	5	55	34	38
F.C. Stoneywood	27	15	5	7	56	30	35
Mugiemoss	27	11	7	9	43	44	29
Sunnybank	27	12	4	11	41	36	28
Inverurie Locos	27	8	9	10	41	55	25
Fraserburgh Utd.	27	10	4	13	36	50	24
Ellon Utd.	27	7	5	15	44	64	19
East End	27	4	10	13	29	53	18
Buchanhaven Hearts	27	2	7	18	24	67	11

Promoted: Rosslyn Sport & Lewis Utd.
Relegated: East End & Buchanhaven Hearts

	Winners	Runners-Up
McLeman Cup:	Turriff Utd.	Inverurie Loco
Archibald Cup:	Rosslyn Sport	Stonehaven
Duthie Cup:	Banks o' Dee	Rosslyn Sport
Morrison Trophy:	Banks o' Dee	Mugiemoss
Watson Cup:	F C Stoneywood	Rosslyn Sport
Jimmy Gibb Trophy:	Banks o' Dee	Rosslyn Sport
Harry Johnson Trophy:	Rosslyn Sport	Stonehaven

INTERSPORT DIVISION ONE

	P	W	D	L	F	A	P
Harp	26	15	6	5	50	29	36
Downfield	26	13	6	7	55	36	32
Lochee United	26	13	5	8	53	44	31
North End	26	13	4	9	41	32	30
Forfar West End	26	11	7	8	44	33	29
Jeanfield Swifts	26	10	9	7	51	49	29
Kinnoull	26	11	4	11	40	37	26
Arbroath Vics	26	10	5	11	55	52	25
Bankfoot	26	9	7	10	47	52	25
Perth Celtic	26	9	6	11	41	39	24
Kirrie Thistle	26	9	6	11	46	37	24
Arbroath S.C.	26	7	9	10	35	42	23
East Craigie	26	5	9	12	36	45	19
Carnoustie	26	3	5	18	26	73	11

SCOTTISH BREWERS DIVISION TWO

	P	W	D	L	F	A	P
Broughty Athletic	22	16	3	3	57	23	35
Violet	22	15	3	4	52	30	33
Forfar Albion	22	13	4	5	45	29	30
Blairgowrie	22	10	4	8	60	47	24
Balbeggie	22	9	5	8	50	45	23
Stobswell	22	7	7	8	44	47	21
Scone Thistle	22	8	5	9	41	52	21
Brechin Vics	22	8	4	10	46	46	20
Coupar-Angus	22	7	4	11	44	55	18
St. Josephs	22	7	2	13	41	57	16
Montrose Roselea	22	6	3	13	43	55	15
Luncarty	22	2	4	16	27	64	8

WHISKY DEWAR LEAGUE CUP
Winner: Kirrie Thistle. Runner up: Downfield
INTERSPORT LEAGUE DIVISION ONE
Champions: Harp. Runner up: Downfield
SCOTTISH BREWERS LEAGUE DIVISION TWO
Champions: Broty A. Runners up: Violet
DRYBROUGH CUP FINAL
Winner: North End. Runners up: Lochee United
CURRIE CUP
Winner: Harp. Runner up: Arbroath S.C.
CREAM OF THE BARLEY TROPHY
Winner: Downfield. Runners up: Forfar West End
CRAIG STEPHEN TROPHY
Winner: North End. Runners up: Lochee United
INVERALMOND CUP
Winner: Blairgowrie. Runner up: Violet
WINTER CUP
Winner: Forfar Albion. Runners up: Blairgowrie
ALBERT HERSCHALL TROPHY
Winner: Harp. Runners up: East Craigie
GOOD CONDUCT CUP
Montrose Roslea: Ten Points
RADIO TAY TROPHY
Team with most League goals
Arbroath Vics 55 goals (Div. One). Downfield 55 goals (Div. One)
Blairgowrie 60 goals (Div. One)
PLAYER WITH MOST GOALS - HUTCHISON SHIELD
Division One: Allen Shepherd, Bankfoot
Division Two: Steve Aitken, Montrose Roselea

Leo Hoenig 'snaps' the moment Bonnyrigg Rose take over the Drybrough National Cup for 1985-86.

EAST REGION FINAL LEAGUE TABLES SEASON 1985-86

SECTION 'A'

	P	W	D	L	F	A	P
Whitburn	22	16	3	3	59	26	35
Linlithgow	22	12	4	6	35	19	28
Newtongrange	22	10	6	6	37	28	26
Bonnyrigg Rose	22	8	9	5	47	34	25
Bo'ness	22	9	7	6	37	27	25
Ormiston*	22	11	4	7	42	41	25
Arniston	22	9	3	10	28	29	21
Blackburn	22	8	4	10	26	37	20
Fauldhouse	22	6	7	9	35	42	19
Tranent**	22	3	8	11	28	44	15
Haddington	22	3	7	12	18	42	13
Armadale	22	3	6	13	24	47	12

**One Point Added * One Point Deducted

Relegated Clubs:- Haddington and Armadale

SECTION 'B'

	P	W	D	L	F	A	P
Edinburgh	28	15	8	5	49	25	38
Dalkeith	28	16	6	6	57	38	38
Broxburn	28	13	11	4	60	44	37
Musselburgh	28	12	10	6	53	36	34
Sauchie	28	12	10	6	55	44	34
Camelon	28	15	4	9	48	40	34
Preston	28	15	3	10	46	37	33
Penicuik	28	10	9	9	49	41	29
Stoneyburn	28	12	4	12	48	46	28
Livingston	28	7	14	7	41	45	28
Bathgate	28	10	4	14	50	56	24
West Calder	28	7	8	13	36	50	22
Dunbar	28	5	5	18	32	62	15
Polkemmet	28	4	6	18	41	72	14
Bonnybridge	28	3	6	19	30	59	12

Promoted Clubs:- Edinburgh, Dalkeith, Broxburn and Musselburgh Ath.

TROPHY WINNERS SEASON 1985 - 86

East Region Drybrough Cup	Bonnyrigg Rose Ath.
National Drybrough Cup	Bonnyrigg Rose Ath.
Robertson Homes Cup	Bonnyrigg Rose Ath.
Centenary Cup	Whitburn
Evening News and Laidlaw League Champions Trophy	Whitburn
John McLean Cup	Edinburgh United
Inchview League Cup	Linlithgow Rose
Radio Forth Cup	Linlithgow Rose
M.R.S. Cup	Dalkeith Thistle

AYRSHIRE REGIONAL JUNIOR F.A.
WESTERN SCOTTISH OMNIBUS LEAGUES

1st Division

	P	W	D	L	F	A	P
Auchinleck Talbot	20	12	6	2	40	24	30
Irvine Meadow	20	11	6	3	30	17	28
Kilbirnie Ladeside	20	9	8	3	40	25	26
Cumnock Juniors	20	10	4	6	40	26	24
Glenafton Athletic	20	10	4	6	32	23	24
Craigmark Bruntonians	20	8	3	9	29	30	19
Ardrossan Winton R.	20	6	6	8	23	26	18
Annbank United	20	7	2	11	33	34	16
Darvel Juniors	20	6	3	11	24	35	15
Largs Thistle	20	6	3	11	28	40	13
Muirkirk Juniors	20	2	3	15	24	63	7

2nd Division

	P	W	D	L	F	A	P
Whitletts Victoria	22	15	4	3	51	23	34
Hurlford United	22	12	5	5	56	34	29
Troon	22	11	6	5	47	28	28
Beith Juniors	22	12	4	6	47	32	28
Kello Rovers	22	11	3	8	57	43	25
Kilwinning Rangers	22	10	4	8	44	38	24
Ardeer Thistle	22	9	4	9	43	40	22
Dalry Thistle	22	10	2	10	34	34	22
Saltcoats Victoria	22	7	4	11	29	43	18
Lugar Boswell Thistle	22	6	4	12	33	54	16
Maybole Juniors	22	5	3	14	34	58	13
Irvine Victoria	22	2	1	19	21	69	5

Jackie Scarlett Cup	-	Cumnock Juniors
Drybrough Cup	-	Wilwinning Rangers
McEwans Lager Cup	-	Glenafton Athletic
Cunninghame District Cup		Irvine Meadow
Blaney Trophy	-	Cumnock Juniors
Whyte & Mackay Cup	-	Auchinleck Talbot (for the 7th time in 8 seasons)
Scottish Junior Cup	-	Auchinleck Talbot

FIFE REGION JUNIOR F.A.
TENNENT CALEDONIAN LEAGUE

	P	W	D	L	F	A	P
Oakley United	34	26	4	4	101	33	58*
Glenrothes	34	25	3	6	90	32	53
Hill of Beath H.	34	22	7	5	84	41	51
Kelty Hearts	34	20	10	4	94	38	48**
St. Andrews United	34	18	7	9	71	38	43
Thornton Hibs	34	18	6	10	78	51	42
Kirkcaldy YM	34	19	2	13	74	68	40
Jubilee Athletic	34	12	11	11	56	46	35
Dundonald Bluebell	34	13	7	14	75	72	33
Leven	34	12	9	13	68	67	33
Clackmannan	34	13	7	14	74	79	33
Lochore Welfare	34	10	6	18	42	71	26
Comrie Colliery	34	8	8	18	53	84	24
Newburgh	34	9	6	19	46	79	24
Crossgates Primrose	34	8	7	19	58	83	23
Tulliallan Thistle	34	6	9	19	43	81	21
Lochgelly Albert	34	3	7	24	47	138	13
Halbeath	34	3	6	25	53	106	12

* 2 points awarded ** 2 points deducted

TROPHY WINNERS AND RUNNERS UP

Tennent Caledonian League	Champions	- Oakley United FC
	Runners up	- Glenrothes FC
Sports Shop (Fife) Cup	Winners	- Glenrothes FC
	Runners up	- Hill of Beath Hawthorn FC
Cowdenbeath Cup	Winners	- Kelty Hearts FC
	Runners up	- Oakley United FC
Fife Drybrough Cup	Winners	- Hill of Beath Hawthorn FC
	Runners up	- Halbeath FC
Laidlaw Shield	Winners	- Hill of Beath Hawthorn FC
	Runners up	- Dundonald Bluebell FC
Rosslyn Trophy (Highest goal scorers - League)	Winners	- Oakley United FC
Montrave Cup (Good Conduct)	Winners	- Comrie Colliery FC

CENTRAL (TROPHY CENTRE) LEAGUE

PREMIER DIVISION	P	W	D	L	F	A	P
Pollok Juniors	26	17	6	3	79	36	40
Kilsyth Rangers	26	16	6	4	65	57	38
Baillieston Juniors	26	13	8	5	63	45	34
East Kilbride Thistle	26	9	9	8	43	37	27
Shotts Bon Accord	26	10	7	9	44	51	27
Petershill	26	11	4	11	60	47	26
Yoker Athletic	26	8	9	9	40	46	25
Port Glasgow Juniors	26	9	7	10	48	52	25
Glasgow Perthshire	26	9	7	10	54	67	25
Larkhall Thistle	26	9	5	12	49	62	23
Forth Wanderers	26	7	8	11	44	53	22
Neilston Juniors	26	9	4	13	49	60	22
Lesmahagow Juniors	26	6	4	16	39	54	16
Benburb	26	4	6	16	31	61	14

Relegated to 1st Division: Benburb, Lesmahagow Juniors

Larkhall - 2 points deducted and relegated

1st DIVISION	P	W	D	L	F	A	P
Shettleston Juniors	26	19	2	5	49	27	40
Ruth Glencairn	26	14	9	3	49	30	37
Blantyre Victoria	26	15	6	5	50	27	36
Lanark United	26	10	9	7	35	30	29
Renfrew Juniors	26	10	9	7	33	30	29
Johnstone Burgh	26	9	10	7	37	28	28
Vale of Leven	26	8	12	6	43	35	28
Kirk Rob Roy	26	10	5	11	41	41	25
Arthurlie	26	9	7	10	44	53	25
Cumbernauld United	26	9	6	11	40	38	24
Bellshill Athletic	26	6	7	13	39	47	19
Stonehouse Violet	26	7	5	14	37	50	19
Maryhill Juniors	26	3	7	16	32	63	13
St. Roch's	26	5	2	19	28	58	12

2nd DIVISION	P	W	D	L	F	A	P
Cambuslang Rangers	24	20	1	3	86	28	41
Glenboig Juniors	24	14	3	7	62	42	31
Vale of Clyde	24	11	8	5	49	37	30
St. Anthony's	24	10	8	6	33	28	28
Dunipace Juniors	24	10	8	6	44	41	28
Ashfield	24	11	4	9	47	40	26
Carluke Rovers	24	10	5	9	38	44	25
Thorniewood United	24	9	4	11	39	48	22
Greenock Juniors	24	8	5	11	34	43	21
Coltness United	24	6	6	12	32	44	18
Blantyre Celtic	24	4	10	10	33	44	18
Wishaw Juniors	24	5	5	14	18	31	15
Royal Albert	24	1	7	16	23	68	9

Promoted to Division 1: Cambuslang Rangers, Glenboig Juniors, Vale of Clyde and St. Anthony's

Promoted to Premier Division: Shettleston Juniors, Ruth Glencairn, Blantyre Victoria, Lanark United

Relegated to 2nd Division: St. Roch's, Maryhill Juniors, Stonehouse Violet, Bellshill Athletic

Play-Off Winners of 1st and 2nd Divisions at Southcroft Park

Shettleston Juniors	1	Cambuslang Rangers	1

Replay - at South Croft Park

Shettleston Juniors	2	Cambuslang Rangers	1

After extra time
(1-1 after 90 minutes)

Tom Brown Trophy at Fir Park, Motherwell

Arthurlie	2	Yoker Athletic	3

Drybrough Cup at Greenfield Park

Larkhill Thistle	2	Lanark United	1

After extra time
(1-1 after 90 minutes)

Evening Times Cup Winners Cup, Greenfield Park, Shettleston

Pollok	1	Shettleston Juniors	0

ABACUS WELSH LEAGUE

Secretary: Walter Williams, 39 Tynewydd, Whitechurch, Cardiff CF4 1NQ.
Telephone (0222) 627722(H)

BARRY TOWN REIGN SUPREME

It has been more than 50 years since a club completed a season in the Welsh League without defeat. The last occasion was in 1932-3 when Llanelly finished the season with a record of 19 wins and three draws in 22 fixtures, scoring 100 goals and conceeding only 16 in winning the championship by five points from Swansea Town. Now Barry Town have equalled that record of remaining undefeated for a whole season but their record of 23 wins and nine draws in 32 fixtures, scoring 84 goals along the way, is much more of an accomplishment due to the extra fixtures, and will take some beating. Manager Richie Morgan (the former Cardiff City captain and manager) says that they intend to try and do the same in the coming season. As each game progressed last season each game took on the significance of a cup-tie, and their final game of the season so nearly proved to be their downfall Barry Town drew 1-1 at Maesteg Park on a rain-soaked Tudor Park pitch. After falling behind they left it until twelve minutes from full time before Martin Goldsmith (another player with Cardiff City connections) scored the all-important equaliser.

Since dropping down from the Southern League, when the Welsh League reorganised their divisions and formed a National Division, Barry Town have been almost invincable. They have been champions for the past four seasons now.

In the Premier Division the race for the Championship continued right through until the final games of the season. Both Sully and A.F.C. Cardiff were neck and neck, and both clubs completed the season on the same May evening. Sully were top and needed a win over Afan Lido, fighting to avoid the drop down to Division One, as A.F.C. Cardiff were only a point behind, with a better goal difference (+71 compared to Sully's +70) and they were at home to Clydach, who had no interest in either promotion or relegation. Sully took a 1-0 lead at half time, through Gary Davies, who then increased it to 2-0 early in the second half. But their nerves got the better of them and they ended up conceeding two late goals. There were a number of tense moments before the news came through that A.F.C. Cardiff had been held to a goal-less draw. Considering their form over the previous couple of seasons, both Sully and A.F.C. Cardiff were expecting to play in the National Division this season. Although promotion and relegation takes place between Division One and the Premier Division, entry into the National Division is by invitation only. The Management Committee decided to send out invitations to the current 17 clubs, and to invite the two biggest clubs in the Central Wales League (Aberystwyth Town and Newtown) to compete in the National Division in 1986-7. Although at one time it seemed likely that both the Central Wales clubs would accept their invitations, both decided to stay in the Central Wales League for the coming season. Newtown F.C. added that they would like to be invited next summer, indicating that they would then be ready to accept the invitation. The decisions of these two clubs, who had contested the Welsh Intermediate Cup—which replaced the former Welsh Amateur Cup some years ago, came as a blow to the Abacus Welsh League's efforts to make their top division a truly national one.

At the time of writing both Sully and A.F.C. Cardiff were still trying to force the hand of the Management Committee into reassessing the situation so things might still change for the coming season.

Even more recently there has been a call by some of the bigger non-league clubs in Wales for the F.A. of Wales to take over the running of the National Divison of the Abacus Welsh League in an effort to make it a truly national Welsh League with the aim of trying to get a second Welsh club into regular European competition via the UEFA Cup.

With the continuing demise of the fortunes of the four Welsh clubs in the Football League I wonder how long it will be before they decided that it would be in their best interests, and those of Welsh football in general, to return to their roots and play their first XI's in the Welsh League!

NATIONAL DIVISION

		Home					Away					
	P	W	D	L	F	A	W	D	L	F	A	Pts
Barry Town	32	14	2	0	51	14	9	7	0	33	12	78
Bridgend Town	32	7	4	5	32	22	12	2	2	37	20	63
Ebbw Vale	32	10	3	3	34	18	9	2	5	37	26	62
Brecon Cor.	32	8	5	3	38	20	9	5	2	21	9	61
Cwybran Town	32	9	3	4	37	24	7	4	5	31	19	55
Briton Ferry	32	7	5	4	34	24	8	4	4	32	26	54
Milford United	32	10	1	5	28	14	6	4	6	34	27	53
Ton Pentre	32	4	3	9	30	27	9	3	4	42	24	45
Haverfordwest	32	6	6	4	33	22	4	9	3	16	18	45
Pembroke	32	5	5	6	27	20	6	4	6	24	36	42
Maesteg Park	32	5	7	4	17	12	4	6	6	17	19	40
Blaenrhondda	32	5	6	5	32	38	2	4	10	16	44	31
Llanelli	32	5	4	7	31	28	2	5	9	20	37	30
Pontlanfraith	32	4	3	9	26	36	4	2	10	24	39	29
Caerleon	32	5	4	7	23	28	1	4	11	15	40	26
Caerau	32	1	5	10	11	43	2	2	12	21	51	16
Port Talbot	32	2	5	9	16	43	0	4	12	13	53	15

PREMIER DIVISION

		Home					Away					
	P	W	D	L	F	A	W	D	L	F	A	Pts
Sully	34	13	4	0	60	17	15	0	2	44	17	88
A.F.C. Cardiff	34	14	2	1	43	8	13	4	0	44	8	87
Cardiff Cor.	34	12	0	5	41	19	7	3	7	35	32	60
Taffs Wells	34	7	3	7	33	31	11	2	4	42	20	59
Pontlottyn	34	9	5	3	25	19	7	2	8	21	25	55
Newport Co.	34	9	2	6	43	25	7	2	8	25	30	52
Blaenavon	34	9	3	5	40	26	5	1	11	23	34	46
Clydach U.	34	6	4	7	28	31	6	5	6	23	21	45
Ammanford T.	34	7	4	6	23	22	5	5	7	21	32	45
Newport YMCA	34	6	4	7	20	26	5	4	8	13	20	41
Ferndale A.	34	9	1	7	43	24	3	2	12	19	47	39
Abercynon A.	34	5	8	4	16	16	2	8	7	18	28	37
Spencer Works	34	6	3	8	26	28	4	4	9	20	28	37
Afan Lido	34	6	4	7	21	28	3	6	8	20	37	37
South Glam	34	6	4	7	25	34	3	5	9	21	46	36
Merthyr Tydfil	34	4	5	8	19	26	5	3	9	24	40	35
Aberaman	34	5	4	8	24	33	1	6	10	15	45	28
Tondu Robins	34	3	4	10	18	32	4	2	11	17	38	27

DIVISION ONE

		Home					Away					
	P	W	D	L	F	A	W	D	L	F	A	Pts
S. Wales Const.	30	12	2	1	42	7	11	3	1	46	17	74
Abergavenny	30	13	2	0	50	12	10	3	2	45	25	74
Skewen Ath.	30	10	0	5	24	12	9	2	4	22	17	59
B.P.	30	9	1	5	26	19	8	1	6	24	21	53
Carmarthen T.	30	10	2	3	35	17	4	6	5	25	25	50
Treharris A.	30	7	6	2	35	23	6	2	7	20	24	47
Tonyrefail Wel.	30	9	1	5	31	23	5	3	7	25	25	46
Pontyclun	30	6	3	6	18	16	7	3	5	28	26	45
Morriston T.	30	9	2	4	37	27	4	2	9	15	25	43
Garw Ath.	30	8	2	5	23	25	4	2	9	12	22	40
Panteg	30	6	4	5	27	20	4	2	9	19	29	36
Ynysybwl	30	4	5	6	26	34	2	3	10	19	35	26
Seven Sisters	30	3	5	7	22	29	2	3	10	29	46	23
Pontardawe A.	30	2	1	12	18	37	4	4	7	17	28	23
Tynte Rovers	30	2	6	7	17	38	2	2	11	15	38	20
Trelewis	30	3	2	10	13	34	1	3	11	12	41	17

S.A. BRAIN CHALLENGE CUP

Winners: Pembroke Boro'; Runners-up: Cwmbran Town

ABACUS YOUTH TROPHY

Winners: A.F.C. Cadiff; Runners-up: Merthyr Tydfil

WELSH LEAGUE — NATIONAL DIVISION

Number of Clubs competing		**16**	**17**	**17**
Season		**83-84**	**84-85**	**85-86**
1	Barry Town	1	1	1
2	Blaenrhondda	5	12	12
3	Brecon Corinthians	10	8	4
4	Bridgend Town	7	2	2
5	Briton Ferry Athletic	6	10	6
6	Caerao	11	11	16
7	Caeleon	2	5	15
8	Cwybran Town	12	15	5
9	Ebbw Vale	15	16	3
10	Haverfordwest	4	4	9
11	Llanelli	8	9	13
12	Maesteg Park	3	6	11
13	Milford United	16	17	7
14	Pembroke Borough	14	14	10
15	Pontllanfraith	13	13	14
16	Ton Pentre	9	7	8
17	Port Talbot Athletic	—	3	17

WELSH LEAGUE NATIONAL DIVISION — PAST CHAMPIONS

Max. Pts.	**Season**	**1st**		**2nd**		**3rd**		**4th**	
90	1983/84	68	Barry Town	62	Caerleon	53	Maesteg Park	49*	Haverfordwest
96	1984/85	71	Barry Town	66	Bridgend	63	Port Talbot	62	Haverfordwest
96	1985/86	78	Barry Town	63	Bridgend	62	Ebbw Vale	61	Brecon

* Goal Average/Difference

BARRY TOWN

President:
Chairman: Neil O'Halloran
Manager: Ritchie Morgan
Secretary: Alan Whelan
Address & Tel. No. 166 Jenner Road, Barry, S. Glam CF6 8HR.
Address and Tel. No. of ground: Jenner Park, Barry. Tel. 721171
Simple ground directions: Junction for Cardiff West from M4, follow signs for Cardiff airport to Barry outskirts. 1st left after 2nd roundabout on entering Barry

No. of seats: 180 **Covered accommodation:** 2,000 **Capacity:** 6,000
Year formed: **Nickname:** **Floodlights:** August 1986
Club colours: Red shirts, white shorts, white socks **Change colours:** All white
Day for midweek home matches: Tuesday **Club metal badges:** No
Previous Leagues: Southern League (1980/81)
Clubhouse details: Open every evening, Saturday & Sunday lunchtime
Past players who progressed into the Football League: Derrick Tapscutt, Dai Ward (Arsenal), Robert Delgardo (Carlisle), Ian Lowe and Phil Green (Happy Valley, Hong Kong, 1985-86 season)
Programme details: 16 pages, 20p **Programme editor:** John A. Lowrie
Local newspapers & Tel. No.
Major Honours: Welsh League Nat Div Winners, Welsh Cup Winners 1953-4

BRIDGEND TOWN

President:
Chairman: Colin Smart
Manager:
Secretary: Philip Dauncey
Address & Tel. No. Oakbrook Est., Llanharan, Pontyclun, Mid. Glam. Llantrisant 226251
Address and Tel. No. of ground: Coychurch Road, Bridgend. Tel. 55097
Simple ground directions: Leave M4 at Pencoed, turn left at Waterton Cross. Second right under railway bridge
No. of seats: 200 **Covered accommodation:** — **Capacity:** 2,000
Year formed: 1954 as Bridgend Victoria, 1959 changed to Bridgend Town **Nickname:** **Floodlights:**
Club colours: Sky blue shirts and socks, white shorts **Change colours:**
Day for midweek home matches: **Club metal badges:** No
Previous Leagues: Southern League
Clubhouse details: Yes. Bridgend 63483
Past players who progressed into the Football League:
Programme details: Yes **Programme editor:** Philip Dauncey
Local newspapers & Tel. No.
Major Honours: Welsh Cup Quarter Final, Southern League Champions 1979-80, Midland Div 1979-80, Div 1 North R/U 1977-8; Welsh League Champions 1968-9, 1972-3

BLAENRHONDDA

President: Roger Matthews
Chairman: Michael Ryan
Manager: Lyndon Davies
Secretary: Mal Hall
Address & Tel. No. 61 Margaret Street, Treherbert. Treorchy 771424
Address and Tel. No. of ground: Blaenrhondda Park. Treorchy 774772
Simple ground directions: Treorchy-Treherbert-Tynewydd-Blaenrhondda
No. of seats: None **Covered accommodation:** 300 **Capacity:** 10,000
Year formed: **Nickname:** **Floodlights:** 1986
Club colours: Blue/blue/blue **Change colours:** Red/red/red
Day for midweek home matches: Wednesday **Club metal badges:** No
Previous Leagues: Welsh League
Clubhouse details: 1986
Past players who progressed into the Football League: John Emanuel

Programme details: 18 page, advert. **Programme editor:** Mal Hall
Local newspapers & Tel. No.
Major Honours: Runners-up to Barry Town 1982-3

BRECON CORINTHIANS

President: David Morgan
Chairman: Ken Parry
Manager: Alan Mullins
Secretary: Terry Harley
Address & Tel. No. 75 The Watton, Brecon Powys. Tel 4568
Address and Tel. No. of ground: Rich Field, The Watton, Brecon. Tel 4033
Simple ground directions: Head for town centre, turn at Rich Way Road

No. of seats: 70 **Covered accommodation:** 1 stand **Capacity:** 2,000
Year formed: **Nickname:** Corries **Floodlights:** Yes
Club colours: Red shirts, shorts and socks **Change colours:** Blule shirts, shorts and socks
Day for midweek home matches: Tuesday **Club metal badges:**
Previous Leagues: Brecon & District League
Clubhouse details: 9 Lion Street, Brecon
Past players who progressed into the Football League: Chris Williams (Cardiff City)

Programme details: 8 page, 20p **Programme editor:** Tam Thomson
Local newspapers & Tel. No. Brecon & Radnor Express, Western Mail
Major Honours: Welsh League Div 1 Champions, Welsh League Cup (Brains Cup) 1981-2, Welsh Intermediate Cup Runners-up 1984-5

BRITON FERRY ATHLETIC

President: Bil Cossins
Chairman: Graham Jenkins
Manager: Alwyn Mainwaring
Secretary: Samuel Jones
Address & Tel. No. 54 Ruskin Street, Briton Ferry. 813401
Address and Tel. No. of ground: Old Road, Briton Ferry. 812458
Simple ground directions: Main road from Neath

No. of seats: Nil
Covered accommodation:
Capacity: 2,000
Year formed: 1928
Nickname:
Floodlights: No
Club colours: Red and green quarters
Change colours: Blue
Day for midweek home matches: Wednesday
Club metal badges: No
Previous Leagues:
Clubhouse details: Bar, lounge etc.
Past players who progressed into the Football League: Carl Harris, Roy John, Clayton Blackmore, Harold Williams (all Welsh internationals)
Programme details: Excellent
Programme editor: Ron Griffiths
Local newspapers & Tel. No. Evening Post
Major Honours: Welsh League Champions Div 1 1971-2, Div 2 1937-8, 1938-9, 1939-40, 1946-7; Welsh Amateur Cup Finalists 1937-8

CAERAO

President: M.W. Smith
Chairman: M Dawkins
Manager: P. Llewllyn
Secretary: Davis Lewis
Address & Tel. No. 19a Hermon Road. 0656 734388
Address and Tel. No. of ground: Humphreys Ter Calrau
Simple ground directions: 2 miles from Maesteg

No. of seats: None
Covered accommodation: Yes
Capacity: 3,000
Year formed: 1901
Nickname:
Floodlights: Next season
Club colours:
Change colours:
Day for midweek home matches: Wednesday
Club metal badges: No
Previous Leagues:
Clubhouse details: On ground
Past players who progressed into the Football League: Len McCarthys (Portsmouths), Tudor Martin (Newport), Glyn (Legs) Williams (Cardiff)
Programme details:
Programme editor:
Local newspapers & Tel. No. SW Echo
Major Honours: Beat Willington 5-3 English Amateur Cup Winnes, match played Maesteg rugby field in 1950

CAERLEON

President: H.N. Nigclasson
Chairman: J. Hopkins
Manager: Alex Beattie
Secretary: Len Blakemore
Address & Tel. No. 33 Tanhouse Drive, Caerleon
Address and Tel. No. of ground: Coldbath Road. 420074
Simple ground directions: 200 yards from main road (common).
No. of seats:
Covered accommodation: 200
Capacity:
Year formed:
Nickname: Romans
Floodlights:
Club colours: Green
Change colours: Tangerine
Day for midweek home matches: Wednesday
Club metal badges:
Previous Leagues:
Clubhouse details: Changing rooms rear, bar front
Past players who progressed into the Football League: Several
Programme details: Yes
Programme editor: C. Hughes
Local newspapers & Tel. No. South Wales Argus
Major Honours: Welsh Amateur Cup 1966, Runners-up Welsh National 1983-4

CUMBRIAN TOWN

President: John Colley
Chairman: George Thorneycroft
Manager: Gwyn Williams
Secretary: Clive Edwards
Address & Tel. No. 21 Dunraven Road, Llanyranon, Cwmbran, Gwent. Cwmbran 65372
Address and Tel. No. of ground: Cwmbran Stadium. Cwmbran 66192/66193
Simple ground directions: Henllys Way, Cwmbran (Cwmbran Stadium Leisure Centre)
No. of seats: 2,000
Covered accommodation: 1,500
Capacity: 8,000
Year formed:
Nickname: The Town
Floodlights: Yes
Club colours: White/thin black lined jersey, black shorts, white socks
Change colours: Red jerseys/blue shorts
Day for midweek home matches: Wednesday
Club metal badges: No
Previous Leagues: Gwent County, Mon Senior
Clubhouse details:
Past players who progressed into the Football League: Simon King, Mark Waite

Programme details: Home matches only
Programme editor: Chairman
Local newspapers & Tel. No. Free Press (Pontypool), Argus (Newport)
Major Honours: 3rd Welsh Premier, Runners-up 1st Div-SA Brains Finalists 1985-6. Performance—losing to Hereford United 4-3 (Welsh Cup) 1983-4

Ebbw Vale beat Caeran 5-2 in the Welsh League (Wrexham Area). (Photo: Leo Hoenig)

Brymbo Steelworks 2 Chirk AAA 1. (Photo: Leo Hoenig)

Cardiff City take an early lead at Caerleon in the Third round of the Welsh Cup. The Football League club eventually won 3-2. (Photo: Leo Hoenig)

An Ebbw Vale freekick goes round the wall (but misses). Seven days previously this fixture, now in bright sunshine was abandoned after ten minutes due to a waterlogged pitch.
(Photo: Leo Hoenig)

A picturesque background impresses as Ruthin Town beat Hawkesbury Villa 4-0 in a Welsh League match (Wrexham area). (Photo: Leo Hoenig)

Ray McHale, now with Scarborough, heads the first goal of his hat-trick in Swansea City's 6-2 victory at Haverfordwest County. (Photo: Leo Hoenig)

EBBW VALE

President: John James
Chairman: Cyril Rogers
Manager:
Secretary: D. Coughlin
Address & Tel. No. 107 Mount Pleasant Road, Ebbw Vale, Gwent. 305993
Address and Tel. No. of ground: Eugene Cross Park
Simple ground directions:
No. of seats: 1,000 **Covered accommodation:** 8,000 **Capacity:** 22,000
Year formed: **Nickname:** **Floodlights:**
Club colours: Amber and black **Change colours:**
Day for midweek home matches: **Club metal badges:**
Previous Leagues:
Clubhouse details:
Past players who progressed into the Football League:
Programme details: **Programme editor:**
Local newspapers & Tel. No.
Major Honours: Welsh Challenge Cup Winners 1926-7, 1955-6, 1956-7, Finalists 1928-9; League Runners-up 1927-8, League Champions 1952-3; Senior Cup Winners 1924-5, 1926-7, 1928-9, 1932-3, 1945-6, 1950-1

HAVERFORDWEST COUNTY

President:
Chairman: John Thomas
Manager: Micky Lenihan
Secretary: Clifford Saies
Address & Tel. No. 46 Wesley Place, Trecwn, Haverfordwest, Dyfed SA62 5XR. Letterston 840083
Address and Tel. No. of ground: The Bridge Meadow, Haverfordwest, Dyfed SA61 2XE. Haverfordwest 2082
Simple ground directions: A40 from Carmathen, third left at roundabout

No. of seats: 600 **Covered accommodation:** Yes **Capacity:** 3,000
Year formed: **Nickname:** The Bluebirds **Floodlights:** No
Club colours: Blue shirts/white shorts/blue socks **Change colours:** White shirts/white shorts/white socks
Day for midweek home matches: No preference **Club metal badges:** None
Previous Leagues:
Clubhouse details: Yes. Members only. Membership 400
Past players who progressed into the Football League: John Gwyther (Notts Forrest), Cliff Pawlett (Portsmouth)
Programme details: Yes **Programme editor:** Clifford Saies
Local newspapers & Tel. No. West Wales Guardian, Western Telegraph, County Echo, West Wales Evening Post
Major Honours: Welsh League Premier Division Champions 1956-7, 1980-1; Welsh League Premier Division Runners-up 1969-70, 1970-71; Welsh League First Division Champions 1955-6, 1979-80; Welsh League Challenge Cup Winners 1960-1; West Wales F.A. Senior Challenge Cup Winners 1981-2; Pembrokeshire League First Division Champions 1960-1, Second Division Runners-up 1954-5, Third Division Runners-up 1980-1; Pembrokeshire League Wiltshire Cup Winners 1969-70

LLANELLI

President: Llanelli Town Mayor
Chairman: J.N. Daniels
Manager: A. Davies
Secretary: D.A. Chappell
Address & Tel. No. c/o Stebonheath Park. Home tel. no. Llanelli 753391
Address and Tel. No. of ground: Stebonheath Park, Llanelli. Llanelli 772973
Simple ground directions:

No. of seats: 600 **Covered accommodation:** 600 **Capacity:** 10,000
Year formed: **Nickname:** **Floodlights:** No
Club colours: All red **Change colours:** All royal blue
Day for midweek home matches: Wednesday **Club metal badges:** No
Previous Leagues: Southern League
Clubhouse details: Open every night and Saturday afternoons
Past players who progressed into the Football League:
Programme details: First team only **Programme editor:** A. Evans
Local newspapers & Tel. No. Llanelli Star (weekly on Fridays)
Major Honours: Welsh League Champions 1970-1, 1976-7, 1977-8

MAESTEG PARK

President:
Chairman: Jack Bridge
Manager: Brian Carpenter
Secretary: David Griffiths
Address & Tel. No. 3 Padley's Close, Maesteg, CF34 OTX
Address and Tel. No. of ground: Tudor Park, St Davids Place, Maesteg. 0656 732092
Simple ground directions:
No. of seats: **Covered accommodation:** 200 **Capacity:** 2,000
Year formed: 1945 **Nickname:** The Park **Floodlights:** Yes
Club colours: Royal blue **Change colours:** Yellow/red
Day for midweek home matches: Wednesday **Club metal badges:** Yes
Previous Leagues: Port Talbot and Bridgend Leagues 1963-4
Clubhouse details: Large modern clubhouse, seating capacity o.k. Concert hall 300
Past players who progressed into the Football League: Chris Pile (Fulham)

Programme details: 10 pages **Programme editor:** Secretary
Local newspapers & Tel. No. Glamorgan Gazette
Major Honours: 1st Div Champions 1978-9, South Wales Senior Cup Winners

MILFORD UNITED

President: G.R. Davies
Chairman: R.G. Hicks
Manager: Dixie Hale
Secretary: F.R. Lowe
Address & Tel. No. 17 Milton Crescent, Pill, Milford Haven, Pembrokeshire, Dyfed.
Address and Tel. No. of ground: Marble Hall Road, Milford Haven. Tel 3691
Simple ground directions: First turning right on entering Milford Haven, easy from railway station
No. of seats: None **Covered accommodation:** 400 **Capacity:**
Year formed: 1885 **Nickname:** The Robins **Floodlights:** None
Club colours: Red shirts, white shorts, red/white top **Change colours:** Blue/black shirts, black shorts, black socks with blue top
Day for midweek home matches: **Club metal badges:**
Previous Leagues:
Clubhouse details: Spacious/situated on ground
Past players who progressed into the Football League: Billy Lloyd (Swindon Town), Hugh Best (Chester, Cardiff), Marwood Marchant (Cardiff, Tottenham), Roley Williams (Cardiff), Frank Donovan (Swansea), John Gwytmer (Notts Forest, Swansea)
Programme details: At all senior games **Programme editor:**
Local newspapers & Tel. No. Western Telegraph, H'west 2551; West Wales Guardian, H'west 2357
Major Honours: West Wales Senior Cup Winners 1937-8, 1978-9, 1985-6, Runners-up 1982-3; Welsh League Runners-up 1948-9; Welsh Challenge Cup Runners-up 1936-7, 1946-7, 1949-50, 1956-7, 1957-8, Winners 1946-7

PEMBROKE BOROUGH

President:
Chairman:
Manager:
Secretary: Des Shanklin
Address & Tel. No. 7 Paunter Street, Orange Gardens, Pembroke, Dyfed. Pembroke 683084
Address and Tel. No. of ground: London Road, Pembroke Dock. Pembroke 682239
Simple ground directions:
No. of seats: **Covered accommodation:** **Capacity:**
Year formed: **Nickname:** **Floodlights:**
Club colours: Black and white shirts and socks, black shorts **Change colours:**
Day for midweek home matches: **Club metal badges:** No
Previous Leagues: None
Clubhouse details: Yes
Past players who progressed into the Football League:
Programme details: Yes **Programme editor:** Secretary
Local newspapers & Tel. No.
Major Honours: Welsh League Challenge Cup Winners 1953-4, 1958-9, Finalists 1961-2

PONTLLANFRAITH

President: H.G. Wade
Chairman:
Manager: Graham Pullin
Secretary: D.P. Chiplin
Address & Tel. No. 26 Glannant Street, Cwmfelinfach, Ynysddu, Newport, Gwent. Ynysddu 349
Address and Tel. No. of ground: Islwyn Park, Pontllanfraith, Blackwood, Gwent.
Simple ground directions:
No. of seats: 500 **Covered accommodation:** Yes **Capacity:** 5,000
Year formed: Reformed 1964 **Nickname:** **Floodlights:**
Club colours: Royal blue **Change colours:** Black and white stripes
Day for midweek home matches: Tuesday **Club metal badges:**
Previous Leagues: South Wales Amateur League
Clubhouse details: No
Past players who progressed into the Football League:
Programme details: Yes **Programme editor:**
Local newspapers & Tel. No. South Wales Argus
Major Honours: Welsh Amateur League Runners-up 2nd Div 1965-6, 1st Division Runners-up 1969-70; League Runners-up 1980-1; S.A. Brain Challenge Cup Winners

PORT TALBOT ATHLETIC

President:
Chairman:
Manager:
Secretary: Tom Heycock
Address & Tel. No. 8 Daffodil Close, Sandfields Est., Port Talbot, W. Glam SA12 7AF. Port Talbot 898744
Address and Tel. No. of ground: Victoria Road, Aberavon, Port Talbot. Port Talbot 882465
Simple ground directions: On left off main road to Aberavon from Port Talbot centre
No. of seats: None **Covered accommodation:** 2,000 **Capacity:** 4,000
Year formed: **Nickname:** **Floodlights:** No
Club colours: Blue **Change colours:**
Day for midweek home matches: Wednesday **Club metal badges:** No
Previous Leagues:
Clubhouse details: Yes
Past players who progressed into the Football League:
Programme details: Yes **Programme editor:** Secretary
Local newspapers & Tel. No. South Wales Post, Port Talbot Guardian
Major Honours:

TON PENTRE

President: I.C. Pursey, M.B.E.
Chairman: Ken Jones
Manager: Des Bartle
Secretary: Paul Willoughby
Address & Tel. No. 37 Bailey St., Ton Pentre, Rhondda, Mid Glam CF41 7EN. Tonypandy 438281
Address and Tel. No. of ground: Ynys Park, Ton Row, Ton Pentre, Rhondda
Simple ground directions: A4058 Pontypridd to Treorchy Plain Road, turn at Thames Rico Garage. Station Ton Pentre ¼ mile from ground

No. of seats: 680
Covered accommodation: 3 Stands
Capacity: 6,000
Year formed: 1935
Nickname: Bulldogs
Floodlights: Yes
Club colours: All red
Change colours: All blue
Day for midweek home matches: Wednesday
Club metal badges: No
Previous Leagues:
Clubhouse details: Adjacent to ground, large hall and large bar
Past players who progressed into the Football League: Gil Reece, Ray Bishop
Programme details: Match day (all games)
Programme editor: Stephen Lowe
Local newspapers & Tel. No. Rhondda Leader, Western Mail, South Wales Echo
Major Honours: Welsh League Champions 1981-2

Welsh Cup Third round action as Milford attack and Merthyr's star international goalkeeper Garry Wager saves. Merthyr won this home tie 5-0. (Photo: Alan Bunce)

A general view of the Bridge Meadow ground and over the town to the Castle. There is a stone circle in the corner of the ground from which this photo was taken. (Photo: Leo Hoenig)

A fine action photo of Wrexham's Dia Davies as he safely handles a high ball in his area in the 1-1 Welsh Cup Final draw at the Racecourse ground. (Photo: Leo Hoenig)

Hectic action as Kidderminster attack at Wrexham. (Photo: Leo Hoenig)

WELSH CUP 1985-86

Round 1

Llanrwst United v. B.S.C. (Shotton) 1-3
Flint Town v. Connah's Quay Nomads 3-3, 3-2
Conwy United v. Holywell Town 2-3
Bethesda Athletic v. Llanfairpwll 1-1, 2-3
Blaenau Ffestiniog v. Llandudno Amateurs 2-0
Pwllheli & District v. Pilkingtons (St. Asaph) 2-1
Rhos United v. Portmadoc
(Walkover - Rhos United F.C.)
Druids United v. Mold Alexandra 2-2, 1-9
Grapes (Moss) v. Denbigh Town 1-0
Cefn Albion v. Brymbo Steelworks 1-1, 2-4
Chirk AAA v. Rhos Aelwyd 1-0
Bala Town v. Gresford Athletic 1-2
Llandrindod Wells v. Newtown 0-1
Machynlleth v. Caersws 2-7
Oswestry Town v. Llanidloes Town 3-1
Aberystwyth Town v. Presteigne St. Andrews 3-1
Kidderminster Harriers v. Montgomery Town 2-0
Knighton Town v. Rhayader Town 1-1, 0-3
Afan Lido v. Taffs Well 0-1
Ammanford Town v. South Glamorgan Institute 2-4
Ferndale Athletic v. Spencer Works 2-1
Abercynon Athletic v. Pontawdawe Athletic 5-0
Aberaman v. BP Llandarcy 3-1
Newport YMCA v. Abergavenny Thursdays 0-3

Round 2

Lex XI v. Colwyn Bay 2-0
Oswestry Town v. Newtown 1-0
Caernarfon Town v. Towyn 2-0
B.S.C. Shotton v. Holywell Town 0-1*
*Protest, Holywell dismissed from comp.
Brymbo Steelworks v. Rhayadar Town 2-0
Chirk AAA v. Kidderminster Harriers 2-2, 1-10
Worcester City v. Rhos United 2-1 a.e.t.
Caersws v. Flint Town United 1-1, 2-1 a.e.t.
Mold Alexandra v. Aberystwyth Town 3-1
Gresford Athletic v. Pwllheli & District 2-3
Grapes (Moss) v. Rhyl (at Rhyl) 0-5
Blaenau Ffestiniog v. Llanfairpwll 0-3
Pembroke Borough v. AFC Cardiff 0-4
Taffs Well v. Barry Town 1-2
Caerleon v. Cardiff Corinthians 1-0
Ferndale Athletic v. Ebbw Vale 1-2
Ton Pentre v. Abergavenney Thursdays 1-1, 2-1
Caerau v. Brecon Corinthians 0-0, 2-5
Aberaman v. Maesteg Park 1-3
Milford United v. Llanelli 2-0
Cwmbran Town v. Sully 1-2
Bridgend Town v. South Glam. Institute 2-2, 1-0
Abercynon Athletic v. Briton Ferry Athletic
(At Briton) 1-1, 0-1
Pontllanfraith v. Haverfordwest County 0-1
Port Talbot Athletic v. Merthyr Tydfil 0-6

Round 3

Caernarfon Town v. Caersws 0-1
Hereford United v. Bangor City 2-0
Llanfairpwll v. Pwllheli & District 3-1
Kidderminster Harriers v. Shrewsbury Town 3-1
Brymbo Steelworks v. Mold Alexandra 2-3
Rhyl v. B.S.C. Shotton 1-2
Worcester City v. Wrexham 1-2
Oswestry Town v. Lex XI 5-2
Ton Pentre v. Newport County 2-4
Brecon Corinthians v. Bridgend Town 2-2, 0-2
Caerleon v. Cardiff City 2-3
AFC Cardiff v. Sully 2-2, 9-10
(after penalties, 1-1 a.e.t.)
Briton Ferry Athletic v. Ebbw Vale 0-1
Merthyr Tydfil v. Milford United 5-0
Haverfordwest County v. Swansea City 2-6
Maesteg Park v. Barry Town 0-2

Round 4

Cardiff City v. Mold Alexandra 4-1
Wrexham v. Bridgend Town 8-0
Hereford United v. BSC Shotton 10-1
Barry Town v. Oswestry Town 6-3
Merthyr Tydfil v. Ebbw Vale 2-0
Newport County v. Kidderminster Harriers 3-3, 1-2
Llanfairpwll v. Caersws 0-2
Sully v. Swansea City 1-2

Round 5

Merthyr Tydfil v. Hereford United 1-3
Wrexham v. Caersws 3-0
Cardiff City v. Barry Town 0-0, 2-0
Swansea City v. Kidderminster Harriers 1-1, 0-4

Semi-Finals

Wrexham v. Cardiff City
1st Leg at Wrexham, 15.4.86, 4-1
2nd Leg at Cardiff, 22.4.86, 2-1
Aggregate 6-2 to Wrexham.

Kidderminster Harriers v. Hereford United
1st Leg at Kidderminster 7.4.86, 4-1
2nd Leg at Hereford 22.4.86, 1-3
Aggregate 5-4 to Kidderminster Harriers

Final

Wrexham v. Kidderminster Harriers 1-1
at Wrexham 18.5.86 a.e.t. (90 mins. 1-1)

Replay: at Kidderminster 21.5.86, 2-1 to Wrexham

An excellent action shot of Mark Rosegreen who played so well for Kidderminster Harriers in the Welsh Cup final at Wrexham. (Photo: Leo Hoenig)

Hectic midfield action at Aggborough as Kidderminster pack the spectators in for the replay won 2-1 by Wrexham. (Photo: Leo Hoenig)

CHANNEL ISLANDS FOOTBALL

JERSEY'S YEAR

It was very much Jersey's year in Channel Islands football. In fact, it was the red and white's most successful season on the inter-island front for many years as they carried off five of the seven most important trophies.

In the Muratti Cup competition, Guernsey scored a 7-0 home win over Alderney in the semi-final, but in the final were beaten 3-2 by Jersey at Springfield.

With only five minutes to go it was 2-2 but then Jersey brought on Tony Salaun and the substitute proceeded to hit a spectacular winning goal with virtually his first touch of the ball.

The result squared the series with Jersey and Guernsey now both having won the Vase 34 times.

Jersey also won the Upton Park Cup when their champion club, the Wanderers, beat Vale Rec. 3-2 at the Track in Guernsey, also with a late goal.

The match-winner in this match was Carlos Lampreia, Jersey-born but of Portuguese descent, who was only playing because Wanderers' regular centre-forward was 'stranded' on the mainland.

Jersey also won Guernsey's Jeremie Cup when, in an all-Jersey final, First Tower United beat St Peter 2-1, but in the final of Jersey's own Wheway Cup, Tower were beaten 2-0 by Vale Rec.

The Junior Muratti was also won by Jersey, 3-2 at the Track, but Guernsey won the schoolboys' match yet again 3-0 at Springfield.

Prior to the senior Muratti, both Jersey and Guernsey embarked on successful mainland trips. Jersey drew with the Army at Aldershot and beat the RAF at Uxbridge, while Guernsey beat the Metropolitan Police and Whyteleafe and lost only narrowly to a Crystal Palace XI at Mitcham.

GUERNSEY REPRESENTATIVE RESULTS

Guernsey v Royal Naval Air Command	3-2
Met. Police v Guernsey	1-2
Crystal Palace XI v Guernsey	4-3
Whyteleafe v Guernsey	1-2
Guernsey v Sheffield United	1-9

JERSEY REPRESENTATIVE RESULTS

Army v Jersey	2-2
RAF V Jersey	0-2
Jersey v Sheffield United	1-5
Jersey v Tottenham Hotspur	0-7

HAMPSHIRE SENIOR CUP

Christchurch v Vale Rec.	2-3
Fareham Town v Vale Rec.	3-3
Vale Rec. v Fareham Town	0-2

Guernsey's Northerners are to compete in a county competition—the Dorset Senior Cup—this season for the first time.

CI club champions Jersey Wanderers pictured after their first Upton Park Cup triumph since 1968 and first on Guernsey soil since 1948 Photo: Guernsey Evening Press

MURATTI CUP FINAL *(Attendance: 1,800)*
Jersey 3 (Le Moignan, Dewhurst, Salaun), **Guernsey 2** (K. Le Tissier, Hunter) Referee. M. James (Horsham)
Jersey: M. Le Blancq, A. Campbell, S. A'Court, P. Harzo, J. Corrigan, R. Crick (capt.), P. Vincenti, P. Taylor, C. Le Moignan, N. Livesey, S. Dewhurst. Sub. A. Salaun
Guernsey: C. Hamon, G. Smith, P. Blondel (capt.), M. Le Tissier, M. Marley, C. Dyer, M. Culverwell, C. Fallaize, N. Hunter, K. Le Tissier. Subs. G. de Carteret, A. Bougourd

UPTON PARK CUP *(Attendance: 605)*
Vale Rec. 2 (M. Hamon, de la Mare), **Jersey Wanderers 3** (Blampied, A'Court, Lampreia)
Referee: M. Bodenham (Brighton)
Vale Rec. C. Hamon, I. Ozanne, P. Blondel, M. Marley, A. Robin, C. Le Tissier, L. Graham, C. Dyer, M. Le Tissier, A. Bougourd, M. Hamon. Sub. P. de la Mare
Wanderers: S. Carylon, J. Whelan, M. Stratford, S. A'Court, R. Norman, G. Mourant, A. Salaun, K. Maguire, A. Blampied, C. Lampreia, C. Le Moignan

Guernsey boy Matthew Le Tissier, formerly of Vale Rec., enjoyed a highly successful first season as an apprentice professional with Southampton. He scored more than 40 goals and won two England youth caps, the first in a tournament at Cannes in France

Chairman Jim Thompson (left) celebrates the birth of the GM Vauxhall Conference

A MESSAGE FROM GENERAL MOTORS

General Motors' philosophy regarding sponsorship goes much deeper than the pure commercial considerations of vehicle sales and product awareness. The Corporation tries to ensure that its involvement makes a positive contribution to the sport or activity.

In the case of football GM's first involvement was with the Football Association 2 years ago commencing with the sponsorship of The GM National School at Lilleshall. This school trains selected boys in the 14-16 years of age bracket, who have the potential to be future England players. The first graduates are now returning to their clubs and will take with them well developed skills, as well as a positive sportsmanlike approach to the game. In addition GM sponsors the General Motors FA Charity Shield each year, which last year provided four worthy charities with minibuses from the proceeds, as well as cash donations to others.

It was during the difficult period of crowd problems that GM decided to sponsor the grassroots 'Non League' football, believing that these clubs had the right attitude to the game and a good balance of social activities to complement the game of football and attract local family people.

The first venture was with the Vauxhall Opel League a year ago and as this was so successful we jumped at the opportunity of sponsoring the former Gola League, renaming it the GM Vauxhall Conference. We have encouraged our dealers to link up with clubs to help the clubs to be successful and to sell more cars.

Our confidence has now been fully justified, as these leagues have now been adopted into a promotion/relegation structure linked right through to the top level of the game in England.

Our involvement in the GM Vauxhall Conference does not mean that we will want to alter the policies and administration in any way. We just think that we might be able to help the Confrence to achieve more of the things it wants to do over the next two years contract and hopefully for a long time to come.

A. MACKAY — Manager Corp. and Industry Relations

FINAL LEAGUE TABLE: 1985-1986

	P	W	D	L	F	A	Pts
Gillingham	9	6	0	3	26	11	18
Wealdstone	9	5	2	2	28	23	17
Enfield	9	4	2	3	21	24	14
Dagenham	9	4	3	2	14	17	14*
Orient	9	4	1	4	12	15	13
Wycombe	9	4	1	4	19	18	12*
Wimbledon	9	3	2	4	23	16	11
Southend	9	3	2	4	20	29	11
Brentford	9	3	1	5	26	19	10
Barnet	9	2	0	7	15	32	6
Dartford	**RECORD EXPUNGED**						

*** No points goal-less draw.**

CAPITAL FOOTBALL LEAGUE
FINAL LEAGUE TABLE 1984-85 SEASON

CLUB	P	W	D	L	F	A	Pts
Wealdstone	7	6	0	1	29	5	18
Brentford	7	5	1	1	20	17	16
Dagenham	7	4	1	2	18	15	13
Enfield	5	3	0	2	9	13	9
Wimbledon	6	2	2	2	15	16	8
Barnet	5	1	1	3	8	14	4
Gillingham	6	1	0	5	10	18	3
Orient	7	0	1	6	9	20	1

Matches not played:
Enfield v Barnet
Barnet v Gillingham
Enfield v Wimbledon

The Management Committee decided that due to unforseen circunstances that had occurred this season, these fixtures would be allowed to remain unplayed.

A lively new competition, instigated by Wealdstone has brought League and Non-League Clubs together in London over the last two years.

For their centenary match against the Vauxhall-Opel League, Hungerford Town signed Viv Richards and Ian Botham to add a little glamour to their line-up! Here Viv signs the League form during the Somerset Weston Festival on the day that the football club had hired an entertainment marquee.

1985-86 LEAGUE TABLES

ANGLIAN COMBINATION

Premier Division

	P	W	D	L	F	A	Pts
aton	30	25	2	3	77	17	52
St Andrews	30	15	8	7	69	41	38
Poringland	30	17	3	10	82	43	37
Gristn Res.	30	14	9	7	48	36	37
Wroxnam	30	15	5	10	69	49	35
Yar. Res.	30	13	7	10	52	44	33
Coltshl HV	30	12	9	9	39	33	33
Newton Flot	30	12	8	10	46	44	32
Fakenham	30	10	11	9	47	42	31
Lkfd Rang.	30	10	6	14	63	70	26
Diss	30	10	5	15	51	57	25
Dereham	30	9	5	16	37	55	23
Overstrand	30	8	7	15	33	58	23
Blofield	30	8	4	18	37	71	20
Lowt. Res.	30	6	6	18	30	75	18
Thtfd Rov.	30	5	7	18	31	76	17

Division 1

Wyndhm Twn	30	22	5	3	99	38	49
Beccles	30	23	3	4	84	31	49
Swaffham	30	14	7	9	51	37	35
Harleston	30	14	7	9	52	50	35
Carrow	30	12	10	8	52	43	34
O. Broad	30	13	6	11	63	53	32
Bradenham	30	11	10	9	61	51	32
Wells	30	12	7	11	48	48	31
Hempnall	30	10	9	11	49	47	29
Bungay	30	11	7	12	52	54	29
Reepham	30	9	9	12	44	46	27
Kirkley	30	9	8	13	52	65	26
Wyndhm O B	30	9	4	17	41	58	22
Holt	30	7	7	16	47	63	21
CEYMS	30	7	5	18	39	75	19
Lakenhth	30	4	2	24	35	110	10

	P	W	D	L	F	A	Pts
1 Achilles	30	19	8	3	77	29	46
2 Westerfield	30	17	7	6	68	46	41
3 RSSC Ransomes	30	16	7	7	67	37	39
4 Sutton	30	16	7	7	69	46	39
5 Haughley	30	13	10	7	75	45	36
6 Hadleigh	30	12	10	8	55	43	34
7 Grundisburgh	30	12	8	10	46	40	32
8 Whitton	30	12	6	12	49	51	30
9 Ipswich Utd	29	9	8	12	49	55	26
10 Halesworth Town	30	11	4	15	42	55	26
11 Leiston	29	7	10	12	46	46	24
12 Willis Faber	30	8	7	15	42	56	23
13 Old Newton	30	8	7	15	39	53	23
14 B. T. Research	30	8	7	15	55	82	23
15 Crane Sports	30	8	5	17	42	82	21
16 Coplestonians	30	3	9	18	30	85	15

KIDDERMINSTER & DISTRICT LEAGUE

	P	W	D	L	F	A	Pts
Springvale Rovers	26	18	4	4	68	32	40
Star Aluminium	26	18	3	5	73	37	39
Lye Town Res.	26	16	6	4	58	31	38
Brintons	26	15	3	8	57	37	33
Tenbury United	26	14	5	7	52	32	33
Wooferton	26	14	4	8	84	52	32
Two Gates	26	14	3	9	53	39	31
Plough Trysull	26	9	6	11	51	55	24
Highley Welfare	26	8	6	12	50	60	22
Ludlow Colts	26	7	6	13	61	64	20
Areley Kings	26	7	4	15	51	73	18
Kinver	26	7	4	15	51	73	18
Chaddesley	26	3	3	20	35	91	9
Stourport Swifts Res.	26	2	1	23	20	100	5

ESSEX & SUFFOLK BORDER LEAGUE

Premier Division

	P	W	D	L	F	A	Pts
Hatfield Peverel	28	22	2	4	71	23	46
Stowmarket Tn Res.	28	17	5	6	57	21	39
Sudbury Tn Res.	28	16	6	6	53	31	38
Bramston	28	16	4	8	68	50	36
Tiptree United Res.	28	12	8	8	42	26	32
Sudbury Wanderers	28	13	5	10	48	42	31
Long Melford	28	13	3	11	41	40	30
Felixstowe Tn Res.	28	12	6	10	33	39	30
Bury Town Reserves	28	10	7	11	53	42	27
Rowhedge	28	11	3	14	49	62	25
Haverhill Rovers Res.	28	10	4	14	47	57	24
Braintree Tn Res.	28	8	4	16	41	56	20
Brantham Ath. Res.	28	4	10	14	34	75	18
Earls Colne	28	5	5	18	24	55	15
Clacton Town Res.	28	2	5	21	22	64	9

Relegated: Clacton Town Reserves.

THE LINCOLNSHIRE STANDARD GROUP F L

	P	W	D	L	F	A	Pts
Louth United	32	26	1	5	102	29	53
Cleethorpes Borough	32	21	6	5	65	24	48
Gainsborough Town	32	20	6	6	70	27	46
Ross Sports	32	15	7	10	61	38	37
Immingham Town	32	14	9	9	48	44	37
Skegness Town	32	13	9	10	56	41	35
Ruston Bucyrus	32	13	8	11	52	44	34
Grimsby SHFS	32	13	8	11	54	49	34
Nettleham	32	12	9	11	50	47	33
Crowle United	32	13	5	14	43	49	31
Ruston Sports	32	13	4	15	48	55	30
Sleaford Town	32	10	10	12	34	47	30
Mablethorpe Ath.	32	10	9	13	35	47	29
Messingham Trinity	32	9	1	22	44	91	19
Lincoln Claytons—4	32	8	4	20	33	60	16
Market Rasen Town	32	5	5	22	40	89	15
Brigg White Horse	32	4	5	23	37	92	13

PETERBOROUGH & DISTRICT LEAGUE

Premier Division

	P	W	D	L	F	A	Pts
Perkins	30	22	4	4	106	34	48
Somersham Town	30	20	5	5	70	29	45
Ortonians	30	18	6	6	51	28	42
Wisbech Town Res.	30	16	6	8	67	51	38
Downham Town	30	13	7	10	58	36	33
Leverington Sports	30	13	7	10	67	53	33
Huntingdon United	30	12	8	10	75	52	32
Deeping Rangers	30	11	9	10	45	38	31
Whittlesey United	30	9	11	10	50	49	29
Yaxley	30	10	7	13	47	59	27
Pinchback United	30	7	10	13	40	51	24
Parson Drove Untd	30	7	9	14	32	46	23
Warboys Town	30	9	5	16	41	70	23
Kings Lynn Res.	30	6	9	15	39	64	21
Eye United	30	6	7	17	33	92	19
Phorphres Sports	30	4	4	22	30	99	12

AMATEUR FOOTBALL ALLIANCE
SEASON 1985-86
Cup Competition Finals

Senior
Old Esthameians v Old Ignatians 2-1
Greenland Memorial
Liverpool Victoria v Parkfield 4-1
Essex Senior
Old Brentwoods v O. Fairlopians.... 2*:1*:10p-2*:1*:11p
Middlesex Senior
Enfield Old Grammarians v St. Mary's College 2-0
Surrey Senior
O. Bromleians v Carshalton 2-1
Intermediate
Hassocks 2nd v Nat.West Bank 2nd 2-0
Essex Intermediate
Old Parmiterians 2nd v Old Parkonians 2nd 2-0
Kent Intermediate
Lloyds Bank 2nd v Bank of America 4*-3*
Middlesex Intermediate
Winchmore Hill 2nd v Lensbury 2nd 1-5

Surrey Intermediate
O. Salesians 2nd v Nat.West Bank 2nd 1-0
Junior
Civil Service 3rd v Kew Association 3rd 1*:2-1*:1
Minor
Lloyds Bank 4th v Barclays Bank 4th 2-0
Senior Novets
Nat.West Bank 5th v Barclays Bank 5th 4-2
Intermediate Novets
O. Salvatorians 6th v O. Parmiterians 6th 3-0
Junior Novets
Nat.West Bank 'D' v Old Esthameians 7th 4-2
Veterans'
Eastbourne Town v Old Wulfrunians 2-0

(* denotes after extra time)
P = penalties

AMATEUR FOOTBALL ALLIANCE
Senior Cup 1985-86

1st Round Proper
Wandsworth Borough v Midland Bank 1-2
O. Esthameians v O. Reptonians 6-0
Hale End Athletic v Bourneside Sports 2-4
O. Fairlopians v O. Edmontonians 2-1*
Kew Association v Cardinal Manning O.B. 2-3
O. Grammarians v S. Bank Polytechnic 2-4
St. Mary's College v British Petroleum 4-0
Corinthian w/d v Lloyds Bank .... w/o
Crouch End Vampires v O. Parmiterians 2-4
Ibis v O. Lyonians 5-0
Broomfield v O. Tollingtonians 3-1
O. Stationers v Southgate County 0-2*
Orange Hill O.B. v O. Parkonians 0-3
O. Camdenians v O. Bealonians 1-3
O. Aloysians v O. Salesians 1-0
Leyton Co. O.B. v Enfield O.G. 0-10
O. Finchleians v O. Colfeians 3-1
Parkfield v O. Chigwellians 3-2
O. Vaughanians v Civil Service 3-1
O. Wersthamians v O. Woodhouseians 2-4
Nat.West Bank v Derbyshire Amateur 4-0
O. Monovians v Ulysses 1-2
West Wickham v Lensbury 2-1
Winchmore Hill v Shene O.G. 1-0
O. Wokingians v O. Bromleians 0-1
Albanian v O. Actonians Assn. 2-6
Cuaco v Norsemen 3-2
O. Greenfordians v O. Hamptonians 3-0
Carshalton v O. Latymerians 3-0
Lancing O.B. v O. Ignatians 0-4
Colposa v O. Tiffinians 4-0
O. Kingsburians v O. Sinjuns 2-3

2nd Round Proper
Midland Bank v O. Esthameians 1-2
Bourneside Sports v O. Fairlopians 0-0*:1*:0-1
Cardinal Manning O.B. v S. Bank Polytechnic 1-3
St. Mary's College v Lloyds Bank 2-1
O. Parmiterians v Ibis 2-3*
Broomfield v Southgate County 4-4*:4-5*
O. Parkonians v O. Bealonians 0-1
O. Aloysians v Enfield O. Gramms. 1-0
O. Finchleians v Parkfield 3-1
O. Vaughanians v O. Woodhouseians 3-1
Nat.West Bank v Ulysses 0-1
West Wickham v Winchmore Hill 3-1
O. Bromleians v O. Actonians Assn. 2-0
Cuaco v O. Greenfordians 0-1*
Carshalton v O. Ignatians 2-4
Colposa v O. Sinjuns 0-3
3rd Round Proper
O. Fairlopians v O.O. Esthameians 1-1:0-1:
S. Bank Polytechnic v St. Mary's College 3:2*-3:1*
Ibis v Southgate County 2-0
O. Bealonians v O. Aloysians 1-2
O. Finchleians v O. Vaughanians 3-0
Ulysses v West Wickham 1-0
O. Bromleians v O. Greenfordians 5-1
O. Ignatians v O. Sinjuns 2-1
4th Round Proper
O. Esthameians v O. Finchleians 2-0
S. Bank Polytechnic v Ulysses 3-2*
Ibis v O. Bromleians 2-0
D. Aloysians v O. Ignatians 1-2*
Semi-Finals
O. Esthameians v S. Bank Polytechnic 1-0
O. Bromleians v O. Ignatians 0-1*

(* denotes after extra time)

SOUTHERN AMATEUR LEAGUE SENIOR SECTION

Division One

	P	W	D	L	F	A	Pts
NatWest Bank	22	12	7	3	30	19	31
Lensbury	22	11	7	4	39	33	29
Old Salesians	22	9	7	6	35	30	25
West Wickham	22	8	8	6	27	18	24
Old Esthameians	22	8	8	6	32	26	24
Norsemen	22	8	8	6	28	24	24
Old Stationers	22	7	7	8	33	34	21
Winchmore Hill	22	5	10	7	30	37	20
South Bank Poly.	22	6	7	9	33	33	19
Carshalton	22	8	3	11	36	38	19
Old Bromleians	22	8	2	12	29	35	18
Midland Bank	22	2	6	14	20	45	10

Division Two

	P	W	D	L	F	A	Pts
Old Actonians Ass.	22	17	4	1	64	19	38
End Vampires	22	14	7	1	67	22	35
Old Parkonians	22	16	2	4	50	22	34
Barclays Bank	22	11	3	8	40	36	25
Kew Association	22	9	5	8	27	31	23
E. Barnet Old Grams.	22	8	6	8	34	32	22
Civil Service	22	8	3	11	33	38	19
Alleyn Old Boys	22	5	6	11	31	58	16
Lloyds Bank	22	6	3	13	30	49	15
Polytechnic	22	3	7	12	23	35	13
Old Westmin. Citizens	22	4	5	13	27	48	13
Southgate Olympic	22	4	3	15	26	62	11

Division Three

	P	W	D	L	F	A	Pts
Ibis	22	13	6	3	50	30	32
Broomfield	22	13	3	6	57	31	29
Cuaco	22	13	3	6	47	27	29
Pearl Assurance	22	10	6	6	41	31	26
Merton	22	10	5	7	41	41	25
Alexandra Park	22	9	2	11	41	41	20
British Petroleum	22	10	0	12	44	48	20
Bank of England	22	7	5	10	43	39	19
Brentham	22	6	5	11	35	52	17
Old Latymerians	22	7	3	12	43	64	17
Old Lyonians	22	6	4	12	24	38	16
Reigate Priory	22	6	2	14	23	47	14

(Also 212 Reserve Teams and below in 19 further Divisions)

MIDLAND AMATEUR ALLIANCE

Division One

	P	W	D	L	F	A	Pts
Old Elizabethans	22	18	3	1	84	18	39
Chilwell	22	12	5	5	62	39	29
Hall Park	22	11	4	7	60	40	26
Derbyshire Amateurs	22	10	6	6	41	39	26
Peoples College	22	10	3	9	54	46	23
Wollaton	22	10	2	10	45	38	22
Magdala Amateurs	22	5	8	9	39	52	18
Lady Bay	22	7	4	11	32	58	18
Wilford	22	7	3	12	37	51	17
Nottinghamshire	22	6	4	12	35	57	16
Sherwood Amateurs	22	4	0	18	26	75	8

Division Two

	P	W	D	L	F	A	Pts
Old Elizabethan 2nd.	22	16	3	3	57	28	35
Wollaton 2nd.	22	14	3	5	69	22	31
Charnos	22	14	3	5	60	36	31
Brunts Old Boys	22	14	2	6	49	30	30
Beeston O.B.A.	22	13	3	6	70	25	29
Heanor Amateurs	22	10	2	10	36	37	22
Woodthorpe	22	8	4	10	32	41	20
Derb. Amateurs 2nd.	22	7	4	11	40	40	18
Kingswood	22	8	1	13	45	53	17
Old Bemrosians	22	6	2	14	38	71	14
Wilford 2nd	22	4	3	15	30	61	11
Chesterfield Ramblers	22	2	2	18	16	98	6

(Also 34 other Teams in Three further Divisions)

ARTHUR DUNN CUP

Final: Old Brentwoods 1, Old Cholmeleians 0

LONDON BANKS F.A.

Division One

	P	W	D	L	F	A	Pts
Royal Bank of Scotland	18	10	3	5	61	31	23
Samuel Montagu	18	10	3	5	47	31	23
Coutts & Co.	18	8	6	4	30	29	22
Bank of America	18	8	5	5	33	35	21
Hong Kong Bank	18	8	3	7	29	29	19
Morgan Guaranty	18	8	1	9	24	36	17
Nat. West Bank 'A'	18	5	5	8	33	40	15
Standard Chartered Bank	18	5	4	9	32	39	14
Citibank	18	5	4	9	27	37	14
Bankers Trust Co.	18	5	2	11	34	43	12

Division Two

	P	W	D	L	F	A	Pts
Royal Bank of Scot. Res.	18	14	2	2	70	25	30
Nat. West Bank 'B'	18	11	2	5	49	33	24
Chase Manhattan Bank	18	11	1	6	45	31	23
Man. Hanover Trust	18	10	0	8	63	40	20
Lloyds Bank International	18	9	2	7	43	44	20
Hill Samuel	18	9	0	9	43	47	18
C. Hoare & Co.	18	6	4	8	51	59	16
Midland Bank 'A'	18	6	2	10	32	56	14
Swiss Bank Corpn.	18	6	0	12	37	53	12
Kleinwort Benson	18	0	3	15	21	66	3

Division Three

Bank of Ireland	18	12	5	1	65	24	29
Banque Nationale de Paris	18	12	2	4	46	24	26
Royal Bank of Scotland 3rd	18	18	6	4	42	31	22
Grindlays Bank	18	9	4	5	39	29	22
Bank of Scotland	18	7	5	6	34	42	19
Coutts & Co. 2nd	18	4	7	7	34	41	15
Westpac Banking Corpn.	18	5	5	8	28	38	15
Nat. West Bank 'C'	18	5	3	10	31	36	13
Bank of America 2nd.	18	3	5	10	26	47	11
Citibank 2nd.	18	1	6	11	27	60	8

Division Four

	P	W	D	L	F	A	Pts
Allied Irish	16	16	0	0	105	15	32
Polytechnic	16	10	1	5	49	24	21
Nat. West Bank 'D'	16	8	5	3	37	32	21
Cent. Trustee Savings Bank	16	6	3	7	45	43	15
Standard Chart. Bank 2nd.	16	5	5	6	22	32	15
Royal Bank of Scotland 4th	16	6	2	6	40	51	14
Barclays Bank 'A'	16	5	3	8	41	48	13
Manufrs Han. Trust 2nd.	16	3	1	12	26	72	7
Morgan Guaranty 2nd.	16	2	2	12	20	68	6

(also 35 other Teams in 4 further Divisions)

LONDON INSURANCE FOOTBALL LEAGUE

Division One

	P	W	D	L	F	A	Pts
Liverpool Victoria	18	14	4	0	73	24	32
Bowring	18	14	2	2	53	21	30
Eagle Star	16	12	2	2	69	20	26
Gaflac	18	7	5	6	40	49	19
Temple Bar	16	7	2	7	39	30	16
Granby	17	6	2	9	39	41	14
Sedgwick	14	4	4	6	31	30	12
Sun Alliance	16	3	3	10	18	48	9
Colonial Mutual	17	2	2	13	21	64	6
Medical Sickness	18	1	2	15	13	69	4

Division Two

Temple Bar 2nd	18	16	0	2	76	24	32
Bowring 2nd	18	12	2	4	51	38	26
Namulua	18	11	3	4	71	37	25
Hill Samuel I.S.	18	8	4	6	61	45	20
Sun Alliance 2nd	18	7	3	8	52	45	17
Sedgwick 2nd.	18	7	3	8	49	58	17
Liverpool Victoria 2nd.	18	7	2	9	34	38	16
Guardian Royal Ex.	18	5	1	12	42	63	11
Municipal	18	4	1	13	30	75	9
Gaflac 2nd	18	3	1	14	38	81	7

(Also 20 other Teams in two further Divisions)

THE OLD BOYS' AMATEUR FOOTBALL LEAGUE

Premier Division

	P	W	D	L	F	A	Pts
Enfield Old Gram.	20	15	3	2	56	24	33
Old Aloysians	19	14	1	4	49	27	27*
Old Ignatians	20	10	5	5	45	23	25
Old Kingsburians	20	8	4	8	37	37	20
Old Fincunians	19	9	3	7	35	28	19*
Old Sinjuns	20	8	3	9	36	40	19
Phoenix O.B.	20	8	2	10	26	37	18
Orange Hill O.B.	20	7	3	10	35	40	17
Old Neadonians	20	7	1	12	42	54	15
Old Highburians	20	4	3	13	23	52	11
Old Buckwellains	20	4	2	14	29	51	10

Senior Division One

	P	W	D	L	F	A	Pts
Cardinal Manning O.B.	22	17	2	3	48	21	36
Clapham O. Xaverians	22	16	3	3	61	24	35
Old Wodingians	22	10	6	6	47	29	26
Old Greenfordians	22	9	5	7	43	30	23
Old Suttonians	22	8	7	7	46	39	23
Latymer O.B.	22	8	7	7	47	42	23
Old Josephians	22	8	7	7	38	37	23
Old Minchendenians	22	6	6	9	40	50	18
Old Salvatorians	22	7	3	12	36	44	17
Old Camdenians	22	7	3	12	44	65	17
Old Tollingtonians	22	5	2	15	26	47	12
Old Uxonians	22	2	5	15	15	63	9

Senior Division Two (A)

	P	W	D	L	F	A	Pts
Old Vaughanians	20	15	2	3	62	34	32
Old Isleworthians	20	14	3	3	56	24	31
Wood Green Old Boys	20	10	5	5	43	39	25
Old Sinjuns 2nd	20	9	4	7	39	42	22
Shene Old Gram.	20	7	7	6	37	36	21
Old Danes	20	7	4	9	40	43	18
Old Thorntonians	20	7	3	10	38	35	17
Chertsey O. Salesians	19	6	5	8	28	28	17
Enfield O. Gram. 2nd	20	7	2	11	32	46	16
John Fisher O.B.	20	5	1	14	40	44	11
Leyton County O.B.	19	3	2	14	20	64	4*

Senior Division Two (B)

	P	W	D	L	F	A	Pts
Old Candenians 2nd	20	13	5	2	57	35	31
Old Addeyans	20	9	7	4	45	30	25
Old Hamptonians	19	11	5	3	37	25	25*
Old Westhamians	20	10	4	6	56	44	24
Old Tenisonians	20	8	6	6	41	32	22
Glyn O.B.	20	8	3	9	32	31	19
Old Manorians	19	7	4	8	39	32	16*
Old Paludians	20	6	4	10	27	37	16
Old Tiffinians	20	4	7	9	40	45	15
Old Aloysians 2nd	20	5	3	12	28	57	13
Clapham O. Xavs. 2nd	22	3	2	15	24	58	8

(* points deducted per Rule)
[Also 247 other Teams in 22 further Divisions]

REPRESENTATIVE MATCHES

v Army F.A. Trial XI	Drawn 2-2
v United Hospitals Centenary XI	Won 1-0
v Cambridge University	Won 1-0
v Oxford University	Won 1-0
v Kent County F.A.	Won 3-1
v Royal Navy	Lost 0-2
v London University	Won 2-1
v Royal Air Force	Cancelled
v Sussex County FA	Cancelled
v Football Association XI	Cancelled

SOUTHERN OLYMPIAN LEAGUE

Senior Section

Division One

	P	W	D	L	F	A	Pts
St Mary's College	18	11	5	2	33	14	27
Old Grammarians	18	11	4	3	39	19	26
Old Parmiterians	18	11	2	5	46	19	24
Witan	18	10	3	5	44	32	23
Albanian	18	10	3	5	36	29	23
Old Bealonians	18	6	4	8	30	27	16
Old Fairlopians	17	5	4	8	23	33	14
Fulham Compton O. B.	17	4	2	11	30	42	10
Bourneside	18	3	4	11	26	58	10
Mill Hill Village	18	2	1	15	22	56	5

Division Two

	P	W	D	L	F	A	Pts
Old Monovians	18	13	5	0	52	22	31
Old Woodhouseians	18	11	3	4	44	29	25
Old Colfeians	18	9	6	3	32	21	24
Parkfield	18	8	4	6	51	37	20
Old Finchleians	18	8	3	7	57	39	19
Wandsworth Borough	18	7	1	10	47	60	15
Hadley	18	4	6	8	31	38	14
Old Edmontonians	18	3	7	8	32	46	13
Old Wilsonians	18	2	6	10	32	58	10
City of Lon. Poly. OSA	18	4	1	13	32	60	9

Division Three

	P	W	D	L	F	A	Pts
Southgate County	18	16	1	1	55	18	33
Centymca	18	11	5	2	57	27	27
Hampstead Heathens	18	8	6	4	41	41	22
Hale End Athletic	18	8	4	6	34	29	20
Ealing Association	18	7	2	9	32	31	16
Tansley	18	5	6	7	39	40	16
Old Owens	18	4	6	8	29	41	14
Duncombe Sports	18	4	4	10	31	42	12
London Welsh	18	4	3	11	27	51	11
Economicals	18	4	1	13	40	65	9

Division Four

	P	W	D	L	F	A	Pts
Inland Revenue	16	12	3	1	57	19	27
Birkbeck College	16	12	2	2	52	14	26*
Academicals	16	7	5	4	43	25	19
Elms	16	6	6	6	46	35	17
Brent	16	5	5	6	36	37	15
Mayfield Athletic	16	6	1	9	45	42	13
London Airways	16	4	3	9	25	45	11
Conoco	16	3	2	11	33	69	8
Westerns	16	3	2	11	24	75	8

(* points deducted per Rule)
[Also 150 Reserve Teams and below in 10 other Divisions]

UNIVERSITY OF LONDON INTER-COLLEGIATE LEAGUE & CUP

Premier Division

	P	W	D	L	F	A	Pts
Queen Mary College	16	11	5	0	3	15	27
University College	16	9	5	2	41	17	23
The London Hos. M.C.	16	9	4	3	43	25	22
R. Holl. & Bed. New Col.	16	9	1	6	41	32	19
Goldsmiths' College	16	7	4	5	36	28	18
Imperial College	16	8	1	7	38	28	17
King's Q. Elizabeth College	16	5	1	10	23	31	11
Char. C. & W. Hos. M.S.	16	3	1	12	17	47	7
St. Thomas's Hospital M.S.	16	0	0	16	16	65	0

London School of Economics .... Record Expunged

UNIVERSITY MATCH

Wednesday, 11th December, 1985. At Wembley Stadium
OXFORD 0, CAMBRIDGE 2.—H.T. 0-1
Evans 29, Earl 48.

Oxford University: S. Crummett* (Manchester G.S./S.E.H.), G. Box* (Maidstone G.S./Oriel) (Captain), I. King (Bluecoats School, Liverpool/Queen's), D. Taylor (Burnley, Habergham H.S./Christ Church), B. Aitkenhead (Corsham School/Corpus Christi)

D. Smith* (Bradfield/New College), G. Link (Hampton/Pembroke), G. Harper@ (Abingdon/S.B.H.), A. Bird (St. Albans/Queen's), I. Gazidis* (Manchester G.S./S.E.H.), D. Hunter* (Q.E.G.S., Blackburn/Oriel). Substitutes: A. Anson (Oulder Hill C.S./Exeter) 78 minutes for Bird, R. Sidebottom (Lytham St. Annes H.S./Pembroke) 83 minutes for Smith. *Blue @Cambridge Blue 1982/3/4.

Cambridge University: M. Potts* (Haberdasher's Aske's, Elstree/Queens') [Captain]; A. Spurling (Tonbridge/Trinity Hall), G. Baker* (Wolverhampton G.S./St. Catherine's), S. Lant (Heaton College/Selwyn), R. Girdlestone* (Hampton/St. John's), G. Bell [Q.E.G.S. Gainsborough/St. Catherine's), P. Earl (Wymondham College/Trinity), B. Randall* (Redden Court School/Downing), C. Elliott* (Forest/Girton), S. Rouse (Corsham School/Robinson), C. Evans* (Wolverhampton G.S./Fitzwilliam). Substitutes: T. Warner (International School, Geneva/Churchill), 77 minutes for Rouse, R. Sismey (Hampton/Trinity), 85 minutes for Earl.

(Missing Oxford player [between Taylor and Smith], B. Aitkenhead [Corsham School/Corpus Christi]).

Referee: D. G. Frampton, Dorset.

There have been better University matches, but this was no fault of Cambridge, who had the more direct side and deserved to win. Oxford by contrast, were too intricate in their approach to the game and their close passing inevitably foundered on a determined defence.

Cambridge also had the best forward on view in Evans and it was he who opened the scoring after twenty-nine minutes when he ended a long run by shooting accurately past the advancing Crummett. This was the only score of the first half, when Oxford played their best football.

A quick goal came after the interval by Earl, who shot home strongly after Oxford had failed to clear a long throw by Baker. Thereafter, Oxford's pretty patterns continued ineffectively and Cambridge always looked likely to increase their lead. It was all reather disappointing for a small crowd of some 5,000.

Best for Cambridge were Baker, Lant, Girdlestone, Earl, Elliott and Evans. Oxford had few stars on the day, but Taylor and Gazidis worked hard.

BILL MITCHELL

ARTHURIAN LEAGUE

SEASON 1985-86

Premier Division

	P	W	D	L	F	A	Pts
Old Chigwellians	16	12	2	2	46	22	26
Old Malvernians..........	16	9	3	4	25	15	21
Lancing Old Boys........	16	8	5	3	31	21	21
Old Brentwoods	16	8	2	5	44	26	18
Old Cholmeleians........	16	6	4	6	25	26	16
Old Carthusians	16	5	5	6	33	34	15
Old Reptonians	16	5	2	9	24	41	12
Old Harrovians	16	3	3	9	21	35	9
Old Foresters...............	16	2	0	14	24	53	4

Division One

Old Etonians	16	9	5	2	46	27	23
Old Ardinians.............	16	10	2	4	44	27	22
Old Salopians	16	7	4	5	43	34	18
Old Bradfieldians	16	7	2	7	24	28	16
Old Wykehamists	16	6	3	7	27	25	15
Old Westminsters	16	5	4	7	25	29	14
Old Citizens................	16	6	1	9	26	48	13
Old Aldenhamians.......	16	4	4	8	27	28	12
Old Wellingburians......	16	4	3	9	23	39	11

Division Two—8 Teams—Won by Old Cholmeleians 2nd.
Division Three—9 Teams—Won by Old Bradfieldians 2nd.
Division Four—8 Teams—Won by Old Foresters 3rd.
Division Five—7 Teams—Won by Old Carthusians 3rd.

NON-LEAGUE FOOTBALL PUBLICATIONS

Once again Tony Incenzo, the editor of Pyramid has kindly agreed to review the Non-League publications that have been sent to his office during the year.

I have personally been particularly impressed with Altrincham's F.A. Trophy brochure "All the King's Men" (available from the club for a suitable donation) and Bob Barton's excellent 'Non-League' book along with the well-established contributions to semi-professional football from Tony's 'Pyramid', 'The Bureau of Non-League Football', 'The Association of Football Statisticians and 'The FPD'.

I am also pleased to announce that Mike Berry will be publishing a new Semi-Professional Monthly.

PYRAMID Magazine received some very interesting publications from the world of non-League football during 1985-86.

Kings of Amateur Soccer is the **Official Centenary History of Bishop Auckland F.C.** It tells the story of the club's six Wembley finals in eight years, using interesting anecdotes and nostaslgic photographs. Copies are available at £2.95 (plus 55p pp) from North Press, 28 Cockton Hill Road, Bishop Auckland, DL14 6AH.

The 1984-85 **F.A. Vase Review** has entitled **Felixstowe Town to Wembley.** It tells the story of the competition, at matches from the first round to the final, looking at the action on the field and 'behind the scenes' events. Price £1.25 (plus 18p p + p) from Tony Incenzo, 31 Tarling Road, London, N2 8LB.

Supermarine of the Hellenic League produced an excellent season's review. This 40 page booklet contains comment, articles and a wealth of statistics on the club's 1984-85 campaign. Send 40p (plus SAE) to George Ransom at 7 Maidens Close, Watchfield, Nr. Swindon, SN6 8TJ.

A 1984-85 review was produced by **St. Albans City**. This 12 page booklet contains photos, narrative, results and statistics from the season. Copies are available at 57p each (inc. p + p) from D. Taverner, 34 Langley Crescent, St. Albans, Herts.

The Worthing F.C. 1984-85 Yearbook consists of 76 pages, and is professionally printed with information on the club and the Vauxhall-Opel League in general. Write to **Worthing F.C.**, c/o 18 Mansfield Road, Hove, E. Sussex, BN3 5NN, enclosing £1 plus an A5 sized SAE.

Sutton United's Guide to Non-League Football gives information about and directions to all the grounds in the Gola, Southern, V-O-L and Multipart Leagues. A must for all groundhoppers, at £1.50 (p + p free) from Dave Farebrother, 24 Lumley Road, Surrey SM3 8NN. Also available from Dave (at 30p plus A4 sized SAE) are copies of Sutton's excellent **Touchliner magazine**, which are full of club news, statistics and historical items.

The Road to Wembley by Tony Incenzo is the 1984- 85 F.A. Cup Review. The book covers a match in every round of the competition, with special features on the non-League clubs. For your copy, send £2.50 (including p + p) to Wembley Way Publications, FREEPOST, 35 Chetwynd Road, London NW5 1BX.

A splendid club handbook was produced by the supporters' association at **Dartford**. The most unique feature is a list of the club's F.A. Cup results and attendances over the last 40 years. Copies may be obtained from Gary Hills at 90 Fleet Road, Dartford, Kent, DA2 6JF, price £1.50 (including p + p).

Another excellent publication is the **Scarborough F.C.** Supporters' Association 1985 Yearbook. This contains 32 pages and is professionally produced with interesting photographs. Please send £1.20 (including p + p) to Steve Adamson, 16 Bracken Hill, Scarborough, N. Yorks YO12 6HB.

A word about the two national non-League football magazines. **The Bureau of Non-League Football** is a monthly publication which lists up-to-date tables from both national and local cups. It is available on subscription at £6.50 (September to May) from 173 Leytonstone Road, London E15.

PYRAMID Magazine is also published monthly. It contains 'behind the scenes' news from every League in the non- League pyramid, plus all the fixtures each month. The subscription rate (10 issues) is £8 — cheques/POs payable to PYRAMID and sent c/o Fisher Athletic F.C., Surrey Docks Stadium, Salter Road, London SE16.

Supporter is the monthly magazine of the **Leyton-Wingate** Supporters' Club. It contains club news, views and statistics, and copies are available at 35p from Shaun Sherrick at Flat 5, 492 Leabridge Road, Leyton, London E10.

An unusual, but praiseworthy publication was the 1984-85 **Review of the Scottish Qualifying Cup**. The 44-page booklet contains match reports and statistics from every game, and is illustrated with match programme covers. Copies from Keith Anderson, 136 Balgillo Road, Dundee, DD5 3EB, enclosing £1.25 (plus 18p p + p).

The latest **Review of Non-League Football in Herts** is well-worth having. It contains an amazing 172 pages, giving league tables, cup results and a review of match programmes. Please send £1 (p + p free) to Derek Fieldsend, 42 Rodney Crescent, Hoddesden, Herts, EN11 9EW.

The monthly magazine of the **Frickley Athletic** Supporters' Club is called Bluesman. Apart from all the club news and statistics, there are guest articles and a look at old Frickley programmes. Priced at 35p (plus SAE) from Steve Berry at 11 Walnut Drive, Pontefract, W. Yorks WF8 4NR.

Another superb brochure is **'84-85: The Double Year"** This is a 32-page, glossy brochure with exciting photos and match reports from the season in which **Wealdstone** won the Gola League and F.A. Trophy. Excellent value at £2 (post free) from Peter Worby at 20 Oak Coppice Close, Bishopstone, Near Eastleigh, Hants.

David Webster has compiled a booklet entitled **A Historical Look at the Midland Counties League 1889 to 1982.** This contains all the past Midland League tables, plus a look at past teams and several other items. Please send £1.50 (plus 25p postage) to David at Low Ash Farm Cottage, Stubbing Lane, Worrall, Sheffield, S30 3AP.

The Football Programme Directory is a monthly magazine catering not only for programme collectors, but for others connected with our national game. There are plenty of mentions of the non-League scene. The annual subscription of £6 (12 issues) should be sent to the FPD at 66 Southend Road, Wickford, Essex, SS11 8EN.

The bi-monthly reports of the **Association of Football Statisticians** also mention non-League football regularly. The yearly subscription is £7.20, payable to the AFS at 22 Bretons, Basildon, Essex, SS15 5BY.

A centenary handbook has been produced by **AFC Totton.** The 66 page publication includes the reproduction of "Official Team Card Number 30" for a match against Basingstoke. Copies can be obtained from P.R. Chilcott at 7 Popes Lane, Totton, Southampton, at £3.20 (including p + p).

Bob Barton's **Northumbrian Football Year Book 1985-86** has a non-League section of nearly 100 pages, with a review of all the local league and cup competitions. It is priced at £2.95 ad Bob's new address is 319 Bedfont Lane, Feltham, Middx.

The most striking publication to arise at our office is Bob Barton's second **Non-League Book**. There are more than 600 pages, reviewing the statistics of every major league in the United Kingdom. Good value at £11.95 from Bob at the address above.

Soccer Smiles is a 44 page booklet of 70 football cartoons that has been published by Supermarine F.C. The contents are very humorous, and many have a non-League flavour. This unique collection is available at 75p (including p + p) from George Ransom at 7 Maidens Close, Watchfield, Nr. Swindon, Wilts, SN6 8TJ.

The Sussex Non-League Football Annual 1985-86 contains 100 pages, covering every level of football in the county. There is a complete Sussex County League directory, which contains an array of details. Please send £1.50 (plus 25p p + p) to Peter Wallis at 9 Stockwell Court, London Road, Burgess Hill, West Sussex, RH15 9RS.

At **Welling** there is a supporters' magazine called **United Review.** This consists of 12 pages of news, photos and match reports. Copies are available by sending a SAE plus another 17p stamp to Andy Legg at 136 Wickham Lane, Abbey Wood, London SE2 0XP.

Meanwhile, **Pink 'N Blue Review** is the new supporters' magazine at Dulwich. You can obtain a copy by sending 25p (plus SAE) to Mishi Morath, 106 Wolverton, Alvey Street, Walworth, London SE17 2AF.

The Away Day Boys' Review is published by the lads at Barnet. The contents are zany and controversial, and copies of the magazine are on sale on the terraces at Underhill.

Stourbridge issued an excellent handbook covering the last five years. The statistical section — including five years of attendances — is particularly interesting. The 40-page production is available at 80p (plus A5 sized SAE) from A. Hill at 17 The Warings, Wombourne, West Midlands, WV5 0DQ. (Cheques payable to Stourbridge FC Supporters' Club).

The supporters are Wealdstone also published a fascinating booklet entitled **'Wem-ber-ley... Wem-ber-ley..."** to celebrate their F.A. Trophy win in 1984-85. The 20-page publication contains match reports by the fans themselves on each stage of Wealdstone's Trophy trail. Please send 50p (plus 25p postage) to Sudhir Pawal at 37, Grange Road, Kenton, Harrow, Middx. HA1 2PR.

All-in-all, it has been another fine season for non-League publicity. The people involved in the production of the above- mentioned publications must be congratulated on the high standard of their work.

Tony Incenzo (Editor, Pyramid Magazine)

THE ELEVENTH WIRRAL PROGRAMME CLUB NON-LEAGUE PROGRAMME SURVEY

The standard of Football Programmes for clubs outside the Football League has never been higher and I am sure the encouragement given by Ian Runham with his survey on behalf of the Wirral Programme Club has had a lot to do with this. The club is a non profit making organisation and any entries for next year's Non-League competition should be sent to Ian at 3 Tansley Close, West Kirby, Wirral, Merseyside, L48 9XH.

THE NATIONAL TOP 30

1. Braintree T 165, 2. Lancing 142, 3. Highgate U 132, 4= Stalybridge C, Three Bridges 130, 6. Gresley Rovers 126, 7= Accrington Stanley, Ash U 120, 9= Sutton Coldfield T, Farnborough T, Banstead A 119, 12. Canvey Island 116, 13. VS Rugby 114, 14= Wealdstone, Yeovil T, Rustington 112, 17= Witton A, Andover, Cobham 111, 20= Enfield, Port of Bristol 110, 22= Kettering T, Oxford C, Oakwood, Harrogate T 109, 26= Nuneaton B, Chelmsford C, Sutton U, Kingstonian, Hampton, St. Albans C 108.

INDIVIDUAL LEAGUE RESULTS

League & No. of Entries	First
Gola 22	Wealdstone 112
Multipart 20	Witton A 111
Eastern Counties 12	Braintree T 165
Southern Overall 48	Sutton Coldfield 119
Southern Prem. Div.	Chelmsford C 108
Southern Div. 1 Mid.	Sutton Coldfield 119
Southern Div. 1 South	Andover 111
Vauxhall-Opel Overall 71	Banstead A, Farnborough T 119
Vauxhall-Opel Prem. Div.	Farnborough T 119
Vauxhall-Opel Div. 1	Oxford C 109
Vauxhall-Opel Div. 2 North	Clapton 94
Vauxhall-Opel Div. 2 South	Banstead A 119
Western Overall 26	Barnstaple 99
Western Prem. Div.	Barnstaple T 99
Western Div. 1	Glastonbury 78
N.W. Counties Overall 29	Stalybridge 130
N.W. Div. 1	Stalybridge C 130
N.W. Divs. 2,3	Kirkby T 83
N. Co. East Overall 36	Harrogate T 109
N. Co. Prem. Div.	Belper T 95
N. Co. Div. 1.	Harrogate T 109
N. Co. Div. 2.	Pickering T 90
N. Co. Div. 3.	Eccleshill U 98
Northern Overall 26	North Shields 101
Northern Div. 1.	North Shields 101
Northern Div. 2.	Guisborough T 99
West Midlands Overall 28	Gresley Rovers 126
West Midlands Prem. Div.	Gresley Rovers 126
West Midlands Div. 1.	Wolverhampton C 93
West Midlands Div. 2.	Bloxwich T 83
United Co. Overall 18	Brackley T 100
United Co. Prem. Div.	Brackley T 100
United Co. Div. 1.	Baker Perkins 85
Sussex Co. Overall 22	Lancing 142
Sussex Co. Div. 1.	Lancing 142
Sussex Co. Divs. 2,3	Oakwood 109
South Midlands Overall 116	Winslow U 84
South Midlands Prem. Div.	Winslow U 84
South Midlands Div. 1.	Biggleswade T 65

London Spartan Overall 116	Redhill 81
London Spartan Prem. Div.	Redhill 81
London Spartan Senior	Corinthian Cas. 74
Scotland Overall 20	Kinnoull Jun. 88
Scotland Highland League	Caledonian, Fraserburgh =82
Scotland Junior League	Kinnoull Jun. 88
Wales Overall 21	Cefn A 92
Wales Welsh League	Cwmbran T, Sully =68
Wales Nat. Lg.	Wrexham Cefn A 92
Kent 12	Whitstable T 73
Hellenic Overall 10	Penhill 96
Hellenic Prem. Div.	Wallingford T 95
Hellenic Div. 1.	Penhill 96
South Western 11	Appledore/BAAC 54
Midland Comb. Overall 10	Highgate U 132
Midland Prem. Div.	Highgate U 132
Midland Div. 1.	Shelfield U 67
Hampshire Overall 12	Romsey T 90
Hampshire Div. 1.	Romsey T 90
Hampshire Divs. 2,3	West Wight 76
Combined Co. 9	Ash U 120
Herts. Senior 8	Elliott Star 93
Essex Srnior 9	Canvey Island 116
Staffs Senior 7	Hednesford Prog. 86
Mid Cheshire 7	Grove U 80
Peterborough 3	Pinchbeck U, Warboys T =85
Wearside 4	Eppleton C.W. 69
Anglian Comb. 5	Wymondham T 82
Central Midlands 4	Thorpe Acre Hallam 92
Notts Alliance 3	Basford U 82
Leicestershire 5	Wigston T 79
Gloucestershire Co. 6	Port of Bristol 110
West Sussex 4	Rustington 112
Dorset Combination 3	Portland U 56
Glos. Senior North 3	Wilton Rovers 64
Schools, Youth teams 7	Didcot Boys 73
Other Leagues 29	Bitton 96
Sunday Clubs 57	Billericay TSC 104
Reserve Programmes 6	Sutton Coldfield T 80

BIG MATCH FOOTBALL PROGRAMME SURVEY 1985-86

OTHER NATIONAL SEMI FINALS

1st. F.A. Vase. Wisbech Town v Southall
2nd. F.A. Trophy. Kettering Town v Runcorn
3rd. F.A. Vase. Southall v Wisbech Town

REPRESENTATIVE

1st. F.A. XI v Multipart League at Witton Albion
2nd. F.A. XI v Vauxhall Opel League at Metropolitan Police
3rd. English Fire Service v R.A.F. at London Fire Brigade Sports Centre

BEST NON LEAGUE SPECIAL 1985-1986

Wisbech Town v Southall F.A. Vase Semi Final
2nd. Ottery St. Mary v Queens Park Rangers Friendly
3rd Ottery St. Mary v Nottingham Forest Friendly

SOUTHERN LEAGUE PREMIER DIVISION FIXTURES 1986-87

	Alvechurch	Aylesbury U.	Basingstoke T.	Bedworth U.	Bromsgrove Rovers	Cambridge C.	Chelmsford C.	Corby T.	Crawley T.	Dartford	Dudley T.	Fareham T.	Fisher Athletic	Folkestone	Gosport Boro	King's Lynn	Redditch U.	Salisbury	Shepshed Charterhouse	Willenhall T.	Witney T.	Worcester C.
Alvechurch		8.11	11.4	25.4	18.4	18.10	4.10	27.9	16.8	21.2	3.9	25.8	29.11	24.1	28.3	7.2	26.12	6.9	7.3	13.12	3.1	10.1
Aylesbury U	4.4		14.3	3.1	27.9	10.1	6.9	2.9	1.11	13.12	21.2	21.3	15.11	28.2	18.4	25.8	2.5	18.10	24.1	29.11	26.12	7.2
Basingstoke T	1.11	20.12		18.10	3.1	14.2	28.3	16.8	2.5	7.3	6.12	10.1	18.4	30.8	22.11	4.4	24.1	26.12	25.8	9.9	27.9	25.4
Bedworth U	27.12	23.8	21.2		11.4	1.11	15.11	1.1	31.1	11.10	28.3	28.2	13.12	7.2	14.3	2.9	29.11	17.1	20.4	20.9	30.8	25.10
Bromsgrove Rovers	1.1	9.9	25.10	22.11		15.11	23.8	27.12	6.12	31.1	11.10	14.3	28.2	21.3	30.8	17.1	2.9	20.9	4.4	7.2	25.4	20.4
Cambridge C.	28.2	11.10	8.11	2.5	28.3		26.12	29.11	7.2	17.1	13.12	24.1	25.10	3.1	21.2	18.4	6.9	14.3	3.9	16.8	25.8	20.9
Chelmsford C	21.3	31.1	11.10	8.9	14.2	20.4		28.2	1.1	13.9	25.8	6.12	8.11	27.9	10.1	1.11	16.8	13.12	27.12	11.4	22.11	30.8
Corby T	8.9	30.8	17.1	18.4	1.11	7.3	3.1		4.10	15.11	31.1		20.9	25.4	6.12	26.12	7.2	23.8	2.5	21.2	28.3	4.4
Crawley T	14.2	25.4	29.11	8.11	25.8	27.9	18.4	10.1		28.3	3.1	25.10	24.1	26.12	11.10	30.8	14.3	15.11	28.2	4.4	13.12	2.9
Dartford	30.8	16.8	20.9	24.1	4.10	4.4	14.3	11.4	9.9		7.2	22.11	26.12	18.4	8.11	28.2	18.10	3.1	14.2	25.8	10.1	6.12
Dudley T.	25.10	27.12	6.9	27.9	2.5	11.4	24.1	18.10	21.3	23.8		20.12	10.1	15.11	28.2	29.11	8.11	4.4	1.1	20.4	14.2	14.3
Fareham T.	31.1	17.1	3.9	16.8	29.11	23.8	7.2	13.12	7.3	25.4	20.9		28.3	1.11	26.12	15.11	3.1	18.4	18.10	6.9	4.4	21.2
Fisher Athletic	20.12	7.3	1.1	4.4	18.10	9.9	25.4	21.3	27.12	20.4	1.11	27.9		2.9	7.2	4.10	23.8	21.2	6.9	17.1	6.12	31.1
Folkestone	23.8	20.9	27.12	25.8	6.9	22.11	21.2	8.11	20.4	1.1	7.3	11.4	11.10		25.10	13.12	17.1	28.3	6.12	31.1	14.3	9.9
Gosport Boro	20.9	1.1	21.3	6.9	7.3	20.12	29.11	14.2	17.1	27.12	16.8	20.4	2.5	4.4		18.10	13.12	31.1	23.8	15.11	2.9	1.11
King's Lynn	11.10	6.12	23.8	10.1	21.2	1.1	7.3	20.4	20.12	6.9	10.9	14.2	14.3	2.5	11.4		28.3	25.4	27.9	25.10	24.1	27.12
Redditch U	20.4	22.11	15.11	7.3	10.1	6.12	4.4	25.10	20.9	21.3	25.4	30.8	14.2	20.12	25.8	31.1		9.9	1.11	27.12	11.10	1.1
Salisbury	6.12	14.2	20.4	20.12	24.1	27.12	1.9	25.8	11.4	2.5	30.8	1.1	16.8	10.1	27.9	8.11	28.2		22.11	21.3	25.10	11.10
Shepshed C'house	17.1	25.10	31.1	26.12	13.12	30.8	20.9	14.3	21.2	29.11	18.4	10.9	3.1	16.8	25.4	21.3	11.4	7.2		11.10	8.11	15.11
Willenhall T	14.3	28.3	28.2	6.12	8.11	25.4	18.10	20.12	23.8	2.9	26.12	2.5	30.8	14.2	24.1	3.1	27.9	1.11	10.1		18.4	4.10
Witney T	15.11	20.4	7.2	21.3	16.8	31.1	2.5	6.9	18.10	1.11	17.1	27.12	11.4	29.11	9.9	20.9	21.2	7.3	20.12	1.1		23.8
Worcester C	2.5	11.4	13.12	14.2	26.12	21.3	17.1	24.1	6.9	27.9	22.11	8.11	25.8	18.10	3.1	16.8	18.4	29.11	28.3	7.3	28.2	

N.B. Fixtures are subject to alterations for reasons of weather, Cup-ties, etc.

G.M. VAUXHALL CONFERENCE FIXTURES 1986-87

	Altrincham	Barnet	Bath City	Boston U.	Cheltenham T.	Dagenham	Enfield	Frickley Ath.	Gateshead U.	Kettering T.	Kidderminster H.	Maidstone U.	Northwich Vic.	Nuneaton Boro	Runcorn	Scarborough	Stafford R.	Sutton U.	Telford U.	Wealdstone	Welling U.	Weymouth
Altrincham		1.11	16.8	30.8	18.10	25.4	17.1	13.12	9.9	22.11	3.1	2.5	25.8	4.10	21.2	23.9	26.12	14.3	14.2	4.4	29.11	20.9
Barnet	31.1		14.2	23.9	14.3	2.5	26.12	8.11	18.4	4.4	6.12	25.8	3.1	9.9	29.11	18.10	7.3	30.8	4.10	30.9	19.8	17.2
Bath City	28.3	14.4		14.3	30.9	11.10	22.11	2.5	17.1	20.9	25.8	9.9	21.2	20.4	31.1	4.4	6.9	23.9	6.12	7.3	23.8	1.1
Boston U.	11.4	3.9	28.2		21.3	23.8	27.9	26.12	15.10	14.2	6.9	31.1	18.4	8.10	1.11	6.12	17.1	20.9	27.8	17.9	3.1	22.11
Cheltenham T	18.4	23.8	8.10	4.4		28.2	1.11	7.3	22.11	25.8	26.12	28.3	14.2	6.12	10.1	31.1	15.10	3.1	24.9	6.9	25.4	3.9
Dagenham	8.11	11.4	27.9	8.9	30.8		22.9	18.10	29.11	14.3	28.3	18.4	16.8	13.9	7.2	7.3	3.1	6.10	17.1	14.2	26.12	18.8
Enfield	11.10	1.1	13.12	8.11	7.2	2.9		23.8	16.8	16.9	11.4	30.9	20.9	18.10	6.9	10.1	2.5	20.4	28.3	29.11	14.2	7.3
Frickley Ath.	10.1	21.2	30.8	1.1	20.4	6.12	25.4		25.8	9.9	1.11	16.8	14.10	27.9	7.10	14.2	23.9	29.11	13.9	31.1	21.3	4.4
Gateshead U	3.9	20.9	11.4	13.12	2.5	21.3	31.1	1.10		21.2	24.1	18.10	6.12	10.1	17.9	1.1	20.4	8.11	14.3	4.10	28.2	6.9
Kettering T	23.8	17.1	20.8	2.5	29.11	6.9	6.12	3.9	3.1		8.10	4.10	24.1	24.9	11.4	28.2	28.3	18.4	7.3	1.1	18.10	8.11
Kidderminster H	18.8	16.8	15.9	7.3	1.1	10.1	30.8	20.9	14.2	29.9		14.3	29.11	31.1	1.9	18.4	27.4	7.2	4.4	13.12	8.11	4.10
Maidstone U	27.9	13.12	3.1	13.9	11.4	17.9	8.10	17.1	7.3	21.3	28.2		25.4	14.2	11.10	6.9	1.11	26.12	22.11	20.8	3.9	23.8
Northwich Vic.	1.10	6.9	10.1	4.10	13.12	22.11	28.2	20.8	24.9	20.4	23.8	8.11		7.3	1.1	3.9	17.9	11.4	7.2	1.11	14.3	18.10
Nuneaton Boro	28.2	7.2	1.9	29.9	15.9	21.2	4.4	6.9	1.11	13.12	13.10	29.11	28.3		14.3	16.8	11.4	23.8	26.12	20.9	17.1	3.1
Runcorn	6.12	28.3	13.9	16.8	8.11	4.10	3.1	25.10	19.8	25.4	23.9	30.8	26.12	2.5		25.8	14.2	18.10	18.4	28.2	20.9	17.1
Scarborough	8.10	22.11	4.10	20.8	17.1	20.9	14.3	17.9	26.12	1.11	21.3	7.2	10.9	30.8	20.4		13.12	21.2	3.1	23.8	11.4	2.5
Stafford Rangers	1.1	10.1	29.11	18.10	20.9	31.1	4.10	7.2	7.10	30.8	9.9	21.2	4.11	19.8	23.8	8.11		6.12	25.4	21.3	18.4	14.3
Sutton U	6.9	28.2	1.11	10.1	4.10	30.9	19.8	28.3	4.4	14.10	22.11	1.1	17.1	14.4	7.3	25.4	24.1		16.8	2.9	16.9	13.12
Telford U	25.10	21.3	8.11	29.11	19.8	13.12	21.2	28.2	23.8	10.1	20.4	20.9	7.10	1.1	30.9	14.10	2.9	31.1		2.5	6.9	11.4
Wealdstone	13.9	20.4	18.10	7.2	21.2	26.8	18.4	3.1	28.3	26.12	17.1	23.9	30.8	8.11	22.11	24.1	16.8	9.9	27.9		7.10	6.12
Welling U	7.3	15.10	7.2	21.2	16.8	1.1	10.9	4.10	30.8	31.1	2.5	20.4	4.4	18.3	13.12	28.3	22.11	11.3	1.11	10.1		24.9
Weymouth	7.2	8.10	26.12	28.3	10.9	1.11	13.9	18.4	25.4	16.8	21.2	10.1	31.1	25.8	27.9	29.11	28.2	21.3	30.8	11.10	1.10	

N.B. Fixtures are subject to alterations for reasons of weather, Cup-ties, etc.

MULTIPART LEAGUE FIXTURES 1986-87

	Bangor City	Barrow	Burton Albion	Buxton	Caernarfon	Chorley	Gainsborough	Goole Town	Horwich RMI	Hyde United	Macclesfield	Marine	Matlock Town	Morecambe	Mossley	Oswestry	Rhyl	South Liverpool	Southport	Witton Albion	Workington	Worksop
Bangor City	—	17.1	1.11	28.3	26.12	20.9	4.10	18.10	30.8	7.3	13.9	10.9	23.8	15.11	6.12	20.4	24.9	31.1	21.2	20.8	25.4	3.1
Barrow	25.10	—	3.1	6.12	28.2	14.3	11.4	14.2	9.9	18.4	30.8	25.8	10.1	30.9	14.10	2.5	21.3	16.8	23.9	24.1	26.12	8.11
Burton Alb	21.3	4.10	—	10.9	15.11	21.2	1.1	27.12	25.4	4.4	20.9	8.11	20.4	31.1	25.10	15.10	17.1	30.8	6.12	7.3	16.8	25.8
Buxton	8.11	7.3	7.10	—	4.4	21.3	30.9	2.9	2.5	25.10	25.8	16.8	1.1	27.12	16.9	6.9	31.1	18.4	28.2	23.8	17.1	22.7
Caernarfon T. A.	25.8	18.10	18.4	20.9	—	25.4	8.11	31.1	22.11	10.1	16.8	7.3	28.3	21.2	6.9	3.9	1.1	8.10	27.12	17.9	24.1	2.5
Chorley	22.11	19.8	24.1	3.1	19.9	—	25.10	18.4	26.12	8.11	4.4	14.2	28.2	16.9	7.3	28.3	30.8	2.5	10.1	14.10	30.9	23.8
Gainsborough Tr.	10.1	6.9	26.1	28.10	21.3	16.8	—	15.8	3.1	8.10	24.1	18.4	23.9	1.11	28.3	7.3	20.9	21.2	18.10	2.5	15.11	9.9
Goole Town	28.2	28.3	30.9	14.10	30.8	28.10	20.4	—	24.1	9.9	10.1	25.4	16.9	25.10	19.8	21.3	8.11	3.1	23.8	22.11	6.12	26.12
Horwich RMI	27.12	6.10	6.9	22.9	11.4	20.4	4.4	21.2	—	20.9	15.11	17.1	16.8	1.9	31.1	23.8	18.10	7.3	1.1	6.12	3.11	21.3
Hyde Utd	29.9	31.1	1.9	18.8	23.8	17.1	5.9	15.11	14.3	—	27.4	4.10	6.12	6.9	20.4	26.12	21.2	18.10	1.11	13.12	3.1	28.3
Macclefield T	27.9	16.9	11.4	21.2	30.9	6.9	2.9	7.3	28.3	1.1	—	31.1	14.2	23.8	17.1	18.8	27.12	8.11	24.3	20.4	14.10	25.4
Marine	16.9	27.12	23.8	15.11	19.8	18.10	28.2	6.9	30.9	11.4	6.12	—	14.3	1.1	21.2	21.10	8.10	24.1	20.4	2.9	28.3	19.1
Matlock T.	11.4	1.11	19.8	26.12	3.1	25.8	14.10	4.11	25.10	21.3	9.9	30.8	—	17.1	25.4	31.1	18.4	15.11	20.9	21.2	7.3	30.9
Morecambe	24.1	25.4	10.1	30.8	6.12	8.10	14.2	14.3	18.4	28.2	18.10	21.3	4.4	—	26.12	3.1	16.8	23.9	9.9	8.11	25.8	20.9
Mossley	16.8	4.4	14.2	10.1	22.9	1.1	27.12	6.10	8.11	25.8	28.2	20.9	24.1	2.5	—	22.11	8.9	21.3	30.8	11.4	18.4	18.10
Oswestry T.	8.10	15.11	20.2	24.1	14.2	27.12	6.12	20.9	10.1	30.8	18.4	24.9	18.10	11.4	14.3	—	25.8	10.9	25.4	1.1	4.4	16.8
Rhyl	3.9	23.8	28.3	11.4	20.4	15.11	14.3	2.5	14.2	24.1	1.11	15.10	6.9	4.10	3.1	17.9	—	26.12	20.8	1.10	25.10	28.2
South Liverpool	1.1	20.4	22.11	25.4	15.10	6.12	23.8	17.1	17.9	14.2	14.3	25.10	27.12	20.8	3.9	1.10	4.4	—	28.3	10.1	28.2	6.9
Southport	18.4	2.9	14.3	14.2	25.10	11.4	17.1	4.4	25.8	16.8	3.1	28.12	4.10	14.10	30.4	8.11	7.3	28.10	—	6.9	16.9	24.1
Witton Alb	14.2	20.9	18.10	14.3	28.10	23.9	30.8	16.8	28.2	29.11	26.12	3.1	8.10	28.3	15.11	17.1	25.4	25.8	31.1	—	9.9	18.4
Workington	6.9	1.1	2.5	18.10	14.3	3.9	31.1	11.4	20.8	27.12	24.9	22.11	8.11	20.4	23.8	21.2	10.1	20.9	8.10	21.3	—	14.2
Worksop T.	14.3	21.2	17.9	20.4	17.1	31.1	20.8	1.1	15.10	24.9	8.10	4.4	3.9	7.3	5.11	25.10	6.12	11.4	15.11	27.12	30.8	—

VAUXHALL OPEL PREMIER DIVISION FIXTURES 1986-87

	Barking	Bishop's Stortford	Bognor Regis	Bromley	Carshalton	Croydon	Dulwich Hamlet	Farnborough Town	Harrow Borough	Hayes	Hendon	Hitchin Town	Kingstonian	St. Albans City	Slough Town	Tooting & Mitcham	Walthamstowe	Windsor & Eton	Wokingham Town	Worthing	Wycombe W.	Yeovil Town
Barking	—	4.11	20.9	14.2	16.2	28.2	19.8	4.10	1.11	24.1	9.9	28.3	10.1	27.12	14.3	15.11	26.8	30.8	16.8	25.4	29.11	18.10
Bishop's Stortford	2.9	—	7.3	25.4	21.3	6.12	8.11	31.1	6.9	20.9	11.10	1.1	18.4	22.11	23.8	20.4	13.12	14.2	4.4	3.1	21.2	17.1
Bognor Regis T.	7.2	18.10	—	24.11	6.9	1.11	1.9	3.1	13.12	18.4	21.2	23.8	27.9	14.3	31.1	4.4	27.12	29.11	15.11	25.8	17.1	28.2
Bromley	27.9	29.11	16.9	—	1.1	7.10	31.1	17.1	23.8	11.10	25.11	3.1	21.2	18.4	13.12	2.9	8.11	4.4	7.3	7.2	6.9	21.3
Carshalton A.	30.9	1.11	24.1	26.8	—	9.9	15.11	18.10	29.11	16.8	10.1	14.3	4.11	28.2	14.2	20.9	30.8	4.10	27.12	13.2	28.3	18.4
Croydon	11.10	2.5	21.3	15.11	31.1	—	1.1	23.8	17.1	25.10	29.11	7.3	8.11	4.4	6.9	13.12	1.9	18.4	21.2	27.9	3.1	18.8
Dulwich Hamlet	6.12	27.12	3.11	8.9	8.12	11.4	—	28.2	18.4	10.1	30.8	1.11	29.9	16.8	4.10	14.2	18.10	20.9	24.1	14.3	25.4	28.3
Farnborough Town	21.2	13.9	16.8	30.8	7.3	10.1	11.10	—	27.9	1.1	16.12	8.11	13.12	24.1	25.4	28.3	11.4	1.11	29.11	2.9	7.2	16.9
Harrow Borough	21.3	24.1	25.4	10.1	8.11	30.8	4.4	14.2	—	27.12	11.4	30.9	16.8	4.11	6.12	24.11	20.9	18.10	9.9	28.2	7.10	1.1
Hayes	6.9	7.2	28.3	28.2	3.1	14.3	23.8	26.8	19.8	—	1.11	31.1	29.11	15.11	18.10	17.1	2.5	30.9	27.9	4.4	2.9	13.2
Hendon	31.1	28.2	8.11	14.3	23.8	25.4	17.1	4.4	24.2	21.3	—	2.9	22.11	26.8	20.9	2.9	14.2	27.12	18.4	18.10	6.12	3.1
Hitchin Town	13.12	25.8	10.1	16.8	4.4	18.10	21.3	27.12	25.10	9.9	4.11	—	11.4	14.2	7.10	28.2	29.11	24.1	30.8	15.11	18.4	20.9
Kingstonian	23.8	15.11	14.2	6.12	2.5	20.9	16.12	14.3	3.1	7.10	28.3	25.4	—	18.10	17.1	26.8	4.4	28.2	1.11	31.1	19.8	6.9
St Albans City	25.10	19.8	11.4	28.3	11.10	20.4	3.1	6.9	2.9	21.2	1.1	27.9	7.3	—	8.11	29.11	21.3	13.12	7.2	17.1	31.1	23.8
Slough Town	11.4	10.1	13.9	27.12	27.9	24.1	21.2	15.11	28.3	7.3	7.2	19.8	30.8	30.9	—	1.11	16.8	4.11	26.8	29.11	11.10	9.12
Tooting & Mitcham	18.4	11.4	22.11	4.11	19.8	16.9	27.9	6.12	21.2	30.8	24.1	12.10	1.1	25.4	21.3	—	9.9	16.8	10.1	27.12	7.3	8.11
Walthamstowe A.	1.1	28.3	18.8	29.9	17.1	3.11	7.3	18.4	7.2	6.12	27.9	21.2	25.10	1.11	3.1	31.1	—	14.3	11.10	6.9	23.8	22.11
Windsor & Eton	17.1	27.9	20.4	11.4	21.2	28.3	7.2	21.3	7.3	8.11	19.8	6.9	11.10	6.12	2.9	3.1	15.11	—	16.9	23.8	1.1	31.1
Wokingham Town	3.1	14.3	6.12	18.10	25.10	4.10	6.9	19.8	31.1	14.2	13.12	17.1	21.3	20.9	1.1	23.8	28.2	25.4	—	11.4	8.11	2.9
Worthing	8.11	16.8	1.1	20.9	16.9	14.2	25.10	4.11	11.10	22.11	7.3	6.12	9.9	30.8	18.4	2.5	24.1	10.1	28.3	—	21.3	4.10
Wycombe W.	4.4	4.10	30.8	24.1	11.4	16.8	13.12	20.9	14.3	14.11	15.11	22.11	27.12	9.9	28.2	18.10	10.1	26.8	30.9	1.11	—	14.2
Yeovil Town	7.3	30.8	11.10	1.11	6.12	27.12	29.11	8.10	15.11	11.4	16.8	7.2	24.1	10.1	4.4	14.3	25.4	13.9	5.11	21.2	27.9	—

STOP PRESS

The first week of August saw the release of a publication entitled 'Non-League North-West'. It is the intention of the publishers to use the following format for what will be a regular magazine:

Clubs covered: The following five Alliance (GMVFC) clubs: Altrincham, Northwich Victoria, Runcorn, Stafford Rangers and Telford United. The following eighteen Northern Premier (Multipart) clubs: Barrow, Burton Albion, Buxton, Caernarfon Town, Chorley, Horwich R.M.I., Hyde United, Marine, Morecambe, Bangor City, Southport, Workington, Macclesfield Town, Witton Albion, Mossley, Rhyl, Owestry Town and South Liverpool. All North West Counties (Bass) clubs. Clubs in the vicinity of the above clubs which are now defunct.

The magazine will consist of: 8 pages (A5 size) (4 on glossy paper, 4 on normal), typesetting will be used accompanied by black and white photography. Each copy will cost 25p but clubs can purchase in bundles of ten upwards at a reduced rate.

10 copies — £2.00 **20 copies — £3.75**

Such bundles are offered post-free and are on a sale or return basis. Individual copies can be purchased at 25p plus 20p postage and packing.

Orders should be sent to: H. JAWAD (Editor), N.L.N.W., 22 Stratford Road, Aigburth, Liverpool L19 3RF.

LEAGUES FEATURED IN THE DIRECTORY

Club's Leagues are listed below so clubs can be traced through the above league index.

INDEX OF CLUBS

A clubs page number may be found by checking the page number of its league.

	League	Comps	Best V or T res.	County
Congleton Town	NWCO	CT	2Q*	CHES
Consett	NTHN	CT	2	DURH
Corby Town	STHN	CT	2*	NHAM
Corinthian	STHN	V	—	KENT
Corinthian Casuals	LNSP	CV	5	SURR
Coundon TT	WEAR	V	4	DURH
Coventry Sporting	STHN	CV	5	BIRM
Cranfield United	SMID	V	—	BEDS
Crawley Town	STHN	CT	2	SUSS
Cray Wanderers	KENT	CV	QF	KENT
Crockenhill	KENT	CV	4*	KENT
Crookes	CMID	V	—	SHEF
Crook Town	NTHN	CT	3	DURH
Croydon	V-OP	CT	2*	SURR
Curzon Ashton	NWCO	CT	2Q*	MANC
Cwmbran Town	WELS	CT	—	WALE
Dagenham	GMVC	CT	W	LOND
Daisy Hill	NWCO	V	P	LANC
Danson (Bexley Borough)	LNSP	CV	P	LOND
Darenth Heathside	KENT	CV	4	KENT
Darlington Cleveland Bridge	NTHN	CV	1	DURH
Dartford	STHN	CT	F	KENT
Darwen	NWCO	CV	1	LANC
Dawdon Colliery Welfare	WEAR	V	—	DURH
Dawlish Town	WEST	V	P	DEVO
Denaby United	NCOE	CV	4	SHEF
Desborough Town	UTDC	CV	5	NHAM
Devizes Town	WEST	CV	QF	WILT
Didcot Town	HELL	V	3	B&B
Diss Town	ANGL	V	4	NORF
Dorchester Town	STHN	CT	3	DORS
Dorking	V-OP	CV	3	SURR
Dover Athletic	STHN	CT	3	KENT
Downham Town	PETE	V	1*	NORF
Downton		V	—	WILT
Droylsden	NWCO	CV	1	MANC
Dudley Town	STHN	CT	2	BIRM
Dulwich Hamlet	V-OP	CT	QF	LOND
Dunstable	STHN	CT	3Q*	BEDS
Durham City	NTHN	CV	P	DURH
Easington Colliery	NTHN	CV	4	DURH
Eastbourne Town	SUSS	CV	5	SUSS
Eastbourne United	V-OP	CV	QF	SUSS
East Grinstead	SUSS	V	3	SUSS
East Ham United	ESSEX	V	QF	LOND
Eastleigh	WESS	CV	4	HAMP
East Thurrock United	ESSX	V	1*	ESSE
Eastwood Hanley	NWCO	CV	3	STAF
Eastwood Town	NCOE	CT	2Q*	NOTT
Eaton Bray United	SMID	V	2*	BEDS
Eccleshall		V	—	STAF
Edgware	LNSP	CV	4	MIDD
Egham Town	V-OP	CV	4	SURR
Ellesmere Port Town & Neston	NWCO	V	3	CHES
Ely City	EAST	CV	2*	CAMB
Emley	NCOE	CV	2	SHEF
Enfield	GMVC	CT	W	MIDD
Eppleton Colliery Welfare	WEAR	CV	3*	DURH
Epsom & Ewell	V-OP	CT	2	SURR
Erith & Belvedere	STHN	CT	P*	KENT
Esh Winning	NTHN	CV	2	DURH
Eton Manor	ESSX	V	2*	ESSE
Evenwood Town	NTHN	CV	P	DURH
Evesham United	MIDC	CV	4*	WORC
Exmouth Town	WEST	CV	SF	DEVO
Eynesbury Rovers	UTDC	V	2	HUNT
Fairford Town	HELL	V	2*	GLOS
Falmouth Town	SWST	V	—	CORN
Fareham Town	STHN	CT	1	HAMP
Farleigh Rovers	COMC	V	XP	SURR
Farnborough Town	V-OP	CT	3Q	HAMP
Farnham Town	COMC	CV	4	SURR
Farsley Celtic	NCOE	CV	4	WRID
Faversham Town	KENT	CV	2*	KENT
Felixstowe Town	EAST	CV	3*	SUFF
Feltham	V-OP	CV	3	MIDD
Ferryhill Athletic	NTHN	CT	2Q*	DURH
Finchley	V-OP	CT	2Q	LOND
Fisher Athletic	STHN	CT	3*	LOND
Flackwell Heath	V-OP	CV	2*	B&B
Fleet Town	COMC	V	2*	HAMP
Fleetwood Hesketh		V	—	LIVE
Fleetwood Town	NWCO	CV	F	LANC
Flight Refuelling	DORS	V	1*	DORS
Flixton	MANC	V	—	MANC
Folkestone	STHN	CT	3Q*	KENT
Ford Motors (Liverpool)	NWCO	V	4	LIVE
Ford United (London)	ESSX	V	3	ESSE
Forest Green Rovers	STHN	CT	3Q	GLOS
Formby	NWCO	CT	1	LIVE
Frecheville Community	NCOE	V	QF	SHEF
Friar Lane OB	LEIC	CV	5F*	LEIC
Frickley Athletic	GMVC	CT	QF	SHEF
Frimley Green	COMC	V	2	SURR
Frome Town	WEST	CT	2	SOME
Fryston Colliery Welfare	NCOE	V	2	WRID
Gainsborough Town	CMID	V	—	LINC
Gainsborough Trinity	MLPT	CT	2*	LINC
Garforth Town	NCOE	CV	3	WRID
Gateshead	GMVC	CT	3	DURH
Gateshead Clark Chapman	WEAR	V	—	DURH
General Chemicals	WCHE	V	—	CHES
Gillingham Town	DORS	V	—	DORS
GKN Sankey	WMID	CV	P*	SHRO
Glastonbury	WEST	CV	1	SOME
Glenside St Gabriels	BRIS	V	1*	GLOS
Glossop	NWCO	CT	2Q	DERB
Gloucester City	STHN	CT	1*	GLOS
Godalming Town	COMC	V	1	SURR
Goole Town	MLPT	CT	QF	WRID
Gorleston	EAST	CV	4*	NORF
Gosforth St Nicholas	NALL	V	—	NHUM
Gosport Borough	STHN	CT	3Q*	HAMP
Graham St Prims	NCOE	V	1	DERB
Grantham	STHN	CT	QF	LINC
Gravesend & Northfleet	STHN	CT	2*	KENT
Grays Athletic	V-OP	CT	2	ESSE
Great Shelford	CAMB	V	XP	CAMB
Great Yarmouth Town	EAST	CV	SF	NORF
Greenwich Borough	KENT	V	3	KENT
Gresley Rovers	WMID	CV	2*	DERB
Gretna	NTHN	CT	2	CUMB
Grimethorpe Miners Welfare	NCOE	V	3	SHEF
Guisborough Town	NTHN	CV	F	NRID
Guiseley	NCOE	CV	QF	WRID
Hadleigh United	SUFF	V	2	SUFF
Hailsham Town	SUSS	CV	1	SUSS
Halesowen Harriers	WMID	V	—	BIRM
Halesowen Town	STHN	CV	W*	BIRM
Hallam	NCOE	V	5	SHEF
Hall Road Rangers	NCOE	V	2	ERID
Halstead Town	ESSX	V	2	ESSE
Hampton	V-OP	CT	1	MIDD
Hanley Town	MDCH	V	—	STAF
Hanwell Town	LNSP	V	3	MIDD
Harefield United	V-OP	CV	4	MIDD
Haringey Borough	V-OP	Cv	QF	LOND
Harlow Town	V-OP	Ct	2*	ESSE
Harrogate Railway	NCOE	V	2	WRID
Harrogate Town	NCOE	CV	3*	WRID
Harrow Borough	V-OP	CT	SF	MIDD
Harwich & Parkeston	EAST	CV	3	ESSE
Harworth Colliery Institute	CMID	CV	3	SHEF
Hastings Town	STHN	CV	2	SUSS
Hatfield Main	NCOE	V	4	WRID
Havant Town	WESS	CV	QF	HAMP
Haverhill Rovers	EAST	CV	2*	SUFF
Hayes	V-OP	CT	QF	MIDD
Haywards Heath	SUSS	CV	P*	SUSS
Hazells (Aylesbury)	HELL	V	3	B&B

	League	Comps	Best V or T res.	County
Heanor Town	CMID	CT	2Q*	DERB
Hebburn Reyrolle	WEAR	V	1	DURH
Hednesford Town	STHN	CT	2	BIRM
Hemel Hempstead	V-OP	CV	5	HERT
Hendon	V-OP	CT	3*	MIDD
Hengrove Athletic	SOMS	V	2	SOME
Herne Bay	KENT	CV	2	KENT
Hertford Town	V-OP	CV	—	HERT
Heswall	WCHE	V	3*	CHES
Heybridge Swifts	V-OP	CV	4*	ESSE
Highgate United	MIDC	CV	P	BIRM
Highworth Town		V	—	WILT
Hinckley Athletic	WMID	CV	4*	LEIC
Hinckley Town	CMID	CV	3	LEIC
Histon	EAST	CV	3	CAMB
Hitchin Town	V-OP	CT	3*	HERT
Hoddesdon Town	SMID	CV	W	HERT
Holbeach United	UTDC	CV	3	LINC
Holmer Green	CHIL	V	—	B&B
Horden Colliery Welfare	NTHN	CT	1*	DURH
Horley Town	COMC	V	2*	SURR
Hornchurch	V-OP	CT	2Q*	ESSE
Horndean	WESS	CV	1	HAMP
Horsham	V-OP	CV	3	SUSS
Horsham YMCA	SUSS	CV	1*	SUSS
Horwich RMI	MLPT	CT	1	LANC
Hounslow	HELL	CV	2	MIDD
Hucknall Colliery Welfare	NOTT	V	QF	NOTT
Hungerford Town	V-OP	CV	SF*	B&B
Hyde United	MLPT	CT	2*	CHES
Hythe Town	KENT	CV	2	KENT
Ilfracombe Town	WEST	V	—	DEVO
Ilkeston Town	NCOE	CT	3	DERB
Immingham Town	LINC	CV	1*	LINC
Irlam Town	NWCO	CV	5	MANC
Irthlingborough Diamonds	UTDC	CV	SF*	NHAM
John Player	NOTT	V	P*	NOTT
Kempston Rovers	UTDC	V	5*	BEDS
Kettering Town	GMVC	CT	F	NHAM
Kettering	CMID	V	—	NHAM
Keynsham Town	WEST	V	2	SOME
Kidderminster Harriers	GMVC	CT	QF*	WORC
Kimberley Town	CMID	V	2*	NOTT
Kingsbury Town	V-OP	CV	4	MIDD
King's Lynn	STHN	CT	2	NORF
Kingstonian	V-OP	Ct	3Q	SURR
Kirkby Town	NWCO	CV	2	LIVE
Kiveton Park	NCOE	V	4	SHEF
Knebworth	SMID	V	P*	HERT
Lancaster City	NWCO	CV	—	LANC
Lancing	SUSS	CV	1*	SUSS
Langford	SMID	V	1*	BEDS
Langley Park Welfare	NTHN	CV	2	DURH
Larkhall Athletic	WEST	V	2*	SOME
Leamington	STHN	CT	QF	BIRM
Leatherhead	V-OP	CT	F	SURR
Leavesden Hospital	HERT	V	1	HERT
Leek Town	NWCO	CT	3	STAF
Leicester United	STHN	CT	3	LEIC
Leighton Town	SMID	V	2	BEDS
Leiston	SUFF	V	—	SUFF
Letchworth Garden City	V-OP	CV	3	HERT
Lewes	V-OP	CT	1	SUSS
Leyland Motors	NWCO	CT	3Q	LANC
Leytonstone/Ilford	V-OP	CT	3*	ESSE
Leyton-Wingate	V-OP	CT	2Q	ESSE
Lincoln United	CMID	V	QF	LINC
Linetype	MDCH	V	2*	CHES
Littlehampton Town	SUSS	CV	3	SUSS
Liversedge	NCOE	V	3	WRID
Llanelli	WELS	CT	1	WALE
London Colney	HERT	V	—	HERT
Long Buckby	UTDC	V	2	NHAM
Long Eaton United	NCOE	CV	2	DERB
Louth United	LINC	V	4	LINC
Lowestoft Town	EAST	CV	2	SUFF

	League	Comps	Best V or T res.	County
Lutterworth Town	LEIC	V	1	LEIC
Lydbrook	GLOS	V	3	GLOS
Lye Town	WMID	CV	P	BIRM
Lymington Town	WESS	CV	1	HAMP
Mablethorpe Athletic	LINC	V	—	LINC
Macclesfield Town	MLPT	CV	W	CHES
Manesteg Park	WELS	CT	2Q	WALE
Maghull	NWCO	V	3	LIVE
Maidenhead Town	HELL	V	2	B&B
Maidenhead United	V-OP	CT	3Q	B&B
Maidstone United	GMVC	CT	QF	KENT
Maine Road	MANC	V	P*	MANC
Malden Town	COMC	V	2	SURR
Malden Vale	COMC	V	3*	SURR
Maldon Town	ESSX	V	2*	ESSE
Maltby Miners Welfare	NCOE	V	2*	SHEF
Malvern Town	WMID	CV	4*	WORC
Mangotsfield United	WEST	CV	2*	GLOS
Marchon Social	CARL	V	P	CUMB
March Town United	EAST	CV	3	CAMB
Marine	MLPT	CT	SF	LIVE
Marlow	V-OP	CV	5	B&B
Marske United	WEAR	V	—	NRID
Massey Ferguson		V	—	BIRM
Matlock Town	MLPT	CT	W	DERB
Melksham Town	WEST	CT	2Q*	WILT
Merseyside Police		V	1	LIVE
Merstham	COMC	CV	3*	SURR
Merthyr Tydfil	STHN	CT	QF	WALE
Metropolitan Police	V-OP	CT	3Q*	LOND
Metropolitan Police (Hayes)	KENT	V	—	KENT
Mickleover RBL		V		DERB
Midland Bank	SAMT	V	1	AFA
Mile Oak Rovers Youth	STHN	CV	2	BIRM
Milton Keynes Borough	SMID	CV	2	B&B
Minehead	WEST	CT	2*	SOME
Mirrlees Blackstone	UTDC	V	1*	LINC
Molesey	V-OP	CV	QF	SURR
Moor Green	STHN	CT	2Q*	BIRM
Morecambe	MLPT	CT	W	LANC
Moreton Town	HELL	V	4	GLOS
Morris Motors	HELL	V	—	OXFO
Mossley	MLPT	CT	F	MANC
Mount Grace (Potters Bar)	HERT	V	—	HERT
Murton	WEAR	CV	1	DURH
Nelson	NWCO	V	1*	LANC
Netherfield	NWCO	CT	2	WEST
New Bradwell St Peter	SMID	V	—	B&B
Newbury Town	V-OP	CV	5	B&B
Newcastle Blue Star	NTHN	CV	W	NHUM
Newhall United	CMID	V	2	DERB
Newmarket Town	EAST	CV	2	SUFF
Newport IOW	WESS	CV	4*	HAMP
Newport Pagnell Town	UTDC	V	2	B&B
Newton	NWCO	V	P*	LIVE
Newton Aycliffe	WEAR	V	P	DURH
Norsemen	SAMT	V	3	AFA
Northallerton Town	NTHN	CV	P*	NRID
Northampton Spencer	UTDC	V	2*	NHAM
North Ferriby United	NCOE	CV	4	ERID
Northfield	MIDC	V	2*	BIRM
North Shields	NTHN	CT	2	NHUM
Northwich Victoria	GMVC	CT	W	CHES
Northwood (London)	LNSP	V	3	MIDD
Norton & Stockton Ancients	NTHN	CV	2	DURH
Nuneaton Borough	GMVC	CT	QF*	BIRM
Nuneaton Athletic	TEES	V	2	NRID
Oakham United	CMID	V	2*	NOTT
Oakwood	SUSS	V	—	SUSS
Odd Down	WEST	V	4	SOME
Oldbury United	WMID	CT	3Q	BIRM
Old Georgians	GLOS	V	QF	GLOS
Oldham Town	NWCO	V	—	MANC
Oldswinford	WMID	CV	1*	BIRM
Ortonians	PETE	V	P	HUNT
Ossett Albion	NCOE	C	—	WRID

	League	Comps	Best V or T res.	County
Ossett Town	NCOE	V	3	WRID
Oswestry Town	MLPT	CT	2	SHRO
Ottery-St-Mary	WEST	CV	3	DEVO
Oxford City	V-OP	CT	3Q*	OXFO
Paget Rangers	MIDC	CV	3*	BIRM
Pagham	SUSS	V	4	SUSS
Patchway		V	—	GLOS
Paulton Rovers	WEST	CV	4	SOME
Peacehaven & Telscombe	SUSS	CV	2	SUSS
Pegasus Juniors	HELL	V	1*	HERE
Pennant	LNSP	V	P	LOND
Penrith	NWCO	CT	1*	CUMB
Peterlee Newtown	NTHN	CT	2Q	DURH
Petersfield United	V-OP	CV	P	HAMP
Pilkington Recreation	NCOE	V	3	WRID
Pirton	SMID	V	1*	HERT
Ponteland United	NALL	V	P	NHUM
Poole Town	STHN	CT	1*	DORS
Portals	WESS	—3	—	HAMP
Port of Bristol	GLOS	V	3	GLOS
Portfield	SUSS	CV	2	SUSS
Portishead	SOMS	V	P*	SOME
Portsmouth Royal Navy	WESS	V	1*	HAMP
Portway Bristol	WEST	V	2	GLOS
Potton United	UTDC	CV	3	BEDS
Poulton Victoria	WCHE	V	—	CHES
Prescot Cables	NWCO	CV	5*	LIVE
Prestwich Heys	NWCO	V	P*	LANC
Princes End United	MIDC	V	—	BIRM
Prudhoe East End	NALL	V	—	NHUM
Racing Club Warwick	MIDC	CV	4	BIRM
Radcliffe Borough	NWCO	CT	1	LANC
Radford Olympic		V	—	NOTT
Radstock Town	WEST	CV	2*	SOME
Rainham Town	V-OP	CV	5	ESSE
Rainworth Miners Welfare	NOTT	V	F	NOTT
Ramsey Town	PETE	V	—	HUNT
Ramsgate	KENT	V	—	KENT
Raunds Town	UTDC	CV	2	NHAM
Rayners Lane	HELL	CV	2	MIDD
Redditch United	STHN	CT	1	BIRM
Redhill	LNSP	CV	4*	SURR
Retford	CMID			
Rhyl	MLPT	CT	1*	WALE
Ringmer	SUSS	CV	3	SUSS
Road-Sea (Southampton)	WESS	CV	5	HAMP
Robinsons DRG	SOMS	V	2	SOME
Rocester		V	—	STAF
Romsey Town	WESS	V	3	HAMP
Rossendale United	CMID	CV	1*	LANC
Rossington Main	CMID	V	XP	SHEF
Rothweel Town	UTDC	CV	4	NHAM
Rowntree Mackintosh	NCOE	V	1*	NRID
Royston Town	V-OP	CV	4*	HERT
RSSC Ransomes	SUFF	V	3	SUFF
Ruislip	STHN	V	—	MIDD
Ruislip Manor	V-OP	CV	3*	MIDD
Runcorn	GMVC	CT	F	CHES
Rushall Olympic	WMIC	CV	4	STAF
Rushden Town	STHN	CV	3*	NHAM
Ryhope Community Ass	NTHN	CT	1	DURH
Rylands	MDCH	V	3*	LIVE
Saffron Walden Town	V-OP	CV	3*	ESSE
St Albans City	V-OP	CT	2	HERT
St Austell	SWST	V	—	CORN
St Blazey	SWST	CV	XP	CORN
St Dominics	LIVE	V	4	LIVE
St Helens Town	NWCO	CV	—	LIVE
St Ives Town	UTDC	V	XP*	HUNT
St Margaretsbury	HERT	V	3	HERT
St Neots Town	UTDC	CV	3	HUNT
Salisbury	STHN	CT	1	WILT
Saltash United	WEST	CT	1	CORN
Sawbridgeworth Town	ESSX	V	3	HERT
Scarborough	GMVC	CT	W*	NRID
Seaham CW Red Star	NTHN	CV	5	DURH
Seaton Delavel Seaton Terrace	NALL	V	2*	NHUM

	League	Comps	Best V or T res.	County
Selby	SMID	V	2	HERT
Sharpness	HELL	CV	5	GLOS
Sheffield	NCOE	V	F	SHEF
Shefford Town	SMID	V	1	BEDS
Sheppey United	STHN	CT	1	KENT
Shepshed Charterhouse	STHN	CT	1	LEIC
Sherborne Town	DORS	V	—	DORS
Shifnal Town	WMID	CV	4*	SHRO
Shildon	NTHN	CT	3Q	DURH
Shillington	SMID	V	4	BEDS
Sholing Sports	WESS	CV	4*	HAMP
Shoreham	SUSS	CV	3*	SUSS
Shortwood United	HELL	CV	5	GLOS
Shotton Comrades	NTHN	V	XP*	DURH
Sittingbourne	KENT	CT	2Q*	KENT
Skegness Town	LINC	V	5	LINC
Skelmersdale United	NWCO	CV	1*	LIVE
Slade Green	KENT	V	1*	KENT
Slough Town	V-OP	CT	SF	B&B
Smethwick Highfield	MIDC	CV	1	BIRM
Soham Town Rangers	EAST	CV	4	CAMB
Solihull Borough	MIDC	V	5	BIRM
Somersham Town	PETE	V	1*	HUNT
Southall	V-OP	CV	F	MIDD
South Bank	NTHN	CT	QF	NRID
South Liverpool	MLPT	CT	2*	LIVE
Southport	MLPT	CT	3	LANC
South Shields	WEAR	V	QF	DURH
Southwick	V-OP	CV	3*	SUSS
Spalding United	NCOE	CV	—	LINC
Spennymoor United	NTHN	CT	SF	DURH
Stafford Rangers	GMVC	CT	W*	STAF
Staines Town	V-OP	CT	2*	MIDD
Stalybridge Celtic	NWCO	CT	2*	CHES
Stamford	UTDC	CV	W	LINC
Stansted	ESSX	V	W	ESSE
Stapenhill	LEIC	V	2	DERB
Staveley Works	NCOE	V	QF	DERB
Stevenage Borough	V-OP	CV	QF	HERT
Steyning Town	SUSS	CV	QF	SUSS
Stockton	NTHN	V	2	NRID
Stotfold	UTDC	V	2*	BEDS
Stourbridge	STHN	CT	QF	BIRM
Stowmarket Town	EAST	CV	4	SUFF
Stratford Town	MIDC	V	4	BIRM
Sudbury Town	EAST	CV	QF	SUFF
Supermarine	HELL	V	3	WILT
Sutton Coldfield Town	STHN	CT	3Q	BIRM
Sutton Town	NCOE	CT	1	NOTT
Sutton United	GMVC	CT	F	SURR
Swanage Town & Herston	WEST	CV	2*	DORS
Swanley Town	LNSP	V	3*	KENT
Tadcaster Albion	NCOE	V	5	WRID
Tamworth	WMID	CV	5	BIRM
Taunton Town	WEST	CT	1*	SOME
Tees Components	TEES	V	P	NRID
Telford United	GMVC	CT	W*	SHRO
Thackley	NCOE	CV	5	WRID
Thames Polytechnic	KENT	V	—	LOND
Thame United	HELL	CV	2*	OXFO
Thanet United	STHN	CT	3	KENT
Thatcham Town	WESS	V	5	B&B
The 61 FC (Luton)	SMID	V	2	BEDS
Thetford Town	EAST	V	1	NORF
Three Bridges	SUSS	CV	5	SUSS
Tilbury	V-OP	CT	3	ESSE
Tiptree United	EAST	CV	3*	ESSE
Tiverton Town	WEST	CV	4	DEVO
Tividale	WMID	CV	4	BIRM
Tonbridge AFC	STHN	CT	1*	KENT
Ton Pentre	WELS	CT	3Q	WALE
Tooting & Mitcham Utd	V-OP	CT	QF	SURR
Torrington	WEST	CV	5	DEVO
Totternhoe		V	—	BEDS
AFC Totton	WESS	CV	5	HAMP
Tow Law Town	NTHN	CT	2	DURH
Tring Town	V-OP	CV	5	HERT
Trowbridge Town	STHN	CT	1*	WILT

	League	Comps	Best V or T res.	County
Tunbridge Wells	KENT	CV	4*	KENT
Uxbridge	V-OP	CT	1	MIDD.
Vauxhall Motors	V-OP	CV	3*	BEDS
VS Rugby	STHN	CT	3Q	BIRM
Wallingford Town	HELL	V	3	B&B
Walsall Borough	MIDC	CV	5	STAF
Walthamstow Avenue	V-OP	CT	3	ESSE
Walton & Hersham	V-OP	CT	3Q*	SURR
Wantage Town	HELL	V	3*	B&B
Ware	V-OP	CV	P*	HERT
Warminster Town	WEST	V	1*	WILT
Warrington Town	NWCO	CV	SF	CHES
Washington	WEAR	V	3	DURH
Waterlook Dock	LIVE	V	4	LIVE
Waterlooville	STHN	CT	2	HAMP
Watton United	ANGL	V	2*	NORF
Wealdstone	GMVC	CT	W	MIDD
Wednesfield Social	WMID	CV	3*	BIRM
Wellingborough Town	STHN	CT	1	NHAM
Wellington	WEST	V	1*	SOME
Welling United	GMVC	CT	3	LOND
Welton Rovers	WEST	CV	1*	SOME
Welworthy Atherl	WESS	—	—	HAMP
Welwyn Garden City	SMID	CV	2	HERT
Wembley	V-OP	CT	3Q*	MIDD
West Allotment Celtic	NALL	V	3	NHUM
West Auckland Town	NTHN	CV	P*	DURH
Westbury United	WEST	CV	3	WILT
Westfields	WMID	V	XP	HERE
West Midlands Police	MIDC	V	4	BIRM
Weston Super Mare	WEST	CT	1	SOME
West Wickham		V	3	AFA
Weymouth	GMVC	CT	QF*	DORS
Whickham	WEST	V	W	DURH
Whitby Town	NTHN	CT	QF	NRID
Whitehawk	SUSS	CV	4	SUSS
Whitley Bay	NTHN	CT	3Q	NHUM
Whitstable Town	KENT	CV	3	KENT

	League	Comps	Best V or T res.	County
Whyteleafe	V-OP	CV	5*	SURR
Wick	SUSS	CV	2	SUSS
Wigmore Athletic	SUSS	V	2*	SUSS
Wigston Fields	LEIC	CV	QF	LEIC
Willenhall Town	STHN	CT	1	BIRM
Wimborne Town	WEST	CV	3	DORS
Winchmore Hill	SAMT	V	1	AFA
Windsor & Eton	V-OP	CT	2*	B&B
Wingate (Durham)	WEAR	V	2*	DURH
Wingate (Herts)	HERT	V	—	HERT
Winsford United	NWCO	CT	QF	CHES
Winslow United	SMID	V	2	B&B
Winterton Rangers	NCOE	—	—	
Wisbech Town	EAST	CV	SF*	CAMB
Witham Town	ESSX	CV	3	ESSE
Witney Town	STHN	CT	2	OXFO
Witton Albion	MLPT	CT	3*	CHES
Wivenhoe Town	V-OP	V	5	ESSE
Woking	V-OP	CT	SF	Surr
Wokingham Town	V-OP	CT	3	B&B
Wolverton Town	V-OP	CV	3*	B&B
Woodford Town	STHN	CV	2*	LOND
Woolley Miners Welfare	NCOE	V	2	SHEF
Wootton Blue Cross	UTDC	CV	3	BEDS
Workington	MLPT	CT	1*	CUMB
Worksop Town	MLPT	CT	2	SHEF
Worsbro Bridge Miners Welfare	NCOE	V	1	SHEF
Worthing	V-OP	CT	3	SUSS
Wotton Rovers		V	—	GLOS
Wren Rovers	NWCO	CV	3*	LANC
Wycombe Wanderers	V-OP	CT	SF	B&B
Wythenshawe Amateurs	MANC	V	5	LANC
Yate Town	HELL	CV	4	GLOS
Yaxley		V	2	HUNT
Yeading	LNSP	CV	2	MIDD
Yeovil Town	V-OP	CT	SF*	SOME
Yorkshire Amateur	NCOE	CV	2	WRID

Best performance details — relate to Trophy or Vase — whichever entered in 1986-87
*Means performance achieved at least twice